HANDLING PROVINCIAL OFFENCE CASES

IN
ONTARIO

2019

John Pearson Allen

of Allen & Allen

&

The Honourable Justice Rick Libman

of the Ontario Court of Justice

THOMSON REUTERS®

ISSN 1719-8283

ISBN 978-0-7798-8983-9

A cataloguing record for this publication is available from Library and Archives Canada.

Printed in Canada by Thomson Reuters.

THOMSON REUTERS

THOMSON REUTERS CANADA, A DIVISION OF THOMSON REUTERS CANADA LIMITED

One Corporate Plaza	Customer Support
2075 Kennedy Road	1-416-609-3800 (Toronto & International)
Toronto, Ontario	1-800-387-5164 (Toll Free Canada & U.S.)
M1T 3V4	Fax 1-416-298-5082 (Toronto)
	Fax 1-877-750-9041 (Toll Free Canada Only)
	Email CustomerSupport.LegalTaxCanada@TR.com

Foreword

Here, perhaps for the first time, is a book that speaks equally to all who have dealings with the Ontario *Provincial Offences Act* (POA).

The prosecutor and defence advocate alike will welcome this new publication. Its clear language and logical format make it easily accessible to the lay person as well.

"Handling Provincial Offence Cases in Ontario" is in some ways a very basic book. The authors, the Honourable Justice Rick Libman of the Ontario Court of Justice, and John P. Allen, Barrister and Solicitor, of the law firm Allen & Allen, take the reader step-by-step through the POA process — from the issuance of the "ticket" or the laying of the charge up to the trial and appeal procedures. Along the way, such fundamental concepts as the types of offences prosecuted under the Act, procedural streams, and the roles of the parties in the courtroom are explained.

The guide also addresses more complex topics, such as *Charter* defences, the classification of offences and hearsay evidence. A full chapter is dedicated to the discussion of the rules of professional conduct and the ethical duties of the prosecutor and the defence advocate in what is commonly referred to as the "people's court".

Well-rounded and carefully-considered, this guide will no doubt prove to be an invaluable addition to the literature already in existence on a subject that touches so many of us in our day-to-day lives.

Justice of the Peace Karen R. Walker

Ontario Court of Justice

Summary Table of Contents

For a detailed Table of Contents, see page vii.

Table of Contents

Chapter 1
THE PROVINCIAL OFFENCES ACT ("POA")

Chapter 2
ROLE OF THE JUSTICE, PROSECUTOR AND DEFENCE ADVOCATE

Chapter 3
PREPARATION FOR TRIAL

Chapter 4
TYPES OF PROVINCIAL OFFENCES

Chapter 5
PROCEDURAL ISSUES

Chapter 6
MENS REA OFFENCES

Chapter 7
STRICT LIABILITY OFFENCES

Chapter 8
ABSOLUTE LIABILITY OFFENCES

Chapter 9
SPECIAL PROCEEDINGS

Chapter 10
TRIALS

Chapter 11
SENTENCING

Chapter 12
APPEALS

Chapter 13
CHECKLISTS

APPENDICES

Table of Cases

l

Introduction

This new publication is a joint collaboration between two authors, Mr. Justice Rick Libman of the Ontario Court of Justice, and John P. Allen of the law firm Allen & Allen, both of whom have extensive experience in the area of the Ontario *Provincial Offences Act*. The format followed is that of a practical guide, but one which is especially designed for use by all those who may come before, or have contact with, the provincial offences court, whether as defendants, agents or prosecutors, students or teachers, witnesses or experts, judges or justices. In this way, this practice guide will apply to a broad range of persons, whose contact with the administration of justice in the province of Ontario will most likely be under the provisions of the *Provincial Offences Act*, and the "peoples' court" which it creates.

This is a basic Guide, then, for the defence and prosecution of Ontario provincial offence cases. Provincial offences range from simple parking infractions to highway traffic accidents, to complex occupational health and safety or environmental or securities offence cases, to give but a few examples. Pursuant to the *Contraventions Act* (Canada), certain federal regulatory offences, such as boating, fishing and wildlife cases, are also prosecuted under the *Provincial Offences Act* where the proceedings are commenced by ticket under Part I or Part II under the *Provincial Offences Act*. Factual and legal issues vary greatly among the different offences.

Use this Guide only as a starting point. It contains checklists, with chapters following the successive steps in a case, including the first client interview, how to gather information such as disclosure, pretrial motions, classification of provincial offences, various defences that may apply, trial procedures, sentencing, and reviews and appeals. A new chapter has also been added to this Guide, concerning ethical issues and obligations of the parties who appear before the provincial offences court: the duty of fairness on the prosecutor, which goes beyond the notion of merely "winning" or "losing" the case; the competency requirements imposed on paralegals, so that their clients fully understand the scope of the representation and their rights; and the importance of testimony from defence and prosecution witnesses which respects the process of the court, and accords with the rules of evidence which applies to provincial and federal regulatory offences.

Bill 108, the *Streamlining of Administration of Provincial Offences Act*, 1997, was enacted and received Royal Assent on June 11, 1998, at which time the legislation came into force. This Bill [S.O. 1998, c. 4] amended the *Provincial Offences Act* to allow the Attorney General to make agreements with municipalities permitting them to undertake courts administration and court support functions for the purposes of the Act. Pursuant to Bill 108, a new Part X was enacted entitled Agreements with Municipalities Concerning Administration Functions and Prosecutions. Under Part X, the Attorney General can authorize municipalities to conduct prosecutions in proceedings under Parts I and II of the *Provincial Offences Act* and in proceedings under the *Contraventions Act* (Canada) that are commenced by ticket under Part I or II of the *Provincial Offences Act*. Contraventions are federal regulatory offences, other than offences for which an offender may be prosecuted only on indictment, which are enforced in Ontario under the *Provincial Offences Act*.

Commencing in March, 1999, the Attorney General entered into agreements with various municipalities, transferring responsibility for administrative functions and the prosecution of charges under Parts I and II of the *Provincial Offences Act*. As of February, 2002, all municipalities in Ontario have taken over the court administration and prosecution of Parts I and II of the *Provincial Offences Act*. A list of the various provincial offences courts throughout Ontario, including telephone and fax numbers, has been added as an Appendix.

For further reference, an annotation of the *Provincial Offences Act* may be found in the *2013 Annotated Ontario Provincial Offences Act*, Segal and Libman (Carswell, 2013); and for a comprehensive text on regulatory offences, see *Regulatory Offences in Canada*, Swaigen (Carswell, 1992), and more recently, *Libman on Regulatory Offences in Canada* (Earlscourt, 2002).

Recent Developments — 2019 Edition

Legislative Update

The *Cannabis Act, 2017*, S.O. 2017, c. 26, Sched. 1, creates a number of new provincial offences related to the purchase, sale and distribution, youth use and place of use for recreational cannabis. The legislation also creates a number of enforcement mechanisms. The legislation is to come into force on proclamation.

A subsequent Act, the *Cannabis Statute Law Amendment Act, 2018*, S.O. 2018, c. 12 was given Royal Assent on 17 October 2018. It amends the *Cannabis Act, 2017*, to permit the Ontario Cannabis Retail Corporation and authorized stores to sell recreational cannabis privately in Ontario. It also makes it an offence for an unlicensed store to claim that it is authorized to sell recreational cannabis. The *Smoke-Free Ontario Act, 2017* and the *Cannabis Act, 2017*, are amended to clarify where the smoking and vaping medical and recreational cannabis is permitted and where it is prohibited, such as in enclosed public places and enclosed workplaces, vehicles and boats. The maximum fine for using cannabis in a prohibited place is $1,000 for a first offence, and $5,000 for a subsequent offence. These are the same fines that apply to smoking tobacco or using an electronic cigarette in a prohibited place.

Recent amendments to the *Highway Traffic Act* of Ontario will result in new issues being raised in provincial offences proceedings in relation to the hand-held device offence under s. 78.1, and new offences being created where careless driving under s. 130 results in death or bodily harm.

Under s. 78.1 (6.1), enacted by S.O. 2017, c. 26, Sched. 4, s. 16, effective date 1 January 2019, the penalty for a first offence for the hand-held device offence is now a fine of not less than $500 and not more than $1,000. For a subsequent offence, the fine is no less than $500 and not more than $2,000; for a second or subsequent additional offence, the penalty is a minimum fine of $500 and maximum fine of $3,000. Pursuant to s. 78.1 (6.2), convictions will also result in mandatory licence suspensions: 3 days for a first offence; 7 days for a first subsequent offence; and 30 days for a second subsequent or an additional subsequent offence. An offence under s. 78.1 committed more than 5 years after a previous conviction under this section is not considered a subsequent offence for the purposes of subs. (6.1) or (6.2): s. 78.1(6.3).

The newly created offence of careless driving causing bodily harm or death is set under s. 130(3). The penalty is a fine of not less than $2,000 and not more than $50,000, and/or imprisonment for up to 2 years. In addition, the person's driver's licence may be suspended for up to 5 years: subs. (4). The amendments also provide that for the careless driving offence under subs. (1) and (3), a person is deemed to drive without reasonable consideration for others using the highway if he/she "drives in a manner that may limit his or her ability to prudently adjust to changing circumstances on the highway": subs. (5). Where there is a conviction for careless driving causing bodily harm or death, it is an aggravating factor on sentencing that the bodily harm or death was caused by a person "who, in the circumstances of the offence, was vulnerable to a lack of due care and attention or reasonable consideration by a driver, including by virtue of the fact that the person was a pedestrian or cyclist": subs. (6). See S.O. 2017, c. 26, Sched. 4, s. 17, effective 1 September 2018.

The expanded use of administrative monetary penalties in place of parking infraction prosecutions under Part II of the *Provincial Offences Act* continues throughout the province. Richmond Hill and Newmarket are amongst the most recent jurisdictions to put such a regime in operation.

Case Law Update

The Supreme Court of Canada's long-awaited decision in *Groia v. Law Society of Upper Canada*, 2018 CSC 27, 2018 SCC 27, 2018 CarswellOnt 8700, 2018 CarswellOnt 8701, 34 Admin. L.R. (6th) 183, 46 C.R. (7th) 227, 424 D.L.R. (4th) 443, [2018] S.C.J. No. 27 (S.C.C.), was released on 1 June 2018. The finding of misconduct against Mr. Groia, a defence lawyer in a *Securities Act* prosecution, was found to be unreasonable. The Court held that defence lawyers must have sufficient latitude to advance their client's right to make full answer and defence by raising arguments about the propriety of state actors' conduct without fear of reprisal. This is not to be taken as endorsing incivility in the name of resolute advocacy; civility and resolute advocacy are not incompatible. To the contrary, civility is often the most effective form of advocacy. Nevertheless, when defining incivility and assessing whether a lawyer's behaviour crosses the line, care must be taken to set a sufficiently high threshold that will not chill the kind of fearless advocacy that is at times necessary to advance a client's cause. Courts and law societies have concurrent jurisdiction to regulate and enforce standards of courtroom behaviour. Improper defence behaviour is not necessarily professional misconduct, be it a function of incivility or incompetence. The Law Society must therefore be careful not to place too much weight on a judge's criticism of defence behaviour. When the impugned behaviour occurs in a courtroom, what, if anything, the judge does about it becomes relevant. Unlike the Law Society, the presiding judge observes the lawyer's behaviour firsthand. This offers the judge a comparatively advantageous position to evaluate the lawyer's conduct relative to the Law Society, who only enters the equation once all is said and done. The judge's reaction is not conclusive, and the Law Society is not barred from reviewing a lawyer's behaviour if the judge does not comment.

Leave to appeal was granted by the Ontario Court of Appeal on a number of issues involving the trial of an unrepresented accused in traffic court. In *R. v. Morillo*, 2018 ONCA 582, 2018 CarswellOnt 10037, 362 C.C.C. (3d) 23, [2018] O.J. No. 3405 (Ont. C.A.), it was held that in respect of leave under s. 131 of the *Provincial Offences Act*, the legal issue raised should be significant and have some broad importance. These same considerations equally apply to leave motions under s. 139. Generally speaking, the implications of the legal issue should go beyond the case at hand. The strength of the proposed grounds of appeal is also a material consideration if there is a real risk that there may have been a miscarriage of justice or a denial of procedural fairness. Appellate courts ought not to take a rigid or technical approach when identifying the grounds of appeal that a self-represented litigant is raising when seeking leave to appeal under s. 139. While self-represented persons are expected to familiarize themselves with relevant legal practices and to prepare their own case, they should not be denied relief on the basis of minor or easily rectified deficiencies in their case. Judges are to facilitate, to the extent possible, access to justice for self-represented persons. Appellate judges should therefore attempt to place the issues raised by a self-represented litigant in their proper legal context. The rule in *W. (D.)* is intended to ensure that reasonable doubt is properly applied where the credibility or reliability of evidence inconsistent with guilt is in issue. The justice of the peace recognized that the *W. (D.)* rule applied and cited it. However, there was strong reason to believe that she then misapplied it as she appeared to have engaged in the very kind of credibility contest reasoning that the rule was intended to prevent, by deciding which competing version of events she preferred. Credibility contests are not properly resolved by choosing one side after carefully giving the other side fair consideration in the context of all of the evidence. They are resolved by ensuring that, even if the evidence inconsistent with guilt is not believed or does not raise a reasonable doubt, no conviction will occur unless the evidence that is accepted proves the guilt of the accused beyond a reasonable doubt. The decision of the justice of the peace failed to make that determination, and there was strong reason to believe that the provincial offences appeal court judge erred by not recognizing that the justice of the peace may have committed such a *W. (D.)* error. When the defendant sought to confront the officer with inconsistencies between his testimony at the retrial and his testimony at the first trial, the justice of the peace refused to allow it. She apparently laboured under the misconception that since retrials are to be determined on their own evidence, no use should be made of testimony taken at the prior trial, even to demonstrate inconsistency. If this is so, she erred in law. It is trite law that prior inconsistent testimony from a first trial can be used to impeach a witness at a retrial. The provincial offences appeal court judge arguably failed to recognize the error. He found that that the defendant's challenge to the officer's evidence was deficient because the defendant did not impeach the officer with transcripts from the first trial. The appeal court judge's ruling also appeared to endorse the public prosecutor's protest at trial that if the defendant wanted to challenge the officer with prior testimony, he needed to have transcripts. This proposition is wrong in law. A party need not have a transcript to cross-examine a witness about their prior inconsistent testimony. The risk in not having a transcript is that if the witness denies making a prior inconsistent statement when asked, that denial cannot be contradicted and hence the contradiction cannot be proved. Put otherwise, the defendant would have been well advised to have had the transcript of the first trial with him for use in cross-examination, but the absence of a transcript does not prevent him from cross-examining the officer about the contradictions he believes to exist. The provincial offences appeal court judge did a commendable job in responding to the defendant's needs as a self-represented litigant. He worked to understand his basis for appeal; he listened carefully and patiently to him and was careful to explain why the appeal had failed. The appeal court judge may nonetheless have erred in law in endorsing the fairness of the manner in which the trial was conducted, by not paying due regard to the fact that the defendant was unrepresented at trial. The fact that this was the defendant's second appeal was not relevant to whether his appeal should be granted. The appeal court judge explained to the defendant that his lack of success could be attributed, in part, to his lack of familiarity with procedures and the proper manner of presenting his case. These comments might fail to allow for the obligation the justice of the peace had to assist the defendant, as an unrepresented litigant, in achieving a functional understanding of proper procedures and the proper manner of presenting a case. A finding that the defendant demonstrated his incompetence with procedures and the manner of presenting arguably called for the provincial offences appeal court judge to consider whether the justice of the peace did enough to assist the defendant in achieving the base level of understanding required. In summary, the special grounds raised by the applicant did not relate to the unsettled state of the law. The legal rules that grid his grounds of appeal are entirely settled and are not in need of determination by this court. The special grounds however arise ironically, from the fact that these errors occurred in a provincial offences court, specifically in traffic court. Traffic courts deal with a high volume of offences. This creates practical pressures to be efficient and economical. Given the low level offences that are prosecuted in these courts, these practical pressures can imperil the proper balance between efficiency and due process. The *W. (D.)* rule is central to the proper conduct of many prosecutions, and it is not without its complexity. This court has yet to affirm the importance of the rule in *W. (D.)*, in traffic court prosecutions, or to provide direct guidance to justices of the peace on its proper application. It was essential in the public interest and for the due administration of justice that leave be granted to accomplish this. Traffic court also sees a significant number of self-represented individuals. This appeal raises issues about the appropriate balance between the justice of the peace's obligation to provide guidance and direction to self-represented litigants, and the demands of trial efficiency in busy traffic courts where the stakes for the accused tend not to be high. It is essential in the public interest and for the due administration of justice that leave be granted to provide this guidance, should the presiding panel consider it appropriate to do so. While the justice of the peace's apparent error in restricting the defendant's ability to cross-examine the officer about his prior testimony does not present special considerations in isolation, however since leave is warranted on the other issues identified, the treatment of this issue may enable this court to give guidance on the importance of compliance with basic rules of evidence in the conduct of traffic offences. Leave to appeal was therefore granted on this issue as well.

It was held in *Halton Region Conservation Authority v. Hanna*, 2018 ONCA 476, 2018 CarswellOnt 7931, [2018] O.J. No. 2695 (Ont. C.A.) that it is well established that sentences imposed by trial courts are entitled to and accorded substantial deference on appellate review. An appellate court is entitled to interfere with the sentence imposed at trial only where the trial court: errs in principle; fails to consider a relevant factor; or errs in considering an aggravating or mitigating factor that has an impact on the sentence imposed, or imposes a sentence that is demonstrably unfit. It was not open to the appeal court judge to simply substitute his view of the nature of the defendant's breach of the regulation for that of the trial court. Findings of fact are the bedrock of sentencing proceedings. They are critical to a determination of the circumstances that may aggravate or mitigate a sentence. In many cases, as here, findings of fact that determine whether an aggravating or mitigating circumstance will have a say in the ultimate sentencing decision will be made on conflicting evidence. And findings of fact are the province of the sentencing judge who is an ear and eyewitness to the conflicting evidence. A reviewing court is not entitled, nor should it be, to interfere with findings of fact made at trial in the absence of palpable and overriding error. In this case the appeal court judge did not identify any palpable and overriding error in the trial court's finding on the critical issue of moral blameworthiness. It follows that the appeal judge was not entitled to interfere with that finding, much less to substitute a contrary finding funded in part by impermissible speculation about one of the defendants' knowledge of applicable residential building restrictions. The appeal judge's decision was therefore flawed by fundamental errors and could not stand.

There was a defect on the information as the offence date was recorded as 2017 instead of 2016. The justice of the peace committed jurisdictional error in quashing the information due to the error without considering whether to amend it under ss. 34 or 36. A justice of the peace may amend the information at any stage of the proceedings, including first appearance. The justice of the peace also erred by failing to give the Crown an opportunity to make submissions. Quashing the information in these circumstances resulted in a miscarriage of justice because it prevented the charge being considered on its merits. See *R. v. Singh*, 2018 ONCA 506, 2018 CarswellOnt 8710, 362 C.C.C. (3d) 161, 28 M.V.R. (7th) 45, [2018] O.J. No. 2943 (Ont. C.A.).

In *R. v. Benson*, 2018 ONCJ 217, 2018 CarswellOnt 5234, [2018] O.J. No. 1748 (Ont. C.J.), the defendant's request for a second adjournment of his trial was denied, and he was told by the presiding justice of the peace that the matter was going to proceed that day. The matter was held down and the defendant left the courtroom. He never returned. When the case was called for trial, and no one appeared, the presiding justice of the peace entered a conviction pursuant to s. 9.1(2). Section 9.1 applies only to Part I matters. The authority to conduct an *ex parte* trial under s. 54 is contained in Part IV and applies in proceedings commenced under Parts I, II or III, but pursuant to s. 9.1(2), it does not apply if s. 9.1(1) does apply. In the instant case, the defendant took the steps to initiate the process and then attended twice, both times to request adjournments. The presiding justice of the peace called the case for trial. It was open to him to treat that precise moment as the time and place appointed for trial. At that time the defendant failed to appear. Despite his earlier appearances, it was open to the presiding justice of the peace to conclude that s. 9.1(1) was applicable. If that was so, it was not open to him to proceed with an *ex parte* trial. To rule otherwise would defeat both the purpose and substance of s. 9.1(1). It is clearly intended to reduce the number of trials and concentrate court resources on those cases where the defendant truly desires to have a trial. It should not be possible for someone to defeat this simply by making one appearance and then leaving the court or declining to participate further.

Faced with a delay resulting from the complexity of a case, the Crown must act reasonably and take steps to implement the plan it has devised to minimize that delay. It is not too stringent a standard in the post-*Jordan* era for the trial judge to impose on the Crown that it be pro-active in its efforts to move the case to trial under the presumptive ceiling while simultaneously being involved in an extensive judicial pre-trial process aimed at resolving the case. There was no basis for appellate interference with the trial judge's decision holding that the Crown failed to develop and follow an adequate plan to minimize the delay arising from the complexity of the case. This conclusion was clearly open to the trial judge and led to his ultimate finding that the Crown had not established exceptional circumstances outside of its control justifying the delay above the presumptive ceiling. See *R. v.*

Nugent, Guillemette and Buckingham, 2018 ONSC 3546, 2018 CarswellOnt 9120, [2018] O.J. No. 3047 (Ont. S.C.J.).

In *R. v. El-Nasrallah*, 2018 ONCJ 161, 2018 CarswellOnt 3644, [2018] O.J. No. 1297 (Ont. C.J.), the trial justice of the peace dismissed the defendant's motion for unreasonable delay where it took 10 months and 24 days for the matter to proceed to trial. It is unreasonable to conclude that the *Morin* framework should still apply to Part I provincial prosecutions. While the *Jordan* framework of a presumptive ceiling must apply to Part I offences, it does not necessarily follow that the presumptive ceiling for Part I offences should be the same as the ceiling for criminal matters. Given the realities of provincial offences Part I proceedings, the fact that there are no significant intake proceedings and the matters tend to be relatively simple and not time consuming, the presumptive ceiling for these type of offences ought to be lower than the ceiling for criminal cases. It is difficult, however, to assign a number to the upper ceiling in the absence of any evidentiary foundation. While the court was unable to identify a clear number for the upper ceiling for Part I proceedings, there was no basis to reduce the ceiling to 10 months. Reducing the upper ceiling by eight months places too much weight on the intake period and not enough weight on the administrative realities of setting trial dates. It is difficult to imagine an upper ceiling for Part I offences that is less than 12 months given the realities of busy courts. Since the delay in the case at bar was well under 12 months, the trial justice of the peace did not err in finding that there was no s. 11(b) violation.

Section 11(b) of the *Charter* was also considered in another provincial offences appeal case, *York (Regional Municipality) v. Tomovski*, 2017 ONCJ 785, 2017 CarswellOnt 18239, 400 C.R.R. (2d) 219, [2017] O.J. No. 6073 (Ont. C.J.), leave to appeal refused 2018 ONCA 57, 2018 CarswellOnt 695 (Ont. C.A.), where it was held that because *Jordan* was decided in the criminal context its narrow *ratio decidendi* — the express or implied legal conclusions necessary to the result on the facts of the case — is silent on whether the same presumptive ceiling applies to non-criminal proceedings. It is important to distinguish the *concept* of a presumptive ceiling and the *number* chosen for it in a particular procedural context. While it is clear the concept applies in Part I proceedings, it is not at all clear the number does. The "realities we currently face" in the Part I process are different realties than the ones reflected in the ceilings set in *Jordan*. Had the Supreme Court used data derived exclusively from Part I and its analogues in the other provinces, its methodology would have generated a lower number of months than 18. Accordingly, the lower overall inherent time requirements of Part I proceedings furnishes a valid legal basis to distinguish *Jordan* to the extent of allowing for a lower presumptive ceiling. A lower ceiling is required to ensure fidelity to the broader principles announced in *Jordan* in this very different procedural context. The *Jordan* court set the presumptive ceilings to meet the requirements of criminal proceedings and implicitly left open the possibility that a different ceiling would apply in this very different context. The ceiling should be lower than the 18-month ceiling applicable in criminal cases; the question of whether the presumptive ceiling should be different for Part III proceedings was not before the court. Accordingly, the appropriate presumptive ceiling for Part I proceedings is in the 13 to 15-month range, and for the purposes of deciding the case at bar the applicable presumptive ceiling is 14 months. However, the court declined to "set" a specific presumptive ceiling for Part I cases generally, as promulgating frameworks and setting ceilings are the responsibility of senior appellate courts, not judges of this court. The net delay in the case of 10 months and 22 days was well below the 14-month ceiling, and as such was presumptively reasonable. Because the case was concluded before *Jordan* was released, the defendant need not demonstrate it took meaningful steps that demonstrate a sustained effort to expedite the proceedings to rebut this presumption. The defendant did have to demonstrate the case took markedly longer than it reasonably should have, however. From the point of view of total delay in fact it did. But the defence was responsible for the majority of that delay and the net delay does not reflect a case that took markedly longer than it should have. It followed that there was no s. 11(b) breach and the justice of the peace erred in concluding otherwise.

It was held in *R. v. 1137749 Ontario Ltd. (operating as Pro-Teck Electric)*, 2018 ONCJ 502, 2018 CarswellOnt 12427, [2018] O.J. No. 4001 (Ont. C.J.) that a justice of the peace sitting in provincial offences court has the authority to pierce the corporate veil in appropriate cases. The authority derives from the implied jurisdiction of the provincial offences court to carry out the legislative scheme. The question, in the context of the present case, really boils down to whether or not the sentencing court should have the power to defeat an effort by a defendant to neuter the court in imposing a just and effective sentence by making that sentence unenforceable, meaningless and illusory. It is simply inconceivable that a justice of the peace conducting a provincial offences trial lacks a very specific power (clearly possessed by other courts) that is essential to avoid a "flagrant" circumvention of justice. The power to pierce the corporate veil will be triggered when failing to act would result in circumvention of justice. On the evidence in this case, once it is clear that the sentencing court had jurisdiction to pierce the corporate veil, the only rational conclusion is that the test for piercing the veil was made out by the principal of the company's wrongful acts in diverting the company's assets by transferring company assets to himself and forming a new company around the same time that charges were laid, such acts being done for the flagrantly unlawful purpose of defeating the course of justice.

In *York (Regional Municipality) v. Martingrove Properties Ltd.*, [2018] O.J. No. 5223 (Ont. C.J.), it was held that the s. 11(b) clock begins to run from the date of an appellant's court's decision. It does not include the period that the defendant indicates he wished to bring an s. 11(b) application. The clock is "reset" after the appeal is complete.

Following the defendant's guilty plea to charges under the *Environmental Protection Act*, the prosecutor and defendant agreed to a term of probation ordered by the court that the defendant be required to have an embedded auditor to review its practices and procedures and make recommendations for future conduct. Section 72(3)(c) provides the authority for making this type of order. See *R. v. Quantex Technologies Inc.*, 2018 ONCJ 546, 2018 CarswellOnt 13407, [2018] O.J. No. 4259 (Ont. C.J.).

In *Halton (Regional Municipality) v. Verigin*, 2018 ONCJ 676, 2018 CarswellOnt 16300, [2018] O.J. No. 5055 (Ont. C.J.), it was held that electronic notes compiled by a police officer may be used to refresh his/her memory , even though the notes have not been in the personal possession of the witness since the time they were recorded up until the time they were reviewed for trial, and the witness could not state that the notes were not accessed by anyone else and/or who could make additions, deletions or other alterations to the notes. The notes had been disclosed and the officer had not attested to the fact that any alterations were, in fact, made. He had an independent recollection. That should itself be enough for the court to proceed to hear such evidence at trial. Though the officer could not truthfully attest to anyone else having access to those notes nor could he say whether someone else had an opportunity to alter such notes, there was no direct evidence led that the notes had been altered nor had the court heard of any additions, deletions or other amendments that had actually been made by others and not the officer himself. In conclusion, it is up to the trier of fact to assess the officer's ability to recall independently from his notes. This is done by consideration of a number of factors including whether or not the officer reads his notes verbatim, and whether or not he attests to having an independent recollection.

In *Weisdorf v. The City of Toronto*, 2019 ONSC 692, 2019 CarswellOnt 1087, [2019] O.J. No. 403 (Ont. S.C.J.), it was held the establishment of an administrative penalty system for certain parking tickets in the City of Toronto rather than prosecution under the *Provincial Offences Act* does not violate ss. 7 or 11 of the *Charter of Rights* since the proceeding to enforce a parking ticket under a by-law does not entail genuinely penal consequences. The City has confronted with a situation that using the court system was not working for the prosecution of parking tickets and using a criminal process for parking tickets was straining the administration of justice's ability to address more serious matters that were truly criminal in nature. The City consulted with ratepayers and made a researched and reasoned decision to implement an administrative penalty system rather than continuing to use the disproportionate and ineffective system in the *Provincial Offences Act* to enforce parking ticket penalties. There was candour, frankness and impartiality in the process. There was no arbitrary or unfair conduct or the exercise of power to serve private purposes at the expense of the public interest.

The interpretation of the relief against minimum fine provision under s. 59(2) of the *Provincial Offences Act* was addressed by the Ontario Court of Appeal in *Ontario*

(Environment, Conservation and Parks) v. Henry of Pelham, 2018 ONCA 999, 2018 CarswellOnt 20638, [2018] O.J. No. 6434 (Ont. C.A.). The Court summarized the guiding principles as follows: (1) Minimum fines establish sentencing floors that apply regardless of ordinary sentencing principles. The imposition of fines *above* the minimum threshold is governed by ordinary sentencing principles, as well as any principles set out in the relevant legislation; (2) Section 59(2) vests a discretionary authority in trial judges to provide relief from minimum fines in exceptional circumstances. The burden is on those seeking the grant of relief to establish that relief is warranted based on the relevant considerations; (3) Section 59(2) applies exceptionally. It will be an unusual case in which the imposition of a minimum fine may be considered "unduly oppressive" or "otherwise not in the interests of justice"; (4) Whether a minimum fine is unduly oppressive will usually depend on consideration of personal hardship. The bar for relief is set very high. Mere difficulty in paying a minimum fine is inadequate to justify discretionary relief; (5) Whether a minimum fine is otherwise not in the interests of justice involves consideration of not only the interests of an individual offender but also the interests of the community protected by the relevant public welfare legislation; (6) The discretion under s. 59(2) cannot be exercised arbitrarily. Trial judges must explain their reasons for invoking s. 59(2), and, in particular, must demonstrate both that the circumstances are exceptional and that it would be unduly oppressive or otherwise not in the interests of justice to apply the minimum fine.

In *R. v. Dennis*, 2019 ONCA 109, 2019 CarswellOnt 2065, [2019] O.J. No. 773 (Ont. C.A.), it was held that the threshold for awarding costs against a lawyer personally in a criminal proceeding is a high one. As stated by the Supreme Court of Canada in *Québec (Directeur des poursuites criminelles et pénales) c. Jodoin*, 2017 CSC 26, 2017 SCC 26, 2017 CarswellQue 3091, 2017 CarswellQue 3092, [2017] 1 S.C.R. 478, 346 C.C.C. (3d) 433, 37 C.R. (7th) 1, 408 D.L.R. (4th) 581, *(sub nom. Quebec (Director of Criminal and Penal Prosecutions) v. Jodoin)* 380 C.R.R. (2d) 285, [2017] S.C.J. No. 26 (S.C.C.), only serious misconduct can justify such a sanction. Costs are awarded on a discretionary basis and appellate courts should only intervene when that discretion is exercised "in an abusive, unreasonable or non-judicial manner." In the instant case, the appellant's counsel requested an adjournment of the appeal hearing without notice to the Crown prosecutor. The Crown prosecutor had interrupted her vacation to attend on the scheduled date to argue the appeal, and had been inconvenienced as a result of the appellant's request for an adjournment. Counsel apologized to the prosecutor and the court. Of his own initiative, the appeal judge asked the Crown prosecutor if she wished to apply for costs under s. 129 of the *Provincial Offences Act*. The appeal court ordered counsel to pay costs personally in the amount of $500 due to his reckless disregard for the other side. The principles described in *Jodoin* ought to apply equally to an order under s. 129. However, while the absence of advance notice of the adjournment request was worthy of adverse comment by the court, the exercise of the appeal judge's discretion was unreasonable and did not meet the threshold for an award of costs against counsel personally. Fundamentally, counsel's behaviour did not warrant the exceptional remedy of a personal costs order. The costs award was vacated.

It is not an error for an appellate court to situate the sentence before it within the usual range of sentences. One cannot begin to measure the demonstrable fitness of a sentence without having an eye to the customary sentencing range. An appeal court errs if it tethers a finding of unfitness to the simple fact that the range is missed, but commits no error by getting a perspective on what a fit sentence looks like by examining comparable cases. The principle of parity requires that sentences should be similar to other sentences imposed on similar offenders for similar offences committed in similar circumstances. This principle is equally applicable to sentencing for regulatory offences and criminal offences. Genuine inability to pay a fine is not a proper basis for imprisonment. As a matter of principle, it must also hold true that the hardship of a fine is not a proper basis for imprisonment either. The appeal court judge was therefore correct in finding that the sentencing justice erred in imposing a jail term because a fine would cause more financial hardship. On this basis alone, the appeal judge was entitled to set aside the sentences of incarceration and to vary the sentences within the limits prescribed by law. However, the appeal judge erred in adopting as a sentencing principle that regulatory offences are concerned with attaining public policy objectives as opposed to punishing moral blameworthiness. This is too crude a formulation and poses a false dichotomy. It is true that regulatory offences are concerned with attaining public policy objectives and the criminal law punishes according to the degree of the offender's moral blameworthiness; however, this does not mean that moral blameworthiness may not also be a relevant sentencing consideration for regulatory offences. The relevance of moral blameworthiness in sentencing for regulatory offences follows necessarily from the application in regulatory offences of the fundamental sentencing principle of proportionality. It is important to appreciate that, despite its application, moral blameworthiness does not operate the same way in sentencing regulatory offenders, as it does in sentencing criminal offenders. This is because regulatory offences tend to reflect lower levels of moral blameworthiness. While both kinds of offences reflect moral blameworthiness, the moral blameworthiness in criminal offences tends to be greater, and that difference must be respected when imposing sentences. See *Ontario (Labour) v. New Mex Canada Inc.*, 2019 ONCA 30, 2019 CarswellOnt 577, 51 C.C.E.L. (4th) 171, [2019] O.J. No. 227 (Ont. C.A.).

In *York (Regional Municipality) v. McGuigan*, 2018 ONCA 1062, 2018 CarswellOnt 22571, [2018] O.J. No. 6916 (Ont. C.A.), the Court of Appeal ruled that trial justice properly ordered the prosecutor to provide disclosure of the testing and operating procedures from the user manual for the device used by the traffic officer to measure the speed of the defendant's vehicle. Even if the justice of the peace had been wrong to order disclosure, the error would not have been jurisdictional in nature. Section 140(1) of the *Provincial Offences Act* confines *certiorari* orders in *POA* matters to situations where an applicant would be entitled to such relief at common law, and for parties to a proceeding, *certiorari* orders are confined to jurisdictional errors. Moreover, *certiorari* should not have been granted in the course of ongoing proceedings. Nor was there a substantial wrong or miscarriage of justice to address, a prerequisite to *certiorari* under s. 141(4) of the Act. Contrary to the application judge's decision, the justice of the peace did not err in making the disclosure order. Where a prosecutor is relying on a speed measuring device to prosecute an offence, it must, on request, disclose the testing and operating procedures set out in the user manual for that device. It is up to the prosecutor to hand such information over on request. The person charged need not bring an application or obtain a court order. This is first party disclosure, not third party disclosure. The charging police force has a corresponding duty to furnish the pertinent passages from the user manual to the prosecutor to enable the prosecutor to discharge its first party disclosure obligations. This is not a crushing administrative task. The disclosure at issue here is not case specific information. The disclosure obligation can therefore be discharged by the prosecutor by posting the relevant content from the user manual online and providing the ticketed driver with the required URL.

1

THE PROVINCIAL OFFENCES ACT ("POA")

1.1 PURPOSE OF THE POA

- It was originally enacted in 1979. Before then, provincial offences were prosecuted by reference to the summary conviction procedures in the federal *Criminal Code*, R.S.C. 1985, c. C-46. The POA seeks to simplify provincial prosecutions, eliminate technical defences, and promote speedy and inexpensive decisions without sacrificing justice.

- Provincial offences are "regulatory" — laws passed for the safety, health or well-being of the community. The "wrongs" tend to be specialized breaches of rules in a regulated activity, and the "players" should expect those rules to be enforced in a less formal manner. In contrast, crimes are wrongs of a general nature — obvious affronts to the community. The criminal accused is facing condemnation by society; the stakes are higher and the procedures stricter.

- In *R. v. Jamieson* (1981), 64 C.C.C. (2d) 550, 1981 CarswellOnt 1105 (Ont. C.A.), MacKinnon A.C.J.O. commented that the *Provincial Offences Act* "was intended to establish a speedy, efficient and convenient method of dealing with offences under Acts of the Legislature and under regulations or by-laws made under the authority of an Act of the Legislature" and that "it is not intended as a trap for the unskilled or unwary but rather, as already stated, as an inexpensive and efficient way of dealing with, for the most part, minor offences." In another early case, *R. v. Hill*, cited below, under the *Provincial Offences Act*, the judge stated that the "underlying philosophy" of this Act "is such as to encourage persons to personally represent themselves at trials of provincial offences".

- "In the spirit of the Statute, Judges and Justices presiding in those courts should approach the proceedings with tolerance and understanding towards such unrepresented persons and should permit certain latitudes in matters of procedure and law, provided no offence be done to basic principles of law and evidence": *R. v. Hill* (June 4, 1987), Nadeau Prov. Ct. J., [1987] O.J. No. 1935 (Ont. Prov. Ct.) at 3. In a recent case, *R. v. Zimmerman* (2005), [2005] O.J. No. 1647, 2005 CarswellOnt 1616, 30 C.R. (6th) 360 (Ont. S.C.J.) at para. 20, Trafford J. observed: "The fairness of trials under the POA, and the appearances of fairness of them, is of critical importance to the administration of justice in Ontario and the public confidence in it, given the nature of the cases tried in that Court each year and given the fact that most ordinary, law abiding citizens have some contact with it in the context of alleged traffic violations."

In *R. v. Messina* (October 28, 2005), Doc. 4860-02-709368, [2005] O.J. No. 4663 (Ont. C.J.), the court set out a number of factors that should be taken into account in most cases when dealing with an "undefended person". If the court concludes that the trial can proceed fairly without representation, it should do the following: (1) determine if the defendant understands the charges and what the case is that he or she has to meet; explain the charge and what the prosecution is required to prove; (2) explain that the prosecution has the onus of proof and that the standard is proof beyond a reasonable doubt; (3) explain briefly the mechanics of the trial, for example, the right of each side to call witnesses, introduce documentary evidence, object to evidence adduced, the choice to testify or not, and that if the person chooses to testify he or she will be cross-examined, and the right to make submissions at the appropriate junctures during the trial; (4) the same should be done if a *voir dire* is held, and if one is held, what a *voir dire* is should be explained; (5) ask if the person needs pen and paper to take notes during the trial; (6) explain the role of the Justice *vis-à-vis* the undefended person, that is, that the Justice is there to ensure that he or she has a fair trial and can offer some guidance regarding the procedures of the trial, but cannot act as the person's advocate; (7) ask if the person has any questions, and tell the person to ask if during the trial there is something that they do not understand; (8) make an order for the exclusion of witnesses.

The trial justice has a duty to assist an unrepresented defendant in the presentation of evidence and to ensure that no inadmissible evidence is presented. Although the defendant indicated that he understood the trial procedure, when it became apparent that in fact he did not, the trial justice failed to explain how the proceedings would unfold, such as telling the defendant that he was entitled to object to the prosecution's evidence; the justice also failed to tell the defendant factors he should consider before testifying on his behalf, as well as the purposes of cross-examination and how to conduct it. By indicating to the defendant that he could explain his side of the story when he testified, the justice would have led the defendant to the conclusion that he had to take the witness stand: *R. v. Rodriguez* 2010 CarswellOnt 10986, [2010] O.J. No. 1665, 214 C.R.R. (2d) 266 (Ont. C.J.).

In *Durham (Regional Municipality) v. Saeed*, 2010 ONCJ 251, 2010 CarswellOnt 4773, [2010] O.J. No. 2860, 213 C.R.R. (2d) 74, 96 M.V.R. (5th) 118 (Ont. C.J.), it was held that the level of assistance which justices of the peace must provide to unrepresented defendants at trials for ticket offences is not the same as for criminal trials or trials under Part III of the *Provincial Offences Act*. The burden of assistance in Part I or II trials is limited to information and assistance necessary for the accused to bring out his/her defence with full force and effect. However, it is not necessary for the justice to articulate to the accused any rules, procedures, rights or burdens that will assist the defence in raising a doubt about the Crown's case. The obligation to follow standard court procedures, hold required voir dires, prevent improper evidence from being led and applying the proper onus and burden of proof is still in place, even if the duty to explain those matters to the accused has been lifted in Part I and II matters. The duty to provide a fair trial and allow an accused to make full answer and defence is fundamental and transcends any derogation of the duties to explain the court process to an accused.

Providing meaningful assistance through the trial process to an unrepresented defendant so that his/her defence is brought out with its full force and effect should neither be the subject of time constraints nor depend upon the nature of the provincial offences proceedings. There is no basis for holding that trial justices conducting proceedings under Part I of the *Provincial Offences Act* should render less assistance to unrepresented defendants than under Part III. The overarching issue for trial justices, in every proceeding, is to ensure that the unrepresented defendant receives a fair trial, and that his/her defence is brought out with its full force and effect; it should be left to the trial justice, who has the advantage of seeing and hearing the unrepresented defendant in person, to determine the length of time that is required for doing so: *R. v. Rijal*, 2010 ONCJ 329, 2010 CarswellOnt 5802, [2010] O.J. No. 3440, 98 M.V.R. (5th) 281, 259 C.C.C. (3d) 227 (Ont. C.J.).

In a case where the defendant has elected to leave the proceedings, which effectively converts the matter into an *ex parte* trial, the court is obligated to ensure fairness in the proceedings in exactly the same way as if the court were presiding over a proceeding involving an unrepresented defendant: *Ontario (Travel Industry Council) v. Baldwin Travel & Tours Ltd.*, 2010 ONCJ 402, 2010 CarswellOnt 6884, [2010] O.J. No. 3859 (Ont. C.J.).

A lawyer who happens to be a defendant before the court should not be treated any differently, and should not appear to be treated any differently, than any other defendant before the court. In dismissing the request of the defendant for an adjournment on the basis of the lack of disclosure, the comments of the court in calling the request disingenuous and smacking of sharp practice gave rise to an appearance of bias. A verbal summary of disclosure materials on a trial date in response to a disclosure request, even in provincial offences procedure, does not meet a minimum standard of disclosure to the defendant: *Durham (Regional Municipality) v. Jagtoo*, 2010 ONCJ 596, 2010 CarswellOnt 9517, [2010] O.J. No. 5334 (Ont. C.J.).

In *Mississauga (City) v. Osman*, 2010 ONCJ 495, 2010 CarswellOnt 8224, [2010] O.J. No. 4618 (Ont. C.J.), a case where the defendant defended himself, it was held that while there was no formal *Charter* application before the court, the unrepresented defendant was appearing in a regulatory court, not a criminal court, and had asked the court to consider the legality of the issue. Since the officer admitted to the search and the nature of the stop and time frame, the court could reasonably infer that the search was indeed warrantless. Given the reason for the stop, and in the absence of any suspicion or evidence on the part of the officer that the defendant was committing a criminal offence, and absent reasonable and probable grounds, the search was not proper in the circumstances. The evidence resulting from the search of phone records was not useable in the trial of the defendant for driving while using a hand-held wireless communication device.

The Ontario Court of Appeal has affirmed the decision that a justice of the peace need not be legally trained to conduct a fair trial of provincial offences charges. The court noted that since its previous decisions on point, the Legislature has further strengthened the justice of the peace bench by mandating minimum education and work experience qualifications, creating an independent appointments committee, and requiring continuing education programs for justices of the peace. It has also provided that upon request, a regional senior judge of the Ontario Court of Justice may decide that a case that would otherwise be heard by a justice of the peace be heard by a judge of the Ontario Court of Justice. See *R. v. Zelinski*, 2011 ONCA 593, 280 C.C.C. (3d) 546, 18 M.V.R. (6th) 210, 2011 CarswellOnt 9540, [2011] O.J. No. 4024 (Ont. C.A.).

It is important that justices of the peace give some type of direction to assist unrepresented defendants in their trial. The court in this case did nothing except to ask the defendant if he was ready to proceed. The court gave him no assistance or direction in the course of the trial. He did not give any instruction as to what issues may be triggered by an officer using his notes and did not invite the defendant to cross-examine on any issue surrounding the acceptance of the notes: *R. v. Kogan*, 2010 ONCJ 662, 2010 CarswellOnt 10421, [2010] O.J. No. 5863 (Ont. C.J.).

In *R. v. Cipriano*, 2011 ONSC 223, 2011 CarswellOnt 89, [2011] O.J. No. 67 (Ont. S.C.J.), it was held that the justice of the peace had no alternative but to declare a mistrial after the defendant's counsel made a complaint against her to the Judicial Council. If she acquitted the defendant, it would have appeared she did so because she was threatened and accused of misconduct; if she found the defendant guilty, it would be said she was angry and biased due to the allegations made and pending against her. Where there are facts and circumstances that clearly give rise to a reasonable apprehension of bias, the court has the ability to address the situation by making use of the remedies of certiorari and mandamus. If the judge who made the original mandamus order in this case had been aware of defence counsel's letter of complaint that was provided to the justice of the peace, it would have been highly doubtful that the original order would have been made. Consequently, the justice of the peace had no alternative but to recuse herself despite the mandamus order to proceed with the trial. There was no basis to stay the charges on the basis of abuse of process.

It was not within the jurisdiction of the justice of the peace to simply indicate that the individual who the defendant wished to assist him at his trial could not appear on the basis that he was not a paralegal licenced by the Law Society. It was open to the justice to make certain inquiries to determine whether or not the person was qualified to be assisting the defendant. It would have been open to the justice of the peace to rule under those circumstances that the individual could not appear in the court: *R. v. Zaltzman*, 2010 ONCJ 667, 2010 CarswellOnt 10523 (Ont. C.J.).

In *Niagara (Regional Municipality) v. DiFruscia*, 2010 ONCJ 427, 2010 CarswellOnt 7104, [2010] O.J. No. 404 (Ont. C.J.), the company was a named defendant in other informations which were being tried before the justice of the peace. It would not have had any reason to believe that it faced any jeopardy with respect to the charges in question. R. DiFruscia Holdings Ltd. was not Rocco DiFruscia. For all legal purposes they were separate entities. Suddenly placing the company in legal jeopardy by amending the information to add its name to the informations was highly prejudicial to the company, especially when done without giving its counsel an opportunity to be heard on that issue. The amendments should not have been made.

There was no evidence to show that the prosecution of the charges was delegated to the Fire Chiefs. The prosecutor, who was properly appointed by the Regional Municipality of Niagara, acted in that capacity throughout the case, and there was no suggestion that he acted improperly at any time. The sentence in the prosecutor's letter that he had received instructions from the Fire Chiefs neither constituted nor indicated that the authority to prosecute the cases had been delegated to the Fire Chiefs; it was very similar to a Crown attorney consulting with the investigating police officer or a complainant before making a decision in a criminal case. As long as the lawyer continues to make the decisions, he/she is still the prosecutor. There was nothing to indicate anything different here. Nor was there anything to suggest that he behaved improperly in any way in his prosecution of the case: *Niagara (Regional Municipality) v. DiFruscia*, 2010 ONCJ 427, 2010 CarswellOnt 7104, [2010] O.J. No. 404 (Ont. C.J.).

The defendant made two adjournment requests to obtain evidence favourable to his case, which were not met with a proper inquiry or reasoned decision. The procedure was not explained to the defendant at the commencement of trial. Had the defendant been able to call at least one of the confirmatory witnesses, he might have been able to raise a reasonable doubt about his guilt. Having been convicted without being afforded a genuine opportunity to be heard, acquittals were entered on appeal. See *R. v. Homma*, 2010 ONCA 698, 2010 CarswellOnt 7923, [2010] O.J. No. 4478 (Ont. C.A.).

The appellant having been convicted for offences of dog running at large, contrary to a City of Toronto by-law, and failing to exercise reasonable precautions to prevent dog from biting or attacking another domestic animal, contrary to the *Dog Owners Liability Act*, should have pursued her appeal rights, and *certiorari* was therefore not available. Her complaints that she was not properly served, that the city official did not have the authority to swear the information, and that city officials trespassed on her property did not affect the jurisdiction of the justice of the peace to try the offences: *R. v. Nilsen*, 2011 CarswellOnt 2681, 2011 ONCA 322, [2011] O.J. No. 1865 (Ont. C.A.), leave to appeal refused 2011 CarswellOnt 10872, 2011 CarswellOnt 10871, 429 N.R. 391 (note), 294 O.A.C. 394 (note), [2011] S.C.C.A. No. 279 (S.C.C.).

The self-represented defendant was advised what would happen on the trial, but the brevity of the explanation might not have provided her with an accurate handle on what she had to do to represent herself. She was confused on the *voir dire* and it did not appear she understood its purpose; after the *voir dire* she waived her right to ask the police officer any questions on the trial proper, although it was clear that she had information that contradicted the officer and would have to present that to him to bolster her submissions. On sentencing, the justice imposed the set fine requested by the Crown, without giving reasons why the defendant's pitch for less than that based on financial considerations was rejected. The findings of guilt were set aside on appeal. See *R. v. Pereira*, 2011 CarswellOnt 6058, [2011] O.J. No. 3271 (Ont. C.J.).

In a case involving a defendant who represented herself at trial, *R. v. Caffrey*, [2011] O.J. No. 6202, 2011 CarswellOnt 15369 (Ont. C.J.), it was held that there was nothing in the transcript that would indicate to the justice of the peace that the defendant was confused or had a problem that required special attention from the justice to address her lack of comfort and familiarity in the system. One of the realities is that in the provincial offences court very few people are in fact represented by paralegals or lawyers. At the commencement of the trial, the justice of the peace asked the defendant if she was ready for trial and she indicated that she was; he courteously addressed her and said the charge would be read and then he would provide her with instructions regarding procedure and he did. While greater instructions could have been given, and have been given on occasion, the appeal court has to be mindful that this was a Part One offence, a highway traffic offence, a rather simple charge and that these courts are the busiest courts with longest lists, and the most unsophisticated litigants. What the justice of the peace did was adequate and there were no questions.

In another case involving an unrepresented defendant, *R. v. Topping*, 2011 ONCJ 483, 2011 CarswellOnt 10230, [2011] O.J. No. 4441 (Ont. C.J.), the appeal court observed that the trial justice was referred to a decision of another trial justice by the defendant that set out the test for the elements of the offence of following too closely, the same offence with which the defendant, who was representing himself, was charged. The trial justice made no reference to this decision in convicting the defendant. However, the defendant was treated in a very fair and even-handed manner by the trial justice. While the trial justice should have made clear to the defendant that he read the case and distinguished it from the defendant's case, or clarified that he disagreed with his colleague's analysis of the law, the other case was distinguishable on the facts and there was a proper basis for the conviction.

In *R. v. Wong*, 2010 ONCJ 636, 2010 CarswellOnt 10221, [2010] O.J. No. 5810 (Ont. C.J.), it was held that the trial justice applied the proper rules of evidence in refusing to admit material that the defendant obtained from the Internet and other sources as to deficiencies on the balcony and parking garage, and the manner in which they should be repaired. Such evidence was not properly supported by calling an engineer or providing an engineer's report, which the prosecutor would then have an opportunity to receive and cross-examine.

It would violate the law of solicitor-client privilege to permit the Crown to question the defendant's legal advisors about all communications related to his application for disability benefits in a prosecution for providing false or misleading information under the *Insurance (Vehicle) Act of British Columbia*. To permit the Crown to ask questions in this area would open up questioning of the legal advisors on virtually the whole of their relationship with the defendant, which was not appropriate or permissible. See *R. v. Sanghera* (2011), 4 M.V.R. (6th) 81, [2010] B.C.J. No. 1943, 2010 CarswellBC 2658, 2010 BCPC 250 (B.C. Prov. Ct.).

In *R. v. Thomas G. Fuller & Sons Ltd.*, 2011 CarswellOnt 4459, (*sub nom.* Ontario (Minister of Labour) v. Black & McDonald Ltd.) 278 O.A.C. 284, (*sub nom.* Ontario (Ministry of Labour) v. Black & McDonald Ltd.) 106 O.R. (3d) 784, [2011] O.J. No. 2615, 2 C.L.R. (4th) 161, 2011 ONCA 440 (Ont. C.A.), the Court of Appeal rejected a challenge to the wording of the counts in an information. It held that the trial judge appeared to have confused a count that is duplicitous with a count that duplicates or overlaps another count. A count is duplicitous if it offends the single transaction rule, that is, it joins separate and distinct offences in the same count. This single transaction rule is codified in s. 25(2). While there were a number of counts in the information, each arising out of the same incident and even overlapping or duplicating each other, this does not create a duplicitous charge. A single incident may give rise to multiple charges. The trial judge should have adjudicated on all the counts and made findings on each of them. If he convicted either or both defendants on all charges, he could then decide whether to conditionally stay one or more charges under the rule against multiple convictions. There is no discretion for the trial judge to reduce the number of counts to one count against each defendant. A trial judge cannot collapse an information by dismissing some of the counts arising out of the same incident. To give a trial judge that discretion would improperly interfere with the Crown's discretion to lay the charges it deems appropriate.

The court further ruled in the *Thomas G. Fuller & Sons Ltd.* case that while the trial judge was concerned from the way the charges were drafted that the defendants would not know the case against them, each count was drafted precisely in the wording of the relevant sections of the Act and the regulation. Offences drafted in the words of a statute or a regulation are presumed to be valid. Under s. 25(6), a defendant is entitled to sufficient particulars of each charge. The five counts in the case complied with s. 25(6). Some particulars were given; neither of the defendants asked for more particulars, and neither claimed that it did not know what it was charged with or that any of the charges failed to disclose an offence. The trial judge erred in dismissing the counts on his own initiative, and he was wrong to do so.

In *Vallance v. Pickering (City)*, [2011] O.J. No. 6107, 2011 ONCJ 771, 2011 CarswellOnt 15358, 17 C.L.R. (4th) 311, 93 M.P.L.R. (4th) 317 (Ont. C.J.), additional reasons at 2012 ONCJ 147, 2012 CarswellOnt 2756, 17 C.L.R. (4th) 323, [2012] O.J. No. 1216 (Ont. C.J.), the trial judge refused to grant a mistrial due to the lateness on receiving replacement disclosure due to its being misplaced by the previous defence representative, and also refused to grant an adjournment to allow the defendant to file a Notice of Constitutional Question or to allow a witness to be recalled for further cross-examination. However, the trial had a long history of delay which was overwhelmingly at the hands of the defendants. Given the context of the delays to that point, and the peripheral benefit to the defence to be gained by the adjournment or recall of the witness, the trial justice's decisions were reasonable.

8

The trial justice had made significant efforts to try to assist the defence in the presentation of their case. There was no miscarriage of justice in the circumstances.

The right to cross-examine witnesses called by the opposing party could hardly be more fundamental to the justice system, particularly in a criminal or quasi-criminal case where the liberty of the defendant may be at issue. Courts ought to tread very carefully when asked to place restrictions on cross-examination in such cases. Counsel have the right to lay the groundwork for further questioning by asking questions in cross-examination that, initially at least, seem to have little connection to the case; only when the relevance of the questions asked becomes increasingly unclear ought counsel for the opposite party or the court on its own motion interfere in the flow of cross-examination by seeking an explanation from the party who is cross-examining. The issue ought to then be determined in the absence of the witness, so that counsel is not forced to "show their hand" unnecessarily to the witness. The trial justice's views of the limits of cross-examination were incorrect, particularly after counsel informed the court of the evidentiary path she was seeking to explore with the witness. See *R. v. Zehr*, [2011] O.J. No. 4493, 2011 ONCJ 516, 2011 CarswellOnt 10607, 21 M.V.R. (6th) 322 (Ont. C.J.).

In *R. v. Butera*, 2011 ONCJ 860, 2011 CarswellOnt 15781, [2011] O.J. No. 6367 (Ont. C.J.), when the defendant, a self-represented individual, indicated that he wished to have a witness present to give evidence, the justice of the peace should have canvassed the possibility of the matter being adjourned so that he could summons or subpoena any witnesses that he wanted and ensure that they were present that day. It would have been open to the justice to inquire as to why the defendant wished to have the police officer present. It would have been open to the justice to point out to the defendant that the evidence he wished to call through the police officer was likely hearsay evidence and likely not be allowed; however, it would appear to be highly likely that the discussion with the defendant would have then led to pointing out that he may wish to subpoena and call the witnesses themselves to give their evidence. The defendant had a statement from a witness that would have helped his cause and there was another witness he could have brought who would also give evidence suggested that he had not entered the road in question. In all the circumstances, the justice erred in not canvassing the possibility of an adjournment.

The notes of the police officer are not evidence; the *viva voce* testimony is the evidence. Failure to put every single action in the notes does not invalidate an otherwise valid case: In *R. v. Goldstein*, 2012 CarswellOnt 7301 (Ont. C.J.).

In *Sproule v. Oshawa (City)* (October 24, 2011), Doc. 2860 999 10 0476 00, [2011] O.J. No. 4732 (Ont. C.J.), it was held that it is the right of the court to control the trial process and to disallow repetitive or irrelevant questions put to witnesses by counsel. While the appeal court may have given more latitude to counsel's questions, he still managed to effectively bring out evidence which tended to show the witness disliked or at least disapproved of the defendant. As a result, the defendant's right to make full answer and defence was not prejudiced.

The location of an offence as particularized in the information is an essential averment. A court cannot legitimately have territorial jurisdiction over a matter unless it knows where the offence took place. In the instant case, the intersection of Queen Street West and Bathurst is a well-known main intersection in downtown Toronto that is capable of immediate and accurate demonstration by resorting to readily accessible sources of indisputable accuracy, and may be judicially noticed by a trial justice without further proof. Any other approach would disregard the plain realities of the situation. See *R. v. Irving*, 2012 ONCJ 234, 2012 CarswellOnt 4914 (Ont. C.J.).

It was further held in *R. v. Irving*, 2012 ONCJ 234, 2012 CarswellOnt 4914 (Ont. C.J.) that when a justice intervenes excessively to assist a prosecutor, this can create a reasonable perception of bias. Extreme care should be taken to ensure that questioning from the bench does not leave an impression of unfairness. The issue is not whether the defendant was in fact prejudiced by the interventions, but whether a reasonable observer might reasonably consider that the defendant has not had a fair trial. The record must be assessed in its totality and the interventions evaluated cumulatively, not as isolated occurrences, from the perspective of a reasonable observer present throughout the trial. Questioning that conveys an impression that a trial justice has placed the authority of his/her office on the side of the prosecution undermines the appearance of trial fairness; however, proper interventions are appropriate. A trial justice has an inherent authority to control the court's process and exercising this authority often requires intervening in proceedings, making comments, giving directions, and asking questions during a trial. In the case at bar, a reasonable observer would not conclude that the whole trial was unfair. The isolated occurrences of instructing both the prosecutor and officer on the correct way to use the rules of evidence to ensure the admissibility of the evidence, and the collaborative way that the justice and prosecutor approached the matter of sentencing, did not detract from the fact that most of the trial proceeded in a conventional fashion, and the conclusions reached were all reasonable. There was no substantial wrong or miscarriage of justice.

In *R. v. Dookie*, 2012 ONCJ 719, 2012 CarswellOnt 14803, [2012] O.J. No. 5740 (Ont. C.J.), it was held that s. 802.1 of the *Criminal Code* which bars agents from appearing to defend persons charged with summary conviction offences punishable by more than six months imprisonment does not violate the s. 15 equality provisions of the *Canadian Charter of Rights and Freedoms*. Parliament has determined that it is not in the interest of defendants that non-lawyers appear to represent individuals who are charged with offences of a certain level of seriousness.

In *R. v. Appiah*, 2012 ONCJ 754, 2012 CarswellOnt 15602, 38 M.V.R. (6th) 173, [2012] O.J. No. 5851 (Ont. C.J.), it was held that a set fine which is an out of court payment is simply a figure that amounts to a reduced fine, and that a justice of the peace had no authority to reduce the penalty for speeding in this fashion as opposed to the fine as set out for speeding under the *Highway Traffic Act*.

The *Highway Traffic Act* offence of driving a motor vehicle while operating a handheld communication device is a strict liability offence: *R. v. Petrovic*, 2012 ONCJ 562, 2012 CarswellOnt 10989, [2012] O.J. No. 4185 (Ont. C.J.).

In a case involving the s. 59 relief from minimum fine provision, *R. v. Clarke*, 2012 ONCJ 627, 2012 CarswellOnt 12469, [2012] O.J. No. 4786 (Ont. C.J.), the court held that the proper application of s. 59(2) requires the court to first find exceptional circumstances before proceeding to the next two considerations, namely, the oppressiveness of the fine and the interests of justice. However, even if the court does not apply s. 59(2), the court may consider the goals and principles of sentencing to arrive at a fit and proper sentence in the circumstances, and the sentence may be less than the minimum fine as set out by the legislature. If after applying the goals and principles of sentencing the court finds that the minimum fine should be imposed, the burden of the fine can be attenuated by granting the offender time to pay. Although there should be deference to fines as set by the legislators, minimum fines are not a one size fits all sentence to be imposed in absolutely every case that comes before the court.

A trial judge has a duty to assist an unrepresented accused to ensure a fair trial. However, the way in which a trial judge assists a self-represented party is a matter of discretion. As an appeal court, the standard of review is that intervention is required only if the trial judge proceeded on a wrong principle or if a miscarriage of justice resulted. To assess this question, it is necessary to have regard to the nature of the charges and/or the circumstances bearing on the conduct of the trial. The trial judge patiently attempted to ensure that the defendant understood the charges that he and his company faced, the law that was applicable to those charges, the nature of the evidence relevant to them, and the process by which evidence could be received and examination and cross-examination conducted. The trial judge gave the defendant considerable latitude to air grievances and raise issues that were not legally relevant to the charges. Importantly, the trial judge made a considerable effort to bring out evidence that was relevant to whether the Crown had discharged its burden to prove the prohibited acts and whether a basis for a due diligence existed. Given that this was not a criminal proceeding, it was not a fair or plausible suggestion to say that the defendant should have been advised that he had a right not to incriminate himself and a right to remain silent. Having proven the prohibited acts, the onus shifted to the defendants to prove a due diligence defence on a balance of probabilities, and the only prospect of making out a defence required the defendant to testify. See *R. v. Ambrosi*, 2012 BCSC 409, 2012 CarswellBC 783, [2012] B.C.J. No. 554 (B.C. S.C.), reversed 2014 BCCA 325, 2014 CarswellBC 2385, 84 C.E.L.R. (3d) 177, 375 D.L.R. (4th) 396, 360 B.C.A.C. 106, 617 W.A.C. 106, [2014] B.C.J. No. 2099 (B.C. C.A.).

In *R. v. Canadian National Railway*, 2012 ONSC 6620, 2012 CarswellOnt 15070, 5 M.P.L.R. (5th) 277, [2012] O.J. No. 5649 (Ont. S.C.J.), it was held that a justice of the peace has jurisdiction to hear and determine the constitutional validity of a by-law. The Superior Court may grant relief for jurisdictional error in such quasi-criminal proceedings, but not for an error within jurisdiction for which an appeal would lie. There must also be a substantial wrong or miscarriage that has occurred. It remained open to the defendant in this case to appeal the decision of the justice of the peace once the trial concluded.

In *R. v. Smith*, 2012 ONCJ 324, 2012 CarswellOnt 6700, 35 M.V.R. (6th) 163, [2012] O.J. No. 2395 (Ont. C.J.), it was held by the Regional Senior Justice who dismissed an application brought by the prosecutor and defence to assign a provincial judge to hear a provincial offences case rather than a justice of the peace that both judges and justices of the peace have jurisdiction to preside at trials of provincial offences. This includes *Highway Traffic Act* charges of careless driving involving a fatality. It is a long and established practice that trials of provincial offences are assigned to justices of the peace in the ordinary course, with some exceptions; while some provincial statutes give the prosecutor the right to require that a judge be assigned, the *Highway Traffic Act* is not one of them. The Regional Senior Justice has the discretion to decide which judicial officer is to hear a case. There are no rules regarding the exercise of such discretion. The issue is not one of competence, and there is no requirement that a trial be heard by the judicial officer most senior in the hierarchy of those having jurisdiction. Relevant considerations in support of the assignment of a judge include cases where there were issues of significant precedent value, a constitutional challenge to the validity of legislation is being put forward, or a broader public interest was engaged. The fact that a fatality is involved does not mandate trial by a judge rather than a justice of the peace.

A trial justice is entitled to exercise a trial management power in the sense of being mindful of the time that the trial proceedings were taking, and those that were following, and limiting the time that could be devoted to opposing an amendment sought by the prosecutor to increase the rate of speed on the certificate of offence. The justice had given the defence representative the opportunity to oppose the amendment, heard his submissions, and ruled that he had been given sufficient time to make his submissions. See *R. v. Kukuy*, 2012 CarswellOnt 14464, [2012] O.J. No. 5310 (Ont. C.J.).

In *R. v. Reid*, 2012 ONCJ 305, 2012 CarswellOnt 6779, 34 M.V.R. (6th) 307, [2012] O.J. No. 2540 (Ont. C.J.), it was held that the defendant's rights under s. 7 of the *Charter of Rights* were violated when he, as an unrepresented accused, at his first drive suspended offence and being deprived of his right to make submissions on sentence was incarcerated for a regulatory offence that he had entered a plea of guilty to in a timely manner, and the justice wholly ignored basic sentencing principles by stating, "I used to give fines. We now impose incarceration." A justice of the peace is required when sentencing someone who is standing before him to allow that person an opportunity to make submissions. It is a basic tenant of the adversarial system of justice and a denial of that right to be heard, which strikes at the heart of fairness, gives rise to the appearance that the fix is in, that the sentence is predetermined. As the sentence had already been served by the defendant, nothing short of a stay of proceedings would remove the prejudice caused by the *Charter* violation; any form of further sentence would only perpetuate and enlarge on the s. 7 violation that occurred.

The defendants were the subject of a private prosecution by an environmental advocacy organization involving regulatory charges that stemmed from birds flying into buildings owned by the defendants. An application by the defendants for production of the organization's internal records respecting its co-operation with the prosecutor in the investigation of the defendant was governed by the third party records disclosure regime set out by the Supreme Court of Canada in *R. v. O'Connor* (1995), 1995 CarswellBC 1098, 1995 CarswellBC 1151, EYB 1995-67073, [1995] 4 S.C.R. 411, 103 C.C.C. (3d) 1, 44 C.R. (4th) 1, 130 D.L.R. (4th) 235, [1996] 2 W.W.R. 153, 68 B.C.A.C. 1, 33 C.R.R. (2d) 1, 191 N.R. 1, 112 W.A.C. 1, [1995] S.C.J. No. 98 (S.C.C.) and *R. v. McNeil*, 2009 SCC 3, 2009 CarswellOnt 116, 2009 CarswellOnt 117, [2009] 1 S.C.R. 66, 238 C.C.C. (3d) 353, 62 C.R. (6th) 1, 301 D.L.R. (4th) 1, 383 N.R. 1, 246 O.A.C. 154, [2009] S.C.J. No. 3 (S.C.C.). The mere assertion that such records were likely relevant to credibility and reliability were not sufficient to justify a disclosure order. See *Podolsky v. Cadillac Fairview Corp.*, 2012 ONCJ 545, 2012 CarswellOnt 10874, 112 O.R. (3d) 22, [2012] O.J. No. 4027 (Ont. C.J.).

In *R. v. Tate* (February 25, 2013), Doc. Newmarket 09-2111, [2013] O.J. No. 1799 (Ont. C.J.), the trial Justice of the Peace took the necessary steps to ensure that the unrepresented defendant was able to put forth her arguments and to determine whether or not she should testify. The trial Justice made sure that the defendant had her disclosure, reviewed it, and had any witnesses present. During the course of the trial, the trial Justice on a number of occasions reminded the defendant that she did have the ability to testify, but she did not take advantage of that opportunity. These were just some of the examples of the Justice intervening and providing assistance to the defendant. The assistance provided by the trial Justice of the Peace was sufficient in these circumstances.

There was a complete failure to provide meaningful assistance to the self-represented defendant. It was apparent from how the defendant spoke throughout the transcript that he needed an interpreter, and that the issue was not properly canvassed by the Justice of the Peace. The defendant was treated with a total and complete lack of respect. There was a total failure by the court and the prosecutor to understand the issue of putting the defendant's case to the witness; even though the defendant did not know it, that was what he was doing when he was presenting statements to the witness. The Justice is supposed to simply explain to the witness, "do you agree with the statement or do you do not agree with the statement", instead of having a battle with the defendant who, unbeknownst to him, was applying the rule in *R. v. Browne & Dunn*, which is what a lawyer and licensed paralegal would have done. There had been a very, very clear miscarriage of justice. See *R. v. Etemadi*, 2013 CarswellOnt 2062, [2013] O.J. No. 2686 (Ont. C.J.).

In *R. v. Wilson*, 2013 ONCJ 313, 2013 CarswellOnt 8034, 49 M.V.R. (6th) 320, [2013] O.J. No. 2767 (Ont. C.J.), affirmed 2014 ONCA 212, 2014 CarswellOnt 3327, 308 C.C.C. (3d) 350, 63 M.V.R. (6th) 1, 317 O.A.C. 314, [2014] O.J. No. 1295 (Ont. C.A.), the trial Justice of the Peace commented, before the evidence was complete and before submissions were made, that the defendant was guilty. However, the trial Justice's interruption of the proceedings was clearly predicated upon his belief that the offence of failing to properly wear a seatbelt was an absolute liability offence. It would have been preferable for the trial Justice to hear all the evidence and the defendant's submissions before articulating his interpretation of the law. He did hear, though, the rest of the evidence and consider the defendant's submissions regarding the nature of the offence, namely, whether failing to properly wear a seatbelt was an absolute liability or strict liability offence, before ultimately deciding the case. In view of the uncertainty of law regarding the issue of strict liability versus absolute liability with respect to the offence, and how the Justice followed through after his interruption of the proceedings, it could not be concluded that the trial Justice of the Peace would not and did not decide the defendant's trial fairly. An informed person viewing the matter realistically and practically having thought the matter through would not think it was more likely than not that the trial Justice consciously or unconsciously would not decide the defendant's trial fairly.

The trial Justice of the Peace did an excellent job in providing guidance to the unrepresented defendant throughout the case. The assistance and guidance was very fulsome at every stage of the trial: *R. v. Zhang* (March 4, 2013), Collins J., [2013] O.J. No. 3232 (Ont. C.J.).

In *R. v. Lo-Hing*, 2013 ONCJ 148, 2013 CarswellOnt 3642, [2013] O.J. No. 1360 (Ont. C.J.), it was held that the Ontario *Evidence Act* governs admissibility of evidence in proceedings under provincial legislation. Under s. 22(1), the defendant, like any other witness, may be questioned on whether he or she has been convicted of a criminal offence, but only to the extent of challenging the credibility of the witness. This questioning is subject to the discretion of the Justice, depending on whether the prejudicial effect of admitting evidence of a prior criminal conviction outweighs its probative value. Similarly, at common law, proof of prior bad acts to impeach the defendant is allowed, but only where the defendant first has put his or her character at issue. Use of prior convictions goes only to credibility of the defendant and cannot be used at trial to determine guilt. On the authority of *Deep v. Wood*, 1983 CarswellOnt 400, 33 C.P.C. 256, 143 D.L.R. (3d) 246, [1983] O.J. No. 23 (Ont. C.A.), s. 22 of the *Evidence Act* extends to regulatory offences convictions. As a result, a witness could be asked if he or she has been convicted, not just of a criminal offence, but also of any regulatory offence. Applying these principles to the matter before the court where the defendant was charged with driving while suspended, the defendant may be asked if he or she has been convicted under the *Highway Traffic Act*, but only where that conviction reflects on the dishonesty or lack of truthfulness of the defendant.

The trial Justice did not allow the self-represented defendant to finish his cross-examination. While the court has a role to play in limiting cross-examination which wastes valuable court time, the defendant was not engaging in cross-examination which was wasting valuable court time. The Justice also erred in restricting the defendant's cross-examination: *R. v. Melrose*, 2013 BCSC 526, 2013 CarswellBC 785, 44 M.V.R. (6th) 78, [2013] B.C.J. No. 592 (B.C. S.C.), leave to appeal allowed 2014 BCCA 148, 2014 CarswellBC 977, 354 B.C.A.C. 106, 605 W.A.C. 106, [2014] B.C.J. No. 659 (B.C. C.A.).

In *R. v. Marriott*, 2013 CarswellOnt 6496, [2013] O.J. No. 2684 (Ont. C.J.), it was held that the prosecutor of a provincial offences matter has an unfettered discretion to withdraw charges prior to plea. In a case where the prosecutor told the defendant he could leave because he would withdraw charges against him in exchange for his guilty plea, the Justice of the Peace should not have imposed a conviction upon deciding not to permit the charge to be withdrawn. The Justice should have adjourned the matters to facilitate the attendance of the defendant in the future. Convicting a person when the prosecutor has telegraphed that it wishes to discontinue the prosecution amounts to a denial of natural justice.

In *R. v. Lucas*, 2013 CarswellOnt 6515, [2013] O.J. No. 2685 (Ont. C.J.), four minutes after court was scheduled to start and the prosecutor had not appeared despite being paged twice, the Justice of the Peace dismissed all 68 charges on the tier for want of prosecution. The prosecutor filed an affidavit on appeal, indicating that he was outside the courtroom at the time, negotiating with a defendant, immediately went towards the courtroom when he saw the Justice appear, and did not hear his name being called as the pager in the hallway was not working. The prosecutor's affidavit showed an apparent lack of any insight into his own contribution to this deplorable affair; it was as if his role in the justice system did not entail certain obligations to the court. One of the prosecutor's duties is to preserve respect for the court. One does not promote such respect by failing to be in attendance when the Justice enters the courtroom. Those in attendance are left with this image of a judicial officer cooling his heels awaiting the arrival of the prosecutor before the machinery of justice can come to life. Had the prosecutor immediately entered the courtroom and then advised the Justice that he required a few more minutes or a recess, it would be routine for judicial officers in these courts to grant such indulgences as provincial offences courts are likely the busiest courts of any courts in the country, bar none. The administration purposely overloads them on the theory that missing witnesses and defendants, illnesses, and resolutions all lead to whittling down the list to a manageable level. The key to making this happen is to give the prosecutor the time and latitude to get a handle on the state of the cases. Every justice of that court is alive to this, and likely none would deny this type of request as it is the most effective way to manage such formidable lists. The Justice in this case was clearly piqued by the prosecutor's absence, which he viewed as wilful, and he likely felt the prosecutor's actions were cumulative. However, it is always an injudicious use of one's discretion to make others suffer the consequences of someone else's actions. Had the Justice instead chosen to dress down the prosecutor in open court, when he did materialize, it was likely warranted. The rocky road taken instead was unacceptable, and led irretrievably to a reversible error of law.

The mere fact that the trial Justice of the Peace was not prepared to address all questions put to the court by an unrepresented litigant who claimed that the *Highway Traffic Act* did not apply to him in no way showed collusion or denial of due process. While the role of the court expands to offer assistance in some degree to an unrepresented party, that does not require the court to depart from the position of neutrality which it must maintain. While the court may indeed be obliged to answer questions about process and law, there are definite limitations to that obligation. A review of the trial transcript did not show that the Justice of the Peace failed to discern the proper balance between aiding the defendant, and either descending into irrelevant or partisan exchanges with him. See *R. v. Bydeley*, 2012 ONCJ 837, 2012 CarswellOnt 17276, [2012] O.J. No. 6407 (Ont. C.J.).

In *R. v. Cassista*, 2013 ONCJ 305, 2013 CarswellOnt 7411, [2013] O.J. No. 2560 (Ont. C.J.), it was held that the defendant claimed that he did not receive a fair trial because the trial Justice of the Peace refused to hear his motions which included an application to stay proceedings on the grounds that the motor vehicle laws under which he was charged applied only to corporations and to those who consent to it. Such arguments by defendants who are identified as an "Organized Pseudo-legal Commercial Argument" (OPCA) litigant are entitled to the shortest possible shrift as they are patently without merit and have never been successful in any court; they are arguments that are not fact or case specific and therefore can have no more merit in one case than in another; that is, none. The only hearing that such arguments are entitled to is to have the court read and appreciate the grounds upon which the motion is based. If the motion contains incomprehensible gibberish or discloses patently ridiculous or meritless arguments or raises known OPCA themes, the court is entitled to dismiss the motion or refuse to hear it, without further inquiry, representation or submission.

There was no basis for holding that the self-represented defendant was not competent to represent himself. He did not testify on appeal, and there was no medical evidence or other evidence suggesting he was suffering from any disability or illness which would have precluded him from acting on his own behalf. The defendant was aware that he was entitled to retain counsel, and there were discussions as to retaining counsel on previous court appearances; a date was selected which accommodated counsel but the defendant appeared on the trial date without counsel, and ready to represent himself. The presiding Justice of the Peace provided explanations and directed the defendant to ask questions, and told him he could give his account later on. He gave a very brief but adequate explanation of the procedures involved. There was no miscarriage of justice. See *R. v. Mcwilliams*, 2012 ONCJ 859, 2012 CarswellOnt 17470 (Ont. C.J.).

In *R. v. Alkhawaji*, 2013 NSSC 233, 2013 CarswellNS 544, 332 N.B.R. (2d) 297, 48 M.V.R. (6th) 267, 1052 A.P.R. 297, [2013] N.S.J. No. 380 (N.S. S.C.), having pled guilty to operating a motor vehicle without insurance, the defendant explained that he had previously spoken to his insurance company and advised that he would be unable to make payments for some time, to which he was told that this would not affect the status of his policy. When the Justice of the Peace informed the defendant that his explanation might constitute the defence of due diligence, the prosecutor objected, and the guilty plea proceedings continued. The defendant had no counsel and there was no indication that he was aware he could ask for an adjournment or seek counsel; his first language was not English. The defendant had no meaningful appreciation of what was meant by due diligence or how he could advance such a defence. It was unreasonable and an error of law for the Justice of The Peace to ask the defendant to confirm his guilty plea while he knew that the defendant still did not understand the nature of the guilty plea.

In *R. v. Rau*, 2013 ONSC 5573, 2013 CarswellOnt 12550, [2013] O.J. No. 4067 (Ont. S.C.J.), an unsuccessful application was brought by the defendant for a stay of proceedings on his charge of failure to stop for police, contrary to the *Highway*

Traffic Act (Ont.), pending the provision of funding for his defence so that he could have legal representation. This appeared to be the first time that such an application had been brought for such a funding order in respect of a *Highway Traffic Act* offence. Although there was a real prospect of imprisonment if the defendant was found guilty, the trial faced by him would be relatively brief, the issues discrete, and the minimum sentence of 14 days' imprisonment was far from the most serious range. The defendant had also demonstrated an understanding of the charges, was able to put forward the facts in an understandable and coherent manner, and had shown an ability to participate effectively in a court proceeding; the case was not of sufficient seriousness or complexity that representation by counsel was essential to a fair trial.

In *R. v. Williams*, 2013 NLTD(G) 103, 2013 CarswellNfld 323, 341 Nfld. & P.E.I.R. 159, 1061 A.P.R. 159, [2013] N.J. No. 299 (N.L. T.D.), the trial judge was held to have acted correctly when he rejected the issue the defendant raised about the lateness of the Crown disclosure. The defendant did not relate the circumstances in which he received the disclosure, which had been sent to him in advance of the trial, and he may not have received it due to his own neglect. If the defendant felt he did not have sufficient time to prepare for trial because he did not receive timely disclosure, he should have brought it to the trial judge's attention when the matter was called and asked him to adjourn the proceedings until he was ready to proceed. The trial judge also acted correctly when he upheld the Crown's objection to the documents that the defendant tries to produce when cross-examining the police officer who stopped him for speeding. The Crown has a right to know what the documents are before halfway through the proceedings so it could inform itself about them, assess their relevance and address any concerns that it might have about them. One of the overarching concerns for a trial judge and one of the main purposes of rules of procedure is to ensure as far as reasonably possible that only relevant evidence is admitted that is probative of the issues raised by the charges. The trial judge achieved the object of the rules when he rejected the documents that the defendant produced from the manufacturer about the calibration of the radar and possibly the tuning forks, which were not served on the Crown with at least 7 days' notice in compliance with s. 28 of the *Canada Evidence Act*.

A recent Ontario case involving an application for a French-language trial and the resulting delay of delay was discussed in *R. v. Byrnes*, 2013 ONCJ 631, 2013 CarswellOnt 16205, 2013 CarswellOnt 16206, 296 C.R.R. (2d) 258, [2013] O.J. No. 5389 (Ont. C.J.), where the defendant immediately requested a French trial by ticking off the box on the Notice of Intention to Appear to indicate his intention and by filing the Notice with the court. However, his request for a French trial was overlooked, and therefore his trial could not proceed on the trial date. While this oversight was an administrative error, this error amounted to a breach of the defendant's language rights. Moreover, the defendant should not have been expected by the trial judge to have required an interpreter. As a French-speaking defendant, he did not require the assistance of an interpreter at his French trial. Perhaps an interpreter would have been necessary to assist any English-speaking witnesses the prosecutor wished to call, but it would be the responsibility of the prosecutor, not the defendant, to make the appropriate arrangements for these witnesses. By indicating on the Notice that he wished to proceed in French, the defendant properly completed the Notice and satisfied all of his obligations on the language issue. The 8-month delay between the date the defendant requested a French trial until the date the trial began amounted to a breach of the defendant's right to have a trial within a reasonable time for two reasons. First, had he requested a trial in English, his matter could have been heard within 5 months; second, no effort was made to immediately secure a date for the French trial, due to his matter being adjourned a further 3 months to a pre-scheduled date for French trials, despite the fact that there were several intervening dates available for English trials. The practice of having only 2 pre-scheduled days set aside each year for French trials in the provincial offences court, one in the Spring and one in the Fall, is problematic from a case management perspective, and unfair because it is unresponsive to the individual requirements of a specific case. The fact that this system appeared to apply only to French-speaking defendants was a clear contravention of s. 16(1) of the Charter and as such, unacceptable. Even if this general process for scheduling French trials was constitutionally sound, the effect of slavishly continuing with the pre-scheduled French dates in the defendant's case, even after the trial had commenced before a specific Justice of the Peace, led to unacceptable delays. The result was that a routine speeding trial was commenced 9 months after the offence date, heard in 6-month instalments over a period of 13 months, and only concluded 22 months after the offence date.

It was also held in *R. v. Byrnes*, 2013 ONCJ 631, 2013 CarswellOnt 16205, 2013 CarswellOnt 16206, 296 C.R.R. (2d) 258, [2013] O.J. No. 5389 (Ont. C.J.), that the defendant did not enter a plea because the Justice of the Peace believed that the Charter application should be heard and decided before the plea was entered. This was incorrect, as the defendant should have been required to enter a plea before the Charter application commenced. If the defendant refused to do so, the court should have deemed his plea to be not guilty, and made this entry on the information. A "best practices" approach would entail having the defendant arraigned prior to hearing the Charter application because it is only after arraignment that the Justice of the Peace is formally seized with the matter. Arraignment includes having the charge read, asking the defendant how he pleads, guilty or not guilty, and noting the plea on the information. To do otherwise and commence a Charter application prior to arraignment or midway through arraignment and prior to plea being entered, would allow a party who received an unfavourable decision on the Charter to request that the trial commence before a different Justice of the Peace since the first one was not seized. If this were to happen, the parties would be able to re-argue the

Charter application since the new Justice of the Peace would not be bound by the original Charter decision. This absurd legal outcome and case management headache would be properly prevented by having the plea entered and noted on the information prior to addressing the Charter application.

A fine should not be perceived simply as a licensing fee for illegal conduct. Not every strict liability provincial offence is of the same seriousness or poses the same threat to the welfare of the public. Every case will have aggravating and mitigating factors, and a fit sentence should reflect the circumstances surrounding the unlawful conduct and the offender's personal circumstances. Where the prosecutor cites four cases with widely disparate sentences, this hardly establishes an accepted range of sentence but rather demonstrates that the appropriate penalty will be determined by considering all the mitigating and aggravating factors based on the facts of the particular case and the personal circumstances of an offender. Having decided that a fine is an appropriate disposition, the trial judge should only impose a fine that is within the offender's ability to pay, bearing in mind that he may extend the time for payment. It is an error to fail to inquire about a defendant's ability to pay before imposing fines. The failure of the Justice of the Peace to give any reasons explaining the quantum of fines he imposed was an error. See *Real Estate Council of Ontario v. Wang*, 2013 ONCJ 515, 2013 CarswellOnt 13174, [2013] O.J. No. 4294 (Ont. C.J.).

In *Real Estate Council of Ontario v. Wang*, 2013 ONCJ 515, 2013 CarswellOnt 13174, [2013] O.J. No. 4294 (Ont. C.J.), it was further held that when defendants are not represented by counsel or a paralegal, the trial Justice of the Peace must conduct a plea comprehension inquiry to ensure that the pleas were voluntary and informed, and that the facts necessary to establish all of the essential elements of the offences were admitted. When the facts are read in by the prosecutor, the Justice of the Peace must ask the defendants if they agree with the facts as read in. When a defendant pleads guilty but indicates he wants to give an explanation, the Justice must determine whether the defendant is really admitting the facts as alleged.

The person who laid the complaint against the defendants had also sued them in Small Claims Court, and the claim was under appeal in Superior Court. The trial Justice of the Peace was in error in declining to let the defendant cross-examine the complainant on her dealings with the defendant because he did not want to ''step on the [Superior Court's] feet''. The civil proceedings that were then outstanding should not have prevented the defendant from cross-examining the witness about the facts pertaining to one of the counts. The trial Justice should also have assisted the unrepresented defendant to frame a proper question to elicit the evidence he was seeking, rather than cutting him off when he was questioning the complainant and stating that he was giving evidence rather than asking questions: *Real Estate Council of Ontario v. Wang*, 2013 ONCJ 515, 2013 CarswellOnt 13174, [2013] O.J. No. 4294 (Ont. C.J.).

It was held in *R. v. Jamieson*, 2013 ONCA 760, 2013 CarswellOnt 17714, 118 O.R. (3d) 327, 304 C.C.C. (3d) 64, 53 M.V.R. (6th) 1, 297 C.R.R. (2d) 58, 297 C.R.R. (2d) 243, 313 O.A.C. 313, [2013] O.J. No. 5836 (Ont. C.A.), leave to appeal refused 2014 CarswellOnt 14802, 2014 CarswellOnt 14803 (S.C.C.) that the Notice of Intention to Appear (NIA) option in the offence notice clearly warns a defendant that failing to appear at the trial will result in a conviction. The defendant must exercise the option to appear on the offence notice and deliver it to the court office, so he or she does not retain a copy; but, in order to make an intelligent choice among the options provided, a defendant who chooses the option of appearing must have read, understood and signed the NIA, which includes the warning. If, as in this case, the defendant opts to file a NIA, then, for the purposes of entering a plea and having a trial, a Notice of Trial (NT) containing the time and place of the trial is issued, which contains a second clear warning of the consequences of failing to appear at trial. These *Provincial Offences Act* forms are clear. They fully informed the defendant of the consequences of failing to appear at trial. There is no systemic flaw in the scheme under the Act and particularly, the operation of the failure to appear at trial provision which results in a default conviction due to the defendant's absence. Section 11(d) of the *Charter of Rights* does not impose on the legislature an additional obligation to warn the defendant again of the consequences of failing to appear for trial if the trial is adjourned. The warnings on the NIA and the NT are clear, and there is nothing on the NT that might lead a defendant to assume that any of the conditions for trial are changed by an adjournment, apart from the date and possibly the time of the trial. The warning on the NT does not disappear. The defendant need only listen to what the Justice says when an adjournment is granted about the date and time of the trial; in this case the defendant was given peremptory warnings on more than one occasion that the matter would proceed at the next trial date, whether or not the defendant was present, and that no further adjournments would be granted. It is reasonable to expect that such a defendant would use basic common sense and would understand that the initial warnings regarding the consequences of failing to appear also apply to the future trial date. While the NT might be improved by an additional warning that states that the initial warning also applies if the trial is adjourned and the defendant does not appear on the date and at the time to which the trial is adjourned, it is not constitutionally required.

There is no jurisdiction to impose concurrent fines on sentencing. While a court may impose concurrent custodial sentences for two or more counts, where the sentence is a fine the court must impose separate fines for each count while ensuring that the overall fine is appropriate: *Ontario (Ministry of Labour) v. Flex-N-Gate Canada Co.*, 2014 ONCA 53, 2014 CarswellOnt 673, 119 O.R. (3d) 1, 315 O.A.C. 66, [2014] O.J. No. 261 (Ont. C.A.).

A trial judge is not bound by a joint submission. The imposition of a fit sentence is ultimately the trial judge's responsibility. Trial judges must, however, give

21

considerable weight to joint submissions. A trial judge should not reject joint submissions unless the joint submission is contrary to the public interest and the sentence would bring the administration of justice into disrepute. That standard is applicable regardless of whether a trial judge is inclined to go above or below the sentence proposed in the joint submission. In the instant case, the proposed sentence was definitely not contrary to the public interest, nor could it bring the administration of justice into disrepute. In those circumstances, the decision to undercut the joint submission constituted a reversible error. See *R. v. Pynappels*, 2014 ONCJ 15, 2014 CarswellOnt 334, [2014] O.J. No. 152 (Ont. C.J.).

In *R. v. Farrage*, 2014 ONSC 564, 2014 CarswellOnt 1090, [2014] O.J. No. 448 (Ont. S.C.J.) it was held that the sentencing judge clearly felt that the joint submission for the minimum penalty was manifestly inadequate based on the submissions in support of the guilty plea. The court expressly recognized that a joint submission should not be lightly overridden. Counsel for the defendant proceeded to make further submissions after the court advised that there must be a suspension of driving privileges in addition to the minimum fine. There was no request to hold the matter down or adjourn to another date for further evidence or submissions. There was no error of law and no basis to interfere with the sentence imposed.

In *R. v. Petrecca*, 2013 ONCJ 744, 2013 CarswellOnt 18653, [2013] O.J. No. 6160 (Ont. C.J.), the information charging the defendant with stunt driving by driving in a manner that indicates an intention to cause some or all of the tires to lose traction referenced the section of the *Highway Traffic Act* but not the regulation, and the information omitted the words "while turning". The Justice of the Peace raised the issue of whether the information was improper, proceeded to find that it was, and after refusing to grant an amendment, dismissed the charge. Even if the information was not proper, the Justice of the Peace erred in not granting an amendment. The underlying philosophy of the *Provincial Offences Act* is to ensure that technical objections do not impede the determination of a case on its merits. Counsel for the defendant would certainly have known or ought to have known the case to be met, as was apparent from the fact that the defendant's legal representative did not raise the issue. There would have been no prejudice in granting the amendment.

An appearance of bias may be an inadvertent consequence of the exercise of the amendment powers referenced in s. 34(2), particularly when that power is exercised or referenced unilaterally the Justice of the Peace. Restraint should be exercised in the use of the amendment powers particularly when the Justice of the Peace, absent a motion by the prosecution, is acting on his or her own initiative. As stated by the Ontario Court of Appeal in *R. v. Winlow*, 2009 ONCA 643, 2009 CarswellOnt 5208, (*sub nom.* York (Regional Municipality) v. Winlow) 99 O.R. (3d) 337, 86 M.V.R. (5th) 171, 265 O.A.C. 326, [2009] O.J. No. 3691 (Ont. C.A.), Justices of the Peace are not encouraged to amend on their own motion. See *R. v. Strati*, 2014 ONCJ 139, 2014 CarswellOnt 3624, [2014] O.J. No. 1413 (Ont. C.J.).

Given the serious professional and punitive consequences of a finding of contempt, the contempt citation process should be used sparingly, if at all: *R. v. Strati*, 2014 ONCJ 139, 2014 CarswellOnt 3624, [2014] O.J. No. 1413 (Ont. C.J.).

Every witness who does not understand the language of the proceedings has a right to the assistance of an interpreter. It was clear from reading a few pages of the evidence of a civilian witness at the *ex parte* trial that he was struggling with English, and it was not clear if he understood all the questions. The witness seemed to have understood some of them, but some of his answers were difficult to follow and the prosecutor had to keep going in and clarifying. It is really unsafe for a court to rely on this type of evidence where an interpreter is clearly needed, and base a conviction on it: *R. v. Demasi*, 2013 CarswellOnt 18133, [2013] O.J. No. 6109 (Ont. C.J.).

In *R. v. Demasi*, 2013 CarswellOnt 18133, [2013] O.J. No. 6109 (Ont. C.J.), at the *ex parte* trial of the defendant who was charged with offences under the *Dog Owners' Liability Act*, statements attributed to the defendant were admitted without a voir dire being held to determine their voluntariness. This included information as to the defendant's identification. This was not one of those circumstances in which an officer has a statutory authority to ask for this information. There should have been a voir dire into the voluntariness of these utterances. Identification is crucial in cases where the defendant is the owner. In addition, where the defendant advised that when his ex-wife returned home the dogs were in the front yard, this was not hearsay but a type of admission, such that voluntariness should have been addressed. There should also have been a voluntariness voir dire into the defendant's admission that the dogs belonged to him. While the justice would have likely found the statements were voluntary had voir dires been done correctly, these were very serious procedural errors and a new trial was required.

The defendant was charged with driving a commercial motor vehicle with no brake lights for which the set fine was $200. However, the set fine indicated on the certificate of offence was $85, which was the set fine for the offence involving a vehicle that is not a commercial motor vehicle. As the set fine was incorrect, it was not complete and regular on its face and ought to have been quashed by the Justice of the Peace. It seemed an unfortunate waste of everyone's time and court resources to require such a simple case with an obvious defect to have to go through two levels of court (first instance and appeal) before the result dictated by law is achieved. It is inappropriate for an officer of the court who is aware that a court is about to make an error by not quashing a certificate of offence that is not complete and regular to fail to bring his/her concern to the court's attention. The party should not be required to lie in the weeds clutching a notice of appeal. There is no downside but rather an upside of eliminating these concerns by permitting a defendant or his/her representative to make a conditional appearance, without thereby being considered to be present, in this narrow and unique situation. To be clear, the very summary nature of default proceedings is not to be altered; rather, this would simply provide an opportunity for one having some knowledge of the particular certificate of offence to point out what might otherwise be overlooked. It would not be a matter for argument, nor would it trigger otherwise inapplicable amending powers. Once so informed, the court would make its determination to convict or quash as the case may be. Any disagreement with that decision would be a matter to be addressed on appeal. See *R. v. Rodrigues*, 2013 ONCJ 719, 2013 CarswellOnt 18477, 62 M.V.R. (6th) 331, [2013] O.J. No. 6041 (Ont. C.J.).

In *R. v. Khalid*, 2014 ONCJ 125, 2014 CarswellOnt 3296, 20 M.P.L.R. (5th) 171, [2014] O.J. No. 1257 (Ont. C.J.), it was held that the trial Justice's interventions and interruptions, while numerous, were all directed to curtailing what he perceived as pursuit of irrelevant matters, a characterization which was borne out on the record. The Provincial Offences Court is a very busy place and like all courts, has limited time and resources. Increasingly, it is required to deal with what might be called nuisance trials or nonsense trials, where there is no real issue on any substantive matter but the proceedings become greatly inflated or prolonged by misinformed or mischievous litigants who pursue irrelevant or manifestly meritless defences, file endless bogus motions alleging (often falsely) petty or irrelevant grievances dressed up as *Charter* violations, and generally treat the court as their playground or their stage on which to play lawyer. It is essential that the court retain the power to deal with these practices with a firm hand. With the benefit of hindsight, it would have been preferable if the trial Justice had simply allowed the defendant to bring out his evidence and then deal with its irrelevance at the end of the case. This would have been less time consuming and disruptive. However, the Justice did not err in taking the approach that was followed as the Justice was entitled to curtail any excursion at all into irrelevant areas and to keep doing so in the face of persistence. If there was any error in doing so, it could have had no effect on the verdict, given the relevant facts were clear, undisputed and un-defendable. A claim of reasonable apprehension of bias cannot be based on conduct and rulings that the trial Justice was entitled to make.

A Justice of the Peace has no jurisdiction to examine a certificate of offence for defects and quash it when the defendant is pleading guilty to an offence: *York (Regional Municipality) v. Datoo*, 2014 CarswellOnt 18598, [2014] O.J. No. 3469 (Ont. S.C.J.).

In *Guelph (City) v. Louws*, 2013 ONSC 7903, 2013 CarswellOnt 17958, [2013] O.J. No. 5861 (Ont. S.C.J.), it was held that the declaration of a mistrial, like the declaration of a stay, should be granted only as a last resort, in the clearest of cases and where no remedy short of that relief will adequately redress the actual harm occasioned. The Justice of the Peace erred in declaring a mistrial rather than ruling on the motion brought before her. The fact that the Justice was of the view that the prosecution had been blindsided by the deliberate absence of the defendant was not ground for declaring a mistrial.

The Traffic Court Commissioner made no definitive findings and agreed to hear submissions when reminded by counsel. A reasonable and informed observer, taking into account the nature of the interaction between the Commissioner and counsel, as well as the submissions subsequently made by counsel and the reasons given by the Commissioner, would not conclude that the Commissioner was partial or had prejudged the case. Rather, a reasonable and informed observer would conclude that the Commissioner, having been reminded of his duty to hear submissions of the parties, did so, and then made a decision based on the evidence and the submissions. See *R. v. Berry*, 2014 ABQB 379, 2014 CarswellAlta 1039, [2014] A.J. No. 675 (Alta. Q.B.).

The prosecutor's comment to the defendant while she was being cross-examined that her opportunity to give evidence was now over, she was now subject to cross-examination, was a total misrepresentation of what cross-examination is. Cross-examination is an opportunity for the person to answer questions given by the other side while still giving evidence. The use of the statement by the prosecutor to cut off an answer was also inappropriate. See *R. v. Shuttleworth*, 2013 ONCJ 749, 2013 CarswellOnt 18654, [2013] O.J. No. 6164 (Ont. C.J.).

In *R. v. Mustakinovski*, 2013 ONCJ 804, 2013 CarswellOnt 18940, [2013] O.J. No. 6397 (Ont. C.J.), at the beginning of the trial the defendant did not mention he was waiting for a lawyer or agent or anyone else, and confirmed that he was ready to proceed when asked by the Justice. He also confirmed that he had read and understood the prosecution materials. It was only during cross-examination that the defendant stated that he had spoken to counsel but when this person did not show up he chose to proceed with the trial. There was no evidence that a lawyer or licensed paralegal had been retained. The Justice of the Peace was right to accept the indication by the defendant that he was ready to proceed to trial, and did not err in failing to cross-examine him or his trial preparation or suggest he apply for another adjournment when there was no basis for such a suggestion and he plainly wanted the matter to proceed.

In most situations where a defendant or an appellant is asked whether they would like an interpreter and they say no, that should be enough to satisfy the informational component of individuals being advised that they have this right and the court should be able to rely on that. There is an additional responsibility on courts if they do not understand submissions that are being presented and if they do not understand what a defendant representing himself is saying. This goes beyond the right to an interpreter. It is simply the obligation to ask questions. Where there are signs that what the appellant was explaining as a defendant was not being understood by the Justice of the Peace, that does not mean he has to provide an interpreter, but the issue does have to be canvassed again, as sometimes even when an individual says that they do not need an interpreter, there are signs of difficulty expressing himself such that the decision-maker has difficulty understanding the submissions. The trial Justice in the instant case also failed to provide a general explanation of the process before the arraignment. This constituted a serious omission and failure to provide meaningful assistance to a self-represented litigant. See *R. v. Bakth*, 2014 CarswellOnt 4868, [2014] O.J. No. 1795 (Ont. C.J.).

In *R. v. Poonia*, 2014 BCSC 1526, 2014 CarswellBC 2393, 69 M.V.R. (6th) 263, [2014] B.C.J. No. 2092 (B.C. S.C.), it was held that while a Judicial Justice of the Peace has some latitude to depart from the procedures that may be customary in criminal trials, evidence still may not be admitted unless the Justice has determined that it is relevant, credible and trustworthy. The procedure of a voluntariness voir dire is specifically designed for that purpose. In the instant case, no voir dire was held, and the Judicial Justice of the Peace did not hear the fresh evidence submitted on appeal as to the defendant being told by the officer at the beginning of their interview that the officer would decide whether to lay charges under the *Criminal Code* or proceed instead under the *Motor Vehicle Act* (B.C.). This is the sort of evidence that the Crown would have been obliged to lead on the voir dire, if one had been held. It would then have been up to the Judicial Justice of the Peace to determine if the words used by the officer constituted an inducement or a threat affecting the voluntariness of the statement. In this case, no voir dire was held, and the Judicial Justice of the Peace never heard this evidence. He therefore had no proper basis for determining whether the statement was voluntary, and accordingly, whether it was reliable. Without holding a voir dire, he could not fulfil his mandate of admitting only evidence that was relevant, credible and trustworthy.

The Justice of the Peace was alive to the nature of the evidence tendered at the defendant's trial for using property zoned residential as a tourist establishment, and was able to distinguish permissible hearsay from what was not. Although much of what the neighbours said about their conversations with the persons who were staying at the properties was hearsay, their observations of the coming and going of people, as well as the time periods that they stayed, were not hearsay. Those observations of what the neighbours saw was direct evidence upon which the trial

Justice could act. Whatever the many visitors to the property may have told the neighbours about where they were from and what they were doing was hearsay, and could not be used as proof of the essential elements of the offence charged. However, this hearsay evidence could only provide context and narrative and provide the grounds for belief by the neighbours that the property was being put to illegal use. See *Kingston (City) v. Patry* (August 9, 2011), Doc. Kingston 090175, 090176, [2011] O.J. No. 6667 (Ont. C.J.).

In *Kingston (City) v. Patry* (August 9, 2011), Doc. Kingston 090175, 090176, [2011] O.J. No. 6667 (Ont. C.J.) at the defendant's trial for using property zoned residential as a tourist establishment, the Justice commented that he preferred to live in a single family house rather than an apartment building. Generally speaking, a judicial officer should refrain from expressing personal preferences or making comments on his personal lifestyle. However, the Justice's comments did not reflect bias or give rise to a reasonable apprehension of bias. A reasonable and right-minded person fully informed of all the circumstances of the case would not come to the conclusion that the Justice would not decide the issue before him fairly. In expressing where he preferred to live, the Justice did not in any way indicate that he was against rental properties or vacation houses. To the contrary, he was in favour of those types of properties so long as they were in compliance with the zoning by-law. Such an expression of preference for his residence could not in way be construed as an expression or demonstration of bias against the defendant.

Before rejecting the range of sentence suggested by the prosecutor and imposing a higher fine, the Justice should have given cogent reasons for doing so and then explained why, in his view, fines within the suggested range would be contrary to the public interest or would otherwise bring the administration of justice into disrepute: *Kingston (City) v. Patry* (August 9, 2011), Doc. Kingston 090175, 090176, [2011] O.J. No. 6667 (Ont. C.J.).

In *Mangov v. Toronto (City)*, 2014 ONCJ 351, 2014 CarswellOnt 10104, [2014] O.J. No. 3477 (Ont. C.J.), at the beginning of the trial, the Justice of the Peace initiated an inquiry about potential resolution, and asked the agent why his client did not want to resolve the case. If there had been any resolution discussions conducted earlier, the Justice should have refrained from making inquiries into it when it was clear the matter was proceeding to trial. The defendant was entitled to an impartial and unbiased adjudicator who could decide the case on the evidence, not one who seemed to assume he was guilty from the beginning. This was exacerbated by the Justice encouraging the defence to speak to the prosecutor about resolution before the start of the trial. A reasonable person hearing these comments would only conclude that the court was predisposed to conviction on speeding trials. There was a substantial apprehension of bias. Subsequently, the Justice curtailed cross-examination of the officer on the laser manual, although there was nothing unfocused or prolix to the questioning. A reasonable person could interpret the court's comments as indicating that the cross-examination regarding his operation of the laser was predetermined in the mind of the Justice as being of no value and a waste of time.

The trial Justice of the Peace refused to allow the defendant to file a copy of the laser manual he received in disclosure as an exhibit at trial. If properly identified and there was a foundation laid for its introduction, the manual could be entered as an exhibit. No rule of evidence required a copy of the manual to be certified as a true copy. It was not necessary to make the manual an exhibit in order for the defendant to have continued cross-examining the officer once the proper foundation had been laid. There is nothing wrong in making portions of the manual an exhibit at trial further to this type of cross-examination; it is often done on consent of the parties, and may be of assistance to the trial Justice to have a written copy to assist him or her in following the testimony of the witness. It is the testimony of the police officer, however, that is the evidence, not the exhibit itself. There is very little gained in making the entire manual an exhibit at trial, even with the consent of the parties, as it contains much that is totally irrelevant. If it is made an independent exhibit, it is incumbent on the Justice to review the whole manual. See *Mangov v. Toronto (City)*, 2014 ONCJ 351, 2014 CarswellOnt 10104, [2014] O.J. No. 3477 (Ont. C.J.).

Likewise, in *R. v. Giorgio*, 2014 ONCJ 372, 2014 CarswellOnt 11249, [2014] O.J. No. 3827 (Ont. C.J.), the Justice interrupted the defendant on his sixth question cross-examining the police officer, and expressed skepticism about his cross-examination, given his lack of expertise about the radar unit. One does not need to be a radar expert to cross-examine the use of a radar unit on the basis of the manufacturer's manual. Non-expert counsel engage in this exercise routinely, and often with great success. Apart from the correctness of the Justice's suggestion, it could dissuade a reasonable lay cross-examiner from persisting in a legitimate area of inquiry, which it did in this case. The defendant's lack of persistence resulted in a less than full examination of what appeared to be the viable means of attacking the Crown's case on the speeding charge, to the defendant's disadvantage. The defendant was unduly restricted in his effort to cross-examine the officer.

The trial Justice accepted the radar manual into evidence as an exhibit, although he expressed skepticism about the relevance of the defendant's cross-examination in this area given his lack of radar unit expertise. The record was clear that its admission by the Justice was not equivalent to its being given any weight by him at the trial. See *R. v. Giorgio*, 2014 ONCJ 372, 2014 CarswellOnt 11249, [2014] O.J. No. 3827 (Ont. C.J.).

In *R. v. Giorgio*, 2014 ONCJ 372, 2014 CarswellOnt 11249, [2014] O.J. No. 3827 (Ont. C.J.), the trial Justice did not believe the defendant's testimony that he monitored his speedometer frequently and did not go over the speed limit. On the second charge of failing to surrender his driver's licence, the defendant stated that he eventually did produce the licence to the officer that day. The Justice of the Peace did not accept the defendant's testimony and was not left in doubt by it. The finding of credibility against the defendant on the speeding charge influenced or was effectively carried over to the Justice's assessment of the conflicting evidence on the other charge. Such a carry-over is permissible. The successful impugning of a witness's credibility in a collateral matter of fact at trial can properly be taken into account in assessing the witness's credibility in the matter of fact at issue.

The Justice of the Peace committed a jurisdictional error by dismissing the charge after a not guilty plea without having a trial. Section 46(1) provides that if the defendant pleads not guilty, as the defendant in this case did, the court *shall* hold a trial. Section 46(3) permits the prosecutor and defendant to examine and cross-examine witnesses at trial. The Justice did not hold a trial or even ask if the prosecutor had evidence to call. He immediately dismissed the charge due to lack of court time. This is not a trial. Neither of the parties was permitted to exercise their right to examine witnesses. When a plea of guilty was entered the Justice of the Peace was required to conduct a trial. That trial would start by asking the prosecutor to call her witness, not by immediately dismissing the charge. In the circumstances, what occurred was a substantial wrong and a miscarriage of justice. The Justice of the Peace proceeded without jurisdiction to dismiss a charge that was validly before the court. Because of his personal preference to avoid being seized with a case, a charge was dismissed. It would be a dangerous precedent to have charges dismissed on that basis, a precedent that should be put to rest at the earliest possible date. See *Brampton (City) v. Singh*, 2014 ONSC 2626, 2014 CarswellOnt 5532, 73 Admin. L.R. (5th) 341, [2014] O.J. No. 2005 (Ont. S.C.J.).

It was further held in *Brampton (City) v. Singh*, 2014 ONSC 2626, 2014 CarswellOnt 5532, 73 Admin. L.R. (5th) 341, [2014] O.J. No. 2005 (Ont. S.C.J.) that the Justice of the Peace erred in refusing the prosecutor's adjournment and compounded that failure by failing to give reasons. While the authority to grant an adjournment is discretionary, it must be exercised judiciously. Judicial discretion, however, is subject to review. Reasons are required so the public knows why a decision was made, the parties understand the decision, and it permits appellate review. Here, no reasons were given, just a refusal to grant the adjournment. Subject to one possible explanation, the public, the parties and the appellate court would be left to speculate why the adjournment application was refused; it was *possible* that the defendant taking a day off work had some impact on the decision. If that were so, an adjournment application should not be refused based solely on the defendant being prejudiced because he took a day off work in the absence of a *Charter* s. 11(b) application *if* that was the motivation for the refusal. It could not be ignored that only 80 days had elapsed since the date that the defendant was charged and there was no indication when the next court date would be. Automatically dismissing an adjournment application on a first trial date 80 days after being charged when the case could not be reached is not determining the adjournment application judiciously.

The decision whether to grant or refuse an adjournment is a matter that lies within the discretion of the trial judge. That discretion will not be interfered with on appeal unless it has been demonstrated that it was exercised injudiciously. The trial Justice in this case was faced with a choice: to grant yet another adjournment and show the administration of justice to be a toothless tiger that is helpless to control its own trial process or to refuse the adjournment and proceed to judgment against a defendant who had had more than ample opportunity to present full answer and defence, but chose to decline by absenting himself. In refusing to grant the adjournment sought by the defendant's son the Justice made the right choice. See *R. v. Choudhry*, 2014 ONCJ 631, 2014 CarswellOnt 16599, [2014] O.J. No. 5642 (Ont. C.J.).

In *York (Regional Municipality) v. Martinez*, 2014 ONSC 6305, 2014 CarswellOnt 15699, [2014] O.J. No. 5277 (Ont. S.C.J.), it was held that the Justice of the Peace quashed the certificate of offence as not being complete and regular on its face in the face of not only compelling but binding authority to the contrary. Once the Superior Court has spoken on an issue, the lower courts are bound to follow these dictates whether they like them or not. This includes the Justices of the Peace of the Province. It is especially so in the context of their extraordinary *ex parte* deliberations exercised under s. 9(2) of the *Provincial Offences Act* where they enjoy ungoverned and unobserved scope to quash the proceedings.

The Justice of the Peace should have asked the defendant whether he had any questions of the officer or submissions to make as to the police officer's notes when the officer asked to use his notes to refresh his memory. The defendant did cross-examine the officer on numerous points, but did not assert that there were any discrepancies between the officer's testimony at trial and the notes disclosed to the defence. The failure to ask the defendant whether he wished to ask questions at that point, or make submissions, did not impact trial fairness as the prosecution provided a proper foundation for the police officer to refer to the notes. See *R. v. Zuccarini*, 2014 ONCJ 571, 2014 CarswellOnt 15457, [2014] O.J. No. 5234 (Ont. C.J.).

In *R. v. Zuccarini*, 2014 ONCJ 571, 2014 CarswellOnt 15457, [2014] O.J. No. 5234 (Ont. C.J.), the defendant had been given notice of the potential amendment to the certificate charging speeding to conform to evidence of speed at trial in the disclosure and on the day of trial by the prosecution. An adjournment was offered to the defendant, which was declined. The trial was also held down for the defendant to consider his position and consult with others, after which the defendant decided to proceed with the trial. The trial Justice found there was no prejudice to the defendant caused by the amendment, and it had no impact on the defendant's defence to the speeding charge. The reasons of the trial Justice demonstrated that he considered and applied the test with respect to granting amendments. There was no evidence of legal error or miscarriage of justice.

There was common ground among the parties that there is a duty of disclosure in trials conducted under Part I of the *Provincial Offences Act*, and that an unrepresented accused must be informed of his right to disclosure. It was also conceded by the City that as a self-represented litigant, the defendant was not adequately informed of his right to disclosure and that significant evidence, in the form of a video recording, has now been lost. On the basis of those concessions the appeal was allowed and an acquittal entered. Given this order, it was unnecessary to consider issues, including constitutional issues, regarding the method and timing of providing notice of the right to disclosure to unrepresented litigants in trials under Part I. It was also unnecessary to consider the nature of the assistance required to be provided by Justices of the Peace to unrepresented litigants in such trials. See *R. v. Ul-Rashid*, 2014 ONCA 896, 2014 CarswellOnt 18386, 70 M.V.R. (6th) 181 (Ont. C.A.).

In *R. v. King*, 2014 ONCJ 695, 2014 CarswellOnt 18016, [2014] O.J. No. 6140 (Ont. C.J.), it was held that the Justice of the Peace was entitled to refuse the defendant's representative from acting as an agent at the defendant's first trial date after the agent indicated there was no plea and that he was looking for an answer to a number of writs he filed, as well as that he was not defending anyone but looking for an answer to his writs. However, it was wrong then to simply treat the case as if the defendant failed to appear for his trial and was deemed to not wish to dispute the charge after having been issued a notice of the time and place for trial. Essentially, the defendant did wish to dispute the charge and attempted to appear through his agent but that agent was disqualified by the court from acting. In such circumstances, fairness dictates that the trial be adjourned so that the defendant could attend personally or through another agent. The Justice of the Peace should have treated the matter no differently from a case where a defendant sent an unknowledgeable and ill-instructed family member as an agent. The defendant should not suffer the consequences of any ill-advised conduct of the agent that resulted in the agent's disqualification.

One of the important steps in any process is the right to make submissions. Where that was not afforded to the defendant's legal representative, a new trial must be ordered: *R. v. Al-Kerwi*, 2015 CarswellOnt 2299, [2015] O.J. No. 769 (Ont. C.J.).

It is not up to the defence to make a request for disclosure more than once. They did not need to bring a motion for production as they were led to believe by the prosecutor the disclosure they had requested was not available. It was only after hearing the testimony of the officer did they realize there had been a lack of follow-up on their request for disclosure. They were entitled to raise the issue of lack of disclosure at that time. However, the defendant's counsel should have brought a non-disclosure application rather than a motion to dismiss the charge. The remedy for non-disclosure is not to dismiss a charge but rather to stay the charge. The Justice of the Peace was in error when she granted a dismissal rather than a stay, however, her logic and reasons for doing so were not a palpable and overriding error. The Justice of the Peace reached the right result but granted an inappropriate remedy. A new trial at this stage would not serve any useful purpose and would cause further inconvenience and expense for the defendant. The order made at trial was set aside and a stay of proceedings entered in lieu of ordering a new trial. See *R. v. Hawdon*, 2014 CarswellOnt 5067 (Ont. C.J.).

A matter is appropriate to be assigned to a Judge instead of a Justice of the Peace where there are issues of significant precedent value, where a constitutional challenge regarding the validity of the legislation is being put forward, where a broader public interest is engaged, or where there are complex legal arguments to be litigated. The mere fact that a *Charter* infringement is raised on the application does not give rise to the exercise of discretion in having the matter heard by a Judge. *Charter* applications are frequently brought in provincial offences matters, and Justices of the Peace have the education, training, and the ability to make decisions with regard to allegations of infringements of rights under the *Charter*. However, in the particular case the trial before a Justice of the Peace would not be efficient or particularly effective. At best, having regard to the issues to be determined, the broader public importance of such a decision, and likelihood of an appeal, the Justice of the Peace would be engaged primarily in hearing evidence, and creating an evidentiary record that would be of some use to a judge of the Ontario Court of Justice on appeal. It would not significantly impact upon the time a judge would have to be scheduled to hear the legal arguments on an appeal: *R. v. Corbiere*, 2015 ONCJ 54, 2015 CarswellOnt 1751, (*sub nom.* R. ex rel. Waterloo (Regional Municipality) v. Corbiere) 328 C.R.R. (2d) 306, [2015] O.J. No. 644 (Ont. C.J.).

In *R. v. Kande*, 2015 ONCJ 131, 2015 CarswellOnt 3595, 76 M.V.R. (6th) 319, [2015] O.J. No. 1246 (Ont. C.J.), it was held that the test to be applied in a trial in absentia is very different from the test to be applied in an application for a non-suit. The test on an application for a non-suit is whether or not there is any evidence upon which a reasonable jury properly instructed could return a verdict of guilty. In answering this question, the presiding justice is not permitted to weigh or consider the quality of the evidence. He is simply to determine if there is "some" evidence upon which the jury "could" convict. That is very different from the test to be applied at the conclusion of a trial in absentia. A defendant who does not appear for his trial is still presumed to be innocent. In the *ex parte* proceedings, the prosecutor must prove the defendant's guilt beyond a reasonable doubt according to the generally applicable evidentiary and procedural rules.

It was further held in *R. v. Kande*, 2015 ONCJ 131, 2015 CarswellOnt 3595, 76 M.V.R. (6th) 319, [2015] O.J. No. 1246 (Ont. C.J.) that a trial is an adversarial process, not an investigative process by the Justice into the charge against the defendant. The prosecutor, counsel and paralegals are primarily responsible for putting their respective cases before the court, and examining and cross-examining witnesses. A Justice may intervene and may ask questions and, in fact, should do so where necessary. There are, however, certain definite limits on that right. A Justice should only intervene and ask questions of a witness to clear up an ambiguity, explore a matter left vague by the witness's answers or ask questions which should have been asked by counsel or agent in order to bring out some relevant matter. Prudence and the resulting judicial restraint must be all the greater where the defendant is a witness. The test for determining whether a trial Justice's interventions have compromised the appearance of trial fairness is an objective one and asks "whether a reasonably minded person who had been present throughout the trial would consider that the defendant has not had a fair trial." The issue is not whether the defendant was, in fact, prejudiced by the interventions, but whether the defendant or a reasonable observer might reasonably consider that the defendant had not had a fair trial. The record must be addressed in its totality and interventions evaluated cumulatively, not as isolated occurrences, from the perspective of a reasonable observer throughout the trial. In the instant case, it was clearly appropriate for the presiding Justice to clarify the situation where the defendant was referring to St. Louis rather than St. Catherines. His other questions, however, appeared to be designed to assist in proving the case against the defendant. The Crown was already represented by a lawyer who was there to present the Crown's case. There was no need for the presiding Justice to assist him in that regard. It could also not be ignored that the defendant might not have chosen to testify at all, thereby exposing himself to cross-examination by the Justice but for the pressure created by the Justice's comments during the non-suit ruling. A reasonably minded person who had been present throughout the trial would consider that the defendant did not have a fair trial.

The defendant completed the Notice of Intention to appear at trial and did not request an interpreter. At trial he did not raise the issue of an interpreter. He went on to conduct the trial in the English language. He asked questions and had the opportunity to present his version of the events. He indicated during the trial that he had a lack of familiarity with legal words. However, this stated lack of familiarity did not impact on the trial. While there was little doubt that a lawyer or paralegal could have conducted a more effective trial, that is not the test. The trial Justice did not run afoul of the guidance from the Supreme Court of Canada in *R. v. Tran*, 1994 CarswellNS 24, 1994 CarswellNS 435, EYB 1994-67408, [1994] 2 S.C.R. 951, 133 N.S.R. (2d) 81, 92 C.C.C. (3d) 218, 32 C.R. (4th) 34, 117 D.L.R. (4th) 7, 380 A.P.R. 81, 23 C.R.R. (2d) 32, 170 N.R. 81, [1994] S.C.J. No. 16 (S.C.C.) assessing the need for interpretation. The Justice did an admirable job of explaining the process and providing guidance throughout the trial. Nothing on the record should have necessarily triggered an inquiry on the part of the trial Justice as to the need for interpreter assistance. See *R. v. Aulakh*, 2015 ONCJ 156, 2015 CarswellOnt 3978, (*sub nom.* Durham (Regional Municipality) v. Aulakh) [2015] O.J. No. 1462 (Ont. C.J.).

The Notice of Trial contained a coloured stamp alerting the recipient that there is disclosure available. A simple request triggers the preparation and provision of disclosure. This disclosure procedure properly balances the obligation to provide disclosure with the reality that there are thousands of ticket offence matters in the Region of Durham. While this procedure strikes a proper balance between the proper administration of disclosure and the rights of a defendant, there are some circumstances where the procedure could potentially impact negatively on the fair trial rights of a defendant. The process is not a balm for circumstances that impact in this manner. What works generally in many circumstances may at times require some flexibility on the part of the court or prosecutor in order to mitigate any negative impact on a fair trial. In this case the defendant did not request disclosure and it was provided on the day of trial. The trial Justice did not canvass whether or not he wished an adjournment to prepare his defence; the defendant did not request an adjournment or request time to consult with an agent or counsel. The provision of disclosure on the trial date is a troubling issue. This is an example where the procedure that works well in general could cause harm to the fair trial interest of a defendant. Where a defendant is provided disclosure on the morning of trial, it would be a more cautious approach for the court to canvass whether the defendant is prepared to proceed and provide guidance on the appropriate remedy, such as an adjournment or recess. The appropriate mindset is a concern for a fair trial — not a fault-finding exercise, that is, the defendant did not request disclosure, therefore, it is his or her fault and there is nothing to be done. In this case, the Justice addressed the issue in an appropriate manner by permitting a recess for the defendant to review the two pages of officer notes related to a highway traffic offence. The defendant was also permitted to speak with the prosecutor and determine what he wished to do. A recess was one available appropriate option. After the recess, the court asked the defendant what he wished to do. He indicated that he wished to have a trial because his side was different. The defendant did not give any indication that he was not in a position to proceed. See *R. v. Aulakh*, 2015 ONCJ 156, 2015 CarswellOnt 3978, (*sub nom.* Durham (Regional Municipality) v. Aulakh) [2015] O.J. No. 1462 (Ont. C.J.).

The word "proceeding" which is not defined in the *Provincial Offences Act* does not mean trial, such that all trials in the Provincial Offences Court must take place within six months of the date of the alleged offence occurring. "Proceeding" in the context of limitations law, means the entire case from the legal process that begins through to final disposition. The "commencement" of a proceeding is the issuance of process, in this case, by the police officer filing the certificate of offence. In this case, the certificate of offence was served on the date of the offence and filed within seven days thereafter, well within the six month limitation period. There was no limitations issue in the case and the Provincial Offences Court was correct to dismiss the applicant's preliminary motion. The proper course for the applicant to challenge the Justice's ruling dismissing his preliminary motion was an appeal to a Provincial Judge in the Ontario Court of Justice, and not by way of extraordinary equitable relief to the Superior Court of Justice. See *Torok v. Ontario*, 2015 ONSC 3100, 2015 CarswellOnt 7080, 336 O.A.C. 17, [2015] O.J. No. 2472 (Ont. Div. Ct.).

In *York (Regional Municipality) v. Lorman*, 2015 ONSC 6486, 2015 CarswellOnt 15914, 46 M.P.L.R. (5th) 153, [2015] O.J. No. 5449 (Ont. S.C.J.), during the course of the arraignment, the Justice of the Peace noted that the certificate of offence had the incorrect municipality. The prosecutor requested that the matter be held down so that he could call evidence from the investigating police officer as to the correct municipality and request an amendment to the certificate of offence. However, on her own volition, the Justice quashed the certificate, notwithstanding that there was no proper motion by the defendant, who was unrepresented, to do so. The spirit and intent of the *Provincial Offences Act*, and prosecutions conducted thereunder, is to ensure that technical objections do not impede a verdict on the merits. The Act sets up a process pursuant to which provincial offences matters can be dealt with in a speedy, efficient and convenient way. In a situation where the defendant appears for trial, the provisions of s. 9(1) governing defective certificates where the defendant does not appear for trial do not apply; where the defendant attends, s. 36 governs what the court must do, namely, it is up to the defendant and not the court to bring a motion to quash. The practice of Justices of the Peace bringing their own motion to quash in these circumstances has been disapproved of by the court. Justices of the Peace, like judges of the Superior Court, are human and may not always like the decision of an appellate court. Fundamentally, however, justices and judges must abide by the decisions of the higher court whether they like it or not. The Justice's decision to quash the certificate of offence where there was no motion by the defendant to do so was a clear error of law. It was clear from her earlier decisions that she knew she did not have the jurisdiction to quash the certificate of offence yet she proceeded to do what she knew she had no jurisdiction to do, and thus challenged the prosecution to appeal. Her decision to proceed in the manner she did reflects not only an error of law that was jurisdictional in nature, but a lack of appreciation of the principle of *stare decisis*. An order of *mandamus* and certiorari quashing the order of the Justice of the Peace was issued.

Although the violation ticket functions as the information in proceedings under the *Offence Act* (B.C.), the type of vehicle or model of vehicle being driven is not an essential element of the offence and is not something that needs to be proven beyond a reasonable doubt on a charge of speeding. See *R. v. Mohammad*, 2015 BCSC 2525, 2015 CarswellBC 3946, [2015] B.C.J. No. 2944 (B.C. S.C.).

In *York (Regional Municipality) v. Sekelyk* (September 22, 2015), Doc. CV-15-123505-00, [2015] O.J. No. 4889 (Ont. S.C.J.), the Justice of the Peace was held to have erred in quashing the certificate of offence on the defendant's guilty plea due to the omission of the municipality. It is the overall philosophy of the *Provincial Offences Act* (Ont.) that technical objections not impede the determination of a verdict on the merits. In other circumstances, the failure of the certificate to identify the municipality would be a material, not technical matter. In the instant case, however, there were full particulars of the time and place of the alleged offence, the nature of the offence, speeding, and the place alleged, together with the immediate circumstances under which the notice and offence occurred. As a result, it could not be said that the failure to have included the name of the municipality could impair the defendant's appreciation of the offence he was alleged to have committed. The justice erred in striking the plea and quashing the certificate, rather the process to amend the certificate should have been allowed to unfold.

The right to be tried within a reasonable period of time includes the right to be sentenced within a reasonable period of time. While justices of the peace are responsible for one of the busiest courts in the province and understandably, on occasion, may, like many judges, need extra time to prepare reasons for sentence, on the facts of this case where there was a joint submission on sentence, one might speculate that the reasons for sentence would be relatively brief and perhaps delivered orally at the time of accepting the plea. A delay in imposing sentence of nine and one-half months was not a prompt sentence and unwarranted in the circumstances. See *York (Regional Municipality) v. Newhook*, 2015 ONSC 6587, 2015 CarswellOnt 16978, [2015] O.J. No. 5766 (Ont. S.C.J.).

It was further held in *York (Regional Municipality) v. Newhook*, 2015 ONSC 6587, 2015 CarswellOnt 16978, [2015] O.J. No. 5766 (Ont. S.C.J.) that the discretion of the court as to whether it will accept or reject the guilty plea is a discretion that has to be exercised judicially. It is not a discretion that can be exercised on an arbitrary whim. In situations where it is evident on the face of the record that the discretion has not been exercised judicially, such a discretion amounts to an error of law. There was no reason in law why the Justice should reject the guilty plea that was being proposed by the prosecutor and the defence. She made no inquiries of the prosecutor or defendant with respect to the reasonableness of the proposed plea. Even if there was some legal basis in law for the Justice to consider the appropriateness of the guilty plea, there was no reason why it should take nearly a year for the court to consider whether the guilty pleas should be accepted. An order for *mandamus* issued directing the Justice to accept a guilty plea to the amended offence and to enter a conviction.

1.2 OFFENCES PROSECUTED UNDER THE POA

- The POA applies to all offences under any provincial statute, including the prosecution of parking, licensing, employment, health, building code, environmental and securities law offences.

- Pursuant to the *Contraventions Act* (Canada), certain federal regulatory offences are also enforced under the POA where the proceedings are commenced by ticket under Part I or II of the POA. The listing of offences is contained in the schedule of offences under the *Contraventions Act* and includes offences under the *Canadian Environmental Protection Act*, the *Canada Shipping Act* and the *Fisheries Act*.

1.3 PROCEDURAL STREAMS

- There are three procedural "streams" for provincial offences: Part I (Minor Offences), Part II (Parking Infractions), Part III (Serious Offences).

- The Prosecutor chooses which stream to follow depending on the seriousness and complexity of the allegations.

1.4 PART I OF THE POA — MINOR OFFENCES

- Most minor offences (including traffic tickets but not parking tickets) are prosecuted by a certificate of offence.
- The maximum fine is $1,000 and there is no imprisonment: section 12(1).

- The defendant must be personally served within 30 days of the alleged offence with either a summons or an offence notice: section 3(3).

- If a summons is served, the defendant must appear in court.

- If an offence notice is served, the defendant may plead:
  - Guilty in writing with full payment of the fine: section 8(1);
  - Guilty "with representations" as to penalty, to be made before a justice: section 7(1);
  - Not guilty and have a trial: section 5(1); or
  - Dispute the charges in writing, if the defendant lives outside a designated jurisdiction where the charges were laid: section 6(1).
- If none of the above is plead within 15 days, or if the defendant fails to appear for trial, he or she is deemed not to dispute the charges and, provided the certificate of offence is complete and regular on its face, the defendant can be convicted in his or her absence: sections 9, 9.1.
- The *Good Government Act, 2009,* S.O. 2009, c. 33, s. 1(18) raised the maximum fine limit for Part I offences to $1,000, effective 15 December 2009. The transition provision set out in new s. 12(1.1) makes it clear that the new fine ceiling of $1,000 applies only to Part I offences committed on or after the Royal Assent date of 15 December 2009 when new s. 12(1) came into force.
- Reg. 950 (Proceedings Commenced by Certificate of Offence) has been amended by O. Reg. 106/11, which was made and filed on 31 March 2011. This regulation revokes a number of sections and forms under Reg. 950. It came into force on 31 March 2012. Pursuant to O. Reg. 108/11, made and filed 31 March 2011, new forms have been provided in respect of Part I and Part II provincial offences proceedings.
- O. Reg. 67/12 (Electronic Documents and Remote Meetings), effective 3 May 2012, has put in place a new method of dealing with remote meetings and sentencing hearings under s. 5.1(2) of the *Provincial Offences Act* which allows the defendant to request a meeting with the prosecutor by sending the offence notice to the court office specified in it. This new regulation allows the meeting to occur by electronic method. A defendant may attend a meeting with the prosecutor by electronic method if the distance between the defendant's residence and the location indicated on the offence notice is greater than the distance indicated on the

offence notice: O. Reg. 67/12, s. 7(1). Similarly, a prosecutor may attend a meeting with the defendant by electronic method if the distance between the prosecutor's office and the location indicated on the offence notice is greater than the distance indicated on the offence notice: O. Reg. 67/12, s. 7(2). If the prosecutor or defendant indicates that he/she will attend the meeting by electronic method, the other person may also attend by electronic method, regardless of the distance between the residence or office location and the location indicated on the offence notice: O. Reg. 67/12, s. 7(4). The distance indicated on the offence notice shall not be greater than 75 kilometres; it may be a shorter distance than 75 kilometres: O. Reg. 67/12, s. 7(3). If an agreement has been reached with the prosecutor after a meeting held under s. 5.1 of the Act, whether the meeting was in person or by electronic method, the appearance to enter a plea and make submissions on sentence may be by electronic method, including audio and telephone conference: O. Reg. 67/12, s. 8. A justice of the peace has the discretion to order the defendant or prosecutor to appear in person if the justice is satisfied that the interests of justice require it: *Provincial Offences Act*, s. 83.1(5).

It was held in *R. v. Jamieson*, 2013 ONCA 760, 2013 CarswellOnt 17714, 118 O.R. (3d) 327, 304 C.C.C. (3d) 64, 53 M.V.R. (6th) 1, 297 C.R.R. (2d) 58, 297 C.R.R. (2d) 243, 313 O.A.C. 313, [2013] O.J. No. 5836 (Ont. C.A.), leave to appeal refused 2014 CarswellOnt 14802, 2014 CarswellOnt 14803 (S.C.C.) that the Notice of Intention to Appear (NIA) option in the offence notice clearly warns a defendant that failing to appear at the trial will result in a conviction. The defendant must exercise the option to appear on the offence notice and deliver it to the court office, so he or she does not retain a copy; but, in order to make an intelligent choice among the options provided, a defendant who chooses the option of appearing must have read, understood and signed the NIA, which includes the warning. If, as in this case, the defendant opts to file a NIA, then, for the purposes of entering a plea and having a trial, a Notice of Trial (NT) containing the time and place of the trial is issued, which contains a second clear warning of the consequences of failing to appear at trial. These *Provincial Offences Act* forms are clear. They fully informed the defendant of the consequences of failing to appear at trial. There is no systemic flaw in the scheme under the Act and particularly, the operation of the failure to appear at trial provision which results in a default conviction due to the defendant's absence. Section 11(d) of the *Charter of Rights* does not impose on the legislature an additional obligation to warn the defendant again of the consequences of failing to appear for trial if the trial is adjourned. The warnings on the NIA and the NT are clear, and there is nothing on the NT that might lead a defendant to assume that any of the conditions for trial are changed by an adjournment, apart from the date and possibly the time of the trial. The warning on the NT does not disappear. The defendant need only listen to what the Justice says when an adjournment is granted about the date and time of the trial; in this case the defendant was given peremptory warnings on more than one occasion that the matter would proceed at the next trial date, whether or not the defendant was present, and that no further adjournments would be granted. It is reasonable to expect that such a defendant would use basic common sense and would understand that the initial warnings regarding the consequences of failing to appear also apply to the future trial date. While the NT might be improved by an additional warning that states that the initial warning also applies if the trial is adjourned and the defendant does not appear on the date and at the time to which the trial is adjourned, it is not constitutionally required.

A Justice of the Peace has no jurisdiction to examine a certificate of offence for defects and quash it when the defendant is pleading guilty to an offence: *York (Regional Municipality) v. Datoo*, 2014 CarswellOnt 18598, [2014] O.J. No. 3469 (Ont. S.C.J.).

If a defendant has a ticket and wants to exercise his/her option within 15 days, the defendant has to exercise this option within 15 days by making delivery, whatever it takes, of the document which exercises such option. It must be emphatically and actively exercised within 15 days. It is not to be extended by those provisions relating to notices to be given or delivered. See *R. v. Hicks*, 2014 ONCJ 468, 2014 CarswellOnt 12621, [2014] O.J. No. 4291 (Ont. C.J.). **Note:** Leave to appeal has been granted in this case: see *R. v. Hicks*, 2014 ONCA 756, 2014 CarswellOnt 15073, [2014] O.J. No. 5174 (Ont. C.A.).

In *R. v. Song*, 2014 BCSC 1502, 2014 CarswellBC 2349, [2014] B.C.J. No. 2054 (B.C. S.C.), it was held that if a person pays a violation ticket, the person is deemed to have pleaded guilty to the alleged contravention. In order to set aside the guilty plea, there must be exceptional circumstances. The onus is on the offender seeking to have the plea set aside to show the guilty plea is invalid and that allowing the plea to stand would result in a miscarriage of justice. The defendant failed to demonstrate that his plea was involuntary or that it was equivocal or uninformed. Neither was there a miscarriage of justice as the defendant failed to show that he had a good defence to the speeding charge.

In *York (Regional Municipality) v. Martinez*, 2014 ONSC 6305, 2014 CarswellOnt 15699, [2014] O.J. No. 5277 (Ont. S.C.J.), it was held that the Justice of the Peace quashed the certificate of offence as not being complete and regular on its face in the face of not only compelling but binding authority to the contrary. Once the Superior

Court has spoken on an issue, the lower courts are bound to follow these dictates whether they like them or not. This includes the Justices of the Peace of the Province. It is especially so in the context of their extraordinary *ex parte* deliberations exercised under s. 9(2) of the *Provincial Offences Act* where they enjoy ungoverned and unobserved scope to quash the proceedings.

There was common ground among the parties that there is a duty of disclosure in trials conducted under Part I of the *Provincial Offences Act*, and that an unrepresented accused must be informed of his right to disclosure. It was also conceded by the City that as a self-represented litigant, the defendant was not adequately informed of his right to disclosure and that significant evidence, in the form of a video recording, has now been lost. On the basis of those concessions the appeal was allowed and an acquittal entered. Given this order, it was unnecessary to consider issues, including constitutional issues, regarding the method and timing of providing notice of the right to disclosure to unrepresented litigants in trials under Part I. It was also unnecessary to consider the nature of the assistance required to be provided by Justices of the Peace to unrepresented litigants in such trials. See *R. v. Ul-Rashid*, 2014 ONCA 896, 2014 CarswellOnt 18386, 70 M.V.R. (6th) 181 (Ont. C.A.).

In *R. v. King*, 2014 ONCJ 695, 2014 CarswellOnt 18016, [2014] O.J. No. 6140 (Ont. C.J.), it was held that the Justice of the Peace was entitled to refuse the defendant's representative from acting as an agent at the defendant's first trial date after the agent indicated there was no plea and that he was looking for an answer to a number of writs he filed, as well as that he was not defending anyone but looking for an answer to his writs. However, it was wrong then to simply treat the case as if the defendant failed to appear for his trial and was deemed to not wish to dispute the charge after having been issued a notice of the time and place for trial. Essentially, the defendant did wish to dispute the charge and attempted to appear through his agent but that agent was disqualified by the court from acting. In such circumstances, fairness dictates that the trial be adjourned so that the defendant could attend personally or through another agent. The Justice of the Peace should have treated the matter no differently from a case where a defendant sent an unknowledgeable and ill-instructed family member as an agent. The defendant should not suffer the consequences of any ill-advised conduct of the agent that resulted in the agent's disqualification.

One of the important steps in any process is the right to make submissions. Where that was not afforded to the defendant's legal representative, a new trial must be ordered: *R. v. Al-Kerwi*, 2015 CarswellOnt 2299, [2015] O.J. No. 769 (Ont. C.J.).

In *R. v. Agasiyants*, 2015 ONCJ 142, 2015 CarswellOnt 3304, [2015] O.J. No. 1214 (Ont. C.J.), it was held that an issue of insufficient or failed jurisdiction may properly be litigated as a ground for appealing a conviction. It was a conviction registered in an Early Resolution Meeting which was the subject of complaint. The recourse to appellate relief is not governed by the manner or forum in which a conviction is registered, but only by the manner in which proceedings are commenced. In this case, proceedings were commenced by a certificate of offence under Part I. The appeal was properly before the court. Although the grounds might suggest that there was no jurisdiction in the Justice of the Peace on the Early Resolution Meeting to enter the conviction, the complaint comes down to one, commonly heard in the Provincial Offences Appeal Court, that the Appellant had no notice of the proceedings in which she was convicted. Her complaint was exacerbated by her assertion that she never requested an early resolution meeting on her request for re-opening. There was an absence of any evidence showing notice to the defendant of the Early Resolution Meeting, directed by the Justice of the Peace on the re-opening application. In the absence of notice as directed to the defendant of a proceeding which directly affected her rights, and given her assertion, uncontested, that she was unaware of the proceeding, the re-opening was not properly constituted and the conviction must be set aside.

The Notice of Trial contained a coloured stamp alerting the recipient that there is disclosure available. A simple request triggers the preparation and provision of disclosure. This disclosure procedure properly balances the obligation to provide disclosure with the reality that there are thousands of ticket offence matters in the Region of Durham. While this procedure strikes a proper balance between the proper administration of disclosure and the rights of a defendant, there are some circumstances where the procedure could potentially impact negatively on the fair trial rights of a defendant. The process is not a balm for circumstances that impact in this manner. What works generally in many circumstances may at times require some flexibility on the part of the court or prosecutor in order to mitigate any negative impact on a fair trial. In this case the defendant did not request disclosure and it was provided on the day of trial. The trial Justice did not canvass whether or not he wished an adjournment to prepare his defence; the defendant did not request an adjournment or request time to consult with an agent or counsel. The provision of disclosure on the trial date is a troubling issue. This is an example where the procedure that works well in general could cause harm to the fair trial interest of a defendant. Where a defendant is provided disclosure on the morning of trial, it would be a more cautious approach for the court to canvass whether the defendant is prepared to proceed and provide guidance on the appropriate remedy, such as an adjournment or recess. The appropriate mindset is a concern for a fair trial — not a fault-finding exercise, that is, the defendant did not request disclosure, therefore, it is his or her fault and there is nothing to be done. In this case, the Justice addressed the issue in an appropriate manner by permitting a recess for the defendant to review the two pages of officer notes related to a highway traffic offence. The defendant was also permitted to speak with the prosecutor and determine what he wished to do. A recess was one available appropriate option. After the recess, the court asked the defendant what he wished to do. He indicated that he wished to have a trial because his side was different. The defendant did not give any indication that he was not in a position to proceed. See *R. v. Aulakh*, 2015 ONCJ 156, 2015 CarswellOnt 3978, (*sub nom.* Durham (Regional Municipality) v. Aulakh) [2015] O.J. No. 1462 (Ont. C.J.).

The Ontario Court of Appeal ruled that the appeal in the *Hicks* decision abated due to the death of the appellant before the appeal could be argued. This appeal involved the interpretation of the offence notice and the calculation of the 15 days to deliver the request for trial form, otherwise a conviction would be entered on the fail to respond docket. The court held that a decision in the matter would have province-wide implications for the validity of convictions under Part I of the *Provincial Offences Act*, but without a better factual record it would not be in the interests of justice to hear the appeal. As a result, the judgment in the court below was stayed: see *R. v. Hicks*, 2016 ONCA 291, 2016 CarswellOnt 5971, [2016] O.J. No. 2061 (Ont. C.A.).

In *R. v. Garwal*, 2016 ONCJ 217, 2016 CarswellOnt 5933, 99 M.V.R. (6th) 151, [2016] O.J. No. 1997 (Ont. C.J.), the defendant was charged with speeding, and following a resolution meeting pleaded guilty to disobeying a sign. The parties jointly submitted that the appropriate sentence was to impose the set fine of $85. The imposition of the set fine was held to be contrary to the public interest or would bring the administration of justice into disrepute as set fines are statutorily reserved for cases that do not go to trial, or where there were mitigating factors. Imposing the set fine would also not respect the legislative intent that proceedings proceed economically and efficiently. A defendant should not have the benefit of both the public cost required to ensure a right to trial as well as a reduced fine after conviction on the day of trial. As the defendant had no record of similar offences, and there were no aggravating factors, imposing a fine of $100 would be sufficiently punitive.

In *R. v. Wei*, 2017 ONCJ 878, 2017 CarswellOnt 20869, [2017] O.J. No. 6785 (Ont. C.J.), the defendant was prosecuted for disobeying a stop sign, commenced by means of a certificate of offence. The disclosure involved the notes of an officer and a video recording. The Part I *Provincial Offences Act* procedure is simplified and the maximum penalty is a $1,000 fine. The set fine for disobey stop sign is $85. In this context, it was appropriate for the justice of the peace to hold the trial down briefly to permit review of disclosure before trial. This practice is not uncommon for Part I provincial offences litigation, and is reasonable in light of the simplified procedure under it.

In *Ontario (Ministry of Labour) v. Nault*, 2018 ONCJ 321, 2018 CarswellOnt 7680, [2018] O.J. No. 2568 (Ont. C.J.), the court noted that in respect of the use of "short-form wording" or "abbreviated wording" to describe a particular regulatory offence, ss. 13(1)(b) and 13(2) of the *Provincial Offences Act* authorize the Lieutenant Governor in Council by regulation to specify a word or expression that can be used on a form, such as on a certificate of offence, to designate that offence, and that the specified word or expression, if used on the form, would be sufficient for all purposes to describe the offence designated by such word or expression. However, those statutory provisions do not require the compulsory use of that prescribed word or expression to describe the offence. In addition, where the regulations do not authorize the use of a word or expression (short-form wording) to describe an offence in a form, then by virtue of s. 13(3) the offence may be described in accordance with s. 25 of the Act. And in the situation where "short-form wording" has not been legally created to describe a particular regulatory offence, s. 25(3) specifically provides that where an offence is identified in a count, but the count fails to set out one or more of the essential elements of the offence, then a reference to the provision creating or defining the offence shall be deemed to incorporate all the essential elements of the offence. The present proceedings had been commenced with a Part I certificate of offence. The charge that had been laid in both of the defendants' certificates was identical and expressed as "worker operate equipment in a manner that may endanger himself or another worker." Under s. 3(2), a provincial offences officer may issue to an accused either an offence notice indicating the set fine for the offence or a summons without a set fine in respect to the Part I certificate of offence. The list of authorized "short-form wordings" for specific regulatory offences are those found and prescribed in O. Reg 950, for which s. 13(2) of the Act has authorized that the use of short-form wordings used in a charge set out in a certificate of offence is sufficient to describe that offence. Consequently, as the defendants were issued a summons setting out the charge in respect to a certificate of offence, then according to s. 5(1) of the regulation, a "short-form wording" may be used on the summons to describe the offence. However, in regard to the offence in question, there was no "short-form wording" that has been legally created to describe the particular charge under any of the *Occupational Health and Safety Act* schedules of charges. As such, where authorized short-form wordings do not exist for a particular regulatory offence, then the wording or expression used to describe the offence in the certificate of offence of "worker operate equipment in a manner that may endanger himself or another worker" has to comply with the requirements of s. 25 of the *Provincial Offences Act*, which sets out the standards for describing and providing the necessary information about the offence that the accused has been charged with committing. In that regard, the defendants had defended themselves at trial in regard to the charge on the basis that they were not actually operating equipment, namely a forklift, as had been specifically expressed in the charge in their respective certificates of offence. Therefore, in fairness to the defendants, and since the doctrine of surplusage did not apply and because no application to amend the charge had been brought by the prosecution, then the defendants' respective charges would be treated as having been particularized by the Ministry of Labour to one of those specific five circumstances set out under the section for which the provision can be contravened by a worker, namely of "operating or using equipment in a manner that may endanger the worker or others."

In *York (Regional Municipality) v. Bouaziz-Caruso*, [2019] O.J. No. 638 (Ont. C.J.), the defence representative had asked for disclosure several weeks before, but by the trial date it had not been handed out. The trial justice denied the adjournment, finding that any suggestion the defendant did not receive the notice of trial in advance was hearsay. The justice held the matter down to permit the trial agent to review disclosure and the defendant present, however she did not attend. Where a second trial date adjournment is denied, it is appropriate for the justice of the peace to hold the trial down briefly to permit the review of disclosure before trial. This practice is not uncommon for Part I litigation, and is reasonable in light of the simplified procedure contemplated under the Act.

On a charge of holding a handheld communication device, the timing of this offence at this particular date and time of day is not an essential element of the certificate of the offence. On the witness stand, the officer testified to the time being 17 minutes different from the time he wrote on the ticket some months early. This difference in time did not affect the officer's vision nor observations of the offence being committed. Weather conditions were not at issue nor did the difference in time materially change or influence the observations nor the preparation of a defence to this charge. In short, there would be no prejudice from adopting one time over the other. See *R. v. Romero*, 2018 ONCJ 892, 2018 CarswellOnt 22011, [2018] O.J. No. 6833 (Ont. C.J.).

In *York (Regional Municipality) v. McGuigan*, 2018 ONCA 1062, 2018 CarswellOnt 22571, [2018] O.J. No. 6916 (Ont. C.A.), the Court of Appeal ruled that trial justice properly ordered the prosecutor to provide disclosure of the testing and operating procedures from the user manual for the device used by the traffic officer to measure the speed of the defendant's vehicle. Even if the justice of the peace had been wrong to order disclosure, the error would not have been jurisdictional in nature. Section 140(1) of the *Provincial Offences Act* confines *certiorari* orders in *POA* matters to situations where an applicant would be entitled to such relief at common law, and for parties to a proceeding, *certiorari* orders are confined to jurisdictional errors. Moreover, *certiorari* should not have been granted in the course of ongoing proceedings. Nor was there a substantial wrong or miscarriage of justice to address, a prerequisite to *certiorari* under s. 141(4) of the Act. Contrary to the application judge's decision, the justice of the peace did not err in making the disclosure order. Where a prosecutor is relying on a speed measuring device to prosecute an offence, it must, on request, disclose the testing and operating procedures set out in the user manual for that device. It is up to the prosecutor to hand such information over on request. The person charged need not bring an application or obtain a court order. This is first party disclosure, not third party disclosure. The charging police force has a corresponding duty to furnish the pertinent passages from the user manual to the prosecutor to enable the prosecutor to discharge its first party disclosure obligations. This is not a crushing administrative task. The disclosure at issue here is not case specific information. The disclosure obligation can therefore be discharged by the prosecutor by posting the relevant content from the user manual online and providing the ticketed driver with the required URL.

1.5 PART II OF THE POA — PARKING INFRACTIONS

- Parking tickets can be proceeded by a certificate of parking infraction.

- Parking infractions are usually created by municipalities, carrying a fixed and relatively minor monetary penalty.
- There are special rules for serving the parking infraction notice: section 15.

- The defendant has two options:

    - Pay the fine out-of-court: section 16.

    - Deliver a notice of intention to appear for trial: sections 17, 17.1.

- If the defendant fails to respond within 15 days, the court may send a notice of impending conviction. If the defendant again fails to respond within 15 days, or fails to appear for trial, provided the certificate of parking infraction is complete and regular on its face, the defendant can be convicted in his or her absence: sections 18, 18.1, 18.2, 18.4.

- Reg. 949 (Parking Infractions) has been amended by O. Reg. 107/11, which was made and filed on 31 March 2011. This regulation revokes a number of sections and forms under Reg. 949. It came into force on 31 March 2012. Pursuant to O. Reg. 108/11, made and filed 31 March 2011, new forms have been provided in respect of Part I and Part II provincial offences proceedings.

In *Toronto (City) v. Braganza* (2011), 91 M.P.L.R. (4th) 276, [2011] O.J. No. 5445, 21 M.V.R. (6th) 104, 2011 ONCJ 657, 2011 CarswellOnt 13681, 250 C.R.R. (2d)

60 (Ont. C.J.), it was held that the discontinuance of the lower voluntary payment does not impact in any way on the set fine. The certificate of parking infraction with the $30 set fine was therefore complete and regular on its face.

The court also observed in this case that the defendant received a parking infraction notice for the offence "park — fail to display receipt in windshield," without any reference to the by-law creating offence. However, if the defendant requests a trial, s. 17(5) requires that the by-law be set out in the notice of trial. The golden rule is that the defendant be reasonably informed of the transaction alleged against him; the obvious fact was that these are parking tickets, the least serious infraction in the system of law enforcement. Given the Supreme Court's approval of the statutory scheme in *R. c. Richard*, REJB 1996-95675, [1996] S.C.J. No. 43, 1996 CarswellNB 465, 1996 CarswellNB 464, 463 A.P.R. 161, 182 N.B.R. (2d) 161, 39 C.R.R. (2d) 219, 140 D.L.R. (4th) 248, 110 C.C.C. (3d) 385, 203 N.R. 8, [1996] 3 S.C.R. 525, 3 C.R. (5th) 1, 23 M.V.R. (3d) 1 (S.C.C.), and the lower constitutional scrutiny for minor regulatory offences with small monetary penalties, it is reasonable to require a defendant to decide whether to request a trial based on the wording in the parking infraction notice of the offence without the by-law number. Section 11(a) of the *Charter of Rights* which requires the defendant to be informed without unreasonable delay of the specific offence was not violated in the circumstances.

Also held in this case was that bilingual signs are not required in Toronto, as held in *R. v. Petruzzo*, [2011] O.J. No. 2203, 2011 ONCA 386, 2011 CarswellOnt 3239, 278 O.A.C. 130, 11 M.V.R. (6th) 201 (Ont. C.A. [In Chambers]). Therefore a defendant who receives a parking ticket in Toronto is precluded from arguing that since neither signs nor parking infraction notices are bilingual, they are void for non-compliance with the *French Language Services Act* and the *Provincial Offences Act*. Reg. 949, s. 8 which governs parking infractions and allows forms under Part II of the *Provincial Offences Act* to be in English, French or both English and French, is a valid regulation which actually promotes the French language by permitting a municipality to use French only forms. There can be no conflict between a regulation in the *Provincial Offences Act* that permits forms to be in English or French and a section in the *French Language Services Act* that permits exemptions. The legislation must be read as a whole, and absent a constitutional right to all services in French in Ontario, or a quasi-constitutional status for the *French Language Services Act*, s. 8 of Reg. 949 is valid.

In *Weisdorf v. The City of Toronto*, 2019 ONSC 692, 2019 CarswellOnt 1087, [2019] O.J. No. 403 (Ont. S.C.J.), it was held the establishment of an administrative penalty system for certain parking tickets in the City of Toronto rather than prosecution under the *Provincial Offences Act* does not violate ss. 7 or 11 of the *Charter of Rights* since the proceeding to enforce a parking ticket under a by-law does not entail genuinely penal consequences. The City has confronted with a situation that using the court system was not working for the prosecution of parking tickets and using a criminal process for parking tickets was straining the administration of justice's ability to address more serious matters that were truly criminal in nature. The City consulted with ratepayers and made a researched and reasoned decision to implement an administrative penalty system rather than continuing to use the disproportionate and ineffective system in the *Provincial Offences Act* to enforce parking ticket penalties. There was candour, frankness and impartiality in the process. There was no arbitrary or unfair conduct or the exercise of power to serve private purposes at the expense of the public interest.

1.6 PART III OF THE POA — SERIOUS OFFENCES

- Serious provincial offences are prosecuted under Part III.

- The maximum fine is $5,000, unless the charging Act allows for a greater penalty or imprisonment: section 61.

- The complainant must swear the truth of the allegations before a justice in a document called "information": section 23.

- If the justice accepts that the complainant has reasonable and probable grounds for believing that the defendant committed an offence, then the justice will endorse the information: section 24.

- The justice must then decide whether to confirm or issue a summons to appear, or whether to issue a warrant for the arrest of the defendant: section 24.

- The defendant must appear in court, if properly served.

Where a consent to the institution of proceedings is required by statute, but is lacking, the statutory authority to issue process under s. 24(1) is not engaged. Satisfaction of a condition precedent to its exercise is lacking: *R. v. Alrifai*, 2008 ONCA 564, 64 M.V.R. (5th) 159, 2008 CarswellOnt 4338, [2008] O.J. No. 2870, (*sub nom.* Alrifai v. Ontario) 235 C.C.C. (3d) 374, 64 M.V.R. (5th) 159 (Ont. C.A.), affirming, 48 M.V.R. (5th) 144, 2007 CarswellOnt 2913, [2007] O.J. No. 1805 (Ont. S.C.J.).

In Vaughan (City) v. Antorisa Investments Ltd., 2010 CarswellOnt 10648, [2010] O.J. No. 3351 (S.C.J.), it was held that when the original information charging the offence is not available, the justice of the peace can rely on a certified copy of the information, under the authority of s. 29 of the *Evidence Act* (Ont.) which allows a court to receive in evidence a certified copy of an official and public document. The certified copy of the information should have been received by the justice of the peace as sufficient evidence that an original information was in existence.

The charge against the defendant is defined by the contents of the information, not the summons. The contents of the summons do not constitute evidence before the court which can be used to contradict the evidence of the police officer in the proceeding as to the time of the subject offence: *R. v. Kahnamoui*, 2010 ONCJ 330, 2010 CarswellOnt 5992, [2010] O.J. No. 3497 (Ont. C.J.).

There is jurisdiction to proceed on a copy of the information where the information had obviously been before the court on previous occasions. Defence counsel had appeared without objection, there was no evidence that it had been destroyed, there was a summons which required the information to have been sworn, and the presumption of regularity applied. See *R. v. Toronto (City)*, 2011 ONCJ 131, 2011 CarswellOnt 2022, [2011] O.J. No. 1293, 58 C.E.L.R. (3d) 300 (Ont. C.J.).

Similarly, in *R. v. Protech Roofing Waterproofing Ltd.*, [2011] O.J. No. 5360, 2011 CarswellOnt 13100, 285 C.C.C. (3d) 55 (Ont. S.C.J.), it was held that s. 21 of the *Provincial Offences Act* states that proceedings are commenced by swearing an information. Nowhere does the Act state the original information must still be in existence for the court to have jurisdiction to deal with a charge. The fact that court endorsements were not present on the photocopy did not detract from the fact that a photocopy of the information was present and available to the court. There was no evidence that the defendant was prejudiced in making full answer and defence; the administration of justice would be brought into disrepute if the court sanctioned the termination of a proceeding due to a procedural irregularity that caused no prejudice to the defendant. An order of mandamus was issued to compel the court to proceed with the charge as contained in the information that was originally sworn.

The court did not lose jurisdiction to try the matter because the original information was lost. Relying on a duplicate information which was sworn was not an error of law, and worked no injustice to the defendant. See *R. v. Fujitec Canada Inc.*, 2013 ONSC 497, 2013 CarswellOnt 1312, [2013] O.J. No. 536 (Ont. S.C.J.).

A person who has laid a private information under Part III of the *Provincial Offences Act* may act as prosecutor and also be a witness at trial: *Strachan v. Szewcyk*, 2013 ONCJ 402, 2013 CarswellOnt 10266, [2013] O.J. No. 3445 (Ont. C.J.).

In *R. v. De Boerr*, 2013 ONSC 2988, 2013 CarswellOnt 6324, 10 M.P.L.R. (5th) 336, [2013] O.J. No. 2268 (Ont. S.C.J.), it was held that the illegibility of the signatures in the summons issued under the *Provincial Offences Act* did not render them invalid since the presumption of regularity applied. The fact that it was unclear whether a Judge or Justice of the Peace signed the summonses did not affect the applicability of the presumption; a summons may be signed by the holder of either of these judicial offices. In each instance, the summons would be valid.

In *R. v. Rau*, 2013 ONSC 5573, 2013 CarswellOnt 12550, [2013] O.J. No. 4067 (Ont. S.C.J.), an unsuccessful application was brought by the defendant for a stay of proceedings on his charge of failure to stop for police, contrary to the *Highway Traffic Act* (Ont.), pending the provision of funding for his defence so that he could have legal representation. This appeared to be the first time that such an application had been brought for such a funding order in respect of a *Highway Traffic Act* offence. Although there was a real prospect of imprisonment if the defendant was found guilty, the trial faced by him would be relatively brief, the issues discrete, and the minimum sentence of 14 days' imprisonment was far from the most serious range. The defendant had also demonstrated an understanding of the charges, was able to put forward the facts in an understandable and coherent manner, and had shown an ability to participate effectively in a court proceeding; the case was not of sufficient seriousness or complexity that representation by counsel was essential to a fair trial.

In *R. v. Petrecca*, 2013 ONCJ 744, 2013 CarswellOnt 18653, [2013] O.J. No. 6160 (Ont. C.J.), the information charging the defendant with stunt driving by driving in a manner that indicates an intention to cause some or all of the tires to lose traction referenced the section of the *Highway Traffic Act* but not the regulation, and the information omitted the words "while turning". The Justice of the Peace raised the issue of whether the information was improper, proceeded to find that it was, and after refusing to grant an amendment, dismissed the charge. Even if the information was not proper, the Justice of the Peace erred in not granting an amendment. The underlying philosophy of the *Provincial Offences Act* is to ensure that technical objections do not impede the determination of a case on its merits. Counsel for the defendant would certainly have known or ought to have known the case to be met, as was apparent from the fact that the defendant's legal representative did not raise the issue. There would have been no prejudice in granting the amendment.

A s. 22 summons is intended to be an expeditious process to allow the defendant to be summoned to court in answer to an allegation of an offence, the summons being delivered prior to the swearing of the Part III information for that offence. There is a clear presumption in the *Provincial Offences Act* in favour of release pending disposition. A plain language reading of s. 22 shows that it is intended to be a more expeditious process for bringing a defendant to court as long as the officer has, obviously, reasonable and probable grounds to believe that a person has committed an offence, and the officer encountered that person at or near the place of the offence. Section 22 does not create an obligation to serve a particular kind of summons in a certain way; it creates an option, an alternative to a s. 24 summons, a convenience, especially when the presence of reasonable and probable grounds, the officer and the offender all coincide at the scene and the officer is ready at that stage to issue a summons. Section 22 does not require that the issuance of the summons coincide with the formation of grounds. The phrase "at or near" in s. 22 is a descriptor of the offender, not the time or place of service. The section links the finding of the defendant "at or near" the place of the offence to the formation of the reasonable and probable grounds. If they coincide then a s. 22 summons is possible. In the event that the defendant should have been served with a second summons under s. 24, any technical defect in the process would be cured by the broad curative powers under s. 90 of the Act. See *R. v. Quibell*, 2014 ONCJ 312, 2014 CarswellOnt 9236, [2014] O.J. No. 3244 (Ont. C.J.).

In *Tenny v. Ontario*, 2015 ONCA 841, 2015 CarswellOnt 18196, 333 C.C.C. (3d) 173, 344 O.A.C. 1, [2015] O.J. No. 6313 (Ont. C.A.), it was held that section 26(3) of the *Provincial Offences Act* clearly and unambiguously authorizes service of a summons on an individual outside Ontario, and outside Canada.

There is no requirement that a corporate defendant be served at its registered business address. A corporation can be served at "an address held out by it to be its address" according to s. 26(4)(b)(ii). A corporation could have any number of such addresses, if it conducted its business at multiple locations. See *R. v. Weston Iron Design Inc.* (April 7, 2015), Doc. M98/14, [2015] O.J. No. 6131 (Ont. S.C.J.).

In *R. v. Cvokic*, 2017 ONCJ 517, 2017 CarswellOnt 11822, [2017] O.J. No. 3930 (Ont. C.J.), it was held as per s. 21(1) of the *Provincial Offences Act*, the exception to obtain the Attorney General's consent to prosecute is triggered when the Part I or II certificates have been filed. In the defendant's case, the Part I certificate was not filed so there was no required Attorney General consent. In the result, the defendant's Part III charge was valid.

The justice of the peace at the defendant's first appearance in court noted that the date of the offence on the information was a date in the future, and determined that the information was "no good" as a result. It is important to remember that an important goal of the *Provincial Offences Act* is that matters are tried on their merits, hence, the very broad powers of amendment where there is no prejudice to the accused. While the question of whether to amend an information is a question of law, this does not relieve the court from its obligation to proceed properly and in accordance with law to arrive at a decision whether to grant an amendment. Clearly, this information was defective in substance or form. It contained an obvious error which required an amendment. No trial evidence was necessary to ascertain this error. The fact that this was at the first appearance did not oust the court's jurisdiction to consider whether to amend the information. Even if the lack of the officer's signature amounted to a substantive defect, there was jurisdiction for the court to amend the information. There was no opportunity for the Crown to adduce evidence to support the amendment or to make submissions as to why the amendment should be made. This was a fatal error. Clearly, the presiding justice did not conduct the proceeding in accordance with natural justice. In proceeding in this manner, the learned judge exceeded his jurisdiction. Not granting the application for prerogative review would, in the circumstances of the case, result in a substantial wrong to society which expects and is entitled to have these matters heard on the merits unless an amendment is rejected after both parties have an opportunity to deal with and the presiding judge gives full consideration of the matters relevant to an amendment application. See *R. v. Singh*, 2017 ONSC 7593, 2017 CarswellOnt 20895, [2017] O.J. No. 6807 (Ont. S.C.J.), affirmed 2018 ONCA 506, 2018 CarswellOnt 8710, 362 C.C.C. (3d) 161, 28 M.V.R. (7th) 45 (Ont. C.A.).

2

ROLE OF THE JUSTICE, PROSECUTOR AND DEFENCE ADVOCATE

2.1 THE JUSTICE

- The justice may be a Provincial Court Judge, to be addressed as "Your Honour", "His Honour", or "Her Honour". Serious provincial offence cases are decided by a Provincial Court Judge. Prior to their appointment, a Judge must have been a lawyer for at least ten years, and new appointments are recommended by the Judicial Appointments Advisory Committee. A Judge wears a black robe with a red sash across the front.

- The justice may be a Justice of the Peace, to be addressed as "Your Worship", "His Worship", or "Her Worship". Currently, there are no formal requirements for an appointment. If passed, the *Access to Justice Act* would establish minimum qualifications — a university degree or community college diploma, or an equivalency, including life experience, and at least ten years work experience. A Justice of the Peace wears a black robe with a green sash across the front.

- For a list of the names of the Judges and Justices of the Peace in the Ontario Court of Justice, and the regions across the province in which they preside, see the website of the Ontario Court of Justice: *www.ontariocourts.on.ca/ ocj.htm.*

There is no authority which requires a judge to monitor the progress of a Crown's case and notify the Crown of any deficiencies. This is in contrast to the duty placed on a judge to provide some level of assistance to an unrepresented accused, especially with regard to potential *Charter* defences, for which an unrepresented defendant would be unaware. The court went on to observe that subject to some specific admission made on the record, a defendant is free to bring an application for a directed verdict of acquittal at the conclusion of the Crown's case. If the defendant's application succeeds, the case is over; if unsuccessful the defendant will be given the option as to whether or not to call a defence; if the defendant decides not to call any evidence by way of defence, he/she can argue that the Crown has failed to meet its burden to prove an essential element of the case to the requisite degree of proof. Because a defendant may proceed in this fashion however, does not oblige him/her to do so. A failure to bring a motion for a directed verdict is not an admission of any sufficiency in, or lack of sufficiency thereof, in a Crown's case. See *R. v. Herzog*, 2008 ONCJ 72, 2008 CarswellOnt 1090, [2008] O.J. No. 757 (Ont. C.J.).

A trial is a nullity due to non-compliance with s. 45(1) where the defendant is not asked whether he pleaded guilty or not guilty to the offence: *R. v. McLaughlin*, 2011 ONCJ 224, 2011 CarswellOnt 3631, [2011] O.J. No. 2373 (Ont. C.J.).

In the course of a trial, the justice of the peace is required only to permit admissible evidence onto the record. A trial is not a free-for-all. The defendant cannot ask every question that comes to his/her mind, or make any statement he/she wishes. The justice of the peace appropriately controlled the trial process having regard to the rules of evidence, materiality and relevance. She made no error in the trial process. See *R. v. Towers*, [2011] O.J. No. 6206, 2011 CarswellOnt 15393 (Ont. C.J.).

In *R. v. Walls*, 2010 NBQB 69, 2010 CarswellNB 148, 919 A.P.R. 164, 356 N.B.R. (2d) 164 (N.B. Q.B.), it was held that reasoning through disposition is a forbidden method of verdict determination. Absent circumstances in which similar fact evidence is properly admissible to help support a finding of guilt, a trial judge cannot infer that a defendant has committed the alleged offence simply because he has done the same thing on previous occasions in the past. However, that is not to say that the defendant's previous record is not relevant; it is relevant to the trial judge's assessment of his credibility as a witness. There was nothing in the evidence that tended to support a conclusion that the trial judge used the prior record of the defendant for driving a motor vehicle on a highway without a seatbelt for any other reason than credibility assessment on his trial for the same charge. In fact, he carried out a detailed assessment of the credibility of both witnesses. The trial judge's comment about the defendant having a prior record came at the appropriate time in the judgment, in the midst of the credibility assessment process. There was no evidence that it was used to draw an inference that because he had been convicted of the same offence in the past he must have committed the offence in question. The use of the record by the trial judge did not constitute palpable and overriding error.

There is a strong presumption of impartiality on the part of judicial officers. An allegation of reasonable apprehension of bias is a serious one. The apprehension of bias must be a reasonable one, held by reasonable and right minded persons, asking

"What would an informed person, viewing the matter realistically and practically ... conclude?" The fact that the findings made by the trial judge were adverse to the defendant were not indicative of bias. See *R. v. Nichols*, [2012] O.J. No. 179, 2012 ONCJ 24, 2012 CarswellOnt 498 (Ont. C.J.).

The trial justice conducted his own research in concluding that similar cow-share programs were functioning lawfully in large parts of the world. By conducting the proceedings in this manner, the trial justice assumed the multi-faceted role of advocate, witness and judge; he put the appearance of impartiality at risk, if not actually comprising that appearance, which produced a fundamental disconnect between the case presented by counsel and the case constructed by the trial justice. It also created a real risk of inaccurate fact-finding by introducing raw statistical information and forms of opinion on a wide variety of topics, none of which was analyzed or tested in any way: *R. v. Schmidt*, 2011 ONCJ 482, 2011 CarswellOnt 10564, 248 C.R.R. (2d) 91, [2011] O.J. No. 4272 (Ont. C.J.), affirmed 2014 ONCA 188, 2014 CarswellOnt 2796, 119 O.R. (3d) 145, 304 C.R.R. (2d) 126, 318 O.A.C. 53, [2014] O.J. No. 1074 (Ont. C.A.).

In *R. v. Calero*, 2011 CarswellOnt 15428, [2011] O.J. No. 6205 (Ont. C.J.), the appeal court noted that in reviewing the evidence of the police officer, the justice of the peace stated that he was confused as to whether the officer was qualified on the radar device in question. If the justice did have questions he should have directed that the officer be questioned on this point or asked the question. It was absolutely inconsistent for the trial justice to dismiss the matter on the basis that the prosecution had failed to prove the qualifications of the officer operating the speed detection device in view of the previous finding of fact that on a *prima facie* basis he was satisfied the device was operating accurately. This error of law was palpable and overriding; it was contrary to the administration of justice and the interests of the state to allow an acquittal on these facts to stand. The public has considerable investment in the enforcement of the *Highway Traffic Act* and where such matters come before courts there is an expectation that matters will be dealt with fairly, expeditiously and efficiently. A trial should not be likened to a game of "Snakes and Ladders" where traps and snares cause a litigant to tumble off the playing field for reasons totally unexpected and unanticipated. It is the goal of the administration of justice to have trials based upon meritorious defences with both sides being given the opportunity to fully participate by making complete and thorough examinations of witnesses and complete argument.

The defendant should have been provided with full disclosure of the testing procedures in advance of the trial. In addition, the interruption of the cross-examination of the defendant when he was questioning the officer resulted in the conviction being quashed on appeal. See *R. v. Cerisano*, 2012 CarswellOnt 4585, [2012] O.J. No. 1864 (Ont. C.J.).

A trial judge has a duty to assist an unrepresented accused to ensure a fair trial. However, the way in which a trial judge assists a self-represented party is a matter of discretion. As an appeal court, the standard of review is that intervention is required only if the trial judge proceeded on a wrong principle or if a miscarriage of justice resulted. To assess this question, it is necessary to have regard to the nature of the charges and/or the circumstances bearing on the conduct of the trial. The trial judge patiently attempted to ensure that the defendant understood the charges that he and his company faced, the law that was applicable to those charges, the nature of the evidence relevant to them, and the process by which evidence could be received and examination and cross-examination conducted. The trial judge gave the defendant considerable latitude to air grievances and raise issues that were not legally relevant to the charges. Importantly, the trial judge made a considerable effort to bring out evidence that was relevant to whether the Crown had discharged its burden to prove the prohibited acts and whether a basis for a due diligence existed. Given that this was not a criminal proceeding, it was not a fair or plausible suggestion to say that the defendant should have been advised that he had a right not to incriminate himself and a right to remain silent. Having proven the prohibited acts, the onus shifted to the defendants to prove a due diligence defence on a balance of probabilities, and the only prospect of making out a defence required the defendant to testify. See *R. v. Ambrosi*, 2012 BCSC 409, 2012 CarswellBC 783, [2012] B.C.J. No. 554 (B.C. S.C.), reversed 2014 BCCA 325, 2014 CarswellBC 2385, 84 C.E.L.R. (3d) 177, 375 D.L.R. (4th) 396, 360 B.C.A.C. 106, 617 W.A.C. 106, [2014] B.C.J. No. 2099 (B.C. C.A.).

In *R. v. Canadian National Railway*, 2012 ONSC 6620, 2012 CarswellOnt 15070, 5 M.P.L.R. (5th) 277, [2012] O.J. No. 5649 (Ont. S.C.J.), it was held that a justice of the peace has jurisdiction to hear and determine the constitutional validity of a by-law. The Superior Court may grant relief for jurisdictional error in such quasi-criminal proceedings, but not for an error within jurisdiction for which an appeal would lie. There must also be a substantial wrong or miscarriage that has occurred. It remained open to the defendant in this case to appeal the decision of the justice of the peace once the trial concluded.

The defendant was not entitled to disclosure of materials that were in the nature of "same incident complaint" disclosure following his complaints against the officers involved in his arrest who issued him violation tickets for riding a bicycle without a headlight after he was stopped while riding his bicycle home from work along an alley way around midnight. In view of the minor natures of the charges against the defendant, the results of the internal police investigation dismissing his complaints, the public and privacy interests, and in some cases privilege attaching to the records which included compelled statements, the report of the investigator and communications to the Crown or investigators which were sent on a without prejudice basis, the accused's claims for a disclosure order were outweighed. See *R.*

v. Taing, 2011 ABPC 165, 2011 CarswellAlta 2564, 520 A.R. 27, [2011] A.J. No. 611 (Alta. Prov. Ct.).

In *R. v. Smith*, 2012 ONCJ 324, 2012 CarswellOnt 6700, 35 M.V.R. (6th) 163, [2012] O.J. No. 2395 (Ont. C.J.), it was held by the Regional Senior Justice who dismissed an application brought by the prosecutor and defence to assign a provincial judge to hear a provincial offences case rather than a justice of the peace that both judges and justices of the peace have jurisdiction to preside at trials of provincial offences. This includes *Highway Traffic Act* charges of careless driving involving a fatality. It is a long and established practice that trials of provincial offences are assigned to justices of the peace in the ordinary course, with some exceptions; while some provincial statutes give the prosecutor the right to require that a judge be assigned, the *Highway Traffic Act* is not one of them. The Regional Senior Justice has the discretion to decide which judicial officer is to hear a case. There are no rules regarding the exercise of such discretion. The issue is not one of competence, and there is no requirement that a trial be heard by the judicial officer most senior in the hierarchy of those having jurisdiction. Relevant considerations in support of the assignment of a judge include cases where there were issues of significant precedent value, a constitutional challenge to the validity of legislation is being put forward, or a broader public interest was engaged. The fact that a fatality is involved does not mandate trial by a judge rather than a justice of the peace.

Absent a miscarriage of justice or an obvious *Charter* violation, it is not the role of the justice of the peace in provincial offences court to intervene in an *ex parte* trial and speculate on possible technical defences to the charge, nor is it the role of the justice of the peace to play devil's advocate. These courts are busy courts. To require the prosecution to lead evidence on uncontested matters that should be common knowledge to any reasonable person would strangle the administration of justice and bring the provincial offences court to a halt. The overall scheme of the *Provincial Offences Act* and its overriding purpose is intended to be informal and user friendly. The courts hearing *Provincial Offences Act* matters should get to the merits of the charges and not be unduly concerned with legal technicalities or procedural formalities. See *R. v. Mitchell-Carson*, 2006 CarswellOnt 10253, [2006] O.J. No. 5676 (Ont. C.J.).

In *R. v. Huxtable*, 2012 ONCJ 611, 2012 CarswellOnt 12396, [2012] O.J. No. 4583 (Ont. C.J.), it was held that the justice erred in law by accepting proof of ownership of the defendant's motor vehicle through the evidence of the police officer, as opposed to certified documents from the Ministry of Transportation showing that the defendant was the registered owner of the vehicle. While the purpose of the *Provincial Offences Act* is to provide a procedure for the prosecution of provincial offences that reflects the distinction between such offences and criminal offences, the jurisprudence is well settled that the same rules of evidence do apply. In both civil and criminal cases, the best evidence rule has historically been applied when a document is adduced as evidence for the truth of its contents. The rule simply stated is that a party must produce the best evidence that the nature of a case will allow. This means that if the original document is available, it should be produced. If the original has been destroyed or is otherwise unavailable, the contents of the document can be proved by using a copy or other secondary evidence. Photocopies are acceptable if the person who made the copies testifies that they are true copies. The issue in the instant case, however, was not the identity of the driver, in which case production of a driver's licence constitutes an admission which is an exception to the hearsay rule and as such can be used as evidence of the truth of its contents, but rather the identity of the registered owner. The justice of the peace erred when he permitted this fact to be established through the investigating officer's evidence. Such evidence was hearsay and not admissible, and it was not the best evidence.

A trial justice is entitled to exercise a trial management power in the sense of being mindful of the time that the trial proceedings were taking, and those that were following, and limiting the time that could be devoted to opposing an amendment sought by the prosecutor to increase the rate of speed on the certificate of offence. The justice had given the defence representative the opportunity to oppose the amendment, heard his submissions, and ruled that he had been given sufficient time to make his submissions. See *R. v. Kukuy*, 2012 CarswellOnt 14464, [2012] O.J. No. 5310 (Ont. C.J.).

In *R. v. Reid*, 2012 ONCJ 305, 2012 CarswellOnt 6779, 34 M.V.R. (6th) 307, [2012] O.J. No. 2540 (Ont. C.J.), it was held that the defendant's rights under s. 7 of the *Charter of Rights* were violated when he, as an unrepresented accused, at his first drive suspended offence and being deprived of his right to make submissions on sentence was incarcerated for a regulatory offence that he had entered a plea of guilty to in a timely manner, and the justice wholly ignored basic sentencing principles by stating, "I used to give fines. We now impose incarceration." A justice of the peace is required when sentencing someone who is standing before him, to allow that person an opportunity to make submissions. It is a basic tenant of the adversarial system of justice and a denial of that right to be heard, which strikes at the heart of fairness, gives rise to the appearance that the fix is in, that the sentence is pre-determined. As the sentence had already been served by the defendant, nothing short of a stay of proceedings would remove the prejudice caused by the *Charter* violation; any form of further sentence would only perpetuate and enlarge on the s. 7 violation that occurred.

The defendants were the subject of a private prosecution by an environmental advocacy organization involving regulatory charges that stemmed from birds flying into buildings owned by the defendants. An application by the defendants for production of the organization's internal records respecting its co-operation with the prosecutor in the investigation of the defendant was governed by the third party records disclosure regime set out by the Supreme Court of Canada in *R. v. O'Connor* (1995), 1995 CarswellBC 1098, 1995 CarswellBC 1151, EYB 1995-67073, [1995] 4 S.C.R. 411, 103 C.C.C. (3d) 1, 44 C.R. (4th) 1, 130 D.L.R. (4th) 235, [1996] 2 W.W.R. 153, 68 B.C.A.C. 1, 33 C.R.R. (2d) 1, 191 N.R. 1, 112 W.A.C. 1, [1995] S.C.J. No. 98 (S.C.C.) and *R. v. McNeil*, 2009 SCC 3, 2009 CarswellOnt 116, 2009 CarswellOnt 117, [2009] 1 S.C.R. 66, 238 C.C.C. (3d) 353, 62 C.R. (6th) 1, 301 D.L.R. (4th) 1, 383 N.R. 1, 246 O.A.C. 154, [2009] S.C.J. No. 3 (S.C.C.). The mere assertion that such records were likely relevant to credibility and reliability were not sufficient to justify a disclosure order. See *Podolsky v. Cadillac Fairview Corp.*, 2012 ONCJ 545, 2012 CarswellOnt 10874, 112 O.R. (3d) 22, [2012] O.J. No. 4027 (Ont. C.J.).

In *Oshawa (City) v. Carter* (December 21, 2012), Rosenberg J., [2012] O.J. No. 6291 (Ont. C.J.) the officer who conducted an inspection of the defendant's property for compliance with a proper standards order conducted another inspection of the property two days before the trial. The notes were not disclosed as the Crown was unaware of the inspection; the officer's notebook subsequently went missing. However, this notebook did not refer to the subject matter of the proceeding before the court. Given that the trial justice appropriately made an order that the witness could not refer in her testimony to the notes in the missing book, there was virtually no prejudice to the defendant as a result of the failure to disclose the notes.

In *R. v. Marriott*, 2013 CarswellOnt 6496, [2013] O.J. No. 2684 (Ont. C.J.), it was held that the prosecutor of a provincial offences matter has an unfettered discretion to withdraw charges prior to plea. In a case where the prosecutor told the defendant he could leave because he would withdraw charges against him in exchange for his guilty plea, the Justice of the Peace should not have imposed a conviction upon deciding not to permit the charge to be withdrawn. The Justice should have adjourned the matters to facilitate the attendance of the defendant in the future. Convicting a person when the prosecutor has telegraphed that it wishes to discontinue the prosecution amounts to a denial of natural justice.

In *R. v. Lucas*, 2013 CarswellOnt 6515, [2013] O.J. No. 2685 (Ont. C.J.), four minutes after court was scheduled to start and the prosecutor had not appeared despite being paged twice, the Justice of the Peace dismissed all 68 charges on the tier for want of prosecution. The prosecutor filed an affidavit on appeal, indicating that he was outside the courtroom at the time, negotiating with a defendant, immediately went towards the courtroom when he saw the Justice appear, and did not hear his name being called as the pager in the hallway was not working. The prosecutor's affidavit showed an apparent lack of any insight into his own contribution to this deplorable affair; it was if his role in the justice system did not entail certain obligations to the court. One of the prosecutor's duties is to preserve respect for the court. One does not promote such respect by failing to be in attendance when the Justice enters the courtroom. Those in attendance are left with this image of a judicial officer cooling his heels awaiting the arrival of the prosecutor before the machinery of justice can come to life. Had the prosecutor immediately entered the courtroom and then advised the Justice that he required a few more minutes or a recess, it would be routine for judicial officers in these courts to grant such indulgences as provincial offences courts are likely the busiest courts of any courts in the country, bar none. The administration purposely overloads them on the theory that missing witnesses and defendants, illnesses, resolutions, all lead to whittling down the list to a manageable level. The key to making this happen is to give the prosecutor the time and latitude to get a handle on the state of the cases. Every justice of that court is alive to this, and likely none would deny this type of request as it is the most effective way to manage such formidable lists. The Justice in this case was clearly piqued by the prosecutor's absence, which he viewed as wilful, and he likely felt the prosecutor's actions were cumulative. However, it is always an injudicious use of one's discretion to make others suffer the consequences of someone else's actions. Had the Justice instead chosen to dress down the prosecutor in open court, when he did materialize, it was likely warranted. The rocky road taken instead was unacceptable, and led irretrievably to a reversible error of law.

A Justice of the Peace has jurisdiction to dismiss a charge under s. 53 of the prosecutor fails to appear, however there is no jurisdiction for the Justice to "withdraw" a charge. A withdrawal of a charge before a plea is entered is a matter that is solely within the discretion of the prosecutor. The prosecutor's failure to appear in this case was because he misdiarized the court date. See *Strachan v. Szewcyk*, 2013 ONCJ 402, 2013 CarswellOnt 10266, [2013] O.J. No. 3445 (Ont. C.J.).

In *R. v. Bydeley*, 2012 ONCJ 837, 2012 CarswellOnt 17276, [2012] O.J. No. 6407 (Ont. C.J.), it was held that there was no reasonable apprehension of bias on account of alleged collusion between the trial Justice of the Peace and the prosecutor and the police officer because they were "all under the employ of those who have a hand in forming these statutes" under which the defendant was charged with a highway traffic offence. There was no such appearance in the trial, and such a serious allegation should not be made lightly. The judiciary, which includes the presiding Justice of the Peace at trial, is a third branch of government, whose independence is maintained by the appointments process on through the appeals process. That the prosecutor and the police witness are paid by the same municipal government, albeit through different legislated authorities, is of no moment in a consideration of entitlement to fair trial.

The mere fact that the trial Justice of the Peace was not prepared to address all questions put to the court by an unrepresented litigant who claimed that the *Highway Traffic Act* did not apply to him in no way showed collusion or denial of due process. While the role of the court expands to offer assistance in some degree to an unrepresented party, that does not require the court to depart from the position of neutrality which it must maintain. While the court may indeed be obliged to answer questions about process and law, there are definite limitations to that obligation. A review of the trial transcript did not show that the Justice of the Peace failed to discern the proper balance between aiding the defendant, and either descending into irrelevant or partisan exchanges with him. See *R. v. Bydeley*, 2012 ONCJ 837, 2012 CarswellOnt 17276, [2012] O.J. No. 6407 (Ont. C.J.).

In *R. v. Cassista*, 2013 ONCJ 305, 2013 CarswellOnt 7411, [2013] O.J. No. 2560 (Ont. C.J.), it was held that the defendant claimed that he did not receive a fair trial because the trial Justice of the Peace refused to hear his motions which included an application to stay proceedings on the grounds that the motor vehicle laws under which he was charged applied only to corporations and to those who consent to it. Such arguments by defendants who are identified as an "Organized Pseudo-legal Commercial Argument" (OPCA) litigant are entitled to the shortest possible shrift as they are patently without merit and have never been successful in any court; they are arguments that are not fact or case specific and therefore can have no more merit in one case than in another; that is, none. The only hearing that such arguments are entitled to is to have the court read and appreciate the grounds upon which the motion is based. If the motion contains incomprehensible gibberish or discloses patently ridiculous or meritless arguments or raises known OPCA themes, the court is entitled to dismiss the motion or refuse to hear it, without further inquiry, representation or submission.

There was no basis for holding that the self-represented defendant was not competent to represent himself. He did not testify on appeal, and there was no medical evidence or other evidence suggesting he was suffering from any disability or illness which would have precluded him from acting on his own behalf. The defendant was aware that he was entitled to retain counsel, and there were discussions as to retaining counsel on previous court appearances; a date was selected which accommodated counsel but the defendant appeared on the trial date without counsel, and ready to represent himself. The presiding Justice of the Peace provided explanations and directed the defendant to ask questions, and told him he could give his account later on. He gave a very brief but adequate explanation of the procedures involved. There was no miscarriage of justice. See *R. v. Mcwilliams*, 2012 ONCJ 859, 2012 CarswellOnt 17470 (Ont. C.J.).

In *R. v. Alkhawaji*, 2013 NSSC 233, 2013 CarswellNS 544, 332 N.B.R. (2d) 297, 48 M.V.R. (6th) 267, 1052 A.P.R. 297, [2013] N.S.J. No. 380 (N.S. S.C.), having pled guilty to operating a motor vehicle without insurance, the defendant explained that he had previously spoken to his insurance company and advised that he would be unable to make payments for some time, to which he was told that this would not affect the status of his policy. When the Justice of the Peace informed the defendant that his explanation might constitute the defence of due diligence, the prosecutor objected, and the guilty plea proceedings continued. The defendant had no counsel and there was no indication that he was aware he could ask for an adjournment or seek counsel; his first language was not English. The defendant had no meaningful appreciation of what was meant by due diligence or how he could advance such a defence. It was unreasonable and an error of law for the Justice of The Peace to ask the defendant to confirm his guilty plea while he knew that the defendant still did not understand the nature of the guilty plea.

In *R. v. Williams*, 2013 NLTD(G) 103, 2013 CarswellNfld 323, 341 Nfld. & P.E.I.R. 159, 1061 A.P.R. 159, [2013] N.J. No. 299 (N.L. T.D.), the trial judge was held to have acted correctly when he rejected the issue the defendant raised about the lateness of the Crown disclosure. The defendant did not relate the circumstances in which he received the disclosure, which had been sent to him in advance of the trial, and he may not have received it due to his own neglect. If the defendant felt he did not have sufficient time to prepare for trial because he did not receive timely disclosure, he should have brought it to the trial judge's attention when the matter was called and asked him to adjourn the proceedings until he was ready to proceed. The trial judge also acted correctly when he upheld the Crown's objection to the documents that the defendant tries to produce when cross-examining the police officer who stopped him for speeding. The Crown has a right to know what the documents are before halfway through the proceedings so it could inform itself about them, assess their relevance and address any concerns that it might have about them. One of the overarching concerns for a trial judge and one of the main purposes of rules of procedure is to ensure as far as reasonably possible that only relevant evidence is admitted that is probative of the issues raised by the charges. The trial judge achieved the object of the rules when he rejected the documents that the defendant produced from the manufacturer about the calibration of the radar and possibly the tuning forks, which were not served on the Crown with at least 7 days' notice in compliance with s. 28 of the *Canada Evidence Act*.

A recent Ontario case involving an application for a French-language trial and the resulting delay was discussed in *R. v. Byrnes*, 2013 ONCJ 631, 2013 CarswellOnt 16205, 2013 CarswellOnt 16206, 296 C.R.R. (2d) 258, [2013] O.J. No. 5389 (Ont. C.J.), where the defendant immediately requested a French trial by ticking off the box on the Notice of Intention to Appear to indicate his intention and by filing the Notice with the court. However, his request for a French trial was overlooked, and therefore his trial could not proceed on the trial date. While this oversight was an administrative error, this error amounted to a breach of the defendant's language rights. Moreover, the defendant should not have been expected by the trial judge to have required an interpreter. As a French-speaking defendant, he did not require the assistance of an interpreter at his French trial. Perhaps an interpreter would have been necessary to assist any English-speaking witnesses the prosecutor wished to call, but it would be the responsibility of the prosecutor, not the defendant, to make the appropriate arrangements for these witnesses. By indicating on the Notice that he wished to proceed in French, the defendant properly completed the Notice and satisfied all of his obligations on the language issue. The 8-month delay between the date the defendant requested a French trial until the date the trial began amounted to a breach of the defendant's right to have a trial within a reasonable time for two reasons. First, had he requested a trial in English, his matter could have been heard within 5 months; second, no effort was made to immediately secure a date for the French trial, due to his matter being adjourned a further 3 months to a pre-scheduled date for French trials, despite the fact that there were several intervening dates available for English trials. The practice of having only 2 pre-scheduled days set aside each year for French trials in the provincial offences court, one in the Spring and one in the Fall, is problematic from a case management perspective, and unfair because it is unresponsive to the individual requirements of a specific case. The fact that this system appeared to apply only to French-speaking defendants was a clear contravention of s. 16(1) of the Charter and as such, unacceptable. Even if this general process for scheduling French trials was constitutionally sound, the effect of slavishly continuing with the pre-scheduled French dates in the defendant's case, even after the trial had commenced before a specific Justice of the Peace, led to unacceptable delays. The result was that a routine speeding trial was commenced 9 months after the offence date, heard in 6-month instalments over a period of 13 months, and only concluded 22 months after the offence date.

It was also held in *R. v. Byrnes*, 2013 ONCJ 631, 2013 CarswellOnt 16205, 2013 CarswellOnt 16206, 296 C.R.R. (2d) 258, [2013] O.J. No. 5389 (Ont. C.J.), that the defendant did not enter a plea because the Justice of the Peace believed that the Charter application should be heard and decided before the plea was entered. This was incorrect, as the defendant should have been required to enter a plea before the Charter application commenced. If the defendant refused to do so, the court should have deemed his plea to be not guilty, and made this entry on the information. A "best practices" approach would entail having the defendant arraigned prior to hearing the *Charter* application because it is only after arraignment that the Justice of the Peace is formally seized with the matter. Arraignment includes having the charge read, asking the defendant how he pleads, guilty or not guilty, and noting the plea on the information. To do otherwise and commence a *Charter* application prior to arraignment or midway through arraignment and prior to plea being entered, would allow a party who received an unfavourable decision on the *Charter* to request that the trial commence before a different Justice of the Peace since the first one was not seized. If this were to happen, the parties would be able to re-argue the

Charter application since the new Justice of the Peace would not be bound by the original *Charter* decision. This absurd legal outcome and case management headache would be properly prevented by having the plea entered and noted on the information prior to addressing the *Charter* application.

A fine should not be perceived simply as a licensing fee for illegal conduct. Not every strict liability provincial offence is of the same seriousness or poses the same threat to the welfare of the public. Every case will have aggravating and mitigating factors, and a fit sentence should reflect the circumstances surrounding the unlawful conduct and the offender's personal circumstances. Where the prosecutor cites four cases with widely disparate sentences, this hardly establishes an accepted range of sentence but rather demonstrates that the appropriate penalty will be determined by considering all the mitigating and aggravating factors based on the facts of the particular case and the personal circumstances of an offender. Having decided that a fine is an appropriate disposition, the trial judge should only impose a fine that is within the offender's ability to pay, bearing in mind that he may extend the time for payment. It is an error to fail to inquire about a defendant's ability to pay before imposing fines. The failure of the Justice of the Peace to give any reasons explaining the quantum of fines he imposed was an error. See *Real Estate Council of Ontario v. Wang*, 2013 ONCJ 515, 2013 CarswellOnt 13174, [2013] O.J. No. 4294 (Ont. C.J.).

In *Real Estate Council of Ontario v. Wang*, 2013 ONCJ 515, 2013 CarswellOnt 13174, [2013] O.J. No. 4294 (Ont. C.J.), it was further held that when defendants are not represented by counsel or a paralegal, the trial Justice of the Peace must conduct a plea comprehension inquiry to ensure that the pleas were voluntary and informed, and that the facts necessary to establish all of the essential elements of the offences were admitted. When the facts are read in by the prosecutor, the Justice of the Peace must ask the defendants if they agree with the facts as read in. When a defendant pleads guilty but indicates he wants to give an explanation, the Justice must determine whether the defendant is really admitting the facts as alleged.

The person who laid the complaint against the defendants had also sued them in Small Claims Court, and the claim was under appeal in Superior Court. The trial Justice of the Peace was in error in declining to let the defendant cross-examine the complainant on her dealings with the defendant because he did not want to "step on the [Superior Court's] feet". The civil proceedings that were then outstanding should not have prevented the defendant from cross-examining the witness about the facts pertaining to one of the counts. The trial Justice should also have assisted the unrepresented defendant to frame a proper question to elicit the evidence he was seeking, rather than cutting him off when he was questioning the complainant and stating that he was giving evidence rather than asking questions: *Real Estate Council of Ontario v. Wang*, 2013 ONCJ 515, 2013 CarswellOnt 13174, [2013] O.J. No. 4294 (Ont. C.J.).

It was held in *R. v. Jamieson*, 2013 ONCA 760, 2013 CarswellOnt 17714, 118 O.R. (3d) 327, 304 C.C.C. (3d) 64, 53 M.V.R. (6th) 1, 297 C.R.R. (2d) 58, 297 C.R.R. (2d) 243, 313 O.A.C. 313, [2013] O.J. No. 5836 (Ont. C.A.), leave to appeal refused 2014 CarswellOnt 14802, 2014 CarswellOnt 14803 (S.C.C.) that the Notice of Intention to Appear (NIA) option in the offence notice clearly warns a defendant that failing to appear at the trial will result in a conviction. The defendant must exercise the option to appear on the offence notice and deliver it to the court office, so he or she does not retain a copy; but, in order to make an intelligent choice among the options provided, a defendant who chooses the option of appearing must have read, understood and signed the NIA, which includes the warning. If, as in this case, the defendant opts to file a NIA, then, for the purposes of entering a plea and having a trial, a Notice of Trial (NT) containing the time and place of the trial is issued, which contains a second clear warning of the consequences of failing to appear at trial. These *Provincial Offences Act* forms are clear. They fully informed the defendant of the consequences of failing to appear at trial. There is no systemic flaw in the scheme under the Act and particularly, the operation of the failure to appear at trial provision which results in a default conviction due to the defendant's absence. Section 11(d) of the *Charter of Rights* does not impose on the legislature an additional obligation to warn the defendant again of the consequences of failing to appear for trial if the trial is adjourned. The warnings on the NIA and the NT are clear, and there is nothing on the NT that might lead a defendant to assume that any of the conditions for trial are changed by an adjournment, apart from the date and possibly the time of the trial. The warning on the NT does not disappear. The defendant need only listen to what the Justice says when an adjournment is granted about the date and time of the trial; in this case the defendant was given peremptory warnings on more than one occasion that the matter would proceed at the next trial date, whether or not the defendant was present, and that no further adjournments would be granted. It is reasonable to expect that such a defendant would use basic common sense and would understand that the initial warnings regarding the consequences of failing to appear also apply to the future trial date. While the NT might be improved by an additional warning that states that the initial warning also applies if the trial is adjourned and the defendant does not appear on the date and at the time to which the trial is adjourned, it is not constitutionally required.

There is no jurisdiction to impose concurrent fines on sentencing. While a court may impose concurrent custodial sentences for two or more counts, where the sentence is a fine the court must impose separate fines for each count while ensuring that the overall fine is appropriate: *Ontario (Ministry of Labour) v. Flex-N-Gate Canada Co.*, 2014 ONCA 53, 2014 CarswellOnt 673, 119 O.R. (3d) 1, 315 O.A.C. 66, [2014] O.J. No. 261 (Ont. C.A.).

A trial judge is not bound by a joint submission. The imposition of a fit sentence is ultimately the trial judge's responsibility. Trial judges must, however, give considerable weight to joint submissions. A trial judge should not reject joint submissions unless the joint submission is contrary to the public interest and the sentence would bring the administration of justice into disrepute. That standard is applicable regardless of whether a trial judge is inclined to go above or below the sentence proposed in the joint submission. In the instant case, the proposed sentence was definitely not contrary to the public interest, nor could it bring the administration of justice into disrepute. In those circumstances, the decision to undercut the joint submission constituted a reversible error. See *R. v. Pynappels*, 2014 ONCJ 15, 2014 CarswellOnt 334, [2014] O.J. No. 152 (Ont. C.J.).

In *R. v. Farrage*, 2014 ONSC 564, 2014 CarswellOnt 1090, [2014] O.J. No. 448 (Ont. S.C.J.) it was held that the sentencing judge clearly felt that the joint submission for the minimum penalty was manifestly inadequate based on the submissions in support of the guilty plea. The court expressly recognized that a joint submission should not be lightly overridden. Counsel for the defendant proceeded to make further submissions after the court advised that there must be a suspension of driving privileges in addition to the minimum fine. There was no request to hold the matter down or adjourn to another date for further evidence or submissions. There was no error of law and no basis to interfere with the sentence imposed.

In *R. v. Petrecca*, 2013 ONCJ 744, 2013 CarswellOnt 18653, [2013] O.J. No. 6160 (Ont. C.J.), the information charging the defendant with stunt driving by driving in a manner that indicates an intention to cause some or all of the tires to lose traction referenced the section of the *Highway Traffic Act* but not the regulation, and the information omitted the words "while turning". The Justice of the Peace raised the issue of whether the information was improper, proceeded to find that it was, and after refusing to grant an amendment, dismissed the charge. Even if the information was not proper, the Justice of the Peace erred in not granting an amendment. The underlying philosophy of the *Provincial Offences Act* is to ensure that technical objections do not impede the determination of a case on its merits. Counsel for the defendant would certainly have known or ought to have known the case to be met, as was apparent from the fact that the defendant's legal representative did not raise the issue. There would have been no prejudice in granting the amendment.

Given the serious professional and punitive consequences of a finding of contempt, the contempt citation process should be used sparingly, if at all: *R. v. Strati*, 2014 ONCJ 139, 2014 CarswellOnt 3624, [2014] O.J. No. 1413 (Ont. C.J.).

Every witness who does not understand the language of the proceedings has a right to the assistance of an interpreter. It was clear from reading a few pages of the evidence of a civilian witness at the *ex parte* trial that he was struggling with English, and it was not clear if he understood all the questions. The witness seemed to have understood some of them, but some of his answers were difficult to follow and the prosecutor had to keep going in and clarifying. It is really unsafe for a court to rely on this type of evidence where an interpreter is clearly needed, and base a conviction on it: *R. v. Demasi*, 2013 CarswellOnt 18133, [2013] O.J. No. 6109 (Ont. C.J.).

In *R. v. Demasi*, 2013 CarswellOnt 18133, [2013] O.J. No. 6109 (Ont. C.J.), at the *ex parte* trial of the defendant who was charged with offences under the *Dog Owners' Liability Act*, statements attributed to the defendant were admitted without a voir dire being held to determine their voluntariness. This included information as to the defendant's identification. This was not one of those circumstances in which an officer has a statutory authority to ask for this information. There should have been a voir dire into the voluntariness of these utterances. Identification is crucial in cases where the defendant is the owner. In addition, where the defendant advised that when his ex-wife returned home the dogs were in the front yard, this was not hearsay but a type of admission, such that voluntariness should have been addressed. There should also have been a voluntariness voir dire into the defendant's admission that the dogs belonged to him. While the justice would have likely found the statements were voluntary had voir dires been done correctly, these were very serious procedural errors and a new trial was required.

The defendant was charged with driving a commercial motor vehicle with no brake lights for which the set fine was $200. However, the set fine indicated on the certificate of offence was $85, which was the set fine for the offence involving a vehicle that is not a commercial motor vehicle. As the set fine was incorrect, it was not complete and regular on its face and ought to have been quashed by the Justice of the Peace. It seemed an unfortunate waste of everyone's time and court resources to require such a simple case with an obvious defect to have to go through two levels of court (first instance and appeal) before the result dictated by law is achieved. It is inappropriate for an officer of the court who is aware that a court is about to make an error by not quashing a certificate of offence that is not complete and regular to fail to bring his/her concern to the court's attention. The party should not be required to lie in the weeds clutching a notice of appeal. There is no downside but rather an upside of eliminating these concerns by permitting a defendant or his/ her representative to make a conditional appearance, without thereby being considered to be present, in this narrow and unique situation. To be clear, the very summary nature of default proceedings is not to be altered; rather, this would simply provide an opportunity for one having some knowledge of the particular certificate of offence to point out what might otherwise be overlooked. It would not be a matter for argument, nor would it trigger otherwise inapplicable amending powers. Once so informed, the court would make its determination to convict or quash as the case may be. Any disagreement with that decision would be a matter to be addressed on appeal. See *R. v. Rodrigues*, 2013 ONCJ 719, 2013 CarswellOnt 18477, 62 M.V.R. (6th) 331, [2013] O.J. No. 6041 (Ont. C.J.).

In *R. v. Khalid*, 2014 ONCJ 125, 2014 CarswellOnt 3296, 20 M.P.L.R. (5th) 171, [2014] O.J. No. 1257 (Ont. C.J.), it was held that the trial Justice's interventions and interruptions, while numerous, were all directed to curtailing what he perceived as pursuit of irrelevant matters, a characterization which was borne out on the record. The Provincial Offences Court is a very busy place and like all courts, has limited time and resources. Increasingly, it is required to deal with what might be called nuisance trials or nonsense trials, where there is no real issue on any substantive matter but the proceedings become greatly inflated or prolonged by misinformed or mischievous litigants who pursue irrelevant or manifestly meritless defences, file endless bogus motions alleging (often falsely) petty or irrelevant grievances dressed up as *Charter* violations, and generally treat the court as their playground or their stage on which to play lawyer. It is essential that the court retain the power to deal with these practices with a firm hand. With the benefit of hindsight, it would have been preferable if the trial Justice had simply allowed the defendant to bring out his evidence and then deal with its irrelevance at the end of the case. This would have been less time consuming and disruptive. However, the Justice did not err in taking the approach that was followed as the Justice was entitled to curtail any excursion at all into irrelevant areas and to keep doing so in the face of persistence. If there was any error in doing so, it could have had no effect on the verdict, given the relevant facts were clear, undisputed and un-defendable. A claim of reasonable apprehension of bias cannot be based on conduct and rulings that the trial Justice was entitled to make.

A Justice of the Peace has no jurisdiction to examine a certificate of offence for defects and quash it when the defendant is pleading guilty to an offence: *York (Regional Municipality) v. Datoo*, 2014 CarswellOnt 18598, [2014] O.J. No. 3469 (Ont. S.C.J.).

In *R. v. Bou-Saleh*, 2014 BCSC 1099, 2014 CarswellBC 1745, [2014] B.C.J. No. 1251 (B.C. S.C.), it was held that the trial judge conflated determining whether the defence of necessity should be considered with determining whether the Crown had proved its case. The trial judge should have considered whether the defence of necessity had an air of reality without extensively reviewing the defendant's credibility. The trial judge's gatekeeping function at this stage is limited to determining only if the defence can be considered. Once it is determined that the defence has an air of reality, then his credibility should be extensively analysed. The trial judge further erred by expecting the defendant to provide evidence corroborating his own testimony. The trial judge's comment that the defendant failed to call corroborative evidence was tantamount to suggesting there was an onus on him to produce such evidence. An instruction that indicates there is an onus on an accused to provide corroborative evidence of his testimony is an error.

Where the Crown withdraws the charge, there is no jurisdiction for the court to deal with the issue of costs. In any event, taking the case at its highest it would not be appropriate to order costs as this was not a matter of abuse or flagrant impropriety on the part of the police or court: *York (Regional Municipality) v. Perza*, 2014 ONCJ 257, 2014 CarswellOnt 6968, 331 C.R.R. (2d) 222, [2014] O.J. No. 2499 (Ont. C.J.).

If a defendant has a ticket and wants to exercise his/her option within 15 days, the defendant has to exercise this option within 15 days by making delivery, whatever it takes, of the document which exercises such option. It must be emphatically and actively exercised within 15 days. It is not to be extended by those provisions relating to notices to be given or delivered. See *R. v. Hicks*, 2014 ONCJ 468, 2014 CarswellOnt 12621, [2014] O.J. No. 4291 (Ont. C.J.). **Note:** Leave to appeal has been granted in this case: see *R. v. Hicks*, 2014 ONCA 756, 2014 CarswellOnt 15073, [2014] O.J. No. 5174 (Ont. C.A.).

In *R. v. 1676929 Ontario Inc.*, 2014 ONCJ 370, 2014 CarswellOnt 11139, 318 C.R.R. (2d) 93, 28 M.P.L.R. (5th) 124, [2014] O.J. No. 3785 (Ont. C.J.), it was held that a Justice of the Peace presiding at a trial under the *Provincial Offences Act* is a "court of competent jurisdiction" and therefore has the jurisdiction to grant remedial relief pursuant to s. 24(1) of the *Charter of Rights*, but does not have the declaratory power to hold a law constitutionally invalid and of no force and effect. Only a Superior Court Judge has the jurisdiction to formally declare legislation constitutionally invalid.

In *Guelph (City) v. Louws*, 2013 ONSC 7903, 2013 CarswellOnt 17958, [2013] O.J. No. 5861 (Ont. S.C.J.), it was held that the declaration of a mistrial, like the declaration of a stay, should be granted only as a last resort, in the clearest of cases and where no remedy short of that relief will adequately redress the actual harm occasioned. The Justice of the Peace erred in declaring a mistrial rather than ruling on the motion brought before her. The fact that the Justice was of the view that the prosecution had been blindsided by the deliberate absence of the defendant was not ground for declaring a mistrial.

The Traffic Court Commissioner made no definitive findings and agreed to hear submissions when reminded by counsel. A reasonable and informed observer, taking into account the nature of the interaction between the Commissioner and counsel, as well as the submissions subsequently made by counsel and the reasons given by the Commissioner, would not conclude that the Commissioner was partial or had prejudged the case. Rather, a reasonable and informed observer would conclude that the Commissioner, having been reminded of his duty to hear submissions of the parties, did so, and then made a decision based on the evidence and the submissions. See *R. v. Berry*, 2014 ABQB 379, 2014 CarswellAlta 1039, [2014] A.J. No. 675 (Alta. Q.B.).

In *R. v. Shuttleworth*, 2013 ONCJ 749, 2013 CarswellOnt 18654, [2013] O.J. No. 6164 (Ont. C.J.), it was held that the photographs taken by the defendant that showed the same scene as at the time of the offence should have been admissible. The issue was not when the photographs were taken; the issue was whether or not the photographs showed an accurate depiction of the scene at the time that the offence was alleged to have occurred. The defendant should also have been given an opportunity, if she wishes to present those photographs to the police officer and ask him if they depicted the scene accurately as of the date of the alleged offence.

In *R. v. Mustakinovski*, 2013 ONCJ 804, 2013 CarswellOnt 18940, [2013] O.J. No. 6397 (Ont. C.J.), at the beginning of the trial the defendant did not mention he was waiting for a lawyer or agent or anyone else, and confirmed that he was ready to proceed when asked by the Justice. He also confirmed that he had read and understood the prosecution materials. It was only during cross-examination that the defendant stated that he had spoken to counsel but when this person did not show up he chose to proceed with the trial. There was no evidence that a lawyer or licensed paralegal had been retained. The Justice of the Peace was right to accept the indication by the defendant that he was ready to proceed to trial, and did not err in failing to cross-examine him or his trial preparation or suggest he apply for another adjournment when there was no basis for such a suggestion and he plainly wanted the matter to proceed.

In most situations where a defendant or an appellant is asked whether they would like an interpreter and they say no, that should be enough to satisfy the informational component of individuals being advised that they have this right and the Court should be able to rely on that. There is an additional responsibility on courts if they do not understand submissions that are being presented and if they do not understand what a defendant representing himself is saying. This goes beyond the right to an interpreter. It is simply the obligation to ask questions. Where there are signs that what the appellant was explaining as a defendant was not being understood by the Justice of the Peace, that does not mean he has to provide an interpreter, but the issue does have to be canvassed again, as sometimes even when an individual says that they do not need an interpreter, there are signs of difficulty expressing himself such that the decision-maker has difficulty understanding the submissions. The trial Justice in the instant case also failed to provide a general explanation of the process before the arraignment. This constituted a serious omission and failure to provide meaningful assistance to a self-represented litigant. See *R. v. Bakth*, 2014 CarswellOnt 4868, [2014] O.J. No. 1795 (Ont. C.J.).

In *R. v. Poonia*, 2014 BCSC 1526, 2014 CarswellBC 2393, 69 M.V.R. (6th) 263, [2014] B.C.J. No. 2092 (B.C. S.C.), it was held that while a Judicial Justice of the Peace has some latitude to depart from the procedures that may be customary in criminal trials, evidence still may not be admitted unless the Justice has determined that it is relevant, credible and trustworthy. The procedure of a voluntariness voir dire is specifically designed for that purpose. In the instant case, no voir dire was held, and the Judicial Justice of the Peace did not hear the fresh evidence submitted on appeal as to the defendant being told by the officer at the beginning of their interview that the officer would decide whether to lay charges under the *Criminal Code* or proceed instead under the *Motor Vehicle Act* (B.C.). This is the sort of evidence that the Crown would have been obliged to lead on the voir dire, if one had been held. It would then have been up to the Judicial Justice of the Peace to determine if the words used by the officer constituted an inducement or a threat affecting the voluntariness of the statement. In this case, no voir dire was held, and the Judicial Justice of the Peace never heard this evidence. He therefore had no proper basis for determining whether the statement was voluntary, and accordingly, whether it was reliable. Without holding a voir dire, he could not fulfil his mandate of admitting only evidence that was relevant, credible and trustworthy.

The Justice of the Peace was alive to the nature of the evidence tendered at the defendant's trial for using property zoned residential as a tourist establishment, and was able to distinguish permissible hearsay from what was not. Although much of what the neighbours said about their conversations with the persons who were staying at the properties was hearsay, their observations of the coming and going of people, as well as the time periods that they stayed, were not hearsay. Those observations of what the neighbours saw was direct evidence upon which the trial Justice could act. Whatever the many visitors to the property may have told the neighbours about where they were from and what they were doing was hearsay, and could not be used as proof of the essential elements of the offence charged. However, this hearsay evidence could only provide context and narrative and provide the grounds for belief by the neighbours that the property was being put to illegal use. See *Kingston (City) v. Patry* (August 9, 2011), Doc. Kingston 090175, 090176, [2011] O.J. No. 6667 (Ont. C.J.).

In *Kingston (City) v. Patry* (August 9, 2011), Doc. Kingston 090175, 090176, [2011] O.J. No. 6667 (Ont. C.J.) at the defendant's trial for using property zoned residential as a tourist establishment, the Justice commented that he preferred to live in a single family house rather than an apartment building. Generally speaking, a judicial officer should refrain from expressing personal preferences or making comments on his personal lifestyle. However, the Justice's comments did not reflect bias or give rise to a reasonable apprehension of bias. A reasonable and right-minded person fully informed of all the circumstances of the case would not come to the conclusion that the Justice would not decide the issue before him fairly. In expressing where he preferred to live, the Justice did not in any way indicate that he was against rental properties or vacation houses. To the contrary, he was in favour of those types of properties so long as they were in compliance with the zoning by-law. Such an expression of preference for his residence could not in way be construed as an expression or demonstration of bias against the defendant.

Before rejecting the range of sentence suggested by the prosecutor and imposing a higher fine, the Justice should have given cogent reasons for doing so and then explained why in his view, fines within the suggested range would be contrary to the public interest or would otherwise bring the administration of justice into disrepute: *Kingston (City) v. Patry* (August 9, 2011), Doc. Kingston 090175, 090176, [2011] O.J. No. 6667 (Ont. C.J.).

In *Mangov v. Toronto (City)*, 2014 ONCJ 351, 2014 CarswellOnt 10104, [2014] O.J. No. 3477 (Ont. C.J.), at the beginning of the trial, the Justice of the Peace initiated an inquiry about potential resolution, and asked the agent why his client did not want to resolve the case. If there had been any resolution discussions conducted earlier, the Justice should have refrained from making inquiries into it when it was clear the matter was proceeding to trial. The defendant was entitled to an impartial and unbiased adjudicator who could decide the case on the evidence, not one who seemed to assume he was guilty from the beginning. This was exacerbated by the Justice encouraging the defence to speak to the prosecutor about resolution before the start of the trial. A reasonable person hearing these comments would only conclude that the court was predisposed to conviction on speeding trials. There was a substantial apprehension of bias. Subsequently, the Justice curtailed cross-examination of the officer on the laser manual, although there was nothing unfocused or prolix to the questioning. A reasonable person could interpret the court's comments as indicating that the cross-examination regarding his operation of the laser was predetermined in the mind of the Justice as being of no value and a waste of time.

The trial Justice of the Peace refused to allow the defendant to file a copy of the laser manual he received in disclosure as an exhibit at trial. If properly identified and there was a foundation laid for its introduction, the manual could be entered as an exhibit. No rule of evidence required a copy of the manual to be certified as a true copy. It was not necessary to make the manual an exhibit in order for the defendant to have continued cross-examining the officer once the proper foundation had been laid. There is nothing wrong in making portions of the manual an exhibit at trial further to this type of cross-examination; it is often done on consent of the parties, and may be of assistance to the trial Justice to have a written copy to assist him or her in following the testimony of the witness. It is the testimony of the police officer, however, that is the evidence, not the exhibit itself. There is very little gained in making the entire manual an exhibit at trial, even with the consent of the parties, as it contains much that is totally irrelevant. If it is made an independent exhibit, it is incumbent on the Justice to review the whole manual. See *Mangov v. Toronto (City)*, 2014 ONCJ 351, 2014 CarswellOnt 10104, [2014] O.J. No. 3477 (Ont. C.J.).

Likewise, in *R. v. Giorgio*, 2014 ONCJ 372, 2014 CarswellOnt 11249, [2014] O.J. No. 3827 (Ont. C.J.), the Justice interrupted the defendant on his sixth question cross-examining the police officer, and expressed skepticism about his cross-examination, given his lack of expertise about the radar unit. One does not need to be a radar expert to cross-examine the use of a radar unit on the basis of the manufacturer's manual. Non-expert counsel engage in this exercise routinely, and often with great success. Apart from the correctness of the Justice's suggestion, it could dissuade a reasonable lay cross-examiner from persisting in a legitimate area of inquiry, which it did in this case. The defendant's lack of persistence resulted in a less than full examination of what appeared to be the viable means of attacking the Crown's case on the speeding charge, to the defendant's disadvantage. The defendant was unduly restricted in his effort to cross-examine the officer.

The trial Justice accepted the radar manual into evidence as an exhibit, although he expressed skepticism about the relevance of the defendant's cross-examination in this area given his lack of radar unit expertise. The record was clear that its admission by the Justice was not equivalent to its being given any weight by him at the trial. See *R. v. Giorgio*, 2014 ONCJ 372, 2014 CarswellOnt 11249, [2014] O.J. No. 3827 (Ont. C.J.).

In *R. v. Giorgio*, 2014 ONCJ 372, 2014 CarswellOnt 11249, [2014] O.J. No. 3827 (Ont. C.J.), the trial Justice did not believe the defendant's testimony that he monitored his speedometer frequently and did not go over the speed limit. On the second charge of failing to surrender his driver's licence, the defendant stated that he eventually did produce the licence to the officer that day. The Justice of the Peace did not accept the defendant's testimony and was not left in doubt by it. The finding of credibility against the defendant on the speeding charge influenced or was effectively carried over to the Justice's assessment of the conflicting evidence on the other charge. Such a carry-over is permissible. The successful impugning of a witness's credibility in a collateral matter of fact at trial can properly be taken into account in assessing the witness's credibility in the matter of fact at issue.

The Justice of the Peace committed a jurisdictional error by dismissing the charge after a not guilty plea without having a trial. Section 46(1) provides that if the defendant pleads not guilty, as the defendant in this case did, the court *shall* hold a trial. Section 46(3) permits the prosecutor and defendant to examine and cross-examine witnesses at trial. The Justice did not hold a trial or even ask if the prosecutor had evidence to call. He immediately dismissed the charge due to lack of court time. This is not a trial. Neither of the parties was permitted to exercise their right to examine witnesses. When a plea of guilty was entered the Justice of the Peace was required to conduct a trial. That trial would start by asking the prosecutor to call her witness, not by immediately dismissing the charge. In the circumstances, what occurred was a substantial wrong and a miscarriage of justice. The Justice of the Peace proceeded without jurisdiction to dismiss a charge that was validly before the court. Because of his personal preference to avoid being seized with a case, a charge was dismissed. It would be a dangerous precedent to have charges dismissed on that basis, a precedent that should be put to rest at the earliest possible date. See *Brampton (City) v. Singh*, 2014 ONSC 2626, 2014 CarswellOnt 5532, 73 Admin. L.R. (5th) 341, [2014] O.J. No. 2005 (Ont. S.C.J.).

It was further held in *Brampton (City) v. Singh*, 2014 ONSC 2626, 2014 CarswellOnt 5532, 73 Admin. L.R. (5th) 341, [2014] O.J. No. 2005 (Ont. S.C.J.) that the Justice of the Peace erred in refusing the prosecutor's adjournment and compounded that failure by failing to give reasons. While the authority to grant an adjournment is discretionary, it must be exercised judiciously. Judicial discretion, however, is subject to review. Reasons are required so the public knows why a decision was made, the parties understand the decision, and it permits appellate review. Here, no reasons were given, just a refusal to grant the adjournment. Subject to one possible explanation, the public, the parties and the appellate court would be left to speculate why the adjournment application was refused; it was *possible* that the defendant taking a day off work had some impact on the decision. If that were so, an adjournment application should not be refused based solely on the defendant being prejudiced because he took a day off work in the absence of a *Charter* s. 11(b) application *if* that was the motivation for the refusal. It could not be ignored that only 80 days had elapsed since the date that the defendant was charged and there was no indication when the next court date would be. Automatically dismissing an adjournment application on a first trial date 80 days after being charged when the case could not be reached is not determining the adjournment application judiciously.

The decision whether to grant or refuse an adjournment is a matter that lies within the discretion of the trial judge. That discretion will not be interfered with on appeal unless it has been demonstrated that it was exercised injudiciously. The trial Justice in this case was faced with a choice: to grant yet another adjournment and show the administration of justice to be a toothless tiger that is helpless to control its own trial process or to refuse the adjournment and proceed to judgment against a defendant who had had more than ample opportunity to present full answer and defence, but chose to decline by absenting himself. In refusing to grant the adjournment sought by the defendant's son the Justice made the right choice. See *R. v. Choudhry*, 2014 ONCJ 631, 2014 CarswellOnt 16599, [2014] O.J. No. 5642 (Ont. C.J.).

In *York (Regional Municipality) v. Martinez*, 2014 ONSC 6305, 2014 CarswellOnt 15699, [2014] O.J. No. 5277 (Ont. S.C.J.), it was held that the Justice of the Peace quashed the certificate of offence as not being complete and regular on its face in the face of not only compelling but binding authority to the contrary. Once the Superior Court has spoken on an issue, the lower courts are bound to follow these dictates whether they like them or not. This includes the Justices of the Peace of the Province. It is especially so in the context of their extraordinary *ex parte* deliberations exercised under s. 9(2) of the *Provincial Offences Act* where they enjoy ungoverned and unobserved scope to quash the proceedings.

The Justice of the Peace should have asked the defendant whether he had any questions of the officer or submissions to make as to the police officer's notes when the officer asked to use his notes to refresh his memory. The defendant did cross-examine the officer on numerous points, but did not assert that there were any discrepancies between the officer's testimony at trial and the notes disclosed to the defence. The failure to ask the defendant whether he wished to ask questions at that point, or make submissions, did not impact trial fairness as the prosecution provided a proper foundation for the police officer to refer to the notes. See *R. v. Zuccarini*, 2014 ONCJ 571, 2014 CarswellOnt 15457, [2014] O.J. No. 5234 (Ont. C.J.).

In *R. v. Zuccarini*, 2014 ONCJ 571, 2014 CarswellOnt 15457, [2014] O.J. No. 5234 (Ont. C.J.), the defendant had been given notice of the potential amendment to the certificate charging speeding to conform to evidence of speed at trial in the disclosure and on the day of trial by the prosecution. An adjournment was offered to the defendant, which was declined. The trial was also held down for the defendant to consider his position and consult with others, after which the defendant decided to proceed with the trial. The trial Justice found there was no prejudice to the defendant caused by the amendment, and it had no impact on the defendant's defence to the speeding charge. The reasons of the trial Justice demonstrated that he considered and applied the test with respect to granting amendments. There was no evidence of legal error or miscarriage of justice.

In *R. v. Hawdon*, 2014 CarswellOnt 5067 (Ont. C.J.), it was held that it is not up to the defence to make a request for disclosure more than once. Neither was it necessary for the defence to bring a motion for production as they were led to believe by the prosecutor that the disclosure requested was not available. The Justice was entitled to make finding of lack of disclosure once she heard the evidence of the investigating officer. The defence should have brought an application to stay the charge for nondisclosure rather than a motion to dismiss the charge. The Justice should not have dismissed the charge but granted a stay of proceedings due to non-disclosure.

There was common ground among the parties that there is a duty of disclosure in trials conducted under Part I of the *Provincial Offences Act*, and that an unrepresented accused must be informed of his right to disclosure. It was also conceded by the City that as a self-represented litigant, the defendant was not adequately informed of his right to disclosure and that significant evidence, in the form of a video recording, has now been lost. On the basis of those concessions the appeal was allowed and an acquittal entered. Given this order, it was unnecessary to consider issues, including constitutional issues, regarding the method and timing of providing notice of the right to disclosure to unrepresented litigants in trials under Part I. It was also unnecessary to consider the nature of the assistance required to be provided by Justices of the Peace to unrepresented litigants in such trials. See *R. v. Ul-Rashid*, 2014 ONCA 896, 2014 CarswellOnt 18386, 70 M.V.R. (6th) 181 (Ont. C.A.).

In *R. v. King*, 2014 ONCJ 695, 2014 CarswellOnt 18016, [2014] O.J. No. 6140 (Ont. C.J.), it was held that the Justice of the Peace was entitled to refuse the defendant's representative from acting as an agent at the defendant's first trial date after the agent indicated there was no plea and that he was looking for an answer to a number of writs he filed, as well as that he was not defending anyone but looking for an answer to his writs. However, it was wrong then to simply treat the case as if the defendant failed to appear for his trial and was deemed to not wish to dispute the charge after having been issued a notice of the time and place for trial. Essentially, the defendant did wish to dispute the charge and attempted to appear through his agent but that agent was disqualified by the court from acting. In such circumstances, fairness dictates that the trial be adjourned so that the defendant could attend personally or through another agent. The Justice of the Peace should have treated the matter no differently from a case where a defendant sent an unknowledgeable and ill-instructed family member as an agent. The defendant should not suffer the consequences of any ill-advised conduct of the agent that resulted in the agent's disqualification.

One of the important steps in any process is the right to make submissions. Where that was not afforded to the defendant's legal representative, a new trial must be ordered: *R. v. Al-Kerwi*, 2015 CarswellOnt 2299, [2015] O.J. No. 769 (Ont. C.J.).

It is not up to the defence to make a request for disclosure more than once. They did not need to bring a motion for production as they were led to believe by the prosecutor the disclosure they had requested was not available. It was only after hearing the testimony of the officer did they realize there had been a lack of follow-up on their request for disclosure. They were entitled to raise the issue of lack of disclosure at that time. However, the defendant's counsel should have brought a non-disclosure application rather than a motion to dismiss the charge. The remedy for non-disclosure is not to dismiss a charge but rather to stay the charge. The Justice of the Peace was in error when she granted a dismissal rather than a stay, however, her logic and reasons for doing so were not a palpable and overriding error. The Justice of the Peace reached the right result but granted an inappropriate remedy. A new trial at this stage would not serve any useful purpose and would cause further inconvenience and expense for the defendant. The order made at trial was set aside and a stay of proceedings entered in lieu of ordering a new trial. See *R. v. Hawdon*, 2014 CarswellOnt 5067 (Ont. C.J.).

A matter is appropriate to be assigned to a Judge instead of a Justice of the Peace where there are issues of significant precedent value, where a constitutional challenge regarding the validity of the legislation is being put forward, where a broader public interest is engaged, or where there are complex legal arguments to be litigated. The mere fact that a *Charter* infringement is raised on the application does not give rise to the exercise of discretion in having the matter heard by a Judge. *Charter* applications are frequently brought in provincial offences matters, and Justices of the Peace have the education, training, and the ability to make decisions with regard to allegations of infringements of rights under the *Charter*. However, in the particular case the trial before a Justice of the Peace would not be efficient or particularly effective. At best, having regard to the issues to be determined, the broader public importance of such a decision, and likelihood of an appeal, the Justice of the Peace would be engaged primarily in hearing evidence, and creating an evidentiary record that would be of some use to a judge of the Ontario Court of Justice on appeal. It would not significantly impact upon the time a judge would have to be scheduled to hear the legal arguments on an appeal: *R. v. Corbiere*, 2015 ONCJ 54, 2015 CarswellOnt 1751, (*sub nom.* R. ex rel. Waterloo (Regional Municipality) v. Corbiere) 328 C.R.R. (2d) 306, [2015] O.J. No. 644 (Ont. C.J.).

In *R. v. Kande*, 2015 ONCJ 131, 2015 CarswellOnt 3595, 76 M.V.R. (6th) 319, [2015] O.J. No. 1246 (Ont. C.J.), it was held that the test to be applied in a trial in absentia is very different from the test to be applied in an application for a non-suit. The test on an application for a non-suit is whether or not there is any evidence upon which a reasonable jury properly instructed could return a verdict of guilty. In answering this question, the presiding justice is not permitted to weigh or consider the quality of the evidence. He is simply to determine if there is "some" evidence upon which the jury "could" convict. That is very different from the test to be applied at the conclusion of a trial in absentia. A defendant who does not appear for his trial is still presumed to be innocent. In the *ex parte* proceedings, the prosecutor must prove the defendant's guilt beyond a reasonable doubt according to the generally applicable evidentiary and procedural rules.

It was further held in *R. v. Kande*, 2015 ONCJ 131, 2015 CarswellOnt 3595, 76 M.V.R. (6th) 319, [2015] O.J. No. 1246 (Ont. C.J.) that a trial is an adversarial process, not an investigative process by the Justice into the charge against the defendant. The prosecutor, counsel and paralegals are primarily responsible for putting their respective cases before the court, and examining and cross-examining witnesses. A Justice may intervene and may ask questions and, in fact, should do so where necessary. There are, however, certain definite limits on that right. A Justice should only intervene and ask questions of a witness to clear up an ambiguity, explore a matter left vague by the witness's answers or ask questions which should have been asked by counsel or agent in order to bring out some relevant matter. Prudence and the resulting judicial restraint must be all the greater where the defendant is a witness. The test for determining whether a trial Justice's interventions have compromised the appearance of trial fairness is an objective one and asks "whether a reasonably minded person who had been present throughout the trial would consider that the defendant has not had a fair trial." The issue is not whether the defendant was, in fact, prejudiced by the interventions, but whether the defendant or a reasonable observer might reasonably consider that the defendant had not had a fair trial. The record must be addressed in its totality and interventions evaluated cumulatively, not as isolated occurrences, from the perspective of a reasonable observer throughout the trial. In the instant case, it was clearly appropriate for the presiding Justice to clarify the situation where the defendant was referring to St. Louis rather than St. Catherines. His other questions, however, appeared to be designed to assist in proving the case against the defendant. The Crown was already represented by a lawyer who was there to present the Crown's case. There was no need for the presiding Justice to assist him in that regard. It could also not be ignored that the defendant might not have chosen to testify at all, thereby exposing himself to cross-examination by the Justice but for the pressure created by the Justice's comments during the non-suit ruling. A reasonably minded person who had been present throughout the trial would consider that the defendant did not have a fair trial.

The defendant completed the Notice of Intention to appear at trial and did not request an interpreter. At trial he did not raise the issue of an interpreter. He went on to conduct the trial in the English language. He asked questions and had the opportunity to present his version of the events. He indicated during the trial that he had a lack of familiarity with legal words. However, this stated lack of familiarity did not impact on the trial. While there was little doubt that a lawyer or paralegal could have conducted a more effective trial, that is not the test. The trial Justice did not run afoul of the guidance from the Supreme Court of Canada in *R. v. Tran*, 1994 CarswellNS 24, 1994 CarswellNS 435, EYB 1994-67408, [1994] 2 S.C.R. 951, 133

N.S.R. (2d) 81, 92 C.C.C. (3d) 218, 32 C.R. (4th) 34, 117 D.L.R. (4th) 7, 380 A.P.R. 81, 23 C.R.R. (2d) 32, 170 N.R. 81, [1994] S.C.J. No. 16 (S.C.C.) assessing the need for interpretation. The Justice did an admirable job of explaining the process and providing guidance throughout the trial. Nothing on the record should have necessarily triggered an inquiry on the part of the trial Justice as to the need for interpreter assistance. See *R. v. Aulakh*, 2015 ONCJ 156, 2015 CarswellOnt 3978, (*sub nom.* Durham (Regional Municipality) v. Aulakh) [2015] O.J. No. 1462 (Ont. C.J.).

The Notice of Trial contained a coloured stamp alerting the recipient that there is disclosure available. A simple request triggers the preparation and provision of disclosure. This disclosure procedure properly balances the obligation to provide disclosure with the reality that there are thousands of ticket offence matters in the Region of Durham. While this procedure strikes a proper balance between the proper administration of disclosure and the rights of a defendant, there are some circumstances where the procedure could potentially impact negatively on the fair trial rights of a defendant. The process is not a balm for circumstances that impact in this manner. What works generally in many circumstances may at times require some flexibility on the part of the court or prosecutor in order to mitigate any negative impact on a fair trial. In this case the defendant did not request disclosure and it was provided on the day of trial. The trial Justice did not canvass whether or not he wished an adjournment to prepare his defence; the defendant did not request an adjournment or request time to consult with an agent or counsel. The provision of disclosure on the trial date is a troubling issue. This is an example where the procedure that works well in general could cause harm to the fair trial interest of a defendant. Where a defendant is provided disclosure on the morning of trial, it would be a more cautious approach for the court to canvass whether the defendant is prepared to proceed and provide guidance on the appropriate remedy, such as an adjournment or recess. The appropriate mindset is a concern for a fair trial — not a fault-finding exercise, that is, the defendant did not request disclosure, therefore, it is his or her fault and there is nothing to be done. In this case, the Justice addressed the issue in an appropriate manner by permitting a recess for the defendant to review the two pages of officer notes related to a highway traffic offence. The defendant was also permitted to speak with the prosecutor and determine what he wished to do. A recess was one available appropriate option. After the recess, the Court asked the defendant what he wished to do. He indicated that he wished to have a trial because his side was different. The defendant did not give any indication that he was not in a position to proceed. See *R. v. Aulakh*, 2015 ONCJ 156, 2015 CarswellOnt 3978, (*sub nom.* Durham (Regional Municipality) v. Aulakh) [2015] O.J. No. 1462 (Ont. C.J.).

In *R. v. Leung*, 2015 ONCJ 413, 2015 CarswellOnt 11727, [2015] O.J. No. 4118 (Ont. C.J.), it was held that the power to grant an adjournment is a discretionary one, reviewable on appeal if that discretion was not exercised judicially. The conditions required for an adjournment because of absence of a witness are threefold: (a) that the absent witness is material to the case; (b) that the party asking for an adjournment is not guilty of laches or an omission; (c) that there is a reasonable expectation that the witness can attend at the future trial date. The trial Justice did not consider, however, in his rulings whether the adjournment was *bona fides*, the fact that the Crown's case was closed and that no witnesses would be inconvenienced, when the trial could have been completed, the impact of the failure to grant the adjournment, whether the adjournment would have prejudiced the Crown who opposed the adjournment, especially given that the Crown case was completed, and whether the expanded testimony of the officer was properly something that required a rebuttal by the accused in order to make full answer and defence as he was entitled to do. It did not appear that the adjournment request was fairly listened to as the Justice dismissed the adjournment application twice, the first time summarily and then a second time after more submissions. The effect of denying the adjournment was to deny the defendant the opportunity to call a defence, which amounted to a miscarriage of justice.

Although a sentencing judge ordinarily has a discretion to exercise in imposing sentence, the Legislature can limit that discretion or eliminate it altogether. As a result, the Justice of the Peace was without jurisdiction to reduce a fixed fine under the municipal parking by-law. See *Toronto (City) v. Iron Mountain Canada Corp.*, 2015 ONCJ 444, 2015 CarswellOnt 12336, [2015] O.J. No. 4298 (Ont. C.J.).

In *R. v. Kee*, 2013 ONCJ 830, 2013 CarswellOnt 19000, [2013] O.J. No. 6455 (Ont. C.J.), affirmed 2015 ONCA 730, 2015 CarswellOnt 16415, 127 O.R. (3d) 518, 89 M.V.R. (6th) 177, 342 O.A.C. 1 (Ont. C.A.), it was held that the Justice of the Peace erred in imposing the fine without giving the defendant any opportunity to make submissions on this issue. The fine imposed should have proportionality to fines for other like offences.

The failure of the Justice of the Peace to allow an adjournment to allow the defendant to properly present his photographic evidence was an overriding and palpable error. The evidence could clearly have the potential of allowing the trier of fact to come to a different decision in the case. See *R. v. Niu*, 2015 ONCJ 379, 2015 CarswellOnt 10609, [2015] O.J. No. 3757 (Ont. C.J.).

In *R. v. Hughes*, 2015 ABQB 508, 2015 CarswellAlta 1464, [2015] A.J. No. 870 (Alta. Q.B.), it was held that the Traffic Commissioner did not breach any of the defendant's entitlements as a self-represented accused. He provided her with all appropriate information. While he did not allow her to contest the photographs entered through the police witness at the time they were being entered, he did allow her to fully cross-examine the police witness concerning the photos. He did not allow the defendant to put forward the *Police Act*, however, because the issue of jurisdiction had been decided against her, evidence relating to that Act was irrelevant. The Traffic Commissioner did not, as the defendant contended, neglect to finish the trial; rather, he convicted her, sentenced her, and then left the room.

The Justice of the Peace should not have jumped into the arena in an effort to broker or facilitate a resolution of the matter. Rather, he had an obligation to maintain impartiality as the trial Justice. His comments about the prosecutor offering the defendant a plea to a reduced speed were, on their face, suggestive of a bias or lack of even-handedness, even though this was not put forward as a ground of appeal. See *R. v. Abdille*, 2015 CarswellOnt 4299, [2015] O.J. No. 1563 (Ont. C.J.).

In *R. v. Khan*, 2015 ONCJ 221, 2015 CarswellOnt 5975, [2015] O.J. No. 2096 (Ont. C.J.), it was held that an unlicensed paralegal cannot conduct trials or appeals of provincial offences under the supervision of a lawyer licensed by the Law Society of Upper Canada. The conduct of trials or appeals involves providing legal services, which only licensed lawyers and paralegals can do under the *Law Society Act* and the by-laws made under it; these functions cannot be delegated to non-licensees. This does not prevent a friend or family member, however, from attending with a defendant at a trial or an appeal to assist the defendant.

An endorsement that a matter proceed "peremptory" should not be given undue emphasis however, the Justice of the Peace is entitled to control the process in that court and in dealing with limited trial time, trial backlogs, and the necessity to effectively manage the court, she is in the best position to make an assessment whether a trial should proceed. However, it is clear that the judge should make comment on the record of the reasons for denying the adjournment. It is an unwritten rule that every request for an adjournment for purposes of retaining counsel should be granted on the first occasion; it is not clear whether this rule would apply for the purposes of retaining a paralegal since that is a relationship far different than retaining a lawyer. In any event, there was a virtual lack of effort and delay by the defendant in taking steps to retain a paralegal. At best it might be described as an "inquiry" not a "step" to engage a paralegal. The risk of scheduling another trial date and wasting expensive and scarce court resources, having the investigating officer attend, triggering concerns about delay to trial, all hung over the head of the Justice of the Peace as she made her decision. Her reasons conveyed that the accused failed to convey diligence, and the endorsements of the court should be respected. No injustice or miscarriage of justice was endured by the defendant. The defendant had a trial and had no evidence to offer which would assist him. He had no potentially valid defence grounded on the merits. See *R. v. Petrosian*, 2014 CarswellOnt 19053, [2014] O.J. No. 6508 (Ont. C.J.).

In *R. v. Ward*, 2015 ONCJ 369, 2015 CarswellOnt 10460, [2015] O.J. No. 3726 (Ont. C.J.), it was held that the test on a motion for non-suit is "whether there is any evidence upon which a reasonable jury properly instructed could return a verdict of guilty." At this stage the judicial officer presiding over the trial does not weigh or consider the quality of the evidence — but rather he or she simply decides if there is "some" evidence upon which a jury "could" convict. There was no basis to interfere with the decision of the trial Justice dismissing the non-suit motion as clearly there was some evidence establishing the necessary elements of the offence.

A review of the transcript showed that there was a careful consideration by the trial Justice of the poorly-framed arguments of counsel with regard to the *Charter* issue, and an equally careful consideration of the evidence of the one witness at trial. There was no basis for the argument that there was an apprehension of bias on the part of the trial Justice. See *R. v. Baksh*, 2015 ONCJ 235, 2015 CarswellOnt 6482, [2015] O.J. No. 2271 (Ont. C.J.).

In *R. v. Duminuco*, 2015 BCSC 1965, 2015 CarswellBC 3110, [2015] B.C.J. No. 2331 (B.C. S.C.), it was held that the misspelling of the defendant's name on the ticket was of no particular significance in light of the fact that she appeared before the judicial justice of the peace and acknowledged that she was the person charged in the ticket, entered a not guilty plea, proceeded through a hearing, which included evidence from the police officer that the person seated in court was indeed the person who had committed the offence and to whom he had issued the ticket.

When the paralegal was not present for the second scheduled trial date, the Justice of the Peace set the matter down to be heard later in the day, and then forced the trial to proceed in the paralegal's absence. The paralegal should have arranged his absence with the prosecution or should have been there. While the conviction was set aside on appeal, it was not likely to be tolerated a third time; the appeal court expected the prosecutor to flag the issue, and the date would likely be set to proceed whether or not the defendant's representative appears. See *R. v. Sayed-Zada*, 2015 CarswellOnt 15571, [2015] O.J. No. 5265 (Ont. C.J.).

In *R. v. Raza*, 2015 ONCJ 545, 2015 CarswellOnt 15164, [2015] O.J. No. 5183 (Ont. C.J.), it was held that it is only after the prosecution has formally closed its case that a motion for a non-suit can be brought. In this case, the issue on the non-suit motion was whether there was any evidence of identification of the defendant as the driver. Regardless of the ultimate evidentiary value of the testimony of the officer as to identifying the driver by looking at his valid driver's licence, the officer had testified that the defendant was the driver of the car. This was some evidence of identification that would pass the non-suit phase.

In *R. v. Leung*, 2015 BCSC 2044, 2015 CarswellBC 3240, [2015] B.C.J. No. 2418 (B.C. S.C.), it was held that trial judges, including Judicial Justices of the Peace hearing trials for traffic violations under the *Highway Traffic Act*, have an obligation to ensure that self-represented individuals understand not only the procedure to be followed but also the nature of the burden of proof and the elements of the offence. Moreover, convictions ought only to be entered when all the elements of the offence have been made out.

When the prosecution asked for the minimum penalty of $200, the Justice of the Peace stated that she would never impose that amount, prior to hearing anything about the circumstances of the defendant. This position does not reflect the proper role of a Justice in sentencing. A minimum sentence is an expression of governmental policy; the Justice's sentencing discretion does not entitle her to disregard a clear statement of legislative intent. The Justice was required to impose the minimum sentence unless the defendant showed exceptional circumstances that justified relief under s. 59(2) of the *Provincial Offences Act*. See *York (Regional Municipality) v. Dave*, 2015 ONCJ 481, 2015 CarswellOnt 13983, [2015] O.J. No. 4651 (Ont. C.J.).

It was further held in *York (Regional Municipality) v. Dave*, 2015 ONCJ 481, 2015 CarswellOnt 13983, [2015] O.J. No. 4651 (Ont. C.J.) that the warning to the prosecutor that the court would never impose the statutory minimum fine reasonably gave rise to an apprehension of bias. The justice also commented to the prosecutor when he attempted to cite a case that he was not going to be permitted "to take advantage of somebody who is here without counsel." There was nothing in the record that suggested the prosecutor was attempting to gain an advantage by citing a case. Indeed, it was the prosecutor's responsibility to do so. If the defendant needed to see a copy of the case or time to consider the prosecutor's position, that could be accommodated by the presiding justice. The comments of the court in relation to the prosecutor's submissions added to the reasonable apprehension of bias.

In *R. v. Gochko*, 2015 ONCJ 555, 2015 CarswellOnt 15350, [2015] O.J. No. 5213 (Ont. C.J.), the Justice of the Peace was most fair and provided considerable assistance to the defendant. There was nothing wrong or unfair in the trial he had. While the defendant was initially served offence notices, which the officer admitted included the wrong charge, a Part III information was sworn, and the defendant was issued a summons. When the defendant appeared, he attorned to the jurisdiction of the court. He was arraigned at trial on the two counts of the information correctly and without objection. When this issue arose, the Justice made careful inquiries that the defendant was properly prepared to meet the charges he was arraigned on, which the defendant acknowledged he was.

In *York (Regional Municipality) v. Lorman*, 2015 ONSC 6486, 2015 CarswellOnt 15914, 46 M.P.L.R. (5th) 153, [2015] O.J. No. 5449 (Ont. S.C.J.), during the course of the arraignment, the Justice of the Peace noted that the certificate of offence had the incorrect municipality. The prosecutor requested that he matter be held down so that he could call evidence from the investigating police officer as to the correct municipality and request an amendment to the certificate of offence. However, on her own volition, the Justice quashed the certificate, notwithstanding that there was no proper motion by the defendant, who was unrepresented, to do so. The spirit and intent of the *Provincial Offences Act*, and prosecutions conducted thereunder, is to ensure that technical objections do not impede a verdict on the merits. The Act sets up a process pursuant to which provincial offences matters can be dealt with in a speedy, efficient and convenient way. In a situation where the defendant appears for trial, the provisions of s. 9(1) governing defective certificates where the defendant does not appear for trial do not apply; where the defendant attends, s. 36 governs what the court must do, namely, it is up to the defendant and not the court to bring a motion to quash. The practice of Justices of the Peace bringing their own motion to quash in these circumstances has been disapproved of by the court. Justices of the Peace, like judges of the Superior Court, are human and may not always like the decision of an appellate court. Fundamentally, however, justices and judges must abide by the decisions of the higher court whether they like it or not. The Justice's decision to quash the certificate of offence where there was no motion by the defendant to do so was a clear error of law. It was clear from her earlier decisions that she knew she did not have the jurisdiction to quash the certificate of offence yet she proceeded to do what she knew she had no jurisdiction to do, and thus challenged the prosecution to appeal. Her decision to proceed in the manner she did reflects not only an error of law that was jurisdictional in nature, but a lack of appreciation of the principle of *stare decisis*. An order of *mandamus* and certiorari quashing the order of the Justice of the Peace was issued.

The police officer while testifying seemed, on several occasions, to control the cross-examination with little or no intervention on the part of the judge. It was only after numerous examples of such inappropriate conduct that the Crown prosecutor himself felt the need to intervene, but this was too little too late. The police officer's conduct during the cross-examination as well as the almost total lack of reaction on the part of the judge in this regard, when added to the exchanges between the judge himself and the accused, resulted in the appearance of an unfair trial. See *R. c. Robichaud*, 2016 NBBR 26, 2016 NBQB 26, 2016 CarswellNB 45, 2016 CarswellNB 48, (*sub nom. R. v. Robichaud*) 445 N.B.R. (2d) 54, 1166 A.P.R. 54, [2016] A.N.B. No. 30, [2016] N.B.J. No. 30 (N.B. Q.B.).

In *R. v. Gagne* (November 9, 2015), Doc. 14-0672, [2015] O.J. No. 6344 (Ont. S.C.J.), it was held that the Crown has the discretion to pursue through legitimate means a vigorous prosecution, which includes cooperative and effective real-time consultation with police as the prosecution unfolds. Such consultation may include having an investigating officer present at counsel table. However, where the officer was to be a witness at the proceeding, the officer was not permitted to sit at counsel table as an exception to the order excluding witnesses. It was open to the Crown to have the witness testify first and then sit at counsel table after his testimony, or have another instructing officer sit at counsel table.

There was considerable merit to the argument that the court failed to give adequate assistance to the unrepresented accused. He was a commercial truck driver; his first language was not English. In any event it was clear that as he was unrepresented he would need assistance from the Court. That assistance was not forthcoming. Indeed, the court was obstructive and hypercritical. See *R. v. Sango*, 2015 BCSC 2377, 2015 CarswellBC 3744, [2015] B.C.J. No. 2816 (B.C. S.C.).

In *R. v. Rhodes*, 2015 BCSC 2437, 2015 CarswellBC 3791, [2015] B.C.J. No. 2841 (B.C. S.C.), it was held that Judicial justices are required under the *Provincial Court Act* (B.C.) to swear an oath of office before entering on the duties of their office. They are not required to restate that oath of office before hearing a specific case. A failure to do so when requested by a litigant does not deprive them of their statutory jurisdiction. A fair trial is one which satisfies the public interest in getting at the truth, while preserving procedural fairness to the accused. The clearing of the courtroom and the justice's interventions did not render the trial unfair or interfere with the defendant's right to make full answer and defence. There was no evidence about the basis for clearing the court before the defendant's case proceeded, nor was there evidence that the trial was not otherwise open to the public.

Trial judges should not reject joint submissions unless the proposed sentence is contrary to the public interest and would bring the administration of justice into disrepute. This high threshold ensures that both parties have confidence in resolving the case without a trial and that the many factors that were considered in arriving at the joint position are respected. The finding that the joint submission in the instant case was unreasonable and likely to bring the administration of justice into disrepute was in error. The minor variation of $15 the court ultimately arrived at shows that there was nothing about the original submission that would justify interference by the court. The rejection of the joint submission was unreasonable and arbitrary, and contrary to binding authority including three prior cases involving the same Justice. See *R. v. Alakoozi*, 2015 ONCJ 763, 2015 CarswellOnt 20504, [2015] O.J. No. 6938 (Ont. C.J.).

In *York (Regional Municipality) v. Sekelyk* (September 22, 2015), Doc. CV-15-123505-00, [2015] O.J. No. 4889 (Ont. S.C.J.), the Justice of the Peace was held to have erred in quashing the certificate of offence on the defendant's guilty plea due to the omission of the municipality. It is the overall philosophy of the *Provincial Offences Act* (Ont.) that technical objections not impede the determination of a verdict on the merits. In other circumstances, the failure of the certificate to identify the municipality would be a material, not technical matter. In the instant case, however, there were full particulars of the time and place of the alleged offence, the nature of the offence, speeding, and the place alleged, together with the immediate circumstances under which the notice and offence occurred. As a result, it could not be said that the failure to have included the name of the municipality could impair the defendant's appreciation of the offence he was alleged to have committed. The justice erred in striking the plea and quashing the certificate, rather the process to amend the certificate should have been allowed to unfold.

The right to be tried within a reasonable period of time includes the right to be sentenced within a reasonable period of time. While justices of the peace are responsible for one of the busiest courts in the province and understandably, on occasion, may, like many judges, need extra time to prepare reasons for sentence, on the facts of this case where there was a joint submission on sentence, one might speculate that the reasons for sentence would be relatively brief and perhaps delivered orally at the time of accepting the plea. A delay in imposing sentence of nine and one-half months was not a prompt sentence and unwarranted in the circumstances. See *York (Regional Municipality) v. Newhook*, 2015 ONSC 6587, 2015 CarswellOnt 16978, [2015] O.J. No. 5766 (Ont. S.C.J.).

It was further held in *York (Regional Municipality) v. Newhook*, 2015 ONSC 6587, 2015 CarswellOnt 16978, [2015] O.J. No. 5766 (Ont. S.C.J.) that the discretion of the court as to whether it will accept or reject the guilty plea is a discretion that has to be exercised judicially. It is not a discretion that can be exercised on an arbitrary whim. In situations where it is evident on the face of the record that the discretion has not been exercised judicially, such a discretion amounts to an error of law. There was no reason in law why the Justice should reject the guilty plea that was being proposed by the prosecutor and the defence. She made no inquiries of the prosecutor or defendant with respect to the reasonableness of the proposed plea. Even if there was some legal basis in law for the Justice to consider the appropriateness of the guilty plea, there was no reason why it should take nearly a year for the court to consider whether the guilty pleas should be accepted. An order for *mandamus* issued directing the Justice to accept a guilty plea to the amended offence and to enter a conviction.

The Ontario Court of Appeal ruled that the appeal in the *Hicks* decision abated due to the death of the appellant before the appeal could be argued. This appeal involved the interpretation of the offence notice and the calculation of the 15 days to deliver the request for trial form, otherwise a conviction would be entered on the fail to respond docket. The court held that a decision in the matter would have province-wide implications for the validity of convictions under Part I of the *Provincial Offences Act*, but without a better factual record it would not be in the interests of justice to hear the appeal. As a result, the judgment in the court below was stayed: see *R. v. Hicks*, 2016 ONCA 291, 2016 CarswellOnt 5971, [2016] O.J. No. 2061 (Ont. C.A.).

The justice of the peace erred by stating, "After listening closely to both the officer and the defendant, I believe the prosecutor has proven the case of followed too closely in accordance with section 158(1) of the *Highway Traffic Act*." A *W.D.* analysis was required in these circumstances. While judges are deemed to know what the case of *W.D.* means, the *W.D.* analysis was not done here. It is not a matter of believing one or the other, but where the defence has called evidence, if the defendant is believed in what he says, he must be acquitted. If the defendant generally is believed or if the trying judge or justice is left in doubt from his evidence or the evidence as a whole, then there has to be an acquittal whether or not the judge or justice believes the officers. See *R. v. McConnell Rodrigues*, 2016 CarswellOnt 9712, [2016] O.J. No. 3252 (Ont. C.J.).

In *R. v. Madussi*, 2016 ONCJ 309, 2016 CarswellOnt 8526, [2016] O.J. No. 2843 (Ont. C.J.), the justice of the peace drew an inference from the evidence of the Crown witness that the light was green when she entered the intersection and was still green after the collision, and that she heard the accused tell someone that she went through a light when she should not have. There was some evidence that the light was red when the defendant went through it. The justice properly refused a motion for a non-suit in these circumstances. However, the justice of the peace cannot take judicial notice of the operation of a traffic light, namely, that if the light on one street is green, the light on the crossing street will be red, as this does not allow for instances such as mechanical failure or blown out bulbs.

The defence raised an objection when the police officer began to testify about the speed measuring device based on the fact that the officer had made no record in his note-book about testing the device. It is trite law that contemporaneous notes may be used by a witness as an aide memoire when testifying in court. However, there is no requirement that a police officer's notes must be complete or written in a particular way, or comprehensively set out every detail. There may be circumstances where the omission of some crucial fact from the notes could cast doubt on the reliability or credibility of a police officer's testimony, but that was not the case here. The officer testified from memory, which he was entitled to do, and the trial justice accepted that evidence. The defence had full opportunity to cross-examine the police officer regarding the testing of the device, but only asked one question about the test that was performed on the device to ensure that it was working. The officer responded by describing the testing procedure in detail; the defence asked no further questions. The justice of the peace noted in her decision that there was "little cross-examination" on this issue, and that there was no defence evidence that suggested the device "was not working properly and tested properly." In the circumstances, the defendant received a fair trial, and there was no basis for concluding that he did not. See *R. v. Zacharias*, 2016 ONCJ 458, 2016 CarswellOnt 12095, [2016] O.J. No. 3975 (Ont. C.J.).

In *R. v. Hadi*, 2016 ONCJ 447, 2016 CarswellOnt 11897, [2016] O.J. No. 3890 (Ont. C.J.), the defendant was given a DVD of the in-car recording in advance of his trial, but there was no audio on that recording. The arresting officer had forgotten to put the audio pack on before he left his car. When the defendant was told this by the justice of the peace, he refused to accept this explanation, and declined to participate in his trial for improper right turn and failing to surrender his driving licence. The Crown's duty to disclose what is in its possession also applies to the police who must provide relevant disclosure to the Crown to be further disclosed to the defence. However, the Crown cannot disclose what it does not have. There was no issue in this case of any lost or destroyed disclosure; the disclosure issue was properly resolved by the justice of the peace who explained to the defendant in plain terms that the audio was not there and he could not be given what was never created in the first place. There could be no other possible decision the justice of the peace could have made. The DVD was played in court at the accused's trial. The fact that there was no audio on the recording was made apparent to the justice of the peace. It was also made clear to him that his copy was the same as that in the possession of the Crown. Despite this, the accused continued to refuse to participate. Having a fair trial means that a defendant receives a fair *opportunity* to make full answer and defence. If the defendant chooses not to make use of this opportunity, there is little that the justice system can do.

The trial justice of the peace did not err in the exercise of his discretion in refusing the defendant's request to adjourn his peremptory trial date. The basis of the adjournment request was that the defendant was not given a copy of the in-car DVD with audio; however, there was no audio on the recording as the officer had not activated the audio pack before leaving his car. However, the defendant refused to accept this explanation. The defendant had been told this before the trial date, and when the justice explained this to him, he refused to participate in the trial. Given the past history of the case and the position taken by the defendant on the audio issue, the justice was entitled to dismiss the adjournment request. See *R. v. Hadi*, 2016 ONCJ 447, 2016 CarswellOnt 11897, [2016] O.J. No. 3890 (Ont. C.J.).

In *R. v. Hadi*, 2016 ONCJ 447, 2016 CarswellOnt 11897, [2016] O.J. No. 3890 (Ont. C.J.), the justice of the peace explained the basic procedure to the defendant, asked a few questions of the arresting officer, consistently inquired of the defendant if he wanted to be involved in his trial despite his adamant refusal, and showed patience given what was transpiring. In addition, he acquitted the accused on the charge of failing to identify himself to the police officer based upon a legal technicality that was raised on the court's own motion. There was no unfairness at the defendant's trial, nor did the justice of the peace's conduct raise any concern about a reasonable apprehension of bias.

A reasonable standard of bias was not established when the justice of the peace threatened to start the case without counsel for the defence being present, even though the justice was aware that counsel was in another courtroom. This statement constituted an outburst of frustration when the parties were not ready to proceed at the appointed time. His comment that if the party wished to bring in hearsay, that's fine, did not constitute bias. However, when the justice pronounced sentence without giving the defence an opportunity to be heard, this was improper. Counsel for the defence was right in assuming that any submissions from him at that point would be a wasted exercise. As a result, sentencing submissions were presented by the parties on appeal. See *R. v. Mr. Ice Man Ltd.*, 2016 ONCJ 372, 2016 CarswellOnt 9849, [2016] O.J. No. 3308 (Ont. C.J.).

In *R. v. Sahadeo*, 2016 ONCJ 122, 2016 CarswellOnt 3721, [2016] O.J. No. 1252 (Ont. C.J.), on the date his trial was scheduled to take place, the paralegal for the defendant appeared and requested an adjournment. When the request was refused, the paralegal advised the presiding justice that he was instructed not to participate in the proceedings any further. The paralegal then left the courtroom. Upon the defendant being paged with no response, a deemed not to dispute conviction was entered. The decision to grant or refuse the adjournment was discretionary, and will not be interfered with on appeal unless the discretion was not exercised judicially, or where it has resulted in a miscarriage of justice. In this case, the need for the adjournment for disclosure could easily have been obviated by the defendant far in advance of the trial. While the justice of the peace was correct to refuse the adjournment, a conviction should not have been imposed under s. 9.1 as it could not be said that the defendant had failed to appear at the time and place appointed for trial. He did appear by instructing an agent to attend, as permitted by s. 50; the provisions of s. 54(1) did not apply in this case. The defendant had appeared by agent, the prosecution was ready, and the trial should have proceeded. The fact that the defendant had instructed his agent to "walk away" did not mean that the agent had any right to do so. A paralegal, like counsel, can only withdraw with the leave of the court. The defendant demonstrated a complete lack of diligence by failing to ensure that he had the necessary disclosure. He ought to have either appeared personally or else sent a properly instructed agent. The agent, who appeared, had not been properly instructed and was initially unable to articulate the reason for which he was seeking an adjournment. The application itself was entirely without merit and should not have been brought; for his part, the agent should not have agreed to act for the defendant without proper instructions.

The defendant's request for an adjournment on the grounds that he wanted to retain new counsel was not reasonable in the particular circumstances of the case. It was consistent with his numerous prior requests for adjournments which resulted in the lengthy history of the case. A previous adjournment had been granted so that he could obtain new counsel upon informing the court that his counsel had been disbarred and therefore no longer able to represent him; subsequent adjournments were also granted, and the case had been marked peremptory. There had been a 9-month interval from the adjournment of the first trial date to the peremptory trial date. The defendant was completely familiar with the charges, and was well acquainted with the alleged deficiencies including what was required to rectify the deficiencies with respect to his property. When the defendant left the court to protest the refusal to grant the adjournment, an *ex parte* trial was held, after which the defendant was found guilty. Upon the defendant returning to court on the day of sentencing at which time he asked for the charges to be withdrawn, dismissed and the proceedings stayed, the court ruled that it was *functus* to do so, having registered a conviction in his absence. See *R. v. Melnyk*, 2016 ONCJ 331, 2016 CarswellOnt 8877, [2016] O.J. No. 2998 (Ont. C.J.).

In *R. v. Garwal*, 2016 ONCJ 217, 2016 CarswellOnt 5933, 99 M.V.R. (6th) 151, [2016] O.J. No. 1997 (Ont. C.J.), the defendant was charged with speeding, and following a resolution meeting pleaded guilty to disobeying a sign. The parties jointly submitted that the appropriate sentence was to impose the set fine of $85. The imposition of the set fine was held to be contrary to the public interest or would bring the administration of justice into disrepute as set fines are statutorily reserved for cases that do not go to trial, or where there were mitigating factors. Imposing the set fine would also not respect the legislative intent that proceedings proceed economically and efficiently. A defendant should not have the benefit of both the public cost required to ensure a right to trial as well as a reduced fine after conviction on the day of trial. As the defendant had no record of similar offences, and there were no aggravating factors, imposing a fine of $100 would be sufficiently punitive.

The trial justice raised the issue of a directed verdict of acquittal without being asked by the self-represented defendant. By failing to ask for submissions and raising the matter as she did, the trial justice fell into error. There may be times when a trial court raises concerns it has about an issue in the Crown evidence. This is a heightened concern when, as here, the accused is unrepresented by counsel. When the trial proceeds in an unrepresented manner, the trial judge has a duty to raise concerns about proof on his or her own. That said, the trial court must first ask for submissions from all parties so that the court does not step into the fray. That was not done in this case. See *York (Regional Municipality) v. Grayson* (April 15, 2016), Doc. Newmarket 4911-999-00-9389233Z, [2016] O.J. No. 5250 (Ont. C.J.).

In *R. v. Webb*, 2016 BCPC 294, 2016 CarswellBC 2789, [2016] B.C.J. No. 2089 (B.C. Prov. Ct.), it was held that judicial notice may be taken of a matter that is so notorious as not to be the subject of dispute among reasonable men or so capable of immediate accuracy by resort to readily accessible sources of indisputable accuracy. Having regard to the officer's testimony of having observed the disputant vehicle's momentum while he was travelling on Highway 1 at the Surrey/Langley border, with the disputant on the 192 on-ramp of Highway 1 approaching to merge westbound, judicial notice was taken that both cities border each other and are within the province of British Columbia. It cannot but be notorious to persons in the Lower Mainland of British Columbia that the location described is in British Columbia. The officer testified he stopped the vehicle on the highway at the location after its speed was estimated and a radar reading was taken and served the disputant with the violation ticket in question. The court was also shown a video of that stop on the highway.

The parties brought an application on consent to have the trial heard before a judge rather than a justice of the peace. *Charter* applications are frequently heard by justices of the peace in provincial offences court. Although a challenge to a by-law may not be an everyday occurrence in these courts, it is also within the ordinary realm of decisions made by justices of the peace. Their education and training is now such that it cannot be stated that the issues presented in the instant case were too complex and should be handed over to a judge. An appeal of a Part I matter heard by a judge would be to another judge of the Ontario Court of Justice, thus it could be inferred that it was not contemplated by the legislators that a Part I matter would be heard by a judge, resulting in an appeal being heard by a colleague of the same court. The fact that there are a considerable number of counts does not make these cases factually complex. There was no legal complexity or broader public interest warranting the scheduling of these charges before a judge. See *Mississauga (City) v. Uber Canada Inc.*, 2016 ONCJ 461, 2016 CarswellOnt 12510, 362 C.R.R. (2d) 8, [2016] O.J. No. 4088 (Ont. C.J.).

In *R. v. Madussi*, 2016 ONCJ 309, 2016 CarswellOnt 8526, [2016] O.J. No. 2843 (Ont. C.J.), it was held that the justice of the peace made an error of law to state that she can take judicial notice of the operation of a traffic light. This does not allow for mechanical failure or blown out bulbs and so on. If the justice had simply stated that she took judicial notice of how the traffic lights work, the appeal would be successful. However, the justice went further and found an inference from the evidence of the principal Crown witness that the light was green when she entered the intersection and was still green after the collision, and that she heard an admission by the defendant that she told someone that she went through a light that she should not have. In all of the circumstances, there was some evidence upon which the trier of fact could convict, and the justice of the peace was correct to dismiss the motion for directed verdict.

The adjournment application was not framed as being based on the unavailability of the defendant's counsel of choice, but instead it was based on the unavailability of a witness that the defendant's counsel wanted to cross-examine. The witness was not a material witness, and was not being called by the Crown, which has a discretion with respect to what witnesses it chooses to call. Accordingly, the defendant would not have been in a position to cross-examine the witness in any event. If the defendant wanted to call the witness to give evidence in direct, it was his responsibility to ensure that the witness was present on the date of trial. The justice's discretionary decision not to permit an adjournment because the witness was not present was entitled to deference on appeal. See *R. v. Gao*, 2016 BCSC 1606, 2016 CarswellBC 2406, [2016] B.C.J. No. 1838 (B.C. S.C.).

In *R. v. Gao*, 2016 BCSC 1606, 2016 CarswellBC 2406, [2016] B.C.J. No. 1838 (B.C. S.C.), the police officer produced his notes from the back of the violation ticket, but did not produce a report to Crown counsel related to potential criminal charges that may have arisen out of the traffic stop. No such charges were ultimately laid. The officer did not believe the information to be relevant, and did not intend to rely on it; no disclosure requests had previously been made. Based on the immateriality of the issue of whether the defendant's driver's licence was fraudulent or not, the fact that the defendant's counsel had access to the information in question before the hearing, and the lack of previous disclosure requests from counsel appearing on the trial date or over the 14-month period between the violation ticket and the date of the trial, the justice did not err in refusing the defendant's request for disclosure.

The justice of the peace made no reference to whether the due diligence defence was made out in a case where the defendant was unrepresented. This issue should have been canvassed at trial. The defendant's explanation as to the reasons he did not produce his motor vehicle permit and insurance card was not fully developed in his evidence. His explanation was brief and imperfectly communicated. It was also very apparent that probably due to his youth, character and emotional state, he was not his own best advocate. But he was unrepresented. Greater assistance should have been offered to him to develop the reason why he did not follow the officer's request. See *R. v. Sathialingam*, 2016 ONCJ 703, 2016 CarswellOnt 19182, [2016] O.J. No. 6250 (Ont. C.J.).

It was further held in *R. v. Sathialingam*, 2016 ONCJ 703, 2016 CarswellOnt 19182, [2016] O.J. No. 6250 (Ont. C.J.) that the justice of the peace was fair and offered to help the unrepresented defendant in relation to the offence of speeding. The video from the in-car camera of the police cruiser had been disclosed. The prosecutor stated that she was not going to introduce it as part of her case; however, she had it ready to go in her computer if the defendant wanted to introduce the evidence. This was all explained repeatedly by the justice of the peace to the defendant. The defendant's main point at trial was that the video did not capture any information from the radar device as to his speed. He pointed this out to the justice of the peace on the monitor that was set up in court. The defendant eventually decided that he did not want to play the video for the court. The defendant was fairly treated, his right to play the video was patiently explained to him, and the video itself neither advanced the prosecution or the defence case. In an *ex parte* trial for driving without insurance, the defendant appeared at court before the trial was completed, but indicated his attendance to the court only after he was found guilty and sentence was imposed. The justice of the peace informed the defendant that he was *functus officio* and there was nothing further he could do in the matter. In these circumstances, although the court accepted the justice's statement that he was *functus*, even if he was incorrect, there had been no miscarriage of justice as fresh evidence tendered on appeal by the Crown demonstrated that the defendant did not have valid insurance at the time of the offence, contrary to his assertion before the court. See *R. v. Simpson*, 2016 ONCA 212, 2016 CarswellOnt 3884, [2016] O.J. No. 1381 (Ont. C.A.).

In *Oshawa (City) v. 536813 Ontario Ltd.*, 2016 ONCJ 665, 2016 CarswellOnt 18205, 60 M.P.L.R. (5th) 343, [2016] O.J. No. 5925 (Ont. C.J.), it was held that the jurisdiction to award costs is necessary for any court of law to control its processes and maintain the integrity of the court's processes and public confidence in the administration of justice. There is no principled reason to have jurisdiction to award costs for a *Charter* breach, but not following a ruling on a constitutional question. The ability to award costs as a sanction responsive to the unacceptable standard of prosecution is inherent jurisdiction of any court of law to control its own process, is reasonably necessary given the mandate of the Provincial Court to decide constitutional issues, and in order for the court to discharge its mandate. For these reasons, the Provincial Offences Court has jurisdiction to award costs in a case involving a constitutional challenge. It was appropriate to make such an order where the prosecution refused to accept the clear jurisprudence giving the federal government exclusive jurisdiction over the field of aeronautics under the constitutional doctrine of interjurisdictional immunity. The witnesses revealed their bias in favour of their employer, the City of Oshawa, by the manner in which they conducted themselves at the trial. Also at the trial, the prosecution inappropriately attempted to use privileged resolution negotiations against the defendant. While the City of Oshawa has an obligation to prosecute in the public interest, in this case the broad public interest appeared to be overtaken by its self-serving interests.

A joint submission should normally be accepted unless the sentencing judge "is satisfied that the recommended disposition would be contrary to the public interest and would bring the administration of justice into disrepute": *R. v. Thompson*, 2013 ONCA 202, 2013 CarswellOnt 3920, 305 O.A.C. 42, [2013] O.J. No. 1546 (Ont.

C.A.). It is an error in principle not to conduct a thoughtful analysis of why the proposed joint submission falls prey to that, and it is an error by sentencing judge not to "forewarn counsel of his intentions or provide them with an opportunity to respond": *Thompson*, para. 16. Neither of those was done in any of the cases in question. As such, the trial justice of the peace erred in imposing a sentence lower than the joint submission. A sentence of $200 was only $115 above the statutory minimum fine. There was no reason why the sentence imposed of $85 was so markedly different than the joint submission. All of the defendants had their charges reduced from speeding to a lesser charge. A $200 fine was a benefit to the accused. So were the saved demerit points. The *quid pro quo* should have been apparent and, if it wasn't, the prosecutor should have been given an opportunity to explain it. See *York (Regional Municipality) v. Sun*, 2016 ONCJ 240, 2016 CarswellOnt 6700, [2016] O.J. No. 2243 (Ont. C.J.).

In a similar case, *R. v. Pellicci*, 2017 ONCJ 85, 2017 CarswellOnt 2788, [2017] O.J. No. 188 (C.J.), it was held that resolution without trial is essential to the efficient and fair operation of the system of provincial offences courts in the province. The resolutions in these cases involved reductions in charges, reductions in fines or both. Some resolutions avoided administrative penalties such as driving demerit points. Others avoided conviction on offences which would trigger serious insurance consequences. Despite those benefits, the joint submissions as to sentence were rejected. Justice of the peace may depart from joint submissions, but the ability to do so is prescribed by law. The appropriate test is a strict one — whether the proposed sentence would bring the administration of justice into disrepute or would otherwise be contrary to the public interest. The phrase "otherwise contrary to the public interest" does not lower the standard. It is an error of law for the presiding justice of the peace to tell the courtroom that there could be no agreements as to sentence, simply to assert judicial independence, and to lower the fine proposed without explaining why the submitted fine was inappropriate or why the minor variance to the set fine amount was necessary. Justices of the peace do have the ultimate responsibility to impose a fit sentence, but that responsibility must be exercised according to the limits imposed by statute and following the framework provided by appellate courts. Where an accused receives the benefit of resolution to a reduced charge and reduced fine and agrees they can pay that amount, a sentencing court should not further reduce the fine due to concerns about ability to pay not founded in the evidence. A general sympathy for an accused person is not a sufficient basis to interfere with a joint proposal.

An application to intervene in a proceeding under the *Dog Owners' Liability Act* for a destruction order was considered in *R. v. Robert*, 2016 ONCJ 697, 2016 CarswellOnt 19181, [2016] O.J. No. 6249 (Ont. C.J.). It was held that Rule 7(6) of the *Provincial Offences Act* Rules limits "applications" and "motions" to those which, in Rule 7(1) "are provided for by the Act". Nowhere in Part IV of the

Provincial Offences Act, or anywhere else in the *Provincial Offences Act*, is there any mention of a motion or an application for intervener status. Therefore Rule 7(6) of the *Provincial Offences Act* Rules cannot give any authority to deal with other applications or motions, such as applications for intervener status, which are not so mentioned within the *Provincial Offences Act* itself. To appoint the applicants as interveners, without formally being so appointed, in order to aid the defendants in obtaining evidence on the behaviour of dogs would be an inappropriate intervention on the part of the court. It is not the court's job to assist the defendants in mounting their defence by means of appointing interveners, if the court otherwise does not find it necessary for those interveners to be appointed. Neither was it necessary to appoint the applicants as amicus in order for the court to carry out its duties and obligations effectively and efficiently. The applicants did not have a unique interest in the matter. From both a legal and practical perspective, the applicant's interests appeared to be quite similar to the defendants. While the applicants were passionate about the good work they did on behalf of dogs, this did not make them or their perspective unique with respect to the case or make their submissions distinctive.

The presiding justice's dismissal of a disclosure motion did not give rise to a reasonable apprehension of bias or require the declaration of a mistrial on the basis that the justice misapprehended what was allegedly not to have been disclosed by the prosecution. The defendant failed to meet its burden to satisfy the high threshold to justify disqualification. See *R. v. Shan*, 2016 ONCJ 663, 2016 CarswellOnt 18212, [2016] O.J. No. 5935 (Ont. C.J.).

There was no prosecutorial misconduct due to "vetting the file erroneously". In the initial redacted duty notes, there was no evidence that any error was intentional or done for some nefarious purpose. Any inconsistency in the notes could have been clarified well in advance of the trial. Instead, the defence chose to raise the issue only during cross-examination. The Crown's position resisting disclosure of the radar manual did not amount to prosecutorial misconduct. The Crown's error in disclosure of the initial notes was unintentional, and the error was remedied by providing further disclosure in advance of the disclosure motion and trial. This did not amount to a standard of misconduct that justified an award of costs against the prosecution. See *R. v. Shan*, 2016 ONCJ 663, 2016 CarswellOnt 18212, [2016] O.J. No. 5935 (Ont. C.J.).

In *R. v. Wadood*, 2017 ONCA 45, 2017 CarswellOnt 554, 344 C.C.C. (3d) 265, 6 M.V.R. (7th) 181, [2017] O.J. No. 245 (Ont. C.A.), it was held that a police officer is entitled to change the information on the certificate of offence after giving the offence notice to the motorist, but before filing the certificate with the court. In one case, the officer added the name of the municipality after noticing that the certificate of offence did not contain this information after the defendant drove off after being given the ticket; in the other case the officer realized that he had written the incorrect year on the certificate of offence, and corrected it before filing it with the court. Both accused failed to appear for their trial. As a result, they were deemed to not dispute their charges. The justice of the peace in each case concluded that the certificate of offence was complete and regular on its face, and the defendants were convicted. Although s. 90 of the *Provincial Offences Act* does not authorize an officer to amend the certificate after serving the offence notice, but before filing the certificate with the court, nothing in the *Provincial Offences Act* prevents an officer from doing so. Whether an amendment will invalidate a conviction depends on the nature of the amendment and its impact on a defendant. In these cases, each amendment did no more than correct a minor clerical error on the certificate; neither of the defendants was misled or prejudiced by the amendment. Thus the validity of the proceeding against each of the defendants was preserved by s. 90. If the officer amends the certificate, and the variance between the certificate and the offence notice comes before the court, then the presiding judge will have to decide whether the defendant was misled or prejudiced by the amendment. If not, then s. 90 will validate the proceeding.

In *R. v. Boukaras*, 2017 ONCJ 608, 2017 CarswellOnt 14000, [2017] O.J. No. 4275 (Ont. C.J.), it was held that the justice of the peace committed reversible legal error in dismissing the charge because the officer had no independent recollection of the events that brought the defendant to court. He failed to take into account the evidentiary rule of past recollection recorded and dismissed the charge without reason. The officer's notes, which were made an exhibit, were properly admitted into evidence as record of his past recollection of the incident that brought the defendant to court. The notes were entered as a record of a past recollection and became evidence themselves as an exception to the hearsay rule, the four conditions for admissibility having been met, namely, (1) the past recollection must have been recorded in a reliable way; (2) the record must have been made or reviewed within a reasonable time; (3) at the time the witness testified he/she had no memory of the recorded events; and (4) the witness was able to say that he/she was being truthful at the time the assertions were recorded. Since the officer had no recollection of the events he had recorded, cross-examination might well have been more limited than if he had an independent recollection of the events and used his notes to refresh his memory. However, this was no reason to dismiss the charge.

The court is entitled to ask focused questions of either party to obtain the benefit of their submissions on particular issues. While part of the discussion regarding sensors and technical aspects of the red light equipment was off topic, it was not referred to in the reasons of the justice of the peace and played no part in the court's decision. Nothing in the proceedings gave rise to a reasonable apprehension of bias. See *R. v. Balanzin*, 2017 ONCJ 88, 2017 CarswellOnt 2787, [2017] O.J. No. 983 (Ont. C.J.).

The officer made notes on the back a ticket, which is fairly consistent with the way in which summary offence tickets occur and how they are dealt with by investigating officers. It is not a criminal case. There is usually not a lengthy report prepared because they are summary offence tickets; they are dealt with in a much more informal manner because of the fact that, although there may well be some serious consequences to them, they are not criminal cases. A "can-say" is exactly what that title specifies. It is what the expectation is that the witness can say. It is not a sworn declaration. It is not a videotaped statement. It is not a handwritten statement by whoever the person is, with their signature at the bottom. It is reasonably expected to be as accurate as one can hope it to be, from information that is provided, to give some assistance to understanding what occurred. Considering all of the evidence in respect of the matter involves what is heard from all of the witnesses on the witness stand, the way in which they answered the questions, and if they had any difficulty in recalling the details. If there was difficulty, the court must consider whether or not there is any evidence for that, whether or not they had notes that they referred to, and whether or not those notes were of assistance to them. See *R. v. Skookum*, 2017 YKTC 65, 2017 CarswellYukon 147, [2017] Y.J. No. 441 (Y.T. Terr. Ct.), affirmed 2019 YKSC 8, 2019 CarswellYukon 14 (Y.T. S.C.).

In *Cape Breton (Regional Municipality) v. Morrison*, 2017 NSSC 347, 2017 CarswellNS 970, 18 M.V.R. (7th) 264, [2017] N.S.J. No. 526 (N.S. S.C.), it was held that whether it was the defence at trial who raised the issue of identity or whether the issue was raised by the court, it does not change or alter the Adjudicator's role, which was to base his decision on the evidence before him. Regardless of whether the defence raised the issue, the Crown's burden remained the same, that is, to prove the essential elements of the offence. It should not have come as a total surprise to the Crown that the court might have a concern as to proof of identity on the evidence. There was no legal authority that would preclude the trier of fact from making a finding based on the evidence before them. It is not an error of law for a trial judge not to provide an opportunity to the Crown to re-open its case where no such opportunity is sought by the party seeking to re-open. While there was some evidence of identity, whether it was sufficient for a jury properly instructed to infer guilt was not clear to the Adjudicator, who in his reasons turned his mind as to whether each element of the offence had been proven.

At the trial, the police officer who testified indicated in chief that he had a conversation with the defendant after pulling him over, but indicated to the judicial justice of the peace that he was not proposing to enter into a *voir dire* to prove the voluntariness of those statements, and so the statements were never found to be voluntary and, hence, admissible at any point during the trial. Nevertheless, when he was cross-examined by the police officer, the police officer did cross-examine on the basis of the statements which he made at the scene following being pulled over. It appeared from the transcript and from the Reasons for Judgment that the judicial justice of the peace relied on the discrepancies in those statements and the differences between what they consist of and what the defendant was saying before him in making a finding of guilt against him. In those circumstances, given that inadmissible evidence was used as a critical part of the finding of the judicial justice, it was necessary that the convictions be set aside and a new trial ordered. See *R. v. Duncan*, 2017 BCSC 1936, 2017 CarswellBC 2967, [2017] B.C.J. No. 1936 (B.C. S.C.).

In *R. v. Friedinger*, 2017 BCSC 2026, 2017 CarswellBC 3080, 18 M.V.R. (7th) 135, [2017] B.C.J. No. 2242 (B.C. S.C.), the police officer was permitted to clarify his evidence at least graphically after he had appeared to have completed his evidence. However, the ability afforded to the defendant to respond to that clarification was somewhat limited and he was refused an ability to respond in more complete form during final submissions. In addition, when identification is put in issue, if a presiding judge is going to conclude that identification has been established on the evidence that should be stated clearly in the reasons, and reasons for coming to that conclusion should be given. That was not done here. If one looked at the issue at trial as being — did the police ticket the right driver — then the evidence of the accused person, the defendant, should be evaluated in the context of the *W. (D.)* criteria. It was not clear that occurred in the hearing. In sum, the hearing suffered from a congeries of defects that made it unsafe to uphold the finding of guilt or finding that the offence occurred.

By the time the matter came for hearing, the transcripts of earlier court appearances had yet to be completed. The defence anticipated that the transcripts would be required for the hearing of the *Charter* s. 11(b) argument, and the attending prosecutor agreed. On that understanding the defence requested an adjournment, which was refused by the trial justice of the peace who was mistaken in his understanding of the procedural history of the case. While the justice was quite right in saying that trial dates were dates when a trial should happen, that does not mean that the principles of fairness and due process might not require the adjournment on the trial date. In denying the request for adjournment the justice effectively denied the defendant the opportunity to be heard on the alleged *Charter* breach. In the circumstances, the justice erred in law in refusing the requested adjournment based on a palpable and overriding mistake as to the underlying facts, and further erred in law in denying the defendant the right to be heard on the alleged *Charter* breach. See *R. v. Ahmad*, 2017 CarswellOnt 19495, 394 C.R.R. (2d) 374, [2017] O.J. No. 6319 (Ont. C.J.).

The justice of the peace at the defendant's first appearance in court noted that the date of the offence on the information was a date in the future, and determined that the information was "no good" as a result. It is important to remember that an important goal of the *Provincial Offences Act* is that matters are tried on their merits, hence, the very broad powers of amendment where there is no prejudice to the accused. While the question of whether to amend an information is a question of law, this does not relieve the court from its obligation to proceed properly and in accordance with law to arrive at a decision whether to grant an amendment. Clearly, this information was defective in substance or form. It contained an obvious error which required an amendment. No trial evidence was necessary to ascertain this error. The fact that this was at the first appearance did not oust the court's jurisdiction to consider whether to amend the information. Even if the lack of the officer's signature amounted to a substantive defect, there was jurisdiction for the court to amend the information. There was no opportunity for the Crown to adduce evidence to support the amendment or to make submissions as to why the amendment should be made. This was a fatal error. Clearly, the presiding justice did not conduct the proceeding in accordance with natural justice. In proceeding in this manner, the learned judge exceeded his jurisdiction. Not granting the application for prerogative review would, in the circumstances of the case, result in a substantial wrong to society which expects and is entitled to have these matters heard on the merits unless an amendment is rejected after both parties have an opportunity to deal with and the presiding judge gives full consideration of the matters relevant to an amendment application. See *R. v. Singh*, 2017 ONSC 7593, 2017 CarswellOnt 20895, [2017] O.J. No. 6807 (Ont. S.C.J.), affirmed 2018 ONCA 506, 2018 CarswellOnt 8710, 362 C.C.C. (3d) 161, 28 M.V.R. (7th) 45 (Ont. C.A.).

In *Oshawa (City) v. 536813 Ontario Limited*, 2017 ONCJ 836, 2017 CarswellOnt 19439, 72 C.L.R. (4th) 140, 69 M.P.L.R. (5th) 313, [2017] O.J. No. 6428 (Ont. C.J.), the trial justice ordered costs against the "Prosecution", the "City of Oshawa" and the "Prosecutor, the City of Oshawa". While the costs order did not specifically detail the names of the prosecutors, it appeared from a review of the judgments that the trial justice sought to punish both the prosecutors *in personam* and the entity known as the City of Oshawa. There is a high test for ordering costs. Costs against the prosecution are relatively rare in criminal and quasi-criminal litigation — costs against the prosecution in the absence of a proven breach of the *Charter of Rights* rarer still. The trial justice erred by ordering costs in the amount of $111,000 plus HST. Given the serious ramifications of such a finding to the proper administration of justice, the perception of justice, the public perception of the City of Oshawa, and the impact on the individual prosecutors in the case, a clear evidentiary basis was required. The evidentiary record did not support a finding that the conduct of the prosecutors constituted "a marked and unacceptable departure from the reasonable standards expected of the prosecution." Nor did the evidentiary record justify costs against the City of Oshawa. There was no basis in evidence to find that the prosecution was directed by the municipality for self-interest and financial gain. The trial judge erred in co-mingling perceived motives associated with the municipality and the approach taken by the prosecution team appearing at trial. The court succumbed to error by dislodging the independent role of the prosecutor and impugning prosecutorial standards in the absence of evidence to support such findings.

There was no evidence, on consideration of the entirety of the trial record, that the defendant was prejudiced in any way by the late receipt of disclosure. The defendant chose not to pick up the disclosure from the prosecutor's office until the morning of trial. His request for a stay of proceedings was quite properly refused, as the defendant failed to exercise due diligence in picking up the available disclosure until the morning of trial. The appropriate remedy, in these circumstances, at its highest, would have been an adjournment of the trial, but no adjournment was requested by the defendant. It was not part of the function of the presiding justice of the peace to advise the defendant that the appropriate remedy for the "late" provision of disclosure was an adjournment rather than a stay of proceedings as the defendant proposed. At the outset of the trial, the justice of the peace explained the trial process, and was informed that the defendant had received legal advice and had some experience in conducting a trial. The trial itself was straightforward and consisted of only one witness. The defendant was asked if he wished to give evidence and declined to do so. Reasonable assistance was provided to the defendant at trial and his fair trial interests were preserved and respected by the presiding justice of the peace as a consequence. See *R. v. Popovici*, 2017 CarswellOnt 21731, [2017] O.J. No. 5697 (C.J.).

In *R. v. Popovici*, 2017 CarswellOnt 21731, [2017] O.J. No. 5697 (C.J.), the defendant was not given an opportunity to make submissions as to penalty and may not have been aware of the prosecutor's entitlement to request an "amendment up" of the amount of the applicable fine by virtue of the amendment provisions of the *Provincial Offences Act*. The court must ensure that the defendant understands the consequences of the amendment and is given a reasonable opportunity to make submissions as to why the amendment should not be granted. As the amendment, if granted, would invariably result in the imposition of a more enhanced financial sanction, fairness dictated that the unrepresented defendant be given a fair opportunity to respond to the request for enhanced penalty. On the record, it did not appear that the defendant understood his jeopardy of the amendment that was granted. More importantly, he was not given an opportunity to make submissions as to penalty generally.

The defendant applied to adjourn the trial, both on the date of the filed application and on the trial date, primarily due to the unavailability of retained representation. The decision to grant or deny an adjournment is a discretionary exercise. Where this discretion is exercised judicially and fails to result in a miscarriage of justice, the decision should not be interfered with on review. The right to representation of choice is not absolute. This is particularly resonant for *Highway Traffic Act* litigation in the general Toronto area where available counsel and paralegals are legion. Given the previously granted defence application to adjourn, it was reasonable for the court to expect that any representation retained by the defendant was available on the second trial date. The defendant demonstrated little or no diligence in this regard. In denying the application to adjourn, the learned justice considered the previously granted defence adjournment application. The trial was endorsed peremptory to proceed. It was appropriate to deny the application in the circumstances. See *R. v. Wei*, 2017 ONCJ 878, 2017 CarswellOnt 20869, [2017] O.J. No. 6785 (Ont. C.J.).

In *R. v. Wei*, 2017 ONCJ 878, 2017 CarswellOnt 20869, [2017] O.J. No. 6785 (Ont. C.J.), the defendant was prosecuted for disobeying a stop sign, commenced by means of a certificate of offence. The disclosure involved the notes of an officer and a video recording. The Part I *Provincial Offences Act* procedure is simplified and the maximum penalty is a $1,000 fine. The set fine for disobey stop sign is $85. In this context, it was appropriate for the justice of the peace to hold the trial down briefly to permit review of disclosure before trial. This practice is not uncommon for Part I provincial offences litigation, and is reasonable in light of the simplified procedure under it.

Application of s. 54 of the *Provincial Offences Act* is not restricted to Part III prosecutions commenced by laying of information. Section 54 applies to all proceedings commenced under the Act, and it explicitly includes certificate proceedings commenced under Part I by way of notice of trial, which fit the defendant in the case at bar. Both ss. 9.1 and 54, however, only permit a conviction *in absentia* where the defendant does not "appear" for trial. The Act does not seem to contemplate a scenario where the defendant "appears" for trial by way of an agent who later withdraws after being denied an adjournment. This unfortunate practice is more prevalent in provincial offences courts than it should be and merits comment. The defence cannot by its conduct thwart the court's direction that a trial will proceed as scheduled. The defendant was placed on notice by no less than three justices of the peace that the trial would proceed in November; when the adjournment application was denied in October, the defence was expected to enter its plea on the trial date. In sending an agent without instructions to enter a guilty plea or to defend the trial, the defence by its conduct endeavoured to subvert the explicit direction of the court. Once the adjournment was denied, the defence ought to have been fixed with the expectation of arraignment. If there was any intention to defend the charge, the defence should have attended the second trial date prepared to do so. The learned justice did not err in conducting an *ex parte* trial under s. 54 in the circumstances. Section 54 affords the absent defendant an appropriate measure of procedural fairness. The prosecution is required to prove the defendant was notified or compelled to attend trial. Evidence must be led to satisfy the standard of proof. The procedure employed was fair and consistent with the due administration of justice. See *R. v. Wei*, 2017 ONCJ 878, 2017 CarswellOnt 20869, [2017] O.J. No. 6785 (Ont. C.J.).

In *Groia v. Law Society of Upper Canada*, 2018 CSC 27, 2018 SCC 27, 2018 CarswellOnt 8700, 2018 CarswellOnt 8701, 34 Admin. L.R. (6th) 183, 46 C.R. (7th) 227, 424 D.L.R. (4th) 443, [2018] S.C.J. No. 27 (S.C.C.), the finding of misconduct against Mr. Groia, a defence lawyer in a *Securities Act* prosecution, was found to be unreasonable. The court held that defence lawyers must have sufficient latitude to advance their client's right to make full answer and defence by raising arguments about the propriety of state actors' conduct without fear of reprisal. This is not to be taken as endorsing incivility in the name of resolute advocacy; civility and resolute advocacy are not incompatible. To the contrary, civility is often the most effective form of advocacy. Nevertheless, when defining incivility and assessing whether a lawyer's behaviour crosses the line, care must be taken to set a sufficiently high threshold that will not chill the kind of fearless advocacy that is at times necessary to advance a client's cause. Courts and law societies have concurrent jurisdiction to regulate and enforce standards of courtroom behaviour. Improper defence behaviour is not necessarily professional misconduct, be it a function of incivility or incompetence. The Law Society must therefore be careful not to place too much weight on a judge's criticism of defence behaviour. When the impugned behaviour occurs in a courtroom, what, if anything, the judge does about it becomes relevant. Unlike the Law Society, the presiding judge observes the lawyer's behaviour firsthand. This offers the judge a comparatively advantageous position to evaluate the lawyer's conduct relative to the Law Society, who only enters the equation once all is said and done. The judge's reaction is not conclusive, and the Law Society is not barred from reviewing a lawyer's behaviour if the judge does not comment.

The failure to deal with the *W. (D.)* analysis by the learned justice of the peace was a fatal error. The accused does not have to testify if the Crown prosecutor leads the accused's statement as part of their case. The learned justice of the peace must address that issue when that happens. See *R. v. Hayle*, 2018 ONCJ 402, 2018 CarswellOnt 9568, [2018] O.J. No. 3151 (Ont. C.J.).

In *Mississauga (City) v. Sekhon*, 2018 ONCJ 306, 2018 CarswellOnt 7286, [2018] O.J. No. 2468 (Ont. C.J.), it was held that an *ex parte* trial is still a trial. It must be conducted fairly and must have the appearance of being conducted fairly, by an impartial judicial officer. Just because a defendant is not present does not mean a conviction is inevitable. The presumption of innocence still applies, as does the burden of proof beyond a reasonable doubt. In some ways, it is even more important for a justice to remain above the fray in an *ex parte* trial because nobody is there to speak for the defendant. Reading the justice's comments as a whole would lead a reasonably informed member of the public to conclude that the appellant's conviction was a foregone conclusion from the outset. A provincial offences court is the only interaction that most Ontarians will have with the Ontario Court of Justice. Proceedings in provincial offences courts are necessarily less formal than they are in criminal court. However, a court of record is not the place for a judicial officer to engage in sarcasm or self-aggrandizing humour. Nor is it meant to be used as a soapbox to express the judicial officer's personal views.

There was no basis for the defendant's argument that no law can affect or seek to control his behaviour unless he has actually caused someone actual harm, given the authority of the Provincial Legislature to enact legislation regulating the operation of motor vehicles by individuals on a highway. Neither was there any basis for the argument that the justice of the peace was an administrator without authority to hear such trials under the *Highway Traffic Act*. The justice of the peace derived her authority from s. 39(2) of the *Courts of Justice Act* which states that "A justice of the peace may preside over the Ontario Court of Justice in a proceeding under the *Provincial Offences Act*." Section 1(1) of that Act defines "justice" as a "provincial judge or a justice of the peace." See *R. v. Corsi*, 2018 ONCJ 252, 2018 CarswellOnt 6328, [2018] O.J. No. 2142 (Ont. C.J.).

In *R. v. Galbraith*, 2018 ONCJ 138, 2018 CarswellOnt 3347, 404 C.R.R. (2d) 371, [2018] O.J. No. 1189 (Ont. C.J.), a written request for disclosure was sought four times by the defendant for her speeding trial, and she received assurances from administration that her requests had been forwarded to the office of the prosecution. She did not receive an answer to her requests. The prosecution policy concerning the provision of disclosure in the jurisdiction was usually two weeks after receipt of a written request. The delay in providing disclosure in a timely manner to the defendant in this case was due to staffing changes in the office of the prosecution. The prosecution delay in providing disclosure was due to a mistake and did not violate her right to a fair trial under s. 11(d) of the *Charter of Rights*, nor was any prejudice demonstrated such that the late disclosure did not violate the right to make full answer and defence under s. 7 of the *Charter*. The time elapsed since the date of the offence to the proposed date of trial was seven months, well below the presumptive ceiling for unreasonable delay established in *R. v. Jordan*. There was no negligence on the part of the prosecutor that justified an order of costs either as a *Charter* remedy or due to procedural irregularities under s. 90 of the *Provincial Offences Act*. The defendant had chosen to attend the Early Resolution meeting and there were a total of two court appearances to date. Section 24(1) of the *Charter* confers a broad remedial mandate and the widest possible discretion on a court to craft remedies that must be easily available for violations of *Charter* rights. The remedy in the instant case was an adjournment to a date for trial and no order for costs.

At the beginning of his trial, the defendant argued he was denied Crown disclosure despite two requests for it. At the start of his trial, the prosecutor gave some disclosure, but the defendant asked for more. The prosecutor was not in a position to provide it at that time. The defendant then asked the justice of the peace for a stay of proceedings due to this failure to make proper disclosure. He was not allowed to make submissions on this point, including his presenting four binding cases that he wished to present. However, the defendant did not give any notice he was bringing a stay application. By not giving such a notice, the justice of the peace understandably was not prepared to hear the stay application on the merits at that time. The justice of the peace was within his right to try and control the proceedings before him, and he did not overstep the appropriate boundaries of that. At the end of the day, while the justice of the peace did not accede to the defendant's request for a stay or listen to the whole of his submissions, he adjourned the trial in order that disclosure be made. The justice of the peace specifically left it open for the defendant to bring his stay application on the new trial date, present any evidence he wished, and to make his submissions. When the whole of the proceedings was assessed, there was no denial of natural justice or an unfair hearing. The justice of the peace was also correct in not ordering a stay of proceedings at this time. The remedy that he chose was to grant an adjournment so that proper disclosure could be made. This was a fit remedy for Crown non-disclosure. The justice of the peace did not preclude the defendant from asking for a stay of proceedings upon the resumption of the trial. No substantial wrong or miscarriage of justice resulted from this decision. See *City of Toronto v. Riddell*, 2018 ONSC 2048, 2018 CarswellOnt 4860, [2018] O.J. No. 1643 (Ont. S.C.J.), affirmed *Toronto (City) v. Riddell*, 2019 ONCA 103, 2019 CarswellOnt 2272, [2019] O.J. No. 823 (Ont. C.A.).

In *Reginella v. R.*, 2018 ONCJ 198, 2018 CarswellOnt 4918, [2018] O.J. No. 1547 (Ont. C.J.), the learned justice of the peace denied the adjournment request brought by the defendant on the trial date due to disclosure not being received mainly on the bases that the Crown witnesses were present, the Crown was ready to proceed and that the defendant had not brought an application or motion for an adjournment prior to the trial date. The learned justice of the peace exercised his discretion judicially in refusing to grant the adjournment on the trial date. He properly considered that there would be an inconvenience to witnesses as being a factor and that the defendant or his agent had not brought an application for an adjournment prior when they realized that the disclosure had not been received. The learned justice of the peace did not consider any irrelevant factors in this decision. Clearly, there was an onus on the defendant and his agent to follow up by way of direct contact with the trial date when the disclosure had not been received. In addition to not being any adjournment request, the defendant or his agent did not bring an application for a stay of proceedings based on a failure of the prosecution to provide disclosure. In the circumstances, the trial was fair. The defendant was represented; he chose not to attend the trial. The defendant's agent could have renewed his request for an adjournment at the close of the prosecution's case so that the defendant or any defence witnesses could testify. Such a request was not made. The appeal court had not been advised that even though disclosure was received subsequent to the trial, there was something of substance in that disclosure that may have assisted the defendant in his defence.

The applicant sought as part of first party records disclosure the disciplinary records and employment file for the police officer who charged him with driving while holding or using a hand-held communication device. Although the applicant had failed to comply with the 30-day notice requirements in s. 141(1) of the *Provincial Offences Act*, s. 85 provides for a broad curative power to extend time for service. The court should exercise the power to extend the times prescribed in s. 141(1) unless to do so would prejudice the other parties. In the present case, the justice of the peace refused the applicant's request for the disciplinary records on the basis that those records were irrelevant and the applicant will have the opportunity to explore the subject in cross-examination. While the reasons for the refusal were not extensive, the decision was one that clearly fell within the jurisdiction of the justice of the peace. As the applicant will be able to explore the matter in cross-examination of the officer, it could not be said that the decision will have a fundamentally important impact on the fairness of the trial. In addition, such pre-trial rulings can always be reconsidered by the justice of the peace who presides over the trial should the evidence warrant disclosure. The disciplinary records may take on more relevance based on how the questions are answered by the witness in cross-examination. However, evidence of historical drug use by an officer who has seemingly satisfied his superiors that he is fit to resume his duties has marginal relevance at this point. How far the applicant can go in cross-examination on this issue and if there will be any merit to some form of documentary disclosure will be determined at trial. The Crown had specifically stated that it had considered the disciplinary records in question and had fulfilled its "gate-keeping" function that they do not form part of first party disclosure. Not every finding of police misconduct by an officer involved in a matter will be relevant to the accused's case and it is certainly not the case that a *McNeil* report should be provided as a matter of course in all provincial offences prosecutions. The applicant had been aware of the Crown's position that an *O'Connor* application was the proper procedure to determine if some or all of the disciplinary records should be produced. The applicant had ignored the Crown's position, and chose to proceed with the application. There was an upcoming trial date for the matter and this date could be impacted if the applicant commenced an *O'Connor* application at this late date. The impact that such an application could have on the trial date was a matter for the discretion of the trial judge. See *Mian v. City of Ottawa*, 2018 ONSC 2131, 2018 CarswellOnt 5388, [2018] O.J. No. 1773 (Ont. S.C.J.).

It was held in *R. v. 1137749 Ontario Ltd. (operating as Pro-Teck Electric)*, 2018 ONCJ 502, 2018 CarswellOnt 12427, [2018] O.J. No. 4001 (Ont. C.J.) that a justice of the peace sitting in provincial offences court has the authority to pierce the corporate veil in appropriate cases. The authority derives from the implied jurisdiction of the provincial offences court to carry out the legislative scheme. The question, in the context of the present case, really boils down to whether or not the sentencing court should have the power to defeat an effort by a defendant to neuter the court in imposing a just and effective sentence by making that sentence unenforceable, meaningless and illusory. It is simply inconceivable that a justice of the peace conducting a provincial offences trial lacks a very specific power (clearly possessed by other courts) that is essential to avoid a "flagrant" circumvention of justice. The power to pierce the corporate veil will be triggered when failing to act would result in circumvention of justice. On the evidence in this case, once it is clear that the sentencing court had jurisdiction to pierce the corporate veil, the only rational conclusion is that the test for piercing the veil was made out by the principal of the company's wrongful acts in diverting the company's assets by transferring company assets to himself and forming a new company around the same time that charges were laid, such acts being done for the flagrantly unlawful purpose of defeating the course of justice.

While giving his evidence, the defendant was trying to explain where the police vehicles were parked in the gas station parking lot and which lane his vehicle was in when he was told to pull over. He asked if he could explain it in a diagram. The Judicial Justice agreed he could do so. The defendant referred to the diagram as he gave his evidence. The Judicial Justice's failure in the case to have the diagram marked as an exhibit prevented proper appellate review of the reasons for conviction in the context of the evidence adduced at trial. Trials in Traffic Court are almost invariably more expeditious than criminal trials in Provincial Court or Supreme Court because they do not engage the same penalty structure and potential for imprisonment, but the record should be created and preserved with the same diligence in Traffic Court as it is in the other courts. See *R. v. Singh*, 2018 BCSC 1325, 2018 CarswellBC 2088, [2018] B.C.J. No. 1325 (B.C. S.C.).

In *R. v. Masoumi*, 2018 ONCJ 576, 2018 CarswellOnt 14043, [2018] O.J. No. 4392 (Ont. C.J.), it was held that there was no air of reality to the claim that the court's conduct in past proceedings involving paralegals and agents gave rise to a reasonable apprehension of bias in the present proceeding. An allegation of hostility towards a paralegal in a different matter, totally unsubstantiated, who is not representing the defendant before the court does not rise to the level of cogent evidence sufficient to rebut the presumption of judicial impartiality. Even accepting for the sake of argument that a justice's exercise of the power to determine where individuals sit in the courtroom could potentially give rise to a reasonable expectation of bias, the past practice of the court in refusing to allow agents to sit at a table reserved for lawyers at a time when agents were not licensed paralegals could not give rise to a reasonable apprehension of bias in the instant proceedings. After the Law Society began issuing licences for paralegals, the court's practice had been to permit paralegals to sit at counsel table, and there was no evidence that the agent in the instant proceedings had been prevented by the court from sitting at counsel table at any time.

In *Halton (Regional Municipality) v. Verigin*, 2018 ONCJ 676, 2018 CarswellOnt 16300, [2018] O.J. No. 5055 (Ont. C.J.), it was held that electronic notes compiled by a police officer may be used to refresh his/her memory , even though the notes have not been in the personal possession of the witness since the time they were recorded up until the time they were reviewed for trial, and the witness could not state that the notes were not accessed by anyone else and/or who could make additions, deletions or other alterations to the notes. The notes had been disclosed and the officer had not attested to the fact that any alterations were, in fact, made. He had an independent recollection. That should itself be enough for the court to proceed to hear such evidence at trial. Though the officer could not truthfully attest to anyone else having access to those notes nor could he say whether someone else had an opportunity to alter such notes, there was no direct evidence led that the notes had been altered nor had the court heard of any additions, deletions or other amendments that had actually been made by others and not the officer himself. In conclusion, it is up to the trier of fact to assess the officer's ability to recall independently from his notes. This is done by consideration of a number of factors including whether the or not the officer reads his notes verbatim, and whether or not he attests to having an independent recollection.

The applicant sought to have a party, M, who was not a licensed paralegal or lawyer, act as his agent on the appeal. The judge ruled that M could not appear as the applicant's agent for that appeal. At that point the applicant requested an adjournment which was not granted. Eventually the matter was adjourned because of time constraints. A judge may bar a person from acting as agent if that person is not competent and does not understand and comply with the duties and responsibilities of an agent. The judge found that M may not understand and properly comply with the duties and responsibilities of an agent, and gave examples of no advance warning to the courts or to the prosecution that he would be appearing and arguing matters before the court as agent, or that he was the one who drafted the Notice of Constitutional Issues. An agent cannot argue that he/she understands and will comply with the duties and obligations of an agent, and then have the principal argue that certain actions were his, and not the agent's. M clearly knew that this issue would arise. He came armed with case law and argument on this point. Yet it was not until the case actually commenced that the appellant advised the court and the Crown that the appellant wished to have M act for him as an agent. The reasonable conclusion was that the appellant and M decided to ambush the

Crown and put it at a disadvantage. The judge's decision to disqualify M from acting as an agent did not constitute a substantial wrong or miscarriage of justice. Neither did the decision of the appeal court to grant an adjournment constitute a substantial wrong or miscarriage of justice. The appellant knew that the issue of M being permitted to act as an agent would be a live issue at the appeal. He knew or should have known that it was possible that M would be disqualified, and therefore he should have been prepared to proceed on his own with the appeal at that time. The appellant could not argue that he was surprised that he was required to proceed, when, in fact, he was the person who failed to give advance notice to the Crown, which notice would have resulted in the Crown advising in advance of its objection. See *R. v. Vanravenswaay*, 2018 ONSC 5348, 2018 CarswellOnt 15064, [2018] O.J. No. 5348 (Ont. S.C.J.).

In *York (Regional Municipality) v. 1085638 Ontario Limited*, 2018 ONCJ 658, 2018 CarswellOnt 16164, [2018] O.J. No. 5003 (Ont. C.J.), it was held that the decision to adjourn a proceeding is one in the discretion of the trial judge. The judicial officer must listen to the request and consider various factors, including the length of time of the proposed adjournment. The longer the period of time, the greater the likelihood the adjournment should not be granted as the likelihood of prejudice to the defence increases. What was clear on the record was that the justice of the peace tried to accommodate an adjournment for sentencing submissions if it was only going to be for a short time. After poring over the court calendar with the assistance of the trial coordinator it was clear that it couldn't. By that time the charges were 12 years and 5 years old, respectively, the court was clearly uncomfortable with yet another delay in the case at the penultimate stage, and ruled that submissions should be heard. Given that counsel were advised two months previously that they should be ready to do just that on the return date, the decision was not unfair. There was also no evidence on the appeal about what evidence would have been heard had the adjournment been granted. No fresh evidence was sought to be tendered on the hearing of the appeal. No error in principle was identified in the reasons for sentence. Absent an error in principle sentencing decisions are entitled to deference. Despite denying the adjournment, the court received submissions on sentence from both the prosecution and defence. The defendants received very substantial fines — $60,000 in total. That said, this was a legal sentence, and the defendants had a history of previous convictions relating to the very issue of non-compliance with municipal orders.

The defendant's concern about the prejudicial effect of evidence that had been adduced from leading questions put by the prosecutor to their own witnesses and the elicitation of irrelevant hearsay, bad character, and lay opinion evidence into the trial, had to be viewed in context and its intended use in the trial. Any prejudicial effect of the impugned evidence had been lessened as this was a non-jury trial and the charges involved strict liability regulatory offences in which the prosecution can elicit evidence in their case-in-chief to rebut a defence of due diligence or other anticipated defences. After considering the impugned evidentiary issues and the context in which the prosecutor's impugned comments, language and tone were used and what had been occurring in the trial at the time, the cumulative effect of the prosecutor's conduct, although not ideal and of perfect comportment, did not go beyond aggressive or abusive as to cause the defendant to receive an unfair trial, since the defendant's trial was a non-jury trial for which the trier would be cognizant of applying the relevant legal principles and law, and would also be able to disabuse and give no weight to any hearsay, bad character, opinion, or any other irrelevant prejudicial evidence, nor put any weight on any inappropriate, sarcastic, or demeaning comments, made by the prosecutor about the defendant's memory, business practices, or personal lifestyle, or to improperly use the impugned evidence or the immoderate comments of the prosecutor as proof of guilt. Accordingly, the defendant's right to a fair trial had not been prejudiced by the cumulative effect of the prosecutor's conduct in eliciting the impugned evidence, nor by the prosecutor's impugned comments, language or tone, that would be manifested, perpetuated or aggravated through the conduct of the trial, or by its outcome. Neither was the cumulative effect of the prosecutor's conduct such that it reached a degree of unfairness or vexatiousness that contravenes notions of fundamental justice, nor was it the type of conduct in which the justice system would find it necessary to intervene so that it would leave the impression that it condones conduct that offends society's sense of fair play and decency. Therefore, the prosecutor's conduct during the trial had not undermined the integrity of the justice system that would be manifested, perpetuated or aggravated through the conduct of the trial, or by its outcome. See *Ontario (Electrical Safety Authority) v. Broomfield*, 2018 ONCJ 640, 2018 CarswellOnt 15732, [2018] O.J. No. 4893 (Ont. C.J.).

In *York (Regional Municipality) v. Bouaziz-Caruso*, [2019] O.J. No. 638 (Ont. C.J.), the defence representative had asked for disclosure several weeks before, but by the trial date it had not been handed out. The trial justice denied the adjournment, finding that any suggestion the defendant did not receive the notice of trial in advance was hearsay. The justice held the matter down to permit the trial agent to review disclosure and the defendant present, however she did not attend. Where a second trial date adjournment is denied, it is appropriate for the justice of the peace to hold the trial down briefly to permit the review of disclosure before trial. This practice is not uncommon for Part I litigation, and is reasonable in light of the simplified procedure contemplated under the Act.

A printout of every keystroke entered by all individuals involved in the investigation of the defendant was not required for him to make full answer and defence on a charge of driving a motor vehicle while prohibited. However, the defendant was entitled to be provided with all broadcast communications relevant to the vehicle investigation and vehicle stop, including communications from dispatch and any officer, and all communications between the officers themselves. See *R. v. Kooner*, 2018 BCPC 355, 2018 CarswellBC 3542, [2018] B.C.J. No. 7038 (B.C. Prov. Ct.).

In *R. v. Kanoon*, 2018 ONCJ 793, 2018 CarswellOnt 19132, [2018] O.J. No. 5948 (Ont. C.J.), the defendant did not accept the facts underpinning the guilty plea. Whether this was an oversight on the part of the justice of the peace, the conviction should not have been registered. The bulk of participants in the provincial offences court proceedings are unsophisticated, and unfamiliar with court proceedings. In these instances, a more detailed plea inquiry is required. This is especially so, when as in this case, the defendant expressed that he had something to say about the facts, and had already relayed that information to someone. It was incumbent upon the presiding justice of the peace to seek clarification and to ensure that the facts were truly being accepted as accurate and supportive of the guilty plea. Additionally, with respect to the specific offence alleged in the matter, the justice of the peace should have advised the parties that there was a potential defence of due diligence and incorporated this into the plea inquiry.

The rule in *Browne v. Dunn* is not merely a procedural rule but a rule of trial fairness. It stands for the proposition that if counsel is going to challenge the credibility of a witness by calling contradictory evidence, the witness must be given the chance to address the contradictory evidence in cross-examination while he or she is in the witness box. More often than not, the rule in *Browne v. Dunn* arises and is invoked in situations where the defendant is unrepresented, as occurred in the instant case. The defendant's testimony as to removing his label/sticker from his vehicle was evidence that should have been put to the prosecution witness so that the officer could have been cross-examined with regard to that evidence. The proper remedy was to permit the officer to be recalled for this purpose. See *R. v. Hartlieb*, 2018 ONCJ 810, 2018 CarswellOnt 19435, [2018] O.J. No. 6080 (Ont. C.J.).

In *R. v. Dennis*, 2019 ONCA 109, 2019 CarswellOnt 2065, [2019] O.J. No. 773 (Ont. C.A.), it was held that the threshold for awarding costs against a lawyer personally in a criminal proceeding is a high one. As stated by the Supreme Court of Canada in *Québec (Directeur des poursuites criminelles et pénales) c. Jodoin*, 2017 CSC 26, 2017 SCC 26, 2017 CarswellQue 3091, 2017 CarswellQue 3092, [2017] 1 S.C.R. 478, 346 C.C.C. (3d) 433, 37 C.R. (7th) 1, 408 D.L.R. (4th) 581, (*sub nom.* Quebec (Director of Criminal and Penal Prosecutions) v. Jodoin) 380 C.R.R. (2d) 285, [2017] S.C.J. No. 26 (S.C.C.), only serious misconduct can justify such a sanction. Costs are awarded on a discretionary basis and appellate courts should only intervene when that discretion is exercised "in an abusive, unreasonable or non-judicial manner." In the instant case, the appellant's counsel requested an adjournment of the appeal hearing without notice to the Crown prosecutor. The Crown prosecutor had interrupted her vacation to attend on the scheduled date to argue the appeal, and had been inconvenienced as a result of the appellant's request for an adjournment. Counsel apologized to the prosecutor and the court. Of his own initiative, the appeal judge asked the Crown prosecutor if she wished to apply for costs under s. 129 of the *Provincial Offences Act*. The appeal court ordered counsel to pay costs personally in the amount of $500 due to his reckless disregard for the other side. The principles described in *Jodoin* ought to apply equally to an order under s. 129. However, while the absence of advance notice of the adjournment request was worthy of adverse comment by the court, the exercise of the appeal judge's discretion was unreasonable and did not meet the threshold for an award of costs against counsel personally. Fundamentally, counsel's behaviour did not warrant the exceptional remedy of a personal costs order. The costs award was vacated.

In *York (Regional Municipality) v. McGuigan*, 2018 ONCA 1062, 2018 CarswellOnt 22571, [2018] O.J. No. 6916 (Ont. C.A.), the Court of Appeal ruled that trial justice properly ordered the prosecutor to provide disclosure of the testing and operating procedures from the user manual for the device used by the traffic officer to measure the speed of the defendant's vehicle. Even if the justice of the peace had been wrong to order disclosure, the error would not have been jurisdictional in nature. Section 140(1) of the *Provincial Offences Act* confines *certiorari* orders in *POA* matters to situations where an applicant would be entitled to such relief at common law, and for parties to a proceeding, *certiorari* orders are confined to jurisdictional errors. Moreover, *certiorari* should not have been granted in the course of ongoing proceedings. Nor was there a substantial wrong or miscarriage of justice to address, a prerequisite to *certiorari* under s. 141(4) of the Act. Contrary to the application judge's decision, the justice of the peace did not err in making the disclosure order. Where a prosecutor is relying on a speed measuring device to prosecute an offence, it must, on request, disclose the testing and operating procedures set out in the user manual for that device. It is up to the prosecutor to hand such information over on request. The person charged need not bring an application or obtain a court order. This is first party disclosure, not third party disclosure. The charging police force has a corresponding duty to furnish the pertinent passages from the user manual to the prosecutor to enable the prosecutor to discharge its first party disclosure obligations. This is not a crushing administrative task. The disclosure at issue here is not case specific information. The disclosure obligation can therefore be discharged by the prosecutor by posting the relevant content from the user manual online and providing the ticketed driver with the required URL.

2.2 THE PROSECUTOR

- The Prosecutor may be a lawyer with the Ministry of the Attorney General, a lawyer with another branch of the

Provincial Government, or an independent agent acting for the Provincial Government.

- Bill 108, the *Streamlining of Administration of Provincial Offences Act, 1997*, was enacted and received Royal Assent on June 11, 1998, at which time the legislation came into force. This Bill [S.O. 1998, c. 4] amends the *Provincial Offences Act* to allow the Attorney General to make agreements with municipalities permitting them to undertake courts' administration and court support functions for the purposes of the Act. Pursuant to Bill 108, a new Part X is enacted which is entitled Agreements With Municipalities Concerning Administration Functions and Prosecutions. Under Part X, the Attorney General can authorize municipalities to conduct prosecutions in proceedings under Parts I and II of the *Provincial Offences Act* and in proceedings under the *Contraventions Act* (Canada) that are commenced by ticket under Part I or II of the *Provincial Offences Act*. Contraventions are federal regulatory offences, other than offences for which an offender may be prosecuted only on indictment, which are enforced in Ontario under the *Provincial Offences Act*.

- Commencing in March, 1999, the Attorney General entered into agreements with various municipalities, transferring responsibility for administrative functions and the prosecution of charges under Parts I and II of the *Provincial Offences Act*. As of February, 2002, all municipalities in Ontario have taken over the court administration and prosecution of Parts I and II of the *Provincial Offences Act*. A list of the various provincial offences courts throughout Ontario, including telephone and fax numbers, has been added as an Appendix.

In *R. v. Miceli*, 2006 ONCJ 67, [2006] O.J. No. 727, 2006 CarswellOnt 1548 (Ont. C.J.), it was held that it is well recognized that the Crown's prosecutorial discretion is almost absolute. Decisions to prosecute or plea-bargain are a result of professional judgment as to the strength of the evidence, the availability of resources, the visibility of the crime and the likely deterrent effect. Even if it were able to collect, understand and balance all of these factors, a court would find it nearly impossible to lay down guidelines to be followed by prosecutors.

In another recent case, *R. v. Baxter*, 2006 ONCJ 313, [2006] O.J. No. 3512, 2006 CarswellOnt 5294 (Ont. C.J.), the court held that in the absence of any wrong doing or malicious intent, the Crown has the discretion to call the list as he or she sees fit.

In *R. v. Figueli*, 2010 CarswellOnt 7262, [2010] O.J. No. 4122 (Ont. C.J.), it was held that with respect to any regulatory or criminal offences, one set of facts can be the basis for more than one charge. There is no rule that the defendant has to be charged with one or the other as long as it is clear on the information what the accusations are that a defendant has to reply or respond to defend himself against. In the context of the case, it was clear that all the parties knew that they were dealing with stunt driving. That was what the prosecutor was prosecuting and that is what the defendant was being defended for. It was clear that the charge and the basis of the charge had been disclosed and he had an opportunity to defend himself, an opportunity to make a full and fair defence and was represented by a licensed paralegal.

There was no evidence to show that the prosecution of the charges was delegated to the Fire Chiefs. The prosecutor, who was properly appointed by the Regional Municipality of Niagara, acted in that capacity throughout the case, and there was no suggestion that he acted improperly at any time. The sentence in the prosecutor's letter that he had received instructions from the Fire Chiefs neither constituted nor indicated that the authority to prosecute the cases had been delegated to the Fire Chiefs; it was very similar to a Crown attorney consulting with the investigating police officer or a complainant before making a decision in a criminal case. As long as the lawyer continues to make the decisions, he/she is still the prosecutor. There was nothing to indicate anything different here. Nor was there anything to suggest that he behaved improperly in any way in his prosecution of the case: *Niagara (Regional Municipality) v. DiFruscia*, 2010 ONCJ 427, 2010 CarswellOnt 7104, [2010] O.J. No. 404 (Ont. C.J.).

In *R. v. Martin Grove Properties Ltd.*, 2011 ONCA 711, 90 M.P.L.R. (4th) 226, 2011 CarswellOnt 12226, [2011] O.J. No. 4992 (Ont. C.A.), leave to appeal refused 2012 CarswellOnt 6765, 2012 CarswellOnt 6766, 426 N.R. 389 (note), 302 O.A.C. 397 (note) (S.C.C.) it was held that the subject matter of the proceedings for the purpose of the *Building Code Act* was the failure to comply with the order made in March, 2008, and the omission of which took place at the earliest after May, 2008, when the defendant allegedly failed to comply with the terms of the order. The charge, which was laid in January, 2009, was therefore laid within the one year statutory limitation period. The fact that there were other orders issued related to the same underlying acts of the defendant might be relevant to an argument that the prosecution was an abuse of process, but did not preclude the municipality from instituting the prosecution. The fact that the municipality had other remedies for failure to comply with orders did not preclude resort to prosecution.

The prosecutor in a *Provincial Offences Act* matter is no less a "minister of justice" than their brothers or sisters in a criminal court, and indeed may have a higher call of duty in that many of the judicial officers they appear before were lay persons before their appointment to the bench. They may also have an added role in assisting the bench in understanding novel or arcane aspects of the law, of evidence or of procedure. In other words, they are more than merely a representative of one of the parties in a litigation. See *R. v. Zehr*, [2011] O.J. No. 4493, 2011 ONCJ 516, 2011 CarswellOnt 10607, 21 M.V.R. (6th) 322 (Ont. C.J.).

In *R. v. Marriott*, 2013 CarswellOnt 6496, [2013] O.J. No. 2684 (Ont. C.J.), it was held that the prosecutor of a provincial offences matter has an unfettered discretion to withdraw charges prior to plea. In a case where the prosecutor told the defendant he could leave because he would withdraw charges against him in exchange for his guilty plea, the Justice of the Peace should not have imposed a conviction upon deciding not to permit the charge to be withdrawn. The Justice should have adjourned the matters to facilitate the attendance of the defendant in the future. Convicting a person when the prosecutor has telegraphed that it wishes to discontinue the prosecution amounts to a denial of natural justice.

In *R. v. Lucas*, 2013 CarswellOnt 6515, [2013] O.J. No. 2685 (Ont. C.J.), four minutes after court was scheduled to start and the prosecutor had not appeared despite being paged twice, the Justice of the Peace dismissed all 68 charges on the tier for want of prosecution. The prosecutor filed an affidavit on appeal, indicating that he was outside the courtroom at the time, negotiating with a defendant, immediately went towards the courtroom when he saw the Justice appear, and did not hear his name being called as the pager in the hallway was not working. The prosecutor's affidavit showed an apparent lack of any insight into his own contribution to this deplorable affair; it was if his role in the justice system did not entail certain obligations to the court. One of the prosecutor's duties is to preserve respect for the court. One does not promote such respect by failing to be in attendance when the Justice enters the courtroom. Those in attendance are left with this image of a judicial officer cooling his heels awaiting the arrival of the prosecutor before the machinery of justice can come to life. Had the prosecutor immediately entered the courtroom and then advised the Justice that he required a few more minutes or a recess, it would be routine for judicial officers in these courts to grant such indulgences as provincial offences courts are likely the busiest courts of any courts in the country, bar none. The administration purposely overloads them on the theory that missing witnesses and defendants, illnesses and resolutions, all lead to whittling down the list to a manageable level. The key to making this happen is to give the prosecutor the time and latitude to get a handle on the state of the cases. Every justice of that court is alive to this, and likely none would deny this type of request as it is the most effective way to manage such formidable lists. The Justice in this case was clearly piqued by the prosecutor's absence, which he viewed as wilful, and he likely felt the prosecutor's actions were cumulative. However, it is always an injudicious use of one's discretion to make others suffer the consequences of someone else's actions. Had the Justice instead chosen to dress down the prosecutor in open court, when he did materialize, it was likely warranted. The rocky road taken instead was unacceptable, and led irretrievably to a reversible error of law.

A Justice of the Peace has jurisdiction to dismiss a charge under s. 53 of the prosecutor fails to appear, however there is no jurisdiction for the Justice to "withdraw" a charge. A withdrawal of a charge before a plea is entered is a matter that is solely within the discretion of the prosecutor. The prosecutor's failure to appear in this case was because he misdiarized the court date. See *Strachan v. Szewcyk*, 2013 ONCJ 402, 2013 CarswellOnt 10266, [2013] O.J. No. 3445 (Ont. C.J.).

A person who has laid a private information under Part III of the *Provincial Offences Act* may act as prosecutor and also be a witness at trial: *Strachan v. Szewcyk*, 2013 ONCJ 402, 2013 CarswellOnt 10266, [2013] O.J. No. 3445 (Ont. C.J.).

In *R. v. Bydeley*, 2012 ONCJ 837, 2012 CarswellOnt 17276, [2012] O.J. No. 6407 (Ont. C.J.), it was held that there was no reasonable apprehension of bias on account of alleged collusion between the trial Justice of the Peace and the prosecutor and the police officer because they were "all under the employ of those who have a hand in forming these statutes" under which the defendant was charged with a highway traffic offence. There was no such appearance in the trial, and such a serious allegation should not be made lightly. The judiciary, which includes the presiding Justice of the Peace at trial, is a third branch of government, whose independence is maintained by the appointments process on through the appeals process. That the prosecutor and the police witness are paid by the same municipal government, albeit through different legislated authorities, is of no moment in a consideration of entitlement to fair trial.

An appearance of bias may be an inadvertent consequence of the exercise of the amendment powers referenced in s. 34(2), particularly when that power is exercised or referenced unilaterally by the Justice of the Peace. Restraint should be exercised in the use of the amendment powers particularly when the Justice of the Peace, absent a motion by the prosecution, is acting on his or her own initiative. As stated by the Ontario Court of Appeal in *R. v. Winlow*, 2009 ONCA 643, 2009 CarswellOnt 5208, (*sub nom.* York (Regional Municipality) v. Winlow) 99 O.R. (3d) 337, 86 M.V.R. (5th) 171, 265 O.A.C. 326, [2009] O.J. No. 3691 (Ont. C.A.),

Justices of the Peace are not encouraged to amend on their own motion. See *R. v. Strati*, 2014 ONCJ 139, 2014 CarswellOnt 3624, [2014] O.J. No. 1413 (Ont. C.J.).

Given the serious professional and punitive consequences of a finding of contempt, the contempt citation process should be used sparingly, if at all: *R. v. Strati*, 2014 ONCJ 139, 2014 CarswellOnt 3624, [2014] O.J. No. 1413 (Ont. C.J.).

The defendant was charged with driving a commercial motor vehicle with no brake lights for which the set fine was $200. However, the set fine indicated on the certificate of offence was $85, which was the set fine for the offence involving a vehicle that is not a commercial motor vehicle. As the set fine was incorrect, it was not complete and regular on its face and ought to have been quashed by the Justice of the Peace. It seemed an unfortunate waste of everyone's time and court resources to require such a simple case with an obvious defect to have to go through two levels of court (first instance and appeal) before the result dictated by law is achieved. It is inappropriate for an officer of the court who is aware that a court is about to make an error by not quashing a certificate of offence that is not complete and regular to fail to bring his/her concern to the court's attention. The party should not be required to lie in the weeds clutching a notice of appeal. There is no downside but rather an upside of eliminating these concerns by permitting a defendant or his/her representative to make a conditional appearance, without thereby being considered to be present, in this narrow and unique situation. To be clear, the very summary nature of default proceedings is not to be altered; rather, this would simply provide an opportunity for one having some knowledge of the particular certificate of offence to point out what might otherwise be overlooked. It would not be a matter for argument, nor would it trigger otherwise inapplicable amending powers. Once so informed, the court would make its determination to convict or quash as the case may be. Any disagreement with that decision would be a matter to be addressed on appeal. See *R. v. Rodrigues*, 2013 ONCJ 719, 2013 CarswellOnt 18477, 62 M.V.R. (6th) 331, [2013] O.J. No. 6041 (Ont. C.J.).

The prosecutor's comment to the defendant while she was being cross-examined that her opportunity to give evidence was now over, she was now subject to cross-examination, was a total misrepresentation of what cross-examination is. Cross-examination is an opportunity for the person to answer questions given by the other side while still giving evidence. The use of the statement by the prosecutor to cut off an answer was also inappropriate. See *R. v. Shuttleworth*, 2013 ONCJ 749, 2013 CarswellOnt 18654, [2013] O.J. No. 6164 (Ont. C.J.).

Before rejecting the range of sentence suggested by the prosecutor and imposing a higher fine, the Justice should have given cogent reasons for doing so and then explained why, in his view, fines within the suggested range would be contrary to the public interest or would otherwise bring the administration of justice into disrepute: *Kingston (City) v. Patry* (August 9, 2011), Doc. Kingston 090175, 090176, [2011] O.J. No. 6667 (Ont. C.J.).

The trial Justice of the Peace refused to allow the defendant to file a copy of the laser manual he received in disclosure as an exhibit at trial. If properly identified and there was a foundation laid for its introduction, the manual could be entered as an exhibit. No rule of evidence required a copy of the manual to be certified as a true copy. It was not necessary to make the manual an exhibit in order for the defendant to have continued cross-examining the officer once the proper foundation had been laid. There is nothing wrong in making portions of the manual an exhibit at trial further to this type of cross-examination; it is often done on consent of the parties, and may be of assistance to the trial Justice to have a written copy to assist him or her in following the testimony of the witness. It is the testimony of the police officer, however, that is the evidence, not the exhibit itself. There is very little gained in making the entire manual an exhibit at trial, even with the consent of the parties, as it contains much that is totally irrelevant. If it is made an independent exhibit, it is incumbent on the Justice to review the whole manual. See *Mangov v. Toronto (City)*, 2014 ONCJ 351, 2014 CarswellOnt 10104, [2014] O.J. No. 3477 (Ont. C.J.).

In *R. v. Zuccarini*, 2014 ONCJ 571, 2014 CarswellOnt 15457, [2014] O.J. No. 5234 (Ont. C.J.), the defendant had been given notice of the potential amendment to the certificate charging speeding to conform to evidence of speed at trial in the disclosure and on the day of trial by the prosecution. An adjournment was offered to the defendant, which was declined. The trial was also held down for the defendant to consider his position and consult with others, after which the defendant decided to proceed with the trial. The trial Justice found there was no prejudice to the defendant caused by the amendment, and it had no impact on the defendant's defence to the speeding charge. The reasons of the trial Justice demonstrated that he considered and applied the test with respect to granting amendments. There was no evidence of legal error or miscarriage of justice.

There was common ground among the parties that there is a duty of disclosure in trials conducted under Part I of the *Provincial Offences Act*, and that an unrepresented accused must be informed of his right to disclosure. It was also conceded by the City that as a self-represented litigant, the defendant was not adequately informed of his right to disclosure and that significant evidence, in the form of a video recording, has now been lost. On the basis of those concessions the appeal was allowed and an acquittal entered. Given this order, it was unnecessary to consider issues, including constitutional issues, regarding the method and timing of providing notice of the right to disclosure to unrepresented litigants in trials under Part I. It was also unnecessary to consider the nature of the assistance required to be provided by Justices of the Peace to unrepresented litigants in such trials. See *R. v. Ul-Rashid*, 2014 ONCA 896, 2014 CarswellOnt 18386, 70 M.V.R. (6th) 181 (Ont. C.A.).

When the paralegal was not present for the second scheduled trial date, the Justice of the Peace set the matter down to be heard later in the day, and then forced the trial to proceed in the paralegal's absence. The paralegal should have arranged his absence with the prosecution or should have been there. While the conviction was set aside on appeal, it was not likely to be tolerated a third time; the appeal court expected the prosecutor to flag the issue, and the date would likely be set to proceed whether or not the defendant's representative appears. See *R. v. Sayed-Zada*, 2015 CarswellOnt 15571, [2015] O.J. No. 5265 (Ont. C.J.).

It was further held in *York (Regional Municipality) v. Dave*, 2015 ONCJ 481, 2015 CarswellOnt 13983, [2015] O.J. No. 4651 (Ont. C.J.) that the warning to the prosecutor that the court would never impose the statutory minimum fine reasonably gave rise to an apprehension of bias. The justice also commented to the prosecutor when he attempted to cite a case that he was not going to be permitted "to take advantage of somebody who is here without counsel." There was nothing in the record that suggested the prosecutor was attempting to gain an advantage by citing a case. Indeed, it was the prosecutor's responsibility to do so. If the defendant needed to see a copy of the case or time to consider the prosecutor's position, that could be accommodated by the presiding justice. The comments of the court in relation to the prosecutor's submissions added to the reasonable apprehension of bias.

The police officer while testifying seemed, on several occasions, to control the cross-examination with little or no intervention on the part of the judge. It was only after numerous examples of such inappropriate conduct that the Crown prosecutor himself felt the need to intervene, but this was too little too late. The police officer's conduct during the cross-examination as well as the almost total lack of reaction on the part of the judge in this regard, when added to the exchanges between the judge himself and the accused, resulted in the appearance of an unfair trial. See *R. c. Robichaud*, 2016 NBBR 26, 2016 NBQB 26, 2016 CarswellNB 45, 2016 CarswellNB 48, (*sub nom.* R. v. Robichaud) 445 N.B.R. (2d) 54, 1166 A.P.R. 54, [2016] A.N.B. No. 30, [2016] N.B.J. No. 30 (N.B. Q.B.).

In *R. v. Gagne* (November 9, 2015), Doc. 14-0672, [2015] O.J. No. 6344 (Ont. S.C.J.), it was held that the Crown has the discretion to pursue through legitimate means a vigorous prosecution, which includes cooperative and effective real-time consultation with police as the prosecution unfolds. Such consultation may include having an investigating officer present at counsel table. However, where the officer was to be a witness at the proceeding, the officer was not permitted to sit at counsel table as an exception to the order excluding witnesses. It was open to the Crown to have the witness testify first and then sit at counsel table after his testimony, or have another instructing officer sit at counsel table.

In *R. v. Zacharias*, 2016 ONCJ 458, 2016 CarswellOnt 12095, [2016] O.J. No. 3975 (Ont. C.J.), the prosecution disclosed the police officer's notes and complied with some special disclosure requests of the defence. However, there were two letters from the defence requesting "if this is a speeding offence, the testing times of this device before and after the subject enforcement". The prosecution did not respond to that request. Prior to the trial, the prosecution and the defence discussed the testing of the device outside of court. The prosecution apparently disclosed the fact that the police officer had tested the device, but testing times were not provided. When the trial commenced, the defence stated that it was ready to proceed to trial. If the defence had been dissatisfied with the disclosure, it should have raised the issue as a pre-trial motion. If the lateness of the disclosure created a preparation problem for the defence, they should have requested an adjournment. However, the defence was ready to proceed to trial, and they so advised the court. There was no basis for concluding that the defendant did not receive a fair trial.

The Crown should not have more procedural rights than the accused. The accused could not attach the condition to his plea that it was dependent on the ruling against him being upheld; likewise, the Crown should not be participating in a process by which facts are agreed to and charges are withdrawn, conditional upon a ruling being upheld. The defendant entered the plea of guilty knowing that the state of law was that they were thereby forestalling the Crown's potential appeal. The Crown also knew this and actively participated notwithstanding. This should have been expected to be a final resolution of the matter. To allow the Crown to proceed to appeal the original ruling through a sentence appeal offends that expectation of finality. It would place the defendant in a position where they were potentially prejudiced by the fact of their plea and any revisitation of the issue of their guilt. See *Ontario (Ministry of Labour) v. Ontario Power Generation*, 2016 ONCJ 299, 2016 CarswellOnt 8272, [2016] O.J. No. 2725 (Ont. C.J.).

In *Oshawa (City) v. 536813 Ontario Ltd.*, 2016 ONCJ 665, 2016 CarswellOnt 18205, 60 M.P.L.R. (5th) 343, [2016] O.J. No. 5925 (Ont. C.J.), it was held that the jurisdiction to award costs is necessary for any court of law to control its processes and maintain the integrity of the court's processes and public confidence in the administration of justice. There is no principled reason to have jurisdiction to award costs for a *Charter* breach, but not following a ruling on a constitutional question. The ability to award costs as a sanction responsive to the unacceptable standard of prosecution is inherent jurisdiction of any court of law to control its own process, is reasonably necessary given the mandate of the Provincial Court to decide constitutional issues, and in order for the court to discharge its mandate. For these reasons, the Provincial Offences Court has jurisdiction to award costs in a case involving a constitutional challenge. It was appropriate to make such an order where the prosecution refused to accept the clear jurisprudence giving the federal government exclusive jurisdiction over the field of aeronautics under the constitutional doctrine of interjurisdictional immunity. The witnesses revealed their bias in favour of their employer, the City of Oshawa, by the manner in which they conducted themselves at the trial. Also at the trial, the prosecution inappropriately attempted to use privileged resolution negotiations against the defendant. While the City of Oshawa has an obligation to prosecute in the public interest, in this case the broad public interest appeared to be overtaken by its self-serving interests.

There was no prosecutorial misconduct due to "vetting the file erroneously". In the initial redacted duty notes, there was no evidence that any error was intentional or done for some nefarious purpose. Any inconsistency in the notes could have been clarified well in advance of the trial. Instead, the defence chose to raise the issue only during cross-examination. The Crown's position resisting disclosure of the radar manual did not amount to prosecutorial misconduct. The Crown's error in disclosure of the initial notes was unintentional, and the error was remedied by providing further disclosure in advance of the disclosure motion and trial. This did not amount to a standard of misconduct that justified an award of costs against the prosecution. See *R. v. Shan*, 2016 ONCJ 663, 2016 CarswellOnt 18212, [2016] O.J. No. 5935 (Ont. C.J.).

The *Stronger, Fairer Ontario Act (Budget Measures) 2017* (Bill 177) was given Royal Assent on 14 December 2017. This legislation, S.O. 2017, c. 34, contains Schedule 35, which makes numerous substantive changes to the *Provincial Offences Act*. These include that the definition of "prosecutor" in s. 1(1) is amended to include persons acting on behalf of a municipality under a transfer agreement.

In *Oshawa (City) v. 536813 Ontario Limited*, 2017 ONCJ 836, 2017 CarswellOnt 19439, 72 C.L.R. (4th) 140, 69 M.P.L.R. (5th) 313, [2017] O.J. No. 6428 (Ont. C.J.), the trial justice ordered costs against the "Prosecution", the "City of Oshawa" and the "Prosecutor, the City of Oshawa". While the costs order did not specifically detail the names of the prosecutors, it appeared from a review of the judgments that the trial justice sought to punish both the prosecutors *in personam* and the entity known as the City of Oshawa. There is a high test for ordering costs. Costs against the prosecution are relatively rare in criminal and quasi-criminal litigation — costs against the prosecution in the absence of a proven breach of the *Charter of Rights* rarer still. The trial justice erred by ordering costs in the amount of $111,000 plus HST. Given the serious ramifications of such a finding to the proper administration of justice, the perception of justice, the public perception of the City of Oshawa, and the impact on the individual prosecutors in the case, a clear evidentiary basis was required. The evidentiary record did not support a finding that the conduct of the prosecutors constituted "a marked and unacceptable departure from the reasonable standards expected of the prosecution." Nor did the evidentiary record justify costs against the City of Oshawa. There was no basis in evidence to find that the prosecution was directed by the municipality for self-interest and financial gain. The trial judge erred in co-mingling perceived motives associated with the municipality and the approach taken by the prosecution team appearing at trial. The court succumbed to error by dislodging the independent role of the prosecutor and impugning prosecutorial standards in the absence of evidence to support such findings.

Faced with a delay resulting from the complexity of a case, the Crown must act reasonably and take steps to implement the plan it has devised to minimize that delay. It is not too stringent a standard in the post-*Jordan* era for the trial judge to impose on the Crown that it be pro-active in its efforts to move the case to trial under the presumptive ceiling while simultaneously being involved in an extensive judicial pre-trial process aimed at resolving the case. There was no basis for appellate interference with the trial judge's decision holding that the Crown failed to develop and follow an adequate plan to minimize the delay arising from the complexity of the case. This conclusion was clearly open to the trial judge and led to his ultimate finding that the Crown had not established exceptional circumstances outside of its control justifying the delay above the presumptive ceiling. See *R. v. Nugent, Guillemette and Buckingham*, 2018 ONSC 3546, 2018 CarswellOnt 9120, [2018] O.J. No. 3047 (Ont. S.C.J.), leave to appeal allowed 2018 ONCA 1014, 2018 CarswellOnt 20709 (Ont. C.A.).

In *R. v. Galbraith*, 2018 ONCJ 138, 2018 CarswellOnt 3347, 404 C.R.R. (2d) 371, [2018] O.J. No. 1189 (Ont. C.J.), a written request for disclosure was sought four times by the defendant for her speeding trial, and she received assurances from administration that her requests had been forwarded to the office of the prosecution. She did not receive an answer to her requests. The prosecution policy concerning the provision of disclosure in the jurisdiction was usually two weeks after receipt of a written request. The delay in providing disclosure in a timely manner to the defendant in this case was due to staffing changes in the office of the prosecution. The prosecution delay in providing disclosure was due to a mistake and did not violate her right to a fair trial under s. 11(d) of the *Charter of Rights*, nor was any prejudice demonstrated such that the late disclosure did not violate the right to make full answer and defence under s. 7 of the *Charter*. The time elapsed since the date of the offence to the proposed date of trial was 7 months, well below the presumptive ceiling for unreasonable delay established in *R. v. Jordan*. There was no negligence on the part of the prosecutor that justified an order of costs either as a *Charter* remedy or due to procedural irregularities under s. 90 of the *Provincial Offences Act*. The defendant had chosen to attend the Early Resolution meeting and there were a total of two court appearances to date. Section 24(1) of the *Charter* confers a broad remedial mandate and the widest possible discretion on a court to craft remedies that must be easily available for violations of *Charter* rights. The remedy in the instant case was an adjournment to a date for trial and no order for costs.

In *York (Regional Municipality) v. 1085638 Ontario Limited*, 2018 ONCJ 658, 2018 CarswellOnt 16164, [2018] O.J. No. 5003 (Ont. C.J.), it was held that the decision to adjourn a proceeding is one in the discretion of the trial judge. The judicial officer must listen to the request and consider various factors, including the length of time of the proposed adjournment. The longer the period of time, the greater the likelihood the adjournment should not be granted as the likelihood of prejudice to the defence increases. What was clear on the record was that the justice of the peace tried to accommodate an adjournment for sentencing submissions if it was only going to be for a short time. After poring over the court calendar with the assistance of the trial coordinator it was clear that it couldn't. By that time the charges were 12 years and 5 years old, respectively, the court was clearly uncomfortable with yet another delay in the case at the penultimate stage, and ruled that submissions should be heard. Given that counsel were advised two months previously that they should be ready to do just that on the return date, the decision was not unfair. There was also no evidence on the appeal about what evidence would have been heard had the adjournment been granted. No fresh evidence was sought to be tendered on the hearing of the appeal. No error in principle was identified in the reasons for sentence. Absent an error in principle sentencing decisions are entitled to deference. Despite denying the adjournment, the court received submissions on sentence from both the prosecution and defence. The defendants received very substantial fines — $60,000 in total. That said, this was a legal sentence, and the defendants had a history of previous convictions relating to the very issue of non-compliance with municipal orders.

The defendant's concern about the prejudicial effect of evidence that had been adduced from leading questions put by the prosecutor to their own witnesses and the elicitation of irrelevant hearsay, bad character, and lay opinion evidence into the trial, had to be viewed in context and its intended use in the trial. Any prejudicial effect of the impugned evidence had been lessened as this was a non-jury trial and the charges involved strict liability regulatory offences in which the prosecution can elicit evidence in their case-in-chief to rebut a defence of due diligence or other anticipated defences. After considering the impugned evidentiary issues and the context in which the prosecutor's impugned comments, language and tone were used and what had been occurring in the trial at the time, the cumulative effect of the prosecutor's conduct, although not ideal and of perfect comportment, did not go beyond aggressive or abusive as to cause the defendant to receive an unfair trial, since the defendant's trial was a non-jury trial for which the trier would be cognizant of applying the relevant legal principles and law, and would also be able to disabuse and give no weight to any hearsay, bad character, opinion, or any other irrelevant prejudicial evidence, nor put any weight on any inappropriate, sarcastic, or demeaning comments, made by the prosecutor about the defendant's memory, business practices, or personal lifestyle, or to improperly use the impugned evidence or the immoderate comments of the prosecutor as proof of guilt. Accordingly, the defendant's right to a fair trial had not been prejudiced by the cumulative effect of the prosecutor's conduct in eliciting the impugned evidence, nor by the prosecutor's impugned comments, language or tone, that would be manifested, perpetuated or aggravated through the conduct of the trial, or by its outcome. Neither was the cumulative effect of the prosecutor's conduct such that it reached a degree of unfairness or vexatiousness that contravenes notions of fundamental justice, nor was it the type of conduct in which the justice system would find it necessary to intervene so that it would leave the impression that it condones conduct that offends society's sense of fair play and decency. Therefore, the prosecutor's conduct during the trial had not undermined the integrity of the justice system that would be manifested, perpetuated or aggravated through the conduct of the trial, or by its outcome. See *Ontario (Electrical Safety Authority) v. Broomfield*, 2018 ONCJ 640, 2018 CarswellOnt 15732, [2018] O.J. No. 4893 (Ont. C.J.).

In *York (Regional Municipality) v. McGuigan*, 2018 ONCA 1062, 2018 CarswellOnt 22571, [2018] O.J. No. 6916 (Ont. C.A.), the Court of Appeal ruled that trial justice properly ordered the prosecutor to provide disclosure of the testing and operating procedures from the user manual for the device used by the traffic officer to measure the speed of the defendant's vehicle. Even if the justice of the peace had been wrong to order disclosure, the error would not have been jurisdictional in nature. Section 140(1) of the *Provincial Offences Act* confines *certiorari* orders in *POA* matters to situations where an applicant would be entitled to such relief at common law, and for parties to a proceeding, *certiorari* orders are confined to jurisdictional errors. Moreover, *certiorari* should not have been granted in the course of ongoing proceedings. Nor was there a substantial wrong or miscarriage of justice to address, a prerequisite to *certiorari* under s. 141(4) of the Act. Contrary to the application judge's decision, the justice of the peace did not err in making the disclosure order. Where a prosecutor is relying on a speed measuring device to prosecute an offence, it must, on request, disclose the testing and operating procedures set out in the user manual for that device. It is up to the prosecutor to hand such information over on request. The person charged need not bring an application or obtain a court order. This is first party disclosure, not third party disclosure. The charging police force has a corresponding duty to furnish the pertinent passages from the user manual to the prosecutor to enable the prosecutor to discharge its first party disclosure obligations. This is not a crushing administrative task. The disclosure at issue here is not case specific information. The disclosure obligation can therefore be discharged by the prosecutor by posting the relevant content from the user manual online and providing the ticketed driver with the required URL.

2.3 THE DEFENCE

- The defendant may be represented by a lawyer or agent (paralegal). The defendant may also represent himself or herself in person.

- On October 27, 2005, the Attorney General of Ontario unveiled the *Access to Justice Act*. It received Royal Asset on October 19, 2006. Its initiatives include the regulation of paralegals in POA and summary criminal trials. Paralegals are required to complete an approved college program and pass a licensing examination, adhere to a code of conduct, carry insurance and contribute to a compensation fund. There is also a process for receiving and investigating consumer complaints which is similar to the system for lawyers. Paralegals found to have engaged in misconduct are subject to penalties, including the possible loss of their licence.

- Subsection 50(3) of the *Provincial Offences Act*, which provided a justice of the peace with the authority to bar an agent from representing a defendant, has been repealed. The revised section states that a justice of the peace now may not bar a lawyer or a licensed paralegal from representing a defendant, but may bar a person such as a friend or family member who is not a professional licensed under the *Law Society Act*.

Justice Casey rejected a constitutional challenge to the Law Society's authority to regulate non-lawyers in the recent case, *R. v. Toutissani*, 2008 CarswellOnt 1688, [2008] O.J. No. 1174, 2008 ONCJ 139 (Ont. C.J.), leave to appeal refused 2008 CarswellOnt 5424, 256 O.A.C. 390 (note), 2008 CarswellOnt 5425, 390 N.R. 390 (note) (S.C.C.). It was argued that since Parliament's criminal law power has granted an agent the right to appear in summary conviction proceedings, the provincial legislature lacks the authority to circumscribe or place limits upon that right through the paralegal licensing regime under the *Law Society Act*. Justice Casey found that both legislative schemes were valid, that is, the *Criminal Code* provisions respecting appearance by agents, and the provincial regulations establishing rules regarding non-lawyers who appear in court. Since a person could, at the same time, comply with both the provisions of the *Criminal Code* and the *Law Society Act*, there was no impermissible conflict between the two pieces of legislation. A person who obtains a licence under the Law Society's by-laws is permitted by both the federal and provincial enactments to represent defendants in summary conviction matters. Parliament's purpose in permitting defendants on summary convictions to be represented by non-lawyers is furthered by the provincial legislation. Since the defendant's representative on the *Immigration Act* charges before the court had not complied with the licensing requirements of the *Law Society Act*, he was not permitted to appear for the defendant.

For cases dealing with the issue of the propriety of an agent appearing on behalf of the defendant, see generally *R. v. Romanowicz* (1999), 26 C.R. (5th) 246, [1999] O.J. No. 3191, 1999 CarswellOnt 2671, 178 D.L.R. (4th) 466, 124 O.A.C. 100, 138 C.C.C. (3d) 225, 45 O.R. (3d) 506, 45 O.R. (3d) 532 (Fr.), 45 M.V.R. (3d) 294 (Ont. C.A.), and *R. v. Morden* (2000), [2000] O.J. No. 873, 2000 CarswellOnt 1037 (Ont. C.J.) which considers the appearance of an agent under the *Provincial Offences Act*. These cases hold that the disqualification of the agent who represents the defendant is a serious matter, and should only be considered by the court where it is necessary to protect the proper administration of justice.

In *Thibaudeau v. Ontario (Justice of the Peace)*, 2008 CarswellOnt 5935, 2008 ONCA 702, [2008] O.J. No. 3966 (Ont. C.A.), the Court of Appeal affirmed the ruling of the Superior Court of Justice, reported at (2007), 2007 CarswellOnt 7550, (*sub nom.* Thibaudeau v. Stafford) 88 O.R. (3d) 113 (Ont. S.C.J.), holding that the trial justice of the peace has jurisdiction to conduct an inquiry and bar an agent from appearing before him or her at a future time, following the completion of the trial. The decision of the trial judge in this case was rendered prior to s. 50(3) being amended due to the paralegal practitioner licensing regime now in place in Ontario. Under the current s. 50(3), the justice may only bar representatives who are not licensed under the *Law Society Act*.

In *Hill v. Toronto (City)*, 2007 ONCJ 253, 48 M.V.R. (5th) 55, (*sub nom.* Toronto (City) v. Hill) 221 C.C.C. (3d) 189, 2007 CarswellOnt 3578, [2007] O.J. No. 2232 (Ont. C.J.), it was held that allegations made by a paralegal agent on appeal that a paralegal agent at trial had not acted properly, so as to amount to professional incompetence or to have otherwise contributed to a miscarriage of justice, must be made only after careful consideration. More particularly, such allegations should only be brought forward after the appeal agent has satisfied himself or herself, by means of personal investigations or inquiries, that there is some factual foundation for the allegation, apart from the instructions of the appellant. There must also be afforded to the trial agent a fair opportunity to respond, specifically by providing notice to the trial agent of the allegations being made before the appeal court, and ensuring that a record of this response is placed before the appeal court so that a proper assessment of the allegations may be made by the judge on appeal. Such a procedure or protocol, which places on the paralegal agent on appeal the obligation to investigate and furnish the paralegal trial agent with an opportunity to respond, and thus the appeal court with a proper basis to evaluate such allegations, reflects the need to ensure fairness, openness, and transparency in the provincial offences court, which is so aptly regarded as the "people's court" given the pervasive nature of public welfare/regulatory offences. At the same time, it is in keeping with the new responsibilities of ethical behaviour now mandated by the Law Society of Upper Canada for paralegal practitioners, which includes the required standard of a "competent paralegal", pursuant to the Paralegal Rules of Conduct.

It would be unfair and unseemly to permit counsel to continue to represent the defendant and thus be in a position to cross-examine a witness who was elderly, unsophisticated and vulnerable, in the same proceeding in which he formerly represented him. The conflict of interest arose as counsel had formerly acted for a codefendant facing *Occupational Health and Safety Act* charges arising from the same accident, against whom the prosecution had been stayed and was now a Crown witness: *R. v. Con-Drain Co. (1983) Ltd.*, 2008 ONCJ 114, 2008 CarswellOnt 1424, [2008] O.J. No. 1012, 172 C.R.R. (2d) 299 (Ont. C.J.).

There was no evidence of any breakdown of solicitor-client confidence or communication, and no reason for the court to believe that the defendant wished counsel to be removed. In fact, counsel candidly admitted that the request, which followed its unsuccessful motion for an adjournment, was for the protection of the interests of the defendant. The motion to be removed as counsel which flew in the face of counsel's duty was dismissed: *Ontario (Travel Industry Council) v. Baldwin Travel & Tours Ltd.*, 2010 ONCJ 402, 2010 CarswellOnt 6884, [2010] O.J. No. 3859 (Ont. C.J.).

In *R. v. Dobson*, 2010 ONCJ 161, 2010 CarswellOnt 2744, [2010] O.J. No. 1823 (Ont. C.J.), it was held that the licensed paralegal who entered a guilty plea in the defendant's absence, on the basis of boilerplate instructions in the retainer agreement authorizing the paralegal to negotiate a plea on the defendant's behalf, did not constitute valid instructions to enter the guilty plea. The instruction was not case specific, included no duty to ensure the facts were admitted by the client, did not indicate that the plea was voluntary, or that the client was aware of the plea. The record keeping practices of the paralegal provided no confidence that she could accurately reconstruct the events that led to the plea; her independent memory was unreliable and she altered the documents in anticipation of the appeal.

The presiding justice of the peace erred when she insisted that the police officer close his notebook before giving his evidence after reading his notes but before answering any questions. It is not necessary to force every witness to close their notebook or set it aside in order to prevent the witness from reading from it:

Mississauga (City) v. Vattiata, 2010 ONCJ 588, 2010 CarswellOnt 9341, 6 M.V.R. (6th) 128, [2010] O.J. No. 5283 (Ont. C.J.).

In *R. v. Cipriano*, 2011 ONSC 223, 2011 CarswellOnt 89, [2011] O.J. No. 67 (Ont. S.C.J.), it was held that the justice of the peace had no alternative but to declare a mistrial after the defendant's counsel made a complaint against her to the Judicial Council. If she acquitted the defendant, it would have appeared she did so because she was threatened and accused of misconduct; if she found the defendant guilty, it would be said she was angry and biased due to the allegations made and pending against her. Where there are facts and circumstances that clearly give rise to a reasonable apprehension of bias, the court has the ability to address the situation by making use of the remedies of *certiorari* and mandamus. If the judge who made the original mandamus order in this case had been aware of defence counsel's letter of complaint that was provided to the justice of the peace, it would have been highly doubtful that the original order would have been made. Consequently, the justice of the peace had no alternative but to recuse herself despite the mandamus order to proceed with the trial. There was no basis to stay the charges on the basis of abuse of process.

It was not within the jurisdiction of the justice of the peace to simply indicate that the individual who the defendant wished to assist him at his trial could not appear on the basis that he was not a paralegal licenced by the Law Society. It was open to the justice to make certain inquiries to determine whether or not the person was qualified to be assisting the defendant. It would have been open to the justice of the peace to rule under those circumstances that the individual could not appear in the court: *R. v. Zaltzman*, 2010 ONCJ 667, 2010 CarswellOnt 10523 (Ont. C.J.).

The justice of the peace was wrong in law to refuse to allow the officer to use his notes to refresh his memory because they were a photocopy rather than the original copy of the notes: *R. v. Thom*, [2010] O.J. No. 4607, 2010 ONCJ 492, 2010 CarswellOnt 8163, 5 M.V.R. (6th) 140 (Ont. C.J.).

Similarly, in *Durham (Regional Municipality) v. Zhu*, [2011] O.J. No. 1797, 2011 CarswellOnt 2614, 2011 ONCJ 193 (Ont. C.J.), it was held that a police officer is entitled to refresh his memory by using the electronic notes he had typed into a computer about the offence.

The rules of evidence are as strict for regulatory matters as they are for *Criminal Code* matters. It was an error for the trial justice to conclude that the officer's evidence was credible on the basis that she did not believe she was entitled to take into account the lack of notes with respect to the officer's observations, given that criminal case law in evidentiary issues did not apply to regulatory offences. See *R.*

v. Vandemunt, [2011] O.J. No. 5783, 2011 ONCJ 844, 2011 CarswellOnt 15626 (Ont. C.J.).

In a case involving the burden of proof at a speeding trial, the appeal court judge held that the trial justice reversed the onus on the defence to produce some kind of evidence that would raise a doubt, whereas there is no requirement to produce evidence, or to give evidence. The defence needs to do nothing more than require the case to be proven beyond a reasonable doubt, and it is quite permissible for the court to fully accept the speedometer or the radar evidence, but that is only one piece of evidence, and it is not sufficient and not appropriate to ignore the standard of proof in a case like this, and the onus of proof on the prosecutor, and somehow hold that the defence has an obligation to produce evidence to the contrary. See *R. v. Timushev*, 2011 CarswellOnt 7425, [2011] O.J. No. 3518 (Ont. C.J.).

In *R. v. Dookie*, 2012 ONCJ 719, 2012 CarswellOnt 14803, [2012] O.J. No. 5740 (Ont. C.J.), it was held that s. 802.1 of the *Criminal Code* which bars agents from appearing to defend persons charged with summary conviction offences punishable by more than six months imprisonment does not violate the s. 15 equality provisions of the *Canadian Charter of Rights and Freedoms*. Parliament has determined that it is not in the interest of defendants that non-lawyers appear to represent individuals who are charged with offences of a certain level of seriousness.

Amendments have been made to the Commissioners for Taking Affidavits Act, R.S.O. 1990, c. C.17, effective 31 December 2012, which will add licensed paralegals to the list of persons who are commissioners for oaths by virtue of their position, and indicated as such by O. Reg. 386/12. This amendment will not come into force, however, until 1 July 2013. Currently, the list includes lawyers who are licensed to practice law in Ontario, as well as judges and justices of the peace. Under s. 9 of the Act, every oath and declaration is to be taken by the deponent in the presence of the party administering the oath or declaration, and this party, which will now include licensed paralegals, must satisfy himself/herself of the genuineness of the signature of the deponent or declarant, and shall administer the oath or declaration in the manner required by law before signing the jurat or declaration.

Defence counsel on appeal alleged that there was a conflict on the part of trial counsel who had previously acted for the prosecuting authority in a prosecution of a case dealing with a similar issue in which the prosecution had not been successful. The competency of trial counsel was also challenged on the basis of a failure to provide the court with evidence including a photograph which purported to show a laneway many years earlier in the area where a laneway now existed. However, even if such evidence had been submitted, it did not support the position that the laneway existed previously, or even if it did exist that it existed to the degree in place at the time the charges were laid. Any conflict that may have existed was for the authority to raise, as they had been previously represented by trial counsel on an unrelated matter involving similar issues. There was nothing on the record to call into question the competence of trial counsel. Decisions about evidence and submissions are within the realm of trial counsel; there was nothing to indicate that such decisions were wrong, let alone negligent, and there was nothing to suggest the actions of trial counsel compromised his duties and ethical responsibilities, nor did his actions compromise the rights of the defendants. See *R. v. Geil*, 2012 ONCJ 740, 2012 CarswellOnt 15014, [2012] O.J. No. 5655 (Ont. C.J.), leave to appeal refused 2013 ONCA 457, 2013 CarswellOnt 8921, [2013] O.J. No. 3087 (Ont. C.A.).

In *Niagara (Regional Municipality) v. Kosyatchkov*, 2013 ONSC 713, 2013 CarswellOnt 992, [2013] O.J. No. 424 (Ont. S.C.J.), it was held that the legislation permits but does not require the use of a prescribed word or phrase to describe the offence. If a prescribed word is used, the offence is sufficiently described. Since the prescribed word "speeding" was not written in this case, one of two things followed: the certificate had to meet the requirements of s. 25 of the *Provincial Offences Act* governing counts in an information, or if it did not, the justice was obliged to amend it unless to do so would have failed to satisfy the ends of justice. The certificate in the case at bar did in fact provide sufficient detail of the circumstances of the alleged offence to give the defendant reasonable information with respect to the act or omission to be proved against the defendant and to identify the transaction referred to, and was thus in compliance with s. 25. An amendment, had one been required, would not have occasioned any prejudice. The certificate should not therefore have been quashed. Neither was any need for the justice to inquire into the matter in the first place. The defendant was appearing to defend the charge. Accordingly, sections 9 and 9.1 of the Act, which require a justice to examine the certificate before convicting an absent defendant who is not disputing the charge, or who is deemed not to dispute the charge, had no application. The defendant was represented, and had obviously given thought to how he wanted to proceed. There was no reason to depart from the normal procedure in which the party who complains of an inadequate information asks the court to quash it, amend it or order particulars.

In *R. v. Bilinski*, 2013 ONSC 2824, 2013 CarswellOnt 8723, [2013] O.J. No. 2984 (Ont. S.C.J.) Justice Durno rejected the notion that a person who retains a paralegal is now entitled to the effective assistance of counsel. He held that the differences between paralegals and counsel remain, and that there is a "clear distinction" between the representation that an accused person is entitled to when they retain a lawyer, as opposed to a paralegal. In terms of whether there should be a lesser standard of competency that applies where an accused person retains a paralegal in a criminal trial, the court acknowledged that this issue was more "problematic". On one hand, the so-called middle ground test could not simply be that the paralegal is entitled to make "more mistakes than a lawyer". Justice Durno pointed out that the focus of the test must still be on the quality of the representation, and whether a miscarriage of justice resulted. Justice Durno went on to dispose of the "middle-ground standard of representation" by ruling that he was not satisfied on the basis of the record before him that the Law Society's regulation of paralegals had given rise to this standard of competency, especially for paralegals who had been grandfathered. He did comment, though, that there may be evidence which could support such a middle ground, particularly with respect to paralegals who were not the subject of grandfathering. However, such evidence had not been presented to the court and His Honour observed that the question of whether there should be a new standard is best determined on the basis of a full record, including "all the requirements for those grandfathered and those who were not".

In *R. v. Rau*, 2013 ONSC 5573, 2013 CarswellOnt 12550, [2013] O.J. No. 4067 (Ont. S.C.J.), an unsuccessful application was brought by the defendant for a stay of proceedings on his charge of failure to stop for police, contrary to the *Highway Traffic Act* (Ont.), pending the provision of funding for his defence so that he could have legal representation. This appeared to be the first time that such an application had been brought for such a funding order in respect of a *Highway Traffic Act* offence. Although there was a real prospect of imprisonment if the defendant was found guilty, the trial faced by him would be relatively brief, the issues discrete, and the minimum sentence of 14 days' imprisonment was far from the most serious range. The defendant had also demonstrated an understanding of the charges, was able to put forward the facts in an understandable and coherent manner, and had shown an ability to participate effectively in a court proceeding; the case was not of sufficient seriousness or complexity that representation by counsel was essential to a fair trial.

A recent Ontario case involving an application for a French-language trial and the resulting delay of delay was discussed in *R. v. Byrnes*, 2013 ONCJ 631, 2013 CarswellOnt 16205, 2013 CarswellOnt 16206, 296 C.R.R. (2d) 258, [2013] O.J. No. 5389 (Ont. C.J.), where the defendant immediately requested a French trial by ticking off the box on the Notice of Intention to Appear to indicate his intention and by filing the Notice with the court. However, his request for a French trial was overlooked, and therefore his trial could not proceed on the trial date. While this oversight was an administrative error, this error amounted to a breach of the defendant's language rights. Moreover, the defendant should not have been expected by the trial judge to have required an interpreter. As a French-speaking defendant, he did not require the assistance of an interpreter at his French trial. Perhaps an interpreter would have been necessary to assist any English-speaking witnesses the prosecutor wished to call, but it would be the responsibility of the prosecutor, not the defendant, to make the appropriate arrangements for these witnesses. By indicating on the Notice that he wished to proceed in French, the defendant properly completed the Notice and satisfied all of his obligations on the language issue. The 8-month delay between the date the defendant requested a French trial until the date the trial began amounted to a breach of the defendant's right to have a trial within a reasonable time for two reasons. First, had he requested a trial in English, his matter could have been heard within 5 months; second, no effort was made to immediately secure a date for the French trial, due to his matter being adjourned a further 3 months to a pre-scheduled date for French trials, despite the fact that there were several intervening dates available for English trials. The practice of having only 2 pre-scheduled days set aside each year for French trials in the provincial offences court, one in the Spring and one in the Fall, is problematic from a case management perspective, and unfair because it is unresponsive to the individual requirements of a specific case. The fact that this system appeared to apply only to French-speaking defendants was a clear contravention of s. 16(1) of the Charter and as such, unacceptable. Even if this general process for scheduling French trials was constitutionally sound, the effect of slavishly continuing with the pre-scheduled French dates in the defendant's case, even after the trial had commenced before a specific Justice of the Peace, led to unacceptable delays. The result was that a routine speeding trial was commenced 9 months after the offence date, heard in 6-month instalments over a period of 13 months, and only concluded 22 months after the offence date.

It was also held in *R. v. Byrnes*, 2013 ONCJ 631, 2013 CarswellOnt 16205, 2013 CarswellOnt 16206, 296 C.R.R. (2d) 258, [2013] O.J. No. 5389 (Ont. C.J.), that the defendant did not enter a plea because the Justice of the Peace believed that the *Charter* application should be heard and decided before the plea was entered. This was incorrect, as the defendant should have been required to enter a plea before the *Charter* application commenced. If the defendant refused to do so, the court should have deemed his plea to be not guilty, and made this entry on the information. A "best practices" approach would entail having the defendant arraigned prior to hearing the *Charter* application because it is only after arraignment that the Justice of the Peace is formally seized with the matter. Arraignment includes having the charge read, asking the defendant how he pleads, guilty or not guilty, and noting the plea on the information. To do otherwise and commence a *Charter* application prior to arraignment or midway through arraignment and prior to plea being entered, would allow a party who received an unfavourable decision on the *Charter* to request that the trial commence before a different Justice of the Peace since the first one was not seized. If this were to happen, the parties would be able to re-argue the *Charter* application since the new Justice of the Peace would not be bound by the original *Charter* decision. This absurd legal outcome and case management headache would be properly prevented by having the plea entered and noted on the information prior to addressing the *Charter* application.

The person who laid the complaint against the defendants had also sued them in Small Claims Court, and the claim was under appeal in Superior Court. The trial Justice of the Peace was in error in declining to let the defendant cross-examine the complainant on her dealings with the defendant because he did not want to "step on the [Superior Court's] feet". The civil proceedings that were then outstanding should not have prevented the defendant from cross-examining the witness about the facts pertaining to one of the counts. The trial Justice should also have assisted the unrepresented defendant to frame a proper question to elicit the evidence he was seeking, rather than cutting him off when he was questioning the complainant and stating that he was giving evidence rather than asking questions: *Real Estate Council of Ontario v. Wang*, 2013 ONCJ 515, 2013 CarswellOnt 13174, [2013] O.J. No. 4294 (Ont. C.J.).

Given the serious professional and punitive consequences of a finding of contempt, the contempt citation process should be used sparingly, if at all: *R. v. Strati*, 2014 ONCJ 139, 2014 CarswellOnt 3624, [2014] O.J. No. 1413 (Ont. C.J.).

The defendant was charged with driving a commercial motor vehicle with no brake lights for which the set fine was $200. However, the set fine indicated on the certificate of offence was $85, which was the set fine for the offence involving a vehicle that is not a commercial motor vehicle. As the set fine was incorrect, it was not complete and regular on its face and ought to have been quashed by the Justice of the Peace. It seemed an unfortunate waste of everyone's time and court resources to require such a simple case with an obvious defect to have to go through two levels of court (first instance and appeal) before the result dictated by law is achieved. It is inappropriate for an officer of the court who is aware that a court is about to make an error by not quashing a certificate of offence that is not complete and regular to fail to bring his/her concern to the court's attention. The party should not be required to lie in the weeds clutching a notice of appeal. There is no downside but rather an upside of eliminating these concerns by permitting a defendant or his/ her representative to make a conditional appearance, without thereby being considered to be present, in this narrow and unique situation. To be clear, the very summary nature of default proceedings is not to be altered; rather, this would simply provide an opportunity for one having some knowledge of the particular certificate of offence to point out what might otherwise be overlooked. It would not be a matter for argument, nor would it trigger otherwise inapplicable amending powers. Once so informed, the court would make its determination to convict or quash as the case may be. Any disagreement with that decision would be a matter to be addressed on appeal. See *R. v. Rodrigues*, 2013 ONCJ 719, 2013 CarswellOnt 18477, 62 M.V.R. (6th) 331, [2013] O.J. No. 6041 (Ont. C.J.).

In *R. v. Sarkozy*, 2014 ONCA 481, 2014 CarswellOnt 8357, [2014] O.J. No. 2964 (Ont. C.A.), it was held that there was conflicting evidence on almost every material aspect of the alleged communications between the accused and the paralegal she retained to assist her on the *Highway Traffic Act* charges she faced. At the end of the day, there was, at the very least, a misunderstanding that led both the accused and the paralegal to not attend the accused's trial. As a result, the trial proceeded *ex parte*, leading to the accused's convictions on both charges. The apparent unfairness at the trial proceeding was not cured by what occurred at the appeal hearing, which also proceeded in the accused's absence, and the accused has not had her day in court. In these circumstances, the interests of justice require that the accused's conviction be set aside and a new trial ordered to avoid a miscarriage of justice.

In *Mangov v. Toronto (City)*, 2014 ONCJ 351, 2014 CarswellOnt 10104, [2014] O.J. No. 3477 (Ont. C.J.), at the beginning of the trial, the Justice of the Peace initiated an inquiry about potential resolution, and asked the agent why his client did not want to resolve the case. If there had been any resolution discussions conducted earlier, the Justice should have refrained from making inquiries into it when it was clear the matter was proceeding to trial. The defendant was entitled to an impartial and unbiased adjudicator who could decide the case on the evidence, not one who seemed to assume he was guilty from the beginning. This was exacerbated by the Justice encouraging the defence to speak to the prosecutor about resolution before the start of the trial. A reasonable person hearing these comments would only conclude that the court was predisposed to conviction on speeding trials. There was a substantial apprehension of bias. Subsequently, the Justice curtailed cross-examination of the officer on the laser manual, although there was nothing unfocused or prolix to the questioning. A reasonable person could interpret the court's comments as indicating that the cross-examination regarding his operation of the laser was predetermined in the mind of the Justice as being of no value and a waste of time.

The trial Justice of the Peace refused to allow the defendant to file a copy of the laser manual he received in disclosure as an exhibit at trial. If properly identified and there was a foundation laid for its introduction, the manual could be entered as an exhibit. No rule of evidence required a copy of the manual to be certified as a true copy. It was not necessary to make the manual an exhibit in order for the defendant to have continued cross-examining the officer once the proper foundation had been laid. There is nothing wrong in making portions of the manual an exhibit at trial further to this type of cross-examination; it is often done on consent of the parties, and may be of assistance to the trial Justice to have a written copy to assist him or her in following the testimony of the witness. It is the testimony of the police officer, however, that is the evidence, not the exhibit itself. There is very little gained in making the entire manual an exhibit at trial, even with the consent of the parties, as it contains much that is totally irrelevant. If it is made an independent exhibit, it is incumbent on the Justice to review the whole manual. See *Mangov v.*

Toronto (City), 2014 ONCJ 351, 2014 CarswellOnt 10104, [2014] O.J. No. 3477 (Ont. C.J.).

The Justice of the Peace should have asked the defendant whether he had any questions of the officer or submissions to make as to the police officer's notes when the officer asked to use his notes to refresh his memory. The defendant did cross-examine the officer on numerous points, but did not assert that there were any discrepancies between the officer's testimony at trial and the notes disclosed to the defence. The failure to ask the defendant whether he wished to ask questions at that point, or make submissions, did not impact trial fairness as the prosecution provided a proper foundation for the police officer to refer to the notes. See *R. v. Zuccarini*, 2014 ONCJ 571, 2014 CarswellOnt 15457, [2014] O.J. No. 5234 (Ont. C.J.).

In *R. v. King*, 2014 ONCJ 695, 2014 CarswellOnt 18016, [2014] O.J. No. 6140 (Ont. C.J.), it was held that the Justice of the Peace was entitled to refuse the defendant's representative from acting as an agent at the defendant's first trial date after the agent indicated there was no plea and that he was looking for an answer to a number of writs he filed, as well as that he was not defending anyone but looking for an answer to his writs. However, it was wrong then to simply treat the case as if the defendant failed to appear for his trial and was deemed to not wish to dispute the charge after having been issued a notice of the time and place for trial. Essentially, the defendant did wish to dispute the charge and attempted to appear through his agent but that agent was disqualified by the court from acting. In such circumstances, fairness dictates that the trial be adjourned so that the defendant could attend personally or through another agent. The Justice of the Peace should have treated the matter no differently from a case where a defendant sent an unknowledgeable and ill-instructed family member as an agent. The defendant should not suffer the consequences of any ill-advised conduct of the agent that resulted in the agent's disqualification.

One of the important steps in any process is the right to make submissions. Where that was not afforded to the defendant's legal representative, a new trial must be ordered: *R. v. Al-Kerwi*, 2015 CarswellOnt 2299, [2015] O.J. No. 769 (Ont. C.J.).

It is not up to the defence to make a request for disclosure more than once. They did not need to bring a motion for production as they were led to believe by the prosecutor the disclosure they had requested was not available. It was only after hearing the testimony of the officer did they realize there had been a lack of follow-up on their request for disclosure. They were entitled to raise the issue of lack of disclosure at that time. However, the defendant's counsel should have brought a non-disclosure application rather than a motion to dismiss the charge. The remedy for non-disclosure is not to dismiss a charge but rather to stay the charge. The

Justice of the Peace was in error when she granted a dismissal rather than a stay, however, her logic and reasons for doing so were not a palpable and overriding error. The Justice of the Peace reached the right result but granted an inappropriate remedy. A new trial at this stage would not serve any useful purpose and would cause further inconvenience and expense for the defendant. The order made at trial was set aside and a stay of proceedings entered in lieu of ordering a new trial. See *R. v. Hawdon*, 2014 CarswellOnt 5067 (Ont. C.J.).

In *R. v. Khan*, 2015 ONCJ 221, 2015 CarswellOnt 5975, [2015] O.J. No. 2096 (Ont. C.J.), it was held that an unlicensed paralegal cannot conduct trials or appeals of provincial offences under the supervision of a lawyer licensed by the Law Society of Upper Canada. The conduct of trials or appeals involves providing legal services, which only licensed lawyers and paralegals can do under the *Law Society Act* and the by-laws made under it; these functions cannot be delegated to non-licensees. This does not prevent a friend or family member, however, from attending with a defendant at a trial or an appeal to assist the defendant.

When the paralegal was not present for the second scheduled trial date, the Justice of the Peace set the matter down to be heard later in the day, and then forced the trial to proceed in the paralegal's absence. The paralegal should have arranged his absence with the prosecution or should have been there. While the conviction was set aside on appeal, it was not likely to be tolerated a third time; the appeal court expected the prosecutor to flag the issue, and the date would likely be set to proceed whether or not the defendant's representative appears. See *R. v. Sayed-Zada*, 2015 CarswellOnt 15571, [2015] O.J. No. 5265 (Ont. C.J.).

In *York (Regional Municipality) v. McGee*, 2015 ONCJ 479, 2015 CarswellOnt 13985, [2015] O.J. No. 4776 (Ont. C.J.), the provincial offences appeal court ruled that the decisions of the paralegal at trial amounted to ineffective assistance. On the day of trial she was given the matter by another agent in her office, and had little direct contact with the defendant and was under the impression he was nervous and might not wish to testify at his trial. The paralegal proceeded to conduct the trial in his absence even though he was in her office in the same building just steps away. The paralegal did not advise the presiding justice of the peace that the defendant was in the building or request that the matter be held down while she determined whether he wished to participate. However, the defendant did want to be present at his trial. He had a right to be present and the right to give evidence if he chose to do so. While the competency standard for now regulated paralegals in provincial offences matters had not been fully determined, on any measure the breach of the defendant's right to be present at his trial resulted in a miscarriage of justice.

The police officer while testifying seemed, on several occasions, to control the cross-examination with little or no intervention on the part of the judge. It was only after numerous examples of such inappropriate conduct that the Crown prosecutor himself felt the need to intervene, but this was too little too late. The police officer's conduct during the cross-examination as well as the almost total lack of reaction on the part of the judge in this regard, when added to the exchanges between the judge himself and the accused, resulted in the appearance of an unfair trial. See *R. c. Robichaud*, 2016 NBBR 26, 2016 NBQB 26, 2016 CarswellNB 45, 2016 CarswellNB 48, (*sub nom.* R. v. Robichaud) 445 N.B.R. (2d) 54, 1166 A.P.R. 54, [2016] A.N.B. No. 30, [2016] N.B.J. No. 30 (N.B. Q.B.).

In *R. v. Gagne* (November 9, 2015), Doc. 14-0672, [2015] O.J. No. 6344 (Ont. S.C.J.), it was held that the Crown has the discretion to pursue through legitimate means a vigorous prosecution, which includes cooperative and effective real-time consultation with police as the prosecution unfolds. Such consultation may include having an investigating officer present at counsel table. However, where the officer was to be a witness at the proceeding, the officer was not permitted to sit at counsel table as an exception to the order excluding witnesses. It was open to the Crown to have the witness testify first and then sit at counsel table after his testimony, or have another instructing officer sit at counsel table.

In *R. v. Zacharias*, 2016 ONCJ 458, 2016 CarswellOnt 12095, [2016] O.J. No. 3975 (Ont. C.J.), the prosecution disclosed the police officer's notes and complied with some special disclosure requests of the defence. However, there were two letters from the defence requesting "if this is a speeding offence, the testing times of this device before and after the subject enforcement". The prosecution did not respond to that request. Prior to the trial, the prosecution and the defence discussed the testing of the device outside of court. The prosecution apparently disclosed the fact that the police officer had tested the device, but testing times were not provided. When the trial commenced, the defence stated that it was ready to proceed to trial. If the defence had been dissatisfied with the disclosure, it should have raised the issue as a pre-trial motion. If the lateness of the disclosure created a preparation problem for the defence, they should have requested an adjournment. However, the defence was ready to proceed to trial, and they so advised the court. There was no basis for concluding that the defendant did not receive a fair trial.

The defendant was represented by a licensed paralegal who entered a guilty plea on his behalf. The defendant claimed that the paralegal did not have his authority to do so, and launched a complaint against him. He also notified the paralegal of the date of his appeal, but the paralegal did not attend. A licensed paralegal is an officer of the court and has a duty to come forward with an explanation because he presented himself in court as someone who had the authority from the defendant to plead guilty to a serious offence under the *Highway Traffic Act*, and be subjected to a thousand dollar fine and licence suspension. The defendant presented evidence that the paralegal acted without authority. As the paralegal failed to comply despite being given numerous opportunities to explain the guilty plea he entered on the defendant's behalf while indicating that he had authority to do so, there was strong evidence that he did not have such authority. The guilty plea was set aside on appeal and a new trial ordered. See *R. v. Ezati*, 2016 CarswellOnt 8435, [2016] O.J. No. 2819 (Ont. C.J.).

Similarly, in *R. v. Antone*, 2016 ONCJ 316, 2016 CarswellOnt 8634, [2016] O.J. No. 2872 (Ont. C.J.), the defendant was not present when his legal representative entered a plea of guilty on his behalf. No plea inquiry was done by the justice of the peace as the defendant was not present and there was no discussion regarding the agent's authority to enter a plea on behalf of her client. However, it was clear from the information presented to the appeal court that the plea had not been arranged on the defendant's behalf with his knowledge and consent. Upon finding out that he had been found guilty, the defendant took steps to set aside the conviction and explain his circumstances. There was merit to his claim that at no time did he provide an informed consent to enter a guilty plea to the charge of driving while suspended and that the possible consequences of the conviction and six months driving suspension were not explained to him. Neither did the agent review disclosure with him. The notes in the Crown file indicated that upon the defendant paying his outstanding fines, a plea to the lesser offence of driving without a licence would have been accepted. A number of attempts were made to have the agent appear before the appeal court and explain her actions, but she did not appear. It appeared that she had been completely negligent in her representation of the defendant. It would be a miscarriage of justice to allow the conviction to stand in these circumstances.

A reasonable standard of bias was not established when the justice of the peace threatened to start the case without counsel for the defence being present, even though the justice was aware that counsel was in another courtroom. This statement constituted an outburst of frustration when the parties were not ready to proceed at the appointed time. His comment that if the party wished to bring in hearsay, that's fine, did not constitute bias. However, when the justice pronounced sentence without giving the defence an opportunity to be heard, this was improper. Counsel for the defence was right in assuming that any submissions from him at that point would be a wasted exercise. As a result, sentencing submissions were presented by the parties on appeal. See *R. v. Mr. Ice Man Ltd.*, 2016 ONCJ 372, 2016 CarswellOnt 9849, [2016] O.J. No. 3308 (Ont. C.J.).

The Crown should not have more procedural rights than the accused. The accused could not attach the condition to his plea that it was dependent on the ruling against him being upheld; likewise, the Crown should not be participating in a process by which facts are agreed to and charges are withdrawn, conditional upon a ruling being upheld. The defendant entered the plea of guilty knowing that the state of law was that they were thereby forestalling the Crown's potential appeal. The Crown also knew this and actively participated notwithstanding. This should have been expected to be a final resolution of the matter. To allow the Crown to proceed to appeal the original ruling through a sentence appeal offends that expectation of finality. It would place the defendant in a position where they were potentially prejudiced by the fact of their plea and any revisitation of the issue of their guilt. See *Ontario (Ministry of Labour) v. Ontario Power Generation*, 2016 ONCJ 299, 2016 CarswellOnt 8272, [2016] O.J. No. 2725 (Ont. C.J.).

In *R. v. Sahadeo*, 2016 ONCJ 122, 2016 CarswellOnt 3721, [2016] O.J. No. 1252 (Ont. C.J.), on the date his trial was scheduled to take place, the paralegal for the defendant appeared and requested an adjournment. When the request was refused, the paralegal advised the presiding justice that he was instructed not to participate in the proceedings any further. The paralegal then left the courtroom. Upon the defendant being paged with no response, a deemed not to dispute conviction was entered. The decision to grant or refuse the adjournment was discretionary, and will not be interfered with on appeal unless the discretion was not exercised judicially, or where it has resulted in a miscarriage of justice. In this case, the need for the adjournment for disclosure could easily have been obviated by the defendant far in advance of the trial. While the justice of the peace was correct to refuse the adjournment, a conviction should not have been imposed under s. 9.1 as it could not be said that the defendant had failed to appear at the time and place appointed for trial. He did appear by instructing an agent to attend, as permitted by s. 50; the provisions of s. 54(1) did not apply in this case. The defendant had appeared by agent, the prosecution was ready, and the trial should have proceeded. The fact that the defendant had instructed his agent to "walk away" did not mean that the agent had any right to do so. A paralegal, like counsel, can only withdraw with the leave of the court. The defendant demonstrated a complete lack of diligence by failing to ensure that he had the necessary disclosure. He ought to have either appeared personally or else sent a properly instructed agent. The agent, who appeared, had not been properly instructed and was initially unable to articulate the reason for which he was seeking an adjournment. The application itself was entirely without merit and should not have been brought; for his part, the agent should not have agreed to act for the defendant without proper instructions.

It is inconceivable that a defence lawyer would conduct a trial in the absence of a client that they had never met. An agent should never have accepted a retainer he did not intend to honour; the sub-agent should not have conducted a trial on behalf of a defendant he never met. In the circumstances, neither should have been permitted to hold themselves out as the defendant's representatives in the matter. On behalf of the administration of justice, the matter was remitted back for a new trial. See *R. v. Martin*, 2016 CarswellOnt 6784 (Ont. C.J.).

An application to intervene in a proceeding under the *Dog Owners' Liability Act* for a destruction order was considered in *R. v. Robert*, 2016 ONCJ 697, 2016 CarswellOnt 19181, [2016] O.J. No. 6249 (Ont. C.J.). It was held that Rule 7(6) of the *Provincial Offences Act* Rules limits "applications" and "motions" to those which, in Rule 7(1) "are provided for by the Act". Nowhere in Part IV of the *Provincial Offences Act*, or anywhere else in the *Provincial Offences Act*, is there any mention of a motion or an application for intervener status. Therefore Rule 7(6) of the *Provincial Offences Act* Rules cannot give any authority to deal with other applications or motions, such as applications for intervener status, which are not so mentioned within the *Provincial Offences Act* itself. To appoint the applicants as interveners, without formally being so appointed, in order to aid the defendants in obtaining evidence on the behaviour of dogs would be an inappropriate intervention on the part of the court. It is not the court's job to assist the defendants in mounting their defence by means of appointing interveners, if the court otherwise does not find it necessary for those interveners to be appointed. Neither was it necessary to appoint the applicants as amicus in order for the court to carry out its duties and obligations effectively and efficiently. The applicants did not have a unique interest in the matter. From both a legal and practical perspective, the applicant's interests appeared to be quite similar to the defendants. While the applicants were passionate about the good work they did on behalf of dogs, this did not make them or their perspective unique with respect to the case or make their submissions distinctive.

The presiding justice's dismissal of a disclosure motion did not give rise to a reasonable apprehension of bias or require the declaration of a mistrial on the basis that the justice misapprehended what was allegedly not to have been disclosed by the prosecution. The defendant failed to meet its burden to satisfy the high threshold to justify disqualification. See *R. v. Shan*, 2016 ONCJ 663, 2016 CarswellOnt 18212, [2016] O.J. No. 5935 (Ont. C.J.).

There was no prosecutorial misconduct due to "vetting the file erroneously". In the initial redacted duty notes, there was no evidence that any error was intentional or done for some nefarious purpose. Any inconsistency in the notes could have been clarified well in advance of the trial. Instead, the defence chose to raise the issue only during cross-examination. The Crown's position resisting disclosure of the radar manual did not amount to prosecutorial misconduct. The Crown's error in disclosure of the initial notes was unintentional, and the error was remedied by providing further disclosure in advance of the disclosure motion and trial. This did not amount to a standard of misconduct that justified an award of costs against the prosecution. See *R. v. Shan*, 2016 ONCJ 663, 2016 CarswellOnt 18212, [2016] O.J. No. 5935 (Ont. C.J.).

On 1 December 2017, a motion was passed by the benchers of the Law Society of Ontario that Convocation endorse the proposition that licensed paralegals be regarded as officers of the court in every court of record in Ontario in which a paralegal is authorized to provide legal services.

The defendant applied to adjourn the trial, both on the date of the filed application and on the trial date, primarily due to the unavailability of retained representation. The decision to grant or deny an adjournment is a discretionary exercise. Where this discretion is exercised judicially and fails to result in a miscarriage of justice, the decision should not be interfered with on review. The right to representation of choice is not absolute. This is particularly resonant for *Highway Traffic Act* litigation in the general Toronto area where available counsel and paralegals are legion. Given the previously granted defence application to adjourn, it was reasonable for the court to expect that any representation retained by the defendant was available on the second trial date. The defendant demonstrated little or no diligence in this regard. In denying the application to adjourn, the learned justice considered the previously granted defence adjournment application. The trial was endorsed peremptory to proceed. It was appropriate to deny the application in the circumstances. See *R. v. Wei*, 2017 ONCJ 878, 2017 CarswellOnt 20869, [2017] O.J. No. 6785 (Ont. C.J.).

Application of s. 54 of the *Provincial Offences Act* is not restricted to Part III prosecutions commenced by laying of information. Section 54 applies to all proceedings commenced under the Act, and it explicitly includes certificate proceedings commenced under Part I by way of notice of trial, which fit the defendant in the case at bar. Both ss. 9.1 and 54, however, only permit a conviction *in absentia* where the defendant does not "appear" for trial. The Act does not seem to contemplate a scenario where the defendant "appears" for trial by way of an agent who later withdraws after being denied an adjournment. This unfortunate practice is more prevalent in provincial offences courts than it should be and merits comment. The defence cannot by its conduct thwart the court's direction that a trial will proceed as scheduled. The defendant was placed on notice by no less than three justices of the peace that the trial would proceed in November; when the adjournment application was denied in October, the defence was expected to enter its plea on the trial date. In sending an agent without instructions to enter a guilty plea or to defend the trial, the defence by its conduct endeavoured to subvert the explicit direction of the court. Once the adjournment was denied, the defence ought to have been fixed with the expectation of arraignment. If there was any intention to defend the charge, the defence should have attended the second trial date prepared to do so. The learned justice did not err in conducting an *ex parte* trial under s. 54 in the circumstances. Section 54 affords the absent defendant an appropriate measure of procedural fairness. The prosecution is required to prove the defendant was notified or compelled to attend trial. Evidence must be led to satisfy the standard of proof. The procedure employed was fair and consistent with the due administration of justice. See *R. v. Wei*, 2017 ONCJ 878, 2017 CarswellOnt 20869, [2017] O.J. No. 6785 (Ont. C.J.).

In *Groia v. Law Society of Upper Canada*, 2018 CSC 27, 2018 SCC 27, 2018 CarswellOnt 8700, 2018 CarswellOnt 8701, 34 Admin. L.R. (6th) 183, 46 C.R. (7th) 227, 424 D.L.R. (4th) 443, [2018] S.C.J. No. 27 (S.C.C.), the finding of misconduct against Mr. Groia, a defence lawyer in a *Securities Act* prosecution, was found to be unreasonable. The court held that defence lawyers must have sufficient latitude to advance their client's right to make full answer and defence by raising arguments about the propriety of state actors' conduct without fear of reprisal. This is not to be taken as endorsing incivility in the name of resolute advocacy; civility and resolute advocacy are not incompatible. To the contrary, civility is often the most effective form of advocacy. Nevertheless, when defining incivility and assessing whether a lawyer's behaviour crosses the line, care must be taken to set a sufficiently high threshold that will not chill the kind of fearless advocacy that is at times necessary to advance a client's cause. Courts and law societies have concurrent jurisdiction to regulate and enforce standards of courtroom behaviour. Improper defence behaviour is not necessarily professional misconduct, be it a function of incivility or incompetence. The Law Society must therefore be careful not to place too much weight on a judge's criticism of defence behaviour. When the impugned behaviour occurs in a courtroom, what, if anything, the judge does about it becomes relevant. Unlike the Law Society, the presiding judge observes the lawyer's behaviour firsthand. This offers the judge a comparatively advantageous position to evaluate the lawyer's conduct relative to the Law Society, who only enters the equation once all is said and done. The judge's reaction is not conclusive, and the Law Society is not barred from reviewing a lawyer's behaviour if the judge does not comment.

In *R. v. Bazdar*, 2018 ONCJ 318, 2018 CarswellOnt 7677, [2018] O.J. No. 2571 (Ont. C.J.), it was held that the net delay of 16 months and 19 days fell below the presumptive ceiling of 18 months and was presumptively reasonable when applying the test set out in *Jordan*. The applicant's agent did nothing exceptional to expedite the proceeding. The proceedings moved along in the manner in which matters commenced under Part I proceeding. On the contrary, the agent did not make all efforts to request full disclosure in that he ought to have requested all disclosure including any DVD evidence that was available. The charges were straightforward as was the disclosure.

In *Reginella v. R.*, 2018 ONCJ 198, 2018 CarswellOnt 4918, [2018] O.J. No. 1547 (Ont. C.J.), the learned justice of the peace denied the adjournment request brought by the defendant on the trial date due to disclosure not being received mainly on the bases that the Crown witnesses were present, the Crown was ready to proceed and that the defendant had not brought an application or motion for an adjournment prior to the trial date. The learned justice of the peace exercised his discretion judicially in refusing to grant the adjournment on the trial date. He properly considered that there would be an inconvenience to witnesses as being a factor and that the defendant or his agent had not brought an application for an adjournment prior when they realized that the disclosure had not been received. The learned justice of the peace did not consider any irrelevant factors in this decision. Clearly, there was an onus on the defendant and his agent to follow up by way of direct contact with the trial date when the disclosure had not been received. In addition to not being any adjournment request, the defendant or his agent did not bring an application for a stay of proceedings based on a failure of the prosecution to provide disclosure. In the circumstances, the trial was fair. The defendant was represented; he chose not to attend the trial. The defendant's agent could have renewed his request for an adjournment at the close of the prosecution's case so that the defendant or any defence witnesses could testify. Such a request was not made. The appeal court had not been advised that even though disclosure was received subsequent to the trial, there was something of substance in that disclosure that may have assisted the defendant in his defence.

In *R. v. Masoumi*, 2018 ONCJ 576, 2018 CarswellOnt 14043, [2018] O.J. No. 4392 (Ont. C.J.), it was held that there was no air of reality to the claim that the court's conduct in past proceedings involving paralegals and agents gave rise to a reasonable apprehension of bias in the present proceeding. An allegation of hostility towards a paralegal in a different matter, totally unsubstantiated, who is not representing the defendant before the court does not rise to the level of cogent evidence sufficient to rebut the presumption of judicial impartiality. Even accepting for the sake of argument that a justice's exercise of the power to determine where individuals sit in the courtroom could potentially give rise to a reasonable expectation of bias, the past practice of the court in refusing to allow agents to sit at a table reserved for lawyers at a time when agents were not licensed paralegals could not give rise to a reasonable apprehension of bias in the instant proceedings. After the Law Society began issuing licences for paralegals, the court's practice had been to permit paralegals to sit at counsel table, and there was no evidence that the agent in the instant proceedings had been prevented by the court from sitting at counsel table at any time.

The applicant sought to have a party, M, who was not a licensed paralegal or lawyer, act as his agent on the appeal. The judge ruled that M could not appear as the applicant's agent for that appeal. At that point the applicant requested an adjournment which was not granted. Eventually the matter was adjourned because of time constraints. A judge may bar a person from acting as agent if that person is not competent and does not understand and comply with the duties and responsibilities of an agent. The judge found that M may not understand and properly comply with the duties and responsibilities of an agent, and gave examples of no advance warning to the courts or to the prosecution that he would be appearing and arguing matters before the court as agent, or that he was the one who drafted the Notice of Constitutional Issues. An agent cannot argue that he/she understands and will comply with the duties and obligations of an agent, and then have the principal argue that certain actions were his, and not the agent's. M clearly knew that this issue would arise. He came armed with case law and argument on this point. Yet it was not until the case actually commenced that the appellant advised the court and the Crown that the appellant wished to have M act for him as an agent. The reasonable conclusion was that the appellant and M decided to ambush the Crown and put it at a disadvantage. The judge's decision to disqualify M from acting as an agent did not constitute a substantial wrong or miscarriage of justice. Neither did the decision of the appeal court to grant an adjournment constitute a substantial wrong or miscarriage of justice. The appellant knew that the issue of M being permitted to act as an agent would be a live issue at the appeal. He knew or should have known that it was possible that M would be disqualified, and therefore he should have been prepared to proceed on his own with the appeal at that time. The appellant could not argue that he was surprised that he was required to proceed, when, in fact, he was the person who failed to give advance notice to the Crown, which notice would have resulted in the Crown advising in advance of its objection. See *R. v. Vanravenswaay*, 2018 ONSC 5348, 2018 CarswellOnt 15064, [2018] O.J. No. 5348 (Ont. S.C.J.).

In *York (Regional Municipality) v. 1085638 Ontario Limited*, 2018 ONCJ 658, 2018 CarswellOnt 16164, [2018] O.J. No. 5003 (Ont. C.J.), it was held that the decision to adjourn a proceeding is one in the discretion of the trial judge. The judicial officer must listen to the request and consider various factors, including the length of time of the proposed adjournment. The longer the period of time, the greater the likelihood the adjournment should not be granted as the likelihood of prejudice to the defence increases. What was clear on the record was that the justice of the peace tried to accommodate an adjournment for sentencing submissions if it was only going to be for a short time. After poring over the court calendar with the assistance of the trial coordinator it was clear that it couldn't. By that time the charges were 12 years and 5 years old, respectively, the court was clearly uncomfortable with yet another delay in the case at the penultimate stage, and ruled that submissions should be heard. Given that counsel were advised two months previously that they should be ready to do just that on the return date, the decision was not unfair. There was also no evidence on the appeal about what evidence would have been heard had the adjournment been granted. No fresh evidence was sought to be tendered on the hearing of the appeal. No error in principle was identified in the reasons for sentence. Absent an error in principle sentencing decisions are entitled to deference. Despite denying the adjournment, the court received submissions on sentence from both the prosecution and defence. The defendants received very substantial fines — $60,000 in total. That said, this was a legal sentence, and the defendants had a history of previous convictions relating to the very issue of non-compliance with municipal orders.

In *York (Regional Municipality) v. Bouaziz-Caruso*, [2019] O.J. No. 638 (Ont. C.J.), the defence representative had asked for disclosure several weeks before, but by the trial date it had not been handed out. The trial justice denied the adjournment, finding that any suggestion the defendant did not receive the notice of trial in advance was hearsay. The justice held the matter down to permit the trial agent to review disclosure and the defendant present, however she did not attend. Where a second trial date adjournment is denied, it is appropriate for the justice of the peace to hold the trial down briefly to permit the review of disclosure before trial. This practice is not uncommon for Part I litigation, and is reasonable in light of the simplified procedure contemplated under the Act.

The rule in *Browne v. Dunn* is not merely a procedural rule but a rule of trial fairness. It stands for the proposition that if counsel is going to challenge the credibility of a witness by calling contradictory evidence, the witness must be given the chance to address the contradictory evidence in cross-examination while he or she is in the witness box. More often than not, the rule in *Browne v. Dunn* arises and is invoked in situations where the defendant is unrepresented, as occurred in the instant case. The defendant's testimony as to removing his label/sticker from his vehicle was evidence that should have been put to the prosecution witness so that the officer could have been cross-examined with regard to that evidence. The proper remedy was to permit the officer to be recalled for this purpose. See *R. v. Hartlieb*, 2018 ONCJ 810, 2018 CarswellOnt 19435, [2018] O.J. No. 6080 (Ont. C.J.).

In *R. v. Dennis*, 2019 ONCA 109, 2019 CarswellOnt 2065, [2019] O.J. No. 773 (Ont. C.A.), it was held that the threshold for awarding costs against a lawyer personally in a criminal proceeding is a high one. As stated by the Supreme Court of Canada in *Québec (Directeur des poursuites criminelles et pénales) c. Jodoin*, 2017 CSC 26, 2017 SCC 26, 2017 CarswellQue 3091, 2017 CarswellQue 3092, [2017] 1 S.C.R. 478, 346 C.C.C. (3d) 433, 37 C.R. (7th) 1, 408 D.L.R. (4th) 581, (*sub nom.* Quebec (Director of Criminal and Penal Prosecutions) v. Jodoin) 380 C.R.R. (2d) 285, [2017] S.C.J. No. 26 (S.C.C.), only serious misconduct can justify such a sanction. Costs are awarded on a discretionary basis and appellate courts should only intervene when that discretion is exercised "in an abusive, unreasonable or non-judicial manner." In the instant case, the appellant's counsel requested an adjournment of the appeal hearing without notice to the Crown prosecutor. The Crown prosecutor had interrupted her vacation to attend on the scheduled date to argue the appeal, and had been inconvenienced as a result of the appellant's request for an adjournment. Counsel apologized to the prosecutor and the court. Of his own initiative, the appeal judge asked the Crown prosecutor if she wished to apply for costs under s. 129 of the *Provincial Offences Act*. The appeal court ordered counsel to pay costs personally in the amount of $500 due to his reckless disregard for the other side. The principles described in *Jodoin* ought to apply equally to an order under s. 129. However, while the absence of advance notice of the adjournment request was worthy of adverse comment by the court, the exercise of the appeal judge's discretion was unreasonable and did not meet the threshold for an award of costs against counsel personally. Fundamentally, counsel's behaviour did not warrant the exceptional remedy of a personal costs order. The costs award was vacated.

In *York (Regional Municipality) v. McGuigan*, 2018 ONCA 1062, 2018 CarswellOnt 22571, [2018] O.J. No. 6916 (Ont. C.A.), the Court of Appeal ruled that trial justice properly ordered the prosecutor to provide disclosure of the testing and operating procedures from the user manual for the device used by the traffic officer to measure the speed of the defendant's vehicle. Even if the justice of the peace had been wrong to order disclosure, the error would not have been jurisdictional in nature. Section 140(1) of the *Provincial Offences Act* confines *certiorari* orders in *POA* matters to situations where an applicant would be entitled to such relief at common law, and for parties to a proceeding, *certiorari* orders are confined to jurisdictional errors. Moreover, *certiorari* should not have been granted in the course of ongoing proceedings. Nor was there a substantial wrong or miscarriage of justice to address, a prerequisite to *certiorari* under s. 141(4) of the Act. Contrary to the application judge's decision, the justice of the peace did not err in making the disclosure order. Where a prosecutor is relying on a speed measuring device to prosecute an offence, it must, on request, disclose the testing and operating procedures set out in the user manual for that device. It is up to the prosecutor to hand such information over on request. The person charged need not bring an application or obtain a court order. This is first party disclosure, not third party disclosure. The charging police force has a corresponding duty to furnish the pertinent passages from the user manual to the prosecutor to enable the prosecutor to discharge its first party disclosure obligations. This is not a crushing administrative task. The disclosure at issue here is not case specific information. The disclosure obligation can therefore be discharged by the prosecutor by posting the relevant content from the user manual online and providing the ticketed driver with the required URL.

2.4 RULES OF PROFESSIONAL CONDUCT

- The Law Society regulates Ontario's lawyers to ensure a competent and ethical bar. It will also regulate paralegals under proposed Bill 14 — *Access to Justice Act*. The Rules of Professional Conduct must be interpreted and applied with common sense. As stated in section 1.03(1)(f) of the

Rules, they do not address every situation, and should be observed in spirit as well as in the letter.

- This is a brief summary of some of the rules for the courtroom advocate. See the Rules on the Law Society website: *www.lsuc.on.ca.*

- If you have any doubt about what to do in a situation, contact an experienced lawyer and seek guidance.

- The *Paralegal Rules of Conduct* governing paralegal practitioners were approved at the March, 2007 convocation of the Law Society of Upper Canada. These rules impose new responsibilities of ethical behaviour on paralegal practitioners, including the required standard of a "competent paralegal": rule 3.01(1). Other rules of note include rule 2.01 which imposes a requirement of integrity and civility on paralegals in connection with the provision of legal services which are made available to the public. A paralegal is to be "honest and candid" when advising clients (rule 3.02(1)) and is expected to treat tribunals and other licensees with "candour, fairness, courtesy and respect." (rule 4.01(1)). Under rule 6.01(1), paralegals are to "encourage public respect for, and try to improve, the administration of justice". Moreover, according to rule 6.01(2) paralegals are to "take care not to weaken or destroy public confidence in legal institutions or authorities by making irresponsible allegations or comments".

- The effect of these rules is discussed in *Hill v. Toronto (City)*, 2007 ONCJ 253, 48 M.V.R. (5th) 55, (*sub nom.* Toronto (City) v. Hill) 221 C.C.C. (3d) 189, 2007 CarswellOnt 3578, [2007] O.J. No. 2232 (Ont. C.J.). Case law decided before the implementation of the *Paralegal Rules of Conduct* indicates that once a paralegal practitioner undertakes to provide legal services and representation to a client, it is under an obligation to ensure that the client is clearly informed of any limits upon its retainer; it is also obliged to ensure that the client is made aware of the necessity to appear in court for trial. Failure to discharge either obligation results in breach of duty to the client and supports a finding of negligence: see *Hamilton v. X-Copper Legal Services Inc.* (2005), [2005] O.J. No. 2463, 2005 CarswellOnt 3344 (Ont. S.C.J.).

- By-Law 4, effective May 1, 2007, governs licensing requirements for paralegal practitioners. The Class P1 licence authorizes licence holders to provide legal services in Ontario. The scope of activities permitted under the Class P1 licence includes: representing a party, in the case of a proceeding in the Small Claims Court, before the Small Claims Court; in the case of a proceeding under the *Provincial Offences Act,* before the Ontario Court of Justice; and, in the case of a proceeding under the *Criminal Code,* before a summary conviction court: sections 5, 6. It is anticipated that the first licences will be issued in early 2008 following the licensing examination process which is sched- uled to commence in January 2008. The ability to appear on summary conviction matters before the Ontario Court of Justice in Ontario is consistent with the practice in other provinces: see, for example, *Law Society (Manitoba) v. Pollock,* 2007 MBQB 51, [2007] 5 W.W.R. 147, 37 C.P.C. (6th) 125, 153 C.R.R. (2d) 131, 2007 CarswellMan 80, [2007] M.J. No. 67, 213 Man. R. (2d) 81 (Man. Q.B.), affirmed 2008 CarswellMan 238, [2008] 7 W.W.R. 493, 2008 MBCA 61, 54 C.P.C. (6th) 4, 427 W.A.C. 273, 228 Man. R. (2d) 273 (Man. C.A.).

- The Law Society of Upper Canada's By-Law 4 was subse- quently amended so as to disqualify suspended lawyers from applying for a paralegal licence. This amendment includes lawyers who have been suspended for both disciplinary and administrative (such as non-payment of fees) reasons. However, it does not include lawyers who have been disbarred.

Justice Casey rejected a constitutional challenge to the Law Society's authority to regulate non-lawyers in the recent case *R. v. Toutissani,* 2008 ONCJ 139, [2008] O.J. No. 1174 (C.J.), leave to appeal refused 2008 CarswellOnt 5424, 2008 CarswellOnt 5425, 256 O.A.C. 390 (note), 390 N.R. 390 (note) (S.C.C.). It was argued that since Parliament's criminal law power has granted an agent the right to appear in summary conviction proceedings, the provincial legislature lacks the authority to circumscribe or place limits upon that right through the paralegal licensing regime under the *Law Society Act.* Justice Casey found that both legislative schemes were valid, that is, the *Criminal Code* provisions respecting appearance by agents, and the provincial regulations establishing rules regarding non-lawyers who appear in court. Since a person could, at the same time, comply with both the provisions of the *Criminal Code* and the *Law Society Act,* there was no impermissible conflict between the two pieces of legislation. A person who obtains a licence under the Law Society's by-laws is permitted by both the federal and provincial enactments to represent defendants in summary conviction matters. Parliament's purpose in permitting defendants on summary convictions to be represented by non-lawyers is furthered by the provincial legislation. Since the defendant's representative on the *Immigration Act* charges before the court had not complied with the licensing requirements of the *Law Society Act*, he was not permitted to appear for the defendant.

In *Chancey v. Dharmadi* (2007), 86 O.R. (3d) 612, [2007] O.J. No. 2852, 2007 CarswellOnt 4664, 44 C.P.C. (6th) 158 (Ont. Master), the court considered the issue as to whether a paralegal could be forced to reveal communications and the file in a civil proceeding regarding a collision where the paralegal defended the same party before the provincial offences court. Master Dash ruled that class privilege, such as solicitor-client privilege, is a form of privilege in which there is a *prima facie* presumption that the communications are inadmissible or not subject to disclosure in criminal or civil proceedings. The problem with recognizing a class privilege respecting paralegal-client communications at this time is that a class requires specific identifiable actors. Paralegal licensing is in progress, but as of yet there are no licensed paralegals. There is no principled reason why a class privilege should not be extended to paralegal-client communications, once communications with an identifiable group, namely paralegals licensed by the Law Society, begin. Once licensing of paralegals is in effect, the court may, in an appropriate case, revisit the idea of granting a class privilege to communications between a client and a paralegal licensed by the Law Society to provide legal services, rather than requiring the court to engage in a case by case analysis respecting each such communication. The communications in the instant case between the defence paralegal and the client, including the agent's entire file, were protected by privilege.

- *Paralegal Professional Conduct Guidelines* have been developed by the Law Society to assist paralegals in understanding and complying with the *Paralegal Rules of Conduct*. These Guidelines are to be considered along with the *Rules*, the *Law Society Act*, By-Laws made under the Act, and other relevant case law or legislation. The Guidelines are available in electronic form, and are directly linked to the *Rules* on the law Society's website. There are 22 separate Guidelines, ranging from the Law Society and its Disciplinary Authority (Guideline 22), to Professionalism — Integrity and Civility (Guideline 1), Undertakings (Guideline 3), Harassment and Discrimination (Guideline 4) and Competence (Guideline 6). A number of amendments have also been made to the *Paralegal Rules of Conduct*, the majority of which deal with matters related to affiliations and multi-discipline practices. Other amendments made in 2008 concern advertising and marketing. The Law Society has also put in place a Practice Management Helpline in the form of a confidential telephone service in order to provide assistance in interpreting the *Paralegal Rules of Conduct* and Law Society By-Laws.

In *R. v. Kronshteyn*, 2008 CarswellOnt 4600 (Ont. C.J.), the court set aside a conviction and ordered a new trial where evidence was placed before the court by the trial agent that he misunderstood the defendant's instructions due to a language barrier, and erroneously entered guilty to a lesser charge.

In *R. v. Fuentes*, 2008 ONCJ 598, 2008 CarswellOnt 7068, [2008] O.J. No. 4677 (Ont. C.J.), it was held that it is the client's right to meet with the person who represents him so there will be no misunderstanding as to what occurs in court. It is mandatory that whomever the licensed paralegal hires meets with the client where a paralegal informs the client that another paralegal will represent the client in court. It is not sufficient for the paralegal to merely tell the other agent what the client wants or said. Where the second paralegal pleaded the client guilty without ever speaking to the client, and a licence suspension was imposed, the conviction could not stand.

In *R. v. Chin*, 2009 CarswellOnt 1563, 2009 ONCJ 180 (Ont. C.J.), the retained paralegal had written instructions from the defendant to do his "best" with his speeding charge. The file was passed to another paralegal, who gave it to an employee in his firm. A guilty plea was negotiated to the charge for a lesser fine. Although the defendant was not happy with the result and sought to have the guilty plea set aside, the signed written instructions were sufficient to uphold the guilty plea.

Licensed paralegals are not permitted to represent defendants who are charged under the *Criminal Code* with the offence of impaired driving when the offence date is after 1 July 2008, this being the time when the maximum term of imprisonment for the offence on summary conviction was increased from 6 months to 18 months.

Section 802.1 of the *Criminal Code* prohibits a non-lawyer from representing a defendant if he/she is liable to a term of imprisonment of greater than 6 months, and the non-lawyer is not authorized to do so pursuant to a program approved by the Lieutenant Governor in Council. There is no such program under s. 802.1 in Ontario authorizing representation; the Law Society has advised that paralegals may only provide legal services to clients in a proceeding under the *Criminal Code* before a summary conviction court where permitted by the *Criminal Code*. There is therefore no jurisdiction, under the common law or otherwise, to permit a paralegal to appear on a summary conviction matter where the punishment is greater than 6 months imprisonment: *R. v. Laurie*, [2009] O.J. No. 3860, 89 M.V.R. (5th) 301, 2009 ONCJ 428, 2009 CarswellOnt 5524 (Ont. C.J.).

Note: The *Laurie* decision is not a provincial offences matter, but is of practical importance to paralegals as they may appear before judges of the Ontario Court of Justice under the *Provincial Offences Act*, and as summary conviction trial courts so long as the punishment period does not exceed 6 months. Law Society By Law 7.1, ss. 1, 5(1)(b), 6(1)(b), allows a licensed paralegal to appear "in respect of a scheduling or other related routine administrative matter before an adjudicative body" when a defendant is represented by a lawyer. It has also been held that where a defendant who is represented by a lawyer authorizes his/her lawyer to appear by means of a duly executed designation under s. 650.01 of the *Criminal Code*, a licensed paralegal may appear in court for the purpose of routine remands for indictable offences: *R. v. L. (G.Y.)*, [2009] O.J. No. 3089, 246 C.C.C. (3d) 112, 2009 CarswellOnt 4350 (Ont. S.C.J.).

The retained paralegal who had another matter in the same courthouse spoke to a second paralegal and asked him to speak to the matter on his behalf. However, when the justice asked whether the second paralegal had spoken with the defendant, he replied that he had not but that he had received instructions from the retained paralegal. The justice refused to permit the second paralegal to appear and dealt with the certificate on the deemed not to dispute docket instead. In the circumstances, the justice erred in proceeding in this manner, and in not adjourning the matter to allow the retained paralegal to attend and speak to the matter: *R. v. Metselaar*, [2009] O.J. No. 1691, 2009 CarswellOnt 2241 (Ont. C.J.), additional reasons at 2009 CarswellOnt 5462 (Ont. C.J.).

The conduct of the paralegal before the trial judge was characterized by questionable conduct of the defence, questionable decision making, and discourtesy throughout the proceedings. The deficiencies in representation included instances of failing to request disclosure, not being aware of what was in the possession of the defendant, failing to lead evidence, failing to attempt to prevent hearsay and opinion evidence from being adduced, failing to properly introduce relevant documentary evidence, and failing to respond fully and effectively to the court's ruling regarding its disallowing leading questions on cross-examination. Consequently, the conduct of the trial resulted in a miscarriage of justice as the fundamental missteps made by the paralegal deprived the defendants of a full and fair trial: *R. v. 20207000 Ontario Inc.*, [2009] O.J. No. 838, 42 C.E.L.R. (3d) 129, 2009 CarswellOnt 1045, 2009 ONCJ 76 (Ont. C.J.).

The licensed paralegal was not barred from appearing in court to represent the defendant where the paralegal representing the defendant was unable to continue the trial due to an emergency, but had given the other instructions. The defendant had also spoken to the other paralegal practitioner and consented to being represented by him: *R. v. Hajivasilis*, 2009 CarswellOnt 3781, 2009 ONCJ 310 (Ont. C.J.), affirmed 2012 CarswellOnt 2632, 2012 ONCJ 110, [2012] O.J. No. 859 (Ont. C.J.), reversed on other grounds 2013 ONCA 27, 2013 CarswellOnt 508, 114 O.R. (3d) 337, 41 M.V.R. (6th) 175, 302 O.A.C. 65, [2013] O.J. No. 253 (Ont. C.A.).

It would be unfair and unseemly to permit counsel to continue to represent the defendant and thus be in a position to cross-examine a witness who was elderly, unsophisticated and vulnerable, in the same proceeding in which he formerly represented him. The conflict of interest arose as counsel had formerly acted for a codefendant facing *Occupational Health and Safety Act* charges arising from the same accident, against whom the prosecution had been stayed and was now a Crown witness: *R. v. Con-Drain Co. (1983) Ltd.*, 2008 ONCJ 114, 2008 CarswellOnt 1424, [2008] O.J. No. 1012, 172 C.R.R. (2d) 299 (Ont. C.J.).

There was no evidence of any breakdown of solicitor-client confidence or communication, and no reason for the court to believe that the defendant wished counsel to be removed. In fact, counsel candidly admitted that the request, which followed its unsuccessful motion for an adjournment, was for the protection of the interests of the defendant. The motion to be removed as counsel which flew in the face of counsel's duty was dismissed: *Ontario (Travel Industry Council) v. Baldwin Travel & Tours Ltd.*, 2010 ONCJ 402, 2010 CarswellOnt 6884, [2010] O.J. No. 3859 (Ont. C.J.).

In *R. v. Dobson*, 2010 ONCJ 161, 2010 CarswellOnt 2744, [2010] O.J. No. 1823 (Ont. C.J.), it was held that the licensed paralegal who entered a guilty plea in the defendant's absence, on the basis of boilerplate instructions in the retainer agreement authorizing the paralegal to negotiate a plea on the defendant's behalf, did not constitute valid instructions to enter the guilty plea. The instruction was not case specific, included no duty to ensure the facts were admitted by the client, did not indicate that the plea was voluntary, or that the client was aware of the plea. The record keeping practices of the paralegal provided no confidence that she could accurately reconstruct the events that led to the plea; her independent memory was unreliable and she altered the documents in anticipation of the appeal.

A lawyer who happens to be a defendant before the court should not be treated any differently, and should not appear to be treated any differently, than any other defendant before the court. In dismissing the request of the defendant for an adjournment on the basis of the lack of disclosure, the comments of the court in calling the request disingenuous and smacking of sharp practice gave rise to an appearance of bias. A verbal summary of disclosure materials on a trial date in response to a disclosure request, even in provincial offences procedure, does not meet a minimum standard of disclosure to the defendant: *Durham (Regional Municipality) v. Jagtoo*, 2010 ONCJ 596, 2010 CarswellOnt 9517, [2010] O.J. No. 5334 (Ont. C.J.).

In *R. v. Figueli*, 2010 CarswellOnt 7262, [2010] O.J. No. 4122 (Ont. C.J.), it was held that with respect to any regulatory or criminal offences, one set of facts can be the basis for more than one charge. There is no rule that the defendant has to be charged with one or the other as long as it is clear on the information what the accusations are that a defendant has to reply or respond to defend himself against. In the context of the case, it was clear that all the parties knew that they were dealing with stunt driving. That was what the prosecutor was prosecuting and that is what the defendant was being defended for. It was clear that the charge and the basis of the charge had been disclosed and he had an opportunity to defend himself, an opportunity to make a full and fair defence and was represented by a licensed paralegal.

In *R. v. Cipriano*, 2011 ONSC 223, 2011 CarswellOnt 89, [2011] O.J. No. 67 (Ont. S.C.J.), it was held that the justice of the peace had no alternative but to declare a mistrial after the defendant's counsel made a complaint against her to the Judicial Council. If she acquitted the defendant, it would have appeared she did so because she was threatened and accused of misconduct; if she found the defendant guilty, it would be said she was angry and biased due to the allegations made and pending against her. Where there are facts and circumstances that clearly give rise to a reasonable apprehension of bias, the court has the ability to address the situation by making use of the remedies of *certiorari* and mandamus. If the judge who made the original mandamus order in this case had been aware of defence counsel's letter of complaint that was provided to the justice of the peace, it would have been highly doubtful that the original order would have been made. Consequently, the justice of the peace had no alternative but to recuse herself despite the mandamus order to proceed with the trial. There was no basis to stay the charges on the basis of abuse of process.

It was not within the jurisdiction of the justice of the peace to simply indicate that the individual who the defendant wished to assist him at his trial could not appear on the basis that he was not a paralegal licenced by the Law Society. It was open to the justice to make certain inquiries to determine whether or not the person was qualified to be assisting the defendant. It would have been open to the justice of the peace to rule under those circumstances that the individual could not appear in the court: *R. v. Zaltzman*, 2010 ONCJ 667, 2010 CarswellOnt 10523 (Ont. C.J.).

There was no evidence to show that the prosecution of the charges was delegated to the Fire Chiefs. The prosecutor, who was properly appointed by the Regional Municipality of Niagara, acted in that capacity throughout the case, and there was no suggestion that he acted improperly at any time. The sentence in the prosecutor's letter that he had received instructions from the Fire Chiefs neither constituted nor indicated that the authority to prosecute the cases had been delegated to the Fire Chiefs; it was very similar to a Crown attorney consulting with the investigating police officer or a complainant before making a decision in a criminal case. As long as the lawyer continues to make the decisions, he/she is still the prosecutor. There was nothing to indicate anything different here. Nor was there anything to suggest that he behaved improperly in any way in his prosecution of the case: *Niagara (Regional Municipality) v. DiFruscia*, 2010 ONCJ 427, 2010 CarswellOnt 7104, [2010] O.J. No. 404 (Ont. C.J.).

In *R. v. Dookie*, 2012 ONCJ 719, 2012 CarswellOnt 14803, [2012] O.J. No. 5740 (Ont. C.J.), it was held that s. 802.1 of the *Criminal Code* which bars agents from appearing to defend persons charged with summary conviction offences punishable by more than six months imprisonment does not violate the s. 15 equality provisions of the *Canadian Charter of Rights and Freedoms*. Parliament has determined that it is not in the interest of defendants that non-lawyers appear to represent individuals who are charged with offences of a certain level of seriousness.

- Amendments have been made to the *Commissioners for Taking Affidavits Act*, R.S.O. 1990, c. C.17, effective 31 December 2012, which will add licensed paralegals to the list of persons who are commissioners for oaths by virtue of their position, and indicated as such by O. Reg. 386/12. This amendment will not come into force, however, until 1 July 2013. Currently, the list includes lawyers who are licensed to practice law in Ontario, as well as judges and justices of the peace. Under s. 9 of the Act, every oath and declaration is to be taken by the deponent in the presence of the party administering the oath or declaration, and this party, which will now include licensed paralegals, must satisfy himself/ herself of the genuineness of the signature of the deponent or declarant, and shall administer the oath or declaration in the manner required by law before signing the jurat or declaration.

In *R. v. Bilinski*, 2013 ONSC 2824, 2013 CarswellOnt 8723, [2013] O.J. No. 2984 (Ont. S.C.J.) Justice Durno rejected the notion that a person who retains a paralegal is now entitled to the effective assistance of counsel. He held that the differences between paralegals and counsel remain, and that there is a "clear distinction" between the representation that an accused person is entitled to when they retain a lawyer, as opposed to a paralegal. In terms of whether there should be a lesser standard of competency that applies where an accused person retains a paralegal in a criminal trial, the court acknowledged that this issue was more "problematic". On one hand, the so-called middle ground test could not simply be that the paralegal is entitled to make "more mistakes than a lawyer". Justice Durno pointed out that the focus of the test must still be on the quality of the representation, and whether a miscarriage of justice resulted. Justice Durno went on to dispose of the "middle ground standard of representation" by ruling that he was not satisfied on the basis of the record before him that the Law Society's regulation of paralegals had given rise to this standard of competency, especially for paralegals who had been grandfathered. He did comment, though, that there may be evidence which could support such a middle ground, particularly with respect to paralegals who were not the subject of grandfathering. However, such evidence had not been presented to the court and His Honour observed that the question of whether there should be a new standard is best determined on the basis of a full record, including "all the requirements for those grandfathered and those who were not".

Given the serious professional and punitive consequences of a finding of contempt, the contempt citation process should be used sparingly, if at all: *R. v. Strati*, 2014 ONCJ 139, 2014 CarswellOnt 3624, [2014] O.J. No. 1413 (Ont. C.J.).

The defendant was charged with driving a commercial motor vehicle with no brake lights for which the set fine was $200. However, the set fine indicated on the certificate of offence was $85, which was the set fine for the offence involving a vehicle that is not a commercial motor vehicle. As the set fine was incorrect, it was not complete and regular on its face and ought to have been quashed by the Justice of the Peace. It seemed an unfortunate waste of everyone's time and court resources to require such a simple case with an obvious defect to have to go through two levels of court (first instance and appeal) before the result dictated by law is achieved. It is inappropriate for an officer of the court who is aware that a court is about to make an error by not quashing a certificate of offence that is not complete and regular to fail to bring his/her concern to the court's attention. The party should not be required to lie in the weeds clutching a notice of appeal. There is no downside but rather an upside of eliminating these concerns by permitting a defendant or his/ her representative to make a conditional appearance, without thereby being considered to be present, in this narrow and unique situation. To be clear, the very summary nature of default proceedings is not to be altered; rather, this would simply provide an opportunity for one having some knowledge of the particular certificate of offence to point out what might otherwise be overlooked. It would not be a matter for argument, nor would it trigger otherwise inapplicable amending powers. Once so informed, the court would make its determination to convict or quash as the case may be. Any disagreement with that decision would be a matter to be addressed on appeal. See *R. v. Rodrigues*, 2013 ONCJ 719, 2013 CarswellOnt 18477, 62 M.V.R. (6th) 331, [2013] O.J. No. 6041 (Ont. C.J.).

- The *Paralegal Rules of Conduct* and the lawyers' *Rules of Professional Conduct* have been amended by Convocation, effective 1 October 2014, by implementing the Federation of Law Societies of Canada's Model Code of Professional Conduct. The *Paralegal Professional Conduct Guidelines* have also been amended.

There was conflicting evidence on almost every material aspect of the alleged communications between the accused and the paralegal she retained to assist her on the *Highway Traffic Act* charges she faced. At the end of the day, there was, at the very least, a misunderstanding that led both the accused and the paralegal to not attend the accused's trial. As a result, the trial proceeded *ex parte*, leading to the accused's convictions on both charges. The apparent unfairness at the trial proceeding was not cured by what occurred at the appeal hearing, which also proceeded in the accused's absence, and the accused has not had her day in court. In these circumstances, the interests of justice require that the accused's conviction be set aside and a new trial ordered to avoid a miscarriage of justice. See *R. v. Sarkozy*, 2014 ONCA 481, 2014 CarswellOnt 8357, [2014] O.J. No. 2964 (Ont. C.A.).

In *R. v. Khan*, 2015 ONCJ 221, 2015 CarswellOnt 5975, [2015] O.J. No. 2096 (Ont. C.J.), it was held that an unlicensed paralegal cannot conduct trials or appeals of provincial offences under the supervision of a lawyer licensed by the Law Society of Upper Canada. The conduct of trials or appeals involves providing legal services, which only licensed lawyers and paralegals can do under the *Law Society Act* and the by-laws made under it; these functions cannot be delegated to non-licensees. This does not prevent a friend or family member, however, from attending with a defendant at a trial or an appeal to assist the defendant.

In *York (Regional Municipality) v. McGee*, 2015 ONCJ 479, 2015 CarswellOnt 13985, [2015] O.J. No. 4776 (Ont. C.J.), the provincial offences appeal court ruled that the decisions of the paralegal at trial amounted to ineffective assistance. On the day of trial she was given the matter by another agent in her office, and had little direct contact with the defendant and was under the impression he was nervous and might not wish to testify at his trial. The paralegal proceeded to conduct the trial in his absence even though he was in her office in the same building just steps away. The paralegal did not advise the presiding justice of the peace that the defendant was in the building or request that the matter be held down while she determined whether he wished to participate. However, the defendant did want to be present at his trial. He had a right to be present and the right to give evidence if he chose to do so. While the competency standard for now regulated paralegals in provincial offences matters had not been fully determined, on any measure the breach of the defendant's right to be present at his trial resulted in a miscarriage of justice.

On 1 December 2017, a motion was passed by the benchers of the Law Society of Ontario that Convocation endorse the proposition that licensed paralegals be regarded as officers of the court in every court of record in Ontario in which a paralegal is authorized to provide legal services.

The defendant applied to adjourn the trial, both on the date of the filed application and on the trial date, primarily due to the unavailability of retained representation. The decision to grant or deny an adjournment is a discretionary exercise. Where this discretion is exercised judicially and fails to result in a miscarriage of justice, the decision should not be interfered with on review. The right to representation of choice is not absolute. This is particularly resonant for *Highway Traffic Act* litigation in the general Toronto area where available counsel and paralegals are legion. Given the previously granted defence application to adjourn, it was reasonable for the court to expect that any representation retained by the defendant was available on the second trial date. The defendant demonstrated little or no diligence in this regard. In denying the application to adjourn, the learned justice considered the previously granted defence adjournment application. The trial was endorsed peremptory to proceed. It was appropriate to deny the application in the circumstances. See *R. v. Wei*, 2017 ONCJ 878, 2017 CarswellOnt 20869, [2017] O.J. No. 6785 (Ont. C.J.).

Application of s. 54 of the *Provincial Offences Act* is not restricted to Part III prosecutions commenced by laying of information. Section 54 applies to all proceedings commenced under the Act, and it explicitly includes certificate proceedings commenced under Part I by way of notice of trial, which fit the defendant in the case at bar. Both ss. 9.1 and 54, however, only permit a conviction *in absentia* where the defendant does not "appear" for trial. The Act does not seem to contemplate a scenario where the defendant "appears" for trial by way of an agent who later withdraws after being denied an adjournment. This unfortunate practice is more prevalent in provincial offences courts than it should be and merits comment. The defence cannot by its conduct thwart the court's direction that a trial will proceed as scheduled. The defendant was placed on notice by no less than three justices of the peace that the trial would proceed in November; when the adjournment application was denied in October, the defence was expected to enter its plea on the trial date. In sending an agent without instructions to enter a guilty plea or to defend the trial, the defence by its conduct endeavoured to subvert the explicit direction of the court. Once the adjournment was denied, the defence ought to have been fixed with the expectation of arraignment. If there was any intention to defend the charge, the defence should have attended the second trial date prepared to do so. The learned justice did not err in conducting an *ex parte* trial under s. 54 in the circumstances. Section 54 affords the absent defendant an appropriate measure of procedural fairness. The prosecution is required to prove the defendant was notified or compelled to attend trial. Evidence must be led to satisfy the standard of proof. The procedure employed was fair and consistent with the due administration of justice. See *R. v. Wei*, 2017 ONCJ 878, 2017 CarswellOnt 20869, [2017] O.J. No. 6785 (Ont. C.J.).

In *Groia v. Law Society of Upper Canada*, 2018 CSC 27, 2018 SCC 27, 2018 CarswellOnt 8700, 2018 CarswellOnt 8701, 34 Admin. L.R. (6th) 183, 46 C.R. (7th) 227, 424 D.L.R. (4th) 443, [2018] S.C.J. No. 27 (S.C.C.), the finding of misconduct against Mr. Groia, a defence lawyer in a *Securities Act* prosecution, was found to be unreasonable. The court held that defence lawyers must have sufficient latitude to advance their client's right to make full answer and defence by raising arguments about the propriety of state actors' conduct without fear of reprisal. This is not to be taken as endorsing incivility in the name of resolute advocacy; civility and resolute advocacy are not incompatible. To the contrary, civility is often the most effective form of advocacy. Nevertheless, when defining incivility and assessing whether a lawyer's behaviour crosses the line, care must be taken to set a sufficiently high threshold that will not chill the kind of fearless advocacy that is at times necessary to advance a client's cause. Courts and law societies have concurrent jurisdiction to regulate and enforce standards of courtroom behaviour. Improper defence behaviour is not necessarily professional misconduct, be it a function of incivility or incompetence. The Law Society must therefore be careful not to place too much weight on a judge's criticism of defence behaviour. When the impugned behaviour occurs in a courtroom, what, if anything, the judge does about it becomes relevant. Unlike the Law Society, the presiding judge observes the lawyer's behaviour firsthand. This offers the judge a comparatively advantageous position to evaluate the lawyer's conduct relative to the Law Society, who only enters the equation once all is said and done. The judge's reaction is not conclusive, and the Law Society is not barred from reviewing a lawyer's behaviour if the judge does not comment.

In *R. v. Masoumi*, 2018 ONCJ 576, 2018 CarswellOnt 14043, [2018] O.J. No. 4392 (Ont. C.J.), it was held that there was no air of reality to the claim that the court's conduct in past proceedings involving paralegals and agents gave rise to a reasonable apprehension of bias in the present proceeding. An allegation of hostility towards a paralegal in a different matter, totally unsubstantiated, who is not representing the defendant before the court does not rise to the level of cogent evidence sufficient to rebut the presumption of judicial impartiality. Even accepting for the sake of argument that a justice's exercise of the power to determine where individuals sit in the courtroom could potentially give rise to a reasonable expectation of bias, the past practice of the court in refusing to allow agents to sit at a table reserved for lawyers at a time when agents were not licensed paralegals could not give rise to a reasonable apprehension of bias in the instant proceedings. After the Law Society began issuing licences for paralegals, the court's practice had been to permit paralegals to sit at counsel table, and there was no evidence that the agent in the instant proceedings had been prevented by the court from sitting at counsel table at any time.

The applicant sought to have a party, M, who was not a licensed paralegal or lawyer, act as his agent on the appeal. The judge ruled that M could not appear as the applicant's agent for that appeal. At that point the applicant requested an adjournment which was not granted. Eventually the matter was adjourned because of time constraints. A judge may bar a person from acting as agent if that person is not competent and does not understand and comply with the duties and responsibilities of an agent. The judge found that M may not understand and properly comply with the duties and responsibilities of an agent, and gave examples of no advance warning to the courts or to the prosecution that he would be appearing and arguing matters before the court as agent, or that he was the one who drafted the Notice of Constitutional Issues. An agent cannot argue that he/she understands and will comply with the duties and obligations of an agent, and then have the principal argue that certain actions were his, and not the agent's. M clearly knew that this issue would arise. He came armed with case law and argument on this point. Yet it was not until the case actually commenced that the appellant advised the court and the Crown that the appellant wished to have M act for him as an agent. The reasonable conclusion was that the appellant and M decided to ambush the Crown and put it at a disadvantage. The judge's decision to disqualify M from acting as an agent did not constitute a substantial wrong or miscarriage of justice. Neither did the decision of the appeal court to grant an adjournment constitute a substantial wrong or miscarriage of justice. The appellant knew that the issue of M being permitted to act as an agent would be a live issue at the appeal. He knew or should have known that it was possible that M would be disqualified, and therefore he should have been prepared to proceed on his own with the appeal at that time. The appellant could not argue that he was surprised that he was required to proceed, when, in fact, he was the person who failed to give advance notice to the Crown, which notice would have resulted in the Crown advising in advance of its objection. See *R. v. Vanravenswaay*, 2018 ONSC 5348, 2018 CarswellOnt 15064, [2018] O.J. No. 5348 (Ont. S.C.J.).

The defendant's concern about the prejudicial effect of evidence that had been adduced from leading questions put by the prosecutor to their own witnesses and the elicitation of irrelevant hearsay, bad character, and lay opinion evidence into the trial, had to be viewed in context and its intended use in the trial. Any prejudicial effect of the impugned evidence had been lessened as this was a non-jury trial and the charges involved strict liability regulatory offences in which the prosecution can elicit evidence in their case-in-chief to rebut a defence of due diligence or other anticipated defences. After considering the impugned evidentiary issues and the context in which the prosecutor's impugned comments, language and tone were used and what had been occurring in the trial at the time, the cumulative effect of the prosecutor's conduct, although not ideal and of perfect comportment, did not go beyond aggressive or abusive as to cause the defendant to receive an unfair trial, since the defendant's trial was a non-jury trial for which the trier would be cognizant of applying the relevant legal principles and law, and would also be able to disabuse and give no weight to any hearsay, bad character, opinion, or any other irrelevant prejudicial evidence, nor put any weight on any inappropriate, sarcastic, or demeaning comments, made by the prosecutor about the defendant's memory, business practices, or personal lifestyle, or to improperly use the impugned evidence or the immoderate comments of the prosecutor as proof of guilt. Accordingly, the defendant's right to a fair trial had not been prejudiced by the cumulative effect of the prosecutor's conduct in eliciting the impugned evidence, nor by the prosecutor's impugned comments, language or tone, that would be manifested, perpetuated or aggravated through the conduct of the trial, or by its outcome. Neither was the cumulative effect of the prosecutor's conduct such that it reached a degree of unfairness or vexatiousness that contravenes notions of fundamental justice, nor was it the type of conduct in which the justice system would find it necessary to intervene so that it would leave the impression that it condones conduct that offends society's sense of fair play and decency. Therefore, the prosecutor's conduct during the trial had not undermined the integrity of the justice system that would be manifested, perpetuated or aggravated through the conduct of the trial, or by its outcome. See *Ontario (Electrical Safety Authority) v. Broomfield*, 2018 ONCJ 640, 2018 CarswellOnt 15732, [2018] O.J. No. 4893 (Ont. C.J.).

In *York (Regional Municipality) v. Bouaziz-Caruso*, [2019] O.J. No. 638 (Ont. C.J.), the defence representative had asked for disclosure several weeks before, but by the trial date it had not been handed out. The trial justice denied the adjournment, finding that any suggestion the defendant did not receive the notice of trial in advance was hearsay. The justice held the matter down to permit the trial agent to review disclosure and the defendant present, however she did not attend. Where a second trial date adjournment is denied, it is appropriate for the justice of the peace to hold the trial down briefly to permit the review of disclosure before trial. This practice is not uncommon for Part I litigation, and is reasonable in light of the simplified procedure contemplated under the Act.

In *R. v. Dennis*, 2019 ONCA 109, 2019 CarswellOnt 2065, [2019] O.J. No. 773 (Ont. C.A.), it was held that the threshold for awarding costs against a lawyer personally in a criminal proceeding is a high one. As stated by the Supreme Court of Canada in *Québec (Directeur des poursuites criminelles et pénales) c. Jodoin*, 2017 CSC 26, 2017 SCC 26, 2017 CarswellQue 3091, 2017 CarswellQue 3092, [2017] 1 S.C.R. 478, 346 C.C.C. (3d) 433, 37 C.R. (7th) 1, 408 D.L.R. (4th) 581, (*sub nom.*

Quebec (Director of Criminal and Penal Prosecutions) v. Jodoin) 380 C.R.R. (2d) 285, [2017] S.C.J. No. 26 (S.C.C.), only serious misconduct can justify such a sanction. Costs are awarded on a discretionary basis and appellate courts should only intervene when that discretion is exercised "in an abusive, unreasonable or non-judicial manner." In the instant case, the appellant's counsel requested an adjournment of the appeal hearing without notice to the Crown prosecutor. The Crown prosecutor had interrupted her vacation to attend on the scheduled date to argue the appeal, and had been inconvenienced as a result of the appellant's request for an adjournment. Counsel apologized to the prosecutor and the court. Of his own initiative, the appeal judge asked the Crown prosecutor if she wished to apply for costs under s. 129 of the *Provincial Offences Act*. The appeal court ordered counsel to pay costs personally in the amount of $500 due to his reckless disregard for the other side. The principles described in *Jodoin* ought to apply equally to an order under s. 129. However, while the absence of advance notice of the adjournment request was worthy of adverse comment by the court, the exercise of the appeal judge's discretion was unreasonable and did not meet the threshold for an award of costs against counsel personally. Fundamentally, counsel's behaviour did not warrant the exceptional remedy of a personal costs order. The costs award was vacated.

2.5 DUTIES OF THE PROSECUTION

- Duty to the Truth:
    - As prosecutor, you must fairly present all material facts and law, so the Justice can make the right decision.
    - You are a minister of justice — you neither win nor lose; nor seek false conviction — if the Justice accepts an explanation and acquits the defendant, you have acted with honour.
- Duty to be Fair:
    - You must disclose all potentially relevant evidence and witnesses to the defence, whether tending to show guilt or innocence.
    - If the defendant is unaware of a potential defence (especially if unrepresented), advise the defendant, bring the issue to the attention of the court, and deal with it openly and fairly.
    - Beware of "tunnel vision" — ignoring evidence which may seem peripheral, but which could lead to other reasonable explanations.

- If there is no reasonable prospect of conviction, or if the prosecution is no longer in the public interest, withdraw the case — it squanders precious time and resources; it causes the defendant unnecessary personal and financial hardship; see section 3.1, "Charge Screening by the Prosecutor" in Chapter 3.

- Advocacy:
  - Be a strong advocate; do not meekly accept any defence or witness assertion; vigorously test the evidence and let the impartial Justice determine the truth at trial.

The prosecutor is permitted to ask leading questions when questioning defence witnesses: *R. v. 20207000 Ontario Inc.*, [2009] O.J. No. 838, 42 C.E.L.R. (3d) 129, 2009 CarswellOnt 1045, 2009 ONCJ 76 (Ont. C.J.).

The prosecutor made sentencing submissions to the court and was a forceful advocate, painting the defendant's conduct as serious and deserving of significant sanction. Similarly, counsel for the defendant energetically advocated his client's position. In an adversary system, that is the function of counsel. The justice is left to make findings of fact and apply the relevant law to those findings. That the justice can be persuaded by the passionate submission of counsel is obvious; however, there was no basis for finding that those submissions, particularly of the prosecutor, amounted to misleading the court. The prosecutor confirmed that he was authorized to conduct the prosecution on behalf of the Workplace Safety and Insurance Board, and although the defence counsel sought production of the retainer agreement, the justice was entitled to rule that the prosecutor was not required to produce it: *R. v. Long Lake Forest Products Inc.*, [2009] O.J. No. 2193, 2009 CarswellOnt 3054, 2009 ONCJ 241 (Ont. C.J.).

Leading questions are questions that suggest an answer or assume a state of facts that is in dispute. The "either or" questions used by the prosecutor were not leading because they did not suggest the answer. The Crown, in meeting the challenge of a child reluctant to respond, asked binary questions that gave her a choice between alternatives; they did not, however, suggest an answer. See *R. v. W. (E.M.)*, 2011 SCC 31, 2011 CarswellNS 392, 2011 CarswellNS 393, [2011] 2 S.C.R. 542, 305 N.S.R. (2d) 1, 270 C.C.C. (3d) 464, 335 D.L.R. (4th) 89, 966 A.P.R. 1, 417 N.R. 171, [2011] S.C.J. No. 31 (S.C.C.).

The prosecutor's comment to the defendant while she was being cross-examined that her opportunity to give evidence was now over, she was now subject to cross-examination, was a total misrepresentation of what cross-examination is. Cross-examination is an opportunity for the person to answer questions given by the other side while still giving evidence. The use of the statement by the prosecutor to cut off an answer was also inappropriate. See *R. v. Shuttleworth*, 2013 ONCJ 749, 2013 CarswellOnt 18654, [2013] O.J. No. 6164 (Ont. C.J.).

The Justice of the Peace should have asked the defendant whether he had any questions of the officer or submissions to make as to the police officer's notes when the officer asked to use his notes to refresh his memory. The defendant did cross-examine the officer on numerous points, but did not assert that there were any discrepancies between the officer's testimony at trial and the notes disclosed to the defence. The failure to ask the defendant whether he wished to ask questions at that point, or make submissions, did not impact trial fairness as the prosecution provided a proper foundation for the police officer to refer to the notes. See *R. v. Zuccarini*, 2014 ONCJ 571, 2014 CarswellOnt 15457, [2014] O.J. No. 5234 (Ont. C.J.).

There was common ground among the parties that there is a duty of disclosure in trials conducted under Part I of the *Provincial Offences Act*, and that an unrepresented accused must be informed of his right to disclosure. It was also conceded by the City that as a self-represented litigant, the defendant was not adequately informed of his right to disclosure and that significant evidence, in the form of a video recording, has now been lost. On the basis of those concessions the appeal was allowed and an acquittal entered. Given this order, it was unnecessary to consider issues, including constitutional issues, regarding the method and timing of providing notice of the right to disclosure to unrepresented litigants in trials under Part I. It was also unnecessary to consider the nature of the assistance required to be provided by Justices of the Peace to unrepresented litigants in such trials. See *R. v. Ul-Rashid*, 2014 ONCA 896, 2014 CarswellOnt 18386, 70 M.V.R. (6th) 181 (Ont. C.A.).

2.6 DUTIES OF THE DEFENCE ADVOCATE

- Duty to Your Client:
  - You must defend your client's rights.
  - You must advocate your client's personal advantage, as perceived by your client.
  - Your client decides how to plead to the charge; not you.
  - You must accept your client's version of events if, after candidly discussing its credibility, your client insists it is true. If you do not know it is false, let the impartial Justice determine the truth at trial.

- If you have promised to represent your client, you cannot simply quit — you must give your client reasonable notice so your client can hire another qualified advocate.

- If you have told the court that you act for your client, you will also need the court's permission to "get off the record"; the court may deny your request if a new advocate would require an adjournment to prepare, and if the delay would unduly inconvenience the court or witnesses.

- If you are not a lawyer, tell your client and the court. On passage of Bill 14 — *Access to Justice Act*, only lawyers and paralegals licensed by the Law Society will be able to represent defendants under the *Provincial Offences Act*. Bill 14 is consumer protection legislation; your client should know what qualifications you have.

- Know your client's expectations, how they wish to plead, what they expect to pay, and advise your client how long the trial or resolution will likely take; if possible, get your client's instructions in writing.

- If your client will not be attending court (and has not been summonsed or ordered to appear), and if you will be appearing as agent or counsel on their behalf, get clear instructions in writing.

- Be Competent:

  - Do not accept a case because you need the "experience" — it is your client's experience that is important; imagine finding out, after an unsuccessful medical procedure, that your surgeon had never performed the operation before, did it without supervision, as a "learning experience".

  - Keep current on changes in the law and procedure; the Law Society mandates continuing legal education for lawyers; on passage of Bill 14 — *Access to Justice Act*, it will also mandate continuing legal education for paralegals.

- Be Prepared:

  - Know the evidence, the inferences likely to be drawn by the Justice, the rules and law that apply, and the likely outcome; advise your client honestly and candidly; do not encourage false hope, but equally, do not discourage a legitimate defence just to enter an easy guilty plea; and consider section 10.2.5 in Chapter 10 regarding credibility evidence.

- Disclose Any Conflict of Interest to Your Client and to the Court:
- You cannot serve two masters.
- How can you effectively represent co-defendants, if one could argue that the other is more responsible?
- How can you fairly cross-examine a witness who is a former client, who earlier provided you with damaging personal information?

- Duty to the Truth:
  - You cannot knowingly obstruct or distort the truth.
  - You cannot misrepresent evidence, facts, law, rulings or precedents, to the court, prosecutor, or authorities.
  - If you know your client is obstructing or distorting the truth, you must persuade them to stop; if they continue, seek permission from the court to withdraw from the case; but give the court minimal reasons; anything more would unnecessarily reveal your client's confidential discussions.

- Confidential Discussions:
  - Everything your client tells you is confidential.
  - But if you have reasonable grounds to believe there is an imminent risk to an identifiable person, or identifiable group of persons, of death or serious bodily harm, including serious psychological harm that substantially interferes with the health or well-being of the person(s), you should disclose enough information to prevent the harm (but no more). If there is time, before doing so, contact an experienced lawyer and request guidance; if there is more time, ask the lawyer to obtain a judicial order for you to disclose the information, presumably on notice to your client.
  - If you have reasonable grounds for believing that a dangerous situation is likely to develop at a court facility, you must inform the local police force and give particu-

lars; if there is time, before doing so, contact an experienced lawyer and request guidance in order to minimize any disclosure of your client's confidential information.

- Right to Silence:
  - If the truth is not your client's friend, remain silent on an issue; what your client has told you is confidential and your client retains the right to remain silent.
  - "Physician, do no harm" is ascribed to Hippocrates; it certainly applies to the advocate; if the prosecution has insufficient evidence to prove an element of its case, do not mention it during trial, but point to the deficiency in summation.
  - Silence only applies to facts and evidence; it does not apply to the law; if you are aware of a law or binding authority, you must disclose it to the Justice.
  - Sometimes your client is required to disclose information to the authorities — see section 3.2.5 under "Initial Advice" in Chapter 3.

- A Client who Confesses to You in Private:
  - What if your client voluntarily confesses the elements of the charge to you in private, can you do more than remain silent in court? Yes, as long as you do not obstruct or distort the truth.
  - You may treat your client's "not guilty" plea as a challenge to the prosecution to "prove it", not a proclamation of innocence.
  - You may take objection to the jurisdiction of the court, the constitutionality of the law, the form of charge, the admissibility of evidence, or other so-called "technical" defences.
  - You may test the observation and credibility of prosecution witnesses, to suggest they did not see "it" (which is different than suggesting "it" did not happen).
  - You may argue that the evidence as a whole fails to prove the charge.

- But you may not set up an affirmative case, or introduce or suggest evidence inconsistent with your client's admissions.
- Beware of Becoming a Witness:
  - An advocate is someone who communicates their client's defence in court; not one who handles evidence outside of court. If you touch, record, gather or handle evidence, just like anyone else, you may become a material witness.
  - For example, if your client leaves evidence or third-party documents in your office, and the history or state of that evidence becomes relevant, you may land in the witness box. Your client's communications are privileged, but the physical or documentary evidence deposited in your office is not.
  - You cannot conceal relevant evidence; you cannot retain it for the purpose of suppressing its use by the prosecution.
  - If you interview a witness who says something relevant, you could be compelled to testify about the conversation.
  - If you do become a material witness, you can no longer act as advocate at trial.
  - How can you assist your client by gathering evidence, yet not become a witness? Have someone else from your office, or perhaps an investigator, gather the evidence. Or, if you must be involved, have a credible person also attend, so they can witness the conversation. Or, ask permission of the witness to record or videotape the conversation; hopefully, your testimony won't be necessary.
- Appeals:
  - Should your client be convicted, get written instructions if they do not wish to file an appeal.
  - If you are appeal counsel, and you allege inadequate representation by the trial advocate, give written notice of the alleged deficiencies to the trial advocate (such as a copy of the appeal documents), so the trial advocate can properly address such allegations.

- In seeking to quash a conviction on the basis of ineffective assistance of counsel, an appellant must:

  - Establish the material facts on a balance of probabilities;

  - Demonstrate that counsel's acts or omissions were incompetent as measured against a reasonableness standard; and

  - Demonstrate that the ineffective representation caused a miscarriage of justice: *R. v. W. (R.)*, (2006), 2006 CarswellOnt 1189, 207 C.C.C. (3d) 137, 207 O.A.C. 280, [2006] O.J. No. 807 (Ont. C.A.), at para. 75, leave to appeal refused (2007), 2007 CarswellOnt 6160, 2007 CarswellOnt 6161 (S.C.C.).

It is an error of law for the justice to order the defendant to testify before the court in order to contradict an explanation given by the paralegal representing him as to the reasons the paralegal did not appear in court on time. In doing so, the justice did not take into account issues of privilege, such as the private communications between the defendant and his representative. While the court was entitled to bring to the attention of the paralegal its displeasure with the party's lateness and the allegedly false explanation for same, there were other alternatives for doing so, such as addressing the paralegal directly upon his arrival in court. Involving the defendant in the process raised questions about the fairness of the trial: *R. v. 20207000 Ontario Inc.*, [2009] O.J. No. 838, 42 C.E.L.R. (3d) 129, 2009 CarswellOnt 1045, 2009 ONCJ 76 (Ont. C.J.).

The conduct of the paralegal before the trial judge was characterized by questionable conduct of the defence, questionable decision making, and discourtesy throughout the proceedings. The deficiencies in representation included instances of failing to request disclosure, not being aware of what was in the possession of the defendant, failing to lead evidence, failing to attempt to prevent hearsay and opinion evidence from being adduced, failing to properly introduce relevant documentary evidence, and failing to respond fully and effectively to the court's ruling regarding its disallowing leading questions on cross-examination. Consequently, the conduct of the trial resulted in a miscarriage of justice as the fundamental missteps made by the paralegal deprived the defendants of a full and fair trial: *R. v. 20207000 Ontario Inc.*, [2009] O.J. No. 838, 42 C.E.L.R. (3d) 129, 2009 CarswellOnt 1045, 2009 ONCJ 76 (Ont. C.J.).

The prosecutor made sentencing submissions to the court and was a forceful advocate, painting the defendant's conduct as serious and deserving of significant sanction. Similarly, counsel for the defendant energetically advocated his client's position. In an adversary system, that is the function of counsel. The justice is left to make findings of fact and apply the relevant law to those findings. That the justice can be persuaded by the passionate submission of counsel is obvious; however, there was no basis for finding that those submissions, particularly of the prosecutor, amounted to misleading the court. The prosecutor confirmed that he was authorized to conduct the prosecution on behalf of the Workplace Safety and Insurance Board, and although the defence counsel sought production of the retainer agreement, the justice was entitled to rule that the prosecutor was not required to produce it: *R. v. Long Lake Forest Products Inc.*, [2009] O.J. No. 2193, 2009 CarswellOnt 3054, 2009 ONCJ 241 (Ont. C.J.).

The defendant had represented himself very poorly, but had the justice allowed him to complete his explanation of why he needed more time to retain counsel, there may have been grounds for the justice to take the position that he did in refusing the adjournment. There was also evidence that the defendant truly did not understand he needed counsel for the trial date. The swift and continued retention of the paralegal by the defendant after he was notified of the need for representation was inconsistent with the view held by the justice that he knew he needed representation for the initial trial date and was not diligent in exercising his right to retain a representative. The justice prejudged the defendant's adjournment request and ignored relevant evidence; his conduct of the case created a reasonable apprehension of bias. A mistrial should have been allowed once the representative appeared: *R. v. Armstrong*, [2009] O.J. No. 4143, 2009 CarswellOnt 6057 (Ont. C.J.).

It would violate the law of solicitor-client privilege to permit the Crown to question the defendant's legal advisors about all communications related to his application for disability benefits in a prosecution for providing false or misleading information under the *Insurance (Vehicle) Act of British Columbia*. To permit the Crown to ask questions in this area would open up questioning of the legal advisors on virtually the whole of their relationship with the defendant, which was not appropriate or permissible. See *R. v. Sanghera*, 2010 BCPC 250, 2010 CarswellBC 2658, [2010] B.C.J. No. 1943, 4 M.V.R. (6th) 81 (B.C. Prov. Ct.).

In *R. v. Bashir* (September 13, 2011), E.N. Libman J., [2011] O.J. No. 5403 (Ont. C.J.), the defence representative made a tactical decision not to indicate prior to the fourth trial date that disclosure was outstanding and that an adjournment would be sought. When the trial justice refused a further adjournment, he discontinued his involvement in the process by asking no questions of the witness or making any submissions in the remainder of the proceeding. In these circumstances, it would not be appropriate to reward this conduct of the behaviour of the defence representative with an adjournment at trial, or overturn the trial justice's decision, where there was a tactical decision to request disclosure, not follow it up, wait until the trial date to complain about it, and on the trial date find that the disclosure/adjournment request was being dismissed.

In *R. v. Dookie*, 2012 ONCJ 719, 2012 CarswellOnt 14803, [2012] O.J. No. 5740 (Ont. C.J.), it was held that s. 802.1 of the *Criminal Code* which bars agents from appearing to defend persons charged with summary conviction offences punishable by more than six months imprisonment does not violate the s. 15 equality provisions of the *Canadian Charter of Rights and Freedoms*. Parliament has determined that it is not in the interest of defendants that non-lawyers appear to represent individuals who are charged with offences of a certain level of seriousness.

Amendments have been made to the *Commissioners for Taking Affidavits Act*, 1990, c. C.17, effective 31 December 2012, which will add licensed paralegals to the list of persons who are commissioners for oaths by virtue of their position, and indicated as such by O. Reg. 386/12. This amendment will not come into force, however, until 1 July 2013. Currently, the list includes lawyers who are licensed to practice law in Ontario, as well as judges and justices of the peace. Under 9 of the Act, every oath and declaration is to be taken by the deponent in the presence of the party administering the oath or declaration, and this party, which will now include licensed paralegals, must satisfy himself/herself of the genuineness of the signature of the deponent or declarant, and shall administer the oath or declaration in the manner required by law before signing the jurat or declaration.

Defence counsel on appeal alleged that there was a conflict on the part of trial counsel who had previously acted for the prosecuting authority in a prosecution of a case dealing with a similar issue in which the prosecution had not been successful. The competency of trial counsel was also challenged on the basis of a failure to provide the court with evidence including a photograph which purported to show a laneway many years earlier in the area where a laneway now existed. However, even if such evidence had been submitted, it did not support the position that the laneway existed previously, or even if it did exist that it existed to the degree in place at the time the charges were laid. Any conflict that may have existed was for the authority to raise, as they had been previously represented by trial counsel on an unrelated matter involving similar issues. There was nothing on the record to call into question the competence of trial counsel. Decisions about evidence and submissions are within the realm of trial counsel; there was nothing to indicate that such decisions were wrong, let alone negligent, and there was nothing to suggest the actions of trial counsel compromised his duties and ethical responsibilities, nor did his actions compromise the rights of the defendants. See *R. v. Geil*, 2012 ONCJ 740, 2012 CarswellOnt 15014, [2012] O.J. No. 5655 (Ont. C.J.), leave to appeal refused 2013 ONCA 457, 2013 CarswellOnt 8921, [2013] O.J. No. 3087 (Ont. C.A.).

The defendant was represented by a licensed paralegal who entered a guilty plea on his behalf. The defendant claimed that the paralegal did not have his authority to do so, and launched a complaint against him. He also notified the paralegal of the date of his appeal, but the paralegal did not attend. A licensed paralegal is an officer of the court and has a duty to come forward with an explanation because he presented himself in court as someone who had the authority from the defendant to plead guilty to a serious offence under the *Highway Traffic Act*, and be subjected to a thousand dollar fine and licence suspension. The defendant presented evidence that the paralegal acted without authority. As the paralegal failed to comply despite being given numerous opportunities to explain the guilty plea he entered on the defendant's behalf while indicating that he had authority to do so, there was strong evidence that he did not have such authority. The guilty plea was set aside on appeal and a new trial ordered. See *R. v. Ezati*, 2016 CarswellOnt 8435, [2016] O.J. No. 2819 (Ont. C.J.).

Similarly, in *R. v. Antone*, 2016 ONCJ 316, 2016 CarswellOnt 8634, [2016] O.J. No. 2872 (Ont. C.J.), the defendant was not present when his legal representative entered a plea of guilty on his behalf. No plea inquiry was done by the justice of the peace as the defendant was not present and there was no discussion regarding the agent's authority to enter a plea on behalf of her client. However, it was clear from the information presented to the appeal court that the plea had not been arranged on the defendant's behalf with his knowledge and consent. Upon finding out that he had been found guilty, the defendant took steps to set aside the conviction and explain his circumstances. There was merit to his claim that at no time did he provide an informed consent to enter a guilty plea to the charge of driving while suspended and that the possible consequences of the conviction and six months driving suspension were not explained to him. Neither did the agent review disclosure with him. The notes in the Crown file indicated that upon the defendant paying his outstanding fines, a plea to the lesser offence of driving without a licence would have been accepted. A number of attempts were made to have the agent appear before the appeal court and explain her actions, but she did not appear. It appeared that she had been completely negligent in her representation of the defendant. It would be a miscarriage of justice to allow the conviction to stand in these circumstances.

In *R. v. Sahadeo*, 2016 ONCJ 122, 2016 CarswellOnt 3721, [2016] O.J. No. 1252 (Ont. C.J.), on the date his trial was scheduled to take place, the paralegal for the defendant appeared and requested an adjournment. When the request was refused, the paralegal advised the presiding justice that he was instructed not to participate in the proceedings any further. The paralegal then left the courtroom. Upon the defendant being paged with no response, a deemed not to dispute conviction was entered. The decision to grant or refuse the adjournment was discretionary, and will not be interfered with on appeal unless the discretion was not exercised judicially, or where it has resulted in a miscarriage of justice. In this case, the need for the adjournment for disclosure could easily have been obviated by the defendant far in advance of the trial. While the justice of the peace was correct to refuse the adjournment, a conviction should not have been imposed under s. 9.1 as it could not be said that the defendant had failed to appear at the time and place appointed for trial. He did appear by instructing an agent to attend, as permitted by s. 50; the provisions of s. 54(1) did not apply in this case. The defendant had appeared by agent, the prosecution was ready, and the trial should have proceeded. The fact that the defendant had instructed his agent to "walk away" did not mean that the agent had any right to do so. A paralegal, like counsel, can only withdraw with the leave of the court. The defendant demonstrated a complete lack of diligence by failing to ensure that he had the necessary disclosure. He ought to have either appeared personally or else sent a properly instructed agent. The agent, who appeared, had not been properly instructed and was initially unable to articulate the reason for which he was seeking an adjournment. The application itself was entirely without merit and should not have been brought; for his part, the agent should not have agreed to act for the defendant without proper instructions.

It is inconceivable that a defence lawyer would conduct a trial in the absence of a client that they had never met. An agent should never have accepted a retainer he did not intend to honour; the sub-agent should not have conducted a trial on behalf of a defendant he never met. In the circumstances, neither should have been permitted to hold themselves out as the defendant's representatives in the matter. On behalf of the administration of justice, the matter was remitted back for a new trial. See *R. v. Martin*, 2016 CarswellOnt 6784 (Ont. C.J.).

2.7 DUTY OF ALL ADVOCATES

- Duty to the Court:
  - Do not misrepresent evidence, facts, law, rulings or precedents.
  - Do not express your personal views — they are irrelevant and prejudicial.
  - Keep your promises ("undertakings") to the court or opponent.
  - Do not disparage the Justice, the decision, your opponent, the witnesses or other parties outside court; your remedy is an appeal.
- Duty to Witnesses:

- Do not demean or humiliate a witness; do not suggest a fact without a good faith belief in its truth; do not misrepresent what a witness is saying; do not ask a witness or defendant to comment on the credibility of another witness — credibility is for the Justice to decide.

- Do not discourage a witness from testifying; do not suggest they change their evidence; do not coach a witness how to testify; do not communicate with your witness when being cross-examined.

- You may refresh a witness's memory with their earlier statement before trial; but if the witness says there is an error in their earlier statement, do not discourage the witness from changing their evidence (and if you are the prosecutor, disclose the contradictory statements to the defence).

- Speak to witnesses in the presence of a police officer or appropriate third person; or, with the consent of the witness, record the interview, so the impartial Justice can assess the credibility of the witness at trial.

- If the defendant or witness is represented, do not communicate with them directly, unless with the consent of their representative.

- Use Common Sense:

  - Does a tactic seem unfair?

  - Does it pass the "smell test"?

  - The Law Society Rules of Professional Conduct must be interpreted and applied with common sense. They do not address every situation, and must be observed in spirit as well as in the letter. Personal ethics cannot be checked at the courtroom door.

  - If you have any doubt about what to do in a situation, immediately seek guidance from an experienced lawyer.

3

PREPARATION FOR TRIAL

3.1 CHARGE SCREENING BY THE PROSECUTOR

- The Province of Ontario, Ministry of Attorney General, Crown Policy Manual (March 21, 2005) requires prosecutors who are conducting criminal prosecutions to screen every charge as soon as practicable after the charge arrives at the Crown's office and prior to setting a date for trial or preliminary hearing. According to the Charge Screening Directive, when considering whether or not to continue the prosecution of a charge, the first step is for the prosecutor to determine whether there is a reasonable prospect of conviction. Where it is determined that there is no reasonable prospect of conviction, at any stage of the proceeding, the prosecution of that charge is to be discontinued.

- Even where there is a reasonable prospect of conviction, the prosecutor is required to go on and consider whether it is in the public interest to discontinue the prosecution, notwithstanding the existence of a reasonable prospect of conviction. The Crown Policy Manual advises that no public interest, however compelling, will warrant prosecuting an individual where there is no reasonable prospect of conviction.

- Provincial offences, of course, are not the same as criminal offences. Indeed, the purpose of the *Provincial Offences Act* is to set out a procedure which reflects this very difference. However, the charge screening process that applies to provincial offences is based on the same principles as those governing criminal offences. As a result, the prosecutor is required to screen provincial offences charges in order to determine the following: whether a *prima facie* case exists, whether there is a reasonable prospect of conviction, and, whether it is in the public interest that the prosecution be continued. (Ministry of Attorney General of Ontario, POA Transfer Project 2001, Handbook for POA Prosecutors, Section 3.2, Charge Screening)

173

- The requirements of reasonable prospect of conviction and public interest have been discussed above. The requirement of determining whether there is a *prima facie* case requires that the prosecutor should ensure the following:
  - that there is evidence on all the essential elements of the charge which, if believed and answered, would warrant a finding of guilt;
  - that there are no jurisdictional obstacles which would constitute a fatal flaw to the prosecution of the charge; and
  - that where the defendant has been served with an offence notice, ensuring that that the certificate of offence is sufficient on its face, and if not, determining whether the defect can be cured by an amendment. (Handbook for POA Prosecutors, Section 3.2.2(a))

- The obligation to screen charges is on-going. Prosecutors are to discontinue a prosecution if it becomes apparent at any stage of the proceedings that a reasonable prospect of conviction no longer exists, or that it is not in the public interest to continue the prosecution.

- In the case of prosecutions brought on behalf of municipalities, there are "Principles of Transfer" which require that the fundamental tenets of procedural fairness and natural justice be affirmed and upheld. While the municipal partner may establish its own prosecutorial policies, such policies must be consistent with provincial policies and not contrary to the law. As a result, both provincial and municipal prosecutors engage in the practice of charge screening of provincial offences.

3.2 PREPARATION BY THE DEFENCE

3.2.1 CLIENT INTERVIEW

- Gather all information that may be relevant to both trial and sentencing.
- If the client is calling from a police station, ensure privacy, and gather as much information as possible from the officer-in-charge.

- Does the client wish to be interviewed in the presence of a third person?
  - Consider that the solicitor-client privilege may no longer apply and the third person could be forced to testify about the interview.

3.2.2 DOCUMENTS TO OBTAIN

- Obtain copies of the following:
  - Documents served on your client;
  - All relevant correspondence and notes;
  - Employment or business records;
  - Photographs or diagrams.

3.2.3 DETERMINE OFFENCE(S) CHARGED

- The *Provincial Offences Act* is the procedure by which offences under other provincial Acts and certain federal regulatory offences governed by the *Contraventions Act (Canada)* are prosecuted.
- Refer to the charging Act and compare its wording with the charges laid against your client.
- Recognize the illegal "acts" alleged. Later chapters analyze defences that might be available.

3.2.4 SAMPLE QUESTIONS FOR CLIENT

(a) Background Questions

- Obtain and accurately record the following background details from your client.
  1. Name, date of birth, address, and telephone number(s).
  2. First language — would an interpreter be helpful?
  3. Marital status, with names and ages of spouse and any children — does the client support dependants?
  4. Immigration status and residence history.
  5. Education history and plans.
  6. Employment history and source(s) of income.

7. Ability to pay fine (and your fees).

8. Mental and/or physical health and treatment.

9. Criminal and/or provincial record of offences (or other relevant governmental record of misconduct), with explanations, if any.

10. Bail, probation, or other court or administrative orders or agreements in effect — with contact person to confirm compliance, if necessary.

11. Charges outstanding.

12. Character references — does your client want family, friends, or an employer to know of the charge(s)?

(b) The Allegations

- Obtain and accurately record the following details about the allegations against your client.

  1. Client's version of the allegations and evidence.

  2. Co-defendant? Get details.

  3. Steps taken to comply with the law (reasonable care).

  4. Steps that could have been taken, with reasons for not doing so.

  5. Industry standards for reasonable care.

  6. Was the client impaired by alcohol or drugs? Was anyone else impaired?

  7. Did the client impede the investigation?

  8. Names, phone numbers, and addresses of all potential witnesses, both favourable and unfavourable.

  9. Details of all contact with the authorities, and whether rights (such as the right to counsel) were given.

  10. Date, time, and place of next court appearance.

(c) Corporate Defendants

- Both individuals and corporations can be charged under various provincial offences.

- Determine the current directors, officers and shareholders of the corporation. Obtain their names, phone numbers, and addresses.

- Determine the directors and officers in the latest filing at the Companies and Personal Property Security Branch of the Ministry of Consumer and Business Services under the *Corporations Information Act*, R.S.O. 1990, c. C.39. Obtain their names, phone numbers, and addresses.

- Review corporate minutes book.

- Consider corporate by-laws and resolutions.

- Who are the directing minds of the corporation?

3.2.5 INITIAL ADVICE

- Advise your client not to communicate with anyone else about the allegations or to provide samples, documents, or other information. *Even if your client has an explanation demonstrating innocence, it is better to wait and present that evidence before an impartial court bound by the rules of procedural fairness.*

- Advise your client that anything said now can be used *against* him or her at trial (as an admission or to impeach credibility), and nothing said now can be used *for* him or her at trial (prior consistent statements are generally inadmissible).

- In some circumstances, your client may be required to disclose information to the authorities.

  - Under the *Highway Traffic Act*, R.S.O. 1990, c. H.8, s. 199, every person in charge of a motor vehicle who is directly or indirectly involved in an accident shall, if the accident results in personal injuries or in damage apparently in excess of the regulated amount, report the accident forthwith to the nearest police officer with particulars, including: the persons involved, the extent of the injuries or damage, and other necessary information for the police officer's accident report.

  - Under the *Environmental Protection Act*, R.S.O. 1990, E.19, ss. 158(7) and 167, every person responsible for a source of contaminant shall furnish such information as a provincial officer requires for the purposes of the Act or Regulations.

- Under the *Occupational Health and Safety Act*, R.S.O. 1990, c. O.1, ss. 51 *et. seq.* and 62(3), employers must report to the Provincial Director particulars of serious work-site accidents within stipulated times, and no person shall neglect or refuse to provide the inspector with information required in the exercise of his or her duties.

- Nevertheless, advise your client not to disclose any information to anyone until *after* you consider *precisely* what must be disclosed, and when and how to disclose it. Do not be unnecessarily rushed.

- In some circumstances, you might consider disclosing certain information *after receiving full disclosure* of the allegations and evidence against your client.

  - Determine whether, under law, an adverse inference can be drawn from your client's failure to disclose information before trial. *For example, if the defence is alibi, particulars must be disclosed sufficiently before trial to allow the authorities time to investigate. However, during the initial interview, advise your client to remain silent, since the authorities can be advised after you receive full disclosure of the prosecutor's case (and after you, as counsel, privately confirm the truth of the alibis).*

  - Though a defendant provides the police with sufficient notice of an alibi prior to trial to permit the police to investigate the alibi witness, an adverse inference may be drawn where the opportunity for meaningful investigation is lost due to the passage of time and the fading memory of the alibi witness: *R. v. Mearow* (2006), 2006 Carswel-lOnt 6140 (Ont. C.A.).

- Many regulatory offences provide "due diligence" or "reasonable care" defences (*see Chapter 7 for details*). *For example, in an on-going pollution spill case, your client may appear more diligent if there is full and timely disclosure to the authorities of the contaminant's problems, with requests for professional assistance and follow-up.*

- As to the powers of search warrants and investigations, *see Chapter 10.*

3.2.6 FIRST APPEARANCE

- Arrange for a sufficient retainer before confirming that you are counsel or agent of record to the court.

- Determine whether the client was properly served. (*See Chapter 5 for details*.)

  - If not, consider appearing in court without your client to argue improper service. (But research the law first; by appearing, your client may be taken to have attorned to the jurisdiction of the court.)

3.3 FURTHER DISCLOSURE FOR THE DEFENCE

3.3.1 DISCLOSURE FROM THE PROSECUTION

In *R. v. Stinchcombe* (1991), 68 C.C.C. (3d) 1, [1992] 1 W.W.R. 97, [1991] 3 S.C.R. 326, 83 Alta. L.R. (2d) 193, 8 C.R. (4th) 277 (S.C.C.), the Supreme Court of Canada held that, in an indictable criminal trial, if the defence requests disclosure, the Crown must disclose all information it proposes to use at trial plus all information which *may* assist the defence.

- Initial disclosure must be done as soon as practicable and before trial.

- The request for disclosure must be made in writing to the Prosecutor's Office at the particular court location [See Sample Request Forms in Appendix C].

- The Prosecutor's Office will then make a formal request for disclosure from the police officer in charge [See Request for Disclosure in Appendix C].

- The disclosure material from the Prosecutor's Office will be faxed to the defendant, or to his or her agent, provided they confirm receipt of same [See Disclosure Facsimile Message Form and the Faxing Instruction Sheet in Appendix C]. Alternatively, the disclosure material must be picked up at the Prosecutor's Office at the court location.

- The Crown has the onus of justifying untimely or refusal of disclosure.

- Disclosure is a continuing obligation on the Crown.

- The Crown can refuse to disclose certain information if privileged, but this discretion is reviewable by the trial judge.

In *R. v. Stinchcombe*, Justice Sopinka did not decide whether the same disclosure duties applied to summary conviction or provincial offences. In Ontario, however, the Attorney General's policy is to provide disclosure of provincial offences upon request. See also: *R. v. Fineline Circuits Ltd.* (1991), 10 C.R. (4th) 241 (Ont. Prov. Ct.).

In *Ontario v. 974649 Ontario Inc.*, 2001 CarswellOnt 4251, 47 C.R. (5th) 316 (*sub. nom.* R. v. 974649 Ontario Inc.) [2001] 3 S.C.R. 575, 56 O.R. (3d) 359 (headnote only), 2001 CarswellOnt 4252, (*sub nom.* R. v. 974649 Ontario Inc.) [2001] S.C.J. No. 79, (*sub nom.* R. v. 974649 Ontario Inc.) 2001 SCC 81, (*sub nom.* R. v. 974649 Ontario Inc.) 206 D.L.R. (4th) 444, (*sub nom.* R. v. 974649 Ontario Inc.) 159 C.C.C. (3d) 321, (*sub nom.* R. v. 974649 Ontario Inc.) 88 C.R.R. (2d) 189, (*sub nom.* R. v. 974649 Ontario Inc.) 279 N.R. 345, (*sub nom.* R. v. 974649 Ontario Inc.) 154 O.A.C. 345 (S.C.C.), the Supreme Court of Canada concluded that the justice of the peace acting as a trial justice under the *Provincial Offences Act* possessed the power to order legal costs against the Crown as a remedy for *Charter* breaches arising from untimely disclosure. The costs were awarded on the defendants' disclosure motion which was brought as a result of the Crown's failure to disclose a copy of the Prosecution Approval Form relating to charges laid under the *Occupational Health and Safety Act*. If defendants were deprived of this remedy, a provincial offences court may be confined to two extreme options for relief — a stay of proceedings or a mere adjournment — neither of which may be appropriate and just in the circumstances.

- Consider adjourning the case at the first court appearance for a matter of weeks. This procedure will enable you to:

    - Order and review disclosure with your client before setting a trial date.

    - Assist the court's schedule (and avoid any later adjournments) by advising how long the trial will take and whether you expect any pre-trial motions.

In *Toronto (City) v. Canada Land Corp.*, 2006 ONCJ 421, [2006] O.J. No. 4489, 2006 CarswellOnt 6959 (Ont. C.J.), the court discussed the issue of the Crown's obligation to make give disclosure of "will-say" statements to the defence. It was held that generally, in provincial offences prosecutions commenced under Part I, there would be no need to provide will-says for officers or investigators who have made notes and they are disclosed to the defendant; even in relatively uncomplicated prosecutions commenced under Part III for more serious offences, there would be usually no need for the prosecution to provide a will-say statement for any officers or investigators or civilian witnesses, when the investigating officer has made notes or has taken a statement from a witness and recorded it in his notes, and those notes have been disclosed to the defence. However, even if the prosecution is not obligated to disclose will-says under the present *Stinchcombe* parameters, especially for uncomplicated regulatory prosecutions, the court may still order the prosecution provide such will-says when due to the particular circumstances of a case it is necessary to ensure that the accused or defendant is accorded a fair trial, or that it will provide useful information to the court and is necessary for managing the trial.

While the Crown disclosed the officer's collision reconstruction report prior to the trial, it failed to disclose the amended report. The defence had not completed its cross-examination of the officer, and the Crown's case was not concluded. The appropriate remedy was not a stay of proceedings, but an order for production of the revised report, and an adjournment to allow the defence to review the revised report with leave to recall Crown witnesses. This remedy removed any prejudice to the defence due to non-disclosure: *R. v. Soo*, 2008 ABPC 221, 2008 CarswellAlta 1077, [2008] A.J. No. 881, 74 M.V.R. (5th) 108 (Alta. Prov. Ct.).

The Crown's duty to disclose information is relevant to defences that are directly related to one of the elements of the offence, but not a defence that is a constitutional challenge to the validity of legislation or its applicability. A constitutional challenge does not constitute a reasonably possible defence in the context of the duty to disclose: *Tenascon c. Québec (Juge de la Cour du Québec)* (2007), EYB 2007121464, 2007 CarswellQue 5968, 2007 CarswellQue 13626, [2007] J.Q. No. 6991, 2007 QCCA 946, 2007 QCCA 947, (*sub nom.* R. v. Commanda) [2008] 3 C.N.L.R. 311 (Que. C.A.), leave to appeal refused (2008), 2008 CarswellQue 3557, 2008 CarswellQue 3558, [2007] S.C.C.A. No. 476, (*sub nom.* R. v. Commanda) 387 N.R. 382 (note) (S.C.C).

The Crown cannot be expected to disclose information before trial whose relevance first becomes apparent during the trial itself, and the prosecution cannot be expected to disclose what it does not have. At the same time, the Crown cannot deliberately refrain from making inquiries because of a fear that it may learn about relevant evidence that it would have to disclose: *R. v. Horan*, 2008 CarswellOnt 4801, 2008 ONCA 589, 240 O.A.C. 313, 60 C.R. (6th) 46, 237 C.C.C. (3d) 514, [2008] O.J. No. 3167 (Ont. C.A.), at para. 27 [ONCA].

The defendant's right to make full answer and defence is paramount to any interest the owner of the radar manual may have in the copyright over the manual. It is not reasonable for the prosecutor to expect that the defendant should purchase a copy of the manual from the manufacturer or distributor. The prosecutor was therefore ordered to provide to the defendants a photocopy of the pages of the user and installation manual relating to testing procedures and operation of the unit. It would be of assistance to have available at trial a certified copy of the applicable manual that could be referred to by the prosecutor or defendant, or in appropriate circumstances the court. There was no basis, however, to order disclosure of the full OPP radar Basic Operator Manual used to conduct initial and recertification courses: *Millar v. Thunder Bay (City)*, 2009 CarswellOnt 6246, 2009 ONCJ 485 (Ont. C.J.).

Disclosure is fundamental and related to the right to make full answer and defence. However, the production of the radar unit's owner's manual would not have had any meaningful capacity to further the defendant's fair trial right; the log of the officer on the alleged offence date, including all tickets he had issued that day, was irrelevant. There was no air of reality to the defendant's suggestion that a copy of the servicing log of the radar unit would have any meaningful capacity to advance his defence to the charge of speeding: *Quebec (Director of Public Prosecution) v. Semenoff*, 2009 QCCQ 8424, 2009 CarswellQue 9378, [2009] Q.J. No. 9600, EYB 2009-163936 (C.Q.).

The defendant was not denied her disclosure rights where she did not complain at the time of trial that she did not see the officer's notes until the morning of the trial. If objections such as this were made in time then the court could have considered the remedy of an adjournment to overcome any prejudice suffered by the defendant. There was no evidence that the defendant in this case suffered any prejudice in the circumstances: *R. v. Davis*, 2010 CarswellOnt 10619, [2010] O.J. No. 5027 (C.J.).

In *R. v. Murray*, 2010 NSSC 296, 2010 CarswellNS 476, 293 N.S.R. (2d) 264, 98 M.V.R. (5th) 245, 928 A.P.R. 264, [2010] N.S.J. No. 419 (N.S. S.C.), it was held that the prosecutor in a speeding case must disclose the ticketing officer's statement on the reverse of the prosecutor's copy of the ticket, and any other relevant statements in the possession of the prosecutor. This must be done on the request of the accused, but the prosecutor must inform an unrepresented accused of his right to make the request when a plea of not guilty is entered.

Under s. 46(2) of the *Provincial Offences Act*, the defendant is entitled to make full answer and defence. The ability to exercise that right depends in large part on disclosure of information relevant to the charge; it does not depend upon disclosure of events after charges were laid. The failure to provide timely disclosure of internal e-mails relating to the request for searches to be conducted or on correspondence between a potential witness and the Crown relating to that witness' vacation does not impact on the defendant's ability to make full answer and defence: *R. v. Hanna*, 2010 ONCJ 552, 2010 CarswellOnt 8899, [2010] O.J. No. 5075 (Ont. C.J.).

A lawyer who happens to be a defendant before the court should not be treated any differently, and should not appear to be treated any differently, than any other defendant before the court. In dismissing the request of the defendant for an adjournment on the basis of the lack of disclosure, the comments of the court in calling the request disingenuous and smacking of sharp practice gave rise to an appearance of bias. A verbal summary of disclosure materials on a trial date in response to a disclosure request, even in provincial offences procedure, does not meet a minimum standard of disclosure to the defendant: *Durham (Regional Municipality) v. Jagtoo*, 2010 ONCJ 596, 2010 CarswellOnt 9517, [2010] O.J. No. 5334 (Ont. C.J.).

The defendant should have been provided with full disclosure of the testing procedures in advance of the trial. In addition, the interruption of the cross-examination of the defendant when he was questioning the officer resulted in the conviction being quashed on appeal. See *R. v. Cerisano*, 2012 CarswellOnt 4585, [2012] O.J. No. 1864 (Ont. C.J.).

In *Ontario v. O.P.S.E.U.*, 2012 ONSC 2078, 2012 CarswellOnt 6293, 44 Admin. L.R. (5th) 340, 219 L.A.C. (4th) 151, [2012] O.J. No. 2356 (Ont. Div. Ct.), the court hearing a judicial review application was concerned with a case where the Crown employed inspectors who had broad investigative powers and lawyers who conducted prosecutions under the *Occupational Health and Safety Act*, and thereby had a dual function as employer and prosecutor. However, the Crown's disclosure obligations as a prosecutor did not arise from the collective agreement, and the collective agreement could not prevent its duty to disclose the inspector's records to the accused. There was no reason to believe that an inspector's criminal record would have less bearing on an accused's right to make full answer and defence in regulatory proceedings than a police officer's criminal record in criminal prosecutions. The Grievance Settlement Board's finding that the accused had to bring an *O'Connor* application for disclosure seriously prejudiced the rights of the accused.

In *Oshawa (City) v. Carter* (December 21, 2012), Rosenberg J., [2012] O.J. No. 6291 (Ont. C.J.), the officer who conducted an inspection of the defendant's property for compliance with a proper standards order conducted another inspection of the property two days before the trial. The notes were not disclosed as the Crown was unaware of the inspection; the officer's notebook subsequently went missing. However, this notebook did not refer to the subject matter of the proceeding before the court. Given that the trial justice appropriately made an order that the witness could not refer in her testimony to the notes in the missing book, there was virtually no prejudice to the defendant as a result of the failure to disclose the notes.

The denial of the defendant's request for disclosure with regard to the speed measuring device and the officer's qualifications for using that device affected the fairness of the trial. There was a reasonable possibility that the non-disclosure of the requested information would impair the right of the defendant to make full answer and defence. See *R. v. Melrose*, 2013 BCSC 526, 2013 CarswellBC 785, 44 M.V.R. (6th) 78, [2013] B.C.J. No. 592 (B.C. S.C.), leave to appeal allowed 2014 BCCA 148, 2014 CarswellBC 977, 354 B.C.A.C. 106, 605 W.A.C. 106, [2014] B.C.J. No. 659 (B.C. C.A.).

Production of a template that contained all of the officer's investigative notes constitutes full and complete disclosure of the officer's anticipated evidence at the defendant's speeding trial: *R. v. Law*, 2013 ONCJ 533, 2013 CarswellOnt 13859, [2013] O.J. No. 4554 (Ont. C.J.).

The trial Justice of the Peace refused to allow the defendant to file a copy of the laser manual he received in disclosure as an exhibit at trial. If properly identified and there was a foundation laid for its introduction, the manual could be entered as an exhibit. No rule of evidence required a copy of the manual to be certified as a true copy. It was not necessary to make the manual an exhibit in order for the defendant to have continued cross-examining the officer once the proper foundation had been laid. There is nothing wrong in making portions of the manual an exhibit at trial further to this type of cross-examination; it is often done on consent of the parties, and may be of assistance to the trial Justice to have a written copy to assist him or her in following the testimony of the witness. It is the testimony of the police officer, however, that is the evidence, not the exhibit itself. There is very little gained in making the entire manual an exhibit at trial, even with the consent of the parties, as it contains much that is totally irrelevant. If it is made an independent exhibit, it is incumbent on the Justice to review the whole manual. See *Mangov v. Toronto (City)*, 2014 ONCJ 351, 2014 CarswellOnt 10104, [2014] O.J. No. 3477 (Ont. C.J.).

In *R. v. Jukes*, 2014 ONCJ 438, 2014 CarswellOnt 12208, [2014] O.J. No. 4182 (Ont. C.J.), it was held that there was no evidence that relevant information was not disclosed or that the accused was not given time to prepare for documents he received. The Justices of the Peace throughout dealt with the many disclosure requests and adjournment requests in a generous and appropriate manner.

In *R. v. Hawdon*, 2014 CarswellOnt 5067 (Ont. C.J.), it was held that it is not up to the defence to make a request for disclosure more than once. Neither was it necessary for the defence to bring a motion for production as they were led to believe by the prosecutor that the disclosure requested was not available. The Justice was entitled to make finding of lack of disclosure once she heard the evidence of the investigating officer. The defence should have brought an application to stay the charge for non-disclosure rather than a motion to dismiss the charge. The Justice should not have dismissed the charge but granted a stay of proceedings due to non-disclosure.

There was common ground among the parties that there is a duty of disclosure in trials conducted under Part I of the *Provincial Offences Act*, and that an unrepresented accused must be informed of his right to disclosure. It was also conceded by the City that as a self-represented litigant, the defendant was not adequately informed of his right to disclosure and that significant evidence, in the form of a video recording, has now been lost. On the basis of those concessions the appeal was allowed and an acquittal entered. Given this order, it was unnecessary to consider issues, including constitutional issues, regarding the method and timing of providing notice of the right to disclosure to unrepresented litigants in trials under Part I. It was also unnecessary to consider the nature of the assistance required to be provided by Justices of the Peace to unrepresented litigants in such trials. See *R. v. Ul-Rashid*, 2014 ONCA 896, 2014 CarswellOnt 18386, 70 M.V.R. (6th) 181 (Ont. C.A.).

The Notice of Trial contained a coloured stamp alerting the recipient that there is disclosure available. A simple request triggers the preparation and provision of disclosure. This disclosure procedure properly balances the obligation to provide disclosure with the reality that there are thousands of ticket offence matters in the Region of Durham. While this procedure strikes a proper balance between the proper administration of disclosure and the rights of a defendant, there are some circumstances where the procedure could potentially impact negatively on the fair trial rights of a defendant. The process is not a balm for circumstances that impact in this manner. What works generally in many circumstances may at times require some flexibility on the part of the court or prosecutor in order to mitigate any negative impact on a fair trial. In this case the defendant did not request disclosure and it was provided on the day of trial. The trial Justice did not canvass whether or not he wished an adjournment to prepare his defence; the defendant did not request an adjournment or request time to consult with an agent or counsel. The provision of disclosure on the trial date is a troubling issue. This is an example where the procedure that works well in general could cause harm to the fair trial interest of a defendant. Where a defendant is provided disclosure on the morning of trial, it would be a more cautious approach for the court to canvass whether the defendant is prepared to proceed and provide guidance on the appropriate remedy, such as an adjournment or recess. The appropriate mindset is a concern for a fair trial — not a fault-finding exercise, that is, the defendant did not request disclosure, therefore, it is his or her fault and there is nothing to be done. In this case, the Justice addressed the issue in an appropriate manner by permitting a recess for the defendant to review the two pages of officer notes related to a highway traffic offence. The defendant was also permitted to speak with the prosecutor and determine what he wished to do. A recess was one available appropriate option. After the recess, the Court asked the defendant what he wished to do. He indicated that he wished to have a trial because his side was different. The defendant did not give any indication that he was not in a position to proceed. See *R. v. Aulakh*, 2015 ONCJ 156, 2015 CarswellOnt 3978, (*sub nom.* Durham (Regional Municipality) v. Aulakh) [2015] O.J. No. 1462 (Ont. C.J.).

In *R. v. Zacharias*, 2016 ONCJ 458, 2016 CarswellOnt 12095, [2016] O.J. No. 3975 (Ont. C.J.), the prosecution disclosed the police officer's notes and complied with some special disclosure requests of the defence. However, there were two letters from the defence requesting "if this is a speeding offence, the testing times of this device before and after the subject enforcement". The prosecution did not respond to that request. Prior to the trial, the prosecution and the defence discussed the testing of the device outside of court. The prosecution apparently disclosed the fact that the police officer had tested the device, but testing times were not provided. When the trial commenced, the defence stated that it was ready to proceed to trial. If the defence had been dissatisfied with the disclosure, it should have raised the issue as a pre-trial motion. If the lateness of the disclosure created a preparation problem for the defence, they should have requested an adjournment. However, the defence was ready to proceed to trial, and they so advised the court. There was no basis for concluding that the defendant did not receive a fair trial.

In *R. v. Hadi*, 2016 ONCJ 447, 2016 CarswellOnt 11897, [2016] O.J. No. 3890 (Ont. C.J.), the defendant was given a DVD of the in-car recording in advance of his trial, but there was no audio on that recording. The arresting officer had forgotten to put the audio pack on before he left his car. When the defendant was told this by the justice of the peace, he refused to accept this explanation, and declined to participate in his trial for improper right turn and failing to surrender his driving licence. The Crown's duty to disclose what is in its possession also applies to the police who must provide relevant disclosure to the Crown to be further disclosed to the defence. However, the Crown cannot disclose what it does not have. There was no issue in this case of any lost or destroyed disclosure; the disclosure issue was properly resolved by the justice of the peace who explained to the defendant in plain terms that the audio was not there and he could not be given what was never created in the first place. There could be no other possible decision the justice of the peace could have made. The DVD was played in court at the accused's trial. The fact that there was no audio on the recording was made apparent to the justice of the peace. It was also made clear to him that his copy was the same as that in the possession of the Crown. Despite this, the accused continued to refuse to participate. Having a fair trial means that a defendant receives a fair *opportunity* to make full answer and defence. If the defendant chooses not to make use of this opportunity, there is little that the justice system can do.

In *R. v. Sahadeo*, 2016 ONCJ 122, 2016 CarswellOnt 3721, [2016] O.J. No. 1252 (Ont. C.J.), on the date his trial was scheduled to take place, the paralegal for the defendant appeared and requested an adjournment. When the request was refused, the paralegal advised the presiding justice that he was instructed not to participate in the proceedings any further. The paralegal then left the courtroom. Upon the defendant being paged with no response, a deemed not to dispute conviction was entered. The decision to grant or refuse the adjournment was discretionary, and will not be interfered with on appeal unless the discretion was not exercised judicially, or where it has resulted in a miscarriage of justice. In this case, the need for the adjournment for disclosure could easily have been obviated by the defendant far in advance of the trial. While the justice of the peace was correct to refuse the adjournment, a conviction should not have been imposed under s. 9.1 as it could not be said that the defendant had failed to appear at the time and place appointed for trial. He did appear by instructing an agent to attend, as permitted by s. 50; the provisions of s. 54(1) did not apply in this case. The defendant had appeared by agent, the prosecution was ready, and the trial should have proceeded. The fact that the defendant had instructed his agent to "walk away" did not mean that the agent had any right to do so. A paralegal, like counsel, can only withdraw with the leave of the court. The defendant demonstrated a complete lack of diligence by failing to ensure that he had the necessary disclosure. He ought to have either appeared personally or else sent a properly instructed agent. The agent, who appeared, had not been properly instructed and was initially unable to articulate the reason for which he was seeking an adjournment. The application itself was entirely without merit and should not have been brought; for his part, the agent should not have agreed to act for the defendant without proper instructions.

In *R. v. Gao*, 2016 BCSC 1606, 2016 CarswellBC 2406, [2016] B.C.J. No. 1838 (B.C. S.C.), the police officer produced his notes from the back of the violation ticket, but did not produce a report to Crown counsel related to potential criminal charges that may have arisen out of the traffic stop. No such charges were ultimately laid. The officer did not believe the information to be relevant, and did not intend to rely on it; no disclosure requests had previously been made. Based on the immateriality of the issue of whether the defendant's driver's licence was fraudulent or not, the fact that the defendant's counsel had access to the information in question before the hearing, and the lack of previous disclosure requests from counsel appearing on the trial date or over the 14-month period between the violation ticket and the date of the trial, the justice did not err in refusing the defendant's request for disclosure.

The presiding justice's dismissal of a disclosure motion did not give rise to a reasonable apprehension of bias or require the declaration of a mistrial on the basis that the justice misapprehended what was allegedly not to have been disclosed by the prosecution. The defendant failed to meet its burden to satisfy the high threshold to justify disqualification. See *R. v. Shan*, 2016 ONCJ 663, 2016 CarswellOnt 18212, [2016] O.J. No. 5935 (Ont. C.J.).

There was no prosecutorial misconduct due to "vetting the file erroneously". In the initial redacted duty notes, there was no evidence that any error was intentional or done for some nefarious purpose. Any inconsistency in the notes could have been clarified well in advance of the trial. Instead, the defence chose to raise the issue only during cross-examination. The Crown's position resisting disclosure of the radar manual did not amount to prosecutorial misconduct. The Crown's error in disclosure of the initial notes was unintentional, and the error was remedied by providing further disclosure in advance of the disclosure motion and trial. This did not amount to a standard of misconduct that justified an award of costs against the prosecution. See *R. v. Shan*, 2016 ONCJ 663, 2016 CarswellOnt 18212, [2016] O.J. No. 5935 (Ont. C.J.).

There was no evidence, on consideration of the entirety of the trial record, that the defendant was prejudiced in any way by the late receipt of disclosure. The defendant chose not to pick up the disclosure from the prosecutor's office until the morning of trial. His request for a stay of proceedings was quite properly refused, as the defendant failed to exercise due diligence in picking up the available disclosure until the morning of trial. The appropriate remedy, in these circumstances, at its highest, would have been an adjournment of the trial, but no adjournment was requested by the defendant. It was not part of the function of the presiding justice of the peace to advise the defendant that the appropriate remedy for the "late" provision of disclosure was an adjournment rather than a stay of proceedings as the defendant proposed. At the outset of the trial, the justice of the peace explained the trial process, and was informed that the defendant had received legal advice and had some experience in conducting a trial. The trial itself was straightforward and consisted of only one witness. The defendant was asked if he wished to give evidence and declined to do so. Reasonable assistance was provided to the defendant at trial and his fair trial interests were preserved and respected by the presiding justice of the peace as a consequence. See *R. v. Popovici*, 2017 CarswellOnt 21731, [2017] O.J. No. 5697 (C.J.).

In *R. v. Wei*, 2017 ONCJ 878, 2017 CarswellOnt 20869, [2017] O.J. No. 6785 (Ont. C.J.), the defendant was prosecuted for disobeying a stop sign, commenced by means of a certificate of offence. The disclosure involved the notes of an officer and a video recording. The Part I *Provincial Offences Act* procedure is simplified and the maximum penalty is a $1,000 fine. The set fine for disobey stop sign is $85. In this context, it was appropriate for the justice of the peace to hold the trial down briefly to permit review of disclosure before trial. This practice is not uncommon for Part I provincial offences litigation, and is reasonable in light of the simplified procedure under it.

3.3.2 REVIEW DISCLOSURE WITH CLIENT

- Fully review the disclosure materials received from the prosecutor with your client.
    - There may be explanations for certain conduct.
    - Your client may recall evidence or witnesses who were not previously considered relevant.
    - Your client may recall evidence which contradicts what the prosecutor's witnesses say.

3.3.3 REQUEST FURTHER DISCLOSURE

- Do you have reason to believe that the prosecutor, or other governmental official, has undisclosed relevant information, physical evidence, or samples?
    - If so, write a letter to the prosecutor detailing the information required before trial. Perhaps you need duplicate samples for independent testing.
    - Where an accused was charged with speeding and sought disclosure of the radar operating manual, the maintenance record of the unit and the officer's training record for the unit, the Crown was ordered to provide sufficient information to answer the relevant information of what the officer would be in a position to testify to: *R. Makuch* (1996), 192 A.R. 299 (Alta. Prov. Ct.).

It is not up to the defence to make a request for disclosure more than once. They did not need to bring a motion for production as they were led to believe by the prosecutor the disclosure they had requested was not available. It was only after hearing the testimony of the officer did they realize there had been a lack of follow-up on their request for disclosure. They were entitled to raise the issue of lack of disclosure at that time. However, the defendant's counsel should have brought a non-disclosure application rather than a motion to dismiss the charge. The remedy for non-disclosure is not to dismiss a charge but rather to stay the charge. The Justice of the Peace was in error when she granted a dismissal rather than a stay, however, her logic and reasons for doing so were not a palpable and overriding error. The Justice of the Peace reached the right result but granted an inappropriate remedy. A new trial at this stage would not serve any useful purpose and would cause further inconvenience and expense for the defendant. The order made at trial was set aside and a stay of proceedings entered in lieu of ordering a new trial. See *R. v. Hawdon*, 2014 CarswellOnt 5067 (Ont. C.J.).

In *R. v. Zacharias*, 2016 ONCJ 458, 2016 CarswellOnt 12095, [2016] O.J. No. 3975 (Ont. C.J.), the prosecution disclosed the police officer's notes and complied with some special disclosure requests of the defence. However, there were two letters from the defence requesting "if this is a speeding offence, the testing times of this device before and after the subject enforcement". The prosecution did not respond to that request. Prior to the trial, the prosecution and the defence discussed the testing of the device outside of court. The prosecution apparently disclosed the fact that the police officer had tested the device, but testing times were not provided. When the trial commenced, the defence stated that it was ready to proceed to trial. If the defence had been dissatisfied with the disclosure, it should have raised the issue as a pre-trial motion. If the lateness of the disclosure created a preparation problem for the defence, they should have requested an adjournment. However, the defence was ready to proceed to trial, and they so advised the court. There was no basis for concluding that the defendant did not receive a fair trial.

In *R. v. Gao*, 2016 BCSC 1606, 2016 CarswellBC 2406, [2016] B.C.J. No. 1838 (B.C. S.C.), the police officer produced his notes from the back of the violation ticket, but did not produce a report to Crown counsel related to potential criminal charges that may have arisen out of the traffic stop. No such charges were ultimately laid. The officer did not believe the information to be relevant, and did not intend to rely on it; no disclosure requests had previously been made. Based on the immateriality of the issue of whether the defendant's driver's licence was fraudulent or not, the fact that the defendant's counsel had access to the information in question before the hearing, and the lack of previous disclosure requests from counsel appearing on the trial date or over the 14-month period between the violation ticket and the date of the trial, the justice did not err in refusing the defendant's request for disclosure.

There was no prosecutorial misconduct due to "vetting the file erroneously". In the initial redacted duty notes, there was no evidence that any error was intentional or done for some nefarious purpose. Any inconsistency in the notes could have been clarified well in advance of the trial. Instead, the defence chose to raise the issue only during cross-examination. The Crown's position resisting disclosure of the radar manual did not amount to prosecutorial misconduct. The Crown's error in disclosure of the initial notes was unintentional, and the error was remedied by providing further disclosure in advance of the disclosure motion and trial. This did not amount to a standard of misconduct that justified an award of costs against the prosecution. See *R. v. Shan*, 2016 ONCJ 663, 2016 CarswellOnt 18212, [2016] O.J. No. 5935 (Ont. C.J.).

In *R. v. Bazdar*, 2018 ONCJ 318, 2018 CarswellOnt 7677, [2018] O.J. No. 2571 (Ont. C.J.), it was held that the net delay of 16 months and 19 days fell below the presumptive ceiling of 18 months and was presumptively reasonable when applying the test set out in *Jordan*. The applicant's agent did nothing exceptional to expedite the proceeding. The proceedings moved along in the manner in which matters commenced under Part I proceeding. On the contrary, the agent did not make all efforts to request full disclosure in that he ought to have requested all disclosure including any DVD evidence that was available. The charges were straightforward as was the disclosure.

In *R. v. Galbraith*, 2018 ONCJ 138, 2018 CarswellOnt 3347, 404 C.R.R. (2d) 371, [2018] O.J. No. 1189 (Ont. C.J.), a written request for disclosure was sought four times by the defendant for her speeding trial, and she received assurances from administration that her requests had been forwarded to the office of the prosecution. She did not receive an answer to her requests. The prosecution policy concerning the provision of disclosure in the jurisdiction was usually two weeks after receipt of a written request. The delay in providing disclosure in a timely manner to the defendant in this case was due to staffing changes in the office of the prosecution. The prosecution delay in providing disclosure was due to a mistake and did not violate her right to a fair trial under s. 11(d) of the *Charter of Rights*, nor was any prejudice demonstrated such that the late disclosure did not violate the right to make full answer and defence under s. 7 of the *Charter*. The time elapsed since the date of the offence to the proposed date of trial was 7 months, well below the presumptive ceiling for unreasonable delay established in *R. v. Jordan*. There was no negligence on the part of the prosecutor that justified an order of costs either as a *Charter* remedy or due to procedural irregularities under s. 90 of the *Provincial Offences Act*. The defendant had chosen to attend the Early Resolution meeting and there were a total of two court appearances to date. Section 24(1) of the *Charter* confers a broad remedial mandate and the widest possible discretion on a court to craft remedies that must be easily available for violations of *Charter* rights. The remedy in the instant case was an adjournment to a date for trial and no order for costs.

At the beginning of his trial, the defendant argued he was denied Crown disclosure despite two requests for it. At the start of his trial, the prosecutor gave some disclosure, but the defendant asked for more. The prosecutor was not in a position to provide it at that time. The defendant then asked the justice of the peace for a stay of proceedings due to this failure to make proper disclosure. He was not allowed to make submissions on this point, including his presenting four binding cases that he wished to present. However, the defendant did not give any notice he was bringing a stay application. By not giving such a notice, the justice of the peace understandably was not prepared to hear the stay application on the merits at that time. The justice of the peace was within his right to try and control the proceedings before him, and he did not overstep the appropriate boundaries of that. At the end of the day, while the justice of the peace did not accede to the defendant's request for a stay or listen to the whole of his submissions, he adjourned the trial in order that disclosure be made. The justice of the peace specifically left it open for the defendant to bring his stay application on the new trial date, present any evidence he wished, and to make his submissions. When the whole of the proceedings was assessed, there was no denial of natural justice or an unfair hearing. The justice of the peace was also correct in not ordering a stay of proceedings at this time. The remedy that he chose was to grant an adjournment so that proper disclosure could be made. This was a fit remedy for Crown non-disclosure. The justice of the peace did not preclude the defendant from asking for a stay of proceedings upon the resumption of the trial. No substantial wrong or miscarriage of justice resulted from this decision. See *City of Toronto v. Riddell*, 2018 ONSC 2048, 2018 CarswellOnt 4860, [2018] O.J. No. 1643 (Ont. S.C.J.), affirmed *Toronto (City) v. Riddell*, 2019 ONCA 103, 2019 CarswellOnt 2272, [2019] O.J. No. 823 (Ont. C.A.).

In *Reginella v. R.*, 2018 ONCJ 198, 2018 CarswellOnt 4918, [2018] O.J. No. 1547 (Ont. C.J.), the learned justice of the peace denied the adjournment request brought by the defendant on the trial date due to disclosure not being received mainly on the bases that the Crown witnesses were present, the Crown was ready to proceed and that the defendant had not brought an application or motion for an adjournment prior to the trial date. The learned justice of the peace exercised his discretion judicially in refusing to grant the adjournment on the trial date. He properly considered that there would be an inconvenience to witnesses as being a factor and that the defendant or his agent had not brought an application for an adjournment prior when they realized that the disclosure had not been received. The learned justice of the peace did not consider any irrelevant factors in this decision. Clearly, there was an onus on the defendant and his agent to follow up by way of direct contact with the trial date when the disclosure had not been received. In addition to not being any adjournment request, the defendant or his agent did not bring an application for a stay of proceedings based on a failure of the prosecution to provide disclosure. In the circumstances, the trial was fair. The defendant was represented; he chose not to attend the trial. The defendant's agent could have renewed his request for an adjournment at the close of the prosecution's case so that the defendant or any defence witnesses could testify. Such a request was not made. The appeal court had not been advised that even though disclosure was received subsequent to the trial, there was something of substance in that disclosure that may have assisted the defendant in his defence.

In *York (Regional Municipality) v. Bouaziz-Caruso*, [2019] O.J. No. 638 (Ont. C.J.), the defence representative had asked for disclosure several weeks before, but by the trial date it had not been handed out. The trial justice denied the adjournment, finding that any suggestion the defendant did not receive the notice of trial in advance was hearsay. The justice held the matter down to permit the trial agent to review disclosure and the defendant present, however she did not attend. Where a second trial date adjournment is denied, it is appropriate for the justice of the peace to hold the trial down briefly to permit the review of disclosure before trial. This practice is not uncommon for Part I litigation, and is reasonable in light of the simplified procedure contemplated under the Act.

A printout of every keystroke entered by all individuals involved in the investigation of the defendant was not required for him to make full answer and defence on a charge of driving a motor vehicle while prohibited. However, the defendant was entitled to be provided with all broadcast communications relevant to the vehicle investigation and vehicle stop, including communications from dispatch and any officer, and all communications between the officers themselves. See *R. v. Kooner*, 2018 BCPC 355, 2018 CarswellBC 3542, [2018] B.C.J. No. 7038 (B.C. Prov. Ct.).

In *York (Regional Municipality) v. McGuigan*, 2018 ONCA 1062, 2018 CarswellOnt 22571, [2018] O.J. No. 6916 (Ont. C.A.), the Court of Appeal ruled that trial justice properly ordered the prosecutor to provide disclosure of the testing and operating procedures from the user manual for the device used by the traffic officer to measure the speed of the defendant's vehicle. Even if the justice of the peace had been wrong to order disclosure, the error would not have been jurisdictional in nature. Section 140(1) of the *Provincial Offences Act* confines *certiorari* orders in *POA* matters to situations where an applicant would be entitled to such relief at common law, and for parties to a proceeding, *certiorari* orders are confined to jurisdictional errors. Moreover, *certiorari* should not have been granted in the course of ongoing proceedings. Nor was there a substantial wrong or miscarriage of justice to address, a prerequisite to *certiorari* under s. 141(4) of the Act. Contrary to the application judge's decision, the justice of the peace did not err in making the disclosure order. Where a prosecutor is relying on a speed measuring device to prosecute an offence, it must, on request, disclose the testing and operating procedures set out in the user manual for that device. It is up to the prosecutor to hand such information over on request. The person charged need not bring an application or obtain a court order. This is first party disclosure, not third party disclosure. The charging police force has a corresponding duty to furnish the pertinent passages from the user manual to the prosecutor to enable the prosecutor to discharge its first party disclosure obligations. This is not a crushing administrative task. The disclosure at issue here is not case specific information. The disclosure obligation can therefore be discharged by the prosecutor by posting the relevant content from the user manual online and providing the ticketed driver with the required URL.

3.3.4 APPLICATION FOR FURTHER DISCLOSURE

The right to disclosure derives from section 7 of the *Charter of Rights*, which states that: "Everyone has the right to life, liberty and security of the person and the right not to be deprived thereof except in accordance with the principles of fundamental justice." It may be that the nature and extent of disclosure depends on the threat to a person's liberty: for example, the Crown may have to investigate and disclose more in a murder case than in a parking infraction case.

- Bring an application to the court for further disclosure, if necessary.

  - Include a notice of application with a supporting affidavit from someone other than the defendant and you (perhaps your secretary) detailing the correspondence with the prosecutor and the reasons to believe that the authorities have undisclosed relevant material.

  - Be prepared to argue that you need full and timely disclosure because a conviction would seriously impair your client's liberty within the meaning of section 7 of the *Charter*.

- Where the defendant has established an infringement of his right to disclosure, on an application to the superior court, the application judge should not order a stay of proceedings as the stay is a drastic remedy unless it is not possible to remedy through reasonable means the prejudice to the defendant's right to make full answer and defence. See: *R. v. Arcand* (2004), [2004] O.J. No. 5017, 2004 CarswellOnt 5160, 10 C.E.L.R. (3d) 161, 125 C.R.R. (2d) 144, 193 O.A.C. 16, 192 C.C.C. (3d) 57, 73 O.R. (3d) 758 (Ont. C.A.).

Trial judge erred in staying proceedings at the outset of the trial based on late disclosure without at least considering adjourning the application to the completion of the trial and without actual evidence of prejudice arising from the late disclosure. (*R. v. Johnson*, [2007] O.J. No. 2228, 2007 CarswellOnt 3583, (*sub nom.* R. v. J. (N.)) 225 O.A.C. 13, 2007 ONCA 419 (Ont. C.A.)).

- Book the return date for your application well before trial. That way, should the material be disclosed, you will have time to review or test it.

- Ordinarily, in cases of non-disclosure, a stay of proceedings is only justified if the non-disclosure either irreparably prejudices the defendant's ability to make full answer and defence, or irreparably harms the integrity of the administration of justice: *R. v. Knox* (2006), 2006 CarswellOnt 3042, [2006] O.J. No. 1976, 209 C.C.C. (3d) 76, 80 O.R. (3d) 515, 31 M.V.R. (5th) 60, 211 O.A.C. 164, 142 C.R.R. (2d) 99 (Ont. C.A.).

While it would have been preferable for the Crown to have been more forthcoming with disclosure, the defendant was in possession of all he needed prior to trial and was not prejudiced by the Crown's conduct: *R. v. Arcand*, 2008 CarswellOnt 4971, [2008] O.J. No. 3294, 2008 ONCA 595, 240 O.A.C. 286, 238 C.C.C. (3d) 204, 92 O.R. (3d) 444, 38 C.E.L.R. (3d) 1, 178 C.R.R. (2d) 199 (Ont. C.A.), leave to appeal refused, [2008] S.C.C.A. No. 449, 2008 CarswellOnt 7740, 2008 CarswellOnt 7741, 180 C.R.R. 375 (note), 257 O.A.C. 399 (note), 393 N.R. 399 (note) (S.C.C.).

The Crown is not prohibited from continuing its investigation during the trial if that is seen as necessary. However, there is a continuing obligation to disclose. The disclosure complaints raised by the defence at trial related to the timing of the disclosure, and did not fall within the category of those most serious violations which would warrant a stay of proceedings: *R. v. Vastis*, [2008] O.J. No. 354, 35 C.E.L.R. (3d) 109, 2008 CarswellOnt 861, 2008 ONCJ 44 (Ont. C.J.).

There is an obligation to disclose when additional information is received. Section 7 is not violated where disclosure was made and the Crown continued to respond to requests for disclosure, albeit not perfectly: *R. v. Rosso*, [2008] O.J. No. 5720, 2008 CarswellOnt 9038, 2008 ONCJ 756 (Ont. C.J.).

In *R. v. Ball*, 2013 BCSC 710, 2013 CarswellBC 1040, [2013] B.C.J. No. 821 (B.C. S.C.), it was held that the accused sought disclosure of violation tickets issued to other vehicles by other officers in the same area at the same time on the date of the offence to advance the defence that the officer could have been mistaken about her speed because she had actually targeted another vehicle. However, the accused is not entitled to a particular kind of disclosure or a specific form of investigation; neither does she have a constitutional right incidental to the right to make full answer and defence. She has no constitutional right to direct the conduct of a police investigation of which she is the target. Nor can she achieve that objective by way of a disclosure demand requiring the police undertake investigatory work. The ticket and the notes on the back of it were provided to the defendant, and indicated the correct speeds registered. While the officer noticed an error when she was preparing for the court proceedings, but did not mention it to the accused's counsel, this amounted to a failure to disclose. However, the accused failed to demonstrate that she suffered actual prejudice to her ability to make full answer and defence.

Prior to trial, the defendant's legal representative requested disclosure and was provided with it. He then sent a fax to the prosecutor stating that the notes were not clear enough to read and to "please resend". On the trial date, the paralegal requested an adjournment, which was denied. Where a defendant feels he is missing something and there is no response, he has to make some noise about it. In this case, a month intervened between the second disclosure request and the trial date, yet the paralegal's office did nothing about it. Given that the trial date was set, the trial time set aside, the witnesses were present, and the failure complained about was only with respect to a portion of the disclosure that was recapitulated in the witness statements, the trial Justice of the Peace did not err in refusing to grant the adjournment. See *R. v. Abdi*, 2012 ONCJ 782, 2012 CarswellOnt 16436, [2012] O.J. No. 6221 (Ont. C.J.).

In *R. v. Bydeley*, 2012 ONCJ 837, 2012 CarswellOnt 17276, [2012] O.J. No. 6407 (Ont. C.J.), the defendant sought disclosure in relation to a large number of issues that related to his assertion that as he was not a "person" the *Highway Traffic Act* did not apply to him. He did receive disclosure prior to trial, but claimed he had not been given items which reflected his unique perspective on the law, for example, reference to "the law . . . that permits the officer to infringe upon my human rights to travel and detain me". Clearly the law requires disclosure of items in possession of the Crown which might reasonably assist the defendant in making full answer and defence. The trial Justice of the Peace dismissed the request for further disclosure. No showing of possible relevance was shown in relation to the matters which might conceivably have been subject to disclosure.

In *R. v. Williams*, 2013 NLTD(G) 103, 2013 CarswellNfld 323, 341 Nfld. & P.E.I.R. 159, 1061 A.P.R. 159, [2013] N.J. No. 299 (N.L. T.D.), the trial judge was held to have acted correctly when he rejected the issue the defendant raised about the lateness of the Crown disclosure. The defendant did not relate the circumstances in which he received the disclosure, which had been sent to him in advance of the trial, and he may not have received it due to his own neglect. If the defendant felt he did not have sufficient time to prepare for trial because he did not receive timely disclosure, he should have brought it to the trial judge's attention when the matter was called and asked him to adjourn the proceedings until he was ready to proceed. The trial judge also acted correctly when he upheld the Crown's objection to the documents that the defendant tried to produce when cross-examining the police officer who stopped him for speeding. The Crown has a right to know what the documents are before halfway through the proceedings so it could inform itself about them, assess their relevance and address any concerns that it might have about them. One of the overarching concerns for a trial judge and one of the main purposes of rules of procedure is to ensure as far as reasonably possible that only relevant evidence is admitted that is probative of the issues raised by the charges. The trial judge achieved the object of the rules when he rejected the documents that the defendant produced from the manufacturer about the calibration of the radar and possibly the tuning forks, which were not served on the Crown with at least 7 days' notice in compliance with s. 28 of the *Canada Evidence Act*.

3.3.5 DISCOVERY FROM THIRD PARTIES

- Is there another governmental department or private organization with information which might be relevant?

- If so, write or phone the organization to find out how to get the information. The information may be public, requiring only a request.

- The information may be confidential — perhaps the organization cannot even confirm whether they have information. If the information is confidential because of the privacy of a third party, you might:

  - Bring an application to the court for production and release of the organization's records.
    - Include a notice of application and a supporting affidavit in an application record.
    - The affidavit should be sworn by someone other than the defendant or you (perhaps your secretary).
    - It should detail the grounds to believe that the organization has relevant information — "fishing expeditions" are generally not permitted, especially when there are legitimate privacy rights at stake.

- Book a return date for your application well before trial. That way, should the records be disclosed, you will have time to review.

- Serve the application record on the prosecutor, on the third party whose privacy right is at stake, and on any other legally interested party.

- Serve a copy on the organization with the records.

- Serve a summons requiring the keeper of the records (you must find out who this person is) or his or her "designate" to appear in court on the date of your application along with the records.

- At the application, you must persuade the justice there are reasonable grounds to believe that the undisclosed records *may* assist your defence (of course, you won't know for sure because you haven't seen the records).

- The justice may balance your client's right to make full answer and defence (under section 7 of the *Charter*) with other privacy rights.

- The justice may even decide to look at the records in private before releasing them to you.

- Ontario cases are somewhat uncertain on the procedure to utilize, and whether to follow a process analogous to the statutory scheme in the *Criminal Code* for disclosure of third party records which followed the *O'Connor* decision.

- The two-stage test in *R. v. O'Connor* (1995), [1996] 2 W.W.R. 153, 44 C.R. (4th) 1, 103 C.C.C. (3d) 1, [1995] 4 S.C.R. 411 (S.C.C.) was taken regarding business records of the corporate victim: *R. v. Caporicci* (1998), 1998 CarswellOnt 1185, [1998] O.J. No. 1123 (Ont. Prov. Div.).

- The Court of Appeal for Ontario has recently stated that where there are third party records, which the defence wishes to have produced, a written application should be brought using the procedure laid down in *R. v. O'Connor*. See: *R. v. Arcand* (2004), [2004] O.J. No. 5017, 2004 CarswellOnt 5160, 10 C.E.L.R. (3d) 161, 125 C.R.R. (2d) 144, 193 O.A.C. 16, 192 C.C.C. (3d) 57, 73 O.R. (3d) 758 (Ont. C.A.).

- For an example of a provincial offences case where disclosure was ordered of records in the possession of a third party, see *R. v. Dare Foods Ltd.*, [2004] O.J. No. 3949, 2004 ONCJ 201, 2004 CarswellOnt 3906 (Ont. C.J.); and *R. v. Dare Foods Ltd.*, [2004] O.J. No. 3951, 2004 ONCJ 202, 2004 CarswellOnt 3908 (Ont. C.J.). The case involved a prosecution under the *Occupational Health and Safety Act*. The justice held that there was jurisdiction for the court to order production of a coroner's records respecting the deceased person, following the procedure in *R. v. O'Connor*.

The procedure set out in *R. v. O'Connor* (1995), 1995 CarswellBC 1098, 1995 CarswellBC 1151, EYB 1995-67073, [1995] S.C.J. No. 98, [1996] 2 W.W.R. 153, [1995] 4 S.C.R. 411, 44 C.R. (4th) 1, 103 C.C.C. (3d) 1, 130 D.L.R. (4th) 235, 191 N.R. 1, 68 B.C.A.C. 1, 112 W.A.C. 1, 33 C.R.R. (2d) 1 (S.C.C.) provides a general mechanism at common law for ordering production of any record beyond the possession or control of the prosecuting Crown. The procedure is not limited to only those cases where a third party has an expectation of privacy in the targeted documents: *R. v. McNeil*, [2009] S.C.J. No. 3, 2009 CarswellOnt 116, 2009 CarswellOnt 117, 383 N.R. 1, 301 D.L.R. (4th) 1, 62 C.R. (6th) 1, 238 C.C.C. (3d) 353, [2009] 1 S.C.R. 66, 2009 SCC 3, 246 O.A.C. 154 (S.C.C.), at para. 11 [SCC].

Evidence of previous incident reports concerning items being thrown from bridges onto highways in the County in question did not meet the "likely relevant" threshold in *R. v. O'Connor* (1995), 1995 CarswellBC 1098, 1995 CarswellBC 1151, EYB 1995-67073, [1995] S.C.J. No. 98, [1995] 4 S.C.R. 411, [1996] 2 W.W.R. 153, 44 C.R. (4th) 1, 103 C.C.C. (3d) 1, 130 D.L.R. (4th) 235, 191 N.R. 1, 68 B.C.A.C. 1, 112 W.A.C. 1, 33 C.R.R. (2d) 1 (S.C.C.). There was no evidence before the court that any items had been thrown from the Sixth Line bridge immediately prior to the motor vehicle collision: *R. v. Parke*, 2010 ONCJ 583, 2010 CarswellOnt 9331, [2010] O.J. No. 5256 (Ont. C.J.).

The defendants were the subject of a private prosecution by an environmental advocacy organization involving regulatory charges that stemmed from birds flying into buildings owned by the defendants. An application by the defendants for production of the organization's internal records respecting its co-operation with the prosecutor in the investigation of the defendant was governed by the third party records disclosure regime set out by the Supreme Court of Canada in *R. v. O'Connor* (1995), 1995 CarswellBC 1098, 1995 CarswellBC 1151, EYB 1995-67073, [1995] 4 S.C.R. 411, 103 C.C.C. (3d) 1, 44 C.R. (4th) 1, 130 D.L.R. (4th) 235, [1996] 2 W.W.R. 153, 68 B.C.A.C. 1, 33 C.R.R. (2d) 1, 191 N.R. 1, 112 W.A.C. 1, [1995] S.C.J. No. 98 (S.C.C.) and *R. v. McNeil*, 2009 SCC 3, 2009 CarswellOnt 116, 2009 CarswellOnt 117, [2009] 1 S.C.R. 66, 238 C.C.C. (3d) 353, 62 C.R. (6th) 1, 301 D.L.R. (4th) 1, 383 N.R. 1, 246 O.A.C. 154, [2009] S.C.J. No. 3 (S.C.C.). The mere assertion that such records were likely relevant to credibility and reliability were not sufficient to justify a disclosure order. See *Podolsky v. Cadillac Fairview Corp.*, 2012 ONCJ 545, 2012 CarswellOnt 10874, 112 O.R. (3d) 22, [2012] O.J. No. 4027 (Ont. C.J.).

In *Ontario v. O.P.S.E.U.*, 2012 ONSC 2078, 2012 CarswellOnt 6293, 44 Admin. L.R. (5th) 340, 219 L.A.C. (4th) 151, [2012] O.J. No. 2356 (Ont. Div. Ct.), the court hearing a judicial review application was concerned with a case where the Crown employed inspectors who had broad investigative powers and lawyers who conducted prosecutions under the *Occupational Health and Safety Act*, and thereby had a dual function as employer and prosecutor. However, the Crown's disclosure obligations as a prosecutor did not arise from the collective agreement, and the collective agreement could not prevent its duty to disclose the inspector's records to the accused. There was no reason to believe that an inspector's criminal record would have less bearing on an accused's right to make full answer and defence in regulatory proceedings than a police officer's criminal record in criminal prosecutions. The Grievance Settlement Board's finding that the accused had to bring an *O'Connor* application for disclosure seriously prejudiced the rights of the accused.

The applicant sought as part of first party records disclosure the disciplinary records and employment file for the police officer who charged him with driving while holding or using a hand-held communication device. Although the applicant had failed to comply with the 30-day notice requirements in s. 141(1) of the *Provincial Offences Act*, s. 85 provides for a broad curative power to extend time for service. The court should exercise the power to extend the times prescribed in s. 141(1) unless to do so would prejudice the other parties. In the present case, the justice of the peace refused the applicant's request for the disciplinary records on the basis that those records were irrelevant and the applicant will have the opportunity to explore the subject in cross-examination. While the reasons for the refusal were not extensive, the decision was one that clearly fell within the jurisdiction of the justice of the peace. As the applicant will be able to explore the matter in cross-examination of the officer, it could not be said that the decision will have a fundamentally important impact on the fairness of the trial. In addition, such pre-trial rulings can always be reconsidered by the justice of the peace who presides over the trial should the evidence warrant disclosure. The disciplinary records may take on more relevance based on how the questions are answered by the witness in cross-examination. However, evidence of historical drug use by an officer who has seemingly satisfied his superiors that he is fit to resume his duties has marginal relevance at this point. How far the applicant can go in cross-examination on this issue and if there will be any merit to some form of documentary disclosure will be determined at trial. The Crown had specifically stated that it had considered the disciplinary records in question and had fulfilled its "gate-keeping" function that they do not form part of first party disclosure. Not every finding of police misconduct by an officer involved in a matter will be relevant to the accused's case and it is certainly not the case that a *McNeil* report should be provided as a matter of course in all provincial offences prosecutions. The applicant had been aware of the Crown's position that an *O'Connor* application was the proper procedure to determine if some or all of the disciplinary records should be produced. The applicant had ignored the Crown's position, and chose to proceed with the application. There was an upcoming trial date for the matter and this date could be impacted if the applicant commenced an *O'Connor* application at this late date. The impact that such an application could have on the trial date was a matter for the discretion of the trial judge. See *Mian v. City of Ottawa*, 2018 ONSC 2131, 2018 CarswellOnt 5388, [2018] O.J. No. 1773 (Ont. S.C.J.).

In *York (Regional Municipality) v. McGuigan*, 2018 ONCA 1062, 2018 CarswellOnt 22571, [2018] O.J. No. 6916 (Ont. C.A.), the Court of Appeal ruled that trial justice properly ordered the prosecutor to provide disclosure of the testing and operating procedures from the user manual for the device used by the traffic officer to measure the speed of the defendant's vehicle. Even if the justice of the peace had been wrong to order disclosure, the error would not have been jurisdictional in nature. Section 140(1) of the *Provincial Offences Act* confines *certiorari* orders in *POA* matters to situations where an applicant would be entitled to such relief at common law, and for parties to a proceeding, *certiorari* orders are confined to jurisdictional errors. Moreover, *certiorari* should not have been granted in the course of ongoing proceedings. Nor was there a substantial wrong or miscarriage of justice to address, a prerequisite to *certiorari* under s. 141(4) of the Act. Contrary to the application judge's decision, the justice of the peace did not err in making the disclosure order. Where a prosecutor is relying on a speed measuring device to prosecute an offence, it must, on request, disclose the testing and operating procedures set out in the user manual for that device. It is up to the prosecutor to hand such information over on request. The person charged need not bring an application or obtain a court order. This is first party disclosure, not third party disclosure. The charging police force has a corresponding duty to furnish the pertinent passages from the user manual to the prosecutor to enable the prosecutor to discharge its first party disclosure obligations. This is not a crushing administrative task. The disclosure at issue here is not case specific information. The disclosure obligation can therefore be discharged by the prosecutor by posting the relevant content from the user manual online and providing the ticketed driver with the required URL.

3.3.6 INTERVIEW WITNESSES

- Gather evidence from all potential witnesses, both favourable and unfavourable. Even the prosecutor's witnesses, who may be convinced your client is guilty, should be questioned. You may learn new information that was not disclosed.

- If you suspect that witnesses may change their story, and should you wish to "pin them down", follow one of the procedures listed below.

  - Interview them in the presence of an investigator or reliable person from your office.

  - Record the interview, with the witness' consent, if possible.

  - Have the witness sign or swear a statement.

- Consider that if the witness changes his or her story, then you will need evidence to contradict him or her at trial, but do whatever procedure is most comfortable for the witness.

Prudent and experienced counsel will not engage in interviews with an opposing witness and, in particular, a complainant, without having a third party witness present: *R. v. Bevan*, 2009 CarswellOnt 6191, 2009 ONCJ 487 (Ont. C.J.).

A defendant who does not testify is not a witness and is not eligible for costs under s. 60(2). Such costs are for witness fees and expenses. Had the defendant who lived in Montreal and travelled to Thunder Bay for his trial testified, he would have been a witness and such an order would have been available to the court; however, the prosecution's witness did not appear for trial, and the case was withdrawn. The trial justice therefore did not have jurisdiction to order $100 costs payable to the defendant. See *Thunder Bay (City) v. Singh-Sidhu*, 2016 ONSC 4889, 2016 CarswellOnt 12987, [2016] O.J. No. 4284 (Ont. S.C.J.).

3.3.7 EXPERT ADVICE

- An expert will assist in understanding the issues and where to focus your strategy. And of course, you may want the expert to test samples or testify at trial.

- Hire an investigator, if you can afford to. The investigator should be licensed, reliable, and willing to testify in court if necessary.

- It is also important to consider whether the expert has been qualified by the court to testify before, or if his/her expertise has not been accepted. It is only a properly qualified expert that will be permitted to testify. In *R. v. Mohan*, [1994] 2 S.C.R. 9, 89 C.C.C. (3d) 402, EYB 1994-67655, 1994 CarswellOnt 66, 1994 CarswellOnt 1155, [1994] S.C.J. No. 36, 29 C.R. (4th) 243, 71 O.A.C. 241, 166 N.R. 245, 114 D.L.R. (4th) 419, 18 O.R. (3d) 160 (note) (S.C.C.) at 414 [C.C.C.], the Supreme Court of Canada stated that in order to qualify as an expert, the evidence must be given by a witness who is shown to have acquired "special or peculiar knowledge through study or experience" of the matters on which the witness undertakes to testify. You should also consider whether the expert you are consulting and con- sidering calling as a witness has been called to testify before by the defence, or the prosecutor, or both, as this may be relevant to the issue of bias or independence of the expert.

The trial judge did not err in refusing to permit a witness tendered by the defence to testify as an expert at the sentencing hearing. The justice of the peace rejected the proposed expert witness on the basis that the witness had no legal training and was seeking to opine about the legislation from a paralegal perspective. The justice's decision that the witness was more of an advocate than an expert was supportable on the evidence: *R. v. Long Lake Forest Products Inc.*, [2009] O.J. No. 2193, 2009 CarswellOnt 3054, 2009 ONCJ 241 (Ont. C.J.).

In *R. v. Wong*, 2010 ONCJ 636, 2010 CarswellOnt 10221, [2010] O.J. No. 5810 (Ont. C.J.), it was held that the trial justice applied the proper rules of evidence in refusing to admit material that the defendant obtained from the Internet and other sources as to deficiencies on the balcony and parking garage, and the manner in which they should be repaired. Such evidence was not properly supported by calling an engineer or providing an engineer's report, which the prosecutor would then have an opportunity to receive and cross-examine.

3.3.8 JUDICIAL PRE-TRIAL CONFERENCES

- The *Good Government Act, 2009,* S.O. 2009, c. 33, s. 1(38), effective 15 December 2009, enacts a new judicial pre-trial conference procedure. As is the case under s. 625.1 of the *Criminal Code*, the prosecutor, defendant or the court on its own motion, acting under s. 45.1(1), may apply for a justice to order that a pre-trial conference be held between the prosecutor and the defendant, or a representative of the defendant. It is contemplated that the justice of the court presiding over the pre-trial conference will have the parties discuss matters that "to promote a fair and expeditious trial, would be better decided before the start of the proceedings" and to make arrangements for decisions on such matters: s. 45.1(2).

- Pre-trial meetings with judges or justices, as opposed to informal meetings between the prosecutor and defence representative only, are an effective way to resolve matters with the input of a judicial officer. The court, who will not be the judge presiding at the trial, can express an opinion, which is not binding, to help the parties narrow the issues in dispute, or resolve the matter by a guilty plea. It is helpful for the client to be available in order to discuss the results of the judicial pre-trial meeting in a timely manner, *e.g.*, the pre-trial conference meeting might be scheduled on the same day as an appearance in court, or a few days before the next court appearance.

4

TYPES OF PROVINCIAL OFFENCES

4.1 CLASSIFICATION SCHEME

- In *R. v. Sault Ste. Marie (City)*, [1978] 2 S.C.R. 1299, 7 C.E.L.R. 53, 3 C.R. (3d) 30, 40 C.C.C. (2d) 353, 1978 CarswellOnt 24, 1978 CarswellOnt 594, 85 D.L.R. (3d) 161, 21 N.R. 295 (S.C.C.), the Supreme Court of Canada classified all offences, both regulatory and criminal, as either:
  - *Mens rea* offences,
  - Strict liability offences, or
  - Absolute liability offences.

4.1.1 *MENS REA* OFFENCES

- The prosecution must prove beyond a reasonable doubt that the defendant committed the illegal act(s).

- The prosecution must also prove beyond a reasonable doubt that the defendant had a particular state of mind.

- The state of mind depends on the offence. For example, it might be intent, knowledge, or recklessness.

- The prosecution can prove the defendant's state of mind in two ways:
  - Admissions by the defendant as to his or her state of mind; and
  - Inferences about the defendant's state of mind based on the common sense principle that people normally intend the natural consequences of their actions.

4.1.2 STRICT LIABILITY OFFENCES

- The prosecution must prove beyond a reasonable doubt that the defendant committed the illegal act(s).

- The defendant must then prove, on a balance of probabilities, that he or she took reasonable care not to commit the illegal act(s), or that he or she made a reasonable mistake of fact which, if true, would have rendered the act(s) lawful.

In *North Bay (City) v. Viens*, 2018 ONCJ 564, 2018 CarswellOnt 13852, [2018] O.J. No. 4309 (Ont. C.J.), it was held that the offence of driving a motor vehicle left of centre while upon a curve in the roadway is a strict liability offence.

The offence of disobeying a sign is a strict liability offence: *West Nipissing (Municipality) v. Langlois*, 2018 ONCJ 802, 2018 CarswellOnt 19297, [2018] O.J. No. 6036 (Ont. C.J.).

The offence of drive hand-held communication device invites of no possible exception to enforcement; it is not complex in nature; the penalty does not carry with it the possibility of incarceration; and the precise language of the legislation does explicitly use wording such as "shall" which purports an offence of absolute liability when read in its totality: see *R. v. Fernandes-Salema*, 2019 ONCJ 67, 2019 CarswellOnt 1801, [2019] O.J. No. 667 (Ont. C.J.).

However, recent amendments to the *Highway Traffic Act* have resulted in a higher minimum fine for the hand- held communication device offence as well as a licence suspension in the event of conviction. This has led to the offence being categorized as being strict liability in nature: *R. v. Loewen*, 2018 ONCJ 850, 2018 CarswellOnt 20501, [2018] O.J. No. 6393 (Ont. C.J.).

4.1.3 ABSOLUTE LIABILITY OFFENCES

- The prosecution must prove beyond a reasonable doubt that the defendant committed the illegal act(s).
- The defendant is liable whether or not he or she was at fault.

4.2 CLASSIFICATION OF OFFENCES

- Provincial offences are presumed to be strict liability offences.
- The offence is *mens rea* and not strict liability, however, if the provincial offence clearly requires proof of a particular state of mind. *For example, section 16 of the Discriminatory Business Practices Act, R.S.O. 1990, c. D.12, states that: Every person who, knowingly furnishes false information in*

an investigation under this Act, fails to comply with any order or assurance of voluntary compliance made or entered into under this Act; or obstructs a person making an investigation is guilty of a provincial offence. Clearly, the Prosecutor must prove the defendant's knowledge, and so it is a mens rea offence.

- The offence is absolute liability, if the provincial offence clearly excludes the defence of reasonable care and clearly indicates that guilt requires only proof of the illegal act(s). To determine if this is the clear intent of the legislation, courts consider the following: (See John Swaigen, *Regulatory Offences in Canada* (Carswell, 1992) pp. 38-42):

  - The overall regulatory pattern adopted by the Legislature. *For example, the purpose of the statute, its legislative history, and its relationship with other provincial laws.*

  - The subject-matter of the legislation. *For example, the class of persons protected by the law, the extent of the harm to them if the offence is committed, and the extent to which other remedies are available.*

  - The importance of the penalty. *For example, the harshness of the penalty, and the difficulty of complying with the legislation.*

  - The precision of the language used. *For example, whether the legislation clearly rejects the defence of reasonable care.*

  - The effect on the defendant's *Charter* rights. *See below for further discussion.*

- As Swaigen points out, the categorization process is not consistent and there is a "lack of any rationality" (See John Swaigen, *Regulatory Offences in Canada* (Carswell, 1992) p. 52). Some statutes employ all three types of offences, as is the case in the *Ontario Highway Traffic Act*: willfully avoiding police while being pursued (*mens rea* offence); failing to yield to pedestrians (strict liability offence); speeding (absolute liability offence). See further *Libman on Regulatory Offences in Canada* (Earlscourt, 2002) for examples of offences under various provincial, federal and municipal statutes which have been classified as *mens rea* offences (Chapter 4.3), absolute liability offences (Chapter 5.6), and strict liability offences (Chapter 6.5).

- The Supreme Court of Canada has recently confirmed that the issue of classification of the offence has become "a question of statutory interpretation", and that regulatory offences usually fall in the category of strict liability offences. See *Lévis (Ville) c. Tétreault*, 2006 SCC 12, [2006] 1 S.C.R. 420, (*sub nom.* Lévis (City) v. Tétreault) 266 D.L.R. (4th) 165, (*sub nom.* Lévis (City) v. Tétreault) 346 N.R. 331, J.E. 2006-818, 36 C.R. (6th) 215, 31 M.V.R. (5th) 1, 207 C.C.C. (3d) 1, 2006 CarswellQue 2911, 2006 CarswellQue 2912, [2006] S.C.J. No. 12 (S.C.C.).

Another recent example of how the classification of offences analysis is used by the courts is provided by the Ontario Court of Appeal in *Brampton (City) v. Kanda*, 2008 CarswellOnt 79, [2008] O.J. No. 80, 41 M.P.L.R. (4th) 199, (*sub nom.* R. v. Kanda) 233 O.A.C. 118, 53 C.R. (6th) 331, 2008 ONCA 22, 56 M.V.R. (5th) 1, (*sub nom.* R. v. Kanda) 227 C.C.C. (3d) 417, (*sub nom.* R. v. Kanda) 88 O.R. (3d) 732, (*sub nom.* R. v. Kanda) 289 D.L.R. (4th) 304 (Ont. C.A.). In this case, the Court of Appeal determined that the offence of driving while a passenger under 16 years old fails to properly wear a seat belt is a strict liability offence for which the due diligence defence is available. In coming to this conclusion the Court examined the overall regulatory pattern of the legislation, the subject matter, penalty, and precision of the language.

- The classification of strict liability struck an appropriate balance between encouraging drivers to be vigilant about the safety of child passengers and not punishing those who exercise due diligence with respect to children's seatbelts: *Brampton (City) v. Kanda*, 2008 CarswellOnt 79, [2008] O.J. No. 80, 41 M.P.L.R. (4th) 199, (*sub nom.* R. v. Kanda) 233 O.A.C. 118, 53 C.R. (6th) 331, 2008 ONCA 22, 56 (5th) 1, (*sub nom.* R. v. Kanda) 227 C.C.C. (3d) 417, (*sub nom.* R. v. Kanda) 88 O.R. (3d) 732, (*sub nom.* R. v. Kanda) 289 D.L.R. (4th) 304 (Ont. C.A.).

The word "shall" in a traffic offence does not necessarily mean absolute liability: *R. v. Dillman*, 2008 CarswellOnt 1596, [2008] O.J. No. 1120, 68 M.V.R. (5th) 272, 2008 ONCJ 101 (Ont. C.J.).

Section 19.2 of the Manitoba *Legislative Assembly and Executive Council Conflict of Interest Act* is an absolute liability offence because it has a stringent code of conduct for senior public servants, and because no relief is given to senior public servants who commit an offence through inadvertence. A similar analysis might be applied in Ontario statutes: *R. v. Kupfer*, [2008] M.J. No. 276, 2008 CarswellMan 405, 232 Man. R. (2d) 98, 2008 MBQB 203 (Man. Q.B.).

Failing to yield at a crosswalk, in Ontario, is an absolute liability offence: *R. v. Kelleher* (2008), 2008 CarswellOnt 8609, 2009 ONCJ 54, [2009] O.J. No. 670 (Ont. C.J.).

In *R. v. Raham*, 2010 ONCA 206, 2010 CarswellOnt 1546, [2010] O.J. No. 1091, 99 O.R. (3d) 241, 213 C.R.R. (2d) 336, 260 O.A.C. 143, 92 M.V.R. (5th) 195, 253 C.C.C. (3d) 188, 74 C.R. (6th) 96 (Ont. C.A.), the Ontario Court of Appeal held that the *Highway Traffic Act* offence of "stunt driving" by driving in excess of 50 km per hour is a strict liability offence. Although speeding *simpliciter* is an absolute liability offence, stunt driving by excessive speed is a strict liability offence. The Court of Appeal rejected lower court decisions which held that there was no factual possibility of a due diligence defence because it was unrealistic for a person to speed at 50 kilometres per hour over the speed limit without knowing that they were already speeding to some extent. The Court of Appeal held that reasonable steps must be taken to avoid committing the offence charged, not acting lawfully in a broader sense. For example, a driver who relies on a speedometer indicating a rate of speed well below 50 km per hour over the speed limit, might succeed on a due diligence defence if there was evidence that the speedometer, unknown to the driver, was malfunctioning.

The recently created offence of driving with a hand held communication device, contrary to the *Highway Traffic Act*, is an absolute liability offence: *R. v. Chadwick*, 2011 ONCJ 402, 2011 CarswellOnt 8302, 25 M.V.R. (6th) 324, [2011] O.J. No. 3748 (Ont. C.J.).

Changing lane not in safety in Ontario is a strict liability offence: *York (Regional Municipality) v. Clarke*, 2011 ONCJ 272, 2011 CarswellOnt 3636, [2011] O.J. No. 2336 (Ont. C.J.).

The law is that there is a presumption in favour of treating regulatory offences as strict liability offences unless there is compelling legislative direction to categorize them as either *mens rea* or absolute liability offences: *R. v. Spasojevic*, 2012 ONCJ 693, 2012 CarswellOnt 14163, [2012] O.J. No. 5319 (Ont. C.J.); *R. v. 555034 Ontario Ltd.*, 2013 ONCJ 20, 2013 CarswellOnt 473, [2013] O.J. No. 279 (Ont. C.J.).

The offence of an owner permitting someone to drive his motor vehicle on a highway while the vehicle was not insured is a strict liability offence. See *Wawanesa Mutual Insurance Co. v. S.C. Construction Ltd.*, 2012 ONSC 353, 2012

CarswellOnt 593, 108 O.R. (3d) 762, 7 C.C.L.I. (5th) 95, 28 M.V.R. (6th) 91, [2012] I.L.R. I-5250, [2012] O.J. No. 316 (Ont. S.C.J.); *R. v. Ikponmwosa*, 2011 ONCJ 149, 2011 CarswellOnt 2067, 13 M.V.R. (6th) 301, [2011] O.J. No. 1367 (Ont. C.J.); *R. v. Huxtable*, 2011 CarswellOnt 13397 (Ont. C.J.); *R. v. Akinkuade*, 2011 CarswellOnt 15858 (Ont. C.J.) (permitting a motor vehicle to be operated without insurance and producing false evidence).

Failing to yield to traffic on a through highway is a strict liability offence: *R. v. Walker*, 2012 ONCJ 485, 2012 CarswellOnt 9257 (Ont. C.J.), as is the offence of failing to stop on right for emergency vehicle: *R. v. Metni*, 2012 ONCJ 134, 2012 CarswellOnt 2752, [2012] O.J. No. 1126 (Ont. C.J.).

The offence of driver with a class G2 driver's licence driving with more than 0% alcohol in his system, contrary to s. 6(1) of O. Reg. 340/94 made under the *Highway Traffic Act*, is a strict liability offence for which the defence of due diligence is available: *Tut v. RBC General Insurance Co.*, 2011 ONCA 644, 2011 CarswellOnt 10626, 107 O.R. (3d) 481, 1 C.C.L.I. (5th) 186, 342 D.L.R. (4th) 464, 19 M.V.R. (6th) 188, 285 O.A.C. 100, [2011] O.J. No. 4509 (Ont. C.A.).

Another example of a common strict liability offence is making an unsafe turn: *R. v. Benedict*, 2012 ONCJ 169, 2012 CarswellOnt 3951, [2012] O.J. No. 1394 (Ont. C.J.); *R. v. Gill*, 2012 ONCJ 473, 2012 CarswellOnt 9117 (Ont. C.J.). Operating an unsafe motor vehicle is also a strict liability offence: *R. v. Crowe*, 2012 ONCJ 411, 2012 CarswellOnt 8594 (Ont. C.J.), as is driving while under suspension: *R. v. Nikbakht*, 2011 ONCJ 861, 2011 CarswellOnt 15780, [2011] O.J. No. 6366 (Ont. C.J.).

Recent examples of *Highway Traffic Act* offences held to be absolute liability in nature include: disobeying a stop sign: *R. v. Lapointe*, 2011 ONCJ 20, 2011 CarswellOnt 324 (Ont. C.J.); *R. v. Harris*, 2011 ONCJ 150, 2011 CarswellOnt 2069, [2011] O.J. No. 1366 (Ont. C.J.); failing to stop for a red light: *R. v. Johnston*, 2011 ONCJ 215, 2011 CarswellOnt 2704 (Ont. C.J.).

The offence of speeding being an absolute liability offence, the trial justice was in error in accepting the evidence of the mechanical defect as a defence to the strict liability offence of speeding: *R. v. Grewal*, 2011 CarswellOnt 15193, [2011] O.J. No. 6118 (Ont. C.J.). See also *R. v. Cerisano*, 2011 CarswellOnt 15681, [2011] O.J. No. 6351 (Ont. C.J.) holding that speeding and failing to surrender insurance card are absolute liability offences.

The *Highway Traffic Act* offence of driving a motor vehicle while operating a handheld communication device is a strict liability offence: *R. v. Petrovic*, 2012 ONCJ 562, 2012 CarswellOnt 10989, [2012] O.J. No. 4185 (Ont. C.J.).

The offence of failing to use a crosswalk, contrary to s. 144(22) of the *Highway Traffic Act* has been held to be an absolute liability offence: *R. v. Anderson*, 2012 ONCJ 781, 2012 CarswellOnt 16437, 40 M.V.R. (6th) 342, [2012] O.J. No. 6217 (Ont. C.J.). Other examples of absolute liability offence under this statute are failing to stop for a red light: *R. v. Scetto*, 2013 ONCJ 236, 2013 CarswellOnt 5453, [2013] O.J. No. 2043 (Ont. C.J.), and disobey sign: *R. v. Ali*, 2013 ONCJ 618, 2013 CarswellOnt 15916, [2013] O.J. No. 5338 (Ont. C.J.).

In *R. v. Grech-Vennare*, 2013 ONCJ 278, 2013 CarswellOnt 6808, [2013] O.J. No. 2387 (Ont. C.J.), the court ruled that, contrary to cases treating the offence of driving a motor vehicle while using a cell phone to be a strict liability offence, it was one of absolute liability.

Failing to surrender a permit for a motor vehicle is a strict liability offence: *R. v. Ko*, 2013 ONCJ 451, 2013 CarswellOnt 11752, [2013] O.J. No. 3826 (Ont. C.J.).

In *R. v. Tate* (February 25, 2013), Doc. Newmarket 09-2111, [2013] O.J. No. 1799 (Ont. C.J.), the following offences under the *Smoke-Free Ontario Act* were held to be strict liability in nature: displaying tobacco by means of countertop display; failure to post age restriction and health warning signs; selling improperly packaged tobacco; selling tobacco without a health warning on the package; offering to sell cigarettes in packages of less than 20.

The offence of failing to properly wear a seatbelt is a strict liability offence: *R. v. Wilson*, 2013 ONCJ 313, 2013 CarswellOnt 8034, 49 M.V.R. (6th) 320, [2013] O.J. No. 2767 (Ont. C.J.), affirmed 2014 ONCA 212, 2014 CarswellOnt 3327, 308 C.C.C. (3d) 350, 63 M.V.R. (6th) 1, 317 O.A.C. 314, [2014] O.J. No. 1295 (Ont. C.A.). The Court of Appeal subsequently ruled that this is a strict liability offence and dismissed the appeal: *R. v. Wilson*, 2014 ONCA 212, 2014 CarswellOnt 3327, 308 C.C.C. (3d) 350, 63 M.V.R. (6th) 1, 317 O.A.C. 314, [2014] O.J. No. 1295 (Ont. C.A.).

Drive under licence of other jurisdiction while suspended in Ontario, drive while under suspended licence, and improper number plate light are strict liability offences: *R. v. Mahamed*, 2013 ONCJ 647, 2013 CarswellOnt 16406, [2013] O.J. No. 5432 (Ont. C.J.). The offence of displaying a licence that has been suspended or altered is also a strict liability offence: *R. v. Kell*, 2013 ONCJ 637, 2013 CarswellOnt 16122, [2013] O.J. No. 5425 (Ont. C.J.).

The charge of failure to be civil and well-behaved as the driver or operator of a taxi cab is a strict liability offence: *R. v. Khan*, 2014 ONCJ 68, 2013 CarswellOnt 18703, 55 M.V.R. (6th) 163, 18 M.P.L.R. (5th) 315, [2014] O.J. No. 687 (Ont. C.J.).

The traffic bylaw offence of parking in excess of time on meter is absolute liability in nature: *R. v. Pereira*, 2014 ONCJ 188, 2014 CarswellOnt 5150, [2014] O.J. No. 1912 (Ont. C.J.).

Driving an overweight vehicle during freeze-up and carrying an excessive load are strict liability offences: *R. v. Lakeside Rat Rapids Enterprises Ltd.*, 2014 ONCJ 187, 2014 CarswellOnt 5148, [2014] O.J. No. 1910 (Ont. C.J.).

Driving while suspended is a strict liability offence: *R. v. Lamanna*, 2014 ONCJ 544, 2014 CarswellOnt 14524, [2014] O.J. No. 4901 (Ont. C.J.); *R. v. Alfano*, 2014 ONCJ 99, 2014 CarswellOnt 2551, [2014] O.J. No. 1007 (Ont. C.J.).

In *R. v. Miller*, 2014 ONCJ 782, 2014 CarswellOnt 18997, [2014] O.J. No. 4805 (Ont. C.J.), it was held that driving or permitting a motor vehicle to be driven without insurance is a strict liability offence.

Turning not in safety is a strict liability offence: *R. v. Hawdon*, 2014 CarswellOnt 5067 (Ont. C.J.).

The offence of owner/operator of a motor vehicle on a highway without insurance, contrary to the *Compulsory Automobile Insurance Act*, is a strict liability offence: *R. v. Correia*, 2015 ONCJ 276, 2015 CarswellOnt 7735, 49 C.C.L.I. (5th) 300, [2015] O.J. No. 2705 (Ont. C.J.); *R. v. Ward*, 2015 ONCJ 369, 2015 CarswellOnt 10460, [2015] O.J. No. 3726 (Ont. C.J.).

Careless driving contrary to s. 130 of the *Highway Traffic Act* is a strict liability offence for which the defence of due diligence is available: *R. v. Li* (June 24, 2015), Doc. 9494481B, [2015] O.J. No. 3363 (Ont. C.J.); *R. v. Anene*, 2016 ONCJ 115, 2016 CarswellOnt 3239, [2016] O.J. No. 1110 (Ont. C.J.). The same is true for the strict liability offence of driving while suspended: *R. v. Quick*, 2015 CarswellOnt 15761, [2015] O.J. No. 5433 (Ont. C.J.).

In *R. v. Goldhawk*, 2015 ONCJ 626, 2015 CarswellOnt 17114, [2015] O.J. No. 5764 (Ont. C.J.), it was held that the offence of unsafe turn is a strict liability offence.

The *Highway Traffic Act* offences of driving a motor vehicle without a valid permit and overweight vehicle are strict liability in nature: *Durham (Regional Municipality) v. D. Crupi & Sons Ltd.*, 2015 ONCJ 488, 2015 CarswellOnt 15126, [2015] O.J. No. 4872 (Ont. C.J.).

Failure to surrender a driver's licence for inspection contrary to s. 33(3) of the *Highway Traffic Act* is a strict liability offence: *R. v. Davidson*, 2015 ONCJ 764, 2015 CarswellOnt 20519, [2015] O.J. No. 7072 (Ont. C.J.).

It was held in *R. v. Clemmer*, 2016 ONCJ 87, 2016 CarswellOnt 2187, 100 C.E.L.R. (3d) 253, 67 R.P.R. (5th) 156, [2016] O.J. No. 774 (Ont. C.J.) that operating an all-terrain vehicle in a provincial park without written authorization is a strict liability offence.

Permitting alteration of property without a permit contrary to the *Ontario Heritage Act*, and permitting development without approval contrary to the *Conservation Authorities Act*, are strict liability offences: *R. v. Robati* (March 12, 2015), Doc. Richmond Hill 11-0021, 11-0256, [2015] O.J. No. 6934 (Ont. C.J.), affirmed (December 15, 2015), Kenkel J., [2015] O.J. No. 6646 (Ont. C.J.).

Driving while suspended is a strict liability offence for which the defence of due diligence is available: *R. v. Lococo* (October 29, 2015), Doc. Niagara Falls 14-0739, [2015] O.J. No. 7186 (Ont. C.J.), affirmed (April 18, 2016), Doc. St. Catharines 2111-999-14-0739, [2016] O.J. No. 2391 (Ont. C.J.).

The offence of driving carelessly is a strict liability offence. See *R. v. Sturgeon*, 2016 ONCJ 391, 2016 CarswellOnt 10451, [2016] O.J. No. 3523 (Ont. C.J.); *R. v. Howarth*, 2016 ONCJ 516, 2016 CarswellOnt 13653, [2016] O.J. No. 4522 (Ont. C.J.), reversed on other grounds 2017 ONCJ 856, 2017 CarswellOnt 20342 (Ont. C.J.); *R. v. Shergill*, 2016 ONCJ 163, 2016 CarswellOnt 4638, 97 M.V.R. (6th) 322, [2016] O.J. No. 1503 (Ont. C.J.), leave to appeal refused [2016] O.J. No. 4294 (C.A. [In Chambers]).

The offence of distracted driving set out in s. 78.1(1) of the *Highway Traffic Act* is an absolute liability offence, which requires the prosecutor to prove the *actus reus* of the offence beyond a reasonable doubt in order to sustain a conviction: *R. v. Srecko*, 2016 ONCJ 499, 2016 CarswellOnt 13023, [2016] O.J. No. 4329 (Ont. C.J.) at para. 22.

In *R. v. Metric Excavating*, 2016 ONCJ 575, 2016 CarswellOnt 14876, [2016] O.J. No. 4917 (Ont. C.J.), it was held that the offence of driving a heavy vehicle on a prohibited highway is a strict liability offence.

Failing to wear a proper helmet while driving a motorcycle has been held to be a strict liability offence: *Kawartha Lakes (City) v. Mortensen*, [2015] O.J. No. 982 (C.J.).

It has been held that failing to surrender a permit for a motor vehicle and failing to surrender an insurance card are strict liability offences: *R. v. Sathialingam*, 2016 ONCJ 703, 2016 CarswellOnt 19182, [2016] O.J. No. 6250 (Ont. C.J.).

4.3 *CHARTER* ISSUES IN CLASSIFYING OFFENCES

Section 7 of the *Charter* states: "Every person has the right to life, liberty and security of the person and the right not to be deprived thereof except in accordance with the principles of fundamental justice".

- It is a principle of fundamental justice that the morally innocent should not be convicted. *An absolute liability offence, which can punish those who did not intend to commit the act, and even those who take all reasonable precautions not to commit the act, can punish the morally innocent. See: Reference re s. 94(2) of the Motor Vehicle Act (British Columbia) (1985), 48 C.R. (3d) 289, 23 C.C.C. (3d) 289, [1985] 2 S.C.R. 486, 69 B.C.L.R. 145, 36 M.V.R. 240, [1986] 1 W.W.R. 481 (S.C.C.).*

- An absolute liability offence is only contrary to *Charter* section 7, however, where the defendant's "liberty" is at stake. *Courts generally only see liberty at stake when there is a possibility of imprisonment or probation upon conviction. If punishment for the offence does not include the possibility of imprisonment, then even though a morally innocent defendant may be convicted, his or her section 7 Charter right is likely not breached.*

- If an absolute liability offence breaches section 7 of the *Charter*, and if it is not a reasonable limit under section 1 of the *Charter*, then by virtue of section 52(1), the offence is unconstitutional and of no force or effect.

- However, courts are loathe to render provincial statutes of no force or effect. *More likely, where prison is a possibility, the court will interpret what might otherwise be an absolute liability offence as a strict liability offence, thereby keeping it constitutional. That way, the defendant can still prove (on a balance of probabilities) that he or she is morally innocent (because he or she took reasonable care). See: R. v. Rube*

(1992), 75 C.C.C. (3d) 575, [1992] 3 S.C.R. 159, 74 B.C.L.R. (2d) 1, [1993] 1 W.W.R. 385 (S.C.C.).

4.4 CONCLUSION

- Research the law on the section of the statute with which your client is charged.
  - Is it a *mens rea* offence?
  - Is it strict liability?
  - Is it absolute liability?
- If the offence is absolute liabilty, and if there is a possibility of prison, consider challenging the law as unconstitutional. However, be prepared for the court to re-interpret the offence as strict liability so that it remains constitutional.
- Note that in some statutes, such as the *Highway Traffic Act* of Ontario, all three types of offences may be charged, such as speeding and failing to stop for a red light or stop sign, which are absolute liability offences; willfully avoiding the police while being pursued, which is a *mens rea* offence; and strict liability offences like careless driving and driving while suspended.
- For a list of offences which have been classified in these various categories, see *Libman on Regulatory Offences in Canada* (Saltspring Island B.C.: Earlscourt Legal Press, 2002): Chapter 4.3 — Examples of *Mens Rea* Offences, Chapter 5.6 — Examples of Absolute Liability Offences, Chapter 6.5 — Examples of Strict Liability Offences.

5

PROCEDURAL ISSUES

5.1 JURISDICTIONAL DEFENCES

5.1.1 TIMING

- Jurisdictional defences should be raised before your client pleads. In effect, you are challenging the right of the court to hear the case.

Where the defendant was served with a notice of trial, but the court house was closed on the trial date due to a power failure, the court regained jurisdiction over the person by mailing out a fresh notice of trial. It is apparent that the legislative intent of the *Provincial Offences Act* was to ensure that technical objections do not impede the arrival of a verdict on the merits, and that it was intended to be a speedy, efficient and convenient way of dealing with provincial offences matters. See: *York (Regional Municipality) v. Scarcello*, 2004 CarswellOnt 6077, (*sub nom.* R. v. Scarcello) [2004] O.J. No. 1002 (Ont. S.C.J.).

5.1.2 TERRITORIAL JURISDICTION

- Proceedings shall be heard in the county or district in which the offence occurred, or in an adjoining county or district if the court's sittings are reasonably close to where the offence occurred (provided that the adjoining place of sitting is named in the summons or offence notice): section 29.

- The court may transfer the proceedings to any other territory upon motion by the defendant or prosecutor, if it is in the interests of justice to do so: section 29(4).

- Some provincial acts allow trials in places other than where the offence occurred. *For example, under section 68 of the Occupational Health and Safety Act, R.S.O. 1990, c. O.1, the informant may elect trial in the county or district in which the accused is resident or carries on business.*

In *R. v. Fortese* (September 25, 2008), Ferguson J., [2008] O.J. No. 5159 (Ont. S.C.J.), it was held that a police officer has jurisdiction to lay a charge for an offence committed anywhere in Ontario. There is no provision in the *Provincial Offences*

Act that requires a proceeding to be commenced in the county, district or regional municipality where the offence occurred. The place of the offence only becomes relevant if the defendant appears and disputes the charge, in which case the court must consider the possible application of s. 29 governing the venue of the proceeding. However, where the defendant fails to appear for trial, the justice was required to proceed in the defendant's absence and enter a conviction and impose sentence pursuant to s. 9.1. If the court does nothing, when it is required to act, the court commits jurisdictional error.

The location of an offence as particularized in the information is an essential averment. A court cannot legitimately have territorial jurisdiction over a matter unless it knows where the offence took place. In the instant case, the intersection of Queen Street West and Bathurst is a well-known main intersection in downtown Toronto that is capable of immediate and accurate demonstration by resorting to readily accessible sources of indisputable accuracy, and may be judicially noticed by a trial justice without further proof. Any other approach would disregard the plain realities of the situation. See *R. v. Irving*, 2012 ONCJ 234, 2012 CarswellOnt 4914 (Ont. C.J.).

In *R. v. Howse*, 2012 ONCJ 517, 2012 CarswellOnt 9877, 37 M.V.R. (6th) 327, [2012] O.J. No. 3772 (Ont. C.J.), it was held that s. 29 starts with the presumption that, as in the instant case, the trial shall take place at the court sitting in the county or district where the offence occurred. However, s. 29(2) states that a trial may take place in an adjoining county or district when it is reasonably convenient to hold the trial there and the notice of trial directs the defendant to that court location. Offences that take place within a short distance of a boundary between two municipalities, as in the case of offences on a common road, may in any event be prosecuted in either municipality.

The Canadian Forces Military Police Officer did not have authority to issue a violation ticket to the defendant for proceeding through a red light except on lands owned or occupied by the Department of National Defence. See *R. v. Hubert*, 2012 BCPC 459, 2012 CarswellBC 4155, [2012] B.C.J. No. 2786 (B.C. Prov. Ct.).

The trial of the offence committed in St. Catharines was held in Welland due to the availability of trial dates in Welland. There was nothing to suggest an unfairness resulted because the trial was held in Welland. Both locations were in the District of Niagara. See *R. v. Adan* (August 24, 2015), Doc. St. Catharines 2111-999-00-4283824A-00, [2015] O.J. No. 5711 (Ont. C.J.).

5.1.3 LIMITATION PERIODS

- A limitation period begins to run from the moment that the offence has ceased. If the offence continues over a period of time (for example, an ongoing pollution offence), the limitation period begins from the moment of the last offending behaviour.

- The issue involving the breach or observance of the limitation period for the commencement of proceedings against the defendant, including applying the discoverability rule, is a question of fact which ought to be left to the trial judge. See: *R. v. Windsor Utilities Commission* (2005), [2005] O.J. No. 474, 2005 CarswellOnt 493, 13 C.E.L.R. (3d) 156 (Ont. S.C.J.), affirmed (2005), [2005] O.J. No. 3370, 2005 CarswellOnt 3513 (Ont. C.A.).

In determining the six month limitation period that applies to the *Child and Family Services Act* offence of failing to report suspicion of harm to a child forthwith, the interpretation placed on the provision should be the one that best promotes the purpose of the Act which is the protection of children. The interpretation that best ensures that childcare workers understand that their obligation is to report any suspicion forthwith is the one that emphasizes the timeliness of the report. The offence in question is a single offence, rather than a continuing offence, and the limitation period thus starts on the date that the alleged harm took place, and not the date when it came to light: *R. v. Newton-Thompson*, [2009] O.J. No. 2161, 2009 CarswellOnt 2973, 2009 ONCA 449, 244 C.C.C. (3d) 338, 249 O.A.C. 320, 67 C.R. (6th) 243, (*sub nom.* Ontario (Attorney General) v. Newton-Thompson) 97 O.R. (3d) 112 (Ont. C.A.).

A specific enactment specifying that there was to be no limitation period under the *Workplace Safety and Insurance Act* is not the same as a situation "where no limitation period is prescribed." There was no limitation period for prosecuting an offence under s. 149 of the legislation, hence the six month limitation period under s 76 of the *Provincial Offences Act* did not apply since the statute specifically addressed limitation periods: *R. v. Commercial Spring & Tool Co.*, [2009] O.J. No. 3839, 2009 CarswellOnt 5589 (Ont. S.C.J.).

(a) In the Charging Act

- Many provincial statutues contain limitation periods, beyond which no charge can be laid. For example,

- Under the *Occupational Health and Safety Act, supra,* section 69 prohibits any prosecution more than one year after the last act or default.

- Under the *Dangerous Goods Transportation Act,* R.S.O. 1990, c. D.1, section 4(3) prohibits any prosecution more than two years after the date of the alleged offence.

- Under the *Ontario Water Resources Act,* R.S.O. 1990, c. O.40, section 94 prohibits any prosecution more than two years after (a) the day on which the offence was committed; and (b) the day on which evidence of the offence first came to the attention of a Director (Provincial Officer) appointed under the Act.

In *R. v. Martin Grove Properties Ltd.,* 2011 ONCA 711, 90 M.P.L.R. (4th) 226, 2011 CarswellOnt 12226, [2011] O.J. No. 4992 (Ont. C.A.), leave to appeal refused 2012 CarswellOnt 6765, 2012 CarswellOnt 6766, 426 N.R. 389 (note), 302 O.A.C. 397 (note) (S.C.C.), it was held that the subject matter of the proceedings for the purpose of the *Building Code Act* was the failure to comply with the order made in March, 2008, and the omission of which took place at the earliest after May, 2008, when the defendant allegedly failed to comply with the terms of the order. The charge, which was laid in January, 2009, was therefore laid within the one year statutory limitation period. The fact that there were other orders issued related to the same underlying acts of the defendant might be relevant to an argument that the prosecution was an abuse of process, but did not preclude the municipality from instituting the prosecution. The fact that the municipality had other remedies for failure to comply with orders did not preclude resort to prosecution.

The offence of failing to comply with a property standards order is such that, if the trial court finds that the order was not complied with by the governing date or dates set out therein, it would be open to find that the offence was a continuing one. When the officer did a further inspection of the property and determined that compliance with the order remained outstanding at that time, charging the defendants with the offence four months later was well within the limitation period allowed. See *Oshawa (City) v. Carter* (December 21, 2012), Rosenberg J., [2012] O.J. No. 6291 (Ont. C.J.).

In *Pigeon v. Ontario (Ministry of Natural Resources),* 2014 ONSC 236, 2014 CarswellOnt 297, [2014] O.J. No. 134 (Ont. S.C.J.), it was held that where the defendant was charged with transporting an animal taken in contravention of a statute or regulation from one province or territory to another, contrary to s. 7(2) of the federal *Wild Animal and Plant Protection and Regulation of International Trade Act,* an Ontario court has jurisdiction to determine, according to the evidence, whether wildlife was killed in Nunavut or the Northwest Territories, contrary to the law of those jurisdictions. The fact that the limitation period has expired in those two jurisdictions does not prohibit an Ontario court from determining whether an offence took place outside Ontario for the purposes of a prosecution in Ontario.

(b) In the POA, Section 76

- Where no limitation period is prescribed in the charging Act, the limitation period is six months after the date of the alleged offence.

- A limitation may be extended by a justice with the consent of the defendant.

- In some cases, the defendant may consider it to be in his/her interests to consent to the extension of a limitation period under section 76 of the *Provincial Offences Act*. An example is where a driving charge under the *Criminal Code* will be withdrawn in exchange for a guilty plea to a driving offence under a provincial statute, such as the *Highway Traffic Act*. The prosecutor's consent is also required in such a situation: see section 45(4) of the *Provincial Offences Act*.

The word "proceeding" which is not defined in the *Provincial Offences Act* does not mean trial, such that all trials in the Provincial Offences Court must take place within six months of the date of the alleged offence occurring. "Proceeding" in the context of limitations law, means the entire case from the legal process that begins through to final disposition. The "commencement" of a proceeding is the issuance of process, in this case, by the police officer filing the certificate of offence. In this case, the certificate of offence was served on the date of the offence and filed within seven days thereafter, well within the six month limitation period. There was no limitations issue in the case and the Provincial Offences Court was correct to dismiss the applicant's preliminary motion. The proper course for the applicant to challenge the Justice's ruling dismissing his preliminary motion was an appeal to a Provincial Judge in the Ontario Court of Justice, and not by way of extraordinary equitable relief to the Superior Court of Justice. See *Torok v. Ontario*, 2015 ONSC 3100, 2015 CarswellOnt 7080, 336 O.A.C. 17, [2015] O.J. No. 2472 (Ont. Div. Ct.).

5.1.4 PROPER SERVICE

(a) Part I: Minor Offences

- A youth must be summoned (section95) within 30 days of the offence (section 3(3)) and a copy must be delivered to the youth's parent(s) (section 96).

- An adult defendant must be served with an offence notice or a summons to appear within 30 days of the offence: section 3(3).

- Proof of service may be:

  - Admitted by the defendant;

  - Certified by the provincial offences officer who issued the certificate of offence; or

  - By affidavit of service in the prescribed form: section 3(4-8).

In *R. v. Singh* (2000), 2000 CarswellOnt 5360, 16 M.V.R. (4th) 141 (Ont. C.J.), where the certificate of offence as filed included no proof of service on the defendant, it was held that the language of section 3 (5) is mandatory in requiring the issuing officer, who performed service of the certificate, to certify service on the certificate of offence. In the circumstances, the failure to comply with section 3(5) rendered the certificate incomplete, and irregular on its face for the purpose of section 9(1).

- There may be special rules for service under the particular charging Act.

Failure to serve the offence notice personally on the defendant is an irregularity only. Placing the ticket in the mailbox and drawing the defendant's attention to the ticket is sufficient service: *London (City) v. Erdesz*, [2009] O.J. No. 1008, 2009 CarswellOnt 1314 (Ont. S.C.J.).

(b) Part II: Parking Offences

- The provincial offences officer may serve the *owner* of the vehicle in two ways:

  - Affixing the notice in a conspicuous place at the time of the alleged infraction; or

- Delivering the notice personally to the person having care and control of the vehicle at the time of the alleged infraction: section 15(4).

- The provincial offences officer may serve the *operator* of the vehicle by delivering it to him or her personally at the time of the alleged infraction: section 15(5).

- The provincial offences officer shall certify on the certificate of parking infraction that the notice was served on the person charged with the date and method of service: section 15(6).

- If done so, the certificate is proof of service unless there is evidence to the contrary: section 15(7).

In *Toronto (City) v. Weingust*, 2006 ONCJ 23, 18 M.P.L.R. (4th) 182, 2006 CarswellOnt 461, [2006] O.J. No. 341 (Ont. C.J.), it was held that the provision of parking spaces on city streets is a reasonable and rational use of a service for which the city is permitted to charge a fee.

(c) Part III: Serious Offences

(i) Requirements of the Summons

- The defendant is ordered to appear in court by a summons. The summons shall:

  - Be directed to the defendant;

  - Set out briefly the offence; and

  - "Require the defendant to attend court at a time and place stated there in to attend there after as required by the court in order to be dealt with according to law": section 26(1).

While a provincial offences appeal court has the power to grant an award of costs, such orders are not ordinarily granted. Although s. 34 of the *Provincial Offences Act* gives the prosecutor the ability to seek, and the court the power to grant, an amendment to an Information, an amendment to change the name of the defendant is not contemplated by this provision. Section 26 requires that a defendant must be named in and served with a summons setting out the charge against it. Section 54 provides that a defendant can be convicted *in absentia* where the prosecutor proves that the summons or notice of trial was served on the defendant. Amending the Information to change the name of the defendant in the absence of the defendant runs contrary to these provisions. At the very least, the prosecutor should have

223

requested an adjournment of the trial to properly serve a summons or notice of trial on the defendant. In failing to do so, the prosecutor carelessly disregarded the procedural safeguards afforded to the defendant under the *Provincial Offences Act*. Section 129(a) grants the court discretion to make any order with respect to costs that it considers "just and reasonable". In this case the defendant was convicted without ever being issued a summons or served with a notice that it had ever been charged; it had no opportunity to argue at trial whether it should have been named as a defendant, or given an opportunity to defend the charge on its merits. In addition, through no fault of its own, it was required to retain counsel to bring the appeal and have the conviction quashed. In the unusual circumstances of the case, fairness demanded that the defendant be relieved of the financial burden of the costs of the appeal and application by being fully compensated. See *R. v. 1820419 Ontario Inc.*, 2013 ONCJ 10, 2013 CarswellOnt 275, [2013] O.J. No. 143 (Ont. C.J.).

(ii) Service of the Summons *Before* an Information is Laid

- A provincial offences officer may serve a person with a summons in the prescribed form before an information is laid where:

  - An offence was committed; and

  - The officer believes, on reasonable and probable grounds, that the person whom the officer finds at or near the place where the offence was committed, committed the offence: section 22.

(iii) Service of the Summons *After* an Information is Laid

- Where an information is laid before serving a summons:

  - The justice shall issue a summons in the prescribed form: section 24(1)(a).

  - The summons shall be served by a provincial offences officer by:
    - Delivering it personally to the person to whom it is directed, or
    - If that person cannot conveniently be found, by leaving it for the person at the person's last known or usual place of abode with an inmate thereof who appears to be at least 16 years of age: section 26(2).

(iv) Additional Means of Service *After* an Information is Laid

- Where the person does not reside in Ontario, the summons shall be deemed to have been duly served seven days after it has been sent by registered mail to the person's last known or usual place of abode: section 26(3).

- Service on a corporation may be effected by delivering the summons personally (section 26(4-6)):

  - In the case of a municipal corporation, to the mayor, warden, reeve or other executive officer of the corporation or person apparently in charge of a branch thereof.

  - In the case of any other corporation, to the manager, secretary or other executive officer of the corporation or person apparently in charge of a branch thereof; or

  - By mailing the summons by registered mail to the corporation at an address held out by the corporation to be its address, in which case the summons shall be deemed to have been duly served seven days after the day of mailing.

  - A justice may, upon motion and upon being satisfied that service cannot be effectively made on a corporation in the above manner, authorize another method of service that has are as on able likelihood of coming to the attention of the corporation.

- Service of a summons may be proved by statement under oath or affirmation.

- For a youth, a copy of the summons must be delivered to the parent(s): section 96.

5.2 CONSTITUTIONAL DEFENCES

- Under the *Constitution Act* (British North America Act), only the federal government can create criminal offences. If a provincial offence is in pith and substance criminal, then it is un-constitutional and the defendant cannot be convicted.

- Provinces, however, can prohibit conduct which is incidentally criminal if the purpose of the law is to regulate a provincial power. For example, the *Ontario Securities Act*, R.S.O. 1990, c. S.5, s. 122, as amended, creates offences regarding the misrepresentation of securities information. These offences may incidentally be criminal fraud, especially where the defendant knowingly or recklessly disseminated false information. However, the purpose of the provincial offences is to regulate the securities industry, which is a provincial power, and so the offences are constitutional.

- The offence of soliciting a stopped car while on a roadway, pursuant to the *Safe Streets Act*or section 177 of the *Highway Traffic Act*, constitutes valid provincial legislation, regulating the interaction of pedestrians and vehicles on the roadways, in the interests of public safety, efficient circulation, and public enjoyment of public thorough fares. *R. v. Banks*, 2007 CarswellOnt 111, 39 M.V.R. (5th) 1, [2007] O.J. No. 99, 220 O.A.C. 211, 150 C.R.R. (2d) 239, 216 C.C.C. (3d) 19, 2007 ONCA 19, 275 D.L.R. (4th) 640, 44 C.R. (6th) 244, 84 O.R. (3d) 1 (Ont. C.A.) (Ont. C.A.), leave to appeal refused (2007), 2007 CarswellOnt 5670, 2007 CarswellOnt 5671, [2007] S.C.C.A. No. 139, 156 C.R.R. (2d) 376 (note) (S.C.C.).

In *R. v. Sibernagel*, 2000 BCCA 251, 2000 CarswellBC 764, 139 B.C.A.C. 7, 227 W.A.C. 7 (B.C. C.A.), leave to appeal refused (2000), 2000 CarswellBC 2171, 2000 CarswellBC 2172, 263 N.R. 396 (note), 151 B.C.A.C. 160 (note), 249 W.A.C. 160 (note) (S.C.C.), the Court of Appeal found that the justice of the peace was not bound as a matter of stare decisis by co-ordinate orders of other justices of local jurisdiction in respect of a constitutional issue. Absent authority from above, a finding as to constitutionality was properly made on a case-by-case basis.

5.2.1 NOTICE OF CONSTITUTIONAL CHALLENGE

- Serve a notice of challenge on the Attorney General, the prosecutors' office, and the court with proof of service, should you wish to challenge the constitutional validity or applicability of a provincial law.

- Do this as soon as practicable, and in any event, no later than 15 days before trial. (See *Courts of Justice Act*, R.S.O. 1990, c. C.43, s. 109, as amended.)

- As the notice requirements under section 109(1) are mandatory, it is inappropriate for the justice of the peace to summarily dispense with service of the notice as he or she lacks jurisdiction to waive these procedural requirements.

See: *R. v. Dickson*, [2004] O.J. No. 4710, 2004 CarswellOnt 4794, 2004 ONCJ 279 (Ont. C.J.).

The parties must make sure all the relevant documents are properly before the court, including affidavits which are signed. In one recent case, the trial judge was found to have erred in dismissing the defendant's constitutional challenge on the basis that the defendant's affidavit was not properly executed and signed: *R. v. Bodik*, 2008 CarswellOnt 1948 (Ont. C.J.).

Where the Notice of Constitutional Question was not served properly or within the time limits prescribed by the legislation, the court considered there was no reason to make any rulings on the validity of the specific requests in the order sought, and the defendant's constitutional challenge was denied: *R. v. Harizanov*, 2008 ONCJ 690, 2008 CarswellOnt 8208, [2008] O.J. No. 5430 (Ont. C.J.).

Where a by-law or statutory provisions is being attacked for its constitutionality, the s. 109 notice requirement must be fulfilled; otherwise, a challenged law cannot be adjudged invalid nor a remedy granted if this requisite notice is not given: *Adult Entertainment Assn. of Canada v. Ottawa (City)* (2007), 156 C.R.R. (2d) 61, 283 D.L.R. (4th) 704, 224 O.A.C. 267, 2007 CarswellOnt 3190, 2007 ONCA 389, [2007] O.J. No. 2021, 33 M.P.L.R. (4th) 1 (Ont. C.A.); *Toronto (City) v. Zanzibar Tavern Inc.*, [2007] O.J. No. 3381, 2007 CarswellOnt 5642, 2007 ONCJ 401, 37 M.P.L.R. (4th) 216 (Ont. C.J.).

The trial justice of the peace erred in granting the defendant's motion at trial to give constitutional relief with respect to the stunt driving provisions of the *Highway Traffic Act* in the absence of not only any notice to the prosecution as required by the *Courts of Justice Act*, but in effect without any legal argument on the merits. The prosecution was entitled to rely on the notice provisions of the *Courts of Justice Act*, which not only go to the issue of proper notice, but would have resulted in a proper foundation, including legal argument being put before the court: *R. v. De Sousa*, 2010 ONCJ 207, 2010 CarswellOnt 4242, [2010] O.J. No. 2529 (Ont. C.J.).

In *R. v. Vellone*, 284 O.A.C. 388, 2011 CarswellOnt 14646, 2011 ONCA 785, 108 O.R. (3d) 481, 25 M.V.R. (6th) 1, 250 C.R.R. (2d) 351, [2011] O.J. No. 5708 (Ont. C.A.), it was held that by virtue of s. 95(3) of the *Courts of Justice Act*, the s. 109 requirement that parties give prior notice of constitutional questions and remedies applies to proceedings under the *Provincial Offences Act*. The wording of s. 109 and the *Courts of Justice Act* parallels the wording of of s. 32(1) of the *Charter of Rights*. Section 109 refers to the Government of Canada and the Government of Ontario; the Supreme Court has consistently held that municipal levels of government come within the meaning of "government" in s. 32(1) of the

Charter. Against this back drop of statutory wording and case law, the term "Government of Ontario" in s. 109 of the *Courts of Justice Act* should be construed to parallel s. 32(1)(b) of the *Charter* as it would not make sense to say that *Charter* s. 32(1) includes municipal action as action of the Government of Ontario, but s. 109 of the *Courts of Justice Act* does not. The component of s.109 requiring people in the position of the defendant, who was charged with a speeding ticket and prosecuted by a municipality, to notify the Attorney General of Ontario of his s. 11(b) *Charter* challenge serves a number of important purposes. The notice requirement enables the Government of Ontario to decide whether to exercise its right to take over a case under the *Provincial Offences Act*; it also furthers the Government of Ontario's important interest in monitoring the performance of municipalities under memoranda of Understanding. Notice to the Attorney General of Ontario of a s. 11(b) challenge, or an avalanche of such notices, provides the Government of Ontario with important data about key components of the provincial justice system. The appeal judge therefore erred by holding that the defendant did not need to provide notice of his *Charter* s. 11(b) claim to the Attorney General of Ontario pursuant to s. 109 of the *Courts of Justice Act*. **Note:** The Court of Appeal did not address the different issue in the *Vellone* case of notice to the municipal prosecutor. It did note, however, that the Law Commission of Ontario, in its Final Report on *Modernizing the Provincial Offences Act: A New Framework and Other Reforms* (Toronto: Law Commission of Ontario, 2011) , has recommended that s. 109 of the *Courts of Justice Act* be amended so that it requires service of a Notice of Constitutional Question on prosecutors in all *Provincial Offences Act* matters, and that a Notice of Constitutional Question be served on a municipal prosecutor when a party seeks relief under s. 24(1) of the *Charter of Rights* relating to an act or omission of a municipality.

Neither of the grounds sought to be raised by the defendant in the leave application concerning the section of the *Highway Traffic Act* under which he should have been charged, and the requirement that traffic signs in the City of Toronto should be bilingual, had been raised at trial. He also had not served a notice of constitutional question challenging the constitutionality of the *French Languages Services Act*. See *R. v. Petruzzo*, 2011 ONCA 386, 2011 CarswellOnt 3239, [2011] O.J. No. 2203, 11 M.V.R. (6th) 201, 278 O.A.C. 130 (Ont. C.A. [In Chambers]).

The Ministry of the Attorney General of Canada does not have to be served with a Notice of Constitutional Question on a *Highway Traffic Act* (Ont.) charge alleging a s. 11(b) *Charter* application breach. It is not an application to strike down legislation, in which case notice would be required: *R. v. Szewczyk*, 2014 ONCJ 467, 2014 CarswellOnt 12597, [2014] O.J. No. 4294 (Ont. C.J.).

5.2.2 VOID FOR VAGUENESS DEFENCE

- It is a principle of fundamental justice that citizens be able to foresee whether their conduct might be illegal. If an offence is too vague, then it is in effect nothing but governmental discretion cloaked in legal terminology.

However, in *Canada v. Pharmaceutical Society (Nova Scotia)*, 15 C.R. (4th) 1, (*sub nom.* R. v. Nova Scotia Pharmaceutical Society) [1992] 2 S.C.R. 606, (*sub nom.* R. v. Nova Scotia Pharmaceutical Society) 74 C.C.C. (3d) 289 (S.C.C.). Justice Gonthier cautioned against using too rigorous a standard for legislative clarity. In some situations, valid governmental legislation cannot be straight-jacketed "by requiring the law to achieve a degree of precision to which the subject-matter does not lend itself" (at 313). See also: *Reference re ss. 193 and 195(1)(c) of the Criminal Code (Canada)*, 56 C.C.C. (3d) 65, 77 C.R. (3d) 1, [1990] 1 S.C.R. 1123, [1990] 4 W.W.R. 481 (S.C.C.).

- Generally, provided the law delineates an area of risk which can be determined by a reasoned analysis of previous court judgments, the law is sufficiently clear (*Nova Scotia, supra,* at 311).

The definition of "pit bull" under the Ontario legislation banning pit bulls was held to be sufficient to delineate the area of risk, and provide a sufficient basis for intelligible debate and interpretation: *Cochrane v. Ontario (Attorney General)*, 179 C.R.R. (2d) 310, 242 O.A.C. 192, 61 C.R. (6th) 374, 2008 ONCA 718, 2008 CarswellOnt 6229, 92 O.R. (3d) 321, 301 D.L.R. (4th) 414, [2008] O.J. No. 4165 (Ont. C.A.), leave to appeal refused, [2009] S.C.C.A. No. 105, 2009 CarswellOnt 3390, 2009 CarswellOnt 3389, 262 O.A.C. 395 (note), 398 N.R. 398 (note) (S.C.C.).

In another Ontario case, a municipal by-law regulating adult entertainment parlours was held not to be unconstitutionally vague. In the court's view, there was no basis for concluding that the by-law was so lacking in precision "as not to give sufficient guidance for legal debate." Moreover, the by-law did sufficiently limit law enforcement discretion since physical contact between dancers and patrons was prohibited while services were being provided. Hence, there was no need to interpret what conduct constituted an offence: *Toronto (City) v. Zanzibar Tavern Inc.*, [2007] O.J. No. 3381, 2007 CarswellOnt 5642, 2007 ONCJ 401, 37 M.P.L.R. (4th) 216 (Ont. C.J.).

There is no fundamental right to ride a motorcycle as one would like to without any limits. A regulation limiting the heights of handle bars for the purposes of public safety is neither void for vagueness nor contrary to the principles of fundamental justice: *Waterloo (Regional Municipality) v. Hampton*, 2012 ONCJ 838, 2012 CarswellOnt 17281, [2012] O.J. No. 6418 (Ont. C.J.).

In *Mississauga (City) v. 1094388 Ontario Ltd.*, 2014 ONCJ 674, 2014 CarswellOnt 19114, 325 C.R.R. (2d) 128, [2014] O.J. No. 6061 (Ont. C.J.), the court ruled that deciding whether a regulatory law is impermissibly vague should generally be considered after the evidence is heard in a regulatory prosecution, and only in rare and exceptional cases should the vagueness question be considered in a motion to quash the information before any evidence is heard.

5.2.3 *CHARTER OF RIGHTS* DEFENCES

- The *Charter of Rights* is the supreme law of Canada. Any in consistent law is, to the extent of the inconsistency, of no force and effect: *Charter*, section 52(1).

- Some of the rights in the *Charter* which maybe impinged by a provincial law are:

  - Freedom of conscience and religion: *Charter*, section 2(a).

In *R. v. Westover*, 2013 ONCJ 472, 2013 CarswellOnt 11933, 49 M.V.R. (6th) 336, [2013] O.J. No. 3904 (Ont. C.J.), it was held that the regulation of the highway sin Ontario is a necessary function of government. As a result, any infringement of rights and freedoms, including freedom of religion, association or movement that might occur in regard to this *Charter* s. 2(a) right was justifiable under s. 1. As a result, even if the accused had a sincere religious belief that he should not abide by the rules and regulations related to motor vehicles and highways, and thus not have a proper validation sticker for his motor vehicle, he was not exempt from the licensing requirements under the *Highway Traffic Act* (Ont.).

  - Freedom of thought, belief, opinion and expression, including freedom of the press and other media of communication: *Charter*, section 2(b).

In *R. v. Glad Day Bookshops Inc.* (2004), [2004] O.J. No. 1766, 2004 CarswellOnt 1688, 239 D.L.R. (4th) 119, 118 C.R.R. (2d) 209, 183 C.C.C. (3d) 449, 70 O.R. (3d) 691 (Ont. S.C.J.), the defendant was charged with distributing an adult sex film that was not approved by the Ontario Film Review Board (OFRB) pursuant to the *Theatre Act* and Regulations. The charges were dismissed as the statutory scheme requiring prior approval of the films was overly broad in applying to expressive material, and thereby violated section 2(b) of the *Charter*. In response to this decision, the Regulations under the *Theatres Act* were amended as of July 5, 2004, and narrowed the criteria the OFRB could use to review and approve film.

In *Smiley v. Ottawa (City)*, 2012 ONCJ 479, 2012 CarswellOnt 9222, 100 M.P.L.R. (4th) 306, [2012] O.J. No. 3391 (Ont. C.J.), it was held that issuing trespass notices to occupiers of a federal park managed by the National Capital Commission did not amount to an infringement of the protesters' *Charter* s. 2(b) and (c) rights that could not be justified under s. 1 While the expressive activity of the defendants conformed to the intent of furthering their *Charter* rights, values and purposes, usage of public parks must be balanced with the larger community's use of the park and facilities, and the larger issues of health and safety. Protesters can access public parks, as any citizen, during the normal hours of operation of the public place to express them selves, but are subject to reasonable limits such as the bylaws prescribed. Although the location may have been opportune for the protesters, the occupation interrupted the lawful use of the property by downtown workers, local residents, tourists to the city, and any other park user. Such a use is not only important to the park authority, it is very important to citizens and visitors to the Nation's Capital in the very core of the city.

- Freedom of peaceful assembly: *Charter*, section 2(c).

In *R. v. Behrens*, [2004] O.J. No. 5135, 2004 CarswellOnt 5315, 2004 ONCJ 327,126 C.R.R. (2d) 50 (Ont. C.J.), the defendants were convicted under the *Trespass to Property Act* for taking part in a demonstration at Queen's Park, after being served with trespass notices following an early demonstration. A recognized category of parliamentary privilege was the ejection of "strangers" from the legislature and its grounds. The issue of trespass notices fell under the Speaker's parliamentary privilege, and the court lacked any jurisdiction to review that action, even on the basis of a *Charter* argument that a conviction would be an infringement of their *Charter* freedom of peaceful assembly right.

In *Smiley v. Ottawa (City)*, 2012 ONCJ 479, 2012 CarswellOnt 9222, 100 M.P.L.R. (4th) 306, [2012] O.J. No. 3391 (Ont. C.J.), it was held that issuing trespass notices to occupiers of a federal park managed by the National Capital Commission did not amount to an infringement of the protesters' *Charter* s. 2(b) and (c) rights that could not be justified under s. 1 While the expressive activity of the defendants conformed to the intent of furthering their *Charter* rights, values and purposes, usage of public parks must be balanced with the larger community's use of the park and facilities, and the larger issues of health and safety. Protesters can access public parks, as any citizen, during the normal hours of operation of the public place to express them selves, but are subject to reasonable limits such as the bylaws prescribed. Although the location may have been opportune for the protesters, the occupation interrupted the lawful use of the property by downtown workers, local residents, tourists to the city, and any other park user. Such a use is not only important to the park authority, it is very important to citizens and visitors to the Nation's Capital in the very core of the city.

- Freedom of association: *Charter*, section 2(d).

- Life, liberty and security of the person and the right not to be deprived thereof except in accordance with the principles of fundamental justice: *Charter*, section 7.

- Equal protection and equal benefit of the law without discrimination, except for laws designed to assist the disadvantaged: *Charter*, section 15.

Where legislation is intended to promote the safe use of public places without the danger or harassment posed by the interaction with those who solicit in an aggressive manner, such provisions do not have the effect of restricting expression with in the meaning of section 2(b) of the *Charter*. See *Safe Streets Act, 1999*, S.O. 1999, c. 8.

The prohibition against aggressive solicitation of persons on streets under the *Safe Streets Act, 1999*, and on roadways under subsection 177(2) of the *Highway Traffic Act* was not in violation of freedom of expression under section 2(d) of the *Charter*. See *R. v. Banks* (2005), [2005] O.J. No. 98, 2005 CarswellOnt 115, 17 M.V.R. (5th) 93, 126 C.R.R. (2d) 189, 248 D.L.R. (4th) 118, 192 C.C.C. (3d) 289, 27 C.R. (6th) 296 (Ont. S.C.J.), affirmed, 2007 CarswellOnt 111, 39 M.V.R. (5th) 1, [2007] O.J. No. 99, 220 O.A.C. 211, 150 C.R.R. (2d) 239, 216 C.C.C. (3d) 19, 2007 ONCA 19, 275 D.L.R. (4th) 640, 44 C.R. (6th) 244, 84 O.R. (3d) 1 (Ont. C.A.), leave to appeal refused (2007), 2007 CarswellOnt 5670, 2007 CarswellOnt 5671, [2007] S.C.C.A. No. 139, 156 C.R.R. (2d) 376 (note) (S.C.C.), reversing (2001), 55 O.R. (3d) 374, 2001 CarswellOnt 2757, 45 C.R. (5th) 23, 86 C.R.R. (2d) 104, 205 D.L.R. (4th) 340 (Ont. C.J.).

- *For the right against unreasonable search and seizure, and the right to counsel, see Chapter 10.*

In *Cochrane v. Ontario (Attorney General)*, [2008] O.J. No. 4165, 2008 CarswellOnt 6229, 301 D.L.R. (4th) 414, 92 O.R. (3d) 321, 2008 ONCA 718, 61 C.R. (6th) 374, 242 O.A.C. 192, 179 C.R.R. (2d) 310 (Ont. C.A.), leave to appeal refused 2009 CarswellOnt 3389, 2009 CarswellOnt 3390, [2009] S.C.C.A. No. 105, 262 O.A.C. 395 (note), 398 N.R. 398 (note) (S.C.C.), the province's legislation banning pit bull dogs was up held in the face of a number of constitutional challenges under the *Charter*. One issue concerned the admissibility under s. 19(1) of the Act of a document from a veterinarian stating that the dog was a pit bull as proof of that fact, in the absence of evidence to the contrary. In rejecting an attack on this provision as a violation of the presumption of innocence, the court stated that this provision did not amount to a legal prescription which alters the burden of proof. Sections 39 and 46 of the *Provincial Offences Act* give trial judges a discretion to allow for cross-examination of the veterinarian who signed the certificate; it was to be assumed that this discretion would be exercised in a way that is consistent with *Charter* rights. There was no reason to suppose that leave to conduct a cross-examination of the veterinarian, if sought by the defendant, would be improperly denied.

Ontario's legislation banning pit bull dog attacks, which was upheld as constitutional by the Ontario Court of Appeal in *Cochrane v. Ontario (Attorney General)*, 179 C.R.R. (2d) 310, 242 O.A.C. 192, 61 C.R. (6th) 374, 2008 ONCA 718, 2008 CarswellOnt 6229, 92 O.R. (3d) 321, 301 D.L.R. (4th) 414, [2008] O.J. No. 4165 (Ont. C.A.) was the subject of an application for leave to appeal to the Supreme Court of Canada. The Supreme Court dismissed the application, thus preventing any further challenge to the legislation: [2009] S.C.C.A. No. 105, 2009 CarswellOnt 3390, 2009 CarswellOnt 3389, 262 O.A.C. 395 (note), 398 N.R. 398 (note) (S.C.C.).

When the Crown has come into possession of a defence document that is protected by solicitor-client and litigation privilege, prejudice will be presumed. The presumption is rebuttable by the Crown. In such circumstances, it does not necessarily follow that the charges should be stayed where a lesser remedy can solve the problem: *R. v. Bruce Power Inc.*, [2009] O.J. No. 3016, 98 O.R. (3d) 272, 254 O.A.C. 335, 245 C.C.C. (3d) 315, 2009 CarswellOnt 4157, 2009 ONCA 573 (Ont. C.A.).

The Crown is not prohibited from continuing its investigation during the trial if that is seen as necessary. However, there is a continuing obligation to disclose. The disclosure complaints raised by the defence atrial related to the timing of the disclosure, and did not fall within the category of those most serious violations which would warrant a stay of proceedings: *R. v. Vastis*, [2008] O.J. No. 354, 35 C.E.L.R. (3d) 109, 2008 CarswellOnt 861, 2008 ONCJ 44 (Ont. C.J.).

There is an obligation to disclose when additional information is received. Section 7 is not violated where disclosure was made and the Crown continued to respond to requests for disclosure, albeit not perfectly: *R. v. Rosso*, [2008] O.J. No. 5720, 2008 CarswellOnt 9038, 2008 ONCJ 756 (Ont. C.J.).

In *R. v. Hawdon*, 2014 CarswellOnt 5067 (Ont. C.J.), it was held that it is not up to the defence to make a request for disclosure more than once. Neither was it necessary for the defence to bring a motion for production as they were led to believe by the prosecutor that the disclosure requested was not available. The Justice was entitled to make finding of lack of disclosure once she heard the evidence of the investigating officer. The defence should have brought an application to stay the charge for non-disclosure rather than a motion to dismiss the charge. The Justice should not have dismissed the charge but granted a stay of proceedings due to non-disclosure.

The Ontario Court of Appeal has decided in *R. v. Michaud*, 2015 ONCA 585, 2015 CarswellOnt 13209, 127 O.R. (3d) 81, 328 C.C.C. (3d) 228, 22 C.R. (7th) 246, 82 M.V.R. (6th) 171, 341 C.R.R. (2d) 89, 339 O.A.C. 41, [2015] O.J. No. 4540 (Ont. C.A.), leave to appeal refused 2016 CarswellOnt 7197, 2016 CarswellOnt 7198 (S.C.C.) that truck speed limiters deprived the defendant of his rights to security of the person in a manner that violated one of the principles of fundamental justice, overbreadth. Truck speed limiters might be rational in some cases, but the legislation overreached in its effect in others. The government's goals in enacting the speed limiter legislation were to improve highway safety by preventing accidents and reducing the severity of collisions, and to reduce greenhouse gas emissions. Those objectives are pressing and substantial. There was proportionality between the deleterious and salutary effects of the legislation, since the public benefits associated with improved highway safety exceed the detrimental effects on the s. 7 rights of truck drivers. The breach of the defendant's s. 7 *Charter* right was therefore justified under s. 1.

There was no abuse of process as a result of a pattern of late disclosure or as a result of the Crown changing their trial tactics and witnesses which is an exercise of prosecutorial discretion. In addition, a mere allegation that other persons could or should be charged is insufficient to establish prosecutorial conduct amounting to an abuse of process. See *Ontario (Ministry of the Attorney General) v. McLellan*, 2015 ONCJ 165, 2015 CarswellOnt 15077, (*sub nom.* Ontario v. McLellan) 332 C.R.R. (2d) 1, [2015] O.J. No. 1562 (Ont. C.J.).

In *Niagara (Reg. Mun.) v. Busch*, 2017 ONCJ 547, 2017 CarswellOnt 12346, (*sub nom.* R. v. Busch) 394 C.R.R. (2d) 147, [2017] O.J. No. 4166 (Ont. C.J.), it was held that the defendant's right to a fair public hearing by an independent and impartial tribunal is achieved through his trial, and not during the police investigation leading to his charges.

5.3 SUFFICIENCY OF THE CHARGES

- Like jurisdictional defences, an objection to an information or certificate for a defect apparent on its face should be made *before* the defendant pleads: section 36(1).

- After the plea, the objection can only be raised with leave of the court: section 36(1).

- The court shall not quash an information or certificate unless an amendment or particulars would fail to satisfy the ends of justice: section 36(2): See Appendix A.

- The requirement to provide sufficient detail in the wording of a charge for a provincial offence is set out in section 25(6), the legislation which governs the prosecution of provincial offences in Ontario. If the wording of a charge for a provincial offence is not sufficiently detailed, a court may order the prosecution furnish particulars under section 35 where the court finds that it is necessary for a fair trial. For a recent case considering this issue, see *Toronto (City) v. Canada Land Corp.*, 2006 ONCJ 421, [2006] O.J. No. 4489, 2006 CarswellOnt 6959 (Ont. C.J.).

Where the defendant was charged with discharging effluent into water, contrary to s. 30(1) of the *Ontario Water Resources Act*, the information was not deficient but the prosecutor was required to provide particulars of water courses that may have been impaired, such that the information was more specific than "any waters in Ontario": *R. v. Inco Ltd.*, 2007 ONCJ 656, 2007 CarswellOnt 8854, [2007] O.J. No. 5212 (Ont. C.J.).

A certificate of offence which uses the prescribed words "being intoxicated in a public place" provides the defendants with reasonable information of the transactions alleged against them. The defendants had all the information they needed to make the decision as to whether to proceed to trial or let the proceedings go by default: *Thunder Bay (City) v. Kamenawatamin*, 2009 CarswellOnt 1873, [2009] O.J. No. 1422 (Ont. S.C.J.).

The short form wording on the certificate of offence was adequate to provide the necessary information to the defendant about the charge where it stated, "Permit operation of commercial motor vehicle not equipped with working speed limiting device" and referred to the charging section of the statute, but omitted to setout the regulation. See *Ontario (Ministry of Transportation) v. Don's Triple F Transport Inc.*, 2012 ONCA 536, 2012 CarswellOnt 9883, 291 C.C.C. (3d) 530, 38 M.V.R. (6th) 8, 295 O.A.C. 114, [2012] O.J. No. 3754 (Ont. C.A.).

In *Niagara (Regional Municipality) v. Kosyatchkov*, 2013 ONSC 713, 2013 CarswellOnt 992, [2013] O.J. No. 424 (Ont. S.C.J.), it was held that the legislation permits, but does not require the use of a prescribed word or phrase to describe the offence. If a prescribed word is used, the offence is sufficiently described. Since the prescribed word "speeding" was not written in this case, one of two things followed: the certificate had to meet the requirements of s.25 of the *Provincial Offences Act* governing counts in an information, or if it did not, the justice was obliged to amend it unless to do so would have failed to satisfy the ends of justice. The certificate in the case at bar did in fact provide sufficient detail of the circumstances of the alleged offence to give the defendant reasonable information with respect to the act or omission to be proved against the defendant and to identify the transaction referred to, and was thus in compliance with s. 25. An amendment, had one been required, would not have occasioned any prejudice. The certificate should not therefore have been quashed. Neither was any need for the justice to inquire into the matter in the first place. The defendant was appearing to defend the charge. Accordingly, sections 9 and 9.1 of the Act, which require a justice to examine the certificate before convicting an absent defendant who is not disputing the charge, or who is deemed not to dispute the charge, had no application. The defendant was represented, and had obviously given thought to how he wanted to proceed. There was no reason to depart from the normal procedure in which the party who complains of an inadequate information asks the court to quash it, amend it or order particulars.

The officer stroked out the title and certification box and fine boxes on the summons upon charging the defendant with a certificate of offence for careless driving. The stroking out of the fine box did not invalidate the document since the fine boxes were redundant as the defendant did not have the option of paying a fine on an out-of-court basis. As for the certification box, while the officer had an obligation to certify on the certificate that he had personally served the summons on the defendant, and stroking out the certification box removed his ability to certify service, he testified that he served the summons on the defendant. However, in striking out the title of the document, he fundamentally altered the substance of the prescribed Form 1 set out in the regulation. The removal of the title indicated that the officer intended it not to be a certificate of offence. As a result, the document before the court purporting to charge the defendant with careless driving was not a certificate of offence in Form 1, and the court had no jurisdiction to proceed on an invalid charge. See *R. v. Djurcik*, 2012 ONCJ 436, 2012 CarswellOnt 8757, [2012] O.J. No. 3211 (Ont. C.J.).

In *Ontario (Ministry of Labour) v. Nault*, 2018 ONCJ 321, 2018 CarswellOnt 7680, [2018] O.J. No. 2568 (Ont. C.J.), the court noted that in respect of the use of "short-form wording" or "abbreviated wording" to describe a particular regulatory offence, ss. 13(1)(b) and 13(2) of the *Provincial Offences Act* authorize the Lieutenant Governor in Council by regulation to specify a word or expression that can be used on a form, such as on a certificate of offence, to designate that offence, and that the specified word or expression, if used on the form, would be sufficient for all purposes to describe the offence designated by such word or expression. However, those statutory provisions do not require the compulsory use of that prescribed word or expression to describe the offence. In addition, where the regulations do not authorize the use of a word or expression (short-form wording) to describe an offence in a form, then by virtue of s. 13(3) the offence may be described in accordance with s. 25 of the Act. And in the situation where "short-form wording" has not been legally created to describe a particular regulatory offence, s. 25(3) specifically provides that where an offence is identified in a count, but the count fails to set out one or more of the essential elements of the offence, then a reference to the provision creating or defining the offence shall be deemed to incorporate all the essential elements of the offence. The present proceedings had been commenced with a Part I certificate of offence. The charge that had been laid in both of the defendants' certificates was identical and expressed as "worker operate equipment in a manner that may endanger himself or another worker." Under s. 3(2), a provincial offences officer may issue to an accused either an offence notice indicating the set fine for the offence or a summons without a set fine in respect to the Part I certificate of offence. The list of authorized "short-form wordings" for specific regulatory offences are those found and prescribed in O. Reg 950, for which s. 13(2) of the Act has authorized that the use of short-form wordings used in a charge set out in a certificate of offence is sufficient to describe that offence. Consequently, as the defendants were issued a summons setting out the charge in respect to a certificate of offence, then according to s. 5(1) of the regulation, a "short-form wording" may be used on the summons to describe the offence. However, in regard to the offence in question, there was no "short-form wording" that has been legally created to describe the particular charge under any of the *Occupational Health and Safety Act* schedules of charges. As such, where authorized short-form wordings do not exist for a particular regulatory offence, then the wording or expression used to describe the offence in the certificate of offence of "worker operate equipment in a manner that may endanger himself or another worker" has to comply with the requirements of s. 25 of the *Provincial Offences Act*, which sets out the standards for describing and providing the necessary information about the offence that the accused has been charged with committing. In that regard, the defendants had defended themselves at trial in regard to the charge on the basis that they were not actually operating equipment, namely a forklift, as had been specifically expressed in the charge in their respective certificates of offence. Therefore, in fairness to the defendants, and since the doctrine of surplusage did not apply and because no application to amend the charge had been brought by the prosecution, then the defendants' respective charges would be treated as having been particularized by the Ministry of Labour to one of those specific five circumstances set out under the section for which the provision can be contravened by a worker, namely of "operating or using equipment in a manner that may endanger the worker or others."

An appeal may be brought against the order of the justice of the peace dismissing the application to quash the information. This is to be distinguished from the case where the Superior Court declines to exercise its jurisdiction to hear an interlocutory appeal of a motion to quash, prior to the final disposition of the charge on the merits. There was no merit to the defendant's motion to quash the information. It had no foundation in law or fact, but nonetheless served to substantially lengthen the proceedings. The justice of the peace made no error of law. He correctly held that the amendments that came into force made no substantive change to the limitation period created under the *Insurance Act*, that the limitation period was based on when the knowledge underlying the offence first came to the attention of the Superintendent. He properly dismissed the application to quash because the information was laid within a period of two years of when the facts first came to the knowledge of the Superintendent. See *Ontario (Superintendent of Financial Services) v. Dies*, 2018 ONCJ 641, 2018 CarswellOnt 15738, [2018] O.J. No. 4894 (Ont. C.J.).

5.3.1 COMMON OBJECTIONS

- Common objections include:
  - That the charging document does not clearly identify the alleged wrong so the defendant can adequately prepare for full answer and defence. Furthermore, whatever the verdict, the defendant must be protected from being charged again for the same wrong — and so the offence must be clearly stated: See *R. v. WIS Development Corp.*, [1984] 1 S.C.R. 485, 31 Alta. L.R. (2d) 289, 40 C.R. (3d) 97, 12 C.C.C. (3d) 129 (S.C.C.).
  - The charging document should indicate the date, time and place of the offence.
  - The charging document shall set out each offence in separate counts.
  - The charging document must comply with the signing rules. For example, an information must be sworn, a certificate must be certified, etc.
- As for general requirements, see section 25 of the POA reproduced in Appendix A.

The prosecutor was entitled to proceed with the charge of failing to obey a traffic sign. There was no obligation to change the charging section to the more specific provision dealing with intersections: *R. v. Petruzzo*, 2011 ONCA 386, 2011

CarswellOnt 3239, [2011] O.J. No. 2203, 11 M.V.R. (6th) 201, 278 O.A.C. 130 (Ont. C.A. [In Chambers]).

The ticket issued to the defendant was not rendered invalid by its reference to an enactment that had been repealed and replaced by another statute. Thus the offence as particularized in the ticket did reference an appropriate authorized charge. However, the ticket was defective by failing to particularize the deficiency being alleged by the Crown: the defendant was entitled to know what specific inadequacy the Crown was alleging with regard to his tail lights, and the deficiency must be one of those set out in the statute. The provisions in the regulation did not allow for a shot gun or multiple approach to the charge. See *R. v. Pott*, 2011 SKQB 141, 2011 CarswellSask 237, [2011] S.J. No. 216, 12 M.V.R. (6th) 178, 372 Sask. R. 197 (Sask. Q.B.).

In *R. v. Lacroix*, 2011 ONCJ 270, 2011 CarswellOnt 3627, [2011] O.J. No. 2332 (Ont. C.J.), the charge indicated that the offence occurred on "Britannia Road" in the City of Mississauga whereas the correct name for the road was actually "Britannia Road West." However, an amendment could be made to remedy this defect. The amendment did not cause irremediable prejudice or cause injustice, since the defendant knew the road he was on at least contained the words "Britannia Road". Quashing the information or dismissing the charge due to the omission of the word "West" would in the circumstances cause injustice, considering the merits of the case.

In *R. v. Thomas G. Fuller & Sons Ltd.*, 2011 CarswellOnt 4459, (*sub nom.* Ontario (Minister of Labour) v. Black & McDonald Ltd.) 278 O.A.C. 284, (*sub nom.* Ontario (Ministry of Labour) v. Black & McDonald Ltd.) 106 O.R. (3d) 784, [2011] O.J. No. 2615, 2 C.L.R. (4th) 161, 2011 ONCA 440 (Ont. C.A.), the Court of Appeal rejected a challenge to the wording of the counts in an information. It held that the trial judge appeared to have confused a count that is duplicitous with a count that duplicates or overlaps another count. A count is duplicitous if it offends the single transaction rule, that is, it joins separate and distinct offences in the same count. This single transaction rule is codified in s. 25(2). While there were a number of counts in the information, each arising out of the same incident and even overlapping or duplicating each other, this does not create a duplicitous charge. A single incident may give rise to multiple charges. The trial judge should have adjudicated on all the counts and made findings on each of them. If he convicted either or both defendants on all charges, he could then decide whether to conditionally stay one or more charges under the rule against multiple convictions. There is no discretion for the trial judge to reduce the number of counts to one count against each defendant. A trial judge cannot collapse an information by dismissing some of the counts arising out of the same incident. To give a trial judge that discretion would improperly interfere with the Crown's discretion to lay the charges it deems appropriate.

The court further ruled in the *Thomas G. Fuller & Sons Ltd.* case that while the trial judge was concerned from the way the charges were drafted, that the defendants would not know the case against them, each count was drafted precisely in the wording of the relevant sections of the Act and the Regulation. Offences drafted in the words of a statute or a regulation are presumed to be valid. Under s. 25(6), a defendant is entitled to sufficient particulars of each charge. The five counts in the case complied with s. 25(6). Some particulars were given; neither of the defendants asked for more particulars, and neither claimed that it did not know what it was charged with or that any of the charges failed to disclose an offence. The trial judge erred in dismissing the counts on his own initiative, and he was wrong to do so.

In *R. v. Siguencia-Vargas*, 2011 ONCJ 805, 2011 CarswellOnt 14848, [2011] O.J. No. 6080 (Ont. C.J.), it was held that the set fine is a component of the certificate of offence that is required for the certificate to be considered to be "complete and regular on its face". The set fine should not be considered mere surplusage but rather its importance lies in the fact that it is the penalty component of the charge which can impact a defendant if it is incorrect. For the defendant to be successful in his application to quash the certificate, the defendant must show prejudice which can be inferred or other wise and that the proposed amendment can be made without an injustice being done; the onus is on the defendant to make the arguments and support these arguments with evidence.

While the defendant did not do this in the instant case, at the same time the prosecution, when responding to the defendant's request in court, did not make a request for the amendment but rather made reference to the amendment in written submissions. This was prejudicial to the defendant as the defendant did not know what the set fine might be so it could make a proper and informed determination of what approach it would take, i.e., pay the fine, plead guilty, or undertake the added expense of going to trial. As a result, a proper request to amend the certificate in court for both the court and defendant to consider was not done by the prosecution. The certificate was quashed as it was not proper and regular on its face, and the failure to make the amendment request would cause prejudice to the defendant.

In *York (Regional Municipality) v. Lorman*, 2015 ONSC 6486, 2015 CarswellOnt 15914, 46 M.P.L.R. (5th) 153, [2015] O.J. No. 5449 (Ont. S.C.J.), during the course of the arraignment, the Justice of the Peace noted that the certificate of offence had the incorrect municipality. The prosecutor requested that he matter be held down so that he could call evidence from the investigating police officer as to the correct municipality and request an amendment to the certificate of offence. However, on her own volition, the Justice quashed the certificate, notwithstanding that there was no proper motion by the defendant, who was unrepresented, to do so. The spirit and intent of the *Provincial Offences Act*, and prosecutions conducted thereunder, is to ensure that technical objections do not impede a verdict on the merits. The Act sets up a process pursuant to which provincial offences matters can be dealt with in a speedy, efficient and convenient way. In a situation where the defendant appears for trial, the provisions of s. 9(1) governing defective certificates where the defendant does not appear for trial do not apply; where the defendant attends, s. 36 governs what the court must do, namely, it is up to the defendant and not the court to bring a motion to quash. The practice of Justices of the Peace bringing their own motion to quash in these circumstances has been disapproved of by the court. Justices of the Peace, like judges of the Superior Court, are human and may not always like the decision of an appellate court. Fundamentally, however, justices and judges must abide by the decisions of the higher court whether they like it or not. The Justice's decision to quash the certificate of offence where there was no motion by the defendant to do so was a clear error of law. It was clear from her earlier decisions that she knew she did not have the jurisdiction to quash the certificate of offence yet she proceeded to do what she knew she had no jurisdiction to do, and thus challenged the prosecution to appeal. Her decision to proceed in the manner she did reflects not only an error of law that was jurisdictional in nature, but a lack of appreciation of the principle of *stare decisis*. An order of *mandamus* and certiorari quashing the order of the Justice of the Peace was issued.

In *York (Regional Municipality) v. Sekelyk* (September 22, 2015), Doc. CV-15-123505-00, [2015] O.J. No. 4889 (Ont. S.C.J.), the Justice of the Peace was held to have erred in quashing the certificate of offence on the defendant's guilty plea due to the omission of the municipality. It is the overall philosophy of the *Provincial Offences Act* (Ont.) that technical objections not impede the determination of a verdict on the merits. In other circumstances, the failure of the certificate to identify the municipality would be a material, not technical matter. In the instant case, however, there were full particulars of the time and place of the alleged offence, the nature of the offence, speeding, and the place alleged, together with the immediate circumstances under which the notice and offence occurred. As a result, it could not be said that the failure to have included the name of the municipality could impair the defendant's appreciation of the offence he was alleged to have committed. The justice erred in striking the plea and quashing the certificate, rather the process to amend the certificate should have been allowed to unfold.

5.3.2 DIVIDING COUNTS

- Section 33 outlines the power to divide counts: See Appendix A.

5.3.3 AMENDMENTS

- Section 34 outlines the power to amend a charging document: See Appendix A.

- The broad curative powers under section 34 include the ability to amend at any stage of the proceeding, including after the Crown closes its case. See *R. v. Larizza* (2006), 2006 ONCJ 400, 2006 CarswellOnt 6795 (Ont. C.J.). The focus of the amendment analysis can only be the potential of prejudice or injustice to the defendant: *R. v. Vanier* (2005), 2005 ONCJ 318, [2005] O.J. No. 5466, 2005 CarswellOnt 7358 (Ont. C.J.).

- What emerges as a consistent theme in case law relating to amendments is the prejudice that could be occasioned to a defendant in mounting a defence: *R. v. Silverstrone* (2007), [2007] O.J. No. 4855, 2007 CarswellOnt 8006 (Ont. S.C.J.).

Conversely, in *Ontario (Ministry of Labour) v. Thomas Fuller Construction Co.*, 2008 CarswellOnt 6044, 2008 ONCJ 487, [2008] O.J. No. 4004 (Ont. C.J.), the court permitted an amendment that added the entry "(1958)"so that the correct name of the corporate entity being charged would be set out. Relevant considerations in making the amendment included the fact that no evidence had been taken at trial, the circumstances of the case were serious as a fatality was involved, there was no prejudice to the defendant given the close relationship of the corporate entities, the expiry of any limitation period was not in itself sufficient to prevent an amendment, and there was no injustice since the defendant had been fully apprised of the circumstances of the case since the date of the fatality. There was no evidence that there had been a considered decision to charge Fuller, as opposed to Fuller (1958), and the decision was more likely a product of confusion or mistake that resulted from the complex corporate organization of the Fuller Group.

The actual rate of speed matters only on penalty and it is open to the prosecutor to seek an amendment under s. 34 of the *Provincial Offences Act* to "amend up" the rate of speed to that recorded at the time of the offence from the lesser speed stated in the certificate of offence. Defendants have no vested right to insist on a trial only on the charge named on the certificate of offence. However, the trial court can "amend up" a certificate only if the evidence supports the amendment. Ideally, the defendant should receive notice of a proposed amendment before the day of trial, however in provincial offences proceedings this ideal will not always be practical. If, for practical reasons, notice of the amendment can only be given on the day of trial, then it would be far preferable that the notice be given before the trial begins and that the defendant then be given a reasonable opportunity to consider how to respond. The broad amendment power in s. 34(2) contemplates that notice of the amendment can be made during or even at the conclusion of the evidence; the later during the proceedings that the defendant is given notice of the proposed amendment, the greater the risk of prejudice if the amendment is granted: *R. v. Winlow*, 2009 ONCA 643, 2009 CarswellOnt 5208, (*sub nom.* York (Regional Municipality) v. Winlow) 99 O.R. (3d) 337, 86 M.V.R. (5th) 171, 265 O.A.C. 326, [2009] O.J. No. 3691 (Ont. C.A.).

In a case of "amending up" at a speeding trial, the best practice is to make sure that the accused party is aware that an amendment could well take place, and that amendment could result in a higher charge and, if the evidence supports it, a higher penalty: *R. v. Monachino*, [2009] O.J. No. 5997 (C.J.). See also *R. v. Zimmer*, 2010 ONCJ 177, 2010 CarswellOnt 3809, [2010] O.J. No. 2247 (Ont. C.J.) where it was held that if a court routinely amends up to a rate of speed that is other than the one charged, it leaves it open to abuse, where high rates of speed could be alleged that were not in fact obtained as readings.

The charge was so badly drafted that it failed to give fair notice to the defendant of the nature of the charge or the penalties that may be imposed. It failed to allege the *Traffic Safety Act*, which was the proper statute, and also failed to allege the proper sections. The court could not amend the charge as it was a nullity which was incapable of amendment: *R. v. Kocsis*, 2010 SKQB 311, 2010 CarswellSask 547, 1 M.V.R. (6th) 115, 364 Sask. R. 19, [2010] S.J. No. 489 (Sask. Q.B.).

In *Greater Sudbury (City) v. Boivin*, 2010 ONCJ 463, 2010 CarswellOnt 7750, [2010] O.J. No. 4404 (Ont. C.J.), the trial justice refused the prosecutor's amendment upon the completion of the Crown's case to change the offence charged from failing to travel in a marked lane of traffic to failing to share half the road way. Although the prosecutor had informed the defendant prior to trial of its intention to seek the amendment, it was held that the proposed amendment could not be made without injustice being done. The justice was fully entitled to exercise her judicial discretion and arrive at the conclusion that she did.

In *York (Regional Municipality) v. Scarcelli*, 2010 ONSC 4560, 2010 CarswellOnt 10645, [2010] O.J. No. 5026, it was held that when the defendant appears for trial, s. 34 allows an amendment of a certificate of offence to state the municipality where the offence occurred, and s. 9.1 does not apply. There is an anomaly in the jurisdiction of a justice of a peace to cure a defect on the face of a certificate of offence depending upon whether or not the accused appears in court or not. Once the defendant appeared in court, the justice had the authority to amend the certificate of offence, and the failure to do so was an error.

Similarly, *York (Regional Municipality) v. Talabe*, 2011 ONSC 955, 2011 CarswellOnt 832, [2011] O.J. No. 654 (Ont. S.C.J.), it was considered that the error in the set fine did not impede the defendant's ability to mount a defence, impair trial fairness, affect the jurisdiction of the court or alter the fact that the justice had the authority to impose a fine of up to $1,000 upon conviction. In such circumstances, and particularly in the absence of any other evidence of prejudice, the certificate should have been amended. The tension created under the *Provincial Offences Act* is that a defendant who fails to appear is in a much more favourable position than a defendant who answers to the charge, even though both may have identical errors on the certificates issued to them. However, the defendant had placed himself in jeopardy of having a higher amount imposed once all the evidence was heard by the trier of fact.

In *Niagara (Regional Municipality) v. DiFruscia*, 2010 ONCJ 427, 2010 CarswellOnt 7104, [2010] O.J. No. 404 (Ont. C.J.), the company was a named defendant in other informations which were being tried before the justice of the peace. It would not have had any reason to believe that it faced any jeopardy with respect to the charges in question. R. DiFruscia Holdings Ltd. was not Rocco DiFruscia. For all legal purposes they were separate entities. Suddenly placing the company in legal jeopardy by amending the information to add its name to the informations was highly prejudicial to the company, especially when done without giving its counsel an opportunity to be heard on that issue. The amendments should not have been made.

In *York (Regional Municipality) v. Yu*, 2011 ONCJ 246, 2011 CarswellOnt 3632, [2011] O.J. No. 2372 (Ont. C.J.), it was held that when uncertainty may have existed regarding one of the elements of the offence (the operative posted limit) it would be difficult to conclude an amendment to the offence notice in order to comply with the evidence, and could have resulted in the defendant being misled or prejudiced in any way. Such an amendment could also be made in these circumstances with out an injustice being done and without offending the statutory preconditions referenced in s. 34(4)(a)-(d).

Likewise, it was held that there was nothing inherently unfair which would expose the defendant to an injustice if the requested "amending up" was granted at his speeding trial. The prosecution had provided notice of its intention to seek the amendment well in advance of the trial date; there was no misleading the defendant or prejudice brought on by lack of or late notification. See *Durham (Regional Municipality) v. Galluzo*, 2011 ONCJ 367, 2011 CarswellOnt 6256, [2011] O.J. No. 3267 (Ont. C.J.). For other cases where the speed was "amended up", see *Waterloo (Regional Municipality) v. Bydeley*, 2010 ONCJ 740, 2010 CarswellOnt 10824, [2010] O.J. No. 6063 (Ont. C.J.); *Durham (Regional Municipality) v. Zhu*, 2011 ONCJ 193, 2011 CarswellOnt 2614, [2011] O.J. No. 1797 (Ont. C.J.).

In *R. v. Lacroix*, 2011 ONCJ 270, 2011 CarswellOnt 3627, [2011] O.J. No. 2332 (Ont. C.J.), the charge indicated that the offence occurred on "Britannia Road" in the City of Mississauga whereas the correct name for the road was actually "Britannia Road West." However, an amendment could be made to remedy this defect. The amendment did not cause irremediable prejudice or cause injustice, since the defendant knew the road he was on at least contained the words "Britannia Road". Quashing the information or dismissing the charge due to the omission of the word "West" would in the circumstances cause injustice, considering the merits of the case.

Where the operator of a commercial motor vehicle was stopped and charged with entering inaccurate information in a daily log, but the certificate of offence alleged the offence on such date where as the in accurate entry had been made four days previously, s. 34(3) specifically provides that a variance between the certificate and evidence at trial with respect to the time of the offence is not material. The offence was therefore made out upon proof that the accused entered inaccurate information or falsified information in the daily log. See *R. v. Motovylets* (2011), 20 M.V.R. (6th) 332, [2011] O.J. No. 4094, 2011 CarswellOnt 9236, 2011 ONCJ 427 (Ont. C.J.).

In *R. v. Siguencia-Vargas*, 2011 ONCJ 805, 2011 CarswellOnt 14848, [2011] O.J. No. 6080 (Ont. C.J.), it was held that the set fine is a component of the certificate of offence that is required for the certificate to be considered to be "complete and regular on its face". The set fine should not be considered mere surplusage but rather its importance lies in the fact that it is the penalty component of the charge which can impact a defendant if it is incorrect. For the defendant to be successful in his application to quash the certificate, the defendant must show prejudice which can be inferred or otherwise and that the proposed amendment can be made without an injustice being done; the onus is on the defendant to make the arguments and support these arguments with evidence. While the defendant did not do this in the instant case, at the same time the prosecution, when responding to the defendant's request in court, did not make a request for the amendment but rather made reference to the amendment in written submissions. This was prejudicial to the defendant as the defendant did not know what the set fine might be so it could make a proper and informed determination of what approach it would take, i.e., pay the fine, plead guilty, or undertake the added expense of going to trial. As a result, a proper request to amend the certificate in court for both the court and defendant to consider was not done by the prosecution. The certificate was quashed as it was not proper and regular on its face, and the failure to make the amendment request would cause prejudice to the defendant.

The amendment of the information at the defendant's *ex parte* trial for speeding to raise the rate of speed and elevate the charge exposed him to greater prejudice, and should not have been made in the absence of notice to the defendant so that he would have a chance to be heard: *R. v. Wheaton*, 2011 NLTD(G) 148, 2011 CarswellNfld 416, 316 Nfld. & P.E.I.R. 356, 24 M.V.R. (6th) 112, 982 A.P.R. 356, [2011] N.J. No. 386 (N.L. T.D.).

As long as the defendant knows the case he has to meet, or is given an adjournment if the amendment results in a charge which takes him by surprise, there is no justification under the Act for quashing instead of amending the information. The only instance where an information cannot be amended is where it is so badly drafted that it fails to give the defendant reasonable information with respect to the charge and to identify the transaction referred to, thus giving the defendant no possibility of full answer and defence at trial. In this case, while the count in the information listed the wrong subsection of the Mining Regulation which cited the definition section rather than the requirement to guard the moving parts of the machine, the parties conducted themselves under the assumption that the correct subsection was in issue and examined and cross examined the witnesses on the issue of guarding. The amendment sought would not therefore have prejudiced the defendant. The defendant had full opportunity to meet all of the issues raised by the charge and the defence would not have been conducted any differently had the amended charge been before the trial court. See *R. v. Preston Sand & Gravel Co.*, 2009 ONCJ 779, 2009 CarswellOnt 9834, [2009] O.J. No. 6399 (Ont. C.J.).

The trial justice erred in dismissing the prosecutor's motion to amend the certificate of offence prior to the date of trial so as to correct the set fine and total payable, holding that the defect was a fatal flaw that could not be amended. Although the motion to amend was not served personally or by mail or other method set out under s. 87(1) of the *Provincial Offences Act* (Ont.), being served by fax, the defendant was properly served through his legal representative. He was a ware of the issue and was made aware of the opportunity to answer the remedy and resist the remedy sought. Instead he did nothing and his technical argument regarding service of the motion failed. See *York (Regional Municipality) v. Burnett* (July 4, 2012), Doc. New market CV-12-0846000, [2012] O.J. No. 3239 (Ont. S.C.J.).

In *R. v. Howse*, 2012 ONCJ 517, 2012 CarswellOnt 9877, 37 M.V.R. (6th) 327, [2012] O.J. No. 3772 (Ont. C.J.), it was held the trial justice was entitled to amend the certificate of offence to conform to the evidence that the speeding stop was made on Highway 9, not Highway 10 as set out in the certificate of offence. Such amendments are expressly permitted at any stage of a proceeding, and are consistent with the thrust of the *Provincial Offences Act* (Ont.) in focusing on the merits of trials and not technical objections. The amendment was obvious and proper and called for no more explanation than that given by the presiding justice.

A trial justice is entitled to exercise a trial management power in the sense of being mindful of the time that the trial proceedings were taking, and those that were following, and limiting the time that could be devoted to opposing an amendment sought by the prosecutor to increase the rate of speed on the certificate of offence. The justice had given the defence representative the opportunity to oppose the amendment, heard his submissions, and ruled that he had been given sufficient time to make his submissions. See *R. v. Kukuy*, 2012 CarswellOnt 14464, [2012] O.J. No. 5310 (Ont. C.J.).

In *R. v. Calleja*, 2013 ONCJ 7, 2013 CarswellOnt 94, 39 M.V.R. (6th) 162, [2013] O.J. No. 116 (Ont. C.J.), the defendant was charged with failing to yield to a pedestrian, contrary to s. 140(1)(a) of the *Highway Traffic Act*, whereas the accident took place at an intersection, such that the better charging section would have been fail to yield to a pedestrian within a crosswalk, contrary to s. 144(7). It was open to the trial justice of the peace to amend the certificate of offence at any stage of the proceedings to reflect the more perfectly suited section of the *Highway Traffic Act*, s. 144(7), as this pedestrian was struck down at a lighted intersection. There would have been no error in law if such an amendment had been made. It would be open as well to the appeal court to amend the certificate at the appeal stage of the proceedings, although it was unnecessary to do so.

While a provincial of fences appeal court has the power to grant an award of costs, such orders are not ordinarily granted. Although s. 34 of the *Provincial Offences Act* gives the prosecutor the ability to seek, and the court the power to grant, an amendment to an Information, an amendment to change the name of the defendant is not contemplated by this provision. Section 26 requires that a defendant must be named in and served with a summons setting out the charge against it. Section 54 provides that a defendant can be convicted *in absentia* where the prosecutor proves that the summons or notice of trial was served on the defendant. Amending the Information to change the name of the defendant in the absence of the defendant runs contrary to these provisions. At the very least, the prosecutor should have requested an adjournment of the trial to properly serve a summons or notice of trial on the defendant. In failing to do so, the prosecutor carelessly disregarded the procedural safeguards afforded to the defendant under the *Provincial Offences Act*. Section 129(a) grants the court discretion to make any order with respect to costs that it considers "just and reasonable". In this case the defendant was convicted without ever being issued a summons or served with a notice that it had ever been charged; it had no opportunity to argue at trial whether it should have been named as a defendant, or given an opportunity to defend the charge on its merits. In addition, through no fault of its own, it was required to retain counsel to bring the appeal and have the conviction quashed. In the unusual circumstances of the case, fairness demanded that the defendant be relieved of the financial burden of the costs of the appeal and application by being fully compensated. See *R. v. 1820419*

Ontario Inc., 2013 ONCJ 10, 2013 CarswellOnt 275, [2013] O.J. No. 143 (Ont. C.J.).

The omission of the name of the municipality on the certificate of offence does not result in a jurisdictional defect that cannot be cured by an amendment. The amending provisions are to be given a broad and purposive analysis. The proposed amendment did not create a new offence in law, but rather amplified the broader location of the offence as set out in the certificate. As such the exact municipality was descriptive rather than substantive. The location of the offence had been set out. See *R. v. Cyr*, 2013 ONCJ 143, 2013 CarswellOnt 3485, [2013] O.J. No. 1331 (Ont. C.J.).

In *R. v. Petrecca*, 2013 ONCJ 744, 2013 CarswellOnt 18653, [2013] O.J. No. 6160 (Ont. C.J.), the information charging the defendant with stunt driving by driving in a manner that indicates an intention to cause some or all of the tires to lose traction referenced the section of the *Highway Traffic Act* but not the regulation, and the information omitted the words "while turning". The Justice of the Peace raised the issue of whether the information was improper, proceeded to find that it was, and after refusing to grant an amendment, dismissed the charge. Even if the information was not proper, the Justice of the Peace erred in not granting an amendment. The underlying philosophy of the *Provincial Offences Act* is to ensure that technical objections do not impede the determination of a case on its merits. Counsel for the defendant would certainly have known or ought to have known the case to be met, as was apparent from the fact that the defendant's legal representative did not raise the issue. There would have been no prejudice in granting the amendment.

An appearance of bias may be an inadvertent consequence of the exercise of the amendment powers referenced in s. 34(2), particularly when that power is exercised or referenced unilaterally by the Justice of the Peace. Restraint should be exercised in the use of the amendment powers particularly when the Justice of the Peace, absent a motion by the prosecution, is acting on his or her own initiative. As stated by the Ontario Court of Appeal in *R. v. Winlow*, 2009 ONCA 643, 2009 CarswellOnt 5208, (*sub nom.* York (Regional Municipality) v. Winlow) 99 O.R. (3d) 337, 86 M.V.R. (5th) 171, 265 O.A.C. 326, [2009] O.J. No. 3691 (Ont. C.A.), Justices of the Peace are not encouraged to amend on their own motion. See *R. v. Strati*, 2014 ONCJ 139, 2014 CarswellOnt 3624, [2014] O.J. No. 1413 (Ont. C.J.).

In *R. v. Zuccarini*, 2014 ONCJ 571, 2014 CarswellOnt 15457, [2014] O.J. No. 5234 (Ont. C.J.), the defendant had been given notice of the potential amendment to the certificate charging speeding to conform to evidence of speed at trial in the disclosure and on the day of trial by the prosecution. An adjournment was offered to the defendant, which was declined. The trial was also held down for the defendant to consider his position and consult with others, after which the defendant decided to proceed with the trial. The trial Justice found there was no prejudice to the defendant caused by the amendment, and it had no impact on the defendant's defence to the speeding charge. The reasons of the trial Justice demonstrated that he considered and applied the test with respect to granting amendments. There was no evidence of legal error or miscarriage of justice.

The violation ticket under which the defendant was charged contained a correct statement of the alleged contravention, but the section quoted as supporting that statement was incorrect. The defendant pleaded not guilty to the charge and the Crown led evidence and closed its case, after which the defendant brought a no evidence motion. It was not appropriate to allow the Crown at the close of its case to amend the section under which the defendant was charged. This was a simple error. If the Crown had read the section before trial, it surely would have concluded there was an error and amended the charge before the defendant made his plea. The defendant based his plea and position at trial on the charge he had to face. See *R. v. Gauthier*, 2012 BCPC 562, 2012 CarswellBC 4464, [2012] B.C.J. No. 3071 (B.C. Prov. Ct.).

The defendant proceeded upon his defence based upon the charge as laid, and it was to that means of committing the offences that his defence was based. The defence and Crown and trial court were in complete error as to what constituted an appropriate defence to the charge as laid, and the defence raised by the defendant could not have been entertained but for this means of committing the offence and the error in law made. The by-law contained at least 14 exemptions from the application of the by-law. The defendant had been misled in his defence. There was real prejudice. It would be manifestly unfair to the defendant to allow such an amendment on appeal and then decide the case on the record before the court. The Justice made very few findings of fact pertaining to these issues. If the amendment had been sought at the outset or during the trial, the court would have been in the position of assessing the specific prejudice and, in the appropriate case, would have granted an adjournment to ameliorate the prejudice, if that was possible. Such an amendment would have been routinely granted if sought before the end of the Crown's case. The trial Justice would have been in a good position to decide whether an adjournment be granted, or indeed whether Crown witnesses should be recalled for further cross-examination. The matter was remitted for trial and the information amended for the re-trial: *R. v. 1533904 Ontario Ltd.*, 2015 ONCJ 75, 2015 CarswellOnt 2388, [2015] O.J. No. 827 (Ont. C.J.).

In *York (Regional Municipality) v. Lorman*, 2015 ONSC 6486, 2015 CarswellOnt 15914, 46 M.P.L.R. (5th) 153, [2015] O.J. No. 5449 (Ont. S.C.J.), during the course of the arraignment, the Justice of the Peace noted that the certificate of offence had the incorrect municipality. The prosecutor requested that he matter be held down so that he could call evidence from the investigating police officer as to the correct municipality and request an amendment to the certificate of offence. However, on her own volition, the Justice quashed the certificate, notwithstanding that there was no proper motion by the defendant, who was unrepresented, to do so. The spirit and intent of the *Provincial Offences Act*, and prosecutions conducted thereunder, is to ensure that technical objections do not impede a verdict on the merits. The Act sets up a process pursuant to which provincial offences matters can be dealt with in a speedy, efficient and convenient way. In a situation where the defendant appears for trial, the provisions of s. 9(1) governing defective certificates where the defendant does not appear for trial do not apply; where the defendant attends, s. 36 governs what the court must do, namely, it is up to the defendant and not the court to bring a motion to quash. The practice of Justices of the Peace bringing their own motion to quash in these circumstances has been disapproved of by the court. Justices of the Peace, like judges of the Superior Court, are human and may not always like the decision of an appellate court. Fundamentally, however, justices and judges must abide by the decisions of the higher court whether they like it or not. The Justice's decision to quash the certificate of offence where there was no motion by the defendant to do so was a clear error of law. It was clear from her earlier decisions that she knew she did not have the jurisdiction to quash the certificate of offence yet she proceeded to do what she knew she had no jurisdiction to do, and thus challenged the prosecution to appeal. Her decision to proceed in the manner she did reflects not only an error of law that was jurisdictional in nature, but a lack of appreciation of the principle of *stare decisis*. An order of *mandamus* and certiorari quashing the order of the Justice of the Peace was issued.

In *York (Regional Municipality) v. Sekelyk* (September 22, 2015), Doc. CV-15-123505-00, [2015] O.J. No. 4889 (Ont. S.C.J.), the Justice of the Peace was held to have erred in quashing the certificate of offence on the defendant's guilty plea due to the omission of the municipality. It is the overall philosophy of the *Provincial Offences Act* (Ont.) that technical objections not impede the determination of a verdict on the merits. In other circumstances, the failure of the certificate to identify the municipality would be a material, not technical matter. In the instant case, however, there were full particulars of the time and place of the alleged offence, the nature of the offence, speeding, and the place alleged, together with the immediate circumstances under which the notice and offence occurred. As a result, it could not be said that the failure to have included the name of the municipality could impair the defendant's appreciation of the offence he was alleged to have committed. The justice erred in striking the plea and quashing the certificate, rather the process to amend the certificate should have been allowed to unfold.

In *R. v. Zarrinkamar*, 2016 BCSC 1272, 2016 CarswellBC 1936, [2016] B.C.J. No. 1476 (B.C. S.C.), it was held that in light of the late amendment of the traffic violation notice to essentially change the nature of the charge, without providing adequate explanation of what was happening to the defendant, and apparently effectively laying a new charge outside of the limitation period, there was a flawed procedure which placed the defendant in jeopardy of a conviction which he should not have had to face.

At the start of the trial for speeding, the prosecutor informed the defendant that he would seek to have the certificate amended to indicate that the defendant was travelling at a greater speed than the one recorded in the certificate. Before granting an amendment, the court must consider the evidence at trial, the circumstances of the case, whether the defendant had been misled or prejudiced, and whether the amendment would cause any injustice to be done. Ideally, the defendant should receive notice of the proposed amendment before the day of the trial. If notice of the amendment can only be done on the day of trial, it would be far preferable that notice be given before the trial begins so that the defendant has a reasonable opportunity to consider how to respond. In the instant case, the prosecutor gave no formal notice of the request to "amend up", and no settlement discussions were held prior to the day of trial. The defendant was not aware of the *R. v. Winlow*, 2009 ONCA 643, 2009 CarswellOnt 5208, (*sub nom.* York (Regional Municipality) v. Winlow) 99 O.R. (3d) 337, 86 M.V.R. (5th) 171, 265 O.A.C. 326, [2009] O.J. No. 3691 (Ont. C.A.) decision, and was given no opportunity to request an adjournment or fully digest the consequences of the case, and was therefore placed at a disadvantage. The trial judge refused to grant the amendment. There is no requirement that the justice accede to the Crown's request and amend the speed to comply with the evidence, the operative word being "may" in the decision to amend. The justice considered all of the appropriate circumstances in declining to grant the amendment. See *Kenora (City) v. Romyn*, 2016 ONCJ 198, 2016 CarswellOnt 5517, 3 M.V.R. (7th) 329, [2016] O.J. No. 1875 (Ont. C.J.).

In *R. v. Wadood*, 2017 ONCA 45, 2017 CarswellOnt 554, 344 C.C.C. (3d) 265, 6 M.V.R. (7th) 181, [2017] O.J. No. 245 (Ont. C.A.), it was held that a police officer is entitled to change the information on the certificate of offence after giving the offence notice to the motorist, but before filing the certificate with the court. In one case, the officer added the name of the municipality after noticing that the certificate of offence did not contain this information after the defendant drove off after being given the ticket; in the other case the officer realized that he had written the incorrect year on the certificate of offence, and corrected it before filing it with the court. Both accused failed to appear for their trial. As a result, they were deemed to not dispute their charges. The justice of the peace in each case concluded that the certificate of offence was complete and regular on its face, and the defendants were convicted. Although s. 90 of the *Provincial Offences Act* does not authorize an officer to amend the certificate after serving the offence notice, but before filing the certificate with the court, nothing in the *Provincial Offences Act* prevents an officer from doing so. Whether an amendment will invalidate a conviction depends on the nature of the amendment and its impact on a defendant. In these cases, each amendment did no more than correct a minor clerical error on the certificate; neither of the defendants was misled or prejudiced by the amendment. Thus the validity of the proceeding against each of the defendants was preserved by s. 90. If the officer amends the certificate, and the variance between the certificate and the offence notice comes before the court, then the presiding judge will have to decide whether the defendant was misled or prejudiced by the amendment. If not, then s. 90 will validate the proceeding.

The justice of the peace at the defendant's first appearance in court noted that the date of the offence on the information was a date in the future, and determined that the information was "no good" as a result. It is important to remember that an important goal of the *Provincial Offences Act* is that matters are tried on their merits, hence, the very broad powers of amendment where there is no prejudice to the accused. While the question of whether to amend an information is a question of law, this does not relieve the court from its obligation to proceed properly and in accordance with law to arrive at a decision whether to grant an amendment. Clearly, this information was defective in substance or form. It contained an obvious error which required an amendment. No trial evidence was necessary to ascertain this error. The fact that this was at the first appearance did not oust the court's jurisdiction to consider whether to amend the information. Even if the lack of the officer's signature amounted to a substantive defect, there was jurisdiction for the court to amend the information. There was no opportunity for the Crown to adduce evidence to support the amendment or to make submissions as to why the amendment should be made. This was a fatal error. Clearly, the presiding justice did not conduct the proceeding in accordance with natural justice. In proceeding in this manner, the learned judge exceeded his jurisdiction. Not granting the application for prerogative review would, in the circumstances of the case, result in a substantial wrong to society which expects and is entitled to have these matters heard on the merits unless an amendment is rejected after both parties have an opportunity to deal with and the presiding judge gives full consideration of the matters relevant to an amendment application. See *R. v. Singh*, 2017 ONSC 7593, 2017 CarswellOnt 20895, [2017] O.J. No. 6807 (Ont. S.C.J.), affirmed 2018 ONCA 506, 2018 CarswellOnt 8710, 362 C.C.C. (3d) 161, 28 M.V.R. (7th) 45 (Ont. C.A.).

In *R. v. Popovici*, 2017 CarswellOnt 21731, [2017] O.J. No. 5697 (C.J.), the defendant was not given an opportunity to make submissions as to penalty and may not have been aware of the prosecutor's entitlement to request an "amendment up" of the amount of the applicable fine by virtue of the amendment provisions of the *Provincial Offences Act*. The court must ensure that the defendant understands the consequences of the amendment and is given a reasonable opportunity to make submissions as to why the amendment should not be granted. As the amendment, if granted, would invariably result in the imposition of a more enhanced financial sanction, fairness dictated that the unrepresented defendant be given a fair opportunity to respond to the request for enhanced penalty. On the record, it did not appear that the defendant understood his jeopardy of the amendment that was granted. More importantly, he was not given an opportunity to make submissions as to penalty generally.

There was a defect on the information as the offence date was recorded as 2017 instead of 2016. The justice of the peace committed jurisdictional error in quashing the information due to the error without considering whether to amend it under ss. 34 or 36. A justice of the peace may amend the information at any stage of the proceedings, including first appearance. The justice of the peace also erred by failing to give the Crown an opportunity to make submissions. Quashing the information in these circumstances resulted in a miscarriage of justice because it prevented the charge being considered on its merits. See *R. v. Singh*, 2018 ONCA 506, 2018 CarswellOnt 8710, 362 C.C.C. (3d) 161, 28 M.V.R. (7th) 45, [2018] O.J. No. 2943 (Ont. C.A.).

In *Ontario (Ministry of Labour) v. Nault*, 2018 ONCJ 321, 2018 CarswellOnt 7680, [2018] O.J. No. 2568 (Ont. C.J.), the court noted that in respect of the use of "short-form wording" or "abbreviated wording" to describe a particular regulatory offence, ss. 13(1)(b) and 13(2) of the *Provincial Offences Act* authorize the Lieutenant Governor in Council by regulation to specify a word or expression that can be used on a form, such as on a certificate of offence, to designate that offence, and that the specified word or expression, if used on the form, would be sufficient for all purposes to describe the offence designated by such word or expression. However, those statutory provisions do not require the compulsory use of that prescribed word or expression to describe the offence. In addition, where the regulations do not authorize the use of a word or expression (short-form wording) to describe an offence in a form, then by virtue of s. 13(3) the offence may be described in accordance with s. 25 of the Act. And in the situation where "short-form wording" has not been legally created to describe a particular regulatory offence, s. 25(3) specifically provides that where an offence is identified in a count, but the count fails to set out one or more of the essential elements of the offence, then a reference to the provision creating or defining the offence shall be deemed to incorporate all the essential elements of the offence. The present proceedings had been commenced with a Part I certificate of offence. The charge that had been laid in both of the defendants' certificates was identical and expressed as "worker operate equipment in a manner that may endanger himself or another worker." Under s. 3(2), a provincial offences officer may issue to an accused either an offence notice indicating the set fine for the offence or a summons without a set fine in respect to the Part I certificate of offence. The list of authorized "short-form wordings" for specific regulatory offences are those found and prescribed in O. Reg 950, for which s. 13(2) of the Act has authorized that the use of short-form wordings used in a charge set out in a certificate of offence is sufficient to describe that offence. Consequently, as the defendants were issued a summons setting out the charge in respect to a certificate of offence, then according to s. 5(1) of the regulation, a "short-form wording" may be used on the summons to describe the offence. However, in regard to the offence in question, there was no "short-form wording" that has been legally created to describe the particular charge under any of the *Occupational Health and Safety Act* schedules of charges. As such, where authorized short-form wordings do not exist for a particular regulatory offence, then the wording or expression used to describe the offence in the certificate of offence of "worker operate equipment in a manner that may endanger himself or another worker" has to comply with the requirements of s. 25 of the *Provincial Offences Act*, which sets out the standards for describing and providing the necessary information about the offence that the accused has been charged with committing. In that regard, the defendants had defended themselves at trial in regard to the charge on the basis that they were not actually operating equipment, namely a forklift, as had been specifically expressed in the charge in their respective certificates of offence. Therefore, in fairness to the defendants, and since the doctrine of surplusage did not apply and because no application to amend the charge had been brought by the prosecution, then the defendants' respective charges would be treated as having been particularized by the Ministry of Labour to one of those specific five circumstances set out under the section for which the provision can be contravened by a worker, namely of "operating or using equipment in a manner that may endanger the worker or others."

At the start of the trial, before any testimony or evidence had been entered, the prosecution brought an application to amend the start date for the alleged offence in one of the counts from "January 2, 2012" to "August 8, 2011". The decision whether to grant this decision was reserved until the evidence for this particular charge was complete. Section 34 of the *Provincial Offences Act* provides that the court may at any stage of the proceedings amend the information as may be necessary, if it appears that the information fails to state, or states defectively, anything that is requisite to charge the offence, is in any way defective in substance or in form, or if the matters to be alleged in the proposed amendment are disclosed by the evidence taken at the trial. But, in considering whether or not an amendment should be made, consideration of the evidence taken on the trial, the circumstances of the case, whether the defendant has been misled or prejudiced in the defendant's defence by a variance, error or omission, and whether, having regard to the merits of the case, the proposed amendment can be made without injustice being done. Having regard to the evidence adduced at trial, the defendant would not have been misled or prejudiced in regard to the defendant's defence by the proposed amendment, nor would there be injustice if the proposed amendment were to be made in regard to the merits of the case, as the defendant himself would have known that he had received a cheque from the party who was the subject of the count with a particular date, as well as a copy of the cheque had been disclosed to the defendant in the prosecution's disclosure prior to the trial commencing. In addition, the issue of the proposed amendment to the count had also been raised at the judicial pre-trial conference, so that the defendant would not have been surprised about the application by the prosecution for that proposed amendment. In the result, the amendment was granted. See *Ontario (Electrical Safety Authority) v. Broomfield*, 2018 ONCJ 640, 2018 CarswellOnt 15732, [2018] O.J. No. 4893 (Ont. C.J.).

5.3.4 PARTICULARS

- The court may order that a particular, further describing any matter relevant to the proceeding, be furnished to the defendant.
- This may be done before or during a trial.
- The court must be satisfied that it is necessary for a fair trial: section 35: See Appendix A.

In *R. v. EFCO Canada Co.*, 2012 ONSC 149, 2012 CarswellOnt 514, [2012] O.J. No. 134 (Ont. S.C.J.), it was observed that the Crown must prove what is alleged. The charge did not particularize that the accused used untested components but rather that he designed plans for falsework which was incapable of resisting the load. The fact that the clip was untested did not mean the falsework could not carry the load. The use of the untested component was not an essential element of the charge, as particularized. The grounds for the guilt or innocence of the defendant, given the particularization of the charge, were dependent upon the evidence before the trial judge as to the bridge collapse and whether the falsework was capable of carrying the likely load.

The location of an offence as particularized in the information is an essential averment. A court cannot legitimately have territorial jurisdiction over a matter unless it knows where the offence took place. In the instant case, the intersection of Queen Street West and Bathurst is a well-known main intersection in downtown Toronto that is capable of immediate and accurate demonstration by resorting to readily accessible sources of indisputable accuracy, and may be judicially noticed by a trial justice without further proof. Any other approach would disregard the plain realities of the situation. See *R. v. Irving*, 2012 ONCJ 234, 2012 CarswellOnt 4914 (Ont. C.J.).

The information part of an offence notice must clearly state the offence for which an individual is charged. Whether one was charged as an owner or driver of trucks that were operating overweight would engage different evidence to be led by the Crown and different defences available to the accused. It was not clear on the face of the charge, as particularized, what the basis of the offence was that the accused was alleged to have committed. See *R. v. Reimer*, 2012 MBQB 292, 2012 CarswellMan 691, 285 Man. R. (2d) 217, [2012] M.J. No. 381 (Man. Q.B.).

Neither changing a lane not in safety nor a charge of failing to drive in a marked lane is a lesser and included offence of the offence of careless driving. The defendant had no way of knowing that she was facing the possibility of defending herself against either of these two alternative charges. The case proceeded by way of information, which could have been particularized but was not. There is therefore no recitation of particulars that could cover all the essential elements of another offence. While the defendant may well have committed the offence of starting from a stopped position not in safety or failing to yield to traffic on a through highway, and the court very likely would have convicted her of one of these offences, she was not so charged. The court would not therefore find her guilty of either of these offences, or of the careless driving offence of which she was charged. See *R. v. Abdo*, 2015 ONCJ 44, [2015] O.J. No. 449 (Ont. C.J.).

In *Ontario (Ministry of Labour) v. Nault*, 2018 ONCJ 321, 2018 CarswellOnt 7680, [2018] O.J. No. 2568 (Ont. C.J.), the court noted that in respect of the use of "short-form wording" or "abbreviated wording" to describe a particular regulatory offence, ss. 13(1)(b) and 13(2) of the *Provincial Offences Act* authorize the Lieutenant Governor in Council by regulation to specify a word or expression that can be used on a form, such as on a certificate of offence, to designate that offence, and that the specified word or expression, if used on the form, would be sufficient for all purposes to describe the offence designated by such word or expression. However, those statutory provisions do not require the compulsory use of that prescribed word or expression to describe the offence. In addition, where the regulations do not authorize the use of a word or expression (short-form wording) to describe an offence in a form, then by virtue of s. 13(3) the offence may be described in accordance with s. 25 of the Act. And in the situation where "short-form wording" has not been legally created to describe a particular regulatory offence, s. 25(3) specifically provides that where an offence is identified in a count, but the count fails to set out one or more of the essential elements of the offence, then a reference to the provision creating or defining the offence shall be deemed to incorporate all the essential elements of the offence. The present proceedings had been commenced with a Part I certificate of offence. The charge that had been laid in both of the defendants' certificates was identical and expressed as "worker operate equipment in a manner that may endanger himself or another worker." Under s. 3(2), a provincial offences officer may issue to an accused either an offence notice indicating the set fine for the offence or a summons without a set fine in respect to the Part I certificate of offence. The list of authorized "short-form wordings" for specific regulatory offences are those found and prescribed in O. Reg 950, for which s. 13(2) of the Act has authorized that the use of short-form wordings used in a charge set out in a certificate of offence is sufficient to describe that offence. Consequently, as the defendants were issued a summons setting out the charge in respect to a certificate of offence, then according to s. 5(1) of the regulation, a "short-form wording" may be used on the summons to describe the offence. However, in regard to the offence in question, there was no "short-form wording" that has been legally created to describe the particular charge under any of the *Occupational Health and Safety Act* schedules of charges. As such, where authorized short-form wordings do not exist for a particular regulatory offence, then the wording or expression used to describe the offence in the certificate of offence of "worker operate equipment in a manner that may endanger himself or another worker" has to comply with the requirements of s. 25 of the *Provincial Offences Act*, which sets out the standards for describing and providing the necessary information about the offence that the accused has been charged with committing. In that regard, the defendants had defended themselves at trial in regard to the charge on the basis that they were not actually operating equipment, namely a forklift, as had been specifically expressed in the charge in their respective certificates of offence. Therefore, in fairness to the defendants, and since the doctrine of surplusage did not apply and because no application to amend the charge had been brought by the prosecution, then the defendants' respective charges would be treated as having been particularized by the Ministry of Labour to one of those specific five circumstances set out under the section for which the provision can be contravened by a worker, namely of "operating or using equipment in a manner that may endanger the worker or others."

5.4 JOINDER AND SEVERANCE

5.4.1 THE POA

- Section38 outlines the power for joint or separate trials of defendants or charges. See Appendix A.
- Section 38 of the POA states that the court may:
    - *Before* trial direct that separate counts, informations or certificates be tried *together* or that persons who are charged separately be tried *together*, where it is satisfied that the ends of justice so require.
    - *Before or during* the trial direct that separate counts, informations or certificates be tried *separately* or that persons who are charged jointly or being tried together be tried *separately*, where it is satisfied that the ends of justice so require.

5.4.2　TRYING MATTERS TOGETHER

- Reasons that the defence may wish to try matters *together* may include the situations listed below:

  - Two defendants are charged separately for the same incident. If the matters are joined together, each defendant is a non-compellable witness by the prosecution under section 46(5) and *Charter* section 11(c).Otherwise, the prosecutor might compel each defendant to testify against the other.

  - The defence may seek to join charges where they can be tried together with out prejudice, and the defence wishes to coordinate its witnesses to testify on both matters.

In *Ontario (Ministry of Labour) v. Intracorp Developments (Lombard) Inc.* (2002), 2002 CarswellOnt 1134, [2002] O.J. No. 1209 (Ont. S.C.J.), the justice of the peace exceeded his jurisdiction under section 90(2) in awarding costs to the defendants where the Crown failed to charge both defendants on one information, and brought a motion pursuant to section 38(1) to try the defendants together. Although one of the defendants opposed the motion which was ultimately granted, such omission did not amount to a defect or irregularity as required under section 90: See Appendix A.

- There is statutory authority under section 38 to order that charges within provincial legislation be tried together. The factual underpinnings, the potential for inconsistent verdicts, the potentially common defences, and the issue of judicial resources weigh in favour of this decision. With regard to a joint trial of criminal and provincial hunting charges in the same proceeding, there is no statutory authority that permits this; neither is there statutory prohibition against the same. The administration of justice would be best served by the hunting charges being tried in the same court as the criminal charges, given the factual and legal nexus between the sets of charges. However, there was no consent by the parties on the procedure that could be implemented to ensure that the proper administration of justice actually occurred. The potential for inconsistency would be alleviated by the trial proceedings on the criminal charges and the hunting charges being heard by the same trial judge, but in two separate proceedings. See *R. v. Krisza*, 2007 ONCJ 471, 2007 CarswellOnt 6729, [2007] O.J. No. 4018 (Ont. C.J.).

The two defendants were charged with the same offence: passenger fails to wear complete seatbelt assembly, contrary to the *Highway Traffic Act*. The agent for the defendants brought a motion so that the matters should be heard jointly, which was granted. Both counts arose from the same set of circumstances, and it was an expeditious way to proceed: *R. v. Nikiforos* (June 4, 2008), Tahiri J.P., [2008] O.J. No. 3180 (Ont. C.J.).

A joint trial was ordered for eight defendants who were charged with hunting offences. The factors weighing in favour of a joint trial were the factual circumstances surrounding the allegations, the potential for in consistent verdicts, the potentially common defences, and the issue of judicial resources: *R. v. Deardorff*, 2008 CarswellOnt 6494, 2008 ONCJ 550, [2008] O.J. No. 4389 (Ont. C.J.).

As the defendants were each separately charged with the offence of driving on a closed highway within minutes of each other, by the same officer, at the same location, and as they were both represented by the same licensed paralegal, their trials were heard jointly at their request: *R. v. Filice*, 2011 ONCJ 833, 2011 CarswellOnt 15546, [2011] O.J. No. 6257 (Ont. C.J.).

In *R. v. Brown*, 2012 ONCJ 122, 2012 CarswellOnt 4046, [2012] O.J. No. 1294 (Ont. C.J.), the defendant was tried fort wo offences under the *Ontario New Home Warranty Protection Act* on two separate informations related to two separate properties that were heard together and resulted in convictions. There was no evidence to suggest that due to proceeding in this manner the justice was in any way biased against the defendant. Cases involving numerous allegations of fraud or theft relating to different complainants and distinct time periods are often tried together as a matter of course. Where there is a significant degree of commonality between the offences alleged, namely, the same defendant, same investigator, same offences alleged and same jurisdiction, the "ends of justice" in s. 38 do not require that separate informations proceed to trial separately.

In *Lake Simcoe Region Conservation Authority v. Saad*, 2016 ONCJ 328, 2016 CarswellOnt 8763, [2016] O.J. No. 2937 (Ont. C.J.), of the four informations before the court each contained a single charge under the *Conservation Authorities Act*. All of them stemmed from facts arising on the same property. As a result, all four counts against the defendants, who were the landowners, were heard together in one trial.

In *R. v. Sciascia*, 2016 ONCA 411, 2016 CarswellOnt 8328, 131 O.R. (3d) 375, 336 C.C.C. (3d) 419, 350 O.A.C. 86, [2016] O.J. No. 2789 (Ont. C.A.), affirmed 2017 CSC 57, 2017 SCC 57, 2017 CarswellOnt 18247, 2017 CarswellOnt 18248, [2017]

2 S.C.R. 539, 355 C.C.C. (3d) 553, 41 C.R. (7th) 275, 417 D.L.R. (4th) 1, 17 M.V.R. (7th) 1, [2017] S.C.J. No. 57 (S.C.C.), the Court of Appeal considered the propriety of holding a joint trial under the *Provincial Offences Act* and the *Criminal Code*. It was held that in combination, the joinder provisions of the *Criminal Code* and s. 34(2) of the *Interpretation Act* make it clear that a *Criminal Code* information cannot include a count charging a provincial offence to which the *Provincial Offences Act* applies. The *Provincial Offences Act* also permits joinder of several offences in a single information. Unlike the *Criminal Code*, however, the *Provincial Offences Act*, in its s. 1(1), defines "offence" as "an offence under an Act of the Legislature." From this definition it follows that a *Provincial Offences Act* information cannot include counts charging *Criminal Code* offences. The joint trial of the *Criminal Code* summary conviction information and the *Provincial Offences Act* information therefore amounted to a procedural irregularity. However, there was no prejudice to the due administration of justice as a result. The joint trial coincided with the positions advanced by counsel on both sides of the case. Joinder avoided unnecessary duplication and depletion of judicial resources, inconvenience to witnesses, and the prospect of inconsistent verdicts. This was an appropriate case to apply the provisos in s. 686(1)(b)(iv) of the *Criminal Code* governing procedural irregularities at trial which do not cause prejudice to the party, and s. 120(1)(b)(iii) of the *Provincial Offences Act* where an appeal may be dismissed due to there being no substantial wrong or miscarriage of justice despite there being a wrong decision on a question of law. Although the *Provincial Offences Act* contains no provision comparable to s. 686(1)(b)(iv), the legal nature of the error is sufficient to bring it within the reach of s. 120(1)(b)(iii).

In *Oshawa (City) v. Shek*, 2018 ONCJ 699, 2018 CarswellOnt 17148, [2018] O.J. No. 5294 (Ont. C.J.), the charges in the matters had been brought on eight separate informations under the *Building Code Act* and *Ontario Fire Code*. Each of the two defendants was charged with the same 4 counts — one count per information. The prosecution requested one trial, wherein the court would hear the case against both defendants with respect to all of the charges at the same time. The two defendants were co-owners of the three properties in question. All three properties were part of the same land parcel. The court was satisfied that the defendants had identical interests in each of the properties, each of the four charges having been brought against each of the defendants, three of the four sets of charges were of a similar nature and the fourth charge was related to one of the properties named in one of the other three charges. All of the charges were being brought and prosecuted by the City of Oshawa. Having eight separate trials would not be efficient and would result in duplicative evidence, exhibits and submissions. As well, separate trials for each defendant on the same charge had the potential to lead to contrary outcomes for each of the two defendants, outcomes that are less than desirable in the interests of justice. A significant amount of judicial and court resources would be spent to have each charge against each of the defendants heard in separate proceedings. There was no prejudice to the defendants or other obstacles that might otherwise prevent them from bringing full answer and defence to each of the charges within one proceeding. Given the relationship of the defendants to the properties, the nexus of the properties as parts of the same land parcel and the similarity of the charges, there was no need for this to occur in the circumstances. The ends of justice were best met by granting joinder and hearing all of the charges at the same time.

5.4.3 TRYING MATTERS SEPARATELY

- Reasons that the defence may wish to try matters *separately* may include the situations listed below:
  - The defendant may wish to testify regarding one count but not expose him- or herself to cross-examination on another.
  - Where there are a number of defendants, one defendant might be prejudiced by an admission against another which is hearsay and inadmissible against the first.
  - Where the evidence is complex and there is a danger that the judge will inadvertently lump together distinct issues to the prejudice of the defence, consider trying the matters separately.

5.5 *RES JUDICATA*

- *Before pleading*, the defendant may argue that the charge being faced is in fact and in law the same offence for which he has already been tried.
- This common law rule against "double jeopardy" is now enshrined in section 11(h) of the *Charter* which states the following:

  > Any person charged with an offence has the right, if finally acquitted of the offence, not to be tried for it again and, if finally found guilty and punished for the offence, not to be tried or punished for it again.

The defendant cannot be convicted of both stunt driving due to driving more than 50 kilometres over the speed limit, and the offence of speeding, due to the rule precluding multiple convictions for the same *delict*: *R. v. Skimming-Quesnel*, 2011 ONCJ 376, 2011 CarswellOnt 8344, [2011] O.J. No. 3799 (Ont. C.J.); *R. v. Stickles*, 2011 ONCJ 128, 2011 CarswellOnt 1892, [2011] O.J. No. 1265 (Ont. C.J.).

Where a finding of guilt is imposed for careless driving, and speeding was an integral part of the findings which led to finding the defendant's action constituted careless driving, proceedings should be conditionally stayed for the lesser speeding offence. See *R. v. Kropf*, 2010 ONCJ 663, 2010 CarswellOnt 10468, [2010] O.J. No. 5864 (Ont. C.J.).

A withdrawal of charges is not the same as an acquittal and cannot give rise to a plea of autrefois acquit: *R. v. 136567 Ontario Ltd.*, 2010 ONCJ 712, 2010 CarswellOnt 10543, [2010] O.J. No. 5913 (Ont. C.J.).

In *R. v. Thomas G. Fuller & Sons Ltd.*, 2011 CarswellOnt 4459, (*sub nom.* Ontario (Minister of Labour) v. Black & McDonald Ltd.) 278 O.A.C. 284, (*sub nom.* Ontario (Minister of Labour) v. Black & McDonald Ltd.) 106 O.R. (3d) 784, [2011] O.J. No. 2615, 2 C.L.R. (4th) 161, 2011 ONCA 440 (Ont. C.A.), the Court of Appeal ruled that the application of the rule in *Kienapple* against multiple convictions does not result in an acquittal; it results in a conditional stay. Therefore, assuming the trial judge had made findings of guilt on all five counts, even if he applied *Kienapple* to counts 1, 2 and 4, at most he could have ordered a conditional stay. He could not have acquitted the defendants or dismissed the charges against them. And once the appeal court judge overturned the findings of guilt on counts 3 and 5, the conditional stays on counts 1, 2 and 4 would have been set aside and the findings of guilt on these counts restored.

In *R. v. Quinn*, 2013 ONCJ 89, 2013 CarswellOnt 2308, [2013] O.J. No. 893 (Ont. C.J.), it was held that the issue of estoppel did not apply to preclude the defendant from being charged with offences under the *Consumer Protection Act* where the victim had obtained a judgment in Small Claims Court based on the same contract and circumstances which gave rise to the charges. The charges were not the same issues int he civil proceedings. As well, Her Majesty the Queen was a party to the charges but not to the civil proceedings.

In *Immeubles Jacques Robitaille inc. c. Québec (Ville)*, 2014 CSC 34, 2014 SCC 34, 2014 CarswellQue 3559, 2014 CarswellQue 3560, [2014] 1 S.C.R. 784, 308 C.C.C. (3d) 334, 370 D.L.R. (4th) 595, 22 M.P.L.R. (5th) 1, 457 N.R. 136, [2014] S.C.J. No. 34 (S.C.C.), it was held that in the public law context, promissory estoppel requires proof of a clear and unambiguous promise made to a citizen by a public authority in order to induce the citizen to perform certain acts. The citizen must also have relied on the promise and acted on it by changing his or her conduct. However, the estoppel doctrine must yield to an overriding public interest and may not be invoked to prevent the application of an express legislative provision. In the instant case, the zoning by-law regulating the operation of a commercial parking lot was clear and did not authorize the municipality to consent to a non-conforming use. The doctrine of estoppel could not be relied on as a defence in a regulatory offence. Moreover, the fact that both civil and penal proceedings were available to municipalities to enforce zoning by-laws does not constitute an injustice. Each proceeding is clearly defined; each has different purposes. Neither results in *res judicata* in relation to the other. The mere possibility of a civil proceeding being unsuccessful does not raise a reasonable doubt as to the guilt of the defendant in a penal proceeding.

5.6 OTHER PROCEDURAL DEFENCES[*]

5.6.1 ABUSE OF PROCESS

- The court may stay (i.e. "stop") a prosecution which amounts to an abuse of process.

- The power is derived from the common law, which is preserved by section 80 of the POA, as well as the principles of fundamental justice in section 7 of the *Charter*.

- The power to stay a prosecution is only exercised in the "clearest of cases" to prevent "oppressive or vexatious proceedings": see *R. v. Jewitt*, 21 C.C.C. (3d) 7, [1985] 2 S.C.R. 128, [1985] 6 W.W.R. 127, 47 C.R. (3d) 193 (S.C.C.); and *R. v. Young* (1984), 46 O.R. (2d) 520, 40 C.R. (3d) 289, 13 C.C.C. (3d) 1 (Ont. C.A.) at 31.

- The alleged abuse must be by the prosecution, or other executive branch of the government: *R. v. Miles of Music Ltd.* (1989), 48 C.C.C. (3d) 96, 31 O.A.C. 380, 23 C.I.P.R. 16, 24 C.P.R. (3d) 301, 69 C.R. (3d) 361, 74 O.R. (2d) 518 (Ont. C.A.), but see the dissent of Blair J.A. and the reasons of Tarnopolsky J.A.

- Examples of abuse include:

    - Successive prosecutions for the same offence amounting to an oppression of the defendant: *R. v. Keyowski*, [1988]1 S.C.R. 657, [1988] 4 W.W.R. 97, 40 C.C.C. (3d) 481, (*sub nom.* Keyowski v. R.) 62 C.R. (3d) 349 (S.C.C.).

    - Delay in the laying of charges with the deliberate intention of impairing the defendant's ability to make full answer and defence: *Young, supra* at 31-32.

---

[*] For a detailed discussion of the procedural defences which are noted in the following sections, see *Libman on Regulatory Offences in Canada* (Earlscourt, 2002), Chapter 8.

- Unfair breach of an agreement not to prosecute to the prejudice of the defendant: *R. v. D. (E.)* (1990), 57 C.C.C. (3d) 151, 73 O.R. (2d) 758, 78 C.R. (3d) 112 (Ont. C.A.) at 163-168.

- Entrapment — when:

  - The authorities provide someone with an opportunity to commit an offence without acting on a reasonable suspicion that he or she is already engaged in criminal activity or in the course of a *bona fide* inquiry; or

  - Although having such a reasonable suspicion or acting in the course of a *bona fide* inquiry, going beyond providing an opportunity and inducing the commission of an offence: *R. v. Mack* (1988), 44 C.C.C. (3d) 513, [1988] 2 S.C.R. 903, [1989] 1 W.W.R. 577, 67 C.R. (3d) 1 (S.C.C.).

- A prosecution brought *solely* to collect a civil debt: *R. v. Leroux* (1928), 62 O.L.R. 336, 50 C.C.C. 52 (Ont. C.A.); *R. v. Lee* (1956), 114 C.C.C. 371 (Alta. S.C.); appeal to S.C.C. quashed; but proceedings are not stayed merely because the victim has asked the accused to repay a debt: *R. v. Laird* (1983), 4 C.C.C. (3d) 92 (Ont. H.C.).

Entrapment may not be considered before there is a finding of guilt. It requires a two-stage trial. At the first stage, the trier of fact must determine whether the accused is guilty of the alleged act. At the second stage, the judge considers the claim of entrapment and the conduct of the state: *R. v. Imoro*, 2010 ONCA 122, 2010 CarswellOnt 771, [2010] O.J. No. 586, 72 C.R. (6th) 292, 328 D.L.R. (4th) 128, 207 C.R.R. (2d) 146, 264 O.A.C. 362, 251 C.C.C. (3d) 131 (Ont. C.A.), affirmed 2010 SCC 50, 2010 CarswellOnt 8420, 2010 CarswellOnt 8421, [2010] S.C.J. No. 50, 408 N.R. 141, 269 O.A.C. 46, 80 C.R. (6th) 27, [2010] 3 S.C.R. 62, 224 C.R.R. (2d) 1, 263 C.C.C. (3d) 296, 328 D.L.R. (4th) 126 in *obiter* (at para. 24).

The provision in s. 80 of the *Provincial Offences Act* "except in so far as they are . . . inconsistent with . . . any other Act" is significant. Doctrines developed in the criminal law context should not automatically be applied, or applied without modification, in the wholly different regulatory context. Government authorities can use random test shopping to monitor compliance with the *Smoke Free Ontario Act*, without a reasonable suspicion that the person monitored is engaged in illegal activity. Random test shopping is the most effective way to achieve the government's purpose of ensuring compliance with the statute and deterring future illegal sales of tobacco. This does not mean that government authorities' discretion to use test shopping is unfettered or unreviewable by the courts. Test shopping may be done randomly; but it must be done in good faith. It must be used for a proper purpose and carried out bona fide and without discrimination. If it is not, if it is done in bad faith, then courts retain jurisdiction to stay proceedings under the general abuse of process doctrine of which entrapment is one aspect: *R. v. Clothier*, 2011 ONCA 27, 2011 CarswellOnt 112, 266 C.C.C. (3d) 19, 330 D.L.R. (4th) 125, 273 O.A.C. 162, [2011] O.J. No. 102 (Ont. C.A.).

There was no evidence to show that the prosecution of the charges was delegated to the Fire Chiefs. The prosecutor, who was properly appointed by the Regional Municipality of Niagara, acted in that capacity throughout the case, and there was no suggestion that he acted improperly at any time. The sentence in the prosecutor's letter that he had received instructions from the Fire Chiefs neither constituted nor indicated that the authority to prosecute the cases had been delegated to the Fire Chiefs; it was very similar to a Crown attorney consulting with the investigating police officer or a complainant before making a decision in a criminal case. As long as the lawyer continues to make the decisions, he/she is still the prosecutor. There was nothing to indicate anything different here. Nor was there anything to suggest that he behaved improperly in any way in his prosecution of the case: *Niagara (Regional Municipality) v. DiFruscia*, 2010 ONCJ 427, 2010 CarswellOnt 7104, [2010] O.J. No. 404 (Ont. C.J.).

Abuse of process concerns the improper exercise of Crown discretion and is available in regulatory prosecutions under provincial statutes. The test for abuse of process is whether the proceedings would violate the fundamental principles which under lie the community's sense of fair play and decency, or whether the proceedings were oppressive or vexatious. It is only in the clearest of cases that the power to stay proceedings will be exercised as a remedy for an abuse of process. The actions of the Ministry of Natural Resources officials in the case to proceed with a prosecution rather than an administrative proceeding did not amount to an abuse of process. See *R. v. Buchanan Forest Products Ltd.*, 2007 ONCJ 630, 2007 CarswellOnt 8720, [2007] O.J. No. 5222 (Ont. C.J.).

The Crown's repudiation of a plea agreement is an exercise of core prosecutorial discretion and is not to be regarded as a contractual undertaking. It is reviewable by the courts only if the process by which it was made constitutes an abuse of process: *R. v. Nixon*, [2011] 2 S.C.R. 566, 2011 CarswellAlta 989, 2011 CarswellAlta 988, [2011] S.C.J. No. 34, [2011] 7 W.W.R. 429, 41 Alta. L.R. (5th) 221, 271 C.C.C. (3d) 36, 517 W.A.C. 18, 502 A.R. 18, 335 D.L.R. (4th) 565, 237 C.R.R. (2d) 333, 85 C.R. (6th) 1, 13 M.V.R. (6th) 1, 417 N.R. 274, 2011 SCC 34 (S.C.C.).

In *R. v. Martin Grove Properties Ltd.,* 2011 ONCA 711, 90 M.P.L.R. (4th) 226, 2011 CarswellOnt 12226, [2011] O.J. No. 4992 (Ont. C.A.), leave to appeal refused 2012 CarswellOnt 6765, 2012 CarswellOnt 6766, 426 N.R. 389 (note), 302 O.A.C. 397 (note) (S.C.C.), it was held that the subject matter of the proceedings for the purpose of the *Building Code Act* was the failure to comply with the order made in March,2008, and the omission of which took place at the earliest after May, 2008, when the defendant allegedly failed to comply with the terms of the order. The charge, which was laid in January, 2009, was therefore laid within the one year statutory limitation period. The fact that there were other orders issued relating to the same underlying acts of the defendant might be relevant to an argument that the prosecution was an abuse of process, but did not preclude the municipality from instituting the prosecution. The fact that the municipality had other remedies for failure to comply with orders did not preclude resort to prosecution.

In an abuse of process case where the defence of entrapment was raised, *R. v. Schmidt,* 2011 ONCJ 482, 2011 CarswellOnt 10564, 248 C.R.R. (2d) 91, [2011] O.J. No. 4272 (Ont. C.J.), affirmed 2014 ONCA 188, 2014 CarswellOnt 2796, 119 O.R. (3d) 145, 304 C.R.R. (2d) 126, 318 O.A.C.53, [2014] O.J. No.1074 (Ont. C.A.), it was held that entrapment occurs when the authorities provide a person with an opportunity to commit an offence without a reasonable suspicion the person is already committing an offence or without making a *bona fide* inquiry to confirm a prohibited activity was already taking place. In this case the authorities had a reasonable basis to suspect raw milk products were being supplied by the defendant to others. The investigators were therefore making a *bona fide* inquiry to confirm the activity in question was taking place when through the use of an undercover investigator the defendant was prevailed upon to supply unpasteurized milk.

It did not constitute an abuse of process to prosecute the defendant for operating a garage contrary to a municipal by-law on the basis that the enforcement officer stated under cross-examination that in her opinion the charge should not have been laid. The by-law enforcement officer was not an expert witness, and her opinion did not meet the test for granting a stay of proceedings only in the clearest of cases. See *Vaughan (City) v. Antorisa Investments Ltd.,* 2012 CarswellOnt 11137, [2012] O.J. No. 3584 (Ont. C.J.), affirmed 2013 ONCA 287, 2013 CarswellOnt 5143, [2013] O.J. No.1997 (Ont. C.A.).

The accused failed to establish, on a balance of probabilities, that the police officers who investigated and arrested him for riding a bicycle with out a head light used excessive force such that they violated his rights to fundamental justice or engaged in cruel or unusual punishment. The defendant exaggerated and was overly dramatic; his version of events became less specific during cross-examination. The injuries that he suffered could have been caused by the gritty reality of a lawful take down. See *R. v. Taing*, 2012 ABPC 236, 2012 CarswellAlta 1423, 546 A.R. 386, [2012] A.J. No. 866 (Alta. Prov. Ct.).

Issuing multiple orders to comply under the *Building Code Act* and laying charges for non-compliance do not meet the test for abuse of process. The evidence relied on by the defendant to establish that there was lost evidence which compromised its ability to defend the charge of failing to comply fell far short of the required standard; the record required the court to speculate that such evidence was available, and in any event that evidence was not relevant to any issue in the trial of the alleged failure to comply. The fact that a corporation has been charged with or even convicted of failing to comply with an order under the *Building Code Act* in the past in relation to the same structure does not in and of itself amount to an abuse of process. Even if the City was negligent in putting the wrong municipal address on the order or was too slow in enforcing the orders, these matters did not approach the level of misconduct required to establish abuse of process. The actions of the City, particularly when viewed in the context of municipal enforcement of land use requirements, did not offend societal notions of fair play and decency. See *York (Regional Municipality) v. Martingrove Properties Ltd.* (October 28, 2015), Doc. Newmarket 999-09-0071, [2015] O.J. No. 6952 (Ont. C.J.), leave to appeal refused (March 29, 2016), Doc. M45752, [2016] O.J. No. 1582 (Ont. C.A.).

The ability to stop vehicles on a random basis for general highway safety purposes was not consistent with the officer's clearly stated purpose and cannot be used to bolster, support or substitute for the true purpose of her stop, that being the finding of a vehicle that had been speeding at an earlier point in time. Given the officer's articulated purpose, there was no rational basis for stopping the defendant's car. It would be disingenuous in the extreme to claim, after the fact, that the purpose in stopping the defendant was not as originally stated — the investigation of a previously committed *Motor Vehicles Act* offence — but rather a random motor vehicle safety check. The stopping of the defendant was not objectively reasonable as there was nothing wrong with his driving at the time he was stopped, and the officer was not claiming to be out conducting random safety checks. The suspicion that the defendant was the driver of the vehicle previously observed by the officer could not rationally be elevated to objectively reasonable grounds for the stop. Further, there was nothing that stopping the defendant's vehicle could have been done to further an investigation into a speeding offence. The stop was therefore arbitrary and violated s. 9 of the *Charter*. While it could not be clearly found that the officer was operating in bad faith, the stop was not made with objectively reasonable grounds. Ultimately, the impact upon the defendant, while not egregious, was not trivial. There is a societal interest in keeping the streets safe and investigating *Motor Vehicles Act* breaches, but these investigations must be for rational and clearly articulated purposes. Here, the officer's stated purpose and subsequent stopping of the defendant did not comport with the requirement that it be objectively reasonable. The appropriate remedy was the exclusion of evidence flowing from the arbitrary stop. However, a new trial was ordered on appeal on the basis that the trial judge erred by not permitting the officer to be recalled which would have permitted the Crown to ask the officer questions about the reasons for her stop. The defence had not flagged the issue of arbitrary detention while the officer gave evidence. See *R. v. Rowat*, 2018 YKTC 20, 2018 CarswellYukon 41, 26 M.V.R. (7th) 146, [2018] Y.J. No. 38 (Y.T. Terr. Ct.), reversed 2018 YKSC 50, 2018 CarswellYukon 103 (Y.T. S.C.).

The defendant's concern about the prejudicial effect of evidence that had been adduced from leading questions put by the prosecutor to their own witnesses and the elicitation of irrelevant hearsay, bad character, and lay opinion evidence into the trial, had to be viewed in context and its intended use in the trial. Any prejudicial effect of the impugned evidence had been lessened as this was a non-jury trial and the charges involved strict liability regulatory offences in which the prosecution can elicit evidence in their case-in-chief to rebut a defence of due diligence or other anticipated defences. After considering the impugned evidentiary issues and the context in which the prosecutor's impugned comments, language and tone were used and what had been occurring in the trial at the time, the cumulative effect of the prosecutor's conduct, although not ideal and of perfect comportment, did not go beyond aggressive or abusive as to cause the defendant to receive an unfair trial, since the defendant's trial was a non-jury trial for which the trier would be cognizant of applying the relevant legal principles and law, and would also be able to disabuse and give no weight to any hearsay, bad character, opinion, or any other irrelevant prejudicial evidence, nor put any weight on any inappropriate, sarcastic, or demeaning comments, made by the prosecutor about the defendant's memory, business practices, or personal lifestyle, or to improperly use the impugned evidence or the immoderate comments of the prosecutor as proof of guilt. Accordingly, the defendant's right to a fair trial had not been prejudiced by the cumulative effect of the prosecutor's conduct in eliciting the impugned evidence, nor by the prosecutor's impugned comments, language or tone, that would be manifested, perpetuated or aggravated through the conduct of the trial, or by its outcome. Neither was the cumulative effect of the prosecutor's conduct such that it reached a degree of unfairness or vexatiousness that contravenes notions of fundamental justice, nor was it the type of conduct in which the justice system would find it necessary to intervene so that it would leave the impression that it condones conduct that offends society's sense of fair play and decency. Therefore, the prosecutor's conduct during the trial had not undermined the integrity of the justice system that would be manifested, perpetuated or aggravated through the conduct of the trial, or by its outcome. See *Ontario (Electrical Safety Authority) v. Broomfield*, 2018 ONCJ 640, 2018 CarswellOnt 15732, [2018] O.J. No. 4893 (Ont. C.J.).

5.6.2 OFFICIALLY INDUCED ERROR

- Section 81 of the POA states that: "Ignorance of the law is no excuse for committing the offence".

However, the Ontario Court of Appeal in *R. v. Cancoil Thermal Corp.* (1986), 27 C.C.C. (3d) 295, 11 C.C.E.L. 219, 52 C.R. (3d) 188 (Ont. C.A.) at 303 held that:

> The defence of officially induced error is available as a defence to an alleged violation of a regulatory statute where an accused has reasonably relied upon the erroneous legal opinion or advice of an official who is responsible for the administration or enforcement of the particular law.
>
> In order for the accused to successfully raise this defence, he must show that he relied on the erroneous legal opinion of the official and that his reliance was reasonable. The reasonableness will depend upon several factors including the efforts he made to ascertain the proper law, the complexity or obscurity of the law, the position of the official who gave the advice, and the clarity, definitiveness and reasonableness of the advice given.

- The error must be one of law and not of fact.

- The defendant must take reasonable steps to specifically direct the official's attention to the situation in which the official's opinion is being relied upon.

- The defendant must provide full disclosure to the official of the surrounding circumstances: *R. v. Cancoil Thermal Corp.* (1988), 1 C.O.H.S.C. 169 (Ont. Prov. Offences Ct.), also digested at 4 W.C.B. (2d) 385.

- The defendant has the burden of proving an officially induced error, on a preponderance of evidence.

- The defence of officially induced error is not available where the defendant was unable to ascertain the existence of a regulation and where there was no erroneous advice given: *Halton Region Conservation Authority v. Cristiano* (1992), 10 C.E.L.R. (N.S.) 154 (Ont. Prov. Div.).

- The defence is in the nature of an excuse which entitles a stay of proceedings rather than an acquittal if six elements are shown: (1) an error of law or of mixed law and fact was made; (2) the person who committed the act considered the legal consequences of his or her actions; (3) the advice obtained came from an appropriate official; (4) the advice was reasonable; (5) the advice was erroneous; and (6) the person relied on the advice in committing the act. See: *Lévis (Ville) c. Tétreault*, 2006 CarswellQue 2911, 2006 Carswell-

Que 2912, [2006] S.C.J. No. 12, 36 C.R. (6th) 215, 2006 SCC 12, 31 M.V.R. (5th) 1, (*sub nom.* Lévis (City) v. Tétreault) 346 N.R. 331, 207 C.C.C. (3d) 1, [2006] 1 S.C.R. 420, (*sub nom.* Lévis (City) v. Tétreault) 266 D.L.R. (4th) 165 (S.C.C.).

The defence of officially induced error does not apply where there is no reliance on anything said by anyone other than advice from the defendant's own solicitor: *R. v. Catena* (February 1, 2008), No. 02-4122, [2008] O.J. No.1806 (Ont. C.J.).

A mistake of law as to whether the *Income Tax Act* applies to an accused person, where the mistake is based on a belief unsupported by the Act, does not negate the fault requirement of tax evasion: *R. v. Klundert* (2008), 2008 CarswellOnt 6718, 2008 ONCA 767, [2008] O.J. No. 4522, 62 C.R. (6th) 90, [2009] 2 C.T.C. 108,93 O.R. (3d)81, 238 C.C.C. (3d) 6, 244 O.A.C. 377 (Ont. C.A.), at paras. 16-22, 28 [ONCA], leave to appeal refused (2009), 2009 CarswellOnt 1883, 2009 CarswellOnt 1884, 396 N.R. 390 (note), [2008] S.C.C.A. No. 522, 260 O.A.C. 398 (note) (S.C.C.).

The defence of officially induced error of law was not established where the defence evidence was self-contradictory and unreasonable in that the defendant produced no corroborative evidence that might have substantiated the important issue of non-enforcement of the by-law. While corroboration was not necessary, one might have thought that the defendant would have a written confirming letter or an extracted minute from a meeting with the municipal officials, given that the city had made it known it would now be enforcing its by-law which prohibited the picking up of passengers without being licensed as a taxi cab owner, the change had occurred approximately one year prior to the charges before the court, and he was aware that he had not received any official accommodation from the city allowing for his actions, which eventually gave rise to the charges in question. See *R. v. Pilgrim Transportation Services Ltd.* (June 1, 2010), Doc. 07-1800, [2010] O.J. No. 3226 (Ont. C.J.).

In another recent decision, *R. v. Sutherland*, 2010 ONSC 2240, 2010 CarswellOnt 2858, 51 C.E.L.R. (3d) 163, [2010] O.J. No. 1797 (Ont. S.C.J.), leave to appeal refused 2011 ONCA 239, 2011 CarswellOnt 1917, [2011] O.J. No. 1295 (Ont. C.A.), it was held that the defence of officially induced error of law did not apply to the facts of the case, given that the defendant's decision to proceed and deposit the fill was based on his discussion with an official who was not charged with the administration of the *Fisheries Act*. He simply went ahead, after making primary inquiries, and ordered the work performed on his property without having regard to the consequences or making sure he complied with the proper permits or permission by the Ministry responsible. Even after being explained the severity of his actions and that the situation should be rectified, he did not comply.

In order for the officially induced error of law defence to be made out, the advice relied upon must meet the definition of reasonableness, that is, it must be clear, definitive, and reasonable to meet the test of reasonableness. Advice from an unnamed source to "read the Act" falls far short of this standard. See *R. v. Willows*, 2010 ONCJ 100, [2010] O.J. No. 1183, 2010 CarswellOnt 1714 (Ont. C.J.).

There was an error of law made by the defendant in publishing an advertisement; it knew or reasonably ought to have considered the legal consequences of its actions in displaying such an advertisement. The advice it received from the appropriate official was not erroneous, neither did it rely upon that advice. Had the defendant relied upon the official's advice for its advertisement, it would not have contravened the legislation. The defence of officially induced error of law had not been proven on a balance of probabilities in these circumstances: *R. v. Almadi Enterprises Inc.*, 2011 ONCJ 332, 2011 CarswellOnt 5585, [2011] O.J. No. 2940, 16 M.V.R. (6th) 319 (Ont. C.J.).

The defence of officially induced error was not made out in a case where a Ministry of Labour inspector had attended the workplace six year earlier following an accident and advised of changes to be made to the machinery to prevent an accident from happening again, but there was no evidence of any steps being taken afterward by the defendant to seek further advice or ascertain the law on the necessity of a gap, even though it was aware of the practice of its employees using their hands to clear jams in the hopper so as not to impede production. See *Ontario (Ministry of Labour) v. Pack All Manufacturing Ltd.* (November 6, 2012), Kehoe J., [2012] O.J. No. 5311 (Ont. C.J.).

In *R. v. Kell*, 2013 ONCJ 637, 2013 CarswellOnt 16122, [2013] O.J. No. 5425 (Ont. C.J.), the defence of officially induced error of law was rejected where the defendant claimed that after being stopped and issued a roadside suspension he contacted the Ministry of Transportation and CAMH to discuss the status of his driving licence. However, the defendant simply believed that registering for a remedial program would ensure the validity of his license. The defendant chose to believe his licence was valid rather than making more fulsome inquiries which would have provided him with information to the contrary.

In *Québec (Autorité des marchés financiers) c. Souveraine, cie d'assurance générale*, 2013 SCC 63, 2013 CarswellQue 11257, 2013 CarswellQue 11258, (*sub nom.* La Souveraine, Compagnie d'assurance générale v. Autorité des marchés financiers) [2013] 3 S.C.R. 756, 305 C.C.C. (3d) 287, 26 C.C.L.I. (5th) 1, 6 C.R.

(7th) 250, 365 D.L.R. (4th) 559, 451 N.R. 113, [2013] S.C.J. No. 63 (S.C.C.), the Supreme Court of Canada ruled that a mistake of law can ground a valid defence only if the mistake was an officially induced error, and if the conditions regarding the application of such a defence are met. No matter how reasonable a mistake of law may be, it cannot, unlike a mistake of fact or an officially induced error, serve as a valid defence in the case of a strict liability offence. The objective of public protection that underlies the creation of regulatory offences militates strongly against accepting a general defence of reasonable mistake of law in this context.

The defendant was charged with failing to obtain a building permit and failing to comply with an order of a building inspector, contrary to the *Building Code Act*. He argued the defence of officially induced error of law. However, the defendant was aware of the permit requirement, and chose to proceed before he had permission. In no way was he misinformed or induced by anyone, official or otherwise to engage in the non-permissible construction. At its highest, the advice he claimed to have received from the Committee of Adjustment might explain why he did not pursue the option to attempt to remedy the situation, but it had nothing to do with his commission of the offences in the first place. The officially induced error defence applies where one commits an offence honestly believing from an official source that it is lawful to do so. Plainly the alleged erroneous advice must precede the commission of the offence. In any event, there was no erroneous advice given to the defendant. Indeed, the City had made it clear throughout that he was non-compliant and in continuing breach of the law. See *R. v. Khalid*, 2014 ONCJ 125, 2014 CarswellOnt 3296, 20 M.P.L.R. (5th) 171, [2014] O.J. No. 1257 (Ont. C.J.).

In *R. v. Lawend*, 2015 ONCJ 205, 2015 CarswellOnt 15076, [2015] O.J. No. 1979 (Ont. C.J.), it was found that the defendant did not meet its burden of proving on a balance of probabilities the defence of officially induced error of law since the supposed information given to the defendant by a person on the telephone was not objectively reasonable, logical or plausible in light of s. 36 of the *Highway Traffic Act* which prohibits anyone with an Ontario driver's licence that has been suspended from using a driver's licence or permit from another jurisdiction while the defendant's Ontario licence is under suspension. In addition, the defendant failed to prove on a balance of probabilities that the person on the telephone had been an appropriate official with the Ministry of Transportation who could properly provide the advice or legal information in question, since not all government people would be able to properly advise or give a legal opinion on a point of law or the legal consequences of a particular action.

The defendant argued that he had tried to pay the fine after returning to the jurisdiction, but had been told by a counter clerk of the Ministry of Transportation when he inquired that there was no fine and his licence was okay. The Justice of the Peace rejected this defence to the charge of driving while suspended, and concluded that the defence was properly served with the notice of suspension. He had failed to advise the Ministry of the changes in his address as required, and had not acted diligently when he was provided information that the system had not indicated an outstanding fine. The Justice rejected the defendant's claim that he was misled by an officially induced error given the status of the official who provided this information. See *R. v. Gochko*, 2015 ONCJ 555, 2015 CarswellOnt 15350, [2015] O.J. No. 5213 (Ont. C.J.).

In *Durham (Regional Municipality) v. D. Crupi & Sons Ltd.*, 2015 ONCJ 488, 2015 CarswellOnt 15126, [2015] O.J. No. 4872 (Ont. C.J.), at first, the defendant was told at the Ministry of Transportation counter that the Ministry would not issue a registration renewal for the impugned motor vehicle because it was "zero" weight class. The defendant decided not to rely solely on this information. In response to the defendant's further queries, the Head Carrier Enforcement Liaison official at the Ministry clearly and concisely provided his erroneous opinion on the law in the matter. For the second time, the defendant was told it was exempt from registering its motor vehicle. Only after taking all of these actions did the defendant then drive the commercial motor vehicle on a highway with no currently validated permit. In these circumstances, the defendant's reliance on the erroneous legal opinion provided by the Ministry of Transportation was reasonable. The defence of officially induced error of law was clearly proven on a balance of probabilities.

Where a citizen is induced to act on the advice of an authorized representative of the state, and that advice is later shown to have been in error and contrary to law, it would be unfair to punish the citizen for the breach. The onus is on the defendant to establish the defence of officially induced error of law on a balance of probabilities. In the instant case, the trial Justice found the defendant's evidence that a municipal enforcement officer told him that he was free to pave was not credible. The statements on the municipality's website could not reasonably have led or contributed to the defendant's error. See *R. v. Robati* (March 12, 2015), Doc. Richmond Hill 11-0021, 11-0256, [2015] O.J. No. 6934 (Ont. C.J.), affirmed (December 15, 2015), Kenkel J., [2015] O.J. No. 6646 (Ont. C.J.).

Similarly, in *R. v. Madan*, 2016 ONCJ 107, 2016 CarswellOnt 2856, [2016] O.J. No. 1024 (Ont. C.J.), it was held that the letter sent by the Ministry which concluded with an invitation to the defendant to contact the writer upon receipt of the letter could not be construed to mean that the defendant's property remediation efforts were complete, and as such did not present the basis for an officially induced error defence. The defendant could not, in good faith, have relied on this information to avoid his obligations in relation to the property.

5.6.3 INADEQUATE DISCLOSURE

- The prosecutor has an obligation to provide timely disclosure to the defence, as described in Chapter 3.

- In the clearest of cases, where the defence has been prejudiced and there are no alternative remedies, the court may stay the proceedings if there is inadequate disclosure.

- The usual remedy consists of one or more of the following:

  - An order compelling the prosecutor to produce the material sought.

  - An adjournment to allow the defendant time to prepare the defence.

  - Where necessary, the recalling of witnesses for further examination.

  - Costs.

In *Ontario v. 974649 Ontario Inc.*, 2001 CarswellOnt 4251, 47 C.R. (5th) 316 (*sub. nom.* R. v. 974649 Ontario Inc.) [2001] 3 S.C.R. 575, 56 O.R. (3d) 359 (headnote only), 2001 CarswellOnt 4252, (*sub nom.* R. v. 974649 Ontario Inc.) [2001] S.C.J. No. 79, (*sub nom.* R. v. 974649 Ontario Inc.) 2001 SCC 81, (*sub nom.* R. v. 974649 Ontario Inc.) 206 D.L.R. (4th) 444, (*sub nom.* R. v. 974649 Ontario Inc.) 159 C.C.C. (3d) 321, (*sub nom.* R. v. 974649 Ontario Inc.) 88 C.R.R. (2d) 189, (*sub nom.* R. v. 974649 Ontario Inc.) 279 N.R. 345, (*sub nom.* R. v. 974649 Ontario Inc.) 154 O.A.C. 345 (S.C.C.), the Supreme Court of Canada concluded that the justice of the peace acting as a trial justice under the *Provincial Offences Act* possessed the power to order legal costs against the Crown as a remedy for *Charter* breaches arising from untimely disclosure. The costs were awarded on the defendants' disclosure motion which was brought as a result of the Crown's failure to disclose a copy of the Prosecution Approval Form relating to charges laid under the *Occupational Health and Safety Act*. If defendants were deprived of this remedy, a provincial offences court maybe confined to two extreme options for relief — a stay of proceedings or a mere adjournment — neither of which may be appropriate and just in the circumstances.

- The awarding of costs against the prosecution in a provincial offences prosecution is considered to be an "exceptional tool" which is reserved for cases which involve a "marked and unacceptable departure from reasonable prosecution standards". See *R. v. Felderhof* (2002), [2002] O.J. No. 4103, 2002 CarswellOnt 5623 (Ont. S.C.J.), additional reasons at (2003), [2003] O.J. No. 393, 2003 CarswellOnt

488 (Ont. S.C.J.), affirmed (2003), 180 C.C.C. (3d) 498, 2003 CarswellOnt 4943, [2003] O.J. No. 4819, 68 O.R. (3d) 481, 10 Admin. L.R. (4th) 229, 235 D.L.R. (4th) 131, 180 O.A.C. 288, 17 C.R. (6th) 20 (Ont. C.A.).

- The justice may declare a mistrial rather than ordering a stay of proceedings where an adjournment or further examination of witnesses is *not* an adequate remedy: *R. v. Fineline Circuits Ltd.* (1991), 10 C.R. (4th) 241 (Ont. Prov. Ct.).

- A stay of proceedings should not normally be ordered as the stay is a drastic remedy, and is reserved for those cases where it is not possible to remedy through reasonable means the prejudice to the defendant's right to make full answer and defence. See *R. v. Arcand* (2004), [2004] O.J. No. 5017, 2004 CarswellOnt 5160, 10 C.E.L.R. (3d) 161, 125 C.R.R. (2d) 144, 193 O.A.C. 16, 192 C.C.C. (3d) 57, 73 O.R. (3d) 758 (Ont. C.A.).

While it would have been preferable for the Crown to have been more forthcoming with disclosure, the defendant was in possession of all he needed prior to trial and was not prejudiced by the Crown's conduct: *R. v. Arcand*, 2008 CarswellOnt 4971, 2008 ONCA 595, 240 O.A.C. 286, 238 C.C.C. (3d) 204, 92 O.R. (3d) 444, 38 C.E.L.R. (3d) 1, [2008] O.J. No. 3294, 178 C.R.R. (2d) 199 (Ont. C.A.), leave to appeal refused (2008), [2008] S.C.C.A. No. 449, 2008 CarswellOnt 7740, 2008 CarswellOnt 7741, 180 C.R.R. 375 (note), 257 O.A.C. 399 (note), 393 N.R. 399 (note) (S.C.C.), leave to appeal refused 2008 CarswellOnt 7740, 2008 CarswellOnt 7741, [2008] S.C.C.A. No. 449, 180 C.R.R. 375 (note), 257 O.A.C. 399 (note), 393 N.R. 399 (note) (S.C.C.).

While an officer's notes cannot be expected to record every minute detail, they must contain a complete and accurate record of the significant events in the investigation so as to enable the Crown to fulfill its obligation to make full disclosure: *R. v. Karunakaran*, 2008 CarswellOnt 5210, 2008 ONCJ 397 (Ont. C.J.), at para. 25 [ONCJ].

The defendant was not deprived of her right to make full answer and defence where she was provided with disclosure of the officer's notes, but which did not include information about the officer's qualifications and training to operate the radar gun: *Durham (Regional Municipality) v. Driscoll-Rogers*, 2008 CarswellOnt 6768, 2008 ONCJ 581, [2008] O.J. No. 4572 (Ont. C.J.).

In *R. v. Zacharias*, 2016 ONCJ 458, 2016 CarswellOnt 12095, [2016] O.J. No. 3975 (Ont. C.J.), the prosecution disclosed the police officer's notes and complied with some special disclosure requests of the defence. However, there were two letters from the defence requesting "if this is a speeding offence, the testing times of this device before and after the subject enforcement". The prosecution did not respond to that request. Prior to the trial, the prosecution and the defence discussed the testing of the device outside of court. The prosecution apparently disclosed the fact that the police officer had tested the device, but testing times were not provided. When the trial commenced, the defence stated that it was ready to proceed to trial. If the defence had been dissatisfied with the disclosure, it should have raised the issue as a pre-trial motion. If the lateness of the disclosure created a preparation problem for the defence, they should have requested an adjournment. However, the defence was ready to proceed to trial, and they so advised the court. There was no basis for concluding that the defendant did not receive a fair trial.

In *R. v. Hadi*, 2016 ONCJ 447, 2016 CarswellOnt 11897, [2016] O.J. No. 3890 (Ont. C.J.), the defendant was given a DVD of the in-car recording in advance of his trial, but there was no audio on that recording. The arresting officer had forgotten to put the audio pack on before he left his car. When the defendant was told this by the justice of the peace, he refused to accept this explanation, and declined to participate in his trial for improper right turn and failing to surrender his driving licence. The Crown's duty to disclose what is in its possession also applies to the police who must provide relevant disclosure to the Crown to be further disclosed to the defence. However, the Crown cannot disclose what it does not have. There was no issue in this case of any lost or destroyed disclosure; the disclosure issue was properly resolved by the justice of the peace who explained to the defendant in plain terms that the audio was not there and he could not be given what was never created in the first place. There could be no other possible decision the justice of the peace could have made. The DVD was played in court at the accused's trial. The fact that there was no audio on the recording was made apparent to the justice of the peace. It was also made clear to him that his copy was the same as that in the possession of the Crown. Despite this, the accused continued to refuse to participate. Having a fair trial means that a defendant receives a fair *opportunity* to make full answer and defence. If the defendant chooses not to make use of this opportunity, there is little that the justice system can do.

In *R. v. Galbraith*, 2018 ONCJ 138, 2018 CarswellOnt 3347, 404 C.R.R. (2d) 371, [2018] O.J. No. 1189 (Ont. C.J.), a written request for disclosure was sought four times by the defendant for her speeding trial, and she received assurances from administration that her requests had been forwarded to the office of the prosecution. She did not receive an answer to her requests. The prosecution policy concerning the provision of disclosure in the jurisdiction was usually two weeks after receipt of a written request. The delay in providing disclosure in a timely manner to the defendant in this case was due to staffing changes in the office of the prosecution. The prosecution delay in providing disclosure was due to a mistake and did not violate her right to a fair trial under s. 11(d) of the *Charter of Rights*, nor was any prejudice demonstrated such that the late disclosure did not violate the right to make full answer and defence under s. 7 of the *Charter*. The time elapsed since the date of the offence to the proposed date of trial was 7 months, well below the presumptive ceiling for unreasonable delay established in *R. v. Jordan*. There was no negligence on the part of the prosecutor that justified an order of costs either as a Charter remedy or due to procedural irregularities under s. 90 of the *Provincial Offences Act*. The defendant had chosen to attend the Early Resolution meeting and there were a total of two court appearances to date. Section 24(1) of the *Charter* confers a broad remedial mandate and the widest possible discretion on a court to craft remedies that must be easily available for violations of *Charter* rights. The remedy in the instant case was an adjournment to a date for trial and no order for costs.

At the beginning of his trial, the defendant argued he was denied Crown disclosure despite two requests for it. At the start of his trial, the prosecutor gave some disclosure, but the defendant asked for more. The prosecutor was not in a position to provide it at that time. The defendant then asked the justice of the peace for a stay of proceedings due to this failure to make proper disclosure. He was not allowed to make submissions on this point, including his presenting four binding cases that he wished to present. However, the defendant did not give any notice he was bringing a stay application. By not giving such a notice, the justice of the peace understandably was not prepared to hear the stay application on the merits at that time. The justice of the peace was within his right to try and control the proceedings before him, and he did not overstep the appropriate boundaries of that. At the end of the day, while the justice of the peace did not accede to the defendant's request for a stay or listen to the whole of his submissions, he adjourned the trial in order that disclosure be made. The justice of the peace specifically left it open for the defendant to bring his stay application on the new trial date, present any evidence he wished, and to make his submissions. When the whole of the proceedings was assessed, there was no denial of natural justice or an unfair hearing. The justice of the peace was also correct in not ordering a stay of proceedings at this time. The remedy that he chose was to grant an adjournment so that proper disclosure could be made. This was a fit remedy for Crown non-disclosure. The justice of the peace did not preclude the defendant from asking for a stay of proceedings upon the resumption of the trial. No substantial wrong or miscarriage of justice resulted from this decision. See *City of Toronto v. Riddell*, 2018 ONSC 2048, 2018 CarswellOnt 4860, [2018] O.J. No. 1643 (Ont. S.C.J.), affirmed *Toronto (City) v. Riddell*, 2019 ONCA 103, 2019 CarswellOnt 2272, [2019] O.J. No. 823 (Ont. C.A.).

In *R. v. Bakshi*, 2018 CarswellOnt 11576, [2018] O.J. No. 3736 (Ont. C.J.), the total delay in the case was 16 months and 28 days, which included a *voir dire* on the lack of production of audio and video recordings in the police cruiser and the lack of an audio recording for the traffic stop. While this delay was under the presumptive ceiling in *Jordan*, the defence did take meaningful steps to expedite the proceedings by bringing two disclosure requests. The matter took markedly longer than it should have, being a trial for drive hand held communication device. This was a simple case. While it was not a minor traffic matter, it was a standard provincial offence matter that is heard on the tier of 40 to 45 matters. The delay falls at the foot of the prosecution as they did not have communication within their office. While there are numerous numbers of cases and there are numerous prosecutors, it is not perfection to track a case where an email comes in that an audio recording is not available to the case that it applies to. There had been unreasonable delay considering the *Jordan* framework as it stands. An order staying the charge was granted.

In *Reginella v. R.*, 2018 ONCJ 198, 2018 CarswellOnt 4918, [2018] O.J. No. 1547 (Ont. C.J.), the learned justice of the peace denied the adjournment request brought by the defendant on the trial date due to disclosure not being received mainly on the bases that the Crown witnesses were present, the Crown was ready to proceed and that the defendant had not brought an application or motion for an adjournment prior to the trial date. The learned justice of the peace exercised his discretion judicially in refusing to grant the adjournment on the trial date. He properly considered that there would be an inconvenience to witnesses as being a factor and that the defendant or his agent had not brought an application for an adjournment prior when they realized that the disclosure had not been received. The learned justice of the peace did not consider any irrelevant factors in this decision. Clearly, there was an onus on the defendant and his agent to follow up by way of direct contact with the trial date when the disclosure had not been received. In addition to not being any adjournment request, the defendant or his agent did not bring an application for a stay of proceedings based on a failure of the prosecution to provide disclosure. In the circumstances, the trial was fair. The defendant was represented; he chose not to attend the trial. The defendant's agent could have renewed his request for an adjournment at the close of the prosecution's case so that the defendant or any defence witnesses could testify. Such a request was not made. The appeal court had not been advised that even though disclosure was received subsequent to the trial, there was something of substance in that disclosure that may have assisted the defendant in his defence.

In *York (Regional Municipality) v. Bouaziz-Caruso*, [2019] O.J. No. 638 (Ont. C.J.), the defence representative had asked for disclosure several weeks before, but by the trial date it had not been handed out. The trial justice denied the adjournment, finding that any suggestion the defendant did not receive the notice of trial in advance was hearsay. The justice held the matter down to permit the trial agent to review disclosure and the defendant present, however she did not attend. Where a second trial date adjournment is denied, it is appropriate for the justice of the peace to hold the trial down briefly to permit the review of disclosure before trial. This practice is not uncommon for Part I litigation, and is reasonable in light of the simplified procedure contemplated under the Act.

A printout of every keystroke entered by all individuals involved in the investigation of the defendant was not required for him to make full answer and defence on a charge of driving a motor vehicle while prohibited. However, the defendant was entitled to be provided with all broadcast communications relevant to the vehicle investigation and vehicle stop, including communications from dispatch and any officer, and all communications between the officers themselves. See *R. v. Kooner*, 2018 BCPC 355, 2018 CarswellBC 3542, [2018] B.C.J. No. 7038 (B.C. Prov. Ct.).

In *York (Regional Municipality) v. McGuigan*, 2018 ONCA 1062, 2018 CarswellOnt 22571, [2018] O.J. No. 6916 (Ont. C.A.), the Court of Appeal ruled that trial justice properly ordered the prosecutor to provide disclosure of the testing and operating procedures from the user manual for the device used by the traffic officer to measure the speed of the defendant's vehicle. Even if the justice of the peace had been wrong to order disclosure, the error would not have been jurisdictional in nature. Section 140(1) of the *Provincial Offences Act* confines *certiorari* orders in *POA* matters to situations where an applicant would be entitled to such relief at common law, and for parties to a proceeding, *certiorari* orders are confined to jurisdictional errors. Moreover, *certiorari* should not have been granted in the course of ongoing proceedings. Nor was there a substantial wrong or miscarriage of justice to address, a prerequisite to *certiorari* under s. 141(4) of the Act. Contrary to the application judge's decision, the justice of the peace did not err in making the disclosure order. Where a prosecutor is relying on a speed measuring device to prosecute an offence, it must, on request, disclose the testing and operating procedures set out in the user manual for that device. It is up to the prosecutor to hand such information over on request. The person charged need not bring an application or obtain a court order. This is first party disclosure, not third party disclosure. The charging police force has a corresponding duty to furnish the pertinent passages from the user manual to the prosecutor to enable the prosecutor to discharge its first party disclosure obligations. This is not a crushing administrative task. The disclosure at issue here is not case specific information. The disclosure obligation can therefore be discharged by the prosecutor by posting the relevant content from the user manual online and providing the ticketed driver with the required URL.

5.6.4 *DE MINIMIS*

- *"De minimis non curat lex"* is Latin for "the law does not concern itself with trifles". In rare circumstances, charges have been dismissed.

- The rationale for the rule is found in *The "Reward"*(1818),165 E.R. 1482, 2 Dods. 265 (Eng. Adm. Ct.):

    > The Court is not bound to a strictness at once harsh and pedantic in the application of statutes. The law permits the qualification implied in the ancient maxim *de minimis non curat lex* — Where there are irregularities of very slight consequence, it does not intend that the infliction of penalties should be inflexibly severe. If the deviation were a mere trifle, which, if continued in practice, would weigh little or nothing on the public interest, it might properly be overlooked.

- It is rarely successful. (It was unsuccessful in *The "Reward"*.)

- Courts generally defer to the power of the legislature to prescribe conduct which might other wise appear trifling, and the power of prosecution, as agent for the Ministry of the Attorney General, to exercise its discretion in using its prosecutorial resources as it deems fit; see section 3.1 in Chapter 3. However, consider the cases discussed below.

In *R. v. Webster* (1981), 10 M.V.R. 310, 15 M.P.L.R. 60 (Ont. Dist. Ct.), the accused was acquitted of parking illegally contrary to a municipal by-law. He parked where parking was prohibited to facilitate snow removal, but there was no snow on the ground. He was acquitted because it was "an absurdity to convict".

In *R. v. Paleshaty* (1949), 96 C.C.C. 147, 9 C.R. 97, [1950] 1 W.W.R. 108 (Man. C.A.), the doctrine was applied to acquit an individual charged with possession of then-illegal alcohol where the accused was found with two bottles containing about ten drops each.

In *R. v. McIntryre Mines Ltd.* (1978), 5 Alta. L.R. (2d) 201 (Alta. Prov. Ct.), the accused was charged with diverting waters, contrary to provincial water resources legislation. The court held that no diversion had been proved. Even if some had been proved, it was so minimal as to be in consequential.

In *R. v. Pang* (1987), 5 W.C.B. (2d) 94 (B.C. Co. Ct.), the principle was applied in the context of a misunderstanding between an individual entering Canada and a Canadian customs official. The visitor was believed to have made a misleading or false declaration and was charged. The charge was dismissed because the misunderstanding was minor and short-lived.

Note, however, that in a recent decision the court considered that the *de minimis* defence does not apply in the cases of public welfare offences or strict liability offences, although this statement was *obiter*: *R. v. Williams Operating Corp.*, [2008] O.J. No. 3736, 2008 CarswellOnt 5646, 39 C.E.L.R. (3d) 66 (Ont. S.C.J.).

If the common law defence of *de minimis* is to apply, it must be offence specific, that is, the conduct must merely be a technical commission of the *actus reus*. The conduct must fall within the words of the offence description but be too trivial or trifling to fall within the range of wrongs which the description was designed to cover. In the instant case, one could hardly describe the almost continuous breach of a condition in the defendant's Certificate of Approval for a number of years as trivial or trifling. Consequently, the *de minimis* defence did not apply. See *R. v. Superior Custom Trailers Ltd.*, 2009 ONCJ 740, 2009 CarswellOnt 9144, [2009] O.J. No. 6104 (Ont. C.J.).

5.6.5 UNREASONABLE DELAY

- Any person charged with an offence has the right to be tried within a reasonable time: *Charter*, section 11(b).

  - The right extends to corporate accused: *R. v. C.I.P. Inc.*, 12 C.R. (4th) 237, [1992] 1 S.C.R. 843, 7 C.O.H.S.C. 1, 71 C.C.C. (3d) 129 (S.C.C.).

  - The right applies equally to regulatory as to criminal offences: *C.I.P.*, *supra*.

- The relevant time for assessing unreasonableness is between the date of charging the defendant and the date of trial.

- The factors in assessing unreasonableness are: see *R. v. Morin*, 71 C.C.C. (3d) 1, 12 C.R. (4th) 1, [1992] 1 S.C.R. 771 (S.C.C.):

  - The length of delay.

- The waiver of time periods (whether the defendant clearly and unequivocally accepted some of the delay with knowledge of his or her Charter rights).

- The reasons for the delay, including:

- Inherent time requirements of the case (a complex trial may take longer to schedule);

- Actions of the defendant;

- Actions of the prosecutor;

- Limitations on institutional resources; and

- Prejudice to the defendant. (*There is a presumption of some prejudice to individuals because of the stress of facing charges, but no presumption for corporations — corporations must establish prejudice for this factor to be considered: see C.I.P., supra*).

In *R. v. J.I. Case Co.* (May 6, 1991), Doc. No. A1858/91 (Ont. Gen. Div.), a 20-month delay before trial constituted a section 11(b) violation where four months would have been reasonable, there was no explanation for the delay by the Crown, no period of delay was caused by the accused, and there was no waiver.

In *R. v. Boise Cascade Canada Ltd.* (1991), 14 W.C.B. (2d) 259 (Ont. Gen. Div.), a delay of 13 months between the laying of charges under the *Occupational Health and Safety Act* against the defendant corporations and the commencement of the trial was considered reasonable.

In *R. v. Hussain* (2005), [2005] O.J. No. 158, 2005 CarswellOnt 1215 (Ont. C.J.), an $11^1/_2$ month delay between the laying of the charges under the *Highway Traffic Act* and the *Compulsory Automobile Insurance Act* and the trial date was sufficiently long to investigate the factors set down in *R. v. Morin*, but where some two months related to a reasonable intake period, the remaining delay was within the guideline of 8 to 10 months set down in *R. v. Morin*.

In *R. v. Farokhshadfar* (April 6, 2001), Libman J., [2001] O.J. No. 6015 (Ont. C.J.), it was held that the very short times which govern *Provincial Offences Act* matters make it clear that "speedy justice" is the hallmark of proceedings under the Act. A period of delay of almost 10 months in sending out the Notice of Trial, when the defendant is required to give his/her intention to elect a trial mode within 15 days, was considered excessive. See further *R. v. Mastroianni* (2000), [2000] O.J. No. 3227, 2000 CarswellOnt 6171 (Ont. C.J.) where the accused's s. 11(b) *Charter* rights were found to have been violated on account of his speeding trial taking place nearly 14 months from the offence date. The same period of 14 months delay was considered excessive in *R. v. Omarzadah* (March 3, 2004), Doc. M30824, [2004] O.J. No. 2212 (Ont. C.A.).

- Absent unusual circumstances, a motion to stay proceedings due to unreasonable delay under section 11(b) of the *Charter of Rights* is ordinarily argued before trial. See *Ontario (Ministry of Labour) v. Pioneer Construction Inc.* (2006), 79 O.R. (3d) 641, 209 O.A.C. 379, 54 C.L.R. (3d) 41, 142 C.R.R. (2d) 81, 2006 CarswellOnt 2900, [2006] O.J. No. 1874 (Ont. C.A.).

- Where a defendant declines an offer for an earlier trial date, the resulting delay is attributable to the defendant rather than to the Crown or to institutional delay. Where the defendant does nothing to move the case forward in a timely way, prejudice is accorded little or no weight: *R. v. M. (N.N.)* (2006), [2006] O.J. No. 1802, 2006 CarswellOnt 2721, 209 C.C.C. (3d) 436, 209 O.A.C. 331, 141 C.R.R. (2d) 95 (Ont. C.A.).

In *R. v. Skolney*, 2006 ONCJ 549, 2006 CarswellOnt 8906, [2006] O.J. No. 5506 (Ont. C.J.), it was held that the trial justice erred in law in dismissing the *Charter of Rights* application on the basis that "section 11(b) is strictly for criminal proceedings". The *Charter* applies to charges under the *Provincial Offences Act.*

A stay of proceedings was set aside on appeal in *R. v. Norwall Group Inc.*, 2008 CarswellOnt 1742, 2008 ONCA 235, [2008] O.J. No. 1222 (Ont. C.A.), reversing 2007 CarswellOnt 3878, [2007] O.J. No. 2397, 161 C.R.R. (2d) 39 (Ont. S.C.J.) where the court considered that there was no evidence of actual, irremediable prejudice to the defendant's ability to make full answer and defence. Neither the nature of the allegations in the charges, nor the fact that the employees no longer worked for the employer, standing alone or together, justified any inference of actual prejudice to the ability to make full answer and defence. The stay of proceedings for unreasonable delay was set aside and the matter remitted to the trial court.

In *R. v. Piskun*, 2008 CarswellOnt 4790, [2008] O.J. No. 3705 (Ont. C.J.), a delay of 13 months in an uncomplicated, straightforward speeding prosecution under the *Highway Traffic Act* was held to be excessive. The court noted that it is the duty of the prosecution to bring an accused person to trial; the state and the prosecution apparatus are required to minimize the prejudice in he rent in delays, in the disposition of criminal litigation, as well as litigation under the *Provincial Offences Act.*

On the other hand, in *Mississauga (City) v. Berbatiotis*, [2007] O.J. No. 4683, 2007 CarswellOnt 7746, 2007 ONCJ 561 (Ont. C.J.), the court ruled that an overall period of 13 and one-half months from the date of the offence of speeding to the time of trial did not violate s. 11(b). Almost 11 months of this period was due to institutional delay. There was an absence of stigma and any real prejudice.

In *R. v. Hale*, 2005 CarswellOnt 10303, 2005 ONCJ 553, [2005] O.J. No. 6368 (Ont. C.J.), the court observed that one of the ways the management of trial work load is accomplished in the provincial offences court is by the holding of judicial pre-trials. The twin goals of the pre-trial process are to resolve matters capable of resolution, or to narrow the issues if no such resolution is possible so that the time required for trial is shortened by agreed statements off act obviating the need for some witnesses to testify. To suggest that the pre-trial process be abolished at the Ontario Court of Justice level because it is not specifically provided for by legislation is to invite chaos at the province's busiest level of court. In a case where there was a delay of 15 months from the laying of the information for careless driving until the start of the scheduled trial, and 5.5 months of this delay was due to setting up and conducting the judicial pre-trial and finding a date that was available for trial from the perspective of an appropriate justice of the peace, the defendant's s. 11(b) rights were violated.

In *R. v. Smith*, 2008 CarswellOnt 4286, 2008 CarswellOnt 4287, 175 C.R.R. (2d) 13, [2008] O.J. No. 2841 (Ont. S.C.J.), it was held that the justice of the peace erred in holding that 8 months was an unreasonable period of time to arrange a trial date for careless driving that resulted in a death. The justice of the peace must consider the public interest in having a full trial on the issues when serious charges are laid and an individual has been killed; the failure of the justice to expressly consider this factor amounted to reversible error. There would be a substantial miscarriage of justice as the public interest in having a full trial would not be met if the error was not corrected.

Apart from the requirements of notice under s. 109 of the *Courts of Justice Act* and the rules of court, the defendant must do more than that to assert his rights before the trial judge. Stating that one wishes to bring at some point a s. 11(b) application is not the same as actually bringing the application. While the defendant does not have to assert the right at every court appearance, at some appropriate stage in the proceedings, that is during the trial process, he must muster the evidence, transcripts of the attendance, evidence of prejudice if any, and present argument to the trier of fact: *R. v. Delvecchio*, 2008 ONCJ 511, 2008 CarswellOnt 6281, 78 M.V.R. (5th) 88, [2008] O.J. No. 4229 (Ont. C.J.).

In *R. v. Vellone*, 284 O.A.C. 388, 2011 CarswellOnt 14646, 2011 ONCA 785, 108 O.R. (3d) 481, 25 M.V.R. (6th) 1, 250 C.R.R. (2d) 351, [2011] O.J. No. 5708 (Ont. C.A.), it was held that by virtue of s. 95(3) of the *Courts of Justice Act*, the s. 109

requirement that parties give prior notice of constitutional questions and remedies applies to proceedings under the *Provincial Offences Act*. The wording of s. 109 and the *Courts of Justice Act* parallels the wording of of s. 32(1) of the *Charter of Rights*. Section 109 refers to the Government of Canada and the Government of Ontario; the Supreme Court has consistently held that municipal levels of government come within the meaning of "government" in s. 32(1) of the *Charter*. Against this back drop of statutory wording and case law, the term "Government of Ontario" in s. 109 of the *Courts of Justice Act* should be construed to parallel s. 32(1)(b) of the *Charter* as it would not make sense to say that *Charter* s.32(1) includes municipal action as action of the Government of Ontario, but s. 109 of the *Courts of Justice Act* does not. The component of s.109 requiring people in the position of the defendant, who was charged with a speeding ticket and prosecuted by a municipality, to notify the Attorney General of Ontario of his s. 11(b) *Charter* challenge serves a number of important purposes. The notice requirement enables the Government of Ontario to decide whether to exercise its right to take over a case under the *Provincial Offences Act*; it also furthers the Government of Ontario's important interest in monitoring the performance of municipalities under memoranda of Understanding. Notice to the Attorney General of Ontario of a s. 11(b) challenge, or an avalanche of such notices, provides the Government of Ontario with important data about key components of the provincial justice system. The appeal judge therefore erred by holding that the defendant did not need to provide notice of his *Charter* s. 11(b) claim to the Attorney General of Ontario pursuant to s. 109 of the *Courts of Justice Act*. **Note:** The Court of Appeal did not address the different issue in the *Vellone* case of notice to the municipal prosecutor. It did note, however, that the Law Commission of Ontario, in its Final Report on *Modernizing the Provincial Offences Act: A New Framework and Other Reforms* (Toronto: Law Commission of Ontario, 2011) , has recommended that s. 109 of the *Courts of Justice Act* be amended so that it requires service of a Notice of Constitutional Question on prosecutors in all *Provincial Offences Act* matters, and that a Notice of Constitutional Question be served on a municipal prosecutor when a party seeks relief unders.24(1) of the *Charter of Rights* relating to an act or omission of a municipality.

An unrepresented defendant requested an adjournment of his first trial date when he applied for disclosure, and at the second trial date raised the issue of delay, which necessitated another adjournment. The original trial date was within a one year period; the proceedings were stayed by the trial judge more than two years after the offence date. However, the justice erred in inferring prejudice from the delay as the defendant had adduced no evidence of prejudice. The criminal justice issue respecting prejudice is an entirely different cultural issue for provincial offences matters which are often strict liability or absolute liability offences: *R. v. Craig*, [2008] O.J. No. 4750, 2008 CarswellOnt 7064 (Ont. C.J.).

In *R. v. Wahabi*, 2010 CarswellOnt 10058, [2010] O.J. No. 5773 (Ont. C.J.), it was held that there was no positive duty on defendants who had no say in the scheduling of their trial to complain about the date in a peremptory fashion, otherwise they will be precluded from arguing s. 11(b) at their trial. The justice erred in holding that by the defendant's failure to seek an earlier trial date than the one and only given to him, his application ought to be viewed in a different manner. Unlike matters that are scheduled in the criminal courts, the defendant's trial was scheduled to him merely by way of a notice of trial being given to him. The type of logic employed by the justice would lead to the situation where individuals would be expected to then have to try to seek different trial dates than the ones that an administrative procedure gives to them. There is no basis for imposing this requirement.

In *R. v. Vollick*, 2010 ONSC 6746, 2010 CarswellOnt 9436, (*sub nom.* Ontario (Ministry of Labour) v. Vollick) 224 C.R.R. (2d) 2, [2010] O.J. No. 5326 (Ont. S.C.J.), it was held that the allowable time frame for bringing an accused charged with a regulatory offence to trial is the same as it would be in the case of a *Criminal Code* offence. The interest of an accused in the availability and reliability of substantiating evidence exists irrespective of the nature of the offence.

The total period of delay from swearing the informations to the date of conviction was between 18 and 21 months. The case did not fall in the category of being simple and straight forward: simple straightforward cases in the provincial offences court do not take ten days to be heard. Cases of that length are the exception, rather than the rule. The same can be said about criminal cases in the Ontario Court of Justice. Counsel also insisted that the full ten days be scheduled together. This further complicated the task of finding early court dates. In these circumstances, the evidence was heard within a very reasonable time considering the inherent time requirements of the case and the limits on institutional resources. The presiding justice of the peace did not err when she concluded that the delay in the hearing of this case did not cause prejudice to the accused such as to warrant a stay of proceedings: *Niagara (Regional Municipality) v. DiFruscia*, 2010 ONCJ 427, 2010 CarswellOnt 7104, [2010] O.J. No. 404 (Ont. C.J.).

The allowable time frame for bringing an accused charged with a regulatory offence to trial is the same as it would be in the case of a *Criminal Code* offence. The interest of an accused in the availability and reliability of substantiating evidence exists irrespective of the nature of the offence: *R. v. Vollick*, 2010 ONSC 6746, 2010 CarswellOnt 9436, [2010] O.J. No. 5326, (*sub nom.* Ontario (Ministry of Labour) v. Vollick) 224 C.R.R. (2d) 2 (Ont. S.C.J.).

Section 11(b) of the *Charter* was violated where there was a total delay of almost 13 months on a speeding charge, and no disclosure was provided at the defendant's first trial date: *R. v. Ferreira*, 2008 CarswellOnt 9748, [2008] O.J. No. 5998 (Ont. C.J.).

However, in *R. v. Matthews*, 2011 ONCJ 506, 2011 CarswellOnt 10488, [2011] O.J. No. 4461 (Ont. C.J.), there was no s. 11(b) violation where there was an overall period of one year and 15 days from the date that the information was sworn until the trial date. The Crown provided all normal disclosure initially in a timely fashion; when it was aware of the expanded disclosure issue the matter was set for a pre-trial. Once the decision was rendered, the Crown provided the manual to the defence on that very date, and diligently sought out the additional materials that were not in its possession, which it provided shortly thereafter. The Crown cannot be expected to disclose more than it has or more than it usually does without direction from the court. Given the reasons for delay in the case, and the lack of any prejudice to the defendant, the delay was not excessive.

There was an overall period of delay of 26 months from the time that the defendant filed his notice of intention to appear at his trial for careless driving under Part I of the *Provincial Offences Act* until the date of the anticipated completion of the trial. The trial date had to be adjourned due to the unavailability of an interpreter to assist the defendant. The inherent time requirement or appropriate intake period for the charge was one month, considering the nature of the charge and the alleged circumstances of the offence, as well as the fact that the defendant filed the offence notice with the court within three days of being served with it. A period of 16 months of the overall 26 months of delay was attributable to limits on institutional resources. The institutional period of delay in the proceeding exceeded the administrative guidelines for trial delay based on institutional or systemic reasons of 6 to 8 months. In balancing the interests of the defendant in seeking his right to be tried with out unreasonable delay with that of society's interest in having trials of matters on their merits, the majority of the delay was due to unacceptable institutional delay for which the prosecution was responsible. The defendant's *Charter* s. 11(b) right was therefore found to be infringed. See *R. v. Sran*, 2012 ONCJ 19, 2012 CarswellOnt 499, [2012] O.J. No. 163 (Ont. C.J.).

Where an earlier or early trial date is offered to the defence and the defence does not accept it, the defence cannot complain about a breach of the right to be tried without unreasonable delay where there is delay occasioned by the refusal of the defence to accept an earlier trial date. The total delay attributable to the prosecution was a period of 4 and one-half months and later 5 and one-half months due to the prosecution witnesses being unavailable due to surgery and attending a funeral. The defence had also sought an adjournment. The total delay attributable to the prosecution was not an amount of delay that would invoke the drastic remedy of a stay of proceedings: *R. v. Albert* (August 2, 2011), J.S. Nadel J., [2011] O.J. No. 4315 (Ont. C.J.).

In *R. v. 1762432 Ontario Inc.*, 2012 ONCJ 80, [2012] O.J. No. 746, 2012 CarswellOnt 2156, 254 C.R.R. (2d) 214 (Ont. C.J.), the information laid against the defendant alleged the breach of the municipal offence of carrying on business of an entertainment establishment without a licence. The overall length of the delay from the date of the charge being laid to the scheduled trial date was 17 months. An intake period of two months is an appropriate period for neutral intake in a case such as this that is not complex. However, the court ran out of time to hear the matter when it was scheduled for trial, which resulted in the holding of a pre-trial, which is normally allotted as neutral delay. Defence counsel was then not available on the next available court date. There was in total Crown delay of 16 days, defence delay of one month, neutral delay of almost 5 months, and institutional delay of 11.5 months. The case presented a routine Part III *Provincial Offences Act* prosecution that was neither complex nor involved serious charges. The acceptable period of institutional delay in the circumstances was 10 months. There is a societal interest in seeing matters proceed to trial, but society also has an interest in ensuring that an accused is able to meet its case with out the prejudice of fading memories. The accused faced a significant fine and other possible sanctions detrimental to its business operations. On balance, its right to go to trial within a reasonable time had been infringed.

The issue of unreasonable delay for Part I offences arose in *R. v. Andrade*, 2011 ONCJ 470, 2011 CarswellOnt 10556, 23 M.V.R. (6th) 18, [2011] O.J. No. 4245 (Ont. C.J.), leave to appeal allowed 2011 ONCA 739, 2011 CarswellOnt 12841, (*sub nom.* R. v. Hariraj) 108 O.R. (3d) 474, 23 M.V.R. (6th) 48, [2011] O.J. No. 5311 (Ont. C.A. [In Chambers]), leave to appeal allowed 2011 CarswellOnt 12924 (Ont. C.A.) where it was held that a reasonable intake period for a traffic ticket, as a general rule, is a period of between 30-45 days. An intake period in the outer range of 45 days will be appropriate where the defendant does not act until the latter part of the 15-day window to respond to his/her ticket and file the notice of intention to appear in court for trial, or the officer does not file with dispatch the certificate of offence or offence notice in the court office, thereby causing court administration to wait a lengthier period before having all the necessary documentation to schedule a trial date. In either case, an intake period or inherent time requirement range of 30 to 45 days should result in provincial offences trials for minor offences being scheduled within approximately two months of the offence date. The constitutionally tolerable period of institutional or systemic delay in the Toronto Region for the type of minor Part I provincial offences cases in question is between 8 to 9 months. Thus the total amount of institutional delay in these cases of 9 months (Andrade) and 10 months (Hariraj) fell at the upper limit and beyond this administrative guideline. Having regard to the totality of the circumstances, the interest of the defendants and society in a prompt trial outweighs the societal interest in bringing the accused persons to trial. The stays of proceedings imposed at trial for unreasonable delay were therefore warranted.

Note: The Court of Appeal has granted leave to appeal in the *Andrade* decision: see *R. v. Andrade*, 2011 CarswellOnt 12841, [2011] O.J. No. 5311, 2011 ONCA 739, (*sub nom.* R. v. Hariraj) 108 O.R. (3d) 474, 23 M.V.R. (6th) 48 (Ont. C.A. [In Chambers]). However, on 10 September 2013 the appellant City of Toronto filed a Notice of Abandonment of Appeal, stating:" The legislative and factual landscapes have changed significantly since this matter was heard at the court below and since leave to appeal was granted. These changes, along with pending changes in practice, will have a direct impact on the issues in this appeal. Therefore, it is not in the interests of justice to continue with this matter."

The trial judge erred in ruling that when the trial did not complete on the trial date and continued to a second trial date, the defendant was precluded from arguing that his s. 11(b) *Charter* right was violated, due to his not having raised the issue prior to arraignment and that the matter should have been brought before the first trial date, regardless of the time it took to continue the trial. The trial judge erred in not hearing submissions on the s. 11(b) motion in the circumstances. See *R. v. Goldenberger*, 2012 CarswellOnt 8528, [2012] O.J. No. 3234 (Ont. C.J.).

In *R. v. Kahlon*, 2012 ONCJ 395, 2012 CarswellOnt 8157, [2012] O.J. No. 2942 (Ont. C.J.), it was held that on its face, the overall period of delay of more 20 months on a charge of failing to stop for a stop sign appeared excessive, and required examination and analysis. However the defendant was ill for his first trial date and the second trial date did not proceed as the defendant's legal representative had not requested disclosure. The matter was then adjourned for a third trial date. Allowing for an intake period of two months in the Toronto Region where there has been a dramatic increase in the provincial offences court list and workloads sincethe20 years following the Supreme Court of Canada's decisions in *Askov* and *Morin*, as well as the period of delay for which the defendant was responsible by not being ready or available for trial, the resulting period of delay of 7 months and 15 days was well within the permissible guidelines.

The defendant's trial date was 13 months due to pure institutional delay. He then sought an adjournment so that he could appear in person, which resulted in another 6 month period of delay, a period of which he did not complain. However, a further postponement was required so that the presiding justice and prosecutor from another jurisdiction could be arranged, given the defendant's familiarity as a local lawyer. The total period of delay that was in issue was approximately 16 months, which was excessive and could not be sanctioned. See *R. v. Barry*, 2011 CarswellOnt 15732, [2011] O.J. No. 6341 (Ont. C.J.).

Institutional delay only starts to run when the parties are ready for trial but the system cannot accommodate them. In addition, more than just a generalized prejudice must be established: *R. v. Goldstein*, 2012 CarswellOnt 7301 (Ont. C.J.).

In *R. v. Gregorczyk*, 2012 ONCJ 99, 2012 CarswellOnt 2502, [2012] O.J. No. 846 (Ont. C.J.), the overall period of delay from the filing of the certificate of offence with the court until the anticipated completion date of the trial of the proceeding for speeding was more than 23 and one-half months, an exceptional period that warranted an inquiry into the reasons for the delay. The defence representative waived 5 months of this period; 1 month was the appropriate intake period having regard to the fact that the defendant requested his trial the day following the offence date. The defendant had, in turn, been responsible for just under a 2 month period of delay due to the intervention of his *Charter* motion. This left a period of institutional delay of 15 and one-half months for which the prosecution was responsible. While the degree of prejudice suffered by the defendant was slight, in the circumstances of the case where the institutional delay significantly exceeded the upper range of the *Morin* administrative guidelines for institutional delay of 10 months, the delay was not justifiable.

There is no mathematical formula for deciding that can be applicable to every case. There is no one size fits all formula that can be applied to every case. Every case has to be reviewed in light of the facts and circumstances and the responsibilities of both parties, the Crown and the Defence. There are certain responsibilities though the Crown is responsible for doing most of the work but the Defence also has to share some responsibility in the matter. The key issue in any s. 11(b) *Charter* application is prejudice. There was no affidavit from the defendant or any other documentation, or any evidence, or any proof that the matter had really upset him or disturbed him mentally. The institutional delay was within reasonable limits. As there was no real prejudice to the defendant and the time lines were within the limit, the resulting delay was not that unreasonable. See *R. v. Spruce*, 2012 CarswellOnt 15648, [2012] O.J. No. 5110 (Ont. C.J.).

In *R. v. Wong*, 2012 ONCJ 589, 2012 CarswellOnt 11922, [2012] O.J. No. 4480 (Ont. C.J.), the defendant's trial for careless driving was set to be commenced within 10 months, and then was adjourned for another 10 months during which time it continued and the defendant brought a motion for unreasonable delay. Part of the delay in the continuation of the trial was caused by the illness and hospitalization of the justice, a period properly characterized as delay associated with the inherent time requirements of the case. The overall length of delay including the time necessitated to argue the *Charter* s. 11(b) motion was 28 months, and this warranted inquiry. Waiver by the defence constituted 8 and one-half months. However, the mere fact that the defendant requested a first attendance meeting with the prosecutor and subsequently requested that it be re-scheduled did not mean that the defendant understood that she was giving up her constitutional right to be tried of the subject offence within a reasonable time. In light of the defendant's prompt action in filing her Notice of Intention to Appear and Request for First Attendance on the date of the alleged offence, an intake period of one month starting on the date of the offence would be reasonable. The subject prosecution was complex, even though it was one commenced under the simplified procedure codified in Part I of the *Provincial Offences Act*. The inherent nature of the prosecution required the reservation of a much longer block of trial time than two hours. The resulting Institutional or systemic period of delay of 9 month sand 23 days fell within the guidelines for constitutionally tolerable institutional delay in Provincial Courts (a period of between 8 and 10 months). There was no evidence of prejudice that the defendant may have suffered as a result of the period of institutional delay which existed in the proceeding. As a result, it had not been established, on the balance of probabilities, that the defendant's right to be tried within a reasonable time under s. 11(b) of the *Charter of Rights and Freedoms* had been infringed.

The defendant's trial date for speeding was just over one year from the time he was charged. The trial justice was not persuaded that either the total amount of delay or the components of it, including a 2-month intake period, violated s. 11(b). The justice was entitled to give importance to the absence of any prejudice. While there was some delay in the time it took court administration to process and issue a notice of trial date, this was merely one factor in the assessment of the overall period of delay. See *R. v. Kukuy*, 2012 CarswellOnt 14464, [2012] O.J. No. 5310 (Ont. C.J.).

Likewise, in *R. v. Szewczyk*, 2012 ONCJ 680, 2012 CarswellOnt 13636, [2012] O.J. No. 5153 (Ont. C.J.), the period of delay from the date of the charge of speeding being laid to the first trial date was just over 12 months. The overall period of delay until the anticipated completion of the trial was 20 and one-half months. The period of time taken to schedule a first attendance appointment did not constitute a waiver by the defendant, although an intake period of 45 days was reasonable given the fact that the defendant waited 13 days to file his Notice of Intention to Appear. The period of delay attributable to institutional or systemic factors amounted to 11 and one-half months. There was no evidence of actual prejudice. Having regard to the absence of prejudice, the period of institutional delay was not so long as to violate the defendant's right to be tried without unreasonable delay.

Another unreasonable delay argument was rejected in *Mississauga (City) v. Lam*, 2012 ONCJ 734, 2012 CarswellOnt 15069, [2012] O.J. No.5594 (Ont. C.J.) where the defendant made a request for a first attendance meeting rather than requesting a trial date after he was stopped and charged with speeding. It took the municipality five months to schedule the first attendance meeting, after which time he was given a trial date, which was almost 13 months after he filed his Notice of Intention to Appear. The overall length of delay was almost 19 months. The first attendance meeting with the municipal prosecutor was not mandatory for the defendant, nor had it been legislated by statute as an option at that time, although subsequently this "first attendance option" had become a legislated option. Considering that the defendant did voluntarily request a first attendance meeting with the prosecutor to discuss the speeding charge for the purposes of resolution, knowing that a trial date would not be scheduled until after the meeting, the delay associated with the scheduling and conducting of the first attendance meeting would be properly characterized as part of the neutral intake period. When this five month period for the first attendance meeting was deducted from the overall length of delay of 18 month sand 29 days, the remaining length of delay was13 months and 29 days, from which 31 days were further deducted as neutral intake period. The resulting period of 6 months and 24 days of institutional or systemic delay was not an excessive or an unreasonable period of delay, such that the defendant's right to a trial within a reasonable time was violated.

A further unreasonable delay argument was made in *R. v. 1762432 Ontario Inc.*, 2012 ONCJ 80, 2012 CarswellOnt 2156, 254 C.R.R. (2d) 214, [2012] O.J. No. 746 (Ont. C.J.), in which it was held that the corporate defendant's right to be tried within a reasonable amount of time was infringed pursuant to s. 11(b) of the *Charter*, leading to a stay. The accused was charged with carrying on business without the requisite license contrary to Chapter 545 of the City of Toronto *Municipal Code*.

The offence occurred on September 18, 2010 and the initial trial date was scheduled for March 28, 2011. Following an adjournment and a judicial pre-trial, the date set for trial was pushed to December 20th, 2011. The overall length of delay was held to be 17 months, of which 12 months were attributed to the Crown and to institutional delay. In assessing whether the delay was reasonable, the court stated that this matter dealt with a routine Part III POA case where an acceptable period of institutional delay would be 10 months. The prejudice incurred by the corporate defendant focused on its two witnesses and on fading memories as one of them was experiencing difficulty recalling specific events as outlined in affidavit evidence. Corporate expansions were put on hold pending resolutions of this case.

In *R. v. Sran*, 2012 ONCJ 19, 2012 CarswellOnt 499, [2012] O.J. No. 163 (Ont. C.J.), the defendant was charged with careless driving pursuant to s. 130 of the *Highway Traffic Act*. The accused was prosecuted under Part I of the POA. The charge was stayed following the s. 11(b) argument. The overall period of institutional delay from the filing of the Notice of Intention to Appear with the court until the anticipated completion date of the trial was held to be 16 months and 7 days. The Applicant applied for a trial within the 15-day window available to file the Notice of Intention to Appear, which the Applicant filed within the first 3 days after the offence occurred. While the Defendant was charged on October 23, 2009, the trial of the charge began on January 26, 2011. At this time, the court embarked on a hearing of the *Charter* application. The trial continued on October 4, 2011, following which it was adjourned to January 3, 2012 for judgment. The court stated that considering the complexity of the case, the disclosure requirement, and the need to provide an interpreter, the reasonable intake period for a case of this calibre was 30 days.

In *R. v. Malcolm*, 2013 ONCJ 86, 2013 CarswellOnt 2315, [2013] O.J. No. 868 (Ont. C.J.), the accused was charged under Part I of the POA with "Pedestrian, Fail to Use Cross-Walk" pursuant to s. 144(12) of the *Highway Traffic Act*. The court ruled the defendant's right to be tried with in a reasonable time had been infringed, staying the charge. The Certificate of Offence was dated November 28, 2011, and the Notice of Intention to Appear was filed promptly by the accused on December 1, 2011. The total period of delay attributable to the Prosecutor and to Institutional delay amounted to 9.5 months. The court stated that based on all the factors, and particularly in light of *Andrade* (supra), the time frame allowing for this minor Part I provincial offence ought to be between 8 and 9 months. The court considered the low level of complexity incurred in this case. During her testimony, the accused described the protracted nature of these proceedings akin to an "open wound taking a while to heal." The court stated that while society has an interest in seeing that these matters proceed to trial, this case deals with a charge laid under Part I of the POA and its low level of complexity does not warrant such a lengthy period of delay.

In *R. v. Ma*, 2013 ONCJ 92, 2013 CarswellOnt 2260, [2013] O.J. No. 888 (Ont. C.J.), it was held that the overall period of delay in the defendant's stunt driving trial was 14 months and 23 days, and therefor warranted an inquiry into the reasonableness of the delay. There was no waiver of any delay by the defendant. The principal reasons for the delay were the Crown's failure to provide adequate disclosure in a timely or efficient manner, and there being no provision of a Mandarin interpreter on two trial dates to assist the defendant. On both these occasions, he flew from British Columbia to Toronto as his university studies in Ontario were completed, and he had returned to his home in British Columbia to live with his parents and look for employment. The defendant has the right to live his life, and that includes returning home after his studies are completed. The prejudice against this defendant in addition to the worry or stress caused by the excessive delay is greater than a typical defendant who resides locally as he was put to the additional expense of travel and accommodation. Looking at the totality of the time, almost 15 months, with almost 11 months attributable for Crown delay to deliver simple disclosure in an expeditious manner, and institutional delay because of availability of trial dates, interpreter and officer scheduling, the scale tipped in favour of deciding the *Charter* s. 11(b) motion in favour of the defendant.

The defendant's trial for following too close was 14.5 months after the offence date. Five months of this period was due to the time required for scheduling the first attendance meeting; the first trial had to be adjourned due to missing disclosure. Throughout the entire time, the defendant represented herself. The total period of delay justified further analysis. The defendant had not received disclosure on the date of the early resolution request nor at the time of the early resolution meeting. At no time was there ever an explicit, unequivocal informed waiver of her right to a speedy trial. Her actions in setting the trial date were diligent. In the circumstances it was appropriate to assign three months as neutral intake period. The total delay attributable to institutional delay and the actions of the Crown amounted to 11.5 months. With respect to the factor of prejudice, the defendant's claim of stress was minimal at best. However, that minimal prejudice must be balanced against the public interest in a fair, efficient and timely process for bringing such matters to trial. The charges were not overly complex and were subject to *Charter* review. The hallmark of Part I provincial offences ought to be speed and efficiency. The total delay exceeded the administrative guideline period. Balancing all of the relevant factors, the defendant's rights under s. 11(b) of the *Charter of Rights* were infringed, and her rights and society's rights to a prompt trial out weighed the societal interests in bringing accused persons to trial. See *R. v. Jair*, 2013 ONCJ 142, 2013 CarswellOnt 3366, 278 C.R.R. (2d) 152, [2013] O.J. No. 1332 (Ont. C.J.).

In *R. v. Malcolm*, 2013 ONCJ 86, 2013 CarswellOnt 2315, [2013] O.J. No. 868 (Ont. C.J.), the total period of delay until the defendant's second trial date for "pedestrian, fail to use cross-walk" was 12 months and 20 days. The relevant period of delay was 3 months of prosecutorial delay sending out the Notice of Trial, and 6.5 months of institutional delay, for a total of 9.5 months. The defence was responsible for 2 months of delay, and neutral delay was fixed at 80 days. There was evidence of actual prejudice because of the delay in proceeding to trial, based on the defendant's testimony of the angst that the delay brought to bear upon her. Society has an interest in seeing accident matters proceed to trial, which in this case was in direct conflict with the accused's right to be tried within a reasonable time. Nevertheless, the charge was laid under Part I of the *Provincial Offences Act*, and taken at its highest, spoke to the behaviour of a pedestrian. There was little, if any, complexity to the case. Society's interest in seeing the matter proceed to trial fell far short of what it would be for a complex criminal matter. Based on all the factors before the court, the time frame permitted for the matter to go to trial should fall at the low end of the *Morin* guidelines. Thus, the defendant's right to go to trial within a reasonable period had been infringed.

The defendant had four trial dates within a two-year time period which resulted in an extraordinary delay that required examination. However, there were three adjournments of trial dates at his request, or in one instance a choice made by him. His argument that he needed adjournments due to the prosecution's delayed disclosure was disingenuous, given the nature of the documents he was seeking which related to his claim that he was not governed by the law since he was not a corporation and a law only applies to those who consent to it. While the trial Justice of the Peace had refused to hear the defendant's motions, including his application for a stay of proceedings due to unreasonable delay, there was no prejudice to him. See *R. v. Cassista*, 2013 ONCJ 305, 2013 CarswellOnt 7411, [2013] O.J. No. 2560 (Ont. C.J.).

In *R. v. Quan*, 2013 ONCJ 699, 2013 CarswellOnt 17576, 59 M.V.R. (6th) 167, [2013] O.J. No. 5766 (Ont. C.J.), the court found that the actions of the defendant should be taken into account in determining what delay is reasonable. It must be remembered that regardless of the nature of the disclosure sought, it was not a failure of proper disclosure that delayed the trial but rather the defendant's decision to bring a late motion seeking disclosure returnable on the date of trial. That delay was attributable to the defendant. There was no suggestion that the delay had interfered with the defendant's ability to have a fair trial as a result of the impairment of the evidence or his ability to meet the case. The total delay from being charged to trial was one year and 25 days, consisting of the inherent requirement of the case — intake and counsel not ready or available for trial (7 months), institutional delay (less than one month), the defendant's delay to the second trial date (4 months). The threshold case for unreasonable delay was not made out. The reasons for delay were in large part attributable to the defendant. Even based on the evidentiary findings of the trial court and the time found by that court to be attributable to limits on institutional resources, the total time found of six months and five days would be below the standard and would not be an unreasonable delay.

A recent Ontario case involving an application for a French-language trial and the resulting delay of delay was discussed in *R. v. Byrnes*, 2013 ONCJ 631, 2013 CarswellOnt 16205, 2013 CarswellOnt 16206, 296 C.R.R. (2d) 258, [2013] O.J. No. 5389 (Ont. C.J.), where the defendant immediately requested a French trial by ticking off the box on the Notice of Intention to Appear to indicate his intention and by filing the Notice with the court. However, his request for a French trial was over looked, and therefore his trial could not proceed on the trial date. While this oversight was an administrative error, this error amounted to a breach of the defendant's language rights. Moreover, the defendant should not have been expected by the trial judge to have required an interpreter. As a French-speaking defendant, he did not require the assistance of an interpreter at his French trial. Perhaps an interpreter would have been necessary to assist any English-speaking witnesses the prosecutor wished to call, but it would be the responsibility of the prosecutor, not the defendant, to make the appropriate arrangements for these witnesses. By indicating on the Notice that he wished to proceed in French, the defendant properly completed the Notice and satisfied all of his obligations on the language issue. The 8-month delay between the date the defendant requested a French trial until the date the trial began amounted to a breach of the defendant's right to have a trial within a reasonable time for two reasons. First, had he requested a trial in English, his matter could have been heard within 5 months; second, no effort was made to immediately secure a date for the French trial, due to his matter being adjourned a further three months to a pre-scheduled date for French trials, despite the fact that there were several intervening dates available for English trials. The practice of having only two pre-scheduled days set aside each year for French trials in the provincial offences court, one in the Spring and one in the Fall, is problematic from a case management perspective, and unfair because it is unresponsive to the individual requirements of a specific case. The fact that this system appeared to apply only to French-speaking defendants was a clear contravention of s. 16(1) of the Charter and as such, unacceptable. Even if this general process for scheduling French trials was constitutionally sound, the effect of slavishly continuing with the pre-scheduled French dates in the defendant's case, even after the trial had commenced before a specific Justice of the Peace, led to unacceptable delays. The result was that a routine speeding trial was commenced 9 months after the offence date, heard in 6 month instalments over a period of 13 months, and only concluded 22 months after the offence date.

In *R. v. Cercone*, 2013 ONCJ 685, 2013 CarswellOnt 17174, 296 C.R.R. (2d) 216, [2013] O.J. No. 5608 (Ont. C.J.), the total delay of 34 months on charges of driving while suspended and speeding was found to be unreasonable. It is the duty of the Crown to bring an accused person to trial. This requires that the prosecution apparatus and the government strive to expedite the trial to minimize the effect that is inherent in delay in the disposition of criminal litigation. There is no constitutional imperative upon the accused to bring himself or herself to trial. The protection of s. 11(b) of the *Charter* is not restricted to those who demonstrate a desire for a speedy resolution by asserting the s. 11(b) right. The Justice of the Peace did not err in deciding that the Crown had failed to demonstrate that the conduct of the defendant in not appearing for the first four times the matter was before the court amounted to waiver under s. 11(b) or an agreement with the pace of the litigation. The onus is on the Crown to prove or establish waiver. A waiver must be clear and unequivocal with full knowledge of the rights the procedure was enacted to protect and of the effect a waiver will have on these rights. The notion of waiver contemplates a choice has been made between available options; where no real choice or option exists there can be no waiver. Agreements to a date within the proceedings in question does not constitute waiver where the agreement can be reached reasonably and fairly characterized as mere acquiescence in the inevitable.

In *R. v. Orgaworld Canada Ltd.*, 2014 ONCA 654, 2014 CarswellOnt 12891, 319 C.R.R. (2d) 335, [2014] O.J. No. 4482 (Ont. C.A.), it was held that the application Judge did not err in declining to entertain the *Charter* s. 24(1) application which was premised on post-trial delay, due to the Justice of the Peace giving his decision about 15 months after the close of submissions. The defendant was entitled to raise the s. 11(b) *Charter* issue of post-hearing delay in an appeal to the Provincial Offences Appeal Court under the *Provincial Offences Act* and had done so. In these circumstances, the application Judge had discretion to decline to entertain the s. 24(1) *Charter* application to the Superior Court, and there was no error in her exercise of discretion. The issue was subsequently argued before the Provincial Offences Appeal Court and was under reserve. While the Crown had argued that the s. 11(b) argument should be entertained because it had not been raised before the Justice of the Peace, the same argument would have been available to the Crown before the application Judge. The defendant, therefore, was under no disadvantage in proceeding in the Provincial Offences Appeal Court. Rather, it would have the advantage of there being a full record.

The Ministry of the Attorney General of Canada does not have to be served with a Notice of Constitutional Question on a *Highway Traffic Act* (Ont.) charge alleging a s. 11(b) *Charter* application breach. It is not an application to strike down legislation, in which case notice would be required: *R. v. Szewczyk*, 2014 ONCJ 467, 2014 CarswellOnt 12597, [2014] O.J. No. 4294 (Ont. C.J.).

In *R. v. Jukes*, 2014 ONCJ 438, 2014 CarswellOnt 12208, [2014] O.J. No. 4182 (Ont. C.J.), it was held that there were four trial dates due to the defendant requesting disclosure of materials that were plainly irrelevant. The trial proceedings showed that the prosecution had disclosed the material essential to the trial at the first instance and the further delays at the request of the defendant could not fairly be attributed to Crown or institutional delay. The accused had also not alleged a breach of his s. 11(b) rights at trial either in formal or informal terms. There was no allegation that the trial would be unfair, given the delay.

The short time lines that govern the *Provincial Offences Act* suggest that speedy justice should be the goal. The delay of 6 months to set the trial date by the courts administration is excessive and is not tolerable. It is also not explained. When this is added to the delay of 5 months from the Notice of Trial to the actual trial date, the total delay of 11 months is unreasonable. Even if no prejudice had been demonstrated, the delay of 11 months for a minor speeding ticket is unreasonable. It is most unsatisfactory that it to take 6 months to schedule a trial for a minor speeding offence, and then another 5 months to the actual trial date. See *R. v. Eschbach*, 2014 ONCJ 598, [2014] O.J. No. 5359 (Ont. C.J.).

In *R. v. Baksh*, 2015 ONCJ 235, 2015 CarswellOnt 6482, [2015] O.J. No. 2271 (Ont. C.J.), it was held that the issue of delay in the first trial was not before the Justice of the Peace at the second trial to decide, as it had come before the appeal court on the first appeal, and a new trial was ordered. If it wove into the timing of the second trial, the Justice had ample ground to find that the history was unclear and the defendant had failed to discharge his burden under s. 11(b).

The total delay period was approximately 19.5 months for the defendant's speeding trial. There had been three previous trial dates set, which did not proceed due to the defendant's disclosure request for some 13 items on the first two trial dates, and the docket being too busy on the third trial date. The motion for unreasonable delay commenced two months after the third trial date and could not be completed until two further court dates. Many of the defendant's positions and submissions pertained to its motion to request disclosure, and were not therefore within the ambit of the unreasonable delay motion. By not following the proper scheduling protocol, the defendant's agent brought the matter to a very busy court without allocating in advance sufficient court time to hear and determine the *Charter* motion. As a result, the three month time period required to hear and conclude the motion was properly considered to be neutral. Having balanced the competing interests and applying the *Charter* s. 11(b) law to the facts before the court, the defendant's right to be tried without unreasonable delay was not infringed. See *R. v. Ghobrial*, 2015 ONCJ 288, 2015 CarswellOnt 15074, [2015] O.J. No. 2802 (Ont. C.J.).

In *Mississauga (City) v. Ciocan*, 2015 ONCJ 293, 2015 CarswellOnt 15332, [2015] O.J. No. 2871 (Ont. C.J.), the defendant's application for a stay of proceedings due to unreasonable delay was not heard until the testimony of the six witnesses had been completed since the application had not been perfected until after the trial had commenced and the prosecution had closed its case. There were four scheduled trial dates. The period from when the defendant filed its Notice of Intention to Appear at the courthouse until the final date of the trial was 29.5 months. The prosecution did not add to the delay by failing to call a witness that the defence wished to call, and then required time to subpoena to court. This witness was not the only witness scheduled to attend court on the first trial date. The defence was aware of the existence of this witness as a potential defence witness since she had talked to the defendant shortly after the collision. Much of the delay in the proceeding had also been caused by the lack of coordination between the Toronto-based paralegal firm and the defendant's trial legal representative, based on their divided responsibilities in the defendant's case. This lack of coordination contributed to the delay in the proceeding, especially in respect to the adjournment of two of the scheduled trial dates. Accordingly, much of the delay was attributable to the defence responsibility and the actions of the defendant's legal representatives in using the defendant's s. 11(b) rights as an offensive weapon. The societal interest in having the defendant's red light charge tried on the merits outweighed the societal and individual interest in the prompt adjudication of the defendant's charge.

The total delay period of over 15 months required an inquiry into the delay as it was excessive. There was a neutral intake period of approximately 2 months. However, the first trial was adjourned at the prosecutor's request because the officer was on leave. A total delay of 12 months to get a *Highway Traffic Act* matter to trial exceeds by a wide margin guidelines in *Morin* or other cases. The inferred prejudice from such a delay outweighs the societal interest in bringing the matter to trial. The Justice of the Peace did not err in staying the charges due to unreasonable delay. See *R. v. Hoac*, 2015 ONCJ 676, 2015 CarswellOnt 18096, [2015] O.J. No. 6222 (Ont. C.J.).

In *R. v. Sooriyapalan* (August 24, 2015), Doc. St. Catharines 2111-999-00-1933093B-00, [2015] O.J. No. 5710 (Ont. C.J.), the accused was charged with speeding and was given a trial date which was then adjourned to allow him to bring his *Charter* application for unreasonable delay. The period of delay for the first trial date was just over 10 months. Taking away a one month period for an intake period, the period of just over 9 months was well within the range of what is not objectionable according to *Morin* and many cases. There was no prejudice other than of being charged.

The totality of the delay was 20.5 months from the charge until the trial date. No actual prejudice was demonstrated by the defendant. There was a neutral 30 day intake period and systemic delay of almost 8 months until the first trial date. The defendant decided to work and not attend court so he was responsible for the delay until the second trial date. Other periods of delay were caused by the prosecutor not providing disclosure and the defendant failing to order the necessary transcripts needed for his *Charter* application. The delay caused by the unexpected illness of the interpreter was neutral. There is a distinction between a defendant not accepting a trial date that is offered and one where the defendant accepts the date, as the defendant did, but when it comes time for the trial date itself made a decision to do something other than attend that trial date. This distinction is especially relevant in proceedings under the *Provincial Offences Act* because trial dates are arbitrarily assigned as opposed to negotiated as they are in the criminal courts. Had the defendant attended his first trial date, an adjournment would have been granted for the disclosure he had requested, and the trial would have proceeded with only a 6 week delay caused by the prosecution. This would have resulted in systemic and prosecution delay of 9.5 months which would not have justified finding the defendant's s. 11(b) right had been breached. See *R. v. Li* (June 24, 2015), Doc. 1211-94944818, [2015] O.J. No. 3364 (Ont. C.J.).

In *R. v. Maxelon*, 2014 ONCJ 711, 2014 CarswellOnt 19111, [2014] O.J. No. 6262 (Ont. C.J.), the defendant was charged with speeding on 31 August 2013, and filed a notice to appear two weeks later through the legal representative she retained. After declining the resolution offered to her on 27 November, her trial date was sent out in

February, 2014 setting a trial date for 13 May 2014. The prosecution applied for an adjournment two weeks before the trial date due to the unavailability of one of the investigating officers, which was granted. The second trial date was set for 19 September 2014. The defence consented to the adjournment, and could be taken as giving implied consent to the length of the adjournment. The overall period of delay was 12 months and 19 days; however, the defendant acquiesced in the last 4 months of the delay. Even if the entire period of time was taken into account, once the intake period and time for the resolution meeting were deducted as neutral period of delay, the actual delay to prejudice the defendant was just under 7 months. The prejudice in this case was minimal. This was a quasi-criminal matter which did not result in her arrest, she did not personally appear in court as she did it through an agent, the penalty is a relatively small fine, although it may impact insurance costs, and the prejudice to the accused is minimal since the evidence in the matter was not affected in any substantial way by the delay given the nature of the charge and the way the evidence is gathered by use of a speed measuring device.

The defendant was charged with nine counts of wilfully collecting and using personal health information without authority in contravention of the *Personal Health Information Protection Act, 2004*. The overall length of delay from the date the information was sworn until the date of the giving of the *Charter* ruling was three years, four months and eight days. The inherent time requirements of the case were found to be almost 9 months, given that the case was fairly complex in certain respects, involving voluminous disclosure, numerous witnesses were likely to be called at trial, three pre-trials were scheduled, and five days of trial time was initially set for the case while there were numerous ongoing resolution discussions. This was not a "run-of-the-mill" *Provincial Offences Act* matter which can be completed with a trial time of one or two hours and minimal intake requirements and no necessity for pre-trials. The time period attributable to the Crown was 16 months and 10 days as a result of the fact that extensive, late disclosure was provided to the defence, resulting in an adjournment of the scheduled trial dates. The time taken for the *Charter* applications was attributable to the defence, a total time period of approximately 11 months. There was nothing excessive that occurred with respect to reasonably accommodating the schedules of Crown counsel, defence counsel and the court. In total, the period of delay attributed to the Crown was 16 months and 10 days, which was lengthy enough to allow for inferred prejudice even in a *Provincial Offences Act* case. The charges against the defendant are not so serious as to warrant extending the *Morin* guidelines to such an extent. The charges were stayed due to the violation of the s. 11(b) *Charter* right against unreasonable delay: *Ontario (Ministry of the Attorney General) v. McLellan*, 2015 ONCJ 165, 2015 CarswellOnt 15077, (*sub nom.* Ontario v. McLellan) 332 C.R.R. (2d) 1, [2015] O.J. No. 1562 (Ont. C.J.).

In *Burlington (City) v. Lacdan*, 2015 ONCJ 502, 2015 CarswellOnt 15125, [2015] O.J. No. 4945 (Ont. C.J.), the court ruled that a s. 11(b) analysis should not be about mathematical computation. It is a balancing exercise between the right of society to have the charges aired in court versus the rights of the individual under the *Charter* — that being to have their matter tried within a *reasonable* period of time. What constitutes a reasonable period of time is subject to interpretation and to the framework analysis under the *Morin* decision. The only accepted remedy from a successful s. 11(b) challenge is a judicial stay of the charge before the court. The court must first ascertain whether or not there has been a breach of those rights. If the breach is evident, then the court must then determine whether or not in the face of that breach, the motion to stay the charge should be granted once balancing the rights of the individual against the rights of society and after having weighed the prejudice to the defendant versus the probative value of proceeding in the face of such a breach. In this case, the court did not accept that there has been a breach of those rights. The entire time period to set the ex parte trial date should not be borne by the Crown or attributed to institutional delay. In assigning the time to the Crown and to any institutional delay, the total delay added up to just over 7 months, plus another month assuming that the defendant was ready for trial. On either period of delay calculation, the resulting 7 or 8 month period was well within the *Morin* suggested boundaries of 8-10 months, all else being equal.

The defendant's first trial date was over 9 months from the time she was charged with failing to stop for a red light. She was ill and did not attend court, leading to her being convicted in her absence. She was granted a re-opening, and given a second trial date 6 months after the re-opening. The trial was adjourned for disclosure to be provided, leading to a third trial date almost 4 months later. However, the matter was not reached and was adjourned for trial three and one-half months later. On this date she attended court with her counsel who brought a s. 11(b) motion, which was adjourned to the following month. The total period of delay of over 24 months was excessive, and there was no waiver by the defendant. Of this period 10 months was comprised of intake and neutral time; the delay attributable to institutional delay was just over 10 months, and the remaining 4 months was attributable to the defendant. There was inferred prejudice due to the length of delay. The case was neither complex nor required more time to prepare; the prosecution anticipated calling the police officer, and the defendant anticipated calling one witness. The low end of the 8 months guideline in *Morin* was exceeded in the circumstances. The defendant's rights to trial within a reasonable period of time had been infringed. See *R. v. Sky*, 2012 ONCJ 875, 2012 CarswellOnt 17600, [2012] O.J. No. 6706 (Ont. C.J.).

In *R. v. Spence-Wilkins*, 2013 ONCJ 815, 2013 CarswellOnt 19045, [2013] O.J. No. 6413 (Ont. C.J.), the defendant was charged under the *Dog Owner's Liability Act* for an incident where a dog killed a cat on a farm. A breach of s. 11(b) of the

Charter is not determined by the application of a mathematical or administrative formula and involves an analysis of the balancing of the rights of the defendant and society. There was a total of 402 days from the date the information was sworn until the date of judgment on the *Charter* motion, consisting of inherent time of 249 days and institutional delay of 153 days or just over 5 months. In all the circumstances there was not a breach of the defendant's right to be tried within a reasonable time. The fact that the trial did not actually take a full day due to the Crown withdrawing one of the counts is of no consequence in these circumstances as there was no unreasonable delay. In addition, that was prosecutorial discretion whether to proceed with that count; decisions are made by the Crown and the defence throughout the proceedings that may or may not affect how long a matter takes to come to trial.

In *R. v. Black and McDonald Ltd.*, 2016 ONCJ 345, 2016 CarswellOnt 9497, [2016] O.J. No. 3107 (Ont. C.J.), it was held that while there had been a delay that justified an inquiry, such delay did not breach the company's fair trial rights. In terms of delay, the institutional delay was within acceptable judicial guidelines. There was no specific actual prejudice to the company that affected its fair trial rights. The inherent time periods requirements of 11 months took place in the context of a case that required a judicial pre-trial, and both defence and Crown were content with the pace of proceedings. The actions of the accused and the Crown accounted for 4 months of the total delay. A period of 5.5 months was considered neutral; during this time both parties continued judicial pre-trials and pre-trial discussions.

The delay of 1 year and 152 days warranted scrutiny by the court. There was not an unreasonable amount of delay attributed to any one party. The 113 days between the notice of intention to appear and first trial date was the intake period; the period of 2 months and 18 days between the first two trial dates was institutional delay. Although the adjournment was a defence request, it was not opposed. The 164 days for the judicial pretrial was inherent delay. The delay in providing the defence with will-say statements of police officers for whom the defence had a synopsis did not interfere with the pre-trial process. The period of 162 days between the end of the judicial pre-trial and the third trial date was institutional delay. These neutral and inherent timelines fell within acceptable limits. The only prejudice claimed by the defence was fading memories of potential witnesses that it made no effort to locate. The societal interest in an adjudication on the merits outweighed the defendant's interest in a prompt trial. See *Ontario College of Trades v. Eastern Power Ltd.*, 2016 CarswellOnt 6485, [2016] O.J. No. 2176 (Ont. C.J.).

In *Oshawa (City) v. 536813 Ontario Ltd.*, 2016 ONCJ 287, 2016 CarswellOnt 7911, 56 C.L.R. (4th) 304, 53 M.P.L.R. (5th) 301, [2016] O.J. No. 2595 (Ont. C.J.), additional reasons 2017 ONCJ 116, 2017 CarswellOnt 3236, 65 M.P.L.R. (5th) 336 (Ont. C.J.), reversed Oshawa (City) v. 536813 Ontario Limited, 2017 ONCJ 836,

2017 CarswellOnt 19439, 72 C.L.R. (4th) 140, 69 M.P.L.R. (5th) 313 (Ont. C.J.), affirmed Oshawa (City) v. 536813 Ontario Limited, 2017 ONCJ 836, 2017 CarswellOnt 19439, 72 C.L.R. (4th) 140, 69 M.P.L.R. (5th) 313 (Ont. C.J.), there was a total delay of 26 months after the charge was laid until the end of the trial. The inherent and intake requirements of the case occurred over almost 6 months; had the prosecution provided disclosure in a more timely fashion, this inherent time period could have been just over 4 months. The defendant waived just under 6 months of delay as well. The institutional delays accounted for a period of time of between 8 and 10 months. At the judicial pre-trial, the suggestion the constitution motion on the issue of division of powers should be heard in the Superior Court created a period of 5 months delay. There was also actual prejudice to the corporation as the Airport Operations manual had undergone revisions, and the prosecutor was unable to produce the version of the manual that was in effect at the time the charge was laid; additionally, as the trial was heard over an almost 4 month period, examination in chief and cross-examination was difficult to follow. The charge was simply a failure on the part of the defendant to obtain a building permit under the Ontario *Building Code Act*. However, there was a significant public or societal interest in having the case heard, especially given the City's insistence that it and the province, not the federal government, have legislative jurisdiction over the defendant's hangar at the Oshawa Airport complex. The question on the doctrine of interjurisdictional immunity was an important one to be determined. Given the complexity of the constitutional issues, along with the societal interest in having the matter heard on the merits, an institutional delay of approximately one year was at the outer boundaries of, but nonetheless within, an acceptable time frame.

In regulatory offences, as opposed to criminal offences, the stigma from conviction is very considerably diminished. Regulatory offences focus on the harmful consequences of otherwise lawful behaviour rather than any kind of moral turpitude. There was no violation of s. 11(b) in the instant case. One and one-half months was intake delay; 2 and three-quarters months was delay for the defence to retain a lawyer; 5 and three-quarters months was institutional delay in order to accommodate the required trial time, and 2 months of the delay was caused by the Crown's adjournment request of the first trial date. The seven and one-half months between the time when the parties were first ready to proceed to trial and the trial date was within the Supreme Court of Canada's guidelines in the *Morin* decision. See *R. v. Gerassimou*, 2016 ONCJ 378, 2016 CarswellOnt 10193, [2016] O.J. No. 3417 (Ont. C.J.).

In *R. v. Priestly Demolition Inc.*, 2016 CarswellOnt 5149 (Ont. C.J.), it was held that although not swift, the court process once commenced moved along in a reasonable fashion from first appearance to judicial pretrial, much of which was an intake period which is neutral. Then from judicial pretrial to trial, there was about 10 months to finish the evidence and submissions. However, there was then some troublesome delay from final submissions to judgment, about 13 months. The first adjournment was apparently due to scheduling problems with the justice and the court; the remaining adjournments were due to the illness of the justice. There was no evidence of prejudice to the defendant caused by the delay over this period. Without further details as to whether it was illness on the day or an extended, or recurring illness, or further information about the availability of the court or the justice, the court could not make any finding except that it was neutral or inherent time, as illnesses of the participants are generally considered to be. The defendant had not met the onus on it for establishing either an unreasonable delay or resulting prejudice.

Applying the Supreme Court of Canada's new framework for unreasonable delay in *R. v. Jordan*, 2016 CSC 27, 2016 SCC 27, 2016 CarswellBC 1864, 2016 CarswellBC 1865, [2016] 1 S.C.R. 631, 335 C.C.C. (3d) 403, 29 C.R. (7th) 235, 398 D.L.R. (4th) 381, 388 B.C.A.C. 111, 358 C.R.R. (2d) 97, 484 N.R. 202, 670 W.A.C. 111, [2016] A.C.S. No. 27, [2016] S.C.J. No. 27 (S.C.C.), the complexities of the case resulted in a presumptive ceiling of 18 months. The overall delay in the case, involving driving while suspended and failing to wear a seatbelt, was just over 17 months. The total amount of time taken to conduct three judicial pre-trial conferences was part of the inherent time requirements, and reduced the total period of delay substantially, such that the actual delay was well below the presumptive ceiling of 18 months. The case did not take markedly longer than it reasonably should have; both sides acted reasonably and expeditiously. The defendant's right to be tried without unreasonable delay was not violated in the circumstances. See *R. v. Ramsay*, 2016 ONCJ 569, 2016 CarswellOnt 14580, [2016] O.J. No. 4841 (Ont. C.J.).

In *Ontario (Ministry of Labour) v. Sterling Crane Division of Procrane Inc.*, 2016 ONCJ 692, 2016 CarswellOnt 19043, 369 C.R.R. (2d) 48, [2016] O.J. No. 6200 (Ont. C.J.), the matter arose out of a serious workplace accident in 2012, and the information against the defendant was laid in May, 2013. The trial continued through 2015 and a conviction registered in 2016. Prior to sentencing, the defendant brought a motion for a stay of proceedings due to unreasonable delay. While the delay exceeded the new presumptive ceiling in *Jordan*, a transitional exceptional circumstance applied. Prejudice could not be proven by the defendant, and there was no s. 11(b) application prior to the start of trial, during the trial or prior to conviction; there were also no efforts to expedite the proceedings as the defendant agreed to all of the agreements, and did not raise the issue of unreasonable delay in a timely manner. The case was proceeding before the court on a timeline and in a manner that both parties accepted as the normal pace, and at the time of trial, the *Morin* decision was still applicable.

The Supreme Court of Canada's framework in *R. v. Jordan*, 2016 CSC 27, 2016 SCC 27, 2016 CarswellBC 1864, 2016 CarswellBC 1865, [2016] 1 S.C.R. 631, 335 C.C.C. (3d) 403, 29 C.R. (7th) 235, 398 D.L.R. (4th) 381, 388 B.C.A.C. 111, 358 C.R.R. (2d) 97, 484 N.R. 202, 670 W.A.C. 111, [2016] A.C.S. No. 27, [2016] S.C.J. No. 27 (S.C.C.), applies equally to the prosecutions of corporations who are charged with regulatory offences like those under the *Occupational Health and Safety Act*. Given that it is not only an accused's interest that is being protected by s. 11(b) but also the community's, the same presumptive ceilings of unreasonable delay must be respected for any accused. See *R. v. Live Nation Canada Inc.*, 2016 ONCJ 735, 2016 CarswellOnt 20178, 372 C.R.R. (2d) 210, [2016] O.J. No. 6591 (Ont. C.J.).

Likewise, in *Mississauga (City) v. Uber Canada Inc.*, 2016 ONCJ 746, 2016 CarswellOnt 20837, 369 C.R.R. (2d) 105, [2016] O.J. No. 6229 (Ont. C.J.), it was held that the right to speedy trial guaranteed under s. 11(b) equally applies to prosecutions brought under regulatory or public welfare statutes as it does to criminal offences. Since the defendant was being prosecuted in the Provincial Offences Court of the Ontario Court of Justice, the 18 month ceiling for provincial courts applies to s. 11(b) applications. Since s. 11(b) protects the fair trial interest of all accused persons, then by implication and by references that the *Jordan* majority had made that its new framework protects the "fair trial interest" of accused persons, the *Jordan* framework would apply to corporations charged with offences. More significantly, since prejudice is no longer a factor under the new *Jordan* framework, and since unreasonable delay is presumed after the ceiling of 18 months is reached in the provincial courts, then a corporation also no longer needs to prove "irremediable prejudice" to their fair trial interests under the new s. 11(b) framework.

In *Ontario (Ministry of Labour) v. Belle-Pak Packaging Inc.*, 2017 ONCJ 811, 2017 CarswellOnt 18898, 399 C.R.R. (2d) 283, [2017] O.J. No. 6226 (Ont. C.J.), it was held that it is well established that s. 11(b) of the *Charter* applies to regulatory matters. Section 11(b) of the *Charter* applies to both regulatory and *Criminal Code* offences. Were *Jordan* not to apply to corporate accused, the end result would be a two tier system for corporate accused and personal defendants. Indeed, as personal and corporate defendants are often jointly charged, inconsistency between defendants could easily occur; moreover, this would dilute the concept of a legal person which includes *inter alia* corporations. The net delay in the instant case was just under 26 months, which was well over the 18-month ceiling for provincial courts which applies to provincial offences court proceedings. The case was not a complex one. The victim was injured while at work; the defendant, his employer, was charged. None of the offences involved novel or complex points of law. Initially the Crown was going to call four witnesses, one of whom was an expert. The Crown called only two witnesses before closing its case: the injured worker and their expert. The delay resulted from the inaccurate assessment of time required for the case as the Crown did not turn its mind to the requirement of two interpreters for three out of four of their witnesses, and how this would prolong the trial. The defendant has a constitutional right to have a trial in a timely fashion. This was not done.

On the other hand, in *R. v. Reid*, 2017 ONCJ 839, 2017 CarswellOnt 19594, [2017] O.J. No. 6489 (Ont. C.J.), the defendant was charged with using a handheld device while driving. The total delay in this case was 10.5 months. This delay was of sufficient length to warrant judicial inquiry. The defendant faced a simple charge and this should have been a relatively straightforward trial which should not have taken more than 30 minutes. The offence of distracted driving is very much in the news these days with reports that it has been contributing significantly to damage to property and to personal injuries arising out of motor vehicle collisions. The offence is often compared to drinking and driving with regard to the serious consequences flowing from these offences. In light of this, balancing the societal interest in a trial on the merits is particularly important in such cases. The delay of just over nine months was well within the guideline especially when one takes into account the absence of prejudice. Under the *Jordan* analysis, the onus is on the defence to show that a delay of less than 18 months is nevertheless unreasonable. Given the level of institutional delay tolerated under the previous approach, a stay of proceedings below the ceiling will be even more difficult to obtain for cases currently in the system.

In *R. v. Bazdar*, 2018 ONCJ 318, 2018 CarswellOnt 7677, [2018] O.J. No. 2571 (Ont. C.J.), it was held that the net delay of 16 months and 19 days fell below the presumptive ceiling of 18 months and was presumptively reasonable when applying the test set out in *Jordan*. The applicant's agent did nothing exceptional to expedite the proceeding. The proceedings moved along in the manner in which matters commenced under Part I proceeding. On the contrary, the agent did not make all efforts to request full disclosure in that he ought to have requested all disclosure including any DVD evidence that was available. The charges were straightforward as was the disclosure.

Faced with a delay resulting from the complexity of a case, the Crown must act reasonably and take steps to implement the plan it has devised to minimize that delay. It is not too stringent a standard in the post-*Jordan* era for the trial judge to impose on the Crown that it be pro-active in its efforts to move the case to trial under the presumptive ceiling while simultaneously being involved in an extensive judicial pre-trial process aimed at resolving the case. There was no basis for appellate interference with the trial judge's decision holding that the Crown failed to develop and follow an adequate plan to minimize the delay arising from the complexity of the case. This conclusion was clearly open to the trial judge and led to his ultimate finding that the Crown had not established exceptional circumstances outside of its control justifying the delay above the presumptive ceiling. See *R. v. Nugent, Guillemette and Buckingham*, 2018 ONSC 3546, 2018 CarswellOnt 9120, [2018] O.J. No. 3047 (Ont. S.C.J.), leave to appeal allowed 2018 ONCA 1014, 2018 CarswellOnt 20709 (Ont. C.A.).

In *R. v. El-Nasrallah*, 2018 ONCJ 161, 2018 CarswellOnt 3644, [2018] O.J. No. 1297 (Ont. C.J.), the trial justice of the peace dismissed the defendant's motion for unreasonable delay where it took 10 months and 24 days for the matter to proceed to trial. It is unreasonable to conclude that the *Morin* framework should still apply to Part I provincial prosecutions. While the *Jordan* framework of a presumptive ceiling must apply to Part I offences, it does not necessarily follow that the presumptive ceiling for Part I offences should be the same as the ceiling for criminal matters. Given the realities of provincial offences Part I proceedings, the fact that there are no significant intake proceedings and the matters tend to be relatively simple and not time consuming, the presumptive ceiling for these type of offences ought to be lower than the ceiling for criminal cases. It is difficult, however, to assign a number to the upper ceiling in the absence of any evidentiary foundation. While the court was unable to identify a clear number for the upper ceiling for Part I proceedings, there was no basis to reduce the ceiling to 10 months. Reducing the upper ceiling by eight months places too much weight on the intake period and not enough weight on the administrative realities of setting trial dates. It is difficult to imagine an upper ceiling for Part I offences that is less than 12 months given the realities of busy courts. Since the delay in the case at bar was well under 12 months, the trial justice of the peace did not err in finding that there was no s. 11(b) violation.

Section 11(b) of the *Charter* was also considered in another provincial offences appeal case, *York (Regional Municipality) v. Tomovski*, 2017 ONCJ 785, 2017 CarswellOnt 18239, 400 C.R.R. (2d) 219, [2017] O.J. No. 6073 (Ont. C.J.), leave to appeal refused 2018 ONCA 57, 2018 CarswellOnt 695 (Ont. C.A.), where it was held that because *Jordan* was decided in the criminal context its narrow *ratio decidendi* — the express or implied legal conclusions necessary to the result on the facts of the case — is silent on whether the same presumptive ceiling applies to non-criminal proceedings. It is important to distinguish the *concept* of a presumptive ceiling and the *number* chosen for it in a particular procedural context. While it is clear the concept applies in Part I proceedings, it is not at all clear the number does. The "realities we currently face" in the Part I process are different realties than the ones reflected in the ceilings set in *Jordan*. Had the Supreme Court used data derived exclusively from Part I and its analogues in the other provinces, its methodology would have generated a lower number of months than 18. Accordingly, the lower overall inherent time requirements of Part I proceedings furnishes a valid legal basis to distinguish *Jordan* to the extent of allowing for a lower presumptive ceiling. A lower ceiling is required to ensure fidelity to the broader principles announced in *Jordan* in this very different procedural context. The *Jordan* court set the presumptive ceilings to meet the requirements of criminal proceedings and implicitly left open the possibility that a different ceiling would apply in this very different context. The ceiling should be lower than the 18-month ceiling applicable in criminal cases; the question of whether the presumptive ceiling should be different for Part III proceedings was not before the court. Accordingly, the appropriate presumptive ceiling for Part I proceedings is in the 13 to 15-month range, and for the purposes of deciding the case at bar the applicable presumptive ceiling is 14 months. However, the court declined to "set" a specific presumptive ceiling for Part I cases generally, as promulgating frameworks and setting ceilings are the responsibility of senior appellate courts, not judges of this court. The net delay in the case of 10 months and 22 days was well below the 14-month ceiling, and as such was presumptively reasonable. Because the case was concluded before *Jordan* was released, the defendant need not demonstrate it took meaningful steps that demonstrate a sustained effort to expedite the proceedings to rebut this presumption. The defendant did have to demonstrate the case took markedly longer than it reasonably should have, however. From the point of view of total delay in fact it did. But the defence was responsible for the majority of that delay and the net delay does not reflect a case that took markedly longer than it should have. It followed that there was no s. 11(b) breach and the justice of the peace erred in concluding otherwise.

In *R. v. Galbraith*, 2018 ONCJ 138, 2018 CarswellOnt 3347, 404 C.R.R. (2d) 371, [2018] O.J. No. 1189 (Ont. C.J.), a written request for disclosure was sought four times by the defendant for her speeding trial, and she received assurances from administration that her requests had been forwarded to the office of the prosecution. She did not receive an answer to her requests. The prosecution policy concerning the provision of disclosure in the jurisdiction was usually two weeks after receipt of a written request. The delay in providing disclosure in a timely manner to the defendant in this case was due to staffing changes in the office of the prosecution. The prosecution delay in providing disclosure was due to a mistake and did not violate her right to a fair trial under s. 11(d) of the *Charter of Rights*, nor was any prejudice demonstrated such that the late disclosure did not violate the right to make full answer and defence under s. 7 of the *Charter*. The time elapsed since the date of the offence to the proposed date of trial was seven months, well below the presumptive ceiling for unreasonable delay established in *R. v. Jordan*. There was no negligence on the part of the prosecutor that justified an order of costs either as a *Charter* remedy or due to procedural irregularities under s. 90 of the *Provincial Offences Act*. The defendant had chosen to attend the Early Resolution meeting and there were a total of two court appearances to date. Section 24(1) of the *Charter* confers a broad remedial mandate and the widest possible discretion on a court to craft remedies that must be easily available for violations of *Charter* rights. The remedy in the instant case was an adjournment to a date for trial and no order for costs.

In *R. v. Bakshi*, 2018 CarswellOnt 11576, [2018] O.J. No. 3736 (Ont. C.J.), the total delay in the case was 16 months and 28 days, which included a *voir dire* on the lack of production of audio and video recordings in the police cruiser and the lack of an audio recording for the traffic stop. While this delay was under the presumptive ceiling in *Jordan*, the defence did take meaningful steps to expedite the proceedings by bringing two disclosure requests. The matter took markedly longer than it should have, being a trial for drive hand held communication device. This was a simple case. While it was not a minor traffic matter, it was a standard provincial offence matter that is heard on the tier of 40 to 45 matters. The delay falls at the foot of the prosecution as they did not have communication within their office. While there are numerous numbers of cases and there are numerous prosecutors, it is not perfection to track a case where an email comes in that an audio recording is not available to the case that it applies to. There had been unreasonable delay considering the *Jordan* framework as it stands. An order staying the charge was granted.

A corporate accused, like the defendant, has the right to be tried within a reasonable time. The issue of delay was raised for the first time on appeal. It was argued that the Reasons for Judgment proved that the justice of the peace completely ignored the cross-examination of the witnesses, the defences put forward by it in their oral submissions at trial and their written argument, and that this is due to the length of time it took for the justice of the peace to render judgment. The case law is clear, only in unusual circumstances can an appellate court entertain a s. 11(b) *Charter* argument even though it was not raised at trial. The failure to make the argument at trial, is, in most cases, fatal. However, where, as in this case, the length of the delay never fully crystallized until the proceedings were completed by the delivery of the Reasons for Judgment of the justice of the peace, and the defendant had every indication during each of the court appearances during the delay that the delivery of the reasons was imminent, it would have been pointless to bring the s. 11(b) application in the Superior Court. Nor would it have been tactically wise for counsel for the defendant to bring a motion for a stay before the justice of the peace based on unreasonable delay. The justice of the peace repeatedly indicated his reasons would be available in the very near future; it is not surprising counsel took him at his word. This, then, was one of those unusual cases where an appellate court can and should entertain a s. 11(b) argument even though the issue was not raised prior to the completion of the proceedings before the justice of the peace. The length of delay was 15 months from the conclusion of counsel's submissions to the Reasons for Judgment. There was nothing in the transcripts that indicated that the actions of the accused, the actions of the Crown, or any limits on institutional resources in any way contributed to the delay. Part of the delay appeared to be the time needed for transcripts to be prepared for the justice of the peace to review as he wrote his decision. This reason for delay is neither unusual nor unreasonable, but the amount of time it took in this case was excessive. It would have been preferable for the Reasons for Judgment to have been completed within six to eight months. The question remained, however, what, if any, prejudice did the defendant suffer from the excessive delay. It could not rely on the presumption of prejudice from delay afforded to an individual accused. In any event, the justice of the peace did not fail to deal with the evidence raised at trial by defence counsel in cross-examination of the Crown witnesses. The justice was alive to each of the issues raised by the defence at trial and dealt with each of those issues. It could not be concluded, therefore, that the justice of the peace forgot relevant evidence or issues due to the delay. As a result, the defendant had not suffered the required "irremediable prejudice." In the absence of any prejudice to the defendant, the interests of society in having a decision on the merits in this case outweighed the interests of the defendant in having a timely decision. See *Ontario (Ministry of the Environment) v. Orgaworld Canada Ltd.*, 2015 CarswellOnt 21087 (Ont. C.J.), leave to appeal refused *R. v. Orgaworld Canada Ltd.*, 2015 CarswellOnt 21086 (Ont. C.A.).

In *York (Regional Municipality) v. Martingrove Properties Ltd.*, [2018] O.J. No. 5223 (Ont. C.J.), it was held that the s. 11(b) clock begins to run from the date of an appellant's court's decision. It does not include the period that the defendant indicates he wished to bring an s. 11(b) application. The clock is "reset" after the appeal is complete.

The net delay in both proceedings under the *Dog Owners' Liability Act* exceeded the threshold of 18 months contemplated for proceedings in the provincial court. In relation to the dog bite incident, the delay would be approximately 19 and one-half months, and in relation to the bite on the child, 20 and one-half months. Assuming that rights to a timely disposition of the matters apply to hearings under s. 161 of the *Provincial Offences Act*, a stay of proceedings for unreasonable delay was not warranted. The lapsed time was not far over the 18 month threshold contemplated by *R. v. Jordan*, apart from allowance for the mistrial and the delay occasioned by the family loss experienced by the court. The particular periods that would be deducted for these reasons would bring the total delay below the 18 month threshold in both cases. See *Halton Hills (Regional Municipality) v. Sciberras*, 2018 ONCJ 555, 2018 CarswellOnt 13684, [2018] O.J. No. 4262 (Ont. C.J.).

In *York (Regional Municipality) v. 1085638 Ontario Limited*, 2018 ONCJ 658, 2018 CarswellOnt 16164, [2018] O.J. No. 5003 (Ont. C.J.), there was no challenge to the delay involving charges under the *Building Code* from 2012 to 2017 when all charges were heard. In rejecting the s. 11(b) application, the trial Justice found that the corporate defendant could not rely on inferred prejudice but had to show actual or real prejudice. The company was found not to have been irremediably prejudiced nor that the prejudice could not be removed or cured pending a fair trial. The s.

11(b) ruling was argued and decided under the rules as they then existed pre-*Jordan*. The court applied the correct test. There was no error in law. There was no mistake or surprise on the part of the defendants going back to 1992 that it was operating outside of zoning law. The trial record left the impression that the defendants simply took the position that non-compliance was the cost of doing business.

The defendant brought a motion for unreasonable delay that was returnable on the date scheduled for judgment on the trial proper. The period from the date the charge was laid to the judgment date was just over two years. The justice of the peace dismissed the s. 11(b) application, holding that the case was not the "most standard or simplest case" and that there had been a number of pre-trial motions. The applicable presumptive ceiling in the case at bar was 18 months as identified in the Supreme Court in *Jordan* for cases tried in the Provincial Court. There is no principled reason to reduce the presumptive ceiling. A wide range of offences are governed by Part III of the *POA*. Many such offences, although regulatory in nature, have many similarities to criminal offences. In some instances, the offences share the same or very similar essential elements to a corresponding criminal offence. Proceedings for Part III offences may be as lengthy and complex as criminal proceedings. There is also a danger in creating a myriad of presumptive ceilings for different types of criminal and regulatory offences. The establishment of a variety of presumptive ceilings (varying by nature of offence, circumstances of the offender, or jurisdiction) may detract from the underlying policy rationales that guided the Supreme Court's findings in *Jordan* which were intended, at least in part, to redress the highly unpredictable and complex nature of the *Morin* analytical framework. The *Jordan* framework is sufficiently flexible to accommodate the wide range of cases tried by criminal and provincial offences courts. On an assessment generous to the defendant, under the *Morin* framework, there was at most 9.5 months of institutional delay, which fell within the *Morin* guidelines. The case was of at least moderate complexity given the number and complexity of the motions and applications. Stepping back from the minutiae what was abundantly clear was that the primary reason that the case took 24 months and 4 days to reach judgment was a result of the frivolous motions initiated by the defendant that used up all of the time initially scheduled for trial. The second major factor was the inaccurate estimate of how long those motions would take. The Crown was prepared to proceed and move the case forward on each occasion and took steps to narrow the issues by narrowing the offence period on the information. The delay was not unreasonable. The justice of the peace correctly dismissed the s. 11(b) application, and, to the extent that the justice of the peace committed any errors in law in reaching his conclusion, there was no miscarriage of justice and no substantial wrong. See *Ontario (Superintendent of Financial Services) v. Dies*, 2018 ONCJ 641, 2018 CarswellOnt 15738, [2018] O.J. No. 4894 (Ont. C.J.).

In *R. v. Madill*, 2019 ONCJ 19, 2019 CarswellOnt 156, [2019] O.J. No. 107 (Ont. C.J.), the justice of the peace erred in calculating the total delay from the date of the swearing of the information to the end of evidence and argument, rather than the "end of trial". Properly calculated, the total delay on which the information was sworn to the date on which judgment was delivered was in excess of 24 months. The trial Crown took the position that if defence counsel was going to challenge the admissibility of the Notice of Project, he was required to file notice, and that an adjournment was the proper remedy in order to permit defence counsel to comply with the notice requirement. In circumstances where at trial, the Crown insisted on compliance with the notice provisions and took the position that an adjournment was the appropriate remedy, it would be unfair, on appeal, to find that defence counsel should have requested a recess to consider the admissibility issue. In this case, the adjournment was granted and requested, with no consideration of other solutions which would have made effective use of court time and reduced delay. In these circumstances, the delay cannot be properly characterized as delay solely due to defence. The *Charter* application was a legitimate application to determine the admissibility of the Notice of Project, which the defendant was entitled to litigate. When the 90-day delay occasioned by exceptional circumstances (the adjournment of the first and second pre-trial) was deducted from the total delay, the net delay of 21 months exceeded the 18-month presumptive ceiling in *Jordan*. As the Crown had not discharged its onus of demonstrating that the delay was not unreasonable, a stay of proceedings was granted.

At trial, the defendant brought a s. 11(b) application complaining of the delay resulting from her adjournment of the first trial. The application was dismissed. A plea of guilty was then entered to a reduced charge. A guilty plea constitutes a waiver, not only of the accused's right to require the prosecution to prove guilt beyond a reasonable doubt, but also of the related procedural safeguards in the trial process. The guilty plea in the instant case disentitles the accused from challenging pre-trial rulings in proceedings before the plea was taken. That applies with stronger reason here where the appellant was permitted to plead to a reduced offence with the benefit of reduced penalty. The appellant's submission to the effect that *R. v. Jordan* imposes absolute timelines such that it doesn't matter whether the defence caused the delay misstates the test. *Jordan* requires the court to begin by deducting defence delay. The timelines are applied after that deduction. In this case, not only did the defence request the delay complained of but the agent at trial specifically confirmed that his client was content with the time to the next trial date despite concerns expressed by the justice of the peace. On either *Jordan* or the prior *R. v. Morin* analysis, there was no merit to the application. See *Yogeswaran v. York (Regional Municipality)*, 2018 ONCJ 819, 2018 CarswellOnt 19741, [2018] O.J. No. 6131 (Ont. C.J.).

5.6.6 PROOF OF BY-LAWS OR SUBORDINATE LEGISLATION

- The basic rule is that judicial notice cannot be taken of municipal by-laws.

- The common law required judicial notice to be taken of public or general statutes but not of private enactments or subordinate legislation such as regulations.

- A copy of a by-law certified by the proper officer of the municipal corporation to be a true copy of the by-law and under the seal of the municipal corporation is admissible in evidence under the *Evidence Act*.

Speed limit signs are *prima facie* proof of compliance with the regulations under the *Highway Traffic Act: R. v. Clark* (1974), 3 O.R. (2d) 716, 18 C.C.C. (2d) 52 (Ont. C.A.).

In *Sproule v. Oshawa (City)* (October 24, 2011), Doc. 2860 999 10 0476 00, [2011] O.J. No. 4732 (Ont. C.J.), it was held that a court cannot take judicial notice of by-laws and that proof of the by-law is an essential element of the case. However, while a certified true copy of the by-law was never formally tendered into evidence, the prosecutor did advice the court at the commencement of the trial that she had a certified true copy of the by-law and would be providing the court with excerpts during submissions; the court confirmed that a true copy of the by law, in its entirety, was present and available, and a copy of it was provided to the court for reference purposes. Although defence counsel asked for the by-law to be made an exhibit, the court did not think this was necessary, and submissions were made on the basis of the by-law being before the court. In these circumstances, there was an implicit agreement between counsel that proof of the by-law was conceded or not in issue, and the court was entitled to proceed as it did, being satisfied that the by-law need not be formally entered into evidence.

The justice of the peace was entitled to take judicial notice of the boundaries of the Town of Caledon, as its boundaries are notorious and defined by provincial statute: *R. v. Howse*, 2012 ONCJ 517, 2012 CarswellOnt 9877, 37 M.V.R. (6th) 327, [2012] O.J. No. 3772 (Ont. C.J.).

When considering whether a fact is suitable for judicial notice, a judge is not to take his or her personal knowledge into account, or profess to know of the fact, or take steps to acquire knowledge of the fact. The speed limit on the relevant portion of the highway in question was so notorious as not to be the subject of dispute among reasonable persons: see *R. v. Abrametz*, 2014 SKCA 84, 2014 CarswellSask 490, 68 M.V.R. (6th) 95, 442 Sask. R. 86, 616 W.A.C. 86, [2014] S.J. No. 438 (Sask. C.A.).

In *R. v. Webb*, 2016 BCPC 294, 2016 CarswellBC 2789, [2016] B.C.J. No. 2089 (B.C. Prov. Ct.), it was held that judicial notice may be taken of a matter that is so notorious as not to be the subject of dispute among reasonable men or so capable of immediate accuracy by resort to readily accessible sources of indisputable accuracy. Having regard to the officer's testimony of having observed the disputant vehicle's momentum while he was travelling on Highway 1 at the Surrey/Langley border, with the disputant on the 192 on-ramp of Highway 1 approaching to merge westbound, judicial notice was taken that both cities border each other and are within the province of British Columbia. It cannot but be notorious to persons in the Lower Mainland of British Columbia that the location described is in British Columbia. The officer testified he stopped the vehicle on the highway at the location after its speed was estimated and a radar reading was taken and served the disputant with the violation ticket in question. The court was also shown a video of that stop on the highway.

5.6.7 BILINGUAL SIGNAGE

- The council of a municipality, which is in a designated area under the *French Language Services Act*, may pass a by-law providing that the administration of the municipality shall be conducted in both English and French, and that all or specified municipal services to the public shall be made available in both languages. See *French Language Services Act*, R.S.O. 1990, c. F.23, s. 14(1).

Where a municipality is designated a bilingual area under the *French Language Services Act*, the issue arises whether the signage under the *Highway Traffic Act* must be bilingual in order to be valid. See *R. v. Myers* (2004), [2004] O.J. No. 4763, 2004 CarswellOnt 5638 (Ont. C.J.), reversed (2005), 2005 CarswellOnt 10019 (Ont. C.J.).

The *Myers* decision regarding unilingual traffic signs in the City of Toronto was held to be wrongly decided in *R. v. Petruzzo*, 2011 ONCA 386, 2011 CarswellOnt 3239, [2011] O.J. No. 2203, 11 M.V.R. (6th) 201, 278 O.A.C. 130 (Ont. C.A. [In Chambers]), where Laskin J.A. ruled that the city was not bound to have signs in French and English as it had not passed a by-law to this effect.

In *Toronto (City) v. Braganza* (2011), 91 M.P.L.R. (4th) 276, [2011] O.J. No. 5445, 21 M.V.R. (6th) 104, 2011 ONCJ 657, 2011 CarswellOnt 13681, 250 C.R.R. (2d) 60 (Ont. C.J.), it was held that bilingual signs are not required in Toronto, as held in

R. v. Petruzzo, 2011 ONCA 386, 2011 CarswellOnt 3239, [2011] O.J. No. 2203, 11 M.V.R. (6th) 201, 278 O.A.C. 130 (Ont. C.A. [In Chambers]). Therefore a defendant who receives a parking ticket in Toronto is precluded from arguing that since neither signs nor parking infraction notices are bilingual, they are void for non compliance with the *French Language Services Act* and the *Provincial Offences Act*. Reg. 949, s. 8 which governs parking infractions and allows forms under Part II of the *Provincial Offences Act* to be in English, French or both English and French, is a valid regulation which actually promotes the French language by permitting a municipality to use French only forms. There can be no conflict between a regulation in the *Provincial Offences Act* that permits forms to be in English or French and a section in the *French Language Services Act* that permits exemptions. The legislation must be read as a whole, and absent a constitutional right to all services in French in Ontario, or a quasi-constitutional status for the *French Language Services Act*, s. 8 of Reg. 949 is valid.

6

MENS REA OFFENCES

6.1 BURDEN OF PROOF

As described in Chapter 4, and as laid down by the Supreme Court in *R. v. Sault Ste. Marie (City)*, [1978] 2 S.C.R. 1299, 7 C.E.L.R. 53, 3 C.R. (3d) 30, 40 C.C.C. (2d) 353, 1978 CarswellOnt 24, 1978 CarswellOnt 594, 85 D.L.R. (3d) 161, 21 N.R. 295 (S.C.C.):

- The prosecution must prove beyond a reasonable doubt that the defendant committed the illegal act(s).

- The prosecution must also prove beyond a reasonable doubt that the defendant had a particular state of mind.

- The state of mind depends on the offence. For example, it might be intent, knowledge, or recklessness.

- The prosecution can prove the defendant's state of mind in two ways:

  - Admissions by the defendant as to his or her state of mind, or

  - Inferences of the defendant's state of mind based on the common sense principle that people normally intend the natural consequences of their actions.

6.2 THE STATE OF MIND

- "Intention" may be an intention to commit particular acts, or an intention to bring about certain results.

- "Knowledge" may refer to knowledge of fairly limited circumstances or actions, or knowledge of the effect of those actions.

- "Recklessness" means an awareness that there is a risk of certain behaviour and then acting in an unacceptable disregard to that risk.

6.3 PARTIES TO THE OFFENCE

- See heading 7.4 in Chapter 7.

6.4 DEFENCES TO THE ELEMENTS OF THE OFFENCE

6.4.1 DEFENCES TO THE ACT ELEMENT

- Is there any reasonable doubt, on the prosecutor's evidence, that your client voluntarily committed the act(s)?

6.4.2 DEFENCES TO THE MENTAL ELEMENT

- Will the justice likely conclude, beyond a reasonable doubt, that your client had the particular state of mind, based on:
  - Your client's admissions, or
  - Inferences that your client intended the natural consequences of his or her act(s)?
- If the prosecutor has strong proof of the act and mental elements, what evidence can you call for the defence? Will it raise a reasonable doubt?

6.5 OTHER DEFENCES

- Section 80 of the POA states:
  - Every rule and principle of the common law that renders any circumstance a justification or excuse for an act or a defence to a charge continues in force and applies in respect of offences, except in so far as they are altered by or inconsistent with this or any other Act.

6.5.1 MISTAKE OF FACT

- If the defendant honestly believed in certain facts which, if true, would have rendered his or her actions legal, then the defendant did not intend to commit the offence. In other words, the defendant has rebutted the presumption of intending the natural consequences of his or her actions.

- A court can properly find wilful blindness where the defendant ". . . suspected the fact, realized its probability, but refrained from obtaining the final confirmation because he or she wanted to be able to deny knowledge": *R. v. Malfara* (2006), 2006 CarswellOnt 3164, 211 O.A.C. 200 (Ont. C.A.), endorsement, following *R. v. Jorgensen,*1995 CarswellOnt 1185, 1995 CarswellOnt 985, [1995] S.C.J. No. 95, [1995] S.C.J. No. 92, EYB 1995-67684, [1995] 4 S.C.R. 55, 43 C.R. (4th) 137, 102 C.C.C. (3d) 97, 129 D.L.R. (4th) 510, 189 N.R. 1, 87 O.A.C. 1, 32 C.R.R. (2d) 189, (*sub nom.* R. v. Hawkins) 25 O.R. (3d) 824 (S.C.C.), at 135 [C.C.C.].

- Generally, a mistake of fact must be honest but not necessarily reasonable.

- As a matter of common sense, a justice may have difficulty believing your client made an honest mistake when a reasonable person in the same situation would not have been mistaken.

- If the defendant honestly believed in mistaken facts because he or she shut his or her mind to the truth, the defendant is "wilfully blind" to the truth and this may be sufficient proof of *mens rea*: *R. v. Sansregret*, (*sub nom.* Sansregret v. R.) [1985] 1 S.C.R. 570, (*sub nom.* Sansregret v. R.) [1985] 3 W.W.R. 701, (*sub nom.* Sansregret v. R.) 45 C.R. (3d) 193, (*sub nom.* Sansregret v. R.) 18 C.C.C. (3d) 223 (S.C.C.).

- "Ignorance of the law by a person who commits an offence is not an excuse for committing the offence": section 81. *But see the defence: "Officially Induced Error" in section 5.6.2 in Chapter 5.*

In *R. v. Filice*, 2011 ONCJ 833, 2011 CarswellOnt 15546, [2011] O.J. No. 6257 (Ont. C.J.), it was held that the defendants had committed the *actus reus* of the offence of driving on a closed highway, and they were wilfully blind to the situation in doing so. The defendants were clearly rationalizing the decision to ignore the clear and understandable wording of the sign. They made decisions to make minimal, if any, inquiries.

6.5.2 INTOXICATION

If your client was so befogged by liquor or other toxic substances that he or she was incapable of forming the required state of mind, then he or she may have a defence.

- Determine exactly what state of mind is required for the offence. *In criminal matters, courts have distinguished between specific and general intent crimes, and have minimized the defence of drunkeness for general intent crimes: R. v. Bernard,* 67 C.R. (3d) 113, 45 C.C.C. (3d) 1, [1988] 2 S.C.R. 833 (S.C.C.). *For general intent crimes, the accused must establish, on a balance of probabilities with expert evidence, that he or she was intoxicated to such an extent as to be in a state akin to insanity or automatism: R. v. Daviault,* 33 C.R. (4th) 165, 93 C.C.C. (3d) 21, [1994] 3 S.C.R. 63 (S.C.C.).

- Distinguish between a client who, because of an intoxicant, did not know what he or she was doing at the time from a client who, because of a hangover, knew but cannot now *remember* what he or she did at the time.

6.5.3 ADDITIONAL DEFENCES

- In addition to the procedural defences in Chapter 5, consider the following defences covered in Chapter 8:

  - Involuntariness;

  - Causation; and

  - Necessity.

6.6 CORPORATE RESPONSIBILITY

The Supreme Court of Canada in *R. v. Sault Ste. Marie (City),* [1978] 2 S.C.R. 1299, 7 C.E.L.R. 53, 3 C.R. (3d) 30, 40 C.C.C. (2d) 353, 1978 CarswellOnt 24, 1978 CarswellOnt 594, 85 D.L.R. (3d) 161, 21 N.R. 295 (S.C.C.), at 371 [C.C.C.] held:

> The element of control, particularly by those in charge of business activities which may endanger the public, is vital to promote the observance of regulation designed to avoid that danger. This control may be exercised by supervision or inspection, by improvement of . . . business methods or by exhorting those whom may be expected . . . to [be] influence[d] or control[led].

- See section 7.3, "Corporate Responsibility" in Chapter 7.

- The requirements which apply to finding a corporation liable for a regulatory offence which is *mens rea* in nature are the same for a finding of liability for the corporation for a *mens rea* criminal offence: *R. v. Knibb,* [1997] 8 W.W.R. 115, 51

Alta. L.R. (3d) 294, 1997 CarswellAlta 466, [1997] No. 513, 198 A.R. 161 (Alta. Prov. Ct.), affirmed [1998] No. 628, 1998 CarswellAlta 489 (Alta. Q.B.).

7
STRICT LIABILITY OFFENCES

7.1 BURDEN OF PROOF

As described in Chapter 4, and as laid down by the Supreme Court in *R. v. Sault Ste. Marie (City)*, [1978] 2 S.C.R. 1299, 7 C.E.L.R. 53, 3 C.R. (3d) 30, 40 C.C.C. (2d) 353, 1978 CarswellOnt 24, 1978 CarswellOnt 594, 85 D.L.R. (3d) 161, 21 N.R. 295 (S.C.C.):

- The prosecution must prove beyond a reasonable doubt that the defendant committed the illegal act(s).
- The defendant must then prove, on a balance of probabilities, that:
  - He or she took reasonable care not to commit the illegal act(s), or
  - He or she made a reasonable mistake of fact which, if true, would have rendered the act(s) lawful.
- A mistake of fact must be reasonable. Normally, the defendant must establish that he or she took all reasonable steps and made all reasonable inquiries to determine the correct information.
- In strict liability cases, the defendant must establish that the mistake of fact was not only an honest one, but that there were reasonable grounds for it.

7.2 CONSIDERATIONS FOR REASONABLE CARE

See the excellent treatise by John Swaigen, entitled *Regulatory Offences in Canada* (Carswell, 1992), Chapters 5, 6 and 7. See also *Libman on Regulatory Offences in Canada* (Earlscourt, 2002) at Chapter 7.3.

7.2.1 ALTERNATIVES

- The defendant must establish, on a balance of probabilities, that there was no reasonable alternative to committing the offence.

- One alternative is to do nothing. If an activity cannot be carried on legally, then it should not be carried on at all. (Economic necessity is not a defence.)

- Some regulations provide that the rules can be deviated from if equivalent or higher standards are followed. For example, Regulation 851, R.R.O. 1990, section 2 under the *Occupational Health and Safety Act* states:

> In applying this Regulation, the composition, design, size and arrangement of any material, object, device or thing may vary from the composition, design, size or arrangement prescribed in this Regulation where the factors of strength, health and safety are equal to or greater than the factors of strength, health and safety in the composition, design, size or arrangement prescribed.

7.2.2 LIKELIHOOD AND GRAVITY OF HARM

- The greater the potential for serious injury, the greater the care required.

- In many businesses, experts make on-going assessments of the probability of minor and serious injuries in order to take special precautions where appropriate.

Due diligence in a traffic offence is a modified objective test — one should appreciate the risk of other drivers speeding, but not necessarily grossly speeding: *R. v. Neal*, [2008] O.J. No. 720, 2008 CarswellOnt 1100, 2008 ONCJ 42, 67 M.V.R. (5th) 277 (Ont. C.J.).

The defendant does not have the onus of demonstrating the precise mechanism by which a prohibited act occurred. Rather, the defence of due diligence is available if the accused can demonstrate that it has exercised due diligence to avoid the specific type of occurrence giving rise to the charges against it: *R. v. Kukuljan*, 2008 CarswellBC 2559, (*sub nom. R. v. Emil K. Fishing Corp.*) 441 W.A.C. 275, (*sub nom. R. v. Emil K. Fishing Corp.*) 262 B.C.A.C. 275, 2008 BCCA 490, [2008] B.C.J. No. 2326 (*sub nom. R. v. Emil K. Fishing Corp.*) 304 D.L.R. (4th) 725 (B.C. C.A.), leave to appeal refused, 2009 CarswellBC 1160, 2009 CarswellBC 1161, (*sub nom. R. v. Emil K. Fishing Corp.*) 396 N.R. 395 (note), (*sub nom. R. v. Emil K. Fishing Corp.*) 283 B.C.A.C. 320 (note), (*sub nom. R. v. Emil K. Fishing Corp.*) 480 W.A.C. 320 (note) (S.C.C.).

In *R. v. Syncrude Canada Ltd.*, 2010 ABPC 229, 2010 CarswellAlta 1157, 489 A.R. 117, [2010] A.J. No. 730, 53 C.E.L.R. (3d) 194, 30 Alta. L.R. (5th) 97, [2010] 12 W.W.R. 524 (Alta. Prov. Ct.), the defendant's due diligence defence was rejected in a case where migratory birds landed in its tailings pond and became heavily oiled.

The court found that management of the company should have been aware of the circumstances that would make it more likely for migratory birds to land on the tailings pond in the spring, including the fact that adverse weather, which was not uncommon during the time in question, would also make it more likely for the birds to land.

In *Ontario (Ministry of Labour) v. 679052 Ontario Ltd.*, 2012 ONCJ 747, 2012 CarswellOnt 15667, [2012] O.J. No. 5849 (Ont. C.J.), it was held that the trial judge had failed to explain how it was foreseeable that an employee would drive a vehicle he was hired to clean only, when his evidence was unequivocal that he was aware that he was not supposed to drive, and that his supervisors would have no reason to believe that he would do so. Due diligence does not require that a supervisor be present for the entire period of time that the employee worked.

In *Ontario (Ministry of Labour) v. Sunrise Propane Energy Group Inc.*, 2013 ONCJ 358, 2013 CarswellOnt 9062, 77 C.E.L.R. (3d) 1, [2013] O.J. No. 3086 (Ont. C.J.), the defendant's due diligence defence was rejected where there was no evidence that it had proper training and supervision procedures in place. It failed to ensure the movement of storage tanks at its facility was carried out in a safe manner. It also failed to prevent the discharge of contaminants from its site.

7.2.3 DEGREE OF SKILL EXPECTED

As stated in *R. v. Placer Developments Ltd.* (1983), 13 C.E.L.R. 42 (Y.T. Terr. Ct.) at 52:

> Anyone choosing to become involved in activities posing a danger to the public, or to the environment, assumes an obligation to take whatever measures may be necessary to prevent harm. . . Unless equipped with the appropriate professional [trade or technical] skills, no one ought to undertake any activity involving a danger to the public. The degree of professional diligence required depends on commonly accepted practices of that specific activity and upon the specific circumstances.

- Staff must be professionally trained, and in some cases, supervised.

7.2.4 INSPECTIONS AND COMPLIANCE PROGRAMS

- Random inspections and testings are the best means to ensure compliance with regulations and policies.

7.2.5 EQUIPMENT AND TECHNOLOGY

- Reasonable care requires adequate technology and regular maintenance. *For example, an operator of a truck, who tries with all possible effort to slam on the brakes for a red light, may still be liable for failing to stop if his brakes were not properly maintained.*

7.2.6 COSTS OF PREVENTION

- If an activity cannot be carried on legally, then it should not be carried on at all. It is the elected legislature which determines the costs and benefits to society of certain activities.

- However, if the defendant reasonably assesses the possibility of mistake as very unlikely, and reasonably assesses the cost of prevention extremely high, then the standard of care set out in the legislation may have been met: see *R. v. Commander Business Furniture Inc.* (1992), 9 C.E.L.R. (N.S.) 185 at 213-217 (Ont. Prov. Ct.), affirmed (February 18, 1994), Doc. 179/93 (Ont. Gen. Div.).

For example, operating a vehicle with excess weight is a strict liability offence. A trucking company may take all reasonable precautions to ensure that its vehicles comply with the weight requirements. However, in very unusual circumstances, its vehicles exceed those requirements (perhaps a grain cargo gains weight in unusually moist environments). If the additional cost to detect for the unusual possibility is prohibitive, perhaps the standard of reasonable care has been met.

7.2.7 WARNINGS

- Once it is known that an existing system fails to prevent an offence, the reasonable person implements a new system.

As Swaigen writes in *Regulatory Offences in Canada* at 122-123:

> The extent to which such earlier incidents will preclude a defence of reasonable care will depend how similar they were to the events before the court, and the extent to which they caused harm on the previous occasion. The effectiveness of warnings to negate a defence of reasonable care will also depend on how clear they were, how forcefully they were communicated, to whom they were communicated, and whether they were directed at the factors that caused the incident before the court.

7.2.8 START-UP PROBLEMS

- Reasonable care requires investigation prior to starting up a business. *For example, before beginning an activity with environmental issues, an environmental audit should be done.*

7.2.9 EVIDENCE OF DUE DILIGENCE

The "accident as *prima facie* breach" theory of breach was adopted on appeal. As per Spence P.C.J. in *R. v. Lonkar Well Testing Ltd.*, 2008 CarswellAlta 521, 93 Alta. L.R. (4th) 181, [2008] A.J. No. 831 (Alta. Prov. Ct.), reversed 2009 CarswellAlta 823, [2009] A.J. No. 604, 473 A.R. 1, 6 Alta. L.R. (5th) 375, 2009 ABQB 345 (Alta. Q.B.), "once a breach has been established, *prima facie*, by virtue of an accident in the workplace despite a statutory regime designed to prevent such occurrences, then it is up to the employer to prove that it complied with the regulations and did all that it reasonably could to prevent the accident from happening": *R. v. Rose's Well Services Ltd.*, 2009 CarswellAlta 8, 2009 ABQB 1, [2009] A.J. No. 7, 467 A.R. 1, 4 Alta. L.R. (5th) 91 (Alta. Q.B).

In a strict liability offence, reasonableness should not be confused with the issue of recklessness or wilful blindness as it impacts upon a *mens rea* offence, which the Crown must disprove beyond a reasonable doubt. The issue of reasonableness and due diligence has to be proved by the defendant on a balance of probabilities: *R. v. Pham*, 2009 CarswellAlta 236, 2009 ABQB 113, [2009] A.J. No. 173, 468 A.R. 111, 56 M.P.L.R. (4th) 254 (Alta. Q.B.).

Documentary support for the accused's mistaken belief is not required to establish a reasonable excuse for failing to comply with an order to register under *Christopher's Law (Sex Offender Registry), 2000*, S.O. 2000, c. 1: *R. v. Sandejas*, 2009 CarswellOnt 1364, 2009 ONCJ 100 (Ont. C.J.), at para. 26 [ONCJ].

In a case where the defendant was charged with the strict liability offence of changing lane not in safety, the court found that she exercised reasonable care where there was evidence that she turned on her left hand turn indicator signal and checked her blind spot: *York (Regional Municipality) v. Clarke*, 2011 ONCJ 272, 2011 CarswellOnt 3636, [2011] O.J. No. 2336 (Ont. C.J.).

Where the defendant had received written notice that his licence had expired and he could be fined if he carried on business as a dealer without it, it would be palpable error to find that he could hold a reasonable belief that his grain dealer's licence was not required. See *R. v. Willows*, 2010 ONCJ 100, 2010 CarswellOnt 1714, [2010] O.J. No. 1183 (Ont. C.J.).

The due diligence claimed by the defendant must be specific to the hazard in issue, that is, the due diligence defence must relate to the commission of the prohibited act, not some broader notion of acting reasonably: *R. v. Prince Metal Products Ltd.* (June 28, 2011), Hoffman J., [2011] O.J. No. 6450 (Ont. C.J.).

In *R. v. Lococo* (October 29, 2015), Doc. Niagara Falls 14-0739, [2015] O.J. No. 7186 (Ont. C.J.), affirmed (April 18, 2016), Doc. St. Catharines 2111-999-14-0739, [2016] O.J. No. 2391 (Ont. C.J.), it was held that the defendant cannot be said to be duly diligent by doing nothing. A suspension of a driving licence becomes mandatory once a fine is unpaid under s. 46(3) of the *Highway Traffic Act*, and one is presumed to know the law under s. 81 of the *Provincial Offences Act*. The defendant has to make a positive demonstration of her efforts in order to be in compliance with the law, and that she did not do.

7.2.10 AFTER-THE-FACT COMPLIANCE

The acts of the defendant beyond the date of the incident are not to be considered by the court in assessing the due diligence defence, otherwise the broader notion of acting reasonably will be taken into account: *R. v. Boyd*, 2010 NSSC 417, 2010 CarswellNS 725, 296 N.S.R. (2d) 164, 940 A.P.R. 164, [2010] N.S.J. No. 585 (N.S. S.C.).

It is incumbent on the defendant to do his homework before he carried out his activities, not after he was charged; due diligence relates to the prevention of the event, meaning precaution and prevention, not correction after the fact, to compensate for an action already taken: *R. v. Sutherland*, 2010 ONSC 2240, 2010 CarswellOnt 2858, 51 C.E.L.R. (3d) 163, [2010] O.J. No. 1797 (Ont. S.C.J.), leave to appeal refused 2011 ONCA 239, 2011 CarswellOnt 1917, [2011] O.J. No. 1295 (Ont. C.A.).

For some unexplained reason, the defendant chose to engage in a rather awkward and lengthy "trial and error" exercise in pursuit of the solution involving the inclusion of containment curtains in the Certificate of Approval, and only after being charged, instead of consulting with the very environmental engineer who had recommended the inclusion of the containment curtains in the first place. In so choosing, it could hardly be said that the defendant established, on a balance of probabilities, that it was acting with "due diligence," "reasonable care" or with "due care". As a result, the defence of due diligence was not available to the defendant in the circumstances of the case. See *R. v. Superior Custom Trailers Ltd.*, 2009 ONCJ 740, 2009 CarswellOnt 9144, [2009] O.J. No. 6104 (Ont. C.J.).

7.3 CORPORATE RESPONSIBILITY

The Supreme Court in *R. v. Sault Ste. Marie (City)*, [1978] 2 S.C.R. 1299, 7 C.E.L.R. 53, 3 C.R. (3d) 30, 40 C.C.C. (2d) 353, 1978 CarswellOnt 24, 1978 CarswellOnt 594, 85 D.L.R. (3d) 161, 21 N.R. 295 (S.C.C.), at C.C.C. 371 held:

> The element of control, particularly by those in charge of business activities which may endanger the public, is vital to promote the observance of regulations designed to avoid that danger. This control may be exercised by supervision or inspection, by improvement of . . . business methods or by exhorting those whom may be expected . . . to [be] influence[d] or control[led].

- The test for control is a factual one. It is based on an assessment of the defendant's position — if the defendant can control the activity, then it should take reasonable care.

- A lender, landlord, or business partner may also be in a position to control illegal activity — if he or she can, he or she should take reasonable care.

- Where a corporation purchased a security guard business, retaining the former general manager, and relied on that manager to employ licensed guards, the defence of due diligence was established in relying on experienced personnel to handle the licensing process. See *R. v. Hi-Tec Security & Investigations Ltd.* (2004), [2004] O.J. No. 779, 2004 CarswellOnt 6080 (Ont. C.J.).

- If a "directing mind" of a corporation commits an offence, then the offence is "identified" with the corporation.

- The "directing mind" was originally a civil law concept, and simply means those who govern or control the activities of the corporation. Who directs the corporation is a question of fact. It may be that different persons have different areas for which they direct the corporation. For example, a marketing manager may "direct" the marketing program, and an engineer on the board of directors may "direct" the design of equipment.

Industry standards are set out to regulate the car sales industry. Industry standards in advertising serve as a consumer protection measure and ensure all dealers act professionally and abide by the same set of rules. The defendant in not following those rules provided itself with an unfair advantage; its advertisement was out of step with the industry standard and the defendant should not be allowed to take advantage of the inequity the non-compliant advertisement created: *R. v. Almadi Enterprises Inc.*, 2011 ONCJ 332, 2011 CarswellOnt 5585, [2011] O.J. No. 2940, 16 M.V.R. (6th) 319 (Ont. C.J.).

The defendant company provided initial training and precautions to new employees that included instructions to stop work at any time if they felt unsafe and notify a supervisor, and not to put their hands in the hopper to clear jams. However, several workers used their hands to clear jams despite these warnings, so as not to impede production. The company was found to lack a safety policy that was sufficient to mitigate against such accidents and therefore lacked due diligence. There was no evidence that the directors of the company fulfilled the requirement to ensure the safety of the employees with respect to the guarding of the hopper. See *Ontario (Ministry of Labour) v. Pack All Manufacturing Ltd.* (November 6, 2012), Kehoe J., [2012] O.J. No. 5311 (Ont. C.J.).

In *R. v. Stratford Chick Hatchery Ltd.*, 2013 ONCJ 47, 2013 CarswellOnt 1254, [2013] O.J. No. 562 (Ont. C.J.), it was held that the due diligence defence failed where the employer had not taken every precaution reasonable in the circumstances for the protection of a worker. Every precaution reasonable in the circumstances includes providing equipment that is adequate to the task for which that equipment is required.

Likewise, the due diligence defence failed in *R. v. 555034 Ontario Ltd.*, 2013 ONCJ 20, 2013 CarswellOnt 473, [2013] O.J. No. 279 (Ont. C.J.), a case where the defendant was charged with offences under the *Fire Protection and Prevention Act*. The overall plan of fire prevention and the supervision of control of the fire prevention and protection equipment were inadequate for the protection of the tenants, and amounted to "a loose, disjointed and haphazard plan without any reasonable form of coordination." There was no proper coordination or arrangement for regular monitoring or maintenance.

In *Ontario (Ministry of Labour) v. Sunrise Propane Energy Group Inc.*, 2013 ONCJ 358, 2013 CarswellOnt 9062, 77 C.E.L.R. (3d) 1, [2013] O.J. No. 3086 (Ont. C.J.), the defendant's due diligence defence was rejected where there was no evidence that it had proper training and supervision procedures in place. It failed to ensure the movement of storage tanks at its facility was carried out in a safe manner. It also failed to prevent the discharge of contaminants from its site.

The due diligence defence also failed in *R. v. Maple Lodge Farms*, 2013 ONCJ 535, 2013 CarswellOnt 13887, [2013] O.J. No. 4582 (Ont. C.J.), a case where the defendant was found not to have put in place sufficient conditions for the humane transportation of chickens to a slaughter facility on two dates in the winter. In coming to this conclusion, the court noted that the defendant had a duty of care to ensure their vehicles and methods met the industry standard, however it did not have a method to accurately measure load temperatures on their trailers.

In *R. v. Strabag Ltd.*, 2013 ONCJ 620, 2013 CarswellOnt 17061, [2013] O.J. No. 6032 (Ont. C.J.), it was held that the fact that the company assessed the *Occupational Health and Safety Act* (Ont.) regulations and interpreted the legislation in such a manner to conclude that a solid lock-down procedure would substitute for a guardrail is not a mistake of fact, but a mistaken interpretation of the law. Exercising due diligence by shutting down the machinery does not provide a defence to failing to install a guardrail.

In *R. v. Pisces Fishery Inc.*, 2016 ONSC 618, 2016 CarswellOnt 959, [2016] O.J. No. 398 (Ont. S.C.J.), it was held that the trial judge erred in failing to consider what a proper system of supervision would consist of, in addition to setting the standard of care in relation to the corporate defendant too low. There was virtually no evidence that the accused's conduct was consistent with what other licensees did; neither was there evidence of a "system" in place so as to address compliance with the requirement for accuracy and completeness of records. The evidence of the defendant did not reveal any system, formal or informal, to address the issue of compliance. In order to demonstrate due diligence, there must be a system of oversight by which the owner of the vessel could reasonably ascertain that the commitments made by it to the Ministry as a term of its licence were being met.

7.4 PARTIES TO AN OFFENCE

- There are a number of ways a defendant can be liable for illegal acts.
  - Where the defendant actually commits the offence: section 77(1)(a).
  - Where the defendant formed a common intention with another person to carry out an unlawful purpose, and where the defendant knew (or ought to have known) that a probable consequence of the unlawful purpose was the commission of the offence: section 77(2).
  - Where the defendant aids or abets another to commit the offence. To "aid" means to do or omit to do anything to facilitate or assist an offence. To "abet" means to instigate or encourage an offence: section 77(1)(b, c). Specific intent is required to find an accused liable as an aider or abettor to an offence of breaching a publication

ban. (*R. v. Helsdon*, [2007] O.J. No. 243, 275 D.L.R. (4th) 209, 2007 CarswellOnt 336, 216 C.C.C. (3d) 1, 2007 ONCA 54, 45 C.R. (6th) 37, 84 O.R. (3d) 544, 220 O.A.C. 302 (Ont. C.A.)).

- Where the defendant counsels or procures another to be a party to an offence, even if the offence was committed in a way different from that which was counselled or procured: section 78(1). Also, the defendant is a party to every offence where he or she knew or ought to have known the offence was likely to be committed as a result of his or her counselling or procuring: section 78(2).

- In addition, some provincial Acts have special provisions making a director or officer liable. See, for example, section 116 of the *Ontario Water Resources Act*, R.S.O. 1990, c. O.40:

   116. (1) Every director or officer of a corporation that engages in an activity that may result in the discharge of any material into or in any waters or any shore or bank thereof or into or in any place that may impair the quality of the water of any waters contrary to this Act or the regulations has a duty to take all reasonable care to prevent the corporation from causing or permitting such unlawful discharge.

   (2) Every person who has a duty under subsection (1) and who fails to carry out that duty is guilty of an offence.

   (3) A director or officer of a corporation is liable to conviction under this section whether or not the corporation has been prosecuted or convicted.

- Where the defendant is an employee, who worked in a manner that endangered others, he may be culpable under the *Occupational Health and Safety Act* for failure to take reasonable care, although he lacked control of the workplace. See *R. v. Campbell* (2004), [2004] O.J. No. 129, 2004 CarswellOnt 116 (Ont. C.J.).

The defence of self-induced intoxication is available to an accused who is charged with aiding and abetting an offence: *R. v. Wobbes*, 2008 CarswellOnt 4528, 235 C.C.C. (3d) 561, 60 C.R. (6th) 31, 2008 ONCA 567, 242 O.A.C. 7, [2008] O.J. No. 2999 (Ont. C.A.), at para. 30 [ONCA].

Where one defendant was driving a pick-up truck in which the other was a passenger, and the vehicle stopped to fire shots at a deer decoy, the actions of the driver enabled the illegal shots to be fired by having the driver's side window of the truck completely down and by stopping the vehicle so the initial shots could be fired, and then re-positioning it and stopping again on the road to allow further shots to be fired. In the circumstances, the driver was as guilty of the offence of illegally discharging a firearm from the vehicle as was the passenger who was the shooter. Both men were parties to the offences: *R. v. Buckton*, [2009] O.J. No. 1338, 2009 ONCJ 130, 2009 CarswellOnt 1759 (Ont. C.J.).

The defendant was charged as the owner with operating a motor vehicle without insurance. A one-person corporation owned by the defendant was the registered owner of the vehicle. However, the evidence did not establish that the defendant had exclusive possession of the vehicle or that it was his exclusive domain and control. The Crown adduced no evidence that the defendant was a director, officer or controlling mind of the corporation; there was no reason to pierce the corporate veil as there was no evidence that the defendant used the corporation to avoid compliance with the *Compulsory Automobile Insurance Act*. The defendant was not the owner of the vehicle and thus not guilty of the offence. Neither was the defendant a party to the offence committed by the corporation as it had not been established that he did anything or omitted to do anything to aid or abet the corporation in not having the vehicle properly insured before it was operated or permitted to be driven. See *Ontario v. Cordoba*, 2016 ONCJ 13, 2016 CarswellOnt 97, 128 O.R. (3d) 594, [2016] O.J. No. 75 (Ont. C.J.).

7.5 EVIDENTIARY ISSUES

7.5.1 TIMING OF EVIDENCE

- The prosecution cannot "split" its case. In its case-in-chief, the prosecutor must adduce all evidence rebutting any defence reasonably anticipated — including the defence of reasonable care.

- The defence's cross-examination of the prosecution witnesses will usually indicate whether reasonable care is in issue.

- Only where new and significantly important issues are raised for the first time in the case for the defence, will the prosecutor be permitted to call rebuttal evidence: see *R. v. Montefort* (1987), 79 N.S.R. (2d) 91, 196 A.P.R. 91 (N.S. C.A.); and *R. v. Lefevre* (1987), 77 N.S.R. (2d) 85, 191 A.P.R. 85 (N.S. C.A.).

7.5.2 SIMILAR ACTS *BEFORE* THE INCIDENT

- Generally, bad character or similar fact evidence is inadmissible in criminal and regulatory proceedings to show a disposition to commit the offence.

- However, where the defence is reasonable care, similar facts may be admitted to show that the defendant was warned in the past and failed to exercise reasonable care. The purpose of the evidence is not to show a disposition to commit the offence, but to rebut the suggestion of reasonable care, and so the evidence is admissible.

7.5.3 ACTS *AFTER* BEING CHARGED

- There are two policy reasons not to admit the evidence, as explained in Swaigen in *Regulatory Offences in Canada* at 191-192:

  - Extra care taken after being charged may imply that the defendant should have taken the same care before the incident. Arguably, the prosecutor should be able prove its case *before* charging the defendant.

  - If extra care after being charged is used against defendants, then there is a disincentive to taking extra care — which is contrary to public policy.

7.6 OTHER DEFENCES

- In addition to the procedural defences in Chapter 5, some of the defences detailed under Chapter 8 for absolute liability offences may apply — especially "causation".

As in the case of all regulatory offences, the prosecution must prove the *actus reus* of a strict liability offence beyond a reasonable doubt. Where it is unable to do so, there is no need for the court to go on and consider the due diligence defence. Hence, in *R. v. Mouland*, 2011 ONCJ 390, 2011 CarswellOnt 8036, [2011] O.J. No. 3491 (Ont. C.J.), the court dismissed a charge of changing lane not in safety where it held that the prosecution failed to prove the element of the *actus reus*, namely, that the defendant failed to execute the subject left-turn, lane change manoeuvre, in a safe manner, beyond a reasonable doubt.

In *R. v. Alfano*, 2014 ONCJ 99, 2014 CarswellOnt 2551, [2014] O.J. No. 1007 (Ont. C.J.), the defence of mistake of fact to the strict liability offence of driving while suspended was rejected as the court held that the defendant did not take reasonable steps to avoid the suspension. If he reasonably believed in a mistaken set of facts, his lack of evidence beyond his own assertion was not enough to convince the court that the mistake of fact was the result of being misled by the clerical staff of the courts on a balance of probabilities standard.

Given the constellation of facts and findings and given the presumption of innocence, the burden of proof and the doctrine of reasonable doubt, it could not be said that the decisions reached by the trial Justice demonstrated palpable and overriding error. In short, she was not convinced to the exclusion of any reasonable doubt that the particulars of the counts were proved. In a strict liability prosecution, a defendant is called upon to demonstrate due diligence only if the Crown has proved the *actus reus* beyond a reasonable doubt. The Crown failed to do so here. While the Justice wrote several pages of reasons explaining why she felt the defendants had been duly diligent, all of this was *obiter dicta* and that portion of her reasons was unnecessary. See *Ontario (Ministry of Labour) v. Dufferin Construction Co.*, 2014 ONCJ 652, 2014 CarswellOnt 17197, [2014] O.J. No. 5866 (Ont. C.J.).

8

ABSOLUTE LIABILITY OFFENCES

8.1 BURDEN OF PROOF

- The prosecution must prove beyond a reasonable doubt that the defendant committed the illegal act(s).
- The defendant is liable whether or not he or she was at fault.

8.2 *CHARTER* ISSUES

- As explained in Chapter 4, any absolute liability with the possibility of imprisonment is contrary to section 7 of the *Charter*, and unless saved as a reasonable limit under section 1, is of no force or effect by section 52(1) of the *Charter*.

8.3 PARTIES TO THE OFFENCE

- See heading 7.4 in Chapter 7.

8.4 PROCEDURAL DEFENCES

- For available defences, see Chapter 5.

8.5 COMMON LAW DEFENCES — GENERALLY

- Section 80 of the POA ensures that every rule and principle of common law continues to be in force as they apply to any justification, excuse or defence to a charge: see *Appendix A*.

There is authority holding that only superior court judges have power to stay proceedings for abuse of process. Even if justices of the peace under the *Provincial Offences Act* have such authority, a stay on the basis of abuse of process should be granted only in the clearest and most exceptional circumstances where to allow the proceeding to continue would tarnish the integrity of the court or prevent trial fairness. That was not the case where before the defendant appeared, he asked for a trial, notwithstanding his complaint about personal service of the offence notice: *London (City) v. Erdesz*, [2009] O.J. No. 1008, 2009 CarswellOnt 1314 (Ont. S.C.J.).

In *R. v. L. (P.R.)*, 2013 ONCJ 322, 2013 CarswellOnt 8107, [2013] O.J. No. 2776 (Ont. C.J.), the defendant was charged with a number of charges under the *Highway Traffic Act*, including speeding, failing to stop for a police officer, failing to signal a lane change and failing to surrender her vehicle permit. She had been diagnosed with a bipolar mood disorder at the time, according to a letter from a psychiatrist. Since the *Provincial Offences Act* does not define what a mental disorder is, it would helpful to consider the mental disorder definition in s. 2 of the *Criminal Code*, which defines a mental disorder as a "disease of the mind". This has been interpreted to be any illness, disorder or abnormal condition that impairs the human mind and its functioning, but does not include normally a self-induced condition caused by alcohol or drugs or transitory mental states such as hysteria or concussion. Before considering the mental disorder defence, the defendant is required to establish an evidentiary basis for the defence so that a properly instructed trier of fact could find that the defendant had acted involuntarily on a balance of probabilities. In the instant case, there was evidence adduced at trial that satisfied the air of reality test. The defendant had been diagnosed with a bipolar mood disorder the year before the offences, and was currently under a Community Treatment Order; she had been recently hospitalized for treatment for her mental disorder. However, there had been no expert evidence provided to the court about the nature and severity of the defendant's bipolar mood disorder, and whether she had been actually suffering from the disorder on the date for which the charges arose or whether she had been in remission. Consequently, the defendant had not met the burden on her to prove the mental disorder defence on a balance of probabilities, or that her actions in operating a motor vehicle were the result of involuntary actions.

8.6 INVOLUNTARINESS DEFENCE

- To some extent, the illegal act(s) must be voluntary and within the control of the defendant.

For example, a driver and passenger are on the highway and, against the driver's will, the passenger slams on the driver's foot, forcing it down on the gas peddle and causing the car to speed. The driver did not commit the act of speeding because he or she did not voluntarily control his or her foot.

In another example, the defendant is drugged by someone, through no fault of the defendant and without his or her knowledge. If he or she becomes incapable of controlling what he or she does, whatever illegal acts occur are not *his or her* acts — they are the involuntary movements of a body beyond his or her control.

See: I. Patient, "Some Remarks about the Element of Voluntariness in Offences of Absolute Liability", [1968] Crim. L.R. 23; see also "The Voluntariness Requirement and the The Doctine of Automatism" Watt J., National Criminal Law Program, Montreal, 1993; see also *R. v. Rabey*, 54 C.C.C. (2d) 1, [1980] 2 S.C.R. 513, 15 C.R. (3d) 225 (Eng.), 20 C.R. (3d) 1 (Fr.) (S.C.C.) per Dickson J. dissenting, cited in *R. v. Parks*, 75 C.C.C. (3d) 287, 303, [1992] 2 S.C.R. 871, 15 C.R. (4th) 289 (S.C.C.) per LaForest J. and voluntariness as it relates to intoxication in *R. v. Daviault*, 33 C.R. (4th) 165, 93 C.C.C. (3d) 21, [1994] 3 S.C.R. 63 (S.C.C.).

In *North Bay (City) v. Viens*, 2018 ONCJ 564, 2018 CarswellOnt 13852, [2018] O.J. No. 4309 (Ont. C.J.), it was held that the offence of driving a motor vehicle left of centre while upon a curve in the roadway is a strict liability offence. While a sudden and intense episode of repeated sneezing and watery eyes can rise to the level to provoke temporary involuntary physical reactions whether caused by an allergy or otherwise, the issue in the instant case was whether there was sufficient evidence that sneezing and watery eyes were of a degree to make the defendant's act of driving into the opposing lane of traffic involuntary. The trial evidence, including the defendant's testimony, did not leave the court with a reasonable doubt on the voluntariness of his conduct.

8.7 CAUSATION DEFENCE

- The Crown must prove beyond a reasonable doubt that the defendant caused the illegal act(s).

- Where the Crown fails to prove the *actus reus* or the "physical action" element of the offence, the defendant is entitled to be found not guilty.

- Causation is the relationship between the defendant and the illegal act(s) which resulted.

- It is not necessary to prove that the defendant was the sole cause of the illegal act(s).

- It is sufficient that the defendant contributed to the illegal act(s), and that the defendant's contribution was outside the "de minimis" range: see *R. v. Smithers* (1977), 34 C.C.C. (2d) 427, [1978] 1 S.C.R. 506, 40 C.R.N.S. 79 (S.C.C.); *R. v. Cribbin* (1994), 89 C.C.C. (3d) 67, 17 O.R. (3d) 548, 28 C.R. (4th) 137 (Ont. C.A.).

A legally blameworthy cause must be "at least a significant" cause and "more than one that is trifling or minor": *R. v. Trakas*, 2008 CarswellOnt 2889, 241 O.A.C. 52, 233 C.C.C. (3d) 172, 2008 ONCA 410, 61 M.V.R. (5th) 159 (Ont. C.A.), at paras. 42-54 [ONCA].

8.8 NECESSITY DEFENCE

"In urgent situations of clear and imminent peril, when compliance with the law is demonstrably impossible" the defendant has the legal excuse of necessity: *Perka v. R.*, 14 C.C.C. (3d) 385, [1984] 2 S.C.R. 232, [1984] 6 W.W.R. 289, 42 C.R. (3d) 113 (S.C.C.) at 400 citing *R. v. Morgentaler (No. 5)* (1975), 20 C.C.C. (2d) 449, [1976] 1 S.C.R. 616, 30 C.R.N.S. 209 (S.C.C.) at 497.

- To use the defence of necessity, the elements listed below must be present.

  - There must be an imminent risk such that the defendant must act to avoid an immediate peril.

  - There must be no reasonable legal alternative to the course of action taken by the defendant.

  - The harm inflicted by the defendant must be less than the harm avoided.

  - The emergency must not be reasonably foreseeable.

- Once the defence provides some evidence of an emergency, then the Crown must prove beyond a reasonable doubt that the necessity excuse does not apply: see *Perka*, *supra*, at 404-405.

- The first and second requirements — imminent peril and no reasonable legal alternative — are evaluated on the "modified objective standard" — an objective standard that takes into account the situation and characteristics of the particular defendant. The third requirement, proportionality, must be measured on an objective standard — i.e. community standards. See: *R. v. Latimer*, 2001 CarswellSask 4, 2001 CarswellSask 5, REJB 2001-21909, [2001] S.C.J. No. 1, [2001] 1 S.C.R. 3, [2001] 6 W.W.R. 409, 2001 SCC 1, 80 C.R.R. (2d) 189, 264 N.R. 99, 39 C.R. (5th) 1, 193 D.L.R. (4th) 577, 150 C.C.C. (3d) 129, 203 Sask. R. 1, 240 W.A.C. 1 (S.C.C.).

- Examples of necessity might include:

- A motorist who exceeds the speed limit, or who drives with a suspended license, or who drives while impaired in order to take an injured person to the hospital: *Perka, supra*, at 393.

- The accused was driving dangerously (a criminal offence) by speeding at 73 miles per hour, but had to in order to avoid being hit by a tail-gating car: see *R. v. Fry* (1977), 36 C.C.C. (2d) 396 (Sask. Prov. Ct.).

- In the case of a police officer who failed to stop at a stop sign, while the defence of necessity was not available on the facts of the case, the court observed that the defence would be available in an appropriate fact situation: *R. v. Walker* (1979), 48 C.C.C. (2d) 126, 5 M.V.R. 114 (Ont. Co. Ct.).

- Shooting a bear contrary to the National Parks Game regulations (a strict liability offence), in order to save a child: see *R. v. Slovack* (1979), [1980] 1 W.W.R. 368 (Alta. Prov. Ct.).

For a recent example of where the defence of duress succeeded, see *R. v. Chu*, 2008 CarswellOnt 3557, 2008 ONCJ 312, [2008] O.J. No. 2733 (Ont. C.J.), a case involving the strict liability offence of selling tobacco to a minor, contrary to the *Smoke Free Ontario Act*, where the court found that the defendant sold the cigarettes to the purchaser and feared for his personal safety.

The necessity defence also succeeded in a case where the defendant was charged with the *Highway Traffic Act* offence of failing to report an accident forthwith, in circumstances where he had been walking in sub-zero weather for several hours in inadequate footwear, and was in the process of warming himself to avoid frost bite prior to reporting the accident to the police: *R. v. Kruchkowsky*, 2008 ONCJ 704, 2008 CarswellOnt 8406, [2008] O.J. No. 5460 (Ont. C.J.).

In another recent case, the court observed that the necessity defence was not formally advanced, although the defence of necessity was suggested by portions of the defendant's testimony. The evidentiary foundation for the defence was insufficient to enable the court to properly determine whether the requirements of the necessity defence had been satisfied: *R. v. Kelleher* (2008), 2008 CarswellOnt 8609, 2009 ONCJ 54, [2009] O.J. No. 670 (Ont. C.J.).

The defence of necessity was not made out in a driving without insurance case where the defendant went to the mechanic's location to resolve the issue regarding his car, and upon being unable to do so, decided to leave with the car rather than having it towed at his expense, which he acknowledged he was unable to afford. It strained credibility to find that he could believe he was in imminent danger of sudden, uncontrolled blood gushing, and that the best alternative presenting least danger to himself and other users of the road would be to get into a car and drive away. See *Ontario v. Kogan*, 2011 ONCJ 58, 2011 CarswellOnt 953, [2011] O.J. No. 693 (Ont. C.J.).

Similarly, in *R. v. Armstrong*, 2011 ONCJ 325, 2011 CarswellOnt 5695, [2011] O.J. No. 2933 (Ont. C.J.), it was held that the defence of necessity did not apply where the defendant suffered a hypoglycaemic episode while driving but the symptoms began before he drove. There were alternatives to ease the symptoms.

The defence of necessity was not made out where the defendant was charged with driving more than 50 kilometres per hour over the speed limit while taking his wife to the hospital to give birth. While the defendant testified that calling an ambulance was not a reasonable alternative because the ambulance would take them to the nearest hospital rather than the hospital where his wife's medical history was known, he could have called 911 and asked the police to escort them to the hospital. This constituted a reasonable alternative available to the defendant which would not have put the defendant, his wife and other members of the public at risk. See *R. v. Paraschiew*, 2012 ONCJ 499, 2012 CarswellOnt 10355 (Ont. C.J.).

In *R. v. Christianson*, 2011 SKQB 390, 2011 CarswellSask 687, 23 M.V.R. (6th) 53, 384 Sask. R. 211, [2011] S.J. No. 653 (Sask. Q.B.), it was held that the accused's decision not to wear a seatbelt while he was operating a city transit bus constituted a reasonable reaction due to the experiences of himself and of others. His experiences, and those of others that had come to his attention in the course of working in the transit industry, provided the accused with reason to believe that his safety might be compromised by wearing his seat belt as he would be unable to defend himself if attacked.

Similarly, in *R. v. Jaspar*, 2012 SKQB 327, 2012 CarswellSask 554, 403 Sask. R. 94, [2012] S.J. No. 518 (Sask. Q.B.), another case involving a bus driver who was found not guilty of failing to wear a seatbelt, it was held that the defendant had a reasonable belief that his safety might be comprised by wearing a seatbelt. There was evidence as to a reported increase in assaults on transit operators who, like the defendant, were obliged to transport people with mental health issues and disabilities. It was noted that compromise of safety encompassed more than mere threats of violence. Accidental injury during the course of operating the bus involved physically disabled persons and their aids which were unwieldy such as crutches, walkers and wheelchairs, and thus also gave rise to safety concerns for persons in the vicinity.

The necessity defence succeeded in *R. v. Anderson*, 2012 BCPC 429, 2012 CarswellBC 3774, [2012] B.C.J. No. 2555 (B.C. Prov. Ct.), a case where the vehicle in which the defendant was a passenger stalled in a dangerous place, and the driver left to go for help. As a result, the defendant decided to coast the vehicle downhill and was able to get it running when he was spotted by the police, but before he could park it in a safe driveway. Although the defendant was prohibited from driving a motor vehicle at the time, the defence of necessity was made out in these circumstances. In considering the alternatives facing the defendant, he could sit and do nothing, hoping that the driver returned soon, or move the vehicle to a safe location. Doing nothing was not necessarily a reasonable alternative because it put other users of the road at risk for personal injury. The harm resulting from a prohibited driver operating a vehicle a short distance to move it to a safer location was not disproportionate to the harm which may have resulted if the vehicle was left in an unsafe location where it might have been struck, causing injury or damage.

Duress is a particular application of the doctrine of necessity, where the circumstance is caused by wrongful threats. The immediacy component of the defence requires a close connection in time between the threat and its execution in such a manner that the accused loses the ability to act freely. In the case at bar, the immediacy requirement of the threat was not present given that the alleged threat of harm to the defendant's parents made by the party he was caught smuggling across the border did not amount to a threat of immediate harm. See *R. v. Mejia*, 2012 ONCJ 571, 2012 CarswellOnt 11159, 12 Imm. L.R. (4th) 103, [2012] O.J. No. 4234 (Ont. C.J.).

In *R. v. Kovnats*, 2013 MBCA 26, 2013 CarswellMan 125, [2013] M.J. No. 101 (Man. C.A.), the defendant was travelling in a lane which required him to turn right at the intersection, but when he came upon the intersection, he thought he saw something in or near it. To avoid a collision, he decided to proceed straight through the intersection. He admitted during his testimony that he was driving too quickly to stop. The defence of necessity was raised at trial on the basis that the reason he disobeyed the traffic control device was to avoid a collision with a cyclist or a pedestrian. However, there was no actual peril or danger. Even if there was, the defendant had a reasonable alternative to committing the offence, namely, applying the brakes and stopping the vehicle before any possible collision.

The defendant's assertion of the defence of necessity was ludicrous in a case where he claimed that he parked his courier vehicle in a disable parking spot due to his having no choice but to leave his vehicle in the accessible spot because the other spots were taken. The defendant was delivering an envelope to city hall; there was underground parking at city hall and under the library next door, and a shopping centre with hundreds if not thousands of parking spaces was across the street. It was an irresistible inference that the defendant left his vehicle in a prohibited place for reasons of expediency. See *1747114 Ontario Inc. v. Mississauga (City)*, 2013 ONCJ 623, 2013 CarswellOnt 15942, 58 M.V.R. (6th) 281, 17 M.P.L.R. (5th) 296, [2013] O.J. No. 5344 (Ont. C.J.).

In *R. v. Khalid*, 2014 ONCJ 125, 2014 CarswellOnt 3296, 20 M.P.L.R. (5th) 171, [2014] O.J. No. 1257 (Ont. C.J.), the defendant was charged with failing to obtain a building permit and failing to comply with an order of a building inspector, contrary to the *Building Code Act*. He argued the defence of necessity on the basis that his basement foundation wall was cracked and there was a serious problem with water leakage that had to be remedied. However, even if the situation required immediate attention and repair, there was no reason why the crack repair had to include creation of a basement entrance or, even if it did, why a permit could not have been obtained for the work. The necessity argument had no merit and was rightly rejected by the trial Justice of the Peace.

In *R. v. Bou-Saleh*, 2014 BCSC 1099, 2014 CarswellBC 1745, [2014] B.C.J. No. 1251 (B.C. S.C.), it was held that the trial judge conflated determining whether the defence of necessity should be considered with determining whether the Crown had proved its case. The trial judge should have considered whether the defence of necessity had an air of reality without extensively reviewing the defendant's credibility. The trial judge's gatekeeping function at this stage is limited to determining only if the defence can be considered. Once it is determined that the defence has an air of reality, then his credibility should be extensively analysed. The trial judge further erred by expecting the defendant to provide evidence corroborating his own testimony. The trial judge's comment that the defendant failed to call corroborative evidence was tantamount to suggesting there was an onus on him to produce such evidence. An instruction that indicates there is an onus on an accused to provide corroborative evidence of his testimony is an error.

The immediate pick-up/drop off zone in front of an airport terminal would require that someone be in attendance at the vehicle at all times in the event of an emergency situation, such as the airport bursts into flames and somebody has to be at those vehicles to move them immediately for the immediate passage of emergency vehicles. That is the intent of the signage. There is no signage that indicates a time limit that two minutes is acceptable or five minutes acceptable, and there is no immediate parking for people who need assistance. The only defence available to the charge would be that of immediate necessity, a life-threatening defence that one had to park there and leave the vehicle because there was basically some life-threatening event that was going to take place if the person did not leave the vehicle there and attend to taking the person in. See *R. v. Luxemburger*, 2014 YKTC 44, 2014 CarswellYukon 86, [2014] Y.J. No. 71 (Y.T. Terr. Ct.).

As one of the main purposes of the *Motor Vehicle Act* is to promote safety on the roads, entry into an HOV lane may be necessary to make a right turn where it is established that entry into a designated right turn lane cannot be done safely because of traffic congestion or otherwise. For example, a driver may establish that he safely entered an HOV lane to make a right turn to avoid having to attempt to enter a highly congested designated right turn lane which could be unsafe. However, on the evidence before the judicial justice, he correctly concluded that where there is a designated exit lane it was not necessary for the defendant to use the HOV lane before entering the marked lane. The evidence was that the defendant had entered the HOV lane several hundred metres before the designated exit lane appeared. See *R. v. Tomkowicz*, 2018 BCSC 43, 2018 CarswellBC 55, 23 M.V.R. (7th) 79, [2018] B.C.J. No. 43 (B.C. S.C.).

9

SPECIAL PROCEEDINGS

9.1 YOUNG PERSONS

Under the POA:

- A "young person" is between 12 and 16: section 93.

- No person under 12 (at the time of the offence) shall be convicted: section 94.

- The young person must appear during the whole trial, with limited exceptions: sections 95, 98.

- Parents are to be notified as soon as practicable: section 96.

- Generally, the young person's identity is not to be published: section 99.

- An absolute discharge is available: section 101.

- The maximum fine is $1,000: section 101.

- Where proceedings are by a certificate under Part I, the maximum fine is $300: section 97.

- A young person shall not be imprisoned, except for a breach of probation (sections 101, 75) and shall not be imprisoned for non-payment of a fine (section 102).

9.2 BAIL HEARINGS

9.2.1 THE LAW

(a) The Officer at the Police Station

- Regarding adult defendants, the arresting police officer, and later the officer-in-charge at the police station, shall release the defendant as soon as practicable, unless there are reasonable and probable grounds to detain in order to:

  - Establish the identity of the defendant;

  - Secure or preserve evidence related to the offence;

- Prevent the continuation of the offence or another offence; or

- The defendant is ordinarily resident outside Ontario, and will not respond to a summons, or to a recognizance without sureties, and/or to a security deposit: sections 149 to 151.

- Regarding young persons, the police must have reasonable and probable grounds to detain in order to:
  - Establish the young person's identity; or
  - Prevent the continuation or repetition of an offence that constitutes a serious danger to the young person or the person or property of another: section 107(2, 3).

- There are rules for notifying the young person's parent(s): section 107(4).

- If an adult or young person is not released, the officer-in-charge shall, as soon as practicable and within 24 hours, bring him or her before a justice.

- With limited exceptions, young persons must be detained separately from adults: section 107(6).

(b) The Justice at the Bail Hearing

- For both young persons and adults, the justice shall release the defendant on an undertaking, unless the prosecutor "shows cause" why a more onerous release or detention is required.

- The justice shall only consider whether the defendant will appear in court. *There is no authority to consider the "public interest" or "the protection or safety of the public" (unlike the "secondary grounds" of a bail hearing under the Criminal Code). And, unlike the police, the justice cannot temporarily detain the defendant to secure or preserve evidence or to prevent the commission of an offence.*

- The justice may order any of the following releases, but the prosecutor must first "show cause" why a less restrictive release is not sufficient. In order of the degree of restriction on the defendant:
  - A recognizance, with appropriate conditions;

- Where the offence is punishable by imprisonment for 12 months or more, a recognizance with conditions and with sureties, or a cash deposit if consented to by the prosecutor;

- If the defendant does not ordinarily reside in Ontario, a recognizance with or without sureties and conditions, plus a cash deposit;

- Detention until trial. (If the defendant is detained, the trial shall be expedited by section 151.)

- The justice's decision and reasons shall be recorded (to allow for an appeal), and the justice may consider any credible or trustworthy information, including hearsay.

- The defendant shall not be examined or cross-examined about the offence charged. (*This may be subject to Charter challenge should the defendant wish to testify about the offence.*)

9.2.2 ACTING FOR THE DEFENDANT AT A BAIL HEARING

- Consider the excellent Practice Guide by D. Garth Burrows, Q.C., *Bail Hearings* (Carswell, 1993).

- All information should have been gathered as described in Chapter 3, including information from the officer-in-charge.

- Speak to the prosecutor before the hearing to get as much disclosure as possible.

  - Is the prosecutor aware of any outstanding charges or a prior record of offences?

- Why does the prosecutor want to detain your client?

  - Is there a record for failing to appear for court? Can that record be explained?

  - Does your client have an alcohol or drug problem? Is your client taking treatment? What evidence can you gather to show improvement?

- Obtain sureties.

  - You must convince the justice that your surety will guarantee the defendant's court appearance.

  - Obtain the following information from the surety:

1. Name? Relation to accused? Age? Phone number?
2. Address? Will the defendant live with the surety?
3. How long has the surety known the defendant?
4. How frequently has the surety seen the defendant?
5. Does the surety know the details of the present charges and prior record of the defendant? If not, you must advise the surety.
6. Ask about the character of the surety — criminal record? Is the surety a responsible person?
7. Does the surety understand his or her duties — a promise to the court to insure that the defendant will appear, and a promise to notify the authorities if the defendant will not appear? (sections 155, 156)
8. How will he or she insure the defendant's appearance?
9. Has he or she ever acted as a surety for the defendant before? If so, did the defendant comply?
10. Does the surety require conditions to the defendant's release?
11. How much money can the surety sign for? What proof can be provided to the justice that the surety can pay that amount if required? Ask about proof of income, property, etc.

9.3 *CHARTER* APPLICATIONS

- By section 109 of the *Courts of Justice Act*, notice of a constitutional question shall be served on the Attorney General of Canada and the Attorney General of Ontario in the following circumstances:

  - The constitutional validity or constitutional applicability of an Act of the Parliament of Canada or the Legislature, of a regulation or by-law made under such an Act or of a rule of common law is in question.

  - A remedy is claimed under subsection 24 (1) of the *Canadian Charter of Rights and Freedoms* in relation to an act or omission of the Government of Canada or the Government of Ontario.

- The notice shall be served as soon as the circumstances requiring it become known and, in any event, at least fifteen days before the day on which the question is to be argued, unless the court orders otherwise.

- If a party fails to give notice in accordance with this section, the Act, regulation, by-law or rule of common law shall not be adjudged to be invalid or inapplicable, or the remedy shall not be granted, as the case may be.

- A court does have some discretion to overlook deficiencies in process when it is in the interests of justice. The requirement of following these rules is an essential safe-guard for the protection of the rights of the public, particularly defendants so that matters may be heard in a fair and impartial manner. See *R. v. Elder-Nilson*, 2006 ONCJ 409, [2006] O.J. No. 4359, 2006 CarswellOnt 6721 (Ont. C.J.).

The parties must make sure all the relevant documents are properly before the court, including affidavits which are signed. In one recent case, the trial judge was found to have erred in dismissing the defendant's constitutional challenge on the basis that the defendant's affidavit was not properly executed and signed: *R. v. Bodik* (2008), 2008 CarswellOnt 1948 (Ont. C.J.).

Apart from the requirements of notice under s. 109 of the *Courts of Justice Act* and the rules of court, the defendant must do more than that to assert his rights before the trial judge. Stating that one wishes to bring at some point a. s. 11(b) application is not the same as actually bringing the application. While the defendant does not have to assert the right at every court appearance, at some appropriate stage in the proceedings, that is during the trial process, he must muster the evidence, transcripts of the attendance, evidence of prejudice if any, and present argument to the trier of fact: *R. v. Delvecchio*, 2008 ONCJ 511, 2008 CarswellOnt 6281, 78 M.V.R. (5th) 88, [2008] O.J. No. 4229 (Ont. C.J.).

In *R. v. Rau*, 2013 ONSC 5573, 2013 CarswellOnt 12550, [2013] O.J. No. 4067 (Ont. S.C.J.), an unsuccessful application was brought by the defendant for a stay of proceedings on his charge of failure to stop for police, contrary to the *Highway Traffic Act* (Ont.), pending the provision of funding for his defence so that he could have legal representation. This appeared to be the first time that such an application had been brought for such a funding order in respect of a *Highway Traffic Act* offence. Although there was a real prospect of imprisonment if the defendant was found guilty, the trial faced by him would be relatively brief, the issues discrete, and the minimum sentence of 14 days' imprisonment was far from the most serious range. The defendant had also demonstrated an understanding of the charges, was able to put forward the facts in an understandable and coherent manner, and had shown an ability to participate effectively in a court proceeding; the case was not of sufficient seriousness or complexity that representation by counsel was essential to a fair trial.

It was held in *R. v. Byrnes*, 2013 ONCJ 631, 2013 CarswellOnt 16205, 2013 CarswellOnt 16206, 296 C.R.R. (2d) 258, [2013] O.J. No. 5389 (Ont. C.J.), that the defendant did not enter a plea because the Justice of the Peace believed that the *Charter* application should be heard and decided before the plea was entered. This was incorrect, as the defendant should have been required to enter a plea before the *Charter* application commenced. If the defendant refused to do so, the court should have deemed his plea to be not guilty, and made this entry on the information. A "best practices" approach would entail having the defendant arraigned prior to hearing the *Charter* application because it is only after arraignment that the Justice of the Peace is formally seized with the matter. Arraignment includes having the charge read, asking the defendant how he pleads, guilty or not guilty, and noting the plea on the information. To do otherwise and commence a *Charter* application prior to arraignment or midway through arraignment and prior to plea being entered, would allow a party who received an unfavourable decision on the *Charter* to request that the trial commence before a different Justice of the Peace since the first one was not seized. If this were to happen, the parties would be able to re-argue the *Charter* application since the new Justice of the Peace would not be bound by the original *Charter* decision. This absurd legal outcome and case management headache would be properly prevented by having the plea entered and noted on the information prior to addressing the *Charter* application.

9.4 OTHER APPLICATIONS

- An application provided for by the POA or the rules under the POA shall be commenced by notice of application. R.R.O. 1990, Regulation 200, amended to O. Reg. 567/00.

- A motion provided for by the Act or these rules shall be commenced by notice of motion.

- There shall be at least three days between the giving of notice of application or notice of motion and the day for hearing the application or motion.

- An applicant or moving party shall file notice of application or notice of motion at least two days before the day for hearing the application or motion.

- Evidence on an application or motion may be given

  - by affidavit;

  - with the permission of the court, orally; or

- in the form of a transcript of the examination of a witness.

- Upon the hearing of an application or motion and whether or not other evidence is given on the application or motion, the justice may receive and base his or her decision upon information the justice considers credible or trustworthy in the circumstances.

- An application or motion may be heard without notice

  - on consent; or

  - where, having regard to the subject-matter or the circumstances of the application or motion, it would not be unjust to hear the application or motion without notice.

10

TRIALS

10.1 PROCEDURE

10.1.1 APPEARANCE FOR TRIAL

- The defendant's appearance for trial is dependent on the procedural "streams" for provincial offences: Part I (Minor Offences), Part II (Parking Infractions), Part III (Serious Offences).

- Where the defendant was served with a notice of trial, but the court house was closed on the trial date due to a power failure, the court retained jurisdiction to proceed with the offence by mailing out a fresh notice of trial. See *York (Regional Municipality) v. Scarcello*, 2004 CarswellOnt 6077, *(sub nom.* R. v. Scarcello) [2004] O.J. No. 1002 (Ont. S.C.J.).

- However, the clerk of the court does not have jurisdiction to adjourn proceedings on account of the absence of the justice of the peace. See *R. v. 1283499 Ontario Inc.* (2003), 65 O.R. (3d) 763, 173 O.A.C. 365, 176 C.C.C. (3d) 522, 2003 CarswellOnt 2497 (Ont. C.A.); *R. v. Colarossi* (2003), [2003] O.J. No. 2629, 2003 CarswellOnt 2496, 65 O.R. (3d) 767 (Ont. C.A.).

In *R. v. Watson* (2007), 2007 CarswellOnt 6283, [2007] O.J. No. 3858 (Ont. C.J.) it was held that the provincial offences court does not lose jurisdiction where a trial is adjourned by a court administrator who is not a judicial officer or a justice of the peace. The court may regain its jurisdiction over the person by mailing out a fresh Notice of Trial, which is certified in the required manner.

The defendant appeared for trial but sought an adjournment which was granted on a peremptory basis; however, no action took place on the adjournment date due to the certificate not being in court. This was the result of the matter being incorrectly recorded on the certificate for a different date, at which time no one appeared, and a default conviction was entered. The court did not lose jurisdiction to deal with the matter due to this administrative error: *R. v. Billingsley*, [2008] O.J. No. 5146, 2008 ONCJ 640, 2008 CarswellOnt 7695 (Ont. C.J.).

(a) Part I: Certificate of Offence

- If a summons is served, the defendant must appear for trial.
- If an offence notice is served, the defendant may plead:
  - Guilty in writing with full payment of the fine: section 8(1);
  - Guilty "with representations" as to penalty, to be made before a justice: section 7(1);
  - Not guilty and appear for trial: section 5(1); or
  - Dispute the charges in writing, if the defendant lives outside a designated jurisdiction where the charges were laid: section 6(1).
- If none of the above is plead within 15 days, or if the defendant fails to appear for trial, he or she is deemed not to dispute the charges and, provided the certificate of offence is complete and regular on its face, the defendant can be convicted in his or her absence: sections 9, 9.1.
- A young person must be summoned for trial: section 95.
  - A notice must be delivered to the parent(s): section 96.
  - The young person must be personally present throughout the trial: section 98.

(b) Part II: Certificate of Parking Infraction

- The defendant has two options:
  - Pay the fine out-of-court: section 16; or
  - Appear for trial by indicating so on the parking infraction notice: section 17.
- If the defendant fails to respond within 15 days, the court may send a notice of impending conviction. If he or she again fails to respond within 15 days, or fails to appear for trial, provided the certificate of parking infraction is complete and regular on its face, the defendant can be convicted in his or her absence: sections 18, 18.1, 18.2, 18.4.

(c) Part III: Information

- The defendant must appear for trial.

10.1.2 MANNER OF DEFENDANT APPEARING FOR TRIAL

- A young person must attend personally throughout the trial: section 98.
- An adult defendant may either attend personally or have a lawyer or agent attend: section 50(1).
- A corporation *must* have a lawyer or agent attend: section 50(2).
- Any defendant may *act* (i.e. be represented) by a lawyer or agent, whether or not the defendant attends: section 82.
- Any agent who is not a lawyer may be barred from representing a defendant if the court finds that the agent is not competent or does not understand and comply with the ethical duties to the court: section 50(3).

In *R. v. Morden* (2000), 2000 CarswellOnt 1037 (Ont. C.J.), it was determined that, although the defendant could choose to be represented by an agent who was not a lawyer, the appellate court has the jurisdiction to allow an appeal if a miscarriage of justice has occurred due to the agent's conduct. Where the agent failed to inquire of the defendant as to whether he wished to testify on his own behalf, the agent's conduct was improper, and a new trial was ordered.

10.1.3 FAILURE OF DEFENDANT TO APPEAR FOR TRIAL

- When the defendant fails to appear for trial and the prosecution proves that procedures for notification were followed (section 54(1)), the court may choose from three alternative procedures:
    - Proceed to hear and determine the case in the absence of the defendant;
    - Adjourn the hearing and issue a summons to appear or a warrant in the prescribed form for the arrest of the defendant; or
    - Choose again from the above if the defendant does not appear in response to the summons or warrant on the date to which the hearing is adjourned: section 54(2).

- Section 54 does not apply to young persons. By section 98(3), a young person must appear throughout the trial.

- Section 54 also does not apply to Part I and Part II offences, where the defendant gave a notice of intention to appear for trial and then failed to appear. In that case, he or she is deemed not to dispute the charges and convicted in his or her absence under sections 9.1 or 18.4.

(a) Compelling the Defendant to Appear for Trial

- The court may order the defendant to attend personally.

- The court may issue a summons in the prescribed form, if it deems it necessary to do so: section 51.

(b) Penalty for Failing to Appear

- Where one is lawfully required to attend the hearing and does not, he or she is guilty of an offence and upon conviction liable to:

  - A fine of not more than $2,000; or

  - Imprisonment for a term of not more than 30 days; or

  - Both: section 42(1).

- If the trial proceeds *ex parte*, then the defendant cannot be prosecuted for failing to appear: section 54(2).

- This section does not apply to young persons: section 98(3).

(c) Excluding the Defendant From the Trial

- The court may remove the defendant if he or she interrupts the proceeding to the extent that his or her attendance is not feasible.

- During the trial of an issue as to whether the defendant is, because of mental disorder, unable to conduct his or her defence, the court is satisfied that failure to exclude the defendant might adversely effect his or her mental health: section 52.

10.1.4 FAILURE OF THE PROSECUTOR TO APPEAR FOR TRIAL

- Where the defendant appears for a hearing and the prosecutor does not, the court may:

  - Dismiss the charge; or

  - Adjourn the hearing to another time: section 53(1).

- There is a similar rule if the prosecutor fails to appear at the resumption of an adjourned hearing: section 53(2).

- Certain costs can be awarded to the defendant: section 60.

- However, these costs are not legal costs of the party, but are costs for witness' fees and expenses. Where the proceeding is under Part I or II of the Act, such costs are not to exceed $100. See section 60(2).

- The defendant can request a certified copy of the order of dismissal to bar any subsequent proceedings by the prosecution.

A "set date" appearance is not a hearing. Thus the justice of the peace erred in dismissing a charge under the authority of s. 53(1) which allows a charge to be dismissed when the prosecutor does not appear at a "hearing". The proper procedure would have been to adjourn the matter to a specific date to permit the court to hear the defendant's motion to dismiss the charges, and permit the prosecutor to attend and explain the reasons for the previous failure to attend. This, in turn, would have given the justice of the peace the relevant information for the proper exercise of the court's jurisdiction. A certified copy of the order for dismissal makes it easier for the defendant to establish the "bar to any subsequent proceeding." Without such a certificate, the defendant may still establish the fact that the order for dismissal was made under s. 53(1): *Ontario (Registrar, Motor Vehicles Dealers Act, 2002) v. Shaikh*, 2011 ONSC 452, 2011 CarswellOnt 259, [2011] O.J. No. 258 (Ont. S.C.J.). **Note:** The prosecutor's subsequent appeal was allowed for substantially the reasons given by the Superior Court Judge on the prerogative remedy application, namely, that the relief under s. 53 sought by the defendant is not available on a set date appearance. The plain wording of s. 53(1) illustrates the intention of the legislature that non-attendance by the prosecution on the date of the hearing (that is, a date when an issue will be judicially considered by the court) may result in the dismissal of the case. See *R. v. Shaikh*, 2011 CarswellOnt 15074, 2011 ONCJ 774, [2011] O.J. No. 5968 (Ont. C.J.).

In *R. v. Lucas*, 2013 CarswellOnt 6515, [2013] O.J. No. 2685 (Ont. C.J.), four minutes after court was scheduled to start and the prosecutor had not appeared despite being paged twice, the Justice of the Peace dismissed all 68 charges on the tier for want of prosecution. The prosecutor filed an affidavit on appeal, indicating that he was outside the courtroom at the time, negotiating with a defendant, immediately went towards the courtroom when he saw the Justice appear, and did not hear his name being called as the pager in the hallway was not working. The prosecutor's affidavit showed an apparent lack of any insight into his own contribution to this deplorable affair; it was if his role in the justice system did not entail certain obligations to the court. One of the prosecutor's duties is to preserve respect for the court. One does not promote such respect by failing to be in attendance when the Justice enters the courtroom. Those in attendance are left with this image of a judicial officer cooling his heels awaiting the arrival of the prosecutor before the machinery of justice can come to life. Had the prosecutor immediately entered the courtroom and then advised the Justice that he required a few more minutes or a recess, it would be routine for judicial officers in these courts to grant such indulgences as provincial offences courts are likely the busiest courts of any courts in the country, bar none. The administration purposely overloads them on the theory that missing witnesses and defendants, illnesses, resolutions, all lead to whittling down the list to a manageable level. The key to making this happen is to give the prosecutor the time and latitude to get a handle on the state of the cases. Every justice of that court is alive to this, and likely none would deny this type of request as it is the most effective way to manage such formidable lists. The Justice in this case was clearly piqued by the prosecutor's absence, which he viewed as wilful, and he likely felt the prosecutor's actions were cumulative. However, it is always an injudicious use of one's discretion to make others suffer the consequences of someone else's actions. Had the Justice instead chosen to dress down the prosecutor in open court, when he did materialize, it was likely warranted. The rocky road taken instead was unacceptable, and led irretrievably to a reversible error of law.

A Justice of the Peace has jurisdiction to dismiss a charge under s. 53 of the prosecutor fails to appear, however there is no jurisdiction for the Justice to "withdraw" a charge. A withdrawal of a charge before a plea is entered is a matter that is solely within the discretion of the prosecutor. The prosecutor's failure to appear in this case was because he misdiarized the court date. See *Strachan v. Szewcyk*, 2013 ONCJ 402, 2013 CarswellOnt 10266, [2013] O.J. No. 3445 (Ont. C.J.).

In *Strachan v. Szewcyk*, 2013 ONCJ 402, 2013 CarswellOnt 10266, [2013] O.J. No. 3445 (Ont. C.J.), it was held that if the prosecutor fails to appear, a Justice of the Peace can award costs pursuant to s. 53(3). However, costs are calculated in accordance with s. 60 which permits witness fees and mileage, and does not give a

Justice of the Peace jurisdiction to order costs for fees and disbursements. Aside from the fact that the informant did not appear in court on the date because he had misdiarized the date, there were no grounds to order costs. The informant did not engage in conduct that warranted an order of costs being made against him. Even assuming that the Justice of the Peace had authority to order costs on a scale wider than provided for under s. 53(3), he should not have made an order of costs against the informant without first directing that the informant be given notice of that application and an opportunity to appear before the court. Procedural fairness required that such notice be given.

10.1.5 ENSURING THE APPEARANCE OF WITNESSES

(a) By Summons

- Before trial, you (or someone from your office) should appear before a justice to show why your witnesses should be summoned for trial.

- If you expect your witnesses to appear without a summons, consider summoning them anyway. They can use the summons as proof to their employer for being absent from work.

- Also, should they become ill or for some reason not appear at trial, you will more likely succeed in a request for an adjournment if your witnesses were summoned, because the presiding justice cannot fault you for not being prepared to proceed.

- The test that the justice will apply before granting a summons to a witness is found in section 39:

    - The justice must be satisfied that the proposed witness can give *material* evidence in the proceeding.

- The summons shall be served by a provincial offences officer as set out in section 26.

- The witness shall attend to give evidence at the proceeding, and re-attend if the proceeding is adjourned: section 39(4).

- If required by the summons, the witness shall bring any writing or other relevant thing in his or her possession or control: section 39(3).

In *Mohtashami v. Toronto (City)*, 2018 ONSC 5460, 2018 CarswellOnt 15568, [2018] O.J. No. 4846 (Ont. S.C.J.), it was held that only in rare cases will courts allow criminal or quasi-criminal proceedings to be delayed or fragmented by interlocutory review. The applicants, who are not defendants, but potential witnesses at a trial laid under the *Provincial Offences Act* for violations of a municipal by-law prohibiting the removal of trees without a permit, admitted that they were likely to give material evidence at trial, but claimed that they were tricked into providing the authorities with the information that they relied on to obtain the summonses. Any negative effect on the administration of justice that would result from compelling the applicants to testify would take place in the context of the defendants' trial. Whether and to what extent the administration of justice's integrity would suffer would depend on a number of factors, including the importance of the applicants' evidence to the prosecution's case and the seriousness of the charges. As a result, the best forum in which to evaluate the harm, if any, that would be caused to the administration of justice is the court in which the defendants are being tried. It is the defendants, not the applicants, whose rights are affected by the trial proceedings. If the conduct of the City authorities somehow compromised the integrity of the trial proceedings, then it is the defendants who will suffer prejudice as a result of the state misconduct. If a remedy is available, it is they who are entitled to it. The Superior Court should not allow a trial to be delayed so that witnesses who have no real interests in the proceedings and who are no risk of suffering any prejudice can embark on a Quixotic quest to remedy some perceived unfairness.

(b) Arrest of a Witness: Section 40

- The judge may issue a warrant for the arrest of the witness where a judge is satisfied upon sworn evidence that:
  - The witness can give material evidence that is necessary; and
    - The witness will not attend if summoned;
    - The witness is evading service of the summons; or
    - The witness was served but failed to attend court: section 40.

(c) A Witness who is in Jail: Section 41

- Prepare an order in the prescribed form, with a supporting affidavit indicating that he or she is a *material* witness, and indicate the jail and estimated release date for the witness.

- Serve a copy of the judge's order on the superintendant of the jail at least one week before trial, so that the jail can make the necessary transportation arrangements.

10.1.6 ADJOURNMENTS: SECTION 49

- The court may adjourn a trial or hearing.

- Where the defendant is in custody, the adjournment may not be longer than eight days without the consent of the defendant.

- The trial or hearing may be resumed before the expiration of the period with the consent of the defendant and prosecutor.

- Where the trial was commenced under Part I or II, the court shall not adjourn to allow the provincial offences officer who completed the certificate to attend to give evidence unless the court is satisfied that the interests of justice require it.

- Where the Crown requested an adjournment of the trial, and the defendants had agreed to the adjournment, the justice of the peace has discretion to grant the adjournment in the absence of the defendants. It was a violation of section 7 of the *Charter* to refuse the adjournment, and convict the defendants. See *R. v. Bednis*, [2004] O.J. No. 3992, 2004 CarswellOnt 3958, 2004 ONCJ 215 (Ont. C.J.).

- Where the party becomes aware of the need for an adjournment before the trial date, e.g., a material witness or the defendant is ill, it is advisable to give notice of the adjournment request to the other side. In the case of an adjournment request by the defendant, the prosecutors' office should be contacted.

- A court need not cater to the convenience of the parties at all costs. However, it is imperative that justice and fairness be addressed when considering a request for an adjournment, a process which requires a weighing or balancing of competing interests. The Crown, in representing the public interest, is as entitled as any litigant to these same considerations of justice and fairness. See *R. v. Baxter*, 2006 ONCJ 313, [2006] O.J. No. 3512, 2006 CarswellOnt 5294 (Ont. C.J.).

The justice of the peace erred in refusing to grant an adjournment on the basis that an associate of the defendant's agent, who appeared on the trial date with instructions to seek an adjournment for disclosure, lacked standing on behalf of the defendant: *R. v. Mangat* (January 31, 2006), G. Trotter J., [2006] O.J. No. 1781 (Ont. C.J.).

- The decision of the justice to exercise his discretion to allow an adjournment at the request of the Crown without affidavit evidence in support did not result in a loss of jurisdiction. If the accused had other complaints that the Crown conduct was abusive, it should be advanced at first instance before the trial court rather than on *a certiorari* application. It would be undesirable to fragment the proceedings with an inter-locutory judicial review: *R. v. Wilson* (March 22, 2006), Doc. 6609/06, [2006] O.J. No. 5653 (Ont. S.C.J.).

While the Crown disclosed the officer's collision reconstruction report prior to the trial, it failed to disclose the amended report. The defence had not completed its cross-examination of the officer, and the Crown's case was not concluded. The appropriate remedy was not a stay of proceedings, but an order for production of the revised report, and an adjournment to allow the defence to review the revised report with leave to recall Crown witnesses. This remedy removed any prejudice to the defence due to non-disclosure: *R. v. Soo*, 2008 ABPC 221, 2008 CarswellAlta 1077, [2008] A.J. No. 881, 74 M.V.R. (5th) 108 (Alta. Prov. Ct.).

An accused has no right to adjourn to get counsel when he has fired counsel to protract the process: *R. v. Maitland Capital Ltd.*, 2008 CarswellOnt 6510, 2008 ONCJ 523, [2008] O.J. No. 4360 (Ont. C.J.).

- The *Good Government Act, 2009,* S.O. 2009, c. 33, s. 1(42), effective 15 December 2009, adds a significant adjournment provision, s. 49(5). This new subs. (5), which gives the *court clerk* the power to adjourn a proceeding on behalf of the court, appears to be in response to the Ontario Court of Appeals' decisions in *R. v. 1283499 Ontario Inc.* (2003), 2003 CarswellOnt 2497, [2003] O.J. No. 2630, 176 C.C.C. (3d) 522, 65 O.R. (3d) 763, 173 O.A.C. 365 (Ont. C.A.) and *R. v. Colarossi* (2003), 65 O.R. (3d) 767, [2003] O.J. No. 2629, 2003 CarswellOnt 2496 (Ont. C.A.), where it was held that the regional senior justice of the peace did not possess the power to delegate jurisdiction to the clerk of the court to adjourn proceedings due to the unavailability of the presiding justice of the peace. Under new subs. (5), the clerk of the court is given the power, on behalf of the court, to adjourn the *first trial date* for a proceeding commenced under Part I or Part II to a date agreed upon by the defendant and the prosecutor in a written agreement filed with the court, *and any proceeding* under the *Provincial Offences Act* or any step under the Act, where no justice is able to attend in person, to a date chosen in accordance with the instructions of a justice.

The justice of the peace erred in denying the prosecution's request for an adjournment, due to the police officer being injured on duty and unavailable for trial, on the basis that special considerations apply where it is a defence witness who was unavailable, given the presumption of innocence. Witnesses, whether they be for the prosecution or for the defence, must be treated equally. It is inappropriate to say that an adjournment due to illness of a witness would be granted if it was a defence witness, but not if it is for a witness for the prosecution: *R. v. Manji*, [2008] O.J. No. 5155, 2008 CarswellOnt 9191 (Ont. C.J.).

An adjournment sought by the Crown two months before the trial date on the basis of unavailability of a civilian witness was rejected due to the inconvenience it would cause to the defendant. The adjournment request was reined on the trial date but was denied without the trial justice providing any reasons. The dismissal of the adjournment request was overturned on appeal as the justice failed to conduct a sufficient investigation into the issue or inquired if a subpoena had been issued: *R. v. McIntyre* (February 28, 2008), V.A. Lampkin J., [2008] O.J. No. 5154 (Ont. C.J.).

There is no absolute right to an adjournment or to any other remedy as a result of lack of disclosure. The trial justice exercised his discretion judicially in holding down the matter to allow the agent to review the disclosure, which was not lengthy, and in considering the history of the matter, which included the defendant appearing in court with an agent on record for trial at an earlier date. The appeal court could not conclude that the justice exercised his discretion incorrectly as to amount to an error of law in refusing the adjournment application: *R. v. Singh* (June 6, 2008), K.L. McLeod J., [2008] O.J. No. 3055 (Ont. C.J.).

The retained paralegal who had another matter in the same courthouse spoke to a second paralegal and asked him to speak to the matter on his behalf. However, when the justice asked whether the second paralegal had spoken with the defendant, he replied that he had not but that he had received instructions from the retained paralegal. The justice refused to permit the second paralegal to appear and dealt with the certificate on the deemed not to dispute docket instead. In the circumstances, the justice erred in proceeding in this manner, and in not adjourning the matter to allow the retained paralegal to attend and speak to the matter: *R. v. Metselaar*, [2009] O.J. No. 1691, 2009 CarswellOnt 2241 (Ont. C.J.), additional reasons at 2009 CarswellOnt 5462 (Ont. C.J.).

The actual rate of speed matters only on penalty and it is open to the prosecutor to seek an amendment under s. 34 of the *Provincial Offences Act* to "amend up" the rate of speed to that recorded at the time of the offence from the lesser speed stated in the certificate of offence. Defendants have no vested right to insist on a trial only on the charge named on the certificate of offence. However, the trial court can "amend up" a certificate only if the evidence supports the amendment. Ideally, the defendant should receive notice of a proposed amendment before the day of trial, however in provincial offences proceedings this ideal will not always be practical. If, for practical reasons, notice of the amendment can only be given on the day of trial, then it would be far preferable that the notice be given before the trial begins and that the defendant then be given a reasonable opportunity to consider how to respond. The broad amendment power in s. 34(2) contemplates that notice of the amendment can be made during or even at the conclusion of the evidence; the later during the proceedings that the defendant is given notice of the proposed amendment, the greater the risk of prejudice if the amendment is granted: *R. v. Winlow*, 2009 ONCA 643, 2009 CarswellOnt 5208, (*sub nom.* York (Regional Municipality) v. Winlow) 99 O.R. (3d) 337, 86 M.V.R. (5th) 171, 265 O.A.C. 326, [2009] O.J. No. 3691 (Ont. C.A.).

The defendant had represented himself very poorly, but had the justice allowed him to complete his explanation of why he needed more time to retain counsel, there may have been grounds for the justice to take the position that he did in refusing the adjournment. There was also evidence that the defendant truly did not understand he needed counsel for the trial date. The swift and continued retention of the paralegal by the defendant after he was notified of the need for representation was inconsistent with the view held by the justice that he knew he needed representation for the initial trial date and was not diligent in exercising his right to retain a representative. The justice prejudged the defendant's adjournment request and ignored relevant evidence; his conduct of the case created a reasonable apprehension of bias. A mistrial should have been allowed once the representative appeared: *R. v. Armstrong*, [2009] O.J. No. 4143, 2009 CarswellOnt 6057 (Ont. C.J.).

In a Newfoundland case, *R. v. Harding*, 2010 CarswellNfld 19, [2010] N.J. No. 24 (N.L. Prov. Ct.), it was held that there is no procedure which allows a trial of a *Highway Traffic Act* matter to be presented "in fax form". In any trial, witnesses give their evidence under oath or solemn affirmation, and are cross-examined. Statements which are not made under oath or solemn affirmation, and which are not subject to cross-examination, are not admissible for the truth of their contents. Such statements fall into the category of inadmissible evidence known as hearsay. The defendant's request for an adjournment, which was faxed to the court, was granted, as the docket was flexible enough to accommodate this request.

In a case of "amending up" at a speeding trial, the best practice is to make sure that the accused party is aware that an amendment could well take place, and that amendment could result in a higher charge and, if the evidence supports it, a higher penalty: *R. v. Monachino*, [2009] O.J. No. 5997 (C.J.). See also *R. v. Zimmer*, 2010 ONCJ 177, 2010 CarswellOnt 3809, [2010] O.J. No. 2247 (Ont. C.J.) where it was held that if a court routinely amends up to a rate of speed that is other than the one charged, it leaves it open to abuse, where high rates of speed could be alleged that were not in fact obtained as readings.

The justice erred in denying the prosecutor's adjournment request without any information as to why the prosecutor was unprepared to proceed to trial that day. An inquiry should be held into, among other things, whether the party applying for the adjournment has been guilty of neglect in procuring the attendance of the witness. However, there was no inquiry into the reasons for the absence of the officer; no opportunity was given to the prosecutor to explain why the officer was not present. To deny the adjournment without such an inquiry and opportunity to make submissions regarding the adjournment request amounts to exercising discretion other than judicially: *R. v. Sljoka*, 2010 CarswellOnt 4413, [2010] O.J. No. 2708 (Ont. C.J.).

It is improper to deny an adjournment request brought by the prosecutor on the basis that, in exercising its discretion, the prosecutor declined to proceed on less serious charges, given the absence of a police witness who was injured and unable to attend court, but sought an adjournment in a case involving a more serious charge. It was held that had the court considered the merits of the application and applied the correct test, the justice would have granted the adjournment request: *R. v. Carrigan*, 2010 CarswellOnt 7781, [2010] O.J. No. 2640 (Ont. C.J.).

The justice erred in refusing the prosecutor's adjournment request, and staying proceedings, on account of the interpreter's non-attendance in court. Where a request for an adjournment is made, the judicial officer is bound to demonstrate that it was fairly listened to and all the relevant factors in deciding whether to grant the adjournment were considered. The goal is to ensure that justice and fairness are done to both sides; this requires enquiry by the court and consideration of the relevant factors before making a decision on the adjournment request. While the issue of language is a factor to consider, the court must make its decision based on all the circumstances. It is an error to stay a matter on the basis that the defendant has the right to be tried on the first appearance and that it was the court's expectation that the trial would take place on the first appearance. The administrative error in not having the interpreter present did not constitute an abuse of process: *Mississauga (City) v. Malik*, 2010 ONSC 2334, 2010 CarswellOnt 2357, [2010] O.J. No. 1606 (Ont. S.C.J.).

In denying the defendant's request for an adjournment on the basis that she was unable to attend court due to a recent operation, the relevant considerations included that the matter had a protracted history with numerous adjournment requests by the defendant. While the adjournment was requested to allow the defendant to attend, instruct counsel and potentially give evidence, the prosecution had ten witnesses present, including civilian witnesses. There was a risk that the witnesses' memory may further erode over the period of any adjournment, and the public interest in having the matters adjudicated would be again delayed, with, simply little confidence that the matters would actually proceed on the next date requested: *Ontario (Travel Industry Council) v. Baldwin Travel & Tours Ltd.*, 2010 ONCJ 402, 2010 CarswellOnt 6884, [2010] O.J. No. 3859 (Ont. C.J.).

The trial justice recognized the reason that the Crown was unable to proceed due to the unavailability of its police witness, and held the matter down to another tier of court to allow the officer to attend. The defence was ready to proceed, and opposed the adjournment on the basis of prejudice. While the officer attended court after the adjournment request was refused and the matter had by then been dismissed, the justice exercised his discretion in a judicial way. The trial justice held that, if the officer was sick or had a family emergency, he would have no problem in granting the adjournment. In this case, however, the absence of the witness was due to scheduling concerns by the police, and the appeal court could see no reason to then disadvantage a defendant who was present and ready for trial: *R. v. Dolman*, 2010 ONCJ 401, 2010 CarswellOnt 7453, [2010] O.J. No. 4290 (Ont. C.J.).

In *R. v. Adebogun*, 2010 SKQB 235, 2010 CarswellSask 408, 357 Sask. R. 201, [2010] S.J. No. 789 (Sask. Q.B.), it was held that the trial judge considered the prejudice to the defendant, and considered that it was brought about as a result of an error of the Crown in not being ready to proceed on the trial date. In refusing the adjournment request, it could not be said that the trial judge refused or failed to consider the positions of the parties, or to have refused or failed to exercise his discretion judicially.

The defendant was not denied her disclosure rights where she did not complain at the time of trial that she did not see the officer's notes until the morning of the trial. If objections such as this were made in time then the court could have considered the remedy of an adjournment to overcome any prejudice suffered by the defendant. There was no evidence that the defendant in this case suffered any prejudice in the circumstances: *R. v. Davis*, 2010 CarswellOnt 10619, [2010] O.J. No. 5027 (C.J.).

A lawyer who happens to be a defendant before the court should not be treated any differently, and should not appear to be treated any differently, than any other defendant before the court. In dismissing the request of the defendant for an adjournment on the basis of the lack of disclosure, the comments of the court in calling the request disingenuous and smacking of sharp practice gave rise to an appearance of bias. A verbal summary of disclosure materials on a trial date in response to a disclosure request, even in provincial offences procedure, does not meet a minimum standard of disclosure to the defendant: *Durham (Regional Municipality) v. Jagtoo*, 2010 ONCJ 596, 2010 CarswellOnt 9517, [2010] O.J. No. 5334 (Ont. C.J.).

The accused has no right to adjourn to get counsel when he has fired counsel to protract the process: *R. v. Maitland Capital Ltd.*, 2008 ONCJ 523, 2008 CarswellOnt 6510, [2008] O.J. No. 4360 (Ont. C.J.).

The defendant made two adjournment requests to obtain evidence favourable to his case, which were not met with a proper inquiry or reasoned decision. The procedure was not explained to the defendant at the commencement of trial. Had the defendant been able to call at least one of the confirmatory witnesses, he might have been able to raise a reasonable doubt about his guilt. Having been convicted without being afforded a genuine opportunity to be heard, acquittals were entered on appeal. See *R. v. Homma*, 2010 ONCA 698, 2010 CarswellOnt 7923, [2010] O.J. No. 4478 (Ont. C.A.).

In *R. v. Bashir* (September 13, 2011), E.N. Libman J., [2011] O.J. No. 5403 (Ont. C.J.), the defence representative made a tactical decision not to indicate prior to the fourth trial date that disclosure was outstanding and that an adjournment would be sought. When the trial justice refused a further adjournment, he discontinued his involvement in the process by asking no questions of the witness or making any submissions in the remainder of the proceeding. In these circumstances, it would not be appropriate to reward this conduct of the behaviour of the defence representative with an adjournment at trial, or overturn the trial justice's decision, where there was a tactical decision to request disclosure, not follow it up, wait until the trial date to complain about it, and on the trial date find that the disclosure/adjournment request was being dismissed.

In *Vallance v. Pickering (City)*, [2011] O.J. No. 6107, 2011 ONCJ 771, 2011 CarswellOnt 15358, 17 C.L.R. (4th) 311, 93 M.P.L.R. (4th) 317 (Ont. C.J.), additional reasons at 2012 ONCJ 147, 2012 CarswellOnt 2756, 17 C.L.R. (4th) 323, [2012] O.J. No. 1216 (Ont. C.J.), the trial judge refused to grant a mistrial due to the lateness on receiving replacement disclosure due to its being misplaced by the previous defence representative, and also refused to grant an adjournment to allow the defendant to file a Notice of Constitutional Question or to allow a witness to be recalled for further cross-examination. However, the trial had a long history of delay which was overwhelmingly at the hands of the defendants. Given the context of the delays to that point, and the peripheral benefit to the defence to be gained by the adjournment or recall of the witness, the trial justice's decisions were reasonable. The trial justice had made significant efforts to try to assist the defence in the presentation of their case. There was no miscarriage of justice in the circumstances.

A defendant has no absolute right to an adjournment of his trial in order to get representation. A trial judge faced with such an application must consider its *bona fides*, whether the defendant has been diligent in attempting to secure representation, and the broader interests of the administration of justice. The defendant not only failed to show diligence, he had done nothing at all to get representation for his trial; the prosecution would be prejudiced to some degree if the adjournment was granted. Granting the adjournment in these circumstances would be tantamount to a declaration that a defendant will always be entitled to adjourn his trial by asserting a last minute wish to be represented. Such a situation would be highly detrimental to the orderly administration of justice. See *Brampton (City) v. Singii*, 2012 ONCJ 276, 2012 CarswellOnt 5978 (Ont. C.J.).

In *R. v. Butera*, 2011 ONCJ 860, 2011 CarswellOnt 15781, [2011] O.J. No. 6367 (Ont. C.J.), when the defendant, a self-represented individual, indicated that he wished to have a witness present to give evidence, the justice of the peace should have canvassed the possibility of the matter being adjourned so that he could summons or subpoena any witnesses that he wanted and ensure that they were present that day. It would have been open to the justice to inquire as to why the defendant wished to have the police officer present. It would have been open to the justice to point out to the defendant that the evidence he wished to call through the police officer was likely hearsay evidence and likely not be allowed; however, it would appear to be highly likely that the discussion with the defendant would have then led to pointing out that he may wish to subpoena and call the witnesses themselves to give their evidence. The defendant had a statement from a witness that would have helped his cause and there was another witness he could have brought who would also give evidence suggested that he had not entered the road in question. In all the circumstances, the justice erred in not canvassing the possibility of an adjournment.

The Crown's witness who was essential to the trial, a police officer, booked a holiday after the trial time was scheduled, but within the timelines permitted by the collective agreement governing police officers which permitted the booking of holidays on four months' notice before the trial, in which case the officer would not be available to attend the trial. In refusing the Crown's adjournment of trial request, it was held that the actions of the police department fell within the category of "neglect" in their duty to endeavour to procure the attendance of witnesses at court. The issue giving rise to the adjournment request was a matter for the Crown and the

Police Department, and not the Court and the Crown or Police. See *R. v. Mojzes*, 2013 BCPC 15, 2013 CarswellBC 179, [2013] B.C.J. No. 135 (B.C. Prov. Ct.).

In *R. v. Schwartz*, 2013 ONCJ 327, 2013 CarswellOnt 8535, [2013] O.J. No. 2819 (Ont. C.J.), it was held that a defendant has a right to a trial but does not have a right to postpone that trial without limit. After three trial dates had been set and two adjournments effectively granted, the Justice before whom the matter came for trial was entitled to insist on the matter proceeding, absent the most compelling circumstances supported by evidence. None was presented. The defendant had been provided an opportunity commensurate with the gravity of the offence, speeding, to have his day in court. Greater harm to the administration of justice would be occasioned if the court was to determine and declare that, under the circumstances and on the vague evidence presented, the trial court was obliged to once again adjourn the trial.

Prior to trial, the defendant's legal representative requested disclosure and was provided with it. He then sent a fax to the prosecutor stating that the notes were not clear enough to read and to "please resend". On the trial date, the paralegal requested an adjournment, which was denied. Where a defendant feels he is missing something and there is no response, he has to make some noise about it. In this case, a month intervened between the second disclosure request and the trial date, yet the paralegal's office did nothing about it. Given that the trial date was set, the trial time set aside, the witnesses were present, and the failure complained about was only with respect to a portion of the disclosure that was recapitulated in the witness statements, the trial Justice of the Peace did not err in refusing to grant the adjournment. See *R. v. Abdi*, 2012 ONCJ 782, 2012 CarswellOnt 16436, [2012] O.J. No. 6221 (Ont. C.J.).

In *R. v. Tate* (February 25, 2013), Doc. Newmarket 09-2111, [2013] O.J. No. 1799 (Ont. C.J.), the Crown's witness became ill with a migraine headache. As a result, the trial Justice of the Peace granted an adjournment, but without consulting the defendant in any great detail about the adjournment request, or about the manner in which the matter was to proceed on the following date. On the return date, the trial continued, and the prosecution essentially went over the qualifying of the officer's notes and took him through some of the evidence given on the prior date. Although, ideally, submissions should have been heard from the defendant, the trial Justice did not err in granting the adjournment or allowing the prosecution to proceed in the manner it did. It seemed the fairest thing to do, and did not cause any prejudice to the defendant.

In *R. v. Williams*, 2013 NLTD(G) 103, 2013 CarswellNfld 323, 341 Nfld. & P.E.I.R. 159, 1061 A.P.R. 159, [2013] N.J. No. 299 (N.L. T.D.), the trial judge was held to have acted correctly when he rejected the issue the defendant raised about the lateness of the Crown disclosure. The defendant did not relate the circumstances in which he received the disclosure, which had been sent to him in advance of the trial, and he may not have received it due to his own neglect. If the defendant felt he did not have sufficient time to prepare for trial because he did not receive timely disclosure, he should have brought it to the trial judge's attention when the matter was called and asked him to adjourn the proceedings until he was ready to proceed. The trial judge also acted correctly when he upheld the Crown's objection to the documents that the defendant tries to produce when cross-examining the police officer who stopped him for speeding. The Crown has a right to know what the documents are before halfway through the proceedings so it could inform itself about them, assess their relevance and address any concerns that it might have about them. One of the overarching concerns for a trial judge and one of the main purposes of rules of procedure is to ensure as far as reasonably possible that only relevant evidence is admitted that is probative of the issues raised by the charges. The trial judge achieved the object of the rules when he rejected the documents that the defendant produced from the manufacturer about the calibration of the radar and possibly the tuning forks, which were not served on the Crown with at least 7 days' notice in compliance with s. 28 of the *Canada Evidence Act*.

In *R. v. Mustakinovski*, 2013 ONCJ 804, 2013 CarswellOnt 18940, [2013] O.J. No. 6397 (Ont. C.J.), at the beginning of the trial the defendant did not mention he was waiting for a lawyer or agent or anyone else, and confirmed that he was ready to proceed when asked by the Justice. He also confirmed that he had read and understood the prosecution materials. It was only during cross-examination that the defendant stated that he had spoken to counsel but when this person did not show up he chose to proceed with the trial. There was no evidence that a lawyer or licensed paralegal had been retained. The Justice of the Peace was right to accept the indication by the defendant that he was ready to proceed to trial, and did not err in failing to cross-examine him or his trial preparation or suggest he apply for another adjournment when there was no basis for such a suggestion and he plainly wanted the matter to proceed.

It was held in *Brampton (City) v. Singh*, 2014 ONSC 2626, 2014 CarswellOnt 5532, 73 Admin. L.R. (5th) 341, [2014] O.J. No. 2005 (Ont. S.C.J.) that the Justice of the Peace erred in refusing the prosecutor's adjournment and compounded that failure by failing to give reasons. While the authority to grant an adjournment is discretionary, it must be exercised judiciously. Judicial discretion, however, is subject to review. Reasons are required so the public knows why a decision was made, the parties understand the decision, and it permits appellate review. Here, no reasons were given, just a refusal to grant the adjournment. Subject to one possible explanation, the public, the parties and the appellate court would be left to speculate why the adjournment application was refused; it was *possible* that the defendant taking a day off work had some impact on the decision. If that were so, an adjournment application should not be refused based solely on the defendant being prejudiced because he took a day off work in the absence of a *Charter* s. 11(b) application *if* that was the motivation for the refusal. It could not be ignored that only 80 days had elapsed since the date that the defendant was charged and there was no indication when the next court date would be. Automatically dismissing an adjournment application on a first trial date 80 days after being charged when the case could not be reached is not determining the adjournment application judiciously.

The decision whether to grant or refuse an adjournment is a matter that lies within the discretion of the trial judge. That discretion will not be interfered with on appeal unless it has been demonstrated that it was exercised injudiciously. The trial Justice in this case was faced with a choice: to grant yet another adjournment and show the administration of justice to be a toothless tiger that is helpless to control its own trial process or to refuse the adjournment and proceed to judgment against a defendant who had had more than ample opportunity to present full answer and defence, but chose to decline by absenting himself. In refusing to grant the adjournment sought by the defendant's son the Justice made the right choice. See *R. v. Choudhry*, 2014 ONCJ 631, 2014 CarswellOnt 16599, [2014] O.J. No. 5642 (Ont. C.J.).

The defendant proceeded upon his defence based upon the charge as laid, and it was to that means of committing the offences that his defence was based. The defence and Crown and trial court were in complete error as to what constituted an appropriate defence to the charge as laid, and the defence raised by the defendant could not have been entertained but for this means of committing the offence and the error in law made. The by-law contained at least 14 exemptions from the application of the by-law. The defendant had been misled in his defence. There was real prejudice. It would be manifestly unfair to the defendant to allow such an amendment on appeal and then decide the case on the record before the court. The Justice made very few findings of fact pertaining to these issues. If the amendment had been sought at the outset or during the trial, the court would have been in the position of assessing the specific prejudice and, in the appropriate case, would have granted an adjournment to ameliorate the prejudice, if that was possible. Such an amendment would have been routinely granted if sought before the end of the Crown's case. The trial Justice would have been in a good position to decide whether an adjournment be granted, or indeed whether Crown witnesses should be recalled for further cross-examination. The matter was remitted for trial and the information amended for the re-trial: *R. v. 1533904 Ontario Ltd.*, 2015 ONCJ 75, 2015 CarswellOnt 2388, [2015] O.J. No. 827 (Ont. C.J.).

In *R. v. Leung*, 2015 ONCJ 413, 2015 CarswellOnt 11727, [2015] O.J. No. 4118 (Ont. C.J.), it was held that the power to grant an adjournment is a discretionary one, reviewable on appeal if that discretion was not exercised judicially. The conditions required for an adjournment because of absence of a witness are threefold: (a) that the absent witness is material to the case; (b) that the party asking for an adjournment is not guilty of laches or an omission; (c) that there is a reasonable expectation that the witness can attend at the future trial date. The trial Justice did not consider, however, in his rulings whether the adjournment was *bona fides*, the fact that the Crown's case was closed and that no witnesses would be inconvenienced, when the trial could have been completed, the impact of the failure to grant the adjournment, whether the adjournment would have prejudiced the Crown who opposed the adjournment, especially given that the Crown case was completed, and whether the expanded testimony of the officer was properly something that required a rebuttal by the accused in order to make full answer and defence as he was entitled to do. It did not appear that the adjournment request was fairly listened to as the Justice dismissed the adjournment application twice, the first time summarily and then a second time after more submissions. The effect of denying the adjournment was to deny the defendant the opportunity to call a defence, which amounted to a miscarriage of justice.

The failure of the Justice of the Peace to allow an adjournment to allow the defendant to properly present his photographic evidence was an overriding and palpable error. The evidence could clearly have the potential of allowing the trier of fact to come to a different decision in the case. See *R. v. Niu*, 2015 ONCJ 379, 2015 CarswellOnt 10609, [2015] O.J. No. 3757 (Ont. C.J.).

An endorsement that a matter proceed "peremptory" should not be given undue emphasis however, the Justice of the Peace is entitled to control the process in that court and in dealing with limited trial time, trial backlogs, and the necessity to effectively manage the court, she is in the best position to make an assessment whether a trial should proceed. However, it is clear that the judge should make comment on the record of the reasons for denying the adjournment. It is an unwritten rule that every request for an adjournment for purposes of retaining counsel should be granted on the first occasion; it is not clear whether this rule would apply for the purposes of retaining a paralegal since that is a relationship far different than retaining a lawyer. In any event, there was a virtual lack of effort and delay by the defendant in taking steps to retain a paralegal. At best it might be described as an "inquiry" not a "step" to engage a paralegal. The risk of scheduling another trial date and wasting expensive and scarce court resources, having the investigating officer attend, triggering concerns about delay to trial, all hung over the head of the Justice of the Peace as she made her decision. Her reasons conveyed that the accused failed to convey diligence, and the endorsements of the court should be respected. No injustice or miscarriage of justice was endured by the defendant. The defendant had a trial and had no evidence to offer which would assist him. He had no potentially valid defence grounded on the merits. See *R. v. Petrosian*, 2014 CarswellOnt 19053, [2014] O.J. No. 6508 (Ont. C.J.).

When the paralegal was not present for the second scheduled trial date, the Justice of the Peace set the matter down to be heard later in the day, and then forced the trial to proceed in the paralegal's absence. The paralegal should have arranged his absence with the prosecution or should have been there. While the conviction was set aside on appeal, it was not likely to be tolerated a third time; the appeal court expected the prosecutor to flag the issue, and the date would likely be set to proceed whether or not the defendant's representative appears. See *R. v. Sayed-Zada*, 2015 CarswellOnt 15571, [2015] O.J. No. 5265 (Ont. C.J.).

The trial justice of the peace did not err in the exercise of his discretion in refusing the defendant's request to adjourn his peremptory trial date. The basis of the adjournment request was that the defendant was not given a copy of the in-car DVD with audio; however, there was no audio on the recording as the officer had not activated the audio pack before leaving his car. However, the defendant refused to accept this explanation. The defendant had been told this before the trial date, and when the justice explained this to him, he refused to participate in the trial. Given the past history of the case and the position taken by the defendant on the audio issue, the justice was entitled to dismiss the adjournment request. See *R. v. Hadi*, 2016 ONCJ 447, 2016 CarswellOnt 11897, [2016] O.J. No. 3890 (Ont. C.J.).

In *R. v. Sahadeo*, 2016 ONCJ 122, 2016 CarswellOnt 3721, [2016] O.J. No. 1252 (Ont. C.J.), on the date his trial was scheduled to take place, the paralegal for the defendant appeared and requested an adjournment. When the request was refused, the paralegal advised the presiding justice that he was instructed not to participate in the proceedings any further. The paralegal then left the courtroom. Upon the defendant being paged with no response, a deemed not to dispute conviction was entered. The decision to grant or refuse the adjournment was discretionary, and will not be interfered with on appeal unless the discretion was not exercised judicially, or where it has resulted in a miscarriage of justice. In this case, the need for the adjournment for disclosure could easily have been obviated by the defendant far in advance of the trial. While the justice of the peace was correct to refuse the adjournment, a conviction should not have been imposed under s. 9.1 as it could not be said that the defendant had failed to appear at the time and place appointed for trial. He did appear by instructing an agent to attend, as permitted by s. 50; the provisions of s. 54(1) did not apply in this case. The defendant had appeared by agent, the prosecution was ready, and the trial should have proceeded. The fact that the defendant had instructed his agent to "walk away" did not mean that the agent had any right to do so. A paralegal, like counsel, can only withdraw with the leave of the court. The defendant demonstrated a complete lack of diligence by failing to ensure that he had the necessary disclosure. He ought to have either appeared personally or else sent a properly instructed agent. The agent, who appeared, had not been properly instructed and was initially unable to articulate the reason for which he was seeking an adjournment. The application itself was entirely without merit and should not have been brought; for his part, the agent should not have agreed to act for the defendant without proper instructions.

The defendant's request for an adjournment on the grounds that he wanted to retain new counsel was not reasonable in the particular circumstances of the case. It was consistent with his numerous prior requests for adjournments which resulted in the lengthy history of the case. A previous adjournment had been granted so that he could obtain new counsel upon informing the court that his counsel had been disbarred and therefore no longer able to represent him; subsequent adjournments were also granted, and the case had been marked peremptory. There had been a 9-month interval from the adjournment of the first trial date to the peremptory trial date. The defendant was completely familiar with the charges, and was well acquainted with the alleged deficiencies including what was required to rectify the deficiencies with respect to his property. When the defendant left the court to protest the refusal to grant the adjournment, an *ex parte* trial was held, after which the defendant was found guilty. Upon the defendant returning to court on the day of sentencing at which time he asked for the charges to be withdrawn, dismissed and the proceedings stayed, the court ruled that it was *functus* to do so, having registered a conviction in his absence. See *R. v. Melnyk*, 2016 ONCJ 331, 2016 CarswellOnt 8877, [2016] O.J. No. 2998 (Ont. C.J.).

The adjournment application was not framed as being based on the unavailability of the defendant's counsel of choice, but instead it was based on the unavailability of a witness that the defendant's counsel wanted to cross-examine. The witness was not a material witness, and was not being called by the Crown, which has a discretion with respect to what witnesses it chooses to call. Accordingly, the defendant would not have been in a position to cross-examine the witness in any event. If the defendant wanted to call the witness to give evidence in direct, it was his responsibility to ensure that the witness was present on the date of trial. The justice's discretionary decision not to permit an adjournment because the witness was not present was entitled to deference on appeal. See *R. v. Gao*, 2016 BCSC 1606, 2016 CarswellBC 2406, [2016] B.C.J. No. 1838 (B.C. S.C.).

By the time the matter came for hearing, the transcripts of earlier court appearances had yet to be completed. The defence anticipated that the transcripts would be required for the hearing of the *Charter* s. 11(b) argument, and the attending prosecutor agreed. On that understanding the defence requested an adjournment, which was refused by the trial justice of the peace who was mistaken in his understanding of the procedural history of the case. While the justice was quite right in saying that trial dates were dates when a trial should happen, that does not mean that the principles of fairness and due process might not require the adjournment on the trial date. In denying the request for adjournment the justice effectively denied the defendant the opportunity to be heard on the alleged *Charter* breach. In the circumstances, the justice erred in law in refusing the requested adjournment based on a palpable and overriding mistake as to the underlying facts, and further erred in law in denying the defendant the right to be heard on the alleged *Charter* breach. See *R. v. Ahmad*, 2017 CarswellOnt 19495, 394 C.R.R. (2d) 374, [2017] O.J. No. 6319 (Ont. C.J.).

There was no evidence, on consideration of the entirety of the trial record, that the defendant was prejudiced in any way by the late receipt of disclosure. The defendant chose not to pick up the disclosure from the prosecutor's office until the morning of trial. His request for a stay of proceedings was quite properly refused, as the defendant failed to exercise due diligence in picking up the available disclosure until the morning of trial. The appropriate remedy, in these circumstances, at its highest, would have been an adjournment of the trial, but no adjournment was requested by the defendant. It was not part of the function of the presiding justice of the peace to advise the defendant that the appropriate remedy for the "late" provision of disclosure was an adjournment rather than a stay of proceedings as the defendant proposed. At the outset of the trial, the justice of the peace explained the trial process, and was informed that the defendant had received legal advice and had some experience in conducting a trial. The trial itself was straightforward and consisted of only one witness. The defendant was asked if he wished to give evidence and declined to do so. Reasonable assistance was provided to the defendant at trial and his fair trial interests were preserved and respected by the presiding justice of the peace as a consequence. See *R. v. Popovici*, 2017 CarswellOnt 21731, [2017] O.J. No. 5697 (C.J.).

The defendant applied to adjourn the trial, both on the date of the filed application and on the trial date, primarily due to the unavailability of retained representation. The decision to grant or deny an adjournment is a discretionary exercise. Where this discretion is exercised judicially and fails to result in a miscarriage of justice, the decision should not be interfered with on review. The right to representation of choice is not absolute. This is particularly resonant for *Highway Traffic Act* litigation in the general Toronto area where available counsel and paralegals are legion. Given the previously granted defence application to adjourn, it was reasonable for the court to expect that any representation retained by the defendant was available on the second trial date. The defendant demonstrated little or no diligence in this regard. In denying the application to adjourn, the learned justice considered the previously granted defence adjournment application. The trial was endorsed peremptory to proceed. It was appropriate to deny the application in the circumstances. See *R. v. Wei*, 2017 ONCJ 878, 2017 CarswellOnt 20869, [2017] O.J. No. 6785 (Ont. C.J.).

In *R. v. Benson*, 2018 ONCJ 217, 2018 CarswellOnt 5234, [2018] O.J. No. 1748 (Ont. C.J.), the defendant's request for a second adjournment of his trial was denied, and he was told by the presiding justice of the peace that the matter was going to proceed that day. The matter was held down and the defendant left the courtroom. He never returned. When the case was called for trial, and no one appeared, the presiding justice of the peace entered a conviction pursuant to s. 9.1(2). Section 9.1 applies only to Part I matters. The authority to conduct an *ex parte* trial under s. 54 is contained in Part IV and applies in proceedings commenced under Parts I, II or III, but pursuant to s. 9.1(2), it does not apply if s. 9.1(1) does apply. In the instant case, the defendant took the steps to initiate the process and then attended twice, both times to request adjournments. The presiding justice of the peace called the case for trial. It was open to him to treat that precise moment as the time and place appointed for trial. At that time the defendant failed to appear. Despite his earlier appearances, it was open to the presiding justice of the peace to conclude that s. 9.1(1) was applicable. If that was so, it was not open to him to proceed with an *ex parte* trial. To rule otherwise would defeat both the purpose and substance of s. 9.1(1). It is clearly intended to reduce the number of trials and concentrate court resources on those cases where the defendant truly desires to have a trial. It should not be possible for someone to defeat this simply by making one appearance and then leaving the court or declining to participate further.

In *R. v. Galbraith*, 2018 ONCJ 138, 2018 CarswellOnt 3347, 404 C.R.R. (2d) 371, [2018] O.J. No. 1189 (Ont. C.J.), a written request for disclosure was sought four times by the defendant for her speeding trial, and she received assurances from administration that her requests had been forwarded to the office of the prosecution. She did not receive an answer to her requests. The prosecution policy concerning the provision of disclosure in the jurisdiction was usually two weeks after receipt of a written request. The delay in providing disclosure in a timely manner to the defendant in this case was due to staffing changes in the office of the prosecution. The prosecution delay in providing disclosure was due to a mistake and did not violate her right to a fair trial under s. 11(d) of the *Charter of Rights*, nor was any prejudice demonstrated such that the late disclosure did not violate the right to make full answer and defence under s. 7 of the *Charter*. The time elapsed since the date of the offence to the proposed date of trial was 7 months, well below the presumptive ceiling for unreasonable delay established in *R. v. Jordan*. There was no negligence on the part of the prosecutor that justified an order of costs either as a *Charter* remedy or due to procedural irregularities under s. 90 of the *Provincial Offences Act*. The defendant had chosen to attend the Early Resolution meeting and there were a total of two court appearances to date. Section 24(1) of the *Charter* confers a broad remedial mandate and the widest possible discretion on a court to craft remedies that must be easily available for violations of *Charter* rights. The remedy in the instant case was an adjournment to a date for trial and no order for costs.

At the beginning of his trial, the defendant argued he was denied Crown disclosure despite two requests for it. At the start of his trial, the prosecutor gave some disclosure, but the defendant asked for more. The prosecutor was not in a position to provide it at that time. The defendant then asked the justice of the peace for a stay of proceedings due to this failure to make proper disclosure. He was not allowed to make submissions on this point, including his presenting four binding cases that he wished to present. However, the defendant did not give any notice he was bringing a stay application. By not giving such a notice, the justice of the peace understandably was not prepared to hear the stay application on the merits at that time. The justice of the peace was within his right to try and control the proceedings before him, and he did not overstep the appropriate boundaries of that. At the end of the day, while the justice of the peace did not accede to the defendant's request for a stay or listen to the whole of his submissions, he adjourned the trial in order that disclosure be made. The justice of the peace specifically left it open for the defendant to bring his stay application on the new trial date, present any evidence he wished, and to make his submissions. When the whole of the proceedings was assessed, there was no denial of natural justice or an unfair hearing. The justice of the peace was also correct in not ordering a stay of proceedings at this time. The remedy that he chose was to grant an adjournment so that proper disclosure could be made. This was a fit remedy for Crown non-disclosure. The justice of the peace did not preclude the defendant from asking for a stay of proceedings upon the resumption of the trial. No substantial wrong or miscarriage of justice resulted from this decision. See *City of Toronto v. Riddell*, 2018 ONSC 2048, 2018 CarswellOnt 4860, [2018] O.J. No. 1643 (Ont. S.C.J.), affirmed *Toronto (City) v. Riddell*, 2019 ONCA 103, 2019 CarswellOnt 2272, [2019] O.J. No. 823 (Ont. C.A.).

In *Reginella v. R.*, 2018 ONCJ 198, 2018 CarswellOnt 4918, [2018] O.J. No. 1547 (Ont. C.J.), the learned justice of the peace denied the adjournment request brought by the defendant on the trial date due to disclosure not being received mainly on the bases that the Crown witnesses were present, the Crown was ready to proceed and that the defendant had not brought an application or motion for an adjournment prior to the trial date. The learned justice of the peace exercised his discretion judicially in refusing to grant the adjournment on the trial date. He properly considered that there would be an inconvenience to witnesses as being a factor and that the defendant or his agent had not brought an application for an adjournment prior when they realized that the disclosure had not been received. The learned justice of the peace did not consider any irrelevant factors in this decision. Clearly, there was an onus on the defendant and his agent to follow up by way of direct contact with the trial date when the disclosure had not been received. In addition to not being any adjournment request, the defendant or his agent did not bring an application for a stay of proceedings based on a failure of the prosecution to provide disclosure. In the circumstances, the trial was fair. The defendant was represented; he chose not to attend the trial. The defendant's agent could have renewed his request for an adjournment at the close of the prosecution's case so that the defendant or any defence witnesses could testify. Such a request was not made. The appeal court had not been advised that even though disclosure was received subsequent to the trial, there was something of substance in that disclosure that may have assisted the defendant in his defence.

In *York (Regional Municipality) v. 1085638 Ontario Limited*, 2018 ONCJ 658, 2018 CarswellOnt 16164, [2018] O.J. No. 5003 (Ont. C.J.), it was held that the decision to adjourn a proceeding is one in the discretion of the trial judge. The judicial officer must listen to the request and consider various factors, including the length of time of the proposed adjournment. The longer the period of time, the greater the likelihood the adjournment should not be granted as the likelihood of prejudice to the defence increases. What was clear on the record was that the justice of the peace tried to accommodate an adjournment for sentencing submissions if it was only going to be for a short time. After poring over the court calendar with the assistance of the trial coordinator it was clear that it couldn't. By that time the charges were 12 years and 5 years old, respectively, the court was clearly uncomfortable with yet another delay in the case at the penultimate stage, and ruled that submissions should be heard. Given that counsel were advised two months previously that they should be ready to do just that on the return date, the decision was not unfair. There was also no evidence on the appeal about what evidence would have been heard had the adjournment been granted. No fresh evidence was sought to be tendered on the hearing of the appeal. No error in principle was identified in the reasons for sentence. Absent an error in principle sentencing decisions are entitled to deference. Despite denying the adjournment, the court received submissions on sentence from both the prosecution and defence. The defendants received very substantial fines — $60,000 in total. That said, this was a legal sentence, and the defendants had a history of previous convictions relating to the very issue of non-compliance with municipal orders.

In *York (Regional Municipality) v. Bouaziz-Caruso*, [2019] O.J. No. 638 (Ont. C.J.), the defence representative had asked for disclosure several weeks before, but by the trial date it had not been handed out. The trial justice denied the adjournment, finding that any suggestion the defendant did not receive the notice of trial in advance was hearsay. The justice held the matter down to permit the trial agent to review disclosure and the defendant present, however she did not attend. Where a second trial date adjournment is denied, it is appropriate for the justice of the peace to hold the trial down briefly to permit the review of disclosure before trial. This practice is not uncommon for Part I litigation, and is reasonable in light of the simplified procedure contemplated under the Act.

10.1.7 MENTAL CAPACITY OF THE DEFENDANT TO CONDUCT A TRIAL: SECTION 44

- Where the court has reason to believe that the defendant suffers from a mental disorder, the issue of the defendant's ability to conduct a defence may be tried.

- If the defendant is unable to conduct a defence, the proceedings are suspended.

- The *Mental Health Act*, R.S.O. 1990, c. M.7 defines "mental disorder" as "any disease or disability of the mind".

- The test is similar to that under the *Criminal Code*, R.S.C. 1985, c. C-46, for the capacity to defend a criminal charge: see *R. v. Taylor* (1992), 77 C.C.C. (3d) 551, 17 C.R. (4th) 371, 11 O.R. (3d) 323 (Ont. C.A.).

- Under the *Criminal Code*,

  - The party raising the issue must prove that the accused is unfit to stand trial on a balance of probabilities.

  - The accused is fit to stand trial, provided the accused understands the nature or object of the proceedings, understands the possible consequences, and can communicate with counsel.

  - The accused must be capable of recounting the necessary facts to his lawyer, but he or she need not be capable of acting in his or her own best interests.

- In addition to the powers to order psychiatric assessments under the POA, under the *Mental Health Act, supra*, there are various powers to order assessments and the detention of dangerous persons.

The issue of mental incapacity to conduct a defence in provincial offences proceedings was considered in *Real Estate Council of Ontario v. Chua*, 2013 ONCJ 251, 2013 CarswellOnt 5845, [2013] O.J. No. 2190 (Ont. C.J.). It was held that the burden is on the person who raises the issue of the defendant's alleged inability to conduct a defence due to mental disorder. The burden, as in criminal cases, is on the defendant to establish he is unfit, given he was the one who claimed at the conclusion of the prosecution that he was unable to conduct a defence to the charges. The test should be the same, given the identical interests at stake whether under the *Criminal Code* or *Provincial Offences Act*. The test is the limited cognitive ability test; it is not a high threshold. The defendant must understand the nature and object of the proceedings and the possible consequences, and be able to communicate with counsel to prepare a defence. It is not necessary that the defendant be capable of acting in his or her best interests. **Note:** In accordance with the procedure under s. 44, the trial proceedings before the Justice of the Peace were suspended so that the issue as to capacity could be determined by a judge, and hearing evidence from a psychiatrist. Upon the judge finding that that the defendant was able to conduct a defence, the suspended proceedings were ordered to continue before the trial Justice of the Peace.

In *R. v. Hanna*, 2015 ONCJ 493, 2015 CarswellOnt 14535, [2015] O.J. No. 4912 (Ont. C.J.), the court considered s. 44 of the *Provincial Offences Act* which provides that where a judge finds a defendant is, because of mental disorder, unable to conduct his or her defence, the judge shall order that the proceeding remain suspended, and where the judge finds that the defendant is able to conduct his or her defence, the judge shall order that the suspended proceeding be continued. "Mental disorder" is not defined under the Act. It is appropriate to use the test under the *Criminal Code* which states that it means a disease of the mind. Unfit to stand trial should also be given the same meaning as that under the *Criminal Code*, that is, the person is "unable on account of mental disorder to conduct a defence ... or to instruct counsel to do so, and, in particular, unable on account of mental disorder to, understand the nature or object of the proceedings, understand the possible consequences of the proceedings or communicate with counsel." The defendant was referred by the court for a psychiatric assessment where the doctor concluded the defendant was unable to stand trial due to a conversion disorder. The court accepted the doctor's conclusions, and the defendant was found unfit to stand trial. The proceedings were ordered to remain suspended under s. 44(3).

Although the doctor was unable to make any formal diagnosis, she believed that the defendant suffered from a "psychotic disorder not otherwise specified". According to the doctor, it was readily apparent that the defendant was extremely disorganized in her thought form, and her ability to focus on matters at hand was impaired; from a psychiatric perspective, her presentation rendered her, likely due to a medical condition, grossly incapable of participating meaningfully in legal proceedings, instructing counsel or assisting in her own defence. It was found on the balance of probabilities that the defendant was unfit to stand trial for driving without insurance. See *R. v. Dudley*, 2016 ONCJ 364, 2016 CarswellOnt 9848, [2016] O.J. No. 3302 (Ont. C.J.).

In *R. v. Kathirkamapillai*, 2016 ONCJ 377, 2016 CarswellOnt 10195, [2016] O.J. No. 3409 (Ont. C.J.), it was held that while there was evidence that the defendant was suffering from depression and anxiety, the medical evidence did not suggest anything to dispute the usual presumption of fitness to stand trial. The defendant's alleged lack of memory of various events was not sufficient to support the contention that he was unable to conduct his defence. The defendant was able to communicate with his counsel, and instruct his counsel, in the assessment of fitness. He had not established, on a balance of probabilities, that due to a mental disorder he was incapable of conducting his defence.

10.1.8 ENTERING THE PLEA

- After preliminary motions are decided (see Chapter 5), the defendant is informed of the substance of the charges and must plead guilty or not guilty: section 45(1).

- If the defendant pleads guilty, the court *may* accept the plea and convict: section 45(2).

  - Where the defendant is unrepresented and may not understand the process, the court can wait for the defendant to admit the essential facts alleged by the prosecutor before convicting the defendant.

- If the defendant pleads not guilty to the offence but guilty to any other offence, whether or not it is an included offence, the court may, with consent of the prosecutor, accept the plea and amend the information or substitute the offence to which the defendant pleads guilty, accordingly: section 45(4).

- If the defendant refuses to plead or does not answer directly, the court will enter a plea of not guilty: section 45(3).

- Prior to the defendant pleading guilty, the justice of the peace may conduct a "plea inquiry" so as to ensure that the guilty plea is being freely and voluntarily made. The defendant will be advised, even in cases where he or she is represented by an agent or another, that it is important the defendant understands that by pleading guilty he or she will be giving up the right to have a trial in the provincial offences court and making the prosecution prove its case in court. The defendant will also be told that the matter of penalty or sentence is exclusively up to the justice of the peace and that while the parties have the right to make submissions as to sentence, only the justice can determine what sentence to impose. See *R. v. Shields* (2002), [2002] O.J. No. 4876, 2002 CarswellOnt 4304 (Ont. C.J.). In cases where a guilty plea is being entered by an agent on behalf of the defendant in the defendant's absence, it is important for the agent to indicate to the court that the defendant has instructed the agent to enter the plea on his or her behalf, and that the defendant is aware of the consequences of the guilty plea but has chosen to be represented by an agent to enter the guilty plea. See *Barrie (City) v. Doherty* (2003), [2003] O.J. No. 1105, 2003 CarswellOnt 1235 (Ont. C.J.).

- To be valid, a guilty plea must be voluntary and unequivocal, and the defendant has to understand the nature of the charges. See *Ontario (Ministry of Consumer & Business Services) v. Whiteside* (2004), 2004 ONCJ 204, 2004 CarswellOnt 3916, [2004] O.J. No. 3972, 25 C.R. (6th) 373 (Ont. C.J.).

The legal principles governing the withdrawal of a guilty plea were canvassed by Trafford J. in *R. v. Jerome*, 2008 CarswellOnt 528, [2008] O.J. No. 407, 65 M.V.R. (5th) 25 (Ont. S.C.J.), a case where the defendant unsuccessfully challenged the validity of her guilty plea to careless driving. The court noted that the appellant has the legal burden of establishing that her plea was invalid, and that the withdrawal of a plea of guilty should be permitted in exceptional circumstances. There is no absolute right to withdraw a plea of guilty. The defendant's plea of guilty to careless driving in the case at bar was informed, voluntary, and unequivocal. Her reasons for entering the plea, namely, to end the stress associated with the accident and the related charges, were considered sufficient and appropriate by her. Those reasons did not vitiate the plea in the circumstances of the case. The plea was an informed admission of guilt, which was made with the knowledge of her right to require the Crown to prove its case. In addition, she admitted the facts alleged by the Crown in support of the plea without any qualification.

The trial justice has a duty to ensure that the defendant's plea of guilty is voluntary, informed and unequivocal. To be informed, the defendant must know the charge and the consequences which the court can impose. However, there is no requirement that the court must inform defendants of all possible consequences of a plea, including administrative and civil consequences: *R. v. Torabi* (September 21, 2007), No. 999-00-86410023-90, [2007] O.J. No. 5402 (Ont. C.J.).

In *R. v. Sholtens*, 2008 CarswellOnt 3605, 2008 ONCJ 282, [2008] O.J. No. 2444 (Ont. C.J.), the appeal court held that where a justice of the peace on his own motion adjourns a sentencing hearing to another date for the purposes of providing reasons as to why he cannot accept the guilty plea, and gives reasons for judgment without providing the prosecutor or unrepresented defendant a real opportunity of making submissions, the proceedings take on the appearance of a public lecture rather than an adversarial process before an impartial decision maker. A reasonable person, reasonably informed, would conclude that that the justice's decision had been arrived at before all the evidence and submissions had been heard. The justice of the peace was bound to follow the law on point and enter a conviction, through the application of the doctrine of *stare decisis*; there was a decision of a judge of the Ontario Court of Justice sitting as an appeal court, indicating that it was appropriate to register a finding of guilt in the circumstances of the case. *Stare decisis* is the glue that binds the court system in Ontario together, and gives purposes to the different levels of court and functions so as to prevent injustice. For a similar case, see *R. c. Bellefeuille*, 2008 CarswellOnt 6641, 2008 ONCJ 575, [2008] O.J. No. 4494 (Ont. C.J.) where the justice of the peace rejected the defendant's guilty plea and erroneously dismissed the charges, rather than set a trial date which was the proper course where a guilty plea is rejected.

In *R. v. Kronshteyn*, 2008 CarswellOnt 4600 (Ont. C.J.), the court set aside a conviction and ordered a new trial where evidence was placed before the court by the trial agent that he misunderstood the defendant's instructions due to a language barrier, and erroneously entered guilty to a lesser charge.

In *R. v. Fuentes*, 2008 ONCJ 598, 2008 CarswellOnt 7068, [2008] O.J. No. 4677 (Ont. C.J.), it was held that it is the client's right to meet with the person who represents him so there will be no misunderstanding as to what occurs in court. It is mandatory that whomever the licensed paralegal hires meets with the client where a paralegal informs the client that another paralegal will represent the client in court. It is not sufficient for the paralegal to merely tell the other agent what the client wants or said. Where the second paralegal pleaded the client guilty without ever speaking to the client, and a licence suspension was imposed, the conviction could not stand.

In *R. v. Dobson*, 2010 ONCJ 161, 2010 CarswellOnt 2744, [2010] O.J. No. 1823 (Ont. C.J.), it was held that the licensed paralegal who entered a guilty plea in the defendant's absence, on the basis of boilerplate instructions in the retainer agreement authorizing the paralegal to negotiate a plea on the defendant's behalf, did not constitute valid instructions to enter the guilty plea. The instruction was not case specific, included no duty to ensure the facts were admitted by the client, did not indicate that the plea was voluntary, or that the client was aware of the plea. The record keeping practices of the paralegal provided no confidence that she could accurately reconstruct the events that led to the plea; her independent memory was unreliable and she altered the documents in anticipation of the appeal.

While the consequences of the defendant's guilty plea in terms of the length of suspension may have been a surprise to the defendant, the fact that he was disqualified from driving was no surprise at all. The guilty plea was unconditional, and from the exchange with the court was informed: *R. v. Pitchford*, 2010 SKQB 400, 2010 CarswellSask 709, 367 Sask. R. 70 (Sask. Q.B.).

In *R. v. Zaltzman*, 2010 ONCJ 667, 2010 CarswellOnt 10523 (Ont. C.J.), the justice failed to take any steps in the form of a plea comprehension process. The defendant was not asked whether he understood that by entering the guilty plea he was giving up the right to a trial. Neither was he asked whether he understood that by entering a guilty plea he would be admitting the essential elements of the offence. The elements of the offence with respect to speeding were never fully disclosed, and the defendant's answer when asked how he wished to plead was equivocal.

- The *Good Government Act, 2009,* S.O. 2009, c. 33, s. 1(37), effective 15 June 2010, enacts a new taking of plea procedure under s. 45. Under subs. (1), it is stated that after being informed of the substance of the information or certificate, the defendant shall be asked whether he/she pleads guilty or not guilty to the offence charged in it. Where the defendant pleads guilty, the court may accept the plea and convict the defendant: subs. (2). These two subsections are essentially the same as current s. 45(1) and (2). However, there is now a plea inquiry requirement set out under subs. (3). A court may accept a guilty plea only where it is satisfied that the defendant is making the plea voluntarily, understands that the plea is an admission of the essential elements of the offence, understands the nature and consequences of the plea, and understands that the court is not bound by any agreement made between the defendant and prosecutor. The failure of the court to *fully inquire* whether the conditions specified in subs. (3) are met does not affect the validity of the plea: subs. (4). It is also stated that where the defendant pleads guilty to an offence other than the offence charged, and whether or not it is an included offence (under s. 55), and whether or not the defendant has pleaded not guilty to the offence charged, the court may, with the prosecutor's consent, accept the guilty plea and accordingly amend the certificate of offence, the certificate of parking infraction or the information, as the case may be, or substitute the offence to which the defendant pleads guilty: subs. (6). The wording of subs. (6), which replaces s. 45(4), expands the scope of this provision to apply to guilty plea proceedings under Parts I and II in addition to those under Part III.

Dissatisfaction with a sentence is not a valid basis on which to withdraw a guilty plea: *R. v. Alexandruk*, 2011 ABQB 475, 2011 CarswellAlta 1297, 520 A.R. 124, 55 Alta. L.R. (5th) 348, [2011] A.J. No. 836 (Alta. Q.B.).

An accused person who does not bother to appear in court in response to a parking charge subjects himself/herself to being deemed not to dispute the charge, on the basis of being indifferent to the charge (as evidenced by the failure to appear), a reasonable and appropriate measure, given the accused person's indifference. However, an accused person who appears in court in response to a parking charge is in a different category. By virtue of the fact that such a person has appeared in court in response to the charge, that person cannot be presumed to be indifferent to the charge. Such a person sometimes is unable or unwilling to communicate either a plea of guilty or a plea of not guilty, in which case the fairer approach is to enter a plea of not guilty and set the matter for trial, as opposed to deeming the person not to dispute the charge. The defendant's effort to read a statement at the time set for entering a plea should not have resulted in his being convicted. See *R. v. Drury*, 2012 SKQB 65, 2012 CarswellSask 55, 389 Sask. R. 299, [2012] S.J. No. 65 (Sask. Q.B.).

In *R. v. Zimmerman*, 2011 CarswellOnt 15344, [2011] O.J. No. 5782 (Ont. C.J.), it was held the unrepresented defendant's plea of "Guilty, but I didn't know" was not an unequivocal plea. It was incumbent on the justice to go into a detailed explanation of the process and the nature and consequences of the guilty plea. It was also important to do so upon the defendant's indication that she was a housewife for most of her life but upon her husband becoming suddenly ill she had become responsible for managing the property. Upon the defendant stating her inability to pay, it was incumbent on the justice to explain that if she was going to make these submissions, she could testify or produce an affidavit. It was not explained how this information could be properly before the court so that the justice could take it into account. This constituted a very serious deficiency in the procedure. The justice is required, by law, to consider the financial circumstances of an individual when imposing a fine.

A Justice of the Peace has no jurisdiction to examine a certificate of offence for defects and quash it when the defendant is pleading guilty to an offence: *York (Regional Municipality) v. Datoo*, 2014 CarswellOnt 18598, [2014] O.J. No. 3469 (Ont. S.C.J.).

In failing to allow the defendant's agent an opportunity to provide submissions on sentencing before rendering his decision, the Justice of the Peace erred in principle. The Justice also erred in relying on the defendant's conduct during the traffic stop as an aggravating factor. The defendant's conduct at the time indicated clearly that he was annoyed at being stopped for speeding, and he expressed himself accordingly; he did not, however, do anything illegal. It may well be that the defendant was rude, but bad manners are not a valid consideration on sentencing. See *R. v. Williston*, 2014 NWTSC 45, 2014 CarswellNWT 47, [2014] N.W.T.J. No. 49 (N.W.T. S.C.).

In *R. v. Song*, 2014 BCSC 1502, 2014 CarswellBC 2349, [2014] B.C.J. No. 2054 (B.C. S.C.), it was held that if a person pays a violation ticket, the person is deemed to have pleaded guilty to the alleged contravention. In order to set aside the guilty plea, there must be exceptional circumstances. The onus is on the offender seeking to have the plea set aside to show the guilty plea is invalid and that allowing the plea to stand would result in a miscarriage of justice. The defendant failed to demonstrate that his plea was involuntary or that it was equivocal or uninformed. Neither was there a miscarriage of justice as the defendant failed to show that he had a good defence to the speeding charge.

Before rejecting the range of sentence suggested by the prosecutor and imposing a higher fine, the Justice should have given cogent reasons for doing so and then explained why, in his view, fines within the suggested range would be contrary to the public interest or would otherwise bring the administration of justice into disrepute: *Kingston (City) v. Patry* (August 9, 2011), Doc. Kingston 090175, 090176, [2011] O.J. No. 6667 (Ont. C.J.).

In *R. v. Ali-Tawfiq*, 2014 ONCJ 727, [2014] O.J. No. 6365 (Ont. C.J.), it was held that while there was no doubt that the defendant's guilty plea was voluntary and unequivocal, the lack of legal representation on a serious charge with complex issues and extensive disclosure for a defendant with limited education and a seemingly limited ability to comprehend the issues caused the court real doubt as to the validity of the plea. As a result, the defendant met his basis of persuasion to establish that the plea of guilty was not fully informed, and the plea was struck.

In *R. v. Quick*, 2016 ONCA 95, 2016 CarswellOnt 1484, 129 O.R. (3d) 334, 26 C.R. (7th) 424, 94 M.V.R. (6th) 42, 345 O.A.C. 237, [2016] O.J. No. 582 (Ont. C.A.), the Ontario Court of Appeal held that for a plea of guilty to be informed, it is not necessary that the defendant understand every conceivable collateral consequence of the plea including consequences that may be legally relevant. What is required is a fact-specific inquiry in each case in order to determine the legal relevance and significance of the collateral consequences to the defendant. The test to be applied is a subjective one. Unawareness of a driver's licence suspension under provincial legislation for a *Criminal Code* driving offence constitutes a clear example of a collateral consequence that may render a guilty plea uninformed.

It was open to the trial judge to consider the absence of any vehicular collision or personal injury as a mitigating factor in imposing sentence. However, even if the learned trial judge should have taken the absence of an accident into account as a mitigating factor, an erroneous consideration of a mitigating factor does not lead to appellate intervention unless the sentence is demonstrably unfit. Considered in light of the maximum available fine of $1,000 under the *Traffic Safety Act* (Sask.) for the offence of failing to stop for a red light, and the fine imposed of $230, the sentence was clearly at the lower end of the range and not demonstrably unfit. By asking an appeal court to take letters of reference and the whole of his circumstances into account, when the defendant declined to do so at trial, the defendant was effectively seeking to have the court impose a different sentence. The trial judge is entitled to deference on an appeal from sentence. An appeal court cannot intervene simply because it would have weighed the relevant factors differently. It may only intervene if the sentence imposed is demonstrably unfit, and in this case it was not. See *R. v. Miller*, 2016 SKQB 35, 2016 CarswellSask 67, [2016] S.J. No. 49 (Sask. Q.B.).

In *York (Regional Municipality) v. Sekelyk* (September 22, 2015), Doc. CV-15-123505-00, [2015] O.J. No. 4889 (Ont. S.C.J.), the Justice of the Peace was held to have erred in quashing the certificate of offence on the defendant's guilty plea due to the omission of the municipality. It is the overall philosophy of the *Provincial Offences Act* (Ont.) that technical objections not impede the determination of a verdict on the merits. In other circumstances, the failure of the certificate to identify the municipality would be a material, not technical matter. In the instant case, however, there were full particulars of the time and place of the alleged offence, the nature of the offence, speeding, and the place alleged, together with the immediate circumstances under which the notice and offence occurred. As a result, it could not be said that the failure to have included the name of the municipality could impair the defendant's appreciation of the offence he was alleged to have committed. The justice erred in striking the plea and quashing the certificate, rather the process to amend the certificate should have been allowed to unfold.

The right to be tried within a reasonable period of time includes the right to be sentenced within a reasonable period of time. While justices of the peace are responsible for one of the busiest courts in the province and understandably, on occasion, may, like many judges, need extra time to prepare reasons for sentence, on the facts of this case where there was a joint submission on sentence, one might speculate that the reasons for sentence would be relatively brief and perhaps delivered orally at the time of accepting the plea. A delay in imposing sentence of nine and one-half months was not a prompt sentence and unwarranted in the circumstances. See *York (Regional Municipality) v. Newhook*, 2015 ONSC 6587, 2015 CarswellOnt 16978, [2015] O.J. No. 5766 (Ont. S.C.J.).

It was further held in *York (Regional Municipality) v. Newhook*, 2015 ONSC 6587, 2015 CarswellOnt 16978, [2015] O.J. No. 5766 (Ont. S.C.J.) that the discretion of the court as to whether it will accept or reject the guilty plea is a discretion that has to be exercised judicially. It is not a discretion that can be exercised on an arbitrary whim. In situations where it is evident on the face of the record that the discretion has not been exercised judicially, such a discretion amounts to an error of law. There was no reason in law why the Justice should reject the guilty plea that was being proposed by the prosecutor and the defence. She made no inquiries of the prosecutor or defendant with respect to the reasonableness of the proposed plea. Even if there was some legal basis in law for the Justice to consider the appropriateness of the guilty plea, there was no reason why it should take nearly a year for the court to consider whether the guilty pleas should be accepted. An order for *mandamus* issued directing the Justice to accept a guilty plea to the amended offence and to enter a conviction.

The defendant was represented by a licensed paralegal who entered a guilty plea on his behalf. The defendant claimed that the paralegal did not have his authority to do so, and launched a complaint against him. He also notified the paralegal of the date of his appeal, but the paralegal did not attend. A licensed paralegal is an officer of the court and has a duty to come forward with an explanation because he presented himself in court as someone who had the authority from the defendant to plead guilty to a serious offence under the *Highway Traffic Act*, and be subjected to a thousand dollar fine and licence suspension. The defendant presented evidence that the paralegal acted without authority. As the paralegal failed to comply despite being given numerous opportunities to explain the guilty plea he entered on the defendant's behalf while indicating that he had authority to do so, there was strong evidence that he did not have such authority. The guilty plea was set aside on appeal and a new trial ordered. See *R. v. Ezati*, 2016 CarswellOnt 8435, [2016] O.J. No. 2819 (Ont. C.J.).

Similarly, in *R. v. Antone*, 2016 ONCJ 316, 2016 CarswellOnt 8634, [2016] O.J. No. 2872 (Ont. C.J.), the defendant was not present when his legal representative entered a plea of guilty on his behalf. No plea inquiry was done by the justice of the peace as the defendant was not present and there was no discussion regarding the agent's authority to enter a plea on behalf of her client. However, it was clear from the information presented to the appeal court that the plea had not been arranged on the defendant's behalf with his knowledge and consent. Upon finding out that he had been found guilty, the defendant took steps to set aside the conviction and explain his circumstances. There was merit to his claim that at no time did he provide an informed consent to enter a guilty plea to the charge of driving while suspended and that the possible consequences of the conviction and six months driving suspension were not explained to him. Neither did the agent review disclosure with him. The notes in the Crown file indicated that upon the defendant paying his outstanding fines, a plea to the lesser offence of driving without a licence would have been accepted. A number of attempts were made to have the agent appear before the appeal court and explain her actions, but she did not appear. It appeared that she had been completely negligent in her representation of the defendant. It would be a miscarriage of justice to allow the conviction to stand in these circumstances.

The Crown should not have more procedural rights than the accused. The accused could not attach the condition to his plea that it was dependent on the ruling against him being upheld; likewise, the Crown should not be participating in a process by which facts are agreed to and charges are withdrawn, conditional upon a ruling being upheld. The defendant entered the plea of guilty knowing that the state of law was that they were thereby forestalling the Crown's potential appeal. The Crown also knew this and actively participated notwithstanding. This should have been expected to be a final resolution of the matter. To allow the Crown to proceed to appeal the original ruling through a sentence appeal offends that expectation of finality. It would place the defendant in a position where they were potentially prejudiced by the fact of their plea and any revisitation of the issue of their guilt. See *Ontario (Ministry of Labour) v. Ontario Power Generation*, 2016 ONCJ 299, 2016 CarswellOnt 8272, [2016] O.J. No. 2725 (Ont. C.J.).

In *R. v. Garwal*, 2016 ONCJ 217, 2016 CarswellOnt 5933, 99 M.V.R. (6th) 151, [2016] O.J. No. 1997 (Ont. C.J.), the defendant was charged with speeding, and following a resolution meeting pleaded guilty to disobeying a sign. The parties jointly submitted that the appropriate sentence was to impose the set fine of $85. The imposition of the set fine was held to be contrary to the public interest or would bring the administration of justice into disrepute as set fines are statutorily reserved for cases that do not go to trial, or where there were mitigating factors. Imposing the set fine would also not respect the legislative intent that proceedings proceed economically and efficiently. A defendant should not have the benefit of both the public cost required to ensure a right to trial as well as a reduced fine after conviction on the day of trial. As the defendant had no record of similar offences, and there were no aggravating factors, imposing a fine of $100 would be sufficiently punitive.

Often when a guilty plea is sought to be withdrawn on appeal, there will be affidavit evidence in support of the submission that the plea was invalid. No such evidence was before the court, and the defendant appeared to have had exposure to the traffic violation system prior to her present situation. The defendant's effective guilty plea by payment of her fine was a plea that was informed by her prior experience and was voluntary and unequivocal. See *R. v. Garra*, 2016 BCSC 1696, 2016 CarswellBC 2542, [2016] B.C.J. No. 1926 (B.C. S.C.).

In *R. v. Mr. Ice Man Ltd.*, 2016 ONCJ 621, 2016 CarswellOnt 16466, [2016] O.J. No. 5443 (Ont. C.J.), there were two errors made, one by the issuing authority, in not issuing the proper gross vehicle weight, and the other by the defendant, in not checking the licence before using it. The government which seeks to impose the fine was in some respects responsible for the circumstances of the offence. This appeared to be a very rare and very exceptional circumstance which was not likely to be repeated; however, the defendant, by simply checking his documents could have avoided the infraction. Taking all of the circumstances into account, it was in the interests of justice to reduce the fine by the proportionate responsibility of the parties: 75 percent by the defendant and 25 percent to the Ministry.

To be a valid guilty plea, the plea must be informed, voluntary and unequivocal. A plea will be informed where the accused person is aware of the nature of the allegations made against him, the effect of his plea and the consequences of entering it. A voluntary plea is the product of an accused's conscious, volitional decision to plead guilty for reasons which he or she regards as appropriate. In this case, the violation ticket indicates on its face that, unless the ticket is disputed within 30 days, the offender will be deemed to have pleaded guilty. On the facts in this case, the defendant paid the ticket within a few days, which is deemed to be a guilty plea. There was no evidence, in the form of sworn evidence, sufficient to support the conclusion that the ticket was paid other than by way of a conscious decision. The defendant's lack of diligence in investigating the circumstances before paying the ticket did not amount to exceptional circumstances to justify allowing the court to exercise its discretion and permitting the defendant to withdraw his guilty plea. See *R. v. Yeghiyan*, 2016 BCSC 1482, 2016 CarswellBC 2237, [2016] B.C.J. No. 1703 (B.C. S.C.).

A joint submission should normally be accepted unless the sentencing judge "is satisfied that the recommended disposition would be contrary to the public interest and would bring the administration of justice into disrepute": *R. v. Thompson*, 2013 ONCA 202, 2013 CarswellOnt 3920, 305 O.A.C. 42, [2013] O.J. No. 1546 (Ont. C.A.). It is an error in principle not to conduct a thoughtful analysis of why the proposed joint submission falls prey to that, and it is an error by sentencing judge not to "forewarn counsel of his intentions or provide them with an opportunity to respond": *Thompson*, para. 16. Neither of those was done in any of the cases in question. As such, the trial justice of the peace erred in imposing a sentence lower than the joint submission. A sentence of $200 was only $115 above the statutory minimum fine. There was no reason why the sentence imposed of $85 was so markedly different than the joint submission. All of the defendants had their charges reduced from speeding to a lesser charge. A $200 fine was a benefit to the accused. So were the saved demerit points. The *quid pro quo* should have been apparent and, if it wasn't, the prosecutor should have been given an opportunity to explain it. See

York (Regional Municipality) v. Sun, 2016 ONCJ 240, 2016 CarswellOnt 6700, [2016] O.J. No. 2243 (Ont. C.J.).

In a similar case, *R. v. Pellicci*, 2017 ONCJ 85, 2017 CarswellOnt 2788, [2017] O.J. No. 188 (C.J.), it was held that resolution without trial is essential to the efficient and fair operation of the system of provincial offences courts in the province. The resolutions in these cases involved reductions in charges, reductions in fines or both. Some resolutions avoided administrative penalties such as driving demerit points. Others avoided conviction on offences which would trigger serious insurance consequences. Despite those benefits, the joint submissions as to sentence were rejected. Justice of the peace may depart from joint submissions, but the ability to do so is prescribed by law. The appropriate test is a strict one — whether the proposed sentence would bring the administration of justice into disrepute or would otherwise be contrary to the public interest. The phrase "otherwise contrary to the public interest" does not lower the standard. It is an error of law for the presiding justice of the peace to tell the courtroom that there could be no agreements as to sentence, simply to assert judicial independence, and to lower the fine proposed without explaining why the submitted fine was inappropriate or why the minor variance to the set fine amount was necessary. Justices of the peace do have the ultimate responsibility to impose a fit sentence, but that responsibility must be exercised according to the limits imposed by statute and following the framework provided by appellate courts. Where an accused receives the benefit of resolution to a reduced charge and reduced fine and agrees they can pay that amount, a sentencing court should not further reduce the fine due to concerns about ability to pay not founded in the evidence. A general sympathy for an accused person is not a sufficient basis to interfere with a joint proposal.

In *York (Regional Municipality) v. 1085638 Ontario Limited*, 2018 ONCJ 658, 2018 CarswellOnt 16164, [2018] O.J. No. 5003 (Ont. C.J.), it was held that the decision to adjourn a proceeding is one in the discretion of the trial judge. The judicial officer must listen to the request and consider various factors, including the length of time of the proposed adjournment. The longer the period of time, the greater the likelihood the adjournment should not be granted as the likelihood of prejudice to the defence increases. What was clear on the record was that the justice of the peace tried to accommodate an adjournment for sentencing submissions if it was only going to be for a short time. After poring over the court calendar with the assistance of the trial coordinator it was clear that it couldn't. By that time the charges were 12 years and 5 years old, respectively, the court was clearly uncomfortable with yet another delay in the case at the penultimate stage, and ruled that submissions should be heard. Given that counsel were advised two months previously that they should be ready to do just that on the return date, the decision was not unfair. There was also no evidence on the appeal about what evidence would have been heard had the adjournment been granted. No fresh evidence was sought to be tendered on the hearing of the appeal. No error in principle was identified in the reasons for sentence. Absent an error in principle sentencing decisions are entitled to deference. Despite denying the adjournment, the court received submissions on sentence from both the prosecution and defence. The defendants received very substantial fines — $60,000 in total. That said, this was a legal sentence, and the defendants had a history of previous convictions relating to the very issue of non-compliance with municipal orders.

In *R. v. Kanoon*, 2018 ONCJ 793, 2018 CarswellOnt 19132, [2018] O.J. No. 5948 (Ont. C.J.), the defendant did not accept the facts underpinning the guilty plea. Whether this was an oversight on the part of the justice of the peace, the conviction should not have been registered. The bulk of participants in the provincial offences court proceedings are unsophisticated, and unfamiliar with court proceedings. In these instances, a more detailed plea inquiry is required. This is especially so, when as in this case, the defendant expressed that he had something to say about the facts, and had already relayed that information to someone. It was incumbent upon the presiding justice of the peace to seek clarification and to ensure that the facts were truly being accepted as accurate and supportive of the guilty plea. Additionally, with respect to the specific offence alleged in the matter, the justice of the peace should have advised the parties that there was a potential defence of due diligence and incorporated this into the plea inquiry.

It is not an error for an appellate court to situate the sentence before it within the usual range of sentences. One cannot begin to measure the demonstrable fitness of a sentence without having an eye to the customary sentencing range. An appeal court errs if it tethers a finding of unfitness to the simple fact that the range is missed, but commits no error by getting a perspective on what a fit sentence looks like by examining comparable cases. The principle of parity requires that sentences should be similar to other sentences imposed on similar offenders for similar offences committed in similar circumstances. This principle is equally applicable to sentencing for regulatory offences and criminal offences. Genuine inability to pay a fine is not a proper basis for imprisonment. As a matter of principle, it must also hold true that the hardship of a fine is not a proper basis for imprisonment either. The appeal court judge was therefore correct in finding that the sentencing justice erred in imposing a jail term because a fine would cause more financial hardship. On this basis alone, the appeal judge was entitled to set aside the sentences of incarceration and to vary the sentences within the limits prescribed by law. However, the appeal judge erred in adopting as a sentencing principle that regulatory offences are concerned with attaining public policy objectives as opposed to punishing moral blameworthiness. This is too crude a formulation and poses a false dichotomy. It is true that regulatory offences are concerned with attaining public policy objectives and the criminal law punishes according to the degree of the offender's moral blameworthiness; however, this does not mean that moral blameworthiness may not also be a relevant sentencing consideration for regulatory offences. The relevance of moral blameworthiness in sentencing for regulatory offences follows necessarily from the application in regulatory offences of the fundamental sentencing principle of proportionality. It is important to appreciate that, despite its application, moral blameworthiness does not operate the same way in sentencing regulatory offenders, as it does in sentencing criminal offenders. This is because regulatory offences tend to reflect lower levels of moral blameworthiness. While both kinds of offences reflect moral blameworthiness, the moral blameworthiness in criminal offences tends to be greater, and that difference must be respected when imposing sentences. See *Ontario (Labour) v. New Mex Canada Inc.*, 2019 ONCA 30, 2019 CarswellOnt 577, 51 C.C.E.L. (4th) 171, [2019] O.J. No. 227 (Ont. C.A.).

At trial, the defendant brought a s. 11(b) application complaining of the delay resulting from her adjournment of the first trial. The application was dismissed. A plea of guilty was then entered to a reduced charge. A guilty plea constitutes a waiver, not only of the accused's right to require the prosecution to prove guilt beyond a reasonable doubt, but also of the related procedural safeguards in the trial process. The guilty plea in the instant case disentitles the accused from challenging pre-trial rulings in proceedings before the plea was taken. That applies with stronger reason here where the appellant was permitted to plead to a reduced offence with the benefit of reduced penalty. The appellant's submission to the effect that *R. v. Jordan* imposes absolute timelines such that it doesn't matter whether the defence caused the delay misstates the test. *Jordan* requires the court to begin by deducting defence delay. The timelines are applied after that deduction. In this case, not only did the defence request the delay complained of but the agent at trial specifically confirmed that his client was content with the time to the next trial date despite concerns expressed by the justice of the peace. On either *Jordan* or the prior *R. v. Morin* analysis, there was no merit to the application. See *Yogeswaran v. York (Regional Municipality)*, 2018 ONCJ 819, 2018 CarswellOnt 19741, [2018] O.J. No. 6131 (Ont. C.J.).

10.1.9 TRIALS WHERE THE DEFENDANT *DOES* APPEAR: SECTION 46

- The defendant has the following procedural rights:
    - The defendant is entitled to make full answer and defence.
    - The prosecutor or defendant, as the case may be, may examine or cross-examine witnesses.

- The court may receive and act upon any facts agreed upon by the defendant and prosecutor without proof or evidence.

- Despite section 8 of the *Evidence Act*, R.S.O. 1990, c. E.23 (EA), the defendant is not a compellable witness for the prosecution: section 46.

10.1.10 TRIALS WHERE THE DEFENDANT DOES *NOT* APPEAR: SECTION 54

- A not guilty plea is entered and the prosecutor must prove its case.

- An *ex parte* trial is still a trial, with all its attendant burdens of proof, formalities and evidentiary requirements.

  - The prosecutor must act fairly and adduce *all* relevant evidence, both indicative of guilt and innocence.

  - The defendant only forfeits the right to be present, to hear and test by cross-examination the evidence of the prosecution witnesses, and to make full answer and defence.

  - The defendant can only be convicted upon legally admissible evidence which establishes proof beyond a reasonable doubt the essential elements of the prosecution's case. See, for example, *R. v. Bandito Video Ltd.* (1986), 52 C.R. (3d) 293 (Ont. Prov. Ct.).

  - An *ex parte* trial, where the defendant does not appear, does not contravene the Charter as the defendant is not deprived of his or her right to be present at trial as he or she need only appear at the time and place fixed for trial: *R. v. Felipa* (1986), 55 O.R. (2d) 362, 27 C.C.C. (3d) 26, 40 M.V.R. 316 (C.A.).

An absent defendant does not give up her right to be convicted only on the basis of legally admissible evidence which establishes beyond a reasonable doubt all essential ingredients of the offences charged. Notwithstanding a lack of any evidence from the defendant, the court is to consider the only other evidence, that is, of the Crown witnesses, to determine whether or not there have been any *Charter* violations and whether any evidence obtained by any such violations should be excluded pursuant to the *Charter: R. v. Dumont*, 2008 CarswellOnt 2186, 2008 ONCJ 173, [2008] O.J. No. 1487 (Ont. C.J.).

Where the trial justice raises the issue of voluntariness at the defendants' *ex parte* trial and dismisses the charge on the basis that the identity of the defendants had not been established, the principles of fundamental justice required that the prosecutor be given an opportunity to make submissions in response to the court's concerns about voluntariness. The inconsistency in the spelling of the name of one of the defendants was a point that should have been presented to the prosecution with an opportunity for submissions to be made: *R. v. Jarecsni*, 2008 CarswellOnt 6779, [2008] O.J. No. 4565 (Ont. C.J.).

The defendant did not appear for the resumption of his hearing and was aware that the matter would proceed without further notice to him. He and his co-defendant were both officers and directors of the company and they allegedly acted together. Separating their matters in any way would be inefficient and simply a waste of court time. It was appropriate for the trial to proceed on an *ex parte* basis: *R. v. Maitland Capital Ltd.*, 2008 CarswellOnt 6508, 2008 ONCJ 521, [2008] O.J. No. 4358 (Ont. C.J.).

The defendant's *Charter* motion for unreasonable delay was adjourned for judgment, at which time a different agent appeared to receive the judgment. The justice questioned the agent's authority to appear for the defendant, and proceeded to find the defendant guilty, rather than continuing the trial. In so doing, the justice erred in law. Under s. 54(1), the justice had the options of either going ahead in the defendant's absence and rendering judgment on the motion, or issuing a summons for the defendant to appear. However, the date was specifically set for judgment on the motion, and there was no indication by the justice that he intended to continue the matter on that day. By not following the procedure set down in s. 54(1), the justice erred in law, resulting in the convictions being set aside: *R. v. Demelo*, 2009 CarswellOnt 7402, [2009] O.J. No. 5079 (Ont. C.J.).

In exercising jurisdiction under s. 9.1 of the *Provincial Offences Act*, R.S.O. 1990, c. P.33, which permits conviction of the accused in absentia where the information is complete and regular on its face, a Justice of the Peace must determine whether the combination of the description of the offence and/or the omission or improper citing of the section number would in all of the circumstances cause confusion in the mind of a reasonable person as to what offence is being charged: *R. v. Stuparayk*, 2009 ONCJ 394, 2009 CarswellOnt 5148 (Ont. C.J.), at para. 24.

Section 54(1)(a) of the *Provincial Offences Act* which permits *ex parte* trials, even when the prosecutor is seeking a period of imprisonment upon conviction, is constitutionally valid and does not violate ss. 7 or 11(d) of the *Charter of Rights and Freedoms*. However, an *ex parte* trial is not automatic, when a defendant fails to appear on a charge under Part III. Where the prosecutor seeks a custodial sentence, the prosecutor would be well-advised to consider whether an *ex parte* proceeding is appropriate: *R. v. Jenkins*, 2010 ONCA 278, 2010 CarswellOnt 2158, [2010] O.J. No. 1517, 99 O.R. (3d) 561, 260 O.A.C. 296, 212 C.R.R. (2d) 137, 93 M.V.R. (5th) 1, 74 C.R. (6th) 117, 253 C.C.C. (3d) 269 (Ont. C.A.), leave to appeal refused 2010 CarswellOnt 7405, 2010 CarswellOnt 7406, 225 C.R.R. (2d) 374 (note), 410 N.R. 395 (note), 279 O.A.C. 399 (note) (S.C.C.).

The rules of evidence still apply at *ex parte* trials. The trial is to proceed just as it would, had the accused been present: *R. v. Villebrun*, 2010 NWTSC 61, 2010 CarswellNWT 59 (N.W.T. S.C.).

In a case where the defendant had elected to leave the proceedings, which effectively converted the matter into an *ex parte* trial, the court was obligated to ensure fairness in the proceedings in exactly the same way as if the court were presiding over a proceeding involving an unrepresented defendant: *Ontario (Travel Industry Council) v. Baldwin Travel & Tours Ltd.*, 2010 ONCJ 402, 2010 CarswellOnt 6884, [2010] O.J. No. 3859 (Ont. C.J.).

In *R. v. Kergan*, 2011 SKPC 115, 2011 CarswellSask 527, 381 Sask. R. 106, [2011] S.J. No. 478 (Sask. Prov. Ct.), it was held that an *ex parte* trial is not the same as a default conviction, and is therefore not subject to the reopening provision for setting aside a default conviction. When a not guilty plea has been entered and the accused then fails to appear for trial, it is not open to the court to simply issue a default conviction; it is open to the court to hear the trial in the absence of the defendant, and then issue a conviction. If the reopening provision for default convictions applied to such trials, the defendant could use it to set aside his conviction and obtain a new trial, and then in theory he could fail to appear for the next trial and again use the procedure to set aside the conviction. The process could go on indefinitely and he could be tried an indefinite number of times. This would be a most unreasonable interpretation of the legislation, and a most unreasonable state of affairs.

In the face of the defendant's fourth motion for prerogative relief, the previous three of which were summarily dismissed or withdrawn, the court was entitled to find that he was intentionally delaying the prosecutions. As the defendant had again absented himself from the proceedings, the court was entitled to proceed on the evidence to convict and sentence him. The defendant was not being deprived of any right to which he was justly entitled by a harsh or arbitrary application of any legal test. See *R. v. Grabowski*, 2011 ABQB 510, 2011 CarswellAlta 1402, 527 A.R. 80, 56 Alta. L.R. (5th) 211, [2011] A.J. No. 913 (Alta. Q.B.).

In *R. v. Borges*, 2011 ONCA 621, 107 O.R. (3d) 377, 281 C.C.C. (3d) 231, 25 M.V.R. (6th) 42, 285 O.A.C. 173, 2011 CarswellOnt 10567,[2011] O.J. No. 4278 (Ont. C.A. [In Chambers]), it was held that s. 131 of the *Provincial Offences Act* is limited to applications for leave to appeal from a decision made by the provincial offences appeal court under s. 116. The decision of the appeal court to deny an extension of time to file an appeal was made under s. 85, and not pursuant to s. 116. Consequently, no "judgment" was rendered under s. 116, and there could be no application for leave to appeal under s. 131. Even if there was jurisdiction, leave to appeal should not be granted as the appeal was without merit. While s. 54, which allows for a conviction in the defendant's absence, requires that the prosecutor prove that the defendant was given notice of the original trial date, it does not require the prosecutor to prove that the defendant received notice of the adjourned date. It is the responsibility of the defendant to ascertain the new date; the court bears no duty of notice beyond announcing the new date, in court, at the time of the adjournment. While the defendant retained counsel initially to represent him at trial, he did not attend on the application of his counsel to be removed as counsel of record. As described in the uncontested affidavit evidence presented on appeal, the defendant was aware of this trial date and that he was facing a jail sentence if convicted. He provided no explanation for his non-attendance at trial. He took no meaningful steps to either appear in person or have someone appear for him at trial, having a two-month period between the removal of his counsel and the trial date. He chose to ignore the charges. Therefore, the trial judge's decision to proceed in his absence was not an error in law, and a review of the transcript of the proceedings did not disclose a miscarriage of justice. See *R. v. Belisle* (February 8, 2011), Doc. Ottawa 08-003698, [2011] O.J. No. 1326 (Ont. C.J.).

In *R. v. Boros*, 2012 ONCJ 156, 2012 CarswellOnt 3709, [2012] O.J. No. 1297 (Ont. C.J.), affirmed 2013 ONCA 263, 2013 CarswellOnt 4834, [2013] O.J. No. 1904 (Ont. C.A.), it was held that the trial court did not lack jurisdiction to proceed with an *ex parte* trial due to the trial transcript not disclosing any testimony about the service of the summons on the defendant. The justice of the peace was simply reading the affidavit of service that was part of the summons; such written proof of service was sufficient under s. 26(6). In the absence of an assertion that the defendant was not notified of the proceedings, there was no reason to doubt the requirements of s. 54(1), permitting an *ex parte* trial, had been met.

At an *ex parte* trial, the prosecutor must prove the defendant's guilt beyond a reasonable doubt according to generally applicable evidentiary rules. In order to prove that the defendant was not a registered builder and had not paid a prescribed fee, the prosecutor relied on the hearsay evidence of the investigator about a computer search he had conducted that the defendant had failed to pay the prescribed fee and was not a registered builder. However, the documents were admissible only if they met the best evidence rule, that "if an original document is available ... you must produce it. You cannot give secondary evidence by producing a copy." This rule applies in both criminal and civil proceedings, and prosecutions for provincial offences. The prosecutor did not explain the failure to produce the original documents the defendant had submitted, and there was no reason to think the original documents were unavailable; no evidence was called as to authenticating the copies that were filed. The investigator's evidence was inadmissible hearsay. It was akin to a traffic officer attempting to prove the suspension of a driver's licence by repeating in evidence what he saw on a police computer screen. See *R. v. Boros*, 2012 ONCJ 156, 2012 CarswellOnt 3709, [2012] O.J. No. 1297 (Ont. C.J.), affirmed 2013 ONCA 263, 2013 CarswellOnt 4834, [2013] O.J. No. 1904 (Ont. C.A.).

In *R. v. Lazaridis*, 2011 ONSC 6833, 2011 CarswellOnt 14026, 32 Admin. L.R. (5th) 326 (Ont. S.C.J.), the defendant applied for prerogative relief in an attempt to attack his conviction and sentence imposed by a properly constituted provincial offences court, acting within its jurisdiction under s. 54 of the Act. There was no suggestion that the warrant of committal was defective on its face in any way, just that it should not have been issued because the proceedings were not carried out in accordance with the Ontario Court of Appeal's decision in *R. v. Jenkins*, released over a year after the issuance of the warrant of committal, where it was held that while *ex parte* proceedings do not infringe the *Charter of Rights*, they ought not to become the norm. Although there was no transcript of proceedings available in order to ascertain whether the prosecutor advised the court that it was seeking a period of imprisonment, failure to abide by the Court of Appeal's cautionary words in proceeding *ex parte* in such circumstances would not deprive a court of jurisdiction to proceed *ex parte* and convict an accused person and then, if appropriate, issue a warrant of committal, although it may turn out to be a fruitful ground of appeal. The defendant's attempt to review his conviction on the basis of an alleged error of law, based on subsequent developments in the law, was therefore clearly barred by s. 141(3) since a right of appeal exists. The ability of the defendant to challenge the underlying conduct leading to his arrest pursuant to the warrant of committal was another matter, and would not be susceptible to review by way of appeal. The Superior Court of Justice has a broad jurisdiction to consider claims for prerogative relief, especially when based on *Charter* grounds. The matter was therefore permitted to proceed to a hearing on the merits. However, while the privative clause in s. 141(3) of the Act does not formally bar this aspect of the claim for prerogative relief, the fact that the defendant has still not pursued the statutory avenue of appeal may be critical in determining whether the relief sought ought to be granted. Relief by way of *certiorari* is discretionary and generally should not be granted when an applicant has failed to avail himself/herself a statutory right of appeal.

Absent a miscarriage of justice or an obvious *Charter* violation, it is not the role of the justice of the peace in provincial offences court to intervene in an *ex parte* trial and speculate on possible technical defences to the charge, nor is it the role of the justice of the peace to play devil's advocate. These courts are busy courts. To require the prosecution to lead evidence on uncontested matters that should be common knowledge to any reasonable person would strangle the administration of justice and bring the provincial offences court to a halt. The overall scheme of the *Provincial Offences Act* and its overriding purpose is intended to be informal and user friendly. The courts hearing *Provincial Offences Act* matters should get to the merits of the charges and not be unduly concerned with legal technicalities or procedural formalities. See *R. v. Mitchell-Carson*, 2006 CarswellOnt 10253, [2006] O.J. No. 5676 (Ont. C.J.).

While a provincial offences appeal court has the power to grant an award of costs, such orders are not ordinarily granted. Although s. 34 of the *Provincial Offences Act* gives the prosecutor the ability to seek, and the court the power to grant, an amendment to an Information, an amendment to change the name of the defendant is not contemplated by this provision. Section 26 requires that a defendant must be named in and served with a summons setting out the charge against it. Section 54 provides that a defendant can be convicted *in absentia* where the prosecutor proves that the summons or notice of trial was served on the defendant. Amending the Information to change the name of the defendant in the absence of the defendant runs contrary to these provisions. At the very least, the prosecutor should have requested an adjournment of the trial to properly serve a summons or notice of trial on the defendant. In failing to do so, the prosecutor carelessly disregarded the procedural safeguards afforded to the defendant under the *Provincial Offences Act.* Section 129(a) grants the court discretion to make any order with respect to costs that it considers "just and reasonable". In this case the defendant was convicted without ever being issued a summons or served with a notice that it had ever been charged; it had no opportunity to argue at trial whether it should have been named as a defendant, or given an opportunity to defend the charge on its merits. In addition, through no fault of its own, it was required to retain counsel to bring the appeal and have the conviction quashed. In the unusual circumstances of the case, fairness demanded that the defendant be relieved of the financial burden of the costs of the appeal and application by being fully compensated. See *R. v. 1820419 Ontario Inc.*, 2013 ONCJ 10, 2013 CarswellOnt 275, [2013] O.J. No. 143 (Ont. C.J.).

The record established that the defendant had proper notice of the proceedings, as an earlier trial date was postponed by a friend on the basis of a non-specified medical note, to a date certain that was brought to the attention of the defendant. He not only had notice of his trial, but was afforded the opportunity to make representations to the court relating to the *ex parte* order, through the friend, in a recess granted to telephone him. This evidence supported the trial judge's exercise of her discretion to proceed on an *ex parte* basis. See *R. v. James*, 2013 NLTD(G) 65, 2013 CarswellNfld 172, 336 Nfld. & P.E.I.R. 355, 1043 A.P.R. 355, [2013] N.J. No. 158 (N.L. T.D.), leave to appeal refused 2014 NLCA 21, 2014 CarswellNfld 119, 347 Nfld. & P.E.I.R. 356, 1080 A.P.R. 356, [2014] N.J. No. 107 (N.L. C.A.).

In *R. v. Steinhoff*, 2013 ONCJ 401, 2013 CarswellOnt 10724, [2013] O.J. No. 3735 (Ont. C.J.), the defendant appeared in court five times to set a trial date for two charges laid under Part III of the *Provincial Offences Act*, including permitting the operation of a motor vehicle to be driven without insurance. On the fifth appearance, the trial was scheduled for six months later. However, the prosecutor informed the defendant that a motion would be brought for an adjournment due to the officer's unavailability. The defendant did not appear at the motion, and was not informed of the new trial date, which was brought forward, instead of being adjourned. The defendant was convicted at her *ex parte* trial. The trial as conducted was unsatisfactory in a number of respects: the lack of notice to the defendant of the trial date; the lack of opportunity to oppose a joint trial with a co-defendant, and the failure to hold a *voir dire* on the one piece of evidence that permitted the prosecutor to obtain a conviction in her absence, namely, her admission that she was the person named in the motor vehicle ownership.

The defendant's right to a fair trial was not infringed due to the Justice of the Peace in set date court endorsing the reverse side of the information charging the defendant with driving while suspended with "*Jenkins* caution given". The *Jenkins* caution arose to minimize the risk of miscarriage of justice through *ex parte* proceedings. In the absence of defendants, before proceeding *ex parte*, prosecutors were advised to carefully present their submissions, including their intent to seek a custodial sentence, as stated by the Ontario Court of Appeal in *R. v. Jenkins*, 2010 ONCA 278, 2010 CarswellOnt 2158, 99 O.R. (3d) 561, 253 C.C.C. (3d) 269, 74 C.R. (6th) 117, 93 M.V.R. (5th) 1, 212 C.R.R. (2d) 137, 260 O.A.C. 296, [2010] O.J. No. 1517 (Ont. C.A.), leave to appeal refused 2010 CarswellOnt 7405, 2010 CarswellOnt 7406, 258 C.C.C. (3d) iv (note), 225 C.R.R. (2d) 374 (note), 410 N.R. 395 (note), 279 O.A.C. 399 (note), [2010] S.C.C.A. No. 223 (S.C.C.). Such a procedure helps the court decide whether or not to proceed *ex parte* or issue a bench summons or warrant. The defendant was present through his paralegal when the prosecutor made the submissions regarding the *Jenkins* caution; the endorsement was made as a record of the prosecutor's obligation and to inform the trial judge in the event that the defendant did not appear in the future, which was a proactive and good faith measure. The decision in *Jenkins* did not hold that an endorsement was synonymous with prior convictions. A custodial sentence was also not solely dependent on prior convictions. The endorsement was therefore not prejudicial to the defendant, nor did it infringe his rights. See *R. v. St. John*, 2014 ONCJ 46, 2014 CarswellOnt 1368, 300 C.R.R. (2d) 335, [2014] O.J. No. 572 (Ont. C.J.).

In *R. v. Sarkozy*, 2014 ONCA 481, 2014 CarswellOnt 8357, [2014] O.J. No. 2964 (Ont. C.A.), there was conflicting evidence on almost every material aspect of the alleged communications between the accused and the paralegal she retained to assist her on the *Highway Traffic Act* charges she faced. At the end of the day, there was, at the very least, a misunderstanding that led both the accused and the paralegal to not attend the accused's trial. As a result, the trial proceeded *ex parte*, leading to the accused's convictions on both charges. The apparent unfairness at the trial proceeding was not cured by what occurred at the appeal hearing, which also proceeded in the accused's absence, and the accused has not had her day in court. In these circumstances, the interests of justice require that the accused's conviction be set aside and a new trial ordered to avoid a miscarriage of justice.

In *R. v. Kande*, 2015 ONCJ 131, 2015 CarswellOnt 3595, 76 M.V.R. (6th) 319, [2015] O.J. No. 1246 (Ont. C.J.), it was held that the test to be applied in a trial in absentia is very different from the test to be applied in an application for a non-suit. The test on an application for a non-suit is whether or not there is any evidence upon which a reasonable jury properly instructed could return a verdict of guilty. In answering this question, the presiding justice is not permitted to weigh or consider the quality of the evidence. He is simply to determine if there is "some" evidence upon which the jury "could" convict. That is very different from the test to be applied at the conclusion of a trial in absentia. A defendant who does not appear for his trial is still presumed to be innocent. In the *ex parte* proceedings, the prosecutor must prove the defendant's guilt beyond a reasonable doubt according to the generally applicable evidentiary and procedural rules.

In *R. v. Sahadeo*, 2016 ONCJ 122, 2016 CarswellOnt 3721, [2016] O.J. No. 1252 (Ont. C.J.), on the date his trial was scheduled to take place, the paralegal for the defendant appeared and requested an adjournment. When the request was refused, the paralegal advised the presiding justice that he was instructed not to participate in the proceedings any further. The paralegal then left the courtroom. Upon the defendant being paged with no response, a deemed not to dispute conviction was entered. The decision to grant or refuse the adjournment was discretionary, and will not be interfered with on appeal unless the discretion was not exercised judicially, or where it has resulted in a miscarriage of justice. In this case, the need for the adjournment for disclosure could easily have been obviated by the defendant far in advance of the trial. While the justice of the peace was correct to refuse the adjournment, a conviction should not have been imposed under s. 9.1 as it could not be said that the defendant had failed to appear at the time and place appointed for trial. He did appear by instructing an agent to attend, as permitted by s. 50; the provisions of s. 54(1) did not apply in this case. The defendant had appeared by agent, the prosecution was ready, and the trial should have proceeded. The fact that the defendant had instructed his agent to "walk away" did not mean that the agent had any right to do so. A paralegal, like counsel, can only withdraw with the leave of the court. The defendant demonstrated a complete lack of diligence by failing to ensure that he had the necessary disclosure. He ought to have either appeared personally or else sent a properly instructed agent. The agent, who appeared, had not been properly instructed and was initially unable to articulate the reason for which he was seeking an adjournment. The application itself was entirely without merit and should not have been brought; for his part, the agent should not have agreed to act for the defendant without proper instructions.

The defendant's request for an adjournment on the grounds that he wanted to retain new counsel was not reasonable in the particular circumstances of the case. It was consistent with his numerous prior requests for adjournments which resulted in the lengthy history of the case. A previous adjournment had been granted so that he could obtain new counsel upon informing the court that his counsel had been disbarred and therefore no longer able to represent him; subsequent adjournments were also granted, and the case had been marked peremptory. There had been a 9-month interval from the adjournment of the first trial date to the peremptory trial date. The defendant was completely familiar with the charges, and was well acquainted with the alleged deficiencies including what was required to rectify the deficiencies with respect to his property. When the defendant left the court to protest the refusal to grant the adjournment, an *ex parte* trial was held, after which the defendant was found guilty. Upon the defendant returning to court on the day of sentencing at which time he asked for the charges to be withdrawn, dismissed and the proceedings stayed, the court ruled that it was *functus* to do so, having registered a conviction in his absence. See *R. v. Melnyk*, 2016 ONCJ 331, 2016 CarswellOnt 8877, [2016] O.J. No. 2998 (Ont. C.J.).

In an *ex parte* trial for driving without insurance, the defendant appeared at court before the trial was completed, but indicated his attendance to the court only after he was found guilty and sentence was imposed. The justice of the peace informed the defendant that he was *functus officio* and there was nothing further he could do in the matter. In these circumstances, although the court accepted the justice's statement that he was *functus*, even if he was incorrect, there had been no miscarriage of justice as fresh evidence tendered on appeal by the Crown demonstrated that the defendant did not have valid insurance at the time of the offence, contrary to his assertion before the court. See *R. v. Simpson*, 2016 ONCA 212, 2016 CarswellOnt 3884, [2016] O.J. No. 1381 (Ont. C.A.).

Application of s. 54 of the *Provincial Offences Act* is not restricted to Part III prosecutions commenced by laying of information. Section 54 applies to all proceedings commenced under the Act, and it explicitly includes certificate proceedings commenced under Part I by way of notice of trial, which fit the defendant in the case at bar. Both ss. 9.1 and 54, however, only permit a conviction *in absentia* where the defendant does not "appear" for trial. The Act does not seem to contemplate a scenario where the defendant "appears" for trial by way of an agent who later withdraws after being denied an adjournment. This unfortunate practice is more prevalent in provincial offences courts than it should be and merits comment. The defence cannot by its conduct thwart the court's direction that a trial will proceed as scheduled. The defendant was placed on notice by no less than three justices of the peace that the trial would proceed in November; when the adjournment application was denied in October, the defence was expected to enter its plea on the trial date. In sending an agent without instructions to enter a guilty plea or to defend the trial, the defence by its conduct endeavoured to subvert the explicit direction of the court. Once the adjournment was denied, the defence ought to have been fixed with the expectation of arraignment. If there was any intention to defend the charge, the defence should have attended the second trial date prepared to do so. The learned justice did not err in conducting an *ex parte* trial under s. 54 in the circumstances. Section 54 affords the absent defendant an appropriate measure of procedural fairness. The prosecution is required to prove the defendant was notified or compelled to attend trial. Evidence must be led to satisfy the standard of proof. The procedure employed was fair and consistent with the due administration of justice. See *R. v. Wei*, 2017 ONCJ 878, 2017 CarswellOnt 20869, [2017] O.J. No. 6785 (Ont. C.J.).

In *R. v. Benson*, 2018 ONCJ 217, 2018 CarswellOnt 5234, [2018] O.J. No. 1748 (Ont. C.J.), the defendant's request for a second adjournment of his trial was denied, and he was told by the presiding justice of the peace that the matter was going to proceed that day. The matter was held down and the defendant left the courtroom. He never returned. When the case was called for trial, and no one appeared, the presiding justice of the peace entered a conviction pursuant to s. 9.1(2). Section 9.1 applies only to Part I matters. The authority to conduct an *ex parte* trial under s. 54 is contained in Part IV and applies in proceedings commenced under Parts I, II or III, but pursuant to s. 9.1(2), it does not apply if s. 9.1(1) does apply. In the instant case, the defendant took the steps to initiate the process and then attended twice, both times to request adjournments. The presiding justice of the peace called the case for trial. It was open to him to treat that precise moment as the time and place appointed for trial. At that time the defendant failed to appear. Despite his earlier appearances, it was open to the presiding justice of the peace to conclude that s. 9.1(1) was applicable. If that was so, it was not open to him to proceed with an *ex parte* trial. To rule otherwise would defeat both the purpose and substance of s. 9.1(1). It is clearly intended to reduce the number of trials and concentrate court resources on those cases where the defendant truly desires to have a trial. It should not be possible for someone to defeat this simply by making one appearance and then leaving the court or declining to participate further.

In *Mississauga (City) v. Sekhon*, 2018 ONCJ 306, 2018 CarswellOnt 7286, [2018] O.J. No. 2468 (Ont. C.J.), it was held that an *ex parte* trial is still a trial. It must be conducted fairly and must have the appearance of being conducted fairly, by an impartial judicial officer. Just because a defendant is not present does not mean a conviction is inevitable. The presumption of innocence still applies, as does the burden of proof beyond a reasonable doubt. In some ways, it is even more important for a justice to remain above the fray in an *ex parte* trial because nobody is there to speak for the defendant. Reading the justice's comments as a whole would lead a reasonably informed member of the public to conclude that the appellant's conviction was a foregone conclusion from the outset. A provincial offences court is the only interaction that most Ontarians will have with the Ontario Court of Justice. Proceedings in provincial offences courts are necessarily less formal than they are in criminal court. However, a court of record is not the place for a judicial officer to engage in sarcasm or self-aggrandizing humour. Nor is it meant to be used as a soapbox to express the judicial officer's personal views.

10.1.11 INCLUDED OFFENCES: SECTION 55

- An included offence is an additional offence to the main charge.

- If the included offence is proved, the defendant may be convicted although the whole offence charged is not proved.

In *R. v. Reiber*, 2007 ONCJ 343, 2007 CarswellOnt 4767, [2007] O.J. No. 2921, 53 M.V.R. (5th) 158 (Ont. C.J.), the court considered section 55 which sets out the concept of an included offence. It is necessary that all of the essential elements of the included offence be part of the original offence. To be an included offence, the accused would necessarily have to commit the included offence in the commission of the offence charged. In the case at bar, the offence of failing to stop for a red light can be committed without committing the offence of failing to stop for an amber light. The essential elements of the amber light offence are not included in the charge of the red light offence.

A lower speed indicated in the certificate of offence is a lesser and included offence of the higher speed. Where the evidence at trial disclosed that a defendant charged with speeding 76 kilometres per hour in a 50 kilometre zone was driving 86 kilometres per hour, the justice of the peace erred by failing to conclude that the speed set out in the certificate of offence was in fact an included offence on the evidence led at trial: *R. v. Mejia*, 2008 CarswellOnt 4439, [2008] O.J. No. 2893 (Ont. C.J.).

For an offence to be an included offence, the essential elements of the included offence must be contained within the original offence or in the count on the charging certificate or information. The count charging the defendant with careless driving made no reference to failing to stop for a red light. As such, the charging certificate did not inform the defendant of the possibility of having to defend herself against the red light charge, nor does the wording of the careless driving enactment in the *Highway Traffic Act* contain the essential elements of the failing to stop for red light offence: *R. v. Richards*, 2009 ONCJ 651, 2009 CarswellOnt 8597, [2009] O.J. No. 5776 (Ont. C.J.).

While the offence of racing under s. 172 of the *Highway Traffic Act* contemplates a more serious breach than simple speeding, it is premised on the fact that speed is an essential ingredient in the offence "race". It is therefore open to the court to register a conviction for speeding as an included offence on a count of racing, given that the element of speed had been proven beyond a reasonable doubt: *R. v. Benson*, 2009 ONCJ 566, 2009 CarswellOnt 7321, [2009] O.J. No. 4956 (Ont. C.J.).

While the defendant's conduct did not make out the offence of careless driving, a conviction was imposed for the lesser and included offence of failing to turn to the left to avoid a collision. Having applied the brakes, the defendant should have turned out either to the left or to the right depending on the situation to avoid the collision, but he did not do so: *R. v. Grzelak*, 2010 CarswellOnt 5483 (Ont. C.J.).

In *R. v. Stevens*, 2010 ONCJ 348, 2010 CarswellOnt 6177, [2010] O.J. No. 3576 (Ont. C.J.), it was held that the offence of speeding contrary to s. 128 of the *Highway Traffic Act* was an included offence of performing a stunt, contrary to s. 172(1) of the *Highway Traffic Act*. See also *R. v. Sanders*, 2009 ONCJ 646, 2009 CarswellOnt 8625, [2009] O.J. No. 5771 (Ont. C.J.) to the same effect.

An included offence is not just a lesser offence, but is one which the defendant necessarily commits in committing the offence with which he or she is charged. In other words, the essential elements of the included offence must be contained within the original offence charged. In the matter before the court, to be considered an included offence, the defendant would necessarily have to commit the included offence of fail to drive in marked lanes (s. 154(1) of the *Highway Traffic Act*) in the commission of the offence with which she was charged, namely, careless driving (s. 130). In light of the court's findings that her motor vehicle crossed over the markings separating the right lane from the left lane, and travelled into the left southbound lane where it sideswiped the victim's vehicle, the provisions of the s. 154(1) offence might reasonably be considered. However, on the facts before the court which included the rate of speed at which the vehicles were travelling, the heavy traffic on a major highway after 5:00 pm at the end of a long weekend, and the good road and weather conditions at the time, the defendant's conduct went beyond the offence of failing to drive in marked lanes, and should be considered as careless driving only. See *Durham (Regional Municipality) v. Wiland*, 2011 ONCJ 225, 2011 CarswellOnt 2844, [2011] O.J. No. 1959 (Ont. C.J.).

The offence of failing to surrender an insurance card is a lesser and included offence of the offence of operating a motor vehicle without insurance: *R. v. Salamon*, 2012 ONCA 176, 2012 CarswellOnt 3336, [2012] O.J. No. 1211 (Ont. C.A.).

It was not open to the court to convict the defendant of failing to stop for a red light on the basis that it is an included offence of careless driving where she was not informed on the charging certificate of any possibility of having to defend herself against a red light offence. See *Mississauga (City) v. Joynt*, 2012 CarswellOnt 8473, [2012] O.J. No. 3236 (Ont. C.J.).

Likewise, the offences of change lane not in safety and fail to drive in marked lane are not lesser and included offences of careless driving: *Greater Sudbury (City) v. McNeil*, 2012 ONCJ 157, 2012 CarswellOnt 3561, [2012] O.J. No. 1315 (Ont. C.J.).

Neither changing a lane not in safety nor a charge of failing to drive in a marked lane is a lesser and included offence of the offence of careless driving. The defendant had no way of knowing that she was facing the possibility of defending herself against either of these two alternative charges. The case proceeded by way of information, which could have been particularized but was not. There is therefore no recitation of particulars that could cover all the essential elements of another offence. While the defendant may well have committed the offence of starting from a stopped position not in safety or failing to yield to traffic on a through highway, and the court very likely would have convicted her of one of these offences, she was not so charged. The Court would not therefore find her guilty of either of these offences, or of the careless driving offence of which she was charged. See *R. v. Abdo*, 2015 ONCJ 44, [2015] O.J. No. 449 (Ont. C.J.).

Where the defendant was charged with speeding 105 km/hr in a posted 60 km/hr zone, it was open to the court to find the defendant guilty of the included offence of speeding 95 kilometres per hour in a posted 60 kilometres per hour zone where based on the totality of the evidence in the proceedings it was proven that the defendant drove her motor vehicle at a rate of speed in excess of the posted speed limit of 60 kilometres per hour, specifically that of 95 kilometres per hour. See *R. v. Abelarde*, 2018 ONCJ 349, 2018 CarswellOnt 8130, [2018] O.J. No. 2747 (Ont. C.J.).

In *R. v. Yilmaz*, 2018 CarswellOnt 14205, [2018] O.J. No. 4438 (Ont. C.J.), it was held the offence of driving with a handheld communication device is not an included offence of careless driving. Without the wording being specifically in the Act, it would be difficult and may very well provide prejudice to the accused in the event that it would be looked at as fundamental and fair to the accused when the charges were read or known.

10.1.12 EXCLUDING THE PUBLIC OR WITNESSES: SECTION 52(2)

- The court may exclude the public or any member of the public from the hearing where the court believes it is necessary to:
  - Maintain order in the courtroom;
  - Protect the reputation of a minor; or
  - Remove an influence that might affect the testimony of a witness.
- However, an order excluding the public, or a member of the public, from the courtroom is an exceptional order as courtrooms are generally open to the public.
- Request an "order excluding witnesses" pursuant to sub-section (c) after your client pleads and before the first witness is called, if you wish to bring out inconsistencies in the prosecution witnesses. If granted, all witnesses shall wait outside the courtroom until summoned to give evidence.
- You might seek an order to protect the defence witnesses. Without such an order, the justice could infer that, because your witnesses heard each other testify, their testimony ought to be given less weight.

10.1.13 PUBLICATION BANS

- In order to protect the reputation of a minor, the court may make an order prohibiting the publication or broadcast of:
  - The identity of the minor; or
  - The evidence or any part of the evidence taken at the hearing.
- The identity of a young person in connection with an offence cannot be published, with some exceptions: section 99.
- Consider the relationship between these sections and the *Charter* section 2(b) right of "freedom of the press and other media of communication".

10.2 EVIDENCE

- The Ontario *Evidence Act*, R.S.O. 1990, c. E.23 applies ("EA").

- Evidence is a complex area of law beyond the scope of this Guide. However, for ease of reference, the following are briefly highlighted: notice rules, documents, number of experts, hearsay, and credibility evidence.

10.2.1 NOTICES REQUIRED UNDER THE EA

- Below follow some examples of Notices required under EA:
  - Seven days notice for business records: EA, section 35(3).
  - Ten days notice for a medical report: EA, section 52(2).
  - Ten days notice for registered land documents: EA, section 53(3).
  - Ten days notice for original of telegram, letter, shipping bill, bill of lading, delivery order, receipt, account or other written instrument used in business or other transactions: EA, section 55(1).

10.2.2 DOCUMENTS

- The following are some examples of documentary rules under the EA:
  - Certified official records: POA, section 47(2).
  - Certified copies of official or public documents in Ontario or certified copies of a document, by-law, rule, regulation or proceeding, or of an entry in a register or other book of a corporation created by charter or statute in Ontario: EA, section 29.
  - Certified copies of public books or documents: EA, section 32.
  - Copies of governmental books and records made in the usual and ordinary course of business: EA, section 31.
  - Business records made in the usual and ordinary course of business: EA, section 35.

- Copies of bank records made in the usual and ordinary course of business: EA, section 33.

- Rules regarding access to bank records: EA, section 33(4).

- Copies of bills of exchange, promissory notes, receipts, instruments: EA, section 34.

- Rules regarding admissibility of electronic records: EA, section 34.1.

Documents that are not admissible in evidence and have not been accepted as exhibits should not be retained by the trial judge to determine what weight will be given to them: *R. v. 20207000 Ontario Inc.*, [2009] O.J. No. 838, 42 C.E.L.R. (3d) 129, 2009 CarswellOnt 1045, 2009 ONCJ 76 (Ont. C.J.).

In *R. v. Wong*, 2010 ONCJ 636, 2010 CarswellOnt 10221, [2010] O.J. No. 5810 (Ont. C.J.), it was held that the trial justice applied the proper rules of evidence in refusing to admit material that the defendant obtained from the Internet and other sources as to deficiencies on the balcony and parking garage, and the manner in which they should be repaired. Such evidence was not properly supported by calling an engineer or providing an engineer's report, which the prosecutor would then have an opportunity to receive and cross-examine.

The short form wording of "careless driving" contrary to the *Highway Traffic Act*, s. 130, on the Certificate of Offence, admitted as a certified statement under s. 48.1 of the *Provincial Offences Act*, cannot support a conviction for the careless driving offence. The words "careless driving" set out a generality but provide no specific actions or the circumstances for the court to assess, as to how the defendant drove "without due care and attention or without reasonable consideration for other persons using the highway." See *R. v. McPherson*, 2012 ONCJ 807, 2012 CarswellOnt 16971, [2012] O.J. No. 6286 (Ont. C.J.).

10.2.3 NUMBER OF EXPERTS

- No more than three expert witnesses can be called by either party without leave: EA, section 12.

10.2.4 HEARSAY

- Any written, oral or gestured statement by someone who is not testifying at trial to prove the truth of the statement is "hearsay" and generally inadmissible.

- The following are exceptions to the hearsay rule:

- An out-of-court admission by the defendant. It is hearsay, but admissible.

- The rationale for admitting admissions by a party without concern for the hearsay rule rests on the theory of the adversary system, and not a necessity/reliability analysis: *R. v. Osmar*, 2007 ONCA 50, [2007] O.J. No. 244, 2007 CarswellOnt 339, 220 O.A.C. 186, 150 C.R.R. (2d) 301, 84 O.R. (3d) 321, 217 C.C.C. (3d) 174, 44 C.R. (6th) 276 (Ont. C.A.) at para. 53 [ONCA], leave to appeal refused (2007), 2007 CarswellOnt 4187, 2007 CarswellOnt 4188, 156 C.R.R. (2d) 373 (note) (S.C.C.).

  - If the Crown tenders the statement of a defendant, it cannot pick and choose those parts of the statement that it would like the court to hear; it must take "the good with the bad," and both the "good" and the "bad" are admitted for their truth, for and against the defendant. Moreover, a party wishing to adduce a statement must put in as much of the statement as is necessary to permit a fair under-standing of the individual utterances: *R. v. Mallory*, 2007 ONCA 46, 2007 CarswellOnt 348, [2007] O.J. No. 236, 220 O.A.C. 239, 217 C.C.C. (3d) 266 (Ont. C.A.), at para. 203.

  - The documentary business records listed above. They are hearsay, but sufficiently reliable to be admissible.

  - There are other exceptions. You should carefully re-search the law in order to deliver persuasive objections to hearsay at trial.

- A hearsay statement may be admitted if it is necessary and reliable. "Necessity" may require that the proponent of the evidence made all reasonable efforts to secure the evidence of the declarant in a manner that also preserves the rights of the other party. "Reliability" may require it to be shown that there is no real concern as to whether the statement is true because of the circumstances in which the statement was made, or where concerns can be met through testing the truth and accuracy of the statements by methods that serve as appropriate substitutes for contemporaneous cross-examination: *R. v. Khelawon*, 2006 CarswellOnt 7825, 2006 CarswellOnt 7826, [2006] S.C.J. No. 57, 355 N.R. 267, 274 D.L.R. (4th) 385, 42 C.R. (6th) 1, 2006 SCC 57,

215 C.C.C. (3d) 161, 220 O.A.C. 338, [2006] 2 S.C.R. 787 (S.C.C.).

At an *ex parte* trial, the prosecutor must prove the defendant's guilt beyond a reasonable doubt according to generally applicable evidentiary rules. In order to prove that the defendant was not a registered builder and had not paid a prescribed fee, the prosecutor relied on the hearsay evidence of the investigator about a computer search he had conducted that the defendant had failed to pay the prescribed fee and was not a registered builder. However, the documents were admissible only if they met the best evidence rule, that "if an original document is available ... you must produce it. You cannot give secondary evidence by producing a copy." This rule applies in both criminal and civil proceedings, and prosecutions for provincial offences. The prosecutor did not explain the failure to produce the original documents the defendant had submitted, and there was no reason to think the original documents were unavailable; no evidence was called as to authenticating the copies that were filed. The investigator's evidence was inadmissible hearsay. It was akin to a traffic officer attempting to prove the suspension of a driver's licence by repeating in evidence what he saw on a police computer screen. See *R. v. Boros*, 2012 ONCJ 156, 2012 CarswellOnt 3709, [2012] O.J. No. 1297 (Ont. C.J.), affirmed 2013 ONCA 263, 2013 CarswellOnt 4834, [2013] O.J. No. 1904 (Ont. C.A.).

In *R. v. Metalore Resources Ltd.*, 2012 ONCJ 518, 2012 CarswellOnt 9744, 72 C.E.L.R. (3d) 52 (Ont. C.J.), the court ruled that the certificate of analysis and report of the analysis of soil and vegetation samples was admissible at trial for the truth of its contents as a business record under the authority of s. 35 of the *Ontario Evidence Act*, and as such an exception to the exclusionary hearsay evidence rule. The document in question constituted a record which was created by a business made on a regular basis. It did not contain any subjective information which might be interpreted in a variety of ways and therefore be considered to be unreliable, and it was made pursuant to a regular business duty associated with the operation of a chemical laboratory.

The evidence of a pamphlet given to a customer by the defendant outlining services provided by the defendant's company was not inadmissible hearsay. The prosecutor tendered the document not for the truth of its contents so as to prove that the vehicle actually needed a power steering flush, but rather to show that this was a service that was offered to the customer with respect to his vehicle. See *Vaughan (City) v. Antorisa Investments Ltd.*, 2012 CarswellOnt 11137, [2012] O.J. No. 3584 (Ont. C.J.), affirmed 2013 ONCA 287, 2013 CarswellOnt 5143, [2013] O.J. No. 1997 (Ont. C.A.).

Negative computer inquires that the accused failed to report a collision to the police does not constitute inadmissible hearsay evidence: *R. v. Saddleback*, 2012 ABQB 670, 2012 CarswellAlta 2037, 548 A.R. 307, 72 Alta. L.R. (5th) 302, [2012] A.J. No. 1184 (Alta. Q.B.), affirmed 2014 ABCA 166, 2014 CarswellAlta 785, 575 A.R. 203, 1 Alta. L.R. (6th) 259, 65 M.V.R. (6th) 189, 612 W.A.C. 203, [2014] A.J. No. 525 (Alta. C.A.).

In *R. v. Huxtable*, 2012 ONCJ 611, 2012 CarswellOnt 12396, [2012] O.J. No. 4583 (Ont. C.J.), it was held that the justice erred in law by accepting proof of ownership of the defendant's motor vehicle through the evidence of the police officer, as opposed to certified documents from the Ministry of Transportation showing that the defendant was the registered owner of the vehicle. While the purpose of the *Provincial Offences Act* is to provide a procedure for the prosecution of provincial offences that reflects the distinction between such offences and criminal offences, the jurisprudence is well settled that the same rules of evidence do apply. In both civil and criminal cases, the best evidence rule has historically been applied when a document is adduced as evidence for the truth of its contents. The rule simply stated is that a party must produce the best evidence that the nature of a case will allow. This means that if the original document is available, it should be produced. If the original has been destroyed or is otherwise unavailable, the contents of the document can be proved by using a copy or other secondary evidence. Photocopies are acceptable if the person who made the copies testifies that they are true copies.

The issue in the instant case, however, was not the identity of the driver, in which case production of a driver's licence constitutes an admission which is an exception to the hearsay rule and as such can be used as evidence of the truth of its contents, but rather the identity of the registered owner. The justice of the peace erred when he permitted this fact to be established through the investigating officer's evidence. Such evidence was hearsay and not admissible, and it was not the best evidence.

In *R. v. Correia*, 2013 ONCJ 562, 2013 CarswellOnt 14204, 25 C.C.L.I. (5th) 311, [2013] O.J. No. 4723 (Ont. C.J.), the prosecutor sought to adduce into evidence as business records materials in the file of an insurance underwriter at the defendant's trial for driving without insurance and knowingly using a false insurance card. However, as the prosecutor was unable to establish that the defendant had been given at least 7 days' notice of its intention to tender the records into evidence, as required by s. 35(2) of the *Ontario Evidence Act*, it argued that the business records were admissible under the statutory exception to the hearsay evidence rule codified in s. 35 of the statute. The court ruled that the admission of the business records, as *prima facie* hearsay in the proceeding, was necessary, and that the evidence may be characterized as meeting the standard of threshold reliability.

In *R. v. Williams*, 2013 NLTD(G) 103, 2013 CarswellNfld 323, 341 Nfld. &
P.E.I.R. 159, 1061 A.P.R. 159, [2013] N.J. No. 299 (N.L. T.D.), the trial judge was
held to have acted correctly when he rejected the issue the defendant raised about
the lateness of the Crown disclosure. The defendant did not relate the circumstances
in which he received the disclosure, which had been sent to him in advance of the
trial, and he may not have received it due to his own neglect. If the defendant felt he
did not have sufficient time to prepare for trial because he did not receive timely
disclosure, he should have brought it to the trial judge's attention when the matter
was called and asked him to adjourn the proceedings until he was ready to proceed.
The trial judge also acted correctly when he upheld the Crown's objection to the
documents that the defendant tried to produce when cross-examining the police
officer who stopped him for speeding. The Crown has a right to know what the
documents are before halfway through the proceedings so it could inform itself
about them, assess their relevance and address any concerns that it might have about
them. One of the overarching concerns for a trial judge and one of the main
purposes of rules of procedure is to ensure as far as reasonably possible that only
relevant evidence is admitted that is probative of the issues raised by the charges.
The trial judge achieved the object of the rules when he rejected the documents that
the defendant produced from the manufacturer about the calibration of the radar and
possibly the tuning forks, which were not served on the Crown with at least 7 days'
notice in compliance with s. 28 of the *Canada Evidence Act*.

The Justice of the Peace was alive to the nature of the evidence tendered at the
defendant's trial for using property zoned residential as a tourist establishment, and
was able to distinguish permissible hearsay from what was not. Although much of
what the neighbours said about their conversations with the persons who were
staying at the properties was hearsay, their observations of the coming and going of
people, as well as the time periods that they stayed, were not hearsay. Those
observations of what the neighbours saw was direct evidence upon which the trial
Justice could act. Whatever the many visitors to the property may have told the
neighbours about where they were from and what they were doing was hearsay, and
could not be used as proof of the essential elements of the offence charged.
However, this hearsay evidence could only provide context and narrative and
provide the grounds for belief by the neighbours that the property was being put to
illegal use. See *Kingston (City) v. Patry* (August 9, 2011), Doc. Kingston 090175,
090176, [2011] O.J. No. 6667 (Ont. C.J.).

In *R. v. Boukaras*, 2017 ONCJ 608, 2017 CarswellOnt 14000, [2017] O.J. No. 4275
(Ont. C.J.), it was held that the justice of the peace committed reversible legal error
in dismissing the charge because the officer had no independent recollection of the
events that brought the defendant to court. He failed to take into account the
evidentiary rule of past recollection recorded and dismissed the charge without
reason. The officer's notes, which were made an exhibit, were properly admitted

into evidence as record of his past recollection of the incident that brought the defendant to court. The notes were entered as a record of a past recollection and became evidence themselves as an exception to the hearsay rule, the four conditions for admissibility having been met, namely, (1) the past recollection must have been recorded in a reliable way; (2) the record must have been made or reviewed within a reasonable time; (3) at the time the witness testified he/she had no memory of the recorded events; and (4) the witness was able to say that he/she was being truthful at the time the assertions were recorded. Since the officer had no recollection of the events he had recorded, cross-examination might well have been more limited than if he had an independent recollection of the events and used his notes to refresh his memory. However, this was no reason to dismiss the charge.

10.2.5 CREDIBILITY EVIDENCE

- The credibility of a witness is affected by a number of factors, *including*:

    - Mental or physical disabilities affecting perception, or the capacity to tell the truth;

    - Bias or partiality towards the case;

    - Inconsistent statements relevant to the case: EA, sections 20, 21;

    - Criminal record; and

    - Discreditable acts or associations.

- All five factors, if the relevance outweighs the prejudice, can be put to a prosecution witness in cross-examination.

- If the witness denies the suggestion in cross-examination, the first four factors can be proved by calling evidence. The final factor is collateral to the central issue of the guilt of the defendant and so the questioner is stuck with the witness' answer. (See: Sopinka, Lederman and Bryant, *The Law of Evidence in Canada*, Second Edition (Butterworths, 1999), at 963-969.)

- If the witness denies a criminal record, you can prove it under section 22 of the EA and section 57(4) of the POA.

- The prosecutor cannot call evidence or suggest that the defendant is the kind of person to commit the offence, unless the defendant first puts into issue his or her good character.

- The court will consider the issue of credibility by asking itself the following three questions:

- First, if you believe the evidence of the accused, you must acquit.

- Second, if you do not believe the testimony of the accused but you are left in reasonable doubt by it, you must acquit.

- Third, even if you are not left in doubt by the evidence of the accused, you must ask yourself whether, on the basis of the evidence you do accept, you are convinced beyond a reasonable doubt by that evidence of the guilt of the accused.

See *R. v. W. (D.)*, [1991] 1 S.C.R. 742, 63 C.C.C. (3d) 397, EYB 1991-67602, 1991 CarswellOnt 80, 1991 CarswellOnt 1015, [1991] S.C.J. No. 26, 3 C.R. (4th) 302, 122 N.R. 277, 46 O.A.C. 352 (S.C.C.).

The trial judge is not obliged to adopt any particular structure in fashioning his/her reasons or a specific order in reviewing the evidence adduced at trial. Neither is the judge required to articulate the *R. v. W.D.* principles at each stage of his/her analysis of the evidence. The jurisprudence of the Supreme Court of Canada confirms that the steps identified in *W.D.* need not be religiously followed or articulated. What is required is that the trier of fact remains focused on the paramount question, namely, whether on the whole of the evidence, the trier of fact is left with a reasonable doubt about the guilt of the accused: *R. v. S. (M.)*, 2008 CarswellOnt 5225, [2008] O.J. No. 3465, 240 O.A.C. 229, 2008 ONCA 616, 237 C.C.C. (3d) 85 (Ont. C.A.).

The failure of a trial judge to sufficiently articulate how credibility concerns were resolved in the reasons for judgment may constitute a reversible error: *R. c. Dinardo*, EYB 2008-133045, 2008 CarswellQue 3451, 2008 CarswellQue 3452, [2008] S.C.J. No. 24, 374 N.R. 198, 57 C.R. (6th) 48, 293 D.L.R. (4th) 375, 231 C.C.C. (3d) 177, 2008 SCC 24, [2008] 1 S.C.R. 788 (S.C.C.).

A trial judge is not required to refer to every piece of evidence led at trial: *R. v. Haller*, 2008 CarswellOnt 3778, 2008 ONCA 517, 61 M.V.R. (5th) 189 (Ont. C.A.), at para. 2 [ONCA].

The appellate court is not given the power to intervene simply because it thinks the trial court did a poor job of expressing itself. Reasons are sufficient if they are responsive to the case's live issues and the parties' key arguments: *R. v. Walker*, 2008 CarswellSask 347, 2008 CarswellSask 348, [2008] S.C.J. No. 34, [2008] 6 W.W.R. 1, 2008 SCC 34, 375 N.R. 228, 57 C.R. (6th) 212, [2008] 2 S.C.R. 245,

310 Sask. R. 305, 423 W.A.C. 305, 294 D.L.R. (4th) 106, 231 C.C.C. (3d) 289 (S.C.C.), at para. 20 [SCC].

The purpose of adhering to the procedure set out in the *W.D.* case is to foreclose an inadvertent shifting of the burden of proof where the complainant and the accused have both testified, and the trial turns on their credibility as witnesses: *R. v. Y. (C.L.)*, [2008] S.C.J. No. 2, 2008 CarswellMan 19, 2008 CarswellMan 20, [2008] 2 W.W.R. 1, 225 Man. R. (2d) 146, 419 W.A.C. 146, [2008] 1 S.C.R. 5, 227 C.C.C. (3d) 129, 53 C.R. (6th) 207, 2008 SCC 2, 370 N.R. 284, 289 D.L.R. (4th) 1 (S.C.C.).

While demeanour is a relevant factor in a credibility assessment, demeanour alone is a notoriously unreliable predictor of the accuracy of evidence given by a witness: *Law Society of Upper Canada v. Neinstein*, 2010 CarswellOnt 1459, 2010 ONCA 193, [2010] O.J. No. 1046, 99 O.R. (3d) 1, 317 D.L.R. (4th) 419, 1 Admin. L.R. (5th) 1, 259 O.A.C. 313 (Ont. C.A.).

10.2.6 CHALLENGING AN OFFICER'S EVIDENCE: PART I AND II OFFENCES

- For Part I offences proceeded by way of a notice of offence and for Part II parking infraction offences, if the defendant intends to challenge an officer's testimony, it must be indicated in the notice sent to the court.

- If so indicated, then the clerk of the court will notify the officer to attend trial.

  - For Part I offences, see section 5.2 and on a reopening, section 11(3-4).

  - For Part II offences, see sections 18.1.2, 19(3).

- This rule does not apply to Part III trials and Part I offences where the defendant is summoned.

The prosecutor is entitled to establish the identity of the defendant by relying on statements in a certificate of offence and certificate of service of summons or offence notice, pursuant to s. 48.1. Subsection 48.1(2) does not state that certificate evidence is inadmissible if the charge is disputed; it is only inadmissible if the defendant has given notice of intention to dispute the evidence of the officer. There is nothing in the *Provincial Offences Act* that prohibits the use of the certificate of offence as evidence just because the defendant chooses to be defended and appears by agent. See *Guelph (City) v. Louws*, 2013 ONSC 7903, 2013 CarswellOnt 17958, [2013] O.J. No. 5861 (Ont. S.C.J.).

The Justice of the Peace should have asked the defendant whether he had any questions of the officer or submissions to make as to the police officer's notes when the officer asked to use his notes to refresh his memory. The defendant did cross-examine the officer on numerous points, but did not assert that there were any discrepancies between the officer's testimony at trial and the notes disclosed to the defence. The failure to ask the defendant whether he wished to ask questions at that point, or make submissions, did not impact trial fairness as the prosecution provided a proper foundation for the police officer to refer to the notes. See *R. v. Zuccarini*, 2014 ONCJ 571, 2014 CarswellOnt 15457, [2014] O.J. No. 5234 (Ont. C.J.).

One of the important steps in any process is the right to make submissions. Where that was not afforded to the defendant's legal representative, a new trial must be ordered: *R. v. Al-Kerwi*, 2015 CarswellOnt 2299, [2015] O.J. No. 769 (Ont. C.J.).

In *York (Regional Municipality) v. Wong*, 2016 ONCJ 370, 2016 CarswellOnt 9854, [2016] O.J. No. 3314 (Ont. C.J.), at the defendant's trial for disobeying a stop sign, neither the prosecution nor the defence chose to play the audio portion of the in-car video. The defence chose not to call evidence at trial as was its right. However, utterances by the defendant that were captured by the audio portion were not evidence, even if their meaning could be ascertained. If the defendant wished to call evidence on this point he could have done so, and that evidence would have been subject to cross-examination so that the court could determine the appropriate weight to give the evidence. Failure to hear non-evidence not called by either party cannot amount to an error. The officer's evidence was straightforward and detailed. It was supported by the in-car video.

10.2.7 COMPELLABILITY OF THE DEFENDANT

- Section 46(5) of the POA and section 11(c) of the *Charter* protect the defendant from being compelled to testify.

10.2.8 PROVING AN EXCEPTION: SECTION 47(3)

- The burden of proving that an authorization, exception, exemption or qualification prescribed by law operates in favour of the defendant is on the defendant, and the prosecutor is not required, except by way of rebuttal, to prove that the authorization, exception or qualification does not operate in favour of the defendant, whether or not it is set out in the information.

- This section places a persuasive burden on the defendant to prove, on a balance of probabilities, that an authorization, exception, exemption or qualification absolves him or her of guilt.

- Arguably, in some circumstances, the defendant must prove his or her innocence, which is contrary to the *Charter* section 11(d) right "to be presumed innocent until proven guilty".

- Supreme Court of Canada and Court of Appeal for Ontario decisions have distinguished between essential and collateral elements of an offence.

  - Some authorities have held that *all* elements of an offence, both essential and collateral, must be proven by the prosecution: see *R. v. Holmes*, 41 C.C.C. (3d) 497, 64 C.R. (3d) 97, [1988] 1 S.C.R. 914, 65 O.R. (2d) 639 (S.C.C.) per Dickson J. for the minority; *R. v. Whyte*, 6 M.V.R. (2d) 138, [1988] 2 S.C.R. 3, [1988] 5 W.W.R. 26, 29 B.C.L.R. (2d) 273, 64 C.R. (3d) 123, 42 C.C.C. (3d) 97 (S.C.C.); *R. v. Schwartz* (1988), 45 C.C.C. (3d) 97, [1989] 1 W.W.R. 289, [1988] 2 S.C.R. 443, 66 C.R. (3d) 251 (S.C.C.) per the minority.

- The better authority, it seems, is that only the essential elements of the offence must be proven by the prosecution, and that it *is* constitutional to require the defendant to prove an exemption on the balance of probabilities: see *Holmes, supra*, per McIntyre J. for the majority; *Schwartz, supra*, per the majority; *R. v. Lee's Poultry Ltd.* (1985), 17 C.C.C. (3d) 539, 43 C.R. (3d) 289 (Ont. C.A.); *Proulx v. Krukowski* (1993), 109 D.L.R. (4th) 606 (C.A.); *Halton Regional Municipality v. Stainton* (1991), 2 O.R. (3d) 170 (Prov. Div.), affirmed (1992), 7 O.R. (3d) 203 (note) (Ont. Prov. Div.).

In a case where the defendants were charged with harvesting timber without a forest resource licence in an area where the defendants held mining claims, the trial court reversed the onus by stating that the Crown had failed to prove that both the defendants did not have an exemption under the *Mining Act* when that onus was on the defendants. The onus was on the defendants to establish an exemption pursuant to s. 47(3) of the *Provincial Offences Act*: *R. v. Wetelainen*, 2008 ONCJ 553, 2008 CarswellOnt 6495, [2008] O.J. No. 4392 (Ont. C.J.).

Although the defendant operated his tractor trailer in a prohibited lane of traffic for a short period of time, the defendant proved, on a balance of probabilities as required by s. 47(3), that he came within the emergency exemption in the regulation. It was established that he had to react quickly to prevent an accident from occurring when the driver of the car he was following suddenly slammed on his brakes. By moving into the prohibited lane of traffic, the defendant avoided a likely accident: *R. v. Gill*, [2009] O.J. No. 1082, 2009 ONCJ 105, 2009 CarswellOnt 1463 (Ont. C.J.).

The evidence was that the defendant company permitted the driver, who was the holder of a Class G licence, to operate a Class F commercial motor vehicle. Pursuant to s. 47(3), the defendant failed to prove that the exception allowing a Class G licence holder to use such a bus for personal purposes without compensation applied. Neither had the defendant provided evidence that anyone had taken steps to ensure that the bus would only be used for such purposes: *Ontario (Ministry of Transportation) v. 457784 Ontario Ltd.*, 83 M.V.R. (5th) 280, 2009 ONCJ 141, 2009 CarswellOnt 1793 (Ont. C.J.).

The onus is on the defendant under s. 47(3) to establish that an appeal has been filed of a property standards order, in a prosecution for failing to comply with such an order. The filing of an appeal constitutes an exception, exemption or qualification prescribed by law which operates in favour of the defendant; there is no burden on the Crown to prove that an appeal has not been filed. See *Ajax (Town) v. Wong*, 2011 ONCJ 352, 2011 CarswellOnt 6315, [2011] O.J. No. 3167 (Ont. C.J.).

In *R. v. Bray*, 2010 ONCJ 98, 2010 CarswellOnt 1706, [2010] O.J. No. 1310 (Ont. C.J.), it was held that the defendant failed to discharge his legal burden of proof under s. 47(3) that his actions in using a "number" plate upon a vehicle other than a "number" plate authorized for use on that vehicle had not been shown to be justified through the operation of the statutory exemption to liability set out in the *Highway Traffic Act*. The transfer application had not been completed and signed by both the persons named in the vehicle portion and the new owner.

Once the prosecution proved that the defendant did not have a G.T.A.A. licence to pick up passengers for hire at Pearson Airport and that he had been banned under the *Trespass to Property Act* by the G.T.A.A. from entering Pearson Airport, the defendant would only be left with two legal ways to enter or be at Pearson Airport. First, in his personal capacity as a traveller, and second, in his capacity as a taxicab driver who had been dropping off a passenger. These two conditions were not essential averments or elements that have to be proven by the prosecution, but were exemptions to the prohibited act set out under s. 2(1)(a) of the *Trespass to Property Act* that had been expressly given to the defendant by the G.T.A.A., which allowed the defendant to be at Pearson Airport despite the non-entry prohibition. Therefore, the prosecution would only need to prove that the defendant did not have a G.T.A.A. licence or permit and that the defendant had been notified and prohibited under the Act from entering Pearson Airport, and that this prohibition had still been in effect on the offence date, and does not need to negative the traveller or employment exemptions to prove beyond a reasonable doubt that the defendant had not been acting under a right or authority conferred by law to be at Pearson Airport, since the onus had been put on the defendant under s. 2(1)(a) of the *Trespass to Property Act* and under s. 47(3) of the *Provincial Offences Act* to prove that he had the express permission from the G.T.A.A. to be at Pearson Airport on the day in question, which could only be done by the defendant proving that he was at the airport in his personal capacity as a traveller or in his capacity as a taxicab driver dropping off a passenger. See *R. v. Shaikh*, 2013 ONCJ 33, 2013 CarswellOnt 1071, [2013] O.J. No. 457 (Ont. C.J.).

In *R. v. Miller*, 2014 ONCJ 782, 2014 CarswellOnt 18997, [2014] O.J. No. 4805 (Ont. C.J.), a *prima facie* case was presented by the Crown which established that the defendant's vehicle was operated by a person who was unable to produce valid proof of insurance. There was no evidence that raised the possibility that the driver was in possession of the vehicle without permission. Insurance was the responsibility of the defendant; any particulars of insurance or permissions regarding the vehicle were within his knowledge. No defence was presented in the case. The Justice of the Peace made the correct findings and decision. The defendant's confusion as to the trial date was not a valid ground to grant the appeal.

In a prosecution for the offence of insecure load-commercial motor vehicle, pursuant to s. 47(3), the onus of proving that the commercial motor vehicle weighed 4,5000 kilograms or less was on the defendant. Even before being enacted in the *Provincial Offences Act*, under the common law, the onus of proving an exception or exemption such as this was upon the defendant. See *R. v. Little*, 2015 ONCJ 52, 2015 CarswellOnt 1583, 74 M.V.R. (6th) 162, [2015] O.J. No. 521 (Ont. C.J.).

The Justice of the Peace did not err in relying on the requirement that the defendant establish any exemption that operates in his favour under s. 47(3) of the *Provincial Offences Act*, in this case if the private school was subject to the *Education Act* it was exempt from the provisions of the *Ontario Fire Code*. If the private school in question had indeed submitted a notice of intention to operate as a private school under s. 16 of the *Education Act*, it would have been a relatively straightforward exercise to establish this fact. See *Oshawa (City) v. 1064145 Ontario Ltd.*, 2015 ONCJ 819, 2015 CarswellOnt 20893, [2015] O.J. No. 1333 (Ont. C.J.).

In *R. v. Charlebois*, 2015 CarswellOnt 7802, [2015] O.J. No. 2805 (Ont. C.J.), it was held that there is an exemption from the prohibition of holding or using a hand-held communication device that the defendant must prove on a balance of probabilities pursuant to s. 47(3). According to the regulation, the exemption is where the device is placed securely in or mounted to the motor vehicle so that it does not move while the vehicle is in motion and the driver can see it at a quick glance and can easily reach it without adjusting his or her driving position. However the defendant failed to prove this exemption, given that the Bluetooth device was not placed securely, nor was it mounted to the motor vehicle so that it did not move when the vehicle was in motion. Instead, the device had fallen from the visor and the defendant picked it up, held it and pressed buttons until the language she was searching for was established. This is the type of distraction that the legislation is attempting to prohibit.

The defendant failed to prove, on a balance of probabilities, that her motor vehicle was insured under a contract of automobile insurance. She therefore failed to establish that the statutory exception, exemption or qualification to liability for the offence of owner/operator of a motor vehicle on a highway without insurance, contrary to the *Compulsory Automobile Insurance Act*, operated in her favour. See *R. v. Correia*, 2015 ONCJ 276, 2015 CarswellOnt 7735, 49 C.C.L.I. (5th) 300, [2015] O.J. No. 2705 (Ont. C.J.).

In *Oshawa (City) v. Le*, 2015 ONCJ 544, 2015 CarswellOnt 15160, [2015] O.J. No. 5180 (Ont. C.J.), it was held that there was no basis for the defendant's submissions that the fortification by-law could only be implemented on public properties, and not private ones. The provision in question expressed the application of the by-law to all land within the City, unless it is expressly exempted by legislation. Under s. 47(3) of the *Provincial Offences Act*, the onus is on the defendant to prove an exemption prescribed by law. There was no authorization, exception, exemption or qualification that afforded the defendants under the by-law in question, or anywhere else prescribed by law. Hence, the defendant's property was subject to the fortification by-law.

A motor vehicle driven on a highway is required to have a currently validated permit. Under s. 47(3), the burden is on the defendant to prove any exemption prescribed by law that may work in its favour. Since the impugned motor vehicle was not a "road building machine" as it did not have its ploughs attached and the defendant testified that it was not such a vehicle, it was a motor vehicle under the definition of the *Highway Traffic Act*. Hence it was not exempt from requiring a currently validated permit. However, the vehicle did have a salter attached, which is a piece of snow clearing equipment. The vehicle was thus within the realm of one which "is equipped with a snow clearing device" and intended to be captured by the exemption to weight contained in the Act. See *Durham (Regional Municipality) v. D. Crupi & Sons Ltd.*, 2015 ONCJ 488, 2015 CarswellOnt 15126, [2015] O.J. No. 4872 (Ont. C.J.).

In *Sault Ste. Marie (City) v. Powley*, 2015 ONCJ 712, 2015 CarswellOnt 19219, 128 O.R. (3d) 390, 92 M.V.R. (6th) 53, [2015] O.J. No. 6640 (Ont. C.J.), it was held that a medical note from a doctor stating that the defendant was unable to wear a seat belt assembly because of his size does not need to set an expiry date, and thus constitutes a medical exemption from wearing a seat belt. Pursuant to s. 47(3) of the *Provincial Offences Act*, the onus is on the defendant to establish an exemption, on a balance of probabilities. As the defendant had established that he met the requirements of the exemption under s. 106(6)(b)(ii) of the *Highway Traffic Act*, the charge was dismissed.

The driver or operator of a motor vehicle on an Ontario highway is required to have in the motor vehicle at all times an insurance card for the motor vehicle or an insurance card evidencing that the operator is insured under a contract of automobile insurance, and to surrender the insurance card to a police officer for reasonable inspection when a demand is made by that police officer to produce that insurance card to the police officer. Section 47(3) provides that the burden of proving that an authorization, exception, exemption or qualification prescribed by law operates in favour of the defendant is on the defendant. The burden was therefore on the defendant, as the owner of the motor vehicle, to prove that his vehicle had been properly insured while the vehicle had been driven on an Ontario highway, as required by s. 3(1) of the *Compulsory Automobile Insurance Act*, in conjunction with the requirement under s. 47(3) that an authorization, exception, exemption or qualification prescribed by law operates in favour of the defendant. As no evidence was presented by the defendant, as the registered owner of the vehicle, of valid insurance for the vehicle at the time the defendant had been operating the vehicle, the prosecution had met its burden of proving that the defendant committed the offence of owner operating a motor vehicle on a highway without insurance. See *Ontario v. Bharath*, 2016 ONCJ 382, 2016 CarswellOnt 10190, [2016] O.J. No. 3416 (Ont. C.J.).

In *R. v. Singh*, 2016 ONCJ 618, 2016 CarswellOnt 16336, 3 M.V.R. (7th) 124, [2016] O.J. No. 5382 (Ont. C.J.), it was held that in their context, the trial justice's comments regarding the lack of defence evidence that the defendant had only driven within a 16-kilometre radius on the day of the accident did not amount to a shifting of the onus of proof, but merely reflected that the onus was on the defendant to establish, on a balance of probabilities, that the regulatory exception under the *Highway Traffic Act* respecting the maintenance of daily log by commercial drivers applied.

In *Niagara (Reg. Mun.) v. Busch*, 2017 ONCJ 547, 2017 CarswellOnt 12346, (*sub nom.* R. v. Busch) 394 C.R.R. (2d) 147, [2017] O.J. No. 4166 (Ont. C.J.), the defendant's pick-up truck was held to fall within the definition of a motor vehicle, and he had not met his onus by proving that his truck attracted the self-propelled implement of husbandry exception. As such, his pick-up truck required a valid vehicle permit, insurance and that he wear his seatbelt when driving it on a highway.

In *R. v. Colaco*, 2018 ONCJ 595, 2018 CarswellOnt 14686, [2018] O.J. No. 4524 (Ont. C.J.), it was held that the defendant had proven on a balance of probabilities that at the material time, she was driving a motor vehicle on a highway, being a highway with a median strip. She was therefore exempt from liability for the subject offence of failing to stop for school bus — meeting, as the presence of a median strip separating traffic travelling in opposite directions on a highway permits drivers to pass a stopped school bus with its red signal lights flashing, which they meet on the highway. Once it is shown that the exemption operates in favour of a defendant, the offence becomes beyond the reach of an accused.

10.2.9 COMMISSION EVIDENCE: SECTION 43

- Upon motion by the defendant or prosecutor, a judge may order a commissioner to take evidence from a witness who:

  - Is outside of Ontario; or

  - Is unlikely to be able to attend trial because of an illness, physical disability, or other good cause.

10.2.10 UNREASONABLE SEARCH AND SEIZURE AND INSPECTIONS

- A justice may issue search warrants on reasonable grounds: section 158. *Section 159 refers to the detention of things seized, and section 160 deals with the seizure of privileged documents.*

- Other provincial Acts provide for "inspections" *without* any evidence of wrong-doing.

- Courts have held that some regulated activities have lower expectations of privacy. *For example, a corporation might reasonably expect a government auditor to periodically review its business records for compliance with the regulations without any suspicion of wrong-doing.* See *Comité paritaire de l'industrie de la chemise c. Sélection Milton*, 4 C.C.E.L. (2d) 214, (*sub nom.* R. v. Potash) 91 C.C.C. (3d) 315, (*sub nom.* Comité paritaire de l'industrie de la chemise c. Potash) [1994] 2 R.C.S. 406 (S.C.C.); *Canada Inc. c. Québec (Procureur général)*, (*sub nom.* Québec (Sousministre du Revenue) c. 143471 Canada Inc.) 31 C.R. (4th) 120, 90 C.C.C. (3d) 1, [1994] 2 S.C.R. 339 (S.C.C.);

Johnson v. Ontario (Minister of Revenue) (1990), 25 M.V.R. (2d) 78, 75 O.R. (2d) 558, 1 C.R.R. (2d) 293 (Ont. C.A.); *R. v. Wholesale Travel Group Inc.,* 67 C.C.C. (3d) 193, 8 C.R. (4th) 145, [1991] 3 S.C.R. 154, 4 O.R. (3d) 799 (note) (S.C.C.).

- If, however, the predominant purpose of a regulatory inquiry is the determination of penal liability, the state is engaged in an adversarial relationship, and the subject of the inquiry must be provided with his or her *Charter* rights: *R. v. Jarvis* (2002), 169 C.C.C. (3d) 1, REJB 2002-35624, 2002 CarswellAlta 1440, 2002 CarswellAlta 1441, [2002] S.C.J. No. 76, [2002] 3 S.C.R. 757, 2002 SCC 73, 2002 D.T.C. 7547, [2003] 1 C.T.C. 135, 6 C.R. (6th) 23, 219 D.L.R. (4th) 233, 295 N.R. 201, [2003] 3 W.W.R. 197, 8 Alta. L.R. (4th) 1, 317 A.R. 1, 284 W.A.C. 1, 101 C.R.R. (2d) 35 (S.C.C.).

Section 8 of the *Charter* guarantees that: "Everyone has the right to be secure against *unreasonable* search or seizure [emphasis added]". Section 24(2) of the *Charter* requires the exclusion of evidence obtained in breach of section 8, if it is established (by the defence on a balance of probabilities) that, having regard to all the circumstances, the admission of the evidence would bring the administration of justice into disrepute.

- The law of search and seizure is complex and should be carefully researched before trial.

- Carefully review the powers of inspection and any legal duties on your client to co-operate with the authorities.

Where the inspector under the *Truck Transportation Act* did not have the authority to direct the defendant's truck to follow him as he had no reasonable grounds to believe that an offence had been committed, the evidence of excessive weight was excluded, and the defendant was acquitted. See *R. v. B. Gottardo Construction Ltd.,* [2004] O.J. No. 2139, 2004 CarswellOnt 2092, 7 M.V.R. (5th) 186, 2004 ONCJ 56 (Ont. C.J.).

- Commercial vehicles operating in a highly controlled industry have a reduced expectation of privacy compared to a private vehicle; therefore, the expectation of privacy in the cargo hold of a commercial vehicle, partially exposed to plain view, is marginal: *R. v. Busat,* 2006 CarswellSask 28, [2006] S.J. No. 42, 33 M.V.R. (5th) 51, 274 Sask. R. 1, 2006 SKQB 36 (Sask. Q.B.), CRWN/2006-038.

- Where a motorist refuses to produce his driver's licence, a police officer is only entitled to arrest without a warrant under section 217 of the *Highway Traffic Act* if the motorist has refused to give other reasonable identification. The officer must make a specific request for identification other than a driver's licence: *R. v. Plummer* (2006), [2006] O.J. No. 4530, 2006 CarswellOnt 7056, 38 M.V.R. (5th) 187, 214 C.C.C. (3d) 84, 217 O.A.C. 201, 45 C.R. (6th) 3, 83 O.R. (3d) 528 (Ont. C.A.).

- A stop based on preventative policing as opposed to another purpose, such as checking for sobriety or documentation pursuant to the *Highway Traffic Act*, violates section 9 of the *Charter*: *R. v. Houben* (2006), 2006 CarswellSask 746, [2007] 2 W.W.R. 195, 39 M.V.R. (5th) 84, 2006 SKCA 129, 214 C.C.C. (3d) 519, [2006] S.J. No. 715, 382 W.A.C. 118, 149 C.R.R. (2d) 244, 44 C.R. (6th) 338, 289 Sask. R. 118 (Sask. C.A.).

The amended search warrant provisions under s. 158.1 of the *Provincial Offences Act* have been proclaimed into force and came into effect on 30 June 2008. These new provisions allow for warrants to be issued by fax by designated justices of the peace, and for a report to be made rather than bringing the actual items seized before a justice.

Tax investigation of criminal activity does not raise *Charter* rights, if the predominant purpose of the investigation is regulatory compliance: *R. v. Tiffin*, [2008] O.J. No. 1525, 2008 CarswellOnt 2424, 57 C.R. (6th) 123, 170 C.R.R. (2d) 151, 235 O.A.C. 52, [2008] 5 C.T.C. 77, 90 O.R. (3d) 575, 232 C.C.C. (3d) 303, 2008 ONCA 306 (Ont. C.A.), affirmed [2008] S.C.C.A. No. 236, 2008 CarswellOnt 7869, 2008 CarswellOnt 7870, 236 C.C.C. (3d) 1 (S.C.C.).

There is a limited expectation of privacy for business records in a regulatory investigation: *Taplin v. Alberta (Securities Commission)*, 2008 CarswellAlta 337, [2008] A.J. No. 286, 442 A.R. 248, 2008 ABQB 173 (Alta. Q.B.).

Evidence was excluded where the police properly stopped a vehicle pursuant to the *Highway Traffic Act*, R.S.O. 1990, c. H.8, but then asked the accused passenger for his identification and ran his name through CPIC. The nature of the detention changed when the police asked the accused for his identification, as they had begun an investigation unrelated to the traffic stop. The accused was being detained by the police and felt compelled to provide his identification. Due to the information available on CPIC, asking for the accused's identification was equivalent to asking him a series of questions regarding his criminal past, his bail status, and any bail conditions by which he was bound: *R. v. Gray*, 2009 CarswellOnt 165, 2009 ONCJ 5, 184 C.R.R. (2d) 347 (Ont. C.J.), at paras. 38, 44-47 [ONCJ].

Although the defendant argued that the search warrant authorized the search of certain buildings and a bus, none of which was actually at the address authorized to be searched under the warrant, both addresses formed part of the farm which was owned and operated by the defendant. Both the defendant's actual residential address and the location at which the search and seizure were conducted were part of the defendant's farm. The alleged error was a mere technicality which had no bearing whatsoever on the validity of the warrant, the search or the seizure. The evidence which was obtained pursuant to the execution of the search warrant was therefore not obtained in a manner that infringed or denied any rights or freedoms guaranteed by the *Charter*: *R. v. Schmidt*, [2009] O.J. No. 605, 2009 CarswellOnt 754, 2009 ONCJ 33 (Ont. C.J.).

In *Mississauga (City) v. Osman*, 2010 ONCJ 495, 2010 CarswellOnt 8224, [2010] O.J. No. 4618 (Ont. C.J.), a case where the defendant defended himself, it was held that while there was no formal *Charter* application before the court, the unrepresented defendant was appearing in a regulatory court, not a criminal court, and had asked the court to consider the legality of the issue. Since the officer admitted to the search and the nature of the stop and time frame, the court could reasonably infer that the search was indeed warrantless. Given the reason for the stop, and in the absence of any suspicion or evidence on the part of the officer that the defendant was committing a criminal offence, and absent reasonable and probable grounds, the search was not proper in the circumstances. The evidence resulting from the search of phone records was not useable in the trial of the defendant for driving while using a hand-held wireless communication device.

The trial judge properly applied the test in *Jarvis* in finding that a routine tax audit did not have as its predominant purpose a criminal investigation which would then engage the obligation of the Canada Revenue Agency to make the defendant aware of his *Charter* rights. The auditor was properly engaged in information gathering; the "to and fro" between the auditor and the defendant did not establish that the auditor was seeking to make out a case for fraud, but rather she was attempting to determine what the actual income tax numbers were in accordance with her obligations in the course of a civil audit under the *Income Tax Act*. Upon it becoming clear to her that the defendant had not been reporting all his income, the auditor ceased questioning him about the unreported income, and her working papers were subsequently transferred to the investigators, who proceeded to obtain a search warrant. See *R. v. Jupp*, 2011 ONSC 3227, 2011 CarswellOnt 4495, [2011] O.J. No. 2528 (Ont. S.C.J.).

In another Ontario case, *R. v. Kuipers*, 2010 ONCJ 755, 2010 CarswellOnt 11021, [2010] O.J. No. 6156 (Ont. C.J.), it was held that there was no evidence as to why the defendant, who was with a group of recreational motorcyclists travelling on a highway, was singled out from the others, as the officer gave no reason in his testimony as to why or how he determined that the defendant appeared to not be wearing "a properly approved helmet." The stop was clearly a selective, discriminatory stop, and not authorized by the *Highway Traffic Act*. It was therefore unlawful and resulted in the arbitrary detention of the defendant, contrary to s. 9 of the *Charter of Rights*.

The court went on to also find that there was a violation of the defendant's *Charter* s. 8 rights in this case. It held in this regard that the seizure of the defendant's helmet after he was stopped by the police while he was riding his motorcycle on the highway constituted a warrantless seizure. The helmet was a "thing" and therefore required a report to a justice, as contemplated by s. 158(1) of the *Provincial Offences Act*. As s. 158.2(2) imposes on the officer making a seizure the mandatory requirement that he either bring the thing seized before a justice or report to a justice, the failure of the officer to do neither denied the defendant the right to have the seizure, detention and continued detention of his helmet judicially determined, as required by the statute. It also denied the defendant the right to have the judicial officer to whom the report should have been made, the opportunity to authorize the examination, testing, inspection or reproduction of the thing seized, as required under s. 159(1.1). The failure of the officer to comply with s. 158.2(2) infringed the defendant's rights against unlawful search and seizure. Any evidence gleaned from the illegal seizure of the helmet must therefore be excluded.

There was no clear evidence that the location searched was the business address of the defendant's outfitting business, and as such it was unclear that the items to be searched for, which were essentially related to his business practices, would be found in that location. Based on this analysis, the defendant's s. 8 *Charter* rights were violated. See *Ontario (Ministry of Natural Resources) v. Gustafson*, 2012 ONCJ 486, 2012 CarswellOnt 9244, [2012] O.J. No. 3428 (Ont. C.J.).

A backyard swimming pool, an exterior amenity the use of which is incidental to the residence, is not a dwelling for the purposes of the *Municipal Act* and *City By-Law*, such that no *Charter* s. 8 issue arose because the City officials were entitled to enter onto the party's property without her consent to determine whether the City's by-laws or its orders or directions were being complied with, pursuant to the City's right of entry by-law: *Davis v. Guelph (City)* (2011), 2011 ONCA 761, 2011 CarswellOnt 13588, 6 C.L.R. (4th) 75, 345 D.L.R. (4th) 1, 92 M.P.L.R. (4th) 163, 286 O.A.C. 127, [2011] O.J. No. 5439, [2012] S.C.C.A. No. 41 (Ont. C.A.), leave to appeal refused 2012 CarswellOnt 6424, 2012 CarswellOnt 6425, 436 N.R. 388 (note), 301 O.A.C. 400 (note), [2012] S.C.C.A. No. 41 (S.C.C.).

The search by the conservation officer of the saddlebag of the off-road vehicle driven by the accused was a breach of his s. 8 *Charter* rights. This search was for the purpose of finding documentation for the off-road vehicle and identification of the defendant; permission was not granted for the search, and the plain view doctrine of search and seizure did not apply. Although this action was a breach of the defendant's *Charter* rights, no evidence was found or seized, so nothing turned on the search. See *Ontario (Ministry of Natural Resources) v. Gustafson*, 2012 ONCJ 484, 2012 CarswellOnt 9188 (Ont. C.J.).

In *Oshawa (City) v. Carter* (December 21, 2012), Rosenberg J., [2012] O.J. No. 6291 (Ont. C.J.), pursuant to the *Building Code Act*, the inspector entered onto the property of an apartment building without a warrant and observed that it was not enclosed as required by the Act. An inspection of property without a warrant may be conducted when an officer produces proper identification. The issue of producing proper identification was not addressed in the evidence, and the justice of the peace concluded that there had not been a violation of the defendant's rights. Had there been any such violation, the prejudice to the defendant would have been so insignificant as to be negligible. The garbage area in question was easily viewable, such that the level of intrusion on the defendant was minimal. The safety and health of the community outweighed the defendant's *Charter* s. 8 rights.

In *R. v. Hunt*, 2013 ONCJ 511, 2013 CarswellOnt 13104, [2013] O.J. No. 4297 (Ont. C.J.), the ITO stated that the police had received a steady stream of complaints about the premises being used as an after-hours bar, which led to the issuance of a search warrant under the *Liquor Licence Act* to search a motorcycle club, when in fact the police could document only eight complaints, all received within the past six months, five of which were from police officers and three of which were from the officer seeking the warrant. Only two of the complaints made reference to an after-hours bar. Such information was extremely misleading and inaccurate. Another paragraph in the ITO stated that the premises were under surveillance throughout the day the warrant was sought, however the officer seeking the warrant had merely driven by in the morning and then again in the early evening. Two drives by were not surveillance or surveillance throughout the day. These two portions of the paragraph were factually incorrect and grossly misleading, and did not constitute full and frank disclosure of material facts. The ITO also set out in the same paragraph that surveillance was conducted because information had been received that an event was being hosted at the premises without identifying the source of the information. It was conceded by the Crown that without that paragraph there would be probably no grounds to get the warrant on that day. The warrant was quashed and the evidence excluded under s. 24(2) of the *Charter*.

In *R. v. Gerassimou*, 2016 ONCJ 378, 2016 CarswellOnt 10193, [2016] O.J. No. 3417 (Ont. C.J.), it was held that the authority for issuing a search warrant under s.

158 is similar to the authority under s. 487 of the *Criminal Code*. There was no disagreement that there were offences that had been committed and that warranted further investigation. It was not in dispute that the defendant's vehicle was involved in a collision, and that a citizen called 911 when they saw no one in the car or in the area; when the police arrived there was no one in the car or vicinity, whoever was operating the vehicle had fled. The airbag had been deployed and the car doors were locked. There was no sign of forced entry, and the defendant had the only key. The question resolves to whether the officer's belief that the defendant's cell phone records would afford evidence of the commission of the offence was reasonable in the circumstances as they were known to the officer or reasonably and honestly believed by her at the time she applied for the search warrant. It was not misleading for the officer to not include information about something she did not observe, namely the absence of any sign of injuries to the defendant when she subsequently interviewed him. There was no evidence of injuries or blood found at the scene. While the information to obtain the warrant did not note that there was no evidence of cell phone usage within the vehicle, it was very clear within the document the purpose for which the information was being sought, and why the affiant believed it would afford evidence of an offence, as it would show that the defendant was in the vicinity of the accident at the time it occurred, a location which was a considerable distance removed from his residence. The omissions alleged were therefore not disingenuous or misleading or false, and would not have materially affected the conclusion to be drawn by the independent reviewer. The officer's belief that the requested cell phone and cell tower records would provide evidence of the commission of the enumerated provincial offences was based on more than mere hope or suspicion, and was at a minimum a reasonable probability, her belief being an honestly founded and held belief. It was reasonable for the justice of the peace to accept the inference that, prima facie, where you find a cell phone, you find its owner. However, the justice erred in issuing the search warrant for production of the actual text or content of all SMS text messages as this could breach the privacy interests of other parties. The request for that information was a clear overreach of the purpose of the application, to gather information about the whereabouts of the defendant's cell phone during the relevant times. The admission of such evidence would tend to bring the administration of justice into disrepute and was excluded.

The police officer's query of the licence plate attached to the defendant's motor vehicle did not constitute a search within the meaning of s. 8 of the *Charter*, since the defendant would not have had a reasonable expectation of privacy over the numbers on the licence plate or any information that may be connected to the licence plate. This conclusion is evidenced from the particular provisions set out in the *Highway Traffic Act* and *Compulsory Automobile Insurance Act* which legally obligate an owner of a motor to provide specific information to the Ministry of Transportation before a licence plate, a vehicle permit, and a validation tag will be issued to the owner of the vehicle, as well as a motorist is required to stop for the police and provide specific documents or information to them upon demand for that document or information. The officer was also legally authorized by the *Highway Traffic Act* to seize or take possession of the validation tag until the facts had been determined, where the officer had testified he removed and seized the licence plate so that he could take it back to the police station to properly remove the apparently fraudulent validation tag that had been taped on the rear licence plate. Since the licence plate and validation tag were the property of the Crown, the officer's action in returning the licence plate to the Ministry of Transportation was not unlawful. See *Ontario v. Bharath*, 2016 ONCJ 382, 2016 CarswellOnt 10190, [2016] O.J. No. 3416 (Ont. C.J.).

In *R. v. Ramsay*, 2016 ONCJ 569, 2016 CarswellOnt 14580, [2016] O.J. No. 4841 (Ont. C.J.), it was held that, applying the Supreme Court of Canada's new framework for unreasonable delay in *R. v. Jordan*, 2016 CSC 27, 2016 SCC 27, 2016 CarswellBC 1864, 2016 CarswellBC 1865, [2016] 1 S.C.R. 631, 335 C.C.C. (3d) 403, 29 C.R. (7th) 235, 398 D.L.R. (4th) 381, 388 B.C.A.C. 111, 358 C.R.R. (2d) 97, 484 N.R. 202, 670 W.A.C. 111, [2016] A.C.S. No. 27, [2016] S.C.J. No. 27 (S.C.C.), the complexities of the case resulted in a presumptive ceiling of 18 months. The overall delay in the case, involving driving while suspended and failing to wear a seatbelt, was just over 17 months. The total amount of time taken to conduct three judicial pre-trial conferences was part of the inherent time requirements, and reduced the total period of delay substantially, such that the actual delay was well below the presumptive ceiling of 18 months. The case did not take markedly longer than it reasonably should have; both sides acted reasonably and expeditiously. The defendant's right to be tried without unreasonable delay was not violated in the circumstances.

The trial judge made a fundamental error in favour of the defendant by accepting the defence assertion that the defendant attended court and was required to attend an early resolution meeting, in the absence of any evidence in support of that assertion. In any event, the time to the resolution meeting should have been excluded from the s. 11(b) calculation of unreasonable delay. Had the trial judge excluded this time period, the trial judge would have inevitably and correctly dismissed the s. 11(b) application. See *Mississauga (City) v. Gordon*, 2016 ONCJ 587, 2016 CarswellOnt 15181, [2016] O.J. No. 5098 (Ont. C.J.).

10.2.11 RIGHT TO COUNSEL

Charter section 10(b) states: "Everyone has the right *on arrest or detention* to retain and instruct counsel without delay and to be informed of that right." [emphasis added]

- A defendant who is arrested or detained must be informed, without delay, of the following:

- The reasons for the arrest or detention;

- That he or she is entitled to speak to a lawyer without delay;

- Information about legal aid and any available duty counsel hotline;

- If there is any indication that the defendant does not understand his or her right to counsel, it should be explained again more clearly;

- The defendant should not be asked any questions dealing with the offence in the meantime, unless there are urgent or dangerous circumstances, or unless he or she understands and clearly says that he or she does not wish to speak to a lawyer; and

- If the defendant wishes to speak to a lawyer, he or she should be given a reasonable opportunity to do so in private.

- The law regarding right to counsel is complex and should be carefully researched before trial.

- The fundamental purpose of section 10(b) is to ensure that detainees are sufficiently informed of their jeopardy and their right to counsel and given a reasonable opportunity to exercise that right. However, the police are not required to provide the defendant's counsel detailed information when first detained, if counsel can obtain that information by other means, including by asking the defendant himself: *R. v. Fitzsimmons* (2006), 2006 CarswellOnt 8086, 39 M.V.R. (5th) 111, [2006] O.J. No. 5079, 84 O.R. (3d) 266, 219 O.A.C. 200, 216 C.C.C. (3d) 141 (Ont. C.A.), leave to appeal refused (2007), [2007] S.C.C.A. No. 81, 2007 CarswellOnt 2863, 2007 CarswellOnt 2864 (S.C.C.).

- See: *R. v. Bartle*, 92 C.C.C. (3d) 289, 33 C.R. (4th) 1, [1994] 3 S.C.R. 173, 6 M.V.R. (3d) 1, 19 O.R. (3d) 802 (note) (S.C.C.); *R. v. Cobham*, 33 C.R. (4th) 73, 6 M.V.R. (3d) 89, [1994] 3 S.C.R. 360, 92 C.C.C. (3d) 333 (S.C.C.); *R. v. Prosper*, 33 C.R. (4th) 85, 6 M.V.R. (3d) 181, [1994] 3 S.C.R. 236, 92 C.C.C. (3d) 353 (S.C.C.); *R. v. Borden*, 33 C.R. (4th) 147, [1994] 3 S.C.R. 145, 92 C.C.C. (3d) 404 (S.C.C.); and *R. v. Pozniak*, 92 C.C.C. (3d) 472, 33 C.R.

(4th) 49, [1994] 3 S.C.R. 310, 6 M.V.R. (3d) 113, 19 O.R. (3d) 802 (note) (S.C.C.).

- Use of tax audit for criminal investigation purposes results in *Charter* violations. (*R. v. Borg* (2007), [2007] O.J. No. 3866, 2007 CarswellOnt 8480, 2007 ONCJ 451, 2008 G.T.C. 1055 (Eng.), 2007 D.T.C. 5671 (Eng.), [2007] G.S.T.C. 154 (Ont. C.J.)).

- A momentary investigatory detention does not trigger section 10(b) of the *Charter*. To require the police to give section 10(b) warnings whenever they momentarily detain a person for routine questioning would be to confuse constitutional vigilance with paranoia: *R. v. Suberu* (2006), 2006 CarswellOnt 3005, 142 C.R.R. (2d) 75 (Ont. S.C.J.), at para. 10, per McIsaac J., sitting as an appeal court, affirmed, 2007 CarswellOnt 430, [2007] O.J. No. 317, 220 O.A.C. 322, 218 C.C.C. (3d) 27, 45 C.R. (6th) 47, 2007 ONCA 60, 151 C.R.R. (2d) 135, 85 O.R. (3d) 127 (Ont. C.A.), affirmed 252 O.A.C. 340, 309 D.L.R. (4th) 114, [2009] 2 S.C.R. 460, 97 O.R. (3d) 480 (note), [2009] S.C.J. No. 33, 245 C.C.C. (3d) 112, 66 C.R. (6th) 127, 390 N.R. 303, 2009 CarswellOnt 4107, 2009 CarswellOnt 4106, 2009 SCC 33, 193 C.R.R. (2d) 96 (S.C.C.). Section 8 held violated where a police officer without lawful justification demands name identification from a passenger detained in a vehicle, and exclusion of evidence under section 24(2) considered in detail. (*R. v. Harris*, [2007] O.J. No. 3185, 87 O.R. (3d) 214, 49 C.R. (6th) 220, 51 M.V.R. (5th) 172, 2007 CarswellOnt 5279, 2007 ONCA 574, 225 C.C.C. (3d) 193, 228 O.A.C. 241 (Ont. C.A.)).

- There is no general right to counsel in proceedings before courts and tribunals. There is however, a possibility that a right to counsel may be recognized in specific and varied situations. *Christie v. British Columbia (Attorney General)*, 2007 SCC 21, 155 C.R.R. (2d) 366, [2007] 1 S.C.R. 873, [2007] 8 W.W.R. 64, 280 D.L.R. (4th) 528, 2007 CarswellBC 1118, 2007 CarswellBC 1117, 2007 G.T.C. 1488 (Eng.), 361 N.R. 322, 66 B.C.L.R. (4th) 1, 2007 G.T.C. 1493 (Fr.), 398 W.A.C. 1, 240 B.C.A.C. 1, 2007 D.T.C. 5229 (Fr.), 2007 D.T.C. 5525 (Eng.) (S.C.C.) at para. 27 [SCC].

- The fact that the accused has spoken to counsel after his or her section 10(b) *Charter* rights were violated does not necessarily immunize any subsequently obtained statements from a section 24(2) analysis. Whether these later statements were obtained in violation of the *Charter* under section 24(2) depends on the "temporal, contextual, and causal connection" between the statements and the original *Charter* breach. *R. v. Lewis*, 2007 ONCA 349, 155 C.R.R. (2d) 94, 219 C.C.C. (3d) 427, 224 O.A.C. 298, 2007 CarswellOnt 2871, 86 O.R. (3d) 46, 48 C.R. (6th) 67 (Ont. C.A.) at para. 31.

Solicitor-client privilege is to be determined by the courts and not administrative boards, generally: *Blood Tribe Department of Health v. Canada (Privacy Commissioner)*, [2008] S.C.J. No. 45, 2008 CarswellNat 2244, 2008 CarswellNat 2245, (*sub nom.* Privacy Commissioner of Canada v. Blood Tribe Department of Health) 2008 C.L.L.C. 210-030, 74 Admin. L.R. (4th) 38, 376 N.R. 327, 294 D.L.R. (4th) 385, 67 C.P.R. (4th) 1, (*sub nom.* Canada (Privacy Commissioner) v. Blood Tribe Department of Health) [2008] 2 S.C.R. 574, 2008 SCC 44 (S.C.C.).

Where a detainee has expressed an intention to exercise his or her s. 10(b) rights, the police must inform that he or she is entitled to a reasonable opportunity to contact a lawyer and that they are required to refrain from taking any statement or requiring the detainee to participate in any potentially incriminating process in the meantime: *R. v. Bell*, 2008 CarswellOnt 1866, 2008 ONCJ 151 (Ont. C.J.), at paras. 37 and 39 [ONCJ].

An accused who is in the company of police officers is not detained for the purposes of the *Charter* simply because the police have reasonable grounds to arrest and have formed the intention to arrest. A broader contextual analysis that accounts for all relevant factors is required to ascertain whether an individual was detained: *R. v. Pomeroy*, 2008 CarswellOnt 3911, [2008] O.J. No. 2550, 2008 ONCA 521, 91 O.R. (3d) 261, 249 O.A.C. 287, 173 C.R.R. (2d) 269 (Ont. C.A.).

Section 10(b) of the *Charter* does not require the presence of a lawyer at the time of a custodial interrogation. In most instances, the initial warning by the police officer, coupled with a reasonable opportunity to consult counsel when the detained person invokes his/her right, satisfies s. 10(b) of the *Charter*. However, the police must give the detained person an additional opportunity to obtain advice from counsel where developments in the course of the investigation make this necessary in order to serve the purpose underlying the *Charter* s. 10(b) right. See *R. v. Sinclair*, 496 W.A.C. 36, 218 C.R.R. (2d) 1, 293 B.C.A.C. 36, 259 C.C.C. (3d) 443, 77 C.R. (6th) 203, [2010] S.C.J. No. 35, [2010] A.C.S. No. 35, [2010] 2 S.C.R. 310, 2010 CarswellBC 2679, 2010 CarswellBC 2664, 2010 SCC 35, 406 N.R. 1, 324 D.L.R.

(4th) 385 (S.C.C.); *R. v. McCrimmon*, 293 B.C.A.C. 144, 218 C.R.R. (2d) 81, 496 W.A.C. 144, 10 B.C.L.R. (5th) 199, 259 C.C.C. (3d) 515, [2010] 12 W.W.R. 1, 77 C.R. (6th) 266, [2010] S.C.J. No. 36, [2010] 2 S.C.R. 402, 2010 CarswellBC 2666, 2010 CarswellBC 2665, 2010 SCC 36, 324 D.L.R. (4th) 458, 406 N.R. 152 (S.C.C.); *R. v. Willier*, 218 C.R.R. (2d) 64, [2010] 12 W.W.R. 385, 259 C.C.C. (3d) 536, 77 C.R. (6th) 283, [2010] A.C.S. No. 37, [2010] S.C.J. No. 37, 37 Alta. L.R. (5th) 1, 497 W.A.C. 1, 490 A.R. 1, [2010] 2 S.C.R. 429, 2010 CarswellAlta 1975, 2010 CarswellAlta 1974, 2010 SCC 37, 324 D.L.R. (4th) 479, 406 N.R. 218 (S.C.C.).

The case law makes it clear that a roadside stop of a vehicle for possible violations of the *Criminal Code* (e.g., impaired driving) or provincial regulatory offences under statutes like the *Highway Traffic Act* (e.g., speeding) is a detention, and that the implicit limitation on the s. 10(b) right to counsel that is inherent to roadside stops is justifiable under s. 1 of the *Charter*. In the present case, the defendant remained detained throughout the time that the police officers processed his speeding infraction. He was not free to leave the scene until this process was completed. In this context, the officer's question about the contents of the box in his vehicle, flowing from his suspicion that the box contained illegal cigarettes, placed the defendant in jeopardy pursuant to the *Tobacco Tax Act* (Ont.). This new jeopardy triggered the defendant's s. 10 rights, especially his right to counsel. The trial judge thus erred in not finding that the defendant's s. 10 rights crystallized when the officer asked him the question about the contents of the box. Before answering the question, which had nothing to do with his speeding offence, he should have been advised of his right to consult counsel. His s. 10(b) *Charter* right was violated in the circumstances. See *R. v. MacDonald*, 2012 ONCA 495, 2012 CarswellOnt 8756, 94 C.R. (6th) 355, 263 C.R.R. (2d) 248, 294 O.A.C. 232, [2012] O.J. No. 3210 (Ont. C.A.).

In *R. v. Smith*, 2012 ONCJ 405, 2012 CarswellOnt 8242, [2012] O.J. No. 2987 (Ont. C.J.), the defendant was charged with failing to comply with the terms of the *Sex Offender Registry* by not providing his registered address within 15 days of changing that address as well as providing false information to a police officer. Although he was given a caution when speaking to the police, it was provided at a much later point in the interview, when the content of the officers' questions indicated that they must have formed reasonable and probable grounds to make an arrest. At this point the issue of detention, either psychological or otherwise, was a live issue. The officers went further and asked for or awaited his responses, then placed him under arrest at which point he was given his *Charter* rights. It was wrong for the police to choose to effectively detain the defendant in order to conduct their investigation without first giving him his rights to counsel and his right to leave without answering any further questions. The defendant's s. 10(a) and s. 10(b) *Charter* rights were violated in the circumstances.

In *R. v. Darteh*, 2014 ONSC 895, 2014 CarswellOnt 1506, 302 C.R.R. (2d) 283, [2014] O.J. No. 638 (Ont. S.C.J.), affirmed 2016 ONCA 141, 2016 CarswellOnt 2489, [2016] O.J. No. 896 (Ont. C.A.), the accused was arrested in the investigation of offences under the *Liquor Licence Act* and *Trespass to Property Act*, and during his initial detention was informed of the reasons for his detention, but was not given his rights to counsel. The term "without delay" in s. 10(b) means "immediately". While there was no detention during the first officer's preliminary questioning of the accused, once the officer finished his preliminary questioning and obtained the accused's health card and decided to make a call on the police radio in order to obtain more information about the accused, the officer knew that a detention had crystallized. At this point, he had sufficient time to step back and begin to make a radio call to the station, so there was also sufficient time to read the accused his s. 10(b) *Charter* rights. The officer gave evidence that he now understood, even in the context of a *Provincial Offences Act* investigation, that the police are obliged to comply with the informational component of s. 10(b) immediately upon detention; the officer's mistake regarding s. 10(b) rights during *Provincial Offences Act* detentions was understandable, given that s. 10(b) rights are suspended during brief roadside detentions under the *Highway Traffic Act*, which is the most common kind of *Provincial Offences Act* investigation.

The most important consideration in all cases is to look for a *quid pro quo* offer by the police officer in determining whether a reasonable doubt has been raised about the suspect's will being overborne by the police officer's inducement to make the statement or admission in question. In considering whether there had been a *quid pro quo* offer made by the police officer to the defendant to improperly induce the defendant to confess or make an admission, the concern was on the officer's testimony that he had provided the defendant with the two options of either the officer charging the defendant with the regulatory offence of owner permitting a motor vehicle to be driven on the highway without insurance, or charging the defendant's brother with a criminal offence of taking motor vehicle without the owner's consent. But since the officer had only provided that two-option scenario to the defendant after the defendant had already made the two inculpatory statements, then it would not have logically or improperly induced the defendant to make those two admissions, since the two inculpatory statements had already been given to the officer before those two options of whom could be charged with an offence had been specified and outlined to the defendant. Moreover, the officer did not have reasonable grounds to believe that the defendant had committed an offence before the officer began speaking to the defendant, and it had only been after the defendant had made the second of the two inculpatory statements that the defendant was in between insurance companies and that he had been presently working on another policy, and that the officer would have had reasonable grounds to charge the defendant with the offence of owner permit motor vehicle to be driven on a highway without insurance. Since the officer did not have reasonable grounds to believe the defendant had committed an offence until the defendant's second inculpatory statement, the officer was not required to caution the defendant to inform him about his right to remain silent. See *R. v. Bakieh*, 2014 ONCJ 155, 2014 CarswellOnt 4157, [2014] O.J. No. 1603 (Ont. C.J.).

While the defendant's routine traffic stop involved a brief roadside detention causing him to be "delayed" or "kept waiting", his s. 10(b) *Charter* rights to retain and instruct counsel and be informed of that right were not triggered. The charges involving the defendant of operating a motor vehicle on a highway without insurance, number plate and fail to wear seat belt, were not arrestable offences, and he was not under arrest. See *Niagara (Reg. Mun.) v. Busch*, 2017 ONCJ 547, 2017 CarswellOnt 12346, (*sub nom*. R. v. Busch) 394 C.R.R. (2d) 147, [2017] O.J. No. 4166 (Ont. C.J.).

10.2.12 VOLUNTARINESS/RIGHT TO SILENCE

- Before the defendant's statement(s) made to a person in authority can be introduced as evidence by the prosecution, it must first be proven *beyond a reasonable doubt* that it was made voluntarily.

  - There can be no threats or promises. A *quid pro quo* offer from the police is an important factor in establishing the existence of a threat or promise, but it is the strength of the inducement, having regard to the particular individual and his or her circumstances, that is to be considered in the overall contextual analysis of voluntariness: *R. v. Spencer*, 2007 SCC 11, [2007] 5 W.W.R. 201, 358 N.R. 278, [2007] S.C.J. No. 11, 44 C.R. (6th) 199, 276 D.L.R. (4th) 565, 2007 CarswellBC 480, 2007 CarswellBC 479, [2007] 1 S.C.R. 500, 392 W.A.C. 1, 237 B.C.A.C. 1, 64 B.C.L.R. (4th) 203, 217 C.C.C. (3d) 353 (S.C.C.), at para. 15 [SCC].

  - It cannot be made in "oppressive circumstances".

  - It cannot be made by a defendant without an "operating mind" (i.e. the defendant must *choose* to make a statement).

- Where the police obtain an involuntary confession from a defendant in an oppressive atmosphere, a subsequent inculpatory statement is tainted where the defendant continues to demonstrate the deleterious effects of the police conduct: *R. v. Bateman* (2006), 2006 CarswellOnt 3417,

[2006] O.J. No. 2562 (Ont. S.C.J.), at paras. 26-28. Right to silence under section 7 of the *Charter* does not prohibit continued police questioning. (*R. v. Singh* (2007), [2007] S.C.J. No. 48, 285 D.L.R. (4th) 583, 225 C.C.C. (3d) 103, 2007 SCC 48, 2007 CarswellBC 2589, 2007 CarswellBC 2588, 73 B.C.L.R. (4th) 1, 51 C.R. (6th) 199, [2008] 1 W.W.R. 191 (S.C.C.)).

- In addition, the section 7 *Charter* right to "life, liberty and security of the person and the right not to be deprived thereof except in accordance with the principles of fundamental justice" includes the right to remain silent.

- As mentioned in Chapter 3, some statutes make it an offence not to disclose regulatory information.

  - Arguably, any such compelled statement is involuntary and contrary to the right to silence.

  - Some courts have upheld the power to compel statements but ruled them inadmissible in a later prosecution.

- The issue is complex and should be carefully researched before trial.

- The voluntariness of the statement in this case was not affected by the lack of a caution or warning, but was affected by the failure to completely record the conversation. The officer admitted that he did not have a full recall of the conversation and his notes were merely skeletal. The lack of complete record left doubt about its voluntariness: *R. v. Shilon*, 2004 CarswellOnt 8947, [2004] O.J. No. 6138, CRWN/2006-188 (S.C.J.).

- Cross-examination on the defendant's failure to tell the police his version of events before trial breached his *Charter* and common law right to silence: *R. v. Kwandahor-Mensah*, 2006 CarswellAlta 182, 380 A.R. 321, 363 W.A.C. 321, 2006 ABCA 59, 205 C.C.C. (3d) 321, [2006] A.J. No. 171 (Alta. C.A.).

- Crown permitted to cross-examine accused on "discovery" evidence given in civil proceeding for the purposes of challenging his credibility (and not for the purpose of incrimination) despite the fact that he was required to participate in that process under the *Rules of Civil Procedure.* (*R. v. Nedelcu* (2007), [2007] O.J. No. 1188, 2007

CarswellOnt 1851, 41 C.P.C. (6th) 357, 46 M.V.R. (5th) 129, 154 C.R.R. (2d) 171 (Ont. S.C.J.)).

- Statements by an accused person must be proved voluntary if they are tendered as proof of the assertions therein. Where an accused is unrepresented, a trial judge has a limited duty to identify and investigate *Charter* issues if they become apparent. The prosecutor should have identified the basis on which the accused's statement to the officer was led — as part of the narrative to explain the process by which the accused was charged or as an admission. Failing that, it would have been preferable, had the justice of the peace required the prosecution to state the basis for the reference to the statement, given that the accused was unrepresented at trial. No substantial wrong or miscarriage of justice could be said to flow from the unqualified reference to the statement as there was ample independent evidence to identify the defendant as the driver of the motor vehicle involved in the incident: See *R. v. Champion*, 2007 ONCJ 319, 2007 CarswellOnt 4515, [2007] O.J. No. 2782, 53 M.V.R. (5th) 52 (Ont. C.J.).

In *R. v. Poonia*, 2014 BCSC 1526, 2014 CarswellBC 2393, 69 M.V.R. (6th) 263, [2014] B.C.J. No. 2092 (B.C. S.C.), it was held that while a Judicial Justice of the Peace has some latitude to depart from the procedures that may be customary in criminal trials, evidence still may not be admitted unless the Justice has determined that it is relevant, credible and trustworthy. The procedure of a voluntariness voir dire is specifically designed for that purpose. In the instant case, no voir dire was held, and the Judicial Justice of the Peace did not hear the fresh evidence submitted on appeal as to the defendant being told by the officer at the beginning of their interview that the officer would decide whether to lay charges under the *Criminal Code* or proceed instead under the *Motor Vehicle Act* (B.C.). This is the sort of evidence that the Crown would have been obliged to lead on the voir dire, if one had been held. It would then have been up to the Judicial Justice of the Peace to determine if the words used by the officer constituted an inducement or a threat affecting the voluntariness of the statement. In this case, no voir dire was held, and the Judicial Justice of the Peace never heard this evidence. He therefore had no proper basis for determining whether the statement was voluntary, and accordingly, whether it was reliable. Without holding a voir dire, he could not fulfil his mandate of admitting only evidence that was relevant, credible and trustworthy.

Based on the evidence that was adduced on the voir dire, which consisted only of the police officer's testimony, it was determined that the defendant's statements had been voluntarily given to the officer beyond a reasonable doubt. The defendant's statements had not been obtained through improper promises, inducements or threats from the officer. In addition, the officer testified that the defendant did not indicate that he did not wish to speak to the officer, that he understood English, that the defendant's answers had been consistent with the officer's questions, and that the defendant had not been under the influence of alcohol or drugs when the statements were given. The officer also testified that the defendant had not been under arrest and he did not have the intention to charge the defendant before he began questioning him. The conversation between them had taken place on the driveway of the defendant's residence, and the officer was still conducting an investigation into the alleged motor vehicle accident at the time of their interaction and conversation. The defendant had not been detained under the *Charter*, since the evidence indicated that the interaction and conversation between the defendant and the officer had been relatively short in duration. See *R. v. Rizvi*, 2014 ONCJ 404, [2014] O.J. No. 3985 (Ont. C.J.).

In *Ontario v. Bharath*, 2016 ONCJ 382, 2016 CarswellOnt 10190, [2016] O.J. No. 3416 (Ont. C.J.), on account of the discrepancy between what the police officer had observed on an apparent valid validation tag that would not expire until the month of December, 2014, on the rear licence plate and that of the information he had received about the permit of the vehicle expiring on February, 2013, the officer decided to activate the emergency roof lights of his cruiser in order to signal the driver of the motor vehicle to stop for further investigation. Accordingly, the officer had clearly expressed and reasonable grounds for stopping the motor vehicle for investigation. As such, the traffic stop he conducted was neither random nor arbitrary, unless it could be established that the officer had an improper purpose as well for stopping the defendant. *Charter* remedies are available for a violation of the right to be free from arbitrary detention under s. 9 when a traffic stop had been proved to be based on racial profiling on a balance of probabilities. However, it was found on the evidence that the police officer's decision to stop the motor vehicle was due to the validation sticker issue, and race had no bearing in that decision. The defendant's testimony, on the other hand, was not reliable or credible. The defendant failed to prove on a balance of probabilities that the traffic stop was due to racial profiling.

10.3 TRIAL STRATEGY

10.3.1 DOES THE PROSECUTION HAVE A CASE?

- Review the prosecution's anticipated evidence.

  - Are all the essential elements of the offence provable?

  - Are any inferences required?

- Are those inferences reasonable?
- Is any of the evidence inadmissible? If so, how does that affect the prosecution's case?

10.3.2 THEORY OF THE CASE

- The prosecutor will adduce evidence and present a "theory" or "story" of what happened. If the story is compelling, then the defence should present a competing "theory of the defence".
- Any question or evidence which neither detracts from your opponent's theory nor advances your theory should be discarded.
- It is risky to attack the adequacy of a police investigation. It may render relevant evidence which the Crown would otherwise not be permitted to adduce. See: *R. v. Mallory*, 2007 ONCA 46, 2007 CarswellOnt 348, [2007] O.J. No. 236, 220 O.A.C. 239, 217 C.C.C. (3d) 266 (Ont. C.A.).

10.3.3 EFFECTIVE PERSUASION

- Present your evidence and examinations in a simple and logical order, to quickly advance your theory of the case. It will be easier for the Justice to follow and remember your evidence.
- In cross-examination, ask only leading questions so as to control the witness' answers.
- In examination-in-chief, use brief directed questions.
  - Get to the point quickly and convincingly — you will project your own competence and advance the believ-ability of your cause.
- It is too late to be discovering evidence.
  - Do not ask a question unless you expect the answer to help.
- There are excellent texts on advocacy, which are both helpful and entertaining.
- Be prepared to make submissions or legal argument at the end of the case which will assist the justice of the peace to find in your favour, e.g., that the prosecution has not proven

> its case beyond a reasonable doubt because of the
> inconsistencies in the witnesses' testimony, or that the
> defendant's evidence is not credible as it fails to meet the *R.
> v. W. (D.)* test in assessing credibility (see section 10.2.5 on
> Credibility Evidence in Chapter 10). Concise submissions
> which are focused and to the point are of great assistance to
> the court. If there are any cases or decisions you are going
> to rely on during your submissions, it is helpful to bring extra
> copies for the other side and the court.

The trial justice did not err in limiting oral submissions on *Charter* applications. The justice has the capacity to request and receive written submissions on any aspect of the litigation; the judicial officer has the right to control its own process and has the trial management power: *R. v. 20207000 Ontario Inc.*, [2009] O.J. No. 838, 42 C.E.L.R. (3d) 129, 2009 CarswellOnt 1045, 2009 ONCJ 76 (Ont. C.J.).

It was held that the justice of the peace made a procedural error in not dealing with the motion for a non-suit at the end of the motion, instead of including it in the body of his judgment. The motion must be dealt with at the end of the arguing of the motion. The justice also erred in ruling that cross-examination should not take place unless there is a basis for it, something that can be proposed to the court, as a legal basis. By requiring the defence to establish some basis for his cross-examination in order to do so, the justice effectively reversed the burden of proof. Clearly the defence has a right to cross-examine at any time and no particular basis has to be established in order to exercise the right to cross-examine: *R. v. Pires*, 2009 CarswellOnt 7403, [2009] O.J. No. 5080 (Ont. C.J.).

The test for a directed verdict of acquittal or non-suit application in a regulatory offence is the same as the test for a directed verdict in criminal matters, namely, whether or not there is any evidence upon which a reasonable jury properly instructed could return a verdict of guilty: *Enbridge Gas Distribution Inc. v. Ontario (Ministry of Labour)*, 2010 ONSC 2013, 2010 CarswellOnt 2305, (*sub nom.* Ontario (Ministry of Labour) v. Enbridge Gas Distribution Inc.) 261 O.A.C. 27, 92 C.L.R. (3d) 145, [2010] O.J. No. 1504 (Ont. S.C.J.), leave to appeal refused 2011 ONCA 13, 2011 CarswellOnt 13, (*sub nom.* Ontario (Ministry of Labour) v. Enbridge Gas Distribution Inc.) 328 D.L.R. (4th) 343, (*sub nom.* Ontario (Minister of Labour) v. Enbridge Gas Distribution Inc.) 272 O.A.C. 347, [2011] O.J. No. 24 (Ont. C.A. [In Chambers]).

In *R. v. Protech Roofing Waterproofing Ltd.*, 2010 ONCJ 591, 2010 CarswellOnt 9474, [2010] O.J. No. 5313 (Ont. C.J.), it was held that the trial justice of the peace erred in granting a directed verdict of acquittal by not considering evidence that could establish the *actus reus* of the offence, and weighing other evidence that was relevant to the due diligence defence. A reasonable jury properly instructed could conclude that the blow torch caused the flash fire that injured a worker, and that the defendant failed to take the necessary precautions to prevent a fire when using a blow torch.

The presiding justice of the peace erred when she insisted that the police officer close his notebook before giving his evidence after reading his notes but before answering any questions. It is not necessary to force every witness to close their notebook or set it aside in order to prevent the witness from reading from it: *Mississauga (City) v. Vattiata*, 2010 ONCJ 588, 2010 CarswellOnt 9341, 6 M.V.R. (6th) 128, [2010] O.J. No. 5283 (Ont. C.J.).

The justice of the peace was wrong in law to refuse to allow the officer to use his notes to refresh his memory because they were a photocopy rather than the original copy of the notes: *R. v. Thom*, [2010] O.J. No. 4607, 2010 ONCJ 492, 2010 CarswellOnt 8163, 5 M.V.R. (6th) 140 (Ont. C.J.). Similarly, in *Durham (Regional Municipality) v. Zhu*, [2011] O.J. No. 1797, 2011 CarswellOnt 2614, 2011 ONCJ 193 (Ont. C.J.), it was held that a police officer is entitled to refresh his memory by using the electronic notes he had typed into a computer about the offence.

The rules of evidence are as strict for regulatory matters as they are for *Criminal Code* matters. It was an error for the trial justice to conclude that the officer's evidence was credible on the basis that she did not believe she was entitled to take into account the lack of notes with respect to the officer's observations, given that criminal case law in evidentiary issues did not apply to regulatory offences. See *R. v. Vandemunt*, [2011] O.J. No. 5783, 2011 ONCJ 844, 2011 CarswellOnt 15626 (Ont. C.J.).

The justice of the peace erred in not allowing the officer to use the pre-printed form to refresh his memory, which contained information about the testing of the radar device in question: *R. v. Fountas*, 2012 ONCJ 267, 2012 CarswellOnt 5949, [2012] O.J. No. 2517 (Ont. C.J.).

11

SENTENCING

11.1 RANGE OF SENTENCES

11.1.1 UNDER THE CHARGING ACT

- The maximum penalty in the charging Act takes precedence over the maximum penalty in the POA: section 61.

- Some charging Acts have severe penalties. For example:

  - The maximum under section 122 of the Securities Act, R.S.O. 1990, c. S.5, amended 2002, for the misrepresentation of securities information is a fine up to $5,000,000, or imprisonment for five years less a day, or both.

  - The maximum under section 116 of the *Consumer Protection Act*, S.O. 2002, Chapter 30, Schedule A, is a fine up to $50,000 ($250,000 for a corporation), or imprisonment for two years less a day, or both.

  - The maximum under section 66(2) of the *Occupational Health and Safety Act*, R.S.O. 1990, c. O.1, for a corporation failing to comply with the Act or regulations, is a fine up to $500,000.

In *R. v. Macrodyne Technologies Inc.*, [2003] O.J. No. 3582, 2003 CarswellOnt 3438 (Ont. C.J.), the corporate defendant pleaded guilty to a charge relating to the death of a worker operating an overhead crane, where the worker was not a competent person as defined in the Act. The defendant was sentenced to a fine of $130,000 to be paid over a period of three years. Although the actual and potential harm was significant, the defendant pleaded guilty, and had attempted to remedy the issues of training.

11.1.2 UNDER THE POA

- If no maximum punishment is set out in the charging Act, the maximum penalty is a $5,000 fine for offences proceeded under Part III: section 61.

- If the offence is proceeded under Part I (certificate of offence), and *regardless* of the maximum penalty in any charging Act,

  - If the defendant was summoned, the maximum penalty is a $1,000 fine and no imprisonment: section 12(1); and

  - If the defendant was served with an offence notice, the maximum penalty is a $1,000 fine and no imprisonment, and there are further limits to any results following a conviction: section 12(2).

- For young persons, regardless of the maximum penalty in any charging Act, except for breach of probation (section 75(d)), the maximum penalty is a $1,000 fine (section 101). For offences proceeded under Part I or Part II, the maximum fine is $300 fine, and an absolute discharge is available: section 97.

11.2 OPTIONS IN SENTENCING

11.2.1 REDUCING MINIMUM FINES AND IMPRISONMENT IN EXCEPTIONAL CIRCUMSTANCES

- Only penalties specifically declared as minimums should be regarded as such: section 59(1).

- The court may impose a fine that is less than the prescribed minimum or suspend the sentence where it finds exceptional circumstances exist such that imposing the minimum would be:

  - Unduly oppressive; or

  - Otherwise not in the interests of justice: section 59(2).

In *R. v. McComb*, [2004] O.J. No. 4765, 2004 CarswellOnt 4807, 2004 ONCJ 289 (Ont. C.J.), the sentence was suspended where the defendant was convicted of an offence under the *Compulsory Automobile Insurance Act*, which was an absolute liability offence, and the defendant was not trying to avoid paying or having appropriate coverage for his vehicle. Pursuant to section 59(2), it would be inappropriate and not in the interest of justice to fine him.

- The court may impose a fine of not more than $5,000 in lieu of imprisonment where the minimum penalty prescribed includes imprisonment: section 59(3).

- Under section 59(2), there exists a limited degree of flexibility in exceptional circumstances where the minimum fine could be unduly oppressive or otherwise not in the interest of justice. It may well have been in this case that the justice hearing the matter could have exercised some discretion under section 59(2), but he was not given the benefit of exceptional circumstances because the accused was not present to relay the exceptional circumstances to him. Having failed to do so, he cannot be heard now to complain of the imposition of less than the maximum fines that could have been imposed. See *R. v. Mundy*, 2007 ONCJ 449, 2007 CarswellOnt 6599, [2007] O.J. No. 3954 (Ont. C.J.).

Section 59(2) does not create an unfettered discretion. In the absence of exceptional circumstances, it is not sufficient to reduce the minimum fine out of a degree of compassion for the defendant: *R. v. Zhang* (2007), 2007 CarswellOnt 9713 (Ont. C.J.).

Exceptional circumstances ought not to be defined so rigidly or so narrowly that they refer to some catastrophic circumstances. Different members of society have different capacities to pay, and there should not be a disproportionate burden on those who are struggling to pay a fine while others could pay using the resources available to them. On the other hand, the sentence must be such that it is sufficiently onerous that there is an incentive to pay the vehicle insurance, as opposed to not paying the insurance and risking a penalty: *R. v. Nemtsov*, 2009 CarswellOnt 3321 (Ont. C.J.).

The fines for speeding under s. 128(14) of the *Highway Traffic Act* are fixed and are derived simply by multiplying the number of kilometers per hour over the speed limit by the appropriate dollar figure. The courts have no discretion to reduce these fines: *R. v. Winlow*, 2009 ONCA 643, 2009 CarswellOnt 5208, (*sub nom.* York (Regional Municipality) v. Winlow) 99 O.R. (3d) 337, 86 M.V.R. (5th) 171, 265 O.A.C. 326, [2009] O.J. No. 3691 (Ont. C.A.).

Section 59(2) provides a limited degree of flexibility in exceptional circumstances where the minimum fine would be unduly oppressive or otherwise not in the interest of justice. The fact that the minimum fine is beyond the offender's present means is not to be considered as an exceptional circumstance. Failing to impose the minimum fine in the absence of exceptional circumstances would be an error in principle: *R. v. Kadiroglu*, 2009 CarswellOnt 6306, 82 C.C.L.I. (4th) 152, 89 M.V.R. (5th) 272 (Ont. C.J.).

In *R. v. Nerian*, 2010 CarswellOnt 881, 2010 ONCJ 46, 92 M.V.R. (5th) 157 (Ont. C.J.), it was held that in determining sentence, aggravating and mitigating factors are relevant. It is also appropriate for the trial justice to take into consideration aggravating factors in the s. 59(1) assessment. "Exceptional circumstances" that are unduly oppressive or otherwise not in the interest of justice cannot be assessed without reference to these factors. The financial circumstances of the defendant must also necessarily factor into whether relief against the minimum fine is necessary in order to prevent an oppressive result.

The justice erred in principle imposing a fine of $7,500 rather than the minimum fine of $5,000 sought by the prosecutor, upon convicting the defendant at an *ex parte* trial, without giving any reasons for doing so. Fairness dictates that trial justices should not impose a greater sentence than the one requested by the prosecutor in an *ex parte* trial without giving good reasons for doing so. Where the defendant seeks to lower the minimum fine pursuant to s. 59(2) but fails to make out a case for a fine below the statutory minimum, the defendant has potential remedies under s. 69 of the *Provincial Offences Act*: *R. v. Jenkins*, 2010 ONCA 278, 2010 CarswellOnt 2158, [2010] O.J. No. 1517, 99 O.R. (3d) 561, 260 O.A.C. 296, 212 C.R.R. (2d) 137, 93 M.V.R. (5th) 1, 74 C.R. (6th) 117, 253 C.C.C. (3d) 269 (Ont. C.A.), leave to appeal refused 2010 CarswellOnt 7405, 2010 CarswellOnt 7406, 225 C.R.R. (2d) 374 (note), 410 N.R. 395 (note), 279 O.A.C. 399 (note) (S.C.C.).

In *R. v. Ade-Ajayi*, 2011 ONCA 192, 2011 CarswellOnt 1477, 97 C.C.L.I. (4th) 183, 14 M.V.R. (6th) 9, [2011] O.J. No. 1016 (Ont. C.A.), it was held that appeals to the Court of Appeal under the *Provincial Offences Act* are very much the exceptions, and particularly so with respect to sentence. Trial judges must decide whether the circumstances of a particular case call for something less than the minimum fine. The court will not "second guess" that assessment absent factors that meet the leave to appeal criteria set out in s. 139.

While a minimum fine of $5,000 for driving without insurance is something that many people would find painful, the intention of the legislature was to impose a penalty that would in fact be painful. The purpose of setting a minimum fine of $5,000 is to make it clear to people that they are not supposed to operate a motor vehicle that is not covered by a policy of insurance; the penalty is not to be viewed as some sort of licence fee or alternative to obtain insurance. This is clear when one looks and sees how quickly the minimum raises if someone comes back charged with further similar offences: *R. v. Boronka*, 2010 ONCJ 665, 2010 CarswellOnt 10524, [2010] O.J. No. 5920 (Ont. C.J.).

There is no jurisdiction to impose a fine for speeding lower than the fine set out for speeding in s. 128(14) of the *Highway Traffic Act*, or to suspend sentence for the offence of speeding: *R. v. Street* (April 22, 2010), Doc. 1556008A-00, [2010] O.J. No. 5951 (Ont. C.J.).

However, the opposite conclusion was reached in *R. v. Doroz* (2011), 16 M.V.R. (6th) 156, 2011 CarswellOnt 3874, [2011] O.J. No. 2540, 2011 ONCJ 281 (Ont. C.J.), where it was held that in exceptional circumstances, it is open to the justice to suspend the passing of sentence in lieu of the set fine for speeding.

The idea behind the high level of minimum fines for the offence of driving without insurance is to make it more financially onerous to offend the legislation than to bear the required cost of insurance premiums. A reduction in the minimum fine should not lightly be imposed: *R. v. Ade-Ajayi*, 2011 ONCA 192, 2011 CarswellOnt 1477, 97 C.C.L.I. (4th) 183, 14 M.V.R. (6th) 9, [2011] O.J. No. 1016 (Ont. C.A.).

In *R. v. Stickles*, 2011 ONCJ 128, 2011 CarswellOnt 1892, [2011] O.J. No. 1265 (Ont. C.J.), it was held that the clear intent of the minimum fine for stunt driving was to deter everyone from engaging in what was seen to be dangerous and undesirable behaviour. The emphasis should be on the word "everyone". In the absence of exceptional circumstances such that to impose the minimum fine would be unduly oppressive or otherwise not in the interest of justice, the court should impose the minimum fine.

A justice of the peace has the jurisdiction to order a suspension of a driver's licence of a person charged by certificate of offence under Part I of the *Provincial Offences Act* (Ont.). A licence suspension fits within the "actions or results" outlined in s. 12(2) of the Act as consequences of conviction, and is separate and apart from the monetary penalties that can be imposed under s. 128(14) of the *Highway Traffic Act*. See *Durham (Municipality) v. Muia*, 2012 ONCJ 229, 2012 CarswellOnt 5592, 32 M.V.R. (6th) 352, 32 M.V.R. (6th) 352, [2012] O.J. No. 1711 (Ont. C.J.).

In *R. v. Appiah*, 2012 ONCJ 754, 2012 CarswellOnt 15602, 38 M.V.R. (6th) 173, [2012] O.J. No. 5851 (Ont. C.J.), it was held that a set fine which is an out of court payment is simply a figure that amounts to a reduced fine, and that a justice of the peace had no authority to reduce the penalty for speeding in this fashion as opposed to the fine as set out for speeding under the *Highway Traffic Act*.

In a case involving the s. 59 relief from minimum fine provision, *R. v. Clarke*, 2012 ONCJ 627, 2012 CarswellOnt 12469, [2012] O.J. No. 4786 (Ont. C.J.), the court held that the proper application of s. 59(2) requires the court to first find exceptional circumstances before proceeding to the next two considerations, namely, the oppressiveness of the fine and the interests of justice. However, even if the court does not apply s. 59(2), the court may consider the goals and principles of sentencing to arrive at a fit and proper sentence in the circumstances, and the sentence may be less than the minimum fine as set out by the legislature. If after applying the goals and principles of sentencing the court finds that the minimum fine should be imposed, the burden of the fine can be attenuated by granting the offender time to pay. Although there should be deference to fines as set by the legislators, minimum fines are not a one size fits all sentence to be imposed in absolutely every case that comes before the court.

The trial justice in the sentencing process seemed highly attuned that this was truly one of the rare circumstances where the minimum fine under the *Compulsory Automobile Insurance Act* could be reduced having regard to the discretionary powers given to a sitting trial judge under the *Provincial Offences Act*. She correctly reviewed the situation, and applied the principles enunciated in *R. v. Fagbemi* to determine that this was truly a special circumstance of driving, namely the defendant's belief that his truck was a self-propelled implement of husbandry, which he insured as such, which entitled him to a reduction in the fine substantially below the minimum fine of $5000. In doing so the trial justice made a merciful and lenient decision which should not be disturbed on appeal. See *R. v. McClary* (October 18, 2012), Pockele J., [2012] O.J. No. 6306 (Ont. C.J.).

The defendant, an "Organized Pseudo-legal Commercial Argument" (OPCA) litigant, was given the minimum fine of $5,000 following his conviction for driving without insurance. The inference was clear that the defendant did not accept that he was bound by law to insure his motor vehicle. It was very likely that he would continue to hold this attitude and continue to own and operate his vehicle without insurance. The need for specific deterrence was therefore augmented. While the defendant had appealed his sentence, and not the Crown, the court would not increase the sentence on its own initiative; however, in the future trial courts should give serious consideration to elevated fines, licence suspensions, and vehicle impoundment in cases such as this. See *R. v. Cassista*, 2013 ONCJ 305, 2013 CarswellOnt 7411, [2013] O.J. No. 2560 (Ont. C.J.).

In *R. v. E. (A.)*, 2013 ONCA 713, 2013 CarswellOnt 15932, 118 O.R. (3d) 98, 28 C.C.L.I. (5th) 1, [2013] O.J. No. 5299 (Ont. C.A.), it was noted that there was conflicting authority on whether the Court of Appeal has jurisdiction to hear the appeals of some of the matters on which the applicant was seeking leave to appeal because he was denied an extension of time in which to appeal by the courts below. This issue had also been considered by single members of the court in applications for leave to appeal, and a panel of the court had referred to the issue but declined to resolve it. In the particular circumstances of the case, where the applicant was apparently suffering from, and was now being treated for, a serious mental illness which was not known by the courts below, and had been convicted four times for operating motor vehicles without insurance which resulted in very significant fines, an extension of time in which to appeal was granted, as was leave to appeal. Significant minimum fines for the offence of operating a motor vehicle without insurance may well have a good public policy justification, particularly in acting as a general deterrent. It is nonetheless in the public interest to determine whether in the particular circumstances of any individual defendant some accommodation should be made for individuals with significant personal disabilities. Numerous authorities set out the appropriate factors that a court should consider in determining whether to extend the time in which to appeal under s. 85 of the *Provincial Offences Act*. Among the appropriate factors, it is usually significant whether: the applicant has demonstrated a *bona fide* intention to appeal within the prescribed appeal period; the applicant has accounted for or explained the delay in initiating the appeal; and the proposed appeal has merit. And in some circumstances it will be significant whether: the consequences of the conviction are out of all proportion to the penalty imposed; the Crown will be prejudiced; and the applicant has taken the benefit of the judgment. In the final analysis, the principal consideration is whether the applicant has demonstrated that justice requires that the time be extended. It is important to note that these are all factors, not preconditions. It was at least arguable that the provincial judge did not appear to take these factors into account. After this dismissal, the applicant was prevented from having the provincial offences appeal court consider the totality of the fines and surcharges. In the particular circumstances of the case, the due administration of justice is implicated, and as a consequence the broader public interest issues involved were not considered.

In *R. v. Farrage*, 2014 ONSC 564, 2014 CarswellOnt 1090, [2014] O.J. No. 448 (Ont. S.C.J.) it was held that the sentencing judge clearly felt that the joint submission for the minimum penalty was manifestly inadequate based on the submissions in support of the guilty plea. The court expressly recognized that a joint submission should not be lightly overridden. Counsel for the defendant proceeded to make further submissions after the court advised that there must be a suspension of driving privileges in addition to the minimum fine. There was no request to hold the matter down or adjourn to another date for further evidence or submissions. There was no error of law and no basis to interfere with the sentence imposed.

In *York (Regional Municipality) v. Benatar* (July 25, 2014), Doc. 4911-997-13-30080503-00, [2014] O.J. No. 3697 (Ont. C.J.), it was held that a court may impose a fine below the statutory minimum or suspend the passing of sentence where it is satisfied that exceptional circumstances exist such that to impose the minimum fine would be unduly oppressive or otherwise not in the interests of justice. The question whether a minimum penalty is unduly harsh is largely a question of economic fact which requires consideration of the defendant's ability to pay. If making a determination as to the basis of "unduly oppressive" factor, a Justice of the Peace should, first, so enunciate, and second, hold a brief hearing, including receiving evidence under oath from the defendant, permitting cross-examination by the

Crown, hearing submissions from both parties, and making a finding of fact with respect to whether or not the minimum penalties are unduly oppressive. This is the proper procedure for Justice of the Peace to follow when acting under s. 59(2) of the *Provincial Offences Act*.

Speeding fines cannot be reduced below the fixed statutory amounts. There is no jurisdiction to suspend the passing of sentence as this effectively means imposing a fine of zero dollar. See *York (Regional Municipality) v. Haque* (June 20, 2014), Doc. Newmarket 4911-999-00-5956043Z-00, [2014] O.J. No. 3629 (Ont. C.J.).

It is an error of law to grant relief against a minimum fine on the basis of submissions, not evidence: *R. v. Lakeside Rat Rapids Enterprises Ltd.*, 2014 ONCJ 187, 2014 CarswellOnt 5148, [2014] O.J. No. 1910 (Ont. C.J.).

Although a sentencing judge ordinarily has a discretion to exercise in imposing sentence, the Legislature can limit that discretion or eliminate it altogether. As a result, the Justice of the Peace was without jurisdiction to reduce a fixed fine under the municipal parking by-law. See *Toronto (City) v. Iron Mountain Canada Corp.*, 2015 ONCJ 444, 2015 CarswellOnt 12336, [2015] O.J. No. 4298 (Ont. C.J.).

In *R. v. Ward*, 2015 ONCJ 369, 2015 CarswellOnt 10460, [2015] O.J. No. 3726 (Ont. C.J.), it was held that in this case the trial Justice of the Peace had already considered the application of s. 59(2) and reduced the fine from the statutory minimum of $5,000 to $3,500. This is an exercise of judicial discretion that was available to the Justice. An appellate court is not to interfere with sentencing decisions unless they are manifestly unjust. The facts advanced by counsel at trial were essentially the same factors that were advanced before the appeal court with respect to the defendant's financial circumstances, and had already been taken into account in the decision made by the Justice of the Peace. The result was appropriate. There was no basis to interfere with that decision.

When the prosecution asked for the minimum penalty of $200, the Justice of the Peace stated that she would never impose that amount, prior to hearing anything about the circumstances of the defendant. This position does not reflect the proper role of a Justice in sentencing. A minimum sentence is an expression of governmental policy; the Justice's sentencing discretion does not entitle her to disregard a clear statement of legislative intent. The Justice was required to impose the minimum sentence unless the defendant showed exceptional circumstances that justified relief under s. 59(2) of the *Provincial Offences Act*. See *York (Regional Municipality) v. Dave*, 2015 ONCJ 481, 2015 CarswellOnt 13983, [2015] O.J. No. 4651 (Ont. C.J.).

It was further held in *York (Regional Municipality) v. Dave*, 2015 ONCJ 481, 2015 CarswellOnt 13983, [2015] O.J. No. 4651 (Ont. C.J.) that s. 59(2) permits a justice to impose a fine less than the minimum or a suspended sentence where exceptional circumstances exist so that to impose the fine would be unduly oppressive or where the minimum fine would be otherwise not in the interests of justice. It is not improper for a justice to make inquiries of an unrepresented person to ensure the circumstances of s. 59(2) do not apply. The defendant had numerous expenses with two children in medical school; although the family had taken on those investments, the defendant stated that he had a good job and that his wife was also employed. There was no evidence of undue hardship in relation to the $200 minimum fine, and the justice erred in not imposing it.

It was also held in *York (Regional Municipality) v. Dave*, 2015 ONCJ 481, 2015 CarswellOnt 13983, [2015] O.J. No. 4651 (Ont. C.J.) that the warning to the prosecutor that the court would never impose the statutory minimum fine reasonably gave rise to an apprehension of bias. The justice also commented to the prosecutor when he attempted to cite a case that he was not going to be permitted "to take advantage of somebody who is here without counsel." There was nothing in the record that suggested the prosecutor was attempting to gain an advantage by citing a case. Indeed, it was the prosecutor's responsibility to do so. If the defendant needed to see a copy of the case or time to consider the prosecutor's position, that could be accommodated by the presiding justice. The comments of the court in relation to the prosecutor's submissions added to the reasonable apprehension of bias.

In *R. v. E. (A.)*, 2016 ONCA 243, 2016 CarswellOnt 5024, 95 M.V.R. (6th) 179, 348 O.A.C. 68, [2016] O.J. No. 1704 (Ont. C.A.), the defendant, who had four convictions for driving without insurance, sought relief against the total fines of $17,000 that were imposed. Fresh evidence was tendered on appeal which indicated that the defendant was suffering from a mental illness. It was not in the interests of justice for the defendant to be fully relieved of these fines, so that he could immediately drive again. The specific deterrence purpose of the fines remained essential. However, given his mental illness and its detrimental effect on the defendant's ability to earn an income to pay the fines, it was also in the interests of justice that the total amount of the fines be reduced, so as to give him the opportunity to pay the reduced fines and move on with his life. The fines were reduced to $5,000.

Minimum fines of $1200 for driving while suspended and $750 for driving without insurance were imposed having regard to the circumstances of the defendant as an Aboriginal offender, and the principles set out by the Supreme Court for sentencing in such cases in *R. v. Gladue*, 1999 CarswellBC 778, 1999 CarswellBC 779, [1999] 1 S.C.R. 688, 133 C.C.C. (3d) 385, 23 C.R. (5th) 197, 171 D.L.R. (4th) 385, 121 B.C.A.C. 161, [1999] 2 C.N.L.R. 252, 238 N.R. 1, 198 W.A.C. 161, [1999] A.C.S.

No. 19, [1999] S.C.J. No. 19 (S.C.C.) and *R. v. Ipeelee*, 2012 SCC 13, 2012 CarswellOnt 4376, 2012 CarswellOnt 4375, [2012] 1 S.C.R. 433, 113 O.R. (3d) 320 (note), 280 C.C.C. (3d) 265, 91 C.R. (6th) 1, 318 B.C.A.C. 1, [2012] 2 C.N.L.R. 218, 428 N.R. 1, 288 O.A.C. 224, 541 W.A.C. 1, [2012] S.C.J. No. 13 (S.C.C.). While the over-riding focus of the *Gladue* principles is on the over-incarceration of Aboriginal offenders, and the case at bar did not involve a request for custody, the drive suspended conviction does allow for both monetary and custodial dispositions and as such, at least the possibility of custody is open for the court to consider, the position of the Crown notwithstanding. It was clear that the defendant had suffered from the effects of alcohol abuse, and had a family history that included being subjected to the residential school system. He had a long history of driving without first obtaining a licence and indeed continuing to drive while that licence was suspended administratively, as a result of an alcohol related driving offence. At the same time, he had not, apparently, been involved in motor vehicle accidents which resulted in loss as a result of property damage or injury to individuals. It was clear that the defendant had not treated driving as a privilege; he had never even qualified to be licensed, and must take a series of steps toward any eventual goal he may have in regard to driving. The first step for him is to stop driving while not permitted. The minimum fines sought by the Crown would exceed a level that would be onerous to the accused, and would likewise be oppressive in the circumstances. Having regard to s. 59(2), and remaining mindful of the many unfortunate circumstances which were reflected in the defendant's background as a member of the First Nations community, it was appropriate to reduce the minimum fines in question. See *R. v. Henry*, 2016 ONCJ 146, 2016 CarswellOnt 4007, [2016] O.J. No. 1377 (Ont. C.J.).

In *R. v. Priestly Demolition Inc.*, 2016 CarswellOnt 5149 (Ont. C.J.), the court commented that general deterrence is a commonly accepted principle of regulatory offences. The fail to report offence was characterized by the justice of the peace as a misunderstanding, which implied her acceptance of a certain less culpable corporate state of mind. Something less than the minimum fine was not appropriate. There were clearly not exceptional circumstances that would warrant the exercise of the discretion under s. 59, either on the grounds of being an oppressive amount or in the interest of justice. This was not a "technical" breach: it was just a breach of the reporting obligation with a mix of factors, good and bad, to consider with respect to penalty. The absence of exceptional circumstances certainly justified not imposing lower than the minimum fine; something greater than the minimum fine should have been imposed, especially in light of the post-offence conduct and the preponderance of aggravating as opposed to mitigating factors, and the grounds for specific deterrence.

In *R. v. Mr. Ice Man Ltd.*, 2016 ONCJ 621, 2016 CarswellOnt 16466, [2016] O.J. No. 5443 (Ont. C.J.), there were two errors made, one by the issuing authority, in not issuing the proper gross vehicle weight, and the other by the defendant, in not checking the licence before using it. The government which seeks to impose the fine was in some respects responsible for the circumstances of the offence. This appeared to be a very rare and very exceptional circumstance which was not likely to be repeated; however, the defendant, by simply checking his documents could have avoided the infraction. Taking all of the circumstances into account, it was in the interests of justice to reduce the fine by the proportionate responsibility of the parties: 75 percent by the defendant and 25 percent to the Ministry.

The mandatory minimum sentences imposed on the defendant gave no consideration at all to his ability to pay or to the enormous gap in time between his previous convictions and the present convictions, a gap of 15 years. Before considering s. 59(2), the existence and length of the gap should have led to sentences much closer to the $10,000 mandatory minimum than the sentences imposed on the defendant on each occasion. Any consideration of s. 59(2) must keep in mind the language of the section, what circumstances of the defendant are presented as being "exceptional" and the legislative purpose underlying the particular mandatory minimum sentence that the defendant seeks to undercut. The case law is very clear that the minimum sentences in s. 2(1) of the *Compulsory Automobile Insurance Act* are harsh, oppressive, even draconian. However, they are so for a reason. There is nothing inadvertent in the mandatory minimum fines. People operating motor vehicles put other people at risk; people operating motor vehicles can easily cause great harm to other people. The mandatory minimum fines are intended to avoid the risk that a driver will choose not to obtain insurance on the theory that, if he gets caught, any penalty will be less than the cost of the insurance. The mandatory minimum sentences are designed to discourage all drivers from even considering that line of thinking. "Exceptional" and "oppressive" are lower standards than "catastrophic". A person's ability to pay may, in some cases, contribute to a determination that s. 59(2) should be engaged to a defendant's benefit. The analysis under s. 59(2) should take into account the fact that a very harsh penalty may be less harsh if a very long time is granted for the fine to be paid. There is no bright line that delineates where "oppressive" or "exceptional" or "otherwise in the interests of justice" begins. Every case must be determined on its merits, keeping in mind not only the mitigating potential of s. 59(2), but also the legitimate goals of the legislature and society's legitimate interest in ensuring that people who choose to drive have a powerful incentive to make sure that they are properly insured. See *R. v. Anderson*, 2016 ONCJ 758, 2016 CarswellOnt 21172, 5 M.V.R. (7th) 131, [2016] O.J. No. 6858 (Ont. C.J.).

The interpretation of the relief against minimum fine provision under s. 59(2) of the *Provincial Offences Act* was addressed by the Ontario Court of Appeal in *Ontario (Environment, Conservation and Parks) v. Henry of Pelham*, 2018 ONCA 999, 2018 CarswellOnt 20638, [2018] O.J. No. 6434 (Ont. C.A.). The Court summarized the guiding principles as follows: (1) Minimum fines establish sentencing floors that apply regardless of ordinary sentencing principles. The imposition of fines *above* the minimum threshold is governed by ordinary sentencing principles, as well as any principles set out in the relevant legislation; (2) Section 59(2) vests a discretionary authority in trial judges to provide relief from minimum fines in exceptional circumstances. The burden is on those seeking the grant of relief to establish that relief is warranted based on the relevant considerations; (3) Section 59(2) applies exceptionally. It will be an unusual case in which the imposition of a minimum fine may be considered "unduly oppressive" or "otherwise not in the interests of justice"; (4) Whether a minimum fine is unduly oppressive will usually depend on consideration of personal hardship. The bar for relief is set very high. Mere difficulty in paying a minimum fine is inadequate to justify discretionary relief; (5) Whether a minimum fine is otherwise not in the interests of justice involves consideration of not only the interests of an individual offender but also the interests of the community protected by the relevant public welfare legislation; (6) The discretion under s. 59(2) cannot be exercised arbitrarily. Trial judges must explain their reasons for invoking s. 59(2), and, in particular, must demonstrate both that the circumstances are exceptional and that it would be unduly oppressive or otherwise not in the interests of justice to apply the minimum fine.

11.2.2 TIME TO PAY A FINE

- A fine becomes due and payable 15 days after its imposition: section 66(1).

- The court will ask the defendant if he or she requires an extension of the 15 days in order to pay the fine: section 66(2).

- Where a fine is imposed in the defendant's absence, the clerk of the court will give the defendant:

    - Notice of the fine;

    - Notice of its due date; and

    - Notice of the defendant's right to make a motion for an extension of the time for payment: section 66(5).

- The defendant may, at any time, request an extension or further extension of time for payment of the fine by:

    - Making a motion in the prescribed form [See Appendix C]; and

    - Filing the motion in the office of the court: section 66(6).

- The motion will be determined by a justice. In respect of the motion, the justice has the same powers as the court has under subsections (3) and (4): section 66(6).

- Where the defendant requests an extension of the time for payment of the fine, the court may:

  - Make inquiries of the defendant, on oath or affirmation, as the court deems necessary. The defendant is not to be compelled to answer: section 66(3).

  - May order periodic payments be made unless it finds that the request for the extension of time is not made in good faith or that it would likely be used to evade payment: section 66(4). [See Appendix C]

Section 66 of the *Provincial Offences Act* requires that the court inquire as to whether the defendant wishes an extension of time to pay a fine, and that unless the court finds that such a request is not made in good faith or that the extension would likely be used to evade payment the court shall grant the time for payment. In the case at bar, the total fines imposed were well above the defendant's total income for the preceding year, and there was no reason to believe that the extension request was being made in bad faith or to evade payment of the fine. In the result, payment of half of the fine imposed was required within 6 months and the remainder within 12 months. See *R. v. Swartz*, 2012 ONCJ 505, 2012 CarswellOnt 9494, [2012] O.J. No. 3648 (Ont. C.J.).

In *R. v. Zimmerman*, 2011 CarswellOnt 15344, [2011] O.J. No. 5782 (Ont. C.J.), it was held the unrepresented defendant's plea of "Guilty, but I didn't know" was not an unequivocal plea. It was incumbent on the justice to go into a detailed explanation of the process and the nature and consequences of the guilty plea. It was also important to do so upon the defendant's indication that she was a housewife for most of her life but upon her husband becoming suddenly ill she had become responsible for managing the property. Upon the defendant stating her inability to pay, it was incumbent on the justice to explain that if she was going to make these submissions, she could testify or produce an affidavit. It was not explained how this information could be properly before the court so that the justice could take it into account. This constituted a very serious deficiency in the procedure. The justice is required, by law, to consider the financial circumstances of an individual when imposing a fine.

11.2.3 FINE OPTION PROGRAM

- The Lieutenant Governor in Council has regulation making authority over programs permitting the payment of fines by means of credits for work performed: section 67.

- Under this authority, he or she may:

  - Prescribe classes of work and the conditions under which they are to be performed;

  - Prescribe a system of credits; and

  - Provide for any matter necessary for the effective administration of the program: section 67.

- Any regulation may limit the program's application to any part or parts of Ontario: section 67.

- According to the annotation to Segal and Libman's *The 2010 Annotated Ontario Provincial Offences Act* (Carswell, 2010) at 348:

  > The applicable rules and regulations for the Fine Option Program are set out in R.R.O. 1990, Reg. 948, as amended by O. Reg. 500/91, section 1. There are currently three fine option districts: the Regional Municipality of Hamilton-Wentworth, the Regional Municipality of Niagara; and the whole of the Territorial District of Kenora. However, this Schedule of Fine Option districts has been revoked effective April 1, 1994: O. Reg. 925/93, sections 1, 2. There is not as yet a program established by the province to permit the payment of fines by means of credit for work performed as contemplated by section 67. An undertaking to satisfy fine payment by earning credits for work performed shall be in Form 1: R.R.O. 1990, Reg. 948, as amended by O. Reg. 500/91, section 1. An undertaking to satisfy fine payment by earning credits for work performed shall be in Form 2.

11.2.4 CIVIL ENFORCEMENT OF FINES

- Section 68 prescribes the manner in which a fine can be used as a civil judgment for collection, and if the fine is not paid within 90 days, section 69.1 permits the disclosure of the fine to a consumer reporting agency.

11.2.5 DEFAULT OF FINE

- Failure to pay a fine may lead to cancellation of a provincial permit, licence, registration, or other privilege: section 69.

- A defaulting defendant may be brought before the court by way of the justice's issuance of a warrant for the arrest of the defendant or the clerk's issuance of a summons if other methods of collecting the fine have failed: section 69(6), (7).

In *R. v. Mitchell* (2001), 2001 CarswellOnt 3767, 30 M.V.R. (4th) 134 (Ont. S.C.J.), it was held that the defendant could not bring a motion under section 69 for relief from the fines. The Justice of the Peace had no common law or inherent power to take on jurisdiction. If the doctrine of attornment existed at all, it could not be relied on in criminal or provincial prosecutions as a basis for assuming jurisdiction. Section 69 does not contemplate or authorize initiating a motion by the defendant.

Defaulted fines, in whole or in part, may be added to the property tax roll, under the authority of s. 441 of the *Municipal Act, 2001*, and the *City of Toronto Act, 2006*, s. 381.1. There is no limitation period for the filing of the certificate of default. Designations are not required to collect parking fines.

Further amendments impacting the *Provincial Offences Act* have been proposed by the *Burden Reduction Act, 2016* (Bill 27). This Bill was given first reading on 27 September 2016. Under Schedule 2, s. 28, new s. 70.1 would be added to the *Provincial Offences Act* which provides for the payment of collection agency costs. It requires that a defendant shall pay the costs that a municipality incurs by using a registered collection agency in good standing under the *Collection and Debt Settlement Services Act* to collect a fine that is in default, but the costs shall not exceed an amount approved by the municipality (s.70.1(1)). For the purpose of making and enforcing payment, costs payable under this section are deemed to be part of the fine that is in default (s. 70.1(2)).

In *Hamilton (City) v. Barbano* (July 28, 2016), Doc. CV-15-53875, [2016] O.J. No. 4011 (Ont. S.C.J.), it was held that s. 69(15)(c) allows a justice of the peace in exceptional circumstances to reduce a fine or order that it does not have to be paid if the justice is satisfied that the person is unable to pay the fine in a reasonable amount of time. However, s. 165(3) of the *Provincial Offences Act* states that this section does not apply to any part of the province that is covered by a municipal transfer agreement. The City in question was covered by such an agreement since 1999. The language in s. 66(6) allowing a justice to order "periodic payments or otherwise" when extending time to pay a fine was not sufficiently broad to allow a justice to invoke the procedure in s. 69(15) to reduce or eliminate fines; the unproclaimed s. 69(14.1) may allow fines to be reduced one day, but it had been passed in 2009 and remained not in effect. The justice's order reducing the total fines payable was quashed, and the matter remitted back for consideration of the issue of extension of time to pay the fines.

11.2.6 COSTS

- Upon conviction, the defendant may have to pay various fees, up to a maximum of $100, which are enforced like a fine: section 60.

- The Provincial Offences Court is restricted in its power to award costs, and does not have jurisdiction to award legal costs. Under section 60, its power is limited to costs in respect of witnesses and costs fixed by regulation (R.R.O. 1990, Reg. 945 as amended).

In *Ontario v. 974649 Ontario Inc.*, 2001 CarswellOnt 4251, 47 C.R. (5th) 316 (*sub. nom.* R. v. 974649 Ontario Inc.) [2001] 3 S.C.R. 575, 56 O.R. (3d) 359 (headnote only), 2001 CarswellOnt 4252, (*sub. nom.* R. v. 974649 Ontario Inc.) [2001] S.C.J. No. 79, (*sub. nom.* R. v. 974649 Ontario Inc.) 2001 SCC 81, (*sub. nom.* R. v. 974649 Ontario Inc.) 206 D.L.R. (4th) 444, (*sub. nom.* R. v. 974649 Ontario Inc.) 159 C.C.C. (3d) 321, (*sub. nom.* R. v. 974649 Ontario Inc.) 88 C.R.R. (2d) 189, (*sub. nom.* R. v. 974649 Ontario Inc.) 279 N.R. 345, (*sub. nom.* R. v. 974649 Ontario Inc.) 154 O.A.C. 345 (S.C.C.), the Supreme Court of Canada concluded that the regulation referred to in section 60(2) is Reg. 945, R.R.O. 1990, which provides for payment of minimum amounts for matters such as fees to cover travel expenses and each day in attendance for witnesses. The word "expenses" used in section 60(2) has the same meaning in section 29(5), and does not include legal fees.

- Section 90 limits the power to award costs to particular procedural breaches.

In *Ontario v. 974649 Ontario Inc.*, 2001 CarswellOnt 4251, 47 C.R. (5th) 316 (*sub. nom.* R. v. 974649 Ontario Inc.) [2001] 3 S.C.R. 575, 56 O.R. (3d) 359 (headnote only), 2001 CarswellOnt 4252, (*sub. nom.* R. v. 974649 Ontario Inc.) [2001] S.C.J. No. 79, (*sub. nom.* R. v. 974649 Ontario Inc.) 2001 SCC 81, (*sub. nom.* R. v. 974649 Ontario Inc.) 206 D.L.R. (4th) 444, (*sub. nom.* R. v. 974649 Ontario Inc.) 159 C.C.C. (3d) 321, (*sub. nom.* R. v. 974649 Ontario Inc.) 88 C.R.R. (2d) 189, (*sub. nom.* R. v. 974649 Ontario Inc.) 279 N.R. 345, (*sub. nom.* R. v. 974649 Ontario Inc.) 154 O.A.C. 345 (S.C.C.), costs were awarded on the defendants' disclosure motion which was brought as a result of the Crown's failure to disclose a copy of the Prosecution Approval Form relating to charges laid under the *Occupational Health and Safety Act*.

In *Ontario (Ministry of Labour) v. Intracorp Developments (Lombard) Inc.* (2002), 2002 CarswellOnt 1134, [2002] O.J. No. 1209 (Ont. S.C.J.), the court held that before legal costs could be awarded under section 90(2), there must be an irregularity or defect in the substance or form of the document compelling the defendant to answer the charges or a variance between the charges set out in the summons and the charge in the information, and the defendant must have been misled by the irregularity, defect or variance. Accordingly, the justice of the peace exceeded his jurisdiction in awarding costs to the defendants where the Crown failed to charge both defendants on one information as such omission did not amount to a defect or irregularity.

11.2.7 SURCHARGE

- Section 60.1 provides for a surcharge if a fine is imposed in respect of a conviction for an offence commenced under Part I or Part III.

- A surcharge is deemed to be a fine for the purpose of enforcing payment: section 60.1(2).

- The surcharge known as the Victim Fine Surcharge consists of a graduated scale of rates, depending on the amount of the fine, and is administered after a fine has been imposed: O. Reg. 161/00.

In *R. v. Henry Heyink Construction Ltd.* (1999), 118 O.A.C. 261, 1999 CarswellOnt 254, [1999] O.J. No. 238 (Ont. C.A.), the Court of Appeal found that it was entirely appropriate for the trial judge in imposing sentence to consider the surcharges and their economic impact in determining the fitness of the sentence. The surcharge is a real life consideration that affects the economic circumstances of the defendant and his or her capacity to pay.

11.2.8 PROBATION

- Where a defendant is convicted of an offence under Part III, the court may suspend sentence and direct the defendant to complete a term of probation with various conditions, having regard to the following factors:

  - The age, character and background of the defendant;

  - The nature of the offence; and

  - The circumstances surrounding its commission: section 72.

- The probation order contains certain statutory conditions, including that the defendant not commit the same offence or any related or similar offence [See copy of Probation Order in Appendix C].

- The court may impose a period of probation of up to two years under subsection 72(4).

- A copy of the probation order must be given to the defendant.

- A probation order may be imposed after a trial held on an *ex parte* basis: the trial justice has jurisdiction to impose probation in the absence of the defendants: *R. v. Viera*, 2007 ONCJ 496, 2007 CarswellOnt 6959, [2007] O.J. No. 4177 (Ont. C.J.).

A justice of the peace is entitled to impose as a condition of probation that the offender not engage directly or indirectly in the business of environmental consulting, under the authority of s. 72(3)(c) of the *Provincial Offences Act* "to prevent similar unlawful conduct": *R. v. Carter*, 2008 CarswellOnt 5301, 39 C.E.L.R. (3d) 1, 2008 ONCA 630, [2008] O.J. No. 3533 (Ont. C.A.), affirming, 2008 CarswellOnt 4339 (Ont. C.J.), varying, 2007 CarswellOnt 9472 (Ont. C.J.).

In *Ontario (Ministry of Labour) v. Creations by Helen Inc.*, 2007 CarswellOnt 9561, 2007 ONCJ 713, [2007] O.J. No. 5560 (Ont. C.J.), it was held that while s. 72(1)(a) authorizes suspending sentence and imposing probation if the proceedings are commenced by information, where the proceedings were instituted by a certificate of offence, there was no jurisdiction for the justice of the peace to place the defendant on a probation order.

In *R. v. Aziz* (February 28, 2008), V.A. Lampkin J., [2008] O.J. No. 5161 (Ont. C.J.), it was held that there is no jurisdiction under the *Provincial Offences Act* to impose a suspended sentence for "ticket offences". Section 59 only applies to minimum fines.

In sentencing the defendant to 90 days' imprisonment for driving while suspended, the court imposed a probation order to assist the defendant deal with his ongoing rehabilitation for alcohol and substance abuse. The defendant was permitted to serve his sentence intermittently so that he could continue with his program; a term of the probation order was that he seek treatment in such programs: *R. v. Myrskog*, 2010 ONCJ 258, 2010 CarswellOnt 4936 (Ont. C.J.).

The defendant was convicted of soliciting following an *ex parte* trial, and had a number of prior convictions for which fines had been imposed, none of which had been paid. However, the trial justice gave no reasons for imposing a jail sentence when the prosecutor sought only probation. A suspended sentence with a period of probation would have been a sound penalty, as it could have incorporated some bolster time for counselling and medical support that the defendant received. Unlike a jail sentence, a period of probation would permit the stability of the defendant's housing to continue. The significance of housing for a person who has been homeless for extended periods of time does not require extensive support in evidence to create a basis in principle for preferring an out of custody sentence. See *R. v. Feldman*, 2013 ONCJ 718, 2013 CarswellOnt 18614, [2013] O.J. No. 6101 (Ont. C.J.).

In *Travel Industry Council of Ontario v. Panorama Travel & Tours Ltd.*, 2014 ONCJ 16, 2014 CarswellOnt 381, [2014] O.J. No. 188 (Ont. C.J.), it was held that in ordering the defendants to both pay restitution of $25,000 and placing them on probation for one year for pleading guilty to trust account violations contrary to the *Travel Industry Act*, the trial Justice of the Peace considered all of the relevant principles of sentence and all of the relevant factors present in the case. The most commonly imposed sentence for similar offences in previous cases had been a fine; imprisonment was clearly not called for in most cases of regulatory offences such as these. Fines will have greater deterrent effect than a restitution order; however, no case suggests that just because a fine has been imposed in most cases, it must be imposed in all cases. While restitution orders should not become the norm in these cases, it could not be said that they would never satisfy the need for deterrence and denunciation. The defendants would lose their house in order to satisfy either fines or restitution orders. It could not be said that two restitution orders for $25,000 provided significantly less deterrent or denunciatory effect than two fines of $15,000 especially where the restitution orders were combined with probation. Any differences that did exist did not constitute reversible error with respect to the sentences imposed on the individual defendants. While from a purely technical standpoint the Justice of the Peace had no jurisdiction to make a probation order in addition to a restitution order, the probation order could be made in conjunction with a suspended sentence, or with a sentence that includes a fine or imprisonment. It would have been permissible for the Justice to accomplish exactly the same result had she suspended the passing of sentence, placed the defendants on probation, and then, in addition to that, made the restitution orders. The sentences were varied to add suspended sentences with probation for one year to achieve this result. The trial Justice was also entitled to take into consideration that for all practical purposes the corporation no longer existed and it would be impossible for anyone to enforce either a fine or a compensation order against it. The corporation was not entitled to be exempted from such a sentence simply because of sentences imposed on the individual defendants, although those sentences would be a factor to be considered; neither was the corporation entitled to be exempted from such a sentence simply because it was not actively carrying on business. It was not exempt even though it had been wound up and its assets liquidated. A fine of $25,000 was imposed against the corporation on appeal in place of a suspended sentence and probation.

In *Real Estate Council of Ontario v. Allen*, 2015 ONCJ 642, 2015 CarswellOnt 17339, [2015] O.J. No. 5924 (Ont. C.J.), it was held that there is statutory authority under s. 74 of the *Provincial Offences Act* to vary the defendant's probation order to provide more time to pay restitution. There is also authority to require the defendant to comply with a free-standing restitution order if authorized by the provincial statute under which the defendant has been found guilty.

The defendants were convicted at an *ex parte* trial of offences under the *Consumer Protection Act* and ordered to pay stand-alone restitution orders in favour of four victims. The restitution term in the probation orders was varied to require the defendants pay a minimum amount in restitution each month in consecutive months for the duration of the probation order or until the total restitution was paid, whichever occurred first. Restitution payments made in satisfaction of the terms of probation or otherwise should be prorated and credited against the stand-alone restitution orders. See *R. v. Storey*, 2016 ONCJ 73, 2016 CarswellOnt 1839, [2016] O.J. No. 690 (Ont. C.J.).

Imposing probation can meet considerations of rehabilitation. In the instant case, the protection of the public is of utmost importance, and more specifically, protection of children, the most vulnerable individuals in our society. Parents who put children in the care of individuals need to be confident in the care that will be provided and that the standard of care will be such as to ensure their safety and protection. The defendants having 28 children in their care without a licence prevented these parents from the comfort of these standards, as demonstrated by the state of the daycare on the date the officers arrived. Given all the considerations, and more importantly, potential harm, a period of 30 days incarceration was required as well as fines of $1500. The defendants were additionally placed on probation for a period of two years, with terms including that they do not commit the same or any related or similar offence or any offence under a statute of Canada or Ontario or any other Province of Canada that is punishable by imprisonment, and not to operate any licensed or unlicensed daycare centres. See *R. v. Panfilova* (March 18, 2016), Doc. Newmarket 4960-13-2837, [2016] O.J. No. 2115 (Ont. C.J.).

Following the defendant's guilty plea to charges under the *Environmental Protection Act*, the prosecutor and defendant agreed to a term of probation ordered by the court that the defendant be required to have an embedded auditor to review its practices and procedures and make recommendations for future conduct. Section 72(3)(c) provides the authority for making this type of order. See *R. v. Quantex Technologies Inc.*, 2018 ONCJ 546, 2018 CarswellOnt 13407, [2018] O.J. No. 4259 (Ont. C.J.).

11.2.9 BREACH OF PROBATION

- Breach of probation is punishable under section 75.

- A defendant may breach the statutory conditions of the probation order in one of two ways:

  - Commit the same or similar offence.

  - Commit an offence under a provincial or federal statute that is punishable by imprisonment.

- Once a defendant has breached a condition of the probation order, section 75 provides for two offences relating to breaching a probation order.

  - For the offence of breach of probation, the defendant must be convicted of an offence that constitutes a breach of the probation order, and the time for appeal has elapsed or any appeal filed has been dismissed or abandoned.

  - For the offence of willfully failing to comply with a probation order, the prosecution must prove to the court that the defendant was aware of the probation order and its conditions, and chose to ignore them.

- Upon conviction under section 75, the court may impose a fine of up to $1,000 or imprisonment of not more than 30 days, or both.

11.2.10 IMPRISONMENT

- The only offence for which a youth can be imprisoned is breach of probation, which has a maximum of 30 days (sections 75, 101), and any sentence for the youth shall be served in open custody (section 103).

- Pre-sentence reports for any defendant can be ordered under section 56 and must be ordered for a youth facing a prison term under section 100(2).

- In determining the sentence to be imposed on a person convicted of an offence, the justice may take into account any time spent in custody by the person as a result of the offence: section 58.

- The term of prison shall, unless otherwise directed, commence on the date taken into custody, though the court may order custody to commence up to 30 days after sentencing: section 63.

- Sentences shall be served consecutively, unless otherwise ordered: section 64.

In *R. v. Seto*, 2010 ONCJ 551, 2010 CarswellOnt 8970, [2010] O.J. No. 5438 (Ont. C.J.), it was held that the justice of the peace did not err in regarding breach of trust as an aggravating factor in sentencing. It is important to get a clear message out to real estate brokers that if they violate their trust they may go to prison. A fine of $20,000 imposed on the company and period of one year's imprisonment on the offender was upheld on appeal.

It was held in *R. v. Nilsson*, 2012 ONCJ 375, 2012 CarswellOnt 7679, [2012] O.J. No. 2750 (Ont. C.J.) that there is no general power to impose a conditional sentence as a punishment where incarceration is available under the *Provincial Offences Act* of Ontario. In this case the trial justice had imposed a house arrest term in sentencing the defendant to jail for multiple counts of driving while suspended.

Imposing probation can meet considerations of rehabilitation. In the instant case, the protection of the public is of utmost importance, and more specifically, protection of children, the most vulnerable individuals in our society. Parents who put children in the care of individuals need to be confident in the care that will be provided and that the standard of care will be such as to ensure their safety and protection. The defendants having 28 children in their care without a licence prevented these parents from the comfort of these standards, as demonstrated by the state of the daycare on the date the officers arrived. Given all the considerations, and more importantly, potential harm, a period of 30 days incarceration was required as well as fines of $1500. The defendants were additionally placed on probation for a period of two years, with terms including that they do not commit the same or any related or similar offence or any offence under a statute of Canada or Ontario or any other Province of Canada that is punishable by imprisonment, and not to operate any licensed or unlicensed daycare centres. See *R. v. Panfilova* (March 18, 2016), Doc. Newmarket 4960-13-2837, [2016] O.J. No. 2115 (Ont. C.J.).

11.2.11 RESTITUTION

A finding of loss is a necessary precondition to the imposition of a restitution order. Where the evidentiary record does not establish that the vendor of the property, in fact, suffered a loss by his payment on closing of the relevant real estate transaction, the restitution order must be set aside. See *R. v. Formosi*, 2012 ONCA 485, 2012 CarswellOnt 8442 (Ont. C.A.).

Sentencing decisions are entitled to considerable deference by appeal courts. The primary objectives of sentencing in the instant case were general and specific deterrence, and warranted the imposition of a jail sentence. The trial judge concluded that the defendant was a predator who preyed upon vulnerable people and that his motive was to take advantage of the consumer for his own benefit, findings that were supported by the evidence presented at trial. The trial judge did not fail to consider a relevant factor and did not overemphasize an appropriate factor. However, some of the counts formed part of the same series of events and it was appropriate for the 15 day jail sentences on these two counts to be made concurrent, rather than consecutive, such that the total sentence of 75 days imprisonment was reduced to 45 days. The defendant did not appeal the probation order imposed requiring him to make restitution in the amount of $29,643, and he had repaid $8,000 of this amount by the time of the appeal hearing. See *R. v. Belisle* (February 8, 2011), Doc. Ottawa 08-003698, [2011] O.J. No. 1326 (Ont. C.J.).

A restitution order was also imposed in *R. v. Perruzza*, 2012 ONCJ 111, 2012 CarswellOnt 2687, [2012] O.J. No. 987 (Ont. C.J.) so that the defendant would not profit from her wrongdoing, at the direct expense of others, while holding a position of trust. Her conduct included making bookings that resulted in a financial loss to the travel agency, not reporting sales, using unauthorized credit card payments and failing to forward consumer payments.

In *Consbec Inc. v. Ontario (Ministry of the Environment)*, 2013 ONCJ 258, 2013 CarswellOnt 5876, 76 C.E.L.R. (3d) 149, [2013] O.J. No. 2220 (Ont. C.J.), it was stated that the requirement that the basis for a court's decision must be ascertainable by those affected by that decision was set out by the Supreme Court of Canada in *R. v. Sheppard*, 2002 SCC 26, 2002 CarswellNfld 74, REJB 2002-29516, [2002] 1 S.C.R. 869, 211 Nfld. & P.E.I.R. 50, 162 C.C.C. (3d) 298, 50 C.R. (5th) 68, 210 D.L.R. (4th) 608, 633 A.P.R. 50, 284 N.R. 342, [2002] S.C.J. No. 30 (S.C.C.). It is a question of accountability not only to the unsuccessful party but to the public. Reasons justify and explain the result. Insufficient reasons can deprive the appellant of a meaningful opportunity to have the correctness of the court's decision reviewed by a court on appeal. That could amount to an error at law. As important as these reasons may be to make clear the basis on which the decision was arrived at, there may be extant on the record of the proceedings an explanation of the path taken by the court when arriving at its decision. While the reasons could have been more fulsome, the Justice of the Peace did take into consideration the evidence introduced at the sentencing hearing as set out in her recitation of the evidence in her reasons. Further, she was at liberty to consider and resolve the conflicts between the theories as advanced by the parties. The court was very much alive to the debate that informed the hearing; on the evidence before the court, the Justice could reach the conclusion that she did, namely, that the blast set off by the defendant was in some way connected to the change in the well water quality. That conclusion, although perhaps not extensively explained, was supported by the evidence at the hearing. The Justice of the Peace therefore arrived at her determination without falling into error of law or principle. It could not be said that the fine imposed and orders for restoration and restitution were demonstrably unfit. The determination of the trial court was entitled to deference by the appeal court.

In *Travel Industry Council of Ontario v. Panorama Travel & Tours Ltd.*, 2014 ONCJ 16, 2014 CarswellOnt 381, [2014] O.J. No. 188 (Ont. C.J.), it was held that in ordering the defendants to both pay restitution of $25,000 and placing them on probation for one year for pleading guilty to trust account violations contrary to the *Travel Industry Act*, the trial Justice of the Peace considered all of the relevant principles of sentence and all of the relevant factors present in the case. The most commonly imposed sentence for similar offences in previous cases had been a fine; imprisonment was clearly not called for in most cases of regulatory offences such as these. Fines will have greater deterrent effect than a restitution order; however, no case suggests that just because a fine has been imposed in most cases, it must be imposed in all cases. While restitution orders should not become the norm in these cases, it could not be said that they would never satisfy the need for deterrence and denunciation. The defendants would lose their house in order to satisfy either fines or restitution orders. It could not be said that two restitution orders for $25,000 provided significantly less deterrent or denunciatory effect than two fines of $15,000 especially where the restitution orders were combined with probation. Any differences that did exist did not constitute reversible error with respect to the sentences imposed on the individual defendants. While from a purely technical standpoint the Justice of the Peace had no jurisdiction to make a probation order in addition to a restitution order, the probation order could be made in conjunction with a suspended sentence, or with a sentence that includes a fine or imprisonment. It would have been permissible for the Justice to accomplish exactly the same result had she suspended the passing of sentence, placed the defendants on probation, and then, in addition to that, made the restitution orders. The sentences were varied to add suspended sentences with probation for one year to achieve this result. The trial Justice was also entitled to take into consideration that for all practical purposes the corporation no longer existed and it would be impossible for anyone to enforce either a fine or a compensation order against it. The corporation was not entitled to be exempted from such a sentence simply because of sentences imposed on the individual defendants, although those sentences would be a factor to be considered; neither was the corporation entitled to be exempted from such a sentence simply because it was not actively carrying on business. It was not exempt even though it had been wound up and its assets liquidated. A fine of $25,000 was imposed against the corporation on appeal in place of a suspended sentence and probation.

In *Real Estate Council of Ontario v. Allen*, 2015 ONCJ 642, 2015 CarswellOnt 17339, [2015] O.J. No. 5924 (Ont. C.J.), it was held that there is statutory authority under s. 74 of the *Provincial Offences Act* to vary the defendant's probation order to provide more time to pay restitution. There is also authority to require the defendant to comply with a free-standing restitution order if authorized by the provincial statute under which the defendant has been found guilty.

The defendants were convicted at an *ex parte* trial of offences under the *Consumer Protection Act* and ordered to pay stand-alone restitution orders in favour of four victims. The restitution term in the probation orders was varied to require the defendants pay a minimum amount in restitution each month in consecutive months for the duration of the probation order or until the total restitution was paid, whichever occurred first. Restitution payments made in satisfaction of the terms of probation or otherwise should be prorated and credited against the stand-alone restitution orders. See *R. v. Storey*, 2016 ONCJ 73, 2016 CarswellOnt 1839, [2016] O.J. No. 690 (Ont. C.J.).

11.3 SUBMISSIONS ON SENTENCE

- The prosecution and defence shall have an opportunity to make submissions as to an appropriate sentence: section 57.

- You, as counsel or agent, should make the submissions and generally your client should remain silent. Anything positive can be said by you, and the risk of your client making matters worse will be greatly reduced.

- However, the justice of the peace may ask the defendant if there is anything he or she wishes to say before sentence is imposed. This is the practice in criminal courts. The defendant may wish to address the court after pleading guilty to make an apology or express remorse for his or her conduct. This can be an effective part of the sentencing process, but the defendant's counsel or agent should discuss this beforehand to ensure that what will be said is appropriate and relevant to the issue of sentencing.

- There have also been some recent cases where the prosecutor has been permitted to tender into evidence a victim impact statement so that the victim's views on sentencing can be communicated to the provincial offences court. See *R. v. Hutchings*, [2004] O.J. No. 3950, 2004 ONCJ 200, 2004 CarswellOnt 3907 (Ont. C.J.); *R. v. Messercola*, [2005] O.J. No. 126, 2005 ONCJ 6, 2005 CarswellOnt 148, 16 M.V.R. (5th) 82 (Ont. C.J.); *R. v.*

> *Robinson*, 2008 CarswellBC 1854, 2008 BCSC 1195, [2008] B.C.J. No. 1691 (B.C. S.C.).

- Consider the following issues in your submissions.
  - General deterrance.
    - How prevalent is the offence in the community?
    - What social interests are at stake?
    - What is the normal range of sentence?
    - What sentence would likely deter others?
  - Specific deterrance.
    - Why did your client commit the offence?
    - Was it done before?
    - What has and can be done to prevent it from happening again?
    - Will the sentence affect his or her dependants, and if so, will it decrease the likelihood of your client repeating the offence?

General deterrence was a key sentencing factor in the case of an aboriginal person who unlawfully hunted moose in partnership with a non-native person contrary to the *Fish and Wildlife Conservation Act*. Each defendant received a fine of at least $5,000, and had their hunting privileges suspended for two years. The illegal hunting had an adverse effect on the local economy, and resulted in an abuse of aboriginal treaty rights. The defendant, who was an aboriginal, committed a breach of trust to his community, and this abuse resulted in tension between the native and non-native communities. See *Ontario (Ministry of Natural Resources) v. Bruyere* (2003), [2003] O.J. No. 5927, 2003 CarswellOnt 6275 (Ont. S.C.J.).

In *R. v. Kang*, 2007 ONCJ 362, 2007 CarswellOnt 5123, [2007] O.J. No. 3085 (Ont. C.J.) Quon J. discussed the use of a pre-sentence report as provided under section 56(1) of the *Provincial Offences Act*. He observed that the purpose of a pre-sentence report is to supply to the court a picture of the offender as a person in society. A probation officer's recommendation for community supervision only means that he is not unsuitable for community supervision: the probation officer, in developing recommendations, does not take into account deterrence and other sentencing objectives that a sentencing court has to consider in finding a fit and suitable sentence for the offender. A pre-sentence report should be confined to portraying the background, family, education, employment record, physical and mental health, associates, social activities, potential, and motivation of the person; its function is not to tell the court what sentence should be imposed.

In an *Occupational Health and Safety Act* case involving two fatalities, the trial judge took account of the impact of the tragic events on the families of the deceased as indicated by his having permitted the widow of one of the deceased workers to read a victim impact statement into the record, even though there is no provision expressly permitting this under the *Provincial Offences Act*: *R. v. Delgant 2000 Ltd.* (2008), 2008 CarswellOnt 1244, [2008] O.J. No. 879 (Ont. S.C.J.).

In *R. v. Sholtens*, 2008 ONCJ 282, 2008 CarswellOnt 3605, [2008] O.J. No. 2444 (Ont. C.J.), the appeal court held that where a justice of the peace on his own motion adjourns a sentencing hearing to another date for the purposes of providing reasons as to why he cannot accept the guilty plea, and gives reasons for judgment without providing the prosecutor or unrepresented defendant a real opportunity of making submissions, the proceedings take on the appearance of a public lecture rather than an adversarial process before an impartial decision maker. A reasonable person, reasonably informed, would conclude that that the justice's decision had been arrived at before all the evidence and submissions had been heard. The justice of the peace was bound to follow the law on point and enter a conviction, through the application of the doctrine of *stare decisis*; there was a decision of a judge of the Ontario Court of Justice sitting as an appeal court, indicating that it was appropriate to register a finding of guilt in the circumstances of the case. *Stare decisis* is the glue that binds the court system in Ontario together, and gives purposes to the different levels of court and functions so as to prevent injustice. For a similar case, see *R. c. Bellefeuille*, 2008 CarswellOnt 6641, 2008 ONCJ 575, [2008] O.J. No. 4494 (Ont. C.J.) where the justice of the peace rejected the defendant's guilty plea and erroneously dismissed the charges, rather than set a trial date which was the proper course where a guilty plea is rejected.

In a sentencing hearing, hearsay evidence that is credible and trustworthy is admissible, unless such evidence is disputed in which event it must be proved by the rules as if in a trial: *R. v. Janes Family Foods Ltd.*, 2008 ONCJ 13, 2008 CarswellOnt 177, 36 C.E.L.R. (3d) 290, [2008] O.J. No. 158 (Ont. C.J.).

The maximum sentence provided for an offence may be appropriate even where the offender is not the worst possible and the offence is not committed in the worst way. If a proper and fit sentence, as determined by the court acting judicially, is at the maximum of the range set by Parliament, then the sentence is fit. The sentencing court must determine the appropriate punishment within the limits established by Parliament: *R. v. Solowan*, 2008 CarswellBC 2396, 2008 CarswellBC 2397, [2008] S.C.J. No. 55, 2008 SCC 62, 299 D.L.R. (4th) 577, 261 B.C.A.C. 27, 440 W.A.C. 27, 70 M.V.R. (5th) 1, (*sub nom.* R. v. S. (K.S.T.)) 237 C.C.C. (3d) 129, 61 C.R. (6th) 268, 381 N.R. 191, [2008] S.C.J. No. 55 (S.C.C.).

In *R. v. Kronshteyn*, 2008 CarswellOnt 4600 (Ont. C.J.), the court set aside a conviction and ordered a new trial where evidence was placed before the court by the trial agent that he misunderstood the defendant's instructions due to a language barrier, and erroneously entered guilty to a lesser charge.

In *R. v. Fuentes*, 2008 ONCJ 598, 2008 CarswellOnt 7068, [2008] O.J. No. 4677 (Ont. C.J.), it was held that it is the client's right to meet with the person who represents him so there will be no misunderstanding as to what occurs in court. It is mandatory that whomever the licensed paralegal hires meets with the client where a paralegal informs the client that another paralegal will represent the client in court. It is not sufficient for the paralegal to merely tell the other agent what the client wants or said. Where the second paralegal pleaded the client guilty without ever speaking to the client, and a licence suspension was imposed, the conviction could not stand.

Victim impact statements may be heard by the court on sentencing under the *Provincial Offences Act*: see *R. v. Delarosbil*, 2008 CarswellOnt 9170 (Ont. C.J.); *R. v. Cory* (2005), 2005 CarswellOnt 8304 (Ont. C.J.); *R. v. Di Franco* (2008), [2008] O.J. No. 879, 78 W.C.B. (2d) 247 (Ont. S.C.J.). However, as the court held in *R. v. Long Lake Forest Products Inc.*, [2009] O.J. No. 2193, 2009 CarswellOnt 3054, 2009 ONCJ 241 (Ont. C.J.), while the justice of the peace was entitled to find that he had jurisdiction to admit into evidence victim impact statements, where the opposing party objects to the admission of portions of such statements, the trial justice should rule upon the objection and determine the issue of admissibility such that any portions which are ruled inadmissible are excluded from the sentencing hearing. Portions of the statements in question were not relevant to the issue before the court as the concerned collateral matters and could have resulted in a lengthy hearing dealing with unrelated workplace issues.

In *R. v. Persaud*, [2009] O.J. No. 1953, 2009 CarswellOnt 2630, 2009 ONCJ 210, 193 C.R.R. (2d) 241 (Ont. C.J.), the court held that the procedural rules governing the trial and sentencing of *Highway Traffic Act* offences are contained in the *Provincial Offences Act*. While these types of offences are regulatory in nature, the same standard of review that is employed in criminal sentencing appeals is applicable and instructive; the principles of sentencing set out in Part XXIII of the *Criminal Code* apply to regulatory proceedings governed by the *Provincial Offences Act*. The justice of the peace erred by the manner in which he rejected the joint submission. Judicial officers are not bound by the submissions of counsel, including joint submissions. However, where a joint submission is placed before a court, it should be accepted unless it is contrary to the public interest and would bring the administration of justice into disrepute. Moreover, before rejecting a joint submission, a judicial officer should inform the parties that the court is considering doing so and afford them the opportunity to justify it. Having done so, the judicial officer may depart from the joint submission where cogent reasons are provided. In other words, the law in Ontario imposes a standard for the rejection of a joint submission, along with the requirement of prior notice to the parties and the opportunity for further dialogue between them and the court.

The fines for speeding under s. 128(14) of the *Highway Traffic Act* are fixed and are derived simply by multiplying the number of kilometers per hour over the speed limit by the appropriate dollar figure. The courts have no discretion to reduce these fines: *R. v. Winlow*, 2009 ONCA 643, 2009 CarswellOnt 5208, (*sub nom.* York (Regional Municipality) v. Winlow) 99 O.R. (3d) 337, 86 M.V.R. (5th) 171, 265 O.A.C. 326, [2009] O.J. No. 3691 (Ont. C.A.).

The prosecutor made sentencing submissions to the court and was a forceful advocate, painting the defendant's conduct as serious and deserving of significant sanction. Similarly, counsel for the defendant energetically advocated his client's position. In an adversary system, that is the function of counsel. The justice is left to make findings of fact and apply the relevant law to those findings. That the justice can be persuaded by the passionate submission of counsel is obvious; however, there was no basis for finding that those submissions, particularly of the prosecutor, amounted to misleading the court. The prosecutor confirmed that he was authorized to conduct the prosecution on behalf of the Workplace Safety and Insurance Board, and although the defence counsel sought production of the retainer agreement, the justice was entitled to rule that the prosecutor was not required to produce it: *R. v. Long Lake Forest Products Inc.*, [2009] O.J. No. 2193, 2009 CarswellOnt 3054, 2009 ONCJ 241 (Ont. C.J.).

In *R. v. Sinclair*, 45 C.E.L.R. (3d) 222, 2009 CarswellOnt 4894 (Ont. C.J.), the appeal court observed that a trial judge should never have recourse to media reports, especially opinion pieces, in order to gauge public sentiment about any issue. A sentencing judge familiar with the community in which the offence has occurred will have a strong sense of the blend of sentencing goals that are just and appropriate for the protection of that community, and thus the sentencing judge will have no need to resort to newspaper clippings. It was also held that the trial judge did not err in preparing, in advance, the structure of a complicated sentencing decision and then deciding on the actual disposition after hearing the oral submissions of counsel. Prior to submissions, the parties had provided extensive argument and case law to the court, and it was obvious that the justice had reviewed this material before the sentencing hearing.

The trial justice's statement to the defendant on convicting him of speeding, "Slow down when you come to Durham Region" did not give rise to a reasonable apprehension of bias. The statement was part of the sentencing caution, and the overwhelmingly reasonable interpretation was that it simply was an exhortation to be careful about not speeding in the future. It could not reasonably have created an apprehension of bias with respect to the trial: *R. v. Sibio*, 2010 ONCJ 315, 2010 CarswellOnt 5542, 99 M.V.R. (5th) 98, [2010] O.J. No. 3242 (Ont. C.J.).

In *R. v. Dobson*, 2010 ONCJ 161, 2010 CarswellOnt 2744, [2010] O.J. No. 1823 (Ont. C.J.), it was held that the licensed paralegal who entered a guilty plea in the defendant's absence, on the basis of boilerplate instructions in the retainer agreement authorizing the paralegal to negotiate a plea on the defendant's behalf, did not constitute valid instructions to enter the guilty plea. The instruction was not case specific, included no duty to ensure the facts were admitted by the client, did not indicate that the plea was voluntary, or that the client was aware of the plea. The record keeping practices of the paralegal provided no confidence that she could accurately reconstruct the events that led to the plea; her independent memory was unreliable and she altered the documents in anticipation of the appeal.

There is no jurisdiction to impose a fine for speeding lower than the fine set out for speeding in s. 128(14) of the *Highway Traffic Act*, or to suspend sentence for the offence of speeding: *R. v. Street* (April 22, 2010), Doc. 1556008A-00, [2010] O.J. No. 5951 (Ont. C.J.).

However, the opposite conclusion was reached in *R. v. Doroz*, 2011 ONCJ 281, 2011 CarswellOnt 3874, [2011] O.J. No. 2540, 16 M.V.R. (6th) 156 (Ont. C.J.), where it was held that in exceptional circumstances, it is open to the justice to suspend the passing of sentence in lieu of the set fine for speeding.

While some of the breaches of the property standards order would not have merited the fine of $7,500 imposed by the trial justice, other breaches did. The fine was not outside the range of fines for offences of this nature, and given the seriousness of at least two of the breaches of the order and the defendant's long term resistance to remedying the defects, it was not unfit. See *Ajax (Town) v. Wong*, 2011 ONCJ 352, 2011 CarswellOnt 6315, [2011] O.J. No. 3167 (Ont. C.J.).

Similarly, in *R. v. Wise*, 2011 ONCJ 366, 2011 CarswellOnt 6477, [2011] O.J. No. 3269 (Ont. C.J.), it was held that while the fines imposed by the justice of the peace constituted significant penalties for selling wildlife without a licence and making a false statement, they were within the range and in the discretion of the justice, and were therefore not manifestly unfit.

The justice of the peace erred in improperly reducing the fine agreed upon in a joint submission where counsel were not advised of the justice's intention to depart from the joint submission, and it was not shown that the joint submission was contrary to the public interest and no reasons were provided for departing from the joint submission: *R. v. Lebovic Enterprises Ltd.*, 2010 ONCJ 631, 2010 CarswellOnt 10072, [2010] O.J. No. 5731 (Ont. C.J.).

The self-represented defendant was advised what would happen on the trial, but the brevity of the explanation might not have provided her with an accurate handle on what she had to do to represent herself. She was confused on the *voir dire* and it did not appear she understood its purpose; after the *voir dire* she waived her right to ask the police officer any questions on the trial proper, although it was clear that she had information that contradicted the officer and would have to present that to him to bolster her submissions. On sentencing, the justice imposed the set fine requested by the Crown, without giving reasons why the defendant's pitch for less than that based on financial considerations was rejected. The findings of guilt were set aside on appeal. See *R. v. Pereira*, 2011 CarswellOnt 6058, [2011] O.J. No. 3271 (Ont. C.J.).

For each of the sentencing considerations under the authority of *R. v. Cotton Felts Ltd.*, 1982 CarswellOnt 1235, 2 C.C.C. (3d) 287, C.E.S.H.G. 95,056, [1982] O.J. No. 178 (Ont. C.A.), the trial justice set out the evidence, his assessment of that evidence and reasons in either accepting or rejecting the evidence. The reasons for sentence also demonstrated that the court considered both mitigating and aggravating factors and the purpose and intent of the *Crown Forest Sustainability Act* recognizing that the offences were public welfare offences. While the fines imposed were significant, they were within the appropriate range, considering all of the circumstances of the case and the purposes of the Act: *R. v. Buchanan Forest Products Ltd.*, 2007 ONCJ 630, 2007 CarswellOnt 8720, [2007] O.J. No. 5222 (Ont. C.J.).

In *R. v. Wong*, 2010 ONCJ 636, 2010 CarswellOnt 10221, [2010] O.J. No. 5810 (Ont. C.J.), it was held on appeal that the reasons that the trial justice provided in imposing a fine of $25,000 for failing to comply with a property standards order, when viewed objectively, were not unreasonable. She took into consideration that the offender delayed or attempted to delay the court proceedings; she took into consideration what repairs were done, and concluded that many of the repairs that were done were minor while some of them were too little too late. The trial justice was entitled to find that lack of remorse was an aggravating factor.

It is trite law that an appropriate sentence cannot be increased to demonstrate the court's displeasure with the manner in which a defence was conducted. Nor can a lack of remorse or continued protestation of innocence be considered in aggravation so as to increase an otherwise appropriate sentence. Clearly, although a plea of guilty may be taken into account in mitigation of sentence, an increased sentence is not justified because the accused has pleaded not guilty, put in motion a full trial, and maintained his/her innocence. A careful review of the trial justice's reasons led to the conclusion that he did, in fact, treat the defendant's plea of not guilty and its insistence upon going to trial as an aggravating circumstance. At the very least, his comments were open to this interpretation. This constituted a fundamental error in principle which ultimately resulted in an increased sentence, thereby making appellate review of the sentence entirely appropriate in the case. See *R. v. Superior Custom Trailers Ltd.*, 2009 ONCJ 740, 2009 CarswellOnt 9144, [2009] O.J. No. 6104 (Ont. C.J.).

In *Vallance v. Pickering (City)*, [2011] O.J. No. 6107, 2011 ONCJ 771, 2011 CarswellOnt 15358, 17 C.L.R. (4th) 311, 93 M.P.L.R. (4th) 317 (Ont. C.J.), additional reasons at 2012 ONCJ 147, 2012 CarswellOnt 2756, 17 C.L.R. (4th) 323, [2012] O.J. No. 1216 (Ont. C.J.), it was held that the individual and corporate defendants were both convicted and fined for offences under the *Building Code*. The individual defendant was effectively the alter-ego of the corporation, and the addition was being built onto his personal property. A double penalty should be avoided in circumstances where an officer and sole director have been convicted of the same offence as the corporation. The principle of totality is exemplified by this principle, and should have been taken into account by the trial justice given the individual defendant's pre-eminent role in the company and the use of the corporation as a vehicle for the ownership of the personal home.

Where the individual and corporate defendant were each fined the statutory minimum of $500 per day for an ongoing offence, for total fines in excess of $402,000, and the individual was the directing mind of the corporation, the trial justice did not improperly "double-up" the fines. The defendants deliberately engaged in illegal operations for substantial gain for almost two years, despite being told to stop; they showed no remorse. Not only was there statutory authority to impose the fines, but it would have been reasonable to impose those fines or even greater ones. The fines imposed were therefore quite reasonable, whether imposed against the individual defendant, or the corporate defendant, or both. See *R. v. Nichols*, [2012] O.J. No. 179, 2012 ONCJ 24, 2012 CarswellOnt 498 (Ont. C.J.).

Parking violations are serious regulatory offences and should be treated as such. Cities and the economic social activities they support cannot function properly if parking regulations are observed only in the breach. It was an error in principle, however, to give strong emphasis in this case to the principle of denunciation. The defendant was not driving the taxi cabs when any of the infractions were committed. There was no evidence before the justice to permit a nexus to be drawn between parking infractions and incidents of both road rage and motor vehicle accidents. In addition, the cumulative amount of the fine failed to give effect to the totality principle. As a result, while the quantum of fine may well have been fit in relation to any one infraction, the total amount of the fine was disproportionate to the blameworthiness of the offender. See *R. v. Jhutty*, [2012] B.C.J. No. 215, 2012 CarswellBC 220, 2012 BCSC 168, 28 M.V.R. (6th) 249 (B.C. S.C. [In Chambers]).

In *R. v. Carloni*, 2012 MBQB 313, 2012 CarswellMan 778, 286 Man. R. (2d) 65, [2012] M.J. No. 428 (Man. Q.B.) the trial judge provided no reasons for his sentence of a $2000 fine plus $200 costs for the offence of failing to complete a stop at a stop sign. The Crown acknowledged that the sentence was unfit as the usual fine for such an offence was $130, and it appeared that the judge after acquitting on the related *Criminal Code* offence of refusing to provide a breath sample at the roadside "compensated" by imposing a disproportionate sentence. The trial judge provided no reasons why the situation called for a significant departure from the usual range of sentence. A sentence must be proportionate to the gravity of the offence and the degree of responsibility of the offender. There was nothing in the defendant's manner of driving, his circumstances or moral blameworthiness that justified the maximum penalty. The sentence was demonstrably unfit. A fine of $130 was substituted in its place.

A justice of the peace has the jurisdiction to order a suspension of a driver's licence of a person charged by certificate of offence under Part I of the *Provincial Offences Act* (Ont.). A licence suspension fits within the "actions or results" outlined in s. 12(2) of the Act as consequences of conviction, and is separate and apart from the monetary penalties that can be imposed under s. 128(14) of the *Highway Traffic Act*. See *Durham (Municipality) v. Muia*, 2012 ONCJ 229, 2012 CarswellOnt 5592, 32 M.V.R. (6th) 352, [2012] O.J. No. 1711 (Ont. C.J.).

Sentencing decisions are entitled to considerable deference by appeal courts. The primary objectives of sentencing in the instant case were general and specific deterrence, and warranted the imposition of a jail sentence. The trial judge concluded that the defendant was a predator who preyed upon vulnerable people and that his motive was to take advantage of the consumer for his own benefit, findings that were supported by the evidence presented at trial. The trial judge did not fail to consider a relevant factor and did not overemphasize an appropriate factor. However, some of the counts formed part of the same series of events and it was appropriate for the 15 day jail sentences on these two counts to be made concurrent, rather than consecutive, such that the total sentence of 75 days imprisonment was reduced to 45 days. The defendant did not appeal the probation order imposed requiring him to make restitution in the amount of $29,643, and he had repaid $8,000 of this amount by the time of the appeal hearing. See *R. v. Belisle* (February 8, 2011), Doc. Ottawa 08-003698, [2011] O.J. No. 1326 (Ont. C.J.).

In *R. v. Brown*, 2012 ONCJ 122, 2012 CarswellOnt 4046, [2012] O.J. No. 1294 (Ont. C.J.), the justice of the peace erred in treating the disposition of another prosecution one month earlier and the fines imposed in that prosecution as aggravating factors on sentence. At the time of the charges in issue, the defendant had an unblemished record and should have therefore been treated as a first offender. The fines imposed were reduced to $15,000 per count, the same fines as imposed in the unrelated prosecution one month prior to trial.

In *R. v. Appiah*, 2012 ONCJ 754, 2012 CarswellOnt 15602, 38 M.V.R. (6th) 173, [2012] O.J. No. 5851 (Ont. C.J.), it was held that a set fine which is an out of court payment is simply a figure that amounts to a reduced fine, and that a justice of the peace had no authority to reduce the penalty for speeding in this fashion as opposed to the fine as set out for speeding under the *Highway Traffic Act*.

The defendant was convicted of contravening a zoning by-law but had purchased the property in its current condition, and was not deliberately flouting the zoning by-law. She was cooperative throughout, admitted the evidence of the prosecution and had not delayed the trial. As there were no aggravating factors, the fine imposed by the trial justice, in addition to a prohibition order, was reduced on appeal from $10,000 to $4,000. See *Stratford (City) v. Thomas*, 2012 ONCJ 613, 2012 CarswellOnt 13287, [2012] O.J. No. 5112 (Ont. C.J.).

In *Ontario (Ministry of Labour) v. Pack All Manufacturing Ltd.* (November 6, 2012), Kehoe J., [2012] O.J. No. 5311 (Ont. C.J.), the justice addressed each of the factors in *R. v. Cotton Felts* and applied them to the circumstances of the case. He expressly stated that each case must be considered on its own facts, and applied each of the relevant factors to the facts of the case. He listed what factors were mitigating and what factors were aggravating, and the sentence imposed was reflective of those considerations. The quantum of fine arrived at, $55,000 on conviction for failing as an employer to ensure that measures and procedures prescribed by the regulation were carried out, following an industrial accident where a worker lost a finger while clearing a jam with his hands in a hopper so as not to impede production, was completely supported on the evidence.

The purposes of fines and sentencing under the regulatory offences scheme is not to punish the offender but to ensure the safety of the public, protection of the process of the regulatory legislation, and respect for the law. An increased fine, therefore, is not in the mode of punishment, but rather as specific deterrence, from which follows protection of the public and respect for the law, by deterring the defendant from committing similar offences in the future. An appellate judge, on a sentence appeal, should give considerable deference to the trial judge's decision, and should only intervene to vary the sentence if the sentence is demonstrably unfit, or clearly unreasonable, or where there has been an error in principle, or the trial judge has over-emphasized relevant factors or under-emphasized relevant factors. See *R. v. Nirta*, 2012 ONCJ 629, 2012 CarswellOnt 12657, [2012] O.J. No. 4793 (Ont. C.J.).

In *R. v. Prince Metal Products Ltd.* (June 28, 2011), Hoffman J., [2011] O.J. No. 6450 (Ont. C.J.), it was held that the responsibility of an appeal court on sentencing is to determine if the sentence imposed is fit and to vary it if it is not. Where the sentence is demonstrably unfit or there has been an error in principle, the appellate court may intervene. Given that general deterrence is the primary sentencing consideration in an industrial accident case involving the death of an employee, greater weight should have been given to this factor in determining the quantum of the fine.

Although a sentencing hearing is not a trial, the onus is on the Crown to prove disputed aggravated facts beyond a reasonable doubt. The defendants had gone ahead and built a lakeside addition despite knowing that such construction was not permitted. If the sentence of a monetary penalty was permitted to stand, others would be easily encouraged to disobey the Conservation Authority and its rules. The sentence imposed was therefore demonstrably unfit. Specific deterrence and general deterrence were the governing sentencing principles. The defendants were ordered to remove the lakeside addition at their own expense and within a reasonable period of time. See *R. v. Hanna*, 2012 ONCJ 715, 2012 CarswellOnt 14491, [2012] O.J. No. 5426 (Ont. C.J.).

In *A. Potvin Construction Ltd. v. Ontario (Workplace Safety & Insurance Board)*, 2011 ONCJ 871, 2011 CarswellOnt 15859, [2011] O.J. No. 6340 (Ont. C.J.), it was held that sentencing decisions are entitled to considerable deference by appellate courts. Section 122(1) allows a court to receive evidence when considering the fitness of a sentence; s. 117(1) allows the court to receive evidence in an appeal, if it considers this to be in the interests of justice. On appeal, the court admitted as fresh evidence the reassessments of the defendant's account by the Workplace Safety and Insurance Board in the amount of $201,241.08. The amount of the reassessment was relevant to a fact in issue, namely that the defendant did not benefit from its illegal actions. It was credible evidence given that it was generated by a governmental agency, and, when considered with the rest of the evidence at trial, was reasonably capable of affecting the sentence imposed by the trial justice who considered that the defendant received a benefit as a result of its false reporting whereas the fresh evidence established that the defendant ultimately did not benefit from its illegal actions. The justice of the peace also committed an error in principle in concluding that the severity of the injury to the worker was an aggravating factor. The justice did correctly consider, however, the following as aggravating factors: the seriousness of the prohibited conduct and defendant's moral blameworthiness; the deprivation or potential deprivation of benefits to the worker; the advantage the corporation or personal defendants gained from their illegal activity; the frequency of the offences; the offences occurred over a long period of time; and the absence of remorse. As a result, the total amount of fines imposed on the defendant of $375,000 was reduced to $309,000.

In *R. v. Reid*, 2012 ONCJ 305, 2012 CarswellOnt 6779, 34 M.V.R. (6th) 307, [2012] O.J. No. 2540 (Ont. C.J.), it was held that the defendant's rights under s. 7 of the *Charter of Rights* were violated when he, as an unrepresented accused, at his first drive suspended offence and being deprived of his right to make submissions on sentence was incarcerated for a regulatory offence that he had entered a plea of guilty to in a timely manner, and the justice wholly ignored basic sentencing principles by stating, "I used to give fines. We now impose incarceration." A justice of the peace is required when sentencing someone who is standing before him to allow that person an opportunity to make submissions. It is a basic tenant of the adversarial system of justice and a denial of that right to be heard, which strikes at the heart of fairness, gives rise to the appearance that the fix is in, that the sentence is predetermined. As the sentence had already been served by the defendant, nothing short of a stay of proceedings would remove the prejudice caused by the *Charter* violation; any form of further sentence would only perpetuate and enlarge on the s. 7 violation that occurred.

The trial court considered the evidence before it, addressed the aggravating and mitigating factors, and applied those factors to the appropriate principles of sentencing. The fines addressed the issues of deterrence and could not be considered harsh or oppressive. The fact that the maximum fine was imposed against one of the defendants was warranted on the basis of the aggravating features present. See *R. v. Geil*, 2012 ONCJ 740, 2012 CarswellOnt 15014, [2012] O.J. No. 5655 (Ont. C.J.), leave to appeal refused 2013 ONCA 457, 2013 CarswellOnt 8921, [2013] O.J. No. 3087 (Ont. C.A.).

In *Kirk v. Lambton (County)*, 2012 ONCJ 809, 2012 CarswellOnt 13915, 4 M.P.L.R. (5th) 304, [2012] O.J. No. 6285 (Ont. C.J.), it was held that there was no *mala fides* on the part of the defendant or blameworthy conduct which would necessitate a higher fine than that imposed by the trial judge after a trial on the merits, namely $950, although the maximum penalty for a first conviction was $25,000. The defendant had been convicted of contravening a zoning by-law by operating a leasing and renting business for which the defence of legal non-conforming use was not available.

A 90-day driving prohibition imposed against a taxi driver who was also fined $196 for speeding was not within the appropriate range, and was reduced to 21 days. The sentencing justice of the peace overemphasized the significance of the defendant's driving record and imposed a sentence that was demonstrably unfit. See *R. v.*

Mirzahossein, 2012 BCSC 982, 2012 CarswellBC 1985, 36 M.V.R. (6th) 139, [2012] B.C.J. No. 1387 (B.C. S.C.).

In *Consbec Inc. v. Ontario (Ministry of the Environment)*, 2013 ONCJ 258, 2013 CarswellOnt 5876, 76 C.E.L.R. (3d) 149, [2013] O.J. No. 2220 (Ont. C.J.), it was stated that the requirement that the basis for a court's decision must be ascertainable by those affected by that decision was set out by the Supreme Court of Canada in *R. v. Sheppard*, 2002 SCC 26, 2002 CarswellNfld 74, REJB 2002-29516, [2002] 1 S.C.R. 869, 211 Nfld. & P.E.I.R. 50, 162 C.C.C. (3d) 298, 50 C.R. (5th) 68, 210 D.L.R. (4th) 608, 633 A.P.R. 50, 284 N.R. 342, [2002] S.C.J. No. 30 (S.C.C.). It is a question of accountability not only to the unsuccessful party but to the public. Reasons justify and explain the result. Insufficient reasons can deprive the appellant of a meaningful opportunity to have the correctness of the court's decision reviewed by a court on appeal. That could amount to an error at law. As important as these reasons may be to make clear the basis on which the decision was arrived at, there may be extant on the record of the proceedings an explanation of the path taken by the court when arriving at its decision. While the reasons could have been more fulsome, the Justice of the Peace did take into consideration the evidence introduced at the sentencing hearing as set out in her recitation of the evidence in her reasons. Further, she was at liberty to consider and resolve the conflicts between the theories as advanced by the parties. The court was very much alive to the debate that informed the hearing; on the evidence before the court, the Justice could reach the conclusion that she did, namely, that the blast set off by the defendant was in some way connected to the change in the well water quality. That conclusion, although perhaps not extensively explained, was supported by the evidence at the hearing. The Justice of the Peace therefore arrived at her determination without falling into error of law or principle. It could not be said that the fine imposed and orders for restoration and restitution were demonstrably unfit. The determination of the trial court was entitled to deference by the appeal court.

Under the *Provincial Offences Act* (Ont.), custodial sentences are rare and represent punishment of last resort, while monetary fines need to be considered proportionately in the light of the seriousness of the offence: *R. v. Blondin*, 2012 ONCJ 826, 2012 CarswellOnt 17153, [2012] O.J. No. 6353 (Ont. C.J.).

In *R. v. Kreklewich*, 2013 SKQB 339, 2013 CarswellSask 663, 429 Sask. R. 257, [2013] S.J. No. 572 (Sask. Q.B.), it was held that when the Justice stated to the defendant that the offence of operating an unregistered vehicle was "zero tolerance", he was incorrectly suggesting to him that it was an absolute liability offence when in fact it was one of strict liability. The defendant entered a guilty plea immediately after the Justice's remark. The Justice's error in law had an impact on the defendant's ability to make full answer and defence to the charge he faced. He believed his lack of knowledge of the vehicle's registration was significant, but he was unable to pursue the issue with the Justice. Had the Justice not been under a misapprehension about the availability of a due diligence defence, the defendant would have had the opportunity to explain what steps, if any, he took to ensure he was operating a registered vehicle. In the circumstances, he did not have that opportunity. As a result, his plea was not informed or unequivocal.

A fine should not be perceived simply as a licensing fee for illegal conduct. Not every strict liability provincial offence is of the same seriousness or poses the same threat to the welfare of the public. Every case will have aggravating and mitigating factors, and a fit sentence should reflect the circumstances surrounding the unlawful conduct and the offender's personal circumstances. Where the prosecutor cites four cases with widely disparate sentences, this hardly establishes an accepted range of sentence but rather demonstrates that the appropriate penalty will be determined by considering all the mitigating and aggravating factors based on the facts of the particular case and the personal circumstances of an offender. Having decided that a fine is an appropriate disposition, the trial judge should only impose a fine that is within the offender's ability to pay, bearing in mind that he may extend the time for payment. It is an error to fail to inquire about a defendant's ability to pay before imposing fines. The failure of the Justice of the Peace to give any reasons explaining the quantum of fines he imposed was an error. See *Real Estate Council of Ontario v. Wang*, 2013 ONCJ 515, 2013 CarswellOnt 13174, [2013] O.J. No. 4294 (Ont. C.J.).

In *Real Estate Council of Ontario v. Wang*, 2013 ONCJ 515, 2013 CarswellOnt 13174, [2013] O.J. No. 4294 (Ont. C.J.), it was further held that when defendants are not represented by counsel or a paralegal, the trial Justice of the Peace must conduct a plea comprehension inquiry to ensure that the pleas were voluntary and informed, and that the facts necessary to establish all of the essential elements of the offences were admitted. When the facts are read in by the prosecutor, the Justice of the Peace must ask the defendants if they agree with the facts as read in. When a defendant pleads guilty but indicates he wants to give an explanation, the Justice must determine whether the defendant is really admitting the facts as alleged.

There is no jurisdiction to impose concurrent fines on sentencing. While a court may impose concurrent custodial sentences for two or more counts, where the sentence is a fine the court must impose separate fines for each count while ensuring that the overall fine is appropriate: *Ontario (Ministry of Labour) v. Flex-N-Gate Canada Co.*, 2014 ONCA 53, 2014 CarswellOnt 673, 119 O.R. (3d) 1, 315 O.A.C. 66, [2014] O.J. No. 261 (Ont. C.A.).

A trial judge is not bound by a joint submission. The imposition of a fit sentence is ultimately the trial judge's responsibility. Trial judges must, however, give considerable weight to joint submissions. A trial judge should not reject joint submissions unless the joint submission is contrary to the public interest and the sentence would bring the administration of justice into disrepute. That standard is applicable regardless of whether a trial judge is inclined to go above or below the sentence proposed in the joint submission. In the instant case, the proposed sentence was definitely not contrary to the public interest, nor could it bring the administration of justice into disrepute. In those circumstances, the decision to undercut the joint submission constituted a reversible error. See *R. v. Pynappels*, 2014 ONCJ 15, 2014 CarswellOnt 334, [2014] O.J. No. 152 (Ont. C.J.).

In *R. v. Farrage*, 2014 ONSC 564, 2014 CarswellOnt 1090, [2014] O.J. No. 448 (Ont. S.C.J.) it was held that the sentencing judge clearly felt that the joint submission for the minimum penalty was manifestly inadequate based on the submissions in support of the guilty plea. The court expressly recognized that a joint submission should not be lightly overridden. Counsel for the defendant proceeded to make further submissions after the court advised that there must be a suspension of driving privileges in addition to the minimum fine. There was no request to hold the matter down or adjourn to another date for further evidence or submissions. There was no error of law and no basis to interfere with the sentence imposed.

In failing to allow the defendant's agent an opportunity to provide submissions on sentencing before rendering his decision, the Justice of the Peace erred in principle. The Justice also erred in relying on the defendant's conduct during the traffic stop as an aggravating factor. The defendant's conduct at the time indicated clearly that he was annoyed at being stopped for speeding, and he expressed himself accordingly; he did not, however, do anything illegal. It may well be that the defendant was rude, but bad manners are not a valid consideration on sentencing. See *R. v. Williston*, 2014 NWTSC 45, 2014 CarswellNWT 47, [2014] N.W.T.J. No. 49 (N.W.T. S.C.).

In *R. v. Karau*, 2014 ONCJ 207, 2014 CarswellOnt 5601, [2014] O.J. No. 2055 (Ont. C.J.), the court commented that the purpose of a *Gladue* report is to provide information to a court about the unique systemic and background factors which bring the Aboriginal offender before the courts. The pre-sentence report submitted was insufficient and deficient for this purpose. A stand-alone *Gladue* report was ordered, or a supplementary report to the pre-sentence report, which would properly address the *Gladue* factors.

Before rejecting the range of sentence suggested by the prosecutor and imposing a higher fine, the Justice should have given cogent reasons for doing so and then explained why, in his view, fines within the suggested range would be contrary to the public interest or would otherwise bring the administration of justice into disrepute: *Kingston (City) v. Patry* (August 9, 2011), Doc. Kingston 090175, 090176, [2011] O.J. No. 6667 (Ont. C.J.).

Although a sentencing judge ordinarily has a discretion to exercise in imposing sentence, the Legislature can limit that discretion or eliminate it altogether. As a result, the Justice of the Peace was without jurisdiction to reduce a fixed fine under the municipal parking by-law. See *Toronto (City) v. Iron Mountain Canada Corp.*, 2015 ONCJ 444, 2015 CarswellOnt 12336, [2015] O.J. No. 4298 (Ont. C.J.).

In *R. v. Kee*, 2013 ONCJ 830, 2013 CarswellOnt 19000, [2013] O.J. No. 6455 (Ont. C.J.), affirmed 2015 ONCA 730, 2015 CarswellOnt 16415, 127 O.R. (3d) 518, 89 M.V.R. (6th) 177, 342 O.A.C. 1 (Ont. C.A.), it was held that the Justice of the Peace erred in imposing the fine without giving the defendant any opportunity to make submissions on this issue. The fine imposed should have proportionality to fines for other like offences.

In *R. v. Ward*, 2015 ONCJ 369, 2015 CarswellOnt 10460, [2015] O.J. No. 3726 (Ont. C.J.), it was held that in this case the trial Justice of the Peace had already considered the application of s. 59(2) and reduced the fine from the statutory minimum of $5,000 to $3,500. This is an exercise of judicial discretion that was available to the Justice. An appellate court is not to interfere with sentencing decisions unless they are manifestly unjust. The facts advanced by counsel at trial were essentially the same factors that were advanced before the appeal court with respect to the defendant's financial circumstances, and had already been taken into account in the decision made by the Justice of the Peace. The result was appropriate. There was no basis to interfere with that decision.

The trial Justice of the Peace rejected a joint submission for a fine of $100 on a guilty plea to start in a stop position not in safety, contrary to the *Highway Traffic Act*, and imposed the set fine of $85 instead, The Justice of the Peace erred in not outlining her reasons why she considered the joint submission contrary to the public interest, or bringing the administration of justice into disrepute; both the prosecution and defence provided ample reasons why the increased fine was being sought. There was a collision with a pedestrian and there was a need for specific deterrence. The joint submission should have been accepted under all the circumstances of the case. See *York (Regional Municipality) v. Chmiel* (July 17, 2015), Doc. Newmarket 4911-999-00-9763334B-00, [2015] O.J. No. 5686 (Ont. C.J.).

In *R. v. Ghajaverest*, 2015 BCSC 1976, 2015 CarswellBC 3127, [2015] B.C.J. No. 2338 (B.C. S.C.), it was held that an appellant who raises the validity of a guilty plea on an appeal bears the onus of showing that the plea was invalid. In this case the appellant paid the ticket the day after or very shortly thereafter the offence was committed. There is no evidence before the court to suggest that she did so by mistake or that she did so involuntarily. Based on the record, there was no miscarriage of justice and no valid grounds for setting the guilty plea aside.

The sentencing Justice instructed himself, properly, on the basis of the controlling authority, *R. v. Cotton Felts Ltd.*, that deterrence was the paramount consideration in sentencing. He carefully considered the competing aggravating and mitigating factors as enumerated by counsel in their written and oral submissions. There was no error in principle that indicated either a failure to consider a relevant sentencing principle, or a failure to give effect to a sentencing principle so identified. See *R. v. Iacono*, 2015 ONCJ 609, 2015 CarswellOnt 17115, [2015] O.J. No. 5819 (Ont. C.J.).

In *R. v. Ontario Corp. 1796926* (August 4, 2015), Doc. Chapleau 140077-01K, 140077-05K, [2015] O.J. No. 5344 (Ont. C.J.), leave to appeal refused 2016 ONCA 612, 2016 CarswellOnt 12253, [2016] O.J. No. 4115 (Ont. C.A.), the defendant interrupted the Justice of the Peace when he started to ask for submissions on sentence, and said that the $20,000 fine sought by the prosecutor would bankrupt the corporation or force it to dissolve. While the Justice did not make a specific inquiry into the ability to pay as contemplated by s. 57(3) of the *Provincial Offences Act*, the Justice attempted to solicit submissions but was interrupted and offered an adjournment so more fulsome submissions could be made. The Justice did not commit an error in principle.

It was further held in *R. v. Ontario Corp. 1796926* (August 4, 2015), Doc. Chapleau 140077-01K, 140077-05K, [2015] O.J. No. 5344 (Ont. C.J.), leave to appeal refused 2016 ONCA 612, 2016 CarswellOnt 12253, [2016] O.J. No. 4115 (Ont. C.A.) that it is an error to decline to impose a fine that might result in the bankruptcy of a corporation. The Justice found that the need for general deterrence was paramount given the unique circumstances and level of civil disobedience. The charges arose out of a demonstration organized by the defendants and was a well-publicised event done to draw attention to the corporation's belief that the Ministry was unlawfully restricting access to lakes. The imposition of a $20,000 fine for an offence for which the maximum fine was $25,000 was not demonstrably unfit in the circumstances of this case and this defendant.

When the prosecution asked for the minimum penalty of $200, the Justice of the Peace stated that she would never impose that amount, prior to hearing anything about the circumstances of the defendant. This position does not reflect the proper role of a Justice in sentencing. A minimum sentence is an expression of governmental policy; the Justice's sentencing discretion does not entitle her to disregard a clear statement of legislative intent. The Justice was required to impose the minimum sentence unless the defendant showed exceptional circumstances that justified relief under s. 59(2) of the *Provincial Offences Act*. See *York (Regional Municipality) v. Dave*, 2015 ONCJ 481, 2015 CarswellOnt 13983, [2015] O.J. No. 4651 (Ont. C.J.).

It was further held in *York (Regional Municipality) v. Dave*, 2015 ONCJ 481, 2015 CarswellOnt 13983, [2015] O.J. No. 4651 (Ont. C.J.) that the warning to the prosecutor that the court would never impose the statutory minimum fine reasonably gave rise to an apprehension of bias. The justice also commented to the prosecutor when he attempted to cite a case that he was not going to be permitted "to take advantage of somebody who is here without counsel." There was nothing in the record that suggested the prosecutor was attempting to gain an advantage by citing a case. Indeed, it was the prosecutor's responsibility to do so. If the defendant needed to see a copy of the case or time to consider the prosecutor's position, that could be accommodated by the presiding justice. The comments of the court in relation to the prosecutor's submissions added to the reasonable apprehension of bias.

A defendant does not face the jeopardy of an increased penalty for a subsequent offence unless he or she has been previously convicted and sentenced for an offence. Before a severer penalty can be imposed for a second or subsequent offence, the second or subsequent offence must have been committed after the first or second conviction, as the case may be, and the second or subsequent conviction must have been made after the first or second conviction, as the case may be; where two offences arising out of the same incident are tried together and convictions are entered on both after trial, they are to be treated as one for the purpose of determining whether a severer penalty applies, either because of a previous conviction or because of a subsequent conviction. The rule operates even where two offences arising out of separate incidents are tried together and convictions are entered at the same time. See *R. v. Zhang*, 2015 ONSC 4128, [2015] O.J. No. 3821 (Ont. S.C.J.), leave to appeal refused 2016 ONCA 473, 2016 CarswellOnt 9380, [2016] O.J. No. 3142 (Ont. C.A.).

It was open to the trial judge to consider the absence of any vehicular collision or personal injury as a mitigating factor in imposing sentence. However, even if the learned trial judge should have taken the absence of an accident into account as a mitigating factor, an erroneous consideration of a mitigating factor does not lead to appellate intervention unless the sentence is demonstrably unfit. Considered in light of the maximum available fine of $1,000 under the *Traffic Safety Act* (Sask.) for the offence of failing to stop for a red light, and the fine imposed of $230, the sentence was clearly at the lower end of the range and not demonstrably unfit. By asking an appeal court to take letters of reference and the whole of his circumstances into account, when the defendant declined to do so at trial, the defendant was effectively seeking to have the court impose a different sentence. The trial judge is entitled to deference on an appeal from sentence. An appeal court cannot intervene simply because it would have weighed the relevant factors differently. It may only intervene if the sentence imposed is demonstrably unfit, and in this case it was not. See *R. v. Miller*, 2016 SKQB 35, 2016 CarswellSask 67, [2016] S.J. No. 49 (Sask. Q.B.).

Trial judges should not reject joint submissions unless the proposed sentence is contrary to the public interest and would bring the administration of justice into disrepute. This high threshold ensures that both parties have confidence in resolving the case without a trial and that the many factors that were considered in arriving at the joint position are respected. The finding that the joint submission in the instant case was unreasonable and likely to bring the administration of justice into disrepute was in error. The minor variation of $15 the court ultimately arrived at shows that there was nothing about the original submission that would justify interference by the court. The rejection of the joint submission was unreasonable and arbitrary, and contrary to binding authority including three prior cases involving the same Justice. See *R. v. Alakoozi*, 2015 ONCJ 763, 2015 CarswellOnt 20504, [2015] O.J. No. 6938 (Ont. C.J.).

The right to be tried within a reasonable period of time includes the right to be sentenced within a reasonable period of time. While justices of the peace are responsible for one of the busiest courts in the province and understandably, on occasion, may, like many judges, need extra time to prepare reasons for sentence, on the facts of this case where there was a joint submission on sentence, one might speculate that the reasons for sentence would be relatively brief and perhaps delivered orally at the time of accepting the plea. A delay in imposing sentence of nine and one-half months was not a prompt sentence and unwarranted in the circumstances. See *York (Regional Municipality) v. Newhook*, 2015 ONSC 6587, 2015 CarswellOnt 16978, [2015] O.J. No. 5766 (Ont. S.C.J.).

It was further held in *York (Regional Municipality) v. Newhook*, 2015 ONSC 6587, 2015 CarswellOnt 16978, [2015] O.J. No. 5766 (Ont. S.C.J.) that the discretion of the court as to whether it will accept or reject the guilty plea is a discretion that has to be exercised judicially. It is not a discretion that can be exercised on an arbitrary whim. In situations where it is evident on the face of the record that the discretion has not been exercised judicially, such a discretion amounts to an error of law. There was no reason in law why the Justice should reject the guilty plea that was being proposed by the prosecutor and the defence. She made no inquiries of the prosecutor or defendant with respect to the reasonableness of the proposed plea. Even if there was some legal basis in law for the Justice to consider the appropriateness of the guilty plea, there was no reason why it should take nearly a year for the court to consider whether the guilty pleas should be accepted. An order for *mandamus* issued directing the Justice to accept a guilty plea to the amended offence and to enter a conviction.

The Prosecutor sought five 30 day concurrent jail sentences for the first set of charges, and five 15 day concurrent jail sentences for the second set of charges, for a total sentence of 45 days' imprisonment under the *Consumer Protection Act*. The trial Justice imposed consecutive jail sentences on all counts instead, for a total sentence of 225 days; the second defendant was convicted of five counts and the prosecutor sought five concurrent 15 day jail sentences, whereas the justice imposed five 15 day consecutive sentences for a total sentence of 75 days' imprisonment. The sentences imposed were unreasonable and would have brought the administration of justice into disrepute. The sentences were varied to direct that the first defendant serve a total sentence of 45 days and the second defendant serve a total sentence of 15 days, both sentences to be served intermittently. See *R. v. Storey*, 2016 ONCJ 73, 2016 CarswellOnt 1839, [2016] O.J. No. 690 (Ont. C.J.).

The defendant who was convicted of three counts of violating a zoning bylaw had sought a minor variation permitting such use, and appealed the refusal of the variance to the Ontario Municipal Board, was not entitled to rely on this as mitigating factor on sentencing. The justice of the peace's critical comments about the Ontario Municipal Board did not raise a reasonable apprehension of bias when considered in the context that defence counsel knew he would be arguing that the application before the Board was a mitigating factor, and no objection was taken to the comments at the time. The sentences imposed, in any event, were reasonable. See *Beaulieu v. Milton (Town)*, 2015 ONCJ 779, 2015 CarswellOnt 20660, [2015] O.J. No. 7121 (Ont. C.J.).

A reasonable standard of bias was not established when the justice of the peace threatened to start the case without counsel for the defence being present, even though the justice was aware that counsel was in another courtroom. This statement constituted an outburst of frustration when the parties were not ready to proceed at the appointed time. His comment that if the party wished to bring in hearsay, that's fine, did not constitute bias. However, when the justice pronounced sentence without giving the defence an opportunity to be heard, this was improper. Counsel for the defence was right in assuming that any submissions from him at that point would be a wasted exercise. As a result, sentencing submissions were presented by the parties on appeal. See *R. v. Mr. Ice Man Ltd.*, 2016 ONCJ 372, 2016 CarswellOnt 9849, [2016] O.J. No. 3308 (Ont. C.J.).

In *R. v. Garwal*, 2016 ONCJ 217, 2016 CarswellOnt 5933, 99 M.V.R. (6th) 151, [2016] O.J. No. 1997 (Ont. C.J.), the defendant was charged with speeding, and following a resolution meeting pleaded guilty to disobeying a sign. The parties jointly submitted that the appropriate sentence was to impose the set fine of $85. The imposition of the set fine was held to be contrary to the public interest or would bring the administration of justice into disrepute as set fines are statutorily reserved for cases that do not go to trial, or where there were mitigating factors. Imposing the set fine would also not respect the legislative intent that proceedings proceed economically and efficiently. A defendant should not have the benefit of both the public cost required to ensure a right to trial as well as a reduced fine after conviction on the day of trial. As the defendant had no record of similar offences, and there were no aggravating factors, imposing a fine of $100 would be sufficiently punitive.

In *R. v. Mr. Ice Man Ltd.*, 2016 ONCJ 621, 2016 CarswellOnt 16466, [2016] O.J. No. 5443 (Ont. C.J.), there were two errors made, one by the issuing authority, in not issuing the proper gross vehicle weight, and the other by the defendant, in not checking the licence before using it. The government which seeks to impose the fine was in some respects responsible for the circumstances of the offence. This appeared to be a very rare and very exceptional circumstance which was not likely to be repeated; however, the defendant, by simply checking his documents could have avoided the infraction. Taking all of the circumstances into account, it was in the interests of justice to reduce the fine by the proportionate responsibility of the parties: 75 percent by the defendant and 25 percent to the Ministry.

There is no requirement that a sentencing judge must mention and distinguish every sentencing case submitted in argument, nor is it reasonable to expect to find a sentencing case that is exactly on all fours with any other single case. The cases are very clear that the overarching sentencing goal for charges involving workplace fatalities is deterrence. Accordingly, sentences must be such that they will not be simply ignored or routinely absorbed by the offending employer in their usual business finances. At the same time, the fines must not be such that the continued existence of the company is jeopardized by the imposition of the fine. The determination a sentencing judge is required to make is not simply an exercise in math or application of a formula. Instead it is a careful weighing of all the factors set out in *R. v. Cotton Felts Ltd.*, 1982 CarswellOnt 1235, 2 C.C.C. (3d) 287, C.E.S.H.G. 95,056, [1982] O.J. No. 178 (Ont. C.A.). There were many cases where similar fines were imposed on similar sized companies in similar circumstances as in the case at bar. There were also some cases where higher and lower fines were imposed. It was very clear that the fine imposed by the trial justice of the peace was well within the range of appropriate fines. See *Ontario (Ministry of Labour) v. R.J.M. Farms Inc.*, [2016] O.J. No. 6695 (C.J.).

The mandatory minimum sentences imposed on the defendant gave no consideration at all to his ability to pay or to the enormous gap in time between his previous convictions and the present convictions, a gap of 15 years. Before considering s. 59(2), the existence and length of the gap should have led to sentences much closer to the $10,000 mandatory minimum than the sentences imposed on the defendant on each occasion. Any consideration of s. 59(2) must keep in mind the language of the section, what circumstances of the defendant are presented as being "exceptional" and the legislative purpose underlying the particular mandatory minimum sentence that the defendant seeks to undercut. The case-law is very clear that the minimum sentences in s. 2(1) of the *Compulsory Automobile Insurance Act* are harsh, oppressive, even draconian. However, they are so for a reason. There is nothing inadvertent in the mandatory minimum fines. People operating motor vehicles put other people at risk; people operating motor vehicles can easily cause great harm to other people. The mandatory minimum fines are intended to avoid the risk that a driver will choose not to obtain insurance on the theory that, if he gets caught, any penalty will be less than the cost of the insurance. The mandatory minimum sentences are designed to discourage all drivers from even considering that line of thinking. "Exceptional" and "oppressive" are lower standards than "catastrophic". A person's ability to pay may, in some cases, contribute to a determination that s. 59(2) should be engaged to a defendant's benefit. The analysis under s. 59(2) should take into account the fact that a very harsh penalty may be less harsh if a very long time is granted for the fine to be paid. There is no bright line that delineates where "oppressive" or "exceptional" or "otherwise in the interests of justice" begins. Every case must be determined on its merits, keeping in mind not only the mitigating potential of s. 59(2), but also the legitimate goals of the legislature and society's legitimate interest in ensuring that people who choose to drive have a powerful incentive to make sure that they are properly insured. See *R. v. Anderson*, 2016 ONCJ 758, 2016 CarswellOnt 21172, 5 M.V.R. (7th) 131, [2016] O.J. No. 6858 (Ont. C.J.).

A joint submission should normally be accepted unless the sentencing judge "is satisfied that the recommended disposition would be contrary to the public interest and would bring the administration of justice into disrepute": *R. v. Thompson*, 2013 ONCA 202, 2013 CarswellOnt 3920, 305 O.A.C. 42, [2013] O.J. No. 1546 (Ont. C.A.). It is an error in principle not to conduct a thoughtful analysis of why the proposed joint submission falls prey to that, and it is an error by sentencing judge not to "forewarn counsel of his intentions or provide them with an opportunity to respond": *Thompson*, para. 16. Neither of those was done in any of the cases in question. As such, the trial justice of the peace erred in imposing a sentence lower than the joint submission. A sentence of $200 was only $115 above the statutory minimum fine. There was no reason why the sentence imposed of $85 was so markedly different than the joint submission. All of the defendants had their charges reduced from speeding to a lesser charge. A $200 fine was a benefit to the accused. So were the saved demerit points. The *quid pro quo* should have been apparent and, if it wasn't, the prosecutor should have been given an opportunity to explain it. See *York (Regional Municipality) v. Sun*, 2016 ONCJ 240, 2016 CarswellOnt 6700, [2016] O.J. No. 2243 (Ont. C.J.).

In a similar case, *R. v. Pellicci*, 2017 ONCJ 85, 2017 CarswellOnt 2788, [2017] O.J. No. 188 (C.J.), it was held that resolution without trial is essential to the efficient and fair operation of the system of provincial offences courts in the province. The resolutions in these cases involved reductions in charges, reductions in fines or both. Some resolutions avoided administrative penalties such as driving demerit points. Others avoided conviction on offences which would trigger serious insurance consequences. Despite those benefits, the joint submissions as to sentence were rejected. Justice of the peace may depart from joint submissions, but the ability to do so is prescribed by law. The appropriate test is a strict one — whether the proposed sentence would bring the administration of justice into disrepute or would otherwise be contrary to the public interest. The phrase "otherwise contrary to the public interest" does not lower the standard. It is an error of law for the presiding justice of the peace to tell the courtroom that there could be no agreements as to sentence, simply to assert judicial independence, and to lower the fine proposed without explaining why the submitted fine was inappropriate or why the minor variance to the set fine amount was necessary. Justices of the peace do have the ultimate responsibility to impose a fit sentence, but that responsibility must be exercised according to the limits imposed by statute and following the framework provided by appellate courts. Where an accused receives the benefit of resolution to a reduced charge and reduced fine and agrees they can pay that amount, a sentencing court should not further reduce the fine due to concerns about ability to pay not founded in the evidence. A general sympathy for an accused person is not a sufficient basis to interfere with a joint proposal.

In *Dabaja v. Ontario (Ontario Motor Vehicle Industry Council)*, 2017 ONCJ 834, 2017 CarswellOnt 19326, 22 M.V.R. (7th) 158, [2017] O.J. No.6834 (Ont. C.J.), it was held that s. 122 of the *Provincial Offences Act* provides that the court shall consider the fitness of the sentence before making any order that may include a dismissal or a variation of the sentence. There is a high threshold that must be met before the court can intervene to vary the sentence. It is settled law that the court should refrain from interfering unless it is satisfied there was an error in principle in coming to the decision on sentence or in these circumstances, the sentence was clearly excessive. There were two errors in principle in the instant case. The first arose as a consequence of the sentencing with the objective of deterring the offender rather than imposing a sanction that would serve as a general deterrence, principally designed to change the behavior of others, commonly known as curb-siders, who tend to have a detrimental effect on the public welfare purpose of the *Motor Vehicle Dealers Act, 2002*. The second error arose by equating past moral blameworthy behavior, namely, fraudulent conduct, with being an unregistered motor vehicle dealer. A fit sentence in the circumstances would be to vary the custodial sentence imposed and vary it to a meaningful fine substantial enough to inform other curb-siders as well as the defendant that similar conduct will have consequences and any belief that the risk of a fine is just the cost of doing business will be realized as short-sighted.

In *R. v. Popovici*, 2017 CarswellOnt 21731, [2017] O.J. No. 5697 (C.J.), the defendant was not given an opportunity to make submissions as to penalty and may not have been aware of the prosecutor's entitlement to request an "amendment up" of the amount of the applicable fine by virtue of the amendment provisions of the

Provincial Offences Act. The court must ensure that the defendant understands the consequences of the amendment and is given a reasonable opportunity to make submissions as to why the amendment should not be granted. As the amendment, if granted, would invariably result in the imposition of a more enhanced financial sanction, fairness dictated that the unrepresented defendant be given a fair opportunity to respond to the request for enhanced penalty. On the record, it did not appear that the defendant understood his jeopardy of the amendment was granted. More importantly, he was not given an opportunity to make submissions as to penalty generally.

In *Halton Region Conservation Authority v. Hanna*, 2018 ONCA 476, 2018 CarswellOnt 7931, [2018] O.J. No. 2695 (Ont. C.A.), it was held that it is well established that sentences imposed by trial courts are entitled to and accorded substantial deference on appellate review. An appellate court is entitled to interfere with the sentence imposed at trial only where the trial court: errs in principle; fails to consider a relevant factor; or errs in considering an aggravating or mitigating factor that has an impact on the sentence imposed, or imposes a sentence that is demonstrably unfit. It was not open to the appeal court judge to simply substitute his view of the nature of the defendant's breach of the regulation for that of the trial court. Findings of fact are the bedrock of sentencing proceedings. They are critical to a determination of the circumstances that may aggravate or mitigate a sentence. In many cases, as here, findings of fact that determine whether an aggravating or mitigating circumstance will have a say in the ultimate sentencing decision will be made on conflicting evidence. And findings of fact are the province of the sentencing judge who is an ear and eyewitness to the conflicting evidence. A reviewing court is not entitled, nor should it be, to interfere with findings of fact made at trial in the absence of palpable and overriding error. In this case, the appeal court judge did not identify any palpable and overriding error in the trial court's finding on the critical issue of moral blameworthiness. It follows that the appeal judge was not entitled to interfere with that finding, much less to substitute a contrary finding funded in part by impermissible speculation about one of the defendants' knowledge of applicable residential building restrictions. The appeal judge's decision was therefore flawed by fundamental errors and could not stand.

The justice of the peace was mindful of the aggravating and mitigating factors, and the other factors he was required to consider including the principles of sentencing, and he considered them. However, he misapplied the sentencing principle of parity by placing too much emphasis on another sentencing decision as a starting point for the consideration of the appropriate fine when that case was clearly distinguishable as that offender had eight prior convictions whereas the defendant had none. This was a first offence for the defendant, a company that attempted to work with the Ministry to solve the odour problem, but failed to do so in a timely fashion. A fine well in excess of the fine imposed on a company that had eight prior convictions was clearly outside the acceptable range and therefore, unreasonable. See *Ontario (Ministry of the Environment) v. Orgaworld Canada Ltd.*, 2015 CarswellOnt 21087 (Ont. C.J.), leave to appeal refused *R. v. Orgaworld Canada Ltd.*, 2015 CarswellOnt 21086 (Ont. C.A.).

It was held in *R. v. 1137749 Ontario Ltd. (operating as Pro-Teck Electric)*, 2018 ONCJ 502, 2018 CarswellOnt 12427, [2018] O.J. No. 4001 (Ont. C.J.) that a justice of the peace sitting in provincial offences court has the authority to pierce the corporate veil in appropriate cases. The authority derives from the implied jurisdiction of the provincial offences court to carry out the legislative scheme. The question, in the context of the present case, really boils down to whether or not the sentencing court should have the power to defeat an effort by a defendant to neuter the court in imposing a just and effective sentence by making that sentence unenforceable, meaningless and illusory. It is simply inconceivable that a justice of the peace conducting a provincial offences trial lacks a very specific power (clearly possessed by other courts) that is essential to avoid a "flagrant" circumvention of justice. The power to pierce the corporate veil will be triggered when failing to act would result in circumvention of justice. On the evidence in this case, once it is clear that the sentencing court had jurisdiction to pierce the corporate veil, the only rational conclusion is that the test for piercing the veil was made out by the principal of the company's wrongful acts in diverting the company's assets by transferring company assets to himself and forming a new company around the same time that charges were laid, such acts being done for the flagrantly unlawful purpose of defeating the course of justice.

The defendant's level of moral culpability for permitting a motor vehicle to be operated without insurance was not that of someone flagrantly defying the law. Her actions were irresponsible, not defiant or deliberate. The justice of the peace also did not identify any aggravating factors above and beyond the facts of the case which could reasonably support the elevated fine of $7,500. This was not a case in which the defendant had a prior conviction for a similar offence, or an otherwise lengthy driving record. This was not a case in which the vehicle was driven a great distance, for a prolonged period, was involved in an accident or was driven by an unlicensed driver. Those are just some examples of possible aggravating factors that could justify an elevated fine. None existed in this case. There was also no suggestion that the minimum fine would be an insignificant consequence for the defendant. Just the opposite. In the circumstances the sentence was unfit. Having regard to the defendant's total income for the year being $7,000, a fine of $3,500 was substituted on appeal. See *R. v. Harry*, 2018 ONCJ 783, 2018 CarswellOnt 18882 (Ont. C.J.).

In *York (Regional Municipality) v. 1085638 Ontario Limited*, 2018 ONCJ 658, 2018 CarswellOnt 16164, [2018] O.J. No. 5003 (Ont. C.J.), it was held that the decision to adjourn a proceeding is one in the discretion of the trial judge. The judicial officer must listen to the request and consider various factors, including the length of time of the proposed adjournment. The longer the period of time, the greater the likelihood the adjournment should not be granted as the likelihood of prejudice to the defence increases. What was clear on the record was that the justice of the peace tried to accommodate an adjournment for sentencing submissions if it was only going to be for a short time. After poring over the court calendar with the assistance of the trial coordinator it was clear that it couldn't. By that time the charges were 12 years and 5 years old, respectively, the court was clearly uncomfortable with yet another delay in the case at the penultimate stage, and ruled that submissions should be heard. Given that counsel were advised two months previously that they should be ready to do just that on the return date, the decision was not unfair. There was also no evidence on the appeal about what evidence would have been heard had the adjournment been granted. No fresh evidence was sought to be tendered on the hearing of the appeal. No error in principle was identified in the reasons for sentence. Absent an error in principle sentencing decisions are entitled to deference. Despite denying the adjournment, the court received submissions on sentence from both the prosecution and defence. The defendants received very substantial fines — $60,000 in total. That said, this was a legal sentence, and the defendants had a history of previous convictions relating to the very issue of non-compliance with municipal orders.

The fine of $10,000 imposed by the justice of the peace was at the lower end of the range of acceptable sentences under the *Insurance Act* which prescribed a maximum fine of $250,000 against a person convicted of a first offence. The offence undoubtedly was one motivated by financial profit. The moral culpability of the defendant was high. The act of making a false statement took place in the context of the defendant providing medical services for financial benefit that he was not entitled to provide and doing so in flagrant disregard of prior court orders. This engaged important social welfare interests. A significant fine was necessary for both specific and general deterrence. The fine was required to be substantial enough to warn others that the offence would not be tolerated and must not appear to be a mere licence fee for illegal activity. The sentence imposed was fit. See *Ontario (Superintendent of Financial Services) v. Dies*, 2018 ONCJ 641, 2018 CarswellOnt 15738, [2018] O.J. No. 4894 (Ont. C.J.).

It is not an error for an appellate court to situate the sentence before it within the usual range of sentences. One cannot begin to measure the demonstrable fitness of a sentence without having an eye to the customary sentencing range. An appeal court errs if it tethers a finding of unfitness to the simple fact that the range is missed, but commits no error by getting a perspective on what a fit sentence looks like by examining comparable cases. The principle of parity requires that sentences should be similar to other sentences imposed on similar offenders for similar offences committed in similar circumstances. This principle is equally applicable to sentencing for regulatory offences and criminal offences. Genuine inability to pay a fine is not a proper basis for imprisonment. As a matter of principle, it must also hold true that the hardship of a fine is not a proper basis for imprisonment either. The appeal court judge was therefore correct in finding that the sentencing justice erred in imposing a jail term because a fine would cause more financial hardship. On this basis alone, the appeal judge was entitled to set aside the sentences of incarceration and to vary the sentences within the limits prescribed by law. However, the appeal judge erred in adopting as a sentencing principle that regulatory offences are concerned with attaining public policy objectives as opposed to punishing moral blameworthiness. This is too crude a formulation and poses a false dichotomy. It is true that regulatory offences are concerned with attaining public policy objectives and the criminal law punishes according to the degree of the offender's moral blameworthiness; however, this does not mean that moral blameworthiness may not also be a relevant sentencing consideration for regulatory offences. The relevance of moral blameworthiness in sentencing for regulatory offences follows necessarily from the application in regulatory offences of the fundamental sentencing principle of proportionality. It is important to appreciate that, despite its application, moral blameworthiness does not operate the same way in sentencing regulatory offenders, as it does in sentencing criminal offenders. This is because regulatory offences tend to reflect lower levels of moral blameworthiness. While both kinds of offences reflect moral blameworthiness, the moral blameworthiness in criminal offences tends to be greater, and that difference must be respected when imposing sentences. See *Ontario (Labour) v. New Mex Canada Inc.*, 2019 ONCA 30, 2019 CarswellOnt 577, 51 C.C.E.L. (4th) 171, [2019] O.J. No. 227 (Ont. C.A.).

12

APPEALS

12.1 RE-OPENING A PART I OR PART II CONVICTION

12.1.1 PART I OFFENCES

- In order for a conviction to be struck out where the defendant was convicted without a hearing
  - The defendant must:
    - Attend at the court office during regular office hours within 15 days of becoming aware of the conviction; and
    - Appear before a justice requesting that the conviction be struck out: section 11(1) [See Record of Re-opening Application in Appendix C].
  - The justice will strike out the conviction if he or she is satisfied by affidavit of the defendant that, through no fault of the defendant [See Affidavit in Support of a Request for Re-opening in Appendix C]:
    - The defendant was unable to appear for a hearing; or
    - A notice or document relating to the offence was not delivered: section 11(1) [See Certificate of Striking Out Conviction in Appendix C].
  - The justice will give the defendant and the prosecutor a notice of trial or proceed under section 7 where the justice strikes out the conviction: section 11(2).
  - The evidence that is required in support of a re-opening request must be an affidavit of the defendant, and not that of an agent. See *Mississauga (City) v. Saleira* (2002), [2002] O.J. No. 5422, 2002 CarswellOnt 5311 (Ont. S.C.J.).

In a case dealing with the delegation of filing and processing notices of appeals from the province to the municipalities, Wake A.C.J. held in *Solda v. Brampton (City)*, 2006 ONCJ 246, 35 M.V.R. (5th) 103, 82 O.R. (3d) 312, 2006 CarswellOnt 4197, [2006] O.J. No. 2801 (Ont. C.J.) that a clerk of the court employed by the province, and a clerk of the court employed by the municipality but assigned to perform some appeal duties by virtue of the Memorandum of Understanding between the municipality and the Attorney General, have concurrent jurisdiction to receive notices of appeal.

The 15-day requirement under s. 11(1) began to run when the defendant had actual knowledge of his conviction. In the instant case, the defendant's agent learned of his client's conviction on January 31, 2008 but was unable to contact his client and inform him of it until February 22, 2008. The defendant's re-opening application on March 4, 2008 was therefore within the time limits prescribed by s. 11(1). While the justice of the peace may have rejected the defendant's explanation that he had lost his ticket, and that the agent, who had been contacted before the conviction was entered, could not obtain information regarding the charge until he received the defendant's authorization, there was evidence in the defendant's affidavit, supplemented by what the justice heard from the defendant and the agent, to support the re-opening decision. The reviewing court was not prepared to say that the exercise of discretion was an error of law. There were no exceptional circumstances to justify an awarding of costs: *Thunder Bay (City) v. Kandiah*, 2008 CarswellOnt 2685, [2008] O.J. No. 1863 (Ont. S.C.J.).

A justice of the peace who convicts a defendant under ss. 9 or 9.1 is not precluded from presiding at a subsequent trial if a re-opening has been granted: *Charron v. Ontario (Justice of the Peace)*, 2008 CarswellOnt 3421, (*sub nom.* Charron v. Squires) 91 O.R. (3d) 305, [2008] O.J. No. 2288 (Ont. S.C.J.).

In *R. v. Kergan*, 2011 SKPC 115, 2011 CarswellSask 527, 381 Sask. R. 106, [2011] S.J. No. 478 (Sask. Prov. Ct.), it was held that an *ex parte* trial is not the same as a default conviction, and is therefore not subject to the reopening provision for setting aside a default conviction. When a not guilty plea has been entered and the accused then fails to appear for trial, it is not open to the court to simply issue a default conviction; it is open to the court to hear the trial in the absence of the defendant, and then issue a conviction. If the reopening provision for default convictions applied to such trials, the defendant could use it to set aside his conviction and obtain a new trial, and then in theory he could fail to appear for the next trial and again use the procedure to set aside the conviction. The process could go on indefinitely and he could be tried an indefinite number of times. This would be a most unreasonable interpretation of the legislation, and a most unreasonable state of affairs.

12.1.2 PART II PARKING OFFENCES

- Section 19(1) and (2) is substantially the same rule for reopening parking infraction cases where the defendant was convicted without a hearing.

12.2 APPEAL PROCEDURE

12.2.1 PART I AND PART II APPEALS

For an *adult* defendant:

- The defendant or prosecutor (or Attorney General by way of intervention) may appeal an acquittal, conviction or sentence to the Ontario Court of Justice: section 135(1).

- The appeal shall be heard by a provincial court judge: section 135(1).

For a *youth* defendant:

- The appeal lies to the Ontario Superior Court of Justice, but the procedures and powers of the court shall be the same as for an adult appeal to the Ontario Court of Justice: section 105.

- The notice of appeal shall:

  - Be in the prescribed form; [See Schedule C]

  - Shall state the reasons why the appeal is taken; and

  - Shall be filed with the court within 30 days of the decision: section 135(2). (The appeal period was increased from 15 days to 30 days by the *Good Government Act, 2009,* S.O. 2009, c. 33, s. 1(57), effective 15 December 2009.)

- The defendant must pay any fine imposed before filing the notice of appeal, unless waived by a judge (section 111), and there is no stay pending appeal, unless a judge so orders (section 112).

- There is no requirement to order transcripts or file a factum.

- The appeal shall be conducted by means of a *review* and the court may "make such inquiries as are necessary to ensure that the issues are fully and effectively defined": section 136. In particular, the court may:

  - Hear and rehear the recorded evidence or any part thereof and may require any party to provide a transcript of the evidence, or any part thereof, or to produce any further exhibit;

- Receive the evidence of any witness whether or not the witness gave evidence at the trial;

- Require the justice presiding at the trial to report in writing on any matter specified in the request; or

- Receive and act upon statements of agreed facts or admissions.

- The appeal court "may affirm, reverse or vary the decision appealed from or where, in the opinion of the court, it is necessary to do so to satisfy the ends of justice, direct a new trial": section 138(1).

- Where a new trial is directed, it will be before a different justice than the one who presided originally, unless the parties consent otherwise: section 138(2).

- In addition, with the consent of the parties, the court may direct that the justice to hear the new trial will be the Provincial Judge hearing the appeal: section 138(2).

- Costs can be awarded: section 138(3).

- With leave, further appeals are to the Court of Appeal for Ontario: section 139.

In *London (City) v. Young*, 2008 CarswellOnt 3091, [2008] O.J. No. 2118, 2008 ONCA 429, 237 O.A.C. 357, 233 C.C.C. (3d) 10, 75 Admin. L.R. (4th) 280, 91 O.R. (3d) 215, 65 M.V.R. (5th) 208 (Ont. C.A.), it was held that no regular avenue of appeal is provided where a proceeding is quashed under s. 9(1) of the *Provincial Offences Act*. If the prosecuting authority or the Attorney General believes a justice has misconstrued what constitutes an error going to the regularity or completeness of the certificate, a prerogative remedy can be sought.

A *Charter* violation was found in a provincial offences appeal case where the trial transcripts took from 15 and one-half months to 27 months to produce. The four appellants had been convicted under Part I Certificate of Offence proceedings. The court ruled that the appellants' fairness of trial rights were compromised due to the delays occasioned in the preparation of the trial transcripts, and resulted in an abuse of process, contrary to s. 7 of the *Charter*. A stay of proceedings was imposed on appeal, and costs were ordered against the prosecutor: *R. v. Ovided*, [2008] O.J. No. 2780, 2008 CarswellOnt 4181, 91 O.R. (3d) 593, 2008 ONCJ 317, 174 C.R.R. (2d) 189 (Ont. C.J.).

The Court of Appeal has jurisdiction to allow an appeal, quash the decision of the provincial judge dismissing the appeal under s. 135 of the *Provincial Offences Act*, as well as the underlying conviction, and to order a new trial. The court's authority for doing this is the result of the combined effect of the definition of "court" in s. 109 and the provisions of s. 138(1). A new trial was necessary to satisfy the ends of justice as the provincial judge treated the hearing for an extension of time as an appeal on the merits, and dismissed the appeal without providing the appellant an opportunity to be heard: *R. v. Baccus*, 2008 CarswellOnt 3726, 2008 ONCA 508, [2008] O.J. No. 2503 (Ont. C.A.).

Once a new trial is ordered under s. 138(2) of the *Provincial Offences Act*, the regulatory authority for setting the new trial date is according to Reg. 200, s. 31(2) which directs the clerk of the court to give notice to the prosecutor of the time and place of trial when a summons is ordered by the appeal court. The return date for the defendant on the summons is expected to be the trial date. O. Reg 722/94, s. 15, also places an obligation on the clerk to provide the appellate court's decision, written reasons and endorsement to the clerk of the Ontario Court of Justice, which includes the Provincial Offences Court and the prosecutor, or if a prosecutor was not present at the appeal, the Crown Attorney: *R. v. Mandina*, [2009] O.J. No. 3822, 2009 CarswellOnt 5497, 2009 ONCJ 423 (Ont. C.J.).

In *R. v. Badesha*, 2010 ONCJ 10, 2010 CarswellOnt 367 (Ont. C.J.), Takach J. dismissed an application to introduce fresh evidence on appeal. The defendant had been convicted of operating a motor cycle without a helmet. It was held that while it may be legitimately argued that at least with respect to some of the requirements of fresh evidence the rules set out by the Supreme Court of Canada in *R. v. Palmer*, 1979 CarswellBC 533, 1979 CarswellBC 541, [1980] 1 S.C.R. 759, 50 C.C.C. (2d) 193, 14 C.R. (3d) 22, 17 C.R. (3d) 34 (Fr.), 106 D.L.R. (3d) 212, 30 N.R. 181, [1979] S.C.J. No. 126 (S.C.C.) should be relaxed in routine Part I offences, the case at bar was not one of them. Applicants wishing to adduce evidence on appeal that was not proffered at trial do not have carte blanche on more straightforward cases. The Ontario Court of Appeal's decision in *R. v. 1275729 Ontario Inc.* (2005), [2005] O.J. No. 5515, 2005 CarswellOnt 7424, 203 C.C.C. (3d) 501, 25 M.V.R. (5th) 157, 205 O.A.C. 359 (Ont. C.A.) respecting the admissibility of fresh evidence for Part III appeals does not stand for the proposition that the factors enumerated in *Palmer* never, in any circumstances, are deserving of consideration in any Part I appeal, regardless of the circumstances of the case or the complexity of the issues before the trial judge. Section 136(3) is permissive rather than mandatory. Clearly, the less complex the case and the more unsophisticated the defendant or applicant, the greater the relaxation of any principles that might be brought to bear on the situation. However, the case before the trial judge was not straightforward and involved complex constitutional issues that occupied both senior experienced counsel and the presiding judge for a number of days and involved volumes of written material and argument. Even in provincial offences court, new evidence is not allowed simply to give an appellant another attempt to convince a judicial officer of his position. Moreover, the evidence sought to be tendered as fresh evidence which related to a survey of Sikh motorcycle riders in British Columbia that did not wear helmets was riddled with the possibility of bias, and could not be expected to have affected the result at trial. The evidence could have been tendered at trial. Whether a rider was Sikh or not was irrelevant to the safety issue of riding motorcycles without a helmet.

An order striking out a conviction and the granting of a re-opening cannot be appealed under s. 135 which only permits an appeal against acquittal, conviction or sentence. The only recourse for the applicant is to seek prerogative remedies pursuant to s. 140(1). When the justice of the peace endorsed the conviction as not being under s. 9.1, that meant there was hearing and the defendant was represented. Administratively, the affidavit in support of a request for reopening ought not to have been put before the justice on the reopening application, given the endorsement of conviction. Public interest dictates that there ought not to be a second trial, but rather an appeal of the first trial. Care should be taken to ensure that applications to reopen are not entertained where there has been a determination on the merits: *London (City) v. Pavar*, 2010 ONSC 3448, 2010 CarswellOnt 3912 (Ont. S.C.J.).

The new extension of time provision under s. 85(2) which limits the number of times that an application for an extension of time for filing of appeal may be brought was discussed in *York (Regional Municipality) v. Sahraeian*, 2011 ONCJ 253, 2011 CarswellOnt 3365, [2011] O.J. No. 2231 (Ont. C.J.). It was held in that case that, effective 15 December 2009, s. 85(2) expressly prohibits more than one application for an extension of time for filing of appeal made in respect of a conviction. In circumstances where a second application to extend the time for the filing of appeal was instituted following the dismissal of the first such application as abandoned, and the second application post-dates the enactment of s. 85(2), the subsequent application(s) is statute barred. Although the appeal did not involve consideration of a request to re-open an un-adjudicated extension request of first instance that had been noted as dismissed as abandoned, should those circumstances arise the *Provincial Offences Act* appeal court judge has jurisdiction to consider such an application even in the absence of specific statutory authority or inherent jurisdiction. In order for an originating (first) application for extension that has been noted dismissed as abandoned to be subsequently re-considered, the applicant must demonstrate that the initial order was made as a result of an error or that the court was operating under some misapprehension of the material facts or without knowledge of all of the material facts when the order was made. If these threshold considerations cannot be met the matter shall not be re-opened; once re-opened, assuming the threshold criteria has been determined to exist, the originating application can then be considered afresh and adjudicated on the merits.

There have also been a number of appeals heard by the Ontario Court of Appeal with respect to s. 85(2), In *R. v. Melaku*, 106 O.R. (3d) 481, 2011 CarswellOnt 11357, 284 C.C.C. (3d) 528, 20 M.V.R. (6th) 22, [2011] O.J. No. 3835 (Ont. C.A. [In Chambers]), it was held that the *Provincial Offences Act* does not provide for an appeal against an unsuccessful application for an extension of time under s. (85)(1) to file a notice of appeal brought before the Ontario Court of Justice sitting as a provincial offences appeal court. Therefore the Court of Appeal has no jurisdiction to grant leave to appeal in such circumstances.

For a similar result, see *R. v. Borges*, 2011 ONCA 621, 107 O.R. (3d) 377, 281 C.C.C. (3d) 231, 25 M.V.R. (6th) 42, 285 O.A.C. 173, 2011 CarswellOnt 10567 [2011] O.J. No. 4278 (Ont. C.A. [In Chambers]), a case dealing with a Part III appeal, and summarized at 12.2.2, *infra*.

Further, in *R. v. Opoku*, [2012] O.J. No. 147, 2012 CarswellOnt 684, 2012 ONCA 22 (Ont. C.A.), a panel of the Ontario Court of Appeal ruled that the test for special leave to appeal under s. 131 is a strict one. No issue essential to the public interest arises in the case where the question is simply the applicant's reason for failing to attend court. Nor is there an issue as to the due administration of justice, given that the applicant has another remedy. It was left for another time to determine whether there is jurisdiction under s. 131 to grant special leave from dismissal of an application for an extension of time when the application was dismissed on the merits. Where the application, however, was dismissed as abandoned, as happened in the instant case, the remedy is an application to the provincial offences appeal court to reopen the application for the extension of time. On the application for leave to reopen, the applicant does not have to meet the strict test for special leave to appeal that applies under s. 131. Rather, it would be for the provincial offences appeal court to apply the appropriate factors for reopening an application for an extension of time. An application to reopen would not violate s. 85(2). Consequently, the application for special leave to appeal was dismissed. **Note:** The leave application in the *Opoku* case was referred to a panel of the Ontario Court of Appeal for determination after first being heard by a single judge of the Ontario Court of Appeal: see *R. v. Opoku*, 2011 ONCA 712, 2011 CarswellOnt 15773 (Ont. C.A. [In Chambers]).

In *R. v. Zehr*, [2011] O.J. No. 4493, 2011 ONCJ 516, 2011 CarswellOnt 10607, 21 M.V.R. (6th) 322 (Ont. C.J.), it was held that the trial justice misapprehended the law and misapplied the law to the facts before him, and as such committed a reversible error. In addition the trial justice improperly interfered with the cross-examination of the sole Crown witness. It was not necessary to the ends of justice to order a new trial. There was a fulsome evidentiary record and the end result of any new trial would not be in doubt given the state of the law as found by the appeal judge concerning Hydro One being a public utility, and that a hydro wire hanging from a pole that was live constituted an emergency, to which the defendant was responding.

At trial, the defendant challenged the constitutional validity of s. 68.1(1) of the *Highway Traffic Act*, which requires commercial trucks to be equipped with speed limiting systems. The Justice of the Peace found in favour of the defendant and struck down the section. On appeal, the Crown sought to adduce evidence of an expert witness as fresh evidence, as did the defendant. The proposed fresh evidence tendered by the Crown consisted of a supplementary affidavit assessing the findings of a safety study that was released after the Crown's expert witness had completed his original affidavit, and after the case had been argued before the presiding Justice of the Peace. There were components of the study that contained new information that could not have been introduced at the trial, and it was relevant to the question of whether the defendant's security of the person was infringed by having his vehicle's speed limited. It also addressed the issue of whether the legislation was arbitrary. The proposed fresh evidence was credible in the sense that it was reasonably capable of belief, and could reasonably be expected to have affected the result. The presiding Justice of the Peace did not choose one expert over the other. His decision as based more on what was not in the evidence before him. Had it been available at trial, the proposed fresh evidence, taken together with the other evidence already presented in the case, could reasonably have affected the result. The impact of the decision regarding the constitutional issue might ultimately be felt well beyond the instant case. Accordingly, it was important that the issue be decided on the basis of all relevant material that might be available. It was therefore in the interests of justice to receive the proposed fresh evidence on the appeal. See *R. v. Michaud*, 2013 ONCJ 213, 2013 CarswellOnt 4910, [2013] O.J. No. 1898 (Ont. C.J.).

In *R. v. E. (A.)*, 2013 ONCA 713, 2013 CarswellOnt 15932, 118 O.R. (3d) 98, 28 C.C.L.I. (5th) 1, [2013] O.J. No. 5299 (Ont. C.A.), it was noted that there was conflicting authority on whether the Court of Appeal has jurisdiction to hear the appeals of some of the matters on which the applicant was seeking leave to appeal because he was denied an extension of time in which to appeal by the courts below. This issue had also been considered by single members of the court in applications for leave to appeal, and a panel of the court had referred to the issue but declined to resolve it. In the particular circumstances of the case, where the applicant was apparently suffering from, and was now being treated for, a serious mental illness which was not known by the courts below, and had been convicted four times for operating motor vehicles without insurance which resulted in very significant fines, an extension of time in which to appeal was granted, as was leave to appeal.

Significant minimum fines for the offence of operating a motor vehicle without insurance may well have a good public policy justification, particularly in acting as a general deterrent. It is nonetheless in the public interest to determine whether in the particular circumstances of any individual defendant some accommodation should be made for individuals with significant personal disabilities. Numerous authorities set out the appropriate factors that a court should consider in determining whether to extend the time in which to appeal under s. 85 of the *Provincial Offences Act*. Among the appropriate factors, it is usually significant whether: the applicant has demonstrated a *bona fide* intention to appeal within the prescribed appeal period; the applicant has accounted for or explained the delay in initiating the appeal; and the proposed appeal has merit. And in some circumstances it will be significant whether: the consequences of the conviction are out of all proportion to the penalty imposed; the Crown will be prejudiced; and the applicant has taken the benefit of the judgment. In the final analysis, the principal consideration is whether the applicant has demonstrated that justice requires that the time be extended. It is important to note that these are all factors, not preconditions. It was at least arguable that the provincial judge did not appear to take these factors into account. After this dismissal, the applicant was prevented from having the provincial offences appeal court consider the totality of the fines and surcharges. In the particular circumstances of the case, the due administration of justice is implicated, and as a consequence the broader public interest issues involved were not considered.

The proper route to be taken by the Crown when it seeks to set aside a decision by a trial court to stay proceedings commenced under the *Provincial Offences Act* on account of unreasonable delay is to be bring an appeal under s. 116(1)(b), and not *certiorari*. A judicial stay of proceedings is tantamount to a dismissal. Challenging the correctness of a judicial stay by way of appeal rather than through an application in the Superior Court is simpler and more straightforward than via prerogative writs. For an accused, particularly one who is self-represented, responding to an appeal is more readily understood than being required to respond to an application for *certiorari* and to follow the procedures of the Superior Court. The interpretation of the term "dismissal" in this manner better achieves the intended purpose of the Act. See *R. v. Courtice Auto Wreckers Ltd.*, 2014 ONCA 189, 2014 CarswellOnt 2797, 308 C.C.C. (3d) 571, 82 C.E.L.R. (3d) 177, 317 O.A.C. 265, [2014] O.J. No. 1145 (Ont. C.A.).

In *R. v. Ul-Rashid*, 2013 ONCA 782, 2013 CarswellOnt 18773, 309 C.C.C. (3d) 468, 313 O.A.C. 324, [2013] O.J. No. 6178 (Ont. C.A.), leave to appeal to the Court of Appeal was granted in a case where the applicant was under the impression that the police officer would provide him with proof of the offence by bringing the videotape to court of his failing to stop at a red light, without him needing to make a request for production. There was conflicting authority on the issues of disclosure obligations in the provincial offences context, and the nature of the duty on Justices of the Peace to assist self-represented defendants. It was in the public interest for the Court of Appeal to decide whether any right to disclosure was breached in this case and to clarify the extent of any assistance that a Justice of the Peace was expected to provide an unrepresented defendant in trial of offences under the *Provincial Offences Act*.

In *R. v. Poonia*, 2014 BCSC 1526, 2014 CarswellBC 2393, 69 M.V.R. (6th) 263, [2014] B.C.J. No. 2092 (B.C. S.C.), it was held that the fresh evidence tendered on appeal was in relation to the alleged inadequacy of disclosure as well as the issue that the Judicial Justice of the Peace should have held a voir dire before admitting the statement of the defendant to the police. These issues go to the fairness of the trial and do not touch directly on the issue of guilt or innocence. The evidence was relevant and admissible for the limited purpose of evaluating the adequacy of the disclosure and for understanding the context in which the Judicial Justice of the Peace admitted the statement of the defendant without holding a voir dire.

In *R. v. Agasiyants*, 2015 ONCJ 142, 2015 CarswellOnt 3304, [2015] O.J. No. 1214 (Ont. C.J.), it was held that an issue of insufficient or failed jurisdiction may properly be litigated as a ground for appealing a conviction. It was a conviction registered in an Early Resolution Meeting which was the subject of complaint. The recourse to appellate relief is not governed by the manner or forum in which a conviction is registered, but only by the manner in which proceedings are commenced. In this case, proceedings were commenced by a certificate of offence under Part I. The appeal was properly before the court. Although the grounds might suggest that there was no jurisdiction in the Justice of the Peace on the Early Resolution Meeting to enter the conviction, the complaint comes down to one, commonly heard in the Provincial Offences Appeal Court, that the Appellant had no notice of the proceedings in which she was convicted. Her complaint was exacerbated by her assertion that she never requested an early resolution meeting on her request for re-opening. There was an absence of any evidence showing notice to the defendant of the Early Resolution Meeting, directed by the Justice of the Peace on the re-opening application. In the absence of notice as directed to the defendant of a proceeding which directly affected her rights, and given her assertion, uncontested, that she was unaware of the proceeding, the re-opening was not properly constituted and the conviction must be set aside.

In *R. v. Michaud*, 2015 ONCA 585, 2015 CarswellOnt 13209, 127 O.R. (3d) 81, 328 C.C.C. (3d) 228, 22 C.R. (7th) 246, 82 M.V.R. (6th) 171, 341 C.R.R. (2d) 89, 339 O.A.C. 41, [2015] O.J. No. 4540 (Ont. C.A.), leave to appeal refused 2016 CarswellOnt 7197, 2016 CarswellOnt 7198 (S.C.C.), it was held that s. 135(1) of the *Provincial Offences Act* provides that an acquittal, conviction or sentence in a proceeding commenced by a Part I certificate of offence may be appealed to the Ontario Court of Justice. Section 136(2) states that such appeals are to be conducted by means of a review; s. 136(3) sets out the appeal court's broad powers of review. The appeal court in this case properly conducted a robust review under s. 136 of the Act. The court was not required to exercise the more limited scope of review applicable to appeals under Part III because the trial involved experienced counsel, expert witnesses and *Charter* arguments. The appeal court was entitled to admit fresh evidence and, having done so, had to consider whether on the whole of the evidence the trial judge's view of the evidence was reasonable. The appeal judge was entitled to come to his own conclusion, based on all the evidence, whether the defendant established on a balance of probabilities that the speed limiter requirement deprived him of his right to security of the person.

In *Brampton (City) v. Robinson*, 2018 ONCJ 839, 2018 CarswellOnt 19919, [2018] O.J. No. 5918 (Ont. C.J.), it was held that subsection 138(1) permits an appeal court "to affirm, reverse or vary the decision appealed from". It appears that the court's jurisdiction to vary the decision appealed from would permit substituting a conviction for a different offence, with the consent of the parties.

12.2.2 PART III APPEALS

(a) Procedure and Forum for Appeal

- The defendant or prosecutor or the Attorney General may, by way of intervention, appeal, as to sentence or in order to conduct a defence, from a conviction or dismissal or from a finding as to ability, because of mental disorder or any other order as to costs (The ability to appeal costs orders was added by the *Good Government Act, 2009,* S.O. 2009, c. 33, s. 1(54), effective 15 December 2009.), where:
  - The proceeding is commenced by information under Part III; and
  - Where the appeal is from the decision of a justice of the peace, to the Ontario Court of Justice presided over by a provincial judge; or
  - Where the appeal is from the decision of a provincial judge, to the Ontario Superior Court of Justice: section 116(1, 2).
- The appellant will give notice of appeal as is provided for by the rules of court: section 116(3) [See Appendix C].

In a case dealing with the delegation of filing and processing notices of appeals from the province to the municipalities, Wake A.C.J. held in *Solda v. Brampton (City)*, 2006 ONCJ 246, 35 M.V.R. (5th) 103, 82 O.R. (3d) 312, 2006 CarswellOnt

4197, [2006] O.J. No. 2801 (Ont. C.J.) that a clerk of the court employed by the province, and a clerk of the court employed by the municipality but assigned to perform some appeal duties by virtue of the Memorandum of Understanding between the municipality and the Attorney General, have concurrent jurisdiction to receive notices of appeal.

In a case involving a Crown appeal against a verdict of acquittal where the provincial offences appeal court substituted verdicts of guilt, the Court of Appeal ruled that it was unfair to permit the Crown to raise a new issue on appeal when the defendant had no notice that this was an issue at trial. A Crown appeal is not the time for the prosecution to advance a new theory of liability. As the errors by the appeal judge infected her assessment of the due diligence defence, the Court of Appeal was not convinced that an appeal court would necessarily have reached the same conclusions on liability in the absence of the errors. A re-hearing of the Crown's appeal in the provincial offences appeal court was ordered: *Ontario (Ministry of Labour) v. Modern Niagara Toronto Inc.*, 2008 CarswellOnt 4799, 2008 ONCA 590, 240 O.A.C. 278, 91 O.R. (3d) 774, (*sub nom.* R. v. Modern Niagara Toronto Inc.) 297 D.L.R. (4th) 156, [2008] O.J. No. 3168 (Ont. C.A.).

The threshold for granting leave under s. 139 of the *Provincial Offences Act* is very high. The section was drafted to eliminate all but appeals on the most significant issues: *R. v. Hemrayeva*, 2010 CarswellOnt 1409, 2010 ONCA 194, 92 M.V.R. (5th) 215, 259 O.A.C. 389 (Ont. C.A. [In Chambers]).

In *R. v. Ade-Ajayi*, 2011 ONCA 192, 2011 CarswellOnt 1477, 97 C.C.L.I. (4th) 183, 14 M.V.R. (6th) 9, [2011] O.J. No. 1016 (Ont. C.A.), it was held that appeals to the Court of Appeal under the *Provincial Offences Act* are very much the exceptions, and particularly so with respect to sentence. Trial judges must decide whether the circumstances of a particular case call for something less than the minimum fine. The court will not "second guess" that assessment absent factors that meet the leave to appeal criteria set out in s. 139.

- The *Good Government Act, 2011*, S.O. 2011, c. 1, which was assented to on 30 March 2011, has made a number of changes to the *Provincial Offences Act*. These include providing authority to the clerk of the court, on notice to the parties, to have an appeal brought before the court for a hearing to determine whether the appeal should be dismissed or abandoned. However, a party that has had an appeal dismissed may apply to have the appeal restored. See sections 128(2) and (3) of the *Provincial Offences Act*.

The appellant having been convicted for offences of dog running at large, contrary to a City of Toronto by-law, and failing to exercise reasonable precautions to prevent dog from biting or attacking another domestic animal, contrary to the *Dog Owners Liability Act*, should have pursued her appeal rights, and *certiorari* was therefore not available. Her complaints that she was not properly served, that the city official did not have the authority to swear the information, and that city officials trespassed on her property did not affect the jurisdiction of the justice of the peace to try the offences: *R. v. Nilsen*, 2011 ONCA 322, 2011 CarswellOnt 2681, [2011] O.J. No. 1865 (Ont. C.A.), leave to appeal refused 2011 CarswellOnt 10872, 2011 CarswellOnt 10871, 429 N.R. 391 (note), 294 O.A.C. 394 (note), [2011] S.C.C.A. No. 279 (S.C.C.).

In *R. v. Thomas G. Fuller & Sons Ltd.*, 2011 CarswellOnt 4459, (*sub nom.* Ontario (Minister of Labour) v. Black & McDonald Ltd.) 278 O.A.C. 284, (*sub nom.* Ontario (Minister of Labour) v. Black & McDonald Ltd.) 106 O.R. (3d) 784, [2011] O.J. No. 2615, 2 C.L.R. (4th) 161, 2011 ONCA 440 (Ont. C.A.), the Court of Appeal ruled that the application of the rule in *Kienapple* against multiple convictions does not result in an acquittal; it results in a conditional stay. Therefore, assuming the trial judge had made findings of guilt on all five counts, even if he applied *Kienapple* to counts 1, 2 and 4, at most he could have ordered a conditional stay. He could not have acquitted the defendants or dismissed the charges against them. And once the appeal court judge overturned the findings of guilt on counts 3 and 5, the conditional stays on counts 1, 2 and 4 would have been set aside and the findings of guilt on these counts restored.

In *R. v. Borges*, 2011 ONCA 621, 107 O.R. (3d) 377, 281 C.C.C. (3d) 231, 25 M.V.R. (6th) 42, 285 O.A.C. 173, 2011 CarswellOnt 10567, [2011] O.J. No. 4278 (Ont. C.A. [In Chambers]), it was held that s. 131 is limited to applications for leave to appeal from a decision made by the provincial offences appeal court under s. 116. The decision of the appeal court to deny an extension of time to file an appeal was made under s. 85, and not pursuant to s. 116. Consequently, no "judgment" was rendered under s. 116, and there could be no application for leave to appeal under s. 131. Even if there was jurisdiction, leave to appeal should not be granted as the appeal was without merit. While s. 54, which allows for a conviction in the defendant's absence, requires that the prosecutor prove that the defendant was given notice of the original trial date, it does not require the prosecutor to prove that the defendant received notice of the adjourned date. It is the responsibility of the defendant to ascertain the new date; the court bears no duty of notice beyond announcing the new date, in court, at the time of the adjournment.

For a similar result, see *R. v. Melaku*, 106 O.R. (3d) 481, 2011 CarswellOnt 11357, 284 C.C.C. (3d) 528, 20 M.V.R. (6th) 22, [2011] O.J. No. 3835 (Ont. C.A. [In Chambers]), a case dealing with a Part I appeal, summarized at 12.2.1, *infra*.

Further, in *R. v. Opoku*, [2012] O.J. No. 147, 2012 CarswellOnt 684, 2012 ONCA 22 (Ont. C.A.), a panel of the Ontario Court of Appeal ruled that the test for special leave to appeal under s. 131 is a strict one. No issue essential to the public interest arises in the case where the question is simply the applicant's reason for failing to attend court. Nor is there an issue as to the due administration of justice, given that the applicant has another remedy. It was left for another time to determine whether there is jurisdiction under s. 131 to grant special leave from dismissal of an application for an extension of time when the application was dismissed on the merits. Where the application, however, was dismissed as abandoned, as happened in the instant case, the remedy is an application to the provincial offences appeal court to reopen the application for the extension of time. On the application for leave to reopen, the applicant does not have to meet the strict test for special leave to appeal that applies under s. 131. Rather, it would be for the provincial offences appeal court to apply the appropriate factors for reopening an application for an extension of time. An application to reopen would not violate s. 85(2). Consequently, the application for special leave to appeal was dismissed. **Note:** The leave application in the *Opoku* case was referred to a panel of the Ontario Court of Appeal for determination after first being heard by a single judge of the Ontario Court of Appeal: see *R. v. Opoku*, 2011 ONCA 712, 2011 CarswellOnt 15773 (Ont. C.A. [In Chambers]).

In *R. v. Houssameddine* (2011), 20 M.V.R. (6th) 161, 2011 CarswellOnt 9764, 2011 ONCJ 473 (Ont. C.J.), it was held that the applicant was entitled to proceed with his appeal in circumstances where he was previously granted an extension of time to file an appeal, but due to an apparent misunderstanding of the requirement to refile the notice of appeal document once the extension of time had been granted, the applicant failed to file another copy of the notice of appeal during the 30 day period for which the extension of time was given. In such factual circumstances, it was open to the court to provide the applicant with relief, in the form of an extension of time of the order it was given, so as to allow him to comply with the ruling granting the extension of time, in the first instance, to file the appeal. The authority to do so is set out in s. 85(1) of the *Provincial Offences Act* and s. 7(1) of the regulations governing Part III appeal proceedings; the making of an order to extend a time period on appeal under these two provisions, s. 85(1) of the Act and s. 7(1) of the appeal rules, is quite distinct from bringing a new, a second or subsequent extension of time application to file an appeal which is barred by s. 85(2).

The appeal court judge erred in allowing the appeal on grounds of appeal that were not raised by the defendant and without giving the prosecutor an opportunity to address the appeal judge's concerns about the admissibility of the evidence, business records, that had been led at the *ex parte* trial that had been held. Both the prosecutor and defendant are entitled to due process. Given the state of the record, fairness required that the parties have an opportunity to present their cases. The matter was remitted to the appeal court to give the parties an opportunity to make submissions on these issues. See *R. v. Boros*, 2013 ONCA 263, 2013 CarswellOnt 4834, [2013] O.J. No. 1904 (Ont. C.A.).

In *R. v. E. (A.)*, 2013 ONCA 713, 2013 CarswellOnt 15932, 118 O.R. (3d) 98, 28 C.C.L.I. (5th) 1, [2013] O.J. No. 5299 (Ont. C.A.), it was noted that there was conflicting authority on whether the Court of Appeal has jurisdiction to hear the appeals of some of the matters on which the applicant was seeking leave to appeal because he was denied an extension of time in which to appeal by the courts below. This issue had also been considered by single members of the court in applications for leave to appeal, and a panel of the court had referred to the issue but declined to resolve it. In the particular circumstances of the case, where the applicant was apparently suffering from, and was now being treated for, a serious mental illness which was not known by the courts below, and had been convicted four times for operating motor vehicles without insurance which resulted in very significant fines, an extension of time in which to appeal was granted, as was leave to appeal. Significant minimum fines for the offence of operating a motor vehicle without insurance may well have a good public policy justification, particularly in acting as a general deterrent. It is nonetheless in the public interest to determine whether in the particular circumstances of any individual defendant some accommodation should be made for individuals with significant personal disabilities. Numerous authorities set out the appropriate factors that a court should consider in determining whether to extend the time in which to appeal under s. 85 of the *Provincial Offences Act*. Among the appropriate factors, it is usually significant whether: the applicant has demonstrated a *bona fide* intention to appeal within the prescribed appeal period; the applicant has accounted for or explained the delay in initiating the appeal; and the proposed appeal has merit. And in some circumstances it will be significant whether: the consequences of the conviction are out of all proportion to the penalty imposed; the Crown will be prejudiced; and the applicant has taken the benefit of the judgment. In the final analysis, the principal consideration is whether the applicant has demonstrated that justice requires that the time be extended. It is important to note that these are all factors, not preconditions. It was at least arguable that the provincial judge did not appear to take these factors into account. After this dismissal, the applicant was prevented from having the provincial offences appeal court consider the totality of the fines and surcharges. In the particular circumstances of the case, the due administration of justice is implicated, and as a consequence the broader public interest issues involved were not considered.

The proper route to be taken by the Crown when it seeks to set aside a decision by a trial court to stay proceedings commenced under the *Provincial Offences Act* on account of unreasonable delay is to bring an appeal under s. 116(1)(b), and not *certiorari*. A judicial stay of proceedings is tantamount to a dismissal. Challenging the correctness of a judicial stay by way of appeal rather than through an application in the Superior Court is simpler and more straightforward than via prerogative writs.

For an accused, particularly one who is self-represented, responding to an appeal is more readily understood than being required to respond to an application for *certiorari* and to follow the procedures of the Superior Court. The interpretation of the term "dismissal" in this manner better achieves the intended purpose of the Act. See *R. v. Courtice Auto Wreckers Ltd.*, 2014 ONCA 189, 2014 CarswellOnt 2797, 308 C.C.C. (3d) 571, 82 C.E.L.R. (3d) 177, 317 O.A.C. 265, [2014] O.J. No. 1145 (Ont. C.A.).

The appeal court's decision to deny the adjournment of the appeal hearing was amply supported by the facts, as the appellant had asked for an adjournment on the day the appeal was to be heard to allow him time to order, prepare and file the remaining transcript. Having decided to deny the adjournment, the appeal court judge had no option but to dismiss the appeal. Such a decision was a matter that fell within the jurisdiction of the court to control its own process. See *Quinte West (Municipality) v. Balroop*, 2016 ONCA 657, 2016 CarswellOnt 13846, [2016] O.J. No. 4614 (Ont. C.A.).

In *R. v. Sciascia*, 2016 ONCA 411, 2016 CarswellOnt 8328, 131 O.R. (3d) 375, 336 C.C.C. (3d) 419, 350 O.A.C. 86, [2016] O.J. No. 2789 (Ont. C.A.), affirmed 2017 CSC 57, 2017 SCC 57, 2017 CarswellOnt 18247, 2017 CarswellOnt 18248, [2017] 2 S.C.R. 539, 355 C.C.C. (3d) 553, 41 C.R. (7th) 275, 417 D.L.R. (4th) 1, 17 M.V.R. (7th) 1, [2017] S.C.J. No. 57 (S.C.C.), the Court of Appeal considered the propriety of holding a joint trial under the *Provincial Offences Act* and the *Criminal Code*. It was held that in combination, the joinder provisions of the *Criminal Code* and s. 34(2) of the *Interpretation Act* make it clear that a *Criminal Code* information cannot include a count charging a provincial offence to which the *Provincial Offences Act* applies. The *Provincial Offences Act* also permits joinder of several offences in a single information. Unlike the *Criminal Code*, however, the *Provincial Offences Act*, in its s. 1(1), defines "offence" as "an offence under an Act of the Legislature." From this definition it follows that a *Provincial Offences Act* information cannot include counts charging *Criminal Code* offences. The joint trial of the *Criminal Code* summary conviction information and the *Provincial Offences Act* information therefore amounted to a procedural irregularity. However, there was no prejudice to the due administration of justice as a result. The joint trial coincided with the positions advanced by counsel on both sides of the case. Joinder avoided unnecessary duplication and depletion of judicial resources, inconvenience to witnesses, and the prospect of inconsistent verdicts. This was an appropriate case to apply the provisos in s. 686(1)(b)(iv) of the *Criminal Code* governing procedural irregularities at trial which do not cause prejudice to the party, and s. 120(1)(b)(iii) of the *Provincial Offences Act* where an appeal may be dismissed due to there being no substantial wrong or miscarriage of justice despite there being a wrong decision on a question of law. Although the *Provincial Offences Act* contains no provision comparable to s. 686(1)(b)(iv), the legal nature of the error is sufficient to bring it within the reach of s. 120(1)(b)(iii).

In *Oshawa (City) v. 536813 Ontario Limited*, 2017 ONCJ 836, 2017 CarswellOnt 19439, 72 C.L.R. (4th) 140, 69 M.P.L.R. (5th) 313, [2017] O.J. No. 6428 (Ont. C.J.), it was held the *Provincial Offences Act* does not explicitly set out a statutory route of appeal from a decision to quash an Information. The trial judge's ruling on the application was not based on a defect in the information or technical procedural irregularities. It was based on a determination of a question of law such that if the defendant was charged subsequently with the same offence, he could plead *autrefois acquit*. The court therefore had jurisdiction to address the prosecution appeal pursuant to s. 116(1)(b) as an appeal against a dismissal of the charge. The trial justice correctly found that the defence of interjurisdictional immunity applied given the record of the application. It is not the role of the appeal court to conduct a trial de novo or substitute alternative views for those held by the trial justice. Consequently, there was no basis to intervene. The trial justice found that the Federal Government power over aerodromes necessarily contemplated the design of an airport, its dimensions, and the specifications associated with related buildings and structures. The defendant's aircraft hangar was such a related building and/or structure. The trial justice held that the Federal Government's jurisdiction over aeronautics was relevant to the proper characterization of the defendant's property, that it was an integral physical part of the Oshawa Airport, and that the use of the property was related to matters of aeronautics and aviation. These findings were available on the evidence and documented in the judgment at trial.

An appeal may be brought against the order of the Justice of the Peace dismissing the application to quash the information. This is to be distinguished from the case where the Superior Court declines to exercise its jurisdiction to hear an interlocutory appeal of a motion to quash, prior to the final disposition of the charge on the merits. There was no merit to the defendant's motion to quash the information. It had no foundation in law or fact, but nonetheless served to substantially lengthen the proceedings. The Justice of the Peace made no error of law. He correctly held that the amendments that came into force made no substantive change to the limitation period created under the *Insurance Act*, that the limitation period was based on when the knowledge underlying the offence first came to the attention of the Superintendent. He properly dismissed the application to quash because the information was laid within a period of 2 years of when the facts first came to the knowledge of the Superintendent. See *Ontario (Superintendent of Financial Services) v. Dies*, 2018 ONCJ 641, 2018 CarswellOnt 15738, [2018] O.J. No. 4894 (Ont. C.J.).

12.2.3 APPEALING A PROVINCIAL OFFENCE — APPEAL POINTERS

- Either the defendant or prosecutor may bring an appeal to challenge the decision of the trial court — the party launching the appeal is called the appellant; the party responding to the appeal is called the respondent; in rare cases the Crown attorney if not the appellant or respondent may intervene and participate in the appeal, as may other third parties, such as an organization or association affected by the decision under appeal, and where permitted to do so such parties to the appeal are called intervenors.

- There are two streams of appeals under the *Provincial Offences Act*:

  - where the trial proceedings are by certificate of offence under Part I of the Act, or certificate of parking infraction under Part II of the Act, the appeal provisions which govern are the more informal requirements set out under sections 135-139;

  - where the trial proceedings are by way of information under Part III of the Act, the appeal provisions which govern are the more formal requirements set out under sections 116-134.

- It is therefore very important to first determine whether the decision being appealed from is in relation to a trial matter under Parts I or II of the *Provincial Offences Act*, or under Part III. Significant differences between the two appeal streams include:

  - Part I and Part II appeals must be filed within 30 days after the decision being appealed from, just like Part III appeals must be filed within 30 days of the decision being appealed from.

  - The forms required to be filed on appeals, such as the Notice of Appeal, are different for the two appeal streams.

  - Part I and Part II appeals are typically heard by a judge of the Ontario Court of Justice whereas Part III appeals are typically heard by a judge of the Ontario Court of Justice if the trial was held before a justice of the peace, but where the trial was held before a judge of the Ontario Court of

Justice the appeal court is the Ontario Superior Court of Justice.

- There are different appeal rules which apply, governing matters such as manner of service of documents: O. Reg. 722/94 for Part I and II appeals, and O. Reg. 723/94 for Part III appeals.

- Further appeals may be brought to the Ontario Court of Appeal, but leave to appeal from a judge of the Court of Appeal is required. There are separate rules which apply to such appeals: O. Reg. 721/94.

- To launch an appeal, the following steps must be followed:

  - Complete a Notice of Appeal in Form 1 under the appropriate appeal rules. Important considerations at this stage include:
    - Is this an appeal against conviction, sentence, or both? The notice of appeal should clearly state this, or the court may decline to allow the appeal to proceed or adjourn it to allow the other side to properly prepare.
    - The basis for the appeal must be stated, e.g., the defendant is appealing the conviction because the justice of the peace entered a conviction which is unreasonable and not supported by the evidence; the prosecutor is appealing the sentence as the fine imposed is not a fit sentence and fails to adequately denounce the defendant's unlawful conduct.
    - It is important for the party bringing the appeal to find out as much information about the trial proceedings as possible, especially where a different party is arguing the appeal than the one who argued the trial — what are grounds for the appeal: did the justice rule evidence admissible or inadmissible that he/she should not have, or did the justice not indicate adequately the basis for finding the defendant guilty, or err in interpreting a legal requirement of the offence or statute? Given the short time periods for bringing the appeal after trial (30 days), there will likely not be a copy of the justice's reasons available for review — what was the basis of the conviction or acquittal? Factual information will also be required as to the name of the justice of the peace who heard the trial, date of decision, location of the court and so on.

- If the appeal is going to involve a question as to the conduct of the parties at trial, e.g., the ground of appeal alleges that the agent did not have authority to plead guilty for the defendant, it is important to contact the party and give him/her an opportunity to provide an explanation as to what happened to the appeal court, such as by swearing an affidavit and being available for examination before the appeal court.
- Where the appeal is not being brought within the required time frames as set out below, the party seeking to appeal must apply for an extension of time and explain to the appeal court the reasons for the delay, including its intention to appeal in time and the merits of the appeal.

- Serve the Notice of Appeal on the other party within the required time frame (30 days for Part I or II appeals; 30 days for Part III appeals).

- File the Notice of Appeal in the court office where the appeal is to be heard within the required time frame (30 days for Part I or II appeals; 30 days for Part III appeals), including proof of service of the Notice of Appeal where necessary (proof of service may be acknowledged in writing on the Notice of Appeal which is filed in the court, otherwise an affidavit of service will be required).

- Order transcripts of the evidence taken at trial for the appeal, including the reasons for judgment and/or sentence — ordinarily 3 copies are required for the appeal — one for the appellant, one for the respondent and one for the court hearing the appeal. Each respondent is entitled to a transcript of the proceedings. The transcript must be ordered from the court reporter or monitor and there will be a fee charged to the party who is appealing the decision. The fee for the transcript is usually based on the number of pages which are transcribed.

- File a certificate in Form 2 regarding trial transcripts with the clerk of the court indicating that the transcript of the evidence has been ordered for Part III appeals. Although there is no similar transcript requirement for Part I and II appeals, it is often of practical assistance to order a trial transcript so that the parties can review in written form the proceedings in the trial court, and not have to rely on the playing of a tape in the appeal court. A transcript will allow the appeal court to better review the trial proceedings and give the parties more time to argue the appeal instead of having to play the tape. Trial transcripts of Part I or II matters are generally shorter than Part III proceedings, although in some cases, such as where the defendant fails to appear for trial or does not respond to the certificate of offence, there will not be a transcript of these "default" proceedings.

- Serve one copy of the trial transcript on the other side and the court, and keep one copy for the arguing of the appeal.

- File cases and/or written argument in the appeal court where appropriate to do so. Although appeals under Parts I or II are informal in nature, it is helpful to the court and good advocacy to bring to court any decisions or a case book that the party is relying on, e.g., a decision of the court ruling that a defect on the certificate renders the document defective in a case where the certificate in question has a similar defect, or a number of decisions showing that the sentence imposed for a similar offence for similar offenders is greater than the one imposed by the justice in the instant case. Written argument or a factum may be required by the court where the issue is novel or involves a new law or has the potential to impact on other cases.

- Attend the appeal court at the time and date specified for arguing the appeal. Attend the appeal court well in advance of the time set for the hearing, as there will usually be several other appeal cases being argued at that time, or motions for extensions of time to file an appeal, or enter into a fine recognizance on appeal rather than paying the fine. Bail pending appeal may also be granted where a period of imprisonment is imposed. There may also be a number of other lawyers or agents at the appeal court, and a number of prosecutors from different municipalities or agencies.

- Other appeal pointers:

  - Prior to arguing an appeal, attend the appeal court to observe the proceedings and see how matters are argued, e.g., does the appeal judge call on the parties to review the trial transcript or grounds of appeal before launching into argument, or does the appeal judge go right to the argument and question the parties about the grounds for the appeal? Attending the appeal court beforehand will also allow the parties to familiarize themselves with where to go in the court to argue the appeal, observe the judge and other parties.

- Speak to the other side in advance of the appeal, to introduce yourself and let the other side know that you are ready for the appeal and to present any cases or written materials, as well as to check that the appropriate materials are in the appeal file, such as a copy of the Notice of Appeal and any transcripts. This may also give the appellant an opportunity to ask the respondent what its position is on the appeal — for example, where the appellant is seeking a new trial as he/she did not show up for trial, but wishes to plead guilty to provide an explanation for speeding although at a lesser speed, the prosecutor may consent to the appellant providing an explanation to the appeal court and having the appeal heard and determined at such time, rather than arguing whether a new trial should be granted.

- The party bringing the appeal generally will have only one opportunity to argue an appeal, as further appeals to the Ontario Court of Appeal and even the Supreme Court of Canada require special grounds of appeal and permission (leave) of the court to do so. The appellant should therefore cast its appeal in its strongest grounds, and remember that the appeal court is to review the proceedings in the court below, and not merely substitute its view of the evidence or the witnesses. As a result, the appellant should be prepared to demonstrate where the trial court made an error by accepting or rejecting the evidence of a witness, or failed to consider a relevant factor, since "a trial is a trial, not a trial run". The appeal court will generally be reluctant to second guess the trial court on findings of fact or credibility, unless they appear not to be supported by the evidence. Where the appellant wishes to argue that the error in the trial court relates to a point of law, such as the interpretation of the essential elements of the offence, it is very helpful to bring decisions of other courts to the appeal court so that other legal authorities are placed before the court for its consideration.

- For the Court of Appeal to grant leave for a further appeal, the legal issue should be of broad public importance. The focus is not on the subject matter of the appeal but on the questions of law to be resolved. For example, the fact that prosecution of securities tipping offences is of public importance is not enough for a leave to be granted. Leave to appeal to the Ontario Court of Appeal will only be granted if the appeal raises questions of law on which the court's guidance is essential in the public interest or for the due administration of justice: *R. v. Rankin*, 2007 ONCA 127, [2007] O.J. No. 719, 2007 CarswellOnt 1045, 221 O.A.C. 184, 216 C.C.C. (3d) 481 (Ont. C.A. [In Chambers]), at para. 30 [ONCA], additional reasons at 2007 CarswellOnt 3698, 2007 ONCA 426, 225 O.A.C. 11, 86 O.R. (3d) 399 (Ont. C.A. [In Chambers]), per Gillese J.A., in chambers.

- If an appellant can show that it was trial counsel and not the appellant who decided that he would not testify at trial, and that the appellant would have testified if he understood that it was his decision, then he will have established a claim of incompetent representation: *R. v. Archer* (2005), 202 C.C.C. (3d) 60, 2005 CarswellOnt 4964, [2005] O.J. No. 4348, 34 C.R. (6th) 271, (*sub nom.* R. v. R.W.A.) 203 O.A.C. 56 (Ont. C.A.), at para. 139 [C.C.C.], followed in *R. v. McKenzie*, 2007 ONCA 470, 2007 CarswellOnt 5294, 228 O.A.C. 182, 51 C.R. (6th) 316 (Ont. C.A.) at paras. 67 & 78 [ONCA].

- Claims of ineffective assistance of counsel at trial based on allegations of inadequate preparation only lead to a miscarriage of justice if it can be shown that the lack of preparation undermined the reliability of the verdict reached at trial: *R. v. Jex*, 2007 ONCA 737, 2007 CarswellOnt 6813, 230 O.A.C. 79 (Ont. C.A.), endorsement.

- See also, Segal and Libman, *The 2010 Annotated Ontario Provincial Offences Act* (Carswell, 2010) at 380-381, for a checklist based on the rules in R.R.O. 1990, Reg. 196 [re-enacted as O. Reg. 723/94].

- The *Good Government Act, 2009,* S.O. 2009, c. 33, s. 1(50), effective 15 December 2009, has enacted a new extension of time provision, which is substantially different from the former version of s. 85. New s. 85(1), however, is cast in language similar to former s. 85, and confirms that, subject to the section, the court may extend any time fixed by the Act, or by regulations under the Act, or rules of court, for doing any thing other than commencing or recommencing a proceeding, whether or not the time has expired. Under new subs. (2), no more than one extension of time for filing an appeal may be brought in respect of a conviction. This will prevent further extensions of time being brought after applications have been dismissed on the merits or dismissed as abandoned. However, the wording of s. 85(2) appears not to specify appeals against sentence. In *R. v. Khan*, 2005 CarswellOnt 2658, 2005 ONCJ 216, 76 O.R. (3d) 387 (Ont. C.J.), it was held that a provincial offences appeal court has jurisdiction to hear a subsequent motion to extend time to appeal notwithstanding that a prior motion had been dismissed for non-appearance of the applicant. The new provision contained in s. 85(2) would seem to apply to such a situation.

In *Hill v. Toronto (City)*, 2007 ONCJ 253, 48 M.V.R. (5th) 55, (*sub nom.* Toronto (City) v. Hill) 221 C.C.C. (3d) 189, 2007 CarswellOnt 3578, [2007] O.J. No. 2232 (Ont. C.J.), it was held that allegations made by a paralegal agent on appeal that a paralegal agent at trial has not acted properly, so as to amount to professional incompetence or to have otherwise contributed to a miscarriage of justice, must be made only after careful consideration. More particularly, such allegations should only be brought forward after the appeal agent has satisfied himself or herself, by means of personal investigations or inquiries, that there is some factual foundation for the allegation, apart from the instructions of the appellant. There must also be afforded to the trial agent a fair opportunity to respond, specifically by providing notice to the trial agent of the allegations being made before the appeal court, and ensuring that a record of this response is placed before the appeal court so that a proper assessment of the allegations may be made by the judge on appeal. Such a procedure or protocol, which places on the paralegal agent on appeal the obligation to investigate and furnish the paralegal trial agent with an opportunity to respond, and thus the appeal court with a proper basis to evaluate such allegations, reflects the need to ensure fairness, openness, and transparency in the provincial offences court, which is so aptly regarded as the "people's court" given the pervasive nature of public welfare/regulatory offences. At the same time, it is in keeping with the new responsibilities of ethical behaviour now mandated by the Law Society of Upper Canada for paralegal practitioners, which includes the required standard of a "competent paralegal", pursuant to the *Paralegal Rules of Conduct*.

A *Charter* violation was found in a provincial offences appeal case where the trial transcripts took from 15 and one-half months to 27 months to produce. The four appellants had been convicted under Part I Certificate of Offence proceedings. The court ruled that the appellants' fairness of trial rights were compromised due to the delays occasioned in the preparation of the trial transcripts, and resulted in an abuse of process, contrary to s. 7 of the *Charter*. A stay of proceedings was imposed on appeal, and costs were ordered against the prosecutor: *R. v. Ovided*, [2008] O.J. No. 2780, 2008 CarswellOnt 4181, 91 O.R. (3d) 593, 2008 ONCJ 317, 174 C.R.R. (2d) 189 (Ont. C.J.).

In *R. v. Kronshteyn*, 2008 CarswellOnt 4600 (Ont. C.J.), the court set aside a conviction and ordered a new trial where evidence was placed before the court by the trial agent that he misunderstood the defendant's instructions due to a language barrier, and erroneously entered guilty to a lesser charge.

To succeed on an incompetence of counsel appeal, there must be a reasonable probability that the verdict would have been different or that the appellant was deprived of a fair trial because of the conduct of counsel: *R. v. Davies*, 2008 CarswellOnt 1673, 2008 ONCA 209, 234 O.A.C. 291, [2008] O.J. No. 1128 (Ont. C.A.), at para. 37 [ONCA].

In *R. v. Fuentes*, 2008 ONCJ 598, 2008 CarswellOnt 7068, [2008] O.J. No. 4677 (Ont. C.J.), it was held that it is the client's right to meet with the person who represents him so there will be no misunderstanding as to what occurs in court. It is mandatory that whomever the licensed paralegal hires meets with the client where a paralegal informs the client that another paralegal will represent the client in court. It is not sufficient for the paralegal to merely tell the other agent what the client wants or said. Where the second paralegal pleaded the client guilty without ever speaking to the client, and a licence suspension was imposed, the conviction could not stand.

Although *Charter* issues not raised at trial cannot normally be initiated by an appellant on appeal, there is an incumbent duty on trial judges to raise *Charter* issues in limited circumstances. In this case, the lawful authority of the investigating officer questioning the passenger on a *Highway Traffic Act* stop was an obvious *Charter* issue, and it was incumbent on the trial judge to enter upon the relevant inquiry. This was particularly so as the conviction in the case was based explicitly on the incriminating statement that the defendant was alleged to have provided to the police officer and the materials which he provided, and which the trial justice determined to be voluntary based on his command of English, and not on any consideration of the applicable legal issues. However, the insufficiency of the trial record made it impossible for the appeal court to make any finding on these issues.

As a result, a new trial was ordered: *R. v. Belous*, 2009 CarswellOnt 5905, 203 C.R.R. (2d) 331 (Ont. C.J.).

In *R. v. Chin*, 2009 CarswellOnt 1563, 2009 ONCJ 180 (Ont. C.J.), the retained paralegal had written instructions from the defendant to do his "best" with his speeding charge. The file was passed to another paralegal, who gave it to an employee in his firm. A guilty plea was negotiated to the charge for a lesser fine. Although the defendant was not happy with the result and sought to have the guilty plea set aside, the signed written instructions were sufficient to uphold the guilty plea.

An extension of time application for an appeal was discussed in *Ontario v. Pomehichuk*, [2009] O.J. No. 2020, 2009 ONCJ 218, 2009 CarswellOnt 2756 (Ont. C.J.). The court held that the general principle expressed in the regulations governing appeals is that the rules shall be construed liberally to obtain as expeditious a conclusion of every proceeding as is consistent with a just determination of the proceeding. This does not mean that notice of an application to extend time to file a notice of appeal against conviction and for authorization to appeal without paying the fine should not be served upon the opposing party. Trials and appeals are important but at the same time parties who seek to contest a result at trial ought not simply presume that latitude will easily be granted to permit the pursuit of an appeal unless there is some basis for excusing the non-compliance with procedures and time limits. Provincial offences appeals are time-consuming and parties who participate should either devote the effort necessary to diligently prepare the appeals in a timely manner or consider accepting the outcome of the trial. Particularly in the face of a lengthy delay in filing an appeal, the appellant bears an onus to show that justice requires that the extension be granted.

The defendant's *Charter* motion for unreasonable delay was adjourned for judgment, at which time a different agent appeared to receive the judgment. The justice questioned the agent's authority to appear for the defendant, and proceeded to find the defendant guilty, rather than continuing the trial. In so doing, the justice erred in law. Under s. 54(1), the justice had the options of either going ahead in the defendant's absence and rendering judgment on the motion, or issuing a summons for the defendant to appear. However, the date was specifically set for judgment on the motion, and there was no indication by the justice that he intended to continue the matter on that day. By not following the procedure set down in s. 54(1), the justice erred in law, resulting in the convictions being set aside: *R. v. Demelo*, 2009 CarswellOnt 7402, [2009] O.J. No. 5079 (Ont. C.J.).

In *R. v. Goodfellow*, 2009 ONCJ 543, [2009] O.J. No. 4915, 2009 CarswellOnt 7253 (Ont. C.J.), it was held that the *Charter* applies to municipal prosecutions.

Costs are rarely awarded in criminal or quasi-criminal cases against the Crown unless there are exceptional circumstances, or fairness requires that the defendant should not be required to carry the financial burden. The instant case was one of those exceptional cases where the prosecution was so flawed and the presentation of evidence was so wrong and the treatment of the defendant was below any reasonable prosecutorial standard that the defendant should be compensated with an award of costs. The appeal Crown properly exercised his jurisdiction and returned the fines imposed, but this only happened after the appeal was launched and there was a complete review of the factum and transcript. While the justice of the peace kept repeating that he was being fair and giving the defendant a great deal of leeway in presenting his case, to an objective observer just the opposite was true. The trial was unfair because of basic misunderstanding of the law respecting the evidence on the part of both the prosecutor and the trier of fact; the trier of fact would misstate the law and be corrected or partially corrected by the prosecutor, or not corrected at all. There was a basic lack of evidence with respect to the enforcement of the by-laws to which the prosecutor and the justice were oblivious. In this rare case, the defendant should not be required to pay the costs of defending the prosecution and more particularly the appeal of these baseless convictions.

Reasons that contain no mention of credibility, display no consideration of reliability, do not indicate any appreciation of the frailties inherent in the testimony of witnesses, and make no reference to the evidence of the accused, preclude meaningful appellate review and constitute a legal error: *R. v. Wadforth* (2009), 254 O.A.C. 295, 2009 CarswellOnt 6104, [2009] O.J. No. 4176, 72 C.R. (6th) 168, 2009 ONCA 716, 247 C.C.C. (3d) 466 (Ont. C.A.), at paras. 72-74.

A stay of proceedings is only available as a remedy in exceptional cases where it is clear that the conduct of the enforcement officers or the Crown is so flagrant and shocking as to constitute the abuse of the court's process. That situation arises where compelling an accused to stand trial would violate the fundamental principles of justice underlying the community sense of fair play and decency or where proceedings would be oppressive and vexatious. Section 7 of the *Charter* will provide a remedy in appropriate circumstances where delay of an appeal proceeding effects the fairness of the trial. In the case at bar, significant portions of the delay were attributable to the appellant, and the overall delay has not affected the fairness of the appeal. This was not a situation where the conduct of the City of Thunder Bay or the Crown amounted to shocking conduct which involved a marked or unacceptable departure from reasonable prosecution standards. See *R. v. Sameluk*, 2011 ONCJ 259, 2011 CarswellOnt 3383, [2011] O.J. No. 2237, 237 C.R.R. (2d) 314 (Ont. C.J.).

The mere fact that with the passage of time it may now be difficult for the Crown to prove its case against the defendant is not a concern to be addressed on an extension of time application where the defendant asserted that he was not the individual charged with the offences and his action, upon receiving notification of the offences, was somewhat supportive of that position. See *R. v. Parsons*, 2012 NLTD(G) 110, 2012 CarswellNfld 262, 327 Nfld. & P.E.I.R. 357, 1015 A.P.R. 357, [2012] N.J. No. 253 (N.L. T.D.).

The prosecutor's application for *certiorari* to quash the decision of a justice of the peace finding the defendant guilty of driving a motor vehicle without having valid insurance was brought in good faith, as the prosecutor had become aware that the defendant did in fact have valid insurance at the relevant time. However, the justice of the peace was within his jurisdiction to proceed the way he did and the course of action he chose was permitted by the statute. Consequently, *certiorari* was simply not available in such circumstances. Instead, there was an avenue of relief available to the defendant, the same that is available to anyone who feels they have been unfairly convicted of an offence, namely, to file an appeal of the conviction, based on the fact that although the justice of the peace was not made aware of it, the defendant did in fact have valid insurance. See *R. v. Schauerte*, 2012 NWTSC 83, 2012 CarswellNWT 92, [2012] N.W.T.J. No. 95 (N.W.T. S.C.).

In *R. v. Canadian National Railway*, 2012 ONSC 6620, 2012 CarswellOnt 15070, 5 M.P.L.R. (5th) 277, [2012] O.J. No. 5649 (Ont. S.C.J.), it was held that a justice of the peace has jurisdiction to hear and determine the constitutional validity of a by-law. The Superior Court may grant relief for jurisdictional error in such quasi-criminal proceedings, but not for an error within jurisdiction for which an appeal would lie. There must also be a substantial wrong or miscarriage that has occurred. It remained open to the defendant in this case to appeal the decision of the justice of the peace once the trial concluded.

There are finality concerns in *Provincial Offences Act* matters and they are an important consideration in all judicial proceedings. The interests of justice require that unnecessary appeals do not further anyone's case. The *Provincial Offences Act* is supposed to be an inexpensive and efficient way of dealing with, for the most part, minor offences. Appeals, second trials heard many months or even years after the original charges are laid do not serve the interest of justice. Finality interest trumps individual interests of defendants in obtaining the legal equivalent of a mulligan. See *R. v. Mitchell-Carson*, 2006 CarswellOnt 10253, [2006] O.J. No. 5676 (Ont. C.J.).

In *R. v. Reid*, 2012 ONCJ 305, 2012 CarswellOnt 6779, 34 M.V.R. (6th) 307, [2012] O.J. No. 2540 (Ont. C.J.), it was held that the defendant's rights under s. 7 of the *Charter of Rights* were violated when he, as an unrepresented accused, at his first drive suspended offence and being deprived of his right to make submissions on sentence was incarcerated for a regulatory offence that he had entered a plea of guilty to in a timely manner, and the justice wholly ignored basic sentencing principles by stating, "I used to give fines. We now impose incarceration." A justice of the peace is required when sentencing someone who is standing before him, to allow that person an opportunity to make submissions. It is a basic tenant of the adversarial system of justice and a denial of that right to be heard, which strikes at the heart of fairness, gives rise to the appearance that the fix is in, that the sentence is pre-determined. As the sentence had already been served by the defendant, nothing short of a stay of proceedings would remove the prejudice caused by the *Charter* violation; any form of further sentence would only perpetuate and enlarge on the s. 7 violation that occurred.

Defence counsel on appeal alleged that there was a conflict on the part of trial counsel who had previously acted for the prosecuting authority in a prosecution of a case dealing with a similar issue in which the prosecution had not been successful. The competency of trial counsel was also challenged on the basis of a failure to provide the court with evidence including a photograph which purported to show a laneway many years earlier in the area where a laneway now existed. However, even if such evidence had been submitted, it did not support the position that the laneway existed previously, or even if it did exist that it existed to the degree in place at the time the charges were laid. Any conflict that may have existed was for the authority to raise, as they had been previously represented by trial counsel on an unrelated matter involving similar issues. There was nothing on the record to call into question the competence of trial counsel. Decisions about evidence and submissions are within the realm of trial counsel; there was nothing to indicate that such decisions were wrong, let alone negligent, and there was nothing to suggest the actions of trial counsel compromised his duties and ethical responsibilities, nor did his actions compromise the rights of the defendants. See *R. v. Geil*, 2012 ONCJ 740, 2012 CarswellOnt 15014, [2012] O.J. No. 5655 (Ont. C.J.), leave to appeal refused 2013 ONCA 457, 2013 CarswellOnt 8921, [2013] O.J. No. 3087 (Ont. C.A.).

In *A. Potvin Construction Ltd. v. Ontario (Workplace Safety & Insurance Board)*, 2011 ONCJ 871, 2011 CarswellOnt 15859, [2011] O.J. No. 6340 (Ont. C.J.), it was held that sentencing decisions are entitled to considerable deference by appellate courts. Section 122(1) allows a court to receive evidence when considering the fitness of a sentence; s. 117(1) allows the court to receive evidence in an appeal, if it considers this to be in the interests of justice. On appeal, the court admitted as fresh evidence the reassessments of the defendant's account by the Workplace Safety and Insurance Board in the amount of $201,241.08. The amount of the reassessment was relevant to a fact in issue, namely that the defendant did not benefit from its illegal actions. It was credible evidence given that it was generated by a governmental agency, and, when considered with the rest of the evidence at trial, was reasonably capable of affecting the sentence imposed by the trial justice who considered that the defendant received a benefit as a result of its false reporting whereas the fresh evidence established that the defendant ultimately did not benefit from its illegal actions. The justice of the peace also committed an error in principle in concluding that the severity of the injury to the worker was an aggravating factor. The justice did correctly consider, however, the following as aggravating factors: the seriousness of the prohibited conduct and a defendant's moral blameworthiness; the deprivation or potential deprivation of benefits to the worker; the advantage the corporation or personal defendants gained from their illegal activity; the frequency of the offences; the offences occurred over a long period of time; and the absence of remorse. As a result, the total amount of fines imposed on the defendant of $375,000 was reduced to $309,000.

(a) Custody Pending Appeal

- An appealing defendant will remain in custody, if already in custody: section 110.

- A judge may order the defendant's release upon any of the conditions prescribed under subsection 150(2): section 110.

In *R. v. Amini*, 2016 ONCJ 116, 2016 CarswellOnt 3366, [2016] O.J. No. 1154 (Ont. C.J.), the defendant was convicted at an *ex parte* trial of one count of engaging in an unfair practice, contrary to the *Consumer Protection Act*, and two counts of carrying on business as a motor vehicle dealer without being registered under the *Motor Vehicle Dealers Act*. A total sentence of approximately 15 months' imprisonment was imposed. The defendant's application to be released from custody pending appeal was dismissed. The grounds of appeal were not viable as the justice of the peace did not err in failing to issue a bench warrant before proceedings for an *ex parte* trial, the defendant's identity was proven, and the trial justice's reasons for convicting were sufficient. There appeared to be no error of law or principle in the decision on sentence. The defendant also failed to establish that his detention was not necessary in the public interest: at the time of sentence, he had already been convicted of a similar set of offences and fined $315,000 which had not been paid, and was awaiting sentencing on a third set of similar charges. There was a need to protect the public from this type of insidious fraud; the defendant kept repeating the same offences, despite new charges, trials, convictions and sentencings. In addition, if the defendant had acted diligently, his appeal could already have been heard. The turnaround time for in-custody appeals can be very short, and high priority would be given to it.

(b) Payment of Fine Pending Appeal

- The defendant must pay in full the fine imposed by the original decision before a notice appeal will be accepted for filing: section 111(1).

- The judge may:
  - Waive the paying of the full fine as prescribed in subsection 111(1) (section 111(2)); and
  - Direct the appellant to enter into a recognizance, to appear on the appeal, in such amount and with or without sureties as the judge deems fits: section 111(2).

(c) Stay Pending Appeal

- The conviction is not stayed by filing of a notice of appeal, unless the judge so orders: section 112.

(d) Attendance and Right to Counsel

- The appellant or respondent may appear and act personally or by counsel: section 118(1).

- The court may impose sentence in the absence of the appellant or respondent: section 118(3).

- Where the appellant or respondent is in custody due to the original decision, he or she is entitled to be present at the hearing of the appeal: section 118(2).

The applicant sought to have a party, M, who was not a licensed paralegal or lawyer, act as his agent on the appeal. The judge ruled that M could not appear as the applicant's agent for that appeal. At that point the applicant requested an adjournment which was not granted. Eventually the matter was adjourned because of time constraints. A judge may bar a person from acting as agent if that person is not competent and does not understand and comply with the duties and responsibilities of an agent. The judge found that M may not understand and properly comply with the duties and responsibilities of an agent, and gave examples of no advance warning to the courts or to the prosecution that he would be appearing and arguing matters before the court as agent, or that he was the one who drafted the Notice of Constitutional Issues. An agent cannot argue that he/she understands and will comply with the duties and obligations of an agent, and then have the principal argue that certain actions were his, and not the agent's. M clearly knew that this issue would arise. He came armed with case law and argument on this point. Yet it was not until the case actually commenced that the appellant advised the court and the Crown that the appellant wished to have M act for him as an agent. The reasonable conclusion was that the appellant and M decided to ambush the Crown and put it at a disadvantage. The judge's decision to disqualify M from acting as an agent did not constitute a substantial wrong or miscarriage of justice. Neither did the decision of the appeal court to grant an adjournment constitute a substantial wrong or miscarriage of justice. The appellant knew that the issue of M being permitted to act as an agent would be a live issue at the appeal. He knew or should have known that it was possible that M would be disqualified, and therefore he should have been prepared to proceed on his own with the appeal at that time. The appellant could not argue that he was surprised that he was required to proceed, when, in fact, he was the person who failed to give advance notice to the Crown, which notice would have resulted in the Crown advising in advance of its objection. See *R. v. Vanravenswaay*, 2018 ONSC 5348, 2018 CarswellOnt 15064, [2018] O.J. No. 5348 (Ont. S.C.J.).

(e) Written Argument

- The appellant or respondent may present his or her case on appeal and argument in writing rather than orally: section 119.

- The court must consider any case or argument when presented in writing: section 119.

(f) Procedural Powers of Appeal Court

- The court may, where it considers it to be in the interest of justice,
  - Order the production of any writing, exhibit or other thing relevant to the appeal (section 117(1)(a));
  - Order any witness who would have been a compellable witness at the trial, whether or not he or she was called at the trial, to:
    - Attend and be examined before the court; or
    - Be examined in the manner provided by the rules of court before a judge of the court, or before any officer of the court or justice of the peace or other person appointed by the court for the purpose (section 117(1)(b));

- Admit, as evidence, an examination that is taken under subclause (b)(ii) (section 117(1)(c));
- Receive the evidence, if tendered, of any witness (section 117(1)(d));
- Order that any question arising on the appeal be referred for inquiry and report to a special commissioner appointed by the court, in the manner provided by the rules of court, that:
  - Involves prolonged examination of writings or accounts, or scientific investigation; and
  - Cannot in the opinion of the court conveniently be inquired into before the court (section 117(1)(e));

and

- Act upon the report of a commissioner who is appointed under clause (e) in so far as the court thinks fit to do so (section 117(1)(f)).
- The appellant or the respondent or their counsel are entitled to cross-examine witnesses and, in any inquiry under clause (1)(e), are entitled to be present during the inquiry and to adduce evidence and to be heard: section 117(2).

(g) Decisional Powers on Appeal Against Conviction Or a Finding of Incapacity to Conduct a Defence

- On the hearing of an appeal against conviction or against a finding as to the ability, because of mental disorder, to conduct a defence, the court may order:
  - The appeal allowed where the court is of the opinion that:
    - The finding should be set aside on the ground that it is unreasonable or cannot be supported by the evidence;
    - The judgment of the trial court should be set aside on the ground of a wrong decision on a question of law; or
    - There was a miscarriage of justice, on any ground: section 120(1)(a).
  - The appeal dismissed where:
    - The court is of the opinion that the appellant, while not properly convicted on a count or part of an information, was properly convicted on another count or part of the information;

- The appeal is not decided in favour of the appellant on any ground mentioned in clause (a); or
- The court finds that no substantial wrong or miscarriage of justice has occurred, although the court is of the opinion that on any ground mentioned in subclause (a)(ii) the appeal might be decided in favour of the appellant: section 120(1)(b).

- Where the court allows an appeal, it shall:
  - Direct a finding of acquittal to be entered, where the appeal is from a conviction;
  - Order a new trial, where the appeal is from a conviction: section 120(2)(a); or
  - Order a new trial, subject to section 44 (the mental disorder provisions) where the appeal is from a finding as to the ability, because of mental disorder, to conduct a defence: section 120(2)(b).

- Where the court dismisses an appeal, it may substitute the decision that in its opinion should have been made and:
  - Affirm the sentence passed by the trial court; or
  - Impose a sentence that is warranted in law: section 120(3).

(h) Decisional Powers on Appeal Against Acquittal

- Where an appeal is from an acquittal, the court may:

  - Dismiss the appeal; or

  - Allow the appeal, set aside the finding, and:
    - Order a new trial; or
    - Enter a finding of guilt with respect to the offence of which, in its opinion, the accused should have been found guilty, and pass the sentence that is warranted in law: section 121.

(i) Decisional Powers on Appeal Against Sentence

- Where an appeal is against sentence, the court shall consider the fitness of the sentence appealed from and may:

  - Dismiss the appeal; or

- Vary the sentence within the limits prescribed by law for the offence of which the defendant was convicted: section 122(1). The court may take into account any time spent in custody by the defendant as a result of the offence.

- Where a court varies a sentence, the new sentence has the same force and effect as if it were a sentence passed by the trial court: section 122(2).

- Where one sentence is passed upon a finding of guilt on two or more counts, the sentence is good if any of the counts would have justified the sentence: section 123.

In *R. v. E. (A.)*, 2016 ONCA 243, 2016 CarswellOnt 5024, 95 M.V.R. (6th) 179, 348 O.A.C. 68, [2016] O.J. No. 1704 (Ont. C.A.), the defendant, who had four convictions for driving without insurance, sought relief against the total fines of $17,000 that were imposed. Fresh evidence was tendered on appeal which indicated that the defendant was suffering from a mental illness. It was not in the interests of justice for the defendant to be fully relieved of these fines, so that he could immediately drive again. The specific deterrence purpose of the fines remained essential. However, given his mental illness and its detrimental effect on the defendant's ability to earn an income to pay the fines, it was also in the interests of justice that the total amount of the fines be reduced, so as to give him the opportunity to pay the reduced fines and move on with his life. The fines were reduced to $5,000.

The accused sought to adduce fresh evidence, on appeal against conviction for careless driving, of a number of reports and notes relating to interactions between him and the investigating police officer. The tenor of the accused's defence was that the officer had an animus towards him, had lied in the past, and that his evidence about his careless driving in this instance was either greatly exaggerated or fabricated. At trial, the accused cross-examined the officer about their past interactions. The trial judge rejected the accused's evidence about his driving, and preferred the evidence of the officer, despite the accused's challenge to his credibility. In determining whether the fresh evidence should be admitted on appeal, especially with a self-represented accused, the first part of the *R. v. Palmer*, 1979 CarswellBC 533, 1979 CarswellBC 541, [1980] 1 S.C.R. 759, 50 C.C.C. (2d) 193, 14 C.R. (3d) 22, 17 C.R. (3d) 34 (Fr.), 106 D.L.R. (3d) 212, 30 N.R. 181, [1979] S.C.J. No. 126 (S.C.C.) test, namely, the evidence should generally not be admitted if, by due diligence, it could have been adduced at trial, may be relaxed. However, the fourth factor in the test, that the evidence, if believed, could reasonably be expected to have affected the outcome of the trial, was not satisfied. While some of the documentation about the accused's past interactions with the police officer was clearly relevant to the charge, and could arguably be used to challenge the officer's credibility and provide evidence of an animus towards the accused, the issue for the accused was that not only was this evidence available at the time of his trial, but he put the substance of this position to the officer and before the court. The fresh evidence application therefore failed, as the accused had not demonstrated that the evidence he sought to admit could reasonably be expected to have affected the result of the trial. See *R. v. Sidhu*, 2016 YKSC 32, 2016 CarswellYukon 84, [2016] Y.J. No. 74 (Y.T. S.C.), leave to appeal refused 2017 YKCA 3, 2017 CarswellYukon 52 (Y.T. C.A.).

In *R. v. Priestly Demolition Inc.*, 2016 CarswellOnt 5149 (Ont. C.J.), the court commented that general deterrence is a commonly accepted principle of regulatory offences. The fail to report offence was characterized by the justice of the peace as a misunderstanding, which implied her acceptance of a certain less culpable corporate state of mind. Something less than the minimum fine was not appropriate. There were clearly not exceptional circumstances that would warrant the exercise of the discretion under s. 59, either on the grounds of being an oppressive amount or in the interest of justice. This was not a "technical" breach: it was just a breach of the reporting obligation with a mix of factors, good and bad, to consider with respect to penalty. The absence of exceptional circumstances certainly justified not imposing lower than the minimum fine; something greater than the minimum fine should have been imposed, especially in light of the post-offence conduct and the preponderance of aggravating as opposed to mitigating factors, and the grounds for specific deterrence.

In an *ex parte* trial for driving without insurance, the defendant appeared at court before the trial was completed, but indicated his attendance to the court only after he was found guilty and sentence was imposed. The justice of the peace informed the defendant that he was *functus officio* and there was nothing further he could do in the matter. In these circumstances, although the court accepted the justice's statement that he was *functus*, even if he was incorrect, there had been no miscarriage of justice as fresh evidence tendered on appeal by the Crown demonstrated that the defendant did not have valid insurance at the time of the offence, contrary to his assertion before the court. See *R. v. Simpson*, 2016 ONCA 212, 2016 CarswellOnt 3884, [2016] O.J. No. 1381 (Ont. C.A.).

It was held in *Halton Region Conservation Authority v. Hanna*, 2018 ONCA 476, 2018 CarswellOnt 7931, [2018] O.J. No. 2695 (Ont. C.A.) that it is well established that sentences imposed by trial courts are entitled to and accorded substantial deference on appellate review. An appellate court is entitled to interfere with the sentence imposed at trial only where the trial court: errs in principle; fails to consider a relevant factor; or errs in considering an aggravating or mitigating factor that has an impact on the sentence imposed, or imposes a sentence that is demonstrably unfit. It was not open to the appeal court judge to simply substitute his view of the nature of the defendant's breach of the regulation for that of the trial court. Findings of fact are the bedrock of sentencing proceedings. They are critical to a determination of the circumstances that may aggravate or mitigate a sentence. In many cases, as here, findings of fact that determine whether an aggravating or mitigating circumstance will have a say in the ultimate sentencing decision will be made on conflicting evidence. And findings of fact are the province of the sentencing judge who is an ear and eyewitness to the conflicting evidence. A reviewing court is not entitled, nor should it be, to interfere with findings of fact made at trial in the absence of palpable and overriding error. In this case the appeal court judge did not identify any palpable and overriding error in the trial court's finding on the critical issue of moral blameworthiness. It follows that the appeal judge was not entitled to interfere with that finding, much less to substitute a contrary finding funded in part by impermissible speculation about one of the defendants' knowledge of applicable residential building restrictions. The appeal judge's decision was therefore flawed by fundamental errors and could not stand.

(j) Appeal Based on Defect in Information or Process

- Unless it is shown that objection was taken at the trial and that, in the case of a variance, an adjournment of the trial was refused although the variance had misled the appellant, judgment shall not be given in favour of an appellant based on:
  - Any alleged defect in the substance or form of an information, certificate or process; or
  - Any variance between the information, certificate or process and evidence adduced at trial: section 124(1).
- The court shall make an order curing the defect where an appeal is based on a defect in a conviction or an order: section 124(2).

(k) Additional Powers for Appeal Court

- The court may make any order that justice requires, where it exercises any of the powers conferred by sections 117 to 124: section 125.

Where a plea of guilty is set aside and the Crown has withdrawn other charges in exchange for the guilty plea, the court may rescind the withdrawal by the Crown of the other counts and direct a new trial on all the counts together: *R. v. K. (S.)* (1995), 1995 CarswellOnt 2340, 24 O.R. (3d) 199, 99 C.C.C. (3d) 376, 82 O.A.C. 132,

[1995] O.J. No. 1627 (Ont. C.A.); *R. v. Yanover (No. 1)* (1985), 1985 CarswellOnt 1114, 9 O.A.C. 93, 20 C.C.C. (3d) 300 (Ont. C.A.).

Where the defendant argued on appeal that it was improperly named as Deneen Allen & Associates rather than Deneen Allen & Associates Ltd. and that the amendment should not be allowed on appeal, the appeal court granted the amendment on the basis that the amendment could have been made at trial if the misnomer was noticed by the prosecutor, the defendant was aware of the charge, and the amendment would not result in the substitution of one corporate entity for another: *Deneen Allen & Associates v. Barrie (City)*, 2008 CarswellOnt 6043, 2008 ONCJ 488, [2008] O.J. No. 4005 (Ont. C.J.).

It is an error of law for a justice sitting as an appeal court on a provincial offences matter to conclude that he did not have jurisdiction to deal with *Charter* arguments: *R. v. Peric*, 2008 CarswellOnt 7217, 2008 ONCA 827 (Ont. C.A. [In Chambers]), per Weiler J.A. The error of law, however, only requires the Court of Appeal to grant leave to appeal if it would result in a miscarriage of justice and undermine public confidence in the administration of justice.

In *A. Potvin Construction Ltd. v. Ontario (Workplace Safety & Insurance Board)*, 2011 ONCJ 871, 2011 CarswellOnt 15859, [2011] O.J. No. 6340 (Ont. C.J.), it was held that sentencing decisions are entitled to considerable deference by appellate courts. Section 122(1) allows a court to receive evidence when considering the fitness of a sentence; s. 117(1) allows the court to receive evidence in an appeal, if it considers this to be in the interests of justice. On appeal, the court admitted as fresh evidence the reassessments of the defendant's account by the Workplace Safety and Insurance Board in the amount of $201,241.08. The amount of the reassessment was relevant to a fact in issue, namely that the defendant did not benefit from its illegal actions. It was credible evidence given that it was generated by a governmental agency, and, when considered with the rest of the evidence at trial, was reasonably capable of affecting the sentence imposed by the trial justice who considered that the defendant received a benefit as a result of its false reporting whereas the fresh evidence established that the defendant ultimately did not benefit from its illegal actions. The justice of the peace also committed an error in principle in concluding that the severity of the injury to the worker was an aggravating factor. The justice did correctly consider, however, the following as aggravating factors: the seriousness of the prohibited conduct and defendant's moral blameworthiness; the deprivation or potential deprivation of benefits to the worker; the advantage the corporation or personal defendants gained from their illegal activity; the frequency of the offences; the offences occurred over a long period of time; and the absence of remorse. As a result, the total amount of fines imposed on the defendant of $375,000 was reduced to $309,000.

On the other hand, fresh evidence was not admitted on appeal in *R. v. Geil*, 2012 ONCJ 740, 2012 CarswellOnt 15014, [2012] O.J. No. 5655 (Ont. C.J.), leave to appeal refused 2013 ONCA 457, 2013 CarswellOnt 8921, [2013] O.J. No. 3087 (Ont. C.A.) where the trial justice did not accept the evidence of the defendant that a laneway had always existed through the wetland, and that it had not changed much except that some gravel had been put on it. In coming to that conclusion, the justice considered the very evidence of the co-defendant who admitted that he had been cleaning the area through the wetland and had made the laneway wider and longer by cleaning bush, trimming branches and putting gravel on the roadway. There was nothing before the appeal court to indicate that the photo sought to be introduced as fresh evidence was not available at the time of trial. In any event, it was clear upon reviewing the photograph that it did not assist the defendants in any productive way as an existing roadway was not readily apparent.

In *R. v. Calleja*, 2013 ONCJ 7, 2013 CarswellOnt 94, 39 M.V.R. (6th) 162, [2013] O.J. No. 116 (Ont. C.J.), the defendant was charged with failing to yield to a pedestrian, contrary to s. 140(1)(a) of the *Highway Traffic Act*, whereas the accident took place at an intersection, such that the better charging section would have been fail to yield to a pedestrian within a crosswalk, contrary to s. 144(7). It was open to the trial justice of the peace to amend the certificate of offence at any stage of the proceedings to reflect the more perfectly suited section of the *Highway Traffic Act*, s. 144(7), as this pedestrian was struck down at a lighted intersection. There would have been no error in law if such an amendment had been made. It would be open as well to the appeal court to amend the certificate at the appeal stage of the proceedings, although it was unnecessary to do so.

It was held in *R. v. Gilchrist*, 2018 ONCA 430, 2018 CarswellOnt 6994, 26 M.V.R. (7th) 181, [2018] O.J. No. 2422 (Ont. C.A.) that under the authority of s. 117(1)(d) it was open to the appellant to adduce evidence of insurance documents to demonstrate the existence of a valid policy of insurance at the time of the traffic stop. A statutory declaration from an employee of the insurance company to this effect would have ben admissible in evidence if tendered at trial, or before the appeal judge, and is admissible in evidence on the appeal before the Court of Appeal.

The applicant sought to have a party, M, who was not a licensed paralegal or lawyer, act as his agent on the appeal. The judge ruled that M could not appear as the applicant's agent for that appeal. At that point the applicant requested an adjournment which was not granted. Eventually the matter was adjourned because of time constraints. A judge may bar a person from acting as agent if that person is not competent and does not understand and comply with the duties and responsibilities of an agent. The judge found that M may not understand and properly comply with the duties and responsibilities of an agent, and gave examples of no advance warning to the courts or to the prosecution that he would be appearing and arguing matters before the court as agent, or that he was the one who drafted the Notice of Constitutional Issues. An agent cannot argue that he/she understands and will comply with the duties and obligations of an agent, and then have the principal argue that certain actions were his, and not the agent's. M clearly knew that this issue would arise. He came armed with case law and argument on this point. Yet it was not until the case actually commenced that the appellant advised the court and the Crown that the appellant wished to have M act for him as an agent. The reasonable conclusion was that the appellant and M decided to ambush the Crown and put it at a disadvantage. The judge's decision to disqualify M from acting as an agent did not constitute a substantial wrong or miscarriage of justice. Neither did the decision of the appeal court to grant an adjournment constitute a substantial wrong or miscarriage of justice. The appellant knew that the issue of M being permitted to act as an agent would be a live issue at the appeal. He knew or should have known that it was possible that M would be disqualified, and therefore he should have been prepared to proceed on his own with the appeal at that time. The appellant could not argue that he was surprised that he was required to proceed, when, in fact, he was the person who failed to give advance notice to the Crown, which notice would have resulted in the Crown advising in advance of its objection. See *R. v. Vanravenswaay*, 2018 ONSC 5348, 2018 CarswellOnt 15064, [2018] O.J. No. 5348 (Ont. S.C.J.).

In *R. v. Dennis*, 2019 ONCA 109, 2019 CarswellOnt 2065, [2019] O.J. No. 773 (Ont. C.A.), it was held that the threshold for awarding costs against a lawyer personally in a criminal proceeding is a high one. As stated by the Supreme Court of Canada in *Québec (Directeur des poursuites criminelles et pénales) c. Jodoin*, 2017 CSC 26, 2017 SCC 26, 2017 CarswellQue 3091, 2017 CarswellQue 3092, [2017] 1 S.C.R. 478, 346 C.C.C. (3d) 433, 37 C.R. (7th) 1, 408 D.L.R. (4th) 581, (*sub nom.* Quebec (Director of Criminal and Penal Prosecutions) v. Jodoin) 380 C.R.R. (2d) 285, [2017] S.C.J. No. 26 (S.C.C.), only serious misconduct can justify such a sanction. Costs are awarded on a discretionary basis and appellate courts should only intervene when that discretion is exercised "in an abusive, unreasonable or non-judicial manner." In the instant case, the appellant's counsel requested an adjournment of the appeal hearing without notice to the Crown prosecutor. The Crown prosecutor had interrupted her vacation to attend on the scheduled date to argue the appeal, and had been inconvenienced as a result of the appellant's request for an adjournment. Counsel apologized to the prosecutor and the court. Of his own initiative, the appeal judge asked the Crown prosecutor if she wished to apply for costs under s. 129 of the *Provincial Offences Act*. The appeal court ordered counsel to pay costs personally in the amount of $500 due to his reckless disregard for the other side. The principles described in *Jodoin* ought to apply equally to an order under s. 129. However, while the absence of advance notice of the adjournment request was worthy of adverse comment by the court, the exercise of the appeal judge's discretion was unreasonable and did not meet the threshold for an award of costs against counsel personally. Fundamentally, counsel's behaviour did not warrant the exceptional remedy of a personal costs order. The costs award was vacated.

It is not an error for an appellate court to situate the sentence before it within the usual range of sentences. One cannot begin to measure the demonstrable fitness of a sentence without having an eye to the customary sentencing range. An appeal court errs if it tethers a finding of unfitness to the simple fact that the range is missed, but commits no error by getting a perspective on what a fit sentence looks like by examining comparable cases. The principle of parity requires that sentences should be similar to other sentences imposed on similar offenders for similar offences committed in similar circumstances. This principle is equally applicable to sentencing for regulatory offences and criminal offences. Genuine inability to pay a fine is not a proper basis for imprisonment. As a matter of principle, it must also hold true that the hardship of a fine is not a proper basis for imprisonment either. The appeal court judge was therefore correct in finding that the sentencing justice erred in imposing a jail term because a fine would cause more financial hardship. On this basis alone, the appeal judge was entitled to set aside the sentences of incarceration and to vary the sentences within the limits prescribed by law. However, the appeal judge erred in adopting as a sentencing principle that regulatory offences are concerned with attaining public policy objectives as opposed to punishing moral blameworthiness. This is too crude a formulation and poses a false dichotomy. It is true that regulatory offences are concerned with attaining public policy objectives and the criminal law punishes according to the degree of the offender's moral blameworthiness; however, this does not mean that moral blameworthiness may not also be a relevant sentencing consideration for regulatory offences. The relevance of moral blameworthiness in sentencing for regulatory offences follows necessarily from the application in regulatory offences of the fundamental sentencing principle of proportionality. It is important to appreciate that, despite its application, moral blameworthiness does not operate the same way in sentencing regulatory offenders, as it does in sentencing criminal offenders. This is because regulatory offences tend to reflect lower levels of moral blameworthiness. While both kinds of offences reflect moral blameworthiness, the moral blameworthiness in criminal offences tends to be greater, and that difference must be respected when imposing sentences. See *Ontario (Labour) v. New Mex Canada Inc.*, 2019 ONCA 30, 2019 CarswellOnt 577, 51 C.C.E.L. (4th) 171, [2019] O.J. No. 227 (Ont. C.A.).

(l) New Trials

- Where a court orders a new trial, it shall:

- Be held in the Ontario Court of Justice;

- Be presided over by a justice other than the justice who tried the defendant in the first instance unless the appeal court directs otherwise: section 126(1).

- Where a court orders a new trial, it may:

  - Make an order for the release of the appellant pending such trial as may be made by a justice under subsection 150(2).

  - The release order may be enforced in the same manner as if it had been made by a justice under that subsection: section 126(2).

(m) Trial *de novo* Before the Appeal Court

- The court may order that the appeal shall be heard by way of a new trial in the appeal court, where, the court, upon the motion of the appellant or respondent, is of the opinion that the interests of justice would be better served by hearing and determining the appeal by holding a new trial in the appeal court, because of the condition of the record of the trial in the trial court or for any other reason: section 127(1).

- For this purpose, this Act applies with necessary modifications in the same manner as to a proceeding in the trial court: section 127(1).

- The appeal court may, for the purpose of hearing and determining an appeal by way of trial *de novo*, permit the evidence of any witness taken before the trial court to be read if that evidence has been authenticated and if:

  - The appellant and respondent consent;

  - The court is satisfied that the attendance of the witness cannot reasonably be obtained; or

  - By reason of the formal nature of the evidence or otherwise the court is satisfied that the opposite party will not be prejudiced: section 127(2).

- Any evidence that is read under the authority of section 127 has the same force and effect as if the witness had given the evidence before the court: section 127(2).

The final transcript of judgment of the presiding justice set out in detail the reasons for his procedural decision on the timing of hearing the stay in proceedings. The missing portions of the transcript were thus not necessary for the hearing of the appeal. There was no realistic possibility that an error of any significance lay within the missing transcript, or that the missing transcript deprived the defendant of any ground of appeal. The interests of justice were not better served by holding a new trial as a result of any gaps in the transcript. See *R. v. Sameluk*, 2011 ONCJ 259, 2011 CarswellOnt 3383, [2011] O.J. No. 2237, 237 C.R.R. (2d) 314 (Ont. C.J.).

(n) Abandonment or Dismissal of Appeal

- The court may order the appeal dismissed, upon proof that notice of an appeal has been given and that,

    - The appellant has failed to comply with any order made under section 110 or 111 or with the conditions of any recognizance entered into under either of those sections; and

    - The appeal has not been proceeded with or has been abandoned: section 128.

The failure of the prosecution to file the transcripts in the required period of time was not excusable in all the circumstances of the matter. Prejudice had been suffered by the defendants by the delay in filing the transcripts. To mount a defence to charges emanating from events in 2004 and 2005 would be very difficult in 2010 or 2011 when a trial would likely be heard. There was no public interest in having the case proceed to the hearing of the appeal: *R. v. 136567 Ontario Ltd.*, 2010 ONCJ 712, 2010 CarswellOnt 10543, [2010] O.J. No. 5913 (Ont. C.J.).

(o) Miscellaneous

- Costs can be awarded under section 129.

    - With leave, further appeals lie to the Ontario Court of Appeal: section 131.

In *Vallance v. Pickering (City)*, 2012 ONCJ 147, 2012 CarswellOnt 2756, 17 C.L.R. (4th) 323, [2012] O.J. No. 1216 (Ont. C.J.), the court dismissed an application for costs on appeal. Although the result in the appeal was identical to the offer to settle made by the City, the case was not an exceptional one such that it merited departing from the rule that each side bear its own costs. While the costs incurred were unnecessary, the City is not in the position of a civil litigant, and defendants should be able to pursue appeal remedies without punitive costs sanctions being imposed in the absence of *mala fides* on their part.

While a provincial offences appeal court has the power to grant an award of costs, such orders are not ordinarily granted. Although s. 34 of the *Provincial Offences Act* gives the prosecutor the ability to seek, and the court the power to grant, an amendment to an Information, an amendment to change the name of the defendant is not contemplated by this provision. Section 26 requires that a defendant must be named in and served with a summons setting out the charge against it. Section 54 provides that a defendant can be convicted *in absentia* where the prosecutor proves that the summons or notice of trial was served on the defendant. Amending the Information to change the name of the defendant in the absence of the defendant runs contrary to these provisions. At the very least, the prosecutor should have requested an adjournment of the trial to properly serve a summons or notice of trial on the defendant. In failing to do so, the prosecutor carelessly disregarded the procedural safeguards afforded to the defendant under the *Provincial Offences Act*. Section 129(a) grants the court discretion to make any order with respect to costs that it considers "just and reasonable". In this case the defendant was convicted without ever being issued a summons or served with a notice that it had ever been charged; it had no opportunity to argue at trial whether it should have been named as a defendant, or given an opportunity to defend the charge on its merits. In addition, through no fault of its own, it was required to retain counsel to bring the appeal and have the conviction quashed. In the unusual circumstances of the case, fairness demanded that the defendant be relieved of the financial burden of the costs of the appeal and application by being fully compensated. See *R. v. 1820419 Ontario Inc.*, 2013 ONCJ 10, 2013 CarswellOnt 275, [2013] O.J. No. 143 (Ont. C.J.).

In *R. v. Gillespie*, 2013 ONCA 275, 2013 CarswellOnt 4985, 44 M.V.R. (6th) 13, [2013] O.J. No. 1910 (Ont. C.A.), it was held that the general rule is that costs are not awarded in provincial offences appeals. This appeal raised a novel issue of public importance and statutory interpretation. It was not appropriate to award costs against a municipality which stood in place of the Crown to represent the public interest.

Similarly, in *R. v. Kazemi*, 2013 ONCA 585, 2013 CarswellOnt 13276, 117 O.R. (3d) 300, 307 C.C.C. (3d) 307, 49 M.V.R. (6th) 179, 311 O.A.C. 76, [2013] O.J. No. 4300 (Ont. C.A.), it was held that the general rule is that no costs are awarded in a *Provincial Offences Act* proceeding. Particularly since the respondent was unsuccessful, it would not be just and reasonable to depart from the general rule in such a case.

In *Durham (Regional Municipality) v. Park* (October 20, 2010), Doc. 999-00-88148699, [2010] O.J. No. 6178 (Ont. S.C.J.), it was held that s. 138(3) confers broad discretion to impose costs incurred on appeal, which is not limited by s. 60 or Regulation 945. Costs incurred on appeal should mean additional costs that would not have been incurred but for the conduct of the appellant. The repeated attendance of the Korean interpreter when the defendant was knowingly not attending the appeal was "unnecessary" or "without necessity". It was appropriate for the court to exercise its discretion in the particular case due to the history of the defendant both at the trial level and the appeal process, in terms of his non-attendances in particular on dates when interpreters were requested.

Likewise, in *R. v. Guan*, 2014 ONCJ 151, 2014 CarswellOnt 4087, [2014] O.J. No. 1539 (Ont. C.J.), the court ruled that an award of costs against the appellant/defendant is appropriate where he did not appear at his trial and the matter proceeded in his absence where counsel chose to proceed in his absence. The appellant requested an interpreter upon filing the filing, but again the appellant did not appear and the matter proceeded by choice of counsel. In the context of his appearance at trial and appeal, it was incumbent on the appellant to advise the court of his non-appearance to avoid unnecessary and waste full costs. The fact that he may have otherwise been occupied on business does not change the fact that unnecessary costs were incurred at his request through counsel.

The costs discussed in s. 60 are costs already incurred for such things as fees and expenses and are imposed as part of a possible sentence. There is no reference to advanced funding. The term "costs" as used in s. 116 cannot be read to include funds necessary to pay the expenses of defence witnesses and defence counsel in advance of the trial. The reference to costs in s. 116(1)(e) refers to the costs as set out in s. 60 of the *Provincial Offences Act* as one could see that an error in an award of costs for fees and expenses already incurred by the defendant upon conviction would need to be addressed by way of an appeal. Where the defendants brought a pre-trial motion alleging a violation of their equality rights under s. 15 of the *Charter of Rights and Freedoms* and sought the remedy of advanced funding for the defence, the dismissal of the motion did not amount to a final order, nor did it amount to a costs order within the meaning of s. 116. Section 116 does not allow for interlocutory appeals. The appeal was dismissed for lack of jurisdiction. See *R. v. Sarazin*, 2014 ONCJ 148, 2014 CarswellOnt 4029, [2014] O.J. No. 1497 (Ont. C.J.).

Where the Crown withdraws the charge, there is no jurisdiction for the court to deal with the issue of costs. In any event, taking the case at its highest it would not be appropriate to order costs as this was not a matter of abuse or flagrant impropriety on the part of the police or court: *York (Regional Municipality) v. Perza*, 2014

ONCJ 257, 2014 CarswellOnt 6968, 331 C.R.R. (2d) 222, [2014] O.J. No. 2499 (Ont. C.J.).

The defendant proceeded upon his defence based upon the charge as laid, and it was to that means of committing the offences that his defence was based. The defence and Crown and trial court were in complete error as to what constituted an appropriate defence to the charge as laid, and the defence raised by the defendant could not have been entertained but for this means of committing the offence and the error in law made. The by-law contained at least 14 exemptions from the application of the by-law. The defendant had been misled in his defence. There was real prejudice. It would be manifestly unfair to the defendant to allow such an amendment on appeal and then decide the case on the record before the court. The Justice made very few findings of fact pertaining to these issues. If the amendment had been sought at the outset or during the trial, the court would have been in the position of assessing the specific prejudice and, in the appropriate case, would have granted an adjournment to ameliorate the prejudice, if that was possible. Such an amendment would have been routinely granted if sought before the end of the Crown's case. The trial Justice would have been in a good position to decide whether an adjournment be granted, or indeed whether Crown witnesses should be recalled for further cross-examination. The matter was remitted for trial and the information amended for the re-trial: *R. v. 1533904 Ontario Ltd.*, 2015 ONCJ 75, 2015 CarswellOnt 2388, [2015] O.J. No. 827 (Ont. C.J.).

In *R. v. Leung*, 2015 ONCJ 413, 2015 CarswellOnt 11727, [2015] O.J. No. 4118 (Ont. C.J.), it was held that the power to grant an adjournment is a discretionary one, reviewable on appeal if that discretion was not exercised judicially. The conditions required for an adjournment because of absence of a witness are threefold: (a) that the absent witness is material to the case; (b) that the party asking for an adjournment is not guilty of laches or an omission; (c) that there is a reasonable expectation that the witness can attend at the future trial date. The trial Justice did not consider, however, in his rulings whether the adjournment was *bona fides*, the fact that the Crown's case was closed and that no witnesses would be inconvenienced, when the trial could have been completed, the impact of the failure to grant the adjournment, whether the adjournment would have prejudiced the Crown who opposed the adjournment, especially given that the Crown case was completed, and whether the expanded testimony of the officer was properly something that required a rebuttal by the accused in order to make full answer and defence as he was entitled to do. It did not appear that the adjournment request was fairly listened to as the Justice dismissed the adjournment application twice, the first time summarily and then a second time after more submissions. The effect of denying the adjournment was to deny the defendant the opportunity to call a defence, which amounted to a miscarriage of justice.

In *R. v. Khan*, 2015 ONCJ 221, 2015 CarswellOnt 5975, [2015] O.J. No. 2096 (Ont. C.J.), it was held that an unlicensed paralegal cannot conduct trials or appeals of provincial offences under the supervision of a lawyer licensed by the Law Society of Upper Canada. The conduct of trials or appeals involves providing legal services, which only licensed lawyers and paralegals can do under the *Law Society Act* and the by-laws made under it; these functions cannot be delegated to non-licensees. This does not prevent a friend or family member, however, from attending with a defendant at a trial or an appeal to assist the defendant.

The defendant was mistaken about how the law applies to him, as his arguments that s. 141 does not apply to him and a statutory right of appeal of his convictions are only available to a "man or a woman consenting to act in the capacity of, or otherwise enter into an association with, a class of person or entity created by statute and subject to the statutes allegedly engaged in this matter" mirror those used by persons identified by other courts in the province and elsewhere as "Organized Pseudo-legal Commercial litigants". The argument that such persons can self-determine which laws of the land apply to them and which do not lacks merit and is spurious. See *R. v. Curle*, 2015 ONSC 1999, 2015 CarswellOnt 4980, [2015] O.J. No. 1714 (Ont. S.C.J.).

The word "proceeding" which is not defined in the *Provincial Offences Act* does not mean trial, such that all trials in the Provincial Offences Court must take place within six months of the date of the alleged offence occurring. "Proceeding" in the context of limitations law, means the entire case from the legal process that begins through to final disposition. The "commencement" of a proceeding is the issuance of process, in this case, by the police officer filing the certificate of offence. In this case, the certificate of offence was served on the date of the offence and filed within seven days thereafter, well within the six month limitation period. There was no limitations issue in the case and the Provincial Offences Court was correct to dismiss the applicant's preliminary motion. The proper course for the applicant to challenge the Justice's ruling dismissing his preliminary motion was an appeal to a Provincial Judge in the Ontario Court of Justice, and not by way of extraordinary equitable relief to the Superior Court of Justice. See *Torok v. Ontario*, 2015 ONSC 3100, 2015 CarswellOnt 7080, 336 O.A.C. 17, [2015] O.J. No. 2472 (Ont. Div. Ct.).

In *R. v. Ward*, 2015 ONCJ 369, 2015 CarswellOnt 10460, [2015] O.J. No. 3726 (Ont. C.J.), it was held that an appellate court does not retry the case but rather reviews the record with a view towards determining whether the trial Justice of the Peace made any errors of fact that are material or were wrong in law in a significant way that would impact upon the results. In this case the trial Justice of the Peace properly examined the evidence and determined that the *actus reus* had been proven and then looked to see if the defendant had either produced the insurance information or had established some reasonably diligent efforts on his part to ensure that the motor vehicle was insured. The Justice of the Peace found that no reasonable actions had been taken by the defendant and accordingly found that the case had been proven by the prosecutor. This was a text book application of the strict liability rules related to provincial offences.

A review of the transcript showed that there was a careful consideration by the trial Justice of the poorly-framed arguments of counsel with regard to the Charter issue, and an equally careful consideration of the evidence of the one witness at trial. There was no basis for the argument that there was an apprehension of bias on the part of the trial Justice. See *R. v. Baksh*, 2015 ONCJ 235, 2015 CarswellOnt 6482, [2015] O.J. No. 2271 (Ont. C.J.).

In *R. v. Iacono*, 2015 ONCJ 609, 2015 CarswellOnt 17115, [2015] O.J. No. 5819 (Ont. C.J.), it was held that there was no reason to depart from the general rule that costs are not awarded in provincial offences appeals. The Crown took the position that a substantial fine should be imposed at trial; it maintained this position on appeal, albeit unsuccessfully. There was nothing exceptional in the Crown's sentencing position, or its conduct throughout the proceedings, in seeking to review a sentence under a statute it prosecutes, albeit infrequently, that merited the awarding of a costs order against it. While the defendant had been subjected to additional time and expense as the result of the appeal proceedings, this was inherent in the nature of the appellate system, which is an integral part of the administration of justice and enhances "the fairness of the process", even though the majority of such appeals are not successful.

The manufacturer' sticker was relevant evidence and accepted as "fresh evidence" on appeal. While a photograph of the sticker could have been made an exhibit by the appellant at trial, he may have thought that it was the responsibility of the police to prove that his vehicle was a motor vehicle and that the police would have gathered this information. The appellant was not a lawyer and appeared to have been unaware that he bore the onus to establish at trial that his vehicle was a "power assisted bicycle" and thereby exempted from the definition of "motor vehicle." The vehicle was referred to as an "e-bike" throughout the proceedings by the officer who also explained that it had an electric motor and a missing pedal. It was accepted by the Justice of the Peace that the evidence established that but for the finding that the bike was missing a pedal, the vehicle being operated by the appellant was a "power assisted bicycle" which would be deemed not to be a motor vehicle under the *Highway Traffic Act*. See *R. v. Woehl*, 2015 ONCJ 597, 2015 CarswellOnt 16367, 90 M.V.R. (6th) 135, [2015] O.J. No. 5587 (Ont. C.J.).

Leave to appeal to the Ontario Court of Appeal was refused in *York (Regional Municipality) v. Tomovski*, 2018 ONCA 57, 2018 CarswellOnt 695, [2018] O.J. No. 357 (Ont. C.A.) where the "decision" of the provincial court appeal judge in this case was that the stay of proceedings should be set aside because there was no breach of s. 11(b) of the *Charter of Rights*. Given his factual finding that the net delay was 10 months and 22 days, the "decision" below would have been the same had the appeal judge not opined that a shorter presumptive delay ceiling applied for Part I POA proceedings. The proposed appeal by the Municipality sought an advisory opinion of the Court of Appeal that was detached from the underlying facts. Ontario courts have repeatedly held that appeals cannot be based on a disagreement with certain determinations within the reasons for judgment. The court could address the important question of the appropriate presumptive delay ceiling for Part I POA proceedings in another case in which the appeal is properly constituted.

Leave to appeal was granted by the Ontario Court of Appeal on a number of issues involving the trial of an unrepresented accused in traffic court. In *R. v. Morillo*, 2018 ONCA 582, 2018 CarswellOnt 10037, 362 C.C.C. (3d) 23, [2018] O.J. No. 3405 (Ont. C.A.), it was held that in respect of leave under s. 131 of the *Provincial Offences Act*, the legal issue raised should be significant and have some broad importance. These same considerations equally apply to leave motions under s. 139. Generally speaking, the implications of the legal issue should go beyond the case at hand. The strength of the proposed grounds of appeal is also a material consideration if there is a real risk that there may have been a miscarriage of justice or a denial of procedural fairness. Appellate courts ought not to take a rigid or technical approach when identifying the grounds of appeal that a self-represented litigant is raising when seeking leave to appeal under s. 139. While self-represented persons are expected to familiarize themselves with relevant legal practices and to prepare their own case, they should not be denied relief on the basis of minor or easily rectified deficiencies in their case. Judges are to facilitate, to the extent possible, access to justice for self-represented persons. Appellate judges should therefore attempt to place the issues raised by a self-represented litigant in their proper legal context. The rule in *W. (D.)* is intended to ensure that reasonable doubt is properly applied where the credibility or reliability of evidence inconsistent with guilt is in issue. The justice of the peace recognized that the *W. (D.)* rule applied and cited it. However, there was strong reason to believe that she then misapplied it as she appeared to have engaged in the very kind of credibility contest reasoning that the rule was intended to prevent, by deciding which competing version of events she preferred. Credibility contests are not properly resolved by choosing one side after carefully giving the other side fair consideration in the context of all of the evidence. They are resolved by ensuring that, even if the evidence inconsistent with guilt is not believed or does not raise a reasonable doubt, no conviction will occur unless the evidence that is accepted proves the guilt of the accused beyond a reasonable doubt. The decision of the justice of the peace failed to make that determination, and there was strong reason to believe that the provincial offences appeal court judge erred by not recognizing that the justice of the peace may have committed such a *W. (D.)* error. When the defendant sought to confront the officer with inconsistencies between his testimony at the retrial and his testimony at the first trial, the justice of the peace refused to allow it. She apparently laboured under the misconception that since retrials are to be determined on their own evidence, no use should be made of testimony taken at the prior trial, even to demonstrate inconsistency. If this is so, she erred in law. It is trite law that prior inconsistent testimony from a first trial can be used to impeach a witness at a retrial. The provincial offences appeal court judge arguably failed to recognize the error. He found that that the defendant's challenge to the officer's evidence was deficient because the defendant did not impeach the officer with transcripts from the first trial. The appeal court judge's ruling also appeared to endorse the public prosecutor's protest at trial that if the defendant wanted to challenge the officer with prior testimony, he needed to have transcripts. This proposition is wrong in law. A party need not have a transcript to cross-examine a witness about their prior inconsistent testimony. The risk in not having a transcript is that if the witness denies making a prior inconsistent statement when asked, that denial cannot be contradicted and hence the contradiction cannot be proved. Put otherwise, the defendant would have been well advised to have had the transcript of the first trial with him for use in cross-examination, but the absence of a transcript does not prevent him from cross-examining the officer about the contradictions he believes to exist. The provincial offences appeal court judge did a commendable job in responding to the defendant's needs as a self-represented litigant. He worked to understand his basis for appeal; he listened carefully and patiently to him and was careful to explain why the appeal had failed. The appeal court judge may nonetheless have erred in law in endorsing the fairness of the manner in which the trial was conducted, by not paying due regard to the fact that the defendant was unrepresented at trial. The fact that this was the defendant's second appeal was not relevant to whether his appeal should be granted. The appeal court judge explained to the defendant that his lack of success could be attributed, in part, to his lack of familiarity with procedures and the proper manner of presenting his case. These comments might fail to allow for the obligation the justice of the peace had to assist the defendant, as an unrepresented litigant, in achieving a functional understanding of proper procedures and the proper manner of presenting a case. A finding that the defendant demonstrated his incompetence with procedures and the manner of presenting arguably called for the provincial offences appeal court judge to consider whether the justice of the peace did enough to assist the defendant in achieving the base level of understanding required. In summary, the special grounds raised by the applicant did not relate to the unsettled state of the law. The legal rules that grid his grounds of appeal are entirely settled and are not in need of determination by this court. The special grounds however arise ironically, from the fact that these errors occurred in a provincial offences court, specifically in traffic court. Traffic courts deal with a high volume of offences. This creates practical pressures to be efficient and economical. Given the low level offences that are prosecuted in these courts, these practical pressures can imperil the proper balance between efficiency and due process. The *W. (D.)* rule is central to the proper conduct of many prosecutions, and it is not without its complexity. This court   has yet to affirm the importance of the rule in *W. (D.)*, in traffic court prosecutions, or to provide direct guidance to justices of the peace on its proper application. It was essential in the public interest and for the due administration of justice that leave be granted to accomplish this. Traffic court also sees a significant number of self-represented individuals. This appeal raises issues about the appropriate balance between the justice of the peace's obligation to provide guidance and direction to self-represented litigants, and the demands of trial efficiency in busy traffic courts where the stakes for the accused tend not to be high. It is essential in the public interest and for the due administration of justice that leave be granted to provide this guidance, should the presiding panel consider it appropriate to do so. While the justice of the peace's apparent error in restricting the defendant's ability to cross-examine the officer about his prior testimony does not present special considerations in isolation, however since leave is warranted on the other issues identified, the treatment of this issue may enable this court   to give guidance on the importance of compliance with basic rules of evidence in the conduct of traffic offences. Leave to appeal was therefore granted on this issue as well.

The appeal judge's reasons disclosed that he understood the applicant was contending her plea of not guilty, coupled with not contesting the facts, was functionally equivalent to a guilty plea. However, he concluded the applicant had instructed trial counsel to proceed on that basis. The applicant could not point to any misapprehension of the evidence by the appeal judge in this regard. Nor did the applicant challenge any of his findings as demonstrating a palpable and overriding error. That she disagreed with the appeal judge's findings did not transform questions of fact into a question of law. The applicant's complaint was fact-based; it did not raise a question of law. The applicant had fallen far short of meeting the very high threshold for granting leave to appeal. See *North Bay (City) v. Vaughan*, 2018 ONCA 319, [2018] O.J. No. 1809 (Ont. C.A.).

In *Ontario (Ministry of the Environment and Climate Change) v. Sunrise Propane Energy Group Inc.*, 2018 ONCA 461, 2018 CarswellOnt 7611, 17 C.E.L.R. (4th) 174, [2018] O.J. No. 2625 (Ont. C.A.), the applicants were tried before a judge of the Ontario Court of Justice and had already had a full appeal to the Superior Court of Justice. A further appeal to the Court of Appeal was not automatic. Leave to appeal was required under s. 131 which sets the bar very high. Under s. 131, the focus is not on whether the subject matter of the case is of interest or importance to the public. In this case clearly it is — the incident at Sunrise was a dramatic, historical event in Toronto. A man lost his life. Many others were affected. Rather,

s. 131 focuses on the significance of the legal issues raised on appeal. The proposed grounds of appeal were fact-laded and did not identify a pure question of law. The contours of the doctrine of officially induced error of law were not engaged by the resolution of this issue at either level of court: for the trial judge, the issue involved the application of a unique factual set of circumstances to a settled body of law; for the appeal judge, the issue involved an assessment of the reasonableness of the trial judge's findings. As for the issue concerning the trial judge's interpretation of compliance with the Ministry of the Environment clean-up order, this was a question of mixed fact and law, not one of law alone. Even if it could be construed as an error of law, it had not been demonstrated that the interpretation of the administrative/enforcement order issued in the case was essential in the public interest or for the due administration of justice in the province.

Section 121 does not empower the court, sitting in appeal, to review the reasons on which a defendant has *succeeded* at trial. The appellant's cross-appeal must, therefore, be dismissed on the basis of lack of jurisdiction. The dismissal, however, does not extinguish the party's entitlement to have its "wrong regulation" defence considered. Given the parties' agreement that the trial court erred in its consideration of the Crown's essential averment that it failed to supply the required signaller on the date of the accident, and that a re-consideration is necessary, that re-consideration ought not to exclude whatever defences it put before the trial court. See *Ontario (Ministry of Labour) v. 614128 Ontario Ltd. (Trisan Construction)*, 2017 ONCJ 935, 2017 CarswellOnt 21438, [2017] O.J. No. 7035 (Ont. C.J.), additional reasons 2018 ONCJ 168, 2018 CarswellOnt 3863 (Ont. C.J.).

In *R. v. Orgaworld Canada Ltd.*, 2015 CarswellOnt 21086 (Ont. C.A.), it was held that the law is settled that a corporation cannot rely on inferred prejudice to support an argument that its s. 11(b) *Charter* rights have been violated. The appeal judge did not err in concluding that the applicant could not rely on inferred prejudice. The factual determination that the applicant had not in fact suffered any prejudice is a question of mixed fact and law. No appeal lies from that determination under s. 131 as it is not a question of law alone. The appeal judge's decision on the continuing offence argument was consistent with the settled jurisprudence. As a result, a hearing in the Court of Appeal on this issue was not essential in the public interest or for the due administration of justice. The construction of whether there was an ambiguity in the letter in question relieving the applicant of any duty to comply with the direction in the letter was factually idiosyncratic. This was not a question of law alone.

The defendant was not entitled to costs following the Crown's successful sentence appeal. Costs would not be appropriate whether the defendant succeeded on the appeal or not. There was absolutely no prosecution misconduct here. There were no exceptional circumstances that would justify freeing the defendant from the financial burden of the proceedings. To the contrary, it came into the appeal with unclean hands. Its principal consciously disgorged the corporation of assets and transferred those assets to himself or to another corporation controlled by him doing precisely what the corporate defendant did, operating out of precisely the same place. The only reasonable conclusion was that that disgorgement was motivated by a desire to deny the prosecution access to assets that belonged to the defendant. See *R. v. 1137749 Ontario Ltd. (operating as Pro-Teck Electric)*, 2018 ONCJ 502, 2018 CarswellOnt 12427, [2018] O.J. No. 4001 (Ont. C.J.).

12.3 REVIEWS TO THE ONTARIO SUPERIOR COURT OF JUSTICE

- Sections 140 through 142 of the POA, sections 1 through 10 of the *Habeas Corpus Act*, R.S.O. 1990 c. H.1, and sections 1 through 11 of the *Judical Review Procedure Act*, R.S.O. 1990, c. J.1, set out the procedures for invoking extraordinary remedies.
- Examples of extraordinary remedies include:
  - *Certiorari*: It is an order to the inferior court to present its record of the proceedings before the Ontario Superior Court of Justice for a review for jurisdictional error(s).

In *Ontario (Ministry of Labour) v. Intracorp Developments (Lombard) Inc.* (2002), 2002 CarswellOnt 1134, [2002] O.J. No. 1209 (Ont. S.C.J.), an application for certiorari was granted where the justice of the peace exceeded his jurisdiction under section 90(2) in awarding costs to the defendants where the Crown brought a motion pursuant to section 38(1) to try the defendants together. Although one of the defendants opposed the motion which was ultimately granted, such omission did not amount to a defect or irregularity as required under section 90.

- Prohibition: It is an order to the inferior court not to exercise or attempt to exercise a power for which it has no jurisdiction. *For example, where the inferior court proceeds under an unconstitutional statute or where the justice is biased.*

In *Enbridge Gas Distribution Inc. v. Ontario* (2005), [2005] O.J. No. 688, 2005 CarswellOnt 691 (Ont. S.C.J.), affirmed (2005), 2005 CarswellOnt 7811 (Ont. C.A.), an application for prohibition was refused where the defendant was charged under both the *Technical Standard and Safety Act* and the *Occupational Health and Safety Act* for a fatal gas explosion. The defendant submitted that the two sets of charges duplicated each other, and arose out of the same delict. Prohibition was available to deal with a jurisdictional error, and where there was an objection with the underlying statute, rather than the content of the information.

- *Mandamus*: It is an order to the inferior court to do that which it is required by law; *for example, where the inferior court declines to exercise its jurisdiction. It is used more by the prosecution.*

- *Habeas Corpus*: It is an order reviewing the detention or imprisonment of a person.

- Extaordinary remedies are not to be brought unless all appeal routes are exhausted: section 141(3).

- At common law, certiorari and prohibition are discretionary remedies and the superior court should generally decline to grant the remedy where there is an adequate appellate remedy. See *R. v. Arcand* (2004), [2004] O.J. No. 5017, 2004 CarswellOnt 5160, 10 C.E.L.R. (3d) 161, 125 C.R.R. (2d) 144, 193 O.A.C. 16, 192 C.C.C. (3d) 57, 73 O.R. (3d) 758 (Ont. C.A.).

- Intervention by the superior court in the middle of a trial defeats not only the integrity of the trial process, but also the efficacy of the appeal process. See *R. v. Felderhof* (2002), [2002] O.J. No. 4103, 2002 CarswellOnt 5623 (Ont. S.C.J.), additional reasons at (2003), [2003] O.J. No. 393, 2003 CarswellOnt 488 (Ont. S.C.J.), affirmed (2003), 180 C.C.C. (3d) 498, 2003 CarswellOnt 4943, [2003] O.J. No. 4819, 68 O.R. (3d) 481, 10 Admin. L.R. (4th) 229, 235 D.L.R. (4th) 131, 180 O.A.C. 288, 17 C.R. (6th) 20 (Ont. C.A.).

- It is clear that it is only in exceptional circumstances that review of a pre-trial ruling, such as a stay application based on section 11(b) of the *Charter*, by way of *certiorari* would be appropriate. Special and exceptional circumstances would involve a palpable infringement of a constitutional right that has taken place or is clearly threatened. See *R. v. 1353837 Ontario Ltd.* (2005), [2005] O.J. No. 166, 2005 CarswellOnt 163 (Ont. S.C.J.).

In *London (City) v. Young*, 2008 CarswellOnt 3091, [2008] O.J. No. 2118, 2008 ONCA 429, 237 O.A.C. 357, 233 C.C.C. (3d) 10, 75 Admin. L.R. (4th) 280, 91 O.R. (3d) 215, 65 M.V.R. (5th) 208 (Ont. C.A.), it was held that no regular avenue of appeal is provided where a proceeding is quashed under s. 9(1) of the *Provincial*

Offences Act. If the prosecuting authority or the Attorney General believes a justice has misconstrued what constitutes an error going to the regularity or completeness of the certificate, a prerogative remedy can be sought.

The public has an interest in the consistent and correct application of *Charter* principles when a justice of the peace acts as trial judge. Where a justice of the peace is a trial judge and there is no other right of appeal under s. 116, *certiorari* should be available to correct errors of law which result in a substantial wrong or miscarriage of justice as set out under s. 141(4). *Certiorari* is not limited to jurisdictional error in these circumstances. The justice of the peace erred in holding that 8 months was an unreasonable period of time to arrange a trial date for careless driving that resulted in a death. The justice of the peace must consider the public interest in having a full trial on the issues when serious charges are laid and an individual has been killed; the failure of the justice to expressly consider this factor amounted to reversible error. There would be a substantial miscarriage of justice as the public interest in having a full trial would not be met if the error was not corrected: *R. v. Smith*, 2008 CarswellOnt 4286, 2008 CarswellOnt 4287, 175 C.R.R. (2d) 13, [2008] O.J. No. 2841 (Ont. S.C.J.).

Extraordinary remedies are discretionary; they do not issue as of right or where no useful purpose would be served by their issuance: *R. v. Alrifai*, 2008 CarswellOnt 4338, [2008] O.J. No. 2870, 64 M.V.R. (5th) 159, (*sub nom.* Alrifai v. Ontario) 235 C.C.C. (3d) 374, 2008 ONCA 564, 242 O.A.C. 88 (Ont. C.A.), affirming 2007 CarswellOnt 2913, 48 M.V.R. (5th) 144, [2007] O.J. No. 1805 (Ont. S.C.J.).

In a recent case involving an administrative process for a "first attendance notice" employed by the City of Brampton, the court ruled that although the justice of the peace quashed the certificate of offence, the entire proceedings were illegal. The certificate of offence was a nullity and the offence notice was illegal as misleading. No substantial wrong or miscarriage of justice therefore resulted by the quashing order: *R. v. Nandalall*, 2008 CarswellOnt 8954 (Ont. S.C.J.).

Where the trial justice erred in quashing the count charging stunt driving in the absence of a defect in the information, the Crown's only recourse was to seek the remedy of *certiorari* and mandamus: *R. v. Saragosa*, 2008 CarswellOnt 7114, [2008] O.J. No. 4848 (Ont. S.C.J.).

In *R. v. Fortese* (September 25, 2008), Ferguson J., [2008] O.J. No. 5159 (Ont. S.C.J.), it was held that a police officer has jurisdiction to lay a charge for an offence committed anywhere in Ontario. There is no provision in the *Provincial Offences Act* that requires a proceeding to be commenced in the county, district or regional municipality where the offence occurred. The place of the offence only becomes relevant if the defendant appears and disputes the charge, in which case the court must consider the possible application of s. 29 governing the venue of the proceeding. However, where the defendant fails to appear for trial, the justice was required to proceed in the defendant's absence and enter a conviction and impose sentence pursuant to s. 9.1. If the court does nothing, when it is required to act, the court commits jurisdictional error.

The refusal or failure of the justice of the peace to hear the prosecution of the serious offences alleged is a substantial wrong. The justice failed to properly exercise her jurisdiction by quashing the counts before her on the reasoning that a "limitation period cannot be indefinite" when "all other offences under the POA have some sort of limitation period": *R. v. Commercial Spring & Tool Co.*, [2009] O.J. No. 3839, 2009 CarswellOnt 5589 (Ont. S.C.J.).

In *R. v. Evans*, 2010 ONSC 645, [2010] O.J. No. 468, 2010 CarswellOnt 607 (Ont. S.C.J.), it was held that once an information has been laid under the *Provincial Offences Act*, ss. 36 (1) and (2) provide a justice with the authority to quash that information in very limited circumstances. There were no defects on the faces of any of the informations in the applications. All of the informations revealed an offence known to law. It was at the time, and is now, an offence to improperly display a disabled parking permit. There was no statutory basis for the quashing of any of the informations. The justices of the peace, therefore, exceeded their jurisdiction in quashing the informations on the basis that the *Highway Traffic Act* did not apply to the shopping plaza parking lots which were private property. Since it could not be said whether the justices of the peace would have reached the same conclusion if they had the benefit of the applicable by-laws, the facts of each case and the submissions of the parties, the reviewing court did not exercise its discretion to decline a prerogative remedy. The applicant was entitled to be given an opportunity to prove its case.

An order striking out a conviction and the granting of a re-opening cannot be appealed under s. 135 which only permits an appeal against acquittal, conviction or sentence. The only recourse for the applicant is to seek prerogative remedies pursuant to s. 140(1). When the justice of the peace endorsed the conviction as not being under s. 9.1, that meant there was hearing and the defendant was represented. Administratively, the affidavit in support of a request for reopening ought not to have been put before the justice on the reopening application, given the endorsement of conviction. Public interest dictates that there ought not to be a second trial, but rather an appeal of the first trial. Care should be taken to ensure that applications to reopen are not entertained where there has been a determination on the merits: *London (City) v. Pavar*, 2010 ONSC 3448, 2010 CarswellOnt 3912 (Ont. S.C.J.).

As the ruling of the justice of the peace to quash the certificate of offence was not an acquittal, conviction or sentence, no appeal was available in respect of it, and therefore the applicant was not prohibited by virtue of s. 141(3) from applying to quash the order in question: *York (Regional Municipality) v. Talabe*, 2011 ONSC 955, 2011 CarswellOnt 832, [2011] O.J. No. 654 (Ont. S.C.J.).

The Ontario Court of Appeal has affirmed the decision that a justice of the peace need not be legally trained to conduct a fair trial of provincial offences charges. The court noted that since its previous decisions on point, the Legislature has further strengthened the justice of the peace bench by mandating minimum education and work experience qualifications, creating an independent appointments committee, and requiring continuing education programs for justices of the peace. It has also provided that upon request, a regional senior judge of the Ontario Court of Justice may decide that a case that would otherwise be heard by a justice of the peace be heard by a judge of the Ontario Court of Justice. See *R. v. Zelinski*, 2011 ONCA 593, 280 C.C.C. (3d) 546, 18 M.V.R. (6th) 210, 2011 CarswellOnt 9540, [2011] O.J. No. 4024 (Ont. C.A.).

Since the justice of the peace dismissed the charges for want of the prosecutor's appearance under s. 53(1) which could be appealed under s. 116(1)(b) , s. 141(3) prohibits the use of a prohibitive writ to challenge the ruling: *Ontario (Registrar, Motor Vehicles Dealers Act, 2002) v. Shaikh*, 2011 ONSC 452, 2011 CarswellOnt 259, [2011] O.J. No. 258 (Ont. S.C.J.). **Note:** The prosecutor's subsequent appeal was allowed for substantially the reasons given by the Superior Court Judge on the prerogative remedy application, namely, that the relief under s. 53 sought by the defendant is not available on a set date appearance. The plain wording of s. 53(1) illustrates the intention of the legislature that non-attendance by the prosecution on the date of the hearing (that is, a date when an issue will be judicially considered by the court) may result in the dismissal of the case. See *R. v. Shaikh*, 2011 ONCJ 774, 2011 CarswellOnt 15074, [2011] O.J. No.5968 (Ont. C.J.).

In *R. v. Cipriano*, 2011 ONSC 223, 2011 CarswellOnt 89, [2011] O.J. No. 67 (Ont. S.C.J.), it was held that the justice of the peace had no alternative but to declare a mistrial after the defendant's counsel made a complaint against her to the Judicial Council. If she acquitted the defendant, it would have appeared she did so because she was threatened and accused of misconduct; if she found the defendant guilty, it would be said she was angry and biased due to the allegations made and pending against her. Where there are facts and circumstances that clearly give rise to a reasonable apprehension of bias, the court has the ability to address the situation by making use of the remedies of certiorari and mandamus. If the judge who made the original mandamus order in this case had been aware of defence counsel's letter of complaint that was provided to the justice of the peace, it would have been highly doubtful that the original order would have been made. Consequently, the justice of the peace had no alternative but to recuse herself despite the mandamus order to proceed with the trial. There was no basis to stay the charges on the basis of abuse of process.

The appellant having been convicted for offences of dog running at large, contrary to a City of Toronto by-law, and failing to exercise reasonable precautions to prevent dog from biting or attacking another domestic animal, contrary to the *Dog Owners Liability Act*, should have pursued her appeal rights, and *certiorari* was therefore not available. Her complaints that she was not properly served, that the city official did not have the authority to swear the information, and that city officials trespassed on her property did not affect the jurisdiction of the justice of the peace to try the offences: *R. v. Nilsen*, 2011 ONCA 322, 2011 CarswellOnt 2681, [2011] O.J. No. 1865 (Ont. C.A.), leave to appeal refused 2011 CarswellOnt 10872, 2011 CarswellOnt 10871, 429 N.R. 391 (note), 294 O.A.C. 394 (note), [2011] S.C.C.A. No. 279 (S.C.C.).

In *R. v. Protech Roofing Waterproofing Ltd.*, [2011] O.J. No. 5360, 2011 CarswellOnt 13100, 285 C.C.C. (3d) 55 (Ont. S.C.J.), it was held that s. 21 of the *Provincial Offences Act* states that proceedings are commenced by swearing an information. Nowhere does the Act state the original information must still be in existence for the court to have jurisdiction to deal with a charge. The fact that court endorsements were not present on the photocopy did not detract from the fact that a photocopy of the information was present and available to the court. There was no evidence that the defendant was prejudiced in making full answer and defence; the administration of justice would be brought into disrepute if the court sanctioned the termination of a proceeding due to a procedural irregularity that caused no prejudice to the defendant. An order of mandamus was issued to compel the court to proceed with the charge as contained in the information that was originally sworn.

Where the defendant's pre-trial application to stay charges for unreasonable delay was dismissed, any error made by the trial justice is a legal error and not one of jurisdiction, such that a reviewing court has jurisdiction to grant judicial review. Society has an interest in the expeditious conduct of criminal and quasi-criminal proceedings without interruption or delay; fragmentation of the trial process and the risk of determination upon an incomplete record favour avoidance of interlocutory review. Judicial review with certiorari for error of law on the face of the record was therefore not available for interlocutory review of a pre-trial ruling in a quasi-criminal matter, and the interests of justice did not support an extension of time for a review hearing on the merits. See *National Direct Response Marketing Canada Inc. v. Travel Industry Council of Ontario*, 2011 ONSC 6157, 2011 CarswellOnt 10778, 249 C.R.R. (2d) 31, 285 O.A.C. 347 (Ont. Div. Ct.).

The trial justice erred in dismissing the prosecutor's motion to amend the certificate of offence prior to the date of trial so as to correct the set fine and total payable, holding that the defect was a fatal flaw that could not be amended. Although the motion to amend was not served personally or by mail or other method set out under s. 87(1) of the *Provincial Offences Act* (Ont.), being served by fax, the defendant was properly served through his legal representative. He was aware of the issue and was made aware of the opportunity to answer the remedy and resist the remedy sought. Instead, he did nothing and his technical argument regarding service of the motion failed. See *York (Regional Municipality) v. Burnett* (July 4, 2012), Doc. Newmarket CV-12-08460-00, [2012] O.J. No. 3239 (Ont. S.C.J.).

In *R. v. Lazaridis*, 2011 ONSC 6833, 2011 CarswellOnt 14026, 32 Admin. L.R. (5th) 326 (Ont. S.C.J.), the defendant applied for prerogative relief in an attempt to attack his conviction and sentence imposed by a properly constituted provincial offences court, acting within its jurisdiction under s. 54 of the Act. There was no suggestion that the warrant of committal was defective on its face in any way, just that it should not have been issued because the proceedings were not carried out in accordance with the Ontario Court of Appeal's decision in *R. v. Jenkins*, released over a year after the issuance of the warrant of committal, where it was held that while *ex parte* proceedings do not infringe the *Charter of Rights*, they ought not to become the norm. Although there was no transcript of proceedings available in order to ascertain whether the prosecutor advised the court that it was seeking a period of imprisonment, failure to abide by the Court of Appeal's cautionary words in proceeding *ex parte* in such circumstances would not deprive a court of jurisdiction to proceed *ex parte* and convict an accused person and then, if appropriate, issue a warrant of committal, although it may turn out to be a fruitful ground of appeal. The defendant's attempt to review his conviction on the basis of an alleged error of law, based on subsequent developments in the law, was therefore clearly barred by s. 141(3) since a right of appeal exists. The ability of the defendant to challenge the underlying conduct leading to his arrest pursuant to the warrant of committal was another matter, and would not be susceptible to review by way of appeal. The Superior Court of Justice has a broad jurisdiction to consider claims for prerogative relief, especially when based on *Charter* grounds. The matter was therefore permitted to proceed to a hearing on the merits. However, while the privative clause in s. 141(3) of the Act does not formally bar this aspect of the claim for prerogative relief, the fact that the defendant has still not pursued the statutory avenue of appeal may be critical in determining whether the relief sought ought to be granted. Relief by way of *certiorari* is discretionary and generally should not be granted when an applicant has failed to avail himself/herself a statutory right of appeal.

The prosecutor's application for *certiorari* to quash the decision of a justice of the peace finding the defendant guilty of driving a motor vehicle without having valid insurance was brought in good faith, as the prosecutor had become aware that the defendant did in fact have valid insurance at the relevant time. However, the justice of the peace was within his jurisdiction to proceed the way he did and the course of action he chose was permitted by the statute. Consequently, *certiorari* was simply not available in such circumstances. Instead, there was an avenue of relief available to the defendant, the same that is available to anyone who feels they have been unfairly convicted of an offence, namely, to file an appeal of the conviction, based on the fact that although the justice of the peace was not made aware of it, the defendant did in fact have valid insurance. See *R. v. Schauerte*, 2012 NWTSC 83, 2012 CarswellNWT 92, [2012] N.W.T.J. No. 95 (N.W.T. S.C.).

In *R. v. Canadian National Railway*, 2012 ONSC 6620, 2012 CarswellOnt 15070, 5 M.P.L.R. (5th) 277, [2012] O.J. No. 5649 (Ont. S.C.J.), it was held that a justice of the peace has jurisdiction to hear and determine the constitutional validity of a by-law. The Superior Court may grant relief for jurisdictional error in such quasi-criminal proceedings, but not for an error within jurisdiction for which an appeal would lie. There must also be a substantial wrong or miscarriage that has occurred. It remained open to the defendant in this case to appeal the decision of the justice of the peace once the trial concluded.

The proper route to be taken by the Crown when it seeks to set aside a decision by a trial court to stay proceedings commenced under the *Provincial Offences Act* on account of unreasonable delay is to be bring an appeal under s. 116(1)(b), and not *certiorari*. A judicial stay of proceedings is tantamount to a dismissal. Challenging the correctness of a judicial stay by way of appeal rather than through an application in the Superior Court is simpler and more straightforward than via prerogative writs. For an accused, particularly one who is self-represented, responding to an appeal is more readily understood than being required to respond to an application for *certiorari* and to follow the procedures of the Superior Court. The interpretation of the term "dismissal" in this manner better achieves the intended purpose of the Act. See *R. v. Courtice Auto Wreckers Ltd.*, 2014 ONCA 189, 2014 CarswellOnt 2797, 308 C.C.C. (3d) 571, 82 C.E.L.R. (3d) 177, 317 O.A.C. 265, [2014] O.J. No. 1145 (Ont. C.A.).

It is well settled that a judge asked to grant certiorari has a discretion to refuse it, and that one ground for refusing is that an appeal would be an adequate remedy. The accused in this case sought certiorari before any trial, and before the facts were ascertained by evidence, yet the accused complained of lack of evidence. If he had gone to trial, he might have been acquitted, or some of the charges might have been dropped; if he was convicted, he could have brought an appeal to the Court of Queen's Bench. The Court of Appeal is especially reluctant to hear appeals partway through a proceeding. See *R. v. Grabowski*, 2014 ABCA 123, 2014 CarswellAlta 478, 572 A.R. 244, 609 W.A.C. 244, [2014] A.J. No. 320 (Alta. C.A.).

In *R. v. Orgaworld Canada Ltd.*, 2014 ONCA 654, 2014 CarswellOnt 12891, 319 C.R.R. (2d) 335, [2014] O.J. No. 4482 (Ont. C.A.), it was held that the application Judge did not err in declining to entertain the *Charter* s. 24(1) application which was premised on post-trial delay, due to the Justice of the Peace giving his decision about 15 months after the close of submissions. The defendant was entitled to raise the s. 11(b) *Charter* issue of post-hearing delay in an appeal to the Provincial Offences Appeal Court under the *Provincial Offences Act* and had done so. In these circumstances, the application Judge had discretion to decline to entertain the s. 24(1) *Charter* application to the Superior Court, and there was no error in her exercise of discretion. The issue was subsequently argued before the Provincial Offences Appeal Court and was under reserve. While the Crown had argued that the s. 11(b) argument should be entertained because it had not been raised before the Justice of the Peace, the same argument would have been available to the Crown before the application Judge. The defendant, therefore, was under no disadvantage in proceeding in the Provincial Offences Appeal Court. Rather, it would have the advantage of there being a full record.

The Justice of the Peace committed a jurisdictional error by dismissing the charge after a not guilty plea without having a trial. Section 46(1) provides that if the defendant pleads not guilty, as the defendant in this case did, the court *shall* hold a trial. Section 46(3) permits the prosecutor and defendant to examine and cross-examine witnesses at trial. The Justice did not hold a trial or even ask if the prosecutor had evidence to call. He immediately dismissed the charge due to lack of court time. This is not a trial. Neither of the parties was permitted to exercise their right to examine witnesses. When a plea of guilty was entered the Justice of the Peace was required to conduct a trial. That trial would start by asking the prosecutor to call her witness, not by immediately dismissing the charge. In the circumstances, what occurred was a substantial wrong and a miscarriage of justice. The Justice of the Peace proceeded without jurisdiction to dismiss a charge that was validly before the court. Because of his personal preference to avoid being seized with a case, a charge was dismissed. It would be a dangerous precedent to have charges dismissed on that basis, a precedent that should be put to rest at the earliest possible date. See *Brampton (City) v. Singh*, 2014 ONSC 2626, 2014 CarswellOnt 5532, 73 Admin. L.R. (5th) 341, [2014] O.J. No. 2005 (Ont. S.C.J.).

It was further held in *Brampton (City) v. Singh*, 2014 ONSC 2626, 2014 CarswellOnt 5532, 73 Admin. L.R. (5th) 341, [2014] O.J. No. 2005 (Ont. S.C.J.) that the Justice of the Peace erred in refusing the prosecutor's adjournment and compounded that failure by failing to give reasons. While the authority to grant an adjournment is discretionary, it must be exercised judiciously. Judicial discretion, however, is subject to review. Reasons are required so the public knows why a decision was made, the parties understand the decision, and it permits appellate review. Here, no reasons were given, just a refusal to grant the adjournment. Subject to one possible explanation, the public, the parties and the appellate court would be left to speculate why the adjournment application was refused; it was *possible* that the defendant taking a day off work had some impact on the decision. If that were so, an adjournment application should not be refused based solely on the defendant being prejudiced because he took a day off work in the absence of a *Charter* s. 11(b) application *if* that was the motivation for the refusal. It could not be ignored that only 80 days had elapsed since the date that the defendant was charged and there was no indication when the next court date would be. Automatically dismissing an adjournment application on a first trial date 80 days after being charged when the case could not be reached is not determining the adjournment application judiciously.

In *York (Regional Municipality) v. Martinez*, 2014 ONSC 6305, 2014 CarswellOnt 15699, [2014] O.J. No. 5277 (Ont. S.C.J.), it was held that the Justice of the Peace quashed the certificate of offence as not being complete and regular on its face in the face of not only compelling but binding authority to the contrary. Once the Superior Court has spoken on an issue, the lower courts are bound to follow these dictates whether they like them or not. This includes the Justices of the Peace of the Province. It is especially so in the context of their extraordinary *ex parte* deliberations exercised under s. 9(2) of the *Provincial Offences Act* where they enjoy ungoverned and unobserved scope to quash the proceedings.

In *R. v. Agasiyants*, 2015 ONCJ 142, 2015 CarswellOnt 3304, [2015] O.J. No. 1214 (Ont. C.J.), it was held that an issue of insufficient or failed jurisdiction may properly be litigated as a ground for appealing a conviction. It was a conviction registered in an Early Resolution Meeting which was the subject of complaint. The recourse to appellate relief is not governed by the manner or forum in which a conviction is registered, but only by the manner in which proceedings are commenced. In this case, proceedings were commenced by a certificate of offence under Part I. The appeal was properly before the court. Although the grounds might suggest that there was no jurisdiction in the Justice of the Peace on the Early Resolution Meeting to enter the conviction, the complaint comes down to one, commonly heard in the Provincial Offences Appeal Court, that the Appellant had no notice of the proceedings in which she was convicted. Her complaint was exacerbated by her assertion that she never requested an early resolution meeting on her request for re-opening. There was an absence of any evidence showing notice to the defendant of the Early Resolution Meeting, directed by the Justice of the Peace on the re-opening application. In the absence of notice as directed to the defendant of a proceeding which directly affected her rights, and given her assertion, uncontested, that she was unaware of the proceeding, the re-opening was not properly constituted and the conviction must be set aside.

The defendant was mistaken about how the law applies to him, as his arguments that s. 141 does not apply to him and a statutory right of appeal of his convictions are only available to a "man or a woman consenting to act in the capacity of, or otherwise enter into an association with, a class of person or entity created by statute and subject to the statutes allegedly engaged in this matter" mirror those used by persons identified by other courts in the province and elsewhere as "Organized Pseudo-legal Commercial litigants". The argument that such persons can self-determine which laws of the land apply to them and which do not lacks merit and is spurious. See *R. v. Curle*, 2015 ONSC 1999, 2015 CarswellOnt 4980, [2015] O.J. No. 1714 (Ont. S.C.J.).

The word "proceeding" which is not defined in the *Provincial Offences Act* does not mean trial, such that all trials in the Provincial Offences Court must take place within six months of the date of the alleged offence occurring. "Proceeding" in the context of limitations law, means the entire case from the legal process that begins through to final disposition. The "commencement" of a proceeding is the issuance of process, in this case, by the police officer filing the certificate of offence. In this case, the certificate of offence was served on the date of the offence and filed within seven days thereafter, well within the six month limitation period. There was no limitations issue in the case and the Provincial Offences Court was correct to dismiss the applicant's preliminary motion. The proper course for the applicant to challenge the Justice's ruling dismissing his preliminary motion was an appeal to a Provincial Judge in the Ontario Court of Justice, and not by way of extraordinary equitable relief to the Superior Court of Justice. See *Torok v. Ontario*, 2015 ONSC 3100, 2015 CarswellOnt 7080, 336 O.A.C. 17, [2015] O.J. No. 2472 (Ont. Div. Ct.).

In *York (Regional Municipality) v. Lorman*, 2015 ONSC 6486, 2015 CarswellOnt 15914, 46 M.P.L.R. (5th) 153, [2015] O.J. No. 5449 (Ont. S.C.J.), during the course of the arraignment, the Justice of the Peace noted that the certificate of offence had the incorrect municipality. The prosecutor requested that he matter be held down so that he could call evidence from the investigating police officer as to the correct municipality and request an amendment to the certificate of offence. However, on her own volition, the Justice quashed the certificate, notwithstanding that there was no proper motion by the defendant, who was unrepresented, to do so. The spirit and intent of the *Provincial Offences Act*, and prosecutions conducted thereunder, is to ensure that technical objections do not impede a verdict on the merits. The Act sets up a process pursuant to which provincial offences matters can be dealt with in a speedy, efficient and convenient way. In a situation where the defendant appears for trial, the provisions of s. 9(1) governing defective certificates where the defendant does not appear for trial do not apply; where the defendant attends, s. 36 governs what the court must do, namely, it is up to the defendant and not the court to bring a motion to quash. The practice of Justices of the Peace bringing their own motion to quash in these circumstances has been disapproved of by the court. Justices of the Peace, like judges of the Superior Court, are human and may not always like the decision of an appellate court. Fundamentally, however, justices and judges must abide by the decisions of the higher court whether they like it or not. The Justice's decision to quash the certificate of offence where there was no motion by the defendant to do so was a clear error of law. It was clear from her earlier decisions that she knew she did not have the jurisdiction to quash the certificate of offence yet she proceeded to do what she knew she had no jurisdiction to do, and thus challenged the prosecution to appeal. Her decision to proceed in the manner she did reflects not only an error of law that was jurisdictional in nature, but a lack of appreciation of the principle of *stare decisis.* An order of *mandamus* and certiorari quashing the order of the Justice of the Peace was issued.

It was held in *York (Regional Municipality) v. Newhook,* 2015 ONSC 6587, 2015 CarswellOnt 16978, [2015] O.J. No. 5766 (Ont. S.C.J.) that the discretion of the court as to whether it will accept or reject the guilty plea is a discretion that has to be exercised judicially. It is not a discretion that can be exercised on an arbitrary whim. In situations where it is evident on the face of the record that the discretion has not been exercised judicially, such a discretion amounts to an error of law. There was no reason in law why the Justice should reject the guilty plea that was being proposed by the prosecutor and the defence. She made no inquiries of the prosecutor or defendant with respect to the reasonableness of the proposed plea. Even if there was some legal basis in law for the Justice to consider the appropriateness of the guilty plea, there was no reason why it should take nearly a year for the court to consider whether the guilty pleas should be accepted. An order for *mandamus* issued directing the Justice to accept a guilty plea to the amended offence and to enter a conviction.

In *Thunder Bay (City) v. Matzov,* 2016 ONSC 4557, 2016 CarswellOnt 12111, 58 M.P.L.R. (5th) 174, [2016] O.J. No. 3982 (Ont. S.C.J.), it was held that the justice of the peace exceeded his jurisdiction by quashing the certificates of offence on the basis that they were either "too vague" or "not specific" on account of the township or municipality where the offence was alleged to have taken place not being shown on the certificate. The certificate of offence was issued to the accused person at the roadside; the place of the alleged offence was therefore within the knowledge of the person charged. No prejudice resulted to the individuals charged at trial. The justice of the peace was therefore incorrect in quashing the certificates of offence as the location of the alleged offences, indicating the highway number and the district, sufficiently identified the location of the alleged offences, and even if the accused wished to dispute the charges, they could be left in no doubt as to the place of the alleged offences as the certificates were served at the roadside where the alleged offences occurred.

A defendant who does not testify is not a witness and is not eligible for costs under s. 60(2). Such costs are for witness fees and expenses. Had the defendant who lived in Montreal and travelled to Thunder Bay for his trial testified, he would have been a witness and such an order would have been available to the court; however, the prosecution's witness did not appear for trial, and the case was withdrawn. The trial justice therefore did not have jurisdiction to order $100 costs payable to the defendant. See *Thunder Bay (City) v. Singh-Sidhu*, 2016 ONSC 4889, 2016 CarswellOnt 12987, [2016] O.J. No. 4284 (Ont. S.C.J.).

In *Hamilton (City) v. Barbano* (July 28, 2016), Doc. CV-15-53875, [2016] O.J. No. 4011 (Ont. S.C.J.), it was held that s. 69(15)(c) allows a justice of the peace in exceptional circumstances to reduce a fine or order that it does not have to be paid if the justice is satisfied that the person is unable to pay the fine in a reasonable amount of time. However, s. 165(3) of the *Provincial Offences Act* states that this section does not apply to any part of the province that is covered by a municipal transfer agreement. The City in question was covered by such an agreement since 1999. The language in s. 66(6) allowing a justice to order "periodic payments or otherwise" when extending time to pay a fine was not sufficiently broad to allow a justice to invoke the procedure in s. 69(15) to reduce or eliminate fines; the unproclaimed s. 69(14.1) may allow fines to be reduced one day, but it had been passed in 2009 and remained not in effect. The justice's order reducing the total fines payable was quashed, and the matter remitted back for consideration of the issue of extension of time to pay the fines.

The presumption of regularity was dispositive of the challenge to the validity of the summonses. The allegation of ineffective service of the Property Standards Orders was an issue for the justice presiding in Provincial Offences Court to determine, not an issue of jurisdiction amendable to relief on an application for an order in lieu of a writ of prohibition. See *R. v. de Boerr*, 2016 ONCA 634, 2016 CarswellOnt 13038, [2016] O.J. No. 4345 (Ont. C.A.).

After the justice of the peace ruled that case was not statute-barred, the defendants applied for *certiorari* to quash the decision. Under s. 141(2.1), the court has a discretion to order that the trial continue, despite the application. Generally speaking, it is best that proceedings run their course before the court is asked to entertain an application for judicial review. In this case, if the order was not granted, the trial would be interrupted at least until the court made its decision on the *certiorari* application. It is only if the application succeeds that there would be any advantage. However, if the application does not succeed, there will have been a delay in proceeding with the trial. That is not in the interests of the parties or in the public interest. If the trial proceeded pending the outcome of the application, there would be no prejudice to the applicants. If they succeeded in the application, the entire proceeding would be quashed; in the alternative, if they are convicted they could raise the same issues on the application as grounds of appeal. On balance, it was in the interests of justice to grant an order that the trial continue forthwith. See *Thomas v. Halton Region Conservation Authority*, 2017 ONSC 514, 2017 CarswellOnt 575, [2017] O.J. No. 274 (Ont. S.C.J.).

The justice of the peace at the defendant's first appearance in court noted that the date of the offence on the information was a date in the future, and determined that the information was "no good" as a result. It is important to remember that an important goal of the *Provincial Offences Act* is that matters are tried on their merits, hence, the very broad powers of amendment where there is no prejudice to the accused. While the question of whether to amend an information is a question of law, this does not relieve the court from its obligation to proceed properly and in accordance with law to arrive at a decision whether to grant an amendment. Clearly, this information was defective in substance or form. It contained an obvious error which required an amendment. No trial evidence was necessary to ascertain this error. The fact that this was at the first appearance did not oust the court's jurisdiction to consider whether to amend the information. Even if the lack of the officer's signature amounted to a substantive defect, there was jurisdiction for the court to amend the information. There was no opportunity for the Crown to adduce evidence to support the amendment or to make submissions as to why the amendment should be made. This was a fatal error. Clearly, the presiding justice did not conduct the proceeding in accordance with natural justice. In proceeding in this manner, the learned judge exceeded his jurisdiction. Not granting the application for prerogative review would, in the circumstances of the case, result in a substantial wrong to society which expects and is entitled to have these matters heard on the merits unless an amendment is rejected after both parties have an opportunity to deal with and the presiding judge gives full consideration of the matters relevant to an amendment application. See *R. v. Singh*, 2017 ONSC 7593, 2017 CarswellOnt 20895, [2017] O.J. No. 6807 (Ont. S.C.J.), affirmed 2018 ONCA 506, 2018 CarswellOnt 8710, 362 C.C.C. (3d) 161, 28 M.V.R. (7th) 45 (Ont. C.A.).

There was a defect on the information as the offence date was recorded as 2017 instead of 2016. The justice of the peace committed jurisdictional error in quashing the information due to the error without considering whether to amend it under ss. 34 or 36. A justice of the peace may amend the information at any stage of the proceedings, including first appearance. The justice of the peace also erred by failing to give the Crown an opportunity to make submissions. Quashing the information in these circumstances resulted in a miscarriage of justice because it prevented the charge being considered on its merits. See *R. v. Singh*, 2018 ONCA 506, 2018 CarswellOnt 8710, 362 C.C.C. (3d) 161, 28 M.V.R. (7th) 45, [2018] O.J. No. 2943 (Ont. C.A.).

Generally, applications for *Charter* relief should be brought to the court hearing the matter. Of course, when the conduct of the trial judge is at issue this is impractical. In such instances, it may be prudent to bring the application before the Superior Court which has constant, complete and concurrent jurisdiction to grant the s. 24(1) *Charter* remedy. However, litigants do not have unfettered access to the Superior Court of Justice. Rather, the court should exercise its discretion to assume jurisdiction where it is appropriate, and where there is no other court in a position to provide an effective remedy. In this case, the appellants had filed a Notice of Appeal to the Ontario Court of Justice and there was a hearing date scheduled for later in the year. It would be imprudent to have appellate decisions from two distinct levels of courts. In all of the circumstances, the court declined to exercise its discretion to hear the matter seeking relief for a violation of s. 11(b) of the *Charter of Rights*. See *Orgaworld v. Her Majesty The Queen in Right of Ontario*, 2014 ONSC 1651, 2014 CarswellOnt 19386 (Ont. S.C.J.).

At the beginning of his trial, the defendant argued he was denied Crown disclosure despite two requests for it. At the start of his trial, the prosecutor gave some disclosure, but the defendant asked for more. The prosecutor was not in a position to provide it at that time. The defendant then asked the justice of the peace for a stay of proceedings due to this failure to make proper disclosure. He was not allowed to make submissions on this point, including his presenting four binding cases that he wished to present. However, the defendant did not give any notice he was bringing a stay application. By not giving such a notice, the justice of the peace understandably was not prepared to hear the stay application on the merits at that time. The justice of the peace was within his right to try and control the proceedings before him, and he did not overstep the appropriate boundaries of that. At the end of the day, while the justice of the peace did not accede to the defendant's request for a stay or listen to the whole of his submissions, he adjourned the trial in order that disclosure be made. The justice of the peace specifically left it open for the defendant to bring his stay application on the new trial date, present any evidence he wished, and to make his submissions. When the whole of the proceedings was assessed, there was no denial of natural justice or an unfair hearing. The justice of the peace was also correct in not ordering a stay of proceedings at this time. The remedy that he chose was to grant an adjournment so that proper disclosure could be made. This was a fit remedy for Crown non-disclosure. The justice of the peace did not preclude the defendant from asking for a stay of proceedings upon the resumption of the trial. No substantial wrong or miscarriage of justice resulted from this decision. See *City of Toronto v. Riddell*, 2018 ONSC 2048, 2018 CarswellOnt 4860, [2018] O.J. No. 1643 (Ont. S.C.J.), affirmed *Toronto (City) v. Riddell*, 2019 ONCA 103, 2019 CarswellOnt 2272, [2019] O.J. No. 823 (Ont. C.A.).

A justice of the peace who is hearing a trial of charges under Part III of the *Provincial Offences Act* is entitled to determine questions of the relevance of evidence and to make disclosure orders, without such decisions being challenged mid-trial. Applications for certiorari should be granted only rarely. Most erroneous rulings made during a trial are appealable only at the end of the trial as part of an appeal against conviction, dismissal or sentence. The test for intervention mid-trial by certiorari under s. 140 is whether the erroneous ruling makes the proceeding "so unfair that the interests of justice require the court to intervene and grant prerogative relief". The application judge erred by failing to consider the substantial wrong or miscarriage of justice test in s. 141(4), and in determining on the merits and mid-trial the issue of whether the earlier orders were relevant to the appellant's defence. Even if the disclosure order were wrong, complying with it does not amount to a substantial wrong or miscarriage of justice. The disclosure order would not preclude the respondent from arguing that the materials disclosed are not in fact relevant and that what was disclosed does not afford a defence. By contrast, the effect of the application judge's order was that any defence based on earlier compliance was effectively taken "off the table". Whether or not the appellant's arguments amounts to a collateral attack on the order to comply, that issue should have been resolved at trial on a proper record, and it was premature for the respondent to bring the issue forward before the trial was concluded. See *York (Municipality) v. Irwin*, 2017 ONCA 906, 2017 CarswellOnt 18374, 68 M.P.L.R. (5th) 179, [2017] O.J. No. 6145 (Ont. C.A.).

The applicant sought as part of first party records disclosure the disciplinary records and employment file for the police officer who charged him with driving while holding or using a hand-held communication device. Although the applicant had failed to comply with the 30-day notice requirements in s. 141(1) of the *Provincial Offences Act*, s. 85 provides for a broad curative power to extend time for service. The court should exercise the power to extend the times prescribed in s. 141(1) unless to do so would prejudice the other parties. In the present case, the justice of the peace refused the applicant's request for the disciplinary records on the basis that those records were irrelevant and the applicant will have the opportunity to explore the subject in cross-examination. While the reasons for the refusal were not extensive, the decision was one that clearly fell within the jurisdiction of the justice of the peace. As the applicant will be able to explore the matter in cross-examination of the officer, it could not be said that the decision will have a fundamentally important impact on the fairness of the trial. In addition, such pre-trial rulings can always be reconsidered by the justice of the peace who presides over the trial should the evidence warrant disclosure. The disciplinary records may take on more relevance based on how the questions are answered by the witness in cross-examination. However, evidence of historical drug use by an officer who has seemingly satisfied his superiors that he is fit to resume his duties has marginal relevance at this point. How far the applicant can go in cross-examination on this issue and if there will be any merit to some form of documentary disclosure will be determined at trial. The Crown had specifically stated that it had considered the disciplinary records in question and had fulfilled its "gate-keeping" function that they do not form part of first party disclosure. Not every finding of police misconduct by an officer involved in a matter will be relevant to the accused's case and it is certainly not the case that a McNeil report should be provided as a matter of course in all provincial offences prosecutions. The applicant had been aware of the Crown's position that an *O'Connor* application was the proper procedure to determine if some or all of the disciplinary records should be produced. The applicant had ignored the Crown's position and chosen to proceed with the application. There was an upcoming trial date for the matter and this date could be impacted if the applicant commenced an *O'Connor* application at this late date. The impact that such an application could have on the trial date was a matter for the discretion of the trial judge. See *Mian v. City of Ottawa*, 2018 ONSC 2131, 2018 CarswellOnt 5388, [2018] O.J. No. 1773 (Ont. S.C.J.).

In *Mohtashami v. Toronto (City)*, 2018 ONSC 5460, 2018 CarswellOnt 15568, [2018] O.J. No. 4846 (Ont. S.C.J.), it was held that only in rare cases will courts allow criminal or quasi-criminal proceedings to be delayed or fragmented by interlocutory review. The applicants, who are not defendants, but potential witnesses at a trial laid under the *Provincial Offences Act* for violations of a municipal by-law prohibiting the removal of trees without a permit, admitted that they were likely to give material evidence at trial, but claimed that they were tricked into providing the authorities with the information that they relied on to obtain the summonses. Any negative effect on the administration of justice that would result from compelling the applicants to testify would take place in the context of the defendants' trial. Whether and to what extent the administration of justice's integrity would suffer would depend on a number of factors, including the importance of the applicants' evidence to the prosecution's case and the seriousness of the charges. As a result, the best forum in which to evaluate the harm, if any, that would be caused to the administration of justice is the court in which the defendants are being tried. It is the defendants, not the applicants, whose rights are affected by the trial proceedings. If the conduct of the City authorities somehow compromised the integrity of the trial proceedings, then it is the defendants who will suffer prejudice as a result of the state misconduct. If a remedy is available, it is they who are entitled to it. The Superior Court should not allow a trial to be delayed so that witnesses who have no real interests in the proceedings and who are no risk of suffering any prejudice can embark on a Quixotic quest to remedy some perceived unfairness.

In *York (Regional Municipality) v. McGuigan*, 2018 ONCA 1062, 2018 CarswellOnt 22571, [2018] O.J. No. 6916 (Ont. C.A.), the Court of Appeal ruled that trial justice properly ordered the prosecutor to provide disclosure of the testing and operating procedures from the user manual for the device used by the traffic officer to measure the speed of the defendant's vehicle. Even if the justice of the peace had been wrong to order disclosure, the error would not have been jurisdictional in nature. Section 140(1) of the *Provincial Offences Act* confines *certiorari* orders in *POA* matters to situations where an applicant would be entitled to such relief at common law, and for parties to a proceeding, *certiorari* orders are confined to jurisdictional errors. Moreover, *certiorari* should not have been granted in the course of ongoing proceedings. Nor was there a substantial wrong or miscarriage of justice to address, a prerequisite to *certiorari* under s. 141(4) of the Act. Contrary to the application judge's decision, the justice of the peace did not err in making the disclosure order. Where a prosecutor is relying on a speed measuring device to prosecute an offence, it must, on request, disclose the testing and operating procedures set out in the user manual for that device. It is up to the prosecutor to hand such information over on request. The person charged need not bring an application or obtain a court order. This is first party disclosure, not third party disclosure. The charging police force has a corresponding duty to furnish the pertinent passages from the user manual to the prosecutor to enable the prosecutor to discharge its first party disclosure obligations. This is not a crushing administrative task. The disclosure at issue here is not case specific information. The disclosure obligation can therefore be discharged by the prosecutor by posting the relevant content from the user manual online and providing the ticketed driver with the required URL.

13

CHECKLISTS

13.1 DEFENDING A PROVINCIAL OFFENCE

- What is the offence charged? How is it worded?

- Is it a *mens rea*, strict liability or absolute liability offence? What must the prosecution prove? (See Chapter 4)

- What evidence is admissible? If some evidence is inadmissible, how does that affect the case? (See section 10.2 "Evidence" and 10.3 "Trial Strategy")

- Are there any *Charter* issues? (See section 5.2 "Constitutional Defences")

- Are there any procedural defences? (See Chapter 5)

- **What is your client's story?**

The Trial:

- **It wasn't me.** (prosecution must prove "identity" beyond a reasonable doubt and the defendant can remain silent)

- **I wasn't there.** (section 3.2.5 "Initial Advice" and the requirement to disclose alibis evidence before trial)

- **I didn't do it.** (proof of *actus reus*; section 8.6 "Involuntariness Defence", section 8.7 "Causation Defence" and section 7.4 "Parties to an Offence")

- **I did it, but I didn't mean to.** (proof of intent — section 6.2 as to "state of mind", section 4.1.1 as to "recklessness" and "awareness of the risk", and section 6.5.2 as to the "intoxication" defence)

- **I did it; I was aware of the risk, but I used reasonable care.** (section 6.5.1 "Mistake of Fact" and section 7.2 "Considerations for Reasonable Care")

- **I had to do it.** (section 8.8 "Necessity Defence")

- **I was told by an official that I could do it.** (section 5.6.2 "Officially Induced Error")

- **It was such a trivial incident that the prosecution ought to be stayed.** (section 5.6.4 "de minimus")

Sentencing:

- **Okay, I did it; it wasn't so trivial; I shouldn't have done it, but I've never done it before.** (first time offenders — in some cases, the emphasis is on rehabilitation rather than punishment)

- **I've done it before, but not for a while. (**the "gap principle" in sentencing may apply)

- **I've done it before, consistently and recently, but I've started treatment or corrective measures.** (if the corrective measures will prevent repetition, then specific deterrence may be partially satisfied)

- **I've done it consistently before; I've failed to break the cycle; I'm not taking treatment; but I plead guilty early — I've saved the prosecution the expense of a trial.** (a guilty plea can be a mitigating circumstance on sentencing)

- **I wish to remain silent.**

Appendix A

Provincial Offences Act

R.S.O. 1990, c. P.33 as am. S.O. 1992, c. 20, ss. 1, 3; 1993, c. 27, Sched. (Fr.); 1993, c. 31, s. 1; 1994, c. 10, s. 23; 1994, c. 17, ss. 130-132; 1994, c. 27, s. 52; 1995, c. 6, s. 7; 1997, c. 30, Sched. D, s. 17; 1998, c. 4, s. 1; 2000, c. 26, Sched. A, s. 13; 2002, c. 17, Sched. C, s. 23, Sched. F, s. 1; 2002, c. 18, Sched. A, s. 15 [s. 15(1) not in force at date of publication. Repealed 2006, c. 21, Sched. F, s. 10.1.]; 2004, c. 22, ss. 7, 8; 2005, c. 18, s. 18; 2006, c. 19, Sched. B, s. 15, Sched. D, s. 18 [Sched. B, s. 15(1) conditions not yet satisfied. Cannot be applied.]; 2006, c. 21, Sched. C, s. 131(1)-(3), (4) (Fr.), (5) (Fr.), (6)-(9), (10) (Fr.), (11), (12), (13) (Fr.), (14)-(19), (20) (Fr.), (21), Sched. E [Sched. E, s. 1 not in force at date of publication.]; 2009, c. 33, Sched. 4, s. 1 [s. 1(45), (46) not in force at date of publication.] [s. 1(31) repealed 2011, c. 1, Sched. 1, s. 8.]; 2011, c. 1, Sched. 1, s. 7; 2015, c. 14, s. 60; 2015, c. 27, Sched. 1, s. 3(1)-(3), (4) (Fr.), (5)-(8); 2017, c. 2, Sched. 2, s. 28; 2017, c. 20, Sched. 2, s. 38; 2017, c. 26, Sched. 3, s. 27; 2017, c. 34, Sched. 35, ss. 1-7, 8 (Fr.), 9, 10 (Fr.), 11-18, 19 (Fr.), 20 (Fr.), 21-23, 24 (Fr.), 25 (Fr.) [ss. 2-7, 11-16, 18(1) not in force at date of publication.]

INTERPRETATION

Definitions

1. (1) In this Act,

"certificate" means a certificate of offence issued under Part I or a certificate of parking infraction issued under Part II;

"court" means the Ontario Court of Justice;

"electronic" and "electronically" have the meanings set out in the *Electronic Commerce Act, 2000*;

"judge" means a provincial judge;

"justice" means a provincial judge or a justice of the peace;

"offence" means an offence under an Act of the Legislature or under a regulation or by-law made under the authority of an Act of the Legislature;

"police officer" means a chief of police or other police officer but does not include a special constable or by-law enforcement officer;

"prescribed" means prescribed by the rules of court;

"prosecutor" means, in respect of a proceeding, the following person, and includes an agent acting on that person's behalf:

1. The Attorney General, subject to paragraphs 2 and 3.

2. In the case of a proceeding to which a transfer agreement made under Part X applies and in which the Attorney General does not intervene, a person acting on behalf of a municipality in accordance with the agreement.

3. The person who issues a certificate or lays an information, if neither the Attorney General nor a person referred to in paragraph 2, or an agent of either of them, acts as prosecutor;

"provincial offences officer" means,

(a) a police officer,

(b) a constable appointed pursuant to any Act,

(c) a municipal law enforcement officer referred to in subsection 101(4) of the *Municipal Act, 2001* or in subsection 79(1) of the *City of Toronto Act, 2006*, while in the discharge of his or her duties,

(d) a by-law enforcement officer of any municipality or of any local board of any municipality, while in the discharge of his or her duties,

(e) an officer, employee or agent of any municipality or of any local board of any municipality whose responsibilities include the enforcement of a by-law, an Act or a regulation under an Act, while in the discharge of his or her duties, or

(f) a person designated under subsection (3);

"representative" means, in respect of a proceeding to which this Act applies, a person authorized under the *Law Society Act* to represent a person in that proceeding;

"set fine" means the amount specified for an offence under section 91.1 by the Chief Justice of the Ontario Court of Justice or by a regional senior judge of that court for the purpose of proceedings under Part I or II.

(2) [Repealed 2002, c. 17, Sched. F, s. 1.]

Designation of provincial offences officers

(3) A minister of the Crown may designate in writing any person or class of persons as a provincial offences officer for the purposes of all or any class of offences.

2000, c. 26, Sched. A, s. 13(6), item 1; 2002, c. 17, Sched. F, s. 1; 2002, c. 18, Sched. A, s. 15(6), item 1; 2006, c. 21, Sched. C, s. 131(1), (2); 2009, c. 33, Sched. 4, s. 1(1); 2015, c. 27, Sched. 1, s. 3(1); 2017, c. 34, Sched. 35, s. 1

Purpose of Act

2. (1) The purpose of this Act is to replace the summary conviction procedure for the prosecution of provincial offences, including the provisions adopted by reference to the *Criminal Code* (Canada), with a procedure that reflects the distinction between provincial offences and criminal offences.

Interpretation

(2) Where, as an aid to the interpretation of provisions of this Act, recourse is had to the judicial interpretation of and practices under corresponding provisions of the *Criminal Code* (Canada), any variation in wording without change in substance shall not, in itself, be construed to intend a change of meaning.

PART I

COMMENCEMENT OF PROCEEDINGS BY CERTIFICATE OF OFFENCE

Certificate of offence

3. (1) In addition to the procedure set out in Part III for commencing a proceeding by laying an information, a proceeding in respect of an offence may be commenced by filing a certificate of offence alleging the offence in the office of the court.

Issuance and service

(2) A provincial offences officer who believes that one or more persons have committed an offence may issue, by completing and signing in the form prescribed under section 13,

(a) a certificate of offence certifying that an offence has been committed; and

(b) either an offence notice indicating the set fine for the offence or a summons.

Proposed Addition — 3(2.1)

Requirements for offence notice

(2.1) An offence notice must comply with the following rules:

1. It must indicate that the notice of intention to appear may be filed in person, in addition to any other methods it may specify.

2. It must indicate that an option of an early resolution meeting with the prosecutor is available, unless it indicates that the notice of intention to appear may be filed by mail.

2017, c. 34, Sched. 35, s. 2 [Not in force at date of publication.]

Service

(3) The offence notice or summons shall be served personally upon the person charged within thirty days after the alleged offence occurred.

(4) [Repealed 2009, c. 33, Sched. 4, s. 1(3).]

Certificate of service

(5) Where service is made by the provincial offences officer who issued the certificate of offence, the officer shall certify on the certificate of offence that he or she personally served the offence notice or summons on the person charged and the date of service.

Affidavit of service

(6) Where service is made by a person other than the provincial offences officer who issued the certificate of offence, he or she shall complete an affidavit of service in the prescribed form.

Certificate as evidence

(7) A certificate of service of an offence notice or summons purporting to be signed by the provincial offences officer issuing it or an affidavit of service under subsection (6) shall be received in evidence and is proof of personal service in the absence of evidence to the contrary.

Officer not to act as agent

(8) The provincial offences officer who serves an offence notice or summons under this section shall not receive payment of any money in respect of a fine, or receive the offence notice for delivery to the court.

1993, c. 31, s. 1(1); 2009, c. 33, Sched. 4, s. 1(2), (3)

Filing of certificate of offence

4. A certificate of offence shall be filed in the office of the court as soon as is practicable, but no later than seven days after service of the offence notice or summons.

2009, c. 33, Sched. 4, s. 1(4)

Having a trial

5. (1) A defendant who is served with an offence notice may give notice of intention to appear in court for the purpose of entering a plea and having a trial of the matter.

Notice of intention to appear in offence notice

(2) If the offence notice includes a part with a notice of intention to appear, the defendant must give notice of intention to appear by,

(a) completing the notice of intention to appear part of the offence notice; and

572

(b) delivering the offence notice to the court office specified in it in the manner provided in the offence notice.

Notice of intention to appear to be filed in person

(3) If the offence notice requires the notice of intention to appear to be filed in person, the defendant must give the notice of intention to appear by,
(a) attending in person or by representative at the court office specified in the offence notice at the time or times specified in the offence notice; and
(b) filing a notice of intention to appear in the form prescribed under section 13 with the clerk of the court.

Specified court office

(4) A notice of intention to appear under subsection (3) is not valid if the defendant files the notice of intention to appear at a court office other than the one specified on the offence notice.

Notice of trial

(5) Where a notice of intention to appear is received under subsection (2) or (3), the clerk of the court shall, as soon as is practicable, give notice to the defendant and the prosecutor of the time and place of the trial.

Rescheduling time of trial

(6) The clerk of the court may, for administrative reasons, reschedule the time of the trial by giving a revised notice to the defendant and the prosecutor within 21 days of giving the notice referred to in subsection (5).

1993, c. 31, s. 1(2); 2009, c. 33, Sched. 4, s. 1(5)

Availability of meeting procedure

5.1 (1) This section applies where the offence notice requires the notice of intention to appear to be filed in person in the form prescribed under section 13.

Option for meeting with the prosecutor

(2) Instead of filing a notice of intention to appear under subsection 5(3), a defendant may request a meeting with the prosecutor to discuss the resolution of the offence by,
(a) indicating that request on the offence notice; and
(b) delivering the offence notice to the court office specified on it within 15 days after the defendant was served with the offence notice.

Notice of meeting time

(3) Where a defendant requests a meeting with the prosecutor under subsection (2), the clerk of the court shall, as soon as is practicable, give notice to the defendant and the prosecutor of the time and place of their meeting.

Rescheduling the meeting time

(4) If the time for the meeting scheduled in the notice under subsection (3) is not suitable for the defendant, the defendant may, at least two days before the scheduled time of the meeting, deliver to the clerk of the court one written request to reschedule the time for the meeting and the clerk shall arrange a new meeting time to take place within 30 days of the time scheduled in the notice under subsection (3).

Notice of rescheduled meeting time

(5) Where a meeting time is rescheduled under subsection (4), the clerk of the court shall, as soon as is practicable, give notice to the defendant and the prosecutor of the rescheduled time and the place of their meeting.

Meeting by electronic method

(6) The defendant and the prosecutor may, if unable to attend in person because of remoteness, attend their meeting by electronic method in accordance with section 83.1.

Agreement on plea of guilty and submissions

(7) At their meeting, the defendant and the prosecutor may agree that,
(a) the defendant will enter a guilty plea to the offence or a substituted offence; and
(b) the defendant and the prosecutor will make submissions as to penalty, including an extension of time for payment.

Appearance before justice

(8) If an agreement is reached under subsection (7), the defendant shall, as directed by the prosecutor,
(a) appear with the prosecutor before a justice sitting in court and orally enter the plea and make submissions; or
(b) appear without the prosecutor before a justice sitting in court within 10 days, enter the plea orally and make the submissions in the form determined by the regulations.

Conviction

(9) Upon receiving the plea and submissions under subsection (8), the justice may,
(a) require the prosecutor to appear and speak to the submissions, if the submissions were submitted under clause (8)(b); and

(b) enter a conviction and impose the set fine or such other fine as is permitted by law in respect of the offence for which the plea was entered.

If no justice available

(10) If no justice is available after the meeting to conduct the proceeding under clause (8)(a), the clerk of the court shall, as soon as practicable, give notice to the defendant and the prosecutor of the time and place for their joint appearance before a justice.

Notice of trial

(11) The clerk of the court shall, as soon as is practicable, give notice to the defendant and the prosecutor of the time and place of the trial if,
(a) an agreement is not reached under subsection (7); or
(b) the justice does not accept the guilty plea and refers the matter to trial.

Rescheduling time of trial

(12) The clerk of the court may, for administrative reasons, reschedule the time of the trial by giving a revised notice to the defendant and the prosecutor within 21 days of giving the notice referred to subsection (11).

Proposed Amendment — 5.1

Early resolution meeting procedure

5.1 (1) This section applies where the offence notice indicates that an option of an early resolution meeting with the prosecutor is available.

Request

(2) Instead of filing the notice of intention to appear, a defendant may request an early resolution meeting with the prosecutor to discuss the resolution of the offence by delivering that request to the court office, by mail or in any other additional manner specified on the offence notice, within 15 days after being served with the offence notice.

Types of early resolution meetings

(3) The defendant may request that the early resolution meeting be conducted,
(a) in person;
(b) in real time by electronic method in accordance with section 83.1; or
(c) through the exchange of written electronic communications in accordance with the regulations, if the offence notice indicates that this option is available.

Written electronic meeting

(4) If the defendant requests an early resolution meeting through the exchange of written electronic communications, the defendant, the prosecutor and the clerk shall comply with the procedure set out in the regulations instead of the procedure set out in subsections (5) to (7).

Notice

(5) If a defendant requests an early resolution meeting described in clause (3)(a) or (b), the clerk of the court shall, as soon as is practicable, give notice to the defendant and the prosecutor of the time and, as applicable, the place or method of their meeting.

Rescheduling of meeting time

(6) If the time for the meeting is not suitable for the defendant, he or she may, at least two days before the scheduled time of the meeting, deliver to the clerk of the court one written request to reschedule the time for the meeting, and the clerk shall arrange a new meeting time to take place within 30 days after the time scheduled in the notice.

Notice of rescheduled meeting time

(7) If a meeting time is rescheduled, the clerk of the court shall, as soon as is practicable, give notice to the defendant and the prosecutor of the rescheduled time and, as applicable, the place or method of their meeting.

Transition

(8) The following rules apply to defendants who were issued an offence notice that requires the notice of intention to appear to be filed in person before the day section 3 of Schedule 35 to the Stronger, Fairer Ontario Act (Budget Measures), 2017 came into force:

1. If the defendant did not meet with the prosecutor in accordance with this section as it read before those amendments came into force, the offence notice is deemed to indicate that an option of an early resolution meeting with the prosecutor is available and the defendant may request an early resolution meeting in accordance with this section.

2. If the defendant met with the prosecutor in accordance with this section as it read before those amendments came into force, their meeting and any agreement made at their meeting shall be dealt with in accordance with this Act as it read at that time.

(9) [Repealed 2017, c. 34, Sched. 35, s. 3. Not in force at date of publication.]

(10) [Repealed 2017, c. 34, Sched. 35, s. 3. Not in force at date of publication.]

(11) [Repealed 2017, c. 34, Sched. 35, s. 3. Not in force at date of publication.]

(12) [Repealed 2017, c. 34, Sched. 35, s. 3. Not in force at date of publication.]

2017, c. 34, Sched. 35, s. 3 [Not in force at date of publication.]

1993, c. 31, s. 1(3); 2006, c. 21, Sched. C, s. 131(3); 2009, c. 33, Sched. 4, s.
1(6)

5.1.1 [Repealed 2009, c. 33, Sched. 4, s. 1(8).]

5.2 [Repealed 2009, c. 33, Sched. 4, s. 1(9).]

Proposed Amendment — 5.2

Early resolution meeting agreements

5.2 (1) A defendant and prosecutor who participate in an early resolution
meeting under section 5.1 may agree that,

(a) the defendant will plead guilty to the offence, a substituted offence or a
substituted allegation related to the offence and,

(i) the defendant will pay the set fine and all applicable costs and
surcharges fixed by the regulations within 15 days, or such other time as
the defendant and prosecutor may agree to, after the conviction date that
will be recorded in accordance with subsection 5.3(4), or

(ii) submissions will be made as to the amount of the fine, the time to pay
the fine, or both; or

(b) the prosecutor will withdraw the charge.

Withdrawal of charge

(2) If the prosecutor agrees to withdraw the charge, he or she shall indicate that
the charge has been withdrawn on the agreement form prescribed under section 13
and file it with the clerk of the court as soon as is practicable.

2017, c. 34, Sched. 35, s. 3 [Not in force at date of publication.]

Proposed Addition — 5.3-5.5

Agreement on plea of guilty, no submissions

5.3 (1) If an agreement described in subclause 5.2(1)(a)(i) is reached, the
defendant shall sign the agreement form prescribed under section 13 and
provide it to the prosecutor, who shall file the form with the clerk of the
court within three days after receiving it.

Failure to file

(2) If the prosecutor does not file a signed agreement form within three days
after receiving it as required by subsection (1), the charge is deemed to be
withdrawn.

Recording of conviction

(3) Subject to an abandonment of the agreement under subsection (7), a clerk of the court who receives a signed agreement form under subsection (1) shall record the conviction in accordance with the agreement as soon as is practicable.

Conviction date

(4) The clerk of the court shall record the conviction date as the earlier of the following days:
1. The day that is 15 days after the day the defendant signed the agreement.
2. The day the defendant pays the set fine and all applicable costs and surcharges.
3. The day the defendant makes the initial payment set out in the agreement.

Fine imposed

(5) The fine is deemed to be imposed as of the conviction date.

Notice

(6) If the defendant has not paid the set fine and all applicable costs and surcharges by the conviction date, the clerk of the court shall give the defendant notice of the fine and its due date and of the defendant's right to make an application for an extension of the time for payment under section 66.0.1.

Abandonment of agreement

(7) The defendant may abandon the agreement within 15 days after the day he or she signed the agreement, if he or she has not made a payment referred to in paragraph 2 or 3 of subsection (4), by filing a notice of intention to abandon an early resolution agreement and appear at trial in the form prescribed under section 13 with the clerk of the court, and in such a case the clerk of the court shall, as soon as is practicable, give notice to the defendant and the prosecutor of the time and place of the trial.

2017, c. 34, Sched. 35, s. 3 [Not in force at date of publication.]

Agreement on plea of guilty, submissions

5.4 (1) If an agreement described in subclause 5.2(1)(a)(ii) is reached, the defendant shall sign the agreement form prescribed under section 13 and, as directed by the prosecutor,
(a) immediately appear with the prosecutor before a justice sitting in court and orally enter the plea and make submissions;
(b) appear with the prosecutor before a justice sitting in court within 10 days to orally enter the plea and make submissions; or
(c) appear without the prosecutor before a justice sitting in court within 10 days, enter the plea orally and make the submissions in the form determined by the regulations.

If proceeding not immediate

(2) If the prosecutor does not direct the defendant to immediately appear before a justice or if no justice is available to immediately conduct the proceeding,
> (a) the prosecutor shall indicate on the agreement form prescribed under section 13 that an appearance before a justice is required and provide it to the clerk of the court; and
> (b) the clerk of the court shall, as soon as is practicable, give notice to the defendant and the prosecutor of the time and place for the proceeding.

Conviction

(3) On receiving the plea and submissions under this section, the justice may,
> (a) at the justice's discretion, require the prosecutor to appear and speak to the submissions if the defendant appears without the prosecutor; and
> (b) enter a conviction and impose the set fine or such other fine as is permitted by law in respect of the offence, and if applicable the allegation related to the offence, for which the plea was entered.
>
> 2017, c. 34, Sched. 35, s. 3 [Not in force at date of publication.]

Notice of trial

5.5 (1) The clerk of the court shall, as soon as is practicable, give notice to the defendant and the prosecutor of the time and place of the trial if,
> (a) an agreement is not reached at the early resolution meeting; or
> (b) the justice does not accept a guilty plea under section 5.4 and sets the matter to trial.

Rescheduling time of trial

(2) The clerk of the court may, for administrative reasons, reschedule the time of a trial under subsection (1) by giving a revised notice to the defendant and the prosecutor within 21 days after giving them notice of the trial.

> 2017, c. 34, Sched. 35, s. 3 [Not in force at date of publication.]

6. [Repealed 2009, c. 33, Sched. 4, s. 1(10).]

Plea of guilty with submissions

7. (1) A defendant who does not have the option of meeting with the prosecutor under section 5.1 and does not wish to dispute the charge in the offence notice, but wishes to make submissions as to penalty, including an extension of time for payment, may attend at the time and place specified in the notice and may appear before a justice sitting in court for the purpose of pleading guilty to the offence and making submissions as to penalty, and the justice may enter a conviction and impose the set fine or such lesser fine as is permitted by law.

Proposed Amendment — 7(1)

Plea of guilty with submissions

(1) A defendant who does not have the option of an early resolution meeting under section 5.1 and does not wish to dispute the charge in the offence notice, but wishes to make submissions as to penalty, including an extension of time for payment, may attend at the time and place specified in the notice and may appear before a justice sitting in court for the purpose of pleading guilty to the offence and making submissions as to penalty, and the justice may enter a conviction and impose the set fine or such lesser fine as is permitted by law.
2017, c. 34, Sched. 35, s. 4 [Not in force at date of publication.]

Submissions under oath

(2) The justice may require submissions under subsection (1) to be made under oath, orally or by affidavit.
2009, c. 33, Sched. 4, s. 1(11)

Payment out of court

8. (1) A defendant who does not wish to dispute the charge in the offence notice may, in the manner indicated on the offence notice, pay the set fine and all applicable costs and surcharges fixed by the regulations.

Effect of payment

(2) Acceptance by the court office of payment under subsection (1) constitutes,
(a) a plea of guilty by the defendant;
(b) conviction of the defendant for the offence; and
(c) imposition of a fine in the amount of the set fine for the offence.
2009, c. 33, Sched. 4, s. 1(12)

Deemed not to dispute charge

9. (1) A defendant is deemed to not wish to dispute the charge where,
(a) at least 15 days have elapsed after the defendant was served with the offence notice and the defendant did not give notice of intention to appear under section 5, did not request a meeting with the prosecutor in accordance with section 5.1 and did not plead guilty under section 7 or 8;

(b) the defendant requested a meeting with the prosecutor in accordance with section 5.1 but did not attend the scheduled meeting with the prosecutor; or

(c) the defendant reached an agreement with the prosecutor under subsection 5.1(7) but did not appear at a sentencing hearing with a justice under subsection 5.1(8).

Action by justice

(2) Where a defendant is deemed to not wish to dispute the charge, a justice shall examine the certificate of offence and shall,

(a) where the certificate of offence is complete and regular on its face, enter a conviction in the defendant's absence and without a hearing and impose the set fine for the offence; or

(b) where the certificate of offence is not complete and regular on its face, quash the proceeding.

Conviction without proof of by-law

(3) Where the offence is in respect of an offence under a by-law of a municipality, the justice shall enter a conviction under clause (2)(a) without proof of the by-law that creates the offence if the certificate of offence is complete and regular on its face.

Proposed Amendment — 9

Deemed not to dispute charge

9. (1) A defendant is deemed to not wish to dispute the charge where,

(a) at least 15 days have elapsed after the defendant was served with the offence notice and the defendant did not give notice of intention to appear under section 5, did not request an early resolution meeting under section 5.1 and did not plead guilty under section 7 or 8;

(b) the defendant requested an early resolution meeting described in clause 5.1(3)(a) or (b) but did not attend the meeting; or

(c) the defendant reached an agreement with the prosecutor in an early resolution meeting under subclause 5.2(1)(a)(ii), but did not appear before a justice as required under section 5.4.

Examination of certificate of offence by clerk

(2) If a defendant is deemed to not wish to dispute the charge in accordance with clause (1)(a) or (b), the clerk of the court shall examine the certificate of offence and,

(a) if it is not defective, as determined by the regulations, enter a conviction in the defendant's absence and without a hearing and impose the set fine for the offence; or

(b) if it is defective, as determined by the regulations, quash the proceeding.

Application to justice

(3) A defendant who is convicted under subsection (2) may, within 15 days after becoming aware of the conviction, make an application to a justice in the prescribed form to strike out the conviction.

Same

(4) On application under subsection (3), the justice shall strike out the conviction if satisfied that the certificate of offence is defective, as determined by the regulations, or is otherwise not complete and regular on its face.

Examination of certificate of offence by justice

(5) If a defendant is deemed to not wish to dispute the charge in accordance with clause (1)(c), the justice shall examine the certificate of offence and,
(a) if it is not defective, as determined by the regulations, and is complete and regular on its face, enter a conviction in the defendant's absence and without a hearing and impose the set fine for the offence; or
(b) if it is defective, as determined by the regulations, or is otherwise not complete and regular on its face, quash the proceeding.

Proof of municipal by-law not required

(6) If the offence is in respect of an offence under a by-law of a municipality, proof of the by-law that creates the offence is not required to enter a conviction and impose a set fine under this section.

2017, c. 34, Sched. 35, s. 5 [Not in force at date of publication.]

2009, c. 33, Sched. 4, s. 1(13)

Failure to appear at trial

9.1 (1) A defendant is deemed to not wish to dispute the charge where the defendant has been issued a notice of the time and place of trial and fails to appear at the time and place appointed for the trial.

Examination by justice

(2) If subsection (1) applies, section 54 does not apply, and a justice shall examine the certificate of offence and shall without a hearing enter a conviction in the defendant's absence and impose the set fine for the offence if the certificate is complete and regular on its face.

Quashing proceeding

(3) The justice shall quash the proceeding if he or she is not able to enter a conviction.

1993, c. 31, s. 1(3); 2009, c. 33, Sched. 4, s. 1(14)

Signature on notice

10. A signature on an offence notice or notice of intention to appear purporting to be that of the defendant is proof, in the absence of evidence to the contrary, that it is the signature of the defendant.

1993, c. 31, s. 1(4)

Reopening—Application to strike out conviction

11. (1) A defendant who was convicted without a hearing may, within 15 days of becoming aware of the conviction, apply to a justice to strike out the conviction.

Striking out the conviction

(2) Upon application under subsection (1), a justice shall strike out a conviction if satisfied by affidavit of the defendant that, through no fault of the defendant, the defendant was unable to appear for a hearing or for a meeting under section 5.1 or the defendant did not receive delivery of a notice or document relating to the offence.

If conviction struck out

(3) If the justice strikes out the conviction, the justice shall,
(a) proceed under section 7, if the offence notice does not require the notice of intention to appear to be filed in person and the defendant wishes to proceed under that section;
(b) direct the clerk of the court to give notice to the defendant and the prosecutor of the time and place of their meeting under subsection 5.1(3), if the offence notice requires the notice of intention to appear to be filed in person and the defendant wishes to proceed under that section; or
(c) direct the clerk of the court to give notice to the defendant and the prosecutor of the time and place of the trial.

Rescheduling time of trial

(4) The clerk of the court may, for administrative reasons, reschedule the time of the trial by giving a revised notice to the defendant and the prosecutor within 21 days of giving the notice referred to clause (3)(c).

(4.1) [Repealed 2009, c. 33, Sched. 4, s. 1(16).]

Certificate

(5) A justice who strikes out a conviction under subsection (2) shall give the defendant a certificate of the fact in the prescribed form.

Proposed Amendment — 11

Reopening—Application to strike out conviction

11. (1) A defendant who was convicted without a hearing may, within 15 days after becoming aware of the conviction, make an application to have the conviction struck out by completing the prescribed form and filing it in the office of the court.

Striking out the conviction

(2) On application under subsection (1), the clerk of the court shall strike out the conviction if satisfied by affidavit of the defendant that, through no fault of the defendant, he or she,

    (a) was unable to attend an early resolution meeting described in clause 5.1(3)(a) or (b);

    (b) was unable to appear for a hearing; or

    (c) did not receive delivery of a notice or document relating to the offence.

Review by justice

(3) If the clerk of the court does not strike out the conviction, he or she shall forward the application to a justice for review, who shall strike out the conviction if he or she determines that the requirements in subsection (2) have been met.

Notice if conviction struck out

(4) If a conviction is struck out under subsection (2) or (3), the clerk of the court shall give notice,

    (a) to the defendant of the time and place to appear under section 7, if the offence notice does not indicate that the option of an early resolution meeting under section 5.1 is available and the defendant wishes to proceed under section 7;

    (b) to the defendant and the prosecutor of the time and, as applicable, the place or method of their early resolution meeting under section 5.1, if the offence notice indicates that the option of an early resolution meeting under that section is available and the defendant wishes to proceed under that section; or

    (c) to the defendant and the prosecutor of the time and place of the trial.

Rescheduling time of trial

(5) The clerk of the court may, for administrative reasons, reschedule the time of the trial by giving a revised notice to the defendant and the prosecutor within 21 days after giving the notice referred to in clause (4)(c).

Certificate

(6) A justice or a clerk of the court who strikes out a conviction under this section shall give the defendant a certificate of the fact in the prescribed form.

Transition

(7) Despite subsection (4), a defendant is eligible to have an early resolution meeting under section 5.1 even if the offence notice does not indicate that the option of an early resolution meeting under that section is available if,

(a) the offence notice was issued before the day section 3 of Schedule 35 to the *Stronger, Fairer Ontario Act (Budget Measures), 2017* came into force; and

(b) the offence notice requires the notice of intention to appear to be filed in person.

2017, c. 34, Sched. 35, s. 6 [Not in force at date of publication.]

1993, c. 31, s. 1(5); 2009, c. 33, Sched. 4, s. 1(15), (16)

Error by municipality

11.1 (1) A municipality or other body may apply to a justice requesting that a conviction be struck out if the defendant was convicted because of an error made by the municipality or other body.

Striking out conviction

(2) On an application by a municipality or other body, if a justice is satisfied that an error was made, the justice shall strike out the conviction.

Notice to defendant

(3) If the justice strikes out the conviction, the municipality or other body shall notify the defendant of that fact.

2009, c. 33, Sched. 4, s. 1(17)

Penalty

12. (1) Where the penalty prescribed for an offence includes a fine of more than $1,000 or imprisonment and a proceeding is commenced under this Part, the provision for fine or imprisonment does not apply and in lieu thereof the offence is punishable by a fine of not more than the maximum fine prescribed for the offence or $1,000, whichever is the lesser.

Transitional

(1.1) Subsection (1) applies only to an offence committed on or after the day subsection 1(18) of Schedule 4 to the *Good Government Act, 2009* comes into force.

Other consequences of conviction

(2) Where a person is convicted of an offence in a proceeding initiated by an offence notice,

(a) a provision in or under any other Act that provides for an action or result following upon a conviction of an offence does not apply to the conviction, except,

(i) for the purpose of carrying out the sentence imposed,

(ii) for the purpose of recording and proving the conviction,

(iii) for the purposes of giving effect to any action or result provided for under the Highway Traffic Act, and

(iv) [Repealed 2004, c. 22, s. 7(2).]

(v) for the purposes of section 22 of the *Smoke-Free Ontario Act, 2017*; and

(b) any thing seized in connection with the offence after the service of the offence notice is not liable to forfeiture.

1994, c. 10, s. 23; 2004, c. 22, s. 7; 2005, c. 18, s. 18; 2009, c. 33, Sched. 4, s. 1(18), (19); 2017, c. 26, Sched. 3, s. 27

Regulations

13. (1) The Lieutenant Governor in Council may make regulations,

(a) [Repealed 2011, c. 1, Sched. 1, s. 7(1).]

(b) authorizing the use in a form prescribed under clause (1.1)(a) of any word or expression to designate an offence;

(c) [Repealed 2011, c. 1, Sched. 1, s. 7(3).]

(d) [Repealed 2009, c. 33, Sched. 4, s. 1(20).]

Same, Attorney General

(1.1) The Attorney General may make regulations,

(a) prescribing the form of certificates of offence, offence notices and summonses and such other forms as are considered necessary under this Part;

Proposed Amendment — 13(1.1)(a)

(a) prescribing the forms that are considered necessary under this Part;
2017, c. 34, Sched. 35, s. 7(1) [Not in force at date of publication.]

(b) respecting any matter that is considered necessary to provide for the use of the forms under this Part.

Proposed Addition — 13(1.1)(c), (d)

(c) establishing and governing a procedure for early resolution meetings under clause 5.1(3)(c) conducted through the exchange of written electronic communications, including, without limiting the generality of the foregoing,

(i) requiring the meetings to be conducted using a prescribed method of exchanging written electronic communications,

(ii) prescribing methods of exchanging written electronic communications that cannot be used to conduct the meetings,

(iii) governing the provision of notice to the defendant and prosecutor,

(iv) governing the process for withdrawing from the meeting and the consequences of such a withdrawal,

(v) governing the timelines and deadlines that must be met by the defendant and prosecutor or the process for determining those timelines and deadlines,

(vi) governing the procedural consequences for failing to meet a timeline or deadline, which may include requiring the clerk of the court to schedule a trial for the offence,

(vii) varying or modifying the application of sections 5.2, 5.3, 5.4 and 5.5 to these meetings, and

(viii) governing transitional matters that may arise in relation to these meetings;

(d) prescribing the characteristics that make a certificate of offence defective for the purposes of section 9.

2017, c. 34, Sched. 35, s. 7(2) [Not in force at date of publication.]

Sufficiency of abbreviated wording

(2) The use on a form prescribed under clause (1.1)(a) of any word or expression authorized by the regulations to designate an offence is sufficient for all purposes to describe the offence designated by such word or expression.

Idem

(3) Where the regulations do not authorize the use of a word or expression to describe an offence in a form prescribed under clause (1.1)(a), the offence may be described in accordance with section 25.

1993, c. 31, s. 1(2), (3), (6); 2009, c. 33, Sched. 4, s. 1(20); 2011, c. 1, Sched. 1, s. 7(1)-(5)

PART II

COMMENCEMENT OF PROCEEDINGS FOR PARKING INFRACTIONS

Definition

14. In this Part, **"parking infraction"** means any unlawful parking, standing or stopping of a vehicle that constitutes an offence.

1992, c. 20, s. 1(1)

Proceeding, parking infraction

14.1 In addition to the procedure set out in Part III for commencing a proceeding by laying an information, a proceeding in respect of a parking infraction may be commenced in accordance with this Part.

1992, c. 20, s. 1(1)

Notice issued

15. (1) A provincial offences officer who believes from his or her personal knowledge that one or more persons have committed a parking infraction may issue,

(a) a certificate of parking infraction certifying that a parking infraction has been committed; and

(b) a parking infraction notice indicating the set fine for the infraction.

Idem

(2) The provincial offences officer shall complete and sign the certificate and notice in the form prescribed under section 20.

Municipal by-laws

(3) If the alleged infraction is under a by-law of a municipality, it is not necessary to include a reference to the number of the by-law on the certificate or notice.

Service on owner

(4) The issuing provincial offences officer may serve the parking infraction notice on the owner of the vehicle identified in the notice,

(a) by affixing it to the vehicle in a conspicuous place at the time of the alleged infraction; or

(b) by delivering it personally to the person having care and control of the vehicle at the time of the alleged infraction.

Service on operator

(5) The issuing provincial offences officer may serve the parking infraction notice on the operator of a vehicle by delivering it to the operator personally at the time of the alleged infraction.

Certificate of service

(6) The issuing provincial offences officer shall certify on the certificate of parking infraction that he or she served the parking infraction notice on the person charged and the date and method of service.

Certificate as evidence

(7) If it appears that the provincial offences officer who issued a certificate of parking infraction has certified service of the parking infraction notice and signed the certificate, the certificate shall be received in evidence and is proof of service unless there is evidence to the contrary.

1992, c. 20, s. 1(1)

Payment out of court

16. A defendant who does not wish to dispute the charge may deliver the notice and amount of the set fine to the place shown on the notice.

1992, c. 20, s. 1(1)

Intention to appear

17. (1) A defendant who is served with a parking infraction notice may give notice of intention to appear in court for the purpose of entering a plea and having a trial of the matter by so indicating on the parking infraction notice and delivering the notice to the place specified in it.

Proceeding commenced

(2) If a defendant gives notice of an intention to appear, a proceeding may be commenced in respect of the charge if it is done within seventy-five days after the day on which the alleged infraction occurred.

Idem

(3) The proceeding shall be commenced by filing in the office of the court,
(a) the certificate of parking infraction; and
(b) if the parking infraction is alleged against the defendant as owner of a vehicle, evidence of the ownership of the vehicle.

Notice of trial

(4) As soon as practicable after the proceeding is commenced, the clerk of the court or a person designated by the regulations shall give notice to the defendant and prosecutor of the time and place of the trial.

Rescheduling time of trial

(4.1) The clerk of the court may, for administrative reasons, reschedule the time of the trial by giving a revised notice to the defendant and the prosecutor within 21 days of giving the notice referred to subsection (4).

Certificate not invalid without by-law number

(5) A certificate of parking infraction issued for an infraction under a by-law of a municipality is not insufficient or irregular by reason only that it does not identify the by-law that creates the offence if the notice of trial given to the defendant identifies the by-law.

 1992, c. 20, s. 1(1); 1993, c. 31, s. 1(7), (8); 2009, c. 33, Sched. 4, s. 1(21)

Application

17.1 (1) This section applies where the parking infraction notice requires the notice of intention to appear to be filed in person at a place specified in the parking infraction notice.

Subss. 17(1), (3) and (4) inapplicable

(2) Subsections 17(1), (3) and (4) do not apply in a municipality in which this section applies.

Filing

(3) A defendant who is served with a parking infraction notice may give notice of intention to appear in court for the purpose of entering a plea and having a trial of the matter by attending in person or by representative at the place specified in the parking infraction notice at the time or times specified in the parking infraction notice and filing a notice of intention to appear with a person designated by the regulations.

Notice

(4) The notice of intention to appear shall be in the form prescribed under section 20.

Proceeding commenced

(5) The proceeding shall be commenced by filing the certificate of parking infraction in the office of the clerk of the court or the person designated by the regulations.

Notice of trial

(6) As soon as practicable after the proceeding is commenced, the clerk of the court or the person designated by the regulations shall give notice to the defendant and the prosecutor of the time and place of the trial.

Rescheduling time of trial

(6.1) The clerk of the court may, for administrative reasons, reschedule the time of the trial by giving a revised notice to the defendant and the prosecutor within 21 days of giving the notice referred to subsection (6).

Evidence required at trial

(7) The court shall not convict the defendant unless the following are presented at the trial:

1. If the parking infraction is alleged against the defendant as owner of a vehicle, evidence of the ownership of the vehicle.

2. A copy of the notice of trial, with the certificate of the person who issued the notice under subsection (6), stating that the notice was given to the defendant and to the prosecutor and stating the date on which this was done.

3. The certificate of parking infraction.

1993, c. 31, s. 1(9); 1994, c. 27, s. 52(1), (2); 2006, c. 21, Sched. C, s. 131(3); 2009, c. 33, Sched. 4, s. 1(22), (23)

Failure to respond

18. (1) The person designated by the regulations may give the defendant a notice of impending conviction if,

(a) at least fifteen days and no more than thirty-five days have elapsed since the alleged infraction occurred;

(b) the defendant has not paid the fine; and

(c) a notice of intention to appear has not been received.

Form of notice

(2) The notice shall be in the form prescribed under section 20.

Contents of notice

(3) The notice shall,

(a) indicate the set fine for the infraction; and

(b) indicate that a conviction will be registered against the defendant unless the defendant pays the set fine or gives notice of an intention to appear in court for the purpose of entering a plea and having a trial of the matter.

1992, c. 20, s. 1(1); 1993, c. 31, s. 1(10), (11)

Intention to appear

18.1 (1) A defendant who receives a notice of impending conviction may give notice of intention to appear in court for the purpose of entering a plea and having a trial of the matter by so indicating on the notice of impending conviction and delivering the notice to the place specified in it.

Proceeding commenced

(2) If a defendant gives notice of an intention to appear after a notice of impending conviction has been given, a proceeding may be commenced in respect

of the charge if it is done within seventy-five days after the day on which the alleged infraction occurred.

Idem

(3) The proceeding shall be commenced by filing in the office of the court,
(a) the certificate of parking infraction; and
(b) if the parking infraction is alleged against the defendant as owner of a vehicle, evidence of the ownership of the vehicle.

Notice of trial

(4) As soon as practicable after the proceeding is commenced, the clerk of the court or a person designated by the regulations shall give notice to the defendant and prosecutor of the time and place of the trial.

Rescheduling time of trial

(5) The clerk of the court may, for administrative reasons, reschedule the time of the trial by giving a revised notice to the defendant and the prosecutor within 21 days of giving the notice referred to subsection (4).
1992, c. 20, s. 1(1); 1993, c. 31, s. 1(12), (13); 2009, c. 33, Sched. 4, s. 1(24)

Application

18.1.1 (1) This section applies where the notice of impending conviction requires the notice of intention to appear to be filed in person at a place specified in the notice of impending conviction.

Subss. 18.1(1), (3) and (4) inapplicable

(2) Subsections 18.1(1), (3) and (4) do not apply in a municipality in which this section applies.

Subss. 17.1(5), (6) and (7) applicable

(2.1) Subsections 17.1(5), (6) and (7) apply to a proceeding begun under this section.

Filing notice of intention to appear

(3) A defendant who receives a notice of impending conviction may give notice of intention to appear in court for the purpose of entering a plea and having a trial of the matter by attending in person or by representative at the place specified in the notice of impending conviction at the time or times specified in the notice of impending conviction and filing a notice of intention to appear with a person designated by the regulations.

Form of notice

(4) The notice of intention to appear shall be in the form prescribed under section 20.

1993, c. 31, s. 1(14); 1994, c. 27, s. 52(3); 2006, c. 21, Sched. C, s. 131(3); 2009, c. 33, Sched. 4, s. 1(25)

18.1.2 [Repealed 2009, c. 33, Sched. 4, s. 1(26).]

No response to impending conviction notice

18.2 (1) A defendant who has been given a notice of impending conviction shall be deemed not to dispute the charge if fifteen days have elapsed since the defendant was given the notice, the fine has not been paid and a notice of intention to appear has not been received.

Request for conviction

(1.1) If subsection (1) applies, the person designated by the regulations may prepare and sign a certificate requesting a conviction in the form prescribed under section 20.

Idem

(2) The certificate requesting a conviction shall state,

(a) that the certificate of parking infraction is complete and regular on its face;

(b) if the defendant is liable as owner, that the person is satisfied that the defendant is the owner;

(c) that there is valid legal authority for charging the defendant with the parking infraction;

(d) that the defendant was given a notice of impending conviction at least fifteen days before the certificate requesting a conviction is filed;

(e) that the alleged infraction occurred less than seventy-five days before the certificate requesting a conviction is filed; and

(f) the prescribed information.

Idem

(3) If the certificate of parking infraction was issued for an infraction under a by-law of a municipality, the certificate requesting a conviction shall also state,

(a) that payment of the set fine has not been made; and

(b) that the defendant has not given notice of intention to appear in court for the purpose of entering a plea and having a trial of the matter.

Idem

(4) A certificate requesting a conviction purporting to be signed by the person authorized to prepare it shall be received in evidence and is proof, in the absence of evidence to the contrary, of the facts contained in it.

Proceeding commenced

(5) A proceeding may be commenced in respect of the charge by filing the certificate requesting a conviction in the office of the court, but only if the certificate is filed within seventy-five days after the alleged infraction occurred.

Recording of conviction

(6) Upon receiving a certificate requesting a conviction, the clerk of the court shall record a conviction and the defendant is then liable to pay the set fine for the offence.

1992, c. 20, s. 1(1); 1993, c. 31, s. 1(15), (16), (17)

Application where ticket defective

18.3 (1) A defendant who is convicted of a parking infraction under section 18.2 may, within fifteen days after becoming aware of the conviction, apply to a justice requesting that the conviction be struck out for the reason that the parking infraction notice is defective on its face.

Idem

(2) On an application by the defendant, if a justice is satisfied that the parking infraction notice is defective on its face, the justice shall strike out the conviction and shall order that the municipality or other body that issued the certificate requesting a conviction pay $25 in costs to the defendant.

1992, c. 20, s. 1(1)

Failure to appear at trial

18.4 (1) A defendant is deemed to not wish to dispute the charge where the defendant has been issued a notice of the time and place of trial and fails to appear at the time and place appointed for the trial.

Examination by justice

(2) If subsection (1) applies, section 54 does not apply, and a justice shall examine the certificate of parking infraction and shall without a hearing enter a conviction in the defendant's absence and impose the set fine for the offence if the certificate is complete and regular on its face.

Owner liability

(3) Despite subsection (2), if the defendant is alleged to have committed the parking infraction as owner of the vehicle involved in the infraction, the justice shall not enter a conviction and impose the set fine unless he or she is satisfied that the defendant is the owner of the vehicle.

Entering conviction

(4) The justice shall enter a conviction with respect to a parking infraction under a by-law of a municipality without proof of the by-law that creates the offence if the justice is satisfied that the other criteria for entering a conviction have been met.

Quashing proceeding

(5) The justice shall quash the proceeding if he or she is not able to enter a conviction.

1992, c. 20, s. 1(1); 1993, c. 31, s. 1(18); 2009, c. 33, Sched. 4, s. 1(27)

Error by municipality

18.5 (1) A municipality or other body may apply to a justice requesting that a conviction respecting a parking infraction be struck out if the defendant was convicted because of an error made by the municipality or other body.

Idem

(2) On an application by a municipality or other body, if a justice is satisfied that an error was made, the justice shall strike out the conviction.

Idem

(3) If the justice strikes out the conviction, the municipality or other body shall notify the defendant of that fact.

1992, c. 20, s. 1(1)

Authority to collect parking fines

18.6 (1) A municipality may collect the fines levied for convictions respecting parking infractions under its by-laws if the municipality,

(a) enters into an agreement with the Attorney General to authorize it; or

(b) enters into a transfer agreement under Part X.

Agreement

(1.1) The Attorney General and a municipality may enter into an agreement for the purpose of clause (1)(a).

Notice to municipality

(2) If a conviction is entered respecting a parking infraction under a by-law of a municipality to which subsection (1) applies, the clerk of the court shall give notice of the conviction to the clerk of the municipality.

Notice of fine

(3) If the clerk of a municipality receives notice of a conviction, the clerk of the municipality or the person designated by the clerk shall give notice to the person

against whom the conviction is entered, in the form prescribed under section 20, setting out the date and place of the infraction, the date of the conviction and the amount of the fine.

If default

(4) If the fine is in default, the clerk of the municipality may send notice to the person designated by the regulations certifying that it is in default.

Idem

(5) If a conviction is entered respecting a parking infraction and the parking infraction is not under a by-law of a municipality to which subsection (1) applies, the clerk of the court shall give notice to the person against whom the conviction is entered of the date and place of the infraction, the date of the conviction and the amount of the fine.

1992, c. 20, s. 1(1); 2009, c. 33, Sched. 4, s. 1(28)

Reopening—Application to strike out conviction

19. (1) A defendant who was convicted of a parking infraction without a hearing may, within 15 days of becoming aware of the conviction, apply to a justice to strike out the conviction.

Striking out the conviction

(2) Upon application under subsection (1), a justice shall strike out a conviction if satisfied by affidavit of the defendant or otherwise that, through no fault of the defendant, the defendant was unable to appear for a hearing or the defendant never received any notice or document relating to the parking infraction.

If conviction struck out

(3) If the justice strikes out the conviction, the justice shall,
(a) if the defendant enters a plea of guilty, accept the plea and impose the set fine; or
(b) direct the clerk of the court to give notice to the defendant and the prosecutor of the time and place of the trial.

Rescheduling time of trial

(4) The clerk of the court may, for administrative reasons, reschedule the time of the trial by giving a revised notice to the defendant and the prosecutor within 21 days of giving the notice referred to in clause (3)(b).

1992, c. 20, s. 1(1); 1993, c. 31, s. 1(19); 2009, c. 33, Sched. 4, s. 1(29)

Regulations

20. (1) The Lieutenant Governor in Council may make regulations,

(a) [Repealed 2011, c. 1, Sched. 1, s. 7(6).]

(b) authorizing the use in a form under this Part of any word or expression to designate a parking infraction;

(c) [Repealed 2011, c. 1, Sched. 1, s. 7(6).]

(d) [Repealed 2011, c. 1, Sched. 1, s. 7(6).]

(e) designating the persons or classes of persons who are required to prepare a notice of impending conviction or a certificate requesting a conviction for municipalities and for other bodies on whose behalf parking infraction notices are issued;

(e.1) designating a person or class of persons for the purposes of subsection 17(4), 17.1(3), 17.1(5), 17.1(6), 18.1(4) or 18.1.1(3);

(f) [Repealed 2015, c. 27, Sched. 1, s. 3(3).]

(g) authorizing Ontario to pay allowances to municipalities and other bodies that issue notices of impending conviction and that collect fines under this Part, providing for the payment of those allowances from the court costs received in connection with the fines levied under this Part and fixing the amount of the allowances;

(h) [Repealed 2009, c. 33, Sched. 4, s. 1(30).]

(i) designating the person to whom a notice certifying that a fine is in default under subsection 18.6(4) is to be sent;

(j) designating municipalities for the purposes of sections 17.1 and 18.1.1.

Same, Attorney General

(1.1) The Attorney General may make regulations,

(a) prescribing the forms that are considered necessary under this Part;

(b) respecting any matter that is considered necessary to provide for the use of the forms under this Part;

(c) prescribing information that is required to be included in a parking infraction notice, a notice of impending conviction or a certificate requesting a conviction;

(d) prescribing the information to be included in a notice certifying that a fine is in default under subsection 18.6(4).

Sufficiency of abbreviations

(2) The use on a form prescribed under clause (1.1)(a) of any word or expression authorized by the regulations to designate a parking infraction is sufficient for all purposes to describe the infraction designated by such word or expression.

Idem

(3) Where the regulations do not authorize the use of a word or expression to describe a parking infraction in a form prescribed under clause (1.1)(a), the offence may be described in accordance with section 25.

1992, c. 20, s. 1(1); 1993, c. 31, s. 1(20), (21); 1994, c. 27, s. 52(4); 2009, c. 33, Sched. 4, s. 1(30); 2011, c. 1, Sched. 1, s. 7(6)-(9); 2015, c. 27, Sched. 1, s. 3(2), (3)

PART III

COMMENCEMENT OF PROCEEDING BY INFORMATION

Commencement of proceeding by information

21. (1) In addition to the procedure set out in Parts I and II for commencing a proceeding by the filing of a certificate, a proceeding in respect of an offence may be commenced by laying an information.

Exception

(2) Where a summons or offence notice has been served under Part I, no proceeding shall be commenced under subsection (1) in respect of the same offence except with the consent of the Attorney General or his or her agent.

Summons before information laid

22. Where a provincial offences officer believes, on reasonable and probable grounds, that an offence has been committed by a person whom the officer finds at or near the place where the offence was committed, he or she may, before an information is laid, serve the person with a summons in the prescribed form.

Information

23. (1) Any person who, on reasonable and probable grounds, believes that one or more persons have committed an offence, may lay an information in the prescribed form and under oath before a justice alleging the offence and the justice shall receive the information.

Multiple defendants

(1.1) For greater certainty, an information laid under subsection (1) may include one or more persons.

Idem

(2) An information may be laid anywhere in Ontario.

2009, c. 33, Sched. 4, s. 1(32)

Procedure on laying of information

24. (1) A justice who receives an information laid under section 23 shall consider the information and, where he or she considers it desirable to do so, hear and consider in the absence of the defendant the allegations of the informant and the evidence of witnesses and,

(a) where he or she considers that a case for so doing is made out,

(i) confirm the summons served under section 22, if any,

(ii) issue a summons in the prescribed form, or

(iii) where the arrest is authorized by statute and where the allegations of the informant or the evidence satisfy the justice on reasonable and probable grounds that it is necessary in the public interest to do so, issue a warrant for the arrest of the defendant; or

(b) where he or she considers that a case for issuing process is not made out,

(i) so endorse the information, and

(ii) where a summons was served under section 22, cancel it and cause the defendant to be so notified.

Summons or warrants in blank

(2) A justice shall not sign a summons or warrant in blank.

Counts

25. (1) Each offence charged in an information shall be set out in a separate count.

Allegation of offence

(2) Each count in an information shall in general apply to a single transaction and shall contain and is sufficient if it contains in substance a statement that the defendant committed an offence therein specified.

Reference to statutory provision

(3) Where in a count an offence is identified but the count fails to set out one or more of the essential elements of the offence, a reference to the provision creating or defining the offence shall be deemed to incorporate all the essential elements of the offence.

Idem

(4) The statement referred to in subsection (2) may be,

(a) in popular language without technical averments or allegations of matters that are not essential to be proved;

(b) in the words of the enactment that describes the offence; or

(c) in words that are sufficient to give to the defendant notice of the offence with which the defendant is charged.

More than one count

(5) Any number of counts for any number of offences may be joined in the same information.

Particulars of count

(6) A count shall contain sufficient detail of the circumstances of the alleged offence to give to the defendant reasonable information with respect to the act or omission to be proved against the defendant and to identify the transaction referred to.

Sufficiency

(7) No count in an information is insufficient by reason of the absence of details where, in the opinion of the court, the count otherwise fulfils the requirements of this section and, without restricting the generality of the foregoing, no count in an information is insufficient by reason only that,

(a) it does not name the person affected by the offence or intended or attempted to be affected;

(b) it does not name the person who owns or has a special property or interest in property mentioned in the count;

(c) it charges an intent in relation to another person without naming or describing the other person;

(d) it does not set out any writing that is the subject of the charge;

(e) it does not set out the words used where words that are alleged to have been used are the subject of the charge;

(f) it does not specify the means by which the alleged offence was committed;

(g) it does not name or describe with precision any person, place, thing or time; or

(h) it does not, where the consent of a person, official or authority is required before proceedings may be instituted for an offence, state that the consent has been obtained.

Idem

(8) A count is not objectionable for the reason only that,

(a) it charges in the alternative several different matters, acts or omissions that are stated in the alternative in an enactment that describes as an offence the matters, acts or omissions charged in the count; or

(b) it is double or multifarious.

Need to negative exception, etc

(9) No exception, exemption, proviso, excuse or qualification prescribed by law is required to be set out or negatived, as the case may be, in an information.

2009, c. 33, Sched. 4, s. 1(33)

Summons

26. (1) A summons issued under section 22 or 24 shall,

(a) be directed to the defendant;

(b) set out briefly the offence in respect of which the defendant is charged; and

(c) require the defendant to attend court at a time and place stated therein and to attend thereafter as required by the court in order to be dealt with according to law.

Service

(2) A summons shall be served by a provincial offences officer by delivering it personally to the person to whom it is directed or if that person cannot conveniently be found, by leaving it for the person at the person's last know or usual place of abode with an inmate thereof who appears to be at least sixteen years of age.

Service outside Ontario

(3) Despite subsection (2), where the person to whom a summons is directed does not reside in Ontario, the summons shall be deemed to have been duly served seven days after it has been sent by registered mail to the person's last known or usual place of abode.

Service on corporation

(4) Service of a summons on a corporation may be effected,

(a) in the case of a municipal corporation by,

(i) delivering the summons personally to the mayor, warden, reeve or other chief officer of the corporation or to the clerk of the corporation, or

(ii) mailing the summons by registered mail to the municipal corporation at an address held out by it to be its address;

(b) in the case of any corporation, other than a municipal corporation, incorporated or continued by or under an Act by,

(i) delivering the summons personally to the manager, secretary or other executive officer of the corporation or person apparently in charge of a branch office of the corporation, or

(ii) mailing the summons by registered mail to the corporation at an address held out by it to be its address;

(c) in the case of corporation not incorporated or continued by or under an Act by,

(i) a method provided under clause (b),

(ii) delivering the summons personally to the corporation's resident agent or agent for service or to any other representative of the corporation in Ontario, or

(iii) mailing the summons by registered mail to a person referred to in subclause (ii) or to an address outside Ontario, including outside Canada, held out by the corporation to be its address.

Date of mailed service

(4.1) A summons served by registered mail under subsection (4) is deemed to have been duly served seven days after the day of mailing.

Substitutional service

(5) A justice, upon motion and upon being satisfied that service cannot be made effectively on a corporation in accordance with subsection (4), may by order authorize another method of service that has a reasonable likelihood of coming to the attention of the corporation.

Proof of service

(6) Service of a summons may be proved by statement under oath or affirmation, written or oral, of the person who made the service.

2009, c. 33, Sched. 4, s. 1(34)

Contents of warrant

27. (1) A warrant issued under section 24 shall,
(a) name or describe the defendant;
(b) set out briefly the offence in respect of which the defendant is charged; and
(c) order that the defendant be forthwith arrested and brought before a justice to be dealt with according to law.

Idem

(2) A warrant issued under section 24 remains in force until it is executed and need not be made returnable at any particular time.

PART IV

TRIAL AND SENTENCING TRIAL

Application of Part

28. This Part applies to a proceeding commenced under this Act.

Territorial jurisdiction

29. (1) Subject to subsection (2), a proceeding in respect of an offence shall be heard and determined by the Ontario Court of Justice sitting in the county or district in which the offence occurred or in the area specified in the transfer agreement made under Part X.

Idem

(2) A proceeding in respect of an offence may be heard and determined in a county or district that adjoins that in which the offence occurred if,
(a) the court holds sittings in a place reasonably proximate to the place where the offence occurred; and
(b) the place of sitting referred to in clause (a) is named in the summons or offence notice.

Transfer to proper county

(3) Where a proceeding is taken in a county or district other than one referred to in subsection (1) or (2), the court shall order that the proceeding be transferred to the proper county or district and may where the defendant appears award costs under section 60.

Change of venue

(4) Where, on the motion of a defendant or prosecutor made to the court at the location named in the information or certificate, it appears to the court that,

(a) if would be appropriate in the interests of justice to do so; or

(b) both the defendant and prosecutor consent thereto,

the court may order that the proceeding be heard and determined at another location in Ontario.

Conditions

(5) The court may, in an order made on a motion by the prosecutor under subsection (3) or (4), prescribe conditions that it thinks proper with respect to the payment of additional expenses caused to the defendant as a result of the change of venue.

Time of order for change of venue

(6) An order under subsection (3) or (4) may be made even if a motion preliminary to trial has been disposed of or the plea has been taken and it may be made at any time before evidence has been heard.

Preliminary motions

(7) The court at a location to which a proceeding is transferred under this section may receive and determine any motion preliminary to trial although the same matter was determined by the court at the location from which the proceeding was transferred.

Delivery of papers

(8) Where an order is made under subsection (3) or (4), the clerk of the court at the location where the trial was to be held before the order was made shall deliver any material in his or her possession in connection with the proceeding forthwith to the clerk of the court at the location where the trial is ordered to be held.

2000, c. 26, Sched. A, s. 13(6), item 2; 2009, c. 33, Sched. 4, s. 1(35)

Justice presiding at trial

30. (1) The justice presiding when evidence is first taken at the trial shall preside over the whole of the trial.

When presiding justice unable to act before adjudication

(2) Where evidence has been taken at a trial and, before making his or her adjudication, the presiding justice dies or in his or her opinion or the opinion of the Chief Justice of the Ontario Court of Justice is for any reason unable to continue, another justice shall conduct the hearing again as a new trial.

When presiding justice unable to act after adjudication

(3) Where evidence has been taken at a trial and, after making his or her adjudication but before making his or her order of imposing sentence, the presiding justice dies or in his or her opinion or the opinion of the Chief Justice of the Ontario Court of Justice is for any reason unable to continue, another justice may make the order or impose the sentence that is authorized by law.

Consent to change presiding justice

(4) A justice presiding at a trial may, at any stage of the trial and upon the consent of the prosecutor and defendant, order that the trial be conducted by another justice and, upon the order being given, subsection (2) applies as if the justice were unable to act.

Delegation

(5) The Chief Justice of the Ontario Court of Justice may delegate the authority to exercise his or her functions under subsection (2) or (3) with respect to justices in a region to the regional senior judge or the regional senior justice of the peace of the region.

2000, c. 26, Sched. A, s. 13(6), item 3; 2002, c. 18, Sched. A, s. 15(6), item 2; 2017, c. 20, Sched. 2, s. 38

Retention of jurisdiction

31. The court retains jurisdiction over the information or certificate even if the court fails to exercise its jurisdiction at any particular time or the provisions of this Act respecting adjournments are not complied with.

Stay of proceeding

32. (1) A proceeding may be stayed at any time before judgment by direction in court given by any of the following persons to the clerk of the court and, on the staying of the proceeding, any recognizance relating to the proceeding is vacated:

1. The Attorney General or his or her agent.
2. In the case of a proceeding to which a transfer agreement made under Part X applies and in which the Attorney General does not intervene, a person acting on behalf of a municipality in accordance with the agreement.

Same

(1.1) The power to stay a proceeding under subsection (1) is in addition to and does not affect the right of the Attorney General, his or her agent or a person acting on behalf of a municipality in accordance with a transfer agreement made under Part X to withdraw a charge.

Recommencement

(2) A proceeding stayed under subsection (1) may be recommenced by direction of the Attorney General, the Deputy Attorney General or a Crown Attorney to the clerk of the court but a proceeding that is stayed shall not be recommenced,

(a) later than one year after the stay; or

(b) after the expiration of any limitation period applicable, which shall run as if the proceeding had not been commenced until the recommencement,

whichever is the earlier.

2017, c. 34, Sched. 35, s. 9

Dividing counts

33. (1) A defendant may at any stage of the proceeding make a motion to the court to amend or to divide a count that,

(a) charges in the alternative different matters, acts or omissions that are stated in the alternative in the enactment that creates or describes the offence; or

(b) is double or multifarious,

on the ground that, as framed, it prejudices the defendant in the defendant's defence.

Idem

(2) Upon a motion under subsection (1), where the court is satisfied that the ends of justice so require, it may order that a count be amended or divided into two or more counts, and thereupon a formal commencement may be inserted before each of the counts into which it is divided.

Amendment of information or certificate

34. (1) The court may, at any stage of the proceeding, amend the information or certificate as may be necessary if it appears that the information or certificate,

(a) fails to state or states defectively anything that is requisite to charge the offence;

(b) does not negative an exception that should be negatived; or

(c) is in any way defective in substance or in form.

Idem

(2) The court may, during the trial, amend the information or certificate as may be necessary if the matters to be alleged in the proposed amendment are disclosed by the evidence taken at the trial.

Variances between charge and evidence

(3) A variance between the information or certificate and the evidence taken on the trial is not material with respect to,

(a) the time when the offence is alleged to have been committed, if it is proved that the information was laid or certificate issued within the prescribed period of limitation; or

(b) the place where the subject-matter of the proceeding is alleged to have arisen, except in an issue as to the jurisdiction of the court.

Considerations on amendment

(4) The court shall, in considering whether or not an amendment should be made, consider,

(a) the evidence taken on the trial, if any;

(b) the circumstances of the case;

(c) whether the defendant has been misled or prejudiced in the defendant's defence by a variance, error or omission; and

(d) whether, having regard to the merits of the case, the proposed amendment can be made without injustice being done.

Amendment, question of law

(5) The question whether an order to amend an information or certificate should be granted or refused is a question of law.

Endorsement of order to amend

(6) An order to amend an information or certificate shall be endorsed on the information or certificate as part of the record and the trial shall proceed as if the information or certificate had been originally laid as amended.

Particulars

35. The court may, before or during trial, if it is satisfied that it is necessary for a fair trial, order that a particular, further describing any matter relevant to the proceeding, be furnished to the defendant.

Motion to quash information or certificate

36. (1) An objection to an information or certificate for a defect apparent on its face shall be taken by motion to quash the information or certificate before the defendant has pleaded, and thereafter only by leave of the court.

Grounds for quashing

(2) The court shall not quash an information or certificate unless an amendment or particulars under section 33, 34 or 35 would fail to satisfy the ends of justice.

Costs on amendment or particulars

37. Where the information or certificate is amended or particulars are ordered and an adjournment is necessary as a result thereof, the court may make an order under section 60 for costs resulting from the adjournment.

Joinder of counts or defendants

38. (1) The court may, before trial, where it is satisfied that the ends of justice so require, direct that separate counts, informations or certificates be tried together or that persons who are charged separately be tried together.

Separate trials

(2) The court may, before or during the trial, where it is satisfied that the ends of justice so require, direct that separate counts, informations or certificates be tried separately or that persons who are charged jointly or being tried together be tried separately.

Issuance of summons

39. (1) Where a justice is satisfied that a person is able to give material evidence in a proceeding under this Act, the justice may issue a summons requiring the person to attend to give evidence and bring with him or her any writings or things referred to in the summons.

Service

(2) A summons shall be served and the service shall be proved in the same manner as a summons under section 26.

Exception

(2.1) Despite subsection (2), a summons served under this section may be served by a person other than a provincial offences officer.

Attendance

(3) A person who is served with a summons shall attend at the time and place stated in the summons to give evidence and, if required by the summons, shall bring with him or her any writing or other thing that the person has in his or her possession or under his or her control relating to the subject-matter of the proceeding.

Remaining in attendance

(4) A person who is served with a summons shall remain in attendance during the hearing and the hearing as resumed after adjournment from time to time unless the person is excused from attendance by the presiding justice.

2009, c. 33, Sched. 4, s. 1(36)

Arrest of witness

40. (1) Where a judge is satisfied upon evidence under oath or affirmation, that a person is able to give material evidence that is necessary in a proceeding under this Act and,

(a) will not attend if a summons is served; or

(b) attempts to serve a summons have been made and have failed because the person is evading service,

the judge may issue a warrant in the prescribed form for the arrest of the person.

Idem

(2) Where a person who has been served with a summons to attend to give evidence in a proceeding does not attend or remain in attendance, the court may, if it is established,

(a) that the summons has been served; and

(b) that the person is able to give material evidence that is necessary,

issue or cause to be issued a warrant in the prescribed form for the arrest of the person.

Bringing before justice

(3) The police officer who arrests a person under a warrant issued under subsection (1) or (2) shall immediately take the person before a justice.

Release on recognizance

(4) Unless the justice is satisfied that it is necessary to detain a person in custody to ensure his or her attendance to give evidence, the justice shall order the person released upon condition that the person enter into a recognizance in such amount and with such sureties, if any, as are reasonably necessary to ensure his or her attendance.

Bringing before judge

(5) Where a person is not released under subsection (4), the justice of the peace shall cause the person to be brought before a judge within two days of the justice's decision.

Detention

(6) Where the judge is satisfied that it is necessary to detain the person in custody to ensure his or her attendance to give evidence, the judge may order that the person be detained in custody to testify at the trial or to have his or her evidence taken by a commissioner under an order made under subsection (11).

Release on recognizance

(7) Where the judge does not make an order under subsection (6), he or she shall order that the person be released upon condition that the person enter into a recognizance in such amount and with such sureties, if any, as are reasonably necessary to ensure his or her attendance.

Maximum imprisonment

(8) A person who is ordered to be detained in custody under subsection (6) or is not released in fact under subsection (7) shall not be detained in custody for a period longer than ten days.

Release when no longer required

(9) A judge, or the justice presiding at a trial, may at any time order the release of a person in custody under this section where he or she is satisfied that the detention is no longer justified.

Arrest on breach of recognizance

(10) Where a person who is bound by a recognizance to attend to give evidence in any proceeding does not attend or remain in attendance, the court may issue a warrant in the prescribed form for the arrest of that person and,

    (a) where the person is brought directly before the court, subsections (6) and (7) apply; and

    (b) where the person is not brought directly before the court, subsections (3) to (7) apply.

Commission evidence of witness in custody

(11) A judge or the justice presiding at the trial may order that the evidence of a person held in custody under this section be taken by a commissioner under section 43, which applies thereto in the same manner as to a witness who is unable to attend by reason of illness.

Order for person in a prison to attend

41. (1) Where a person whose attendance is required in court to stand trial or to give evidence is confined in a prison, and a judge is satisfied, upon evidence under oath or affirmation orally or by affidavit, that the person's attendance is necessary to satisfy the ends of justice, the judge may issue an order in the prescribed form that the person be brought before the court, from day to day, as may be necessary.

Idem

(2) An order under subsection (1) shall be addressed to the person who has custody of the prisoner and on receipt thereof that person shall,
(a) deliver the prisoner to the police officer or other person who is named in the order to receive the prisoner; or
(b) bring the prisoner before the court upon payment of the person's reasonable charges in respect thereof.

Idem

(3) An order made under subsection (1) shall direct the manner in which the person shall be kept in custody and returned to the prison from which he or she is brought.

Penalty for failure to attend

42. (1) Every person who, being required by law to attend or remain in attendance at a hearing, fails without lawful excuse to attend or remain in attendance accordingly is guilty of an offence and on conviction is liable to a fine of not more than $2,000, or to imprisonment for a term of not more than thirty days, or to both.

Proof of failure to attend

(2) In a proceeding under subsection (1), a certificate of the clerk of the court or a justice stating that the defendant failed to attend is admissible in evidence as proof, in the absence of evidence to the contrary, of the fact without proof of the signature or office of the person appearing to have signed the certificate.

Order for evidence by commission

43. (1) Upon the motion of the defendant or prosecutor, a judge or, during trial, the court may by order appoint a commissioner to take the evidence of a witness who is out of Ontario or is not likely to be able to attend the trial by reason of illness or physical disability or for some other good and sufficient cause.

Admission of commission evidence

(2) Evidence taken by a commissioner appointed under subsection (1) may be read in evidence in the proceeding if,
(a) it is proved by oral evidence or by affidavit that the witness is unable to attend for a reason set out in subsection (1);

(b) the transcript of the evidence is signed by the commissioner by or before whom it purports to have been taken; and

(c) it is proved to the satisfaction of the court that reasonable notice of the time and place for taking the evidence was given to the other party, and the party had full opportunity to cross-examine the witness.

Attendance of accused

(3) An order under subsection (1) may make provision to enable the defendant to be present or represented by representative when the evidence is taken, but failure of the defendant to be present or to be represented by representative in accordance with the order does not prevent the reading of the evidence in the proceeding if the evidence has otherwise been taken in accordance with the order and with this section.

Application of rules in civil cases

(4) Except as otherwise provided by this section or by the rules of court, the practice and procedure in connection with the appointment of commissioners under this section, the taking of evidence by commissioners, the certifying and return thereof, and the use of the evidence in the proceeding shall, as far as possible, be the same as those that govern like matters in civil proceedings in the Superior Court of Justice.

2000, c. 26, Sched. A, s. 13(5), item 1; 2006, c. 21, Sched. C, s. 131(6)

Trial of issue as to capacity to conduct defence

44. (1) Where at any time before a defendant is sentenced a court has reason to believe, based on,

(a) the evidence of a legally qualified medical practitioner or, with the consent of the parties, a written report of a legally qualified medical practitioner; or

(b) the conduct of the defendant in the courtroom,

that the defendant suffers from mental disorder, the court may,

(c) where the justice presiding is a judge, by order suspend the proceeding and direct the trial of the issue as to whether the defendant is, because of mental disorder, unable to conduct his or her defence; or

(d) where the justice presiding is a justice of the peace, refer the matter to a judge who may make an order referred to in clause (c).

Examination

(2) For the purposes of subsection (1), the court may order the defendant to attend to be examined under subsection (5).

Finding

(3) The trial of the issue shall be presided over by a judge and,

(a) where the judge finds that the defendant is, because of mental disorder, unable to conduct his or her defence, the judge shall order that the proceeding remain suspended;

(b) where the judge finds that the defendant is able to conduct his or her defence, the judge shall order that the suspended proceeding be continued.

Application for rehearing as to capacity

(4) At any time within one year after an order is made under subsection (3), either party may, upon seven days notice to the other, make a motion to a judge to rehear the trial of the issue and where upon the rehearing the judge finds that the defendant is able to conduct his or her defence, the judge may order that the suspended proceeding be continued.

Order for examination

(5) For the purposes of subsection (1) or a hearing or rehearing under subsection (3) or (4), the court or judge may order the defendant to attend at such place or before such person and at or within such time as are specified in the order and submit to an examination for the purpose of determining whether the defendant is, because of mental disorder, unable to conduct his or her defence.

Idem

(6) Where the defendant fails or refuses to comply with an order under subsection (5) without reasonable excuse or where the person conducting the examination satisfies a judge that it is necessary to do so, the judge may by warrant direct that the defendant be taken into such custody as is necessary for the purpose of the examination and in any event for not longer than seven days and, where it is necessary to detain the defendant in a place, the place shall be, where practicable, a psychiatric facility.

Limitation on suspension of proceeding

(7) Where an order is made under subsection (3) and one year has elapsed and no further order is made under subsection (4), no further proceeding shall be taken in respect of the charge of any other charge arising out of the same circumstance.

Taking of plea

45. (1) After being informed of the substance of the information or certificate, the defendant shall be asked whether the defendant pleads guilty or not guilty of the offence charged in it.

Conviction on plea of guilty

(2) Where the defendant pleads guilty, the court may accept the plea and convict the defendant.

Conditions of accepting plea

(3) A court may accept a plea of guilty only if it is satisfied that the defendant,

(a) is making the plea voluntarily;

(b) understands that the plea is an admission of the essential elements of the offence;

(c) understands the nature and consequences of the plea; and

(d) understands that the court is not bound by any agreement made between the defendant and the prosecutor.

Validity of plea not affected

(4) The failure of a court to fully inquire into whether the conditions set out in subsection (3) are met does not affect the validity of the plea.

Refusal to plead

(5) Where the defendant refuses to plead or does not answer directly, the court shall enter a plea of not guilty.

Plea of guilty to another offence

(6) Where the defendant pleads guilty of an offence other than the offence charged, and whether or not it is an included offence and whether or not the defendant has pleaded not guilty to the offence charged, the court may, with the consent of the prosecutor, accept such plea of guilty and accordingly amend the certificate of offence, the certificate of parking infraction or the information, as the case may be, or substitute the offence to which the defendant pleads guilty.

2009, c. 33, Sched. 4, s. 1(37)

Judicial pre-trial conferences

45.1 (1) On application by the prosecutor or the defendant or on his or her own motion, a justice may order that a pre-trial conference be held between the prosecutor and the defendant or a representative of the defendant.

Matters for consideration

(2) The court, or a justice of the court, shall preside over the pre-trial conference, the purpose of which is to,

(a) consider the matters that, to promote a fair and expeditious trial, would be better decided before the start of the proceedings and other similar matters; and

(b) make arrangements for decisions on those matters.

2009, c. 33, Sched. 4, s. 1(38)

Trial on plea of not guilty

46. (1) If the defendant pleads not guilty, the court shall hold the trial.

Right to defend

(2) The defendant is entitled to make full answer and defence.

Right to examine witnesses

(3) The prosecutor or defendant, as the case may be, may examine and crossexamine witnesses.

Agreed facts

(4) The court may receive and act upon any facts agreed upon by the defendant and prosecutor without proof or evidence.

Defendant not compellable

(5) Despite section 8 of the *Evidence Act*, the defendant is not a compellable witness for the prosecution.

2009, c. 33, Sched. 4, s. 1(39)

Evidence taken on another charge

47. (1) The court may receive and consider evidence taken before the same justice on a different charge against the same defendant, with the consent of the parties.

Certificate as evidence

(2) Where a certificate as to the content of an official record is, by any Act, made admissible in evidence as proof, in the absence of evidence to the contrary, the court may, for the purpose of deciding whether the defendant is the person referred to in the certificate, receive and base its decision upon information it considers credible or trustworthy in the circumstances of each case.

Burden of proving exception, etc.

(3) The burden of proving that an authorization, exception, exemption or qualification prescribed by law operates in favour of the defendant is on the defendant, and the prosecutor is not required, except by way of rebuttal, to prove that the authorization, exception, exemption or qualification does not operate in favour of the defendant, whether or not it is set out in the information.

Exhibits

48. (1) The court may order that an exhibit be kept in such custody and place as, in the opinion of the court, is appropriate for its preservation.

Release of exhibits

(2) Where any thing is filed as an exhibit in a proceeding, the clerk may release the exhibit upon the consent of the parties at any time after the trial or, in the absence of consent, may return the exhibit to the party tendering it after the disposition of any appeal in the proceeding or, where an appeal is not taken, after the expiration of the time for appeal.

Certified evidence—Application

48.1 (1) This section applies to a hearing, including a hearing in the absence of a defendant under section 54, where,

(a) the proceeding for the offence was commenced by certificate under Part I or II; and

(b) the offence is specified by the regulations.

Proposed Amendment — 48.1(1)

Certified evidence—Application

(1) This section applies to a hearing, including a hearing in the absence of a defendant under section 54, if,

(a) the proceeding for the offence was commenced under Part I or II and a set fine has been specified for the offence; or

(b) the offence is specified by the regulations.

2017, c. 34, Sched. 35, s. 11 [Not in force at date of publication.]

Admissibility of certified evidence

(2) The following are admissible in evidence as proof of the facts certified in it, in the absence of evidence to the contrary:

1. A certified statement in a certificate of offence.

2. A certified statement in a certificate of parking infraction.

3. Other types of certified evidence specified by the regulations.

Other provisions on admissibility

(3) For greater certainty, subsection (2) does not affect or interfere with the operation of a provision of this Act or any other Act that permits or specifies that a document or type of document be admitted into evidence as proof of the facts certified in it.

Onus

(4) For greater certainty, this section does not remove the onus on the prosecution to prove its case beyond a reasonable doubt.

No oral evidence

(5) A provincial offences officer who provides certified evidence referred to in subsection (2) in respect of a proceeding shall not be required to attend to give evidence at trial, except as provided under subsection 49(4).

Regulations

(6) The Lieutenant Governor in Council may make regulations,
(a) specifying offences for the purposes of clause (1)(b);
(b) respecting other types of certified evidence for the purposes of paragraph 3 of subsection (2);
(c) respecting restrictions or conditions on the admissibility of evidence under subsection (2).

2009, c. 33, Sched. 4, s. 1(40) 1993, c. 31, s. 1(22)

Adjournments

49. (1) The court may, from time to time, adjourn a trial or hearing but, where the defendant is in custody, an adjournment shall not be for a period longer than eight days without the consent of the defendant.

Early resumption

(2) A trial or hearing that is adjourned for a period may be resumed before the expiration of the period with the consent of the defendant and the prosecutor.

Adjournment

(3) Despite subsection (1) and subject to subsection (4), if the trial is being held in respect of a proceeding commenced under Part I or II, the court shall not adjourn the trial for the purpose of having the provincial offences officer who completed the certificate of offence or the certificate of parking infraction, as the case may be, attend to give evidence unless the court is satisfied that the interests of justice require it.

2009, c. 33, Sched. 4, s. 1(41)

Adjournment where certified evidence

(4) If certified evidence referred to in subsection 48.1(2) is being admitted as evidence in a trial referred to in subsection (1), the court shall not adjourn the trial for the purpose of having any of the following persons attend to give evidence unless the court is satisfied that the oral evidence of the person is necessary in order to ensure a fair trial:
1. The provincial offences officer who completed the certificate of offence or the certificate of parking infraction, as the case may be.
2. Any provincial offences officer who provided certified evidence in respect of the proceeding.

2009, c. 33, Sched. 4, s. 1(41)

Power of clerk to adjourn

(5) The clerk of the court may, on behalf of the court, adjourn,

(a) the first trial date for a proceeding commenced under Part I or Part II to a date agreed to by the defendant and the prosecutor in a written agreement filed with the court; and

(b) any proceeding under this Act or any step in a proceeding under this Act, where no justice is able to attend in person, to a date chosen in accordance with the instructions of a justice.

1993, c. 31, s. 1(23); 2009, c. 33, Sched. 4, s. 1(42)

Appearance by defendant

50. (1) A defendant may appear and act personally or by representative.

Appearance by corporation

(2) A defendant that is a corporation shall appear and act by representative.

Exclusion of representatives

(3) The court may bar any person, other than a person who is licensed under the *Law Society Act*, from appearing as a representative if the court finds that the person is not competent properly to represent or advise the person for whom he or she appears, or does not understand and comply with the duties and responsibilities of a representative.

2006, c. 21, Sched. C, s. 131(7), (8)

Compelling attendance of defendant

51. Although a defendant appears by representative, the court may order the defendant to attend personally, and, where it appears to be necessary to do so, may issue a summons in the prescribed form.

2006, c. 21, Sched. C, s. 131(9)

Excluding defendant from hearing

52. (1) The court may cause the defendant to be removed and to be kept out of court,

(a) when the defendant misconducts himself or herself by interrupting the proceeding so that to continue in the presence of the defendant would not be feasible; or

(b) where, during the trial of an issue as to whether the defendant is, because of mental disorder, unable to conduct his or her defence, the court is satisfied that failure to do so might have an adverse effect on the mental health of the defendant.

Excluding public from hearing

(2) The court may exclude the public or any member of the public from a hearing where, in the opinion of the court, it is necessary to do so,

    (a) for the maintenance of order in the courtroom;

    (b) to protect the reputation of a minor; or

    (c) to remove an influence that might affect the testimony of a witness.

Prohibition of publication of evidence

(3) Where the court considers it necessary to do so to protect the reputation of a minor, the court may make an order prohibiting the publication or broadcast of the identity of the minor or of the evidence or any part of the evidence taken at the hearing.

Failure of prosecutor to appear

    53. (1) Where the defendant appears for a hearing and the prosecutor, having had due notice, does not appear, the court may dismiss the charge or may adjourn the hearing to another time upon such terms as it considers proper.

Idem

(2) Where the prosecutor does not appear at the time and place appointed for the resumption of an adjourned hearing under subsection (1), the court may dismiss the charge.

Costs

(3) Where a hearing is adjourned under subsection (1) or a charge is dismissed under subsection (2), the court may make an order under section 60 for the payment of costs.

Written order of dismissal

(4) Where a charge is dismissed under subsection (1) or (2), the court may, if requested by the defendant, draw up an order of dismissal stating the grounds therefor and shall give the defendant a certified copy of the order of dismissal which is, without further proof, a bar to any subsequent proceeding against the defendant in respect of the same cause.

Conviction in the absence of the defendant

    54. (1) Where a defendant does not appear at the time and place appointed for a hearing and it is proved by the prosecutor, having been given a reasonable opportunity to do so, that a summons was served, a notice of trial was given under Part I or II, an undertaking to appear was given or a recognizance to appear was entered into, as the case may be, or where the defendant does not appear upon the resumption of a hearing that has been adjourned, the court may,

(a) proceed to hear and determine the proceeding in the absence of the defendant; or

(b) adjourn the hearing and, if it thinks fit, issue a summons to appear or issue a warrant in the prescribed form for the arrest of the defendant.

Proceeding arising from failure to appear

(2) Where the court proceeds under clause (1)(a) or adjourns the hearing under clause (1)(b) without issuing a summons or warrant, no proceeding arising out of the failure of the defendant to appear at the time and place appointed for the hearing or for the resumption of the hearing shall be instituted, or if instituted shall be proceeded with, except with the consent of the Attorney General or his or her agent.

2009, c. 33, Sched. 4, s. 1(43)

Included offences

55. Where the offence as charged includes another offence, the defendant may be convicted of an offence so included that is proved, although the whole offence charged is not proved.

SENTENCING

Pre-sentence report

56. (1) Where a defendant is convicted of an offence in a proceeding commenced by information, the court may direct a probation officer to prepare and file with the court a report in writing relating to the defendant for the purpose of assisting the court in imposing sentence.

Service

(2) Where a report is filed with the court under subsection (1), the clerk of the court shall cause a copy of the report to be provided to the defendant or the defendant's representative and to the prosecutor.

2006, c. 21, Sched. C, s. 131(11)

Submissions as to sentence

57. (1) Where a defendant who appears is convicted of an offence, the court shall give the prosecutor and the defendant's representative an opportunity to make submissions as to sentence and, where the defendant has no representative, the court shall ask the defendant if he or she has anything to say before sentence is passed.

Omission to comply

(2) The omission to comply with subsection (1) does not affect the validity of the proceeding.

Inquiries by court

(3) Where a defendant is convicted of an offence, the court may make such inquiries, on oath or otherwise, of and concerning the defendant as it considers desirable, including the defendant's economic circumstances, but the defendant shall not be compelled to answer.

Proof of previous conviction

(4) A certificate setting out with reasonable particularity the finding of guilt or acquittal or conviction and sentence in Canada of a person signed by,

(a) the person who made the adjudication; or

(b) the clerk of the court where the adjudication was made,

is, upon the court being satisfied that the defendant is the person referred to in the certificate, admissible in evidence and is proof, in the absence of evidence to the contrary, of the facts stated therein without proof of the signature or the official character of the person appearing to have signed the certificate.

2006, c. 21, Sched. C, s. 131(12)

Time spent in custody considered

58. In determining the sentence to be imposed on a person convicted of an offence, the justice may take into account any time spent in custody by the person as a result of the offence.

Provision for minimum penalty

59. (1) No penalty prescribed for an offence is a minimum penalty unless it is specifically declared to be a minimum.

Relief against minimum fine

(2) Although the provision that creates the penalty for an offence prescribes a minimum fine, where in the opinion of the court exceptional circumstances exist so that to impose the minimum fine would be unduly oppressive or otherwise not in the interests of justice, the court may impose a fine that is less than the minimum or suspend the sentence.

Idem, re imprisonment

(3) Where a minimum penalty is prescribed for an offence and the minimum penalty includes imprisonment, the court may, despite the prescribed penalty, impose a fine of not more than $5,000 in lieu of imprisonment.

Fixed costs on conviction

60. (1) Upon conviction, the defendant is liable to pay to the court an amount by way of costs that is fixed by the regulations.

Costs respecting witnesses

(2) The court may, in its discretion, order costs towards fees and expenses reasonably incurred by or on behalf of witnesses in amounts not exceeding the maximum fixed by the regulations, to be paid,

(a) to the court or prosecutor by the defendant; or

(b) to the defendant by the person who laid the information or issued the certificate, as the case may be,

but where the proceeding is commenced by means of a certificate, the total of such costs shall not exceed $100.

Costs collectable as a fine

(3) Costs payable under this section shall be deemed to be a fine for the purpose of enforcing payment.

Surcharge

60.1 (1) If a person is convicted of an offence in a proceeding commenced under Part I or III and a fine is imposed in respect of that offence, a surcharge is payable by that person in the amount determined by regulations made under this Act.

Collection

(2) The surcharge shall be deemed to be a fine for the purpose of enforcing payment.

Priorities

(3) Any payments made by a defendant shall be credited towards payment of the fine until it is fully paid and then towards payment of the surcharge.

Part X agreements

(3.1) When an agreement made under Part X applies to a fine, payments made by the defendant shall first be credited towards payment of the surcharge, not as described in subsection (3).

Special purpose account

(4) Surcharges paid into the Consolidated Revenue Fund shall be credited to the victims' justice fund account and shall be deemed to be money received by the Crown for a special purpose.

Same

(4.1) Subsection (4) also applies to payments received under clause 165(5)(a).

(5) [Repealed 1995, c. 6, s. 7(2).]

(6) [Repealed 1995, c. 6, s. 7(2).]

Regulations

(7) The Lieutenant Governor in Council may make regulations,
(a) prescribing the amount of the surcharges or the method by which they are to be calculated;
(b) [Repealed 1995, c. 6, s. 7(2).]
(c) exempting any offence or class of offence from the application of subsection (1).

(8) [Repealed 1995, c. 6, s. 7(2).]

General penalty

61. Except where otherwise expressly provided by law, every person who is convicted of an offence is liable to a fine of not more that $5,000.

Minute of conviction

62. Where a court convicts a defendant or dismisses a charge, a minute of the dismissal or conviction and sentence shall be made by the court, and, upon request by the defendant or the prosecutor or by the Attorney General or his or her agent, the court shall cause a copy thereof certified by the clerk or the court to be delivered to the person making the request.

Time when imprisonment starts

63. (1) The term of imprisonment imposed by sentence shall, unless otherwise directed in the sentence, commence on the day on which the convicted person is taken into custody thereunder, but no time during which the convicted person is imprisoned or out on bail before sentence shall be reckoned as part of the term of imprisonment to which he or she is sentenced.

Idem

(2) Where the court imposes imprisonment, the court may order custody to commence on a day not later than thirty days after the day of sentencing.

Sentences consecutive

64. Where a person is subject to more than one term of imprisonment at the same time, the terms shall be served consecutively except in so far as the court has ordered a term to be served concurrently with any other term of imprisonment.

Authority of warrant

65. (1) A warrant of committal is sufficient authority,

(a) for the conveyance of the prisoner in custody for the purpose of committal under the warrant; and

(b) for the reception and detention of the prisoner by keepers of prisons in accordance with the terms of the warrant.

Conveyance of prisoner

(2) A person to whom a warrant of committal is directed shall convey the prisoner to the correctional institution named in the warrant.

Prisoner subject to rules of institution

(3) A sentence of imprisonment shall be served in accordance with the enactments and rules that govern the institution to which the prisoner is sentenced.

When fine due

66. (1) A fine becomes due and payable fifteen days after its imposition.

Proposed Amendment — 66(1)

When fine due

(1) A fine becomes due and payable 15 days after its imposition unless an extension or agreement under this Act provides otherwise.

2017, c. 34, Sched. 35, s. 12(1) [Not in force at date of publication.]

Extension of time for payment of a fine

(2) Where the court imposes a fine, the court shall ask the defendant if the defendant wishes an extension of the time for payment of the fine.

Inquiries

(3) Where the defendant requests an extension of the time for payment of the fine, the court may make such inquiries, on oath or affirmation or otherwise, of and concerning the defendant as the court considers desirable, but the defendant shall not be compelled to answer.

Granting of extension

(4) Unless the court finds that the request for extension of time is not made in good faith or that the extension would likely be used to evade payment, the court shall extend the time for payment by ordering periodic payments or otherwise.

Notice where convicted in the absence of the defendant

(5) Where a fine is imposed in the absence of the defendant, the clerk of the court shall give the defendant notice of the fine and its due date and of the defendant's right to make a motion for an extension of the time for payment under subsection (6).

Proposed Amendment — 66(5)

Notice where convicted in the absence of the defendant

(5) Where a fine is imposed in the absence of the defendant, the clerk of the court shall give the defendant notice of the fine and its due date and of the defendant's right to make an application for an extension of the time for payment under section 66.0.1.

> 2017, c. 34, Sched. 35, s. 12(2) [Not in force at date of publication.]

Further motion for extension

(6) The defendant may, at any time by motion in the prescribed form filed in the office of the court, request an extension or further extension of time for payment of a fine and the motion shall be determined by a justice and the justice has the same powers in respect of the motion as the court has under subsections (3) and (4).

Proposed Repeal — 66(6)

(6) [Repealed 2017, c. 34, Sched. 35, s. 12(3). Not in force at date of publication.]

Defendant's address

66.1 If a court imposes a fine, grants an extension of time for payment of a fine or deals with a fine under section 69, and the defendant is before the court, the court shall require the defendant to provide the defendant's current address to the clerk of the court.

> 1993, c. 31, s. 1(24)

Proposed Addition — 66.0.1

Application for extension

66.0.1 (1) A defendant may, at any time, make an application for an extension or a further extension of time for payment of a fine by completing the prescribed form and filing it in the office of the court.

Consideration by clerk of the court

(2) The clerk of the court may,
(a) grant the application if he or she is satisfied, having regard to any criteria prescribed under subsection (4), that the application is made in good faith and will not be used to evade payment; or
(b) forward the application to a justice for review.

Review by justice

(3) A justice who reviews the application has the same powers in respect of the application as the court has under subsection 66(3) and shall assess the application in accordance with the criteria set out in subsection 66(4).

Regulations

(4) The Attorney General may make regulations prescribing criteria that the clerk of the court shall consider in determining whether to grant an extension of the time for payment of a fine.

2017, c. 34, Sched. 35, s. 13 [Not in force at date of publication.]

Fee for refused cheque collectable as a fine

66.2 When a person purports to pay a fine by a cheque that the drawee of the cheque refuses to cash and thereby becomes liable to pay a fee in the amount prescribed for the purpose of section 8.1 of the *Financial Administration Act*, the fee shall be deemed to be a fine for the purpose of enforcing payment.

1994, c. 27, s. 52(5)

Regulation for work credits for fines

67. The Lieutenant Governor in Council may make regulations establishing a program to permit the payment of fines by means of credits for work performed, and, for the purpose and without restricting the generality of the foregoing may,
(a) prescribe classes of work and the conditions under which they are to be performed;
(b) prescribe a system of credits;
(c) provide for any matter necessary for the effective administration of the program,

and any regulation may limit its application to any part or parts of Ontario.

Civil enforcement of fines

68. (1) When the payment of a fine is in default, the clerk of the court may complete a certificate in the prescribed form as to the imposition of the fine and the amount remaining unpaid and file the certificate in a court of competent jurisdiction and upon filing, the certificate shall be deemed to be an order or judgment of that court for the purposes of enforcement.

(2) [Repealed 2009, c. 33, Sched. 4, s. 1(44).]

Certificate of discharge

(3) Where a certificate has been filed under subsection (1) and the fine is fully paid, the clerk shall file a certificate of payment upon which the certificate of default is discharged and, where a writ of execution has been filed with the sheriff, the clerk shall file a certificate of payment with the sheriff, upon which the writ is cancelled.

Costs of enforcement

(4) Costs incurred in enforcing the deemed court order or judgment shall be added to the order or judgment and form part of it.

More than one fine

(5) The clerk may complete and file one certificate under this section in respect of two or more fines imposed on the same person.

1993, c. 31, s. 1(25); 1994, c. 27, s. 52(6); 2009, c. 33, Sched. 4, s. 1(44)

Default

69. (1) The payment of a fine is in default if any part of it is due and unpaid for fifteen days or more.

Order on default

(2) A justice of the peace who is satisfied that payment of a fine is in default,
(a) shall order that any permit, licence, registration or privilege in respect of which a suspension is authorized under any Act because of non-payment of the fine be suspended until the fine is paid;
(b) shall order that any permit, licence, registration or privilege in respect of which any Act authorizes a refusal to renew, validate or issue the permit, licence, registration or privilege because of non-payment of the fine not be renewed, validated or issued until the fine is paid; and
(c) may direct the clerk of the court to proceed with civil enforcement under section 68.

Highway Traffic Act permits

(3) If section 7 of the *Highway Traffic Act* authorizes an order or direction under this section that any permit under that Act not be validated or issued because

payment of a fine is in default, a person designated by the regulations who is satisfied that payment of a fine is in default shall direct that until the fine is paid,

    (a) validation of any permit held by the person who has defaulted be refused; and

    (b) issuance of any permit to the person who has defaulted be refused.

Highway Traffic Act restriction

(4) Orders or directions made under this section pursuant to section 7 of the Highway Traffic Act are subject to subsection 7(12) of that Act and any regulations made under section 7 of that Act.

Highway Traffic Act licences

(5) If section 46 of the *Highway Traffic Act* authorizes an order or direction under this section that any licence under that Act be suspended or not be issued because payment of a fine is in default, a person designated by the regulations who is satisfied that payment of a fine is in default shall direct that until the fine is paid,

    (a) if the person who has defaulted holds a licence, the licence be suspended; or

    (b) if the person who has defaulted does not hold a licence, no licence be issued to him or her.

Obtaining convicted person's attendance

(6) A justice may issue a warrant requiring that a person who has defaulted be arrested and brought before a justice as soon as possible if other reasonable methods of collecting the fine have been tried and have failed, or would not appear to be likely to result in payment within a reasonable period of time.

Alternative summons procedure

(7) The clerk of the court that imposed the fine that is in default may issue a summons requiring the person who has defaulted to appear before a justice if the conditions described in subsection (6) exist.

Service of summons

(8) The summons referred to in subsection (7) may be served by regular prepaid mail.

Hearing

(9) If a person who has defaulted in paying a fine is brought before a justice as a result of a warrant issued under subsection (6) or such a person appears before a justice as a result of a summons issued under subsection (7), the justice shall hold a hearing to determine whether the person is unable to pay the fine within a reasonable period of time.

Onus

(10) In a hearing under subsection (9), the onus of proving that the person is unable to pay the fine within a reasonable period of time is on the person who has defaulted.

Adjournment

(11) The justice may adjourn the hearing from time to time at the request of the person who has defaulted.

Warning

(12) When an adjournment is granted, the justice shall warn the person who has defaulted that if the person fails to appear for the resumption of the hearing, the hearing may proceed in the person's absence.

Failure to warn

(13) If a hearing was adjourned and the person who has defaulted does not appear when it is resumed, the hearing may proceed in the person's absence even if the warning required by subsection (12) was not given.

Warrant of committal

(14) If the justice is not satisfied that the person who has defaulted is unable to pay the fine within a reasonable period of time and that incarceration of the person would not be contrary to the public interest, the justice may issue a warrant for the person's committal or may order that such other steps be taken to enforce the fine as appear to him or her to be appropriate.

Proposed Addition—69(14.1)

Inability to pay

(14.1) Despite subsection 165(3), a defendant may, in accordance with the regulations, apply to a justice to reduce or expunge a defaulted fine under subsection (15) where the defendant meets the criteria for inability to pay defined in the regulations.

2009, c. 33, Sched. 4, s. 1(45) [Not in force at date of publication.]

Inability to pay fine

(15) If the justice is satisfied that the person who has defaulted is unable to pay the fine within a reasonable period of time, the justice may,

(a) grant an extension of the time allowed for payment of the fine;

(b) require the person to pay the fine according to a schedule of payments established by the justice;

(c) in exceptional circumstances, reduce the amount of the fine or order that the fine does not have to be paid.

Term of imprisonment

(16) Subject to subsection (17), the term of imprisonment under a warrant issued under subsection (14) shall be for three days, plus,
(a) if the amount that has not been paid is not greater than $50, one day; or
(b) if the amount that has not been paid is greater than $50, a number of days equal to the sum of one plus the number obtained when the unpaid amount is divided by $50, rounded down to the nearest whole number.

Limit

(17) The term of imprisonment shall not exceed the greater of,
(a) ninety days; and
(b) half of the maximum number of days of imprisonment that may be imposed on conviction of the offence that the person who has defaulted was convicted of.

Effect of payments

(18) Subject to subsection (19), a payment in respect of the fine in default that is made after a warrant is issued under subsection (14) shall result in a reduction of the term of imprisonment by the number of days that is in the same proportion to the term as the payment is to the amount in default.

Restriction

(19) A payment that is less than the amount outstanding on the fine shall not result in a reduction of the term of imprisonment unless it is an amount that would reduce the term by a number of days that is a whole number.

Exceptions

(20) Subsections (6) to (19) do not apply if,
(a) the person who has defaulted is less than eighteen years old; or
(b) the fine was imposed on conviction of an offence under subsection 31(2) or (4) of the *Liquor Licence Act*.

Exceptional circumstances

(21) In exceptional circumstances where, in the opinion of the court that imposed the fine, to proceed under subsections (6) to (14) would defeat the ends of justice, the court may order that no warrant be issued under subsection (6) and that no summons be issued under subsection (7).

Regulations

(22) The Lieutenant Governor in Council may make regulations,

(a) designating a person or class of persons for purposes of subsections (3) and (5);

Proposed Addition—69(22)(a.1)

(a.1) prescribing the form and procedure for an application under subsection (14.1);

2009, c. 33, Sched. 4, s. 1(46) [Not in force at date of publication.]

(b) prescribing criteria to be considered by a justice in determining whether a person is unable to pay a fine within a reasonable period of time.

1992, c. 20, s. 1(2); 1993, c. 31, s. 1(26); 2004, c. 22, s. 8; 2015, c. 14, s. 60

Disclosure to consumer reporting agency

69.1 (1) When a fine has been in default for at least 90 days, the Ministry of the Attorney General may disclose to a consumer reporting agency the name of the defaulter, the amount of the fine and the date the fine went into default.

Same

(2) When a fine disclosed to a consumer reporting agency has been paid in full, the Ministry of the Attorney General shall inform the agency of this fact as soon as possible after payment.

1994, c. 17, s. 131

Proposed Addition — 69.2

Order of payment for multiple fines in default

69.2 (1) A person with multiple fines in default shall pay the defaulted fines in order of default date, beginning with the fine that has been in default for the longest period of time.

Older fines in default must be paid in full

(2) A person may not pay any portion of a fine in default until any outstanding older fines in default have been paid in full.

Fines that went into default on same day

(3) For greater certainty, a person's oldest outstanding fines in default may be paid in any order if they went into default on the same day.

Fine that has gone into default multiple times

(4) If a fine has gone into default multiple times, only the most recent default date shall be used to calculate how long it has been in default for the purposes of this section.

Transition

(5) This section applies to any fine that was in default or that went into default on or after the day this section came into force.

2017, c. 34, Sched. 35, s. 14 [Not in force at date of publication.]

Fee where fine in default

70. (1) Where the payment of a fine is in default and the time for payment is not extended or further extended under subsection 66(6), the defendant shall pay the administrative fee prescribed by the regulations.

Fee collectable as a fine

(2) For the purpose of making and enforcing payment, a fee payable under this section shall be deemed to be part of the fine that is in default.

Proposed Amendment — 70

Administrative monetary penalty where fine in default

70. (1) A defendant shall pay the administrative monetary penalty prescribed by the regulations if the payment of his or her fine goes into default.

Administrative monetary penalty not affected if time for payment extended

(2) If a fine goes into default, the obligation to pay an administrative monetary penalty under subsection (1) is not affected by a subsequent extension or further extension of the time for payment of the fine under section 66.0.1.

Multiple administrative monetary penalties possible

(3) For greater certainty, it is possible for a defendant to incur multiple administrative monetary penalties in respect of the same fine if the payment goes into default, the defendant is granted an extension of time for payment and the fine subsequently goes into default again.

Administrative monetary penalty collectable as a fine

(4) For the purpose of making and enforcing payment, an amount payable under this section shall be deemed to be part of the fine that is in default.

Transition

(5) This section applies to any fine that was in default or that went into default on or after the day this section came into force.

2017, c. 34, Sched. 35, s. 15 [Not in force at date of publication.]

Collection agency costs payable

70.1 (1) A defendant shall pay the costs that a municipality incurs by using a registered collection agency in good standing under the Collection and Debt Settlement Services Act to collect a fine that is in default, but the costs shall not exceed an amount approved by the municipality.

Costs collectable as a fine

(2) For the purpose of making and enforcing payment, costs payable under this section shall be deemed to be part of the fine that is in default.

2017, c. 2, Sched. 2, s. 28

Suspension of fine on conditions

71. Where an Act provides that a fine may be suspended subject to the performance of a condition,

(a) the period of suspension shall be fixed by the court and shall be for not more than one year;

(b) the court shall provide in its order of suspension the method of proving the performance of the condition;

(c) the suspension is in addition to and not in lieu of any other power of the court in respect of the fine; and

(d) the fine is not in default until fifteen days have elapsed after notice that the period of suspension has expired is given to the defendant.

Probation order

72. (1) Where a defendant is convicted of an offence in a proceeding commenced by information, the court may, having regard to the age, character and background of the defendant, the nature of the offence and the circumstances surrounding its commission,

(a) suspend the passing of sentence and direct that the defendant comply with the conditions prescribed in a probation order;

(b) in addition to fining the defendant or sentencing the defendant to imprisonment, whether in default of payment of a fine or otherwise, direct that the defendant comply with the conditions prescribed in a probation order; or

(c) where it imposes a sentence of imprisonment on the defendant, whether in default of payment of a fine or otherwise, that does not exceed ninety days, order that the sentence be served intermittently at such times as are specified in the order and direct that the defendant, at all times when he or she is not in confinement pursuant to such order, comply with the conditions prescribed in a probation order.

Statutory conditions of order

(2) A probation order shall be deemed to contain the conditions that,

(a) the defendant not commit the same or any related or similar offence, or any offence under a statute of Canada or Ontario or any other province of Canada that is punishable by imprisonment;

(b) the defendant appear before the court as and when required; and

(c) the defendant notify the court of any change in the defendant's address.

Conditions imposed by court

(3) In addition to the conditions set out in subsection (2), the court may prescribe as a condition in a probation order,

(a) that the defendant satisfy any compensation or restitution that is required or authorized by an Act;

(b) with the consent of the defendant and where the conviction is of an offence that is punishable by imprisonment, that the defendant perform a community service as set out in the order;

(c) where the conviction is of an offence punishable by imprisonment, such other conditions relating to the circumstances of the offence and of the defendant that contributed to the commission of the offence as the court considers appropriate to prevent similar unlawful conduct or to contribute to the rehabilitation of the defendant; or

(d) where considered necessary for the purpose of implementing the conditions of the probation order, that the defendant report to a responsible person designated by the court and, in addition, where the circumstances warrant it, that the defendant be under the supervision of the person to whom he or she is required to report.

Form of order

(4) A probation order shall be in the prescribed form and the court shall specify therein the period for which it is to remain in force, which shall not be for more than two years from the date when the order takes effect.

Notice of order

(5) Where the court makes a probation order, it shall cause a copy of the order and a copy of section 75 to be given to the defendant.

Regulations for community service orders

(6) The Lieutenant Governor in Council may make regulations governing restitution, compensation and community service orders, including their terms and conditions.

Exception

(7) The court shall not make a probation order when an individual has been convicted of an absolute liability offence, unless the order is made in addition to a sentence of imprisonment imposed under section 69 in default of payment of a fine.

1994, c. 27, s. 52(7)

When order comes into force

73. (1) A probation order comes into force,

(a) on the date on which the order is made; or

(b) where the defendant is sentenced to imprisonment other than a sentence to be served intermittently, upon the expiration of that sentence.

Continuation in force

(2) Subject to section 75, where a defendant who is bound by a probation order is convicted of an offence or is imprisoned in default of payment of a fine, the order continues in force except in so far as the sentence or imprisonment renders it impossible for the defendant to comply for the time being with the order.

Variation of probation order

74. The court may, at any time upon the application of the defendant or prosecutor with notice to the other, after a hearing or, with the consent of the parties, without a hearing,

(a) make any changes in or additions to the conditions prescribed in the order that in the opinion of the court are rendered desirable by a change in circumstances;

(b) relieve the defendant, either absolutely or upon such terms or for such period as the court considers desirable, of compliance with any condition described in any of the clauses in subsection 72(3) that is prescribed in the order; or

(c) terminate the order or decrease the period for which the probation order is to remain in force,

and the court shall thereupon endorse the probation order accordingly and, if it changes or adds to the conditions prescribed in the order, inform the defendant of its action and give the defendant a copy of the order so endorsed.

Breach of probation order

75. Where a defendant who is bound by a probation order is convicted of an offence constituting a breach of condition of the order and,

(a) the time within which the defendant may appeal or make a motion for leave to appeal against that conviction has expired and the defendant has not taken an appeal or made a motion for leave to appeal;

(b) the defendant has taken an appeal or made a motion for leave to appeal against the conviction and the appeal or motion for leave has been dismissed or abandoned; or

(c) the defendant has given written notice to the court that convicted the defendant that the defendant elects not to appeal,

or where the defendant otherwise wilfully fails or refuses to comply with the order, the defendant is guilty of an offence and upon conviction the court may,

(d) impose a fine of not more than $1,000 or imprisonment for a term of not more than thirty days, or both, and in lieu of or in addition to the penalty, continue the probation order with such changes or additions and for such extended term, not exceeding an additional year, as the court considers reasonable; or

(e) where the justice presiding is the justice who made the original order, in lieu of imposing the penalty under clause (d), revoke the probation order and impose the sentence the passing of which was suspended upon the making of the probation order.

PART V

GENERAL PROVISIONS

Limitation

76. (1) A proceeding shall not be commenced after the expiration of any limitation period prescribed by or under any Act for the offence or, where no limitation period is prescribed, after six months after the date on which the offence was, or is alleged to have been, committed.

Extension

(2) A limitation period may be extended by a justice with the consent of the defendant.

Electronic court documents

76.1 (1) A document that is required or authorized to be filed, given or delivered to a court office or the clerk of the court under this Act may, in accordance with the regulations, be filed, given or delivered electronically.

(1.1) [Repealed 2015, c. 27, Sched. 1, s. 3(5)].

(1.2) [Repealed 2015, c. 27, Sched. 1, s. 3(5)].

Electronic signature

(2) An electronic document that is filed, given or delivered to a court office or the clerk of the court may be signed electronically in accordance with the regulations.

Electronic copy of paper original

(3) When a document is filed, given or delivered to a court office or the clerk of the court in paper form, the court may create and retain an electronic copy instead of the paper original.

Duty to ensure integrity

(4) A person who creates, retains or reproduces an electronic copy of a paper original for the purposes of subsection (3) shall ensure the integrity of the information contained in the electronic copy.

Power to deal with electronic documents

(5) Anything that the court is required or authorized to do with respect to a document may be done with respect to an electronic document.

Delivery in Person

(6) Nothing in this section limits the operation of a requirement to deliver a document personally or in person to a court office or the clerk of the court.

Regulations

(7) The Lieutenant Governor in Council may make regulations,
(a) governing the electronic filing, giving and delivery of documents to a court office or the clerk of the court;
(b) respecting the electronic signing of electronic documents that are filed, given or delivered to a court office or the clerk of the court;
(c) governing the storage, retention and disposal of computer-readable media used to file, give or deliver documents to a court office or the clerk of the court;
(d) governing the creation, storage, retention, transfer, reproduction, distribution, disposal or use of electronic documents by the court;
(e) respecting the electronic signing or certification of electronic documents by the court.

2015, c. 27, Sched. 1, s. 3(5)

Parties to offence

77. (1) Every person is a party to an offence who,
(a) actually commits it,
(b) does or omits to do anything for the purpose of aiding any person to commit it; or
(c) abets any person in committing it.

Common purpose

(2) Where two or more persons form an intention in common to carry out an unlawful purpose and to assist each other therein and any one of them, in carrying out the common purpose, commits an offence, each of them who knew or ought to have known that the commission of the offence would be a probable consequence of carrying out the common purpose is a party to the offence.

Counselling

78. (1) Where a person counsels or procures another person to be a party to an offence and that other person is afterwards a party to the offence, the person who counselled or procured is a party to the offence, even if the offence was committed in a way different from that which was counselled or procured.

Idem

(2) Every person who counsels or procures another person to be a party to an offence is a party to every offence that the other commits in consequence of the counselling or procuring that the person who counselled or procured knew or ought to have known was likely to be committed in consequence of the counselling or procuring.

Computation of age

79. In the absence of other evidence, or by way of corroboration of other evidence, a justice may infer the age of a person from his or her appearance.

Common law defences

80. Every rule and principle of the common law that renders any circumstance a justification or excuse for an act or a defence to a charge continues in force and applies in respect of offences, except in so far as they are altered by or inconsistent with this or any other Act.

Ignorance of the law

81. Ignorance of the law by a person who commits an offence is not an excuse for committing the offence.

Representation

82. A defendant may act by representative.

2006, c. 21, Sched. C, s. 131(14)

Recording of evidence

83. (1) A proceeding in which evidence is taken shall be recorded.

Evidence under oath or affirmation

(2) Evidence under this Act shall be taken under oath or affirmation, except as otherwise provided by law.

Definition

83.1 (1) In this section,

"electronic method" means video conference, audio conference, telephone conference or other method determined by the regulations.

Appearance by electronic method

(2) Subject to this section, in any proceeding under this Act or any step in a proceeding under this Act, if the appropriate equipment is available at the courthouse where the proceeding occurs,

    (a) a witness may give evidence by electronic method;

    (b) a defendant may appear by electronic method;

    (c) a prosecutor may appear and prosecute by electronic method; and

    (d) an interpreter may interpret by electronic method.

Proposed Addition — 83.1(2.1)

Early resolution meeting equipment

(2.1) If an offence notice indicates that the option of an early resolution meeting under section 5.1 is available, the clerk of the court at the courthouse indicated on the offence notice shall ensure that the courthouse is equipped to allow a defendant or prosecutor who is unable to attend in person because of remoteness to attend by electronic method.

    2017, c. 34, Sched. 35, s. 16(1) [Not in force at date of publication.]

Consent required

(3) A witness may appear by electronic method to give evidence in a proceeding commenced by information under Part III only with the consent of both the prosecutor and the defendant.

Attendance by justice

(3.1) A justice may attend and conduct a sentencing hearing under sections 5.1 and 7 and any other proceeding or any step in a proceeding determined by the regulations, by means of electronic method, if the appropriate equipment is available at the courthouse where the proceeding occurs, and the justice may,

Proposed Amendment — 83.1(3.1) opening words

Attendance by justice

(3.1) A justice may attend and conduct a hearing under sections 5.4 and 7 and any other proceeding or any step in a proceeding determined by the regulations, by means of electronic method, if the appropriate equipment is available at the courthouse where the proceeding occurs, and the justice may,

2017, c. 34, Sched. 35, s. 16(2) [Not in force at date of publication.]

(a) adjourn the sentencing hearing to have the defendant appear in person before the justice for the purpose of ensuring that the defendant understands the plea; and

(b) adjourn any other proceeding or step in a proceeding determined by the regulations if he or she is satisfied that the interests of justice require it or it is necessary for a fair trial.

Limited use of certain electronic methods

(4) Attendance by audio conference or telephone conference may only be used for the purpose of,

(a) attending a pre-trial conference;

(b) attending a meeting between the defendant and the prosecutor under section 5.1; or

Proposed Amendment — 83.1(4)(b)

(b) attending an early resolution meeting between the defendant and the prosecutor under section 5.1; or

2017, c. 34, Sched. 35, s. 16(3) [Not in force at date of publication.]

(c) attending or appearing at any other proceeding or step in a proceeding determined by the regulations.

Appearance in person

(5) The court may order any person described in subsection (2) to appear in person if it is satisfied that the interests of justice require it or it is necessary for a fair trial.

Oaths

(6) Despite the *Commissioners for taking Affidavits Act*, where evidence is given under oath by electronic method, the oath may be administered by the same electronic method.

Regulations

(7) The Lieutenant Governor in Council may make regulations,
(a) respecting the conditions for using any electronic method, including the degree of any remoteness required;
(b) determining proceedings where attendance or appearance may be made by electronic method;
(c) requiring the payment of fees for using electronic methods, fixing the amounts of the fees, and prescribing the circumstances in which and the conditions under which a justice or another person designated in the regulations may waive the payment of a fee.

2009, c. 33, Sched. 4, s. 1(48), (49)

Interpreters

84. (1) A justice may authorize a person to act as interpreter in a proceeding before the justice where the person swears the prescribed oath and, in the opinion of the justice, is competent.

Idem

(2) A judge may authorize a person to act as interpreter in proceedings under this Act where the person swears the prescribed oath and, in the opinion of the judge is competent and likely to be readily available.

Extension of time

85. (1) Subject to this section, the court may extend any time fixed by this Act, by the regulations made under this Act or the rules of court for doing any thing other than commencing or recommencing a proceeding, whether or not the time has expired.

Limit on number of applications

(2) No more than one application for an extension of the time for filing of an appeal may be made in respect of a conviction.

Exception for commencing parking proceeding

(3) A justice may extend the time for commencing a parking proceeding where the court is unable to obtain proof of ownership of the vehicle or to send a notice of impending conviction to the defendant within that time because of extraordinary circumstances, including labour disputes and disruptions of postal services, power services and technological facilities.

2009, c. 33, Sched. 4, s. 1(50)

Penalty for false statements

86. Every person who makes an assertion of fact in a statement or entry in a document or form for use under this Act knowing that the assertion is false is guilty of an offence and on conviction is liable to a fine of not more than $2,000.

Delivery

87. (1) Any notice or document required or authorized to be given or delivered under this Act or the rules of court is given or delivered if,

(a) delivered personally or by mail;

(b) delivered in accordance with a method provided by this Act or the regulations; or

(c) delivered in accordance with a method provided under any other Act or prescribed by the rules of court.

Exception, personal delivery

(1.1) Despite subsection (1), a notice or document shall be delivered personally if this Act or the rules of court require it to be given or delivered personally or in person.

Rebuttable presumption, mail delivery

(2) If a notice or document that is to be given or delivered to a person under this Act is mailed to the person at the person's last known address appearing on the records of the court in the proceeding, there is a rebuttable presumption that the notice or document is given or delivered to the person.

Rebuttable presumption, electronic delivery

(2.1) If a notice or document that is to be given or delivered to a person under this Act is delivered electronically, in accordance with a method provided by the regulations, to an email address or phone number that the person has provided for the purpose of receiving electronic notices or documents, there is a rebuttable presumption that the notice or document is given or delivered to the person.

Regulations

(3) The Lieutenant Governor in Council may make regulations respecting the method of delivery for any notice or document, including additional electronic methods, for the purposes of this Act.

2009, c. 33, Sched. 4, s. 1(51); 2015, c. 27, Sched. 1, s. 3(6); 2015, c. 27, Sched. 1, s. 3(6)-(8)

Civil remedies preserved

88. No civil remedy for an act or omission is suspended or affected for the reason that the act or omission is an offence.

Process on holidays

89. Any action authorized or required by this Act is not invalid for the reason only that the action was taken on a non-juridical day.

Irregularities in form

90. (1) The validity of any proceeding is not affected by,

(a) any irregularity or defect in the substance or form of the summons, warrant, offence notice, parking infraction notice, undertaking to appear or recognizance; or

(b) any variance between the charge set out in the summons, warrant, parking infraction notice, offence notice, undertaking to appear or recognizance and the charge set out in the information or certificate.

Adjournment to meet irregularities

(2) Where it appears to the court that the defendant has been misled by any irregularity, defect or variance mentioned in subsection (1), the court may adjourn the hearing and may make such order as the court considers appropriate, including an order under section 60 for the payment of costs.

Contempt

91. (1) Except as otherwise provided by an Act, every person who commits contempt in the face of a justice of the peace presiding over the Ontario Court of Justice in a proceeding under this Act is on conviction liable to a fine of not more than $1,000 or to imprisonment for a term of not more than thirty days, or to both.

Statement to offender

(2) Before a proceeding is taken for contempt under subsection (1), the justice of the peace shall inform the offender of the conduct complained of and the nature of the contempt and inform him or her of the right to show cause why he or she should not be punished.

Show cause

(3) A punishment for contempt in the face of the court shall not be imposed without giving the offender an opportunity to show cause why he or she should not be punished.

Adjournment for adjudication

(4) Except where, in the opinion of the justice of the peace, it is necessary to deal with the contempt immediately for the preservation of order and control in the courtroom, the justice of the peace shall adjourn the contempt proceeding to another day.

Adjudication by judge

(5) A contempt proceeding that is adjourned to another day under subsection (4) shall be heard and determined by the court presided over by a provincial judge.

Arrest for immediate adjudication

(6) Where the justice of the peace proceeds to deal with a contempt immediately and without adjournment under subsection (4), the justice of the peace may order the offender arrested and detained in the courtroom for the purpose of the hearing and determination.

Barring representative in contempt

(7) Where the offender is appearing before the court as a representative and the offender is not licensed under the *Law Society Act*, the court may order that he or she be barred from acting as representative in the proceeding in addition to any other punishment to which he or she is liable.

Appeals

(8) An order of punishment for contempt under this section is appealable in the same manner as if it were a conviction in a proceeding commenced by certificate under Part I of this Act.

Enforcement

(9) This Act applies for the purpose of enforcing a punishment by way of a fine or imprisonment under this section.

    2000, c. 26, Sched. A, s. 13(6), item 4; 2006, c. 21, Sched. C, s. 131(15)

Set fines—Chief Justice

    91.1 (1) The Chief Justice of the Ontario Court of Justice may specify an amount as the set fine for the purpose of proceedings under Part I or II for any offence.

Regional senior judge

(2) The regional senior judge of the Ontario Court of Justice for a region may specify an amount as the set fine for the purpose of proceedings under Part I or II for an offence under a by-law of a municipality in the region.

Conflict

(3) A set fine specified by the Chief Justice prevails over a set fine specified by a regional senior judge.

2017, c. 34, Sched. 35, s. 17

Regulations

92. The Lieutenant Governor in Council may make regulations,

(a) prescribing any matter referred to in this Act as prescribed by the regulations;

(b) prescribing the form of certificate as to ownership of a motor vehicle given by the Registrar under subsection 210(7) of the *Highway Traffic Act* for the purpose of proceedings under this Act;

(c) providing for the extension of times prescribed by or under this Act or the rules of court in the event of a disruption in postal services;

(d) requiring the payment of fees upon the filing of anything required or permitted to be filed under this Act or the rules and fixing the amounts thereof, and providing for the waiver of the payment of a fee by a justice, or by a judge under Part VII, in such circumstances and under such conditions as are set out in the regulations;

(e) fixing costs payable upon conviction and referred to in subsection 60(1);

(f) fixing the items in respect of which costs may be awarded under subsection 60(2) and prescribing the maximum amounts that may be awarded in respect of each item;

(g) prescribing administrative fees for the purposes of subsection 70(1) for the late payment of fines or classes of fines, and prescribing the classes;

Proposed Amendment — 92(g)

(g) prescribing administrative monetary penalties for the purposes of subsection 70(1) for the late payment of fines or classes of fines, and prescribing the classes;

2017, c. 34, Sched. 35, s. 18(1) [Not in force at date of publication.]

(h) providing for any transitional matter that the Lieutenant Governor in Council considers necessary or advisable in connection with the implementation of the amendments made by Schedule 35 to the *Stronger, Fairer Ontario Act (Budget Measures), 2017.*

2017, c. 34, Sched. 35, s. 18(2)

PART VI

YOUNG PERSONS

Definitions

93. In this Part,

"parent", when used with reference to a young person, includes an adult with whom the young person ordinarily resides;

"young person" means a person who is or, in the absence of evidence to the contrary, appears to be,

(a) twelve years of age or more, but

(b) under sixteen years of age,

and includes a person sixteen years of age or more charged with having committed an offence while he or she was twelve years of age or more but under sixteen years of age.

Minimum age

94. No person shall be convicted of an offence committed while he or she was under twelve years of age.

Offence notice not to be used

95. A proceeding commenced against a young person by certificate of offence shall not be initiated by an offence notice under clause 3(2)(a).

Notice to parent

96. (1) Where a summons is served upon a young person or a young person is released on a recognizance under this Act, the provincial offences officer, in the case of a summons, or the officer in charge, in the case of a recognizance, shall as soon as practicable give notice to a parent of the young person by delivering a copy of the summons or recognizance to the parent.

Where no notice given

(2) Where notice has not been given under subsection (1) and no person to whom notice could have been given appears with the young person, the court may,

(a) adjourn the hearing to another time to permit notice to be given; or

(b) dispense with notice.

Saving

(3) Failure to give notice to a parent under subsection (1) does not in itself invalidate the proceeding against the young person.

Sentence where proceeding commenced by certificate

97. (1) Despite subsection 12(1), where a young person is found guilty of an offence in a proceeding commenced by certificate, the court may,

(a) convict the young person and,

(i) order the young person to pay a fine not exceeding the set fine that would be payable for the offence by an adult, the maximum fine prescribed for the offence, or $300, whichever is the least, or

(ii) suspend the passing of sentence and direct that the young person comply with the conditions prescribed in a probation order; or

(b) discharge the young person absolutely.

Term of probation order

(2) Section 72 applies with necessary modifications to a probation order made under subclause (1)(a)(ii), in the same manner as if the proceeding were commenced by information, except that the probation order shall not remain in force for more than ninety days from the date when it takes effect.

s. 12(2) applies where proceeding initiated by summons

(3) Subsection 12(2) applies with necessary modifications where a young person is convicted of an offence in a proceeding initiated by summons, in the same manner as if the proceeding were initiated by offence notice.

Young person to be present at trial

98. (1) Subject to subsection 52(1) and subsection (2) of this section, a young person shall be present in court during the whole of his or her trial.

Court may permit absence

(2) The court may permit a young person to be absent during the whole or any part of his or her trial, on such conditions as the court considers proper.

Application of ss. 42, 54

(3) Sections 42 and 54 do not apply to a young person who is a defendant.

Failure of young person to appear

(4) Where a young person who is a defendant does not appear at the time and place appointed for a hearing and it is proved by the prosecutor, having been given a reasonable opportunity to do so, that a summons was served, an undertaking to appear was given or a recognizance to appear was entered into, as the case may be, or where the young person does not appear upon the resumption of a hearing that has been adjourned, the court may adjourn the hearing and issue a summons to appear or issue a warrant in the prescribed form for the arrest of the young person.

Compelling young person's attendance

(5) Where a young person does not attend personally in response to a summons issued under section 51 and it is proved by the prosecutor, having been given a reasonable opportunity to do so, that the summons was served, the court may

adjourn the hearing and issue a further summons or issue a warrant in the prescribed form for the arrest of the young person.

Identity of young person not to be published

99. (1) No person shall publish by any means a report,

(a) of an offence committed or alleged to have been committed by a young person; or

(b) of a hearing, adjudication, sentence or appeal concerning a young person who committed or is alleged to have committed an offence,

in which the name of or any information serving to identify the young person is disclosed.

Offence

(2) Every person who contravenes subsection (1) and every director, officer or employee of a corporation who authorizes, permits or acquiesces in a contravention of subsection (1) by the corporation is guilty of an offence and is liable on conviction to a fine of not more than $10,000.

Exceptions

(3) Subsection (1) does not prohibit the following:

1. The disclosure of information by the young person concerned.

2. The disclosure of information by the young person's parent or lawyer, for the purpose of protecting the young person's interests.

3. The disclosure of information by a police officer, for the purpose of investigating an offence which the young person is suspected of having committed.

4. The disclosure of information to an insurer, to enable the insurer to investigate a claim arising out of an offence committed or alleged to have been committed by the young person.

5. The disclosure of information in the course of the administration of justice, but not for the purpose of making the information known in the community.

6. The disclosure of information by a person or member of a class of persons prescribed by the regulations, for a purpose prescribed by the regulations.

Pre-sentence report

100. (1) Section 56 applies with necessary modifications where a young person is convicted of an offence in a proceeding commenced by certificate of offence, in the same manner as if the proceeding were commenced by information.

Pre-sentence report mandatory where imprisonment considered

(2) Where a young person who is bound by a probation order is convicted of an offence under section 75 and the court is considering imposing a sentence of imprisonment, the court shall direct a probation officer to prepare and file with the court a report in writing relating to the defendant for the purpose of assisting the court in imposing sentence, and the clerk of the court shall cause a copy of the report to be provided to the defendant or his or her representative and to the prosecutor.

2006, c. 21, Sched. C, s. 131(16)

Penalties limited

101. (1) Despite the provisions of this or any other Act, no young person shall be sentenced,

(a) to be imprisoned, except under clause 75(d); or

(b) to pay a fine exceeding $1,000.

Sentence where proceeding commenced by information

(2) Where a young person is found guilty of an offence in a proceeding commenced by information, the court may,

(a) convict the young person and,

(i) order the young person to pay a fine not exceeding the maximum prescribed for the offence or $1,000, whichever is less, or

(ii) suspend the passing of sentence and direct that the young person comply with the conditions prescribed in a probation order; or

(b) discharge the young person absolutely.

Term of probation order

(3) A probation order made under subclause (2)(a)(ii) shall not remain in force for more than one year from the date when it takes effect.

No imprisonment for non-payment of fine

102. (1) No warrant of committal shall be issued against a young person under section 69.

Probation order in lieu of imprisonment

(2) Where it would be appropriate, but for subsection (1), to issue a warrant against a young person under subsection 69(3) or (4), a judge may direct that the young person comply with the conditions prescribed in a probation order, where the young person has been given fifteen days notice of the intent to make a probation order and has had an opportunity to be heard.

Term of probation order

(3) A probation order made under subsection (2) shall not remain in force for more than ninety days from the date when it takes effect.

Open custody

103. Where a young person is sentenced to a term of imprisonment for breach of probation under clause 75(d), the term of imprisonment shall be served in a place of open custody designated under section 24.1 of the *Young Offenders Act* (Canada), whether in accordance with section 88 of the *Youth Criminal Justice Act* (Canada) or otherwise.

2006, c. 19, Sched. D, s. 18(1)

Evidence of young person's age

104. In a proceeding under this Act, a parent's testimony as to a young person's age and any other evidence of a young person's age that the court considers credible or trustworthy in the circumstances are admissible.

Appeal

105. Where the defendant is a young person, an appeal under subsection 135(1) shall be to the Superior Court of Justice, but the procedures and the powers of the court and any appeal from the judgment of the court shall be the same as if the appeal were to the Ontario Court of Justice presided over by a provincial judge.

2000, c. 26, Sched. A, s. 13(5), item 2, (6), item 5

Arrest without warrant limited

106. No person shall exercise an authority under this or any other Act to arrest a young person without warrant unless the person has reasonable and probable grounds to believe that it is necessary in the public interest to do so in order to,

(a) establish the young person's identity; or

(b) prevent the continuation or repetition of an offence that constitutes a serious danger to the young person or to the person or property of another.

s. 149 does not apply

107. (1) Section 149 does not apply to a young person who has been arrested.

Release after arrest by officer

(2) Where a police officer acting under a warrant or other power of arrest arrests a young person, the police officer shall, as soon as is practicable, release the young person from custody unconditionally or after serving him or her with a summons

unless the officer has reasonable and probable grounds to believe that it is necessary in the public interest for the young person to be detained in order to,

(a) establish the young person's identity; or

(b) prevent the continuation or repetition of an offence that constitutes a serious danger to the young person or the person or property of another.

Release by officer in charge

(3) Where a young person is not released from custody under subsection (2), the police officer shall deliver the young person to the officer in charge who shall, where in his or her opinion the conditions set out in clause (2)(a) or (b) do not or no longer exist, release the young person,

(a) unconditionally;

(b) upon serving the young person with a summons; or

(c) upon the young person entering into a recognizance in the prescribed form without sureties conditioned for his or her appearance in court.

Notice to parent

(4) Where the officer in charge does not release the young person under subsection (3), the officer in charge shall as soon as possible notify a parent of the young person by advising the parent, orally or in writing, of the young person's arrest, the reason for the arrest and the place of detention.

ss. 150, 151 apply

(5) Sections 150 and 151 apply with necessary modifications to the release of a young person from custody under this section.

Place of custody

(6) No young person who is detained under section 150 shall be detained in any part of a place in which an adult who has been charged with or convicted of an offence is detained unless a justice so authorizes, on being satisfied that,

(a) the young person cannot, having regard to the young person's own safety or the safety of others, be detained in a place of temporary detention for young persons; or

(b) no place of temporary detention for young persons is available within a reasonable distance.

Idem

(7) Wherever practicable, a young person who is detained in custody shall be detained in a place of temporary detention designated under the *Youth Criminal Justice Act* (Canada).

2006, c. 19, Sched. D, s. 18(2)

Functions of a justice of peace limited

108. (1) The functions of a justice with respect to a defendant who is a young person shall be performed only by a judge where a defendant is charged with an offence under section 75.

Exception

(2) Subsection (1) does not apply to the functions of a justice under Parts III and VIII.

1993, c. 31, s. 1(28)

PART VII

APPEALS AND REVIEW

Definitions

109. In this Part,

"counsel" [Repealed 2006, c. 21, Sched. C, s. 131(17).]

"court" means the court to which an appeal is or may be taken under this Part;

"judge" means a judge of the court to which an appeal is or may be taken under this Part;

"sentence" includes any order or disposition consequent upon a conviction and an order as to costs.

2000, c. 26, Sched. A, s. 13(6), item 6; 2006, c. 21, Sched. C, s. 131(17)

Custody pending appeal

110. A defendant who appeals shall, if in custody, remain in custody, but a judge may order his or her release upon any of the conditions set out in subsection 150(2).

Payment of fine before appeal

111. (1) A notice of appeal by a defendant shall not be accepted for filing if the defendant has not paid in full the fine imposed by the decision appealed from.

Exception with recognizance

(2) A judge may waive compliance with subsection (1) and order that the appellant enter into a recognizance to appear on the appeal, and the recognizance shall be in such amount, with or without sureties, as the judge directs.

Simultaneous applications

(3) A defendant may file an application to waive compliance with subsection (1) at the same time as the notice of appeal.

Role of prosecutor

(4) The defendant shall give the prosecutor notice of any application to waive compliance with subsection (1) and the prosecutor shall have an opportunity to make submissions in the public interest in respect of the application.

2009, c. 33, Sched. 4, s. 1(52), (53)

Stay

112. The filing of a notice of appeal does not stay the conviction unless a judge so orders.

Fixing of date where appellant in custody

113. (1) Where an appellant is in custody pending the hearing of the appeal and the hearing of the appeal has not commenced within thirty days from the day on which notice of the appeal was given, the person having custody of the appellant shall make a motion to a judge to fix a date for the hearing of the appeal.

Idem

(2) Upon receiving a motion under subsection (1), the judge shall, after giving the prosecutor a reasonable opportunity to be heard, fix a date for the hearing of the appeal and give such directions as the judge thinks appropriate for expediting the hearing of the appeal.

Payment of fine not waiver

114. A person does not waive the right of appeal by reason only that the person pays the fine or complies with any order imposed upon conviction.

Transmittal of material

115. Where a notice of appeal has been filed, the clerk or local register of the appeal court shall notify the clerk of the trial court of the appeal and, upon receipt of the notification, the clerk of the trial court shall transmit the order appealed from and transmit or transfer custody of all other material in his or her possession or control relevant to the proceeding to the clerk or local registrar of the appeal court to be kept with the records of the appeal court.

APPEALS UNDER PART III

Appeals, proceedings commenced by information

116. (1) Where a proceeding is commenced by information under Part III, the defendant or the prosecutor or the Attorney General by way of intervention may appeal from,

(a) a conviction;

(b) a dismissal;

(c) a finding as to ability, because of mental disorder, to conduct a defence;

(d) a sentence; or

(e) any other order as to costs.

Appeal court

(2) An appeal under subsection (1) shall be,

(a) where the appeal is from the decision of a justice of the peace, to the Ontario Court of Justice presided over by a provincial judge; or

(b) where the appeal is from the decision of a provincial judge, to the Superior Court of Justice.

Notice of appeal

(3) The appellant shall give notice of appeal in such manner and within such period as is provided by the rules of court.

Simultaneous application

(4) Despite subsection (3), the notice of appeal may be filed at the same time as an application under section 85 to extend the time to give notice of appeal.
2000, c. 26, Sched. A, s. 13(5), item 3, (6), item 7; 2009, c. 33, Sched. 4, s. 1(54), (55)

Powers of court

117. (1) The court may, where it considers it to be in the interests of justice, (a) order the production of any writing, exhibit or other thing relevant to the appeal;

(a.1) amend the information, unless it is of the opinion that the defendant has been misled or prejudiced in his or her defence or appeal;

(b) order any witness who would have been a compellable witness at the trial, whether or not he or she was called at the trial,

(i) to attend and be examined before the court, or

(ii) to be examined in the manner provided by the rules of court before a judge of the court, or before any officer of the court or justice of the peace or other person appointed by the court for the purpose;

(c) admit, as evidence, an examination that is taken under subclause (b)(ii);

(d) receive the evidence, if tendered, of any witness;

(e) order that any question arising on the appeal that,

(i) involves prolonged examination of writings or accounts, or scientific investigation, and

(ii) cannot in the opinion of the court conveniently be inquired into before the court,

be referred for inquiry and report, in the manner provided by the rules of court, to a special commissioner appointed by the court; and

(f) act upon the report of a commissioner who is appointed under clause (e) in so far as the court thinks fit to do so.

Rights of parties

(2) Where the court exercises a power under this section, the parties or their representatives are entitled to examine or cross-examine witnesses and, in an inquiry under clause (1)(e), are entitled to be present during the inquiry and to adduce evidence and to be heard.

2006, c. 21, Sched. C, s. 131(18); 2009, c. 33, Sched. 4, s. 1(56)

Right to representation

118. (1) An appellant or respondent may appear and act personally or by representative.

Attendance while in custody

(2) An appellant or respondent who is in custody as a result of the decision appealed from is entitled to be present at the hearing of the appeal.

Sentencing in absence

(3) The power of a court to impose sentence may be exercised although the appellant or respondent is not present.

2006, c. 21, Sched. C, s. 131(19)

Written argument

119. An appellant or respondent may present the case on appeal and argument in writing instead of orally, and the court shall consider any case or argument so presented.

Powers on appeal against conviction

120. (1) On the hearing of an appeal against a conviction or against a finding as to the ability, because of mental disorder, to conduct a defence, the court by order,

(a) may allow the appeal where it is of the opinion that,
(i) the finding should be set aside on the ground that it is unreasonable or cannot be supported by the evidence,
(ii) the judgment of the trial court should be set aside on the ground of a wrong decision on a question of law, or
(iii) on any ground, there was a miscarriage of justice; or
(b) may dismiss the appeal where,

(i) the court is of the opinion that the appellant, although the appellant was not properly convicted on a count or part of an information, was properly convicted on another count or part of the information,

(ii) the appeal is not decided in favour of the appellant on any ground mentioned in clause (a), or

(iii) although the court is of the opinion that on any ground mentioned in subclause (a)(ii) the appeal might be decided in favour of the appellant, it is of the opinion that no substantial wrong or miscarriage of justice has occurred.

Idem

(2) Where the court allows an appeal under clause (1)(a), it shall,

(a) where the appeal is from a conviction,

(i) direct a finding of acquittal to be entered, or

(ii) order a new trial; or

(b) where the appeal is from a finding as to the ability, because of mental disorder, to conduct a defence, order a new trial, subject to section 44.

Idem

(3) Where the court dismisses an appeal under clause (1)(b), it may substitute the decision that in its opinion should have been made and affirm the sentence passed by the trial court or impose a sentence that is warranted in law.

Powers on appeal against acquittal

121. Where an appeal is from an acquittal, the court may by order,

(a) dismiss the appeal; or

(b) allow the appeal, set aside the finding and,

(i) order a new trial, or

(ii) enter a finding of guilt with respect to the offence of which, in its opinion, the person who has been accused of the offence should have been found guilty, and pass a sentence that is warranted in law.

Appeal against sentence

122. (1) Where an appeal is taken against sentence, the court shall consider the fitness of the sentence appealed from and may, upon such evidence, if any, as it thinks fit to require or receive, by order,

(a) dismiss the appeal; or

(b) vary the sentence within the limits prescribed by law for the offence of which the defendant was convicted,

and, in making any order under clause (b), the court may take into account any time spent in custody by the defendant as a result of the offence.

Variance of sentence

(2) A judgment of a court that varies a sentence has the same force and effect as if it were a sentence passed by the trial court.

One sentence on more than one count

123. Where one sentence is passed upon a finding of guilt on two or more counts, the sentence is good if any of the counts would have justified the sentence.

Appeal based on defect in information or process

124. (1) Judgment shall not be given in favour of an appellant based on any alleged defect in the substance or form of an information, certificate or process of any variance between the information, certificate or process and the evidence adduced at trial unless it is shown that objection was taken at the trial and that, in the case of a variance, an adjournment of the trial was refused although the variance has misled the appellant.

Idem

(2) Where an appeal is based on a defect in a conviction or an order, judgment shall not be given in favour of the appellant, but the court shall make an order curing the defect.

Additional orders

125. Where a court exercises any of the powers conferred by sections 117 to 124, it may make any order, in addition, that justice requires.

New trial

126. (1) Where a court orders a new trial, it shall be held in the Ontario Court of Justice presided over by a justice other than the justice who tried the defendant in the first instance unless the appeal court directs that the new trial be held before the justice who tried the defendant in the first instance.

Order for release

(2) Where a court orders a new trial, it may make such order for the release or detention of the appellant pending such trial as may be made by a justice under subsection 150(2) and the order may be enforced in the same manner as if it had been made by a justice under that subsection.

2000, c. 26, Sched. A, s. 13(6), item 8

Appeal by way of new trial

127. (1) Where, because of the condition of the record of the trial in the trial court or for any other reason, the court, upon the motion of the appellant or respondent, is of the opinion that the interests of justice would be better served by hearing and determining the appeal by holding a new trial in the court, the court may order that the appeal shall be heard by way of a new trial in the court and for this purpose this Act applies with necessary modifications in the same manner as to a proceeding in the trial court.

Evidence

(2) The court may, for the purpose of hearing and determining an appeal under subsection (1), permit the evidence of any witness taken before the trial court to be read if that evidence has been authenticated and if,

(a) the appellant and respondent consent;

(b) the court is satisfied that the attendance of the witness cannot reasonably be obtained; or

(c) by reason of the formal nature of the evidence or otherwise the court is satisfied that the opposite party will not be prejudiced,

and any evidence that is read under the authority of this subsection has the same force and effect as if the witness had given the evidence before the court.

Dismissal or abandonment

128. (1) The court may, upon proof that notice of an appeal has been given and that,

(a) the appellant has failed to comply with any order made under section 110 or 111 or with the conditions of any recognizance entered into under either of those sections; or

(b) the appeal has not been proceeded with or has been abandoned,

order that the appeal be dismissed.

Dismissal by justice

(2) Where the clerk of the court considers that an appeal has not been proceeded with or has been abandoned, the clerk may, after giving notice to the parties to the appeal, have the matter brought before a justice sitting in open court to determine whether the appeal has been abandoned and the appeal should be dismissed.

Motion to restore

(3) A party to an appeal that was dismissed under subsection (2) may apply to have the appeal restored.

2011, c. 1, Sched. 1, s. 7(10)

Costs

129. (1) Where an appeal is heard and determined or is abandoned or is dismissed for want of prosecution, the court may make any order with respect to costs that it considers just and reasonable.

Payment

(2) Where the court orders the appellant or respondent to pay costs, the order shall direct that the costs be paid to the clerk of the trial court, to be paid by the clerk to the person entitled to them, and shall fix the period within which the costs shall be paid.

Enforcement

(3) Costs ordered to be paid under this section by a person other than a prosecutor acting on behalf of the Crown shall be deemed to be a fine for the purpose of enforcing its payment.

Implementation of appeal court order

130. An order or judgment of the appeal court shall be implemented or enforced by the trial court and the clerk or local registrar of the appeal court shall send to the clerk of the trial court the order and all writings relating thereto.

Appeal to Court of Appeal

131. (1) A defendant or the prosecutor or the Attorney General by way of intervention may appeal from the judgment of the court to the Court of Appeal, with leave of a judge of the Court of Appeal on special grounds, upon any question of law alone or as to sentence.

Grounds for leave

(2) No leave to appeal shall be granted under subsection (1) unless the judge of the Court of Appeal considers that in the particular circumstances of the case it is essential in the public interest or for the due administration of justice that leave be granted.

Appeal as to leave

(3) No appeal or review lies from a decision on a motion for leave to appeal under subsection (1).

Custody pending appeal

132. A defendant who appeals shall, if the defendant is in custody, remain in custody, but a judge may order his or her release upon any of the conditions set out in subsection 150(2).

Transfer of record

133. Where a motion for leave to appeal is made, the Registrar of the Court of Appeal shall notify the clerk or local registrar of the court appealed from of the motion and, upon receipt of the notification, the clerk or local registrar of the court shall transmit to the Registrar all the material forming the record including any other relevant material requested by a judge of the Court of Appeal.

Application of ss. 114, 117—126, 128(b), 129

134. Sections 114, 117, 118, 119, 120, 121, 122, 123, 124, 125 and 126, clause 128(b) and section 129 apply with necessary modifications to appeals to the Court of Appeal under section 131.

APPEALS UNDER PARTS I AND II

Appeal

135. (1) A defendant or the prosecutor or the Attorney General by way of intervention is entitled to appeal an acquittal, conviction or sentence in a proceeding commenced by certificate under Part I or II and the appeal shall be to the Ontario Court of Justice presided over by a provincial judge.

Application for appeal

(2) A notice of appeal shall be in the prescribed form and shall state the reasons why the appeal is taken and shall be filed with the clerk of the court within 30 days after the making of the decision appealed from, in accordance with the rules of court.

Simultaneous application

(2.1) Despite subsection (2), the notice of appeal may be filed at the same time as an application under section 85 to extend the time to give notice of appeal.

Notice of hearing

(3) The clerk shall, as soon as is practicable, give a notice to the defendant and prosecutor of the time and place of the hearing of the appeal.
2000, c. 26, Sched. A, s. 13(6), item 9; 2009, c. 33, Sched. 4, s. 1(57), (58)

Conduct of appeal

136. (1) Upon an appeal, the court shall give the parties an opportunity to be heard for the purpose of determining the issues and may, where the circumstances warrant it, make such inquires as are necessary to ensure that the issues are fully and effectively defined.

Review

(2) An appeal shall be conducted by means of a review.

Evidence

(3) In determining a review, the court may,

(a) hear or rehear the recorded evidence or any part thereof and may require any party to provide a transcript of the evidence, or any part thereof, or to produce any further exhibit;

(b) receive the evidence of any witness whether or not the witness gave evidence at the trial;

(c) require the justice presiding at the trial to report in writing on any matter specified in the request; or

(d) receive and act upon statements of agreed facts or admissions.

Dismissal on abandonment

137. (1) Where an appeal has not been proceeded with or abandoned, the court may order that the appeal be dismissed.

Dismissal by justice

(2) Where the clerk of the court considers that an appeal has not been proceeded with or has been abandoned, the clerk may, after giving notice to the parties to the appeal, have the matter brought before a justice sitting in open court to determine whether the appeal has been abandoned and the appeal should be dismissed.

Motion to restore

(3) A party to an appeal that was dismissed under subsection (2) may apply to have the appeal restored.

2009, c. 33, Sched. 4, s. 1(59)

Powers of court on appeal

138. (1) Upon an appeal, the court may affirm, reverse or vary the decision appealed from or where, in the opinion of the court, it is necessary to do so to satisfy the ends of justice, direct a new trial.

New trial

(2) Where the court directs a new trial, it shall be held in the Ontario Court of Justice presided over by a justice other than the justice who tried the defendant in the first instance, but the appeal court may, with the consent of the parties to the

appeal, direct that the new trial be held before the justice who tried the defendant in the first instance or before the judge who directs the new trial.

Costs

(3) Upon an appeal, the court may make an order under section 60 for the payment of costs incurred on the appeal, and subsection (3) thereof applies to the order.

2000, c. 26, Sched. A, s. 13(6), item 10

Appeal to Court of Appeal

139. (1) An appeal lies from the judgment of the Ontario Court of Justice in an appeal under section 135 to the Court of Appeal, with leave of a judge of the Court of Appeal, on special grounds, upon any question of law alone.

Grounds for leave

(2) No leave to appeal shall be granted under subsection (1) unless the judge of the Court of Appeal considers that in the particular circumstances of the case it is essential in the public interest or for the due administration of justice that leave be granted.

Costs

(3) Upon an appeal under this section, the Court of Appeal may make any order with respect to costs that it considers just and reasonable.

Appeal as to leave

(4) No appeal or review lies from a decision on a motion for leave to appeal under subsection (1).

2000, c. 26, Sched. A, s. 13(6), item 11

REVIEW

Application for relief in nature of mandamus, prohibition, certiorari

140. (1) On application, the Superior Court of Justice may by order grant any relief in respect of matters arising under this Act that the applicant would be entitled to in an application for an order in the nature of mandamus, prohibition or certiorari.

Notice of application

(2) Notice of an application under this section shall be served on,

(a) the person whose act or omission gives rise to the application;

(b) any person who is a party to a proceeding that gives rise to the application; and

(c) the Attorney General.

Appeal

(3) An appeal lies to the Court of Appeal from an order made under this section.

2000, c. 26, Sched. A, s. 13(5), item 4

Notice re certiorari

141. (1) A notice under section 140 in respect of an application for relief in the nature of certiorari shall be given at least seven days and not more than ten days before the date fixed for the hearing of the application and the notice shall be served within thirty days after the occurrence of the act sought to be quashed.

Filing material

(2) Where a notice referred to in subsection (1) is served on the person making the decision, order or warrant or holding the proceeding giving rise to the application, such person shall forthwith file with the Superior Court of Justice for use on the application, all material concerning the subject-matter of the application.

Motion to continue proceeding

(2.1) Where a notice referred to in subsection (1) is served in respect of an application, a person who is entitled to notice of the application under subsection 140(2) may make a motion to the Superior Court of Justice for an order that a trial in the proceeding giving rise to the application may continue despite the application and the Court may make the order if it is satisfied that it is in the interests of justice to do so.

Where appeal available

(3) No application shall be made to quash a conviction, order or ruling from which an appeal is provided by this Act, whether subject to leave or otherwise.

Substantial wrong

(4) On an application for relief in the nature of certiorari, the Superior Court of Justice shall not grant relief unless the court finds that a substantial wrong or miscarriage of justice has occurred, and the court may amend or validate any decision already made, with effect from such time and on such terms as the court considers proper.

(5) [Repealed 2009, c. 33, Sched. 4, s. 1(60).]

Application for habeas corpus

142. (1) On application, the Superior Court of Justice may by order grant any relief in respect of a matter arising under this Act that the applicant would be entitled to in an application for an order in the nature of *habeas corpus*.

Procedure on application for relief in nature of habeas corpus

(2) Notice of an application under subsection (1) for relief in the nature of *habeas corpus* shall be served upon the person having custody of the person in respect of whom the application is made and upon the Attorney General and upon the hearing of the application the presence before the court of the person in respect of whom the application was made may be dispensed with by consent, in which event the court may proceed to dispose of the matter forthwith as the justice of the case requires.

Idem

(3) Subject to subsections (1) and (2), the *Habeas Corpus Act* applies to applications under this section, but an application for relief in the nature of certiorari may be brought in aid of an application under this section.

Idem

(4) The *Judicial Review Procedure Act* does not apply to matters in respect of which an application may be made under section 140.

Costs

(5) A court to which an application or appeal is made under section 140 or this section may make any order with respect to costs that it considers just and reasonable.

2000, c. 26, Sched. A, s. 13(5), item 6

PART VIII

ARREST, BAIL AND SEARCH WARRANTS ARREST

Officer in charge

143. In this Part, **"officer in charge"** means the police officer who is in charge of the lock-up or other place to which a person is taken after his or her arrest.

Execution of warrant

144. (1) A warrant for the arrest of a person shall be executed by a police officer by arresting the person against whom the warrant is directed wherever he or she is found in Ontario.

Idem

(2) A police officer may arrest without warrant a person for whose arrest he or she has reasonable and probable grounds to believe that a warrant is in force in Ontario.

Arrest without warrant

145. Any person may arrest without warrant a person who he or she has reasonable and probable grounds to believe has committed an offence and is escaping from and freshly pursued by a police officer who has lawful authority to arrest that person, and, where the person who makes the arrest is not a police officer, shall forthwith deliver the person arrested to a police officer.

Use of force

146. (1) Every police officer is, if he or she acts on reasonable and probable grounds, justified in using as much force as is necessary to do what the officer is required or authorized by law to do.

Use of force by citizen

(2) Every person upon whom a police officer calls for assistance is justified in using as much force as he or she believes on reasonable and probable grounds is necessary to render such assistance.

Immunity from civil liability

147. Where a person is wrongfully arrested, whether with or without a warrant, no action for damages shall be brought,

(a) against the police officer making the arrest if he or she believed in good faith and on reasonable and probable grounds that the person arrested was the person named in the warrant or was subject to arrest without warrant under the authority of an Act;

(b) against any person called upon to assist the police officer if such person believed that the police officer had the right to effect the arrest; or

(c) against any person required to detain the prisoner in custody if such person believed the arrest was lawfully made.

Production of process

148. (1) It is the duty of every one who executes a process or warrant to have it with him or her, where it is feasible to do so, and to produce it when requested to do so.

Notice of reason for arrest

(2) It is the duty of every one who arrests a person, whether with or without warrant, to give notice to that person, where it is feasible to do so, of the reason for the arrest.

BAIL

Release after arrest by officer

149. (1) Where a police officer, acting under a warrant or other power of arrest, arrests a person, the police officer shall, as soon as is practicable, release the person from custody after serving him or her with a summons or offence notice unless the officer has reasonable and probable grounds to believe that,

(a) it is necessary in the public interest for the person to be detained, having regard to all the circumstances including the need to,

(i) establish the identity of the person,

(ii) secure or preserve evidence of or relating to the offence, or

(iii) prevent the continuation or repetition of the offence or the commission of another offence; or

(b) the person arrested is ordinarily resident outside Ontario and will not respond to a summons or offence notice.

Release by officer in charge

(2) Where a defendant is not released from custody under subsection (1), the police officer shall deliver him or her to the officer in charge who shall, where in his or her opinion the conditions set out in clauses (1)(a) and (b) do not or no longer exist, release the defendant,

(a) upon serving the defendant with a summons or offence notice;

(b) upon the defendant entering into a recognizance in the prescribed form without sureties conditioned for his or her appearance in court.

Cash bail by non-resident

(3) Where the defendant is held for the reason only that he or she is not ordinarily resident in Ontario and it is believed that the defendant will not respond to a summons or offence notice, the officer in charge may, in addition to anything required under subsection (2), require the defendant to deposit cash or other satisfactory negotiable security in an amount not to exceed,

(a) where the preceeding is commenced by certificate under Part I or II, the amount of the set fine for the offence or, if none, $300; or

(b) where the proceeding is commenced by information under Part III, $500.

Person in custody to be brought before justice

150. (1) Where a defendant is not released from custody under section 149, the officer in charge shall, as soon as is practicable but in any event within twenty-four hours, bring the defendant before a justice and the justice shall, unless a plea of guilty is taken, order that the defendant be released upon giving his or her undertaking to appear unless the prosecutor having been given an opportunity to do so shows cause why the detention of the defendant is justified to ensure his or her appearance in court or why an order under subsection (2) is justified for the same purpose.

Order for conditional release

(2) Subject to subsection (1), the justice may order the release of the defendant,
(a) upon the defendant entering into a recognizance to appear with such conditions as are appropriate to ensure his or her appearance in court;
(b) where the offence is one punishable by imprisonment for twelve months or more, conditional upon the defendant entering into a recognizance before a justice with sureties in such amount and with such conditions, if any, as are appropriate to ensure his or her appearance in court or, with the consent of the prosecutor, upon the defendant depositing with the justice such sum of money or other valuable security as the order directs in an amount not exceeding,
    (i) where the proceeding is commenced by certificate under Part I or II, the amount of the set fine for the offence or, if none, $300, or
    (ii) where the proceeding is commenced by information under Part III, $1,000; or
(c) if the defendant is not ordinarily resident in Ontario, upon the defendant entering into a recognizance before a justice, with or without sureties, in such amount and with such conditions, if any, as are appropriate to ensure his or her appearance in court, and depositing with the justice such sum of money or other valuable security as the order directs in an amount not exceeding,
    (i) where the proceeding is commenced by certificate under Part I or II, the amount of the set fine for the offence or, if none, $300, or
    (ii) where the proceeding is commenced by information under Part III, $1,000.

Idem

(3) The justice shall not make an order under clause (2)(b) or (c) unless the prosecutor shows cause why an order under the immediately preceeding clause should not be made.

Order for detention

(4) Where the prosecutor shows cause why the detention of the defendant in custody is justified to ensure his or her appearance in court, the justice shall order the defendant to be detained in custody until he or she is dealt with according to law.

Reasons

(5) The justice shall include in the record a statement of the reasons for his or her decision under subsection (1), (2) or (4).

Evidence at hearing

(6) Where a person is brought before a justice under subsection (1), the justice may receive and base his or her decision upon information the justice considers credible or trustworthy in the circumstances of each case except that the defendant shall not be examined or cross-examined in respect of the offence with which he or she is charged.

Adjournments

(7) Where a person is brought before a justice under subsection (1), the matter shall not be adjourned for more than three days without the consent of the defendant.

Expediting trial of person in custody

151. (1) Where a defendant is not released from custody under section 149 or 150, he or she shall be brought before the court forthwith and, in any event, within eight days.

Further orders

(2) The justice presiding upon any appearance of the defendant in court may, upon the motion of the defendant or prosecutor, review any order made under section 150 and make such further or other order under section 150 as to the justice seems appropriate in the circumstances.

Appeal

152. A defendant or the prosecutor may appeal from an order or refusal to make an order under section 150 or 151 and the appeal shall be to the Superior Court of Justice.

2000, c. 26, Sched. A, s. 13(5), item 7

Appointment of agent for appearance

153. (1) A person who is released upon deposit under subsection 149(3) or clause 150(2)(c) may appoint the clerk of the court to act as the person's agent, in the event that he or she does not appear to answer to the charge, for the purpose of entering a plea of guilty on the person's behalf and authorizing the clerk to apply the amount so deposited toward payment of the fine and costs imposed by the court upon the conviction, and the clerk shall act as agent under this subsection without fee.

Returns to court

(2) An officer in charge or justice who takes a recognizance, money or security under section 149 or 150 shall make a return thereof to the court.

Returns to sureties

(3) The clerk of the court shall, upon the conclusion of a proceeding, make a financial return to every person who deposited money or security under a recognizance and return the surplus, if any.

Recognizance binds for all appearances

154. (1) The recognizance of a person to appear in a proceeding binds the person and the person's sureties in respect of all appearances required in the proceeding at times and places to which the proceeding is adjourned.

Recognizance binds independently of other charges

(2) A recognizance is binding in respect of appearances for the offence to which it relates and is not vacated upon the arrest, discharge or conviction of the defendant upon another charge.

Liability of principal

(3) The principal to a recognizance is bound for the amount of the recognizance due upon forfeiture.

Liability where sureties

(4) The principal and each surety to a recognizance are bound, jointly and severally, for the amount of the recognizance due upon forfeiture for non-appearance.

Motion by surety to be relieved

155. (1) A surety to a recognizance may, on motion in writing to the court at the location where the defendant is required to appear, ask to be relieved of the surety's obligation under the recognizance and the court shall thereupon issue a warrant for the arrest of the defendant.

Certificate of arrest

(2) When a police officer arrests the defendant under a warrant issued under subsection (1), he or she shall bring the defendant before a justice under section 150 and certify the arrest by certificate in the prescribed form and deliver the certificate to the court.

Vacating of recognizance

(3) The receipt of the certificate by the court under subsection (2) vacates the recognizance and discharges the sureties.

Delivery of defendant by surety

156. A surety to a recognizance may discharge the surety's obligation under the recognizance by delivering the defendant into the custody of the court at the location where he or she is required to appear at any time while it is sitting at or before the trial of the defendant.

Certificate of default

157. (1) Where a person who is bound by recognizance does not comply with a condition of the recognizance, a justice having knowledge of the facts shall endorse on the recognizance a certificate in the prescribed form setting out,

(a) the nature of the default;

(b) the reason for the default, if it is known;

(c) whether the ends of justice have been defeated or delayed by reason of the default; and

(d) the names and addresses of the principal and sureties.

Certificate as evidence

(2) A certificate that has been endorsed on a recognizance under subsection (1) is evidence of the default to which it relates.

Motion for forfeiture

(3) The clerk of the court shall transmit the endorsed recognizance to the local registrar of the Superior Court of Justice and, upon its receipt, the endorsed recognizance constitutes a motion for the forfeiture of the recognizance.

Notice of hearing

(4) A judge of the Superior Court of Justice shall fix a time and place for the hearing of the motion by the court and the local registrar of the court shall, not less than ten days before the time fixed for the hearing, deliver notice to the prosecutor and to each principal and, where the motion is for forfeiture for non-appearance, each surety named in the recognizance, of the time and place fixed for the hearing and requiring each principal and surety to show cause why the recognizance should not be forfeited.

Order as to forfeiture

(5) The Superior Court of Justice may, after giving the parties an opportunity to be heard, in its discretion grant or refuse the motion and make any order in respect of the forfeiture of the recognizance that the court considers proper.

Collection on forfeiture

(6) Where an order for forfeiture is made under subsection (5),

(a) any money or security forfeited shall be paid over by the person who has custody of it to the person who is entitled by law to receive it; and

(b) the principal and surety become judgment debtors of the Crown jointly and severally in the amount forfeited under the recognizance and the amount may be collected in the same manner as money owing under a judgment of the Superior Court of Justice.

2000, c. 26, Sched. A, s. 13(5), item 8

SEARCH WARRANTS

Search warrant

158. (1) A justice may at any time issue a warrant under his or her hand if the justice is satisfied by information upon oath that there are reasonable grounds to believe that there is in any place,

(a) anything on or in respect of which an offence has been or is suspected to have been committed; or

(b) anything that there are reasonable grounds to believe will afford evidence as to the commission of an offence.

Same

(1.1) The search warrant authorizes a police officer or person named in the warrant,

(a) to search the place named in the information for any thing described in clause (1)(a) or (b); and

(b) to seize the thing and deal with it in accordance with section 158.2.

Expiration

(2) Every search warrant shall name a date upon which it expires, which date shall be not later than fifteen days after its issue.

When to be executed

(3) Every search warrant shall be executed between 6 a.m. and 9 p.m. standard time, unless the justice by the warrant otherwise authorizes.

Definition

(4) In this section and in section 158.1,

"place" includes a building and a receptacle.

2002, c. 18, Sched. A, s. 15(2), (3)

Telewarrants—Submission of information

158.1 (1) Where a provincial offences officer believes that an offence has been committed and that it would be impracticable to appear personally before a justice to make application for a warrant in accordance with section 158, the provincial offences officer may submit an information on oath, by a means of telecommunication that produces a writing, to a justice designated for the purpose by the Chief Justice of the Ontario Court of Justice.

Filing of information

(2) The justice who receives an information submitted under subsection (1) shall, as soon as practicable, cause the information to be filed with the clerk of the court, certified by the justice as to time and date of receipt.

Same, alternative to oath

(3) A provincial offences officer who submits an information under subsection (1) may, instead of swearing an oath, make a statement in writing stating that all matters contained in the information are true to his or her knowledge and belief, and the statement is deemed to be made under oath.

Contents of information

(4) An information submitted under subsection (1) shall include,
(a) a statement of the circumstances that make it impracticable for the provincial offences officer to appear personally before a justice;
(b) a statement of the alleged offence, the place to be searched and the items alleged to be liable to seizure;
(c) a statement of the provincial offences officer's grounds for believing that items liable to seizure in respect of the alleged offence will be found in the place to be searched; and
(d) a statement as to any prior application for a warrant under this section or any other search warrant, in respect of the same matter, of which the provincial offences officer has knowledge.

Issuing warrant

(5) A justice to whom an information is submitted under subsection (1) may, if the conditions set out in subsection (6) are met,
(a) issue a warrant to a provincial offences officer conferring the same authority respecting search and seizure as may be conferred by a warrant issued by a justice before whom the provincial offences officer appears personally under section 158; and
(b) require that the warrant be executed within such time period as the justice may order.

Conditions

(6) The conditions referred to in subsection (5) are that the justice is satisfied that the information,

(a) is in respect of an offence and complies with subsection (4);

(b) discloses reasonable grounds for dispensing with an information presented personally; and

(c) discloses reasonable grounds, in accordance with section 158, for the issuance of a warrant in respect of an offence.

Application of s. 158(2) and (3)

(7) Subsections 158(2) and (3) apply to a warrant issued under this section.

Form, transmission and filing of warrant

(8) A justice who issues a warrant under this section shall,

(a) complete and sign the warrant, noting on its face the time, date and place of issuance;

(b) transmit the warrant by the means of telecommunication to the provincial offences officer who submitted the information; and

(c) as soon as practicable after the warrant has been issued, cause the warrant to be filed with the clerk of the court.

Copies

(9) The copy of the warrant that is transmitted to the provincial offences officer and any copies that are made from the transmitted copy have the same effect as the original for all purposes.

Providing or affixing copy when executing warrant

(10) When a provincial offences officer executes a warrant issued under this section,

(a) if the place to be searched is occupied, the provincial offences officer shall, before entering or as soon as practicable thereafter, give a copy of the warrant to any person present and ostensibly in control of the place; and

(b) if the place to be searched is unoccupied, the provincial offences officer shall, on entering or as soon as practicable thereafter, cause a copy of the warrant to be suitably and prominently affixed within the place.

Proof of authorization

(11) In any proceeding in which it is material for a court to be satisfied that a search or seizure was authorized by a warrant issued under this section, the warrant or the related information shall be produced and the court shall verify,

(a) in the case of the warrant, that it is signed by the justice and bears on its face a notation of the time, date and place of issuance;

(b) in the case of the related information, that it is certified by the justice as to time and date of receipt.

Presumption

(12) If the warrant or related information is not produced or if the matters set out in clause (11)(a) or (b) cannot be verified, it shall be presumed, in the absence of evidence to the contrary, that the search or seizure was not authorized by a warrant issued under this section.

2002, c. 18, Sched. A, s. 15(4)

Duty of person who carries out seizure

158.2 (1) Subsection (2) applies when,

(a) a person has, under a warrant issued under this or any other Act or otherwise in the performance of his or her duties under an Act, seized any thing,

(i) upon or in respect of which an offence has been or is suspected to have been committed, or

(ii) that there are reasonable grounds to believe will afford evidence as to the commission of an offence; and

(b) no procedure for dealing with the thing is otherwise provided by law.

Same

(2) The person shall, as soon as is practicable, take the following steps:

1. The person shall determine whether the continued detention of the thing is required for the purposes of an investigation or proceeding.

2. If satisfied that continued detention is not required as mentioned in paragraph 1, the person shall,

i. return the thing, on being given a receipt for it, to the person lawfully entitled to its possession, and

ii. report to a justice about the seizure and return of the thing.

3. If paragraph 2 does not apply, the person shall,

i. bring the thing before a justice, or

ii. report to a justice about the seizure and detention of the thing.

2002, c. 18, Sched. A, s. 15(4); 2006, c. 19, Sched. B, s. 15(2)

Order of justice re things seized

159. (1) When, under paragraph 3 of subsection 158.2(2), a thing that has been seized is brought before a justice or a report in respect of it is made to a justice, he or she shall, by order,

(a) detain the thing or direct it to be detained in the care of a person named in the order; or

(b) direct it to be returned.

Detention pending appeal, etc.

(1.0.1) A direction to return seized items does not take effect for 30 days and does not take effect during any application made or appeal taken in respect of the thing.

Same

(1.1) The justice may, in the order,

(a) authorize the examination, testing, inspection or reproduction of the thing seized, on the conditions that are reasonably necessary and are directed in the order; and

(b) make any other provision that, in his or her opinion, is necessary for the preservation of the thing.

Time limit for detention

(2) Nothing shall be detained under an order made under subsection (1) for a period of more than three months after the time of seizure unless, before the expiration of that period,

(a) upon motion, a justice is satisfied that having regard to the nature of the investigation, its further detention for a specified period is warranted and he or she so orders; or

(b) a proceeding is instituted in which the thing detained may be required.

Motion for examination and copying

(3) Upon the motion of the defendant, prosecutor or person having an interest in a thing detained under subsection (1), a justice may make an order for the examination, testing, inspection or reproduction of any thing detained upon such conditions as are reasonably necessary and directed in the order.

Motion for release

(4) Upon the motion of a person having an interest in a thing detained under subsection (1), and upon notice to the defendant, the person from whom the thing was seized, the person to whom the search warrant was issued and any other person who has an apparent interest in the thing detained, a justice may make an order for the release of any thing detained to the person from whom the thing was seized where it appears that the thing detained is no longer necessary for the purpose of an investigation or proceeding.

Appeal where order by justice of the peace

(5) Where an order or refusal to make an order under subsection (3) or (4) is made by a justice of the peace, an appeal lies therefrom in the same manner as an appeal from a conviction in a proceeding commenced by means of a certificate.

2002, c. 18, Sched. A, s. 15(5); 2006, c. 19, Sched. B, s. 15(3); 2009, c. 33, Sched. 4, s. 1(61)

Examination or seizure of documents where privilege claimed

160. (1) Where under a search warrant a person is about to examine or seize a document that is in the possession of a lawyer and a solicitor-client privilege is claimed on behalf of a named client in respect of the document, the person shall, without examining or making copies of the document,

(a) seize the document and place it, together with any other document seized in respect of which the same claim is made on behalf of the same client, in a package and seal and identify the package; and

(b) place the package in the custody of the clerk of the court or, with the consent of the person and the client, in the custody of another person.

Opportunity to claim privilege

(2) No person shall examine or seize a document that is in the possession of a lawyer without giving him or her a reasonable opportunity to claim the privilege under subsection (1).

Examination of documents in custody

(3) A judge may, upon the motion made without notice of the lawyer, by order authorize the lawyer to examine or make a copy of the document in the presence of its custodian or the judge, and the order shall contain such provisions as are necessary to ensure that the document is repackaged and resealed without alteration or damage.

Motion to determine privilege

(4) Where a document has been seized and placed in custody under subsection (1), the client by or on whose behalf the claim of solicitor-client privilege is made may make a motion to a judge for an order sustaining the privilege and for the return of the document.

Limitation

(5) A motion under subsection (4) shall be by notice of motion naming a hearing date not later than thirty days after the date on which the document was placed in custody.

Attorney General a party

(6) The person who seized the document and the Attorney General are parties to a motion under subsection (4) and entitled to at least three days notice thereof.

Private hearing and scrutiny by judge

(7) A motion under subsection (4) shall be heard in private and, for the purposes of the hearing, the judge may examine the document and, if he or she does so, shall cause it to be resealed.

Order

(8) The judge may by order,
(a) declare that the solicitor-client privilege exists or does not exist in respect of the document;
(b) direct that the document be delivered up to the appropriate person.

Release of document where no motion under subs. (4)

(9) Where it appears to a judge upon the motion of the Attorney General or person who seized the document that no motion has been made under subsection (4) within the time limit prescribed by subsection (5), the judge shall order that the document be delivered to the applicant.

PART IX

ORDERS ON APPLICATION UNDER STATUTES

Orders under statutes

161. Where, by any other Act, a proceeding is authorized to be taken before the Ontario Court of Justice or a justice for an order, including an order for the payment of money, and no other procedure is provided, this Act applies with necessary modifications to the proceeding in the same manner as to a proceeding commenced under Part III, and for the purpose,
(a) in place of an information, the applicant shall complete a statement in the prescribed form under oath attesting, on reasonable and probable grounds, to the existence of facts that would justify the order sought; and
(b) in place of a plea, the defendant shall be asked whether or not the defendant wishes to dispute the making of the order.

2000, c. 26, Sched. A, s. 13(6), item 12

PART X

AGREEMENTS WITH MUNICIPALITIES CONCERNING ADMINISTRATIVE FUNCTIONS AND PROSECUTIONS

Definition

161.1 In this Part,

"transfer agreement" means an agreement under subsection 162(1).

2002, c. 17, Sched. C, s. 23(1)

Agreements

162. (1) The Attorney General and a municipality may enter into an agreement with respect to a specified area, authorizing the municipality to,

(a) perform courts administration and court support functions, including the functions of the clerk of the court, for the purposes of this Act and the *Contraventions Act* (Canada); and

(b) conduct prosecutions,

(i) in proceedings commenced under this Act, and

(ii) in proceedings under the *Contraventions Act* (Canada) that are commenced under this Act.

Application of cl. (1)(a)

(2) Clause (1) (a) also applies to the functions assigned to the clerk of the court by any other Act.

Performance standards and sanctions

(3) Performance standards and sanctions shall be specified in the agreement; the municipality shall meet the standards and is subject to the sanctions for failure to meet them.

Definition

(4) In subsection (3), **"performance standards"** includes standards for the conduct of prosecutions, for the administration of the courts and for the provision of court support services.

1998, c. 4, s. 1(2); 2017, c. 34, Sched. 35, s. 21

Area of application

163. A transfer agreement may specify an area that includes territory outside the municipality.

1998, c. 4, s. 1(2); 2002, c. 17, Sched. C, s. 23(2)

Deposit with clerk

164. (1) When the Attorney General and a municipality have entered into a transfer agreement, a copy of the agreement shall be deposited with the clerk of the municipality and with the clerk of any other municipality that has jurisdiction in the specified area.

Judicial notice

(2) Judicial notice shall be taken of the agreement without the agreement or its deposit being specially pleaded or proved.

Non-compliance

(3) No proceeding is invalidated by reason only of a person's failure to comply with the agreement.

Fair hearing

(4) Without limiting the generality of subsection (3), that subsection does not preserve the validity of the proceeding if the failure to comply with the agreement results in prejudice to the defendant's right to a fair hearing.

1998, c. 4, s. 1(2); 2002, c. 17, Sched. C, s. 23(3)

Collection and enforcement

165. (1) When a transfer agreement is in force, the municipality has power to collect fines levied in respect of proceedings under Parts I, II and III, including costs under section 60, surcharges under section 60.1 and fees referred to in section 66.2, and to enforce their payment; collection and enforcement shall be carried out in the manner specified in the agreement.

Contraventions Act (Canada)

(2) Subsection (1) also applies to fines and fees imposed under the *Contraventions Act* (Canada).

Non-application of s. 69(6-21)

(3) Subsections 69(6) to (21) do not apply to fines that are governed by the agreement.

Fines, etc., payable to municipality

(4) Fines that are governed by the agreement are payable to the municipality and not to the Minister of Finance.

Payments to Minister of Finance

(5) The municipality shall pay to the Minister of Finance, at the times and in the manner specified in the agreement, amounts calculated in accordance with the agreement, in respect of,

(a) surcharges collected by the municipality under section 60.1;

(b) other fine revenues collected by the municipality that constitute money paid to Ontario for a special purpose within the meaning of the *Financial Administration Act*;

(c) costs the Attorney General incurs for adjudication and prosecution, for monitoring the performance of the agreement and for enforcing the agreement; and

(d) fines and fees imposed under the *Contraventions Act* (Canada) and collected by the municipality.

Exception, federal-municipal agreement re parking fines and fees

(6) Despite clause (5)(d), fines and fees imposed under the *Contraventions Act* (Canada) in relation to the unlawful parking, standing or stopping of a vehicle and collected by the municipality shall be paid in accordance with any agreement made under sections 65.2 and 65.3 of that Act.

Payments to another municipality

(7) The municipality acting under a transfer agreement shall pay to another municipality,

(a) the amount of any fine collected by the municipality that was imposed for a contravention of the other municipality's by-law;

(b) the amount of any fine collected by the municipality that was imposed for a contravention of a provincial statute and that would, except for the agreement, be payable to the other municipality; and

(c) the amount of any allowance retained by the municipality that would, except for the agreement, be payable to the other municipality under a regulation made under clause 20(1)(g).

Retention of balance

(8) Despite the *Fines and Forfeitures Act*, the municipality is entitled to retain, as a fee, the balance remaining after payment under subsections (5) and (7).

No other charge

(9) The municipality shall not collect any other charge for acting under a transfer agreement, except in accordance with section 304 of the *Municipal Act, 2001* or section 240 of the *City of Toronto Act, 2006* or with the Attorney General's advance written consent.

Disclosure to consumer reporting agency

(10) When a transfer agreement applies to a fine, section 69.1 applies to the municipality in the same manner as it applies to the Ministry of the Attorney General.

Exception, transitional period

(11) Despite subsection (4), while a regulation made under clause 174(b) is in effect, fines that are governed by the agreement remain payable to the Minister of Finance, who shall,

(a) calculate and retain the appropriate amounts under subsection (5);

(b) make any payments required by subsection (7); and

(c) pay the balance remaining to the municipality in accordance with subsection (8).

1998, c. 4, s. 1(2); 2002, c. 17, Sched. C, s. 23(4)—(7); 2009, c. 33, Sched. 4, s. 1(62)

Definition

165.1 (1) In this section,

"local board" has the same meaning as in the *Municipal Affairs Act*, but does not include a school board or a hospital board.

Special rules, municipal defendant

(2) When a transfer agreement is in effect, the special rules set out in subsection (3) apply to a proceeding if,
  (a) the proceeding is under Part I or III; and
  (b) the defendant is a municipality or one of its local boards.

Same

(3) The special rules referred to in subsection (2) are:
1. The fine is payable to the Minister of Finance and not to the municipality, despite subsection 165(4).
2. The prosecutor may elect to collect and enforce the fine instead of the municipality, despite subsection 165(1) and the provisions of the agreement relating to collection and enforcement.
3. Notice of the election shall be given to the municipal representative named in the agreement for the purpose, or if none is named, to the clerk of the court.
1997, c. 30, Sched. D, s. 17; 2002, c. 17, Sched. C, s. 23(8)

Fines imposed before effective date

166. A transfer agreement may,
  (a) authorize the municipality to collect and enforce the payment of fines that were imposed before the agreement's effective date; and
  (b) provide in what proportions and in what manner the amounts collected are to be shared between the municipality and the Minister of Finance.
1998, c. 4, s. 1(2); 2002, c. 17, Sched. C, s. 23(9)

Special rules

167. (1) When a transfer agreement is in effect, the following rules apply:
1. The clerk of the court may be a municipal employee.
2. Subject to section 29, the court may sit in the location designated by the municipality, which need not be in premises operated by the Province of Ontario for court purposes.
3. The court office shall be in the location designated by the municipality.
4. Despite anything else in this Act, the municipality shall not without the Attorney General's written consent, obtained in advance, assign to a person

other than its own employee a function that the agreement gives to the municipality.

(2) [Repealed 2017, c. 34, Sched. 35, s. 22.]

1998, c. 4, s. 1(2); 2002, c. 17, Sched. C, s. 23(10); 2006, c. 21, Sched. C, s. 131(21); 2017, c. 34, Sched. 35, s. 22

Right to intervene

168. A transfer agreement does not affect the Attorney General's right to intervene in a proceeding and assume the role of prosecutor at any stage, including on appeal.

1998, c. 4, s. 1(2); 2002, c. 17, Sched. C, s. 23(11)

No agency

169. A municipality that acts under a transfer agreement does not do so as an agent of the Crown in right of Ontario or of the Attorney General.

1998, c. 4, s. 1(2); 2002, c. 17, Sched. C, s. 23(12)

Protection from personal liability

170. (1) No proceeding shall be commenced against any person for an act done in good faith in the performance or intended performance of a function under a transfer agreement or for an alleged neglect or default in the performance in good faith of such a function.

Municipality not relieved of liability

(2) Subsection (1) does not relieve a municipality of liability in respect of a tort committed by a person referred to in subsection (1) to which the municipality would otherwise be subject.

1998, c. 4, s. 1(2); 2002, c. 17, Sched. C, s. 23(13)

Order for compliance

171. (1) When a transfer agreement is in effect, the Attorney General may make an order directing the municipality to comply with the agreement within a specified time.

Revocation or suspension

(2) The Attorney General may revoke or suspend the agreement if the municipality does not comply with the order within the specified time.

Protection from personal liability

(3) No proceeding for damages shall be commenced against the Attorney General or an employee of the Ministry of the Attorney General for anything done

or omitted in good faith in connection with the revocation or suspension of a transfer agreement.

1998, c. 4, s. 1(2); 2002, c. 17, Sched. C, s. 23(14), (15)

Review committee

172. A transfer agreement may provide for a review committee whose composition and functions are determined by regulation.

1998, c. 4, s. 1(2); 2002, c. 17, Sched. C, s. 23(16)

Transition, Part III proceedings

173. (1) Unless a transfer agreement provides otherwise, the agreement applies in respect of a proceeding commenced under Part III regardless of when the proceeding was commenced, subject to subsection (2).

Exception

(2) If either of the following applies with respect to a proceeding, the trial and disposition, including sentencing, shall be conducted as if there were no agreement:

1. The trial is scheduled to begin within 60 days after the day on which the agreement begins applying to the proceeding.

2. The trial began before the day the agreement begins applying to the proceeding, but the disposition, including sentencing, is not complete on that day.

1998, c. 4, s. 1(2); 2002, c. 17, Sched. C, s. 23(17); 2017, c. 34, Sched. 35, s. 23

Regulations

174. The Attorney General may, by regulation,

(a) impose obligations in connection with a transfer agreement on a person who is not a party to the agreement;

(b) provide that fines governed by a transfer agreement may, for a transitional period after its effective date, be paid to the Minister of Finance;

(c) determining the composition and functions of a review committee for the purposes of section 172;

(d) provide for the effective implementation of transfer agreements.

1998, c. 4, s. 1(2); 2002, c. 17, Sched. C, s. 23(18)-(20)

Municipal powers

174.1 (1) A municipality has power to enter into and to perform a transfer agreement.

Employees and others

(2) The functions given to a municipality by a transfer agreement or by an agreement under subsection (3) or (7) may be performed,

682

(a) by the municipality's employees;

(b) by a combination of the municipality's employees and the employees of another municipality, if the municipalities have an agreement under subsection (3) or (7); or

(c) by any other person, with the Attorney General's consent, as described in subsection 175(2).

Joint performance agreement between municipalities

(3) A municipality that has entered into a transfer agreement may enter into an agreement with one or more other municipalities for the joint performance, by a joint board of management or otherwise, of the functions given to the first municipality by the transfer agreement.

Attorney General's consent

(4) The joint performance agreement requires the Attorney General's written consent, obtained in advance.

Extra-territorial effect

(5) The power to perform an agreement under subsection (3) may be exercised in an area outside the municipality's territorial limits if that area forms part of the area specified in the agreement.

Intermunicipal agreements

(6) Municipalities may enter into and perform intermunicipal agreements to implement a transfer agreement.

Further agreements

(7) A municipality that has entered into a transfer agreement may enter into an agreement with one or more municipalities for the performance by the other municipality or municipalities of any of the functions given to the first municipality by the transfer agreement and the municipalities have the power to enter into and perform the agreement under this subsection.

Consent

(8) An agreement entered into under subsection (7) requires the Attorney General's written consent.

Extra-territorial effect

(9) The power to perform an agreement under subsection (7) may be exercised in an area outside the municipality's territorial limits.

2002, c. 17, Sched. C, s. 23(21)

Delegation

175. (1) Subject to subsection (2), a municipality has power to assign to any person a function that a transfer agreement gives to the municipality.

Attorney General's consent

(2) An assignment to a person other than the municipality's employee requires the Attorney General's written consent, obtained in advance.

(3) [Repealed 2002, c. 17, Sched. C, s. 23(23).]

1998, c. 4, s. 1(2); 2000, c. 26, Sched. A, s. 13(4); 2002, c. 17, Sched. C, s. 23(22), (23)

Group of municipalities

176. A transfer agreement may also be made with two or more municipalities, and in that case sections 162 to 175 apply with necessary modifications.

1998, c. 4, s. 1(2); 2002, c. 17, Sched. C, s. 23(24)

Appendix A1

Ont. Reg. 67/12 — Electronic Documents and Remote Meetings

made under the *Provincial Offences Act*
O. Reg. 67/12

ELECTRONIC DOCUMENTS

Definitions

1. In this Regulation,

"electronic" and "electronically" have the meanings set out in the *Electronic Commerce Act, 2000*;

"electronic signature" has the meaning set out in the *Electronic Commerce Act, 2000*.

Electronic signing

2. For the purposes of subsection 76.1 (1) of the Act, a document may be signed or endorsed by electronic means if the method of signing results in an electronic signature being in, attached to or associated with the document.

Electronic filing

3. (1) For the purposes of subsection 76.1 (1) of the Act, a document may be filed with a court office by direct electronic transmission if,

(a) the document or the data or information in, attached to or associated with the document is sent to the court office electronically or on a computer-readable medium;

(b) the court office has indicated that the method of sending and the technical specifications of the document are acceptable to it; and

(c) the document or the data or information in, attached to or associated with the document indicates,

(i) the name of the document,

(ii) the form number and version date, if the document is a form,

(iii) the defendant's name,

(iv) for a document relating to a proceeding commenced under Part I or II of the Act,

(A) if a court file number has not been assigned, the offence number and court location code, or

(B) if a court file number has been assigned, either the court file number or the offence number and court location code,

(v) for a document relating to a proceeding commenced under Part III of the Act, the court file number, if one has been assigned.

(2) If a document is filed with a court office in accordance with subsection (1), the clerk of the court office shall ensure that an acknowledgment of receipt is sent to the filer indicating the date of receipt of the document.

Electronic delivery

4. For the purposes of section 87 of the Act, a notice or document is sufficiently given or delivered by an electronic method if,

(a) the notice or document or the data or information in, attached to or associated with the notice or document is sent to the recipient electronically or on a computer-readable medium;

(b) the recipient has indicated that the method of sending and the technical specifications of the document are acceptable to it; and

(c) the document or the data or information in, attached to or associated with the document indicates,

(i) the name of the document,

(ii) the form number and version date, if the document is a form,

(iii) the defendant's name,

(iv) for a document relating to a proceeding commenced under Part I or II of the Act,

(A) if a court file number has not been assigned, the offence number and court location code, or

(B) if a court file number has been assigned, either the court file number or the offence number and court location code,

(v) for a document relating to a proceeding commenced under Part III of the Act, the court file number, if one has been assigned.

Timing of filing or delivery

5. A document that is filed or delivered electronically is deemed to be filed or delivered on the day the document is available to be retrieved and processed by the recipient, even if the recipient is not able, for his or her own technical or other reasons, to retrieve and process it on that day.

Use and retention of electronic documents

6. (1) For every document that is filed under section 3 of this Regulation or retained under subsection 76.1 (1.1) of the Act, a record shall be made of the document such that it is possible to view and print a copy of,

(a) the document, if any, as it looked when it was received from the sender; and

(b) the data and information, if any, in, attached to or associated with the document, as it was when it was received from the sender.

(2) A document filed under section 3 of this Regulation or retained under subsection 76.1 (1.1) of the Act, or an electronic court record that includes the document, may be altered if,

(a) a permanent archive is maintained that specifies the alteration and identifies when and by whom it was made;

(b) the alteration would be required or authorized to be done to the equivalent paper court record or is otherwise authorized by law; and

(c) the record of the document or of the data or information in, attached to or associated with the document, made in accordance with subsection (1), is not altered.

(3) A printed copy of a document filed under section 3 of this Regulation or retained under subsection 76.1 (1.1) of the Act that is used for the purpose of disposing of a charge under the Act shall be deemed under subsection 76.1 (2) of the Act to have been filed as the original document if the printed copy is the only copy printed for the purpose and has marks on it indicating the time and date that it was printed and that it is the original document.

(4) A justice of the peace, judge of the Ontario Court of Justice, judge of the Superior Court of Justice or any other judge may complete and sign by electronic means any electronic document so as to indicate the disposition of the proceeding or reflect an order that was made relating to a step in a proceeding.

(5) The period of time for which a document is to be retained is not affected by whether the document is filed or maintained in an electronic format.

REMOTE MEETINGS

Resolution meeting

7. (1) A defendant may attend the meeting described in subsection 5.1 (2) of the Act by electronic method in accordance with section 83.1 of the Act if the distance between his or her residence and the location indicated on the offence notice is greater than the distance indicated on the offence notice.

(2) A prosecutor may attend the meeting described in subsection 5.1 (2) of the Act by electronic method in accordance with section 83.1 of the Act if the distance between his or her office and the location indicated on the offence notice is greater than the distance indicated on the offence notice.

(3) The distance indicated on the offence notice shall not be greater than 75 kilometres.

(4) If a defendant or prosecutor indicates that he or she will attend the meeting described in subsection 5.1 (2) of the Act by electronic method, as permitted under subsection (1) or (2), the other person may also attend the meeting by electronic

method in accordance with section 83.1 of the Act, regardless of the distance between his or her residence or office and the location indicated on the offence notice.

Sentencing hearings

8. For the purposes of section 83.1 of the Act, an appearance described in subsection 5.1 (8) of the Act is a proceeding where attendance or appearance may be made by electronic method in accordance with section 83.1 of the Act, including by audio conference or telephone conference.

Revocation

9. Ontario Regulation 497/94 is revoked.

Commencement

10. This Regulation comes into force on the day it is filed.

Ont. Reg. 132/14 — Certified Evidence

made under the *Provincial Offences Act*
O. Reg. 132/14

CERTIFIED EVIDENCE

Specified offences

1. (1) Every offence for which there is a set fine, other than an offence referred to in subsection (2), is specified for the purposes of clause 48.1 (1) (b) of the Act.

(2) The following offences for which there is a set fine are not specified for the purposes of clause 48.1 (1) (b) of the Act:

1. Every offence under a provision of an Act, regulation or municipal by-law that, on the offence date indicated in the offence notice, is set out in the Table to Ontario Regulation 339/94 (Demerit Point System) made under the *Highway Traffic Act*.

2. An offence under section 128 of the *Highway Traffic Act*.

Other types of certified evidence

2. The following types of certified evidence are specified for the purposes of paragraph 3 of subsection 48.1 (2) of the Act:

1. A certified copy of a photograph taken by a provincial offences officer.

2. In respect of a document, a certified statement by a provincial offences officer that he or she served the document on the person charged, with the date and method of service indicated.

3. A certified statement by a provincial offences officer respecting the configuration, weight, dimensions or other characteristics of a vehicle inspected by the provincial offences officer.

3. OMITTED (PROVIDES FOR COMING INTO FORCE OF PROVISIONS OF THIS REGULATION).

Ont. Reg. 108/11 — Forms

made under the *Provincial Offences Act*
O. Reg. 108/11 as am. O. Reg. 108/11, s. 16
[s. 16(8), (9) repealed O. Reg. 462/11, s. 4.]; 462/11; 136/14; 291/16; 236/18, ss. 1(1)(Fr.), (2), 2 (Fr.), 3

Forms

1. (1) In this Regulation, when a form is referred to by number, the reference is to the form with that number that is described in the Table of Forms at the end of this Regulation and is available on the Internet through www.ontariocourt forms.on.ca.

(2) A form issued pursuant to Part II of the Act (Commencement of Proceedings for Parking Infractions) may be provided in either English or French or in both languages, whether or not the form shown on www.ontariocourtforms.on.ca is in both languages.

(3) [Repealed O. Reg. 136/14, s. 1.]

(4) [Repealed O. Reg. 136/14, s. 1.]

O. Reg. 462/11, s. 1; 136/14, s. 1

PROCEEDINGS COMMENCED BY CERTIFICATE OF OFFENCE (PART I OF THE ACT)

Certificate of offence

2. (1) A certificate of offence shall be in Form 1.

(2) Despite subsection (1), a certificate of offence issued in proceedings based on evidence obtained through the use of a red light camera system shall be in Form 2.

(2.1) Despite subsection (1), a certificate of offence issued in proceedings based on evidence obtained through the use of a camera system in relation to a contravention of subsection 175(19) or (20) of the *Highway Traffic Act* (duty of drivers when school bus stopped — vehicle owner) shall be in Form 2.1.

O. Reg. 291/16, s. 1

Offence notice

3. (1) An offence notice shall be in Form 3.

(2) Despite subsection (1), an offence notice shall be in Form 4 in those parts of Ontario where the notice of intention to appear is required to be filed in person.

(3) Despite subsections (1) and (2),

(a) an offence notice issued in proceedings based on evidence obtained through the use of a red light camera system shall be in Form 5; and

(b) an offence notice issued in proceedings based on evidence obtained through the use of a camera system in relation to a contravention of subsection 175(19) or (20) of the *Highway Traffic Act* (duty of drivers when school bus stopped — vehicle owner) shall be in Form 5.1.

(4) Despite subsections (1), (2) and (3), in those parts of Ontario where the notice of intention to appear is required to be filed in person,

(a) an offence notice issued in proceedings referred to in clause (3)(a) shall be in Form 6; and

(b) an offence notice issued in proceedings referred to in clause (3)(b) shall be in Form 6.1.

O. Reg. 108/11, s. 16(1), (2); 291/16, s. 2

Summons under Part I of Act

4. A summons under Part I of the Act shall be in Form 7.

Early resolution meeting notice (in person)

4.1 An early resolution meeting notice (in person) shall be in Form 7.1.

O. Reg. 108/11, s. 16(3)

Early resolution meeting notice (electronic method)

4.2 An early resolution meeting notice (electronic method) shall be in Form 7.2.

O. Reg. 108/11, s. 16(3)

Early resolution outcome form (joint submission)

4.3 An early resolution outcome form (joint submission) shall be in Form 7.3.

O. Reg. 108/11, s. 16(3)

Notice of intention to appear

5. A notice of intention to appear shall be in Form 8 in those parts of Ontario where the notice of intention to appear is required to be filed in person.

O. Reg. 108/11, s. 16(4); 291/16, s. 3

Notice of trial under Part I of Act

6. A notice of trial under Part I of the Act shall be in Form 9.

Certificate of striking out conviction

7. (1) A certificate of striking out conviction shall be in Form 103 of Regulation 200 of the Revised Regulations of Ontario, 1990 (*Rules of the*

Ontario Court (Provincial Division) in Provincial Offences Proceedings) made under the *Courts of Justice Act.*

(2) Section 1 does not apply to the form referred to in subsection (1).

Notice of fine and due date

8. (1) A notice of fine and due date under Part I of the Act shall be in Form 10.

(2) Despite subsection (1), Form 10.1, 10.2 or 10.3 may be used instead of Form 10 in The Regional Municipality of York.

O. Reg. 462/11, s. 2; 236/18, s. 1(2)

PARKING INFRACTIONS (PART II OF THE ACT)

Certificate of parking infraction

9. A certificate of parking infraction shall be in Form 11.

Parking infraction notice

10. (1) A parking infraction notice shall be in Form 12.

(2) Despite subsection (1), a parking infraction notice shall be in Form 13 in those municipalities where the notice of intention to appear is required to be filed in person.

O. Reg. 108/11, s. 16(5); 291/16, s. 4

Information set out in certificate or notice

11. A certificate of parking infraction or a parking infraction notice may set out,

(a) more than one infraction as long as each infraction with which a person is charged is clearly indicated on the certificate or notice by a check-mark, an ''x'', a punch hole or by some other means;

(b) information related to the voluntary payment of penalties under by-laws adopted under an Act that authorizes such by-laws.

Notice of intention to appear

12. A notice of intention to appear shall be in Form 8 in those municipalities where the notice of intention to appear is required to be filed in person.

O. Reg. 108/11, s. 16(6); 291/16, s. 5

Notice of trial under Part II of Act

13. A notice of trial under Part II of the Act shall be in Form 9.

Notice of impending conviction, certificate requesting a conviction

14. (1) A notice of impending conviction shall be in Form 14.

(2) Despite subsection (1), a notice of impending conviction shall be in Form 15 in those municipalities where the notice of intention to appear is required to be filed in person.

(3) A certificate requesting a conviction shall be in Form 16 and shall be completed in accordance with the following rules:

1. If the defendant's driver's licence number is available, the defendant's date of birth need not be completed.

2. If the defendant's driver's licence number is not available, the defendant's date of birth must be completed if it is available.

3. If the defendant's driver's licence number or date of birth is available, the registrant identification number for the vehicle need not be completed.

4. If neither the defendant's driver's licence number nor date of birth is available, then the registrant identification number for the vehicle must be completed.

5. If the certificate is issued by a municipality that has entered into an agreement under subsection 18.6(1) of the Act, the defendant's address, sex, driver's licence number and date of birth, the registrant identification number for the vehicle and the by-law number need not be completed.

(4) A notice of impending conviction and a certificate requesting a conviction issued by a municipality shall be prepared by the clerk of the municipality or another employee who is responsible for parking prosecutions.

(5) A notice of impending conviction and a certificate requesting a conviction issued by a ministry shall be prepared by the deputy minister of the ministry or another employee who is responsible for parking prosecutions.

(6) A notice of impending conviction and a certificate requesting a conviction issued by another body shall be prepared by the chief administrator of the body or another employee who is responsible for parking prosecutions.

(7) A facsimile signature of a person mentioned in subsection (4), (5) or (6) is sufficient authentication of a certificate requesting a conviction.

O. Reg. 108/11, s. 16(7); 291/16, s. 6

Notice of fine and due date

15. A notice of fine and due date under Part II of the Act shall be in Form 10.

O. Reg. 462/11, s. 3

Amendments

16. (1) Subsection 3(2) of this Regulation is amended by striking out "designated for the purposes of section 5.1 of the Act" and substituting "where the offence notice requires the notice of intention to appear to be filed in person".

(2) Subsection 3(4) of this Regulation is amended by striking out "designated for the purposes of section 5.1 of the Act" and substituting "where the offence notice requires the notice of intention to appear to be filed in person".

(3) This Regulation is amended by adding the following sections:

4.1 Early resolution meeting notice (in person) — An early resolution meeting notice (in person) shall be in Form 7.1.

4.2 Early resolution meeting notice (electronic method) — An early resolution meeting notice (electronic method) shall be in Form 7.2.

4.3 Early resolution outcome form (joint submission) — An early resolution outcome form (joint submission) shall be in Form 7.3.

(4) Section 5 of this Regulation is amended by striking out "designated for the purposes of section 5.1 of the Act" and substituting "where the offence notice requires the notice of intention to appear to be filed in person".

(5) Subsection 10(2) of this Regulation is amended by striking out "designated for the purposes of section 17.1 of the Act" and substituting "where the parking infraction notice requires the notice of intention to appear to be filed in person".

(6) Section 12 of this Regulation is amended by striking out "designated for the purposes of section 17.1 of the Act" and substituting "where the parking infraction notice requires the notice of intention to appear to be filed in person".

(7) Subsection 14(2) of this Regulation is amended by striking out "designated for the purposes of section 17.1 of the Act" and substituting "where the parking infraction notice requires the notice of intention to appear to be filed in person".

(8) [Repealed O. Reg. 462/11, s. 4.]

(9) [Repealed O. Reg. 462/11, s. 4.]

TABLE OF FORMS
(See Section 1)

Form Number	Form Name	Date of Form
1	Certificate of Offence	November 2, 2011
2	Red Light Camera System Certificate of Offence	March 15, 2014
2.1	Fail to Stop for a School Bus — Owner Liability Certificate of Offence	July 6, 2016
3	Offence Notice	March 15, 2014
4	Offence Notice	November 2, 2011
5	Red Light Camera System Offence Notice	March 15, 2014
5.1	Fail to Stop for a School Bus — Owner Liability Offence Notice	July 6, 2016
6	Red Light Camera System Offence Notice	November 2, 2011
6.1	Fail to Stop for a School Bus — Owner Liability Offence Notice	July 6, 2016
7	Summons	March 17, 2011
7.1	Early Resolution Meeting Notice (In Person)	November 2, 2011
7.2	Early Resolution Meeting Notice (By Electronic Method)	November 2, 2011
7.3	Early Resolution Outcome	November 2, 2011
8	Notice of Intention to Appear	March 15, 2014
9	Notice of Trial	March 15, 2014
10	Notice of Fine and Due Date	January 19, 2018
10	Notice of Fine and Due Date	January 19, 2018
10.1	Notice of Fine and Due Date	January 19, 2018
10.2	Notice of Fine and Due Date	January 19, 2018
10.3	Notice of Fine and Due Date	January 19, 2018
11	Certificate of Parking Infraction	March 17, 2011
12	Parking Infraction Notice	March 15, 2014
13	Parking Infraction Notice	March 17, 2011
14	Notice of Impending Conviction	March 15, 2014
15	Notice of Impending Conviction	March 17, 2011
16	Certificate Requesting Conviction	March 17, 2011
17	[Repealed O. Reg. 462/11, s. 6(4).]	

O. Reg. 462/11, s. 6; 136/14, s. 2; 291/16, s. 7; 236/18, s. 3

Form 1 — Certificate of Offence

Provincial Offences Act

[Editor's Note: Pursuant to section O. Reg. 108/11, s. 1, when a form is referred to by number, the reference is to the form with that number that is described in the Table of Forms at the end of this Regulation and is available on the Internet through www.ontariocourtforms.on.ca. For your convenience, the government form is reproduced below. Form current to November 2, 2011.]

ICON Location Code Code d'emplacement du RIII	Offence number Numéro d'infraction

Form 1, *Provincial Offences Act*, Ontario Court of Justice, O. Reg. 108/11
Formulaire 1, *Loi sur les infractions provinciales, Cour de justice de l'Ontario, Règl. de l'Ont. 108/11*

Certificate of Offence
Procès-verbal d'infraction

I,
Je soussigné(e) _____ (print name / nom en lettres moulées)

believe and certify that on the day of
crois et atteste que le

Y / A	M / M	D / J	Time / heure
2 0			M

Name
Nom _____ (family / nom de famille)

_____ (given / prénom)   _____ (initials / initiales)

Address
Adresse _____ (number and street / numéro et nom de la rue)

(municipality / municipalité)   (P.O. / C.P.)   (province)   (postal code / code postal)

Driver's licence no. / *Nº de permis de conduire*   Juris / Aut. Lég.

Birth date / Date de naissance			Sex / Sexe	Motor vehicle involved / Véhicule impliqué	Collision involved / Collision	Witnesses / Témoins
Y / A	M / M	D / J		☐ N / N	☐ Y / O	☐ Y / O

At
À _____ (municipality / municipalité)

Did commit the offence of
A commis l'infraction de _____

contrary to _____ sect.
contrairement à _____ *l'art.*

Plate no. Nº de la plaque d'immatriculation	Juris Aut. Lég.	Commercial Utilitaire	CVOR IUVU	NSC CNS	Code
		☐ Y / O	☐ Y / O	☐ Y / O	
CVOR No. - NSC No. / Nº de IUVU - Nº du CNS					

And I further certify that I served an offence notice   ☐ Or other service date of:
personally upon the person charged on the offence date.   *Autre date de signification, le :*
J'atteste également qu'à la date de l'infraction, j'ai signifié, en mains propres, un avis d'infraction à la personne accusée.

Signature of issuing Provincial Offences Officer Signature de l'agent des infractions provinciale	Officer No Nº de l'agent	Platoon Peloton	Unit Unité

Set fine of Amende fixée de	Total payable Montant total exigible	Total payable includes set fine, applicable victim fine surcharge and costs. / Le montant total exigible comprend l'amende fixée, la suramende compensatoire applicable et les frais.
$	$	$	

Summons issued. You are required to appear in court on
***Assignation. Vous êtes** tenu(e) de comparaître devant le tribunal le*

Y / A	M / M	D / J	Time / heure
2 0			M

Ct. room / Salle d'audience   at the Ontario Court of Justice POA Office at / à la Cour de justice de l'Ontario. Bureau des infractions provinciales au

Deemed not to dispute charge under s. 9(1)(a) of the *Provincial Offences Act*. Set fine imposed. / *Réputé ne pas contester l'accusation aux termes de l'alinéa 9 (1) (a) de la Loi sur les infractions provinciales. Amende fixée imposée.*

Y / A	M / M	D / J
2 0		

_____ Justice / *Juge*

POA 0847 (November 2, 2011 / 2 novembre 2011) CSD

697

Form 2 — Red Light Camera System Certificate of Offence
Provincial Offences Act

[Editor's Note: Pursuant to section O. Reg. 108/11, s. 1, when a form is referred to by number, the reference is to the form with that number that is described in the Table of Forms at the end of this Regulation and is available on the Internet through www.ontariocourtforms.on.ca. For your convenience, the government form is reproduced below. Form current to March 15, 2014.]

Ontario Court of Justice / Cour de justice de l'Ontario
Province of Ontario / Province de l'Ontario

**RED LIGHT CAMERA SYSTEM
CERTIFICATE OF OFFENCE
*PROCÈS-VERBAL D'INFRACTION –
SYSTÈME PHOTOGRAPHIQUE
RELIÉ AUX FEUX ROUGES***

Offence Number
Numéro de l'infraction

Icon Location Code
Code d'emplacement du RIII

Form 2, *Provincial Offences Act*, O. Reg. 108/11
Formulaire 2, *Loi sur les infractions provinciales*, Règl. de l'Ont. 108/11

I, _____ believe and certify that I have viewed the photographic equivalent of
Je soussigné(e), _____ crois et atteste avoir visionné l'équivalent photographique d'images
images processed from photographic film recorded on the _____ day of _____
développées à partir d'une pellicule photographique enregistrée le _____ jour de _____ (year / année)
at _____ m. that were obtained through the use of a prescribed red light camera system, I have determined
à _____ , qui ont été obtenues au moyen d'un système photographique relié aux feux rouges prescrit. J'ai
that the motor vehicle shown therein bears the Ontario number plate _____ and that
déterminé que le véhicule automobile en question est muni de la plaque d'immatriculation de l'Ontario _____ et que
(name / nom) _____
(address / adresse) _____
was the owner of the motor vehicle bearing the said plate on the date of offence as recorded with the Ministry of Transportation and that:
était le propriétaire du véhicule automobile muni de ladite plaque d'immatriculation à la date de l'infraction, comme elle est enregistrée auprès du ministère des Transports
on the _____ day of _____ , the Defendant, as the owner did commit the offence of failing
et que le _____ jour de _____ (year / année) , le défendeur, en sa qualité de propriétaire, a commis
to stop at a red light at _____
l'infraction d'omettre de s'arrêter à un feu rouge à _____ (intersection location / indiquer l'intersection)
in the _____ ; a designated area pursuant to Ontario Regulation 277/99, as amended, thereby
à _____ (municipality / municipalité) , région désignée conformément au Règlement de l'Ontario 277/99 dans sa version
committing an offence contrary to subsection 144(18.1) and pursuant to section 207 of the *Highway Traffic Act*
modifiée, commettant ainsi une infraction, contrairement au paragraphe 144(18.1) et conformément à l'article 207 du Code de la route.
I further certify and believe that the red light camera system used was (make) _____
Par ailleurs, j'atteste et crois que le système photographique relié aux feux rouges était (marque) _____
(model) _____ a prescribed system pursuant to Ontario Regulation 277/99, as amended, and that the red
(modèle) _____ un système prescrit en vertu du Règlement de l'Ontario 277/99 dans sa version modifiée et
light camera system and the traffic control signal were in operation and functioning properly at the time the photographs referred to herein were taken; that the first and second photographs show the date, time of day, and location at which the photographs were taken; that the first/second photograph in the sequence of two photographs shows a motor vehicle
que le système photographique relié aux feux rouges et les feux de circulation étaient en marche et fonctionnaient adéquatement au moment où les photographies auxquelles il est fait référence ont été prises; que la première et la deuxième photographies indiquent la date et l'heure de la journée, de même que l'endroit où les photographies ont été prises; que la première/deuxième photographie dans la séquence de deux photographies montre un
bearing an Ontario number plate _____ , that the vehicle approached the described intersection at which the
véhicule automobile muni de la plaque d'immatriculation de l'Ontario _____ , que le véhicule s'approchait de l'intersection décrite où le feu de
traffic control signal displayed a circular red indication at the speed of _____ kilometres per hour, that the photographs are sequential and
circulation affichait une indication circulaire rouge à une vitesse de _____ kilomètres l'heure, que les photographies sont séquentielles et
show that the traffic control signal displayed a red indication for _____ seconds in the first photograph, _____ seconds in the
montrent que le feu de circulation était rouge depuis _____ secondes dans la première photographie, _____ secondes dans la
second photograph and that the motor vehicle failed to stop at the intersection.
deuxième photographie et que le véhicule automobile a omis de s'arrêter à l'intersection
I, _____ certify that I mailed Offence Notice # _____ to the Defendant
Je soussigné(e), _____ atteste que j'ai envoyé par la poste l'avis d'infraction n° _____ au défendeur
on the _____ day of _____ at the address of the Defendant on the date of offence as recorded
le _____ jour de _____ (year / année) à l'adresse du défendeur, à la date de l'infraction, comme elle est
with the Ministry of Transportation.
enregistrée auprès du ministère des Transports.

SIGNATURE OF ISSUING PROVINCIAL OFFENCES OFFICER *SIGNATURE DE L'AGENT DES INFRACTIONS PROVINCIALES*	OFFICER NO. *N° DE L'AGENT*	DATE OF ISSUE / *DATE DE DÉLIVRANCE*		
		Y / A	M / M	D / J

SET FINE OF *AMENDE FIXÉE DE*	TOTAL PAYABLE	TOTAL PAYABLE INCLUDES SET FINE, APPLICABLE VICTIM FINE SURCHARGE AND COSTS *LE MONTANT TOTAL EXIGIBLE COMPREND L'AMENDE FIXÉE, LA SURAMENDE COMPENSATOIRE QUI S'APPLIQUE ET LES FRAIS*		
$	$ $ *MONTANT TOTAL EXIGIBLE*			

CONVICTION ENTERED PURSUANT TO SECTION 205.19(1)(a) OF THE *HIGHWAY TRAFFIC ACT*. SET FINE IMPOSED *DÉCLARATION DE CULPABILITÉ INSCRITE CONFORMÉMENT À L'ALINÉA 205.19(1) a) DU CODE DE LA ROUTE. AMENDE FIXÉE IMPOSÉE*		Y / A	M / M	D / J
	JUSTICE / *JUGE*			

POA 0816 (March 15, 2014 / 15 mars 2014) CSD

698

Form 2.1 — Fail to Stop for a School Bus — Owner Liability Certificate of Offence

Provincial Offences Act

[Editor's Note: Pursuant to section O. Reg. 108/11, s. 1, when a form is referred to by number, the reference is to the form with that number that is described in the Table of Forms at the end of this Regulation and is available on the Internet through www.ontariocourtforms.on.ca. For your convenience, the government form is reproduced below. Form current to July 2016.]

Ontario Court of Justice / *Cour de justice de l'Ontario*
Province of Ontario / *Province de l'Ontario*

**FAIL TO STOP FOR A SCHOOL BUS - OWNER LIABILITY
CERTIFICATE OF OFFENCE**
*OMISSION DE S'ARRÊTER POUR UN AUTOBUS SCOLAIRE -
RESPONSABILITÉ DU PROPRIÉTAIRE
PROCÈS-VERBAL D'INFRACTION*

Offence Number / *Numéro de l'infraction*

ICON Location Code / *Code d'emplacement du RIII*

Form 2.1, Provincial Offences Act, O. Reg. 108/11
Formulaire 2.1, Loi sur les infractions provinciales, Régl. de l'Ont. 108/11

I, _____ , believe and certify that on the _____ day of
Je soussigné(e), _____ , *crois et atteste que le* _____ *jour de*

_____ _____ , at _____ a.m./p.m., the motor vehicle bearing the [fill in jurisdiction] number plate
(month / *mois*) (year / *année*) *à* _____ *après-midi/avant-midi, le véhicule automobile muni de la plaque d'immatriculation*

_____ failed to stop for a school bus, and that
de/d' [indiquer la province/le territoire] numéro _____ *a omis de s'arrêter pour un autobus scolaire, et que*

_____
(name / *nom*)

_____
(address / *adresse*)

was the owner of the motor vehicle bearing the said plate on the date of offence and that on the _____ day of
était le propriétaire du véhicule automobile muni de ladite plaque d'immatriculation à la date de l'infraction, et que le _____ *jour de* (month / *mois*)

_____ , the Defendant, as the owner, did commit the offence of failing to stop for a school bus, in the
(year / *année*) , *le défendeur, en sa qualité de propriétaire, a commis l'infraction d'omettre de s'arrêter pour un autobus scolaire dans le/la*

_____ ; thereby committing an offence contrary to subsection [175(19)/175(20)] and pursuant
(municipality / *municipalité*) , *commettant ainsi une infraction prévue au paragraphe [175(19)/175(20)] et conformément*

to section 207 of the *Highway Traffic Act*
à l'article 207 du Code de la route.

I further certify and believe that the school bus was marked as such, in accordance with the definition of 'school bus' in subsection 175(1) of the *Highway Traffic Act*, and that the red signal lights and the school bus stop arm were activated by the school bus driver and were functioning properly and that at the time a motor vehicle bearing
Je crois et j'atteste en outre que l'autobus scolaire était marqué comme tel, conformément à la définition d'« autobus scolaire » au paragraphe 175(1) du Code de la route, et que les feux rouges et le bras d'arrêt de l'autobus scolaire étaient activés par le chauffeur et fonctionnaient correctement et qu'à ce moment, le véhicule automobile muni de la plaque d'immatriculation de/d'

[fill in jurisdiction] number plate _____ approached the school bus from the [rear/front] of the school
[indiquer la province/le territoire] numéro _____ *s'est approché [derrière/devant] l'autobus scolaire dont les feux*

bus with the red signal lights and school bus stop arm activated and proceeded to pass the school bus, failing to stop as required by law
rouges et le bras d'arrêt étaient activés et s'est engagé en [dépassant/croisant] l'autobus, omettant de s'arrêter comme l'exige la loi.

I, _____ , certify that I mailed Offence Notice Number _____
Je soussigné(e), _____ , *atteste que j'ai envoyé par la poste l'avis d'infraction numéro*

_____ to the Defendant on the _____ day of _____ _____ at the address of the Defendant
au défendeur le _____ *jour de* (month / *mois*) (year / *année*) *à l'adresse du défendeur,*

on the date of offence as recorded by jurisdiction transportation ministry/office/records.
à la date de l'infraction, telle qu'elle figure dans les dossiers, au ministère des Transports ou au greffe du territoire de compétence.

SIGNATURE OF ISSUING PROVINCIAL OFFENCES OFFICER *SIGNATURE DE L'AGENT DES INFRACTIONS PROVINCIALES*		OFFICER NUMBER *NUMÉRO DE L'AGENT*	DATE OF ISSUE / *DATE DE DÉLIVRANCE*		
			Y / A	M / M	D / J
SET FINE OF *AMENDE FIXÉE DE* $	TOTAL PAYABLE *MONTANT TOTAL EXIGIBLE* $ $	TOTAL PAYABLE INCLUDES SET FINE, APPLICABLE VICTIM FINE SURCHARGE, AND COSTS *LE MONTANT TOTAL EXIGIBLE COMPREND L'AMENDE FIXÉE, LA SURAMENDE COMPENSATOIRE QUI S'APPLIQUE ET LES FRAIS*			
CONVICTION ENTERED SET FINE IMPOSED *DÉCLARATION DE CULPABILITÉ INSCRITE, AMENDE FIXÉE IMPOSÉE*			Y / A	M / M	D / J
JUSTICE / *JUGE*					

POA-0862-E (2016/07)

Form 3 — Offence Notice

Provincial Offences Act

[Editor's Note: Pursuant to section O. Reg. 108/11, s. 1, when a form is referred to by number, the reference is to the form with that number that is described in the Table of Forms at the end of this Regulation and is available on the Internet through www.ontariocourtforms.on.ca. For your convenience, the government form is reproduced below. Form current to March 15, 2014.]

ICON Location Code	Offence number
Code d'emplacement du RIII	Numéro d'infraction

Form 3, *Provincial Offences Act*, Ontario Court of Justice, O. Reg. 108/11
Formulaire 3, *Loi sur les infractions provinciales, Cour de justice de l'Ontario, Régl. de l'Ont. 108/11*

Offence Notice
Avis d'infraction

(print name / nom en lettres moulées)

believes and certifies that on the day of
croit et atteste que le

	Y / A	M / M	D / J	Time / heure
2 0				M

Name
Nom   *(family / nom de famille)*

(given / prénom)   *(initials / initiales)*

Address
Adresse   *(number and street / numéro et nom de la rue)*

(municipality / municipalité)   *(P.O. / C.P.)*   *(province)*   *(postal code / code postal)*

Driver's licence no. / *N° de permis de conduire*   Juris / *Aut. lég.*

Birth date / *Date de naissance*			Sex / Sexe	Motor vehicle involved / Véhicule impliqué	Collision involved / Collision	Witnesses / Témoins
Y / A	M / M	D / J		☐ N / N	☐ Y / O	☐ Y / O

At
A   *(municipality / municipalité)*

Did commit the offence of
A commis l'infraction de

contrary to _____ sect.
contrairement à _____ *, art.*

Plate no. / *N° de la plaque d'immatriculation*	Juris / Aut. lég.	Commercial / Utilitaire	CVOR / IUVU	NSC / CNS	Code
		☐ Y / O	☐ Y / O	☐ Y / O	

CVOR No. - NSC No. / *N° de l'IUVU - N° du CNS*

And I further certify that I served an offence notice   ☐ Or other service date of:
personally upon the person charged on the offence date   *Autre date de signification, le :*
J'atteste également qu'à la date de l'infraction, j'ai signifié, en mains propres, un avis d'infraction à la personne accusée.

Signature of issuing Provincial Offences Officer / *Signature de l'agent des infractions provinciales*	Officer No. / *N° de l'agent*	Platoon / Peloton	Unit / Unité

Set fine of / *Amende fixée de*	Total payable / *Montant total exigible*	Total payable includes set fine, applicable victim fine surcharge and costs. / *Le montant total exigible comprend l'amende fixée, la suramende compensatoire pour l'aide aux victimes applicable et les frais.*
$ $	$ $	

Important
You have 15 days from the day you receive this notice to choose one of the options on the back of the notice.

Important :
À compter de la réception du présent avis, vous avez 15 jours pour choisir une des options décrites au verso de l'avis.

POA 0848 (March 15, 2014 / 15 mars 2014) CSD

700

Important – If you do not exercise one of the following options within 15 days of receiving this notice, you will be deemed not to dispute the charge and a justice may enter a conviction against you. Upon conviction, additional costs will be added to the total payable. If the fine goes into default, an administrative fee will be added and steps will be taken to enforce your defaulted fine. For example, information may be provided to a consumer reporting agency and for certain offences including speeding, your driver's licence may be suspended.

Important – Si vous n'exercez pas l'une des options suivantes dans un délai de 15 jours à compter de la réception du présent avis, vous serez réputé(e) ne pas contester l'accusation et un juge pourra inscrire une déclaration de culpabilité contre vous. Sur déclaration de culpabilité, des frais additionnels s'ajouteront au montant total exigible. En cas de défaut de paiement de l'amende, des frais d'administration s'ajouteront et des mesures seront prises pour faire exécuter le paiement de votre amende. Par exemple, l'information pourra être transmise à une agence de renseignements sur le consommateur et dans le cas de certaines infractions, dont l'excès de vitesse votre permis de conduire pourra être suspendu.

OPTION 1

Plea of Guilty – Voluntary Payment of Total Payable: I plead guilty and payment of the total payable is enclosed (follow the instructions on the "payment notice").

Plaidoyer de culpabilité – paiement volontaire du montant total exigible : Je plaide coupable et le montant total exigible est joint au présent avis (suivre les instructions figurant sur « l'avis de paiement »).

OPTION 2

Plea of guilty – Submissions as to Penalty: I want to appear before a justice to enter a plea of guilty and make submissions as to penalty (amount of fine or time to pay). **Note: You must attend the court office** shown below within the times and days shown. Bring this notice with you.

Plaidoyer de culpabilité – observations au sujet de la peine : Je désire comparaître devant un juge pour inscrire un plaidoyer de culpabilité et présenter des observations au sujet de la peine (montant de l'amende ou délai de paiement). Remarque : Vous devez vous présenter au greffe du tribunal indiqué ci-après aux dates et heures indiquées. Apportez le présent avis.

Ontario Court of Justice, Provincial Offences Office

Cour de justice de l'Ontario, Bureau des infractions provinciales

OPTION 3

Trial Option, Ontario Court of Justice, Provincial Offences Office

Procès, Cour de justice de l'Ontario, Bureau des infractions provinciales

Notice of intention to appear in court:

Avis d'intention de comparaître devant le tribunal :

☐ I intend to appear in court to enter a plea of not guilty **at the time and place set for the trial** and I wish to have the trial conducted in the English language.

☐ *J'ai l'intention de comparaître devant le tribunal pour inscrire un plaidoyer de non-culpabilité à l'heure et au lieu prévus pour le procès et je désire que le procès se déroule en français.*

I request a _____ language interpreter for the trial. (Leave blank if inapplicable.)

Je demande l'aide d'un interprète en langue _____ pour le procès

(À remplir, s'il y a lieu.)

Note: If you **fail to notify** the court office of **address changes**, you may not receive important notices, e.g., your Notice of Trial. You may be convicted in your absence if you do not attend the trial.

Remarque : Si vous omettez de prévenir le greffe du tribunal de tout changement d'adresse, vous pourriez ne pas recevoir d'importants avis (p. ex., votre avis de procès). Si vous n'assistez pas au procès, vous pourriez être déclaré(e) coupable en votre absence.

_____
Signature

Changes to your address (if applicable): Changement d'adresse (le cas échéant) :

Telephone Number: Numéro de téléphone :

FOR INFORMATION ON ACCESS TO ONTARIO COURTS FOR PERSONS WITH DISABILITIES: [Court to insert information]
POUR OBTENIR DES RENSEIGNEMENTS SUR L'ACCÈS DES PERSONNES HANDICAPÉES AUX TRIBUNAUX DE L'ONTARIO [ajouter l'information]

POA 0848 (March 15, 2014 / 15 mars 2014) CSD

701

Form 4 — Offence Notice

Provincial Offences Act

[Editor's Note: Pursuant to section O. Reg. 108/11, s. 1, when a form is referred to by number, the reference is to the form with that number that is described in the Table of Forms at the end of this Regulation and is available on the Internet through www.ontariocourtforms.on.ca. For your convenience, the government form is reproduced below. Form current to November 2, 2011.]

ICON Location Code	Offence number
Code d'emplacement du RIII	Numéro d'infraction

Form 4, Provincial Offences Act, Ontario Court of Justice, O. Reg. 108/11
Formulaire 4, Loi sur les infractions provinciales, Cour de justice de l'Ontario, Régl. de l'Ont. 108/11

Offence Notice
Avis d'infraction

(print name / nom en lettres moulées)

believes and certifies that on the day of
croit et atteste que le

Y / A	M / M	D / J	Time / heure
2 0			M

Name
Nom

(family / nom de famille)

(given / prénom)   (initials / initiales)

Address
Adresse

(number and street / numéro et nom de la rue)

(municipality / municipalité)   (P.O. / C.P.)   (province)   (postal code / code postal)

Driver's licence no. / N° de permis de conduire   Juris / Aut. Lég

| Birth date / Date de naissance | | | Sex | Motor vehicle involved | Collision involved | Witnesses |
Y / A	M / M	D / J	Sexe	Véhicule impliqué	Collision	Témoins
				☐ N / N	☐ Y / O	☐ Y / O

At
À

(municipality / municipalité)

Did commit the offence of
A commis l'infraction de

contrary to _____ sect.
contrairement à   l'art.

| Plate no | Juris | Commercial | CVOR | NSC | Code |
N° de la plaque d'immatriculation	Aut. Lég	Utilitaire	IUVU	CNS	
		☐ Y / O	☐ Y / O	☐ Y / O	

CVOR No. NSC No. / N° de l'IUVU N° du CNS

And I further certify that I served an offence notice   ☐ Or other service date of:
personally upon the person charged on the offence date   Autre date de signification, le :
J'atteste également qu'à la date de l'infraction, j'ai signifié, en
mains propres, un avis d'infraction à la personne accusée

| Signature of issuing Provincial Offences Officer | Officer No | Platoon | Unit |
Signature de l'agent des infractions provinciales	N° de l'agent	Peloton	Unité

| Set fine of | Total payable | Total payable includes set fine, applicable victim |
Amende fixée de	Montant total exigible	fine surcharge and costs / Le montant total
$ $	$ $	exigible comprend l'amende fixée, la suramende compensatoire pour l'aide aux victimes applicable et les frais

Important:
You have 15 days from the day you receive this notice to choose one of the options on the back of the notice.

Important :
À compter de la réception du présent avis, vous avez 15 jours pour choisir une des options décrites au verso de l'avis.

POA 0849 (Novembre 2, 2011 / 2 novembre 2011) CSD

Important — If you do not exercise one of the following options within 15 days of receiving this notice, you will be deemed not to dispute the charge and a justice may enter a conviction against you. Upon conviction, additional costs will be added to the total payable. If the fine goes into default, an administrative fee will be added and steps will be taken to enforce your defaulted fine. For example, information may be provided to a consumer reporting agency and for certain offences, including speeding, your driver's licence may be suspended.

Important — Si vous n'exercez pas une des options suivantes dans un délai de 15 jours à compter de la réception du présent avis, vous serez réputé(e) ne pas contester l'accusation et un juge pourra inscrire une déclaration de culpabilité contre vous. Sur déclaration de culpabilité, des frais additionnels s'ajouteront au montant total exigible. En cas de défaut de paiement de l'amende, des frais administratifs s'ajouteront et des mesures seront prises pour faire exécuter le paiement de votre amende. Par exemple, l'information peut être transmise à une agence de renseignements sur le consommateur, et dans le cas de certaines infractions, dont l'excès de vitesse, votre permis de conduire peut être suspendu.

OPTION 1 — Plea of Guilty — Voluntary Payment of Total Payable. I plead guilty and payment of the total payable is enclosed (follow the instructions on the "payment notice")

OPTION 1 — Plaidoyer de culpabilité — Paiement volontaire du montant total exigible : Je plaide coupable et le montant total exigible est joint à la présente (suivre les instructions figurant sur « l'avis de paiement »)

OPTION 2 — Early Resolution — Meet with Prosecutor (by choosing this option you do not forego the right to a trial)

OPTION 2 — Résolution rapide — Rencontre avec le poursuivant (si vous choisissez l'option suivante, vous ne renoncez pas au droit d'obtenir un procès) :

☐ I request a meeting with a prosecutor to discuss the possible resolution of the charge. I understand that if I fail to attend the scheduled meeting, I will be deemed not to dispute the charge and may be convicted in my absence.

☐ Je désire une rencontre avec le poursuivant pour discuter du règlement relatif à l'infraction. Je comprends que si je n'assiste pas à la rencontre, je serai réputé(e) ne pas contester l'accusation et un juge pourra inscrire une déclaration de culpabilité contre moi en mon absence.

I request a _____ language interpreter
(Leave blank if inapplicable)

Je demande l'aide d'un interprète de langue _____
(À remplir s'il y a lieu)

☐ I live more than [Court to insert distance of not more than 75 km] from the courthouse listed below and I would like to meet the prosecutor by [Court to insert electronic method(s) available locally].

☐ J'habite à plus de [ajouter la distance désirée jusqu'à concurrence de 75 km] du palais de justice mentionné ci-dessous et j'aimerais que la rencontre avec le poursuivant ait lieu par [ajouter la méthode électronique offerte]

You must send this notice to the Ontario Court of Justice, Provincial Offences Office address below. You will be sent a meeting notice to the address on the file. Notify the court if your address changes.

Vous devez envoyer cet avis au Bureau des infractions provinciales de la Cour de justice de l'Ontario à l'adresse indiquée ci-dessous. Vous recevrez un avis de rencontre à l'adresse figurant au dossier. Vous devez aviser le tribunal si vous changez d'adresse.

OPTION 3 — Trial Option — DO NOT MAIL — I intend to appear in court to plead not guilty and have an English language trial. You or your representative MUST attend in person at the court office shown below within the times and days shown to file a notice of intention to appear in court. Bring this notice with you.

OPTION 3 — Procès — NE PAS ENVOYER PAR LA POSTE — Je désire comparaître devant un juge pour inscrire un plaidoyer de non-culpabilité et subir un procès en français. Vous ou votre représentant DEVEZ vous présenter au greffe du tribunal aux dates et aux heures indiquées pour déposer un avis d'intention de comparaître devant le tribunal. Apportez le présent avis au greffe du tribunal.

Ontario Court of Justice / Cour de justice de l'Ontario
Provincial Offences Office / Bureau des infractions provinciales
[Court to insert Address, Hours of Operation] / [ajouter l'adresse et les heures d'ouverture]

FOR INFORMATION ON ACCESS TO ONTARIO COURTS FOR PERSONS WITH DISABILITIES: [Court to insert information]
POUR PLUS DE RENSEIGNEMENTS SUR L'ACCÈS DES PERSONNES HANDICAPÉES AUX TRIBUNAUX DE L'ONTARIO [ajouter l'information]

POA 0649 (November 2, 2011 / 2 novembre 2011) CSD

Form 5 — Red Light Camera System Offence Notice

Provincial Offences Act

[Editor's Note: Pursuant to section O. Reg. 108/11, s. 1, when a form is referred to by number, the reference is to the form with that number that is described in the Table of Forms at the end of this Regulation and is available on the Internet through www.ontariocourtforms.on.ca. For your convenience, the government form is reproduced below. Form current to March 15, 2014.]

RED LIGHT CAMERA SYSTEM OFFENCE NOTICE
AVIS D'INFRACTION – SYSTÈME PHOTOGRAPHIQUE RELIÉ AUX FEUX ROUGES
Form / Formulaire 5

Provincial Offences Act / Loi sur les infractions provinciales
O. Reg. / Regl de l'Ont. 108/11

ONTARIO COURT OF JUSTICE
COUR DE JUSTICE DE L'ONTARIO

OFFENCE NO. / Nº D'AVIS D'INFRACTION

You / Vous
(Name / Nom)

(Address / Adresse)

being the owner of a motor vehicle displaying
propriétaire d'un véhicule automobile muni de la

Ontario number plate
plaque d'immatriculation de l'Ontario

are charged with the offence of failing to stop at a red light
êtes accusé(e) de l'infraction d'omettre de s'arrêter à un feu rouge

on the   day of   20   at   m.
le   jour de   20   à   h.

at the intersection of
à l'intersection de

Location
Lieu

in the
a   (municipality / municipalité)

as shown in the digitized images set forth in this notice, contrary to subsection 144(18.1) and pursuant to section 207 of the *Highway Traffic Act*,
comme il est indiqué dans les images numérisées présentées dans le présent avis, contrairement au paragraphe 144(18.1) et conformément à l'article 207 du Code de la route.

Photograph or equivalent / photographie ou l'équivalent

The photographs taken by the red light camera system show the vehicle approaching the intersection, at which time the signal had displayed red for
Les photographies prises par le système photographique relié aux feux rouges montrent que le véhicule s'est approché de l'intersection, après que le feu de circulation est devenu rouge depuis

seconds and that vehicle proceeded through the intersection
secondes et que le véhicule a continué à avancer dans

when the light had been red for   seconds
l'intersection, alors que le feu de circulation était rouge depuis   secondes

I believe and certify that the above offence has been committed
Je crois et j'atteste que l'infraction mentionnée ci-dessus a été commise

Signature of Officer issuing this notice
Signature de l'agent qui a délivré l'avis d'infraction

Issuing Officer Number
Matricule de l'agent qui a délivré l'avis d'infraction

Date of Deemed Service
Date de signification présumée

PLEASE NOTE: Section 207 of the *Highway Traffic Act* provides that you, as the owner, are liable for this offence even if you were not the driver at the time, subject to limited exceptions. Neither demerit points nor a driver's licence suspension will result from your conviction for this offence. The provincial offences officer has certified that the red light camera system used in the detection of this offence is a prescribed system used in a designated area and furthermore that it was in proper working order at the time that the photographs obtained were recorded by that system and the traffic signals were in proper working order at the time of the offence. Certified photographs will be tendered in evidence at your trial. You must apply to the justice at trial if you wish to compel the attendance of the Provincial Offences Officer who issued the certificate of offence or who certified the photographs to be tendered at your trial.

Set Fine
Amende fixée
$ $

Total Payable:
Montant total exigible :
(includes set fine, applicable victim fine surcharge and costs)
(comprend l'amende fixée, la suramende compensatoire applicable et les frais)

$ $

REMARQUE : L'article 207 du Code de la route prévoit que vous-même, en tant que propriétaire, êtes responsable de cette infraction, même si vous n'étiez pas le conducteur au moment où celle-ci a été commise, sous réserve de certaines exceptions. Aucune déduction de culpabilité pour la présente infraction n'entraînera aucun point d'inaptitude ni la suspension du conducteur. L'agent des infractions provinciales a attesté que le système photographique relié aux feux rouges utilisé pour détecter l'infraction est un système prescrit et utilisé dans une région désignée. De plus, il a attesté que le système était en bon état de marche au moment de l'infraction, que les photographies obtenues ont été enregistrées par ce système et que les feux de circulation étaient en bon état de marche au moment de l'infraction. Des photographies certifiées seront présentées en preuve lors de votre procès. Vous devez vous adresser au juge du procès si vous désirez obtenir la comparution de l'agent des infractions provinciales qui a délivré le procès-verbal d'infraction ou qui a certifié les photos qui seront présentées en preuve lors de votre procès.

POA 0818 (March 15, 2014 / 15 mars 2014) CSD

704

Important – If you do not exercise one of the following options within 15 days of receiving this notice, you will be deemed not to wish to dispute the charge and a justice may enter a conviction against you. Upon conviction additional costs will be added to the total payable. If the fine goes into default, an administrative fee will be added and the information may be provided to a consumer reporting agency. Steps will be taken to enforce your defaulted fine, including refusal to issue a validation of your vehicle permit or refusal to issue a vehicle permit until the total payable and all additional costs and fees have been paid.

OPTION 1 – Trial Option – Ontario Court of Justice, Provincial Offences Office

NOTICE OF INTENTION TO APPEAR IN COURT:

☐ I intend to appear in court to enter a plea of not guilty **at the time and place set for the trial** and I wish to have the trial conducted in the English language.

I request a .... language interpreter for the trial.

leave blank if inapplicable)

Changes to your address (if applicable):

Telephone number:

OPTION 2 – Plea of Guilty – Submissions as to Penalty

I want to appear before a justice to enter a plea of guilty and make submissions as to penalty (amount of fine or time to pay).

Note: You must attend at the court office shown within the times and days shown. Bring this notice with you.

OPTION 3 – Plea of Guilty – Voluntary Payment of Total Payable

I plead guilty and payment of the total payable is enclosed.

Offence Notice No.

Sign Here

TO PAY: Forward your payment in the self-addressed envelope provided. Sign the plea of guilty (above) and write the number of the offence notice on the front of the cheque or money order. Do not send cash or post-dated cheques. Make the cheque or money order payable to the ONTARIO COURT OF JUSTICE. Dishonoured cheques will be subject to an administrative charge.

Name:
Nom:

Address:
Adresse:

Total Payable
Montant total exigible $ .... $ ....

POA 0818 (March 15, 2014 / 15 mars 2014) CSD

Important – Si vous n'exercez pas l'une des options suivantes dans les 15 jours à compter de la réception du présent avis, vous serez réputé(e) ne pas contester l'accusation et un juge pourra inscrire une déclaration de culpabilité contre vous. Sur déclaration de culpabilité, des frais additionnels s'ajouteront au montant total exigible. En cas de défaut de paiement de l'amende, des frais d'administration s'ajouteront et l'information pourra être transmise à une agence de renseignements sur le consommateur. Des mesures seront prises pour faire exécuter le paiement de votre amende, y compris le refus de validation de votre certificat d'immatriculation ou le refus de délivrance de votre certificat d'immatriculation jusqu'à ce que le montant total exigible et tous les frais additionnels aient été payés.

OPTION 1 – Procès – Cour de justice de l'Ontario, Bureau des infractions provinciales

AVIS D'INTENTION DE COMPARAÎTRE DEVANT LE TRIBUNAL :

☐ J'ai l'intention de comparaître devant le tribunal pour inscrire un plaidoyer de non-culpabilité **à l'heure et au lieu prévus pour le procès** et je désire que le procès se déroule en français.

Je demande l'aide d'un interprète en langue .... pour le procès.

(à remplir, s'il y a lieu)

Changement d'adresse (le cas échéant) :

Numéro de téléphone :

OPTION 2 – Plaidoyer de culpabilité – observations au sujet de la peine

Je désire comparaître devant un juge pour inscrire un plaidoyer de culpabilité et présenter des observations au sujet de la peine (montant de l'amende ou délai de paiement)

Remarque : Vous devez vous présenter au greffe du tribunal aux dates et heures indiquées. Apportez le présent avis.

OPTION 3 – Plaidoyer de culpabilité – paiement volontaire du montant total exigible

Je plaide coupable et le montant total exigible est joint au présent avis.

N° de l'avis d'infraction :

Signez ici

POUR PAYER – Envoyez votre paiement dans l'enveloppe-réponse fournie. Signez le plaidoyer de culpabilité (ci-dessous) et écrivez le numéro de l'avis d'infraction sur le recto du chèque ou du mandat. N'envoyez pas d'espèces ou de chèques postdatés. Libellez le chèque ou mandat à l'ordre de la COUR DE JUSTICE DE L'ONTARIO. Les chèques impayés feront l'objet de frais d'administration.

PAYMENT RETURN SLIP / FICHE DE PAIEMENT

Cheque/Money Order enclosed: ☐   Visa ☐   MasterCard ☐
Chèque ou mandat joint :

Card No.:   Expiry Date: M   Y
N° de carte :   Date d'expiration : M   A

Signature of Cardholder:
Signature du ou de la titulaire :

705

Form 5.1 — Fail to Stop for a School Bus — Owner Liability Offence Notice

Provincial Offences Act

[Editor's Note: Pursuant to section O. Reg. 108/11, s. 1, when a form is referred to by number, the reference is to the form with that number that is described in the Table of Forms at the end of this Regulation and is available on the Internet through www.ontariocourtforms.on.ca. For your convenience, the government form is reproduced below. Form current to July 2016.]

**FAIL TO STOP FOR A SCHOOL BUS - OWNER LIABILITY
OFFENCE NOTICE**
*OMISSION DE S'ARRÊTER POUR UN AUTOBUS SCOLAIRE - RESPONSABILITÉ DU PROPRIÉTAIRE
AVIS D'INFRACTION*

Form 5.1, *Provincial Offences Act*, O. Reg. 108/11
Formule 5.1. *Loi sur les infractions provinciales, Régl. de l'Ont. 108/11*

ONTARIO COURT OF JUSTICE
COUR DE JUSTICE DE L'ONTARIO

OFFENCE NUMBER / *NUMÉRO D'AVIS D'INFRACTION*

You
Vous _____
(Name / *Nom*)   (Address / *Adresse*)

being the owner of a motor vehicle displaying [fill in jurisdiction] number plate
propriétaire d'un véhicule automobile muni de la plaque d'immatriculation numéro de/d: [indiquer la province/le territoire]

_____ are charged with the offence of failing to stop for a school bus on the
êtes accusé(e) de l'infraction d'avoir omis de vous arrêter pour un autobus scolaire le

_____ day of _____ 20____ , at _____ m. at/near _____
jour de   *20*   *à*   *h, à l'intersection de*   (location / *endroit*)

in the
dans le/la _____ contrary to subsection [175(19)/175(20)] of the *Highway Traffic Act* and
(municipality / *municipalité*)   *contrairement au paragraphe [175(19)/175(20)] et*

pursuant to section 207 of the *Highway Traffic Act*
conformément à l'article 207 du Code de la route.

I believe and certify that the above offence has been committed
Je crois et j'atteste que l'infraction mentionnée ci-dessus a été commise

_____
Signature of Officer issuing this notice
Signature de l'agent qui a délivré l'avis d'infraction

Issuing Officer Number: _____
Matricule de l'agent qui a délivré l'avis d'infraction

Date of Deemed Service _____
Date de signification présumée :

PLEASE NOTE: Section 207 of the *Highway Traffic Act* provides that you, as the owner, are liable for this offence even if you were not the driver at the time, subject to limited exceptions. Neither demerit points nor a driver's licence suspension will result from your conviction for this offence. The provincial offences officer viewed images from a camera system used in the detection of this offence. These images may be tendered in evidence at your trial.

Set Fine
Amende fixée
$ _____ $
Total Payable:
Montant total exigible :
(includes set fine, applicable victim fine surcharge and costs)
(comprend l'amende fixée, la suramende compensatoire pour l'aide aux victimes applicable et les frais)
$ _____ $

REMARQUE : L'article 207 du Code de la route prévoit que vous-même, en tant que propriétaire, êtes responsable de cette infraction, même si vous n'étiez pas le conducteur au moment où celle-ci a été commise, sous réserve de certaines exceptions. Votre déclaration de culpabilité pour la présente infraction n'entraînera aucun point d'inaptitude ni la suspension du permis de conduire. L'agent des infractions provinciales a visionné les images d'un système photographique utilisé pour la détection de cette infraction. Ces images pourraient être présentées en preuve à votre procès.

POA 0863-E (2016/07)

Important – If you do not exercise one of the following options within 15 days of receiving this notice, you will be deemed not to wish to dispute the charge and a justice may enter a conviction against you. Upon conviction additional costs will be added to the total payable. If the fine goes into default, an administrative fee will be added and the information may be provided to a consumer reporting agency. Steps will be taken to enforce your defaulted fine, including refusal to issue a validation of your vehicle permit or refusal to issue a vehicle permit until the total payable and all additional costs and fees have been paid.

OPTION 1 - Trial Option - Ontario Court of Justice, Provincial Offences Office

NOTICE OF INTENTION TO APPEAR IN COURT:

☐ I intend to appear in court to enter a plea of not guilty **at the time and place set for the trial** and I wish to have the trial conducted in the English language

I request a _____ *(leave blank if inapplicable)* language interpreter for the trial.

Changes to your address (if applicable):

Telephone number:

OPTION 2 - Plea of Guilty - Submissions as to Penalty

I want to appear before a justice to enter a plea of guilty and make submissions as to penalty (amount of fine or time to pay).

Note: You must attend at the court office shown within the times and days shown. Bring this notice with you.

(Insert court contact information here)

PAYMENT RETURN SLIP / FICHE DE PAIEMENT

OPTION 3 - Plea of Guilty - Voluntary Payment of Total Payable

I plead guilty and payment of the total payable is enclosed.

Offence Notice Number

Sign here

TO PAY: Forward your payment in the self-addressed envelope provided. Sign the plea of guilty (above) and write the number of the offence notice on the front of the cheque or money order. Do not send cash or post-dated cheques. Make the cheque or money order payable to the ONTARIO COURT OF JUSTICE. Dishonoured cheques will be subject to an administrative charge.

Name: / Nom:

Address: / adresse

Total Payable / Montant total exigible $ _____

POA-0663-E (2016/07)

Important – Si vous n'exercez pas l'une des options suivantes dans les 15 jours à compter de la réception du présent avis, vous serez réputé(e) ne pas contester l'accusation et un juge pourra inscrire une déclaration de culpabilité contre vous. Sur déclaration de culpabilité, des frais additionnels s'ajouteront au montant total exigible. En cas de défaut de paiement de l'amende, des frais d'administration s'ajouteront et l'information pourra être transmise à une agence de renseignements sur le consommateur. Des mesures seront prises pour faire exécuter le paiement de votre amende, y compris le refus de délivrance de votre certificat d'immatriculation ou le refus de validation de votre certificat d'immatriculation jusqu'à ce que le montant total exigible et tous les frais additionnels aient été payés.

OPTION 1 - Procès - Cour de justice de l'Ontario, Bureau des infractions provinciales

AVIS D'INTENTION DE COMPARAÎTRE DEVANT LE TRIBUNAL :

☐ J'ai l'intention de comparaître devant le tribunal pour inscrire un plaidoyer de non-culpabilité **aux date, heure et lieu prévus pour le procès** et je désire que le procès se déroule en français.

Je demande l'aide d'un interprète de langue _____ pour le procès *(à remplir, s'il y a lieu)*.

Changement d'adresse (le cas échéant) :

Numéro de téléphone :

OPTION 2 - Plaidoyer de culpabilité - observations au sujet de la peine

Je désire comparaître devant un juge pour inscrire un plaidoyer de culpabilité et présenter des observations au sujet de la peine (montant de l'amende ou délai de paiement).

Remarque : Vous devez vous présenter au greffe du tribunal aux dates et heures indiquées. Apportez le présent avis.

(indiquez ici les coordonnées du greffe)

OPTION 3 - Plaidoyer de culpabilité - paiement volontaire du montant total exigible

Je plaide coupable et le montant total exigible est joint au présent avis.

Numéro de l'avis d'infraction

Signez ici

POUR PAYER : Envoyez votre paiement dans l'enveloppe-réponse fournie. Signez le plaidoyer de culpabilité (ci-dessus) et écrivez le numéro de l'avis d'infraction sur le recto du chèque ou du mandat. N'envoyez pas d'espèces ou de chèques postdatés. Libellez le chèque ou mandat à l'ordre de la COUR DE JUSTICE DE L'ONTARIO. Les chèques impayés feront l'objet de frais d'administration.

Cheque/Money Order enclosed ☐ Visa ☐ MasterCard ☐ / Chèque ou mandat joint :

Card Number: / Numéro de carte :

Expiry Date M _____ Y _____ / Date d'expiration : M _____ A _____

Signature of Cardholder: / Signature du ou de la titulaire

Form 6 — Red Light Camera System Offence Notice

Provincial Offences Act

[Editor's Note: Pursuant to section O. Reg. 108/11, s. 1, when a form is referred to by number, the reference is to the form with that number that is described in the Table of Forms at the end of this Regulation and is available on the Internet through www.ontariocourtforms.on.ca. For your convenience, the government form is reproduced below. Form current to November 2, 2011.]

RED LIGHT CAMERA SYSTEM OFFENCE NOTICE
AVIS D'INFRACTION – SYSTÈME PHOTOGRAPHIQUE RELIÉ AUX FEUX ROUGES
Form 6, Provincial Offences Act, O. Reg. 108/11
Formulaire 6, Loi sur les infractions provinciales, Règl. de l'Ont. 108/11

ONTARIO COURT OF JUSTICE
COUR DE JUSTICE DE L'ONTARIO

OFFENCE NO. / N° D'AVIS D'INFRACTION

You / Vous
(Name / Nom)

(Address / Adresse)

being the owner of a motor vehicle displaying
à titre de propriétaire d'un véhicule automobile affichant

Ontario number plate
le numéro de plaque d'immatriculation de l'Ontario

are charged with the offence of failing to stop at a red light
êtes accusé(e) de l'infraction d'omettre de s'arrêter à un feu rouge

on the ___ day of ___, 20 ___ at ___ m.
le ___ *jour de* ___ à ___ h

at the intersection of
à l'intersection de ___ (location / endroit)

in the
dans le/la ___ (municipality / municipalité)

as shown in the digitized images set forth in this notice, contrary to subsection 144(18.1) and pursuant to section 207 of the *Highway Traffic Act*.
comme le montrent les images numérisées exposées au présent avis, contrairement au paragraphe 144 (18.1) et conformément à l'article 207 du Code de la route.

Photograph or equivalent : *photographie ou l'équivalent*

The photographs taken by the red light camera system show the vehicle approaching the intersection, at which time the signal had displayed red for
Les photographies prises par le système photographique relié aux feux rouges montrent le véhicule qui s'approche de l'intersection, au moment où le feu était rouge depuis

___ seconds and that vehicle proceeded through the
secondes et que le véhicule a franchi

intersection when the light had been red for ___ seconds.
l'intersection alors que le feu était rouge depuis ___ *secondes*

I believe and certify that the above offence has been committed.
Je crois et atteste que l'infraction susmentionnée a été commise.

Signature of Officer issuing this notice
Signature de l'agent qui délivre le présent avis

Issuing Officer Number:
Numéro de l'agent qui délivre le présent avis :

Date of Deemed Service:
Date de signification présumée :

PLEASE NOTE: Section 207 of the *Highway Traffic Act* provides that you, as the owner, are liable for this offence even if you were not the driver at the time, subject to limited exceptions. Neither demerit points nor a driver's licence suspension will result from your conviction for this offence. The provincial offences officer has certified that the red light camera system used in the detection of this offence is a prescribed system, used in a designated area and furthermore that it was in proper working order at the time, that the photographs obtained were recorded by that system and the traffic signals were in proper working order at the time of the offence. Certified photographs will be tendered in evidence at your trial.

Set Fine / Amende fixée
$ ___ $

Total Payable
Montant total exigible
(includes set fine, applicable victim fines surcharge and costs)
(comprend l'amende fixée, la suramende compensatoire pour l'aide aux victimes applicable et les frais)

$ ___ $

VEUILLEZ PRENDRE NOTE L'article 207 du Code de la route prévoit que vous-même, à titre de propriétaire, êtes responsable de cette infraction même si vous ne conduisiez pas le véhicule à ce moment-là, sous réserve d'exceptions restreintes. Une déclaration de culpabilité pour cette infraction ne mènera pas à l'inscription de points d'inaptitude dans votre dossier ou à la suspension de votre permis de conduire. L'agent des infractions provinciales a attesté que le système photographique relié aux feux rouges qui a servi à détecter cette infraction est un système prescrit, utilisé dans une zone désignée. De plus, il a attesté que le système était en bon état de fonctionnement à ce moment-là que les photos obtenues ont été enregistrées par le système et que les feux de circulation fonctionnaient correctement au moment de l'infraction. Des photos certifiées seront présentées en preuve lors de votre procès.

POA 0850 (November 2, 2011 / 2 novembre 2011) CSD

Important – If you do not exercise one of the following options within 15 days of receiving this notice, you will be deemed not to wish to dispute the charge and a justice may enter a conviction against you. Upon conviction additional costs will be added to the total payable. If the fine goes into default an administrative fee will be added and the information may be provided to a consumer reporting agency. Steps will be taken to enforce your defaulted fine, including refusal to issue a validation of your vehicle permit or refusal to issue a vehicle permit until the total payable and all additional costs and fees have been paid.

Important – Si vous n'exercez pas l'une des options suivantes dans les 15 jours à compter de la réception du présent avis, vous serez réputé(e) ne pas contester l'accusation et un juge pourra inscrire une déclaration de culpabilité contre vous. En cas de déclaration de culpabilité, des frais additionnels s'ajouteront au montant total exigible. En cas de défaut de paiement de l'amende, des frais d'administration s'ajouteront et l'information pourra être transmise à une agence de renseignements sur le consommateur. Des mesures seront prises pour faire exécuter le paiement de votre amende, y compris le refus d'une demande de validation ou de délivrance de certificat d'immatriculation jusqu'à ce que le montant total exigible et tous les frais additionnels aient été payés.

OPTION 1 – Trial Option – DO NOT MAIL – I want to appear before a justice to enter a plea of not guilty and to have a trial.

You or your representative MUST attend the court office at the times and days shown to file a notice of intention to appear in court. You cannot set a trial date by mail. Bring this notice to the court office.

OPTION 1 – Option du procès – NE PAS POSTER : Je désire comparaître devant un juge pour inscrire un plaidoyer de non-culpabilité et subir un procès.

Vous ou votre représentant DEVEZ vous présenter au greffe du tribunal aux dates et heures indiquées pour déposer un avis d'intention de comparaître devant le tribunal. Vous ne pouvez pas fixer la date du procès par courrier. Apportez le présent avis au greffe du tribunal.

RETURN SLIP / *BORDEREAU DE RÉPONSE*

Offence Notice No. / *Nº de l'avis d'infraction*

Name / *Nom*

Address / *Adresse*

OPTION 2 – Early Resolution – Meet with Prosecutor (by choosing this option you do not forego the right to a trial):

☐ I request a meeting with a prosecutor to discuss the possible resolution of the charge. I understand that if I fail to attend the scheduled meeting. I will be deemed not to dispute the charge and may be convicted of the offence.

I request a _____ language interpreter.
(Leave blank if inapplicable)

☐ I live more than *[Court to insert distance of not more than 75 km]* from the courthouse listed below and I would like to meet the prosecutor by *[Court to insert electronic method(s) available locally]*.

You will be sent a meeting notice to the address on the file. You must notify the court if your address changes.

OPTION 2 – Résolution rapide – Rencontre avec le poursuivant (si vous choisissez l'option suivante, vous ne renoncez pas au droit d'obtenir un procès) :

☐ Je désire une rencontre avec le poursuivant pour discuter du règlement relatif à l'infraction. Je comprends que si je n'assiste pas à la rencontre, je serai réputé(e) ne pas contester l'accusation et un juge pourra inscrire une déclaration de culpabilité contre moi.

Je demande l'aide d'un interprète de langue _____
(À remplir s'il y a lieu)

☐ J'habite à plus de [ajouter la distance désirée jusqu'à concurrence de 75 km] du palais de justice mentionné ci-dessous et j'aimerais que la rencontre avec le poursuivant ait lieu par [ajouter la méthode électronique offerte].

Vous recevrez un avis de rencontre à l'adresse figurant au dossier. Vous devez aviser le tribunal si vous changez d'adresse.

OPTION 3 – Plea of Guilty – Voluntary Payment of Total Payable: I plead guilty and payment of the total payable is enclosed.

TO PAY Write the number of the offence notice on the front of the cheque or money order. Do not send cash or post-dated cheques. Make the cheque or money order payable to the ONTARIO COURT OF JUSTICE. Dishonoured cheques will be subject to an administrative charge.

OPTION 3 – Plaidoyer de culpabilité – Paiement volontaire du montant total exigible : Je plaide coupable et le montant total exigible est joint à la présente.

POUR PAYER Écrivez le numéro de l'avis d'infraction sur le recto du chèque ou du mandat. N'envoyez pas d'espèces ou de chèques postdatés. Libellez le chèque ou mandat à l'ordre de la COUR DE JUSTICE DE L'ONTARIO. Les chèques impayés donneront lieu à des frais d'administration.

☐ Cheque/Money Order enclosed ☐ Visa ☐ MasterCard Card No _____ Expiry Date: M ___ Y ___
Chèque ou mandat joint *Nº de carte* *Date d'expiration M ___*

Total Payable $ _____ Signature of Cardholder _____
Montant total exigible $ ___ *Signature du titulaire de la carte :*

FORWARD YOUR RETURN SLIP IN THE SELF-ADDRESSED ENVELOPE PROVIDED / *ENVOYEZ VOTRE BORDEREAU DANS L'ENVELOPPE-RÉPONSE FOURNIE.*

POA 0850 (November 2, 2011 / 2 novembre 2011) CSD

Form 6.1 — Fail to Stop for a School Bus — Owner Liability Offence Notice

Provincial Offences Act

[Editor's Note: Pursuant to section O. Reg. 108/11, s. 1, when a form is referred to by number, the reference is to the form with that number that is described in the Table of Forms at the end of this Regulation and is available on the Internet through www.ontariocourtforms.on.ca. For your convenience, the government form is reproduced below. Form current to July 2016.]

FAIL TO STOP FOR A SCHOOL BUS – OWNER LIABILITY
OFFENCE NOTICE
OMISSION DE S'ARRÊTER POUR UN AUTOBUS SCOLAIRE – RESPONSABILITÉ DU PROPRIÉTAIRE
AVIS D'INFRACTION

Form 6.1 *Provincial Offences Act*, O. Reg. 108/11
Formule 6.1, *Loi sur les infractions provinciales, Régl. de l'Ont. 108/11*

ONTARIO COURT OF JUSTICE
COUR DE JUSTICE DE L'ONTARIO

OFFENCE NUMBER / *NUMÉRO D'AVIS D'INFRACTION*

You
Vous

(Name / *Nom*)   (Address / *Adresse*)

being the owner of a motor vehicle displaying [fill in jurisdiction] number plate
propriétaire d'un véhicule automobile muni de la plaque d'immatriculation numéro de/d [indiquer la province/le territoire]

are charged with the offence of failing to stop for a school bus on the
êtes accusé(e) de l'infraction d'avoir omis de vous arrêter pour un autobus scolaire le

_____ day of _____ , 20____ : at _____ m. at/near
jour de _____ 20____ *à* _____ h. *à l'intersection de* _____ (location / *endroit*)

in the
dans le/la _____ (municipality / *municipalité*)

contrary to subsection [175(19)/175(20)] of the *Highway Traffic Act* and
contrairement au paragraphe [175(19)/175(20)] et

pursuant to section 207 of the *Highway Traffic Act*
conformément à l'article 207 du Code de la route

I believe and certify that the above offence has been committed.
Je crois et j'atteste que l'infraction mentionnée ci-dessus a été commise.

Signature of Officer issuing this notice
Signature de l'agent qui a délivré l'avis d'infraction

Issuing Officer Number:
Matricule de l'agent qui a délivré l'avis d'infraction

Date of Deemed Service:
Date de signification présumée

PLEASE NOTE: Section 207 of the *Highway Traffic Act* provides that you, as the owner, are liable for this offence even if you were not the driver at the time, subject to limited exceptions. Neither demerit points nor a driver's licence suspension will result from your conviction for this offence. The provincial offences officer viewed images from a camera system used in the detection of this offence. These images may be tendered in evidence at your trial.

| Set Fine |
| *Amende fixée* |
| $ _____ $ |
| **Total Payable:** |
| ***Montant total exigible :*** |
| (includes set fine, applicable victim fine surcharge and costs) |
| (comprend l'amende fixée, la suramende compensatoire pour l'aide aux victimes applicable et les frais) |
| $ _____ $ |

REMARQUE : L'article 207 du Code de la route prévoit que vous-même, en tant que propriétaire, êtes responsable de cette infraction, même si vous n'étiez pas le conducteur au moment où celle-ci a été commise, sous réserve de certaines exceptions. Votre déclaration de culpabilité pour la présente infraction n'entraînera aucun point d'inaptitude ni la suspension du permis de conduire. L'agent des infractions provinciales a visionné les images d'un système photographique utilisé pour la détection de cette infraction. Ces images pourraient être présentées en preuve à votre procès.

POA-0864-E (2016/07)

Important – If you do not exercise one of the following options within 15 days of receiving this notice, you will be deemed not to wish to dispute the charge and a justice may enter a conviction against you. Upon conviction additional costs will be added to the total payable. If the fine goes into default, an administrative fee will be added and the information may be provided to a consumer reporting agency. Steps will be taken to enforce your defaulted fine, including refusal to issue a validation of your vehicle permit or refusal to issue a vehicle permit until the total payable and all additional costs and fees have been paid.

OPTION 1 - Trial Option – DO NOT MAIL – I want to appear before a justice to enter a plea of not guilty and to have a trial.

You or your representative MUST attend the court office at the times and days shown to file a notice of intention to appear in court. You cannot set a trial date by mail. Bring this notice to the court office.

RETURN SLIP / BORDEREAU DE RÉPONSE

Offence Notice Number / *Numéro de l'avis d'infraction* _____

Name / *Nom* _____

Address / *Adresse* _____

OPTION 2 - Early Resolution - Meet with Prosecutor (by choosing this option you do not forego the right to a trial):

☐ **I request a meeting with a prosecutor to discuss the possible resolution of the charge.** I understand that if I fail to attend the scheduled meeting, I will be deemed not to dispute the charge and may be convicted of the offence.

I request a _____ language interpreter.
(Leave blank if inapplicable)

☐ I live more than *[Court to insert distance of not more than 75 km]* from the courthouse listed below and I would like to meet the prosecutor by *[Court to insert electronic method(s) available locally]*.

You will be sent a meeting notice to the address on the file. You must notify the court if your address changes.

OPTION 3 - Plea of Guilty - Voluntary Payment of Total Payable. I plead guilty and payment of the total payable is enclosed.

TO PAY: Write the number of the offence notice on the front of the cheque or money order. Do not send cash or post-dated cheques. Make the cheque or money order payable to the ONTARIO COURT OF JUSTICE. Dishonoured cheques will be subject to an administrative charge.

Cheque/Money Order enclosed: ☐   Visa ☐   MasterCard ☐
Chèque ou mandat joint :

Total Payable $ _____
Montant total exigible

FORWARD YOUR RETURN SLIP IN THE SELF-ADDRESSED ENVELOPE PROVIDED. / *ENVOYEZ VOTRE BORDEREAU DANS L'ENVELOPPE-RÉPONSE FOURNIE.*

Important – *Si vous n'exercez pas l'une des options suivantes dans les 15 jours à compter de la réception du présent avis, vous serez réputé(e) ne pas contester l'accusation et un juge pourra inscrire une déclaration de culpabilité contre vous. En cas de déclaration de culpabilité, des frais additionnels s'ajouteront au montant total exigible. En cas de défaut de paiement de l'amende, des frais d'administration s'ajouteront et l'information pourra être transmise à une agence de renseignements sur le consommateur. Des mesures seront prises pour faire exécuter le paiement de votre amende, y compris le refus d'une demande de validation ou de délivrance de certificat d'immatriculation jusqu'à ce que le montant total exigible et tous les frais additionnels aient été payés.*

OPTION 1 – Option du procès – NE PAS POSTER : *Je désire comparaître devant un juge pour inscrire un plaidoyer de non-culpabilité et subir un procès.*

Vous ou votre représentant DEVEZ vous présenter au greffe du tribunal aux dates et heures indiquées pour déposer un avis d'intention de comparaître devant le tribunal. Vous ne pouvez pas fixer la date du procès par courrier. Apportez le présent avis au greffe du tribunal.

OPTION 2 - Résolution rapide – Rencontre avec le poursuivant (*si vous choisissez l'option suivante, vous ne renoncez pas au droit d'obtenir un procès*) :

☐ **Je désire une rencontre avec le poursuivant pour discuter du règlement relatif à l'accusation.** *Je comprends que si je n'assiste pas à la rencontre, je serai réputé(e) ne pas contester l'accusation et un juge pourra inscrire une déclaration de culpabilité contre moi.*

Je demande l'aide d'un interprète de langue _____
(À remplir, s'il y a lieu)

☐ *J'habite à plus de [ajouter la distance jusqu'à concurrence de 75 km] du palais de justice mentionné ci-dessous et j'aimerais que la rencontre avec le poursuivant ait lieu par [ajouter la ou les méthodes électroniques offertes].*

Vous recevrez un avis de rencontre à l'adresse figurant au dossier. Vous devez aviser le tribunal si vous changez d'adresse.

OPTION 3 - Plaidoyer de culpabilité - paiement volontaire du montant total exigible . *Je plaide coupable et le montant total exigible est joint à la présente*

POUR PAYER : *Écrivez le numéro de l'avis d'infraction sur le recto du chèque ou du mandat. N'envoyez pas d'espèces ou de chèques postdatés. Libellez le chèque ou mandat à l'ordre de la COUR DE JUSTICE DE L'ONTARIO. Les chèques impayés donneront lieu à des frais d'administration.*

Card Number _____   Expiry Date M ____ Y ____
Numéro de carte :   *Date d'expiration : M ____ A ____*

Signature of Cardholder: _____
Signature du ou de la titulaire de la carte :

POA-0864-E (2016/07)

Form 7 — Summons

Provincial Offences Act

[Editor's Note: Pursuant to section O. Reg. 108/11, s. 1, when a form is referred to by number, the reference is to the form with that number that is described in the Table of Forms at the end of this Regulation and is available on the Internet through www.ontariocourtforms.on.ca. For your convenience, the government form is reproduced below. Form current to March 17, 2011.]

ICON Location Code
Code d'emplacement du RIII

Form 7, *Provincial Offences Act*, Ontario Court of Justice
Formulaire 7, *Loi sur les infractions provinciales. Cour de justice de l'Ontario*

Summons
Assignation

(print name / nom en lettres moulées)

believes and certifies that on the day of
croit et atteste que le

	Y / A	M / M	D / J	Time / heure	
2 0					M

Name
Nom

(family / nom de famille)

(given / prénom) (initials / initiales)

Address
Adresse

(number and street / numéro et nom de la rue)

(municipality / municipalité) (P.O. / C.P.) (province) (postal code / code postal)

Driver's licence no. / *N° de permis de conduire*   Juris / Aut. Lég.

Birth date / *Date de naissance*			Sex / Sexe	Motor vehicle involved / Véhicule impliqué	Collision involved / Collision	Witnesses / Témoins
Y / A	M / M	D / J		☐ N / N	☐ Y / O	☐ Y / O

At
À

(municipality / municipalité)

Did commit the offence of
A commis l'infraction de

contrary to
contrairement à   sect.
l'art.

Plate no N° de la plaque d'immatriculation	Juris Aut. Lég.	Commercial Utilitaire	CVOR IUVU	NSC CNS	Code
		☐ Y / O	☐ Y / O	☐ Y / O	

CVOR No. NSC No. / *N° de l'IUVU N° du CNS*

This is therefore to command you in Her Majesty's name to appear before the Ontario Court of Justice. / *Pour ces motifs, il vous est enjoint, au nom de Sa Majesté, de comparaître devant la Cour de justice de l'Ontario.*

Officer No N° de l'agent	Platoon Peloton	Unit Unité

	Y / A	M / M	D / J	Time / heure	
2 0					M

Ct. room / Salle d'audience   at the Ontario Court of Justice POA Office at / à la Cour de justice de l'Ontario, Bureau des infractions provinciales au

And to attend thereafter as required by the court in order to be dealt with according to law, this summons is served under Part I of the *Provincial Offences Act.*
Et d'être présent(e) par la suite selon les exigences du tribunal, afin d'être traité(e) selon la loi. La présente assignation vous est signifiée conformément à la Partie I de la Loi sur les infractions provinciales

Signature of Provincial Offences Officer / *Signature de l'agent des infractions provinciales*

POA 0861 (March 17, 2011 / 17 mars 2011) CSD

712

Form 7.1 — Early Resolution Meeting Notice—(In Person)

Provincial Offences Act

[Editor's Note: Pursuant to section O. Reg. 108/11, s. 1, when a form is referred to by number, the reference is to the form with that number that is described in the Table of Forms at the end of this Regulation and is available on the Internet through www.ontariocourtforms.on.ca. For your convenience, the government form is reproduced below. Form current to November 2, 2011.]

EARLY RESOLUTION MEETING NOTICE
AVIS DE RENCONTRE POUR RÈGLEMENT RAPIDE
(In Person / *en personne*)

ONTARIO COURT OF JUSTICE
COUR DE JUSTICE DE L'ONTARIO
PROVINCE OF ONTARIO
PROVINCE DE L'ONTARIO

Form / *Formulaire* 7.1
Provincial Offences Act
Loi sur les infractions provinciales
O. Reg. / *Régl. de l'Ont.* 108/11

Offence No.
Nº de l'infraction

Offence Date
Date de l'infraction

Officer No.
Nº de l'agent

(name and address of defendant / *nom et adresse du défendeur*)

This notice will confirm that an early resolution meeting has been scheduled in the (strike out inapplicable) English/French language.
Le présent avis confirme qu'une rencontre pour règlement rapide en (biffer la mention inutile) anglais/français

on the _____ day of _____ , yr. _____ , at _____
a été fixée au _____ *jour de* _____ *an* _____ *à* _____ (time / *heure*)

at _____
à _____ (address / *adresse*)

regarding the offence of _____ section _____
en ce qui concerne l'infraction à _____ (statute / *loi*) *article* _____

A/An _____ language interpreter has been requested.
Un interprète de langue _____ (leave blank if inapplicable / *à remplir, le cas échéant*) *a été demandé.*

You or a representative authorized by you to act on your behalf must appear at the above time. At the time of your meeting, a prosecutor will be available to discuss the charge(s) with you or your representative.
Vous ou un représentant que vous désignerez devez vous présenter à l'heure mentionnée ci-dessus. À l'heure fixée pour votre rencontre, un poursuivant pourra s'entretenir avec vous ou avec votre représentant sur l'accusation ou les accusations.

If you or your representative does not attend the meeting, **you will be deemed to not wish to dispute the charge(s)** and you may be convicted in your absence.
*Si vous ou votre représentant ne vous présentez pas à la rencontre, **vous serez réputé(e) ne pas contester l'accusation ou les accusations** et une déclaration de culpabilité pourra être inscrite contre vous en votre absence.*

Upon conviction, additional costs will be added to the total payable. If the fine goes into default, an administrative fee will be added and steps will be taken to enforce your defaulted fine. For example, information may be provided to a consumer reporting agency and for certain offences, including speeding, your driver's licence may be suspended.
Si vous êtes déclaré(e) coupable, des frais supplémentaires s'ajouteront au montant total à payer. En cas de défaut de paiement de l'amende, des frais administratifs s'ajouteront et des mesures seront prises pour faire exécuter le paiement de votre amende. Par exemple, l'information peut être transmise à une agence de renseignements sur le consommateur, et dans le cas de certaines infractions, dont l'excès de vitesse, votre permis de conduire pourra être suspendu.

You may request in writing that the meeting be rescheduled by [insert description of how and where to send the request.] The court office must receive the request at least 2 working days before the original scheduled appointment. You are entitled to reschedule this meeting only once.
Vous pouvez, pas moins de deux jours ouvrables avant la date de la rencontre, demander, par écrit seulement, que la rencontre soit remise. La demande écrite doit être envoyée [décrire comment et où la demande doit être envoyée]. Vous ne pouvez demander la remise de la rencontre qu'une fois.

Distribution
☐ Defendant / *Défendeur*
☐ Prosecutor / *Poursuivant*
☐ File / *Dossier*

Served by _____ on the _____ day of _____ , yr. _____
Signifié par _____ (Clerk of the Court / *greffier du tribunal*) *le* _____ *jour de* _____ *an* _____

FOR INFORMATION ON ACCESS TO ONTARIO COURTS FOR PERSONS WITH DISABILITIES: [Court to insert information]
POUR PLUS DE RENSEIGNEMENTS SUR L'ACCÈS DES PERSONNES HANDICAPÉES AUX TRIBUNAUX DE L'ONTARIO [ajouter l'information]

POA 0851 (November 2, 2011 / 2 novembre 2011) CSD

Form 7.2 — Early Resolution Meeting Notice—(by electronic method)

Provincial Offences Act

[Editor's Note: Pursuant to section O. Reg. 108/11, s. 1, when a form is referred to by number, the reference is to the form with that number that is described in the Table of Forms at the end of this Regulation and is available on the Internet through www.ontariocourtforms.on.ca. For your convenience, the government form is reproduced below. Form current to November 2, 2011.]

EARLY RESOLUTION MEETING NOTICE
AVIS DE RENCONTRE POUR RÉGLEMENT RAPIDE
(by electronic method / par moyen électronique)

ONTARIO COURT OF JUSTICE
COUR DE JUSTICE DE L'ONTARIO
PROVINCE OF ONTARIO
PROVINCE DE L'ONTARIO

Form / *Formulaire* 7.2
Provincial Offences Act
Loi sur les infractions provinciales
O. Reg. / *Règl. de l'Ont.* 108/11

Offence No.
Nº de l'infraction

Offence Date
Date de l'infraction

Officer No.
Nº de l'agent

(name and address of defendant / nom et adresse du défendeur)

This notice will confirm that an early resolution meeting by electronic method has been scheduled in the (strike out if applicable) English/French language.
Le présent avis confirme qu'une rencontre pour règlement rapide par moyen électronique en (biffer la mention inutile) anglais/français

on the   day of   yr   at
a été fixée au   jour de   an   à   (time / heure)

at
à   (address / adresse)

regarding the offence of   section
en ce qui concerne l'infraction à   (statute / loi)   article

A/An   language interpreter has been requested
Un interprète de langue   (leave blank if inapplicable / À remplir, le cas échéant)   a été demandé.

You or a representative authorized by you to act on your behalf must call   at the above time
Vous ou un représentant que vous désignerez devez téléphoner à   à l'heure mentionnée ci-dessus

At the time of your meeting, a prosecutor will be available to discuss the charge(s) with you or your representative.
À l'heure fixée pour votre rencontre, un poursuivant pourra s'entretenir avec vous ou avec votre représentant sur l'accusation ou les accusations.

If you or your representative does not call at the appointed day and time, **you will be deemed to not wish to dispute the charge(s)** and you may be convicted in your absence.
*Si vous ou votre représentant n'appelez pas à la date et à l'heure fixées, **vous serez réputé(e) ne pas contester l'accusation ou les accusations** et une déclaration de culpabilité pourra être inscrite contre vous en votre absence.*

Upon conviction, additional costs will be added to the total payable. If the fine goes into default, an administrative fee will be added and steps will be taken to enforce your defaulted fine. For example, information may be provided to a consumer reporting agency and for certain offences, including speeding, your driver's licence may be suspended.
Si vous êtes trouvé coupable, des frais supplémentaires s'ajouteront au montant total à payer. Si l'amende est en défaut de paiement, des frais administratifs s'ajouteront et des mesures seront prises pour procéder à l'exécution forcée de votre amende en défaut. Par exemple, les données peuvent être transmises à une agence de renseignements sur la consommation et dans le cas de certaines infractions, dont la conduite en excès de vitesse, votre permis de conduire pourra être suspendu.

You may request in writing that the meeting be rescheduled. The written request must be sent to *[insert description of how and where to send the request]* and it must be received no later than 2 working days prior to the original scheduled appointment. You are entitled to reschedule this meeting only once.
Vous pouvez, pas moins de deux jours ouvrables avant la date de la rencontre, demander, par écrit seulement, que la rencontre soit remise. La demande écrite doit être envoyée [décrire comment et où la demande doit être envoyée]. Vous ne pouvez demander la remise de la rencontre qu'une fois.

Distribution		
☐	Defendant / *Défendeur*
☐	Prosecutor / *Poursuivant*
☐	File / *Dossier*

Served by   on the   day of   , yr
Signifié par   (Clerk of the Court / greffier du tribunal)   le   jour de   an

FOR INFORMATION ON ACCESS TO ONTARIO COURTS FOR PERSONS WITH DISABILITIES   *[Court to insert information]*
POUR PLUS DE RENSEIGNEMENTS SUR L'ACCÈS DES PERSONNES HANDICAPÉES AUX TRIBUNAUX DE L'ONTARIO   [ajouter l'information]

POA 0852 (November 2, 2011 / 2 novembre 2011) CSD

Form 7.3 — Early Resolution Outcome

Provincial Offences Act

[Editor's Note: Pursuant to section O. Reg. 108/11, s. 1, when a form is referred to by number, the reference is to the form with that number that is described in the Table of Forms at the end of this Regulation and is available on the Internet through www.ontariocourtforms.on.ca. For your convenience, the government form is reproduced below. Form current to November 2, 2011.]

Form / *Formulaire* 7.3
Provincial Offences Act
Loi sur les infractions provinciales
O. Reg. / *Règl. de l'Ont.* 108/11

EARLY RESOLUTION OUTCOME
ENTENTE DE RÈGLEMENT RAPIDE

ONTARIO COURT OF JUSTICE
COUR DE JUSTICE DE L'ONTARIO
PROVINCE OF ONTARIO
PROVINCE DE L'ONTARIO

BETWEEN
ENTRE
(Prosecuting Authority / *partie poursuivante*)

And / *et*

Prosecutor
Poursuivant

Defendant
Défendeur

Having scheduled a meeting to discuss the resolution of the following matter
Une rencontre est prévue afin d'examiner le règlement de la question suivante

☐ In person / *en personne* ☐ Electronically / *par Internet* the following agreement has been reached
l'accord suivant est survenu

Offence Number *Numéro de l'infraction*	Offence Description Statute & Section *Description de l'infraction Loi et article*	Guilty Plea *Plaide coupable*	Plead Guilty to Substituted Offence *Plaide coupable à une infraction de substitution*	Substituted Offence *Infraction de substitution* Statute & Section / *Loi et article*	Fine* *Amende** Leave blank if no agreement *Ne rien inscrire s'il n'y a pas entente*	Time to pay *Nombre de jours pour payer*	Withdraw *Retrait*
1		☐	☐				☐
2		☐	☐				☐
3		☐	☐				☐
4		☐	☐				☐
5		☐	☐				☐

*Does not include costs, fees or Victim Fine Surcharge / *Ne comprend pas les frais, les droits ou la suramende compensatoire pour l'aide aux victimes*

Defendant or authorized Representative Signature
Signature du défendeur ou du représentant autorisé :
_____ Signature _____ Date

Prosecutor Signature:
Signature du poursuivant :
_____ Signature _____ Date

☐ Defendant requested a meeting but failed to attend.
Le défendant a demandé une rencontre, mais ne s'est pas présenté.

☐ Meeting occurred, but no resolution. Trial date to be set.
Une rencontre a eu lieu, mais aucun règlement n'est intervenu. Date du procès à fixer.

Prosecutor Signature:
Signature du poursuivant :
_____ Signature _____ Date

(Distribution)

PCA 0663 (November 2, 2011 / *2 novembre 2011*) CSD

715

Form 8 — Notice of Intention to Appear

Provincial Offences Act

[Editor's Note: Pursuant to section O. Reg. 108/11, s. 1, when a form is referred to by number, the reference is to the form with that number that is described in the Table of Forms at the end of this Regulation and is available on the Internet through www.ontariocourtforms.on.ca. For your convenience, the government form is reproduced below. Form current to March 15, 2014.]

NOTICE OF INTENTION TO APPEAR
AVIS D'INTENTION DE COMPARAÎTRE

ONTARIO COURT OF JUSTICE
COUR DE JUSTICE DE L'ONTARIO
PROVINCE OF ONTARIO
PROVINCE DE L'ONTARIO

Form / Formulaire 8
Provincial Offences Act
Loi sur les infractions provinciales

TAKE NOTICE THAT I,
VEUILLEZ PRENDRE AVIS QUE JE SOUSSIGNÉ(E), _____ (defendant's name / nom du défendeur/de la défenderesse)

_____ (current address / adresse actuelle) _____ (street / rue) _____ (apt. / app.)

_____ (municipality / municipalité) _____ (province) _____ (postal code / code postal)

_____ (offence number / numéro de l'infraction) _____ (offence date / date de l'infraction)

wish to give notice of my intention to appear in court to enter a plea of not guilty at the time and place set for the trial respecting the charge set out in the Offence Notice or Parking Infraction Notice.
désire donner avis de mon intention de comparaître devant le tribunal pour inscrire un plaidoyer de non-culpabilité à l'heure et au lieu prévus pour le procès en réponse à l'accusation énoncée dans l'avis d'infraction ou l'avis d'infraction de stationnement.

☐ I intend to appear in court to enter a plea at the time and place set for the trial and I wish that it be held in the English language.

☐ *J'ai l'intention de comparaître devant le tribunal pour inscrire un plaidoyer à l'heure et au lieu prévus pour le procès et je désire que le procès se déroule en français.*

I request a _____ language interpreter for the trial.
(leave blank if inapplicable)

Je demande l'aide d'un interprète en langue _____ *pour le procès.*
(à remplir s'il y a lieu)

Note: If you fail to notify the court office of **address changes** you may not receive important notices e.g. your Notice of Trial. You may be convicted in your absence if you do not attend the trial.

Remarque : *Si vous omettez de prévenir le greffe du tribunal de* **tout changement d'adresse** *vous pourriez ne pas recevoir d'importants avis (p. ex., votre avis de procès). Vous pourriez être déclaré(e) coupable en votre absence si vous n'assistez pas au procès.*

_____ Signature of defendant /
Signature du défendeur/de la défenderesse

_____ (date)

_____ (telephone number / numéro de téléphone)

POA 0913 (March 15, 2014 / 15 mars 2014) CSD

Form 9 — Notice of Trial

Provincial Offences Act

[Editor's Note: Pursuant to section O. Reg. 108/11, s. 1, when a form is referred to by number, the reference is to the form with that number that is described in the Table of Forms at the end of this Regulation and is available on the Internet through www.ontariocourtforms.on.ca. For your convenience, the government form is reproduced below. Form current to March 15, 2014.]

NOTICE OF TRIAL
AVIS DE PROCÈS

ONTARIO COURT OF JUSTICE
COUR DE JUSTICE DE L'ONTARIO
PROVINCE OF ONTARIO
PROVINCE DE L'ONTARIO

Form / Formulaire 9
Provincial Offences Act
Loi sur les infractions provinciales
O. Reg. / Régl de l'Ont. 108/11

Offence No
Nº de l'infraction

Offence Date
Date de l'infraction

Officer No.
Nº de l'agent

D.L. No
Nº de permis de conduire

Plate No.
Nº de plaque d'immatriculation

Enforcement Agency
Organisme chargé de l'exécution

To:
À :

You are charged with the following offence:
Vous êtes accusé(e) de l'infraction suivante :

On the _____ day of _____, yr. _____, at _____ (hour / heure)
Le _____ jour de _____ an _____ à _____

at _____
à

you did commit the offence of
vous avez commis l'infraction de

contrary to _____ (statute / loi) section _____
contrairement à la article

The total payable includes the Set Fine, costs and Victim Fine Surcharge as indicated on your Offence Notice.
Le montant total exigible comprend l'amende fixée, les frais et la suramende compensatoire pour l'aide aux victimes, comme il est indiqué sur votre avis d'infraction.

Total Payable $ _____
Montant total exigible $

TAKE NOTICE that on the _____ day of _____, yr. _____, at _____ (hour / heure)
AVIS VOUS EST DONNÉ que le jour de an à

your trial will be held at: _____ (court address / adresse du tribunal)
votre procès sera tenu à :

Your trial will be held on the date noted above at the Ontario Court of Justice shown. Note that the prosecutor may rely upon certified statements and/or certificate evidence pursuant to section 49.1 of the Provincial Offences Act. You and your witnesses should be ready for your trial at that time. If you do not appear at trial, including any future dates set by the court, you will be deemed not to dispute the charge and the court may convict you in your absence without further notice.

Votre procès se tiendra à la date et à l'heure mentionnées ci-dessus à la Cour de justice de l'Ontario susmentionnée. Prenez note que le poursuivant peut se fonder sur des déclarations attestées et/ou des preuves certifiées conformément à l'article 49.1 de la Loi sur les infractions provinciales. Vos témoins et vous-même devrez être prêts pour votre procès à cette date. Si vous ne comparaissez pas au procès, y compris à toute date future fixée par le tribunal, vous serez réputé(e) ne pas contester l'accusation et le tribunal pourra vous déclarer coupable en votre absence, sans autre avis.

Issued at _____ this _____ day of _____, yr. _____
Délivré à le jour de an

FOR COURT USE ONLY / PARTIE RÉSERVÉE AU TRIBUNAL

I certify that a copy of this Notice was
J'atteste qu'une copie du présent avis a été

☒ sent by mail to Defendant
   envoyée par courrier au défendeur.

☐ given personally to Defendant
   remise en mains propres au défendeur.

☐ sent by mail to Prosecutor
   envoyée par courrier au poursuivant.

☐ given to Prosecutor
   donnée au poursuivant.

_____ Date

_____ Clerk/Justice / Greffière ou greffier/Juge

FOR INFORMATION ON ACCESS TO ONTARIO COURTS FOR PERSONS WITH DISABILITIES: [Court to insert information]
POUR OBTENIR DES RENSEIGNEMENTS SUR L'ACCÈS DES PERSONNES HANDICAPÉES AUX TRIBUNAUX DE L'ONTARIO : [ajouter l'information]]

Guide for Defendants available at www.ontariocourts.ca/OCJ/POAGuide, or contact the court office.
Le Guide du défendeur est consultable à www.ontariocourts.ca/Guide/UPC IC, ou contactez le greffe du tribunal.

POA 0814 (March 15, 2014 / 15 mars 2014) CSD

Form 10 — Notice of Fine and Due Date

Provincial Offences Act

[Editor's Note: Pursuant to section O. Reg. 108/11, s. 1, when a form is referred to by number, the reference is to the form with that number that is described in the Table of Forms at the end of this Regulation and is available on the Internet through www.ontariocourtforms.on.ca. For your convenience, the government form is reproduced below. Form current to June 2019.]

Ontario Court of Justice
Provincial Offences Office

Phone No. / *N° de téléphone*

To / *À*

NOTICE OF FINE AND DUE DATE
AVIS D'AMENDE ET DE DATE D'EXIGIBILITÉ

[name of defendant / *nom du défendeur*]
[address of defendant / *adresse du défendeur*]
[city, province & postal code / *ville, province et code postal*]

You have been convicted of an offence, and a court ordered fine is due.
Vous avez été déclaré(e) coupable d'une infraction et un tribunal vous a ordonné de payer une amende.

Place of Offence *Lieu de l'infraction*	Offence Date (DD/MM/YY) *Date de l'infraction (JJ/MM/AA)*	Offence *infraction*

Due Date (DD/MM/YY) *Date d'exigibilité (JJ/MM/AA)*	Offence No. *N° d'infraction*	Plate No. *N° de plaque d'immatriculation*	Conviction Date (DD/MM/YY) *Date de condamnation (JJ/MM/AA)*	Amount Due / *Montant exigible* $ Includes, costs and Victim - ine Surcharge / *Comprend les dépens et la surcharge compensatoire*

Fines not paid by the due date are subject to an <u>administrative fee of $40.00</u> and any additional applicable costs for enforcement.

If you have already paid the amount due, please disregard this notice.

Si l'amende n'est pas payée au plus tard à la date d'exigibilité, des <u>frais administratifs supplémentaires de 40 $ s'ajouteront</u> ainsi que tout frais additionnel d'exécution.

Si vous avez déjà payé le montant exigible, veuillez ne pas tenir compte du présent avis.

FAILURE TO PAY THIS FINE BY THE DUE DATE MAY RESULT IN ONE OR MORE OF THE FOLLOWING:
- Suspension of your driver's licence or refusal to renew licence plate(s)
- Imposition of a licence reinstatement fee by the Ministry of Transportation
- Additional fees and collection costs
- Informing the Credit Bureau of the debt, which may affect your credit rating.

See reverse side of this form for additional legal measures which may be taken if payment is not received by the due date.

LE DÉFAUT DE PAIEMENT DE L'AMENDE AU PLUS TARD À LA DATE D'EXIGIBILITÉ PEUT ENTRAÎNER UNE OU PLUSIEURS DES ÉVENTUALITÉS SUIVANTES :
- *Suspension de votre permis de conduire ou refus de renouvellement de votre (vos) plaque(s) d'immatriculation;*
- *Imposition de frais de rétablissement du permis par le ministère des Transports;*
- *Frais de recouvrement supplémentaires*
- *Communication à l'agence d'évaluation du crédit des renseignements relatifs à votre dette, ce qui peut nuire à votre cote de solvabilité*

Voir au verso de la formule pour connaître les autres mesures légales pouvant être prises si le montant n'est pas reçu au plus tard à la date d'exigibilité

✄　✄　✄　✄　✄　✄　　✄　✄　✄　✄　　✄　✄

COMPLETE AND DETACH THIS PORTION AND SEND WITH PAYMENT. SEE BACK FOR MAILING AND PAYMENT INSTRUCTIONS.

REMPLISSEZ CETTE PARTIE, DÉTACHEZ-LA ET ENVOYEZ-LA AVEC VOTRE PAIEMENT. LES DIRECTIVES D'ENVOI PAR LA POSTE ET LES MODES DE PAIEMENT SONT INCLUES AU VERSO

[name of defendant / *nom du défendeur*]
[address of defendant / *adresse du défendeur*]
[city, province & postal code / *ville, province et code postal*]
[telephone no. / *n° de tél.*]

999 [offence number] 00

☐ cheque/money order enclosed *chèque/mandat joint*	☐ VISA	☐ MASTERCARD

CARD NUMBER / *NUMÉRO DE LA CARTE*

CARD EXPIRY DATE *DATE D'EXPIRATION*　MONTH *MOIS*　YEAR *ANNÉE*

Conviction Date *Date de condamnation*	Authorized Amount *Montant autorisé*
	$ _____ $

CARDHOLDER'S SIGNATURE
SIGNATURE DU DÉTENTEUR DE LA CARTE

999 [offence number] 00

POA 0954 (January 19, 2018 / 19 janvier 2018) CSD

718

FAIL TO PAY BY THE DUE DATE

May result in:
- Suspension of a driver's licence, and the imposition of a licence reinstatement fee
- Refusal to renew licence plate(s)

Additional legal measures:
- Bank Garnishment – require your bank or other financial institution to deduct from your account (including RRSP funds) the money owing and send it to the court offices;
- Wage Garnishment – require your employer to deduct from your wages the amount owing and send it to the court office;
- Register a lien against real property;
- Addition to municipal tax roll;
- Writ of Seizure and Sale – instruct the enforcement officials of the civil courts to seize and sell some of the property.

You have the right to apply to the court for an extension of time for payment of this fine.

If you have any questions regarding this matter, please contact the Court office at the address shown on the upper left-hand corner of the front of this notice.

LE DÉFAUT DE PAIEMENT AU PLUS TARD À LA DATE D'EXIGIBILITÉ

Peut entraîner :
- la suspension de votre permis de conduire et l'imposition de frais administratifs pour le rétablissement du permis
- le refus de renouvellement de votre (vos) plaque(s) d'immatriculation

Mesures légales supplémentaires :
- Saisie-arrêt de comptes bancaires – Exiger de votre banque ou d'un autre établissement financier de déduire de votre compte (y compris un REER) le montant exigible et de l'envoyer au greffe
- Saisie-arrêt de salaire – Ordonner à votre employeur de déduire de votre salaire le montant exigible et de l'envoyer au greffe
- Inscrire un privilège contre vos biens immobiliers
- Ajouter le montant au rôle des impôts municipaux
- Bref de saisie-exécution – Ordonner aux agents d'exécution des tribunaux civils de saisir et vendre certains de vos biens

Vous avez le droit de présenter au tribunal une demande de prorogation du délai de paiement de l'amende.

Si vous avez des questions à ce sujet, veuillez communiquer avec le greffe, à l'adresse indiquée dans le coin supérieur gauche, sur la première page du présent avis.

HOW TO PAY

- By credit card **Visa** or **MasterCard** through the mail by completing the authorization form on the front of this notice.
- By cheque or money order through the mail along with the bottom portion of this notice.
- In person at any Provincial Offences Office by debit, cheque, money order, credit card or cash.
- Online at: www.paytickets.ca

Dishonoured cheques will be subject to an administrative charge and the amount may be immediately referred to a Private Collection Agency and your driver's licence suspended.

Make Cheque / Money Order payable to:

City of _____

and write the file number on the front of the cheque/money order. Do not send cash or post-dated cheques. If paying by Credit Card, please fully complete and sign the reverse side.

When you mail your payment and this notice, you assume the consequences if, for any reason, the payment is not received in our Court office by the due date.

MODE DE PAIEMENT

- Par carte de crédit **Visa** ou **MasterCard**, par la poste, en remplissant la formule d'autorisation figurant au recto du présent avis.
- Par chèque ou mandat, envoyé par la poste avec la partie inférieure du présent avis.
- En personne, dans n'importe quel Bureau des infractions provinciales, par débit, chèque, mandat, carte de crédit ou en espèces.
- En ligne à : www.paytickets.ca

Les chèques refusés sont assujettis à des frais administratifs et le dossier peut être immédiatement envoyé à une agence de recouvrement privée et votre permis de conduire pourrait être suspendu.

Libellez votre chèque ou mandat à l'ordre de:

Ville de _____

et indiquez le numéro de dossier au recto du chèque/mandat. N'envoyez pas d'argent en espèces ni de chèques postdatés. Si vous payez par carte de crédit, veuillez dûment remplir et signer la partie correspondante au verso.

Lorsque vous envoyez par la poste votre paiement et le présent avis, vous êtes responsable des conséquences si, pour une raison quelconque, le greffe ne reçoit pas votre paiement au plus tard à la date d'exigibilité.

REMEMBER TO KEEP A RECORD OF THIS PAYMENT

MAILING INSTRUCTIONS

Mail payment along with this portion of the notice to:

ONTARIO COURT OF JUSTICE
PROVINCIAL OFFENCE OFFICE

N'OUBLIEZ PAS DE CONSERVER UNE PREUVE DU PAIEMENT

DIRECTIVES D'ENVOI PAR LA POSTE

Envoyez le paiement ainsi que la présente partie de l'avis à la

COUR DE JUSTICE DE L'ONTARIO
BUREAU DES INFRACTIONS PROVINCIALES

FOR INFORMATION ON ACCESS TO ONTARIO COURTS FOR PERSONS WITH DISABILITIES: [Court to insert information]
POUR OBTENIR DES RENSEIGNEMENTS SUR L'ACCÈS DES PERSONNES HANDICAPÉES AUX TRIBUNAUX DE L'ONTARIO [ajouter l'information]

Guide for Defendants available at www.ontariocourts.ca/OCJ/POAGuide, or contact the court office.
Le Guide pour les défendeurs est consultable à www.ontariocourts.ca/OCJ/fr/POAGuide, ou contactez le greffe du tribunal.

POA 0854 (January 19, 2018 / 19 janvier 2018) CSD

Form 10.1 — Notice of Fine and Due Date

Provincial Offences Act

[Editor's Note: Pursuant to section O. Reg. 108/11, s. 1, when a form is referred to by number, the reference is to the form with that number that is described in the Table of Forms at the end of this Regulation and is available on the Internet through www.ontariocourtforms.on.ca. For your convenience, the government form is reproduced below. Form current to June 2019.]

Notice of Fine and Due Date

Form 10.1, Provincial Offences Act, Ontario Court of Justice, O. Reg. 108/11

Unpaid Fine

Ontario Court of Justice
Provincial Offences Office
The Regional Municipality of York,
465 Davis Drive, Suite 200
Newmarket ON L3Y 7T9

Phone No. (905) 898-0425

File No.:

You owe:

You must pay by:

To pay now, go to **www.paytickets.ca**

Re: Notice of Fine and Due Date - If you have already paid the amount due, please disregard this notice

[name of defendant]
[address of defendant]
[city, province & postal code]

PAY NOW

4 out of 5 people convicted in York respond in a timely manner[1].

You have been convicted of the following offence. You are required to pay the above amount by the due date.

Offence	Offence Date	Conviction Date	Place of Offence	Licence Plate No.

SERIOUS LEGAL CONSEQUENCES MAY RESULT IF YOU DO NOT PAY YOUR FINE ON TIME:

- **Loss of your driver's licence**, and a licence reinstatement fee
- An order for your employer to **garnish your wages**
- Property seizure by enforcement officials
- Registration of a lien (possession of your property until the debt is paid)
- An order for your bank to remove the owed funds from your account
- A freeze on renewing your licence plate sticker
- **Downgrading of your credit score** by Credit Bureaus
- **Formal collection proceedings** via Private Collection Agency
- Additional fees, costs and surcharges

HOW TO PAY:

Mail
Send in the bottom portion of this letter (reverse side) to the address above

Online
www.paytickets.ca
Fast and convenient

In Person
Go to any Provincial Offences Court Office

ADDITIONAL INFORMATION:

- Remember to keep a record of your payment
- You have the right to apply to the court for an extension of time for payment of this fine
- If you have any questions, please contact the Court officer at the address shown on the upper left hand corner
- For information on access to Ontario Courts for Services with Disabilities please contact via the address and telephone number in the upper left hand corner

FRANÇAIS AU VERSO.

Pay Online at PayTickets.ca

Guide for Defendants available at www.paytickets.ca/Guide-for-Defendants or contact the court office
Le Guide pour les défendeurs est consultable à www.paytickets.ca/Guide-for-Defendants ou contactez le greffe du tribunal

[1] Assessment made by the Regional Municipality of York
POA-0034 (January 19, 2018 / 19 janvier 2018) CSD - Form 10.1

720

Avis d'amende et de date d'exigibilité
Formulaire 10.1, Loi sur les infractions provinciales, Cour de justice de l'Ontario, Règl. de l'Ont. 108/11

Amende impayée

Cour de Justice de l'Ontario
Bureau des infractions provinciales
Municipalité régionale de York
465 Davis Drive, Suite 200
Newmarket (Ontario) L3Y 7T9

Téléphone : 905 898-0425

N° de dossier :

Vous devez :

Vous devez payer au plus tard le :

Pour payer maintenant, visitez www.paietickets.ca

Objet : Avis d'amende et de date d'exigibilité – Si vous avez déjà payé le montant exigible, veuillez ne pas tenir compte du présent avis.

[nom du défendeur]
[adresse du défendeur]
[ville, province et code postal]

À PAYER SANS DÉLAI

Quatre fois sur cinq, les personnes condamnées à York répondent dans les délais[2].

Vous avez été déclaré(e) coupable d'une infraction et vous devez payer l'amende indiquée ci-dessus au plus tard à la date d'exigibilité.

Infraction	Date de l'infraction	Date de condamnation	Lieu de l'infraction	N° de plaque d'immatriculation

Le défaut de paiement de l'amende au plus tard à la date d'exigibilité peut entraîner des conséquences juridiques graves :

- La **perte de votre permis de conduire** et l'imposition de frais administratifs pour le rétablissement du permis.
- La **saisie de votre salaire**, sur ordre donné à votre employeur.
- La saisie de biens par des agents d'application de la loi.
- L'enregistrement d'un privilège (possession de vos biens jusqu'au remboursement de la dette).

- Le retrait des fonds dus de votre compte, sur ordre donné à votre banque.
- Un gel du renouvellement de votre autocollant de plaque d'immatriculation.
- La **réduction de votre pointage de crédit** auprès des bureaux de crédit.
- Une **procédure officielle de recouvrement** par l'intermédiaire d'une agence de recouvrement privée.
- Des frais, coûts et surtaxes supplémentaires.

Comment payer :

Courrier	En ligne	En personne
Envoyer la partie inférieure de la présente lettre (verso) à l'adresse ci-dessus	www.paietickets.ca *Rapide et pratique!*	Se présenter à un bureau des infractions provinciales

RENSEIGNEMENTS ADDITIONNELS :

- N'oubliez pas de conserver une preuve du paiement.
- Vous avez le droit de présenter au tribunal une demande de prorogation du délai de paiement de l'amende.
- Si vous avez des questions, veuillez communiquer avec le greffe à l'adresse indiquée dans le coin supérieur gauche.
- Pour obtenir des renseignements sur l'accès des personnes handicapées aux tribunaux de l'Ontario, veuillez communiquer avec nous à l'adresse ou au numéro de téléphone figurant dans le coin supérieur gauche.

Paiement en ligne à paietickets.ca

See front side of this page for English.

Le Guide pour les défendeurs est consultable à www.ontario.ca/fr/page/POA/JU/Guide, ou contactez le greffe du tribunal.
Guide for Defendants available at www.ontario.ca/fr/page/POA/JU/Guide, or contact the court office.

---

[2] Évaluation faite par la municipalité régionale de York.
POA 0054 (January 10, 2018 / 10 janvier 2018) CSD - Form 10.1

721

COMPLETE AND DETACH THIS PORTION AND SEND WITH PAYMENT

REMPLISSEZ CETTE PARTIE, DÉTACHEZ-LA ET ENVOYEZ-LA AVEC VOTRE PAIEMENT

NAME AND ADDRESS
NOM ET ADRESSE

[name of defendant / nom du défendeur]
[address of defendant / adresse du défendeur]
[city, province & postal code / ville, province et code postal]
[telephone no. / n° de tél.]

999 [offence number] 00

☐ cheque/money order enclosed payable to
Regional Municipality of York
☐ chèque/mandat ci-joint libellé à l'ordre de
la municipalité régionale de York

☐ VISA   ☐ MASTERCARD

Conviction Date
Date de condamnation

Authorized Amount
Montant autorisé

CARD NUMBER / NUMÉRO DE LA CARTE

CARD EXPIRY DATE
DATE D'EXPIRATION

MONTH
MOIS

YEAR
ANNÉE

CARDHOLDER'S SIGNATURE
SIGNATURE DU DÉTENTEUR DE LA CARTE

Form 10.2 — Notice of Fine and Due Date

Provincial Offences Act

[Editor's Note: Pursuant to section O. Reg. 108/11, s. 1, when a form is referred to by number, the reference is to the form with that number that is described in the Table of Forms at the end of this Regulation and is available on the Internet through www.ontariocourtforms.on.ca. For your convenience, the government form is reproduced below. Form current to June 2019.]

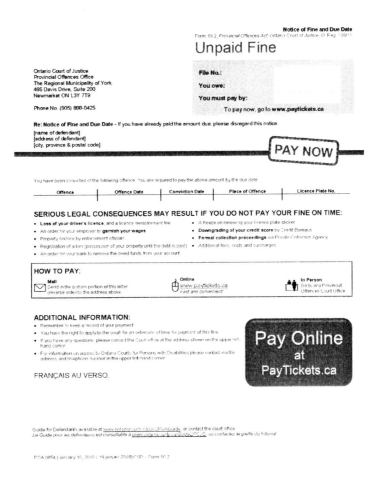

Avis d'amende et de date d'exigibilité
Formulaire 10.2, Loi sur les infractions provinciales, Cour de justice de l'Ontario, Règl. de l'Ont. 108/11

Amende impayée

Cour de Justice de l'Ontario
Bureau des infractions provinciales
Municipalité régionale de York
465 Davis Drive, Suite 200
Newmarket (Ontario) L3Y 7T9

Téléphone : 905 898-0425

N° de dossier :

Vous devez :

Vous devez payer au plus tard le :

Pour payer maintenant, visitez **www.paietickets.ca**

Objet : Avis d'amende et de date d'exigibilité – Si vous avez des questions, veuillez ne pas tenir compte du présent avis.

[nom du défendeur]
[adresse du défendeur]
[ville, province et code postal]

À PAYER SANS DÉLAI

Vous avez été reconnu(e) coupable d'une infraction et vous devez payer l'amende indiquée ci-dessous au plus tard à la date d'expiration.

Infraction	Date de l'infraction	Date de condamnation	Lieu de l'infraction	N° de plaque d'immatriculation

Le défaut de paiement de l'amende au plus tard à la date d'exigibilité peut entraîner des conséquences juridiques graves :

- **La perte de votre permis de conduire** et l'imposition de frais administratifs pour le rétablissement du permis;
- **La saisie de votre salaire** (chez votre donneur d'ordre ou payeur);
- La saisie de biens par des agents d'application de la loi;
- L'enregistrement d'un privilège (possession) de vos biens jusqu'au remboursement complet de la dette);

- Le retrait des fonds dus de votre compte, sur ordre donné à votre banque;
- Un rappel ou renouvellement de votre auto-collant de plaque d'immatriculation;
- **La réduction de votre pointage de crédit** auprès des bureaux de crédit;
- **Une procédure officielle de recouvrement** par l'intermédiaire d'une agence de recouvrement privée;
- Des frais, coûts et autres suppléments supplémentaires.

Comment payer :

Courrier
Envoyer la partie intérieure de la présente lettre (verso) à l'adresse ci-dessus

En ligne
www.paietickets.ca
Rapide et pratique

En personne
Se présenter à un bureau des infractions provinciales

RENSEIGNEMENTS ADDITIONNELS :

- N'oubliez pas de conserver une preuve de paiement.
- Vous avez le droit de présenter au tribunal une demande de prorogation du délai de paiement de l'amende.
- Si vous avez des questions, veuillez communiquer avec le greffe, à l'adresse indiquée dans le coin supérieur gauche.
- Pour obtenir des renseignements sur l'accès des personnes handicapées aux tribunaux de l'Ontario, veuillez communiquer avec nous à l'adresse ou au numéro de téléphone figurant dans le coin supérieur gauche.

Paiement en ligne à paietickets.ca

See front side of this page for English.

Le Guide pour les défendeurs est consultable à www.ontariocourts.ca/ocj/fr/ ou contactez le greffe du tribunal.
Guide for Defendants available at www.ontariocourts.ca/ocj/en/ or contact the court office.

POA 0054 (January 15, 2018 / 19 janvier 2018) C-43 – Form 10.2

If you mail your payment, you assume the consequences if, for any reason, the payment is not received in our Court office by the due date.
Si vous envoyez votre paiement par la poste, vous êtes responsable des conséquences si, pour une raison quelconque, il n'est pas reçu par notre paiement au plus tard à la date d'échéance.

COMPLETE AND DETACH THIS PORTION AND SEND WITH PAYMENT

REMPLISSEZ CETTE PARTIE, DÉTACHEZ LA ET ENVOYEZ LA AVEC VOTRE PAIEMENT

NAME AND ADDRESS
NOM ET ADRESSE

name of defendant / nom du défendeur
address of defendant / adresse du défendeur
city, province & postal code / ville, province et code postal
telephone no. / n° de tél.)

999 (offence number) 80

cheque/money order enclosed payable to
Regional Municipality of York
chèque/mandat ci-joint libellé à l'ordre de
la municipalité régionale de York

VISA

MASTERCARD

Conviction Date
Date de condamnation

Authorized Amount
Montant autorisé

CARD NUMBER / NUMÉRO DE LA CARTE

CARD EXPIRY DATE
DATE D'EXPIRATION

MONTH
MOIS

YEAR
ANNÉE

CARDHOLDER'S SIGNATURE
SIGNATURE DU DÉTENTEUR DE LA CARTE

We are the file number on the front of the cheque/money order. Do not send cash or post-dated cheques. If paying by Credit Card, please fully complete and sign. Dishonoured cheques will be subject to an administrative charge and the amount may be immediately referred to a Private Collection Agency.
Indiquez le numéro de dossier au recto du chèque ou du mandat. N'envoyez pas d'argent en espèces ni de chèques postdatés. Si vous payez par carte de crédit, veuillez dûment remplir et signer la partie correspondante. Les chèques refusés sont assujettis à des frais administratifs et le dossier peut être immédiatement envoyé à une agence de recouvrement privée.

POA 0854 (January 19, 2018 / 19 janvier 2018) CSD – Form 10.2

725

Form 10.3 — Notice of Fine and Due Date
Provincial Offences Act

[Editor's Note: Pursuant to section O. Reg. 108/11, s. 1, when a form is referred to by number, the reference is to the form with that number that is described in the Table of Forms at the end of this Regulation and is available on the Internet through www.ontariocourtforms.on.ca. For your convenience, the government form is reproduced below. Form current to June 2019.]

Avis d'amende et de date d'exigibilité
Formulaire 10.3, Loi sur les infractions provinciales, Cour de justice de l'Ontario, Regl. de l'Ont. 108/11

Amende impayée

Cour de Justice de l'Ontario
Bureau des infractions provinciales
Municipalité régionale de York
465 Davis Drive, Suite 200
Newmarket (Ontario) L3Y 7T9

Téléphone : 905 898-0425

N° de dossier :

Vous devez :

Vous devez payer au plus tard le :

Pour payer maintenant, visitez **www.paietickets.ca**

Objet : Avis d'amende et de date d'exigibilité – Si vous avez déjà payé le montant exigible, veuillez ne pas tenir compte du présent avis.

[nom du défendeur]
[adresse du défendeur]
[ville, province et code postal]

À PAYER SANS DÉLAI

Payez votre amende maintenant ou vous risquez de perdre votre permis de conduire, vos biens pourraient être saisis ou votre employeur peut avoir l'ordre de saisir votre salaire.

Vous avez été déclaré(e) coupable d'une infraction et vous devez payer l'amende indiquée ci-dessus au plus tard à la date d'exigibilité.

Infraction	Date de l'infraction	Date de condamnation	Lieu de l'infraction	N° de plaque d'immatriculation

Le défaut de paiement de l'amende au plus tard à la date d'exigibilité peut entraîner des conséquences juridiques graves :

- La **perte de votre permis de conduire** et l'imposition de frais administratifs pour le rétablissement du permis;
- La **saisie de votre salaire**, sur ordre donné à votre employeur;
- La saisie de biens par des agents d'application de la loi;
- L'enregistrement d'un privilège (possession de vos biens jusqu'au remboursement de la dette);

- Le retrait des fonds dus de votre compte, sur ordre donné à votre banque;
- Un gel du renouvellement de votre autocollant de plaque d'immatriculation;
- La **réduction de votre pointage de crédit** auprès des bureaux de crédit;
- Une **procédure officielle de recouvrement** par l'intermédiaire d'une agence de recouvrement privée;
- Des frais, coûts et surtaxes supplémentaires.

Comment payer :

Courrier
Envoyez la partie inférieure de la présente lettre (verso) à l'adresse ci-dessus

En ligne
www.paietickets.ca
Rapide et pratique!

En personne
Se présenter à un bureau des infractions provinciales

Paiement en ligne à paietickets.ca

RENSEIGNEMENTS ADDITIONNELS :

- N'oubliez pas de conserver une preuve de paiement
- Vous avez le droit de présenter au tribunal une demande de prorogation du délai de paiement de l'amende.
- Si vous avez des questions, veuillez communiquer avec le greffe, à l'adresse indiquée dans le coin supérieur gauche
- Pour obtenir des renseignements sur l'accès des personnes handicapées aux tribunaux de l'Ontario, veuillez communiquer avec nous à l'adresse ou au numéro de téléphone figurant dans le coin supérieur gauche

See front side of this page for English

Le Guide pour les défendeurs est consultable à www.ontariocourts.ca/ScJ/fr/POA, ou contactez le greffe du tribunal.
Guide for Defendants available at www.ontariocourts.ca/ScJ/POAGuide, or contact the court office.

POA 0854 (January 19, 2018 / 19 janvier 2018) CSD - Form 10.3

COMPLETE AND DETACH THIS PORTION AND SEND WITH PAYMENT

REMPLISSEZ CETTE CARTE, DÉTACHEZ-LA ET ENVOYEZ-LA AVEC VOTRE PAIEMENT

NAME AND ADDRESS
NOM ET ADRESSE

999 [offence number] 00

CARD NUMBER / NUMÉRO DE LA CARTE

CARD EXPIRY DATE
DATE D'EXPIRATION

MONTH
MOIS

YEAR
ANNÉE

CARDHOLDER'S SIGNATURE
SIGNATURE DU DÉTENTEUR DE LA CARTE

Form 11 — Certificate of Parking Infraction
Provincial Offences Act

[Editor's Note: Pursuant to section O. Reg. 108/11, s. 1, when a form is referred to by number, the reference is to the form with that number that is described in the Table of Forms at the end of this Regulation and is available on the Internet through www.ontariocourtforms.on.ca. For your convenience, the government form is reproduced below. Form current to March 17, 2011.]

Form 11, *Provincial Offences Act*, Ontario Court of Justice
Formulaire 11, Loi sur les infractions provinciales, *Cour de justice de l'Ontario*

Certificate of Parking Infraction
Procès-verbal d'infraction de stationnement

I,
Je soussigné(e) (Print name / *Nom en lettres moulées*)

believe from my personal knowledge and certify that on the
crois, en me fondant sur ma connaissance directe de faits, et atteste que le day of / *jour de*

, 20 , Time / *À (heure)* **M**

the owner (or operator) of the vehicle upon which was displayed the number plate:
le propriétaire de (ou l'utilisateur) du véhicule portant la plaque d'immatriculation suivante :

Plate No. / *N° de plaque d'immatriculation*	Province	Expiry Date / *Date d'expiration* M / M	Y / A

did commit the parking infraction of:
a commis l'infraction de stationnement de :

at
à

(Municipality / *Municipalité*)

contrary to / *contrairement à* sect. / *l'art.*

I further certify that I: **J'atteste en outre j'ai :**

A. served a parking infraction notice on the owner of the vehicle identified herein by affixing it to the vehicle in a conspicuous place at the time of this alleged infraction or. ☐ A. *signifié un avis d'infraction de stationnement au propriétaire de véhicule ci-identifié en apposant cet avis sur ce véhicule à un endroit bien en vue au moment d'infraction reprochée ou;*

B. served a parking infraction notice on the owner (or operator) of the vehicle identified herein by delivering it personally to the person having care and control (or operator) of the vehicle at the time of the alleged infraction. ☐ B. *signifié un avis d'infraction de stationnement au propriétaire (ou à utilisateur) du véhicule ci-identifié en remettant cet avis en mains propres à la personne qui a la garde et le contrôle (ou à utilisateur) du véhicule au moment de l'infraction reprochée.*

Signature of issuing Provincial Offences Officer / *Signature de l'agent des infractions provinciale*	SET FINE / *AMENDE FIXÉE* $
Officer No / *N° de l'agent*	Unit / *Unité*

Complete only if operator is charged / *Ne remplir que si l'utilisateur est inculpé*

Name of operator / *Nom de l'utilisateur* (Last / *Nom*) (First / *Prénom*) (Middle / *Initiale*)

Address / *Adresse*

(Municipality / *Municipalité*) (Province) (Postal code / *Code postal*)

Driver's licence no. / *N° de permis de conduire*

Birth date / *Date de naissance* Y / A	M / M	D / J	Sex / *Sexe*	Province

POA 0855 (March 17, 2011 / *17 mars 2011*) CSD

Form 12 — Parking Infraction Notice

Provincial Offences Act

[Editor's Note: Pursuant to section O. Reg. 108/11, s. 1, when a form is referred to by number, the reference is to the form with that number that is described in the Table of Forms at the end of this Regulation and is available on the Internet through www.ontariocourtforms.on.ca. For your convenience, the government form is reproduced below. Form current to March 15, 2014.]

Form 12, *Provincial Offences Act*, Ontario Court of Justice
Formulaire 12, Loi sur les infractions provinciales, Cour de justice de l'Ontario

Parking Infraction Notice
Avis d'infraction de stationnement

believes from personal knowledge and certifies that on the _____ day of
crois, en me fondant sur ma connaissance directe de faits, et atteste que le   jour de

_____, 20 _____ . Time
à (heure)   **M**

the owner (or operator) of the vehicle upon which was displayed the number plate:
le propriétaire (ou l'utilisateur) du véhicule portant la plaque d'immatriculation suivante :

Plate No. / *N° de plaque d'immatriculation*	Province	Expiry Date *Date d'expiration* M / M Y / A

did commit the parking infraction of:
a commis l'infraction de stationnement suivante :

at _____
à

(Municipality / *Municipalité*)

contrary to   section
contrairement à   . article

NOTICE   ### AVIS

Within 15 days of the date noted above, choose one of the options on the back of this Notice. If you do not pay the set fine shown below, or if you do not deliver a Notice of Intention to Appear in court, or if you do not appear for trial, you will be deemed not to dispute this charge and a conviction may be entered against you. Upon conviction you will be required to pay the set fine plus court costs. An administrative fee is payable if the fine goes into default and the information may be provided to a credit bureau.

Dans les 15 jours de la date indiquée ci-dessus, veuillez choisir l'une des options figurant au verso du présent avis. Si vous n'acquittez pas le montant de l'amende fixée qui est indiqué ci-dessous ou si vous ne remettez pas un avis d'intention de comparaître devant le tribunal, ou si vous ne comparaissez pas, vous serez réputé(e) ne pas contester cette accusation et une déclaration de culpabilité pourra être inscrite contre vous. Sur déclaration de culpabilité, vous serez tenu(e) de payer l'amende fixée ainsi que les frais judiciaires. Des frais d'administration sont payables en cas de défaut de paiement de l'amende et l'information pourra être transmise à une agence d'évaluation du crédit.

Signature of issuing Provincial Offences Officer *Signature de l'agent des infractions provinciales*	SET FINE *AMENDE FIXÉE*
	$ $
Officer No. / *N° de l'agent*	Unit / *Unité*

POA 0656 (March 15, 2014 / 15 mars 2014) CSD

730

IMPORTANT – Please read carefully – Within 15 days of the date of the Parking Infraction Notice, choose one of the following options. Complete the selected option (sign where necessary) and deliver it (and payment where applicable) to the address shown below. All enquiries concerning this infraction should be made to:

IMPORTANT – Veuillez lire attentivement – Dans les quinze jours qui suivent le date à laquelle vous recevez le présent avis, choisissez l'une des options suivantes. Remplissez l'option choisie (signez là où c'est nécessaire) et remettez l'avis (avec votre paiement, le cas échéant) à l'adresse indiquée ci-dessous. Pour tous renseignements concernant l'infraction, veuillez vous adresser à :

(Address and telephone number of police force or other agency that issued the Parking Infraction Notice / *adresse et numéro de téléphone du corps de police ou d'un autre organisme qui a délivré l'avis d'infraction de stationnement*)

Defendant's Options – Choose One Only
Options du défendeur – N'en choisir qu'une

OPTION 1 Voluntary Payment – I do not wish to dispute the charge and I enclose the amount of the set fine indicated on the front of this notice.
Paiement volontaire – Je ne désire pas contester l'accusation et je joins au présent avis le montant de l'amende fixée qui est indiqué au recto du présent avis.

Signature _____

Write the number of the Parking Infraction Notice on the front of your cheque or money order and make it payable to:
Inscrivez le numéro de l'avis d'infraction de stationnement au recto de votre chèque ou mandat, libellé à l'ordre de :

and mail or deliver your payment along with this notice to the address shown below. Dishonoured cheques will be subject to an administrative charge. An administrative fee is payable if the fine goes into default and the information may be provided to a credit bureau. Please allow sufficient time for your payment to be delivered.
et postez votre paiement ou remettez-le, accompagné du présent avis, à l'adresse indiquée ci-dessous. Les chèques refusés sont assujettis à des frais d'administration. Des frais d'administration s'appliquent également si l'amende reste impayée et l'information pourra être transmise à une agence d'évaluation du crédit. Veuillez prévoir assez de temps pour que votre paiement soit délivré.

OPTION 2 Trial Option – Notice of Intention to Appear in Court
Demande de procès – Avis d'intention de comparaître devant le tribunal :

☐ I intend to appear in court at the time and place set for trial and I wish it to be held in the English language.

☐ *J'ai l'intention de comparaître devant le tribunal aux date, heure et lieu fixés pour le procès et je désire que le procès se déroule en français.*

I request a _____ language interpreter for the trial.
Je demande l'aide d'un interprète en langue ____ *pour le procès.*
(Leave blank if inapplicable.)
(Laissez en blanc si vous n'avez pas besoin d'un interprète.)

Signature _____

Name (Please print) / *Nom (Lettres moulées)*

Address / *Adresse*	Postal code / *Code postal*	Telephone Number / *Numéro de téléphone*

Deliver this signed notice (and payment where applicable) to the:
Remettez le présent avis signé (avec votre paiement, le cas échéant) à :

NOTICE – Ontario Motorists
Failure to pay the fine imposed upon conviction will result in your Ontario Vehicle Permit not being renewed and no new permit being issued to you until the fine and all court costs and fees have been paid.

AVIS – Automobilistes de l'Ontario
Si l'amende imposée sur déclaration de culpabilité est impayée, votre certificat d'immatriculation de l'Ontario ne sera pas renouvelé et aucun nouveau certificat d'immatriculation ne vous sera délivré jusqu'à ce que l'amende, les frais judiciaires et autres frais aient été acquittés en totalité.

POA 0856 (March 15 2014 / 15 mars 2014) CSD

731

Form 13 — Parking Infraction Notice
Provincial Offences Act

[Editor's Note: Pursuant to section O. Reg. 108/11, s. 1, when a form is referred to by number, the reference is to the form with that number that is described in the Table of Forms at the end of this Regulation and is available on the Internet through www.ontariocourtforms.on.ca. For your convenience, the government form is reproduced below. Form current to March 17, 2011.]

Form 13, *Provincial Offences Act*, Ontario Court of Justice
Formulaire 13, *Loi sur les infractions provinciales*, *Cour de justice de l'Ontario*

Parking Infraction Notice
Avis d'infraction de stationnement

believes from personal knowledge and certifies that on the
crois, en me fondant sur ma connaissance directe de faits, et atteste que le

day of
jour de

, 20 , Time
À (heure)

M

the owner (or operator) of the vehicle upon which was displayed the number plate:
le propriétaire de (ou l'utilisateur) du véhicule portant la plaque d'immatriculation suivante :

Plate No. / N° de plaque d'immatriculation	Province	Expiry Date Date d'expiration M / M Y / A

did commit the parking infraction of:
a commis l'infraction de stationnement de :

at
à

(Municipality / Municipalité)

contrary to
contrairement à

section
l'article

NOTICE	**AVIS**
Within 15 days of the date noted above, choose one of the options on the back of this Notice. If you do not pay the set fine shown below, or if you do not deliver a Notice of Intention to Appear in court, or if you do not appear for trial, you will be deemed not to dispute this charge and a conviction may be entered against you. Upon conviction you will be required to pay the set fine plus court costs. An administrative fee is payable if the fine goes into default and the information may be provided to a credit bureau.	*Dans les 15 jours de la date indiquée ci-dessus, veuillez choisir l'une des options figurant au verso de la présente formule. Si vous n'acquittez pas le montant de l'amende fixée qui est indiqué ci dessous ou si vous ne remettez pas un avis d'intention de comparaître ou si vous ne comparaissez pas, vous serez réputé(e)ne pas contester cette accusation et une déclaration de culpabilité pourrait être inscrite contre vous. Sur déclaration de culpabilité, vous serez tenu(e) de payer l'amende fixée ainsi que les frais judiciaires. Des frais administratifs sont payables en cas de défaut de paiement de l'amende et les renseignements pourraient être communiqués à un service d'informations financières.*

Signature of issuing Provincial Offences Officer Signature de l'agent des infractions provinciale	**SET FINE** **AMENDE FIXÉE**
	$ $
Officer No. / N° de l'agent	Unit / Unité

POA 0857 (March 17, 2011 / 17 mars 2011) CSD

732

IMPORTANT – Please read carefully – Within 15 days of the date of the Parking Infraction Notice, choose one of the following options. Complete the selected option (sign where necessary) and deliver it (and payment where applicable) to the address shown below. All enquiries concerning this infraction should be made to:

IMPORTANT – Veuillez lire attentivement – Dans les quinze jours qui suivant le date a laquelle vous recevez le présent avis, choisissez l'une des options suivantes. Remplissez l'option choisie (signez là ou c'est nécessaire) et remettez l'avis (avec votre paiement, le cas échéant) à l'adresse indiquée ci-dessous. Pour tous renseignements concernant l'infraction veuillez vous adresser à :

(Address and telephone number of police force or other agency that issued the Parking Infraction Notice / *adresse et numéro de téléphone du corps de police ou d'une autre agence qui a délivré l'avis d'infraction de stationnement*)

Defendant's Options – Choose One Only
Options du défendeur – N'en choisir qu'une

OPTION 1 Voluntary Payment – I do not wish to dispute the charge and I enclose the amount of the set fine indicated on the front of this notice.
Paiement volontaire – Je ne désire pas contester l'accusation et joins à la présente le montant de l'amende fixée qui est indiquée au recto de cet avis.

Signature _____

Write the number of the Parking Infraction Notice on the front of your cheque or money order and make it payable to:
Inscrivez le numéro de l'avis d'infraction de stationnement au recto de votre cheque ou mandat, libellé à l'ordre de :

and mail or deliver your payment along with this notice to the address shown below. Dishonoured cheques will be subject to an administrative charge. An administrative fee is payable if the fine goes into default and the information may be provided to a credit bureau. Please allow sufficient time for your payment to be delivered.
et postez votre paiement ou remettez-le, accompagné de cet avis, à l'adresse indiquée ci-dessous. Les cheques refusés sont assujettis à des frais administratifs. Des frais administratifs s'appliquant également si l'amende reste impayée et les renseignements pourraient être communiqués à un service d'informations financières. Veuillez prévoir assez de temps pour que votre paiement soit délivré.

OPTION 2 Trial Option – Do Not Mail
Demande de procès – ne pas envoyer par la poste

1. You or your agent MUST attend in person at the office shown below within the times and days shown to file a Notice of Intention to Appear in Court.
Vous devez vous présenter au greffe indiquée ci-dessous, en personne ou par l'intermédiaire d'une représentant, durant les heures et les jours indiqués, pour y déposer un avis d'intention de comparaître.

2. You or your agent must bring this notice with you.
Vous out votre représentant devez apporter le présent avis.

3. **You cannot set a trial date by mail.**
On ne peut pas fixer la date d'un procès par courrier.

4. For your convenience and to save time, you may call the office in advance for an appointment.
Pour gagner du temps, vous pouvez appeler le greffe pour prendre un rendez-vous.

Address / *Adresse*

Change of name or address if applicable / *Changement de nom ou d'adresse (le cas échéant)*

_____
Name (Please print) / *Nom (Lettres moulées)*

_____
Address / *Adresse*   Postal code / *Code postal*

NOTICE – Ontario Motorists
Failure to pay the fine imposed upon conviction will result in your Ontario Vehicle Permit not being renewed and no new permit being issued to you until the fine and all court costs and fees have been paid.

AVIS – Automobilistes de l'Ontario
Si l'amende imposée sur déclaration de culpabilité est impayée, votre certificat d'immatriculation ne sera pas renouvelé aucun nouveau certificat d'immatriculation ne vous sera délivré jusqu'à ce que l'amende, les frais judiciaires et autres frais aient été acquittes en totale.

Form 14 — Notice of Impending Conviction
Provincial Offences Act

[Editor's Note: Pursuant to section O. Reg. 108/11, s. 1, when a form is referred to by number, the reference is to the form with that number that is described in the Table of Forms at the end of this Regulation and is available on the Internet through www.ontariocourtforms.on.ca. For your convenience, the government form is reproduced below. Form current to March 15, 2014.]

NOTICE OF IMPENDING CONVICTION
AVIS DE DÉCLARATION DE CULPABILITÉ IMMINENTE

ONTARIO COURT OF JUSTICE
COUR DE JUSTICE DE L'ONTARIO
PROVINCE OF ONTARIO
PROVINCE DE L'ONTARIO

Form / Formulaire 14
Provincial Offences Act
Loi sur les infractions provinciales

FROM / DE

ADDRESS / ADRESSE

(PLEASE INDICATE CHANGE OF NAME OR ADDRESS HERE IF APPLICABLE)
(VEUILLEZ INSCRIRE TOUT CHANGEMENT DE NOM OU D'ADRESSE, LE CAS ÉCHÉANT)

(NAME AND ADDRESS OF DEFENDANT / NOM ET ADRESSE DU DÉFENDEUR / DE LA DÉFENDERESSE)

To
À

Location	Set Fine Amount	Date of Infraction
Lieu	*Montant de l'amende fixée*	*Date de l'infraction*
Parking Infraction No	Licence Place No	Due Date
N° d'infraction de stationnement	*N° de plaque d'immatriculation*	*Date d'échéance*

The vehicle bearing the licence plate mentioned above was unlawfully parked or stopped.

The amount of the fine indicated on the Parking Infraction Notice has not been paid. Unless payment or a Notice of Intention to Appear in court for the purpose of entering a plea and having a trial of the matter is received by the above due date a conviction will be recorded against you without further notice. On conviction you will be required to pay the set fine plus court costs. An administrative fee is payable if the fine goes into default and the information may be provided to a credit bureau.

If you do not wish to dispute the charge, you may pay the set fine amount above. Write the Parking Infraction Notice number on the front of your cheque or money order and make it payable to.

DO NOT SEND CASH IN THE MAIL

Deliver this form and your payment to the address indicated below. If you would like to request a trial regarding this matter, complete the Notice of Intention to Appear below and deliver this form to the address below.

Please allow sufficient time for your payment or Notice to be delivered. If you have any further questions regarding this Notice, please call

Le véhicule portant la plaque d'immatriculation susmentionnée était stationné ou arrêté illégalement.

Le montant de l'amende inscrit sur l'avis d'infraction de stationnement n'a pas été payé. À moins que le paiement ou un avis d'intention de comparaître devant le tribunal pour inscrire un plaidoyer et faire instruire la question ne soit reçu au plus tard à la date d'échéance susmentionnée, une déclaration de culpabilité sera inscrite contre vous sans autre préavis. Sur déclaration de culpabilité, vous devrez payer l'amende fixée, plus des frais de justice. Vous devrez payer des frais d'administration en cas de non-paiement de l'amende, et l'information pourra être transmise à une agence d'évaluation du crédit.

Si vous ne désirez pas contester l'accusation, vous pouvez payer le montant de l'amende fixée, indiqué ci-dessus. Écrivez le numéro de l'infraction de stationnement au recto de votre chèque ou mandat libellé à l'ordre de

N'ENVOYEZ PAS D'ARGENT COMPTANT PAR LA POSTE

Si vous désirez demander un procès sur cette question, remplissez l'avis d'intention de comparaître ci-dessous. Faites parvenir le présent formulaire et votre paiement ou votre avis d'intention de comparaître à l'adresse suivante

Veuillez prévoir un délai suffisant pour la livraison de votre paiement ou de votre avis. Pour toute autre question sur le présent avis, veuillez appeler

NOTICE OF INTENTION TO APPEAR IN COURT

☐ I intend to appear in court to enter a plea at the time and date set for the trial and I wish to have the trial conducted in the English language.

I request a _____ language interpreter for the trial. (Leave blank if inapplicable.)

AVIS D'INTENTION DE COMPARAÎTRE DEVANT LE TRIBUNAL

☐ *J'ai l'intention de comparaître pour inscrire un plaidoyer aux date et heure fixés pour le procès et je souhaite que le procès se déroule en français.*

Je demande l'aide d'un interprète en langue _____ pour le procès. (Laissez en blanc si vous n'avez pas besoin d'un interprète.)

Signature of Defendant / *Signature du défendeur / de la défenderesse*   (date)   Telephone number / *numéro de téléphone*

POA-055E (March 15, 2014 / 15 mars 2014) CSD

734

Form 15 — Notice of Impending Conviction

Provincial Offences Act

[Editor's Note: Pursuant to section O. Reg. 108/11, s. 1, when a form is referred to by number, the reference is to the form with that number that is described in the Table of Forms at the end of this Regulation and is available on the Internet through www.ontariocourtforms.on.ca. For your convenience, the government form is reproduced below. Form current to March 17, 2011.]

NOTICE OF IMPENDING CONVICTION
AVIS DE DÉCLARATION DE CULPABILITÉ IMMINENTE

ONTARIO COURT OF JUSTICE
COUR DE JUSTICE DE L'ONTARIO
PROVINCE OF ONTARIO
PROVINCE DE L'ONTARIO

Form / Formulaire 15
Provincial Offences Act
Loi sur les infractions provinciales

FROM / *DE*

ADDRESS / *ADRESSE*

(PLEASE INDICATE CHANGE OF NAME OR
ADDRESS HERE IF APPLICABLE)
*(VEUILLEZ INSCRIRE TOUT CHANGEMENT
DE NOM OU D'ADRESSE, LE CAS ÉCHÉANT)*

(NAME AND ADDRESS OF DEFENDANT / *NOM ET ADRESSE DU DÉFENDEUR*)

To / *À*

Location *Lieu*	Set Fine Amount *Montant d'amende fixée*	Date of Infraction *Date de l'infraction*
Parking Infraction No. *N° d'infraction de stationnement*	Licence Plate No. *N° de plaque d'immatriculation*	Due Date *Date d'échéance*

The vehicle bearing the licence plate mentioned above was unlawfully parked or stopped.

The amount of the fine indicated on the Parking Infraction Notice has not been paid. Unless payment or a Notice of Intention to Appear in court for the purpose of entering a plea and having a trial of the matter is received by the above due date a conviction will be recorded against you without further notice. On conviction you will be required to pay the set fine plus court costs. An administrative fee is payable if the fine goes into default and the information may be provided to a credit bureau.

If you do not wish to dispute the charge, you may pay the set fine amount above. Write the Parking Infraction Notice number on the front of your cheque or money order and make it payable to:

Le véhicule portant la plaque d'immatriculation susmentionnée était stationné ou arrêté illégalement.

Le montant de l'amende inscrit sur l'avis d'infraction de stationnement n'a pas été payé. À moins que le paiement ou un avis d'intention de comparaître au tribunal pour inscrire un plaidoyer et faire instruire la question ne soit reçue avant la date d'échéance, une déclaration de culpabilité sera enregistrée contre vous, sans autre avis. Sur déclaration de culpabilité, vous devrez payer l'amende fixée, plus des frais de justice. Des droits administratifs sont exigibles, en cas de non-paiement de l'amende, et de l'information peut être transmise à un service d'informations financières.

Si vous ne désirez pas contester l'accusation, vous pouvez payer le montant d'amende fixée, indiqué ci-dessus. Écrivez le numéro de l'infraction de stationnement au recto de votre chèque ou mandat libellé à l'ordre de

DO NOT SEND CASH IN THE MAIL

Deliver this form and your payment to:

Please allow sufficient time for your payment to be delivered. If you have any further questions regarding this Notice, please call:

If you would like to request a trial regarding this matter please note

1. You or your agent must attend at the office shown below.

2. You or your agent must bring this notice with you.

3. You cannot set a trial date by mail.

4. For your convenience and to save time, you may call in advance for an appointment.

N'ENVOYEZ PAS D'ARGENT COMPTANT PAR LA POSTE

Faites parvenir la présente formule et votre paiement à

Veuillez prévoir un délai suffisant pour la livraison de votre paiement. Pour toute question sur le présent avis, veuillez appeler :

Si vous désirez qu'il y ait un procès sure cette question, veuillez prendre note que :

1. *Votre mandataire ou vous-même devez vous présenter au greffe mentionné ci-dessous.*

2. *Vous mandataire ou vous-même devez apporter cet avis avec vous.*

3. *Vous ne pouvez pas fixer une date pour le procès par courrier.*

4. *Pour gagner du temps, vous pouvez téléphoner à l'avance pour obtenir un rendez-vous.*

(Office address and telephone number)
Please refer, if another court office is closer to you, you may call the above office for further instructions.

(Adresse et numéro de téléphone du greffe)
Veuillez noter que si un autre greffe du tribunal est situé plus près de chez vous, vous pouvez appeler le greffe susmentionné pour d'autres directives.

POA 0812 (March 17, 2011 / 17 mars 2011) CSD

735

Form 16 — Certificate Requesting Conviction Under Section 18.2 of the Provincial Offences Act

Provincial Offences Act

[Editor's Note: Pursuant to section O. Reg. 108/11, s. 1, when a form is referred to by number, the reference is to the form with that number that is described in the Table of Forms at the end of this Regulation and is available on the Internet through www.ontariocourtforms.on.ca. For your convenience, the government form is reproduced below. Form current to March 17, 2011.]

Certificate Requesting a Conviction
Provincial Offences Act Part II

I certify for each of the above listed items that:

(a) The Certificate of Parking Infraction is complete and regular on its face;

(b) If the Defendant is liable as the owner, I am satisfied that the Defendant is the owner of the vehicle plate;

(c) There is valid legal authority for charging the Defendant with the parking infraction

(d) The Defendant was given a Notice of Impending Conviction at least fifteen (15) days before the filing of this Certificate Requesting Conviction; and

(e) The alleged infraction occurred less than seventy-five (75) days before the filing of this Certificate Requesting Conviction.

(For an infraction under by-law of a municipality only)
Strike out if inapplicable

I further certify, for each of the above listed items that is an infraction under a by-law of a municipality:

(f) Payment of the set fine has not been made; and

(g) The Defendant has not given Notice of Intention to appear in court for purpose of entering a plea and having a trial of the matter.

Certificat de demande de déclaration de culpabilité en vertu de la Partie II de la Loi sur les infractions provinciales

Je certifie, pour chaque élément figurant ci-dessus, ce qui suit :

a) *Le procès-verbal d'infraction de stationnement est complet et régulier à sa face même;*

b) *Si le défendeur ou la défenderesse est responsable à titre de propriétaire, je suis convaincu(e) qu'il ou elle est bien propriétaire des plaques d'immatriculation du véhicule;*

c) *Le défendeur ou la défenderesse est accusé(e) de l'infraction de stationnement en vertu d'un pouvoir valide confère par la loi;*

d) *Un avis de déclaration de culpabilité imminente a été donné au défendeur ou à la défenderesse au moins quinze (15) jours avant le dépôt du présent certificat de demande de déclaration de culpabilité; et*

e) *L'infraction reprochée a eu lieu moins de soixante-quinze (75) jours avant le dépôt du présent certificat de demande de déclaration de culpabilité.*

(Pour une infraction prévue par un règlement municipal seulement) *Biffer toute mention inutile*

De plus, je certifie pour chaque élément énoncé ci-dessus que constitue une infraction prévue par un règlement municipal, ce qui suit :

f) *L'amende fixée n'a pas été payée; et*

g) *Le défendeur n'a pas donné d'avis d'intention de comparaître au tribunal pour inscrire un plaidoyer et faire instruire la question.*

_____
Authorized Signature / *Signature autorisée*

Date

FOR COURT USE ONLY

I certify that a conviction has been recorded this date with regard to the above listed items as provided by subsection 18.2(6) of the *Provincial Offences Act.*

RÉSERVÉ AU TRIBUNAL

Je certifie qu'une déclaration de culpabilité a été inscrite à la date d'aujourd'hui à l'égard des éléments énoncés ci-dessus, comme le prévoit le paragraphe 18.2(6) de la Loi sur les infractions provinciales.

_____
Clerk of the Court / *Greffier du tribunal*

Date

POA 0803 (March 17, 2011 / *17 mars 2011*) CSD

Form 17 [Repealed (November 2, 2011).]

Appendix B

Regulations Under the Courts of Justice Act

Rules of the Ontario Court (General Division) and the Ontario Court (Provincial Division) in Appeals Under Section 116 of the Provincial Offences Act — R.R.O. 1990, Reg. 196 [Re-enacted as O. Reg. 723/94]

DEFINITIONS AND INTERPRETATION

Definitions

1. (1) In these rules,

"Act" means the *Provincial Offences Act"*

"appeal court" means the Ontario Court (General Division) or the Ontario Court (Provincial Division), as the case may be, sitting as the appeal court under section 116 of the Act;

"clerk" means the clerk of the Ontario Court (Provincial Division) or the local registrar of the Ontario Court (General Division) to which an appeal is or may be taken under Part VII of the Act;

"file" means file with the clerk;
 "judge" means a judge of the Ontario Court (General Division) or the Ontario Court (Provincial Division), as the case may be, sitting as the appeal court under section 116 of the Act.

Application of rules

(2) These rules apply in respect of appeals to the Ontario Court (General Division) or the Ontario Court (Provincial Division) under section 116 of the Act.

General principle

(3) These rules shall be constructed liberally so as to obtain as expeditious a conclusion of every proceeding as is consistent with a just determination of the proceeding.

Matters not provided for

(4) Where matters are not provided for in these rules, the practice shall be determined by analogy to them.

CALCULATION OF TIME

General

2. (1) In the calculation of time under these rules or an order of the court, except where a contrary intention appears.

(*a*) where there is a reference to a number of days between two events, they shall be counted by excluding the day on which the first event happens and including the day on which the second event happens, even if they are described as clear days or the words "at least" are used;

(*b*) where a period of less than seven days is prescribed, holidays shall not be counted;

(*c*) where the time for doing an act under these rules expires on a holiday, the act may be done on the next day that is not a holiday; and

(*d*) service of a document made after 4 p.m. or at any time on a holiday shall be deemed to have been made on the next day that is not a holiday.

Local time

(2) Where a time of day is mentioned in these rules or in any documents in an appeal, the time referred to shall be taken as the time observed locally.

"Holiday"

(3) For the purposes of subsection (1), "holiday" means,

(*a*) any Saturday or Sunday;

(*b*) New Year's Day;

(*c*) Good Friday;

(*d*) Easter Monday;

(*e*) Victoria Day;

(*f*) Canada Day;

(*g*) Civic Holiday;

(*h*) Labour Day;

(*i*) Thanksgiving Day;

(*j*) Remembrance Day;

(*k*) Christmas Day;

(*l*) Boxing Day; and

(*m*) any special holiday proclaimed by the Governor General or the Lieutenant Governor.

Same

(4) Where,

(*a*) New Year's Day, Canada Day or Remembrance Day falls on a Saturday or Sunday, the following Monday is a holiday;

(*b*) Christmas Day falls on a Saturday or Sunday, the following Monday and Tuesday are holidays;

(*c*) Christmas Day falls on a Friday, the following Monday is a holiday.

NOTICE BY MAIL

3. A notice or document given or delivered by mail shall, unless the contrary is shown, be deemed to be given or delivered on the seventh day following the day on which it was mailed.

SUBSTITUTED SERVICE

4. Where, on motion without notice, it appears to a judge that reasonable efforts have been made without success to give or deliver a notice or document in the manner required by these rules or the Act, or that reasonable efforts would not be successful, the judge may make an order for substituted service of the notice or document in such manner as the judge directs or, where necessary in the interests of justice, may dispense with the giving or delivery of the notice or document upon such terms as the judge considers proper in the circumstances.

SERVICE AND FILING OF NOTICE OF APPEAL

Notice of appeal

5. (1) A notice of appeal shall be in Form 1.

Time for service, appeal by defendant

(2) A defendant who appeals shall serve the notice of appeal on the prosecutor and, if the prosecutor is not acting on behalf of the Crown, on the Crown Attorney within 30 days after the date of the decision appealed from.

Time for service, appeal by prosecutor

(3) A prosecutor who appeals shall serve the notice of appeal on the defendant and, if the prosecutor is not acting on behalf of the Crown, on the Crown Attorney within 30 days after the date of the decision appealed from.

Filing

(4) An appellant shall file the notice of appeal with proof of service within five days after service.

Proof of service

(5) Proof of service of the notice of appeal may be made by affidavit.

Admission of service

(6) Where admission of service is endorsed on the notice of appeal, proof need not be made by affidavit.

APPEAL WHERE FINE IMPOSED

6. A defendant who appeals from a decision imposing a fine shall file with the notice of appeal a receipt for payment of the fine issued by the clerk of the court that imposed the fine, unless the clerk is satisfied that an order has been made under subsection 111(2) of the Act and a recognizance has been entered into by the defendant in accordance with the order.

EXTENSION OR ABRIDGMENT OF TIME

Judge's power

7. (1) A judge may extend or abridge the time for bringing an appeal and for doing any other act in connection with an appeal for which a time is prescribed before or after the expiration of the time prescribed.

Notice

(2) A notice of motion to extend or abridge time shall be given to the opposite party, unless otherwise directed by a judge.

TRANSCRIPTS

Certificate

8. (1) An appellant shall file with the notice of appeal a certificate of the clerk of the Ontario Court (Provincial Division) as to transcript of evidence in Form 2.

Filing and delivery of transcript

(2) An appellant shall file and deliver to the respondent,
(*a*) in an appeal against conviction, dismissal, a finding as to ability to conduct a defence or an order under section 161 of the Act, one copy of the transcript of evidence at trial, including reasons for judgment; and
(*b*) in an appeal against conviction and sentence or sentence only, one copy of the transcript of evidence at trial and submissions on sentencing, including reasons for judgment and sentence, if any.

Transcript to Crown Attorney

(3) Where the Crown Attorney has given notice of intervention after receiving notice of appeal, the appellant shall deliver a copy of the transcript of evidence at trial, including reasons for judgment and sentence, if any, to the Crown Attorney.

Time for filing certificate

(4) An appellant who has been issued a provisional legal aid certificate limited to the filing of a notice of appeal and making a motion for release from custody under

the *Legal Aid Act* shall file a certificate in Form 2 within one month of filing the notice of appeal.

Deemed abandonment

(5) An appellant referred to in subrule (4) who does not file the certificate within one month of filing the notice of appeal or within such longer period of time as a judge may permit shall be deemed to have abandoned the appeal.

RECOGNIZANCES

9. (1) An order for recognizance and recognizance under section 110 of the Act shall be in Form 3.

(2) An order for recognizance under section 111 of the Act shall be in Form 4.

MOTIONS UNDER ACT OR RULES

Notice of motion

10. (1) A motion provided for by the Act or these rules shall be commenced by a notice of motion.

Time for hearing

(2) There shall be at least three days between service of the notice of motion and the day for hearing the motion.

Time for filing notice

(3) The moving party shall file the notice of motion at least two days before the day for hearing the motion.

Evidence

(4) Evidence on a motion may be given,
   (*a*) by affidavit;
   (*b*) with the permission of the court, orally; or
   (*c*) in the form of a transcript of the examination of a witness.

Power of judge

(5) Upon the hearing of a motion, the justice may receive and base his or her decision on information that the justice considers credible or trustworthy in the circumstances, whether or not other evidence is given.

Hearing where notice not served

(6) A motion may be heard without service of a notice of motion,
   (*a*) on consent; or

(*b*) where the motion is made under section 111 or 112 of the Act; or

(*c*) where, having regard to the subject-matter or the circumstances of the motion, it would not be unjust to hear the motion without service of a notice of motion.

Appeal by way of new trial

(7) A person making a motion for an order under section 127 of the Act that an appeal be heard and determined by way of a new trial in the court shall give at least seven days notice of the motion to all other parties to the appeal.

TRANSMISSION OF MATERIAL

s. 115 notice deemed given

11. (1) The clerk of the appeal court shall send a copy of the notice of appeal to the clerk of the Ontario Court (Provincial Division) as the notice required by section 115 of the Act.

Time for transmittal of documents

(2) The clerk of the Ontario Court (Provincial Division) shall transmit the order appealed from and transmit or transfer custody of the other material referred to in section 115 of the Act to the clerk of the appeal court within 10 days after receiving the copy of the notice of appeal.

INTERVENTION OF CROWN ATTORNEY

12. Where a prosecutor is not acting on behalf of the Crown, the Crown Attorney may intervene to act on behalf of the prosecutor or to attend as a party on the appeal.

LISTING OF APPEAL

Appeal list

13. (1) The clerk shall place the appeal on an appeal list for the next sitting of the court at which dates are fixed for hearing appeals as soon as 10 days have elapsed after,

(*a*) the clerk has received the order appealed from and the other material referred to in section 115 of the Act;

(*b*) the appellant has filed a copy of the transcript of evidence at trial, including reasons for judgment or sentence if any; and

(*c*) any other step required by the Act, these rules or the court has been completed.

Notice period

(2) The clerk shall give at least 14 days notice of the date fixed for the hearing of the appeal to the appellant and the respondent and, where the Crown Attorney has filed a notice of intervention, to the Crown Attorney.

Motion under s. 127

(3) Where a motion is made under section 127 of the Act for an order that an appeal be heard and determined by way of a new trial in the court, the clerk shall not place the appeal on an appeal list until the motion has been disposed of and 10 days have elapsed since the disposition of the motion.

DIRECTIONS

> **14.** A party to an appeal may make a motion to the court at any time for directions with respect to the conduct of the appeal.

FACTUMS

Where factum not necessary

> **15.** (1) Unless a judge orders otherwise, a party to an appeal who intends to be present either personally or by counsel at the hearing of the appeal need not file a factum.

Form of factums

(2) Where a factum is requred by order of the court or is filed by a party to an appeal, subrules (3) to (7) apply.

Appellant's factum

(3) An appellant shall prepare an "Appellant's Factum" not exceeding 10 pages in length, excluding the Schedule, and shall file, on or before the date specified in the notice of hearing given under rule 13, one copy of the factum, together with proof of service, on all other parties and persons who have been granted the right to be heard on the appeal.

Same

(4) Except in appeals from sentence only, the appellant's factum shall consist of
(*a*) Part I, entitled "Statement of the Case", containing a statement identifying the appellant, the court in which the proceedings arose, the nature of the charge or charges, the result in that court and the nature of each order to which the appeal relates;
(*b*) Part II, entitled "Summary of the Facts", containing a concise summary of the facts relevant to the issues on the appeal, with such references to the evidence by page and line, or paragraph, as the case may be, as may be necessary;

(*c*) Part III, entitled "Issues and the Law", containing a statement of each issue raised, immediately followed by a concise statement of the law and any authorities relating to that issue;

(*d*) Part IV, entitled "Order Requested", containing a statement of the order that the court is being asked to make; and

(*e*) a Schedule, entitled "Authorities to be Cited", containing a list of the authorities, with citations, to which reference was made in Part III in the order in which they appear in that Part.

Respondent's factum

(5) A respondent shall prepare a "Respondent's Factum" not exceeding 10 pages in length, excluding the Schedule, and shall file, not later than 15 days after receipt of the appellant's factum and not later than 7 days before the date fixed for the hearing of the appeal under rule 13, one copy of the factum, together with proof of service, on all other parties and persons who have been granted the right to be heard on the appeal.

Same

(6) Except in appeals from sentence only, the respondent's factum shall consist of,

(*a*) Part I, entitled "Respondent's Statement as to Facts", containing a statement of the facts in Part II of the appellant's factum that the respondent accepts as correct and those facts with which the respondent disagrees and a concise summary of any additional facts relied on, with such reference to the transcript evidence by page and line or paragraph, as the case may be, as is necessary;

(*b*) Part II, entitled "Response to Appellant's Issues", containing the position of the respondent with respect to each issue raised by the appellant immediately following a concise statement of the law and the authorities relating to that issue;

(*c*) Part III, entitled "Additional Issues", containing a statement of any additional issues raised by the respondent, immediately followed by a concise statement of the law and the authorities relating to those issues;

(*d*) Part IV, entitled "Order Requested", containing a statement of the order that the court will be asked to make; and

(*e*) a Schedule, entitled "Authorities to be Cited", containing a list of the authorities, with citations, referred to in the order in which they appear in Parts II and III.

Paragraphs

(7) The appellant's and the respondent's factum shall be in paragraphs numbered consecutively throughout.

APPEAL IN WRITING

16. An appellant who intends not to be present in person or by counsel at the hearing of the appeal shall file, prior to the date of the hearing,

(*a*) a notice in writing of that intention, unless the appellant has already done so in the notice of appeal; and

(*b*) a statement in writing of the issues and the appellant's arguments on the appeal.

DISMISSAL OF APPEAL

17. The court may dismiss an appeal where the appellant,

(*a*) does not attend in person or by counsel and,

(i) has not indicated in the notice of appeal the appellant's intention not to be present in person or by counsel at the hearing of the appeal,

(ii) has not filed notice in writing of the intention not to be present in person or by counsel at the hearing of the appeal, and

(iii) has not filed a statement in writing of the issues and the appellant's arguments on the appeal;

(*b*) has filed a notice of abandonment;

(*c*) has not filed a transcript of evidence at trial, including reasons for judgment or sentence, if any, within 30 days after receiving notice of completion of the transcript from the clerk of the Ontario Court (Provincial Division);

(*d*) after obtaining an order under subclause 117(1)(*b*)(ii) of the Act for the examination of a witness, has not filed a transcript of the examination within 30 days after receiving notice of completion of the transcription from the other person before whom the witness was examined; or

(*e*) has filed to comply with an order of the court in respect of the appeal.

ABANDONMENT OF APPEALS

Notice of abandonment

18. (1) An appellant who wishes to abandon the appeal may file a notice of abandonment in Form 5.

Signing of notice

(2) The appellant or counsel for the appellant shall sign the notice of abandonment.

Signing by witness

(3) Where the appellant signs the notice of abandonment, the notice must also be signed by another person who witnessed the signing by the appellant.

Affidavit of execution

(4) Where the witness is not counsel for the appellant, the appellant shall file an affidavit of execution by the witness with the notice of abandonment.

Notice to other parties

(5) The clerk shall give a copy of the filed notice of abandonment to each of the other parties to the appeal.

APPEAL RESPECTING RELEASE FROM CUSTODY

Commencing appeal

19. (1) An appeal under section 152 of the Act in respect of release from custody shall be commenced by written notice filed and given to all other parties and, if the Crown Attorney is not a party, to the Crown Attorney.

Grounds for release from custody

(2) On the appeal, the court shall order that the defendant be released from custody pending trial if it is satisfied that the defendant will attend in court for trial.

When order for release takes effect

(3) The court shall provide in the order that the order does not take effect until the defendant,

(*a*) gives an undertaking, either without conditions or with such conditions as the court may order, to attend in court for trial; or

(*b*) enters into a recognizance, with or without sureties, in such amount, with such conditions and before such justice as the court may order either with or without depositing with the justice money or other valuable security specified by the court.

OFFICIAL EXAMINATIONS

Definition, "order"

20. (1) In this rule, "order" means an order under subclause 117(1)(*b*)(ii) of the Act.

Presence of parties, counsel

(2) Except with the consent of the parties or their counsel, the examination of a witness under an order shall take place in the presence of the parties or their counsel.

Tentative appointment

(3) A party who intends to make a motion for an order for the examination of a witness before an official examiner shall obtain a tentative appointment for the examination before making the motion for the order.

748

Certificate of official examiner

(4) Upon the completion of the examination, the party who made the motion for the order shall file a certificate of the official examiner in Form 6.

Notice of completion of transcript

(5) An official examiner who signs and delivers a certificate in Form 6 shall notify each of the parties to the appeal and the clerk when the transcript of the examination is completed.

SPECIAL COMMISSIONER

Appointment

21. (1) Where the court makes an order under clause 117(1)(*e*) of the Act referring a question to a special commissioner for inquiry and report, the court shall, by order, appoint the special commissioner and fix the date on or before which the inquiry shall be completed and the report shall be filed.

Motion for directions

(2) The special commissioner may make a motion to the court for directions in respect of the inquiry or the report, or both.

Filing of report

(3) Upon completion of the report, the special commissioner,
(*a*) shall file the report, together with one copy for each party to the appeal; and
(*b*) shall give notice of the filing of the report to each party to the appeal.

NOTICE OF DECISION OF COURT

22. Immediately after the disposition of an appeal, the clerk shall give notice of the court's decision, including any written reasons and endorsements,
(*a*) to each party to the appeal who was not present in person or by counsel when the decision was made;
(*b*) to the clerk of the Ontario Court (Provincial Division); and
(*c*) to the Crown Attorney, where a prosecutor is not acting on behalf of the Crown.

TRANSITION

Definition, "preceding rules"

23. (1) In this rule, "preceding rules" means the Rules of the Ontario Court (General Division) and the Ontario Court (Provincial Division) in Appeals under Section 116 of the *Provincial Offences Act* (Regulation 196 of the Revised Regulations of Ontario, 1990) as they read on the day before these rules come into force.

Application of rules

(2) These rules apply to all appeals, whether commenced before or after these rules come into force, except in respect of steps taken under the preceding rules.

Power of judge

(3) Despite the repeal of the preceding rules and subrule (2), a judge may make an order that an appeal, or a step in the appeal, be conducted under these rules or the preceding rules or make any order that is considered just in order to secure the fair and expeditious conduct of the appeal.

REVOCATION AND COMMENCEMENT

24. (1) Regulation 196 of the Revised Regulations of Ontario, 1990 is revoked.

(2) This Regulation comes into force on December 12, 1994.

Rules of the Ontario Court (Provincial Division) in Appeals Under Section 135 of the Provincial Offences Act — R.R.O. 1990, Reg. 198 [am. O. Reg. 504/93; Re-enacted as O. Reg. 722/94.]

DEFINITIONS AND INTERPRETATION

Definitions

1. (1) In these rules,

"Act" means the *Provincial Offences Act*;

"appeal court" means the Ontario Court (Provincial Division) sitting as the appeal court under sections 135 of the Act;

"clerk" means the clerk of the Ontario Court (Provincial Division);

"file" means file with the clerk;

"judge" means a judge of the Ontario Court (Provincial Division) sitting as the appeal court under section 135 of the Act.

Application of rules

(2) These rules apply in respect of appeals to the Ontario Court (Provincial Division) under section 135 of the Act.

General principle

(3) These rules shall be construed liberally so as to obtain as expeditious a conclusion of every proceeding as is consistent with a just determination of the proceeding.

Matters not provided for

(4) Where matters are not provided for in these rules, the practice shall be determined by analogy to them.

CALCULATION OF TIME

General

   2. (1) In the calculation of time under these rules or an order of the court, except where a contrary intention appears,

   (*a*) where there is a reference to a number of days between two events, they shall be counted by excluding the day on which the first event happens and including the day on which the second event happens, evy if they are described as clear days or the words "at least" are used;

   (*b*) where a period of less than seven days is prescribed, holidays shall not be counted;

   (*c*) where the time for doing an act under these rules expires on a holiday, the act may be done on the next day that is not a holiday; and

   (*d*) service of a document made after 4 p.m. on or at any time on a holiday shall be deemed to have been made on the next day that is not a holiday.

Local time

(2) Where a time of day is mentioned in these rules or in any documents in an appeal, the time referred to shall be taken as the time observed locally.

"Holiday"

(3) For the purposes of subsection (1), "holiday" means,

   (*a*) any Saturday or Sunday;

   (*b*) New Year's Day;

   (*c*) Good Friday;

   (*d*) Easter Monday;

   (*e*) Victoria Day;

   (*f*) Canada Day;

   (*g*) Civic Holiday;

(*h*) Labour Day;

(*i*) Thanksgiving Day;

(*j*) Remembrance Day;

(*k*) Christmas Day;

(*l*) Boxing Day; and

(*m*) any special holiday proclaimed by the Governor General or the Lieutenant Governor.

Same

(4) Where,

(*a*) New Year's Day, Canada Day or Remembrance Day falls on a Saturday or Sunday, the following Monday is a holiday;

(*b*) Christmas Day falls on a Saturday or Sunday, the following Monday and Tuesday are holidays;

(*c*) Christmas Day falls on a Friday, the following Monday is a holiday.

NOTICE BY MAIL

3. A notice or document given or delivered by mail shall, unless the contrary is shown, be deemed to be given or delivered on the seventh day following the day on which it was mailed.

SUBSTITUTED SERVICE

4. Where, on motion without notice, it appears to a judge that reasonable efforts have been made without success to give or deliver a notice or document in the manner required by these rules or the Act, or that reasonable efforts would not be successful, the judge may make an order for substituted service of the notice or document in such manner as the judge directs or, where necessary in the interests of justice, may dispense with the giving or delivery of the notice or document upon such terms as the judge considers proper in the circumstances.

APPEAL WHERE FINE IMPOSED

5. A defendant who appeals from a decision imposing a fine shall file with the notice of appeal a receipt for payment of the fine issued by the clerk of the court that imposed the fine or state in the notice of appeal that the fine has been paid to a municipality responsible for collecting its own parking fines, unless the clerk is satisfied that an order has been made under subsection 111(2) of the Act and a recognizance has been entered into by the defendant in accordance with the order.

FILING OF NOTICE OF APPEAL

Notice of appeal

6. (1) A notice of appeal shall be in Form 1.

Time and place for hearing

(2) Upon the filing of the notice of appeal, the clerk shall set a time and place for the hearing of the appeal in accordance with section 135 of the Act.

Notice to respondent

(3) The clerk shall give the respondent a copy of the filed notice of appeal and a notice of the time and place of the hearing in Form 2.

Timely notice

(4) Notice of the time and place of the hearing shall be given at least 15 days before the day set for the hearing.

Certificate

(5) A certificate of giving a notice under subrule (3) endorsed on the notice by the clerk shall be received in evidence and, in the absence of evidence to the contrary, is proof that the notice was given.

Interpretation

(6) For the purposes of this rule, where the defendant appeals, the prosecutor is the respondent, and vice-versa.

NOTICE TO CROWN ATTORNEY

Copies to Crown Attorney

7. (1) The clerk shall give the Crown Attorney a copy of each notice or document filed with or issued by the clerk in respect of an appeal under these rules.

Intervention of Crown Attorney

(2) Where a prosecutor is not acting on behalf of the Crown, the Crown Attorney may intervene to act on behalf of the prosecutor or to attend as a party on the appeal.

EXTENSION OR ABRIDGMENT OF TIME

Judge's power

8. (1) A judge may extend or abridge the time for bringing an appeal and for doing any other act in connection with an appeal for which a time is prescribed before or after the expiration of the time prescribed.

Notice

(2) A notice of motion to extend or abridge time shall be given to the opposite party, unless otherwise directed by a judge.

TRANSCRIPTS

Transcript not required

9. (1) Unless a judge orders otherwise, a party to an appeal need not provide a transcript of all or any part of the evidence at trial.

Transcripts required

(2) Where the court orders that a transcript of all or any part of the evidence at trial be provided under clause 136(3)(a) of the Act or a party to an appeal files such a transcript, an appellant shall file and deliver to the respondent,

(*a*) in an appeal against conviction or acquittal, one copy of the transcript of evidence at trial, including reasons for judgment; and

(*b*) in an appeal against conviction and sentence or sentence only, one copy of the transcript of evidence at trial and submissions on sentencing, including reasons for judgment and sentence, if any.

Transcript to Crown Attorney

(3) Where the Crown Attorney has given notice of intervention after receiving notice of appeal, the appellant shall deliver a copy of the transcript of evidence at trial, including reasons for judgment and sentence, if any, to the Crown Attorney.

RECOGNIZANCES

10. (1) An order for recognizance and recognizance under section 110 of the Act shall be in Form 3.

(2) An order for recognizance and recognizance under section 111 of the Act shall be in Form 4.

MOTIONS UNDER ACT OR RULES

Notice of motion

11. (1) A motion provided for by the Act or these rules shall be commenced by a notice of motion.

Time of hearing

(2) There shall be at least three days between service of the notice of motion and the day for hearing the motion.

Time for filing notice

(3) The moving party shall file notice of motion at least two days before the day for hearing the motion.

Evidence

(4) Evidence on a motion may be given,
 (*a*) by affidavit;
 (*b*) with the permission of the court, orally; or
 (*c*) in the form of a transcript of the examination of a witness.

Power of judge

(5) Upon the hearing of a motion, the judge may receive and base his or her decision on information that he or she considers credible or trustworthy in the circumstances, whether or not other evidence is given.

Hearing where notice not served

(6) A motion may be heard without service of a notice of motion,
 (*a*) on consent;
 (*b*) where the motion is made under section 111 or 112 of the Act; or
 (*c*) where, having regard to the subject-matter or the circumstances of the motion, it would not be unjust to hear the motion without service of a notice of motion.

DIRECTIONS

12. A party to an appeal may make a motion to the court at any time for directions with respect to the conduct of the appeal.

DISMISSAL OF APPEAL

13. The court may dismiss an appeal where the appellant,
 (*a*) does not attend in person or by counsel on the day set by the clerk for the hearing of the appeal;
 (*b*) has filed a notice of abandonment;
 (*c*) has not filed a transcript of evidence at trial, including reasons for judgment or sentence, if any, within 30 days after receiving notice of completion of the transcript from the clerk of the Ontario Court (Provincial Division); or
 (*d*) has failed to comply with an order of the court in respect of the appeal.

ABANDONMENT OF APPEALS

Notice of abandonment

14. (1) An appellant who wishes to abandon the appeal may file a notice of abandonment in Form 5.

Signing of notice

(2) The appellant or counsel for the appellant shall sign the notice of abandonment.

Signing by witness

(3) Where the appellant signs the notice of abandonment, the notice must also be signed by another person who witnessed the signing by the appellant.

Affidavit of execution

(4) Where the witness is not counsel for the appellant, the appellant shall file an affidavit of execution by the witness with the notice of abandonment.

Notice to other parties

(5) The clerk shall give a copy of the filed notice of abandonment to each of the other parties to the appeal.

NOTICE OF DECISION OF COURT

Notice of decision on appeal

15. (1) Immediately after the disposition of an appeal, the clerk shall give notice of the court's decision, including any written reasons and endorsements,

(*a*) to each party to the appeal who was not present in person or by counsel when the decision was made;

(*b*) to the clerk of the Ontario Court (Provincial Division); and

(*c*) to the Crown Attorney, where a prosecutor is not acting on behalf of the Crown.

Deemed receipt of notice of trial

(2) Where the appeal court directs a new trial and sets a date for the trial with the consent of the parties, the defendant is deemed to have received notice of trial.

TRANSITION

Definition, "preceding rules"

16. (1) In this rule, "preceding rules" means the Rules of the Ontario Court (Provincial Division) in Appeals under Section 135 of the *Provincial Offences Act* (Regulation 198 of the Revised Regulations of Ontario, 1990) as they read on the day before these rules come into force.

Application of rules

(2) These rules apply to all appeals, whether commenced before or after these rules come into force, except in respect of steps already taken under the preceding rules.

Power of judge

(3) Despite the repeal of the preceding rules and subrule (2), a judge may make an order that an appeal, or a step in the appeal, be conducted under these rules or the preceding rules or make any order that is considered just in order to secure the fair and expeditious conduct of the appeal.

REVOCATION AND COMMENCEMENT

17. (1) Regulation 198 of the Revised Regulations of Ontario, 1990 and Ontario Regulation 504/93 are revoked.

(2) This Regulation comes into force on December 12, 1994.

Rules of the Ontario Court (Provincial Division) in Provincial Offences Proceedings — R.R.O. 1990, Reg. 200 [am. O. Reg. 505/93; O. Reg. 498/94; O. Reg. 567/00]

1. In these rules, "Act" means the *Provincial Offences Act*.

2. (1) These rules apply to proceedings under the Act and a word or term in the Act has the same meaning in these rules as it has in the Act.

(2) In these rules, any reference to electronic process is a reference to the electronic process in force at the time of the coming into force of the *Provincial Offences Statute Law Amendment Act, 1993.*

O. Reg. 498/94, s. 1.

3. These rules shall be construed liberally so as to obtain as expeditious a conclusion of every proceeding as is consistent with a just determination of the proceeding.

4. The following apply to the calculation of a period of time prescribed by the Act, section 205.7 or 205.19 of the *Highway Traffic Act*, these rules or an order of a court:

1. The time shall be calculated by excluding the first day and including the last day of the period.

2. Where a period of less than six days is prescribed, a Saturday or holiday shall not be reckoned.

3. Where the last day of the period of time falls on a Saturday or a holiday, the day next following that is not a Saturday or a holiday shall be deemed to be the last day of the period.

4. Where the days are expressed to be clear days or where the term "at least" is added, the time shall be calculated by excluding both the first day and the last day of the period.

O. Reg. 498/94, s. 2; O. Reg. 567/00, s. 1.

5. A notice or document given or delivered by mail shall, unless the contrary is shown, be deemed to be given or delivered on the seventh day following the day on which it was mailed.

6. For the purpose of proceedings under Part I or II of the Act, the amount of fine set by the court for an offence is such amount as may be set by the Chief Judge of the Ontario Court (Provincial Division).

7. (1) An application provided for by the Act or these rules shall be commenced by notice of application.

(2) A motion provided for by the Act or these rules shall be commenced by notice of motion.

(3) There shall be at least three days between the giving of notice of application or notice of motion and the day for hearing the application or motion.

(4) An applicant or moving party shall file notice of application or notice of motion at least two days before the day for hearing the application or motion.

(5) Evidence on an application or motion may be given,

(*a*) by affidavit;

(*b*) with the permission of the court, orally; or

(*c*) in the form of a transcript of the examination of a witness.

(6) Upon the hearing of an application or motion and whether or not other evidence is given on the application or motion, the justice may receive and base his or her decision upon information the justice considers credible or trustworthy in the circumstances.

(7) An application or motion may be heard without notice,

(*a*) on consent; or

(*b*) where, having regard to the subject-matter or the circumstances of the application or motion, it would not be unjust to hear the application or motion without notice.

(8) Subrules (2) to (5) do not apply in respect of a motion under section 66 of the Act.

8. (1) Where a certificate of parking infraction has been issued in respect of a parking infraction under a municipal by-law without a reference to the number of the by-law that creates the offence, the number of the by-law shall be affixed or appended to the court filing document when the certificate is filed in the office of the court.

(2) Where a certificate of parking infraction has been issued alleging a parking infraction against the defendant as owner of a vehicle, evidence of the ownership of the vehicle shall be affixed or appended to the court filing document when the certificate is filed in the office of the court.

(3) A certificate of parking infraction shall be affixed or appended to the court filing document when the certificate is filed in the office of the court.

(4) Where a defendant delivers a parking infraction notice or notice of impending conviction in respect of an alleged parking infraction under a municipal by-law and gives notice of intention to appear in court for the purpose of entering a plea and having a trial of the matter, the parking infraction notice or notice of impending conviction shall be affixed or appended to the court filing document when the certificate of parking infraction is filed in the office of the court.

(5) Where a defendant files a notice of intention to appear under subsection 17.1(3) or 18.1.1(3) of the Act, the notice of intention to appear shall be affixed or appended to the court filing document when the certificate of parking infraction is filed in the office of the court.

(6) In this rule and subrule 22(2), ''court filing document'' means a document approved by the clerk of the court.

O. Reg. 498/94, s. 3.

9. (1) A provincial offences officer who files a certificate of offence in the office of the court shall file with the certificate of offence a certificate control list, in the form that shall be supplied by the clerk of the court, with the certificate recorded on the list.

(2) A provincial offences officer who files a certificate of parking infraction in the office of the court shall file with it a certificate control list in the form approved by the clerk of the court, with the certificate recorded on the list.

(3) A single certificate control list may be filed with as many certificates of offence as can be accounted for on the certificate control list.

(4) A single certificate control list may be filed with as many certificates of parking infractions as can be accounted for on the certificate control list.

(5) The clerk of the court shall endorse on the certificate control list a receipt for the certificates of offence or certificates of parking infraction filed with the certificate control list.

(6) The clerk of the court shall, on request, give a copy of the receipt to the provincial offences officer who filed the certificate control list.

(7) Subrules (1) to (6) do not apply if a certificate of offence or a certificate of parking infraction is filed in an electronic format.

O. Reg. 498/94, s. 4.

10. A facsimile signature of the person designated by the regulations is sufficient authentication of the certificate requesting a conviction under subsection 18.2(1.1) of the Act.

O. Reg. 505/93, s. 1; O. Reg. 498/94, s. 5.

11. (1) The clerk of the court shall not accept for filing a certificate of offence more than seven days after the day on which the offence notice or summons was served unless the time is extended by the court.

(2) No certificate of offence, certificate of parking infraction or certificate requesting a conviction shall be accepted for filing by direct electronic transmission after the last day prescribed for its filing, unless the time is extended by the court.

O. Reg. 498/94, s. 6.

12. (1) The clerk of the court shall endorse the date of filing in every certificate of offence, certificate of parking infraction or certificate requesting conviction filed in the office of the court, except any such certificate filed in an electronic format.

(2) The clerk of the court shall ensure that the date of filing is indicated on any document filed in an electronic format.

(3) A certificate of offence, certificate of parking infraction or certificate requesting a conviction filed by direct electronic transmission shall be deemed to be filed the day on which the transmission concludes, unless the contrary is shown.

O. Reg. 505/93, s. 2; O. Reg. 498/94, s. 7.

12.1 [Revoked O. Reg. 498/94, s. 8.]

13. (1) On the delivery of an offence notice under section 5 of the Act, a parking infraction notice under subsection 17(1) of the Act or a notice of impending conviction under subsection 18.1(1) of the Act, giving notice of intention to appear in court for the purpose of entering a plea and having a trial of the matter, the clerk of the court shall, where proceedings have been commenced, set a day and time for trial.

(1.1) On the filing of a notice of intention to appear under section 5.1 of the Act, the clerk of the court shall, where proceedings have been commenced, set a day and time for trial.

(2) Where a parking infraction notice issued in respect of an alleged parking infraction under a municipal by-law is received under subsection 17(1) of the Act or a notice of impending conviction for such an infraction is received under subsection 18.1.1(1) of the Act, the clerk of the court shall give notice of the time and place of trial to the defendant and the prosecutor as soon as practicable after the prosecutor has filed the certificate of parking infraction in the office of the court, together with the corresponding parking infraction notice or notice of impending conviction.

(2.1) Where a notice of intention to appear is filed under subsection 17.1(3) or 18.1.1(3) of the Act, the clerk of the court shall give notice of the time and place of trial to the defendant and prosecutor as soon as practicable after the prosecutor has filed the certificate of parking infraction in the office of the court together with the notice of intention to appear.

(3) The clerk of the court shall give notice of the trial to the defendant and prosecutor at least seven days before the day set for trial.

(4) Where a parking infraction is alleged against the defendant as owner of a vehicle, notice of the trial shall be given to the person identified as the holder of the permit, as defined in section 6 of the *Highway Traffic Act*, in the evidence of the ownership of the vehicle affixed or appended to the certificate of parking infraction.

(5) A certificate as to the giving of a notice of trial endorsed on the notice of trial by the clerk of the court shall be received in evidence and, in the absence of evidence to the contrary, is proof of the giving of the notice stated in the certificate.

(6) Where a defendant files a notice of intention to appear under section 5.1 of the Act and it appears that the certificate of offence has not been filed, the clerk of the court shall,

(*a*) provide the defendant with a receipt for the notice; and

(*b*) as soon as practicable after the filing of the certificate of offence, set a day and time for trial and issue the notice of trial.

O. Reg. 505/93, s. 4; O. Reg. 498/94, s. 9.

14. (1) A defendant who attends at the time and place specified in an offence notice for the purpose of taking steps under subsection 7(1) of the Act shall give the offence notice to the office of the court specified in the notice.

(2) The court shall give to a defendant a receipt for an offence notice delivered to the court in accordance with subrule (1).

15. (1) The following matters shall be dealt with only in court:

1. Quashing a proceeding, except under section 9, 18.3 or 18.5 of the Act or under section 205.7 or 205.19 of the *Highway Traffic Act*.

2. Amending an information, a certificate of offence or a certificate of parking infraction.

(2) A justice may dispose of an application under section 18.3 of the Act on the basis of the parking infraction notice and the form of application presented by the applicant.

(3) A justice may dispose of an application under section 18.5 of the Act on the basis of the form of application presented by the applicant, together with any oral submission the applicant wishes to make or the justice wishes to hear.

(4) A justice may dispose of an application under section 19 of the Act on the basis of the notice of fine and due date and the affidavit of the applicant.

O. Reg. 505/93, s. 5; O. Reg. 498/94, s. 10; O. Reg. 567/00, s. 2.

16. A justice shall not quash a proceeding or amend a certificate of offence in respect of a defendant who is appearing before the justice for the purposes of section 7 of the Act.

761

17. Where a defendant appears before a justice under section 7 of the Act and it appears that the certificate of offence has not been filed in the office of the court, the justice may receive the plea of guilty and submissions of the defendant and specify the amount of fine the justice will impose and the time the justice will allow for payment when the certificate of offence is filed and a conviction is entered.

18. Where a defendant appears before a justice under section 7 of the Act and the justice is of the opinion that the certificate of offence is so defective on its face so that it cannot be cured under section 33, 34, 35 or 36 of the Act, the justice shall refuse to accept the plea, shall inform the defendant of the reason for the refusal and shall inform the defendant of the provisions of section 5 or 5.1 of the Act as applicable. O. Reg. 498/94, s. 11.

19. Money paid to the office of the court by a defendant who was served with an offence notice shall be refunded to the defendant if the certificate of offence is not filed in the office of the court named therein within seven days after the day on which the offence notice was served or within such extension of time as may be granted by the court.

20. Where notice is given to the clerk by the prosecutor that the prosecutor does not intend to file a certificate requesting conviction or a certificate of parking infraction that has been issued in respect of a parking infraction under an Act of the Legislature or under a regulation made under the authority of an Act, the prosecutor shall furnish the clerk with the name and address of the person to whom the parking infraction notice was issued and money paid to the office of the court in respect of the alleged parking infraction shall be refunded to that person.

O. Reg. 505/93, s. 6.

21. Every justice shall keep a daily docket, electronically or in the form supplied by the clerk of the court, and shall record the disposition of every proceeding or matter under Part I or II of the Act dealt with by the justice.

O. Reg. 498/94, s. 12.

22. (1) A justice acting under section 7 of the Act who imposes a fine that is less than the set fine or less than the minimum fine prescribed for the offence by the provision that creates the penalty shall endorse on the certificate of offence or the information, as the case may be, the decision and the reasons for the decision.

(1.1) A justice who quashes a proceeding under section 9 or 9.1 of the Act or under section 205.7, 205.11 or 205.19 of the *Highway Traffic Act* shall endorse on the certificate of offence or the information, as the case may be, the decision and the reasons for the decision.

(2) A justice who quashes a proceeding under section 18.4 of the Act shall endorse on the court filing document to which the certificate of parking infraction is affixed or appended the decision and the reasons for the decision.

(2.1) A justice who strikes out a conviction under section 18.3 or 18.5 of the Act shall endorse on the form of application the decision and the reasons for the decision.

(3) In addition to recording the decision on a daily docket, a justice referred to in subrule (1) or (1.1) shall complete a separate report, in the form that shall be supplied by the clerk of the court, of the decision and the reasons for the decision.

(4) A completed report mentioned in subrule (3) forms part of and shall be kept with the records of the court maintained by the clerk of the court.

O. Reg. 505/93, s. 7; O. Reg. 498/94, s. 13; O. Reg. 567/00, s. 3.

22.1 A justice acting under section 9 of the Act or under section 205.7 of the *Highway Traffic Act* may examine by electronic means a certificate of offence that has been filed in an electronic format and may indicate his or her disposition of the proceeding by electronic means. O. Reg. 498/94, s. 14.

23. Upon payment of a fine, the administrative officer of the entity receiving the fine shall, upon request, issue to the defendant a receipt for the payment.

O. Reg. 505/93, s. 8.

24. [Revoked O. Reg. 498/94, s. 15.]

25. A justice who issues a warrant of committal under subsection 69(14) of the Act shall enter the reasons for the warrant in the records of the court.

O. Reg. 498/94, s. 16.

26. Where a person is sentenced to a term of imprisonment and a warrant of committal is issued for custody of the person to commence, under subsection 63(2) of the Act, on a day that is later than the day of sentencing, the clerk of the court, as soon as practicable after the warrant is issued,

(*a*) shall cause to be given or delivered to the person a notice stating the warrant has been issued and specifying the place where and the time within which the person is to surrender into custody; and

(*b*) shall deliver the warrant to the individual who is to accept the custody of the person.

27. (1) The following oath is prescribed for the purpose of subsection 84(1) of the Act:

I, ... do swear (or solemnly affirm) that I am capable of translating and will translate to the best of my skill and ability from

.... to ....

(name of language)   **(name of language)**

.... to ....

(name of language)   **(name of language)**

in this proceeding.

SO HELP ME GOD. (Omit this line in an affirmation).

(2) The following oath is prescribed for the purpose of subsection 84(2) of the Act:

I, ...

do swear (or solemnly affirm) that I am capable of translating and will translate to the best of my skill and ability

from .... to ....

(name of language)   **(name of language)**

.... to ....

(name of language)   **(name of language)**

in proceedings under the *Provincial Offences Act.*

SO HELP ME GOD. (Omit this line in an affirmation).

28. (1) The clerk of the court who receives notice from the clerk of an appeal court that a notice of appeal has been filed shall transmit the order appealed from and transmit or transfer custody of all other material referred to in section 133 of the Act to the clerk of the appeal court within ten days after receiving the notice, to the extent that the clerk of the court receiving notice has the order or the other material in his or her possession.

(1.1) The clerk of the court receiving notice shall direct that any electronic document that has not been previously printed for the purpose of disposing of the charge and that is required as part of an appeal record be printed so as to create an original record, unless the appeal court requests that the document be transmitted to it in an electronic format.

(2) In an appeal from an order made under Part II, if the clerk of the court receiving notice does not have the order or the other material in his or her possession, the clerk may request and the municipality shall provide to the clerk the certificate of parking infraction and proof of ownership of the motor vehicle relating to the prosecution of the matter giving rise to the appeal.

O. Reg. 505/93, s. 9; O. Reg. 498/94, s. 17.

29. Where a transcript of evidence at trial, including reasons for judgment or sentence, is requested from the clerk of the court for the purpose of an appeal, the clerk, (*a*) shall complete and deliver to the person making the request a certificate of preparation of transcript in Form 2 of Regulation 196 of Revised Regulations of Ontario, 1990;

(*b*) shall ensure that the transcript is prepared with reasonable diligence;

(*c*) shall obtain and attach to the transcript a certificate by the person who prepared the transcript that it is an accurate transcription of the evidence and reasons recorded at trial; and

(*d*) shall notify,

(i) the appellant,

(ii) the clerk of the court in which the appeal is taken, and

(iii) if the Crown Attorney is not the appellant or respondent, the Crown Attorney, when the transcript has been completed.

30. The clerk of the court who receives notice of the decision of an appeal court on an appeal from a decision of the court shall give the notice and any written reasons or endorsement included with the notice to the justice whose decision was appealed from.

31. (1) Where, upon an appeal, the appeal court has directed a new trial, upon motion by the prosecutor without notice a justice shall issue a summons to the defendant.

(2) Where a justice issues a summons under subrule (1), the clerk of the court shall, as soon as is practicable, give notice to the prosecutor of the time and place of the trial.

(3) Where the appeal court has directed a new trial and sets a date for the trial with the consent of the parties to the appeal, the defendant shall be deemed to have received notice of trial, and subrules (1) and (2) do not apply.

O. Reg. 498/94, s. 18.

32. (1) An affidavit of service of an offence notice or summons shall be in Form 101.

(2) An affidavit in support of a request under section 11 or 19 of the Act or section 205.13 or 205.23 of the *Highway Traffic Act* shall be in Form 102.

(3) A certificate under section 11 of the Act or section 205.13 or 205.23 of the *Highway Traffic Act* shall be in Form 103.

(4) A summons under section 22 of the Act shall be in Form 104.

(5) An information under section 23 of the Act shall be in Form 105.

(6) A summons under section 24 of the Act shall be in Form 106.

(7) A warrant for arrest under section 24 of the Act shall be in Form 107.

(8) A notice of cancellation of summons under section 24 of the Act shall be in Form 108.

(9) A summons under section 39 of the Act shall be in Form 109.

(10) A warrant under subsection 40(1) of the Act shall be in Form 110.

(11) A warrant under subsection 40(2) of the Act shall be in Form 111.

(12) A recognizance by witness under section 40 of the Act shall be in Form 112.

(13) A warrant under subsection 40(10) of the Act shall be in Form 113.

(14) An order under subsection 40(6) of the Act shall be in Form 114.

(15) An order under section 41 of the Act shall be in Form 115.

(16) A certificate under section 42 of the Act shall be in Form 116.

(17) An order to attend for examination under section 44 of the Act shall be in Form 117.

(18) A warrant to take a defendant into custody under section 44 of the Act shall be in Form 118.

(19) A certificate of execution of a warrant issued under subsection 44(6) of the Act shall be in Form 119.

(20) A summons under section 51 of the Act shall be in Form 120.

(21) An order of dismissal under section 53 of the Act shall be in Form 121.

(22) A summons to a defendant under section 54 of the Act shall be in Form 122.

(23) A warrant under section 54 of the Act shall be in Form 123.

(24) A warrant under subsection 63(2) of the Act shall be in Form 124.

(25) A motion under subsection 66(6) of the Act shall be in Form 125.

(26) An order under subsection 66(6) of the Act extending time for payment of a fine shall be in Form 126.

(27) A certificate of default under section 68 of the Act shall be in Form 127.

(28) [Revoked O. Reg. 498/94, s. 19.]

(29) [Revoked O. Reg. 498/94, s. 19.]

(30) [Revoked O. Reg. 498/94, s. 19.]

(31) An undertaking by a defendant to appear shall be in Form 131.

(32) A probation order under section 72 of the Act shall be in Form 132.

(33) A summons to a defendant where a new trial is ordered by an appeal court shall be in Form 133.

(34) A recognizance under subsection 149(2) of the Act shall be in Form 134.

(35) A recognizance under section 150 of the Act shall be in Form 135.

(36) An order for detention of a defendant under section 150 of the Act shall be in Form 136.

(37) A warrant under section 155 of the Act for the arrest of a defendant shall be in Form 137.

(38) A certificate of arrest under section 155 of the Act shall be in Form 138.

(39) A certificate under subsection 157(1) of the Act as to failure to comply with a condition of a recognizance shall be in Form 139.

(40) An information to obtain a search warrant under section 158 of the Act shall be in Form 140.

(41) A search warrant under section 158 of the Act shall be in Form 141.

(42) A statement under section 161 of the Act shall be in Form 142.

(43) A warrant remanding,
  (a) a witness under subsection 40(6) of the Act; or
  (b) a defendant under subsection 150(4) of the Act, shall be in Form 143.

(44) An order for the release of a defendant under subsection 150(2) of the Act shall be in Form 144.

(45) An order for the release of a person in custody under subsection 40(9) of the Act shall be in Form 145.

(46) A warrant of committal the form of which is not otherwise specified in these rules shall be in Form 146.

(47) An order the form of which is not otherwise specified in these rules shall be in Form 147.

(48) A recognizance under subsection 149(3) of the Act shall be in Form 148.

(49) [Revoked O. Reg. 498/94, s. 19.]

(50) An application under section 18.3 of the Act shall be in Form 150.

(51) An application under section 18.5 of the Act shall be in Form 151.

(52) An application under subsection 19(2) of the Act shall be in Form 152.

(53) An order under subsection 69(21) of the Act shall be in Form 153.
        O. Reg. 505/93, s. 10; O. Reg. 498/94, s. 19; O. Reg. 567/00, s. 4.

Appendix C

Forms

Notice of Motion

NOTICE OF MOTION
AVIS DE MOTION

BETWEEN .... Prosecutor
ENTRE *Poursuivant*

and
et

.... Defendant
Défendeur

TAKE NOTICE that an application will be made by the ....
SACHEZ QU'UNE requête sera déposée par (Prosecutor/Defendant) / *(poursuivant/défendeur)*

on ...., yr ...., before the Ontario Court of Justice
le *an* *devant la Cour de justice de l'Ontario*

at ....
à

in the following matter:
en ce qui concerne l'affaire suivant

....

....

for an Order as follows:
pour une ordonnance comme suit :

....

....

....

....

And further take notice that in support of this application will be read the affidavit of ....
Sachez aussi qu'à l'appui de cette requête sera lu l'affidavit de

...., and such other and further evidence as may be required.
ainsi que d'autres preuves qui s'avéreront nécessaires.

Dated this .... day of ...., yr ....
Fait le *jour de* *an*

at ....
à

Signed _____
Signature

Address ....
Adresse

TO: / Á :
Prosecutor (or Defendant) and Clerk of the Court
Poursuivant (ou Défendeur) et au greffier de la Cour

DISTRIBUTION:

☐   Defendant/Prosecutor
défendeur/poursuivant

☐   Counsel for Defendant/Prosecutor
avocat du défendeur/poursuivant

☐   Agent for Defendant/Prosecutor
mandataire du défendeur/poursuivant

FOR INFORMATION ON ACCESS
TO ONTARIO COURTS
FOR PERSONS WITH DISABILITIES, CALL
1-800-387-4456
TORONTO AREA 416-326-0111

POUR PLUS DE RENSEIGNEMENTS SUR L'ACCÈS
DES PERSONNES HANDICAPÉES
AUX TRIBUNAUX DE L'ONTARIO, COMPOSEZ LE
1-800-387-4456
RÉGION DE TORONTO 416-326-0111

PQA 0007 CSD (rev 11/03)

General Form for Affidavit

Ministry of
the Attorney
General

Ministère du
Procureur
général

GENERAL FORM FOR AFFIDAVIT
FORMULE GÉNÉRALE D'AFFIDAVIT

I,
_____
Je / soussigné(e),

of
_____
de

_____

make oath and say as follows:
déclare sous serment que. _____

_____

_____

_____

_____

_____

_____

_____

_____

_____

_____

_____

_____

_____

_____

_____

_____

_____

_____

_____

_____

_____

_____

_____
Signature

Sworn by the said _____
Déclaré sous serment par

before me _____
devant moi

at _____
dans le/la

on the _____ day of _____ yr. 20 ___
le   *jour de*   *an*

_____
(a commissioner, etc. / commissaire, etc.)

F POA 0006 CSD nf (rev. 06/14)

Notice of Intention to Appear (Form 8)

NOTICE OF INTENTION TO APPEAR
AVIS D'INTENTION DE COMPARAÎTRE

ONTARIO COURT OF JUSTICE
COUR DE JUSTICE DE L'ONTARIO
PROVINCE OF ONTARIO
PROVINCE DE L'ONTARIO

Form / *Formulaire* 8
Provincial Offences Act
Loi sur les infractions provinciales

TAKE NOTICE THAT I,
VEUILLEZ PRENDRE AVIS QUE JE SOUSSIGNÉ(E),

(defendant s name / *nom du défendeur/de la défenderesse*)

(current address / *adresse actuelle*)　　　　(street / *rue*)　　　　(apt. / *app.*)

(municipality / *municipalité*)　　　　(province)　　　　(postal code / *code postal*)

(offence number / *numéro de l'infraction*)　　　　(offence date / *date de l'infraction*)

wish to give notice of my intention to appear in court to enter a plea of not guilty at the time and place set for the trial respecting the charge set out in the Offence Notice or Parking Infraction Notice.
désire donner avis de mon intention de comparaître devant le tribunal pour inscrire un plaidoyer de non-culpabilité à l'heure et au lieu prévus pour le procès en réponse à l'accusation énoncée dans l'avis d'infraction ou l'avis d'infraction de stationnement.

☐ I intend to appear in court to enter a plea at the time and place set for the trial and I wish that it be held in the English language.

☐ *J'ai l'intention de comparaître devant le tribunal pour inscrire un plaidoyer à l'heure et au lieu prévus pour le procès et je désire que le procès se déroule en français.*

I request a _____ language interpreter for the trial.
(leave blank if inapplicable)

Je demande l'aide d'un interprète en langue _____ *pour le procès.*
(à remplir s'il y a lieu)

Note: If you **fail** to notify the court office of **address changes** you may not receive important notices e.g., your Notice of Trial. You may be convicted in your absence if you do not attend the trial.

Remarque : *Si vous **omettez de prévenir** le greffe du tribunal de **tout changement d'adresse**, vous pourriez ne pas recevoir d'importants avis (p. ex., votre avis de procès). Vous pourriez être déclaré(e) coupable en votre absence si vous n'assistez pas au procès.*

Signature of defendant /
Signature du défendeur/de la défenderesse　　　　(date)　　　　(telephone number / *numéro de téléphone*)

POA 0813 (March 15, 2014 / 15 mars 2014) CSD

Disclosure Request Form

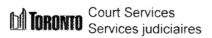

Court Services
Services judiciaires

Disclosure Request
Demande de divulgation

Notice to Counsel / Agent / Defendant
Please be advised that the following information (unless otherwise indicated) is required in full in order to process this request. If you do not have complete and accurate information, it can be obtained from the Courts Administration office. Please ensure this form is delivered to the appropriate court location. Thank you for your co-operation.

Avis au conseiller / avocat / agent / défendeur
Afin de traiter la demande, SVP noter que l'information demandée est requise au complet. Si vous n'avez pas toutes informations exactes et complètes, vous pouvez contacter le bureau administratif du Service de la Cour. Assurez-vous que ce formulaire soit livré à l'emplacement du tribunal approprié. Merci de votre collaboration.

Date:

Defendant **LAST** Name / **Nom** du défendeur:

Defendant FIRST Name / Prénom du défendeur: Initial:
Offences / Infraction(s):

Offence / Ticket / P.O.T. No. /No. de l'infraction / billet:

Offence Date / Date de l'infraction:

Appearance Date / Date de la comparution:

Courtroom / Salle de tribunal:

Time / Heure: ☐ A.M.   ☐ P.M.

Officer in Charge / Agent en charge: Name / Nom:

                                         Number / Numéro:

                                         Division

Requested by / Demandé par:
                               (defendant/défendeur / counsel/conseiller / lawyer/avocat / agent)

Telephone / No. de téléphone:

OFFICE USE ONLY / USAGE INTERNE SEULEMENT

Notified by / Notifié par:

Telephone / No. de téléphone:

Disclosure received / La divulgation reçu: Year/Année _____ Month/Mois _____ Day/Jour _____

Signed / Signature: _____
                   (defendant/défendeur / counsel/conseiller / lawyer/avocat / agent)

Remarks / Remarques:

T DIS REN (rev. (14/Oct)

Provincial Offences Act Part 1 Charges

Prosecution Office, Legal Services
950 Burnhamthorpe Road West, Mississauga L5C 3B4
Phone: 905-615-3200, Ext. 4088
Fax: 905-615-4504

PROVINCIAL OFFENCE ACT PART 1 CHARGES
DISCLOSURE REQUEST

Please complete the information required below upon receiving a trial date and return this form to the Prosecution Office, 950 Burnhamthorpe Rd.West, Mississauga ON L5C 3B4 or fax to 905-615-4504. Once disclosure becomes available it will be forwarded to you by fax transmission or you will be contacted regarding pick-up of this material. Your co-operation and assistance is appreciated.

PLEASE NOTE: REPLACEMENT OF ANY DISCLOSURE MATERIAL PREVIOUSLY PROVIDED WILL BE SUBJECT TO A FEE IN ACCORDANCE WITH THE CITY OF MISSISSAUGA GENERAL FEES AND CHARGES BY-LAW NO. 0539-2004.

Prosecution Office Phone: 905-615-3200 Ext. 4088   Fax: 905-615-4504

DEFENDANT:

CHARGES:

WAS A COLLISION INVOLVED: YES   NO

OFFENCE NO: OFFENCE DATE:

TRIAL DATE: TIME: COURT RM:

OFFICERS BADGE NO: PEEL   OPP

DATE REQUESTED: REQUESTED BY:

ADDRESS

PHONE NO: FAX NO

Picked Up:_____

REQUEST FOR DISCLOSURE

To obtain disclosure please complete the information below and deliver the request by email to poadisclosure@niagararegion.ca or by fax to: 905-734-7816, or in person at the Provincial Offence Court, 3 Cross Street, Welland - Attention: Prosecution Coordinator.

PLEASE ALLOW 8 – 10 WEEKS FOR DELIVERY

DEFENDANT INFORMATION

Name:		
Address:		
Phone # Home:	Work:	Cell:
Email Address:		

CHARGE INFORMATION

Ticket #:	Date of Offence:
Charge:	Police/Agency: ☐ OPP ☐ Niagara Regional Police ☐ Other:
Trial Date:	Time:

DELIVERY REQUEST

☐ Email my disclosure to the email address noted above; or

☐ Fax my disclosure to: _____ ; or

☐ Call me to arrange pick up at 3 Cross Street, Welland

Date: _____	Signature: _____

Probation Order (s. 72)

PROBATION ORDER
ORDONNANCE DE PROBATION
Under Section 72 of the *Provincial Offences Act*
Aux termes de l'article 72 de la Loi sur les infractions provinciales

ONTARIO COURT OF JUSTICE
COUR DE JUSTICE DE L'ONTARIO
PROVINCE OF ONTARIO
PROVINCE DE L'ONTARIO

Form / Formule 132
Courts of Justice Act
Loi sur les tribunaux judiciaires
R.R.O. / R.R.O. 1990
O. Reg. / Règl. de l'Ont. 200

Whereas _____   hereinafter called the Defendant
Attendu que   *ci-après appelé le défendeur*

was convicted of the offence of / *a été reconnu coupable d'avoir commis l'infraction suivant*

contrary to   section
par dérogation à   *article*

by the Ontario Court of Justice at   **5 Ray Lawson Boulevard**
devant la Cour de justice de l'Ontario au(à la)

on the _____ day of _____ , yr. _____   in a proceeding commenced by information.
le   *jour de*   *an*   *à la suite d'une poursuite intentée par voie de dénonciation.*

And whereas on the _____ day of _____ , yr. _____ , the court
Et attendu que   *jour de*   *an*   *le tribunal*
(check applicable box / *cocher ce qui s'applique ici*)

☐ suspended the passing of sentence on the Defendant and directed the Defendant to comply with the conditions set out below.
   a suspendu le prononcé de la peine imposée au défendeur et ordonné que celui-ci conforme aux conditions énumérées ci-dessous.

☐ in addition to   ☐ fining the Defendant
   en plus de   *lui imposer une amende*
                         ☐ sentencing the Defendant to imprisonment
                            le condamner à une peine d'emprisonnement
   directed that the Defendant comply with the conditions set out below.
   a ordonné que celui-ci conforme aux conditions énumérées ci-dessous.

☐ imposed upon the Defendant a sentence of imprisonment that did not exceed ninety days, ordered that the sentence be
   served intermittently and directed that the Defendant comply with the conditions set out below at all times when the
   Defendant is not in confinement under that sentence.
   *a imposée au défendeur une peine d'emprisonnement d'une durée que n'excède pas quatre-vingt-dix jours, a ordonné que
   la peine soit purgée de façon intermittente et a ordonné que le défendeur se conforme aux conditions ci-dessous pendant
   tout le temps qu'il n'est pas détenu aux termes de la condamnation prononcée contre lui.*

Therefore, it is ordered that for the period of _____   commencing
À ces causes, ordre est donné que pour la période de   *qui commence*
(check applicable box / *cocher ce que s'applique ici*)

☐ from the date of this order,
   à compter de la date de cette ordonnance,

☐ from the date of the Defendant's release from custody,
   à compter de la date à laquelle le défendeur a été remis en liberté,

the Defendant shall comply with the following conditions:
le défendeur doit se conformer aux conditions suivantes :

1. The Defendant shall not commit the same offence or any related or similar offence, or any offence under a statute of Canada
   or Ontario or any other province of Canada that is punishable by imprisonment.
   *Le défendeur ne doit pas commettre la même infraction, toute infraction connexe ou semblable ou toute infraction qui, aux
   termes d'une loi du Canada, de l'Ontario ou de toute autre province du Canada, est punissable d'une peine d'emprisonnement.*

2. The Defendant shall appear before the court as and when required.
   Le défendeur doit comparaître devant le tribunal de la façon prescrite et au moment où il est enjoint de le faire.

POA 0132 CSD (rev 11/03) (posted / *affichée* 03/01/05)

3   The Defendant shall notify the court of any change in the Defendant's address.
    Le défendeur doit aviser le tribunal de tout changement d'adresse.

And, in addition, the Defendant / *Et le défendeur doit de plus*
(set out and number additional conditions separately / *énoncer et numéroter les conditions supplémentaires séparément*)

Ordered at   **Brampton, Ontario**
Ordonnance rendue à

th s	day of	, yr.	
ce	*jour de*	*an*	Judge or Justice of the Peace in and for the Province of Ontario / *Juge ou juge de paix et pour la province de l'Ontario*

I certify that the Defendant was given a copy of this probation order on the _____ day of _____ , yr.
Je certifie qu'une copie de cette ordonnance de probation a été remise au défendeur le _____ *jour de* _____ *an*

☐ by personal service
   par voie de signification personnelle

☐ by sending it to the Defendant by mail to
   par courrier à

the Defendant's last known address appearing on the records of the court.
la dernière adresse du défendeur qui est donnée dans les archives du tribunal.

_____
Clerk / *Greffier*

NOTE: Sections 73 and 75 of the *Provincial Offences Act* is as follows:

73   (1)   When order comes into force – A probation order comes into force.
           (a) on the date on which the order is made; or
           (b) where the defendant is sentenced to imprisonment other than a sentence to be served intermittently, upon the expiration of that sentence

     (2)   Continuation in force – Subject to section 75, where a defendant who is bound by a probation order is convicted of an offence or is imprisoned in default of payment of a fine, the order continues in force except in so far as the sentence or imprisonment renders it impossible for the defendant to comply for the time being with the order.

75   Breach of probation order – Where a defendant who is bound by a probation order is convicted of an offence constituting a breach of condition of the order and,

           (a) the time within which the defendant may appeal or make a motion for leave to appeal against that conviction has expired and defendant has not taken an appeal or made a motion for leave to appeal;
           (b) the defendant has taken an appeal or made a motion for leave to appeal against the conviction and the appeal or motion for leave has been dismissed or abandoned, or
           (c) the defendant has given written notice to the court that convicted him/her that the defendant elects not to appeal,

or where the defendant otherwise wilfully fails or refuses to comply with the order, the defendant is guilty of an offence and upon conviction the court may,

           (d) impose a fine of not more than $1,000 or imprisonment for a term of not more than thirty days, or both, and in lieu of or in addition to the penalty, continue the probation order with such changes or additions and for such extended term, not exceeding an additional year, as the court considers reasonable; or

           (e) where the justice presiding is the justice who made the original order, in lieu or imposing the penalty under clause (d), revoke the probation order and impose the sentence the passing of which was suspended upon the making of the probation order

REMARQUE : *Les articles 73 et 75 Loi sur les infractions provinciales se lisent comme suit :*

73   1)   *Une ordonnance de probation entre en vigueur*
           (a) à la date de son émission; ou
           (b) à l'expiration de la peine lorsque le défendeur est condamné à purger la peine d'emprisonnement autrement que d'une façon intermittente.

     2)   *Sous réserve de l'article 75, lorsqu'un défendeur sous le coup d'une ordonnance de probation, est reconnu coupable d'une infraction ou est emprisonné pour défaut de paiement d'une amende, l'ordonnance demeure en vigueur, sauf dans la mesure ou la peine ou l'emprisonnement l'empêchent de se conformer aux dispositions de l'ordonnance.*

75   *Lorsqu'un défendeur qui est sous le coup d'une ordonnance de probation est reconnu coupable d'une infraction qui constitue une violation de conditions de l'ordonnance et*

           (a) que le délai durant lequel il peut interjeter appel de cette condamnation ou demander la permission de la porter en appel est expiré et qu'il n'a pas interjeté appel ou demandé la permission d'en appeler;
           (b) qu'il a interjeté appel de cette condamnation ou qu'il a demandé la permission de la porter en appel et que l'appel ou la permission d'en appeler a été rejeté ou qu'il a abandonné son recours; ou
           (c) qu'il a donné un avis écrit au tribunal qui l'a reconnu coupable, de son choix de ne pas interjeter appel,

           ou, lorsque le défendeur, d'une autre façon fait sciemment défaut ou refuse de se conformer à l'ordonnance, il est coupable d'une infraction, et le tribunal peut, après avoir reconnu sa culpabilité:

           (d) imposer une amende d'au plus 1 000 dollars ou un emprisonnement pour une période d'au plus trente jours ou les deux à la fois et, au lieu de la peine ou en plus de celle-ci, maintenir en vigueur l'ordonnance de probation pour une période n'excédant pas une année supplémentaire, en lui apportant les modifications ou les additions que le tribunal estime raisonnable. ou

           (e) lorsque le juge qui préside le tribunal est celui qui a émis l'ordonnance originale, annuler l'ordonnance de probation et imposer la peine qui a été suspendue lors de l'émission de l'ordonnance de probation, au lieu d'imposer la peine prévue aux termes de l'alinéa d)

POA 0132 CSD (rev. 11/03) (posted / *affichée* 03/01/05)

Motion for Extension of Time to Pay Fine (subs. 66(6))

MOTION FOR EXTENSION OF TIME TO PAY FINE
REQUÊTE PRÉSENTÉE EN VUE D'OBTENIR UNE PROROGATION DU DÉLAI POUR
ACQUITTER LE PAIEMENT D'UNE AMENDE

ONTARIO COURT OF JUSTICE
COUR DE JUSTICE DE L'ONTARIO
PROVINCE OF ONTARIO
PROVINCE DE L'ONTARIO

Under Subsection 66(6) of the *Provincial Offences Act*
Aux termes du paragraphe 66(6) de la Loi sure les infractions provinciales

Form / Formule 125
Courts of Justice Act
Loi sur les tribunaux judiciaires
R.R.O. / R.R.O. 1990
O. Reg. / Règl. de l'Ont. 200

PLEASE PRINT / LETTRES MOULÉES S.V.P.

1. I, _____
Je soussigné(e)

of _____ (occupation / profession)
de

was convicted in Ontario Court of Justice
ai été déclaré coupable devant la Cour de justice de l'Ontario

at _____ on the _____ day of _____ , yr. _____
à _____ *le* _____ *jour de* _____ *an* _____

of the offence of _____
d'avoir commis l'infraction suivante

contrary to _____ section _____
par dérogation à article

and was sentenced to pay a fine of $ _____ (including cost and Victim Fine Surcharge).
et j'ai été condamné à verser une amende de $ *(y compris les frais et la suramende compensatoire).*

2. I was given _____ days/months to pay this amount
J'ai obtenu un délai de *jours (ou mois) pour acquitter ce montant.*

3. I have paid $ _____ in satisfaction of the above amount.
J'ai versé $ *pour qu'ils soient affectés au paiement du montant ci-dessus.*

4. I am unable to pay this amount within the time given for the payment for the following reasons:
Il ne m'est pas possible d'acquitter le montant imposé dans le délai qui m'est accordé pour les raisons suivantes :

_____

_____

5. I hereby apply for an extension of time for payment until
Je formule cette requête en vue d'obtenir une prorogation du délai de paiement jusqu'au

the _____ day of _____ , yr. _____
le *jour de* *an*

6. I am _____ years of age.
Je suis âgé de *ans.*

7. I am / Je
(check one / cochez l'un ou l'autre, selon le cas)
☐ employed. / possède un emploi.
☐ unemployed. / suis sans emploi.

Case Reference Number: _____
Drivers Licence Number: _____
Home Telephone Number: _____

8. (check one / cochez l'un ou l'autre, selon le cas)
☐ This is my first application for an extension.
Je demande une prorogation du délai de paiement pour la première fois.

☐ I previously obtained _____ extension(s) of time for payment, the last of
J'ai déjà obtenu *prorogation(s) du délai de paiement dont la dernière*

which expired/will expire upon the _____ day of _____ , yr. _____
s'est terminée (ou doit se terminer) le *jour de* *an*

Dated at _____
Fait à

this _____ day of _____ , yr. _____   _____
ce *jour de* *an*   Signature

POA 0809 CSD (rev. 11/03)

779

Order Extending Time for Payment

ORDER EXTENDING TIME FOR PAYMENT
ORDONNANCE EN VUE D'OBTENIR UNE PROROGATION DU DÉLAI DE PAIEMENT

ONTARIO COURT OF JUSTICE	Under Section 66 of the *Provincial Offences Act*	Form / *Formule* 126
COUR DE JUSTICE DE L'ONTARIO	*Aux termes de l'article 66 de la Loi sur les infractions provinciales*	*Courts of Justice Act*
PROVINCE OF ONTARIO		*Loi sur les tribunaux judiciaires*
PROVINCE DE L'ONTARIO		R.R.O. / R.R.O. 1990
		O. Reg. / *Régl. de l'Ont.* 200

Upon reading the attached motion of
À la lecture de la requête ci-jointe de

dated the .... day of .... , yr. ....
qui porte la date du   *jour de*   *an*

it is hereby ordered that the time for payment of the fine (including cost and Victim Surcharge) mentioned therein
*j'ordonne, par le présentes, que le délai pour acquitter l'amende (y compris les frais et la suramende compensatoire) dont il est question
dans la requête*

(check appropriate box / *cochez la cas appropriée*)

A ☐ is extended to the .... day of .... , yr ....
   soit prorogé jusqu'au   *jour de*   *an*

B ☐ is extended to the .... day of .... , yr ....
   soit prorogé jusqu'au   *jour de*   *an*

    to allow for the following periodic payments.
    pour permettre les paiements périodiques suivantes :

    ....

    ....

    ....

    ☐ is not extended for the following reasons:
    ne soit pas prorogé pour les raisons suivantes :

    ....

    ....

    ....

    ....

Ordered at .... this .... day of .... , yr ....
Ordonnance rendue à   *ce*   *jour de*   *an*

If extension granted, Defendant's current address:
Si la prorogation est accordée, indiquer l'adresse actuelle du défendeur

....

....

....

....
Justice of the Peace in and for the Province of Ontario
Juge de paix dans et pour la province de l'Ontario

FOR INFORMATION ON ACCESS
TO ONTARIO COURTS
FOR CUSTOMERS WITH DISABILITIES, CALL
1-800-387-4456
TORONTO AREA **416-326-0111**

POUR PLUS DE RENSEIGNEMENTS SUR L'ACCÈS
DES PERSONNES HANDICAPÉES
AUX TRIBUNAUX DE L'ONTARIO, COMPOSEZ LE
1-800-387-4456
RÉGION DE TORONTO **416-326-0111**

POA 0809 CSD (rev. 11/03)

Record of Reopening Application (ss. 11 POA and 205.13 HTA)

RECORD OF REOPENING APPLICATION
DOSSIER DE DEMANDE DE RÉOUVERTURE

ONTARIO COURT OF JUSTICE
COUR DE JUSTICE DE L'ONTARIO
PROVINCE OF ONTARIO
PROVINCE DE L'ONTARIO

Sections 11 of the *Provincial Offences Act* and
205.13 of the *Highway Traffic Act*
*Article 11 de la Loi sur les infractions provinciales et
article 205.13 du Code de la route*

Form / *Formule* **4**

FILE NO / *N° DU DOSSIER* _____

Defendant's Name _____
Nom du défendeur

Current Address _____
Adresse actuelle

On the _____ day of _____ , yr. _____ , an application was made by the Defendant/Representative to
Le jour de an , le défendeur/représentant a fait une demande en vue de la

reopen a conviction entered without a hearing on the _____ day of _____ , yr _____
réouverture de la déclaration de culpabilité faite sans audience, le jour de an

The following notice(s) was/were sent/delivered to the Defendant or Representative:
Les avis suivants ont été envoyés/délivrés au défendeur ou au représentant :

	Yes / *Oui*	No / *Non*	Unknown / *Ne sait pas*
Did the Provincial Offences Officer certify service? *L'agent des infractions provinciales a-t-il confirmé la signification?*	☐	☐	☐
Notice of Trial *Avis de procès*	☐	☐	☐
Early Resolution Meeting Notice *Avis de rencontre pour règlement rapide*	☐	☐	☐
Notice of Fine and Due Date *Avis d'amende et de date d'échéance*	☐	☐	☐
Was a Notice of Intention to Appear filed? *Un avis d'intention de comparaître a-t-il été déposé?*	☐	☐	☐
Was a trial date/early resolution meeting set for the offence? *Une date de procès ou de rencontre pour règlement rapide a-t-elle été fixée?*	☐	☐	☐
Was the defendant or representative present at trial or early resolution meeting? *Le défendeur ou le représentant s'est-il présenté au procès ou à la rencontre pour règlement rapide?*	☐	☐	☐

ORDER OF THE JUSTICE / *ORDONNANCE DU JUGE*

☐ Application denied. _____
Demande rejetée

☐ Conviction struck out. Clerk of the Court is directed to deliver an Early Resolution Meeting Notice to defendant/representative.
Déclaration de culpabilité annulée. On demande au greffier du tribunal de remettre un avis de rencontre pour règlement rapide au défendeur/représentant.

☐ Conviction struck out. Clerk of the Court is directed to deliver a Notice of Trial to defendant/representative.
Déclaration de culpabilité annulée. On demande au greffier du tribunal de remettre un avis de procès au défendeur/représentant.

☐ Conviction struck out. Re-opening to take a guilty plea immediately.
Déclaration de culpabilité annulée. Réouverture pour inscrire un plaidoyer de culpabilité immédiatement.

Other / *Autre*

_____
Justice of the Peace in and for the Province of Ontario
Juge de paix dans la province de l'Ontario et pour cette province

Date _____

FOR INFORMATION ON ACCESS
TO ONTARIO COURTS
FOR PERSONS WITH DISABILITIES CALL
(Court to insert own information)

*POUR PLUS DE RENSEIGNEMENTS SUR L'ACCÈS
DES PERSONNES HANDICAPÉES
AUX TRIBUNAUX DE L'ONTARIO, COMPOSEZ LE
(insérer les coordonnées du tribunal)*

POA 0819a (rev 04/12) CSD

Affidavit in Support of Request for Reopening

AFFIDAVIT IN SUPPORT OF A REQUEST FOR REOPENING
AFFIDAVIT À L'APPUI D'UNE DEMANDE DE RÉOUVERTURE

ONTARIO COURT OF JUSTICE
COUR DE JUSTICE DE L'ONTARIO
PROVINCE OF ONTARIO
PROVINCE DE L'ONTARIO

Under Section 11 or Subsection 19(1) of the *Provincial Offences Act*, or
Section 205.13 or Section 205.23 of the *Highway Traffic Act*
En vertu de l'article 11 ou du paragraphe 19(1) de la Loi sur les infractions
provinciales ou de l'article 205.13 de l'article 205.23 du Code de la route

Form / Formule 102
Courts of Justice Act
Loi sur les tribunaux judiciaires
O. Reg. / Régl. de l'Ont. 200

I
Je soussigné(e), ...

.... (name / nom)

of
de ....

.... (address / adresse)

make oath/affirm and say as follows:
déclare sous serment et affirme ce qui suit :

1. I was convicted without a hearing on the .... day of .... , yr. .... , of the offence of
   J'ai été reconnu(e) coupable sans la tenue d'une audience le jour de an de l'infraction de

   contrary to .... section
   contrairement à la(au) article

2. (a) I was unable to appear at my hearing through no fault of my own because
      Je n'ai pu comparaître à mon audience, sans faute de ma part, parce que :

      ....

      .... (state reason / donner la raison)

   or / ou

   (b) a notice or document relating to the offence was not delivered to me, namely:
      un avis ou un document concernant l'infraction ne m'a pas été livré, notamment :

      ....

      .... (identify document / préciser quel document)

      ....

3. The conviction first came to my attention on the .... day of .... , yr. ....
   J'ai pris connaissance de la déclaration de culpabilité pour la première fois le jour de an

Sworn/Affirmed before me at ....
Fait sous serment/affirmé devant moi à

this .... day of .... , yr. ....
le *jour de* *an*

....
A Commissioner, etc. / Commissaire, etc.   Signature of Defendant / Signature du défendeur/de la défenderesse

NOTE: Section 86 of the *Provincial Offences Act* provides
Every person who makes an assertion of fact in a statement or entry in a document
or form for use under this Act knowing that the assertion is false is guilty of an
offence and on conviction is liable to a fine of not more than $2,000

REMARQUE : Selon l'article 86 de la Loi sur les infractions provinciales
« Est coupable d'une infraction et passible, sur déclaration de culpabilité, d'une
amende d'au plus 2 000 $, quiconque affirme un fit dans une déclaration ou l'inscrit
dans un document ou une formule dont la présent loi prévoit l'usage, et sait que
cette affirmation est fausse »

FOR INFORMATION ON ACCESS
TO ONTARIO COURTS
FOR PERSONS WITH DISABILITIES CALL
1-800-387-4456
TORONTO AREA 416-326-0111

POUR PLUS DE RENSEIGNEMENTS SUR L'ACCÈS
DES PERSONNES HANDICAPÉES
AUX TRIBUNAUX DE L'ONTARIO, COMPOSEZ LE
1-800-387-4456
RÉGION DE TORONTO 416-326-0111

POA 0901 CSD (rev. 11/03)

FORMS

Certificate of Striking Out Conviction

CERTIFICATE OF STRIKING OUT CONVICTION
CERTIFICAT D'ANNULATION DE DÉCLARATION DE CULPABILITÉ

(Section 11 or 19 of the *Provincial Offences Act* or Section 205.13 or
Section 205.23 of the *Highway Traffic Act*)
*(Article 11 ou 19 de la Loi sur les infractions provinciales ou articles
205.13 ou article 205.23 du Code de la route)*

Form / Formule **103**
O. Reg. / Règl. de l'Ont. 200

TO: (Defendant) / AU(À LA)   (Défendeur/Défenderesse)

Offence Number
Numéro d'infraction

Offence Date
Date d'infraction

Statute
Loi

Section
Article

I certify that the conviction entered on the _____ day of _____ , yr 20 _____ , against the Defendant in respect of
J'atteste que la déclaration de culpabilité, enregistrée le   jour de   an   *contre le défendeur ou la défenderesse*
susmentionné(e), en ce qui

the offence described above was struck out by me on the _____ day of _____ , yr. 20 _____ .
concerne l'infraction décrite ci-dessus, a été annulée par moi le   jour de   an

_____
Justice of the Peace in and for the Province of Ontario
Juge de paix dans et pour la province de l'Ontario

POA 0827 CSD (rev 11/03) (CD 0827)

Notice of Appeal [Part I and Part II]

NOTICE OF APPEAL UNDER SECTION 135 OF THE PROVINCIAL OFFENCES ACT
AVIS D'APPEL INTERJETÉ AUX TERMES DE L'ARTICLE 135 DE LA
LOI SUR LES INFRACTIONS PROVINCIALES

ONTARIO COURT OF JUSTICE	Parts I and II of the *Provincial Offences Act*	Form / *Formule* 1
COUR DE JUSTICE DE L'ONTARIO	*Parties I et II de la* Loi sur les infractions provinciales	*Courts of Justice Act*
PROVINCE OF ONTARIO		Loi sur les tribunaux judiciaires
PROVINCE DE L'ONTARIO		O. Reg. / *Régl. de l'Ont.* 722/94

1. Ontario Court of Justice at ....
   Cour de justice de l'Ontario à

2. Appellant is: / *La partie appelante est* :
   ☐ Defendant   ☐ Prosecutor   ☐ Attorney General
       le défendeur (la défenderesse)   *le poursuivant*   *le procureur général*

3. Name of Appellant: ....
   Nom de l'appelant(e) :

   Address for service: ....
   Domicile élu :

4. Counsel for Appellant: Name: ....
   Avocat(e) de l'appelant(e) : *Nom* :

   Address for service: ....
   Domicile élu :

5. Name of Respondent *(if known)*: ....
   Nom de l'intimé(e) (s'il est connu) :

   Address for service ....
   Domicile élu :

6. Counsel for Respondent *(if known)*: ....
   Nom de l'avocat(e) de l'intimé(e) (s'il est connu) :

   Address for service: ....
   Domicile élu

7. Decision of Ontario Court of Justice: / *Décision rendue par la Cour de justice de l'Ontario* :
   (include name of Judge or Justice of Peace appealed from, if known / *inscrire le nom du juge ou du juge de paix dont la décision est portée en appel, s'il est connu*)
   ....
   ....
   ....
   ....
   ....

8. Date of decision: / *Date de la décision* ....

9. The Appellant appeals against: / *L'appelant(e) interjette appel* :
   ☐ Conviction   ☐ Dismissal   ☐ Sentence
       de la déclaration de culpabilité   *du rejet de l'accusation*   *de la sentence*

10. If Appellant is in custody, place where held: ....
    Si l'appelant(e) est sous garde, lieu de détention :

11. (a) Description of offence[1] ....
    Description de l'infraction[1]

    (b) Certificate number *(if known)*: / *Numéro du procès-verbal (s'il est connu)* :
    ....

FOR INFORMATION ON ACCESS
TO ONTARIO COURTS
FOR PERSONS WITH DISABILITIES, CALL
1-800-387-4456
TORONTO AREA 416-326-0111

POUR PLUS DE RENSEIGNEMENTS SUR L'ACCÈS
DES PERSONNES HANDICAPÉES
AUX TRIBUNAUX DE L'ONTARIO, COMPOSEZ LE
1-800-387-4456
RÉGION DE TORONTO 416-326-0111

[1] for example, speeding / *par exemple, excès de vitesse*
POA 0201 (rev. 05/09) CSD

12. (1) Statute[2] ....
    Loi [2]

13. Date of offence: ....
    Date de l'infraction :

14. Plea at trial: ....
    Plaidoyer au procès :

    The plea entered was:
    Le plaidoyer inscrit :
    (check one / cocher la case appropriée)

    ☐ guilty   ☐ not guilty   ☐ not known
       coupable   non coupable   non connu

15. The Appellant wants the appeal court to:
    L'appelant(e) désire que le tribunal d'appel :
    (check one / cocher la case appropriée)

    ☐ Find the Defendant not guilty / Déclare la partie défenderesse non coupable

    ☐ Find the Defendant guilty / Déclare la partie défenderesse coupable

    ☐ Order a new trial / Ordonne la tenue d'un nouveau procès

    ☐ Change the sentence / Modifie la sentence

    ☐ Other / Autre : (specify / préciser) ....

16. The grounds of appeal are: / Les motifs d'appel sont les suivants :

    ....
    ....
    ....
    ....
    ....

Complete No. 17 for *Provincial Offences Act*, Part II, parking Offences where the municipality is collecting its own parking fines.
Remplir le N°17 dans le cas des infractions de stationnement visées par la partie II de la Loi sur les infractions provinciales, lorsque la municipalité perçoit ses propres amendes de stationnement.

17. The fine has been paid in full at: .... on ....
    L'amende a été payée intégralement à   (municipality / municipalité)   le   (date)

18. Date: ....

19. Signature of Appellant or Counsel or Agent: _____
    Signature de l'appelant(e) ou de son avocat(e) ou représentant(e) :

I request a _____ language interpreter for the appeal.
Je demande les services (leave blank if inapplicable / à remplir, le cas échéant) pour l'appel.
d'un interprète de langue

NOTES:

(1) If Appellant's address for service is that of the Appellant's Counsel state Counsel's full address and Appellant's own full address.

(2) Please notify the clerk of the court in writing immediately of any change of address. The court will communicate with you by mail at the address shown by you in this notice unless you notify the court of a change in your address.

(3) This notice of appeal must be filed with the local registrar of the Superior Court of Justice or Ontario Court of Justice.

Sections 111 and 112 of the *Provincial Offences Act* are as follows:

111. (1) A notice of appeal by a Defendant shall not be accepted for filing if the Defendant has not paid in full the fine imposed by the decision appealed from.

(2) A judge may waive compliance with subsection (1) and order that the Appellant enter into a recognizance to appear on the appeal, and the recognizance shall be in such amount, with or without sureties, as the judge directs.

112. The filing of a notice of appeal does not stay the conviction unless a judge so orders.

REMARQUES :

1) Si le domicile élu de l'appelant(e) est celui de son avocat(e), indiquer l'adresse au complet de l'avocat(e) de même que l'adresse au complet de l'appelant(e) lui-même(elle-même).

2) En cas de changement d'adresse, en aviser immédiatement le greffier du tribunal par écrit. Si le tribunal n'est pas avisé, il communiquera avec vous par courrier à l'adresse indiquée au présent avis.

3) Le présent avis d'appel doit être déposé auprès du greffier local de la Cour supérieure de justice ou de la Cour de justice de l'Ontario.

Les articles 111 et 112 de la Loi sur les infractions provinciales se lisent comme suit :

111. 1) L'avis d'appel d'un défendeur n'est pas accepté pour dépôt s'il n'a pas payé intégralement l'amende imposée par la décision portée en appel.

2) Un juge d'appel peut dispenser l'appelant de se conformer au paragraphe (1) et lui ordonner de consentir un engagement à comparaître en appel. Le juge décide du montant de l'engagement, avec ou sans caution.

112. Le dépôt d'un avis d'appel ne suspend pas la déclaration de culpabilité à moins qu'un juge d'appel ne l'ordonne.

[2] for example, *Highway Traffic Act / par exemple, Code de la route*
POA 0201 (rev 05/09) CSD

Notice of Appeal (Form 1) [Part III]

NOTICE OF APPEAL UNDER SECTION 116 OF THE *PROVINCIAL OFFENCES ACT*
AVIS D'APPEL INTERJETÉ EN VERTU DE L'ARTICLE 116 DE LA LOI SUR LES INFRACTIONS
PROVINCIALES

ONTARIO COURT OF JUSTICE	(Part III)	**Form / Formule 1**
COUR DE JUSTICE DE L'ONTARIO	*(Partie III)*	*Courts of Justice Act*
PROVINCE OF ONTARIO		Loi sur les tribunaux judiciaires
PROVINCE DE L'ONTARIO		O.Reg. / Règl. de l'Ont. 723/94

1. Superior/Ontario* Court of Justice / *Cour supérieure de justice/de justice de l'Ontario* at / *à*

2. Appellant is / *La partie appelante est*

   ☐ Defendant
   le défendeur (la défenderesse)

   ☐ Attorney General
   le procureur général

   ☐ Prosecutor
   le poursuivant

3. Name of Appellant:
   Nom de l'appelant(e) :

   Address for service:
   Domicile élu :

4. Counsel for Appellant: Name:
   Avocat(e) de l'appelant(e): Nom :

   Address for service:
   Domicile élu :

5. Name of respondent *(if known)*:
   Nom de l'intimé(e) (s'il est connu) :

   Address for service:
   Domicile élu :

6. Counsel for respondent *(if known)*:
   Nom de l'avocat(e) de l'intimé(e) (s'il est connu) :

   Address for service:
   Domicile élu :

7. Decision of Ontario Court of Justice / *Décision rendue par la Cour de justice de l'Ontario*
   (include name of Judge or Justice of Peace appealed from, if known): / *Inscrire le nom du juge ou du juge de paix dont la décision est portée en appel, s'il est connu) :*

8. Date of decision: / *Date de la décision :*

9. The Appellant appeals against: / *L'appelant(e) interjette appel :*

   ☐ conviction / *de la déclaration de culpabilité*

   ☐ dismissal / *du rejet de l'accusation*

   ☐ finding as to ability to conduct a defense / *de la conclusion quant à la capacité du défendeur (de la défenderesse) d'assurer sa défense*

   ☐ sentence / *de la sentence*

   ☐ order (s. 161 of the P.O.A.) / *de l'ordonnance (art. 161 de la L.I.P.)*

   ☐ any other order as to costs

   by the Ontario Court of Justice / *de la Cour de justice de l'Ontario*

   at
   à/au   (address of court / *adresse du tribunal*)

* Strike out inapplicable /
* *Rayer ce qui ne s'applique pas*

FOR INFORMATION ON ACCESS
TO ONTARIO COURTS
FOR PERSONS WITH DISABILITIES, CALL
1-800-387-4456
TORONTO AREA 416-326-0111

POUR PLUS DE RENSEIGNEMENTS SUR L'ACCÈS
DES PERSONNES HANDICAPÉES
AUX TRIBUNAUX DE L'ONTARIO, COMPOSEZ LE
1-800-387-4456
RÉGION DE TORONTO 416-326-0111

POA 0301 (rev. 12/09) CSD

10. If Defendant is in custody, place where held: _____
    Si l'appelant(e) est sous garde, lieu de détention :

11. (a) Description of offence[1]: / Description de l'infraction[1] : _____

    (b) Information number *(if known)*: _____
        Numéro de la dénonciation (s'il est connu) :

12. (1) Statute[2] / Loi[2] : _____

    (2) Section[3] : / Article[3] : _____

13. Date of offence: / Date de l'infraction : _____

14. Plea at trial / Plaidoyer au procès : _____

15. The grounds for appeal are: / Moyens d'appel :
    (specify the question of law or issue where the appeal is from conviction or acquittal or finding as to ability to conduct a defense or specify the ground for appeal against sentence / préciser la question de droit ou la question en litige lorsqu'il est interjeté appel de la déclaration de culpabilité, de l'acquittement ou de la conclusion quant à la capacité de la partie défenderesse d'assurer sa défense, ou préciser les moyens d'appel contre la sentence)

16. In support of this appeal, the Appellant relies upon the following:
    À l'appui du présent appel, l'appelant(e) se fonde sur les documents suivants :
    (set out documents such as transcript, etc. upon which the Appellant relies / indiquer les documents, tels que les transcriptions, sur lesquels se fonde l'appelant(e))

17. The relief sought is: _____
    Mesure de redressement demandée :

18. The Appellant intends: / Intention de l'appelant(e) :

    ☐ to be present in person or by counsel and to present the issues and the Appellant's arguments orally.
       comparaître en personne ou par l'entremise d'un(e) avocat(e) et débattre les questions en litige et présenter ses arguments oralement.

    ☐ not to be present in person or by counsel and to present the issues and the Appellant's arguments in writing
       ne comparaître ni en personne ni par l'entremise d'un(e) avocat(e) et débattre les questions en litige et présenter ses arguments par écrit.

19. Does the Appellant intend to make a motion for an order that the appeal be heard by way of a new trial in the appeal court?
    L'appelant(e) a-t-il(elle) l'intention de présenter une motion en vue d'obtenir une ordonnance prévoyant la tenue de l'appel sous forme d'un nouveau procès devant le tribunal d'appel?

    ☐ Yes / Oui   ☐ No / Non

20. Date: _____

21. Signature of Appellant or Counsel: _____
    Signature de l'appelant(e) ou de son avocat(e) :

I request a _____ language interpreter for the appeal
Je demande les services   (leave blank if inapplicable / à remplir, le cas échéant)   pour l'appel.
d'un interprète de langue

NOTES:
(1) If Appellant's address for service is that of the Appellant's Counsel, state Counsel's full address and Appellant's own full address.

(2) Please notify the clerk of the court in writing immediately of any change of address. The court will communicate with you by mail at the address shown by you in this notice unless you notify the court of a change in your address.

(3) This court of appeal must be filed with the local registrar of the Superior Court of Justice or Ontario Court of Justice.

REMARQUES :
1) Si le domicile élu de l'appelant(e) est celui de son avocat(e), indiquer l'adresse au complet de l'avocat(e) de même que l'adresse au complet de l'appelant lui-même (elle-même).

2) En cas de changement d'adresse, en aviser immédiatement le greffier du tribunal par écrit. Si le tribunal n'est pas avisé, il communiquera avec vous par courrier à l'adresse indiquée au présent avis.

3) Le présent avis d'appel doit être déposé auprès du greffier local de la Cour supérieure de justice ou de la Cour de justice de l'Ontario.

[1] for example, careless driving / par exemple, conduite imprudente
[2] for example, *Highway Traffic Act* / par exemple, Code de la route
[3] for example, Section 130 / par exemple, article 130

POA 0301 (rev. 12/09) CSD

Notice of Time and Place of Hearing of Appeal (s. 135)

NOTICE OF TIME AND PLACE OF HEARING OF APPEAL
AVIS DE L'HEURE, DE LA DATE ET DU LIEU DE L'AUDITION DE L'APPEL

ONTARIO COURT
OF JUSTICE
PROVINCE OF ONTARIO
*COUR DE JUSTICE
DE L'ONTARIO
PROVINCE DE L'ONTARIO*

Under Section 135 of the *Provincial Offences Act*
Interjeté en vertu de l'article 135 de la Loi sur les infractions provinciales

Form 2
Formule 2
Courts of Justice Act
Loi sur les tribunaux judiciaires
O. Reg. 722/94
Règl. O. 722/94

To/*Destinataires* : ...., appellant/*appelant*

....
(address/*adresse*)

and/*et*

...., respondent/*intimé*

....
(address/*adresse*)

Take notice that the appeal in respect of the/*Avis vous est donné que l'appel relatif à* ....

....

in the Ontario Court of Justice on/*interjeté devant la Cour de justice de l'Ontario le* .... yr./*an* ....

in respect of the charge that/*relativement à l'accusation selon laquelle* ....
(name/*nom*)

of/*de* ....

on or about/*le ou vers le* ...., yr./*an* ....

at/*à* ....

did commit the offence(s) of/*a commis l'infraction (les infractions) suivante(s)* ....

....

....

(set out charges/*indiquer les accusations*)

contrary to/*en violation de l'article* .... section/*article* ....

will be heard in the Ontario Court of Justice at/*sera entendu devant la Cour de justice de l'Ontario à/au*

....

on/*le* ...., yr./*an* ...., at/*à* .... M
(heure)

Given at/*Fait à* ....

on/*le*........ ...., yr./*an* ....

_____
Clerk / *Greffier*

CD 0202 (rev 10/99)

788

Appendix D

List of Provincial Offences Courts in Ontario

Barrie
45 Cedar Pointe Dr.
Barrie, ON L4N 5R7
Tel: 705-739-4291
Fax: 705-739-4292
E-mail: POAExternal.Mail-barrie@barrie.ca

Belleville — Hastings
235 Pinnacle St. — 3rd Floor
Belleville, ON K8N 3A9
Tel: 613-966-0331
Fax: 613-966-7045
Email: poa@hastingscounty.com

Bracebridge — Muskoka
76 Pine Street
Bracebridge, ON P1L 0C4
Tel: 705-645-1231
Fax: 705-645-5319
Email: poa@muskoka.on.ca

Brampton
5 Ray Lawson Blvd.
Brampton, ON L6Y 5L7
Tel: 905-450-4770
Fax: 905-450-4794
E-mail: provincialoffencescourt@brampton.ca

Brantford
102 Wellington Square, P.O. Box 760
Brantford, ON N3T 5R7
Tel: 519-751-9100
Fax: 519-751-0404
Email: brantfordpoa@brantford.ca

Brockville — Leeds & Grenville
32 Wall St., Suite 100
Brockville, ON K6V 4R9
Tel: 613-342-2357
Fax: 613-342-8891
Email: poacourt@uclg.on.ca
TTY/ATS: 613-341-3854
TF: 1-800-539-8685

Caledon East
6311 Old Church Rd.
Caledon, ON L7C 1J6
Tel: 905-584-2273
Fax: 905-584-2861

Cayuga — Haldimand
45 Munsee St. North, P.O. Box 220
Cayuga, ON N0A 1E0
Tel: 905-772-3327
Fax: 905-772-5810

Chatham — Kent
21633 Communication Rd. R.R.#5
Blenheim, ON N0P 1A0
Tel: 519-352-8484
Fax: 519-352-7979
E-mail: CKpoc@chatham-kent.ca

Cobourg — Northumberland
860 William St.
Cobourg, ON K9A 3A9
Tel: 905-372-3329, ext. 5300
Fax: 905-372-6529
Email: poainfo@northumberlandcounty.ca

Cochrane
171 4th Avenue
P.O. Box 1867
Cochrane, ON P0L 1C0
Tel: 705-272-2538
Fax: 705-272-3593

Cornwall — Stormant, Dundas & Glengarry
26 Pitt St., Suite 308
Cornwall, ON K6J 3P2
Tel: 613-933-4301
Fax: 613-933-4161
Email: courtservices@sdgcounties.ca

Durham
605 Rossland Rd. East
P.O. Box 740
Whitby, ON L1N 0B3
Tel: 905-668-3130
Fax: 905-668-3166
Email: poa.courts@durham.ca

Dryden
30 Van Horne Ave, Box 105
Dryden, ON P8N 2Y7
Tel: 807-223-1429
Fax: 807-223-5839
Email: abeaulne@dryden.ca

Elliot Lake
100 Tudhope St., Suite 4
Espanola, ON P5E 1S6
Tel: 705-862-7875
Fax: 705-862-7876

Espanola
100 Tudhope St., Suite 4
Espanola, ON P5E 1S6
Tel: 705-862-7875
Fax: 705-862-7876

Fort Frances
Town Hall (Civic Centre)
320 Portage Ave.
Fort Frances, ON P9A 3P9
Tel: 807-274-1676
Fax: 807-274-0446
Email: dkneisz@fortfrances.ca

Goderich — Huron
1 Courthouse Square
Goderich, ON N7A 1M2
Tel: 519-524-8394, ext. 2
Fax: 519-524-2044
Email: poa@huroncounty.ca

Gore Bay
15 Water Street
P.O. Box 500
Gore Bay, ON P0P 1H0
Tel: 705-282-2837
Fax: 705-282-3076
Email: gorebaypoa@gorebay.ca

Guelph
59 Carden St.
Guelph, ON N1H 2Z9
Tel.: 519-826-0762
Fax: 519-826-6814
TTY/ATS: 519-826-9771
Email: courtservices@guelph.ca

Haileybury — Temiskaming Shores
325 Farr Dr.
P.O. Box 2050
Haileybury, ON P0J 1K0
Tel: 705-672-3221
Fax: 705-672-2911
Email: lregan@temiskamingshores.ca

Halton Region (Burlington — Halton Hills — Milton — Oakville)
2051 Plains Rd. E.
Burlington, ON L7R 5A5
Tel: 905-637-1274
Fax: 905-637-5919
Email: burlingtoncourt@burlington.ca

Hamilton
50 Main St. East
Hamilton, ON L8N 2B7
Tel: 905-540-5592

Fax: 905-540-5730

Kenora
1 Main St. South
Kenora, ON P9N 3X2
Tel: 807-467-2984
Fax: 807-467-8530
Email: poa@kenora.ca

Kingston
362 Montreal Street
Kingston, ON K7K 3H5
Tel: 613-547-8557
Fax: 613-547-8558
TTY/ATS: 613-546-4889
Email: contactus@cityofkingston.ca

Kitchener — Cambridge — Waterloo Region
77 Queen St. North
Kitchener, ON N2H 2H1
Tel: 519-745-9446
Fax: 519-742-1112
TTY/ATS: 519-575-4607

L'Orignal — Prescott Russell
28 Court St., P.O. Box 347
L'Orignal, ON K0B 1K0
Tel: 613-675-4661 ext. 2700
Fax: 613-675-4940
TF: 1-800-667-6307 ext. 2700
Email: lip-poa@prescott-russell.on.ca

Lindsay — Kawartha Lakes
440 Kent St. West
Lindsay, ON K9V 5P2
Tel: 705-324-3962
Fax: 705-324-7991
Email: POAAdmin@kawarthalakes.ca

London
824 Dundas St. E.
London, ON N5W 5R1

Tel: 519-661-1882
Fax: 519-661-1944
Email: POAAdmin@london.ca

Mississauga
950 Burnhamthorpe Rd. W.
Mississauaga, ON L5B 3C4
Tel: 905-615-4500
Fax: 905-615-4038
Email: Court.admin@mississauga.ca

Napanee — Lennox & Addington
97 Thomas Street East
Napanee, ON K7R 4B9
Tel: 613-354-4883
Fax: 613-354-3112
Email: kmcgarvey@lennox-addington.on.ca

Newmarket — York Region
Ontario Court of Justice
465 Davis Dr., Suite 200
Newmarket, ON L3Y 7T9
Tel: 905-898-0425
Fax: 905-898-5218

North Bay
200 McIntyre St. E.
P.O. Box 360
North Bay, ON P1B 8H8
Tel: 705-474-0626, ext: 2146, 2147
Fax: 905-474-8302

Orangeville
55 Zina Street
Orangeville, ON L9W 1E5
Tel: 519-941-5808
Fax: 519-940-3685
Email: Dufferin.poa@caledon.ca

Orillia
575 West Street South, #10
Orillia, ON L3V 7N6

Tel: 705-326-2960
Fax: 705-326-3613
Email: POAExternal.Mail-Orillia@barrie.ca

Ottawa
100 Constellation Cres.
Ottawa, ON K2G 6J8
Tel: 613-580-2665
Fax: 613-580-2664

Owen Sound / Walkerton — Grey Bruce
595 9th Ave. E.
Owen Sound, ON N4K 3E3
Tel: 519-376-3470, ext: 1267
Fax: 519-376-0638
Email: poa@grey.ca

Parry Sound
52 Sequin St.
Parry Sound, ON P2A 1B4
Tel: 705-746-2553
Fax: 705-746-7461

Pembroke — Renfrew
141 Lake Street,
Pembroke, ON K8A 5L8
Tel: 613-735-3482
Fax: 613-735-8484
Email: poaoffice@countyofrenfrew.on.ca

Perth – Lanark
80 Gore St. East
Perth, ON K7H 1H9
Tel: 613-267-3122
Fax: 613-267-5635
Email: POA@perth.ca

Peterborough
99 Simcoe St.
Peterborough, ON K9H 2H3
TF: 1-855-738-3755

Picton — Prince Edward County
332 Main Street
Picton, ON K0K 2T0
Tel: 613-476-2148, ext. 247
Fax: 613-476-8356
Email: alumley@pecounty.on.ca

Richmond Hill — York
Ontario Court of Justice
50 High Tech Rd., 1st floor
Richmond Hill, ON L4B 4N7
Tel: 905-762-2105
Fax: 905-762-2106

Sarnia – Lambton
150 North Christina St., P.O. Box 1060
Sarnia, ON N7T 7K2
Tel: 519-344-8880
Fax: 519-344-9379
Email: poa@county-lambton.on.ca

Sault Ste. Marie
99 Foster Dr., 1st floor
P.O. Box 580
Sault Ste. Marie, ON P6A 5N1
Tel: 705-541-7334
Fax: 705-759-5395

Simcoe — Norfolk
185 Robinson St., Suite 100
Simcoe, ON N3Y 5L6
Tel: 519-426-5870
Fax: 519-427-5900
Email: poa@norfolkcounty.ca

St. Catharines — Niagara Region
71 King St
St. Catharines, ON L2R 3H7
Tel: 905-687-6590
Fax: 905-687-6614
Email: poaenquiries@niagararegion.ca

St. Thomas — Elgin
450 Sunset Dr.
St. Thomas, ON N5R 5V1
Tel: 519-631-1460, ext. 119
Fax: 519-631-5088
E-mail: poa@elgin-county.on.ca

Stratford — Perth
1 Huron St.
Stratford, ON, N5A 5S4
Tel: 519-271-0531, ext. 3
Fax: 519-271-7993
Email: poa@perthcounty.ca

Sudbury
199 Larch Street, Suite 102
Sudbury, ON P3E 5P3
Tel: 705-674-4455
Fax: 705-673-9505
Email: poacourt@greatersudbury.ca

Thunder Bay
101 South Syndicate Ave. (Victoriaville Mall)
P.O. Box 1600
Thunder Bay, ON P7C 6A9
Tel: 807-625-2999
Fax: 807-623-7751

Timmins
220 Algonquin Blvd. E.
Timmins, ON P4N 1B3
Tel: 705-360-2620, option 1
Fax:705-360-2694
Email: poa@timmins.ca

Toronto East
1530 Markham Road, Main Floor
Scarborough, ON M1B 3M4
Tel: 416-338-7320
Email: poacourt@toronto.ca

Toronto South

137 Edward Street
Toronto, ON M5G 2P8
Tel.: 416-338-7320
TTY/ATS: 416-338-7394
Email: poacourt@toronto.ca

Toronto West
York Civic Centre
2700 Eglinton Ave W.
Toronto, ON M6M 1V1
Tel: 416-338-7320
TTY/ATS: 416-338-7394
Email: poacourt@toronto.ca

Welland — Niagara Region
445 East Main St.
Welland, ON L3B 3X7
Tel: 905-687-6590
Fax: 905-687-6614
Email: poaenquiries@niagararegion.ca

Windsor
Westcourt Place
251 Goyeau St., Suite 300
Windsor, ON N9A 6V2
Tel: 519-255-6555
Fax: 519-255-6556

Woodstock — Oxford
P.O. Box 1614
Woodstock, ON N4S 7Y3
Tel: 519-537-4890
Fax: 519-537-3024
Email: poa@oxfordcounty.ca

Index